To Peter Hennessy, in friendship and fellowship

Give them a chance. Give them money. Don't dole them out poetry-books and railway-tickets like babies. Give them the wherewithal to buy these things. When your Socialism comes it may be different, and we may think in terms of commodities instead of cash. Till it comes give people cash, for it is the warp of civilisation, whatever the woof may be.

E. M. Forster, *Howards End* (p. 134)

A time there was, as one may guess,
And as, indeed, earth's testimonies tell,
Before the birth of consciousness
When all went well.

Thomas Hardy, 'Before Life and After', from *Time's Laughingstocks*

We are weak, and writing is difficult, but for my own sake I do not regret this journey, which has shown that Englishmen can endure hardships, help one another, and meet death with as great a fortitude as ever in the past. We took risks, we knew that we took them; things have come out against us, and therefore we have no cause for complaint, but bow to the will of Providence, determined still to do our best to the last.

Captain Robert Falcon Scott, Journal, 29 March 1912

This they all with a joyful mind
Bear through life like a torch in flame,
And falling fling to the host behind –
Play up! play up! and play the game!

Sir Henry Newbolt, '*Vitai Lampada*'

Penny buses, gramophones, bamboo furniture, pleasant Sunday afternoons, Glory Songs, modern language teas, golf, tennis, high school education, dubious fiction, shilling's worth of comic writing, picture postcards, miraculous hair restorers.

T. W. H. Crosland, *The Suburbans* (p. 80)

THE AGE OF DECADENCE

Britain 1880 to 1914

Simon Heffer

1 3 5 7 9 10 8 6 4 2

Random House Books
20 Vauxhall Bridge Road
London SW1V 2SA

Random House Books is part of the Penguin Random House group of companies whose addresses can be found at global.penguinrandomhouse.com.

First published by Random House Books in 2017

www.penguin.co.uk

A CIP catalogue record for this book is available from the British Library.

ISBN 9781847947420

Typeset in 12/14.5 pt Dante MT by Jouve (UK), Milton Keynes
Printed and bound by Clays Ltd, St Ives plc

Penguin Random House is committed to a sustainable future for our business, our readers and our planet. This book is made from Forest Stewardship Council® certified paper.

In the first place I believe in the British Empire, and in the second place I believe in the British race. I believe that the British race is the greatest of governing races that the world has ever seen . . . I believe there are no limits accordingly to its future.

Joseph Chamberlain, speech to the Imperial Institute, London, 11 November 1895

'And yet,' demanded Councillor Barlow, 'what's he done? Has he ever done a day's work in his life? What great cause is he identified with?'

'He's identified,' said the Speaker, 'with the great cause of cheering us all up.'

Arnold Bennett, *The Card* (p. 256)

Our Sovereign Lord the King chargeth and commandeth all persons, being assembled, immediately to disperse themselves, and peaceably to depart to their habitations, or to their lawful business, upon the pains contained in the act made in the first year of King George, for preventing tumults and riotous assemblies. God save the King.

The Form of Proclamation from the Riot Act, 1714

CONTENTS

PART IV
STRIFE

INTRODUCTION

This book is a successor to *High Minds: The Victorians and the Birth of Modern Britain*, which told the history of Britain and the growth of British power from 1838 to 1880. It starts where that finished, with Gladstone beginning his second administration in April 1880; and it ends in July 1914, with a nation fixated on an Ireland on the brink of civil war over Home Rule. It does not deal with the immensely complex question of why Britain went to war in 1914, which the author hopes to cover in a later volume. Although primarily a social, political and cultural history of Britain in the decades before the Great War, *The Age of Decadence* also deals at length with two other matters that profoundly shaped and affected Britain at home: the thirty-year wrangle over Irish Home Rule, whose consequences are still apparent in the twenty-first century, and the late-Victorian and Edwardian expansion and consolidation of the British Empire.

I owe great thanks to many individuals and institutions who assisted me or granted me access to archives during the writing of this book, or who simply discussed questions within it with me and pointed me towards hitherto unknown sources. Extracts from the journals of Bishop Hensley Henson are reproduced by kind permission of the Chapter of Durham Cathedral: I owe a particular debt to Dr Julia Stapleton for alerting me to this source, and to Dr Janet Gunning and Lisa di Tommaso for facilitating access. Andrew Riley and Ceri Humphries, of the Churchill College Archives Centre at Cambridge, helped me with the papers of the 2nd Lord Esher. The Marquess of Salisbury generously granted me access to the papers of his great-great grandfather, the 3rd Marquess. Vicki Perry and Sarah Whale helped me greatly in the Hatfield archives. Sonia Gomes and Gemma Read at the London School of Economics Women's Library helped me with material concerning the campaign for women's suffrage. I should also like to thank the staff of the British Library for assistance with a number of archives, notably those of W. E. Gladstone and Viscount Northcliffe. The staff of the Cambridge University Library, particularly Peter Meadows, helped me with access to the archives of Lord Randolph Churchill. The staff of the Bodleian Library, Oxford, especially Sonja Kujansuu, assisted me with the papers of Herbert Henry Asquith. Simon Gough, Archives Officer at the Parliamentary Archives, enabled access to the papers of David Lloyd George, and I was greatly helped by Dr Mari Takayanagi, Senior Archivist, Parliamentary Archives. I must also thank the staff of the National Archives, Kew.

I much profited from conversations with Professor Lord Hennessy, Professor Brendan Simms, Dr Karina Urbach, Dr Fred Hohler, Leo McKinstry, Dr Andrew Roberts, Professor Roy Foster, Dr Jean Chothia, Jeff Randall, Jonathan Meades, Dr Shruti Kapila, Angus MacKinnon, Julia Richardson, Dr Matthew Butler, Professor Robert Colls, David Frith and His Honour Judge Martin Edmunds QC. I am grateful to Natascha Nel for her design expertise. Mr and Mrs Tom Ward provided peerless hospitality on my visit to the Bodleian Library, for which I salute them. Sue Brealey very kindly read the book in proof, as did Caroline Pretty, and I am much in their debt. Lynn Curtis, who copy-edited the manuscript, saved me from some errors, and any that remain are mine.

I am particularly fortunate in my agent, Georgina Capel, who has been a constant support throughout the writing of this book; and in my editor at Random House, Nigel Wilcockson, whose enthusiasm for the subject and knowledge of it have been as invaluable to me as his magnificent insight and vision about how a book should actually be constructed. In an age when too many authors complain about the indifference of their editors, I am conscious of my great good fortune. I am also grateful to his assistant, Rowan Borchers, for some heavy lifting at a late stage in the process. But as always my greatest debt is to my wife, Diana, not merely for her advanced proofreading skills but also for unquestioningly providing all the practical and metaphysical infrastructure an author could need during a four-year gestation period from conception to birth, and to my sons Fred and Johnnie for their help, tolerance and encouragement.

Simon Heffer, Great Leighs, 10 April 2017

PROLOGUE:
SWAGGER

I

The decades before the Great War appeal to the imagination because of the often romantic glimpses we have of them more than a century later. We sense an era when, it seems, all went well. The first moving pictures show jubilees and state funerals, with kings and emperors in richly decorated uniforms and plumed helmets, personifying the pomp of the period: it was a time of unquestioned British imperial power, and its leaders looked the part. We see film of an age of elegance, with men in silk hats and frock coats, and women in astonishing examples of the milliner's and dressmaker's art, promenading by rivers and in parks, applauding moustachioed cricketers or rowing eights. London and other cities are captured on film too, the new motor-omnibuses mixing in the streets with horse-drawn traffic, everyone busy and bustling. We hear the music of Sir Edward Elgar and Sir Hubert Parry; we still see hotels and office blocks finished then – great Edwardian baroque palaces, which when built rose higher than any such buildings had before thanks to their innovative steel frames. In museums and antique shops we see the beautifully designed everyday objects of the period: the coins, the stamps, the advertisements, the hot water bottles and boot-jacks.

Swagger was the predominant style of the period, and not merely in painting. The pervasiveness of this mixture of opulence, arrogance and ornament and its ability to seduce explains why our conceptions of the age between 1880 and 1914 are rooted, still, so much more in myth than in reality. Swagger reflected the rise of imperial power, and the effects of that on the British psyche. It was evident at Queen Victoria's 1887 Golden Jubilee, but far more so at the 1897 celebrations and the Coronation of King Edward VII in 1902. It caught on among the wealthy, for whom tasteful ostentation became *de rigueur*. It provoked the swagger portrait; shaped the dress of the moneyed classes; influenced the architecture; informed the music of contemporary composers; inspired everyday design; and dominated the personal style of Edward VII and George V. The age developed a love of ceremonial, show and ornament, practised mainly by the rich but lapped up by those who witnessed it, the tens of millions whose lives bore no relation to this elegant Belle Époque fantasy and who existed outside the myth, many of them in a life whose precariousness shamed so wealthy, and advanced, a nation.

Doing things in style was expensive. On 1 January 1905 General Sir Dighton Probyn VC, a hero of the Indian Mutiny but now comptroller of King Edward VII's household, wrote to Arthur James Balfour, the etiolated and exhausted Tory prime minister, expressing outrage at how starved of funds the King – head of the greatest empire in the world – was. His Majesty felt 'disappointment' in paying income tax; and in having to fund State visits out of the civil list.[1] He was used to his friends bankrupting themselves to pay for his private visits to them, but far less sanguine when paying for himself. Visits to Scotland and Ireland in 1903 had cost £12,101 – more than £1 million in early-twenty-first-century prices – and he sought assurances that the Treasury would in future bear such costs, and those of State visits to Britain.

But Probyn's main gripe on behalf of his master was about the state of Windsor Castle and Buckingham Palace: £60,000 had been allowed for work, but Probyn, having consulted the Office of Works, thought the sum needed was nearer twice that. The Ball Room and Supper Room in Buckingham Palace 'must be restored next autumn', he said. 'I doubt if there are two such shabby big State Rooms in any other Court in Europe.'[2] Balfour agreed to find the money to keep up appearances, though begged for a delay to avoid 'a difficult controversy and an inconvenient inquiry' by small-minded MPs, who had recently voted money to maintain Royal residences.[3] In an age before a welfare state, when photographs show ragged children without shoes in the slums of British cities, and when those too worn out to work were consigned to die in workhouses, politicians had to be careful. Beneath the surface, and away from the swagger, the social storm before the international catastrophe was brewing.

II

As the nineteenth century neared its end, so too did the greatest British life of all. Queen Victoria celebrated her Diamond Jubilee in June 1897, just after her seventy-eighth birthday. Few could recall Britain before Victoria, so epic had been her reign. She had emerged from her deep unpopularity of the 1870s and early 1880s to become the sentimental incarnation not just of the British nineteenth century, when it had finally achieved greatness as the world's leading power, but of the whole British past.

A great pageant was set for 22 June, when the Queen would make a progress to St Paul's Cathedral. A committee chaired by the Prince of Wales and including Regy Brett, the future Lord Esher – whose instinct for the pompous was as fine as his organisational skills – had been planning the event in meticulous detail since March. Brett was charged with arranging an opera gala (which the Queen would not attend); for her carriage to stop on the procession so a child could be presented to her; for various loyal addresses to be declaimed; and for the Munshi – the Queen's Indian secretary, adored by her but hated by her household and family – to have three tickets for the best stand.[4] For weeks beforehand newspapers teemed with advertisements offering to rent out rooms, or rather views, along the route, with the cost of places ranging from two guineas to around £20 each, depending on position and whether or not one was under cover. Entrepreneurs threw in luncheon for those wishing to extend the party. The Princess of Wales launched a £25,000 appeal to provide a substantial meal for each of London's destitute. Clerkenwell had an astonishing 40,000 of them; Bethnal Green 14,500 and Shoreditch and Hackney 10,000 each, but such unfortunates as these also lived cheek-by-jowl with the well-to-do: Westminster had 4,500 and Kensington 5,000 to 6,000 – figures that show not merely the extent of poverty at that time within the principal city of the British Empire, but also how impossible it was for the ruling class to remain unaware of the fact.[5] At a shilling a head it would cost £15,000 to feed the estimated 300,000 indigent in the capital alone. Ultimately Thomas Lipton, the tea merchant, covered that part of the cost the Princess of Wales's fund fell short of.

Large contingents of soldiers and sailors paraded throughout Britain and the Empire, displaying the nation's new military power; the fleet was reviewed off Spithead, with 167 ships present, all painted black for the occasion. Crowned heads and representatives from around the world headed to London. There were banquets and conferences for visiting imperial prime ministers and potentates, not just in London, but in great provincial cities too; colonial and imperial troops joined the parades. When the Jubilee hymn was sung in St Paul's Cathedral, an electric signal was sent around the world so at that precise moment people in Australia and elsewhere would know to sing it too. The copes worn by the officiating clergy, it was disclosed, were of a special design, 'chosen with a view to its harmonising with the architecture of the Cathedral'.[6] The vestments were 'of white silk on a gold ground, and have hoods bearing the monogram IHS worked in gold on green velvet and surrounded by rays.'

Ceremony ensured the dignity of the proceedings. *The Times* devoted thousands of words and acres of newsprint to cataloguing to the minute every planned movement of every contingent of soldiers and sailors. When, the week before the great pageant, the Queen and her Court travelled from Balmoral to Windsor, a guard of honour saw off her fifteen-coach, double-engined (the 'Victoria' and the 'Jubilee', specially painted blue and gold) train. It stopped at Aberdeen, where flowers were presented to the Queen, and at Perth, where the public lined the trackside to cheer and wave flags. At Carlisle the London and North Western Railway's finest engine, the 'Queen Empress', painted cream and gold, took over, with the help of another engine, the 'Prince of Wales'.

When the Queen reached Windsor the next morning she found the station approach 'lined with Venetian masts and flags, yellow-fringed crimson cloth, red, blue and white bunting, and trophies of flags and shields bearing Her Majesty's arms and Prince of Wales feathers, while the Royal Standard and Union Jacks have been hoisted above the façade.'[7] This was but a hint of what would come. Paddington Station, through which the Queen would enter London, was lavishly smothered in heraldic devices, Union flags and bunting: as was much of the capital and, indeed, Britain. Temporary triumphal arches strewn with ornaments marked the route from Paddington to Buckingham Palace: the Queen was pleased to note one bore the motto 'Our hearts thy Throne'.[8] The symbolism of royalty, richly wrought, had become the symbolism of power, personal majesty, and the majesty of an entire Empire and the culture of its mother country.

When the Queen reached the Palace her vast European family awaited her, and showered her with diamonds. At dinner for the family, foreign potentates and ambassadors that evening – she sat between the ill-fated Archduke Franz Ferdinand and the Prince of Naples – she wore 'a dress of which the whole front was embroidered in gold, which had been specially worked in India, diamonds in my cap, and a diamond necklace.'[9] A band played in the ballroom while she was pushed around in her wheelchair – she could not stand for long – to greet her guests. So that the splendour could be taken to the people a force of 2,400 officers and men marched from the City of London on the Saturday before the Jubilee pageant, parading through the East End to Bethnal Green and Victoria Park and back. The event also ensured that the city's lowest classes would be impressed by the power and glory of their nation, would identify with it, and have their patriotism stirred.

On 22 June, Jubilee Day, the sun shone. The Queen, escorted by Life Guards and officers of Indian regiments, drove from Buckingham Palace to St Paul's through what *The Times* called 'a storm of acclamation'.[10] It was 'a military and Royal procession of unparalleled grandeur . . . the pageant as a whole was of wonderful splendour and variety, and not to be matched by any of which history holds the record.' Sixteen carriages of foreign and native royalties and dignitaries preceded the Queen's State Carriage, 'drawn by the cream-colour horses, which were gorgeous in their new harness . . . ridden by postilions, with red-coated running footmen at their sides'. The Royal dukes, led by the Prince of Wales, accompanied the carriage, uniformed and on horseback, while 'guns boomed in Hyde Park [and] the bells clanged from St Paul's . . . round by Hyde Park Corner into Piccadilly and past the great houses, the stream of gold and scarlet flowed like a sunlit river.' In the carriage next to the Queen's was her daughter Vicky, the Dowager Kaiserin. She could not ride with the Queen because 'her rank of Empress prevented her sitting with her back to the horses'.[11]

In the sea of colour – the lavishly decorated and flag-draped palaces of St James's Street and Piccadilly, the vast array of uniforms, the finery of princesses and ambassadresses, what the Queen termed 'festoons of flowers across the road and many loyal inscriptions' and a crowd in its finest clothes – the small figure of the Queen stood out, in her customary 'black silk dress trimmed with white lace and a bonnet to match', clutching a parasol.[12] Along the route the dates '1837' and '1897' were picked out in garlands of purple flowers; imperial crowns in red, white and yellow ones. Road, river and railway bridges bore flowers and the Royal cipher. 'Squadron after squadron of cavalry, battery after battery of artillery' marched ahead of the Sovereign.[13] For three hours, from 10.45 to 1.45, the Queen's procession wound its way around London, with stops outside St Paul's and at the Mansion House before going over London Bridge and through the Borough and Southwark to Westminster Bridge.

The approach to St Paul's was lavishly decorated. 'The obelisks in Ludgate Circus were draped in purple and gold cloth, with embossed shields and palms. In Ludgate Hill the columns were surmounted by relief banners of elephants, through whose trunks the line of garlands passed. These elephants . . . were decked with purple and gold trappings, and were mounted on a base of Oriental design,' *The Times* reported.[14] The exotic beasts indicated it was not merely a nation, but an empire, whose glories were celebrated. The next day the Duke of Argyll wrote to the Queen: 'No Sovereign since the fall of Rome could muster subjects from so many and so distant countries all over the world.'[15]

Her carriage, drawn by eight cream horses in gold-plated and morocco harness, pulled up outside St Paul's amid a 'deep, thrilling, prolonged "hurrah!"' and 'the merry peal of the cathedral's bells'. The Queen was not equal to walking to the chancel so 500 choristers complemented the remarkable scene and sang a *Te Deum* on the steps of the building. The Archbishops of Canterbury and York, and several bishops, were at the open-air service 'in rich copes, with their crosiers, the Archbishop of Canterbury and the Bishop of London each holding a very fine one'; and when the 'Old Hundredth' was sung the vast crowd joined in.[16] They then sang 'God Save the Queen', after which the Archbishop of Canterbury, 'departing from the prescriptions of etiquette, called for three cheers for the Queen, and had an enthusiastic response from the entire assembly.' As the procession moved on to the Mansion House, where the Lady Mayoress presented the Queen with a silver basket of orchids, *The Times's* reporter noted that 'never in the long course of its history did the City look gayer or more picturesque than yesterday.'

Such pomp was next witnessed when the Queen was buried on 2 February 1901; she had died at Osborne on 22 January. A show such as never before seen at a monarch's obsequies was felt to be obligatory. The

Victorian cult of death had full expression as the presiding spirit of the British nineteenth century went to her grave. Lady Battersea, Lord Rothschild's daughter and wife of a Liberal politician and property developer, described the atmosphere: 'Black, mourning London, black, mourning England, black, mourning Empire . . . the emptiness of the great city without the feeling of the Queen's living presence in her Empire, and the sensation of universal change haunted me more than any other sensations.'[17]

The obsequies were marked, as *The Times*'s correspondent observed, by 'every circumstance of public ceremonial . . . in accordance with the wishes of the Queen'.[18] She had been conscious of the importance of her own dignity as monarch being represented to her mourning people, and wanted her funeral to project the grandeur of her realm and empire. 'From the moment when the gleam of the white pall and the flash of the golden Crown were seen at the doors of Osborne to that in which her late Majesty's style and titles were proclaimed in St George's Chapel, Windsor, and the stirring prayer "God Save the King" was heard for the first time for two generations from the altar steps of St George's Chapel . . . it was a ceremony of sorrowful splendour from beginning to end.'

As the Queen's mortal remains sailed from the Isle of Wight to Gosport 'a thunder of cannon . . . seemed unending'. A 'mighty fleet' lined up to salute her along the eight miles of the crossing, stretching, it seemed, 'into infinity', 'emblems and instruments alike of her Empire and dominion'. Foreign ships lined up too in salute, including some from the Navy of her grandson, the Kaiser, in whose arms she had died. The coffin was borne through London 'in solemn pomp . . . followed by a train of mourners, Royal and representative, of unprecedented volume and splendour . . . significant of the vast extent of the Empire.' The service was 'of unexampled dignity and beauty'. At Osborne, in London and at Windsor, the Army and Navy were in massed formations. Military bands played sombre marches by Chopin and Beethoven, and pipe bands played laments. The State Crown and a smaller crown lay on cushions at either end of the coffin, with two orbs and a sceptre.

A train brought the coffin from Gosport to Victoria, whence it processed to Paddington via the Mall, St James's, Piccadilly and Marble Arch. Around 32,000 soldiers lined the route; those in the procession wore full dress uniform and decorations, led by their commander-in-chief, Earl Roberts. When the coffin reached the funeral train it was placed on an 'imposing catafalque' in a carriage 'draped in purple and ornamented with white satin rosettes . . . broad purple stripes divided the walls into panels, crowned with a purple garland and held by white rosettes and ribbons.'[19] In Windsor 'the houses were shrouded in purple hangings. The people were clad in the profoundest black.' Life Guardsmen in shining helmets and scarlet cloaks massed below the castle, punctuating the sea of black. There were judges in full-bottomed wigs and robes, heralds in playing-card costumes and Garter knights in robes and decorations.

Only once did the ceremony threaten to come unstuck. A horse pulling the gun carriage carrying the Queen's coffin reared and could not be brought under control. The procession stopped; the King, the Kaiser and the Duke of Connaught, walking behind the gun carriage, waited for calm. In the end all the horses were removed, and bluejackets from the naval guard of honour moved in, picked up the harnesses and used them to pull the carriage. A new tradition was born. As *The Times* put it: 'The honour of drawing the carriage bearing the coffin of the Queen who held sway over the greatest Navy the world has ever seen had, by a rare accident, fallen to the representatives of the service which holds so large a part in the affections of all who own the British name.'[20] The procession was deemed 'the most memorable spectacle in the lives of all who had beheld it.'

By the time of the Coronation of the new King, postponed from June to August 1902 because of his succumbing to appendicitis, the public were not only used to massive displays of pomp, but expected them, and expected the world to be watching. The King was devoted to pageantry and show, and this essential part of the tone of Edwardian Britain took its lead from him. So aware was he of the value of ceremony that, for the first time since Prince Albert's death, he revived the State Procession to open parliament. 'The State coach was exhumed and done up, and the famous cream-coloured horses from Hanover were exercised and drilled to get them into condition,' wrote Sir Lionel Cust, Surveyor and Keeper of the King's Pictures, and a Gentleman Usher.[21] He took part in several such occasions and said that 'each time I felt the same thrill as we entered the House of Lords with its massed robes and uniforms, and the bevies of ladies in diamonds and Court dresses in the galleries above.'[22] The spectacle was awesome, and deliberately so, projecting majesty and imperial power: but Cust found the ride to and from Westminster from Buckingham Palace in an antique coach so boring – the seats were set so far back one could not easily see out of the window – that he and his fellow courtiers played a rubber of bridge *en route*.

III

A feature of the era was that an idea of beauty and grandeur was often found in the design of everyday objects, especially those issued by the state. It was the good fortune of George William de Saulles – chief engraver to the Royal Mint when Edward VII ascended the Throne – not to have designed the Golden Jubilee silver and gold coinage of Queen Victoria minted in the years immediately after 1887. It was roundly criticised, mainly for Sir Edgar Boehm's portrait of the Queen on the obverse. Her Majesty had been depicted flatteringly on the coinage of her youth, designed by William Wyon, as a lovely young girl out of Jane Austen. In her middle years she had been depicted on the copper coinage as a stately but handsomely romantic figure – the famous 'bun' pennies, halfpennies and farthings, that Wyon's son Leonard designed in 1860. However, in Boehm's Jubilee coinage – which *The Times*, with its usual obsequiousness, had described as 'modelled from life . . . lifelike and dignified, the Queen appears crowned and veiled' – she looked sour, chinless and porcine, her over-sized head made all the more glaring by a crown several sizes too small being perched upon it, above a bizarre flowing head-dress.[23]

The Queen was then sixty-eight and not even in the first flush of middle age. Compared with photographs of her at this period the engraving is honest and lifelike, both in physiognomy and demeanour. However, her popularity among her people having recovered considerably by 1887, there was an outcry at this less than idealised representation, and the controversy echoed down the years. Cartoonists seized upon the ridiculous crown about to topple off her head. There had been a long traffic between Boehm, the Mint and Windsor Castle about the effigy, with everyone proclaiming himself unhappy: it recalled the controversy in the 1860s over Marochetti's statue of Prince Albert on the Albert Memorial, resolved only by Marochetti's sudden death and the recommissioning of the statue.[24] This time fate did not intervene, and the effigy circulated on coins for years.

The coins appeared on the day the Golden Jubilee was publicly marked, 21 June 1887, and *The Times* published the first salvo against them a month later, in a letter to the editor. 'The feeblest and most ill-executed specimens of coinage ever sent out from a national mint, except at periods of extreme decadence or distress', proclaimed the writer, Edward J. Poynter.[25] He wanted 'a more simply-treated portrait of Her Majesty without the accessories' – the ridiculous crown, and veil. Poynter added – in case anyone had missed the point – that 'the crying evil is the portrait of the Queen. Here something must be done.' Historians are denied insight into how Boehm felt, because almost all of his papers were destroyed after his sudden death in December 1890, in his studio in the Fulham Road in the presence of his 'pupil' Princess Louise, the Queen's daughter. Rumours of a sexual relationship between the two have never been proved and, in the light of the destruction of Boehm's papers, probably never will be.

Shortly after the Queen's death Evelyn Cecil, a Unionist MP, asked Sir Michael Hicks Beach, Chancellor of the Exchequer and Master of the Mint, whether in view of the 'widespread condemnation of the portrait of Queen Victoria on the coinage first used in 1887, he has satisfied himself that the designing of the new coinage has been entrusted to the best possible artistic workmanship'.[26] Hicks Beach replied that 'the task of designing the effigy of His Majesty on the new coinage has been entrusted to Mr de Saulles, the engraver to the Mint. I think the coinage of 1887 is a warning against entrusting this work to an artist unaccustomed to coinage and engraving.' Cecil fretted about the designs for the reverses of the new coinage, declaring himself pleased with those on the copper coinage since 1895, when the 'bun' coinage had been superseded, and on the silver coinage since 1893, when the Jubilee designs were ended. Hicks Beach promised that 'the whole question of the designs for the new coinage is receiving my careful attention. I do not, as at present advised, think that it will be found desirable to introduce many changes in the present designs on the reverses.'

Yet fortunately for de Saulles, and for the coinage, some of those designs did change. It was announced on 11 December 1901 that the gold and bronze coinage would remain unchanged, as would the silver threepenny and sixpenny coins; but the shilling, florin and half-crown were redesigned to project both the fluidity and grace of de Saulles's expertise, and the peak of imperial, swaggering self-confidence in the

Edwardian age: for the prosaic reason, as Hicks Beach had said on 12 March, that the florin and the half-crown needed to look more distinct from each other. They were close in size and in the last Victorian silver coinage had each borne reverses of heraldic shields. There was a campaign for a decimal coinage – Anthony Trollope had made it the obsession of Plantagenet Palliser in his political novels thirty years earlier – but Balfour had ruled: 'I do not think the country is prepared for any fundamental change such as [that]'.[27] The contentious issue resolved, the design of the new coinage could proceed.

There was great public interest in it, not least because of a widespread feeling that the coinage should reflect national pride. A reader wrote to *The Times* on 28 February to demand that a ship be used on the reverse of some of the coins, following a precedent followed for 300 years from the time of Edward III. 'It would', wrote R. L. Kenyon from his club in Pall Mall, 'represent our connexion with our colonies, the extension of our commerce, the foundation of our strength.'[28] He added that such a design would 'beautify our coins and be a recognition of our colonial empire.'

De Saulles had become Engraver to the Mint in 1893, aged just thirty-one, on the death of Leonard Wyon. His grandfather was Swiss-French and his father a Birmingham glass merchant. Despite this there was criticism of his being commissioned to design King Edward's coinage because he was – the ill-informed critics contended – a foreigner. No less a figure than Alfred Gilbert, Britain's most fashionable sculptor, rushed to his defence, demanding 'fair play' not least because 'art knows no nationality.'[29] In his teens de Saulles trained at the Birmingham School of Art, before being apprenticed to a die-sinker. He began his career as a commercial artist designing labels. In 1884 he secured a post with John Pinches, the medallist and die-engraver, in London. Having learned the art of medalling, he returned to Birmingham in 1888 to work for Joseph Moore, another medallist. The Royal Mint engaged him on the advice of Sir Thomas Brock in 1892, and having seen his work appointed him its chief engraver. It was a demanding job, in an era when the Mint made not only the British coinage – usually redesigned only once in a generation – but also that of many colonies. De Saulles designed the copper coinage for British East Africa and for British Honduras, as well as some of the Indian coinage, and designed and engraved medals.

His first big commission was to engrave dies for the new silver coinage of Queen Victoria in 1893, using designs by Brock. De Saulles's idiom was different from Brock's, and his own coinage designed eight years later would be radically so; however, de Saulles had his first chance with British coinage in 1895, redesigning the reverse of the copper coinage. Replacing Wyon's Amazonian Britannia was a slimmer, more elegant and girlish figure in light, flowing robes. The double florin, or four-shilling piece, introduced uniquely into the Jubilee coinage, had been deeply unpopular because of its similarity in size to the crown, causing incautious shopkeepers to give a shilling too much change, and unlucky shoppers frequently to be swindled of a shilling. The decision to alter the designs of the shilling, florin and half-crown, and the pressing need to ensure the denominations of coins were clearly displayed, gave de Saulles his opportunity to create perhaps the most beautiful coinage in British history.[30]

It was believed that Oscar Roty, the French medallist who designed in the Art Nouveau style and was most noted for the figure of *La Semeuse*, used on French coins and stamps for decades, had influenced de Saulles; also Roty's friend and fellow initiator of the Art Nouveau movement, Jules-Clément Chaplain. Whatever influence these medallists had on de Saulles, the idiom of Art Nouveau, with its fluidity and lack of restraint, was an integral part of Edwardian design in everyday objects, and redolent of the self-confidence and opulence of the era. The engraving of St George slaying the dragon, by Benedetto Pistrucci, first used on the gold coinage of George III in 1817, also inspired de Saulles. At the end of Victoria's reign it was used on the crown as well as on the half-sovereign, sovereign, double-sovereign and five-pound piece.

De Saulles went to Marlborough House on 21 February 1901, a month after the accession, and the King sat for him while the engraver made sketches of the Royal profile. A further sitting took place on 6 June. On 13 January 1902 a Proclamation in the King's name described de Saulles's new coinage. His effigy of the King was on all the obverses. On the reverses, the half-crown showed 'the Ensigns Armorial of the United Kingdom contained in a shield surmounted by the Royal Crown and surrounded by the Garter bearing the motto "Honi Soit Qui Mal y Pense" '; the florin 'the figure of Britannia standing upon the prow of a vessel, her right hand grasping a trident, and her left resting on a shield'; and the shilling 'Our Royal Crest, with the date of the year placed across the Crest'.[31]

The descriptions do not do justice to the designs de Saulles produced. The coat of arms on the half-crown bursts out of the Garter that surrounds it, and threatens to overflow from the coin itself. The font of the lettering is spare, clear and sharp, shorn of High Victorian ornament. On the florin, the figure of Britannia standing – she had always previously been seated – creates an impression of motion: the figure is at the front of her ship, her robes filled with the wind and billowing around and behind her. She, too, bursts from her frame towards the clear line of the edge of the coin. On the shilling, the Royal lion surmounts the Crown. It is a vigorous, arrogant, powerful living beast, and the Crown is sumptuously bejewelled.

Only a nation in its pomp could contemplate a coinage such as this. Its opulence and extravagance were utterly appropriate to the public's sense of self-worth. With de Saulles's coinage, the idea of swagger was inculcated into society, through everyone's pocket or purse. The coinage brought beauty and aesthetics into everyday life. There was nothing token about this currency: the gold coins were gold and the silver ones silver (after the Great War the silver content would be halved; after the Second World War it would be zero). The designs reflected, most fundamentally, the preciousness of the metal they adorned.

De Saulles designed, modelled and engraved his own work, and when he died suddenly in 1903, aged only forty-one, his friends and fellow artists attributed it to overwork undermining an already weak constitution. By then the Edwardian silver coinage was in its second year of minting, and no one wrote to the papers attacking it. De Saulles's idea that an object such as a coin could be a thing of great beauty caught on quickly: more care was taken over the presentation of everything, from the design of shop-fronts to advertisements, from steam engines to sweet-tins.

The new aesthetics also influenced stamp design, particularly when the philatelist George V took an expert interest in those depicting him. The Australian artist and sculptor Bertram Mackennal, who designed the King's stamps, suggested larger dimensions for high-value items so he could adorn them with a ravishing design of Britannia driving a chariot through the waves, next to the King's head in a crowned and draped wreath. The received impression of George V as a boorish oaf is belied by the consultations he had with Mackennal between September 1910 and March 1911, in order to refine the 'Seahorses' design. The monarch was determined that his stamps should befit the nation over which he reigned; and in doing so, he brought a little grandeur into the lives of everyone who bought a stamp.

IV

Architects in the imperial capital and elsewhere in Britain around the turn of the century found patrons eager for new buildings worthy of the world's greatest power. Men such as Sir Aston Webb (perhaps best known for his sub-Gothic design of the Victoria and Albert Museum in London), J. M. Brydon and William Young led the way during the 1890s, creating a vogue for exuberance in architecture that the Great War killed off. Edwardian baroque (or English renaissance) was in part embraced as a reaction against the Gothic, and all it represented about the Victorian age. There was also a perceived link between classicism and opulence at a time of ostentation. Some architects, mainly in provincial practices, but including Edwin Lutyens (who came late to the grand style), carried on building in this way until the 1920s when, like much of the Edwardian legacy, it looked pompous and reactionary. However debased it became as it outstayed its welcome, its first flowering was magnificent, and visually exemplified the Belle Époque and Edwardian style. The Architectural Association's *Notes* recorded in 1898 that 'the possibilities of the style seem infinite . . . who can say that it will not lead to what must be the desire of us all, namely the formulating of a truly English twentieth-century progressive architecture?'[32]

In late-Victorian domestic architecture there was a fashion, in grander houses, for a pastiche of the Queen Anne style. The late-seventeenth and eighteenth centuries inspired Edwardian public buildings: and so was born Edwardian baroque. Wren, Vanbrugh and the architects of the great French chateaux and public buildings of the eighteenth century were major influences. The new buildings' grandeur resided not merely in their ornaments and mouldings. The introduction of steel frames meant they could be built higher and, to maintain proportions, wider. The great Edwardian palaces along London's Millbank, Whitehall, Piccadilly and in the City, are memorials to the wealth of the age. In Whitehall designs such as Young's War Office (begun in 1898) fit in well with the Banqueting Hall, Inigo Jones's masterpiece, having the same Italianate features: columns, domes, lavishly cut arches over windows and doors, pediments, rusticated stonework, *oeil-de-boeuf* windows, richly varied rooftops and chimneys. Brydon's Treasury building on the corner of Parliament Square, built between 1898 and 1912, complements Scott's Foreign Office of forty years earlier.[33] They were also adorned with lavish statuary, which made the Edwardian era a golden age for sculptors. Steel-framed buildings also allowed for much larger windows, and encouraged the evolution from ornate stone edifices to plainer, more utilitarian styles.

Edwardian baroque was not confined to London, its greatest showcase. Manchester had several examples, notably Lancaster House, but also great warehouses such as Asia House and India House. Belfast's City Hall was built in the style; so too the Bristol Museum and Art Gallery, the Liver Building at Liverpool, and the Port of Liverpool Building. The Liver Building, by Walter Aubrey Thomas, was started in 1908 and finished in 1911. It was the first building in Britain made of reinforced concrete; it has the grandeur and some of the ornamentation of Edwardian baroque without the finesse. The Cunard Building on Liverpool's waterfront – the third of the 'Three Graces', begun just before the war began in 1914 – is more authentically baroque, also built of reinforced concrete but embellished with Portland stone flourishes as well as with richly detailed sculptures. Smaller provincial towns also embraced the style: one of the grandest and most ornate baroque revival buildings is John Belcher's Colchester Town Hall, begun in 1897. In Scotland, architects such as Charles Rennie Mackintosh built on a similarly grand scale, though in a more idiosyncratic style that in some ways anticipated modernism.

In London, such buildings and their settings conform with the Edwardians' idea of an imperial capital, the scale and the style of the new streetscape summoning up ideas of the avenues of Vienna, the Unter den Linden in Berlin and the Champs-Élysées in Paris. The most famous introduction of the Edwardian era was the façade of Buckingham Palace, built by Sir Aston Webb in just three months in the summer of 1913, in what *The Buildings of England* calls 'a tasteful but insipid performance in the Louis XVI manner', thus completing John Nash's work of a century earlier and turning a house into a palace.[34] The newly embellished building was the climax of a ceremonial route that ran from Trafalgar Square through the neo-baroque glory of Admiralty Arch (completed a year earlier), along the Mall (lined with the most ornate lamp-posts in London, decorated with little galleons) to the Queen

Victoria Memorial, ending at the Palace itself. The re-fronting was paid for by public subscription, and the money left over built the Victoria Memorial.

The massive monument to the late Queen outside the Palace proclaimed national pride even more than Webb's great façade. Sir Thomas Brock, who conceived the decorated lamp-posts in the Mall, designed it. It took eighteen years – from 1906 to 1924 – to finish. Even in that era of bombast it took a friend at Court to argue for a memorial on so lavish a scale, and that friend was Esher, Secretary to the Office of Works, who had the ear of the King on all matters. Esher's regard for the image of Britain was almost as great as his regard for himself. He had little difficulty in persuading the Sovereign that to honour his late mother in this magnificent way would not merely appeal to the masses who had cheered her at her last jubilee, but would boost Britain's standing.

Brock had proved his credentials when, aged just twenty-seven, he had been commissioned to complete the great statue of Prince Albert on the Albert Memorial after the death of the sculptor J. H. Foley, whose pupil he had been.[35] Having come to the attention of the Royal family he had been asked to make statues of the Queen at both her jubilees; but his work was known to all because, as previously noted, he had designed the veiled head of the Queen on her last coinage. The Victoria Memorial is almost as elaborate as that to her Consort, with Webb filling in the architectural details as Sir George Gilbert Scott had done in Kensington. It was made from 2,300 tons of white Carrara marble (the statues) and Pentelic marble (the plinth). The Queen, enthroned, sits looking down the Mall: above her, 80 feet up, is a gilded winged Victory with Courage and Constancy by her feet, and below, around the Queen, are Charity, Truth and Justice. As at the Albert Memorial, there are classical friezes and bronze groups representing abstracts such as peace, progress, the arts and manufacture. All this was set in a circus, or public space, adorned by much statuary. Through this baroque revival Britain had found its trumpet, and was blowing it.

At the other end of the ceremonial route, Admiralty Arch proclaimed something fundamental to Edwardian *amour propre*: British naval power. Webb had designed this, too, between 1905 and 1907, and it was built at Edward VII's request in stone in 1908–11 as part of the national commemoration of Queen Victoria. The iron gates in the three arches were the largest in Britain; and Brock provided suitable statuary to represent Navigation and Gunnery. The arch's rusticated stone, lavish pediments and pavilioned roofs exemplified the neo-baroque, and the building is, if anything, a finer and more original expression of its grandeur than even Webb's façade at the Palace or the Memorial before it.

Edwardian baroque buildings went up all over prime sites in the capital, transforming its aspects. Parliament Square, for instance, was newly adorned by Methodist Central Hall, an example of the most uncompromising baroque revival, built by Edwin Rickards between 1905 and 1911. In partnership with Henry Vaughan Lanchester he had just built City Hall in Cardiff, a lavishly baroque extravaganza, and the more modest but still Italianate Cardiff Law Courts. What they put in Parliament Square – described by *The Buildings of England* as being 'in a surprisingly worldly Viennese style' and looking as though 'it might almost be a very substantially built *kursaal*' (a public recreation room in a European spa) – was radical in size, ornament and style for a location confronting Westminster Abbey and the Neo-Gothic of the Parliament buildings.[36] It transformed the architectural nature of a vital part of London.

A series of palaces posing as office blocks went up on Millbank, on the south side of the Abbey. From 1903 to 1906 William Caroe, who specialised in Gothic Revival churches, built the almost incomprehensible headquarters for the Church Commissioners, its roofs and windows baroque, its material red brick dressed with stone, its rampant asymmetricality making it resemble a half-finished Loire chateau. Next to it, in stone, more regularly baroque with an ornate cupola among the pavilions on the roof and bedecked with ornament, is the office block built for the Crown Agents, begun in 1912; adjoining it a tobacco company headquarters, begun in 1913, is even mightier because of its steel frame, and even more decorated. The private sector adopted the majestic idea of the architecture of grandeur just as much as the state did, and thus made its contribution to the transformation of the face and scale of London.

This was just as apparent in two other localities: in the City of London, where bankers and merchants displayed their wealth, and in the West End, where richly-wrought theatres and palatial hotels served an increasingly affluent middle- and upper-middle-class clientele, in keeping with the tone of the grand imperial city London had become. In the City, a programme began in the late 1890s of building larger and more palatial premises for financial institutions. The first exercise in this was in Finsbury Circus, by the Great Eastern Railway's terminus at Liverpool Street, where the expiry of numerous residential leases in the 1890s allowed a large area of land to be bought up and developed. Salisbury House, completed in 1901, was the first City building to include lifts. There was no sense of restraint among either clients or architects. Electra House in Moorgate, completed in 1903, deploys what *The Buildings of England* calls 'the full artillery of domes and decorative sculpture . . . to bombastic effect.'[37]

More restrained was the new Central Criminal Court – the Old Bailey – built between 1900 and 1907 on the site of Newgate prison. Edward William Mountford, who had specialised hitherto in town halls and other small institutions, won a competition to design it. The cupola and small dome that crown the building echo the authentic baroque of St Paul's, just up Ludgate Hill, but owe more to the Royal Naval Hospital at Greenwich; the Court's ornamentation and sculpture reach their climax with the gilded figure of Justice holding aloft her scales, projecting the idea of British justice to the world. Pediments, friezes, rustication and pilasters all suggest the majesty of the law: not a uniquely Edwardian concept, but one that this building helpfully institutionalises.

A great international city needed up-to-date amenities for visitors, and ones whose grandeur created the right impression. John James Burnet was knighted in 1914 on completing his Edward VII Galleries at the British Museum, an imposing and monumental stone building with a frontage of high windows amid towering Ionic columns. Edwardian baroque also lent itself to hotels, department stores and theatres. The impresario Richard D'Oyly Carte, the great patron of Gilbert and Sullivan, built the Savoy Theatre in 1881, and less than a decade later decided to complement it with a hotel to rival any in the world: it was the first entirely lit by electricity and contained seventy bathrooms.

The Savoy impressed by its size, but in 1906, after three years of building, the Ritz opened on Piccadilly and impressed by its design as well – it was the largest modern building yet seen in London. Pevsner calls it 'frankly Parisian', and its version of the baroque – an importation of the Beaux Arts style – evokes the Rue de Rivoli or the Place des Vosges, not least in the way César Ritz was allowed to build over the pavement, creating an arcade under his hotel.[38] Its architects, Charles Mewès (a Parisian) and Arthur Davis, thus introduced Beaux Arts architecture to

London: two years later they would start building the less French, but outstandingly baroque, Royal Automobile Club on Pall Mall. Waring and Gillow were hired for the Ritz's interior design, which was pure Louis XVI. And further east along Piccadilly, built from 1905 to 1908, is the Piccadilly Hotel, designed by Richard Norman Shaw in his Late Baroque style, heavily gabled and rusticated.

To the north, Oxford Street was by the Great War dotted with great baroque emporia, much of it grand if ordinary, but with occasional great statements of Edwardian wealth and grandeur: an imposing Doric-columned building of 1906–8 for Mappin and Webb, for instance, and the former Waring and Gillow building of 1901–6 in what Pevsner calls 'riotous Hampton Court Baroque', in which Shaw also had a hand.[39] Oxford Street's baroque jewel was, however, Selfridge's, begun in 1908 for the Chicago retailer, Gordon Selfridge. Taking up a whole block of the West End, his mighty store – without precedent in London – combined Ionic classicism with vast areas of plate glass, the better to display the goods. Cast-iron panels to conceal the steel framing, by the engineer who had built the Ritz, punctuate the walls. Daniel Burnham, an American architect, was largely responsible, his Parisian training obvious in the style of the decorations. The building was not finished until after the war, but it began, and was completed, as a statement of Belle Époque ambition.

As drama increased in popularity, so new theatres appeared all over London's West End. Many theatres of ancient lineage – dating back to the golden age of comedy after the Restoration and in the eighteenth century – were drastically improved to comply with modern regulations after some disastrous fires in theatres around the world in the 1890s. Several fine examples were built in St Martin's Lane – the Coliseum in 1902–4, the Duke of York's in 1891–2 and the Albery in 1902–3. Most had sumptuous French baroque interior decoration, Waring and Gillow undertaking the Albery as they would later do the Ritz. With other theatres opening in the Charing Cross Road in the 1890s and 1900, the approaches to Trafalgar Square were at last elevated to a grandeur echoing the triumphal mood of the times: the Mall, Pall Mall and Whitehall had come first, with Northumberland Avenue filled by stone-faced buildings during the 1870s and 1880s by order of the then Metropolitan Board of Works. That Northumberland House, the grandest Jacobean palace left in London, had been flattened to provide this expression of late-Victorian vanity reminds one that beneath the façade of swagger there was often a philistinism and arrogance that had yet to work themselves out. They would eventually do so in near-apocalyptic circumstances.

V

The calculated ostentation of commercial and public buildings in this period complemented a similar quality in the personal appearance of those wishing to make an impression on society. Dress in late-Victorian and Edwardian England signified rank and, among the middle and lower classes in particular, was a barometer of respectability. No office boy would go out without a hat. Poor dress was seen as a mark of degeneracy and destitution. The rich, however, took the question of clothing to a sometimes absurd extreme. They often changed clothes several times a day, especially when in London. Unlike their inferiors, they had no need to use clothes to advertise their propriety, but rather dressed according to the minutely calibrated rules of their caste. Women's finery was never finer; but stealing the show were the dandies, who used clothes as a personal advertisement and in a spirit of competition.

The rules of how the ruling class dressed were strictly enforced, and the ultimate arbiter from the time when he set up his Court at Marlborough House in the 1860s until his death in 1910 was Edward VII. His otherwise unpretentious son, George V, whose happiest moments were spent shooting game or mounting stamps in his albums, was if anything even harder in his strictures about dress. Nor did this fetish die with the Great War: when in the 1920s an emergency cabinet meeting was called for a bank holiday, the King was horrified to see a picture in the paper of Lord Birkenhead sauntering into Downing Street in a tweed suit and a soft hat, and told the offender so.

What Edward VII, as King and Prince of Wales, said about dress had the force of iron law: his son agreed and never wavered from that law until he died in 1936. That men to this day leave the bottom button undone on a waistcoat was one of Edward VII's initiatives, designed to assist his ever-expanding stomach. He also popularised the dinner jacket, when on his trip to India in 1876 he dined in one on board HMS *Serapis*, but this was only used *en famille* on informal occasions. When a junior Guards officer arrived at the Marlborough Club wearing one and not a tailcoat, the Prince, after staring at him with disgust, said: 'I suppose, my young friend, you are going to a costume ball.'[40]

He supposedly invented the turned-up trouser 'after rolling up his trouser bottoms to walk through fields'.[41] He, like his son after him, was swift to rebuke anyone who forgot any of the multiplicity of rules, most of which were arbitrary. When a private secretary, Fritz Ponsonby, visited an exhibition in a morning coat, the King said: 'I thought everyone must know that a short jacket is always worn with a silk hat at a private view in the morning?'[42] That may have been an example of his sense of humour, which relied on humiliating those who could not answer back. When he saw Lord Rossmore wearing an unsatisfactory hat at Epsom, he asked: 'Well, Rossmore, have you come ratting?'[43] Noting a picture of the Kaiser, in full dress uniform, greeting Queen Victoria, whose private secretaries General Ponsonby and Colonel Bigge were in frock coats and silk hats, the Prince telegraphed her to say: 'I see you were attended by Bishop Ponsonby and Dean Bigge.'[44]

In his obsession with clothing Edward VII lacked a sense of proportion in a way that now seems ridiculous, but which terrified his posse of sycophants who lived, it seemed, mainly to win his approval. Conscious of his status, he dressed to reflect it, and expected those who aspired to his society to follow his rules and thus convey an impression of dignity and grandeur to those outside the charmed circle. Austen Chamberlain once overheard him, while in Scotland, say to his valet '*un costume un peu plus écossais demain*', as if there were gradations of Englishness or Scottishness the monarch had to reflect in his dress.[45] The Earl of Rosebery once dared to attend one of the King's evening parties in trousers rather than knee-breeches, which caused the King to ask whether he was part of the suite of the American Ambassador. Such remarks betray an idea of dress as tribal, and as a means not merely of differentiation from other tribes, but of reflecting an imagined superiority over them. At this height of British power, appearances were very much everything.

Even the King, however, could not override public opinion. His notion that knee-breeches should be worn with evening dress did not catch on. Nor did his fad of having his trousers creased at the sides: even for him, that fashion passed. Having invented the smoking jacket, Edward VII (and his circle) permitted this ensemble only at the most informal evenings in. Most dinners required the uniform of evening tailcoat, white waistcoat, white tie and white gloves, particularly when there were ladies present. If a gentleman dined out, or attended the theatre or opera, a black cloak and silk hat would complete the outfit. Those who dressed any differently were regarded as clearly indicating their membership of a lower class, so rigid were the tribal rules, and such was the importance of conformity.

Edward VII and George V had such clout when it came to dictating what they considered 'proper' dress because of their rank, and especially because of the sycophantic and eager-to-please social circle around the former. The last battle George V fought and almost entirely lost was to maintain the frock coat, a requisite of formal wear since the early nineteenth century, and *de rigueur* for statesmen and the governing class until the Great War. It was steadily supplanted by the more informal morning coat, which was cut away from the waist in almost a diagonal to the tail behind, rather than each half of the coat finishing in a squared-off skirt above the knee.

Victorian society too had its share of dandies. One of the first had been Disraeli, who made his maiden speech in the Commons in 1837 wearing a bottle-green tailcoat (he was, perhaps for other reasons, howled down) but progressed by the 1860s through a black velvet morning coat to a more conventional frock coat. Such men led changes in fashion against mounting conformity – they would include Oscar Wilde, Max Beerbohm and Aubrey Beardsley, all high representatives of decadence. Wilde's biographer cites a letter he wrote aged thirteen, in 1867, expressing dandyish sentiments and praising his scarlet and lilac shirts and a heliotrope tie.[46] Wilde's dandyism then was about expressing his personality; later he used it to swagger, to announce that he had 'arrived'. On his first visit to America in 1882 (when he is alleged to have said he had nothing to declare except his genius), *The New York Times* recorded the spectacle he presented while meeting Lillie Langtry – sometime mistress of the Prince of Wales, and with whom he was on 'my dear Lil' terms – off a ship from England: 'He was dressed as probably no grown man in the world was ever dressed before. His hat was of brown cloth not less than six inches high; his coat was of black velvet; his overcoat was of green cloth, heavily trimmed with fur; his trousers matched his hat; his tie was gaudy and his shirtfront very open, displaying a large expanse of manly chest. A pair of brown cloth gloves and several pimples on his chin completed his toilet.'[47]

After having set out to shock America he then became 'elaborately decorous': though would adorn tribal dress, such as white tie in the evenings, with diamond jewellery.[48] In 1891 Wilde wrote to the editor of *The Daily Telegraph* about men's dress, exercising himself on the subject of buttons: 'We all have more than a dozen useless buttons on our evening coats, and by always keeping them black and of the same colour as the rest of the costume we prevent them being in any way beautiful. Now, when a thing is useless it should be made beautiful, otherwise it has no reason for existing at all . . . the handsome effect produced by servants' liveries is almost entirely due to the buttons they wear.'[49]

The dandyism of politicians – who were the film stars of their day, the subject matter of most cartoons and of fawning social columnists – was by the 1880s and 1890s more conservative than Disraeli's. Joseph Chamberlain, conscious he was a self-made man and a Non-conformist, dressed according to his wealth rather than his notional station; but limited his dandyism to his use of a monocle, and an orchid buttonhole on the silk-faced lapel of his well-cut frock coat. The affectation of the orchid was not prompted by any desire to be showy; Chamberlain loved the flowers, collected varieties of them, and grew them in a hothouse at Highbury Hall, his late-Gothic Revival pile in the suburbs of Birmingham.

Lord Randolph Churchill was flashier, as a duke's son had every right to be, his brightly coloured waistcoats defying the sombre dress code of his colleagues and offsetting his striking physical appearance, which his friend and biographer Rosebery described thus: 'slim and boyish figure, his moustache which had an emotion of its own, his round protruding eye . . .'[50] Some colleagues, annoyed by his trademark bumptiousness and arrogance, considered him overdressed. Another biographer notes that 'he frequently wore a dark blue frock coat, his shirts were coloured, and he wore an exceptional amount of jewellery for a man, noticeably a large ring in the shape of a Maltese cross set with diamonds, one of his wife's gifts to him. He smoked cigarettes heavily, and used a holder with a single diamond in it . . . he appeared to be a young man likely to be more at home in the stalls of the Gaiety than in the councils of the State.'[51]

Even though King Christian IX of Denmark arrived at the Duke of York's wedding in 1893 in a morning coat – which presumably horrified the groom, his grandson and the future George V – the frock coat remained *de rigueur* in the most formal society until the Great War. No minister would attend Buckingham Palace in anything else, unless the occasion were so elevated as to require the full Court dress of tunic and knee-breeches with buckled shoes. Edward VII, while Prince of Wales, had expressed astonishment to the Marquess of Salisbury, when the then prime minister attended upon the Queen wearing the tunic of the privy counsellor's uniform with the trousers of an Elder Brother of Trinity House. The prime minister explained his valet was away, at which the Prince expressed further astonishment that Salisbury had not noticed the error himself. He replied that 'it was a dark morning and I am afraid at the moment my mind must have been occupied by some subject of less importance.'[52] Lady Salisbury remarked that this incident 'nearly caused the death of the Heir to the Crown from consternation.'

The professional classes moved from the frock coat to the morning coat in the 1880s, and by 1900 it was normal wear – with a black silk top hat – for anyone of quality on business in London or in other major cities. Even at the height of summer and on the hottest day the Quality were expected to wear a silk hat and morning coat: when Arthur Lee – a Tory MP, retired army officer and diplomat, and so not from below the salt – was elected to the Hurlingham Club in 1908 he resigned after only one visit, the other members shocked to see him on a boiling day wearing a panama hat and flannel suit while they dressed as if for Ascot.

The middle classes, unless they had pretensions, wore the increasingly ubiquitous lounge suit, which would supersede the morning coat. For the Edwardian dandy the frock coat, however beleaguered, remained the garment of choice, with its silk-faced lapels. Some morning coats had piping around their edges, and the dandy could choose from a range of striped or checked trousers: no dandy would contemplate a lounge suit. It was not until 1926 that George V wore a morning coat, not a frock coat, to the Chelsea Flower Show: by which time even the well-to-do were in lounge suits.

King George was small in stature, and fine clothing helped him project the princely and, later, kingly image necessary. While a devotee of the frock coat long after it had passed from fashion, he would wear grey in the summer – such as at Ascot – and popularised the grey top hat. He followed his father's rules: 'His trousers were creased down the side, his overcoats generally long, his gloves ribbed in black. He pulled his ties through a ring rather than knot them, and kept them in place by a jewelled pin. He preferred boots to shoes and invariably carried a stick.'[53]

While opening parliament in 1911 he was annoyed to see that Viscount Morley, the Lord President and, in his eighth decade, one of the Liberals' elder statesmen, was wearing a frock coat and not privy counsellor's uniform, even though he went to some lengths to close his viscount's robe around him so his solecism might remain unnoticed. A peeress who attended in a hat rather than a tiara received an official rebuke from the Lord Great Chamberlain and was made to write 'a humble apology' to the King, which was accepted.[54] The main victims of his obsession with dress would, however, be his sons, who were on the receiving end of streams of rebukes about wrong clothing or any innovation that corrupted the Edwardian standard: it would be one of the many causes of estrangement between the King and his heir, who would briefly be Edward VIII and who on his accession in 1936 would abolish the requirement to wear a frock coat at Court.

The idea late-Victorian and Edwardian high society had of itself – of its splendour and grandeur – was captured in a genre of portraits that symbolise the era. Sir Joshua Reynolds, over a century earlier, had described the grand style used in portraiture to capture status and nobility, but it was never such a cult as during the Belle Époque. In this era portraits usually showed full-length studies of their subjects, which allowed them to display fine clothing and strike masterful poses. The prime exponent of the genre was John Singer Sargent, an American born in Florence in 1856, who trained in Paris before moving to London. He had embarked on portraiture in 1884 in Paris with his full-length *Portrait of Madame X* (Madame Pierre Gautreau), depicted in a black dress that not only accentuates her waist but is cut so low that it reveals her shoulders and much of her bust. The picture shocked Paris, and work dried up for Sargent there. He thought of giving up painting, but instead headed to London.

For just over twenty years, until he closed his studio largely out of boredom, he was Britain's leading portrait painter; his swagger portraits defined the historical image of the moneyed classes of the era. He was not the only prominent artist to work in this genre – Sir Luke Fildes's portrait of Edward VII in his Coronation robes is the *ne plus ultra* of swagger portraits, and Sir John Lavery's depictions of grand women in their finery are in Sargent's league. Although he remained a master of the portraiture of beautiful women – such as in *Lady Agnew of Lochnaw*, painted in 1892, or *Mrs Waldorf Astor*, from 1909, her bare shoulders and sculptured hair miraculously lit against a black background that displays the sumptuousness of her white dress – it is through his male subjects that Sargent best captures High Edwardian style. When he painted his fellow artist W. Graham Robertson in 1894, the young Robertson insisted on being painted leaning on a malacca cane – a typically insouciant pose – in his fine, ankle-length, fur-collared coat, even though he was painted at the height of summer, showing the link between dandyism and swagger.

Colonel (later General Sir) Ian Hamilton, painted in 1898, stares haughtily out to one side, his huge greatcoat open just enough to reveal the scarlet dress tunic beneath complete with frogging, sash and medals. Joseph Chamberlain, painted two years earlier, leans on a pile of official papers while staring at the painter, his monocle betrayed by just the slightest glint, his orchid the only splash of colour between his high starched collar and the flash of cuff under his long, black frock coat. Lord Russell of Killowen, the Lord Chief Justice, painted in 1899, embodies the full majesty of the law in his scarlet, black and ermine robes, his full-bottomed wig and chain of office. Lord Londonderry, carrying the Great Sword of State at the 1902 Coronation, a riot of scarlet, gold and ermine, shows an expression of almost terrified seriousness to the artist, but is otherwise a monument to aristocratic grandeur. Painted two years later Sir Frank Swettenham, the first Resident-General of the Federated Malay States, clothed in tropical uniform, his sword at his side and with his gold-embellished pith helmet beside him, leans on plushly upholstered furniture draped with silk of red and gold, exuding proconsular might. Earl Roberts, his bright-buttoned greatcoat hanging casually from his right shoulder, in full dress uniform, gilded, besashed, bestarred and bemedalled until his tunic is almost invisible, stares fiercely from his portrait, his field marshal's baton jutting priapically forward and his right leg raised as if on a mounting block. Understated by comparison is the Duke of Connaught, the King's brother, in black dress uniform alleviated by the gold aiguillettes of his tunic and the sash about his waist, leaning on his sword and with the opposing hand on his hip.

The peak of Sargent's portraiture is his 1902 painting of Lord Ribblesdale, a tall, elegant and supremely aristocratic figure just in from the hunting field. The peer wears a calf-length black coat, pinned back behind his right hand thrust in a trouser pocket. He is leaning his weight on his right foot with his left at right-angles to it, both encased in highly polished boots. Ribblesdale is a tall, slim figure, his voluminous breeches and waistcoat hanging loosely on him, a black stock emphasising his aquiline face crowned by a silk hat at a rakish angle. A gloved hand holds a riding crop; his expression is one of disdain verging upon boredom. He is swagger personified.

VI

By coincidence, the English Musical Renaissance, which provided the first domestic composers of international rank since the death of Purcell in 1695, coincided with this heady era of pomp and ostentation, and some of its composers consciously reflected it in their works. Elgar wrote what later generations considered to be the background music to Edwardian swagger. He met his perfect match in a nation fixated on ceremony, tradition (mostly of recent provenance) and ritual as a means of expressing its power and self-belief; and that now required a music of ceremonial to illustrate them. In much of his work between 1901 and 1914 his idiom is self-consciously grand; and while he composed to display his great talents, and to make a living, he also pursued a mission to write music that reflected the culture of the greatest nation, with the greatest empire. He was intensely patriotic, loved pageantry and ceremonial, and loved what such rituals said about England.

The son of a Worcester music-shop proprietor, Elgar struggled at first in a land with no recent tradition of great composers. He began by conducting the orchestra at the county lunatic asylum, and giving music lessons. He married an older woman – a pupil – for love, but because she was a general's daughter, and he the son of a tradesman, the match outraged her family. It was not until the mid-1890s that he began to secure performances of his works; and it was only with the debut of the *Enigma Variations* on 19 June 1899 that Elgar's reputation took off, and he began to prove his detractors wrong. He was fortunate to be a composer of great gifts at a time when, at last, there was a keen demand for English music.

Yet Elgar was not simply a composer who depicted in music the times in which he lived. He was acutely spiritual – his most famous oratorio, *The Dream of Gerontius*, the setting of words by Cardinal Newman, was premiered in 1900: there would be other similar works and, although fired by his Catholicism, they gained huge popularity in a mainly

Protestant culture. He was also highly emotional, forming platonically intense attachments to women, such as the anonymous dedicatee of his Violin Concerto of 1910, for whom the superscription to the score reads, in Spanish, 'Herein is enshrined the soul of . . .' However even that concerto, unequivocally a personal rather than a state work, has from its opening bars the grandeur of tone present in those Elgarian works designed to represent the dignity, importance and majesty of the Edwardian imperial moment – or, as the composer (quoting Shakespeare) put it, the pomp and circumstance of the era. He had a talent for writing music that was either explicitly ceremonial – such as his *Pomp and Circumstance* marches, *Coronation Ode* or *Crown of India* suite – or that could lend itself to ceremony. 'Nimrod', from the *Enigma Variations*, was after the Great War appropriated to reflect the tragedy and loss of the hecatomb of men who never came back.

The marches of that title – four written between 1901/2 and 1907 – have become synonymous with swagger, even though Elgar protested that he merely wanted to show that the ordinary quick march played by bands could be made into an orchestral work. Even without words – tacked on later by A. C. Benson when the first march was adapted into the *Coronation Ode* for the 1902 ceremony – the tune thereafter known as 'Land of Hope and Glory' reflected imperial might, and Elgar knew it: not just because of the name he gave the marches, but because of his conviction that its intrinsic appeal and its connection to the prevailing public mood and sense of national identity would, as he put it in May 1901 to his friend Dora Powell – 'Dorabella' of the *Enigma Variations* – 'knock 'em – knock 'em flat'.[55] When Edward VII (who in 1904 would knight Elgar) congratulated him on the tune later in 1901 – it was premiered on 22 October – Elgar professed to have been carrying it about for twenty years, which shows how innovative he was, and how painfully long his genius had had to wait to be recognised. By 1901, the time was right. August Jaeger, Elgar's publisher, told him the reception constituted 'the greatest success I have ever witnessed over a novelty at a concert.'[56]

By the time of his First Symphony, in 1908, the public mood had become more entrenched and more expectant of the music of grandeur, and audiences loved what they heard. It was far from being the first English symphony – Parry had written four by then, greatly influenced by Brahms, and there was a minor tradition going back to William Boyce in the mid-eighteenth century – but this was the first great symphonic work in that imperial–national idiom Elgar had made his own, one far removed from the inspiration of folk song that drove on his younger brethren such as Vaughan Williams, Holst and Butterworth. By any standards the First Symphony was a masterpiece, and the public saw this at once. It had 100 performances within two years and its stateliness, exuberance, lyricism and, at the very end, triumph, endeared it to audiences. Its ending, when the theme that opened the symphony in understated, serene and stately tones that Elgar marked *nobilmente* returns in a state of glory, struck listeners as an affirmation of life. Elgar described the work as representing 'massive hope in the future' – and almost victory.[57] For the composer, who until the age of forty had only scraped a living and whose talent had been doubted by almost everyone apart from his wife, it was a very personal victory indeed; but his Edwardian music speaks too of the victory of an ideal, and of a great imperial nation.

Elgar inspired the Edwardians not just because he wrote tunes echoing their self-belief, but because his countrymen were proud to have a composer of note again – among his champions was Hans Richter, a Hungarian and one of Europe's leading conductors. It was yet another field where Britain had fought, and prevailed. Forster captured the mood in *Howards End*, when Aunt Juley tries to persuade her German relative, Herr Liesecke, to stay at a concert to hear a *Pomp and Circumstance* march; but her niece, infected with the snobbery that places foreign above British music, says it will not be worth hearing. Juley rebukes her for 'undoing all my work. I am so anxious for him to hear what we are doing in music. Oh, you mustn't run down our English composers, Margaret!'[58]

Elgar's identification with the embodiment of the imperial nation – King Edward himself – had always been strong, and he felt no cynicism about the imperial project, about his national identity or about Britain's place in the world. He was sketching his Second Symphony when, on the morning of 7 May 1910, he heard that the King – not merely his Sovereign but to a great extent his patron and inspiration – had died the previous evening. The swagger in the first movement is muted; the second movement becomes a funeral march for the King, to whose memory the symphony was dedicated. Lady Elgar, looking at the score of the movement in February 1911, just as her husband finished it, called it a 'lament for King Edward'.[59] Whatever Edward VII's failings he had, for

Elgar, embodied what the composer saw as the proper spirit of England – noble, grand, generous, opulent, exciting and inspiring – and the composer was stricken by his death. This new mood of reflection, when the work was first performed on 24 May 1911 in a London preparing for George V's Coronation, dismayed an audience longing for imperial swagger. Elgar said of them: 'They sit there like a lot of stuffed pigs'.[60] The new King's award of the Order of Merit a month later, on the eve of the Coronation, was some consolation.

The sense of swagger in his music did not die with the King – it was back in his symphonic study *Falstaff* of 1913 – but it became inhibited, as if Elgar, more than some in other fields of art, realises the moment has passed, and more than just a king has died. Elgar's influence is apparent in the first movement of Vaughan Williams's *London Symphony* of 1914 – quite unlike the bucolic idiom in which the younger composer wrote at that time, but immediately evocative of the magnificence of the Edwardian city – but that work, too, becomes subdued and almost mournful by its close. When war came Elgar's creativity was depleted, and he found the business of composition a struggle after the death of his wife in 1920, just as he had completed his introspective and almost tragic Cello Concerto. The great imperial adventure had inspired him, in Worcestershire and in London, every bit as much as it had Rhodes or Baden-Powell in Africa, or Curzon in India. Once Edward VII went the personal inspiration to write swagger music declined, and the war killed it.

VII

The obsession with show; the importance of the pose; the decline of the spiritual and the rise of the material; an undue concentration of wealth among a privileged few, many of whose new recruits lacked the philanthropic impulse of an earlier generation – all these provided the stuff of the moral, intellectual and industrial decline that made this an age of decadence. The mid-Victorians had worked relentlessly; had been motivated by religion to acts of philanthropy; had striven to improve the lot of the poor; had transformed Britain's infrastructure, radicalised its education system, reformed its institutions and expanded its empire. But after 1880, until the apocalypse came in 1914, there was among the upper and upper-middle classes a resting on laurels; a decision, literal and metaphorical, to live off dividends rather than work that little bit harder, and improve more. Religion retreated further; the maintenance of appearances brought with it hypocrisy; standards of public conduct and private behaviour returned to where they had been in the eighteenth century, only this time were confronted by enduring Victorian censure. Decay began with the highest in the land and was imitated by the rising middle class. Britain's industrial performance slipped behind first Germany, then America. As its enemies, within and without, sensed its power and its resolve waning, they sought to take advantage. Though still recognised as an awesome power, its cracks were showing; though it had avoided revolution, its common people were increasingly angry and politically motivated; though blessed with the world's most powerful navy, its confidence was sapped by fears of a German invasion for more than a decade before the largely accidental outbreak of the Great War; though called a United Kingdom, a substantial part of it wished to break away. Britain learned, by the first decade of the twentieth century, that being a great power meant inviting rivals and challenges, and with them insecurities.

The change in the British way of life over the thirty-five or so years preceding 1914 was staggering. At the opening of his 1880 novel *The Portrait of a Lady*, Henry James – an American who had made Britain his adoptive home – depicts the ideal, serene existence of the upper-middle class at the height of Victorian self-assurance, on the cusp of that period of growing prosperity and refinement known in Europe as the Belle Époque:

> Under certain circumstances there are few hours in life more agreeable than the hour dedicated to the ceremony known as afternoon tea. There are circumstances in which, whether you partake of the tea or not . . . the situation is in itself delightful . . . The implements of the little feast had been disposed upon the lawn of an old English country-house, in what I should call the perfect middle of a splendid summer afternoon. Part of the afternoon had waned, but much of it was left, and what was left was of the finest and rarest quality. Real dusk would not arrive for many hours; but the flood of summer light had begun to ebb, the air had grown mellow, the shadows were long upon the smooth, dense turf. They lengthened slowly, however, and the scene expressed that sense of leisure still to come which is perhaps the chief source of one's

> enjoyment of such a scene at such an hour. From five o'clock to eight is on certain occasions a little eternity; but on such an occasion as this the interval could be only an eternity of pleasure.[61]

Of the 35,026,108 souls recorded as living in Great Britain and Ireland at the time of the 1881 census only a small fraction knew the 'eternity of pleasure' James described: despite rising living standards and an expanding middle class, wealth was concentrated in the hands of an alarmingly small group. Not least as a result of that, the status quo was under assault: economically, politically, socially and culturally. This is the other side of the myth of late-Victorian and Edwardian self-assurance.

People had been forced to live with tumultuous change ever since the Industrial Revolution, but its tempo was increasing. In 1906 Arnold Bennett, in *Whom God Hath Joined*, described the new, urbanised, bustling Britain: 'Railway stations, institutes, temples, colleges, grave-yards, parks, baths, workshops, theatres, concerts, cafés, pawnshops, emporiums, private bars, unmentioned haunts, courts of justice, banks, clubs, libraries, thrift societies, auction rooms, telephone exchanges, post offices, marriage registries, municipal buildings'.[62] Some of these pre-dated the Belle Époque; all proliferated in it as the population boomed, social mobility created a bigger middle class, and a more demanding populace required and made an infrastructure to exploit the fruits of modernity.

As technology changed people changed, not least because of society's acceptance that to capitalise on the industrial potential of new technologies and processes, workers had to be better educated. The growth of the middle class was one of the great consequences of this programme: but so too were the rise of the Labour movement, the women's suffrage campaign, the pursuit of Irish Home Rule, the demand for an embryonic welfare state, the rise of the popular press, and a revolution in morals that led to more protection for young women and children (though the upper classes became more licentious). Although the Belle Époque is seen as an age of refinement, elegance and order, it was in fact an age of upheaval, radical change and relentless challenges to the social order.

A sense of the speed with which the world moved on between 1880 and 1914 is given by H. G. Wells in his 1909 novel *Tono-Bungay*. 'Only thirty years ago it was,' he wrote, 'and I remember I learnt of the electric light as an expensive, impracticable toy, the telephone as a curiosity, electric traction as a practical absurdity. There was no argon, no radium, no phagocytes – at least to my knowledge, and aluminium was a dear infrequent metal. The fastest ships in the world went then at nineteen knots, and no-one but a lunatic here and there ever thought it possible that men might fly.'[63]

A big agricultural depression further stimulated the growth of an urban society: between 1870 and 1911 2,500,000 acres of land went out of cereal production, with East Anglia being hit exceptionally hard.[64] The population in rural Britain became markedly older on average than that in the towns and cities. The birth rate fell as contraception was more widely practised. In towns, not only did the numbers employed in manufacturing, transport and mining rise sharply, but so too did those in white-collar work, such as management, administration and retailing. The chain store and the department store were born in this age, with big independent department stores opening in baroque palaces, and it saw the start of national retailing chains such as Lipton's the tea merchant, Boots the chemist and Burton's the tailor. The public sector also boosted white-collar employment. There were four times as many government employees in 1914 as in 1870, thanks partly to the growth of state education, but also the rise of local government after 1888.[65]

The growth of industry and a worldwide boom in trade led to the expansion of the City of London, whose manpower had already increased by 67 per cent in the 1870s alone to 363,000 people. London was not merely financing the business of Britain, but also of much of the world. And it was the heart of a great empire and, at the start of the period, of the greatest world power, all of which had a profound effect on British self-confidence and attitudes.

Many trappings of modern life appeared in the decades before the Great War. The first telephone network in Europe, the Telephone Company in London, had opened in 1878, three years after Bell invented the device in America. Other providers opened and amalgamated throughout the 1880s and 1890s. The Post Office took over trunk lines after the 1892 and 1896 Telegraph Acts, government realising the telephone was a strategic resource. Another Act of 1899 allowed municipalities to set up telephone systems. The Post Office took over the National Telephone Company on 1 January 1912, gaining 561,708 subscribers.[66] As well as being wired to the telephone, Britain was being electrified. Godalming was the first town to be illuminated by electric light, on 26 September 1881. A fortnight later the

Savoy Theatre in London became the first public place on earth to be lit electrically. The 1882 Electric Lighting Act allowed local authorities or private companies to set up power supply networks, and power stations began to be built.

There was a technological revolution in transport. Karl Benz patented his first motor-car in January 1886: it is believed the first vehicle was imported to Britain in 1895, providing a stimulus for British engineers and designers to produce their own. By 1904 there were 8,465 motor-cars on British roads, but by 1914 there were 132,000, including taxi cabs: on 22 March 1907 metered taxis had begun operating in London. Horse-drawn buses disappeared in the late 1880s, replaced first by trams. Motor buses appeared in 1898: there were 5,000 by 1904 and 50,000 by 1914.[67] The railway network grew by 50 per cent between 1870 and 1912, mainly because of rural and suburban lines as cities grew and commuting became commonplace.[68] Trains became faster, slashing journey times between Britain's cities: on 9 May 1904 the locomotive 'City of Truro' went over 100 m.p.h. on the Great Western Railway.

The Underground also expanded: on 4 November 1890 the first deep-level tube – part of the Northern line – opened between the City and south London. However it was not until 4 October 1911 that the Underground had its first escalators, at Earls Court. Glasgow opened the first phase of its Metro on 14 December 1896. Local authorities, led by the London County Council (LCC), began to alleviate the pressure on inner cities by building public housing along rail and tram routes. As well as having to cope with motorised traffic, pedestrians also had to deal with bicycles, allowed on roads from July 1888 provided they had bells: Michelin patented the rubber tyre in 1891. The arrival of personal locomotion brought with it risks. Henry Lindfield of Brighton was the first man to die in a car crash on the public highway, when his electric car ran down a hill in Purley and hit a tree on 12 February 1898. The first man killed in a petrol-driven car, Edwin Sewell, died at Harrow on 25 February 1899; his passenger, Major James Richer, followed three days later.

In these years the ordinary lives of the United Kingdom's rapidly growing population – by 1911 there were 45,370,530 people in Britain and Ireland, an increase of over 10 million in thirty years – changed in countless other ways. A great taboo was challenged when the first cremation took place in Britain, of Jeanette Pickersgill at Woking on 26 March 1885. The massive population growth, whose visible consequences were the suburban cemeteries sprawling over the outskirts of London and other towns, made this form of disposal of the dead inevitable, however much many of the living objected to its supposedly heathen associations. The arrival from Australia of the first frozen meat in the winter of 1880 changed both the public's diet and the lives of British farmers, forced to compete as never before. Aspirin was introduced in 1897, supplanting the quack medicines so popular in the nineteenth century.

The invention of recorded sound by Thomas Edison in 1877 led to the arrival of gramophones in the houses of the well-to-do by the turn of the century and, as they became cheaper, into those of the middle classes before the Great War. Voices from history could be captured, changing perspectives on the past for successive generations. Edison made recordings of Gladstone in 1888 and Tennyson, reading 'The Charge of the Light Brigade', in 1890, immortalising the voices of men born six years before Waterloo. Both Asquith and Lloyd George recorded defences of the highly controversial People's Budget of 1909, allowing them to speak to a wider public. Film, similarly, brought great events before the eyes of the general public: Edison opened the first motion picture studio, in New Jersey, in February 1893, and by the turn of the century British audiences were in cinemas watching great events such as the Diamond Jubilee and Edward VII's Coronation procession.

Modernity showed itself in the further mechanisation of armaments, which would have such a devastating effect in the Great War. The Army had used the Maxim gun since the late 1880s but upgraded to the Vickers machine gun in November 1912. Earlier that year, on 13 April, just over eight years after the Wright brothers' first manned flight at Kitty Hawk, four years after the first flight in England (by the Wild West showman Samuel Cody, over Farnborough) and less than three years after Louis Blériot crossed the English Channel by aeroplane, the Royal Flying Corps was formed. Eighteen months later, on 16 October 1913, the Royal Navy's first oil-fired battleship was launched.

Yet for all the greater efficiency of killing machines, people were living longer. Medical science was slowly conquering disease, improved sanitation and better diet produced healthier people, fewer women and children died in childbirth, and anaesthesia had helped widen the range of treatments for hitherto terminal illnesses. On 9 February 1912 *The Times* reported evidence of longevity among the upper-middle classes, at least. 'The notices of death in *The Times* of today include those of 13 persons whose average age was 87 years. Nine were between 80 and 90, and four were 90 and over.'[69]

Such were the radical changes in the everyday existences of the people of the British Isles in the thirty-five years or so before the Great War. This book will describe not just the great political debates and crises that shaped the country in which they lived, but also the changes in culture, attitudes and society that made Britain on the eve of war in July 1914 a very different land from that at the beginning of Mr Gladstone's second administration in April 1880. Prosperity had taken greater hold, but not for all, despite the beginnings of welfarism. The people acquired more power but so, paradoxically, did the state: the tension between the two, in a world being shrunk by technological progress at the same time as its possibilities were becoming ever more infinite, is not the least of the themes of what follows.

PART I

THE WORLD OF THE LATE VICTORIANS

CHAPTER I

THE DECLINE OF THE PALLISERS

I

The power of the aristocracy faded steadily after 1832, when the Reform Act ended its near-monopoly of parliament. The repeal of the Corn Laws in 1846 undermined its wealth. The Industrial Revolution created a class of businessmen whose riches, thanks not least to the growth of free trade, matched or exceeded those of many landed families, and who used them to challenge the aristocracy's political clout and breach its social bastions – the world described in the 1860s and 1870s by Anthony Trollope in his Palliser novels. An agricultural depression from 1873, lasting over twenty years, hit the pockets of the landed classes, though the hardship they felt was nothing compared with their tenants'. Nonetheless, in the early 1890s they retained much of their heft. A few owned vast swathes of the Kingdom – even by 1906 it was estimated that just 882,460 people (out of a population of around 40 million) owned 87 per cent of private property.[1] Aristocrats dominated the House of Commons; the Lords still had a veto over the Commons's wishes, and exercised it in all except Treasury matters. The Church, the judiciary, the magistracy, the Armed Forces and the professions were all dominated by the well-to-do, with 'new money' only slowly gaining a foothold.

Liberalism had broken the landed classes' stranglehold on the Army and the civil service, weakened the Protestant, largely English Ascendancy in Ireland, and opened up Oxford and Cambridge to those who wished to teach in them but would not sign the Church of England's Thirty-nine Articles. After Gladstone retired, a Liberal administration forced the rich to pay more towards the upkeep of the country. Some aristocrats, feeling poor, hunted moneyed American brides; at least 300 such women married into landed families between 1870 and 1914.[2] Social mobility caused numerous old estates to change hands, passing from families who had held them for centuries to the newly rich, especially after the introduction of death duties in 1894. In tandem, the aristocracy became popularly perceived as immoral after scandals embroiled the Prince of Wales, the Duke of Clarence, Sir Charles Dilke, Lord Alfred Douglas and Lord Arthur Somerset.

The enduring reputation of the 1890s is that of a 'naughty' era, an idea popularised in the contemporary music halls and given credence by the louche behaviour of the upper classes. It was the decade of decadence, an idea imported – as it was felt most morally undermining things were – from France, where louche behaviour appeared in certain sections of society to be *de rigueur,* to the envy of many in England where a subtle revolt against Victorian values was starting. By the time Edward VII succeeded in 1901, high society increasingly followed the King's example in taking a flexible view of marriage: a mistress became an indispensable accessory to a man of good breeding, and the *grande horizontale* a feature of high society. At the same time the strong moral code of the new middle class, with its Protestant work ethic, adherence to scripture and rigid sense of propriety, acted as a bulwark against the further spread of decadence, whatever the depravities of the upper and working classes.

The Jack the Ripper murders of 1888 revealed the usually unmentioned and unmentionable proliferation of prostitution, another hobby the highest and lowest classes had in common. A year later the Cleveland Street scandal exposed to public scrutiny something even more shocking to Victorian society, the homosexual underworld, an aspect of society even less visible than prostitution. Hypocrisy on these and other matters seemed rife. Generational tensions – exemplified by those between the Queen and her heir – were often fierce, as those born in the last decades of the century rebelled against the orthodox Victorian morality of their parents. As the aristocracy declined it neglected and ignored ideas of *noblesse oblige* that had fascinated Disraeli and his acolytes. The example the ruling class set became questionable. So began the class tensions that would lead to much unrest before the Great War.

II

William Ewart Gladstone's second administration remained dominated by the traditional governing class, despite mercantile interlopers such as Joseph Chamberlain and John Bright. Gladstone spent the morning of Saturday 24 April 1880 – the first of his second term as prime minister – finishing a memorandum about his audience of Queen Victoria at Windsor the previous day. He was in his seventy-first year, but this would be 'a long day of incessant work' on which, having written his account of kissing hands with a sovereign who did not want him as her prime minister, he saw cabinet colleagues, Liberal party grandees, and wrote in his own hand several letters.[3] That evening the Prince of Wales, who liked him, visited. Gladstone believed he would serve a year or two, rectifying the mistakes (mainly in foreign policy) of the outgoing government, before retiring to enjoy what remained of his old age. Events, and the insistence of colleagues that he stay as a unifying and commanding figure in Liberalism, holding the ring between Whigs and radicals, would wreck this plan.

Domestic reforms had dominated his first premiership, from 1868 to 1874. However, Disraeli's aggrandisement of Britain's empire (he had made the Queen Empress of India in 1876), the scramble for Africa and the need to defend these possessions, meant imperial affairs would assume far greater significance than hitherto. Gladstone rejected the expansionist, imperialist ideas of some of his contemporaries. Nor did he fret about other European powers expanding in regions such as Africa where Britain had already established a presence.

The balance of power in Europe, which had *pro tempore* been settled by the Congress of Berlin in 1878, would be a constant worry, as would the intentions of Russia towards British India. Having made his political comeback not least because of his indignation at barbarism towards Christian minorities in the Ottoman Empire, Gladstone fretted about the instability of Eastern Europe and the Near East. Unrest in Egypt was a powerful distraction because the Suez Canal, opened in 1869, had now become of such strategic importance by shortening the route to India.

Foreign and imperial policy dominated the first cabinet meeting, on 3 May 1880, as did discussion of legislation to pacify Ireland through land and franchise reform: the Irish question would soon come to overwhelm government business. Gladstone exercised caution in his choice of colleagues. He was one of a cabinet of fourteen: of the others, seven were Whigs. Bright, now like Gladstone in his seventies, was no longer the man who had campaigned successfully against the Corn Laws and the Crimean War and for extending the franchise. W. E. Forster, radical in Gladstone's first administration, joined the second as a brooding conservative: a cast of mind his experience as Chief Secretary for Ireland would deepen.

In a cabinet led by a former Tory and populated by Whigs with old money, the only active radical was Chamberlain, in his second parliament as MP for Birmingham, who became President of the Board of Trade: partly because of his success as mayor of his city, but partly because of his role as leader of the radical faction. Although rich from his career as a screw-maker (he had retired in 1874, aged thirty-eight, taking a £100,000 dividend), Chamberlain was a man of the people. His Non-conformism – he was a Unitarian – gave him a considerable electoral base in an industrial area where such religious affiliations were important. He and his associates dominated the National Liberal Federation, founded in 1877, which had played a significant role in propelling Gladstone into Downing Street. The Queen, who hated radicals because she believed they were targeting the Throne, regarded him as 'especially most dangerous'.[4]

Gladstone hoped to buy Chamberlain's compliance by binding him under collective cabinet responsibility, which would require constant monitoring. Before long, his team became known as 'the Cabinet of Incompatibles'.[5] The tensions incompatibility would create, coupled with troubles at home and abroad, meant the legislative and reforming momentum of Gladstone's second administration would never match that of his first. A nation greater in terms of wealth, reach, human capital and influence had experienced a parallel growth in responsibilities and burdens.

Life was altering because of the speed of technological change; this in turn fuelled pressure for social change, forcing government to respond. Growing literacy increased political awareness. Newspapers could communicate ideas rapidly, and radicals could cohere more easily, because of the printed word and ease of rail travel. Wealth was spreading and a new middle class growing up. The world Gladstone had to manage in 1880 was markedly different from that of 1874. As he told Lord Kimberley, the Colonial Secretary, on his first day back, he knew he faced an 'arduous task'.[6]

Yet Gladstone never allowed this, even at what for the nineteenth century was a great age, to sap his intellectual curiosity, nor the vigour with which he exercised it. After long days of political activity, whether in the Commons, dealing face-to-face with colleagues, writing letters to countless correspondents, propitiating ambassadors, dining with great hostesses at their salons, or simply managing the petulance and spite of the Queen, he would refresh himself by reading – the classics, theology, politics or culture – before sleep. This titanic appetite would not diminish until the end of his days in office.

Gladstone had to accommodate men such as the Marquess of Hartington, heir to the dukedom of Devonshire and India Secretary, and other aristocratic Whigs whose attitudes and way of life differed little from those of the landed families who controlled the Tory party. That was led, since Disraeli's defeat, by the Marquess of Salisbury, an arch-Conservative and head of a family that had served the country since Elizabeth I, who wanted as little change as possible. At the far end of Gladstone's party were extreme radicals, levelling Non-conformists compared with whom even such free-thinkers as Bright looked conservative. Gladstone told Chamberlain, on offering him office: 'Your political opinions may on some points go rather beyond what I may call the general measure of the Government; but I hope and believe there can be no practical impediment on this score to your acceptance of my proposal.'[7] When the cabinet ranking was settled Chamberlain was twelfth: the broad church only went so far.

His main radical associate, Sir Charles Dilke, a capable but louche baronet who had aggrieved the Queen in the 1870s by espousing republicanism, was allowed to be under-secretary at the Foreign Office, but only after writing a grovelling apology to Her Majesty explaining himself for his conduct while, as she put it, 'young and foolish' – and provided 'Sir Charles Dilke would not be brought into any contact with me.'[8] Dilke would climb higher, only to see his career dashed on a scandal caused by alleged sexual incontinence: which in retrospect set the tone for an age of decadence distinct from the godly earnestness of the mid-century.

Partly because of Gladstone's earlier reforms, which Disraeli had built upon, the state had grown. Gladstone was determined to rein in public spending and keep taxation low. He took direct charge, appointing himself Chancellor and serving until the burdens of his two high offices overcame him in 1882, when he handed the Treasury over to Hugh

Childers, the Secretary for War. On appointing A. J. Mundella (whom the Queen considered 'one of the most violent Radicals') to be Vice-President of the Board of Education, Gladstone stressed the 'enormous' cost of schools; and warned him this money would not inevitably be well spent.[9] 'I hope you will think it is the duty of the official man representing the department to make vigilant enquiry not only into any augmentation, but into wasteful charges which may have crept in, and into charges also which having been originally necessary may have become needless and therefore wasteful.' There would be further reform, in education and elsewhere: but the emphasis would shift towards management.

There was no clear agenda for domestic policy, other than developing the electoral reform started in 1832 and continued, in panic and opportunism, by Derby and Disraeli in 1867. Their Reform Act had dealt with the new urban masses; the county franchise, affecting their rural cousins, awaited parliament's attention. The spread of education and the growth of trades unions had ensured that the unfranchised working man was informed about precisely what he was being denied, and an expanding working-class movement, mainly urban-based, agitated for him. Most Liberals and even some Tories felt it was inequitable that agricultural workers and the poorest urban-dwellers should be denied the vote; one or two feared insurrection if they were not offered a say in running the country. It was also clear to the Liberals that the raised expectations that social and technological progress had fostered required attention, not least by modernising, and democratising, the medieval framework of local government.

Gladstone's sense of divine motivation drove him. At the opening of parliament on 20 May 1880 he recalled that 'it almost overpowered me as I thought by what deep and hidden agencies I have been brought back into the midst of the vortex of political action and contention.'[10] God, he felt, had given him strength to go on in his eighth decade: 'Looking calmly over this course of experience I do believe that the Almighty has employed me for His purposes in a manner larger or more special than before, and has strengthened me and led me on accordingly, though I must not forget the admirable saying of Hooker that evil ministers of good things are like torches, a light to others, waste and destruction to themselves.'

Gladstone had a reputation for vigour: his recreation was chopping down trees. However, within three months of taking office a fever felled him. On 30 July 1880 he was 'seized with chill and nausea'. By the next day his 'nerves and muscular system' were afflicted and, despite its being the height of summer, he felt intensely cold: 'I had been for three-quarters of an hour not shivering but shaking as a house is shaken by an earthquake.' His wife cancelled a cabinet meeting and sent him to bed, where he spent the next week, his temperature up to 103, with 'strong and prolonged perspirations'. When able to resume his diary he admitted that on his second day in bed 'I thought of the end';[11] Mrs Gladstone read to him from the *Book of Common Prayer*. Had he died the course of British history would have been much changed. He did not take this debilitating illness as a warning to slow down.

The Queen, by early 1881, wrote off her government as 'poor' and fretted about the contents of the speech to be delivered in her name at the opening of the new session in January. Beaconsfield (as Disraeli became when elevated to an earldom in 1876), with towering impropriety, told her that a dictum of Sir William Harcourt, the Home Secretary, that she must read out whatever her ministers wished, was 'only a piece of Parliamentary gossip'.[12] He said she must consider the speech before formally approving it, and there was room for a 'degree of resistance' if she was unhappy. She was placated, and no controversy resulted. The next two sessions were so dominated by Ireland that much remained undone. The public also became more concerned about foreign policy, and not just in the Empire. When the Russo-Turkish War of 1877–8 threatened to drag Britain in, a music-hall song contained the chorus:

We don't want to fight but by Jingo if we do
We've got the ships, we've got the men, we've got the money too.
We've fought the Bear before, and while we're Britons true
The Russians shall not have Constantinople.[13]

A side-effect of jingoism was that it made the masses absurdly proud of their country as a great imperial and military power (it was certainly the former; the latter was debatable). However, the public was easily upset if their government lacked aggression and self-assertion in maintaining that status. This view was shaken by the Second Boer War of 1899–1902, but it still helped fill recruiting stations for Kitchener's Army in 1914.

In Palmerston's day foreign policy was simpler, and more autocratic: by the 1880s it had to take a back seat to domestic considerations, which helps explain some of the miscalculations of that decade, notably the disastrous response to General Gordon's expedition to Khartoum. In a Britain agitating for a third Reform Act, the simplicities by which an elite acted with the permission of a slightly wider elite were consigned to history; the strain of governing was greater than ever, and democracy was to blame. In terms of influence, the main casualty of this new emphasis on the needs of an electorate was the aristocracy.

III

Gladstone's impulse was to further the democratic trend. The government's most important measures were the Representation of the People Act 1884, and the Redistribution of Seats Act 1885, which complemented it. George Otto Trevelyan, who in 1882 became Secretary of State for Ireland, had as an opposition MP proposed franchise reform in 1876. He argued that the right of working-class men to vote, confined under the 1867 Act to those living in towns and renting or owning property worth £10 a year, should be extended to rural areas. He also argued for a redistribution of seats to provide the new constituencies, creating more in rural areas. Disraeli's administration ignored him, well aware that the Tory dominance of county constituencies would end if agricultural labourers could vote.

Once the Liberals returned the momentum for reform, equalling out the franchise between boroughs and counties, became intense. On 30 March 1883 the Commons debated a uniformity of franchise: extending the £10 property qualification to counties, enfranchising agricultural workers on the same basis as industrial ones. The Tories were deeply opposed: most agricultural labourers worked for Tory landowners, and life was hard: if labourers had the vote it was expected they would cast it for candidates who did not represent their masters. The Tories also feared it would lead to universal suffrage for men and, worse, women. Their fears were summed up by the attitude attributed to Chamberlain, the leading reformer, by his friend and biographer J. L. Garvin: doubling the electorate 'would double the power of Liberalism in the State and make Liberalism synonymous with Radicalism.'[14]

Gladstone contemplated this with equanimity. However Hartington, the Whig heir of Palmerston, viewed reform that impinged upon the landed interest as potentially fatal to the social fabric and, more to the point, of the social order. Chamberlain pressed Gladstone to set up a system of local government, based on county councils, throughout the Kingdom. Hartington, aware of the clout the Cavendishes exercised in Derbyshire and around their estates in County Waterford, found the idea of local democracy outside the cities anathematical, and unthinkable in Ireland. County councils would, paradoxically, be established by Salisbury's Conservative administration later in the 1880s, which came to count Hartington as one of its adherents, after the Liberal split over Home Rule.

Chamberlain – who by 1882 the Queen thought an 'evil genius' – refused to make concessions to party unity, or to Hartington's feelings, in his quest for reform. Gladstone's need to keep the radicals happy meant Chamberlain had great leeway under collective responsibility to voice his views.[15] And when Salisbury, the leader of the opposition, chose to visit Chamberlain's Birmingham fiefdom in March 1883 and to tease him for being a cause of strife within the Liberal party, the provocation was too much. Speaking in the city the next day, at a meeting chaired by the party's rising star the Earl of Rosebery, Chamberlain assailed Salisbury and his views, but also attacked everything Hartington and the Whigs around him held dear. After berating Salisbury for his imperial warmongering, Chamberlain attacked the harshness of Tory policies towards Ireland, making a point relevant to the expansion of democratic rights in Great Britain.

He said that the 'unjust rents' extracted under threat of eviction had been 'extorted' from the 'desperate toil' of the Irish, and continued: 'Lord Salisbury constitutes himself the spokesman of a class – of the class to which he himself belongs, "who toil not neither do they spin".'[16] The report of the speech interpolates the words '[cheers and laughter]'. Chamberlain continued that the fortunes of this class 'as in his case, have originated by grants made in times gone by for the services which courtiers rendered kings [loud cheers] and have since grown and increased while they have slept by levying an increased share on all that other men have done by toil and labour to add to the general wealth and prosperity of the country.'

That one phrase – 'They toil not, neither do they spin' – electrified the public, some of whom regarded it as an incitement. Lord Dartmouth, a friend of Salisbury, wrote to *The Times* to protest that Salisbury had had to truncate a visit to Dartmouth's house because duty had compelled him 'to travel up to London at some personal inconvenience in order to be present this morning at the Hertfordshire Quarter Sessions, of which he is chairman.'[17] The Duke of Argyll, writing from the toil of Cannes, described the remark as 'an illiberal attack upon the whole class to which he [Salisbury] belongs', and called the allusions to the source of Salisbury's wealth 'invidious and unjust'.[18] Argyll had served with Gladstone in various administrations since 1852, but had resigned as Lord Privy Seal in 1881 over Ireland. As a representative of the high Whig tendency he would be a constant point of reference for Gladstone during the reform crisis, and a measure of how far policy could go before provoking belligerence from the Tories, with whom Argyll was increasingly in sympathy. Chamberlain had drawn blood, and illustrated the deep divisions marking the discussion of reform.

It was a cry for the greater sharing of power, and wealth, and a naked attack on hereditary privilege. This theme would run through politics until the Great War, and would drive Rosebery's brief administration in 1894–5 to initiate death duties; and once Radical Joe had burned out, felled by a stroke in 1906, the cry was taken up by Lloyd George with equal fervour, and by a Liberal government determined to rein in the hereditary interest and found a welfare state. With this speech Chamberlain confirmed himself in Liberalism as second to Gladstone, which further estranged him from Hartington and fed their enmity: and it signalled the passing of the baton of conscience of the movement from John Bright to Chamberlain. Indeed, when he spoke at a dinner in June 1883 in Birmingham to mark Bright's twenty-five years as an MP for the city, Chamberlain took as his theme, to 'long and tumultuous cheering', the idea that 'every day the country is becoming more Radical and more Democratic.'

He reminded his audience that in 1858 Bright had complained that five out of six adult men had no vote. In 1883, five out of eight still did not. 'This wrong is greatest, of course, in the counties,' he added, saying that only one in seventeen men there could vote. 'There is a vast population of orderly, industrious men who are totally unrepresented,' he continued. 'By a geographical accident they are refused the rights which are conceded to their fellows.' But his demands went beyond rectifying this anomaly: 'We want equal electoral districts [cheers], in order that every vote may have an equal value [hear, hear], and we want, I think, the payment of members [hear, hear], in order that every man who has the capacity to serve his country shall not be excluded for want of means.' He could play his audience like the proverbial violin: 'That is what we want; what we shall get [laughter] is a different matter.'[19]

The Queen, at Balmoral and unwell, delayed her recovery by reading the report of Chamberlain's speech in *The Times*. Sir Henry Ponsonby, her private secretary, wrote to Gladstone. The prime minister had not read the speech until alerted by the Queen's wrath ('my sight does not now allow me to read largely the small type of newspapers'), but told Ponsonby he had now done so 'with deep regret'.[20] Gladstone, used to the Queen rebuking ministers who failed to behave with appropriate deference, sought to defend Chamberlain as one who otherwise had reserves of 'tact and talent'. Chamberlain was instructed to make a speech urgently illustrating his reasonableness, which he attempted at the end of June.

The results were not entirely to Gladstone's satisfaction, for he reminded Chamberlain that 'declarations tending to place [a minister] markedly in advance or in arrear of his colleagues on subjects of high politics, or otherwise delicate, should be made as rarely and reservedly, and if I may so say as reluctantly, as possible.'[21] He specifically warned Chamberlain to conceal his opinions on the 'county suffrage Bill' if he wished any proposal to maintain 'dignity and weight'; and reminded him that he was one of the 'official defenders' of the 'balanced' system under which Britons lived, including 'the rights of the Crown as guaranteed by the constitution'.[22] The Queen took the opportunity to assert her superiority: 'A Cabinet Minister, or indeed any Minister, should not hold such dangerous and improper language . . . The Queen had from the first greatly deprecated Mr Chamberlain's being in the Cabinet, and she must say she thinks her fears have been fully realised.'[23]

Gladstone had signalled support for franchise reform, which would more than double the electorate to 5.5 million men. He asked Sir Henry James, the Attorney-General, to start framing legislation in October 1883.[24] That at least would pacify Chamberlain and his supporters: but Gladstone told his son Herbert that while 'I can, please God, face the suffrage question', he lacked the energy to pursue two other coveted measures 'relating to Local Government in the counties and to a London Municipality.'[25] Keeping Chamberlain sweet was only part of Gladstone's problems; he also had to make sure Hartington kept close, and wrote to him on 22 October that 'the public interests' required action in the following parliamentary session.[26] 'I entertain no doubt that the equalisation of the suffrage is the question of questions for the time . . . it should be the first measure of the season.'

He warned Hartington the measure would fail if it did not embrace Ireland, given the mounting pressure there for Home Rule, and so it would be 'impolitic and inequitable' to leave it out. The question, as he discussed with Trevelyan, was whether to equalise the Irish franchise between counties and boroughs at a lower level than in England, or at the same one. He told Rosebery on 15 November that there would be one bill 'for the three kingdoms, with a heap of Local Government behind it.'[27]

Chamberlain, having been quiet for a few months, chose to speak out on 27 November at a meeting of the National Liberal Federation. Gladstone and Hartington were horrified to read in *The Times* that he had proposed reform in Ireland and a separate measure of redistribution: these matters were being discussed in cabinet and were not common knowledge. The speech also contained, in the words of Eddy Hamilton, Gladstone's private secretary, 'an undercurrent of sneer'.[28] Hearing Chamberlain was about to speak again, Gladstone wrote to him and expressed the 'hope' that 'you will do it with as much reserve on pending and proximate subjects as your conscience will allow.'[29] Chamberlain replied that he thought cabinet had decided to proceed with the Bill, but now realised he was under a misapprehension. The incident was indicative of how different the Liberal cabinet was compared with a decade earlier.

In an attempt to placate Hartington he agreed the NLF speech had been 'provocative', and reminded him the cabinet had decided nothing 'except that if it proceed with the franchise, it will be the franchise alone,' and not to include redistribution in the Bill.[30] Gladstone handled Hartington with deference, aware he was only prime minister because Hartington had turned the post down. 'No other man is in a position resembling that which you hold in the House of Commons,' Gladstone told him, 'for you hold there your commission as Chief, although it is in temporary and accidental abeyance.' Hartington told Gladstone that he, too, thought a decision had been taken at cabinet: but agreed to stay.

Worse would come. Chamberlain, having been prevailed upon to speak positively about the institution of monarchy, then appeared to threaten the House of Lords with unnamed sanctions if they tried to stop a Franchise Bill. Gladstone agreed it would be unwise for the Lords to oppose the will of the people, but the idea of a cabinet minister warning them not to was unpalatable. He told Chamberlain he concurred, but 'it would not have a savoury effect, were I to speak out all I think on that matter.'[31] In addition to his problems with the Irish (see Chapter 5), handling legislation that divided his own party and cabinet was wearing Gladstone down, and he contemplated retirement. This alarmed his colleagues, partly because there was no obvious successor who could unite the Liberals, but also because those who supported him on the franchise wanted him to pilot through the Redistribution Bill. On 1 January 1884 he reassured Lord Derby, the Colonial Secretary and son of the erstwhile prime minister, that he would 'other things permitting . . . remain in the ship with a view to a similar effort for redistribution'.[32]

After Christmas Gladstone consulted James, the Attorney-General, about framing the Bill. On 4 January the cabinet finally agreed a means of proceeding. The separate Redistribution Bill was announced, and it was settled this would best be taken in the session following the reform of the franchise. Gladstone outlined his intention on the first day of the parliamentary session – 5 February 1884 – to bring in a Bill to extend the franchise. The Tories tried to delay its introduction because of war in Egypt and the Sudan (see page 220), which they argued should be the focus of political activity. However, on 28 February Gladstone detailed his Bill, promising it would enfranchise 'capable citizens' such as 'the minor tradesmen of the country, and the skilled labourers and artisans in all the common arts of life'.[33] The Tories had, in 1867, enfranchised the working class in the towns; it made no sense not to do so in the country. And, if the measure entailed some of the 'peasantry' getting the vote, so be it: the consequence would be that the state, and the nation, would be stronger. He also told the House about the Redistribution Bill, which would come separately to avoid the main Bill becoming bogged down, and 'at the earliest date'.[34] If redistribution were part of the main Bill, it would add to the opportunities of reform's opponents to derail it – which is why the Tories argued for a single measure.

Gladstone commended the Bill – the most substantial measure of reform in the nineteenth century – to 'every man favourable to the extension of popular liberty'.[35] The borough franchise would be changed, allowing people with grace-and-favour residences, provided they were householders, to vote as well as freeholders and tenants. This meant that some 'men of high class, who inhabit valuable houses, as the officers of great institutions' would have the vote, rectifying an anomaly.[36] But it also meant that those in tied cottages, or their urban equivalent, would get the vote, enfranchising many of the 'servants of the gentry'. Gladstone termed it 'the service franchise'. The franchise in the counties would operate exactly as in the towns, and as far as possible a similar franchise would operate in Scotland and Ireland. He spoke for an hour and three-quarters, a performance that betrayed no diminution of his intellectual powers in his seventy-fifth year, and judged the reception 'favourable'.[37]

The Conservatives argued that the country had not given the government a mandate to advance this measure at the 1880 election – the only reference to something like it had been Hartington asserting that the existing franchise was 'incomplete'.[38] There were fears, borne out by events, that the reforms as applied to Ireland would cause an overwhelming return of Nationalist MPs, as the newly enfranchised would be preponderantly Catholic supporters of Home Rule: it was suggested that, to protect the rights of the Unionists in Ireland, proportional representation should be adopted there. Gladstone dismissed this: and Charles Stewart Parnell, the Nationalist leader, argued that even if all 103 seats in Ireland returned Nationalists they would still be in a substantial minority in the United Kingdom; and the House of Lords also existed as 'a still further check and safeguard against . . . revolutionary designs'.[39]

The Tories continued their attempt to derail the Bill at second reading. Allowing the Irish to elect Nationalists who were determined to reject England was discussed almost *ad nauseam*. Lord John Manners, son of the Duke of Rutland, said there were 20,000 female farmers in the United Kingdom, and none would qualify for the vote however vast their landholdings and substantial their wealth: yet their labourers, in tied cottages, whose wages these women paid, would – 'every carter, every ploughman, every hedger and ditcher'.[40] There had also been relatively little public interest in the Bill, a point the Tories used to raise doubts about whether there really was, as the Liberals maintained, a strong mandate for it. The main Liberal opponent was George Goschen, fearing a tyranny of an uneducated majority, and indicating the temper that would lead him into the Conservative party and a Unionist government within three years.

The Bill passed its second reading easily, by 340 votes to 210, on 7 April.

Then the trouble started. In committee the Conservatives attempted to introduce a redistribution clause, something that would so complicate the Bill that it would probably fall. Gladstone would not discuss the matter, outraging the Tories. The guillotining of parliamentary debates had been introduced only two years previously, to stop Irish Nationalists using filibusters. Lord Randolph Churchill, the *enfant terrible* of the Tory benches, called Gladstone's obduracy 'the first application, in its most rigid and barbarous form, of the *clôture*'.[41] Churchill asserted that the government secretly intended to postpone redistribution until after the next election: which, if fought with the new franchise on existing boundaries, would allow the Liberals to 'swamp' county constituencies.[42]

Progress was slowed down by events not merely in Ireland, but in Egypt and the Sudan, where British authority was being seriously undermined. The government's majority ensured that the Reform Bill went through the Commons. More radical Liberals, such as Dilke, agitated for a woman franchise, but Gladstone dismissed them: not because he opposed women having the vote, but because he saw it would derail the measure. Some Tories advocated such an amendment too, for which they were accused of opportunism worthy of Disraeli. John Morley, former editor of the influential *Pall Mall Gazette*, who had recently won a by-election and was close to Gladstone, indicated he wanted one man, one vote, irrespective of a property qualification: but accepted the Bill was an important step towards that, a point its opponents understood only too well.

On 26 June the Bill had an unopposed third reading, the Tories walking out rather than forcing a division: Gladstone told MPs, warning the House of Lords not to kill the Bill, that 'even the remote probability of a conflict between the two Houses upon such a question as this I take to be the most serious prospect that has been opened during my recollection since the crisis of the Corn Laws was opened to the view of Parliament. I will not undertake to put a limit to the mischiefs and the difficulties which might result.'[43] Sir Stafford Northcote, the leader of the Tories in the Commons, said he thought Gladstone's speech had not been about the merits of the Bill, but 'upon the question whether the House of Lords is any longer to form a part of the legislature in this country.'[44]

The Tories, who controlled the Upper House, signified they would object to it mainly, but not exclusively, because they could not tolerate the new franchise on old boundaries. There was a deep cynicism behind this plan. The Tories had detected a fissure between Whigs and Radicals; the debate was being conducted against a background of possible national humiliation in Egypt and the Sudan, where General Gordon, who had been sent out to report on the situation and advise on an evacuation, had come under siege in Khartoum. The squabbling accompanying a Redistribution Bill was guaranteed to delay matters until Gladstone's administration might implode.

He foresaw not just the probability of defeat in the Lords, but also the grave constitutional crisis defeat would trigger. He wrote to Edward Benson, who had succeeded Tait as Archbishop of Canterbury, on 2 July, that if Salisbury insisted on defeating the Bill and entering into conflict with the Commons, the situation 'will probably develop itself into a constitutional crisis of such an order as has not occurred since 1832.'[45] He warned Benson and other prelates against backing the Tories, noting the effect it might have on the Church. If a general election were forced the question, Gladstone said, would be 'not only what is to be the constituency of the House of Commons, but what is to be the future of the House of Lords.'

He called in every favour he could to avert the crisis. He wrote to Frederick Temple, the Bishop of Exeter (appointed by Gladstone during his previous administration) and Benson's eventual successor, urging his attendance and apologising for contacting him on a 'merely political matter': but describing the issues at stake as 'so grave and so far reaching' that he begged Temple to consider them.[46] He did, and was translated to the Bishopric of London a year later. In 1883 Gladstone had sought to persuade Alfred Tennyson, the poet laureate and beloved of the Queen, to accept a peerage; he had, after much deliberation, been ennobled four months earlier. On 3 July Gladstone wrote to Tennyson's son, Lionel, to implore him to ensure his father would attend the vote the following week.

The poet himself replied that 'I cannot vote with you and will not vote *against* you.'[47] Distressed, and plagued also by lumbago, Gladstone wrote to Tennyson, telling him the Lords' course was 'essentially suicidal' and that even 'sober-minded' Conservative peers were 'in great dismay' at Salisbury's 'wild' idea to amend the Bill to wreck it.[48] He also warned Tennyson that the ultra-radicals and the Irish Nationalists saw this as a chance to finish off the House of Lords, a likely outcome of the defeat of such a popular measure. This swayed the naturally conservative Tennyson, who said he would vote against the Tory amendment provided Gladstone promised the franchise extension would not be implemented until after a redistribution. Gladstone next worked on Lady Tennyson, telling her 'the House of Lords is the only irresponsible, absolutely irresponsible power known to our constitution. It is madness for Lord Salisbury to raise the question whether 250 gentlemen sitting by birth and responsible to nobody shall override and overrule this nation.'[49]

Earl Cairns, the former Lord Chancellor, leading the assault in the Lords, felt the absence of provision for 'true and fair representation' of the people made the proposals unthinkable.[50] However, the Upper House was far from unanimous against it. The Earl of Fife rejected the Tory claim that this was a fundamental change in the British constitution, but said this further extension of the franchise 'was really the natural outcome of that wise and beneficent measure introduced by their late Leader [Disraeli and the 1867 Act] and which they never ceased to hear lauded as a masterpiece of Conservative statesmanship.'[51] Viscount Powerscourt asked whether the Tories would prefer – given their objections to extending the reform to Ireland – the country were disfranchised altogether and governed as a Crown Colony.

Memories of 1866 and the Hyde Park riots, where the working classes who demanded the franchise had seemed to some – such as Thomas Carlyle – to threaten revolution, remained strong. The Tories claimed their only objection to the Bill was that the redistribution was not part of it, and said they would pass the measure if it were reintroduced in the following session including redistribution. Lord Derby countered this with the claim that an election on the old boundaries would be a 'temporary inconvenience': but it remained an inconvenience that, the Tories feared, would lose them that election.[52] Rosebery, in a speech of deep intelligence and power from the Liberal back benches on the second evening that would propel him to the cabinet two years later, feared the vote would be lost: but said the result would 'not be to reject, but only to retard, the great measure of emancipation now before your Lordships.'[53] However he also warned, as Derby had, that outside the House there were 'a great many rude, honest, simple, ignorant people' who would not understand why they had been denied what they saw as their right.[54]

He sought to invoke the philosophical question of whether, in that age, the Lords could reject such a Bill, sent by the House of Commons on behalf of the people. 'I will not deny,' he said, 'for one moment, the abstract, and if I may so term it, the black-letter right of the House of Lords to reject this Bill; but I do deny that the House of Lords has any moral justification for rejecting this Bill on the second reading.'[55] He felt the Lords should leave the matter alone just as it had long refused to exercise its right to interfere on money Bills. He also reminded them of the storm when the Lords rejected the Reform Bill in 1831. 'You strengthen your prerogative,' he told his fellow peers, 'by narrowing it to what is useful and practical.'[56]

Salisbury addressed directly the question of a dissolution: if that was what it took to ensure a Bill was brought in that embraced redistribution, then so be it. Demonstrations in favour of the Bill were planned in London, but he was unperturbed. 'We know perfectly that demonstrations and expressions of anger can be produced to order by our adversaries so long as the balance at their bankers remains unexhausted,' he said.[57] 'We know that there are plenty of radicals in this country; and if it pleases them to walk up and down the roads, and spend their Sundays in the Parks, and do other things from which they may derive wholesome exercise, and exhibit themselves in the open air, we know that that gives no indication whatever of the real opinion of the majority of the constituencies.' The House was with him, and defeated the government by 205 votes to 146. The Archbishop of Canterbury and all the bishops save three – London, Salisbury and Bangor – voted with the government, as did Tennyson. Echoing language he had used to the poet, Gladstone simply noted in his diary: 'What a suicidal act of the Lords!'[58]

Many Tory MPs and peers agreed: but Salisbury had made a ruthless calculation. He told a clergyman, Canon Malcolm MacColl, that he believed franchise reform without redistribution would cause 'the absolute effacement of the Conservative Party. It would not have reappeared as a political force for thirty years. This conviction . . . greatly simplified the computation of risks.'[59] MacColl was also close to Gladstone, and Salisbury seems to have hoped the message would be relayed to him – including the point that he was prepared to lose his position rather than see his party emasculated. Salisbury put his views to a party meeting at the Carlton Club on 15 July, promising to resign if they did not support him. With some reluctance the party – notably Northcote – did.

Gladstone and his colleagues decided to drive the Bill through by any means. He told the Commons on 10 July that the Bill was of such 'paramount importance' that it was the government's duty to bring the measure before the parliament again.[60] He said the Queen had assented to an autumn session – which would wreck the Tory aristocracy's shooting season – and the Bill would come in again, with a commitment to a Redistribution Bill in the 1885 session that would begin, as usual, early in the new year, within weeks of the end of the emergency session. It was not possible to do both in 1884. Once he had outlined his plans to the Commons Gladstone proceeded to deliver a speech in the Foreign Office, of which a report appeared in the papers the next day, accusing the Tory party of a breach of good faith. He was alleged to have said that offers had been made to the Tory party to reach a compromise, but had been rejected out of hand. What had in fact happened was during the evening of the second day of the Lords debate, Granville, the Foreign Secretary, had made an offer to Cairns to introduce a special resolution committing the government to introducing a redistribution measure in 1885. Cairns had told Salisbury, who said it made no difference: he had always thought this to be the government's intention.

What had most angered Salisbury – and, in the Commons, had angered Randolph Churchill, who accused Gladstone of traducing the Tory leader – was that Gladstone had exposed this confidential communication, and had imputed motives to Salisbury for his rejection of the offer. He had accused Salisbury of saying he could not discuss redistribution 'with a rope round his neck', which Gladstone had called 'a monstrous statement'.[61] The reports also claimed Gladstone had accused Salisbury of regarding the franchise as 'a poison', and of considering those whom it was proposed to enfranchise as 'a set of wild beasts'. Salisbury told the Lords: 'This statement is an utter fabrication, and has not a vestige of foundation'. He had not communicated any opinion to the government 'either by word or by letter', and nor had Cairns done so on his behalf.

This was potentially hugely damaging to Gladstone, who had traded much on his reputation for a character of utter probity, as had others in comparisons made of him with Disraeli. Calm returned, but relations between the two parties were at a new low ebb. The Queen also rebuked Gladstone for what she considered harsh language against the Lords, which Her Majesty believed – on what evidence is unclear – reflected 'the true feeling of the country' far more than the elected House of

Commons.[62] There was a public ferment about the Lords' rejection of the Bill, and no less than the Earl of Shaftesbury – whose career stretched back to the 1820s – announced he had never known such a thing and that 'the crisis of 1832 was nothing whatever in comparison with the crisis in which we are now placed'.[63] He warned peers that if they did not reconsider the Bill it would 'produce a real and permanent breach in the harmony, peace and order of this great country.' He felt opinion had changed since the rejection, and noted that 'many of those who before were adverse are now silent.' To keep the peace, the Bill had become 'an absolute and unqualified necessity.'[64] The Lords agreed to reconsider it, but together with discussion of redistribution.

Elements in the Commons were now intensely hostile, with George Anderson, a Glasgow Liberal MP, asking Gladstone to table a resolution that 'the continuance, unreformed, of a Legislative Chamber of an irresponsible character, and with legislative functions founded largely on accident of birth, is incompatible with wise legislation and antagonistic to the welfare of the people.'[65] This was exactly what Gladstone had feared. He knew such talk horrified the Queen and hardened her sentiments further against him and sections of his party.

These views about the House of Lords were widely held. Under the auspices of the London Trades Council, the working-class movement mobilised for a mass demonstration in London to attack the Lords. In 1866 it had been the urban artisan class, aided and abetted by London's roughs, who had taken to the streets: now it was men from the countryside – agricultural labourers unfranchised after the 1867 Act – who came on 21 July 1884 to march on Hyde Park from the Embankment via Parliament Square. In the park, speakers addressed the multitude from seven separate platforms. Presiding on one was Henry Broadhurst, leader of the Trades Union Congress and a Liberal MP since 1880. He recalled that 'as we passed along Whitehall I remember seeing Lord Carrington and a party of friends standing at an open window in his house. He greeted the procession with enthusiastic cheers, and waved his hand in token of encouragement. Among those at the window was the Prince of Wales, apparently deeply interested in the demonstration and pleased at its imposing appearance. His Royal Highness also waved his hand in recognition of someone known to him in the procession.'[66] Had the Queen known this it would have confirmed all her prejudices about her heir, whom she continued to consider a juvenile delinquent.

Unlike in 1866, the government and the police did all they could to facilitate the demonstration.

Salisbury responded with a speech to a rally of 8,000 in Sheffield on 23 July. He said all the Lords sought was to protect the constitution, which would not be changed by a big demonstration in Hyde Park. Two days later he was burned in effigy at a pro-reform rally in Leicester, one of around 700 meetings before parliament met in October. Most were hostile to the status quo, illustrating the potential for unrest if the Lords threw the Bill out again. Many Tories knew this, and the truce Salisbury had established in the party began to crumble.

Gladstone, however, had to warn Chamberlain again about his language when he made a speech in which he said in public what the prime minister had been saying in private – that the Lords was busy destroying itself. The last thing Gladstone wanted was to provoke further obstructionism when he was trying to arrange a compromise. But Chamberlain, obsessed with getting the vote for the rural working class since the early 1870s, was in no mood to moderate his opinions. He believed that, as in 1831–2, this measure would be driven through only if the peers were intimidated into supporting it: and he intended to play his part. What such a rhetorical campaign did to offend the Queen, the peers and even Whigs in his own party was of no interest to him. He had said in Birmingham the previous January that 'if this great act of justice is frustrated by Lord Salisbury and the hereditary branch of the Legislature, then the Government may appeal with a clear conscience to the people against the Peers'.[67] He now intended to renew that theme, and expand upon it.

He spoke at a dining club in London on 23 July, inveighing against hereditary privilege. The Queen wrote in fury to Gladstone that 'The Queen will yield to no one in TRUE LIBERAL FEELING, but not to destructive [feeling], and she calls upon Mr Gladstone to restrain, as he can, some of his wild colleagues and followers.'[68] Chamberlain was expressing his opinion that 'any just redistribution will be favourable to the Liberal Party,' a sentiment Gladstone regarded as one that 'can only darken and embroil matters'.[69] He tried to warn Chamberlain off provoking either the Queen or the Tory party, but a more virulent assault was to come. On 4 August Chamberlain and Bright addressed an open-air meeting in Birmingham attended by 200,000 people. Chamberlain said of the Lords that 'it has protected every abuse and sheltered every privilege . . . it has denied justice and delayed reform. It is irresponsible without independence, arbitrary without judgment and arrogant without knowledge.'[70] He added that the British were in danger of being 'the only race in the civilised world subservient to the insolent pretensions of an hereditary caste.' For a cabinet minister to attack a base of the constitution, and the hereditary principle, outraged the Queen.

Gladstone asked him to restrain himself, but Chamberlain stonewalled him. His friend and ally Dilke, who took care on the eve of Joe's great speeches to egg his friend on to savage the hereditary caste, nonetheless warned him on 5 August that the Queen was near boiling point. Chamberlain (according to Dilke's record of the conversation) replied that 'she may, if she likes, dismiss me, in which case I will lead an agitation against the Lords in the country'.[71] Dilke, who had reached the cabinet as President of the Local Government Board, said he would resign too in that eventuality: however, it would have been likely that, even in 1884, for the Sovereign to demand the head of a minister for no reason other than his having expressed an opinion with which she did not agree, would have forced the resignation of the entire government.

On 19 August Gladstone sent a memorandum to the Queen about the political situation. It was a highly comprehensive document, making the case for and against his proposals, avoiding the outright advocacy that Gladstone – who handled the Queen far more sensitively than some give him credit for – thought might provoke her into obstructionism. With the Queen having decided that radicals had overrun the Liberal party and were hell-bent on ending hereditary power, Gladstone – writing to the Sovereign in the third person – also thought it prudent to preface his remarks with the observation that 'closely allied with his convictions is an unwillingness to see political power further dissociated from the hereditary principle.'[72] However, he told the Queen he believed the Lords 'cannot afford to enter into a direct conflict with the representative power' and that averting this was 'in the highest degree [in] the interest of the State'.

Feelings were already so strong in his party that the demand for 'organic change in the House of Lords' had, he thought, 'assumed a permanent form' and would persist even if the Franchise Bill were passed in the emergency session.[73] Yet he believed that if the Lords did pass the Bill the clamour would subside; but told her the 'general expectation' was that they would again defeat it. He did not, of course, ask her to persuade

Salisbury to avert a deepening crisis that might cause a constitutional revolution; but did offer further examples of the consequences of a defeat. These would include an early dissolution, a strengthening of the Irish party, the destabilisation of the Tories and the hardening of opinion in the Liberal party about the need to reform the Lords, 'certain to be professed in every Liberal constituency'.[74]

Gladstone concealed within an elaborate show of deference and courtly language a threat to the Queen that if she did not tell her Tory friends to call their dogs off, the social order as she knew it would end – with the monarchy threatened accordingly. He told the Queen he genuinely opposed Lords reform 'for the avoidance of greater evils' – notably the difficulty in finding any satisfactory plan for reform, a problem that persists. He also claimed to see the hereditary principle as 'a barrier against mischief', but warned the monarch that the Lords was too weak to resist an onslaught from the elected Commons. If these things were to be preserved, the Franchise Bill would have to be passed.

The Queen, like the Tory party and some Whigs in Gladstone's ranks, wanted to know why a Redistribution Bill could not be coupled to the Franchise Bill, to ensure the latter was passed? She had Sir Henry Ponsonby, her private secretary, put this question: Gladstone promised to answer it in a speech within days. He wished to do it in his Midlothian constituency, while staying with Rosebery at Dalmeny. The points made privately to the Queen about his sincere belief in the Lords were duly made to an audience of 5,000 at the Edinburgh Corn Exchange on 30 August, in a speech lasting ninety-seven minutes. After it he wrote to the Duke of Argyll to say that in his battle to save the Lords and avert constitutional revolution 'my greatest opponents are the flabby weakness of Northcote & the unrestrained character of Salisbury.'[75] He also stressed, in answer to hints from Balmoral, that a dissolution might be in order if the Lords rejected the Bill again; that 'never will I be a party to dissolving in order to determine whether the Lords or the Commons were right upon the Franchise bill. If I have anything to do with dissolution, it will be a dissolution upon organic change in the House of Lords.'[76] Those now were the stakes.

Argyll urged Gladstone to let the Lords see the detail of a Redistribution Bill before voting on the franchise: however the prime minister remained stubborn that redistribution would be taken separately, in the new session immediately after enacting the Franchise Bill. This annoyed the

Queen, who wanted a compromise to ensure no election would take place on the new franchise unless on new boundaries. On 28 September Gladstone protested his good faith to Argyll, to allay any suspicion of gerrymandering or of an intention to steal partisan advantage: 'So far from wishing to swamp the rural by the urban element I am desirous to sever them by every reasonable means, & to adjust areas with this view.'[77] In his Edinburgh speech his remarks on the glories of the Upper House had been met with icy silence, proving the accuracy of his remarks about feelings among the Liberal rank and file. In case Argyll were minded to be obstructive, or doubted the prime minister's sincerity on this question, Gladstone added, 'I can assure you that in speaking *for* the House of Lords I have sailed very near the wind with audiences I have addressed.' The Grand Old Man could see the world in which he had passed his political career disappearing, and prophetically told Argyll: 'The country is after all strong & sound, though I do not think the men for the next fifty years will have a comfortable time of it.' Argyll acted as a go-between with Salisbury, but he was uncomfortable.

Dilke drew up the redistribution plans, and by late September had sent Gladstone details for approval. Gladstone replied that while he wished to respect the character of certain districts when drawing up new constituency boundaries, he was happy to go further to meet Tory concerns 'if we could thereby effectually promote peace & get the Franchise Bill passed.'[78] This meant he would consider more single-member seats (many urban seats returned two MPs, meaning that there was a chance of electing both a Liberal and a Conservative), and more borough constituencies only if there was evidence of 'local or municipal life' – in other words, a cohesive community. This was to allay Tory fears that many of the rural constituencies that were the basis of their power in the country would be absorbed into others in order to free up numbers to create seats in newly populous areas. He charged Dilke to have private conversations with the opposition to improve the chances of success. But, inevitably, some Tory strongholds would disappear so rural districts, where newly enfranchised farm labourers might elect Liberal MPs, could be established. He warned Rosebery on 30 September that 'if the division [on the Bill] shall go decidedly wrong, I think the chances are that we may be out before Christmas' and added that 'nothing private of a promising kind has yet proceeded from the leaders of the Opposition.'[79] He did, however, take as a sign of hope an article

Salisbury had written in the *National Review*, in which he seemed to support 'Mr Cobden's principle of single-member constituencies'.[80]

The Whiggish tendency annoyed Gladstone as much as the Tories did. There was talk of writing a 'postponing clause' into the Franchise Bill to ensure it could not apply until 1 January 1886: that, the Tories who favoured it argued, would either ensure a Redistribution Bill had been enacted before an election on the new franchise, or it would bring down the government and put Salisbury and his colleagues in. Hartington, writing on 29 September, asked Gladstone whether it might not be better to agree to such an idea now than have the humiliation of the Lords forcing it on the government later, in order to get the Bill.[81] Gladstone slapped Hartington down, saying that 'a prior acceptance of the Clause would probably break up the party' and adding: 'What I feel most strongly is the extremely damaging nature of any debate on the merits of such a clause, & the utter lack, to my mind, of pleas in its favour.'[82]

IV

On Friday 3 October 1884 Lord Randolph Churchill, speaking in Leeds to a crowd estimated at 10,000 and flanked by Tory MPs and grandees from the West Riding, called the Bill 'a mere electioneering manoeuvre', and said Tory objections were made with 'utter impartiality' because it was 'incomplete'.[83] The younger son of the Duke of Marlborough, Churchill was only thirty-five but already a controversial figure with a substantial following in the Tory party, where he was the father of the concept of Tory Democracy: a creed deriving from Disraeli's one-nation conservatism that sought through paternalism and established institutions, rather than by radical change, to improve the lot of working people. He had a reputation as a radical, but also for engaging in naked politicking that relied more on humiliating his opponents – inside his party as well as outside it – than on any deeply held principles. In a speech long on jokes and short on analysis or, for that matter, strict truth – *The Times* called his style 'that homely and elegant vernacular which he enjoys the proud distinction of having introduced into political controversy' – he accused Gladstone of dealing with reform as in 1866, on 'a limited and unfair scale', glossing over the hypocrisy and panic of Disraeli's measure in 1867 as something that had settled the issue.

Inevitably, Churchill did not admit that Disraeli's measure created the long-standing grievance of an unfranchised rural working class that the government sought, at last, to redress. He added that 'the House of Lords is a body of English gentlemen exercising constitutionally constitutional [sic] powers.'[84] He led the field in using ridicule to undermine Gladstone. The previous January he had told an audience in Blackpool that 'for the purposes of recreation he [Gladstone] has selected the felling of trees, and we may usefully remark that his amusements, like his politics, are constantly destructive. The forest laments in order that Mr Gladstone may perspire.'[85]

Salisbury, that same evening in Glasgow, insisted the two Bills be passed together, saying it was his 'firm belief' the Lords would agree.[86] He accused Gladstone of attempting 'numerical legerdemain' and feared the Conservative element in Scottish boroughs would be 'systematically and universally suppressed.' Glasgow, with a population of 487,000, returned just three MPs, whereas the Welsh boroughs of the Non-conformist Liberal heartland, with 483,000, returned fifteen. Salisbury's intervention, apparently on behalf of the unelected House, gave Gladstone an excuse to co-ordinate a wider assault. Aware Chamberlain was about to speak to the National Liberal Federation at Hanley in Staffordshire, Gladstone told him Salisbury had provided 'an excellent subject for denunciation' and that 'you may safely denounce him to your heart's content.'[87]

However, Gladstone was nervous of Radical Joe straying beyond matters the cabinet could agree upon, and added, 'I earnestly hope that you will leave us all elbow room on other questions'. Hartington had spoken in public, with reference to the postponing clause, about a possible 'compromise'. Gladstone reassured Chamberlain that it was 'a word which has never passed my lips', and summoned him to a cabinet two days later – after he would have spoken – with the tacit warning that anything untoward he might say would be considered by his colleagues. Put on notice, Chamberlain handled the compromise question with what Gladstone subsequently termed 'skill & moderation'.[88]

Thousands were left outside when Chamberlain came on stage, and there were several minutes of cheering and hat-waving before he could begin. The chairman, introducing him, was received rapturously when he said that 'the people did not want the Lords to rule and would not allow them.'[89] Their hero said that 'the Tories have lighted a flame throughout the length and breadth of the land which will never be quenched until 2,000,000 of capable citizens have received the final sanction of the law to the rights which are now unjustly withheld from them.' The crowd bore out Gladstone's fears about the state of popular opinion. 'A great wave of excitement has passed over the country,' Chamberlain said. 'The torrent is still rising, and shows no sign of declining. Yesterday it was Scotland; today it is the midland district; tomorrow it will be Wales; and everywhere it is not a party agitation; it is something like a real uprising of the people.'

The trades unions and friendly societies had mobilised, especially in industrial areas, to campaign for reform. They held open meetings; the anti-reform ones, far less numerous, were limited to Tories. Chamberlain characterised these as 'legislation by picnic', where landed estates were specially opened to Tory supporters for events at which the status quo could be reinforced. He said their opponents were 'relying all the time on Conservative fetes and Saturday excursions, personally conducted by members of the aristocracy, enlivened by conjurors, by nigger minstrels, by tight-rope dancing, and by pyrotechnics. It would not be the first time the Tory party had been saved by juggling and by fireworks.'

Because – unlike Churchill – Chamberlain had popular opinion behind him and interlaced his jokes with passages of factual exposition, his barbs were more devastating. He could also be menacing: 'It is one of the great discoveries of modern warfare that the vanquished nation should pay an indemnity to the victors, and I do not wonder that the people are everywhere asking what indemnity is to be extorted from the House of Lords if this contest, which they have rashly provoked, is wantonly prolonged.' His fundamental point remained: 'The Tory party hate the franchise'. It would never be given with 'generosity', he added, and so therefore the people would have to 'extort' it.

In a soaring peroration, Chamberlain said: 'We cannot play with the rights of two millions of people. We cannot tamper with the hopes which have been excited. It is said that the peers will not give way. Then I say neither will the people submit.' He asserted that 'their claim to dictate the laws which we shall make, the way in which we shall govern ourselves – to spoil, delay, even reject measures demanded by the popular voice, passed after due discussion by a majority of the people's House, and receiving the sanction and confirmation of popular assemblies such as this – is a claim contrary to reason, opposed to justice, and which we shall resist to the death.' This was greeted with 'loud and prolonged cheering'. The Queen telegraphed Gladstone when she read the report in *The Times* to profess herself 'shocked'.[90] She told him 'it was impossible for the Government to expect any success being come to if a Cabinet Minister used such language.'[91] She asked Gladstone to proceed, as Hartington had recommended, by compromise, suggesting Hartington negotiate with Salisbury. Gladstone assented, but told her he held out no hopes of success.

The Conservative party organised for the following Monday a vast all-ticket rally at Aston in a hall holding 6,000 people, and invited Northcote and Churchill – medals of whom had been struck specially for the occasion – to address it. The hall was in the middle of a park with an ice-rink, an assembly room and other locations where it was planned to hold four or five meetings simultaneously. Aston had been excluded from the Birmingham constituency on the insistence of the Liberal party after the 1867 Reform Act, and therefore its working men had been deprived of the vote. However, the decision to hold such an event at such a time in an area filled with Chamberlain's militants was an unwise provocation. Also, to create the notion that it was an open meeting, 120,000 tickets were offered to all comers, adding to the risk of a disturbance. A Liberal counter-demonstration marched to some waste ground near the park, with several thousand protesters. Then things turned ugly.

Protesters tried to storm the park, and scaled a wall. It partly collapsed under their weight and thousands without tickets ran in, set off fireworks (including an ingenious display in the shape of Sir Stafford Northcote) and occupied the skating rink. They assailed the platform from which a local MP was due to speak, and what *The Times* called 'a violent struggle' broke out.[92] Chairs were brandished, blows exchanged, and much of the hall smashed up. An attempt was made to hold the meeting, but it was abandoned in a storm of heckling. That was but the *hors d'oeuvre*. The mob stormed the main hall, forcing reporters at the foot of the platform to retreat to the stage with some of the local dignitaries. Rioters joined them and started a fight. Screaming women fled the stage, and the fighting ended only when all chairs had been broken. The protesters had seized control of the hall.

Then Northcote arrived: and when he started to lecture the mob about the importance of obeying the law they howled him down, brandishing not parts of broken furniture, but pictures of Gladstone. He gave up and left the stage, but Churchill, who for all his lack of judgment in speech was not lacking physical courage, jumped up to replace him.

The Times noted that 'the audience immediately set up an immense shout of disapprobation', reflecting Churchill's place as prime enemy of the British working class. With an irony probably lost on those present, Churchill announced: 'I can see that you are among those exceptions to Mr Gladstone's ruling that the people are on his side.' He promised to take an early opportunity of expressing his opinions, and he, too, left the stage.

The smaller assembly rooms had been secured, and he and Northcote addressed a meeting there. Northcote claimed that the logical course on which the government was headed was abolition of the House of Lords, and an undermining of the Commons as an all-powerful prime minister attempted to rule with the support of a bureaucracy. Churchill said what had happened earlier had brought 'a great stigma and a slur' on Birmingham and had damaged the radicals. He added: 'It is to Mr Chamberlain that we owe the scandalous proceedings of tonight [cheers and groans], proceedings which may have been pardonable enough when he was a private individual, but now that he is a Cabinet Minister I say they are disgraceful and scandalous to the last degree.' He accused the radicals of aiming 'to put down their opponents by sheer noise and force, and also to resort to any conceivable dodge to prevent them putting their views before the public.'

Later that evening Churchill chaired an impromptu meeting of the Birmingham Conservative Club, where he raised the temperature still further, suggesting Tories should deny a hearing to leading Liberals such as Chamberlain or Bright when they attempted to speak in Birmingham: 'It is', he told them, 'in your power to collect and organise a body which by careful and assiduous attention at Liberal meetings will so conduct themselves that the Liberals, at least, will begin to perceive that they will do well to leave the Conservative meetings alone.'[93] Churchill stayed on in Birmingham and, in a speech given while opening a bazaar the next day, for good measure accused the Liberals of seeking to corrupt the youth of Britain, having the object 'to exclude entirely from the education given by the State all moral training, and, if possible, even to exclude the Bible from the State schools of England.' Later, addressing a banquet, he again accused Chamberlain of advocating force to silence his opponents: whether or not this was designed to flush Chamberlain out, it had that effect.

The next Saturday, at Newtown in Montgomeryshire, Chamberlain told an audience waving banners proclaiming 'The House of Lords Mended or Ended' that 'I was reading with feelings of infinite disgust' [Churchill's Birmingham speeches] in which he has, more than any other man, degraded political controversy to Billingsgate, and lowered the whole tone of political life.'[94] He branded Churchill's accusations 'groundless' and illustrated the democratic deficit in Britain: in America and France one in four people had the vote; in Germany one in five, but in Britain only one in eleven. He asked – rhetorically – 'Do you intend to govern yourselves, or to be governed by the peers?' But the words that would be twisted were these: 'Speaking at Edinburgh at the end of last year, Lord Randolph Churchill declared that he would not consent to the extension of the franchise unless the Liberals showed that they were in earnest by pulling down railings, or by engaging the police and the military; and, gentlemen, this is the man who is now so indignant because the workmen of Birmingham took him at his word and pulled off the coping of a wall in order to attend a meeting to which they had been invited, and which the Tory managers were endeavouring to palm off as a misrepresentation of the opinion of Birmingham.'

The Queen thought this suggested approval of the riot. She wrote a letter to Gladstone, rife with the heavy underlinings that signified Royal rage, to say that 'if a Cabinet Minister makes use of such language and sets the Prime Minister's injunctions at defiance he ought *not* to *remain* in the *Cabinet*. His language if not disavowed justifies the *worst apprehensions* of the Opposition.'[95] Gladstone said he concurred in the Queen's 'regret and disapprobation', and had at once 'adopted measures which he hopes will have a good result'.[96] He asked Dilke, as Chamberlain's closest associate, to persuade him to qualify a passage in the speech about heading a march to fight Salisbury, and to deny it was an incitement to actual violence. Chamberlain made a half-hearted attempt, writing to a friend (for publication) to say he had merely been trying to expose the absurdity of Salisbury's position, adding: 'In order that I may give no countenance for possible misunderstanding I shall refrain from any further rejoinder though the provocation is great and the occasion tempting.'[97]

This lack of contrition incensed the Queen, who had the consolation of taking her wrath out on Gladstone, who had conceded that 'that letter does not come up to Mr Gladstone's expectations and desires' in the hope of avoiding an eruption.[98] Dilke was pressed again to ask whether more could be done: Chamberlain replied: 'I cannot and *will not* do more.'[99] The eruption followed. 'It is, the Queen thinks, absolutely necessary for the honour of the Government that Mr Gladstone should take a firm stand and separate his name from Mr Chamberlain, with which unfortunately it is too often, wrongly no doubt, connected.'[100] Sailing close to the constitutional wind, she added: 'Mr Chamberlain must restrain his language, or not remain in the Cabinet. In any other Cabinet such freedom of language has not been tolerated.'

If this was intended to restrain Chamberlain and force an apology of which the Sovereign would approve it had the opposite effect: Dilke warned Gladstone the next day that it 'would not take much to make a serious row' – in other words, Radical Joe would walk out of the government, split the party and force the Liberals from office. Gladstone was in an almost impossible position, though he could call the Queen's bluff, which is effectively what happened. For the moment, however, Chamberlain offered no further provocation.

Hartington's conversations did not prove so fruitless as Gladstone had feared. Some Tories realised that the obstinate attitudes of Salisbury and, even more extreme, Churchill were leading the party to catastrophe. If the Lords underwent 'organic change' it would mean excising, partly or completely, the legislative power of the landed interest that remained the backbone of the party; and eventually the Franchise Bill would be passed. Sir Michael Hicks Beach, the former Colonial Secretary and one of Salisbury's main lieutenants in the Commons, became Hartington's interlocutor. There was much agreement on detail, and Hicks Beach pressed home two points on redistribution – the strict separation of rural and urban constituencies, and the creation of single-member seats. The Liberals liked dual-member seats because, being a one-party coalition, they could have a radical and a Whig elected in each place: but it was not something they felt the need to insist upon at the cost of losing the Franchise Bill.

Meanwhile, to Gladstone's distress, the draft redistribution plan was leaked to a newspaper. He appealed to the editors of other papers, in the interests of national stability, not to retail the contents: he thanked Edward Levy-Lawson, proprietor of *The Daily Telegraph*, for having acted in his restraint 'in the interests of all Government, of Government as such, & even of something more & higher' in not having repeated the details.[101] The leak gave Salisbury the chance to observe that the paper had been drawn up with 'purposed unfairness'. Gladstone told Hartington that he suspected Salisbury 'does not want an accommodation for he does not as Lady S told Lady Spencer care for the House of Lords & wd like to be in the House of Commons better.'[102] He hoped his party would make Salisbury see sense. Gladstone told Lord Winmarleigh, a Liberal peer, that a second rejection would 'effectually raise the question of the organic structure of the House of Lords . . . and that question, once raised, will and can only be settled by a great change, which it is my heart's desire if possible to avert.'[103]

When Parliament resumed on 23 October, its mood soured by the rantings during the off-season, Gladstone announced his imminent intention to reintroduce the Bill, as amended in the previous session. The opposition front bench was completely empty. But before the House could proceed Churchill, still bent on mischief, sought to censure Chamberlain for incitement and 'a justification of riot and disorder.'[104] The debate dragged relations between the two parties to a new low. The Queen made it clear she did not want a dissolution. Ponsonby asked Gladstone whether the Lords could not give a second reading to the Franchise Bill but then wait to see the contents of a Redistribution Bill before dealing with the later stages of the legislative process. Gladstone rejected this on the grounds it would change nothing. However, not least because of the Queen's anxiety that a massive constitutional crisis would destabilise the social order and the country, both parties were forced to discuss a way to proceed.

Part of the problem was that Northcote, who led the Tories in the Commons, was no longer trusted by Gladstone, and had a difficult relationship with Salisbury; unless Salisbury himself would engage, the process would stall. The Queen took the initiative, and wrote to her prime minister from Balmoral on 31 October to ask him to arrange for 'the leaders of the parties in both Houses [to] exchange their views personally' on redistribution.[105] 'The Queen believes that were assurance given that the redistribution would not be wholly inimical to the prospects of the Conservative party, their concurrence might be obtained,' she continued. Wishing to have 'this serious crisis' curtailed, 'and knowing how fully Mr Gladstone recognises the great danger that might arise by prolonging the conflict, the Queen earnestly trusts that he will avail himself of such means to obviate it.' Only in provoking the most ghastly confrontation could Gladstone ignore this; and the Queen had written to

Salisbury in identical terms, eliciting his immediate agreement to enter into talks: though Salisbury attempted to soothe the Queen by saying he doubted anyone in the country cared about what was going on – an assertion that was not strictly true.

Dilke represented the government, dealing directly with Salisbury in private meetings in his house in Arlington Street. The two men had sat on the Royal Commission for the Housing of the Working Classes, which Dilke had chaired, and had a cordial relationship. Salisbury, who had recently written an article in the *National Review* making the case for single-member constituencies, demanded them as the price for supporting the Bill, and presented a plan drawn up by Hicks Beach. He believed a Redistribution Bill would divide up counties to form the new constituencies, allowing discrete Tory-voting areas as well as Liberal ones. Dilke, as a radical, felt such a reform would also reduce the influence of the Whigs in his own party and expand that of his faction, and so warmly endorsed Salisbury's proposal. On 5 November Gladstone told Dilke that 'the principle of one member districts is to be generally applied'.[106]

The second reading began the next day. After two days' debate it was given by a majority of 140, and by the end of the week had been read a third time and sent to the Lords. Before it was considered there Gladstone sought and received the cabinet's approval to introduce the Redistribution Bill after the Lords' second reading of the Franchise Bill, exactly the procedure the Queen had, through Ponsonby, urged him to adopt. On 13 November he privately asked Northcote what assurances his party required about the Redistribution Bill, if it were produced before the Franchise Bill went into committee, in return for not 'endangering or retarding the passing of the Franchise Bill'.[107] Having consulted Salisbury, however, Northcote replied that 'the Lords would not pass the Franchise Bill until the seats Bill was before them.'[108] So the discussions ended, and stalemate, or worse, beckoned again.

The position was untenable for both Gladstone and Salisbury. They would have to compromise on timing, with the Redistribution Bill being introduced as soon as the Franchise Bill had gone into committee in the Lords. Salisbury and Northcote visited Gladstone in Downing Street on 19 November for tea and what were believed to be unprecedented discussions between the leaders of two parties about the composition of a Bill. Further compromises about timing and boundary changes were settled upon on 28 November after more secret meetings in Arlington Street that, as well as the two principals, involved Dilke, Hartington and Granville on the government side, and Northcote, the Duke of Richmond and Lord Cairns for the Tories. The Queen was notified, and replied that 'to be able to be of use is all I care to live for now.'[109]

The agreement became known as 'The Arlington Street Compact', and was set out in writing by Dilke on 28 November. The proposals entailed expanding the Commons from 652 seats to 670. The seats needed for the counties with their expanded electorates were found from the disfranchisement of seventy-nine boroughs with fewer than 15,000 voters, whose electors would vote in the surrounding counties instead, four more that contained large stretches of countryside, and two that were deemed corrupt. Another thirty-six boroughs with fewer than 50,000 voters had their representation cut from two MPs to one, and Rutland and Herefordshire each lost a member. Scotland had twelve more MPs but Ireland, whose population had fallen by 40 per cent since the potato famine, retained all its 103 members, Gladstone having no appetite to present the Irish with any further grievances.

This settled, the Lords' second reading happened without a vote. There had been jitters in cabinet, from Hartington and others concerned that undue advantage might be conferred upon the Tories. Dilke trumped objections, not least because, as he noted, 'Chamberlain and I and Mr Gladstone were the only three people who understood the subject, so that the others were unable to fight except in the form known as sweating at large.'[110] The committee stage was over in a single day, 4 December. The Redistribution Bill had its second reading in the Commons, the committee stage postponed until February 1885 to allow three boundaries commissions – England and Wales, Scotland and Ireland – to report.

There was one final hitch, namely the resignation of the Financial Secretary to the Treasury, Leonard Courtney, over the establishment of single-member constituencies in Ireland and the refusal to consider proportional representation. Gladstone tried unsuccessfully to dissuade him. Ironically, although he lost a minister, Gladstone ended up on better terms with Salisbury than previously, because of the integrity and respect with which the two men had conducted their recent negotiations. The two measures went on the statute book, one after the other. The boundaries system pertains in Britain today, so the reform would resonate for a century and beyond. The election in 1885 was fought on the new franchise and the new boundaries. There was also a measure to keep polling stations open until eight o'clock in the evening – they had hitherto closed at four o'clock – so that workers could still exercise their vote.

The most obvious effect was the reduction of the influence of the landed classes and the rise of 'new men', although the aristocratic element would remain strong in cabinets until the Liberal victory of 1906 brought in men from a wider range of backgrounds. Reform also caused more extreme radicals to be elected in 1885, paving the way for the election of the first *de facto* Labour MP in 1892. However, in a parliament where neither main party had an overall majority after 1885, the reform left the Irish party holding the balance of power and using it, somewhat cynically, to put a Conservative government in, albeit for just a few months. By setting a residence qualification, and having a highly contentious lodger franchise that ensured very few lodgers had the vote, the new franchise still left roughly 40 per cent of the adult male population voteless. But it gave the vote to many who would form the rank and file of the nascent Labour movement, eventually splitting the anti-Conservative vote in a fashion that helped ensure that, after a brief interlude of Liberal government between 1892 and 1895, the Tories would hold power until 1905 as Labour candidates entered the field.

V

Archibald Philip Primrose, 5th Earl of Rosebery, bet a friend at Oxford a sovereign that he would marry an heiress, become prime minister and win the Derby. At Epsom on 6 June 1894 he won his wager. His three-year old, Ladas, won the race by a length and a half, having started as the shortest-priced favourite in Derby history, at 2/9. On 5 March he had succeeded the then eighty-four-year-old Gladstone as prime minister. In 1878 he had married Hannah de Rothschild, daughter of Baron Meyer de Rothschild, *châtelaine* of Mentmore and the richest woman in Britain, who saw neither of his other triumphs; she died of typhoid in 1890, weakened by Bright's disease, which would have killed her in any case within two years. Rosebery was grief-stricken and never had the same drive again. The shambles of his fifteen-month premiership, which culminated in the Liberals entering opposition for a decade after 1895, was partly attributable to his distress, but also to his tense relations with some colleagues, notably Sir William Harcourt, the Chancellor of the Exchequer. He was also a martyr to nervous and psychosomatic illnesses.

Rosebery's role in Gladstone's Midlothian Campaign of 1879–80 had endeared him to the Grand Old Man. However, he achieved the highest office mainly because of the Queen, who detested Harcourt, leader of the radical faction and his rival for the leadership. The Queen shared her loathing with most of Harcourt's peers. Asquith called it 'an impossibility' for Harcourt to take over, 'as his colleagues would neither serve under him nor with him,' and Rosebery called him 'a man of many qualities, all marred by a violent, uncontrollable temper.'[111] Had there been a vote either of the party in the country or even just of MPs, Harcourt might have won but as the choice was the cabinet's, the Queen was advised to send for Rosebery, who, because he had many qualities she liked in a Tory, won immediate approval.

The key figure in the opposition to Harcourt was John Morley, who had had the rough end of Harcourt's tongue too often: he thought Harcourt so bad that he would support Rosebery, even though Morley believed the prime minister should sit in the Commons; and even though Rosebery, unlike the Gladstonian Morley, was a devout imperialist. Harcourt's ambitious son Lewis – universally known as Loulou – urged his father to refuse to serve: Harcourt rejected his advice, for fear of being accused of harming the party. But he was outraged – though he believed the government would not last – and his and Rosebery's relationship was toxic. He would succeed Rosebery as leader of the opposition, but would never be prime minister. However, precisely because of Harcourt's clout and Rosebery's weakness, Rosebery needed him. In early 1894, before Rosebery's rise, Harcourt berated colleagues about the naval estimates, hectoring the First Lord of the Admiralty, Spencer, on 26 February and maintaining that the government was 'placed in *very great* difficulties by the delay in settlement' caused by Spencer's refusal to agree cuts, which 'prevents all progress in the arrangements of the Budget'.[112] 'The least you can do for us while you make these immense demands is to tell us their amount . . . that we may make provision to meet them,' he continued. This tone was why colleagues loathed him.

Harcourt was a first-generation Liberal grandee from a profoundly

Tory background, his cast of mind far from Rosebery's Whiggishness. His family had come over with the Conqueror and had served both England and France with distinction. Harcourt's grandfather had been Archbishop of York. Through his father he was related to the Dukes of Bedford, Bridgewater and Sutherland, and traced his descent to the Plantagenets. This lineage enabled him to attack his own caste without accusations of envy: and attack them he did, to raise £5 million, and accomplish what he told Rosebery was 'an act of financial justice to which the Liberal Party are deeply pledged.'[113] His radical motivation had begun in his teens as a reaction against the innate Toryism of his family, and had developed into a protracted means of provoking his Tory opponents and making them appear hostile to the interests of working people: which the landmark measure of his Chancellorship unquestionably did.

On 16 April 1894, introducing his third Budget, Harcourt not only raised income tax – as expected – but revolutionised taxation of estates through death duties. This fell most heavily on the landed interest, and on Tories. Death had long been taxed. There were five separate imposts on the statute book, but most easily avoidable and therefore raising little. Probate Duty had existed since 1694; Account Duty, which taxed gifts between living people, since 1881. Lord North brought in a Legacy Duty in 1780 and Gladstone a Succession Duty in 1853, both of which taxed legatees on a graduated scale according to their closeness to the testator. Goschen brought in Estate Duty in 1889. Some of these duties taxed people, others land; Goschen's taxed both. Harcourt could claim, while raising revenue, to be tidying up an arcane system. Land was not highly taxed compared with other wealth, being valued on the life interest of the holder and not on capital worth. It was changing this system that brought the wrath of the landed classes down upon Harcourt.

The Budget came after acrimonious wrangling between Rosebery and Harcourt. The deficit was fed not least by £3 million more naval expenditure, which Rosebery supported. The idea of graduated death duties was Alfred Milner's, a brilliant civil servant who had studied Irish finances for Gladstone. Rosebery told Harcourt he would be happier about the attack on privilege if its proceeds were to help the masses; he felt that 'proposals of this kind should be introduced with gentleness and high graduation appears to be essentially a war tax.'[114]

Harcourt, confiding in his son, dismissed Rosebery's objections as 'high Tory'. He told Spencer that Rosebery's opposition to death duties 'would have been thought extreme in its Toryism by Lord Eldon' and his arguments 'rubbish'. To Rosebery himself he was even ruder, patronising him for his inexperience and saying he regarded Liberal fortunes and the outcome of the next election 'with philosophic indifference'.[115] Rosebery answered that 'insolence is not argument', but surrendered rather than fight in cabinet. The toxicity of his relationship with Harcourt contributed to the short duration of Rosebery's premiership.

Harcourt abolished Estate, Probate and Account duties and replaced them with a uniform Estate Duty on the capital value of all property passed on at death. Estates under £100 would be exempt. The duty would start at 1 per cent on estates between £100 and £500, rising to 8 per cent on those over £1 million. He modified the Legacy and Succession duties, sweetening the pill by granting a 10 per cent depreciation allowance on land and a 16 per cent one on houses, but that did little to stem the outrage.

In 1877 a Tory, John Bateman, in his work *The Great Landowners of Britain and Ireland*, had in a population of 31 million found only a million freeholders, of whom 850,000 held less than an acre. He defined 2,800 people, 400 of them peers, as 'great landowners', the qualification for this being 3,000 acres and £3,000 a year in rents. However, agricultural land prices fell steadily after Bateman's survey, more than halving between 1875 and 1911.[116] This fall, at a time when the City of London was flourishing as never before as a financial centre, led to members of many landed families seeking new fortunes in business. It also increased the sense of persecution such families felt at their fiscal treatment.

Property owners already paid local taxes, out of which, for example, parishes raised money for workhouses and other poor reliefs. They claimed they were being hit disproportionately hard. At the second reading of the Finance Bill on 7 May, Walter Long, a future Tory minister, said Harcourt's measures 'would go far to complete the ruin which was now rapidly overtaking the agricultural interest.'[117] Arable farmers were harder hit than those with livestock, because of cheap imported grains and cereals, thanks to the opening up of the cultivation of the North American prairies and the relatively cheap cost of transporting foodstuffs. The south-east of England and East Anglia suffered worst, having declined from the 1870s and being predominantly arable. By the early 1890s the livestock farmers of the north and west of England were suffering most, as demand fell for home-produced meat. Successive governments of both parties refused to consider any form of protectionism.

However, even in 1894 a report of the Royal Commission on Agriculture showed that in the corn-growing districts of Essex there was above-average dereliction of farms and of 'farm houses, farm buildings, and labourers' cottages falling into ruin'.[118] Even before death duties, there were sixty farms derelict in the county, and calls for intervention to prevent matters getting worse. Since 1879, 28,222 acres and twenty-eight poles of land in Essex had been returned to landlords by bankrupt or failed tenant farmers; much was now derelict.[119] To compound the problem, tithes were far higher in Essex and other parts where arable farming prevailed: 6s per acre, giving a rate of 6s 4½d per inhabitant, there against 1s 9¼d per acre, or 4½d per inhabitant, in Lancashire.[120]

Some of Harcourt's supporters argued for great estates to be broken up, with parcels of land sold to pay the new duties, ending the transmission of wealth from father to son. Long goaded Harcourt by saying that if that breach of the hereditary principle really was the government's aim then it should be honest about it 'and not proceed by bleeding the land to death.'[121] He argued that if estates broke up, many who depended on the land – not just the rich whom the new taxes targeted, but tenant farmers, labourers, grooms and others working on the land – would lose their livelihoods. Charles Hobhouse, a Wiltshire MP, countered that instead of a man grooming a horse for his master's benefit, with broken-up estates 'it would be open to a man to cultivate some of the land for his own benefit.'[122] The burden of Liberal opinion, however, was that the rich should pay a fair share: and if that entailed selling part of their estates, so be it.

Goschen, Harcourt's predecessor, characterised the proposals as 'a strong form of fiscal robbery' and 'socialistic', saying there was 'no principle of justice' to guide the graduated nature of the tax. He thought the top rate, 8 per cent, very high.[123] He warned Harcourt that 'it is bad finance to set any tax so high that everybody sets about thinking how to evade it.'[124] During his incumbency Treasury officials had warned him against higher death duties because of their adverse effect on the economy: he asked Harcourt whether the advice still prevailed.

A man with an estate of £251,000 would pay £10,400 under existing duties, rising to £17,500 under Harcourt's scheme. However, if the man had four children and gave each assets worth £26,000 in his lifetime, the estate would be so diminished that the Exchequer would receive only £9,000. Thus increasing taxes could raise less revenue: an argument used by economic liberals ever since. Goschen's fundamental argument was about the effect of the duties on the accumulation of capital and wealth creation: without such things, Britain's supremacy as a commercial and economic power was over.

As people gave money away to avoid duties, he argued, the Treasury would have to tax property – less easily disposed of – more heavily than 8 per cent. Capital in businesses far outweighed the value of land; targeting land for higher taxes was illogical. Goschen forecast less money going to charities, thus harming the poor, and estates falling into disrepair. He knew some heirs would break up estates to pay the taxes; but others would be run down and managed by agents until families could afford to live on them again, creating absenteeism.

As the Bill went through the MP for Colchester, Captain Herbert Naylor-Leyland, demanded urgent action on a special report the government had commissioned into the depression in Essex. Matters were now as bad there as in the congested districts of Ireland. Rents unpaid across the county meant economic hardship in the towns, where there was no money to spend, and too many men competing for a shrinking number of jobs as they moved there from the countryside. Essex had, within living memory, been hugely prosperous because of its suitability for corn-growing, which made its current abject state even more shocking. 'The years since 1875 have been a period of accumulated decline,' Naylor-Leyland said, 'nineteen years in which not one year had been a good one, with the exception of 1887.'[125] The previous year, 1893, had been 'the worst season agriculture had ever known'. In twenty-five years prosperity had been shattered, and it was now proposed to tax this diminishing asset even further.

The report described a 360-acre farm that a decade earlier had employed twelve men and several boys and had six teams of horses:

> To-day the abomination of desolation seems to have settled down upon the place. The fields once under the constant dominion of the plough have covered themselves with a coarse profitless herbage . . . The buildings, commodious and substantial in the days of a thriving agriculture, are rapidly succumbing to the decay induced of neglect; doors of which the fastenings have disappeared creak idly in the

> wind, the weather boarding piece by piece is falling away, and there is no hand to replace the tiles, the constant dislodgment of which renders even larger the holes in the roof through which the rain pours to carry on the work of destruction within. The stables are tenantless, the byres are unoccupied, and the farmyard is empty, neither waggon, plough, nor any other implement being visible. The house is deserted, save, indeed, for one room occupied by an aged caretaker, whose shambling gait, as he moves about the desolate premises, seems scarcely out of accord with the air of solitude which reigns over all.[126]

Inevitably, land was cheap: an acre in Essex cost £6 10s, but the cost of making it fit for cultivation was £17, mostly to reinstate drainage. Landlords facing higher taxation were less likely to improve their land. New eviction notices had been issued: more land would become derelict once these farmers left. 'Every class now connected with agriculture in the county is now on the verge of ruin,' Naylor-Leyland said. 'Rents and values are sinking to nothing at all . . . the population are migrating to West Ham and the Metropolis.'

Some Essex landlords had written off rent arrears, invested in new buildings and farming methods, but were still losing money because of the low price of corn. Naylor-Leyland said that even some 'canny Scots' had tried their hand at farming there, and had failed too. There was no duty on imported grain, but a three-sixteenths of a penny duty per hundredweight on grain grown here: he urged Harcourt to scrap this. He also felt the government should use some derelict land to set up a model farm using methods other than crop rotation, to see whether that succeeded. And he wanted the Church to remit the tithe – and if it refused, the government should force it. Most unjust of all, rates were charged to owners of derelict land in Essex as though it were still productive.

Harcourt split hairs in his reply. He said Hunter Pringle, the report's author, had not been appointed by the government or reported to it, but by and to a commission appointed by the government. He also pleaded helplessness, in that Pringle had said corn could not economically be grown until the price rose by 45 per cent: the price was not going to rise, in the foreseeable future, by 45 per cent. Wheat – 58s 8d a quarter in 1873 – was 26s 4d a quarter by 1893.[127] It suited Harcourt to quote Pringle about the failure of farmers to have the foresight to move from arable to livestock rather than persisting with an unprofitable crop.

Another Essex MP, Major Frederic Rasch, was surprised there had not been an outbreak of rick-burning, given how bad things were, and that landlords were now routinely subsidising their tenants. He wanted a ten-year remission of all land taxes. 'There is something very rotten in the state . . . if a tract of land 2,000 acres in extent was to be allowed to become derelict whilst farmers are being ruined, and agricultural labourers were starving within twenty miles of the Palace of Westminster.'[128] Colonel Amelius Lockwood, the MP for Epping, felt the Budget meant Harcourt 'was chastising agriculturalists with whips of a heavier material and imposing heavier burdens.'[129] He suggested that, as the government was pouring investment into African colonies, it might buy some land in Essex and set up a Crown Colony there.

The Times sent a reporter to see the desolation: 'Why it is that within less than an hour's ride of the wealthiest metropolis in the world thousands upon thousands of acres should be steadily undergoing degradation into mere prairie wastes is an economic problem the local interest of which is eclipsed by its national importance?'[130] He computed that 52,663 acres had left cultivation since 1880, partly because of a rise in livestock: but roughly one-third of Essex farmland, 251,564 acres, was grass. Wherever one went, he continued, one found 'the same dismal story of a hopeless fight against adversity'. Between 1879 and 1891 'the landlords lost half their rents and the tenants half their capital.' Whereas ten or twelve millers had formerly attended the Chelmsford Corn Exchange, now there were only two. A Chelmsford baker who used to take thirteen sacks of flour each week now took only one, buying the rest more cheaply from abroad. Even livestock was sent back from market unslaughtered, because imported meat was cheaper.

Harcourt argued that the new middle class with relatively small estates to pass on would pay little tax on them: this was the class described by the Duke of Devonshire as the one 'which has begun to wear a black coat', many of them Liberal voters.[131] When the Finance Bill reached the Lords the outrage was yet more voluble. Lord Feversham called it 'a gospel of plunder' that would 'do great injury to the landed interest of the country'.[132] He, like other peers, was angry that this revolutionary question had been incorporated in the Finance Bill – which by convention the Lords did not defeat, though within fifteen years that idea would be tested to destruction – rather than in a free-standing measure that could be vetoed.

Devonshire said the graduation of the tax 'must have a tendency to diminish the inducement for the accumulation or saving of wealth, must tend to reduce the capital of the country, and, therefore, must exercise a prejudicial influence upon all classes, and most of all upon the working classes.'[133] He believed that 'once the principle is admitted that the State has the first claim upon property which passes by death, and that no one inherits except on condition of the payment of such toll as the State may arbitrarily demand, it is difficult to see why those limits are not capable of indefinite extension until they reach absolute confiscation'.[134]

He argued that great estates were not just about land: they were about works of art and other treasures central to the heritage of the nation. These too would be taxed: they might be sold abroad before the death of the owner, thereby losing them to Britain and losing the Treasury some tax. And the new tax would have a social effect, 'a great direct, and perhaps a still greater indirect, cessation of the employment of labour, and certainly a great dislocation of labour . . . Thus, the persons who will be most affected by the Bill will not be the rich, who will actually have to pay the tax, and to whom these changes may mean nothing but some alteration, more or less complete, in their present mode of life, and some deprivation of luxuries or means of enjoyment, but those who, owing to the operation of the measure, are deprived of their means of subsistence.'[135]

The agricultural depression had already caused some houses to be closed up and estates run down, their owners holing up in London or in Europe, where the strength of sterling meant one could live well on a reduced income: and that was before the new tax. Now, Devonshire claimed, more would want to sell land: but even fewer would want to buy. What remained of the feudal structure of the countryside – essentially, the charitable work that landowners did for tenant farmers unable to pay rents, or to help their families and children in times of need, or to look after those too old or ill to work, would be threatened.

The Tories argued that the Bill had passed in the Commons by so small a majority that it lacked sufficient support, and should be withdrawn. It was not. In one respect Devonshire was wrong: the development of the suburbs in pre-1914 Britain, and the absence of planning laws, meant there were often developers to buy land from estates that adjoined towns and expand housing stock using them. This happened to Cassiobury, the estate of the Earls of Essex in Hertfordshire, part of which was sold for the expansion of Watford in 1908; the death of the 7th Earl in 1916 – run over by a taxi – led not just to the sale of the rest of the estate, but also of its contents (some of which are in the Metropolitan Museum of Art in New York) and, in 1927, the demolition of the neo-Gothic house to sell off its materials: all because the Dowager Countess could not pay her tax bill.

The death duties ratchet, which Harcourt set in motion, operated throughout the twentieth century: an estimated 1,200 country houses in England, or one in six, were demolished in the century after his Act, helped by the absence of laws to protect historic buildings.[136] By 1940 the 8 per cent rate Devonshire had deplored had risen to 65 per cent. Landowners gave estates to their heirs, exploiting a loophole, but this led to some families being penalised after the deaths of the heirs in two world wars, because the heirs had predeceased the original landowner, and sometimes had no heir themselves, leaving the family encumbered with the property and no means of evading duties. Landowners killed in action were not liable to death duties. Other estates were too expensive to run, which was why the Duke of Newcastle abandoned Clumber Park in Nottinghamshire in 1908: it was demolished just before the Second World War.

Death duties were not the sole cause of this destruction, but were an aggravating factor. Between their introduction in 1894 and 1914, thirty estates were valued at £2 million or more, and it was computed that 92 per cent of the nation's wealth was concentrated in the hands of 10 per cent of the adult population. The income-tax threshold was £160 a year, and 88 per cent of people failed to meet it.[137] Death duties were the beginning of a redistributive process that the Liberal government of 1905–16 would continue, and which would take further chunks out of the wealth and privileges of the landed classes. The taxes were also a factor in the further urbanisation of England as land was sold off to pay them; and they increased the need for a welfare state, as part of the landed interest lost its patronage in the rural population, in losing the opportunity to employ and house many of them. Whatever the practical effects of death duties, their introduction derailed a class that had for centuries regarded wealth and privilege as its right.

VI

Although the break up of large estates was, to start with, neither so widespread nor so socially devastating in the years immediately after Harcourt's Budget as had been predicted, the measure confirmed a sense of persecution among the old ruling class. They sensed they were the target of a creed that wanted to end what remained of their privileges. This sense of doom – fulfilled in too many cases by the unforeseen horrors of the Great War, and its effect on landed families – made a substantial cultural impact.

John Galsworthy's novel *The Country House*, set in 1891–2 but written in 1906, anticipates Harcourt's predations with the benefit of hindsight. The narrator relates: '. . . the times were bad and dangerous. There was every chance of a Radical Government being returned, and the country going to the dogs'.[138] One of the main characters, squire of a village in Cambridgeshire, outlines his creed as a landowner and a Tory: 'I believe in my father, and his father, and his father's father, the makers and keepers of my estate; and I believe in myself and my son and my son's son. And I believe that we have made the country, and shall keep the country what it is. And I believe in the Public Schools, and especially the Public School that I was at. And I believe in my social equals and the country house, and in things as they are, for ever and ever. Amen.'[139] The squire's brother, a retired General, when asked if he thinks the Liberals 'will really get in', replies: 'I pray every night to God they won't.'[140] Galsworthy presents a mild caricature of the gentry and aristocracy, whose sons belong to a London club called the Stoics, whose main qualification for membership is that a man has no occupation. 'They who have passed the windows of the Stoics' Club', he writes, 'and seen the Stoics sitting there have haunting visions of the idle landed classes.'[141]

Galsworthy nevertheless had a romantic attachment to the old landed class, which he saw as an embodiment of gentility and service; he was less enamoured of the rising class that he saw usurping them with their recently acquired money. His first Forsyte novel, *The Man of Property*, which deals with the 1880s, would be published in 1906, after three years of arduous writing and re-writing; it dealt with a family risen from modest beginnings in Dorset, through the mercantilism of the late eighteenth and nineteenth centuries, to enter the professions and form an urban upper-middle class who, when wealth permitted, bought country properties for recreation and not to farm. Such people threatened the status quo, however much they sought to ape the aristocracy's manners, and however keen the aristocracy's offspring were to marry into 'new' money such as the Forsyte family represented.

Although, as his friend Edward Garnett wrote, Galsworthy had been through the 'upper-class mills of the Public School, the University and the Bar', he was, nonetheless, 'inwardly seething against the Forsytes' world and their concentrated social pressure.'[142] Joseph Conrad told Galsworthy after reading the book that 'the socialists ought to present you with a piece of plate.'[143] He looked into the souls of his characters in a way of which they themselves were mostly incapable. Writing to the drama critic William Archer in 1913, Galsworthy commented that 'so far as I know Conrad and I are the only two English novelists trying to paint and not narrate – if not physically, then spiritually – and isn't it perhaps just that attempt of ours that makes you read us?'[144] He continued: 'You know, I can't help thinking that in my series *The Man of Property*, *The Country House*, *Fraternity*, *The Patrician*[,] I went a good way towards recording the *Spiritual Conditions* of the various sections of the middle and upper classes, and of their shadows – and *The Island Pharisees* and *A Commentary* help to fill out that general picture.'

Garnett advised Galsworthy to 'write about the English, for you've got it all inside you – all the keys that nobody turns in the locks.'[145] He did just that, writing about his class as an insider but with a perception denied to many of them. Garnett felt Galsworthy stood 'for the best of the upper-class Englishman of his period, ineradicably English in his essential virtues and limitations, in his love of justice, in his reserve, in his amalgam of hardness and compassion, in his fair-mindedness, his caution and instinct for balance, in his poetical romanticism and sentimental leanings.' The growing threat to these virtues is the enduring theme of *The Man of Property*, and occurs throughout the other eight novels in the series written over the next quarter-century. While writing *The Man of Property* Galsworthy told Garnett: 'We both hate the Forsytes and wish their destruction.'[146] The sequence of Forsyte novels, which would not be completed until the early 1930s, was the author's extended lament for a class, a world and a way of life that he renders almost invisible through his extensive documentation of the more self-serving and materialistic types who took their place, and whose attitudes are embodied in his most masterful creation, the inflexible and unimaginative solicitor Soames Forsyte.

While Galsworthy chronicled a class that was moving up, one of the leading playwrights of the day, Sir Arthur Wing Pinero, looked at those on the way down. As Sir Julian Twombley, the eponymous cabinet minister of Pinero's play, puts it in describing his wife's friend and dress designer, in reduced circumstances after the death of her husband, a peer's son: 'It is to be regretted that poor Mrs Gaylustre is forced to follow the modern fashion of increasing her income by devices formerly practised only by the lower middle-classes.'[147] This has compromised Mrs Gaylustre, whom Twombley's son calls 'a sort of society mermaid – half a lady and half a milliner . . . only it bothers you to know where the one leaves off and the other begins.'[148] But Sir Julian, his wife and his son are all in debt and, as in so many of Trollope's novels of the mid-century, up to their eyes in obligations to Jewish money-lenders with names such as Mr Nazareth and Mr Lebanon (who happens to be Mrs Gaylustre's brother, and whom the enterprising milliner introduces to Lady Twombley, with catastrophic results). Lady Twombley tells her errant son that such has been her own extravagance that 'when I creep into that bank now and ask for my passbook I have to hold on to the edge of the counter, I feel so sick and giddy.'[149]

Even in decline, the landed classes determinedly pursued their traditional pleasures. One of their great extravagances, enabled by their and their neighbours' private ownership of vast acreages, was fox hunting. This was a staple country pastime, though as R. S. Surtees had shown as long ago as *Jorrocks' Jaunts and Jollities* in 1838, it was not exclusively aristocratic, but attracted many yeomen either on horseback or as foot-followers: its reputation as a sport of the rich would be enhanced when the future Edward VIII and his circle patronised it in the 1920s at hunts in the east and south Midlands. Women participated on the same basis as men. Game shooting was popular with the aristocracy and landed gentry, attracting an additional cachet through Royal patronage. It expanded in the nineteenth century – the number of gamekeepers in England and Wales rose from 9,000 in 1851 to 23,000 in 1911, so it was an important source of employment for the rural working class – not least because acquiring an estate was an easy way for the newly rich to gain access to the highest society.[150] The social life of Edward VII, when Prince of Wales, revolved between September and January around pheasant- and partridge-shooting, either on his estate at

Sandringham in west Norfolk, or on those of his landed and aristocratic friends who wished to ingratiate themselves with him.

His son George V took the sport even more seriously, and magnates competed to provide him with the best day's shooting – a vulgarity to which new money, seeking endorsement, was susceptible. One such was Edward Levy-Lawson, 1st Lord Burnham and proprietor of *The Daily Telegraph*, the largest selling quality newspaper, who had in 1880 bought the Hall Barn estate near Beaconsfield. On 18 December 1913, to mark his imminent eightieth birthday, Burnham invited the King and his elder son to join five others who between them shot 3,937 pheasant, 3 partridge, 4 rabbits and a pigeon in the day. Legend says the birds were very sporting, and the guns – who also numbered Lord Ilchester, Lord Dalhousie, Lord Herbert Vane Tempest, Lord Charles Fitzmaurice and the Hon. Harry Stonor – were among the finest shots in Britain. But the King was perturbed by the carnage, saying to his son in the train going back to London: 'Perhaps we went a little far today, David.'[151]

It was not, however, the largest bag ever recorded. At Warter Priory, a 14,000-acre estate in the East Riding of Yorkshire, on 5 December 1906 the Hon. C. H. W. Wilson, son of the owner the 1st Lord Nunburnholme – a Hull shipping magnate, known until his elevation earlier that year as Charles Wilson, and brother of the owner of Tranby Croft, scene of one of the great scandals of the 1890s – and seven of his friends (a duke, five peers and the younger son of a duke) shot 4,460 head of game in the day – 3,824 pheasant, 15 partridge, 526 hare, 92 rabbits and 3 various. Such shoots reflected several factors: the improvement in shotgun mechanisms during the nineteenth century, such as the invention of the boxlock in 1875, as well as improvements in shotgun cartridges. Also, the infusion of new money into old estates enabled tens of thousands of birds to be raised each year. However, hunting and shooting were prominent among the activities that created an idea of the aristocracy as being the idle rich.

VII

Queen Victoria was not above understanding the problem of the idle rich herself. She felt that her son and heir, Albert Edward, Prince of Wales, was so lazy, incapable, unreliable and irresponsible that he was into his fifties before she would allow him even to look formally at state papers. He seemed perfectly to embody a class that many outside it regarded as irrelevant to the changing world and no longer making any valuable contribution to the country. The apex of that class, from the mid-1860s until the Queen's death on 22 January 1901, was Marlborough House, the palace in St James's where Albert Edward and his Danish wife Alexandra were quartered. By 1880 the Prince, then nearly forty, was an accomplished adulterer and glutton, the former hobby noted by his circle (and his wife) but never publicly remarked upon, and the latter earning him the nickname 'Tum-tum'. He had been drawn in early adulthood to Paris, and acquired his tastes from French high society. He was the personification of the manners and morals that caused the age in which he prevailed and later reigned to be regarded as one of decadence. He was the object of sycophantic regard from much of the aristocracy, though to his credit broadened out his circle of friends to include 'new money' and, notably, Jews, hitherto considered unsuitable for Royal society. The Marlborough House Set, as his Court became known, came to oppose everything conventional Victorian morality (as personified by the Sovereign) stood for; therefore the Queen deprecated her son and heir, and many of his friends.

Her own prejudices were fed regularly throughout the 1880s and 1890s, as one scandal after another linked the Prince of Wales to disreputable aspects of modern life. His career as an adulterer started soon after his marriage in 1863. Over the years he moved up from strumpets via actresses to the wives of his smart friends. On his marriage his Court quickly separated from the Queen's, moribund since Prince Albert's death and her withdrawal from society. Aristocrats seeking a more traditionally Hanoverian experience felt the magnetic pull of Marlborough House. The Prince's Court had an annexe too. He was obsessed with smoking – which would kill him, aged sixty-eight – and petitioned for the rules of his club, White's, to be changed to allow it. When the vote on this was lost, he and his nicotinomane friends formed their own club, with premises in Pall Mall, which soon had 400 members chosen by the Prince. He visited every day he was in London, and its existence made him even more the kingpin of fashionable society than he already was. The sycophancy it engendered went to his head, immature and rather vacuous as he was.

His first great public scandal was the Mordaunt case of 1870, when a Warwickshire baronet, Sir Charles Mordaunt, sued his wife for divorce, citing two society figures as co-respondents. He had, however, suspected a liaison with the Prince, who not only visited her regularly in the afternoons in London but whom Mordaunt found at his country seat one day, having returned unexpectedly. Lady Mordaunt had a child who she professed was not her husband's. Sir Charles mentioned her friendship with the Prince while in the witness box, saying he had found a cache of letters from His Royal Highness to his wife, and said on oath that 'I warned my wife against continuing acquaintance with His Royal Highness for reasons which governed my own mind.'[152] He continued: 'I had heard in various quarters certain circumstances connected with the Prince's character which caused me to make that remark.'

The Prince had warned the Queen he would have to give evidence in the case, which he did, and she believed his claims of innocence. So, he said, did Gladstone. However, newspapers reporting the case were hidden from the Queen's younger children because the details were 'such as hardly to be readable for any one'.[153] It cannot have amused her to see her son and heir put on record as being of dubious character. Though he swore he had not committed adultery with Lady Mordaunt, few believed him. Gladstone, at the Queen's insistence, wrote to the Prince, reminding him of the importance of a man in his position upholding the principles of family life, by which he meant the Prince should discourage gossip by stopping visiting other men's wives for meetings *à deux*. Writing in 1906, Galsworthy observed, of a man carrying on with the wives of others, 'it was legendary in his class that young men's peccadilloes must be accepted with a certain indulgence.'[154]

The Prince expected this indulgence, and ignored Gladstone's advice. In the spring of 1871 he fathered a child on Lady Susan Vane Tempest, daughter of the Duke of Newcastle. He washed his hands of her; no trace can be found of the child, who may have been stillborn or simply parcelled out to a compliant family; Lady Susan died four years later. Also in 1871, the brother of a Parisian whore who had died during the Siege of Paris tried to blackmail the Prince when letters emerged. That was resolved by a high-speed intervention, but the procession of mistresses and alleged bastards continued throughout the 1870s; at one point Rosebery was asked to lend his London house to the Prince and his brother the Duke of Edinburgh so that they might meet actresses there. Rosebery refused.

Lillie Langtry, the actress who became the Prince's most celebrated mistress, met him in 1877. She had modelled for the painting *Effie Deans* by Sir John Everett Millais. The Prince saw the painting and asked to meet the model; an intermediary invited them to dinner. Mrs Langtry, Jersey-born, was the wife of an Irish landowner. For a year or so the affair flourished; then, when in 1879 a periodical called *Town Talk* wrote that Langtry would divorce his wife and the Prince would be a co-respondent, Langtry sued. He won, but the Prince's name was further blackened. Respectable newspapers printed accounts of the case, retailing all allegations against him. *Town Talk* was a trivial magazine that made money writing about trivial goings-on among trivial people; it was a pity one happened to be the Prince of Wales. The QC who defended its editor, Adolphus Rosenberg, in the libel suit observed: 'Far be it from me to suppose that the Prince of Wales could for a moment depart from the morality which it is his duty to exhibit . . . but, Gentlemen, have not men in high stations fallen before now?'[155] The Prince ended his affair with Mrs Langtry, whose aggrieved husband left her.

There were degeneracies beyond the sexual that made the Prince a poor example to a society flirting with republicanism, and in which an increasingly educated and politically-aware working class was alert to inequalities. He was idle, his life devoted to the pursuit of pleasure – shooting, house parties, travelling, yachting. His self-indulgence offended not only the Queen but many of her subjects. His insistence on luxury created a revolting competition among his 'friends' about who might best entertain him when he visited; one or two bankrupted themselves, throwing lavish balls and shooting parties with browsing and sluicing lasting days at a time. It was absurd behaviour given the debts he and his sycophants ran up; and not in the best taste.

By the end of the 1880s his sexual incontinence was again causing problems. He fell for twenty-eight-year-old Daisy Brooke, an heiress married to the future Earl of Warwick. She was the mistress of Lord Charles Beresford, a naval officer of distinction and Fourth Lord of the Admiralty, much liked by the Prince and part of the Marlborough House Set. It was natural, therefore, that the Prince should pay him the compliment of seducing his mistress. Beresford had a forceful character: he would take on his naval superiors if he thought they were mistaken about policy, and would not hesitate to quarrel with a prince. He took the Prince of Wales's behaviour badly, not least because the Prince had behaved appallingly in one further respect: he had bullied a solicitor to let him see a potentially ruinous letter Lady Brooke had written to

Beresford, but which had fallen into Lady Charles's hands. In January 1890, boiling with rage, Beresford demanded an interview with the Prince, at which they ended up calling each other blackguards. When Beresford refused to give up Lady Brooke, the Prince threw an inkwell at him. But when the Princess of Wales invited Lady Brooke to dinner in July 1891, Lady Charles had her revenge by circulating a pamphlet around society parties detailing events. This pamphlet included the draft of a letter to the Prince from Beresford that had not been sent.

The Prince had ostracised Lord and Lady Charles, enraging Beresford still further. Away at sea, he had drafted the letter; and Lady Charles asked for an interview with Salisbury, the prime minister, to show it to him, given the potential implications of a scandal. Salisbury advised Beresford not to send it, mainly for Lady Charles's sake: he was aware Beresford himself was not without blemish. It included lines such as 'there was only one blackguard in the case at all, and that was YRH.'[156] It also included the threat that 'the first opportunity that occurs to me I shall put my opinion publicly of YRH: and state that you have behaved more like a blackguard and a coward and that I am prepared to prove my words as publicly as I make them either before a Court Martial or in another manner.'

While Beresford held off, and apologised to Salisbury for having troubled him 'on a matter of so scandalous a nature', he remained volatile.[157] He told Salisbury that 'I have received letters from England telling me that Lady Charles has been insulted by a distinguished personage', and that his wife had sent him 'very unhappy letters . . . on the matter'. Beresford felt the Prince could not 'possibly affect my position either in society or professionally' and only his wife's feelings held him back. When Lady Charles's pamphlet started circulating Beresford's brother, Lord Marcus, wrote him a stinging rebuke for the inclusion of a letter 'which you ought never to have allowed to remain in existence'.[158]

Lord Charles 'expressed no horror about this'. Lord Marcus denounced him as not being 'Charlie Beresford the brave sailor who has hitherto been looked up to as the soul of honour.' But then Lord Marcus felt his brother was defaming 'a man who has been the greatest friend to you in the world', and who, he was sure, had not said or done the things Lord Charles believed. He was worried about tarnishing the family name and particularly the effect on their mother, thus far ignorant of the matter. 'I dread reading a newspaper for fear of seeing the publication of your shame and dishonour', he continued, begging his brother to order Lady Charles to withdraw the pamphlet.

Lord Charles was not convinced. He came back from sea in December 1891 having been adopted by the Conservatives to fight the North Kensington seat at the general election, which redoubled his need to force an apology from the Prince. Salisbury's private secretary, Schomberg McDonnell, met him on 16 December. Lord Charles Beresford, who initially refused to see him, agreed to write to the Prince and use 'temperate language as he felt the delicacy of his position with regard to Lady Brooke (which had been fully shewn him by Lord Salisbury)'.[159] McDonnell went to see Francis Knollys, the Prince's secretary, who agreed with him that 'the only way out of the impasse was concession'. This was made harder by the Prince's having forbidden anyone to discuss the matter with Lady Brooke; and by Lady Charles (who had petitioned Sir Henry Ponsonby to inform the Queen: Ponsonby refused) demanding the removal of Lady Brooke from Court, and her absence from London for a year.

On 18 December Charles Beresford wrote to the Prince. 'Your Royal Highness's behaviour to Lady Charles in openly slighting and ignoring her during my absence abroad on duty, and this taking into consideration a certain conspicuous part that Your Royal Highness played in an affair (which in no way concerned you) that unfortunately caused much talk 3 or 4 years ago, has had the result of causing Lady Charles to sell her house and announce her intention to tell her friends and relations that sooner than be humiliated any longer she would rather live abroad.'[160] He denied his wife had circulated the pamphlet ('malicious rumours . . . absolutely devoid of foundation') and called the claim 'a direct intention to damage my wife'. He added that 'all her friends and relations' believed 'such a state of things is brought about entirely by the line of conduct Your Royal Highness has thought to adopt. I now demand an apology from Your Royal Highness on behalf of Lady Charles Beresford, failing which I shall not only apply for an extension of leave, but I shall no longer intervene to prevent these matters becoming public.'

The Prince replied by return that 'I am at a loss to understand how Lady Charles can imagine that I have in any way slighted or spurned her during your absence abroad'. She had been invited to, and had attended, the garden party at Marlborough House the previous summer, and he had shaken hands with and bowed to her as the occasion arose.[161] Beresford curtly dismissed this as inadequate. Salisbury advised it was 'impossible' for the Prince to have further correspondence with Beresford. He also suggested that Lady Charles be advised that 'she had condoned adultery to the fullest extent: but directly she found that she was not invited as often as before to Marlborough House, and she did not receive as much attention from the Pr of Wales as formerly, she at once began to declare her injuries to the world.'[162]

Salisbury proposed a compromise: Beresford would apologise for having 'misinterpreted' the Prince's attitude and for the tone of his letters; the Prince would apologise for having 'inadvertently wounded' Lady Charles. There followed haggling about the exact wording, but the matter was settled by Christmas. The ridiculousness of the episode, and the time wasted on it, emphasises the trivial milieu in which the Prince, and those in his orbit, lived. It hardened Salisbury's view that the heir to the Throne was contemptible, an unfortunate impression for a man who would be his first prime minister to hold.

The scandal most associated with the Prince is not sexual, but about gambling, and known by the name of the country house where it happened, Tranby Croft in the East Riding of Yorkshire. It was owned by Arthur Wilson, a Hull shipping magnate typical of the newly moneyed men the Prince favoured with his society – provided they entertained him lavishly. The Prince was staying for the St Leger, and on the first evening suggested playing baccarat. A game of chance in which the odds were heavily stacked in favour of the house and against individual players, baccarat was usually played in casinos. It required a serious level of mindlessness: when the Royal baccarat scandal ended up in court the solicitor-general, Sir Edward Clarke, described it as 'a most uninteresting mode of losing your own money, or winning somebody else's. There is no room for skill or judgment.'[163] Sandringham had a dedicated baccarat table, as in a casino; at Tranby Croft some whist tables were laid end to end to make one.

In 1866 the High Court had decreed baccarat illegal if played for money, even in a private house. It was typical of the Prince that he should suggest setting up a table and playing for money. He was dealer on the first night, and the players used counters with sums of money printed on them made specially for him, which he carried around with him. Some members of the Wilson family thought they saw another guest,

Lieutenant-Colonel Sir William Gordon-Cumming, cheat by adding to his stake late in the play. Nothing was said, but he was watched on the second night, thought to be cheating again, and confronted. The Prince, to whom he had been close for a decade, decided the weight of evidence was against him. To stop a scandal, the others forced Gordon-Cumming to sign a statement swearing not to play cards again so long as he lived. In return, nothing would be said. He signed, it seems, to end the argument, not because he admitted guilt.

Gordon-Cumming continued to protest his innocence. He had a reputation for arrogance and rudeness, so may have believed he could do as he liked. He had won £225 in two nights – worth perhaps £20,000 today – so had he been cheating it would not merely have been a breach of honour, but one to the pecuniary disadvantage of others. However, Gordon-Cumming had huge Scottish estates and was rich, so did not need to cheat. He was also a prodigious womaniser. He may have sought to proposition Ethel, daughter of Arthur Wilson and wife of one of his accusers, Edward Lycett Green, who perhaps determined to teach him a lesson: but that would not explain why the others rounded on him.

Soon events at Tranby Croft were common knowledge in London society. Gordon-Cumming faced social ruin if he did not clear his name, and would be thrown out of his regiment; so he chose to sue his accusers – the Lycett Greens, Wilson and his wife, and another guest, Berkeley Levett, an officer in the Scots Guards. The Prince was forced to give evidence, to his horror and the Queen's. His courtiers tried, and failed, to have it dealt with by court martial, which further damaged their master's reputation. The popular press thought the Prince shifty in the witness box: the future Sovereign admitted breaking the law by conducting a game of cards. After the case, senior Anglican clergy denounced the example set by the Prince's social circle while the Nonconformists were beside themselves.

Gordon-Cumming lost; his regiment expelled him; society shunned him. He lived until 1930 as an outcast. 'He has committed a mortal offence,' *The Times* wrote. 'Society can know him no more.'[164] When the verdict was given people in the gallery hissed; the Prince was booed in public. He forsook baccarat and confined himself to whist, where a small amount of skill is required. *The Times*, normally reluctant to criticise the Royal family, could hardly avoid it. 'What does concern and indeed distress the public is the discovery that the PRINCE should have been at the baccarat table; that the game was apparently played to please him; that it was played with his counters, specially taken down for the purpose; that his set are a gambling, a baccarat playing set,' it announced. It understood the 'monotony' of Royal existence; but, while everyone was entitled to a private life: 'a Prince of Wales is an exception to that rule. He cannot put off his responsibilities when he puts off his official dress. He is, next to the QUEEN, the most visible embodiment of the Monarchical principle; and any personal default of his gives a shock to the principle which in these democratic days is mischievous, even dangerous.' The paper wished the Prince would sign a declaration to give up cards, as his former friend had.

One of the Prince's biographers has claimed Gordon-Cumming probably did cheat, because many players did.[165] This was because the Prince bullied others into playing while at house parties, to try to win money off them: he may even have cheated himself. Gordon-Cumming never accepted the verdict. The Lord Chief Justice's summing-up was regarded as biased, and to read it today – a point-by-point rebuttal of everything said by Clarke – bears out that view. It does smell as though the establishment sought to protect the House of Saxe-Coburg-Gotha, however little it merited such protection. When the Lord Chief Justice spoke of the need 'to keep our institutions sacred and respectable', he could hardly have advertised his own views more clearly.[166]

The Queen was remarkably restrained in her wrath. She told the Empress Frederick, her daughter, that 'people think good will come of it' because it would be 'a shock to Society'.[167] Yet her expectations of the Prince's set had been more than fulfilled. The son whom she regarded as utterly unfit to succeed her seemed, even at the age of almost fifty, intent on proving her right. She had abdicated, in her widowhood, notional leadership of society; worse, she had abdicated it to a capricious, selfish, hypocritical poltroon shielded from his own poor judgment by the obsequiousness of his Court. He belatedly matured during the 1890s, not least because the Queen's senescence required that he should be entrusted with more duties of state: but he persisted in most of his vices, setting an atrocious example. High society's role in changing British morals was substantial.

The Prince initiated one commendable social revolution: his enthusiastic admission of Jews into his social circle. He lacked a prejudice that disfigured much of the class that otherwise took their lead from him. Admittedly, his enthusiasm for Jews was motivated in part by self-interest: those he befriended had money. They could entertain him in the sybaritic style to which he was accustomed or, more often, help finance his elephantine debts. His Jewish friends also supplied him with information from around Europe, about politics and business, from their own family and commercial networks; this was useful when the Queen forbade him access to government information.

His patronage of Jews had a remarkable effect on society. Money, however recently acquired, became an accepted means of entering it; admission was no longer regulated by birth or land. The first hereditary Jewish peer was Nathan Rothschild, ennobled in 1885; between then and the Great War many peerages were bestowed on new money, subtly changing the character of the House of Lords. The Prince had first met Rothschild at Cambridge in 1861, and his association with the family grew despite attempts by courtiers to stop it. He became close, too, to the Sassoons. Daisy Brooke, the Prince's mistress, made an insightful comment about the difficulties the Marlborough House Set had in accepting Jews: they were resented 'not because we disliked them . . . but because they had brains and understood finance. As a class we did not like brains. As for money, our only understanding of it lay in the spending, not the making of it.'[168] That remark betrays part of the reason for the decline of the old ruling class in the twentieth century.

The Prince understood money-making better than his mistress realised, but had little capacity for doing so. Therefore, he was thought to have negotiated huge loans from Jewish magnates, notably Baron Maurice de Hirsch, said in 1890 to have lent him £600,000. Hirsch rented an estate twenty miles from Sandringham, where he could entertain the Prince in the shooting season. After Hirsch's death the Prince became close to his executor, Ernest – later Sir Ernest – Cassel, whose grand-daughter, Edwina Ashley, would marry Lord Louis Mountbatten in 1921. It is believed Hirsch instructed Cassel to waive the Prince's debts after Hirsch died in 1896. Cassel became the Prince's financial adviser, a role he continued to occupy once the Prince became King. Cassel became hugely rich through investments in Egypt and the Middle East. The King did however use the Jewish connection for more than his own benefit. When, after the Boer War, he sought to fund the King Edward VII Hospital for Officers, it was largely his Jewish friends who paid for it.

While his acceptance of Jews and other representatives of new money broadened and intellectually enriched society, the Prince was always keen to exclude from it, and from the peerage, anyone he felt had standards he imagined unworthy of it. Given his own behaviour there was a strong element of hypocrisy in this. It became even more intense once he was King, and could comment on honours lists. When Sir Henry Campbell-Bannerman, as prime minister, sought a peerage for the long-serving cabinet minister Sir Henry Fowler in 1907, the King objected. He indicated he would approve the elevation 'if you have satisfied yourself that Sir Henry Fowler's eldest son is reputable. When it was proposed to confer a Coronation Peerage on Sir Henry in 1902, the idea had to be abandoned on account of the son's character, and HM imagines that this objection still holds good.'[169] Campbell-Bannerman spoke up for the boy, but Knollys said the King 'cannot, he is afraid, consider the account of young Fowler very satisfactory': so it was postponed.[170] However, Fowler was elevated – as Viscount Wolverhampton – days after Asquith came to power, in May 1908.

VIII

In an age before the tabloid press, when newspapers trod carefully while covering the Royal family, the very highest in the land could generally behave as though George III were still on the Throne. In the post-Palmerston era, however, the oppressive moral tone of the Court on the one hand, and the press's determination to test the limits of possibility on the other, started to change things. It became less easy to conceal lubricious behaviour among those who were well born but lacked the cachet of Royal blood, and some boundaries were crossed at one's peril.

One such case was that of Sir Charles Dilke, an ornament of the Prince of Wales's circle. He came from an ancient Warwickshire family whose seat was at Maxstoke Castle in that county; and Dilkes had sat in parliament since the sixteenth century. A baronet, Dilke was elected for Chelsea as a Liberal in the 1868 general election, aged twenty-five. He advertised himself as on the radical wing of the party by becoming a voice of republicanism at the height of the Queen's unpopularity in the early 1870s. His views angered his constituents and colleagues alike. Rampantly ambitious, he stopped articulating them. The ploy worked, and he found himself – much to the Queen's disgust – a junior minister at the Foreign Office when Gladstone came back in 1880. Because Granville, the Foreign Secretary, was in the Lords, Dilke had a great platform in the Commons. Having turned down the Irish secretaryship after the Phoenix Park murders (see Chapter 5), he reached the top table in December 1882 as President of the Local Government Board, where he devised the 1884 Reform Act and the measures for redistributing seats. But these would be the last achievements of a man once tipped as a future leader of his party.

From 1876 Ellen Eustace Smith, mother-in-law of Dilke's younger brother Ashton, had been Charles Dilke's mistress. Were that not sufficiently complicated her husband, Thomas Eustace Smith, was also a Liberal MP and a close colleague. Another of the Smith daughters, Virginia, was married to Donald Crawford, a Liberal activist twenty-five years her senior, who would become an MP in 1885. Within months of the Crawfords marrying, according to Mrs Crawford, Dilke, operating on some hereditary principle, seduced her she was just nineteen. The affair, she later alleged, continued on and off for the next two and a half years, after Dilke himself had become engaged in 1884 (it was his second marriage: his first wife died in childbirth in 1874). In 1885 Crawford announced he was suing his wife for divorce on the grounds of her adultery with Dilke, who learned, from a mutual friend of Mrs Crawford's and his, of the matter on 18 July on his return from a banquet in his honour at the Reform Club, to mark the Redistribution Act. Divorce had then been legal for just twenty-eight years but was regarded as incompatible with respectable society, and no case had ever implicated a politician.

Dilke told his future wife he believed the scandal had been cooked up 'by a woman who wanted me to marry her'.[171] He sought advice from Chamberlain and from Sir Henry James, the Attorney-General; his biographer reports that in the fortnight after the bombshell his weight fell from 13 stone 13lbs to 12 stone 4lbs. He soon regained his appetite. He just held his hitherto safe seat in Chelsea in November 1885, after his marriage. There were rumours Gladstone had, before the election, sought to deploy patronage to buy Crawford off: if he did, it failed.[172] Dilke told the Prince of Wales of his trouble that autumn; at least in doing so he confided in someone familiar with one of Dilke's hobbies.

He also decided Rosebery had somehow engineered the scandal to remove his main rival for the Foreign Office and, one day, the party leadership. Such was Dilke's paranoia that he wrote to Rosebery on 12 December to say Crawford had claimed Lady Rosebery 'had promised to help him in this case.'[173] Rosebery was outraged at the perceived insult, and slapped down Dilke with the assertion that 'even in this age of lies no human being could have invented so silly a lie as you mention.' Dilke needed as many friends as he could find, and had alienated one of the most influential: Rosebery had little to do with him thereafter.

When Gladstone regained office on 30 January 1886 he felt it impossible to restore Dilke to office. He told him on 2 February of his 'profound regret that any circumstances of the moment should deprive me of the opportunity' of using Dilke, claimed to have no 'want of inward confidence' in him, and a desire that he should still have 'a long and honourable career of public distinction.' Coming ten days before the case was heard, Dilke's exclusion confirmed the view taken of his conduct at the highest level.

The case came to court on 12 February. Mrs Crawford had refused, on the advice of her father, to make a statement to a solicitor. Nor did she give evidence. Nor, on the advice of Chamberlain, did Dilke, who had plenty to hide beyond any misbehaviour with Mrs Crawford. All the judge had to go on was Crawford's account of his wife's confession, and evidence from servants. Crawford told the court Dilke had seduced his wife in a house near Tottenham Court Road in February 1882, and their affair had lasted until the summer of 1884.

The divorce caused a huge scandal. *The Times* devoted over 7,500 words to reporting it. A crowd fought to get in; notabilities for whom seats were reserved in the jury box included Chamberlain and, bizarrely, the Turkish Ambassador. Mrs Crawford's sister – Dilke's sister-in-law – sat in the well of the court. Happily, Dilke's brother had died of tuberculosis in 1883, obviating an especially acute family problem. Dilke, who strongly denied his complicity, had hired the Attorney-General, Sir Charles Russell, and his predecessor, James, to represent him.

The court heard that Crawford had first been warned about Dilke's attentions to his wife in April 1882, in an anonymous letter imploring him to 'beware the Member for Chelsea.'[174] He assumed the writer wished to damage Dilke and burned the letter. A second letter came two years later when Crawford was helping Dilke with the Redistribution Bill; it accused Dilke of having 'ruined' Mrs Crawford. Crawford put this to his wife, who accused her mother of having written it: had that line of questioning been pursued Dilke's ruin would have been even more spectacular. For a time Crawford had been thrown off the scent because he had thought another of his wife's admirers, a Captain Forster, was pursuing her. But Dilke's demeanour convinced him he had something to hide.

Crawford told the court that, in the manner of the times, he wanted to 'horsewhip' Dilke when his wife admitted she had been his mistress until the autumn of 1884 when, she supposed, he had grown tired of her. Crawford had sought, and claimed to have obtained, corroborative evidence from various servants, both his own and Dilke's. Russell, however, claimed there was no case to answer, for the claims of a woman accused of adultery against her alleged seducer were not really evidence at all, and the servants had seen nothing of substance. The judge, Mr Justice Butt, agreed there not 'a shadow of a case' against him, and James asked for Dilke's name to be struck from the petition. The judge ruled Mrs Crawford had committed adultery with Dilke and granted a decree nisi, because he did not wish to 'disbelieve' Crawford. The decree was granted mainly on his evidence; but the judge repeated that there was no admissible evidence that Dilke had committed adultery with her. Mrs Crawford's confession – the judge called it 'an unsworn statement' – was inadmissible, and her refusal to give evidence meant her claims could not be tested by cross-examination.

That was absurd enough: but not so absurd as what Dilke did next. The scandal had cast a cloud over him that he was determined to clear, a cloud the most formidable muck-raking journalist of the day, W. T. Stead, did all he could, in *The Pall Mall Gazette* of which he was editor, to thicken. Stead, who was obsessed with Dilke, kept up his attacks for years. Worse still for Dilke, Stead attacked Chamberlain as the adviser who had got Dilke into this mess by persuading him not to enter the witness box. Chamberlain wrote sulphurously to Stead, accusing him of trying to ruin Dilke in order to boost the circulation of the *Gazette*.

While Dilke's political career was heading for the abyss, that of his closest friend in politics was being damaged by association with him. Chamberlain could not, however, stop giving advice. He suggested Dilke could clear his name either by suing for libel, or by asking the Queen's Proctor to challenge the process to award the decree absolute, on the grounds Mrs Crawford had not told the truth, and no adultery had happened. Anxious to enlist support, Dilke called a meeting attended by an estimated 2,000 voters in Chelsea on 3 May 1886.

Accompanied by his wife, he said he had hoped to avoid a public statement on 'painful topics', but had to stress the 'baselessness' of the charges against him.[175] He blamed 'the unsatisfactory state of the law', and announced he had enlisted the Queen's Proctor. His protestations of innocence seemed to work. One constituent, the Reverend Lawson Forster, told the meeting he thought 'Sir C Dilke is the most ill-used man in England.'

However, because Dilke was no longer part of the case after the decree nisi, his barrister could not cross-examine Mrs Crawford. Dilke asked to be joined to the proceedings, but a judge in chambers rejected his application. He went to the Court of Appeal, who rejected his claim on 30 June. The Queen's Proctor's investigation continued, however, and Mrs Crawford was subpoenaed to appear on 16 July. Thanks to Dilke's asking for the case to be reconsidered the full allegations were aired again, the detail more lurid than ever – an allegation of three-in-a-bed sex including a maidservant was widely reported. Worse, however, was that Dilke was called to give evidence.

He could deny, on oath, the allegations against him. However, Henry Matthews, a former Tory MP representing Crawford, took him to pieces. Twice he asked Dilke whether he had had an affair with Mrs Crawford's mother; twice Dilke refused to answer. Such answers as he would give were prolix and shifty. He was vague about dates, arrangements and how well he knew Mrs Crawford. Matthews exposed Dilke's bizarre habit of cutting sections from his diary with scissors, as if he had things to hide. Dilke said he did this when appointments were cancelled. The jury agreed Mrs Crawford had not lied, and that the decree absolute should be granted. As a consequence Dilke, by protesting his innocence, was finished.

If anything, matters became even worse in the aftermath of the case. Various other women claimed he had pursued them. As well as the ridicule prompted by the threesome rumours, and claims of an interest in exotic sexual practices, he feared being charged with perjury. He lost Chelsea in the general election of July 1886, days before his courtroom *débâcle*. He would devote much of the rest of his life – he died in 1911 – to trying to make the world believe Mrs Crawford had lied. In any case, Dilke's affair with her mother left him vulnerable, and was a dangerous hobby in that age for a man who wanted a political career.

He was re-elected to parliament in 1892, but never held office again.

The Queen had a rare moment of delight at his humiliation. She was so thrilled by Matthews's performance that she urged Salisbury to make him Home Secretary when the Tories regained power in 1886. Matthews, his reputation boosted by his destruction of Dilke, as the Victorian public wallowed in a periodic fit of morality, had been re-elected after an absence from the Commons of twelve years: so Salisbury could oblige. Dilke never left the favour of the Prince of Wales, and in the summer of 1897 found himself and his wife invited to meet the Queen. He asked the Prince what he made of the invitation, and Knollys, on his master's behalf, replied that 'though he understands the reason which prompts you and Lady Dilke to hesitate about going to Windsor tomorrow, he is at the same time of opinion that you should both "obey Her Majesty's commands".'[176] When the Prince became King, Dilke was reabsorbed into the highest Royal circles.

IX

In May 1889 the Earl of Euston, heir to the Dukedom of Grafton, was walking down Piccadilly at about 11 p.m. one evening when a man pressed into his hand a card with '*Poses Plastiques*' – understood to mean a striptease – the name 'C. Hammond' and an address in Cleveland Street, Fitzrovia, printed on it. A week later Euston found the card in his pocket and, after a convivial evening at the Garrick Club, went to the house on a whim. A man opened the door and asked him for a sovereign. As a court later heard, 'he was shown into a parlour, and the man made some indecent proposal. Lord Euston became very indignant and threatened to kick him out of the place, which he himself afterwards left.'[177]

A month later, on 4 July, Constable Hanks of the Metropolitan Police questioned a Post Office telegraph boy, Charles Thomas Swinscow, about a theft of money from his workplace: suspicions were aroused because the boy had fourteen shillings on him, which it was thought he could not have earned reputably. Swinscow said he had made the money performing sexual favours for men at 19 Cleveland Street, and two fellow messenger boys – George Wright and Charles Thickbroom – had also profited in this way, having been procured by Henry Horace Newlove, a Post Office clerk. Thickbroom, in his statement, described events, from which an extract (probably translated from the vernacular by a policeman) will suffice: 'He and I went into the bedroom and undressed, quite naked. We got into bed and played with each other. He did not put his person into me. We got up and he gave me half a sovereign which I gave to the proprietor who gave me four shillings.'[178]

The police arrested Newlove on 6 July. His boss, John Hammond, who had opened the door for Euston, escaped abroad after Newlove alerted him. A man responsible with Hammond for running the brothel, George Veck, escaped detection by dressing as a clergyman, but was arrested at Waterloo on 20 August after a trip to Portsmouth. From 9 July the police watched the house, and noted numbers of young soldiers – other ranks, not officers – visiting. The name of Lord Arthur Somerset, a younger son of the Duke of Beaufort, a major in the Royal Horse Guards, or the Blues, and a Sudan veteran, came to the police's attention. On 25 July boys Newlove had procured were taken to Piccadilly, where they observed Somerset – whom they had known as Mr Brown – and identified him as a client. He would arrange to meet in the brothel men picked up in the street, including young soldiers. His own regiment had a reputation for harbouring guardsmen willing to oblige well-to-do male clients with sexual favours.[179]

Somerset adorned the Marlborough House Set, advising the Prince of Wales on his bloodstock and managing his stables, for which he was made an extra equerry. When a caricature of him appeared in *Vanity Fair* in November 1887 it claimed: 'He hunts much with his father's hounds, he is the best of sons, a true Somerset, a gentleman, a good sportsman, good natured, and of much solid sense. He is favourably regarded by the fair sex, and his irreverent brother officers long ago nicknamed him "Podge".'[180] Probably unknown to the ingratiating writer was that 'Podge' was also homosexual, and interested in very young men, in pursuit of whom – when homosexuality was illegal and he had a position to think of – his 'solid sense' deserted him.

It deserted him, too, when he realised he would be implicated in the Cleveland Street scandal, and he tried to interfere with witnesses, including attempting to bribe a boy to emigrate. It was later proved Somerset had sent three twenty-shilling postal orders to a witness. He went about his normal life, but with police watching him and with government ministers and high officials alerted to the case, because of Somerset's standing. Reality intervened on 7 August: after taking part in a military review during the Kaiser's visit to England, Somerset was interviewed at Knightsbridge barracks by police officers. Sadly, no record of this survives. On 13 August he saw the Prince of Wales off from Charing Cross for a three-week holiday in Homburg.

Somerset would not have known that on 10 August the Director of Public Prosecutions, Sir Augustus Stephenson, the Attorney-General, Sir Richard Webster, and the solicitor-general, Sir Edward Clarke, met in Webster's chambers and agreed that Somerset (and Veck) should be arrested. However, immediately the opinion was delivered, the permanent secretary at the Home Office wrote to Stephenson on behalf of Matthews, the Home Secretary, asking him to 'stay your hand until he [Matthews] has seen Lord Salisbury on Monday.'[181] This smell of political interference upset the DPP, and would linger. Webster then vacillated on Somerset (but not on Veck), telling Stephenson on 17 August that he was unsatisfied with his identification – surprising, as Somerset was a very distinctive-looking man, tall, bald but with a huge ginger moustache – and on 26 August that the evidence needed corroborating. Stephenson countered that the prosecutions against the other men should proceed irrespective of the consequences to anyone else – that is, Somerset. By 29 August Webster was telling him that if Somerset's name came out in this 'horrible case . . . "Brown's" conduct must – and ought to be – brought home to him.'[182] The Home Secretary did not agree, nor did Salisbury who seemed determined to keep the dogs off Somerset.

'Brown', however, had a clear idea of the trouble he was in. His attempt to bribe a witness came before the authorities, but not, it seems, before the police interviewed him for a second time on 22 August. Since his first interview he had sent his solicitor, Arthur Newton, to conduct Newlove's defence; now he paid him to help Veck. He briefed his former schoolfriend Regy Brett, later 2nd Viscount Esher and chief factotum and busybody to King Edward VII; a man whose own peculiar sexual tastes appear to have included his being in love with his younger son. He thanked Brett for seeing 'that fellow yesterday', by whom he seems to have meant the imminently arrested Veck, and complained that Newton's and the other legal costs would probably exceed £1,000.[183] He left for the Villa Imperiale at Homburg, whence he and Brett corresponded often, Brett keeping in regular touch with Newton.

On 2 September Stephenson passed Webster information about the postal orders, adding that Somerset was abroad. 'It is quite possible', he added, '– in my judgment it is probable – that he will not return.'[184]

Somerset would be back, but not for long. While in Homburg he attended the Prince of Wales, at the spa to drink waters supposedly beneficial to the effects of his gluttony. Somerset found them disgusting, but had higher concerns. He wrote to Brett begging him: 'For heaven's sake . . . make Newton keep the expenses down as much as possible.'[185] Newton warned Brett on 5 September that 'the case is concluded so far as the Police Court is concerned and both defendants will next week be committed for trial.'[186] Four days later he sought £500, indicating £1,000 would soon be necessary: Brett persuaded a city friend, Hugh Weguelin, to give Newton £1,200, which he did on 16 September. Somerset minded that the Prince of Wales, and his regiment, would shortly find out about the scandal, since Stead's *Pall Mall Gazette* was already publishing rumours about a compromised peer. On 14 September he wrote to Brett that 'I have even got so far as to wonder what I am to do with myself in case of the worst.'[187]

On 15 September Stephenson, angered by the refusal to pursue Somerset, wrote to Webster to protest that 'in the interest of public justice' he should be charged with conspiring with Hammond to commit buggery, since there was 'direct and overwhelming moral evidence' against him.[188] He also told Webster he felt it his duty to tell the Secretary of State for War about someone 'under War Office control' – Somerset – against whom information was known: not least that he was 'a commissioned officer' seen 'shaking hands with a private soldier at the door of a house known to be frequented by sodomites', even though that was not a criminal offence. Stephenson hinted at the effect of political interference to protect Somerset: 'The public scandal involved in a criminal charge against a man in his position in Society is undoubted. But in my opinion the public scandal in declining to prefer such a charge and in permitting such a man to hold Her Majesty's Commission and remain in English society is much greater.' Webster agreed, but referred it to Salisbury, who wanted the Lord Chancellor, Halsbury, to advise him.

A letter in the Director of Public Prosecution's archives, written on 16 September by Hamilton Cuffe, the Assistant Director, to Stephenson after a meeting with Newton, introduces a further twist, and shows why the matter became of such concern. Newton had warned Cuffe that if Somerset were prosecuted 'a very distinguished personage' would be dragged into the scandal.[189] In his letter, Cuffe had used only the initials of the personage, who was allegedly another Cleveland Street regular:

PAV. They stood for Prince Albert Victor, vacuous twenty-five-year-old elder son of Lord Arthur's master, the Prince of Wales, and after his father the next heir to the Throne. The Prince – known as 'Eddy' – was considered unmanly and effeminate, sufficiently so to make him a credible homosexual according to contemporary opinion, although there is not the slightest evidence he was. He would also be accused of being Jack the Ripper, a preposterous assertion also without evidence, not least because at the time of two murders the Prince was shooting in Scotland, and on another was at Sandringham. He was suffocatingly close to his mother, who indulged both her sons to compensate for the neglect she endured from her adulterous husband.

The letter eventually landed on Salisbury's desk. It may have influenced the decision to delay the warrant for Somerset's arrest long enough for him to flee abroad. Newton may have known the story was fiction, but uttered it to try to protect Somerset. Alternatively, Somerset may have told Newton the story, relying on his solicitor's credulity, knowing the effect it would have when passed on. It is also possible, as one historian has mooted, that the Prince was duped into going to the house, as Euston had been, to see a striptease.[190]

Somerset later wrote to Brett to claim that Prince Eddy's name had been associated with the brothel 'in June or July', independent of any scandalous behaviour Somerset himself had engaged in – he told Brett this in case it helped lessen the disfavour in which the Prince of Wales now held him.[191] 'Nothing', Somerset continued, 'will ever make me divulge anything I know even if I were arrested.' He said if he went into court and had to tell the whole truth '*no one* who called himself a man would *ever* speak to me again.' How far this was a ruse to ensure he was not put in that position one can only conjecture.

The Old Bailey dealt with Newlove and Veck on 18 September. The case had been delayed in the hope that Hammond would join them in the dock: but Inspector Abberline of Scotland Yard, who traced and followed him to Paris, reported that the French police refused to help extradite him. The alleged crime may not have bothered the French, but it outraged the English. The indictment of Newlove read that he had inflicted upon George Wright 'that detestable and abominable crime not to be named among Christians called buggery', which he had undertaken 'feloniously, wickedly, diabolically and against the order of nature'.[192] Veck was also charged with procuring.

Algernon Edward Allies, aged twenty, from Sudbury in Suffolk, gave evidence. He had been a servant at the Marlborough Club until sacked for theft. Somerset took a shine to him, and he was spared prison thanks to his new patrons standing surety. Somerset had Hammond keep the youth in Cleveland Street; promised, but failed, to find him a job; and he was the youth to whom Somerset had written letters and sent the postal orders. Allies, during his stay in Cleveland Street, had referred to Somerset as 'Mr Brown' or 'Captain Brown', but knew his true identity.[193]

The accused pleaded guilty to what the judge called 'misdemeanours' – which technically they were – and which carried lenient sentences. Newlove was given four months' hard labour and Veck nine. A conspiracy charge was considered: but on the morning of their trial Webster telegraphed Cuffe to advise him not to proceed with that. The guilty pleas meant the case ended in half an hour; no opportunity was given to name distinguished clients in court. The serious press largely avoided the case: it was hard to write about it, in the sensibilities of the times, without causing the gravest offence to readers. Cuffe, who held a principled view of the independence of the law from politics, later referred to the case as 'the travesty of justice at which I assisted at the Central Criminal Court'.[194] Suspicions of a cover-up to help Somerset, orchestrated from Westminster, were growing. Cuffe was all the more determined that a warrant for his arrest should be issued. The boys were all sacked from the Post Office, which had its reputation to maintain.

On the day the case came to court, Webster wrote to Salisbury to say: 'I regret that in my opinion there is no doubt about the guilt of the person in question; and that the evidence now laid before me is such that in my judgment some action must be taken.'[195] However, he also suggested – improperly, given his view that Somerset should be prosecuted – that he might be tipped off and disappear, to avoid scandal. 'In view of questions that may be raised I think it safer that an application for a summons should be made but if it were considered wise to make a communication to the military authorities and the person implicated I should not press my own view. I do not think the person in question will face the inquiry.'

Somerset stayed at Welbeck with the Duke of Portland for the St Leger, hearing after he left that he might be arrested. Newton had alerted Brett on 26 September that he had 'received information of the most reliable nature that on Friday (tomorrow) a warrant will be applied for against your friend'.[196] He told Somerset, now at Newmarket looking at horses for the Prince. He fled by a circuitous route to the Hotel Royal at Dieppe, returning (against Newton's advice) within days, having realised it was a false alarm. Avoiding London, he went to Badminton, his father's seat in Gloucestershire. As Somerset fled, Abberline told Cuffe that Newton's clerk, Frederick Taylorson, had on Somerset's orders offered Allies a passage to America, with £15 on landing and £1 a week until he found work. News of this attempt to pervert the course of justice was passed to the Attorney-General, and Allies was interviewed. He was not charged, but wrote to the Duke of Beaufort in July 1890 claiming he was 'destitute', seeking money and asking for Somerset's address 'as I should like to explain myself to him – of all the troubles and anxiety it must have caused you and I should like to impress upon you that it was not entirely my doing.'[197]

The popular press was awash with stories about the scandal – though no one dared mention Prince Eddy – and blaming the police for not arresting Hammond. The *Star*, edited by T. P. O'Connor, a prominent Irish Nationalist MP, led the crusade, having picked up the story at the committal hearings. The police were appalled. They could not fathom why Hammond went unpursued: but Somerset's attempt to suborn a witness could not be ignored. James Monro, Commissioner of the Metropolitan Police, alerted the DPP's office when Somerset returned to London on 5 October to explain himself to his commanding officer (his grandmother had died, taking him to Badminton), and sought permission to arrest him. But all was delayed while Halsbury, holidaying in Braemar, deliberated.

He had in Newlove's and Veck's case advised the DPP that no jury would convict either man of any more serious offence, for want of evidence.[198] Now, he argued that a failed prosecution of Somerset 'would be a most serious injury to the Public morals.' He alluded to Somerset's 'social position' and argued that the 'wide publicity' would 'spread very extensively matter of the most revolting and mischievous kind' which would, he thought, be 'an enormous evil'. For both Somerset and Hammond, Halsbury said that 'if a successful prosecution could be reasonably looked for, and if the sentence could be penal servitude for life, or something which by its terrible severity would strike terror into such wretches as the keeper of such a house or his adult customers, I should take a different view.' But Halsbury believed any such prosecution was doomed, which appalled Cuffe and Stephenson.

On 8 October Somerset attended his grandmother's funeral ('one is almost glad the old Duchess of Beaufort should have died before this all comes to light,' Cuffe told Stephenson).[199] He seems to have been convinced that his brother, the Marquess of Worcester, was spreading rumours about him.[200] Monro wrote again on 10 October to say Somerset was still at Badminton. 'I can only deplore the delay which is being made in high quarters about this horrible case,' he added.[201] The DPP was told that the Colonel of the Blues, Oliver Montagu, knew of the suspicions, as did much of London society: a point proved on 16 October when two senior members of the Prince of Wales's household, Knollys and Probyn, visited the Attorney-General to ask what was known against Somerset. The penny had dropped at Marlborough House. As Salisbury and Halsbury dithered, the police and the DPP lamented that their reputations for efficiency were sullied.

Monro's information was wrong. Somerset had returned to London on 9 October, and rejected Newton's advice to flee abroad. He was warned he would be arrested 'unless he resigns his appointments and goes away' – a phrase that suggests collusion with the authorities.[202] Somerset was getting the point. 'I am afraid things look as black as it is possible for them to,' he told Brett after seeing Newton.[203] He went to Sandringham to discuss horses with the Prince of Wales, and told him of the rumours. That prompted the courtiers' visit to Webster. The Marlborough House Set, learning of the rumours, refused to believe them and closed ranks, tribally, around him: apart from the Earl of Dudley who, Somerset told Brett, 'does not matter a bit.'[204] Perhaps emboldened by this, Somerset wrote on 15 October to Lord Cranbrook, the Lord President of the Council, to rebuke him for spreading 'rumours of the most disgusting nature'.[205]

Probyn and Knollys saw Newton and suggested the police were spreading the rumours about Somerset; Newton tried to disabuse them. His reward was that they advised Somerset to get a better solicitor. They then saw Cuffe, who told them of the substance behind the rumours. The courtiers told him the Prince was 'in a great state' and refusing to believe it.[206] The Prince had Knollys telegraph Salisbury, asking him to see Probyn. That interview took place on 18 October, in a private room at King's Cross Station. Probyn asked whether there was any truth in the rumours about 'sundry persons' – presumably Euston and Prince Albert Victor, who would have been the greater cause of the Prince's agitation –

as well as Somerset.[207] Salisbury admitted there was a case against one – Somerset – but there was insufficient evidence. Probyn, though, heard enough to conclude that the Marlborough House Set had made a profound error of judgment. 'I fear that what you told me last night', he wrote to Salisbury the next day, 'was all too true. I tried to see Ld A after I had seen you, but he was not to be found. This morning I hear from his solicitor that he has gone.'[208]

Somerset saw Knollys on 19 October: then evacuated his office at Marlborough House, deserted Hyde Park Barracks with Montagu's complicity, and headed for Rouen. Montagu's assistance contrasted with the view of some of Somerset's brother officers, who felt he should do the decent thing and shoot himself. He resigned his commission and his appointments. Knollys may have told Somerset what Salisbury had told him. This time he would not be back from France. He wrote to his father – who Probyn told Salisbury was 'broken-hearted' – to explain his departure, but did not admit fault: he said that even just accused of 'this awful crime' he could never live in England again.[209] He wrote to Brett from Rouen to ask him to deal with his furniture and pay off his servants, and said his father's conclusion had been 'God help you'.[210] The Duke had experience of these matters: his second son, Lord Henry Somerset, was holed up in Italy following an obsession with a seventeen-year-old boy that had ended his marriage, and his career as a Tory MP, a decade earlier. 'My poor Father and Mother,' Somerset bleated to Brett. 'I suppose I shall never see them again! Nor shall I see any of my very many friends!'[211] Convinced his letters were being intercepted, he signed himself 'Arthur Short'.

Probyn wrote to Salisbury 'to ask you, to implore of you if it can be managed, to have the prosecution now stopped. It can do no good to prosecute him – he has gone, and will never show his face in England again. He *dare* never come again to this country . . . further publicity will only make matters worse.' He said the Prince 'will be terribly cut up about it. He wrote to me "I don't believe it, any more than I would if they had accused the Archbishop of Canterbury".' Probyn said he urged this course on Salisbury not because he was 'trying to save the man' but because he wanted 'if possible not to increase the fearful disgrace which has fallen upon the family.' By way of an *envoi*, he concluded: 'For the man, in his defence, I can only trust that he is *mad*.'

The Prince gathered from Salisbury that there would be no action, which he applauded for the sake of society and the Somerset family; but it would also help the Prince if one so close to him were not prosecuted on so shocking a charge. He was unaware of the pressure the police and the DPP placed on the government to have justice done to this high personage just as it was to far lowlier ones. The Duke of Beaufort asked Brett to advise Somerset to return home and give himself up; he could not bring himself to tell his wife what had happened.

Seeing the inevitable – and shrewd enough to realise the damage to him and the government if he interfered – Salisbury realised he must try to let justice be done. He delayed approval of a warrant long enough for Somerset to resign his commission rather than be cashiered. This had all been effected by 4 November, but it was not until eight days later, when Allies told the police that Brown was Somerset (whom he had known by his real name at the Marlborough Club), that a warrant was issued for Somerset's arrest. However, the files show that as early as 10 August Webster had given an opinion that 'it is quite clear that "Brown" can be identified' and 'some action must now be taken'.[212] An undated opinion in the same file cautioned against the attempt to charge Somerset with having committed 'acts of gross indecency with . . . Charles Joseph Ernest Thickbroom' during July, since there was no evidence any of the boys had met Somerset since February. There were also doubts about the identification of the man in Piccadilly. It does seem the delays in pursuing Somerset were caused in part by a need for hard evidence.

On 16 November a radical north London newspaper accused Euston of being among the 'distinguished criminals' who had escaped prosecution for 'unspeakable scandals' in Cleveland Street. It said Euston had fled to Peru; and that he and other aristocrats had been allowed to evade justice in order not to 'inculpate more highly-placed and distinguished personages': a reference to Prince Eddy.[213] Lady Waterford, Somerset's sister, asked Brett to have him write to Probyn absolving Prince Eddy from blame: she feared Somerset was using Eddy's name to escape prosecution, blackening the family reputation further. No wonder Brett would confide in his journal a year later that the episode 'ended disastrously for all concerned'.[214]

Euston sued for libel, obtaining judicial permission to bring a criminal and not a civil charge. On 26 November, Ernest Parke, the twenty-nine-year-old editor of the *North London Press*, appeared in court for publishing 'a false and malicious libel of and concerning the Earl of Euston'. A defence barrister was Herbert Henry Asquith, a young MP and a coming man. The court heard that when Euston reached the house he asked when the '*Poses Plastiques*' would take place. 'The man said there was nothing of the sort.' There then followed Euston's threat to kick the man out of his own house after which Euston went home, 'disgusted at having found out such a place.' It was clarified that he had said: 'You infernal scoundrel; if you don't let me out I will knock you down.'

Euston may have been foolish, but he was innocent. His appearance allowed other details to be dragged out, however. The prosecution asked him: 'Is Lord Arthur Somerset a friend of yours?' Euston admitted he saw Somerset often in society, but not since the summer of 1888. Parke was sent for trial to the Old Bailey; but before then something more substantial happened at Bow Street police court. On 23 December Newton, Taylorson and Adolphus de Galla, an interpreter, appeared on a charge of conspiracy to pervert the course of justice 'in respect of offences alleged to have been committed by divers persons at 19 Cleveland Street'.[215] It was stated that the man behind the attempt to suborn witnesses was Lord Arthur Somerset. The case was sent for trial at the Old Bailey, where it did not come on until May 1890.

The day before the men were arraigned the London edition of the *New York Herald* printed a letter signed 'A Member of Parliament' in which it was stated that Prince Eddy, who was in India, 'would shortly be recalled . . . under circumstances peculiarly painful to himself and his family.'[216] This salacious letter served to give the rumour about Prince Eddy even more currency, since it mentioned the writer had heard – 'though I have not actually seen the paper' – that 'a New York journal recently published an article on certain abominable scandals, with a portrait of Prince Albert Victor in the midst of it. If this be so, a more atrocious or a more dastardly outrage was never perpetrated in the press.' The MP demanded the real culprit or culprits – he mentioned Somerset only to say Newton was his legal adviser – be brought to justice, to stop innocent parties being defamed. The Prince of Wales was sufficiently alarmed by the article that he had Knollys cut it out and send it to Salisbury.

Parke pleaded not guilty when his case was heard on 15 January. The house at 19 Cleveland Street had by then become so 'notorious' for the 'nefarious' practices there that the association of anyone's name with it was massively defamatory.[217] The most Euston would admit about his decision to go to Cleveland Street was a 'prurient curiosity': presumably he was expecting a proper, respectable Victorian brothel rather than one full of rent boys. His counsel, confirming he had left the moment Hammond had shown him the menu, claimed the point of giving out the cards was to lure potential blackmail victims.

The libel was highly unfortunate, and not just because it allowed the re-broadcasting of innuendo about Prince Eddy: Parke could have avoided it by the simple procedure of determining that Euston was in Belgravia and not far Peru. Also, there was no warrant for his arrest, and no prospect of one. Parke asserted that Euston had visited 19 Cleveland Street several times since 1887, which was not true either. Various unreliable witnesses were called to claim they had seen Euston there on various occasions: the judge, Sir Henry Hawkins, was far from convinced. The libel was 'of a very atrocious character, if it was not justifiable', he said in his summing-up.[218] After all, the libel imputed to Euston 'heinous crimes revolting to one's notions of all that was decent in human nature': though what these crimes were could only be left to the imagination, as the newspapers spoke just of evidence that was unfit for publication.

Hawkins, making it as clear as he could what verdict the jury should reach, said that not only had Euston's Peruvian jaunt not been proved, it had been disproved. The judge mocked the notion that he had been seen frequently entering 19 Cleveland Street, because the man various witnesses had seen was five feet eight inches or five feet ten inches, whereas Euston was a strapping six feet four inches. And he skewered one witness, John Saul, one of the most notorious male prostitutes in London, by saying that 'a more melancholy spectacle or a more loathsome object' he could not imagine. The case came down to something quite predictable: whether the jury preferred the word of these dregs of society to that of the heir to a dukedom. After retiring for three-quarters of an hour, the jury found Parke guilty. Hawkins rose to the occasion. 'I must say that I think that a more atrocious libel than that of which you have been guilty has never been published by any man in circumstances less justifiable than those in which you have published this libel,' he told Parke. He deserved 'the most condign punishment' for 'this wicked libel', and he hoped the punishment he proposed would deter others minded to publish such 'atrocious' lies about respectable people. He imprisoned him for a year.

Six weeks later, on 28 February, a vote in the Commons on funds for the civil service took an unexpected turn when Henry Labouchere, a trouble-making Liberal MP with a long history of throwing spanners in the works, asked for a reduction in the salaries of 'certain official persons' because they had 'conspired together to defeat the course of justice'.[219] Knollys had first had wind of this potential embarrassment the previous autumn, when Labouchere – whom he had known for some years – warned him of the widespread view that the Prince of Wales had good reason 'for wishing to see the matter [Cleveland Street] hushed up'.[220] Brett had also tried, and failed, to persuade him to stay silent – 'poor AS's family suffer agonies every time his name is mentioned. I am sure you will be as tender towards the feelings of his beloved mother and sister (who have suffered so much) as you can be consistently with the unpleasant necessities of the case,' he wrote on 6 February.[221] The galleries were cleared of strangers. It had been Labouchere's amendment to the Criminal Law Amendment Bill in 1885, at the suggestion of W. T. Stead, that had criminalised all homosexual acts between men (see Chapter 8), and he was mightily unhappy that someone was evading prosecution for what he regarded as these repulsive practices. He alleged interference by high personages 'to prevent their friends being put on trial for a crime in regard to which two persons [Newlove and Veck] were tried and convicted.'

There was, he felt, a climate of degeneracy surpassing any in the past. 'There is no doubt that of late years a certain offence – I will not give it a name – has become more rife than it ever was before,' he said. Parliament knew this and had armed 'the guardians of public morality' to deal with it severely.[222] The 'gross scandal' of Cleveland Street had not been adequately managed, and he wanted a formal investigation. He felt the sentence on Veck had been 'scandalously inadequate' because of his partnership with Hammond.[223] He claimed a deal had been done to silence these men in return for light sentences: 'I think it is pretty clear that the real object was to stop all further disclosures, hush the matter up, and get these men out of the way.' Petty thieves received far longer sentences. He believed the Home Secretary also knew the identities of some of Hammond's clientele, and that the prosecution had happened only at the insistence of the Postmaster-General, Henry Raikes, a clergyman's son who wished to protect the good name of the Post Office.

Hammond had fled to France. Inspector Abberline sought permission to go there to arrest him, but it was declined. Labouchere said that on 25 July Salisbury had told the police 'that the Government could not ask that Hammond should be extradited from France'.[224] At police insistence the matter was reconsidered, but on the day Veck was arrested – 20 August – Salisbury 'decided that it was impossible to move the French Government in the matter': so Hammond remained untouchable.[225] In September Hammond moved to Belgium, and was located by the police; but again they were told there was no offence on the basis of which he could be extradited. He went to Antwerp and boarded a ship for America, accompanied by an English boy 'abstracted from his parents presumably for vile purposes,' Labouchere said.[226] He knew Somerset had paid for Hammond's ticket and for that of his catamite, but did not seem to know that Hammond had also been paid off with £2,000, which was effectively blackmail. He was last heard of living in a brothel in Seattle.

Had the government been seriously inclined to exact retribution, Labouchere continued, it would have secured Hammond's extradition, because treaties with France and with Belgium covered his crimes. But instead he had been allowed to get far away from Britain, because the government wanted no more 'revelations'.[227] Similarly there had, he conjectured, been no attempt to arrest Somerset when his depravity was well known, and when the police knew where he was. Labouchere was indignant that Somerset 'went to his clubs as if nothing had occurred.'[228] He also knew of the King's Cross meeting between Salisbury and Probyn, and asserted – wrongly – that Salisbury had promised that a warrant for Somerset's arrest would be issued immediately.

He came to the point:

> Why did Lord Salisbury interfere in the matter? What right had he to interfere? Was it the business of a Prime Minister and Foreign Secretary to mix himself up in such matters? But if he did intend, or know that a warrant was about to be issued, surely the last thing a man in his official position should have done was to communicate the fact to a friend of Lord A Somerset's. The object, however, is perfectly clear. Lord Salisbury had had his hands forced. Public attention had been drawn to the matter; it became necessary to issue a warrant, and it was intended that a hint should be conveyed to Lord A Somerset to get out of the jurisdiction of the law before the warrant could be served on him.[229]

This had happened, Labouchere implied, only because of Somerset's position. Allowing him to escape dishonour by resigning his commission before the warrant was issued was 'an insult to every officer in the Army and to every man in the country who is anxious that the Army should remain an honoured and an honourable profession.' Worse, he remained a magistrate in two counties. Those who had tried to suborn witnesses had been prosecuted for impeding justice: so, he thought, should Salisbury be, because of his 'criminality'.[230]

Labouchere was convinced the ruling class was engaging in an orgy of sodomy. He believed no policeman would arrest any public figure for the crime because it would wreck the officer's career; so the catamites behaved with impunity too. He warmed to his theme. 'In the streets, in the music halls, you have these wretched creatures openly pursuing their avocation. They are known to the police, yet the police do nothing to stop this sort of thing. It is scandalous that such a state of things should exist in London. There is no capital where it exists more openly . . . These poor and wretched creatures live to minister to the vices of those in a superior station. Is there any man who will not feel indignant that boys employed in one of our public offices should be tempted into indecencies more gross than were ever committed under Louis XV?'[231]

The imputations of a Tory establishment cover-up began to make the government benches restive, and each assertion was greeted with mounting outrage and cries of 'Withdraw!' This only encouraged Labouchere. 'My first charge is that Lord Salisbury and others entered into a criminal conspiracy to defeat the ends of justice,' he proclaimed. He accused the Tories – who had just persecuted Charles Stewart Parnell, the Irish Nationalist Leader, over statements he was alleged to have made in letters that turned out to be forgeries – of operating a double standard.[232]

Webster denied everything. He said that on 25 July the case had been put in the hands of the Treasury solicitor, since when he, as Attorney-General, had directed it. The delays in arrests had been for want of evidence. It had not been until 5 or 6 November that he felt he had enough evidence against Somerset to issue a warrant; and Salisbury categorically denied telling Probyn the warrant would be issued immediately. Labouchere shouted: 'I do not believe Lord Salisbury.' Uproar ensued. The chairman – the House was in committee, chaired by the deputy speaker – ordered him to withdraw. He refused. Tories yelled 'Name!', the procedure by which a member was thrown out. Three times Labouchere refused to withdraw: finally he was ordered to leave the chamber.

Salisbury recounted the King's Cross meeting in the Lords the next day. After admitting the case against Somerset, the rest of the conversation had consisted mainly of expressions of 'absolute disbelief' by Probyn.[233] He was certain Probyn had not tipped Somerset off, allowing him to make his escape; which was true, for Somerset by then was already on his way. Salisbury's biographer, Andrew Roberts, notes that in 1862 Salisbury had written that a white lie was acceptable to help 'a fugitive who is in danger, or a friend who is in trouble'; and he concludes that Salisbury's long friendship with the Duke of Beaufort may have led him to give information to Probyn to pass on, to help Somerset get away.[234] If that was Salisbury's intention, he was too late. With this statement the political argument died down. By January the Prince of Wales would write to Lord Carrington that 'I hardly like to allude any more to the subject of AS as it is really a too painful one to write about – and his subsequent conduct makes me wish he had never existed.'[235]

In May Taylorson pleaded not guilty to conspiring with Newton to pervert the course of justice, and was acquitted. Oddly, Newton pleaded guilty and received six weeks in Holloway, after which he resumed his career. Somerset thought of going to Constantinople to manage the Sultan's horses, but an extradition treaty between Turkey and Britain deterred him. Pathetically, he sought an office job in France working for the Commercial Union. He re-styled himself Mr Somerset, as hotels put up their prices for aristocrats. He even thought of teaching English. Several members of his family, including his mother, continued to urge him to return and face the music, not least because rumours were rife that he had avoided going into court to stop Prince Eddy's name being brought into the case; rumours traced back to Somerset's sister-in-law, Lady Henry Somerset, whose husband was also homosexual, which had left her a little unstable.

Somerset grew a long beard and, having fled Turkey, looked for work in Budapest and then Vienna, where he spent Christmas and was hounded by the police. In Budapest he received an anonymous letter that distressed him. It read, in handwriting that looks consciously disguised: 'Can it be true that you have authorised your sister to say you are innocent and Prince Eddie [sic] – are you determined to add treason and shameful ingratitude to bestiality. For God's [sake] contradict the foul calumnies of your family.'[236] He sent it to Brett, asking him, 'Surely it is not HRH's handwriting on the envelope and Harry Tyrrwhitt's [sic] inside it? Seems impossible, but yet it is posted in the SW district (M House) by someone who knows how to address one properly.' Tyrwhitt-Wilson was another of the Marlborough House Set. Somerset then went to Paris.

During the winter of 1889–90, while Prince Eddy visited India, the Royal family's way of brushing aside the talk about him was for his tour to continue as planned, and for the Queen to create him Duke of Clarence and Avondale and Earl of Athlone on his return. It was seen now that putting Somerset in court would help clear Prince Eddy's name. But he never returned: having rejected the prospect of the Cape because, as he told Brett, he knew too many people there, he moved from Paris to Hyères on the French Riviera, where he lived in a villa with an Englishman, James Neale, until his death in May 1926, the warrant for his arrest still outstanding. Whether in jest or as evidence of continuing denial, his gravestone reads: 'The Memory of the Just is Blessed'.

The Duke of Clarence, formerly known as Prince Eddy, had been born two months prematurely and was a weakling all his life. He chain-smoked Turkish cigarettes and cigars, and was treated for gonorrhea. Late in 1891 he was affianced to Princess May of Teck, the wedding fixed for the following February. However, a day's shooting at Sandringham in January 1892 was followed by his collapse with flu, and death a week later from pneumonia. His grief-stricken brother George, Duke of York, became his father's heir; and Princess May, widowed before she was even married, married George in 1893. Eddy's lavish tomb, an eruption of ornately carved stone by Sir Alfred Gilbert in St George's Chapel at Windsor, is as fabulous a monument to late-Victorian overstatement and the era's lingering cult of death as one could, or could not, wish to see. It is an appropriately overblown memorial to a man who, in his short life, perfectly embodied the growing decadence of the class of which he was so prominent an ornament, and whom the hypocrisy of the age ensured was richly mythologised in death, to keep up appearances.

CHAPTER 2

THE RISE OF THE POOTERS

I

By 1914 Britain was a predominantly industrial nation, and an increasingly middle-class one. Its beleaguered countryside remained overwhelmingly working-class; but among the four-fifths of the population who lived in urban areas, ever more were making their way into the ranks of the bourgeoisie, particularly in the thirty years before 1914. The expansion of industry and commerce brought with it a growth in demand for clerical jobs, which, thanks to the spread of free formal education, could be filled by some of those who would once have been classified as skilled working-class: according to census figures, the numbers of males aged fifteen and over in white-collar jobs rose from 144,035 in 1851 to 918,186 in 1911.[1] In many cases, such workers actually earned less than skilled artisans, and things were made even more difficult for them by the strain and cost of having to keep up appearances, such as by dressing more respectably and moving out of old working-class areas. But other new members of the middle class achieved greater prosperity, and were able to live in greater comfort than their parents or grandparents could ever have dreamed of. Their numbers swelled the new suburbs that grew up around most of the major towns and cities in Britain, notably London, and that were served by a widening, and increasingly affordable, network of public transport.

The expansion in education had an impact on other reaches of the middle class, too. It created a huge demand for teachers, many of them women. It also provided administrators to work in local government – a sector that expanded rapidly after the reforms introduced in 1888. At the top end it helped swell long-established professions such as the law and medicine, and provided personal fortunes to those who led the expansion of industry, and of the banking and commercial enterprises that helped support it. When Paris's position as the world's financial centre was undermined during the Franco-Prussian War, London took over. By the time the 1901 census was prepared, about one-fifth of the population were in middle-class callings, ranging from highly qualified and well-paid professionals – lawyers and doctors, for example – down to clerical staff.

Because of inequality of opportunity in trades and professions men were the main beneficiaries of social mobility, and they pulled their wives and children up with them. A Victorian feminist, Lydia Becker, highlighted the difficulties this presented for women. 'What I most desire', she wrote, 'is to see married women of the middle classes stand on the same terms of equality as prevail in the working classes and the highest aristocracy. A great lady or a factory woman are independent persons – personages – the women of the middle classes are nobodies, and if they act for themselves they lose caste.'[2] Until the professions opened up more to women in the mid-twentieth century, middle-class women, if they married, often endured subservience and stultifying boredom. The independence Becker advocated was only possible for unmarried women with some education. The best an aspirant married woman could hope for was to carve out, as many did, a noble career in charitable work or social service.

Even for men there were limits to class mobility – certainly, at least, in England. While it was estimated that one-third of Glasgow University students in 1911 were working-class, the ancient English universities remained largely closed to those below the middle class, even after the 1902 Education Act created county council-funded grammar schools that allowed working-class children a leg up into some professions.[3] There was also acute class consciousness. Those who managed to climb the ladder lived in fear of falling down again since there was little security of employment. They were anxious, therefore, to preserve their newfound status by identifying with their social superiors rather than their inferiors. White-collar trades unions were formed to protect and improve the conditions of their members, but for the most part the new middle class sought to serve its interests by aping what it considered the virtues of the class immediately above it.

II

The fine gradations of class were rapidly absorbed into the nation's fabric and culture. Arnold Bennett, who chronicled life in the Potteries, explored the ways in which even the smallest nuances of geography had a social significance. In *Anna of the Five Towns* (1902), for example, he describes how 'Trafalgar Road', which stretches 'under many aliases', 'through the Five Towns from end to end', changes markedly along its course: 'Within the municipal limits Bleakridge was the pleasantest quarter of Bursley – Hillport, abode of the highest fashion, had its own government and authority – and to reside "at the top of Trafalgar Road" was still the final ambition of many citizens, though the natural growth of the town had robbed Bleakridge of some of that exclusive distinction which it once possessed.'[4] 'Trafalgar Road,' he goes on, 'in its journey to Bleakridge from the centre of the town, underwent certain changes of character. First came a succession of manufactories and small shops; then, at the beginning of the rise, a quarter of a mile of superior cottages; and lastly, on the brow, occurred the houses of the comfortable-detached, semi-detached, and in terraces, with rentals from 25*l.* to 60*l.* a year . . . Somewhat higher up . . . came an imposing row of four new houses, said to be the best planned and best built in the town, each erected separately and occupied by its owner. The nearest of these four was Councillor Sutton's, valued at 60*l.* a year. Lower down, below Manor Terrace and on the same side, lived the Wesleyan superintendent minister, the vicar of St Luke's Church, an alderman, and a doctor.' This sort of new topography applied to countless towns in late-nineteenth-century Britain.

The newly prosperous classes were fiercely determined to protect their gains. In *Clayhanger*, another Arnold Bennett novel, Osmond Orgreave, the architect friend of Edwin Clayhanger, tells him that 'if trusting to the people means being under the thumb of the British working man . . . you can scratch me out, for one.'[5] Bennett's novels specialise in showing people on their way up – Denry Machin in *The Card* is the most famous example – or those who have newly reached salubriousness, such as the Clayhanger family. He writes of Machin: 'The thrill of being magnificent seized him, and was drenched in a vast desire to be truly magnificent himself.'[6] In his novel of 1906, *Whom God Hath Joined*, Bennett articulates the divide opening up between Lawrence Ridware, a newly risen man, a solicitor's senior clerk, and his older cousin who has clung to the old ways: 'She was one of the needy and undistinguished relations of which a family indomitably ascending in the social scale has almost the right to be ashamed. She stood at the level of Lawrence's grandfather, a potter's fireman of thrifty habits, who died in 1862 . . . she had obstinately refused to rise with Lawrence's father, who had become a traveller and, just before his death, manager, for the historic potting firm of Boones. To be even an errand boy at Boones conferred respectability in the seventies.'[7] 'Respectability' was vital even to the white-collar trades unions: the National Union of Clerks announced in 1909 that 'the clerk has to appear like a gentleman, to pretend to live like a gentleman, and to have the manners of a gentleman' – and thus demanded a minimum wage of thirty-five shillings a week.[8]

The new gentility – the striving for respectability – of this class is also a constant theme of H. G. Wells's novels, which celebrate the end of an era in which social mobility had been limited. Wells remembered his rise up the ladder as marked, when he became an apprentice to a draper in Southsea in 1881, by his acquisition of a morning coat and top hat; he acquired two more top hats of superior quality as he advanced through life, marking 'a phase of social acquiescence' before the Great War, to wear to 'Bond Street picture shows' and the Royal Academy.[9] He adds: 'It was the symbol of complete practical submission to a whole world of social conventions.' Many aspirants yearned to be asked to make that submission, because it indicated they had advanced.

Wells's 1909 novel *Tono-Bungay* – its unusual title being the name of a useless patent medicine whose sales enrich the uncle of the narrator – shows the rise of a youth who should have been apprenticed to a baker but ends up as an aeronautical engineer. Wells infuses his novel with doctrines from the Fabian Society, and in doing so accentuates the difference between two breeds in this new middle class: those whose inherent respectability caused them to know their new place and behave with a conservatism that seemed further to entrench it, and those who refused to know their place but wished to use their new social and economic power to challenge the old order. Wells himself, as we shall see, was firmly in the second camp.

To serve these aspiring middle classes, a vast number of new houses had to be constructed: 150,000 a year between 1898 and 1903, 981,000 in the decade between 1901 and 1911.[10] Many were provided by speculative builders for, and then mostly rented by, the new breed of commuting white-collar workers. These generally took the form of spaciously set houses, predominantly of brick (for the brick industry of the east Midlands these were boom years), with ornate wooden window-frames and porches. Builders' merchants who imitated patterns in architectural catalogues turned out fittings for these houses – woodwork, iron grates, encaustic floor tiles, fancy moulded cornices, stained and leaded glass, and fancy tiles adorning fireplaces – thus giving a remarkably uniform style to houses all over Britain. The late-Victorian and Edwardian home was built and furnished with a conservatism that reflected the desire to conform rather than to break out in new directions.

The established and better-heeled end of the middle classes commissioned architects such as C. F. A. Voysey and Edwin Lutyens to build country houses for them, giving those on the ladder beneath them something to strive for. The houses of the well-to-do were of high specification: Voysey, for example, became renowned for his ironwork on door handles, casements, hinges and locks. Edwardian houses for the affluent were spacious, not just in their living area but in their domestic offices and servants' quarters. Children were given their own space, in imitation of the living arrangements of the landed classes in their country houses. Such arrangements will be familiar to readers of *Mary Poppins* or *Peter Pan*. In *The Railway Children*, Roberta, Phyllis and Peter live in a 'red-brick-fronted villa, with coloured glass in the front door, a tiled passage that was called a hall, a bathroom with hot and cold water, electric bells, french windows, and a good deal of white paint, and "every modern convenience", as the house agents say': 'these three lucky children,' E. Nesbit writes, 'always had everything they needed: pretty clothes, good fires, a lovely nursery with heaps of toys, and a Mother Goose wall-paper.'[11] The establishment also includes a cook, a parlour-maid and a nursemaid, though not the butler, valet, lady's maid and others that would have adorned an aristocratic establishment.

Servants were an integral part of the more well-to-do middle-class home: from a girl who would help out a few times a week to a range of staff in upper-middle-class establishments that could well include a cook, maids, and possibly a governess for the children. The England and Wales Census of 1891 discovered that 16.1 per cent of the working population, or 2.33 million people, were in domestic service. In London a first-class cook could command thirty shillings a week, plus board, a senior housemaid up to twelve shillings and sixpence, while a butler in the finest houses could expect up to £100 a year: further down the hierarchy and in the provinces pay was less and the work harder, especially out of London, because the demand was lower. This was at a time when the average clerical wage in London was £175 8s a year.[12] Not surprisingly, getting out of service was the aim of many in it.

Books and magazines about homes and gardens for all gradations of the middle class built a consensus view of its aesthetics. And from 1908 the *Daily Mail* staged the Ideal Home Exhibition at Olympia in London, striving to set a standard for the domestic lives of its predominantly lower-middle-class readers and encouraging their aspirations. Before they acquired the income to do as they dreamed – the ultimate, often elusive, goal was home ownership, something enjoyed by perhaps one-tenth of the population before the Great War – the aspirant middle class established their credentials by imbibing the values of that class, notably an idea of respectability. Publishers made a fortune out of etiquette manuals, so people could study the manners they wished to emulate, and – in the widespread social paranoia that people had about not being accorded the level of respectability they felt they merited – to acquire manners that would prevent them from being mistaken for their inferiors.

III

For some, these aspiring members of the middle class were an object of mockery, and became victims of the type of snobbery they were dishing out to the class below them. *The Suburbans*, a forgotten pot-boiling work of social observation by a forgotten novelist, T. W. H. Crosland (who became the ghost-writer of Lord Alfred Douglas, Oscar Wilde's lover), dismissively observes how men on the make ape the manners and dress of their betters, and how each suburb has its small contingent of 'professional people – solicitors, chartered accountants, auctioneers and valuers, Civil Servants, and last, but not least, in puffedupness, actors, authors, and journalists. These and the like of them are supposed to set the tone and standardise the manners and ambitions of the great mass of their fellow-dwellers in outward darkness. But what a grubby, limited, old, unhappy, underbred crowd they are!'[13] Crosland was an Olympic standard snob, though at least he recognised the driving force of the new Edwardian suburbs: the desire to be better, or at least to appear better.

He conjectures that 75 per cent of suburban men were 'clerks' and that 'to be told that he is no gentleman breaks the male suburban's heart.'[14]

Other contemporary observers, however, took a more nuanced and sympathetic view. George and Weedon Grossmith's *Diary of a Nobody*, published in 1892 after originating in that middle-class staple *Punch* magazine, is a case in point. It depicts the life of Mr Charles Pooter, a clerk who lives with his wife in a rented six-roomed house (not counting the basement) called The Laurels in Holloway. His desperation to succeed socially almost invariably ends in comic failure. His delight at being asked to a ball at the Mansion House is dashed when he discovers that his ironmonger is also on the guest list. Anxious to behave correctly, he asks advice on how to reply to the invitation and how to dress for the event, but then drinks so much he falls over. His son Lupin, who engages in degeneracies normally associated with the ruling class and who is therefore guilty of getting above his station, is a constant source of worry and embarrassment. And yet, despite such disasters, Pooter eventually does rise, being promoted to chief clerk in his firm and, thanks to bringing in a wealthy new client, being bought the freehold of The Laurels by his employer, Mr Perkupp. His loyalty to his employer, and his hard work, are ultimately rewarded. He is among the early representatives of a class that was to boom in the twentieth century, when what had once been a great industrial working class was reduced to a marginal presence.

The Grossmiths' satire hugely influenced writers such as Bennett and Wells, many of whose novels are about the determination of the lower-middle class to become middle-middle class. Some fictional characters, such as Wells's Mr Polly, rebel against the code of respectability; others, such as Bennett's Denry Machin, embrace it and then manipulate it to force others to look up to them – in Machin's case by personifying 'the great cause of cheering us all up'.[15] Such books proved the British public's ability to laugh at itself, because the types satirised were the types reading the books – newly respectable people in the suburbs, in neat homes with neat gardens.

IV

It was, as already suggested, the availability of a free education that helped equip people such as Mr Pooter to enter the lower-middle class and rise further from that. The brightest, who might pass a scholarship exam or test to enter a selective school, were even more fortunate. Grammar schools, state-funded after the 1902 Education Act, propelled large numbers of boys, and an increasing number of girls, socially upwards, often into the professions or management.

Most children left school at twelve with a basic certificate of competence in core subjects. Middle-class children, on the other hand, were likely to be kept in education rather longer. Those who went to grammar schools (many of which were revived and improved by the Taunton Commission in the 1860s) typically stayed until they were fourteen or sixteen, when they would move into family businesses – as Bennett's Edwin Clayhanger does when, at sixteen, he joins his father's printing business. A few stayed until eighteen and went to university, but it would not be until after the Great War that the old universities would take boys from this tier of schools in larger numbers. Parents with more money were not always self-confident enough socially to send their sons to the schools patronised by the aristocracy and gentry, such as the Clarendon schools – the nine old public schools into whose governance the government had ordered an inquiry in 1861 and which included Eton, Harrow, Winchester and Westminster.[16] From the mid-nineteenth century, however, they were increasingly served by new public schools modelled on the Clarendon schools that educated boys – it was mostly boys until the end of the century – until the age of eighteen, when the brighter ones would go to a university but others would go directly into articles in a profession such as the law. Some of these schools catered for boarders, but many in the great cities were designed for day boys.

In terms of the social mobility that education offered, Scotland was considerably ahead of England. Boys from humble backgrounds had been able to attend Scottish universities since their foundation: even if, like Carlyle when at Edinburgh in the 1810s, it meant walking the seventy-four miles from his home in Dumfriesshire to the capital city at the start of each term, and back again at the end. A similar potential scholar in England – such as Hardy's Jude Fawley, the stonemason who in the 1895 novel *Jude the Obscure* teaches himself Latin and Greek in the hope of going to Oxford – faced far greater obstacles. It would be decades before education for the working class would make a university education possible. The Scots were also in the vanguard of the Mutual Improvement movement, which originated partly in the self-help gospel of Samuel Smiles, and capitalised on a society with higher than average rates of literacy to expand knowledge and learning. Its membership was confined to working men. Ramsay MacDonald, who would be the first Labour prime minister, was the secretary of the Lossiemouth Mutual Improvement Association, which met regularly. In 1884 it debated paying MPs, temperance, emigration, capital punishment, competition and 'Is Novel-Reading Beneficial?'[17] In 1883 the Women's Co-operative Guild was formed as a female equivalent of the Mutual Improvement Societies. This worried some working-class men, who feared they would equip women to question their authority.

Middle-class education was not only extended to boys. In the latter decades of the nineteenth century, increasing provision was made for girls, too. In fact, the middle classes, more than their social superiors, were quick to embrace the idea of their daughters being educated, not least because those girls might be required to earn a living in a way that the daughters of the gentry and aristocracy usually were not. One notable enterprise originating from this impulse was the Girls' Public Day School Company, which grew out of a public meeting held in the Albert Hall in June 1872 by two sisters, Maria Grey and Emily Shirreff, on the need for girls' schools. This was not purely for the benefit of the middle classes; the sisters had founded, in November 1871, the National Union for the Improvement of the Education of Women of All Classes. Princess Louise, the Queen's daughter, became their patron. Harnessing public support, the company opened their first school in Chelsea in 1873.

By 1896 thirty-eight schools, around half of them in London, had opened, though some subsequently failed, and most received government grants. An alumna of one – Philippa Fawcett, from Clapham High School – recorded in 1890 the highest marks of any candidate in the Cambridge Mathematical Tripos, although the university would still not allow women to proceed to degrees (and would not until 1948). In 1906 the Company became a charitable trust, to comply with demands made by the 1902 Education Act for schools receiving government grants to provide more free places. Once state sponsorship of education became formalised in 1902, girls at last had something approaching an equal chance of an education with boys.

V

The aspiring middle class – and upper reaches of the working class – were keen autodidacts, too. Among Ramsay MacDonald's friends were a watchmaker who introduced him to Shakespeare and Dickens and a ragman who in idle moments read a translation of Thucydides. Such individuals were helped by the public libraries and those financed by the co-operative movement that flourished in the late nineteenth century. In working-class homes reading aloud was a popular pastime, whether from weekly serials or the Bible. Books teaching the art of self-improvement were popular: but from the late nineteenth century numerous publishers brought out cheap editions of classic texts of fiction and non-fiction, edited to provide context for those catching up on education later in life.

The 1890s had seen various editions of penny novels, and a forty-volume popular edition of Shakespeare, published by J. M. Dent, who then published the 300-volume Temple Classics. Dent was the Nonconformist son of a painter and decorator from Darlington, who flourished after joining a Mutual Improvement Society in the 1860s. He became a formidable autodidact, reading voraciously, and was eventually apprenticed to a bookbinder in London. In 1904 he launched a concerted attempt to provide an authentic canon for the general reader, as French and German publishers had done in their countries. His ambition was to publish a 1,000-volume series of works out of copyright, for one shilling each: and thus, with Boswell's *Life of Johnson*, the Everyman's Library was born in 1906. It would be fifty years before the thousandth volume was published, by which time the books had become staples of the Workers' Educational Association syllabuses.

The flourishing of the publishing trade in late-Victorian Britain reflected not just the growth of literacy and the desire for information and self-improvement among the skilled artisan and middle classes, but also the greater availability of disposable income for entertainment and leisure. There was a wide range of magazines for men, some of which were part-works aimed at continuing the reader's education; and from the 1870s publishers saw that middle-class women were becoming an impressive market for magazine sales. In 1875 the first aimed at anything other than a social elite, *Weldon's Ladies' Journal*, began publication. In the 1880s *Home Notes*, published by Pearson, and *Home Chat*, from Harmsworth, became hugely popular: by 1895 *Home Chat* sold 186,000 copies a week. *Woman's World* was launched in 1903 and, like *Home Chat* and *Home Notes*, had a clientele who lived respectably but could not afford servants. The editorial matter, therefore, was about how a woman could manage the home and keep up appearances – an essential middle-class preoccupation – without dropping from exhaustion. The aim was also to show how these women could distance themselves from the uncouth working classes from which most had risen.

Women's weeklies also exploited the aspirational climate by encouraging women to improve themselves, and especially their personal appearance, the better to fit in with the class they wished to join. Readers sent in queries about how to look and be better, and appeared willing to accept unequivocally the authority of the hacks who offered advice in reply. One such was Herbert Allingham, in the 1890s in his twenties and son of a publisher, who dispensed help in the *London Journal*. The readers' letters were not published: the answers, written by Allingham, included such gems as 'the face is a very pleasant one although it would not be called exactly good looking' (presumably in response to a photograph sent by a reader) and (to a correspondent called 'Blue-Eyed Nell') the verdict that 'you are decidedly a blonde and delicate greens are the colours that will best suit you.'[18]

Children, especially boys, were targeted too. The Religious Tract Society founded *The Boy's Own Paper* in 1879, to encourage Christian morality among youths into whom it had not been beaten at public school, and to encourage them to read. Sunday schools made bulk orders, and gave copies away in return for regular attendance. There was also a monthly edition with card-like covers aimed at the overseas market, and for British boys to keep rather than throw away or pass on. Until 1912 a Sunday school teacher, George Hutchison, edited it, from his suburban villa in Leytonstone, where he was a pillar of the Baptist creed. However William Gordon, Hutchison's deputy, noted that 'so broad and fundamental was the paper's Christianity that there was never a word to indicate the denomination to which its editor belonged.'[19] Gordon was related by marriage to W. G. Grace, whose cricketing exploits featured frequently in its pages.

Boy's Own adventure stories became popular with young men too: many would read the paper well into adulthood. It championed British, Christian values and the cult of manliness. It also sought to inculcate into its readers the middle-class values on which its commercial success and the future of society – according to its editorial vision – depended. In much of its content *The Boy's Own Paper* pre-empted the Boy Scout movement, and *Scouting for Boys*. The novelist George Gissing analysed the appeal of tales of upper-class life to those born lower down: 'The working classes detest anything that tries to represent their daily life. It isn't because that life is too painful; no, no; it's downright snobbishness.'[20] Also in 1879 James Allingham, founder of *The Christian Globe*, launched *Boy's World*, its masthead motto being 'Overcome evil with good'.[21] Its moral didacticism echoed *The Boy's Own Paper*'s, promising its tone 'will always be to encourage the practice of uprightness, perseverance, sobriety and reverence for virtue and religion.'

A year after *The Boy's Own Paper*'s launch came *The Girl's Own Paper*, also from the Religious Tract Society. It sought to encourage the finer feelings of British girlhood. It too had stories, and sought to educate by publishing information and factual articles, but its view of females was stereotypical: unsurprising given that for its first twenty-seven years a man, Charles Peters, edited it. To encourage refinement, *The Girl's Own Paper* was illustrated with beautiful engravings. It published poetry, and articles on crafts, cookery, etiquette, fashion, health and interior decoration; but also on female heroism, education – Girton College was the subject of an early feature – and women at work. Much advice, though, was rigidly practical: 'Your sedentary life as a dressmaker does not agree with you,' it told a correspondent in October 1886. 'You should try to take more exercise and warming food. Dress in woollen under-clothing, and rub the body well in the morning with a cloth dipped in salt and water.'[22]

The Boy's Own Paper's adventure stories highlighted the deeds of soldiers and sailors, praising the Empire's civilising mission and educating readers about it. Famous heroes wrote articles for the paper, including Baden-Powell, W. G. Grace and Captain Webb, the first man to swim the English Channel. Many of the by-lines belonged to clergymen, underlining the wholesomeness of the content, but there were also stories by renowned writers, such as Jules Verne. Hobbies too – notably stamp, coin, shell and fossil collecting, and bird and butterfly spotting – were extensively covered, and to encourage the Christian virtues of care and kindness boys were urged to keep a pet. They were told how to make models, and even how to build small boats. Some articles dealt with the lives of great men, history or geography, and some with science; there were dense columns of type with few illustrations, for the idea was to read and to concentrate.

Herbert Allingham, who wrote for rival publications, understood the secret of the paper's success: 'A boys' paper must have good serials or it will not do,' he noted, recognising the need to hook readers and have them longing for the next instalment.[23] Serials such as *From Powder Monkey to Admiral* ended in cliffhangers. *The Boy's Own Paper* also gave advice. In November 1890 it told somnambulists: 'Digestion all wrong, and nerves as well. Consult a doctor.' Another suggestion – the question was, doubtless for reasons of taste, not specified – was: 'What you ask about is natural at your age. Take a cold bath every morning.'[24] Another youth advised to take cold baths was told to 'get up earlier'. Smoking was already recognised as an evil, not least for those suffering from pimples.

Some of its most popular stories were about the readers' social superiors at public schools. The school story had the advantage, for both writer and reader, of an august and familiar setting, and a regular cast of characters within a microcosm. It was also a context in which popular themes – notably manliness – could be rehearsed. Publishers soon launched other boys' papers to exploit that niche market. Northcliffe's Amalgamated Press, in the children's market since 1890 with *Comic Cuts* and *Illustrated Chips*, published the first issue of *The Gem* in February 1907, and its first school story the next month. It used a character named Tom Merry, familiar to some readers from a defunct paper called *Pluck*, and whose japes at St Jim's would feature weekly until paper shortages caused *The Gem's* closure in December 1939. The *nom de guerre* of the author was Martin Clifford, which disguised a team of writers, the most prolific of whom during *The Gem's* early years was Charles Hamilton. Hamilton, educated at a very minor private school in Ealing, began writing fiction as soon as he left school in 1895, and was thirty when Tom Merry made his debut.

Hamilton, or Clifford, or Owen Conquest, or Ralph Redway, or Ken King – his aliases numbered around twenty-five – would become probably the world's most prolific author, having written an estimated 100 million words before his death in 1961.[25] His popularity hinged on his best-known pseudonym of all, Frank Richards. When Amalgamated, impressed by the success of *The Gem*, decided to exploit the market further and launched another halfpenny weekly, *The Magnet*, in 1908, Hamilton, alias Richards, was its main author. Each issue carried a long story – usually part of a serial – about the adventures of boys called the Famous Four (subsequently Five) in the Lower Fourth at an old public school in Kent called Greyfriars. Harry Wharton, Frank Nugent, Bob

Cherry and Hurree Jamset Ram Singh – an Indian nabob known as 'Inky' – all displayed values of decency, sportsmanship and loyalty that made them a tough prospect for the bullies, cads and bounders who otherwise populated Greyfriars. A minor character in the first story, William George Bunter, would become one of the great comic inventions of British popular culture, and would in time assume the central role.

Extracts from a number of *The Magnet*, from December 1908, give the flavour. There is snobbery: 'Carberry burst into a laugh. He knew that the Lancashire lad came of extremely poor people, and that only the scholarship he had won by hard work enabled him to come to Greyfriars at all.'[26] There is violence, and manliness in the face of violence: 'Five more cuts he received, each as hard and stinging as the first, but not a sound escaped his lips. But for the drawn, strained look about his lips, and the blaze in his eyes, he might have been a statue standing there, under the blows of the cane, so little did he give a sign of suffering.'[27] And finally, right prevails: 'From the Remove came a long though suppressed chuckle. They had never triumphed so signally over the bully of the Sixth.'[28] The icing on the cake of this particular story is that Harry Wharton very nearly gets expelled because of his refusal to sneak on another boy – but the other boy owns up, because he is 'a decent chap', and Harry is spared.[29]

There is also the ridiculing of Bunter, who has just eaten a huge study tea at his chums' expense, for his lack of proper middle-class values: 'If I hadn't been disappointed about getting a prize in *The Gem* football competition, I should have stood a series of extensive feeds in this study, and shown you what things might be like if we devoted our energies to one important end. As a matter of fact, though, I'm expecting a postal order this evening, and – what are you fellows grinning at?'[30] The Bunter phenomenon was paradoxical, matching Richards's ironic, Wodehousian style. Bunter's role was to embody everything the ideal English public schoolboy was supposed not to be, and everything the less privileged who read about him should not emulate. He was idle, stupid, dishonest, vulgar, conceited, a shirker, a slacker, a coward, a braggart, a glutton and a sponger. No wonder he had such appeal. Richards was shrewd enough to depict masters with character flaws too, and to allow boys free rein within an institution regulated by fagging and corporal punishment, giving much scope for adventures.

The Magnet would run until the Second World War. Just weeks before it folded George Orwell attacked it in his essay 'Boys' Weeklies' in *Horizon*, March 1940. Orwell felt the genre had done serious damage. He objected to the prolix style; the slang; the nicknames; the recycling of plots ('A constantly recurring story is one in which a boy is accused of some misdeed committed by another and is too much of a sportsman to reveal the truth'); and the ossifying effects of the fictional world that made the schools appear entirely unreal.[31] He despised the snobbery ('completely shameless'), the conservatism, and the writing's reactionary flavour. He worried the stories caused their readers to live 'a complete fantasy life' rather than grasp reality. He was perplexed that all foreigners were stereotypes and, usually, objects of ridicule. While the chaps sat round the fires in their studies eating tea after their game of football, 'The King is on his throne and the pound is worth a pound. Over in Europe the comic foreigners are jabbering and gesticulating, but the grim grey battleships of the British Fleet are steaming up the Channel and at the outposts of Empire the monocled Englishmen are holding the niggers at bay.' This was as true, he said, of 1910 as of 1940.

He was annoyed that 'sex is completely taboo, especially in the form in which it actually arises at public schools'. Hamilton lived harmlessly in Broadstairs with his elderly housekeeper, and was devoted to his sister. He, alias Richards, replied to Orwell in a witty, allusive riposte: 'His business', he wrote of the writer, 'is to entertain his readers, make them as happy as possible, give them a feeling of cheerful security, turn their thoughts to healthy pursuits, and above all to keep them away from unhealthy introspection, which in early youth can only do harm.'[32] Orwell had taken the genre too seriously in expecting escapist boys' fiction to adhere to realism; though had not taken its evangelising and moralising aspects seriously enough, given the influence *The Magnet's* values may have had on its readers. Hamilton was unrepentant. When he considered all that had happened since 1908, he happily stuck to an imaginary world that had not moved on ('Probably I am older than Mr Orwell: and I can tell him that the world went very well then'). Foreigners 'are funny', he maintained: 'They lack the sense of humour which is the special gift of our own chosen nation: and people without a sense of humour are always unconsciously funny. Take Hitler, for example . . .'; and as for sex 'surely the less he [the adolescent] thinks about it, at an early age, the better.' This is the authentic voice of the middle-class Edwardian man.

Just as this was a golden age for children's magazines, so too was it one for novels aimed at young readers. Authors spun breathless adventure yarns, set in far-flung parts or at thrilling moments in history, and praising the forging of empire through muscular Christianity. Some writers were considerable figures, such as the exotic Robert Louis Stevenson, a man of genuine literary genius and poetic sensibility who was widely travelled, and who when he turned those talents to writing *Treasure Island*, serialised in a magazine in 1881–2, became a hugely successful children's author. His poems and his 1886 novel *The Strange Case of Dr Jekyll and Mr Hyde* showed he was much more than a children's writer: but in the 1880s he consolidated his reputation as a 'boys'' novelist with works such as *Kidnapped*, *The Black Arrow* and *The Master of Ballantrae*, which accelerated his fame before his fatal brain haemorrhage on Samoa in 1894, when he was just forty-four.

G. A. Henty's more robust, sensationalist yarns attacked the reader's instincts far more directly and coarsely. Henty was a former soldier and war correspondent who had seen much of the nastier parts of the world, from the Crimea to Abyssinia. He wrote over 120 works of historical fiction, from the late 1860s until the early 1900s. His heroes were usually boys or young men, called upon to show exemplary courage in wars or rebellions. He was an unreconstructed imperialist; his books depicted the English as a superior breed and foreigners as suspect, criminal or worse. His stories set on the frontiers of empire show contempt, sometimes bordering on disgust, for the natives any white man has the misfortune to encounter. His books support the status quo, praising the work and stewardship of the aristocracy and objecting to any attempts by the lower orders to assert themselves.

A typical work is *St George for England: A Tale of Cressy and Poitiers*, published in 1885. Its hero is a youth, Walter Somers, raised by his nurse and her husband, a fletcher, after his mother dies in childbirth. Walter is a 'frank, manly young fellow'.[33] He leads the London Apprentices in a tournament against young nobles and wins: it is revealed that Walter's father was a knight. He then fights gallantly against the French. Henty upholds the principle of deference: an apprentice boy did well because he was really a gentleman, and blood will out. And as England is an old country with an old ruling class, the values of the fourteenth century apply in the nineteenth. But Henty knows empire is maintained only by will and force. Walter is told: 'There are some . . . who think that peace is the greatest of blessings, and in some ways, lad, they are no doubt right; but there are many compensations in war. It brings out the noble qualities; it raises men to think that valour and fortitude and endurance and honour are qualities which are something above the mere huckstering desire for getting money, and for ignoble ease and comfort.'[34]

Henty's novels were historically accurate: *St George for England* shows a good grasp of the Hundred Years' War. His books stimulated an interest in and understanding of English history. They are, though, pure propaganda. When the two armies engage at Crécy 'nobly did the flower of English chivalry withstand the shock of the French': while the French are 'impetuous' and 'confused'.[35] The English are noble in victory: 'Contrary to the customs of the times, Walter gave orders to his men not to slay any when resistance had ceased.'[36] His refusal to deploy 'fire and sword' against the vanquished means they show no animosity towards their conquerors. These are all metaphors for empire, and for the way Henty's readers were to go out and govern it.

VI

For the new middle classes, reading had blurred the line between pure recreation and edification. From the 1890s theatre followed a similar path. At one end of the spectrum were the shows that were simply designed to entertain: the operettas of Gilbert and Sullivan; drawing-room comedies or French farce, loosely translated and allowed on stage thanks to the incomprehension of the censor. The provincial middle classes as well as those in London gained greater access to the best professional theatre. In 1879 there were just a dozen touring companies taking West End plays around Britain; by 1901 there were 143.[37] The popularity of their productions in turn led to the formation of amateur dramatic societies all over Britain, matching the new theatres in London's West End and the provinces. The National Operatic and Dramatic Association was founded in 1899 to further the interests of amateur drama.

At the same time, however, more intelligent fare was increasingly becoming available. Sir Henry Irving offered histrionic versions of Shakespeare. Oscar Wilde – very much *sui generis* – wrote well-constructed dramas in which wit and social observation were combined. Arthur Wing Pinero, who had delighted audiences with, mainly, light comedies since the 1880s, started to explore more serious contemporary issues with *The*

Second Mrs Tanqueray in 1893 and *The Notorious Mrs Ebbsmith* in 1895, both of which dealt with the complications of marriage in an age of divorce and moral revisionism. Pinero was an entertainer rather than a social scientist; he confined his explorations of weightier issues to plays about the well-to-do, and for what he considered a good reason: the 'inarticulateness, the inexpressiveness of the English lower-middle and lower classes – their reluctance to analyse, to generalise, to give vivid utterance to their thoughts or emotions' hardly made them, in his view, the stuff of drama.

His works were nevertheless a presage of things to come. In the hands of Bernard Shaw – a prolific playwright who commanded a large following – and, to a lesser extent, John Galsworthy, English drama started to tackle serious social and political questions, even if arguably it remained a little insular: Galsworthy would win the Nobel Prize in Literature in 1932, but he told the critic William Archer, who had compared him as a playwright with the German Gerhart Hauptmann (who also won the Nobel, in 1912), that 'I'm afraid I am disgracefully ignorant', recounting that he had seen just one Hauptmann work, one by Ibsen and 'no modern French plays. On the other hand I have seen a great many modern English plays.'[38] Shaw was rather more adventurous.

One of the most remarkable pre-war figures in the theatre was Harley Granville Barker. He worked at the Court – later the Royal Court – Theatre from 1904 to 1907, in partnership with J. E. Vedrenne, his business manager, and it was here his ambitions to be a director came to fruition. He put on several of Shaw's plays there, and the Court became identified as Shaw's main showcase. He was also a highly-accomplished dramatist in his own right: Shaw regarded him as 'a great poet and dramatist' and the two men would have a rich collaboration.[39] Barker had written for the stage since the late 1890s, but his first great success came in 1905 with *The Voysey Inheritance*, about a man who realises the business he has inherited from his father is built on fraud, the old man having embezzled his clients' money. Writing to Archer on 8 November 1905, Barker said the play ended as it did to emphasise it has been 'about Edward's inheritance and not about his love for the girl. If you could read the thing I am sure you would see this in a moment. Of course they play the last scene six times too slow.'[40] Such subject matter was unusual at the time and consciously challenged those who saw the theatre as pure recreation: but not so much as his next play, *Waste*, would have done had it been allowed past the censor (see Chapter 12).

It was a measure of how far English theatre had come in a very short period that in 1904 Barker should collaborate with Archer in writing a privately circulated manifesto calling for a National Theatre, in which some state subsidy would enable more adventurous and imaginative programming: he was not least persuaded of this by his difficulties in staging Shaw's *Mrs Warren's Profession*, which discussed prostitution. The Court had had an element of adventurous programming, subsidised not just by the success of the Shaw productions but by his generous decision to refuse royalties. The manifesto was 'on no account to be communicated to, or criticised or mentioned in, the Public Press.'[41] It was estimated the project would require £300,000 in funding: around £30 million in early-twenty-first-century values. The idea had widespread support, one of its partisans being Winston Churchill.

It got nowhere. In 1908 the committee merged with one advocating a Shakespeare Memorial National Theatre. The aims of this enterprise were similar: as well as wanting to keep Shakespeare's plays in the repertory it would revive other classical works, produce new plays and stimulate modern drama, and 'prevent recent plays of great merit from falling into oblivion.'[42] Despite a donation in 1909 from Carl Meyer, scion of a Hamburg banking family, the Great War thwarted the project. When in April 1913 the Commons discussed a private member's Bill to establish a National Theatre, it was defeated. Shaw's and Barker's dream would not be achieved in their lifetimes.

The middle-class affluence – and leisure time – that helped build English theatre also contributed to a new form of entertainment that in the twentieth century was to assume a culturally dominant role. Louis le Prince, a French inventor, shot the first known moving picture in Leeds in 1888, using paper film. The following year an Englishman, William Friese-Greene, shot moving pictures in Hyde Park on celluloid, and patented the process the following year. Robert W. Paul, an inventor and instrument maker, and Birt Acres, an expert in photography, made the first 35-millimetre camera, in February 1895. They made the first successful British film, *Incident at Clovelly Cottage*, and then, on 30 March, filmed the Oxford and Cambridge boat race. The first cinema in Britain opened the following year as Paul and Acres (separately: they had fallen out over patent rights) made the first projectors, and the Lumière brothers, who had developed the cinematograph and made what is considered the world's first film in 1894, brought theirs to London. Acres's projector, the Kineopticon, was demonstrated to the Royal

Photographic Society in the Queen's Hall in London on 14 January 1896, the first public film shown in Britain. On the same day that the Lumières demonstrated their wares at the Empire, Leicester Square – 20 February – Paul gave a show with his Theatrograph at the Alhambra.

By 1914 between 7 and 8 million people each week went to 'picture palaces', of which there were by then over a thousand, mostly in the larger cities: Manchester, where the architecture of one or two early examples still survives, had around 100, and Glasgow and Birmingham perhaps half that. Tickets started at threepence and the audience was drawn mainly from the poorer and lower-middle classes: cinemas abounded in the new suburbs where they lived. A mass audience was needed to justify the investment both in films and cinemas, so the shows were short and aimed mostly at the uneducated: though there were newsreels, thanks to which film survives of Queen Victoria's Diamond Jubilee and funeral, and of the Coronations of Edward VII and George V. The old Queen herself ordered a command performance at Osborne in 1898, watching a short film made by a Gosport photographer, Alfred West, of a cruise by HMS *Crescent*.

Around 1910 producers began to release longer films based on popular novels, but by then American films had seduced the audience, as they would for much of the ensuing century. Even before August 1914 the Keystone Cops were popular with British audiences, and Charlie Chaplin's and Fatty Arbuckle's first films were reaching Britain. In 1914 Britain's first film studios were opened by Neptune Films at Elstree, near Borehamwood in Hertfordshire, establishing the site as a place of film and, later, television production.

VII

If the growing ranks of the middle classes provided the audiences for a new, more serious English theatre and for the newly popular cinema, they also helped transform the fortunes of English music. In the early 1880s it was an art form that was largely moribund. The Germans called Britain *Das Land ohne Musik* – the land without music – for good reason. The last British composer of international renown – Purcell – had died in 1695. The eighteenth century had produced Arne and Boyce, the early nineteenth century Sterndale Bennett, all of whom made some impact on native audiences otherwise preoccupied with the Italian and German masters. Britain had no *Kapellmeister* tradition, nor an operatic one sustained by rich patrons. The one contemporary figure to enjoy a limited reputation as a classical composer was Arthur Sullivan, the son of a military bandmaster, but success only really came to him when he started to write comic operettas with the librettist W. S. Gilbert: their first collaboration, *Thespis*, was in 1871, and the first to be produced by Richard D'Oyly Carte, *Trial by Jury*, was presented in 1875.

Nevertheless, although looked down upon by purists, Gilbert and Sullivan showed there was a potential audience for home-grown music. This was, after all, a period when most households from the lower-middle class upwards had a piano; and as towns expanded so did their musical lives, with glee clubs, choirs and choruses. The Promenade concerts that began at the Queen's Hall in London in 1895, under the direction of Henry Wood, reflected a new appetite for classical music and recognition that its market extended beyond the social elite. Although work was still hard – five and a half days a week at least – the late Victorians had the money and time to do more than just exist: and Britain and its culture changed markedly as a result. Ability to play an instrument or to sing became a prized and essential middle-class accomplishment, especially for young women who might pass on their skills either as part of their work as governesses, or as full-time music teachers. The rise of Edward Elgar around the turn of the century was enabled not least by this new consciousness of the joy of music. Elgar himself, appropriately enough, was a product of the solidly lower-middle class – from his family's a music shop in Worcester – and his career represented a magnificent success story for this newly risen social stratum.

The career of a man such as Elgar also brought into relief the question of the future direction of British music. For decades, audiences had been bombarded by the great German composers and the great Italian operas. With a growing appetite among audiences for music in general, however, came a desire for more music that had been written by the British in particular. Elgar was self-taught. For other budding home-grown composers there had long been little in the way of formal training available to them. A grand solution was called for, and it was provided by the foundation in 1882 of the Royal College of Music.

The RCM was built on land purchased with profits from the Great Exhibition of 1851.[43] Stating the objects of the college, its putative president, the Prince of Wales, told Charles Dilke in June 1880 that it would comprise 'in one Institution the most influential persons both social and professional who are interested in music throughout the United Kingdom. The object of the College is in general the advancement of the Art of Music in the United Kingdom, and in particular affording the highest possible class of musical education.'[44] The middle classes would be the main beneficiaries of this project, and its success (and royal patronage) would make the profession of music respectable for those in the middle and upper echelons as well as the lower.

The Prince sought to fulfil his father's aims of a conservatoire in Albertopolis: but the man with the energy actually to realise the idea was George Grove, not himself from a landed background, but a grammar-school boy of drive and talent. Trained as a civil engineer, Grove had been impresario for the concerts given at the Crystal Palace from 1853 to 1873. He then became a publisher. He was also a considerable Bible scholar and music critic, and founded the dictionary of music and musicians that bears his name. Not the least part of Grove's genius, however, was to recruit Hubert Parry, son of a Gloucestershire squire, as a professor, and the man who would succeed him as director in 1895.

At this time Elgar was giving music lessons and conducting the orchestra of a local lunatic asylum, with no hope of having any of his own works performed in a major concert hall. The RCM's purpose was to create composers, and fine musicians, and place them once more at the heart of the national culture, and have British music taken seriously again.

Sullivan had in 1876 been appointed the first Principal of the National Training School for Music (NTSM). He had reluctantly taken the job, believing he had insufficient time for it. When he gratefully resigned in 1881 his successor, John Stainer, found the institution near collapse. London's other conservatoire, the Royal Academy of Music (RAM), was faring little better. Grove wanted both institutions to merge into the new RCM. The Academy declined his offer, but Stainer saw it as the perfect means to achieve the aims the NTSM had been designed for. The Prince of Wales convened a meeting on 28 February 1882 at which he, his brother the Duke of Edinburgh, the Archbishop of Canterbury, Gladstone, Northcote and Rosebery, all appealed for funds – which, happily, poured in. When the Royal Charter was granted, Grove – knighted on the day in May 1883 when the RCM opened – had it specify that the college could award degrees. This immediately elevated the standing of the profession of musician, so much so that the RAM successfully petitioned to award degrees jointly with the RCM.

More than 1,500 people applied to join in its first year; after auditions ninety-two were accepted, fifty on scholarships. The college was not merely seeking to encourage a musical tradition in England by breeding composers, but helping composers by establishing at the RCM an orchestra of a sufficiently high standard to perform their music as they intended. It began life in a small building behind the Albert Hall that had been home to the NTSM, and which later housed the Royal College of Organists, but in 1894 moved across Prince Consort Road to a fine institution in the High Victorian style – one of the last of its type built before the advent of Edwardian baroque – by Sir Reginald Blomfield.

Grove's appointment of Parry to the Chair of Musical History was crucial, and perhaps more than anything made the institution's name and reputation. 'My dear Parry,' he wrote on 30 December 1882, 'I write by desire of the Prince of Wales to ask if you will assist him in his great experiment by taking the Department of Musical History with a seat on the Board of Governors. It is our wish to make lectures an important part of the College course, and into no hands could those on the history and development of music be put with more propriety than into yours. As the College grows I hope that there may be some other opportunity of turning your great abilities – as in Composition – but the lectures will be your cardinal occupation.'[45]

He offered fifteen shillings an hour, adding that: 'when we come to our full strength I am not without hope that that rate may be increased'. Fortunately, Parry had a private income. He was gaining public recognition as a composer, surpassing his near contemporary Sullivan as a writer of classical music. Added to that was a talent Sullivan did not possess, for teaching. Parry's mission was not merely to teach, but to teach in order to make England a cultural power in music to rival European countries. He would take home his pupils' works and pore over them with huge care, looking for moments of genius and inspiration and questioning methods and techniques. He was a superb spotter of talent, and would teach Ralph Vaughan Williams, Gustav Holst, Herbert Howells and Arthur Bliss, among others: and as such, with the overarching vision of Grove and the dedication of Charles Villiers Stanford, the Professor of Composition, he was a father of the English Musical Renaissance. He was, as Grove told him in 1886, above all a man of 'goodness, patience and hard work', *noblesse* on which the RCM depended throughout his thirty-five years as professor and director.[46]

Parry's career as a composer suffered because of the dedication he put into teaching and administration. Nonetheless he wrote five symphonies, other fine orchestral works that have entered the repertoire, and works that have entered the English national consciousness – such as his anthem *I Was Glad*, written for the Coronation of King Edward VII in 1902, his hymn tune 'Repton' set to the words 'Dear Lord and Father of Mankind', and, above all, his setting of Blake's 'And did those feet in ancient time' in the closing phase of his life, in 1916. He also composed several biblical oratorios: Frederick Delius said that if Parry had lived long enough he would have set the whole Bible to music. He imparted his vision of enlightenment through music to his pupils. He told Vaughan Williams to 'write choral music as befits an Englishman and a democrat'.[47] Charles Villiers Stanford, an Irishman, was also a considerable composer, suffering like Parry from being overshadowed by the popular appeal, in his generation, of Elgar: a century later the works of both men are being re-discovered, recorded and performed.

Parry's achievement, despite his debt to the German masters, most notably Brahms, was to inspire his pupils not simply to write 'as befits an Englishman and a democrat' – by which he meant in a distinct national style that was accessible to all – but to use music to articulate an idea of English identity. Led by Vaughan Williams and Holst, they would do this into the second half of the twentieth century. Parry's biographer argues that the stylistic developments in his music made his work increasingly distinctive as 'English', rather than showing dominant continental influences.[48] Parry's claim to greatness rests in his leadership of this area of British culture: a selfless pursuit of beauty and truth that helped create great composers out of impoverished students such as Holst and Howells, and build the English Musical Renaissance that would become a key feature of middle-class life in the early twentieth century.

VIII

Education transformed the opportunities of the emerging middle classes, and widened their cultural horizons. But it wasn't only in the classroom that their minds and futures were shaped. What was played on the sports fields also came to exert an extraordinary influence, not only in terms of instilling a love of games in the British psyche but in shaping broader outlooks and attitudes.

When the reforming Dr Arnold had been headmaster of Rugby in the 1820s and 1830s he had prized godliness and intellect far above sporting prowess. In the course of the 1850s and 1860s, however, sport became viewed not just as a useful form of physical exercise, but as a means to build spirit and to stamp out the moral and physical degeneracy that was felt to threaten the ruling class's dominance. Soon it became subsumed into the doctrine of 'muscular Christianity' and the notion of *mens sana in corpore sano*: a means not simply of exhausting adolescent boys' energies before they were diverted to undesirable activity, and of removing the evils of idleness, but also a method by which upstanding, Christian Englishmen would be created. Sport became a vital adjunct to the school timetable. Recalling his years at Repton in the 1880s, C. B. Fry noted that 'there was never any time to get done the things that one had to do.'[49] A notice in a house at Eton in this era said that 'any lower boy in this house who does not play football once a day and twice on half holiday will be fined half-a-crown and kicked.'[50]

If sport was to instil discipline, then it was also necessary for discipline to be instilled into sport; and so it is scarcely surprising that the late-Victorian and Edwardian periods were marked by the codification of sporting rules. Even prize fighting succumbed. Popular with men of all classes, not least the aristocracy who staked considerable sums on the outcome of particular bouts, it had in the days of bare-knuckle fighting often ended in serious injury for the fighters, who would sometimes box for fifty rounds. In 1865, however, John Chambers wrote a code for professional and amateur boxing matches that stressed the necessity to win in accordance with the rules; 'no holds barred' was not acceptable; gloves were to be worn. The new rules were adopted and championed by the newly formed Amateur Athletic Club, one of whose founders was the twenty-two-year-old Marquess of Queensberry. Bare-knuckle fighting continued for another thirty years or so, the professionals being reluctant to adopt the refinements of amateurs until a formal sporting body persuaded them. By the 1890s, however, professional boxing under the Queensberry Rules had begun in England, under the auspices of the National Sporting Club, founded in London in 1891. In 1909 the Earl of Lonsdale, the NSC's president, presented the first ornamental belt for the winner of a title fight.

Queensberry's rules became a metaphor. It was soon not just boxing, but life in general that it was felt should be conducted according to them. When public-school and university missions opened in the slums of London, hoping to turn boys from the underclass into upright young men, boxing became a core activity. As well as channelling aggression, it taught the need to play by the rules. Indeed fair play became strongly associated with Britain's image, and the projection of British values, while organised sport came to be viewed as one of the great cultural achievements of the late Victorians. It was exported around the world, not just to the Empire. For a time, it distinguished the country from others. It is not surprising that when Britain faced the national humiliation of a long-drawn-out war with the Boers in South Africa, it was compounded by the news that many potential military recruits from among the lower classes were physically unfit to serve: there were manifestly not enough match-fit flannelled fools and muddied oafs to defend Britain. Within the United Kingdom, the growth of national teams in cricket, football and rugby strengthened regional identities. Cricket was seen as an expression of Englishness; Scotland and Wales became famed for their football and rugby teams respectively.

The main beneficiaries of the sporting revolution were men; but women also became participants. Girls' schools emulated boys' in establishing a culture of games. From its origins women played lawn tennis. British schoolgirls first played lacrosse – imported from Canada – at St Leonard's School in Fife in 1890. Hockey was introduced into girls' schools and at Girton College, Cambridge in the 1890s. The first women's cricket club was formed in 1887, although no formal association existed until 1926. English and Scottish women played football as early as 1881, although the game did not become widespread until the Great War.

Some sports were largely middle-class preserves or had strongly middle-class enclaves: for example, the Marylebone Cricket Club, founded in 1787, and the Leander Club for rowing, in 1818. However, the sporting ethos soon spread beyond tight class confines. The MCC may have had an exclusive leadership and membership, providing a comfortable milieu for those who had learned to play cricket at public schools, but it also encouraged the growth of a socially more broadly-based professional sport. For its part, the Leander Club, while sparing gentlemen rowers the prospect of having to compete against stronger, more experienced professional rowers, also encouraged Thames watermen to continue their tradition of rowing.

Other rowing clubs were more assiduous in preserving class distinctions. The Amateur Rowing Association was founded in 1882 by university clubs, and others to serve ex-university and public-school men. Watermen who had sculled on the Thames since childhood were barred from membership and from regattas on grounds of class; not just those who worked as oarsmen but also anyone who earned wages as a labourer or artisan. Some university men who sought to take the Christian message into the slums, however, felt that this was hypocritical, and lent their muscle to the formation in 1890 of the National Amateur Rowing Association for working-class men. Even so, the ARA's class barrier remained until 1937, and the two associations did not merge until 1956. The Amateur Athletic Club, by contrast, sought from the start to have a broad base of members, and did not recruit entirely from public-school and university men.

For working-class enthusiasts sport could be a way to earn a living, not simply a pastime to be pursued for its own sake (see Chapter 3). For middle-class adherents, financial reward was not usually a consideration. Two interlinked nineteenth-century sporting inventions particularly exemplify this: croquet and tennis. The rules for a new game called croquet were registered in 1856. It was soon enthusiastically taken up by the Earl of Essex, who proceeded to give croquet parties at his Hertfordshire house. These were then aped around society and by those who aspired to join it. By 1867 65,000 copies of the game's rules had been sold. The following year the first championship was held in Moreton-in-Marsh. Soon the sport had been adopted wholesale by those in the aspirant middle classes whose new suburban villas or country houses boasted reasonable grounds and a lawn. The All England Croquet Club was formed in Wimbledon the following year.

The craze for this game was, however, soon eclipsed. Two Birmingham men – Major Harry Gem and Augurio Perera, a Spaniard who ran an import business – had invented a new outdoor game in the 1860s, which combined racquets and the Basque game of pelota, and which they first played on Perera's croquet lawn in Edgbaston (Gem gave the credit for the game's invention to Perera). When Perera moved to Leamington Spa in 1872, he and Gem started the first lawn tennis club. The rules of the game were published in 1874 by Major Walter Clopton Wingfield, who developed and sold lawn tennis sets. A lawn at the All England Croquet Club was reserved for tennis from 1875; and it caught on so fast that in 1877, when the first men's singles championship was held, the club changed its name to the All England Croquet and Lawn Tennis Club.

In 1882 the All England Club dropped all reference to croquet, which became a minority sport; croquet clubs gave their lawns over to tennis. Wingfield's rules were constantly revised, so that by the mid-1880s they bore little resemblance to those he had codified. In 1884 the first ladies' singles and men's doubles were introduced at Wimbledon, with ladies' doubles and mixed doubles coming in 1913. Croquet was restored to the club's name in 1899, only this time it was the All England Lawn Tennis and Croquet Club. The mood at the turn of the century, of paying respect to the past before it vanished entirely, was thus enlisted even for a past of very recent date.

IX

No sport captured the national imagination in the decades before the Great War so much as cricket – nor the balance between middle-class amateurism and working-class professionalism. As a summer game of long duration it had an ease that exploited the growth of leisure time. Although attendances at professional games varied from county to county, and declined in the years before the war with some clubs in dire financial straits, Yorkshire would attract crowds of 20,000 or more to three-day matches regularly in the 1890s, excluding members: Kent, Surrey and Lancashire would regularly have gates of more than 12,000.[51] The strong amateur element at the highest level brought elegance and glamour to the sport that inspired schoolboys and men alike. Its code of conduct owed something to chivalry and as such reflected the ancient virtue of *noblesse*. As a pursuit of some antiquity, with its laws and customs settled by the dictatorship of its leading private club – the Marylebone Cricket Club – rather than by a collective, cricket escaped the schisms over professionalism that affected football and rugby by maintaining a consensual divide between amateurs and professionals, or gentlemen and players. Although the game at national and county level was dominated by the middle classes, and especially by ex-public schoolboys, clubs of mainly working-class men formed the Lancashire

League in 1892, and the Bradford League in 1903. The leagues that played in London and the Home Counties, by contrast, were strongly middle-class, and included the old boys XIs of many public and grammar schools.

The MCC's ground at Lord's, in St John's Wood in north-west London, was the home of the sport and attracted a smart clientele, but the first-class game also flourished in industrial cities such as Manchester, Leeds, Birmingham and Nottingham. The long-standing amateur cadre in the northern and midland counties ensured the status quo was not rocked as it had been in football and rugby. As a result, cricket remained a genuinely national English game. The predominant team before the Great War was Yorkshire, where (as in Lancashire) the strong local league system grew up to breed professional players.

Two or three times a year Gentlemen and the Players played each other. The Gentlemen had learned their cricket at public school and then at Oxford, Cambridge or in the Army; they turned out for county sides when not at their businesses or estates or, in many cases, working as schoolmasters; or they lived off a private income. They were only paid expenses, though had other income streams: the 1896 *Wisden*, for example, includes advertisements in which W. G. Grace, not just one of the most famous sportsmen of the age but one of the most famous men in England, Prince Ranjitsinhji and A. C. MacLaren – three of the great amateur batsmen – endorse cricket bats. The greatest cricketing athlete of the age, C. B. Fry – a prodigious batsman who was a good enough footballer to play as an amateur for Southampton in the 1902 FA Cup final, and once for England, and who won a blue for athletics at Oxford as well as for cricket and football – had been a schoolmaster in the 1890s before realising he could earn more in journalism. Earlier in his career, heavily in debt, he had also worked as a nude model. Fry and his friend Ranjitsinhji were the two greatest batsmen of the Edwardian era. No man has ever beaten Fry's feat of scoring six centuries in successive innings as he did in 1901.

County and national captains were always gentlemen. It was the role of the officer class to lead and unthinkable for any amateur to be captained by a social inferior. The players were the NCOs and other ranks, men who escaped a life down a coal mine, in a blast furnace or in the fields thanks to their ability as cricketers. They would come up through local leagues and around their twentieth birthday have their first county match. At Lord's and certain other grounds they did not merely have a dressing room separate from the gentlemen, but would walk on to the field through a separate gate.

Since 1873 there had been an unofficial championship among eight leading county clubs. Because there was no set number of matches it was difficult to judge who was best: the press, or popular acclaim, usually chose the champion county. In response to the growing popularity of the sport, club secretaries, at their annual meeting at Lord's in December 1889 to arrange fixtures, settled on a system to award points to each county and thereby settle on a champion county each year. This ushered in twenty-five seasons in England, from 1890 to 1914, known as cricket's Golden Age. By 1895 the championship had expanded to fourteen teams, and more first-class cricket was played than ever before.

Such was the sport's popularity that its great players became superstars, and their names resonate over a century later: thanks not least to these idols, cricket assumed a central place in English culture from which it has not yet quite been evicted. Dr W. G. Grace was regarded as the country's greatest cricketer: and held that position in 1890 even though he was forty-two, obese, prone to cheating because of a childish obsession with winning, and a complete charlatan as a so-called amateur. The Earl of Sheffield, for example, paid him £3,000, plus expenses, plus the cost of a locum for his medical practice in Bristol, to tour Australia in 1891–2. Fry noted that, for all his faults, 'W. G. was a very kind man', and stories of his tipping admiring urchins who stopped him in the street half-a-crown were legion.[52]

Other names of this era passed from cricket into national consciousness: amateurs such as Fry and Ranjitsinhji, an Indian prince who played for England because India had no test team, and professionals such as Jack Hobbs, Wilfred Rhodes and George Herbert Hirst. Some professionals played until their fifties, until arthritic and worn out, because a life of poverty beckoned when they stopped.

Andrew Ernest Stoddart was an archetypal *Boy's Own* hero. He was the son of a coal owner and wine merchant, and captained England at both Rugby Union and cricket (and, in 1888, in a game of Australian Rules football). Although he was England's leading Rugby Union player, his fame as a batsman eclipsed all else. He first played for Middlesex – the most glamorous county club, and the one for which E. W. Hornung's fictional hero A. J. Raffles, the amateur cracksman, was a spin bowler – in 1885, aged twenty-two. He was considering emigration to Colorado, where his brother had gone to seek his fortune, when on 4 August 1886 he made 485 for Hampstead against the Stoics, the highest score made at that date in a formal match. He had been up dancing and playing cards for most of the previous night, and after his innings played tennis before going to the theatre and out to supper afterwards. His fame travelled around the cricketing world, and soon he was opening with Grace for both England and the Gentlemen.

The highlight of his cricketing career came in 1894–5, when he captained the England team that beat Australia. 'Since the visit of George Parr's XI in 1863–4 no tour of English cricketers to Australia has been from every point of view more brilliantly successful than that of Mr Stoddart's team,' wrote *Wisden*.[53] The English public hung on every ball, made possible by the decision of Stead at *The Pall Mall Gazette* to print long, detailed cable messages when his paper appeared every afternoon. At Sydney in December 1894 what *Wisden* called 'the most sensational match ever played either in Australia or in England' was played over six days. Australia, batting first, made 586, enforced the follow-on and still lost, after being caught on a 'sticky'.[54] The series was closely fought, England finally winning by three matches to two in the last game at Melbourne, an event that caused national rejoicing. The Melbourne *Punch*, with humour quite unlike that of its ponderous London namesake, recorded:

> Then wrote the Queen of England
> Whose hand is blessed by God
> I must do something handsome
> For my dear victorious Stod.[55]

Stoddart was hurt by insinuations in the press that he, too, was a sham amateur. His next tour to Australia, in 1897–8, was less successful, and he never played for England again after it.

When he stopped playing first-class cricket Stoddart became a stockbroker and, when that turned out uncongenial, secretary of the Queen's Club. He started drinking, made an unhappy marriage and got into debt; in April 1915, aged fifty-two, he shot himself. He would not be the last, and was not the first former cricketer to meet such an end: there was (and still is) an unusually high incidence of suicide among former professional cricketers, who as their careers ended became conscious of difficulties in maintaining the lifestyle the game once funded for them: it is the dark back-story to cricket's most glittering era. William Scotton, regarded as the finest left-handed batsman in England, killed himself in a fit of depression in 1893 when Nottinghamshire dropped him, aged thirty-seven. Arthur Shrewsbury, who succeeded Grace as England's greatest batsman, shot himself in 1903, aged forty-seven, when it seemed bad health would prevent his playing again. Fred Bull, who bowled off-breaks for Essex and was a *Wisden* cricketer of the year in 1898, drowned himself off the Lancashire coast in 1910. Another celebrated Essex bowler, Harry Pickett, drowned himself off South Wales in 1907, even though he had seemed content as cricket coach at Clifton College – the type of job many retired players went to. And four days before the Great War broke out Albert Edward Trott, an all-rounder who played for both Australia and England and whose most famous feat was to hit a ball over the pavilion at Lord's in 1899, shot himself.

The golden year of the Golden Age was 1895, when Stoddart returned victorious. Thousands swarmed to matches while millions more followed their heroes' exploits in the press. Stoddart's vice-captain, MacLaren, made the highest score then recorded in first-class cricket when he took 424 off Somerset at Taunton in under eight hours on 15/16 July, the Somerset side having its first season in first-class cricket and fielding nine amateurs, including a doctor and a clergyman. For Grace, whose difficulties with his employers in the Bristol Poor Law Union (who retained his medical services) had prevented him from touring, it was an *annus* all the more *mirabilis* because The Champion was then forty-seven and creaking. Grace began that summer with the unprecedented feat of scoring 1,000 runs in May, in one innings of which he achieved the equally unprecedented feat of his one hundredth first-class century. He ended by having made 2,346 runs in total at an average of fifty-one, only prolonged bad weather preventing him from surpassing his previous season's best of 2,739 in 1871. *The Daily Telegraph*, in league with MCC and Gloucestershire, Grace's county club, had a testimonial for him that raised £9,703 and mocked his amateur status – which Grace had done for decades, constantly creatively accounting for money he made from the game while still being considered a 'Gentleman'.

Wisden called Grace, after his 'Indian Summer' of 1895, 'the greatest cricketer the world has ever seen'.[56] His image – a great, sturdy man with a long curly black beard, his head usually topped with the hooped red-

and-yellow MCC cap – was instantly recognisable, having featured in advertisements for the many commodities both cricketing and non-cricketing that he endorsed. Fry recorded that Grace, for all his might, 'squeaked' when he spoke.[57] His first first-class match was in 1864 and his last in 1908, when he was sixty; statisticians reckon he played between 870 and 878 in all, since the status of some games is unclear. Pitches were poorly prepared and unreliable, and his fame hinged on his ability to play well on even the worst.

Until 1914 crowds poured into grounds, for county matches as well as tests: 30,000 would pack Old Trafford or Headingley for Roses matches between Lancashire and Yorkshire. At Leeds in 1904 there were 78,792 people at George Hirst's benefit match over three days, at which they consumed 135,000 bananas.[58] Crowds of 10,000 at ordinary county matches were quite normal, remarkable numbers considering cricket was played mostly on working days – matches were of three days' duration – and for most working-class people attending a game was a holiday or retirement pursuit.

The game threw up matches that seized the public's imagination and intensified the national obsession with cricket: such as Jessop's match, named after the feet of the Gloucestershire amateur, captain and all-rounder Gilbert Jessop, which was the fifth and final test between England and Australia, at the Oval in August 1902. England needed 263 to win, and had been reduced to 48 for 5 when Jessop – 'The Croucher' – came in. Just five feet seven inches tall but powerfully built, Jessop went up to Cambridge in 1895 hoping to read for the priesthood, but left without taking a degree. He brought reflectiveness and aggression to his cricket, but was believed to be the fastest-scoring batsman ever: the following season he made 286 in three hours against Sussex. Despite England's perilous position, he made no compromises in an innings described as 'an apocalyptic blend of high art and controlled violence'.[59] *Wisden* pronounced that 'a more astonishing display has never been seen'.[60] No other living player could have matched him: 'The rest of the match was simply one *crescendo* of excitement.' He reached 50 in forty-three minutes and 100 in seventy-five off 76 balls, being out for 104 two minutes later, having hit seventeen fours and a five and transformed the game, and scored his runs out of 139 while at the crease. Fry, no mean batsman, described Jessop's feat as 'the greatest innings by a pure hitter ever played'.[61]

However, he was out before victory was secured, with England 187 for

7; and two more wickets left England at 248 for 9, with the last two men in and 15 runs short, a Newboltian moment. Those two men were the Yorkshiremen Hirst – the only player to score 2,000 runs and take 200 wickets in a season – and Rhodes, who although batting at number eleven would by 1909 be opening with Jack Hobbs. Legend – unsubstantiated – has it that Hirst said to Rhodes, on the latter's arrival, 'We'll get 'em in singles.'[62] They did not, but they did get them, and England won by one wicket. The popular press dramatised these events and brought these heroes and their glamour into millions of households. Cricket's part in 'the great cause of cheering us all up' was undisputed. Its culture infused the nation's. Fine writers rhapsodised on it; stories about it left the sports pages and graced the news pages. Poets such as Newbolt and Thompson elevated it, the former allying the game with the moral code of the middle-class ideal:

There's a breathless hush in the Close to-night –
Ten to make and the match to win –
A bumping pitch and a blinding light,
An hour to play and the last man in.
And it's not for the sake of a ribboned coat,
Or the selfish hope of a season's fame,
But his Captain's hand on his shoulder smote –
'Play up! play up! and play the game!'[63]

X

Not all outdoor middle-class pursuits took the form of organised sport. The growth of the railways, which in the second half of the nineteenth century spread into even sparsely populated areas, also facilitated more informal pastimes. Trains took town and city dwellers to the countryside within half an hour for a few pennies, where all that was required for a day's rambling were a pair of stout shoes, a waterproof and a map. Walking tours on the continent became a popular recreation with the better-off in the nineteenth century, and industrialisation caused the middle and working classes to emulate their betters and take exercise in the open air. There was a network of public footpaths and bridleways in most of England, but with almost all land being privately owned walkers risked prosecution for trespass, which limited their activity. The first rambling clubs grew up in the north, and from the early 1880s parliament debated the need for a law to grant the 'right to roam'. The Federation of Rambling Clubs (clubs of all descriptions were a leading fetish of the middle classes, and an expression of their tribalism) was formed in 1905, partly to lobby for better rights of access. Attempts to change the law failed; it was not until 1932, and a mass trespass on Kinder Scout in Derbyshire, that the movement agitated sufficiently for parliament to grant rights of access.

A Scottish blacksmith, Kirkpatrick Macmillan, is credited with inventing the bicycle in 1839: the first, and much faster, chain-driven cycles appeared around 1885. As the roads improved the passion for cycling grew: by the 1890s a million machines a year were manufactured in Britain, the majority going for export.[64] Many people already owned a bike to get cheaply and quickly to their places of work, and the still-quiet countryside attracted hundreds of rambling clubs. Rambling and cycling were popular with women as individual pursuits that did not, in the manner of most sports clubs, exclude them by being male only.

In recreational terms, one technological advance trumped all others. The Edwardian period saw a boom in motoring, though to start with it was a rich man's pursuit. When compulsory registration was introduced in 1904 just 8,500 cars were recorded, but by 1913 the roads were filling up, with 338,000 cars sold that year at an average cost of £340 each, as cars became affordable to more people. Life changed as a result.[65] The Automobile Club of Great Britain was formed in 1897 to oppose the 14 m.p.h. speed limit imposed the previous year, itself an improvement on the 1865 Act that forced 'road locomotives' to have a man walk in front at 4 m.p.h. holding a red flag. With Balfour's help the Motor Car Act of 1903 raised the limit to 20 m.p.h. An offence of reckless driving was created, and the requirement to buy a driving licence: for five shillings and no test required. The Automobile Club started to organise motor sport and because the motor's leading devotee was the King himself, the club became the Royal Automobile Club in 1907. In 1901 it had started mobile patrols of mechanics on motorbikes, useful given the unreliability of early cars. They would salute as a member – identified by the badge on his fender – drove past: failure to salute meant a police speed trap lay ahead. The Automobile Association, founded in 1905, gave the same service.

In the 1880s boating became a craze with the middle classes, with hotels, restaurants and cafés opening along the Thames west of London in towns such as Richmond, Goring, Maidenhead, Marlow and Henley, to accommodate the needs of trippers. The banks of the Thames and other rivers like it are adorned to this day by villas from the 1880s and 1890s in grounds leading down to the river, built by the well-to-do to capitalise upon the new salubriousness of the riverside towns. The atmosphere of the age is exemplified in the phenomenally successful novel of 1889, *Three Men in a Boat*, by the grammar-school boy turned solicitor's clerk Jerome K. Jerome, who fictionalised an account of a real-life fortnight's trip between Kingston and Oxford that he took with two other friends, a banker and a manager in a printing works. Jerome intended the work to be a guidebook for the thousands like him and his friends who had turned the river into a playground: accidentally, it became a comic novel.

Leisure hours could be enjoyed at home, too. Gardening, for example, which had hitherto been the province of big houses and great estates, with vast kitchen gardens and highly architectural hothouses, was taken up by the rising middle class who now had the time, the money – and the space – to enjoy it. Even in towns, many new houses came with plots where small-scale horticulture could be practised, and local councils made allotments available to householders to grow vegetables. Such things became competitive, with flower, fruit and vegetable shows where people could display their produce and win prizes. Meanwhile, for those with a technological bent, there was photography, which was popular with both men and women: the happy consequence of its becoming ever more affordable was that it ensured that late-Victorian and Edwardian Britain was captured before the seismic changes of the twentieth century.

Without doubt, though, one of the most widespread hobbies of the time, and a particular favourite of the middle classes with a few extra shillings to spend, arose out of a bureaucratic reform of 1840. This was when Britain issued the world's first postage stamps, the penny black and the twopenny blue. Because of the engraving and printing processes, stamps seeming identical to non-collectors differed in ways collectors could spot. Various numbered plates were used in printing, or plates broke during the process causing flaws on stamps. The inks used for printing were often fugitive, leading to shade varieties. The paper was watermarked to deter forgery; sometimes it was loaded into presses upside down or the wrong way, reversing, inverting or turning sideways the watermark; and once perforations came in – the first stamps were cut out with scissors – the machines that punched the holes had different gauges, so the number of perforations per stamp could vary. Postal authorities also used postmarks to prevent stamps being re-used, and people began to collect examples of those too.

The hobby had further traction because of the use of stamps in British colonies, mostly printed in London. Schoolboys collected stamps not for varieties (usually beyond their pockets) or for aesthetics but to obtain a window on to the wider world and to follow the British imperial project. As interest in the hobby – the study of stamps had by the 1860s become known as philately, after a word coined in France from the Greek – ballooned in the late nineteenth century, so rarer varieties and those with restricted print runs became highly sought after, with a consequent rise in price and the rise, too, of the stamp dealer.

The most famous was Edward Stanley Gibbons, son of a Plymouth pharmacist, born six weeks after the penny black. Packages arrived from around Britain and the world at Gibbons's father's shop. As a schoolboy Stanley collected stamps and swapped them with friends. A brief spell as a bank clerk fuelled his hobby by giving him access to even more stamps. He went to work in his father's shop, and was allowed to set up a separate counter to buy and sell stamps. When Gibbons *père* died in 1867, Stanley sold up and became a full-time stamp dealer, having issued a price list – the embryonic catalogue – from 1864. In 1874 he relocated to Gower Street in London, and his enterprise grew.

Gibbons fostered both stamp collecting and philately. He published an expanding annual catalogue (more volumes appearing as the number of issues multiplied) but also magazines about the hobby. His and his firm's work in cataloguing stamps by variety played a crucial role in developing philately. In 1890, however, Gibbons sold his business to a twenty-seven-year-old philatelist, Charles Phillips, for £25,000, and retired. He maintained links with Phillips and, during extensive travels, bought stamps for the firm that still bore his name and of which, until his death, he remained chairman.

However, as if to prove stamp collecting was not the mark of a dullard, Gibbons also had five wives, four of whom pre-deceased him at early ages. There has been speculation their ends were not always from natural causes, but encouraged by his early training as a pharmacist. Two wives died of liver ailments, a common effect of poisoning, and another of a wasting condition linked to such a death. His fifth wife survived him, but his will passed his estate to another woman to whom he was not married. He died in 1913, supposedly at his nephew's flat near Oxford Street: but rumours circulated that he died *in flagrante* with his mistress in the Savoy Hotel, his corpse being taken across London concealed in a carpet.

In 1902 the Gibbons company published the early definitive work on the hobby, *Stamp Collecting as a Pastime*, by Edward J. Nankivell, a member of the Philatelic Society of London. The work noted outsiders were 'thunderstruck' at the prices paid for rare stamps, and also that 'stamp collecting has never been more popular than it is today.'[66] Nankivell continued:

> Its votaries are to be found in every city and town of the civilised world. Governments and statesmen recognise, unsolicited, the claims of stamp collecting – the power, the influence, and the wealth that it commands. From a mere schoolboy pastime it has steadily developed into an engrossing hobby for the leisured and the busy of all classes and all ranks of life, from the monarch on his throne to the errand boy in the merchant's office.

The monarch cited was not the King of England, whose pleasures were generally less cerebral; that would change, however, with the accession of his son, George V.

Part of the attraction of stamp collecting was how it crossed class boundaries. Children could soak stamps off letters arriving in the family home and start a collection. 'The average series of used stamps are now so cheap', Nankivell observed, 'that a lad may get together a fairly representative collection for what he ordinarily spends at the tuck shop.'[67] Thus as well as combating childhood obesity, stamp collecting enhanced the lad's knowledge of geography, 'so important to the boys of a great commercial nation'. Those with money could buy complete collections and stockpile them as investments. Some collectors became dealers. But George V gave the hobby – his main pastime apart from shooting and yachting – the royal endorsement and, in the process, assembled one of the finest private collections in the world. 'It is one of the greatest pleasures of my life,' he wrote while Prince of Wales.[68]

Touring colonies from the 1890s onwards, the Prince collected stamps wherever he went: and not merely stamps, but proof sheets and other items of philatelic interest. This went further after 1893, when one of his wedding presents was a collection of 1,500 rare varieties. His uncle and fellow collector, the Duke of Edinburgh, introduced him to John Alexander Tilleard, a solicitor and expert philatelist. Posterity paints him as stupid, but George V's knowledge of the intricacies of stamp design, printing and production put him among the world's leading philatelists; though his official biographer, Sir Harold Nicolson, deprecated the fact that Tilleard's visits to the Prince were more frequent than those of Professor J. R. Tanner, the Cambridge constitutional historian engaged after Prince Eddy's death to educate the Duke of York in Kingship.[69]

Shortly before his death in 1900 the Duke of Edinburgh, in financial difficulties, sold his considerable stamp collection to his brother, the Prince of Wales. This seems to have been an act of charity, as the Prince had no interest in the hobby; he gave the collection to the Duke of York. The Duke became President of the Philatelic Society of London (founded in 1869); and, under his patronage as Prince of Wales, it became in 1906 the Royal Philatelic Society, of which Tilleard was honorary secretary. Such societies sprang up all over the country and, indeed, the Empire.

An old lady read in a newspaper of the Prince's interest in stamps and sent him an album. Her husband had collected stamps since the 1850s and she had found the album after his death. A local dealer had offered her £50 for it, which her doctor advised her not to accept. The Prince told the curator of his stamp collection to send the album back and advise the old lady to put it into a philatelic auction, which she did. He also told his curator to bid anonymously for a rare Bahamas stamp, one of the few colonial ones the Prince lacked. The album realised £7,000 and the Bahamas stamp alone £1,400. The next day Sir Arthur Davidson, the King's equerry, rang the Prince on another matter and finished by saying: 'I know how interested Your Royal Highness is in stamps. Did you happen to see in the newspapers that some damned fool had given as much as £1,400 for one stamp?' The Prince replied: 'I was the damned fool.'[70]

On his accession King George appointed Tilleard court philatelist, at a handsome salary of £750 a year, and he turned the King's collection into the Royal Philatelic Collection, one of the great legacies of his reign. Wherever he travelled he acquired stamps; and his courtiers, if going overseas, were also given instructions of what to buy. At his death in 1936 his collection was estimated at a quarter of a million stamps in 325 albums. Yet it was during his father's reign that George V gave the greatest boost to the hobby, and the stamp trade. He spent a large proportion of his income as Prince of Wales – he made £60,000 a year from the Duchy of Cornwall and £40,000 from a government grant – on stamps. The hobby of millions of small boys was also the hobby of kings, and this king's investment created a stunning national heirloom. His passion also, incidentally, demonstrated – along with his uxoriousness and his immaculate family life – how middle class the Royal family had become.

In *The Suburbans,* T. W. H. Crosland sneered at this clutter of new middle-class pastimes and obsessions. For him this was a world of 'penny buses, gramophones, bamboo furniture, pleasant Sunday afternoons, Glory Songs, modern language teas, golf, tennis, high school education, dubious fiction, shilling's worth of comic writing, picture postcards, miraculous hair restorers, prize competitions, and all other sorts of twentieth-century claptrap'.[71] The middle-class suburbs were enclaves of 'oyster-bars, Methodist chapels, free public libraries, small shops, ha'penny newspapers, cheap music-halls, police and county courts, billiard matches, minor race-meetings, third-class railway carriages, public museums, public baths, indifferent academies for young ladies': 'whatever, in short,' he concluded, 'strikes the superior mind as being deficient in completeness, excellence and distinction may with absolute safety be called suburban.'[72] For the suburbanites themselves, however, this was an era of comfort unimaginable only a couple of generations earlier.

XI

Many in the middle classes were the first generation in their family to be enfranchised – if they were male – and took seriously the civic obligation to participate in the political process. When the Tories first organised as a mass party under Disraeli in the 1870s, with a national network of agents, it was with a view to bringing the new middle classes into the fold: hitherto the Liberal party had been attractive to such people, and Lord Randolph Churchill's Tory Democracy was in part designed to appeal to the new middle classes who might otherwise be drawn to radicalism, as many were in the mid-nineteenth century. This was even more important after the Reform Act of 1884, when many more of the party's natural opponents were given the vote. Supporting the Conservative party was very much a badge of social respectability; though some of the party's associations (such as with the brewing industry, which funded it heavily) drove large groups of the northern middle classes, who supported Non-conformism with its temperance leanings, into the arms of the Liberal party.

The middle classes – particularly higher up the scale, where there were fewer fears about being considered lacking in respectability – remained instrumental in encouraging and organising radical politics, and from the 1880s onwards embraced leftist ideas once associated mainly with the working class. In London and elsewhere debating and philosophical societies were set up for men – and sometimes women. Those on the left in the middle classes were few in number, but their energy and access to the press and intellectual society gave them an influence far in excess of their numbers. Partly as a result of this, and partly because of the policies of their opponents, the questions they championed – notably the conditions of the poor and how to alleviate them – became of central importance in the quarter-century before the Great War.

The Fabian Society was formed in January 1884 by a group who the previous year had set up a less politicised, more utopian grouping called the Fellowship of the New Life, arguing for social change. The Fabians (named after the Roman general Quintus Fabius Maximus Verrucosus, his sobriquet Cunctator meaning 'the delayer') effectively became the political wing of this movement, their doctrine one of incremental rather than revolutionary change, but also one of practicality that dispensed with the Fellowship's sentimentalising of the working class. The Fabians would help the nascent Labour movement mobilise, and would provide much of its doctrinal base.

Once formed, the society became a magnet for progressive intellectuals. George Bernard Shaw, then a jobbing writer, joined early on, and was elected to the executive in January 1885. Born into genteel poverty among the declining Anglo-Irish Ascendancy in Dublin in 1856, Shaw had left school for a mind-numbing clerical job at the age of fifteen. He succeeded in it until the age of twenty, when he left for London and tried to make a living as a writer. He lived off his mother (who was estranged from his father and had moved from Dublin a little earlier) and his savings while applying for jobs, spending his days in the reading room of the British Museum, which he regarded as his university. To ward off starvation he took a job with the Edison Telephone Company in 1879, persuading householders to let telephone wires cross their properties. After a year he returned, full-time and unsuccessfully, to writing, but made friends among fellow radicals and socialists. Socialist magazines began to publish his writings, and he imbibed Karl Marx.

Having met Sidney Webb, the prominent socialist, of whom more below, Shaw edited and contributed to *Fabian Essays in Socialism* in 1889. He and Webb wrote the Fabian manifesto *To Your Tents, O Israel!* in November 1893, which sought to distance Fabianism from a failing Liberal government, and to forge links with the Independent Labour party. Shaw's writings from the 1890s onwards are mostly about promoting and securing progress. He did once stand for election – successfully, for the St Pancras borough council – but felt he could change the world and shape the future better through writing, and speaking: in an age before the broadcast media he became the public face and voice of the Fabians, speaking frequently on platforms and evangelising for his vision of the future.

His first play, *Widowers' Houses* in 1892, was a tale of people horrified to realise they made their money by exploiting the poor. The implication was that most wealth was created in that way, and it caused predictable controversy. *Mrs Warren's Profession*, written the following year, had as its subject a woman who decided that making money by prostitution was far preferable to working in a factory. A suggestion of incest caused the Lord Chamberlain's censor to ban it for public performance until 1925: but it was privately performed from 1902 and made Shaw's name as a dramatist. Mrs Warren was also an entrepreneur: she set up a chain of brothels, the capital provided by apparently respectable men, and used the money to send her daughter to Cambridge. Shaw was a proto-feminist as well as a socialist, and the women in his plays are strong and commanding. In his preface to *Man and Superman* he would write that 'home is the girl's prison and the woman's workhouse.'[73]

His plays before the Great War – notably *John Bull's Other Island*, *Major Barbara*, *The Doctor's Dilemma* and *Pygmalion* – all criticise aspects of class, exploitation and social injustice. Shaw attacks the status quo, and argues for a better future, using satire: as in *Pygmalion*, when Doolittle has offered to sell Eliza, his daughter, to Higgins for £5. Pickering, shocked to witness this, asks the dustman: 'Have you no morals, man?'

to which Doolittle replies, 'Can't afford them, Governor. Neither could you if you was as poor as me.'[74] Shaw constantly strove to promote progress, and in 1913 was a founder of the *New Statesman* as an organ of socialist debate. As a critic, he broadened British taste, championing Ibsen, Wagner and Elgar. The last was an important patronage, as for a serious critic in the early twentieth century to have anything positive to say about British music was brave. Shaw, however, looked always to the future, not the past.

The propagandistic element in Shaw is as much in the prefaces he wrote for his plays as in the plays themselves. Introducing *Major Barbara*, he wrote that Undershaft, the arms dealer who is Barbara's father, has become conscious 'of the irresistible natural truth which we all abhor and repudiate: to wit, that the greatest of our evils, and the worst of our crimes is poverty'.[75] He asserts that the police force exists 'to force the poor man to see his children starve whilst idle people overfeed pet dogs with the money that might feed and clothe them . . . we tolerate poverty as if it were either a wholesome tonic for lazy people or else a virtue to be embraced as St Francis embraced it.'[76] Writing in 1905, he called for a minimum wage and for old age pensions. The latter would come in three years, the former would take almost a century.

Shaw's apostasy from Marxism in joining the Fabians, and using his considerable gifts to promote the society, its methods and doctrines, came as a great disappointment to Henry Hyndman, a well-to-do agitator and the leading socialist of the day, whom we shall meet in the next chapter. Hyndman had made Shaw his protégé and had high hopes for him as a fellow architect of a Marxist-based movement. Where Shaw led, other prominent leftists followed. Annie Besant, the leading female radical and secularist, became a Fabian early on, under Shaw's influence. Later, H. G. Wells and Leonard and Virginia Woolf joined, as did politicians such as Ramsay MacDonald: Wells noted that when he came to London in the 1880s 'Fabianism was Socialism, so far as the exposition of views and policy went. There was no other Socialist propaganda in England worth considering.'[77]

The Fabians became prominent in the 1890s through the partnership of Sidney and Beatrice Webb, who over the next half-century became synonymous with its work and programme. Their own intense and at times parodically earnest view of social science would exemplify the Fabian approach, even if some of their research did not stand up to scrutiny and, as they aged and were taken in by Sovietism, their judgments seemed questionable.

The Webbs were well-heeled, Beatrice more so than Sidney. Her father, Richard Potter, had inherited (and lost, and re-made) a fortune. She had been brought up as one of nine daughters in a grand house in Gloucestershire. Sidney's father had prospered in trade, including as a parfumier, in London. As a teenager in the 1870s Beatrice, brimming with intellectual curiosity and intensely serious, had caught the tail end of the mid-Victorian crisis of faith after the widely-publicised discoveries and theories of Charles Darwin. Religion – in a form like Carlyle's post-Christian deism – would remain a considerable, but diminishing, obsession. As well as being clever she was a beauty, pursued in the early 1880s by Joe Chamberlain, twice widowed and twenty-two years her senior. 'I don't know how it will all end,' she told her diary on 16 March 1884. 'Certainly not in *my happiness*.'[78] She believed he would 'refuse me all freedom of thought', but found him fascinating. A few weeks later she mused: 'Once married, I should of course subordinate my views to my husband's . . . accept implicitly his views of right and wrong. But I cannot shirk the responsibility of using my judgement before I acknowledge his authority.'[79]

The relationship 'died a natural death from the unfitness of things' in July 1884, though she had sporadic lapses over the next three years.[80] The final break came in August 1887 when 'in another moment of suicidal misery [I] told him I cared for him passionately', before telling him not to see her again.[81] On the first day of the next century – 1 January 1901 – Beatrice noted that meeting Joe had been 'the catastrophe of my life'.[82] She was deeply infatuated, while he trifled with her: she was twice pitched into depression, first in 1888 when he married again (Beatrice was then thirty and at the point when most Victorian women of her station might have thought themselves on the shelf), and the second time in 1901 when he was widowed yet again. Beatrice herself was married by then. An effect of the first trauma was that she pitched herself into social work in London's East End to try to forget about him. It profoundly reinforced her political instincts.

She was not a conventional radical. She and her sisters were for a time committed anti-feminists. She was one of 104 women who signed a petition against women's suffrage in 1889 – its argument included the contention that participation in politics was rendered unthinkable 'either by the disabilities of sex, or by strong formations of custom and habit resting ultimately upon physical difference against which it is useless to contend' – but as she moved towards the Labour party her views changed.[83] She was never a suffragette, opposing militancy there as in the union movement, and seemed ambivalent when women obtained the vote. However, she believed in ending the subjection of women to men at home – she would in old age find this, or her interpretation of it, one of the joys of Stalin's Soviet Union. She found this aspect of Chamberlain's character odious: Joe always wore the trousers.

By the late 1880s she was doing missionary work among London's poor for the Charity Organisation Society, and in the more salubrious industrial setting of Bacup in Lancashire. She widely read the literature of poverty and how to relieve it, and concluded that lady-of-the-manor philanthropy was no answer. Bacup was a bastion of the co-operative movement and Beatrice felt it a signal success. It was closely linked to dissenters and Non-conformists, who when given the incentive to look after each other made a conspicuous success of it. Her work in the East End, particularly among Jewish garment workers – she even masqueraded as a jobbing tailor to gather data – caused her to develop a hatred of individualism and competition. On 1 February 1890 this caused her to proclaim to her diary: 'At last I am a socialist!'[84]

She was not, however, a revolutionary. She had read Auguste Comte, whose writings encouraged her to study sociology and made her realise that change pursued by anything other than a gradualist approach risked being inhumane. This was also why she was so interested in the co-operative movement, and decided to write an essay about its history. She needed to consult an expert on the Labour movement and a cousin, Margaret Harkness, knew just the man: and so at Miss Harkness's house in Bloomsbury, on 8 January 1890, thirty-one-year-old Beatrice Potter met thirty-year-old Sidney Webb, a largely self-taught Colonial Office civil servant active in socialist politics since his teens and influenced by Bentham and J. S. Mill, who Sidney believed had died a socialist.

Before the Fabians Sidney had participated in various debating societies – which enjoyed a vogue in *fin-de-siècle* London – and at one, the Zetetical, he met Shaw in 1880. He thought Webb 'the ablest man in England'.[85] Partly under Webb's influence, Shaw decided in 1887 that 'it is time for us to abandon the principle of Individualism, and to substitute that of Socialism, on pain of national decay.'[86] This was not entirely how he saw things himself: he may have been turned against economic individualism, but apart from that he remained an individualist to his core. Around the same time he shocked the Shelley Society by proclaiming that he was 'a Socialist, an Atheist and a Vegetarian.'[87] By then, Shaw and Webb were the presiding geniuses of the Fabians, convinced their brand of socialism could supplant the Marxist ideas of Hyndman and his friends.

Webb's approach to politics was empirical and relied on statistical argument: his first publication, in 1887, *Facts for Socialists*, was effectively an economic handbook with data from official sources that socialists could use to attack the parties of government. His and Beatrice's union was a meeting of minds: he instinctively rejected Marxist analysis but wished the privileged classes would understand their obligations to the poor, and would discharge them. The roots of Sidney's thinking were in Christian socialism, though he was moving smartly away from religion, and, like Beatrice, towards Comte.

Another early meeting between Beatrice and 'Sidney Webb, the socialist' was on 26 April 1890, when she interrogated him about his past. She was impressed by his story of self-improvement, and Sidney – 'the little man' – told her: 'I have done everything I intended to do. I have a belief in my own star.'[88] When he professed that 'you have reduced me to a pulp by your sympathy', Beatrice told him 'you can feel you have humbled me – by making me a socialist.' However, it was only a meeting of minds. She referred to how 'his tiny tadpole body, unhealthy skin, lack of manner, Cockney pronunciation, poverty are all against him. He has the conceit of a man who has raised himself out of the most insignificant surroundings into a position of power . . . this self-important egotism, this disproportionate view of his own position, is at once repulsive and ludicrous.'[89] Yet she also saw him as 'above all a loophole into the socialist party; one of the small body of men with whom I may sooner or later throw in my lot'.

A shared interest in social science, notably in collectivism, co-operation and social policy, would bind them. Sidney persuaded Beatrice to join the Fabians in January 1891, and to make the society a platform for their ideas. In May, in the romantic setting of the Co-operative Congress in Lincoln, Sidney found for the first time that when he placed his hand in Beatrice's she did not pull away. They 'embraced' for the first time that evening.[90] Eventually Beatrice was persuaded by the idea of marriage, though primarily as a partnership by which to further their shared ideals. As she weighed the pros and cons she wrote that 'if I marry, though I shall be drawn to it by affection and gratitude, it will be an act of renunciation of self and not of indulgence of self as it would have been in the other case.'[91] They agreed to become engaged, but in secret. Beatrice's father was mortally ill; nothing could be finalised until he died. The idea of her marrying the 'tadpole' might have killed him. Meanwhile their first joint project would be a history of trade unionism, a subject to which the Fabians had come late, failing to appreciate how the unions could add clout to middle-class theorising and create a proper Labour movement. Once Richard Potter died, the money Beatrice inherited enabled Sidney to retire from the Colonial Office and the pair of them to devote themselves to the improvement of society.

Wells satirised the Webbs as 'two active self-centred people excessively devoted to the public service'.[92] He found their earnestness preposterous, and satirised that too, in *The New Machiavelli*: 'PBP, she boasted, was engraved inside their wedding rings, *Pro Bono Publico*, and she meant it to be no idle threat.'[93] He mocked their response to the reality of socialist politicians: 'Most of them have totally unpresentable wives . . . and they *will* bring them . . . Some of the poor creatures have scarcely learned their table manners.'[94] He could not resist mocking the Fabians too, who by the turn of the century had become steeped in the attitudes of the Webbs. In Wells's novel *Ann Veronica* the heroine's friend Miss Miniver tells her: 'It's the society! . . . It's the centre of the intellectuals! Some of the meetings are wonderful! Such earnest, beautiful women! Such deep-browed men! . . . And to think that there they are making history! There they are putting together the plans of a new world!'[95] When Ann Veronica asks: 'But are these people going to alter everything?' Miss Miniver replies: 'What else can happen? . . . What else can possibly happen – as things are going now?'

Sidney Webb, his retirement funded by his dead father-in-law, decided to learn about public policy and administration, and in 1892 stood in the second elections for the London County Council. Opportunities to organise politically and to participate in politics had been multiplied as a result of Salisbury's restructuring of local government in 1888, which set up county councils, including one in London. Webb took full advantage of this. He sailed under the flag of the Progressive party, which was mainly composed of Liberals and radicals but, as with the Liberal party at Westminster, also harboured those who would slip with ease into the Labour party. Formed in 1888 for the purpose of securing election to local government, the party was endorsed by the Fabians, and in the 1889 elections to the LCC won seventy-two of the 118 available seats (one of these going to Rosebery, returned for the City of London) and had eighteen of the nineteen aldermen. Those elections also saw women councillors elected for the first time. In 1892 the victory was even more pronounced, with eighty-three seats (but just seventeen aldermen).

The Progressive party used London to show what a radical government would do if it ran Britain. For all its socialists it in many ways offered a preview of the Liberal government after 1906. It built municipal housing and in the inner suburbs set out parks and swimming baths. It expanded its Works Department, and set an example by fixing a forty-eight-hour week and paying union rates, which horrified many politicians – notably Salisbury, who in 1894 described the LCC as where 'collectivist and socialistic experiments are tried. It is the place where a new revolutionary spirit finds its instruments and collects its arms.'[96] This was ironic, for Salisbury, as prime minister in 1890, had given the LCC permission to build houses.

Webb was elected for Deptford, one of the most working-class areas of London, and set about implementing another Progressive policy, of improving education. He became head of the technical education board, revelling in the bureaucracy of local government. His civil service experience made him a fine committee man, highly effective at driving through policies. With county-based local government in its infancy and no culture of centralisation in Whitehall, there were no clear guidelines about how and how far power should be exercised, so the opportunity existed to build empires.

Webb did exactly that. He turned the board into what would now be regarded as a local education authority, with the support of Arthur Dyke Acland, the minister in Gladstone's last administration responsible for education. Acland, like Webb an enthusiast for the co-operative movement but unlike him the son of a baronet, understood the importance of supplying the working and lower-middle classes – whose parents could not afford to send them to a school where they would learn to be gentlemen – with an education broader than one that would equip them to work in industry. Acland had sponsored a Bill in 1889 to make county councils in Wales responsible for education – something comparable would not happen in England until 1902 – but with Webb running the London board he set a prototype for the future.

He ensured that history, foreign languages, geography and economics were in the curriculum as well as sciences, and found money for a scholarship system to allow young people from humble origins to aspire to university. He was also instrumental in founding the London School of Economics. On 4 August 1894 Shaw breakfasted with the Webbs and Graham Wallas, a fellow Fabian, social reformer and educationalist, who would lecture at the London School of Economics for more than thirty years. Henry Hunt Hutchinson, a Derby solicitor and member of the society, had shot himself the previous month and left £20,000 to the Fabians to further socialist propaganda. Webb, a trustee of his estate, interpreted this broadly, deciding to propagate socialism by educating young people to evangelise for it. Despite vehement objections from Shaw, who saw Webb's plan as 'an atrocious malversation of the rest of the bequest', he persuaded the society to use half the money to found the London School of Economics, inspired by Webb's visits to the Massachusetts Institute of Technology and the Institut d'Études Politiques de Paris.[97]

Webb did not just view the LSE as a means of providing higher education to the working and middle classes. He saw it as a different kind of institution entirely from the old universities, and newer institutions that had modelled themselves on Oxford and Cambridge. It was also expected that the LSE, by specialising in the social sciences, would provide an intellectual underpinning for the nascent Labour movement, a place that 'would train experts in the task of reforming society.'[98] It would be a modernising institution in the broadest sense, allowing Britain to match European countries whose training in economics and business was superior because of the British focus on classical studies at university level. The LSE would study the modern world, not the ancient: the perfect place to propound the Webbs' obsession with the social sciences, public administration and political economy.

The LSE opened for business in rooms in the Adelphi in 1895, and grew rapidly. Shaw and the Webbs soon fell out about its direction: Shaw said that if Hutchinson's money was being put into the LSE, then 'the collectivist flag must be waved and the *Marseillaise* played.'[99] The Webbs were too high-minded to agree, knowing the independence of the institution ensured its credibility. The lack of partisanship enabled Sidney Webb to persuade the LCC to make a grant of land for the LSE north of the Aldwych, where an urban clearance was under way, and to arrange regular maintenance grants. In 1900 University College London designated the LSE as its economics faculty; and LSE students could receive London University degrees from 1902, the year Rosebery opened the new premises. The institution was not merely a great achievement of the Fabians, but of the Fabian mind. It shaped the future by facilitating the liberal education that would help secure reform: but it also provided much of the intellectual underpinning for the advance of socialist ideas that would seduce some left-wing and even centrist Liberals, but would ultimately defeat the party and push it to third place in a two-party system.

The University of London was also where Leonard Hobhouse, in 1907, became Professor of Sociology, one of the first two such chairs in the country. He was a self-radicalised Liberal, being the son of a clergyman and a Tory who at Marlborough had identified himself with the radical wing of the Liberal party, and had preferred rationalism and agnosticism to Christianity. This advanced secularism also came to characterise that wing of the Liberal party that he would come to influence. Unsurprisingly in this context, Charles Bradlaugh, the radical atheist MP, John Morley, John Bright and John Stuart Mill were his heroes. He was interested in the Fabians, but rejected what he considered to be their elitism and flippancy, the latter being a vice he attributed especially to Shaw, whom he despised. In the years before he acquired his chair in sociology Hobhouse worked full-time at *The Manchester Guardian*, writing leading articles in tandem with C. P. Scott, its editor, with both of them seeking to act as the conscience of a modern Liberal party by forcing it to acknowledge the need to form some sort of consensus with the collective.

Hobhouse rejected Marxism because of its coercive aspects, which was the same reason he dismissed imperialism: but he did believe that individual wealth owed something to the collective, literally and metaphorically; and in his doctrine he drew distinctions between wealth or property that individuals had for their own use, and property they held to exert power or control over others. Hobhouse argued that the powerful owed the acquisition of their power to society, and therefore had an obligation to others. This idea would lie behind Asquith's decision, as Chancellor of the Exchequer, to introduce state pensions, which entailed a redistribution of wealth, and as prime minister to force through that redistribution in the face of massive opposition from the Tories and even his former master, Rosebery, whom Hobhouse also loathed. But then Rosebery, essentially a Whig, was from a Liberal tradition quite other than Hobhouse's. However, for all Hobhouse's influence, the Liberal party would never commit itself so profoundly to state intervention and control as would the nascent Labour party: Liberalism's decline while Labour flourished after the Great War was not least because the public wanted to have that choice.

While Sidney concentrated on forging an educational revolution – with some success – Beatrice researched their trade union history. Aged thirty-seven in 1895, and with a work on the co-operative movement also to research, she had decided against having children, something she later regretted: not least because she felt it was an obligation to society she had failed to discharge. However, the Webbs began to develop social theories that would resonate through the Labour movement for decades, such as the idea of a minimum wage and about duties the individual owed to society. The salon of *bien pensants* for which they would become famous did not develop until the 1900s, when such was its catholicity that it would include A. J. Balfour, Unionist prime minister from 1902 to 1905 and nephew of Lord Salisbury. The genuine working class, for whom the Webbs had such good intentions, were thinner on the ground.

The Webbs and their circle were far from alone in advocating the cause of the working class while keeping them at arm's length: but at least they recognised that there were problems further down society that needed to be addressed. Most in the new middle classes were so relieved to have moved up the ladder that they were only too keen to forget the life and the people they had left behind. However, the working classes would not be forgotten, and now embarked upon their own campaign for social clout and political representation.

CHAPTER 3

THE WORKERS' STRUGGLE

I

Although the Labour movement regarded the 1884 Reform Act as inadequate, given the large proportion of working men still without the vote, it was a key step in its advance to full enfranchisement and, eventually, power. It encouraged the further mobilisation of the working classes; and, together with the growing secularism that came from the rootless nature of many new urban communities, compared with the more traditional ones in rural areas, eroded deference and further undermined the old social order. Local government reforms in 1888 also broadened the base of power (see Chapter 7). Over the next decades, the Labour movement's desire to be a force in its own right would prove unstoppable.

As with the middle class, however, it would be wrong to assume that the working class of the late-Victorian and Edwardian periods was a unified and monolithic group. Nor was it static. The changing economic patterns of the late nineteenth century continually reshaped society. The agricultural decline, caused by the commitment of both Liberal and Conservative governments to free trade, which allowed cheap food (mainly corn) to be imported from America, caused a new migration from the countryside. Cities continued to grow. Unemployment fluctuated. It rose from 2.7 per cent of the workforce in 1872 to 9.1 per cent in 1879, before falling until 1883 to just under 5 per cent (the Board of Trade claimed it was back to 2 per cent, but subsequent analysis repudiated these figures). It then rose in 1885 to 8 per cent. The result was mass protests that threatened the rule of law.[1]

Groups within the working classes were differentiated from one another by skill and pay. But even individuals were likely to experience fluctuations in their relative social status over the course of their lives. The fortunes of working people could be undermined by illness or unemployment. They might experience comparative affluence, but then see it snatched away by the poverty that frequently accompanied old age. The pattern of working-class life was therefore constantly shifting, and many people passed through each of its various levels. At the very bottom were those who by accident or through idleness were incapable of productive work; then there were those who earned money but were feckless in matters of spending or saving it; there were the sick and the elderly, who when their savings were exhausted ended up in the workhouse; and those who earned so modest a living that they could not, without any other imposed or self-inflicted handicap, make ends meet. All this added to unhappiness and agitation. By the late 1880s, even though living standards had risen throughout the second half of the nineteenth century for industrial workers, there was a turbulence in British working-class life not seen since the 1840s.

II

Poverty remained a problem for the whole of society, not merely those who endured it: and to many of those with the good fortune to be at the opposite end of the spectrum, it was a severe embarrassment. Its causes and cures were widely debated. In London, Charles Booth's pioneering work established a poverty line below which the basic necessities of life could not be met. In York, Seebohm Rowntree, second son of the cocoa magnate and a trained chemist, believing his home city to be 'fairly representative of the conditions existing in many, if not most of our provincial towns', conducted his own poverty survey in 1899.[2] He looked at 11,560 families in 388 streets, comprising 46,754 people, out of a total of 75,812 in York. The population had risen nearly fivefold since 1801, thanks to the city's having become a major centre of railway construction and engineering, and the growth of Rowntree's confectionery business. 'Practically every capable boy and girl can find employment in the factories,' he wrote: but he would find family incomes often inadequate to maintain a reasonable standard of living.[3] There was also a form of what Rowntree called secondary poverty in many families with adequate incomes, as they chose to spend their money fruitlessly and even damagingly. Smoking rose, especially among the young, using up their extra earnings.

When visiting houses he noted their and their inhabitants' condition. In one street he described the people variously as 'very clean and respectable', 'tidy', 'very poor but tidy' and 'clean but very poor'. There were also 'untidy, overcrowded', 'untidy, house unsteady' and 'untidy woman, addicted to drink'.[4] He found that 4.2 per cent of people who were neither servants nor in the workhouse lived in households with an income of less than eighteen shillings a week; 52.6 per cent had an income of over thirty shillings a week. Not everyone he visited was poor: 28.8 per cent were of what Rowntree called 'the servant-keeping class'.[5]

Conditions for the poorest class were grim: a sixty-four-year-old man stricken with dropsy lived with his wife – a cleaner – in two rooms (for which they paid half-a-crown a week in rent), sharing a lavatory with eight other families and a cold-water tap with four others.[6] In one block fifteen families shared a lavatory, and slops were emptied in the yard. A widow with five children lived in four rooms surrounded by a slaughterhouse. Rowntree found houses permanently drenched in smoke from nearby factories; undernourished children; drink-sodden parents (in the poorest area there were thirty-nine public houses, or one for every 174 people); houses bereft of possessions because they had been pawned; damp and foul smells were ubiquitous. Consumption, bronchitis, rheumatism and general poor health were common. This was 'life lived under the pressure of chronic want'.[7]

Rowntree found that widows or men too ill to work headed many of the poorest families: though he also found malingerers and 'professional cadgers'.[8] The poorest families were not in a ghetto: they were in all the working-class areas. Their clothing might be superficially tidy, but was inadequate against the cold. For the elderly, if their income stopped and funds ran out before they died, the workhouse was the only option (Rowntree would become a strong advocate for a state pension). Conditions were little better in homes with higher incomes: only when he examined those earning over thirty shillings a week did he find an absence of poverty, except where self-inflicted by drink or gambling. He also noted that the children who did better at school were generally from higher-income families – but that they showed little interest in intellectual questions, and their reading was mainly confined to penny dreadfuls and other cheap fiction. They were largely untroubled by religion.

He also noted 'the monotony which characterises the life of most married women of the working class', a monotony less noticeable in the worst slums where 'the women are constantly in and out of each other's houses'.[9] The wives of working men were 'largely thrown upon their own resources', which were 'sadly limited' and caused the women to become 'hopeless drudges'. Husbands devoted most of their time to their 'mates' and 'seldom' rose 'even to the idea of mental companionship with his wife.'[10] Rowntree found the diet these women prepared included no fruit and few vegetables: dried peas and onions were the exceptions.

He computed the minimum vital expenditure for families of different sizes – seven shillings a week for a single man or woman, eighteen shillings and tenpence for a couple with two children, thirty-seven shillings and fourpence for a couple with eight children (two-thirds of which went on food), and regarded this as the 'poverty line', below which families had too little to live. He calculated that 15.46 per cent of wage-earners in York, or 9.91 per cent of the whole population, lived in poverty based on the level of their income. However, because many families spent wastefully, they endured self-inflicted poverty, causing Rowntree to estimate that 43.4 per cent of wage-earners, or 27.84 per cent of people, were living in secondary poverty. His conclusion was that 'the wages paid for unskilled labour in York are insufficient to provide food, shelter and clothing adequate to maintain a family of moderate size in a state of bare physical efficiency.'[11]

His minimum income assumed a diet 'even less generous than that allowed to able-bodied paupers in the York Workhouse', and that families 'must never purchase a halfpenny newspaper', or a stamp, or 'spend a penny on a railway fare or omnibus': their lives would be mere existence. To do any of these things would mean malnourishment. Disease was prevalent: in 1898 120 people (115 of them under five years old) died of dysentery or diarrhoea in the city, just under one-tenth of total deaths; consumption accounted for 45 of these (all children), 121 died from phthisis (another form of tuberculosis), 36 from measles and 17 from typhoid. Of 1,386 deaths that year, 551 were of children under five. The lower the income, Rowntree found, the shorter and lighter the children.

III

One of the great evils of working-class life – as well as one of its main recreations – was drink. Karl Marx said that drink was the curse of the working classes: Wilde that work was the curse of the drinking classes. The law had in 1830 allowed the opening of beerhouses, which effectively allowed any householder to sell ale, and the effect on drunkenness, public order and productivity had quickly become apparent. It was not until 1869 that the Wine and Beerhouse Act introduced strict licensing laws. The growth of urban and suburban England saw a concomitant growth in the numbers of pubs. In 1890 there were nineteen in Oxford Street in London, and thirty in the Strand. In the capital as a whole in 1896 there was a pub for every 345 people, in Sheffield the ratio was one for 176 and in Manchester it was one for 168.[12] Together England and Wales had 102,000 pubs served by 6,500 breweries by the turn of the century. They sprang up on the main roads out of cities as ports of call, as well as around railway stations.

Although inns had been classless up to and beyond Mr Pickwick's day, by the late nineteenth century few above the middle class used pubs. In London and other cities gentlemen's clubs proliferated so that men could drink in suitable society. The Hon. Algernon Bourke, secretary of White's Club, said in 1896 that 'the class I deal with and the class I associate with and the class I know do not go into public houses.'[13] The middle class did frequent pubs, but generally as families became more prosperous, the code to which they conformed dictated moderation, and they tended to drink in the privacy of their own or someone else's home. By 1900 whenever members of the middle class were to be found in a pub it would be in the saloon bar, where the beer was more expensive and the furnishings likely to be more comfortable. The many working-class people who frequented pubs would colonise the more basic public bar, sometimes called the 'spit and sawdust' because of its absorbent floor covering.

The clientele of pubs was heavily male: in urban areas in particular, women who went into a public bar were not considered respectable, and respectable ones would hardly venture into the saloon without their husbands. Some brewers provided special ladies' bars as they rebuilt lavishly during the 1890s, but these were rare. Towns with a high proportion of women frequenting pubs – such as Seebohm Rowntree found to be the case in York in his 1900 study *Poverty: A Study of Town Life* – were viewed as being on the cusp of degeneracy, because if the woman was not at home minding her children it was unlikely anyone else was. For women the staple drink was gin, or sometimes port and lemon. The popular drinks for men, mild and porter, cost fourpence a quart: the bars where they were drunk became known as four-ale bars. Children were allowed in pubs, but had been unable to buy spirits since 1839 and beer since 1886.

The appeal of alcohol made the men who produced it very powerful. Brewers became a significant political force and a huge financial support to the Tory party – so many were ennobled that they became known as 'the beerage'. In return for their support, the tax on beer was kept down and the licensing laws flexible. The brewers flourished, with several of the bigger ones changing from private to public companies during the 1880s and 1890s: Guinness's share issue in 1886 was much oversubscribed.

Given the level of alcohol consumption in Victorian and Edwardian England this was scarcely surprising. According to one survey in the National Archives, in 1900 every male drinker consumed an estimated 73 gallons of beer a year and two and two-fifths of a gallon of spirits.[14] However, other surveys suggest this may be an exaggeration, though they include the whole adult population and not just men. Every incentive existed for the British working man to drink, and he took it. The pub was an essential part of his life. Here he could not only drink but play darts, cribbage, bar billiards or dominoes while he drank: the existence of a pub on virtually every corner helped bond communities together – many of which would otherwise have been rootless. As breweries made larger profits they improved pubs to attract more customers and to tone down the image of rough establishments for hard drinkers. Surviving examples of the Victorian pub, with lavishly decorated interiors and elaborate woodwork and glasswork – including grand mirrors, tiled walls, panelling and gilding – show the lengths to which breweries went to seem salubrious. Many new pubs conformed to this standard. The higher the specification to which a pub was built, the more the clientele subtly changed.

Drunkenness and the social ills that attended it were a constant issue, even though three Acts of Parliament were passed – in 1864, 1872 and 1874 – to restrict opening hours. Middle-class philanthropists waged war on drunkenness. In working-class families men often handed their wives their wages, who then decided how to allocate them. It was women who led the anti-drinking, or temperance, movement that took root strongly in Non-conformism and the Liberal party. The Band of Hope had been founded in Leeds in 1847 with the aim not of rescuing working-class men or women from drink, but children. By the 1870s, with children now mostly in school and less prone to temptation, the focus moved to men. The British Women's Temperance Association was founded in 1876 in Newcastle-upon-Tyne with the specific aim of stopping men drinking. It, and the economic downturn from 1873, had some effect. Alcohol consumption fell gradually from its 1873 peak of thirty-five gallons per head per annum (calculated to include women and children, hence the much lower figure than for male consumption) to twenty-eight gallons by 1890 and twenty-five by 1910, despite the building of thousands of public houses in new urban areas (consumption of spirits fell by a quarter between 1873 and 1890[15]). The temperance movement opened coffee houses and temperance bars, often next to the pubs. Its activists, often women, would stand outside pubs handing out leaflets to patrons as they entered. However, with beer at twopence a pint, the lure of the pub remained powerful to the drinking classes, even though the law after 1869 punished drunkenness with heavy fines.

IV

If the pub was an essential part of working-class life, so too was another ubiquitous feature of the Victorian and Edwardian city: music hall. Indeed the music hall had its origins in mid-nineteenth-century pubs, where comic singers would entertain drinkers: and, to justify their high salaries, would go and drink with them afterwards to boost bar takings. This was partly why so many performers ended up as alcoholics; Charles Chaplin, father of the comic and actor, drank himself to death aged thirty-seven. As acts became more structured the roles were largely reversed: the music hall became a place primarily of entertainment where people could listen to singers, or be amused by comics, or watch sketches, or be diverted by dancers or jugglers, while eating, drinking and smoking. Its function, according to W. Macqueen-Pope, friend and biographer of Marie Lloyd, was 'to supply the wants of the industrious working class who had little or no entertainment provided for them.'[16]

Music hall's success was such that it created enormous stars: notably Lloyd, a singer and dancer at her peak in the 1890s and 1900s; and Dan Leno, a favourite of King Edward VII, who became the first music-hall act to give a command performance to the King, when he went to Sandringham in November 1901; he became known thereafter as 'the King's jester'. Both came from humble working-class backgrounds. Both enjoyed swift and early success. Both fell prey to alcoholism and illness. Leno had begun in show business as a clog-dancer, before becoming a comedian and comic singer. He recorded some of his songs and monologues for the gramophone between 1901 and 1903, which not only brought his talents to the attention of a wider public but also preserved his voice and humour for later generations. But his father had been an alcoholic and Leno himself started to drink heavily. He suffered an alcohol-related mental breakdown before dying of tertiary syphilis on 31 October 1904, when he was just forty-three.

Marie Lloyd's career began in 1880 when, aged ten, she sang temperance songs to derelicts in the East End of London under the auspices of an urban mission. She turned professional at fifteen and within months was performing all over London. Before she was seventeen she was earning £100 a week, not just for singing, but for her routine of jokes that she often ad-libbed. In the early 1890s she toured the halls of the northern cities; and in 1893, America. Like Leno, she starred annually in pantomime, which was hugely popular at the time. However, despite her temperance roots, she too became an alcoholic, dying of kidney failure aged just fifty-two. By then she had become one of the most beloved women in Britain, her funeral in October 1922 being attended by 50,000 people.

Music hall was to enjoy the patronage not just of the working class but of the well-to-do, particularly in London. Two of Lloyd's songs from the 1880s and 1890s – 'The Boy I Love Is Up in the Gallery' and 'Oh! Mr Porter' – became known to almost everybody, as did perhaps her most famous song, written for her at the end of the Great War a few years before her death, 'My Old Man Said Follow the Van' (or 'Don't Dilly Dally On the Way'), which came to epitomise the idea of music hall to later generations. The Great MacDermott's song, mentioned in Chapter 1, which coined the word 'jingoism', shaped public opinion: it proved immensely popular not only with the general public, but with the Prince of Wales, who ordered a command performance. But music hall very much reflected working-class sensibilities and culture: it dealt with the romance of everyday life and its hardships, it was wryly sceptical, frequently irreverent, and to some minds occasionally obscene.

This was not least because it was also leavened by an extraordinary level of innuendo. Marie Lloyd's biographer notes that her smutty lines went down far better in the West End – she often played the Empire, Leicester Square – than among the prudish audiences of Bethnal Green and Bermondsey. Many working-class audiences were instinctively puritanical, unlike some of the performers, whose own working-class origins and attitudes had been stripped from them by the whirlwind of show business. Music-hall artistes were not constrained in the content of their material by the Lord Chamberlain's censor who, as discussed in Chapter 12, helped retard the progress of English drama. Nevertheless, in 1894 the Social Purity Movement, led by Laura Ormiston Chant, objected so forcefully to Lloyd's act at the Empire, Leicester Square that a hearing was held to consider whether the theatre's licence should be revoked.

Lloyd sang some songs before the licensing committee – 'without an inflection, a nod, wink or smile' – and no one could see any problem.[17] When told she could go, she let rip: 'A fat lot you know about songs and singers . . . Now I'll show you. I'll sing you some of the songs your wives sing in your own drawing-room. They are clean enough, aren't they? All right – you just see what you think.'[18] She then sang 'Come Into the Garden, Maud' – words by Tennyson – to an accompaniment of obscene and suggestive gestures that shocked the committee: Lloyd had proved that for anyone who considered her act 'blue', it was all in the mind. Her biographer protests that 'she never in all her career sang what was known as a "dirty" song, or a line which was really "blue".'[19]

Nevertheless, her 'Oh! Mr Porter' was about a girl who went too far, and such gems as 'She'd Never Had Her Ticket Punched Before' went very close indeed to the knuckle. She would make gestures to her audience – nods, winks, hand signals and lewd poses – that seemed to lend new meaning to her words. Complaints were made about her song 'She Sits Among the Cabbages and Peas'. She therefore changed the title to 'I Sits Among the Cabbages and Leeks', which kept everyone happy, including her.

New stars emerged: such as Harry Champion, whose songs 'I'm Henery the Eighth, I Am' and 'Any Old Iron' became widely known before the Great War, and Harry Fay, whose 1910 hit 'Let's All Go Down the Strand' resounded, like Champion's songs, through the twentieth century. When Lloyd began to fade, her place as Queen of the Music Hall was taken by Florrie Forde, though Forde's leap to real fame would come with the war, when she recorded 'It's a Long Way to Tipperary' and 'Pack Up Your Troubles'. On 1 July 1912 there was a Royal Command Performance for music-hall artistes at the Palace Theatre: but Lloyd was not included (even though 150 others were) because she was considered 'too blue'. Her revenge was to play to a packed house at the Pavilion, at the other end of Shaftesbury Avenue, her billing describing her as 'the Queen of Comediennes' and announcing that 'Every Performance given by Marie Lloyd is a Command Performance by order of the British Public.'[20]

V

The world of the pub and the music hall serves as a reminder that while life for the poorest in late-Victorian and Edwardian Britain was often hand to mouth, skilled workers had both the resources and, increasingly, the leisure time for recreation. In fact, real earnings increased as the nineteenth century drew to its close. Municipalities recognised this more moneyed class by striving to provide some form of recreational facilities for their communities. This was an era of building better, and bigger, and of using the fruits of affluence for public display, not least as one town competed against another for show and pride. Arnold Bennett, describing the park opened in Bursley (based on one of the six towns that merged to form Stoke-on-Trent in 1910) in his novel *Anna of the Five Towns* (1902), wrote:

> The Park rose in terraces from the railway station to a street of small villas almost on the ridge of the hill. From its gilded gates to its smallest geranium-slips it was brand new, and most of it was red. The keeper's house, the bandstand, the kiosks, the balustrades, the shelters – all these assailed the eye with a uniform redness of brick and tile which nullified the pallid greens of the turf and the frail trees.[21]

By the later nineteenth century, workers were also able to take brief holidays. Weekends away remained a luxury of the well-to-do, but the annual Wakes Week allowed some workers and their families a whole week by the sea. The opening of Blackpool Tower on 14 May 1894 was a significant moment in working-class culture. The Lancashire resort, with its vast sands and long seafront, was thirty miles from mill towns such as Blackburn and Burnley. It represented a different world to the hands who took their Wakes Week holidays there while mill towns closed down so plants could be repaired and serviced.

The railway also turned Blackpool, which in the early nineteenth century was a village of 500 souls, into a town whose permanent population in 1901 was 47,000. By the 1880s its seafront was strewn with public houses and fish and chip shops, and it had two piers. Its massive Winter Gardens opened in 1878, and an Opera House Theatre in 1889. In the mid-nineteenth century it had been a middle-class bathing resort, but as the fashion of Wakes Weeks caught on the clientele changed, and so did Blackpool. By 1900 there were enough boarding houses for 250,000 visitors, and an estimated 3 million people a year went to the town.

The growing popularity of seaside holidays created, and changed, resorts all round the coast. Because of its proximity to London, Brighton expanded even more than Blackpool, growing from 7,000 to 120,000 residents during the nineteenth century. Southend too became a focus for day-trippers from London's East End after the railway arrived, having built the longest pier in the world – a mile and a third – to allow pleasure boats to land at low tide. The twenty years after the arrival of the railway in Llandudno in 1858 saw huge development there, the creation of a long promenade, and the establishment of the town as 'The Queen of Welsh Resorts': in Bennett's *The Card*, Denry Machin takes his tiresome girlfriend there, and regrets it. The railway was also the making of Skegness, which from 1908 enticed visitors with a poster that proclaimed 'Skegness is so Bracing'. Meanwhile the upper classes, anxious to avoid the influx of working-class holidaymakers, began to take their holidays abroad, helped by Bradshaw's international timetable and European train travel.

VI

The pastime that perhaps best illustrates the relationship between the social classes – and the differences between them – is association football. It was a sport that had its roots in the public schools. The rules of football had many variants, each school having its own code. Because of problems when old boys sought to play after leaving school the rules had to be standardised, and Cambridge University published a code in 1848. In 1858 an alternative code was developed in Sheffield, where some businessmen set up Sheffield Football Club in 1857. Other northern clubs, with working men rather than ex-school players, adopted them. The formation of the Football Association in 1863, when representatives mainly of schools and old boys' clubs met to standardise the rules, was largely the work of Ebenezer Cobb Morley, a solicitor, oarsman and (in 1862) founder and captain of the Barnes club in London. He drew up the rules, and thereby earned his reputation as the father of the game.

The FA prohibited footballers playing for money, though by the 1870s, when clubs started to attract spectators, some (notably in the northern mill towns) enhanced their performances by illicitly paying players. The FA encouraged the amateur game by introducing a challenge cup for affiliated teams, the first competition held in the 1871–2 season. However, its ruling that all ties had to be played in London was financially prohibitive for northern clubs, and in the early years many did not compete. Eventually, some obtained local sponsorship – Blackburn Olympic, for example, entered the FA Cup in 1882–3, and won it, thanks to financial support from a local ironmaster. It was apparent that football's popularity, as with cricket's, gave it business potential, and like cricket it could sustain both professionals and amateurs.

Wanderers, formed mainly of Old Harrovians and alumni of other major schools, won the first FA Cup final – played at Kennington Oval – beating Royal Engineers 1–0 in 1872. They won five of the first seven finals, Oxford University winning in 1874 and the Engineers in 1875 (beating Old Etonians, who won in 1879 and 1882, the second time beating Blackburn Rovers). Not all clubs had their origins in the Newboltian Close of a Clarendon school or in one of the new imitators where the newly-monied classes educated their sons in emulation of the aristocracy and gentry. Pubs, churches, factories, mills, temperance societies and collieries all generated teams in the last quarter of the nineteenth century.

When Blackburn Olympic – a team of artisans, mill hands and a couple of pub landlords – beat Old Etonians in 1883, they ended amateur dominance of the FA Cup. Thereafter the roll call of winners has a more familiar feel – Blackburn Rovers, Aston Villa, West Bromwich Albion, Wolverhampton Wanderers. Although professionalism was still against

FA rules, Sidney Yates, the ironmaster who funded Olympic, was paying his men £1 a week. When a complaint was made in 1884 that Preston North End was also paying its team the manager, Major William Sudell, admitted it, and that he had imported players – inventing the transfer market – but claimed it was common practice. His side was disqualified, but the damage was done. When Blackburn Rovers won the 1884 cup, Notts County, whom they defeated, complained Rovers' star player was being paid; an investigation showed that he was working as a mechanic.

The flagrant breach of the amateur rule made the status quo impossible. Yates was not the only industrialist to bankroll a club, and other professional outfits threatened to leave the FA and form the British Football Association. The FA had to capitulate to survive, which it did on 20 July 1885. It decided to allow payment of players provided they had been born or had lived for two years within six miles of the club's ground. Football's evolution into a predominantly working-class sport would soon be complete. Payment meant the substantial overhead of a wages bill, and to meet it major clubs, led by Aston Villa, decided in early 1888 to form a league, to play home and away fixtures and draw in more spectators. Thus six Lancashire clubs and six from the midlands formed the Football League, which started in September 1888: by 1914 there would be two divisions of twenty clubs, including some from the south of England.

Football provided a fast-moving form of entertainment, which boys and men could play without expensive kit or pitch preparation. Its support became tribal and fed local patriotism. When Preston North End won the FA Cup in 1889, 30,000 people surrounded the station to greet the team on its return and a band played 'See the Conquering Hero Comes'.[22] By 1900 an estimated 6 million a year went to a football match – perhaps 300,000 watching professional games each Saturday – and half a million played recreationally.[23] There was, though, in the early years a north-south divide because of the professional momentum behind the League clubs, and the view in the less industrialised, more middle-class south that sport should have an amateur base: not least because genuine amateurs believed those paid to train and play in all fixtures would reach a level of skill allowing them to dominate the game.

Having seen how quickly football became professional, effectively ruling out amateurs at the highest level, Rugby Union was determined to avoid the same fate. Again, the north-south divide became apparent, undoing sport's potential as a national and class unifier. Several northern clubs had by 1895 started to pay some players to compensate them for time taken off work. The game's ruling body, the Rugby Football Union, founded in 1871, objected, fearing a repeat of what had happened in football. This ruled out working-class players: the RFU's ruling had less effect on southern clubs, which had more middle-class members, with the resources to play as amateurs. However, as with football, rugby flourished in the northern towns, and its players dominated the game nationally.

Just as the northern football clubs had challenged the FA in 1885, so the northern rugby clubs sought to force the RFU's hand a decade later. There had been ill feeling for years: Leeds and Bradford had been censured for paying players in 1892, but the northern clubs argued that the southern ones were over-represented on the RFU's governing body – and the Union failed to grasp the hardship suffered by players who could not afford to miss work, and whose livelihoods were at stake if they sustained serious injury. A modest proposal by Yorkshire clubs to pay up to six shillings to players who missed work because of training or fixtures was dismissed.

In 1895 the RFU said rugby could not be played on any ground where an admission fee was charged. Yorkshire clubs proposed forming a separate union, and Lancashire clubs announced that they would support this. On 29 August 1895, twenty-two northern clubs met at the George Hotel, Huddersfield, and formed the Northern Rugby Football Union, signalling the determination of a predominantly working-class branch of the sport to settle its own rules and culture and not have another caste impose them. From this evolved Rugby League; rule changes occurred, the most important being the reduction of a side from fifteen to thirteen men in 1906. The sport went professional in 1898, and 200 clubs had left the RFU by 1910 to join the new code. The schism left Rugby Union weakened, since its best players had left to turn professional, and the crowds followed them. Sanctions were taken against any player who had anything to do with the new Union, or played against a team from it. Therefore more clubs in the north crossed the divide. By 1904 the Northern Union had more affiliates than the RFU.

Thus most Rugby Union clubs in England were in the south and the midlands, and fully amateur, while Rugby League dominated Lancashire,

Yorkshire, Cheshire and Cumberland. As well as the geographical divide, rugby was now divided between the middle and upper classes (RFU) and the working class (NRFU); and in 1922 the NRFU became the Rugby Football League, and their game became known as Rugby League thereafter.

Men and boys from the working class came to see playing professional sport as an escape from life in a mill or factory: their social betters saw it, and all amateur organised recreation, as a diversion from evils such as drink, gambling and crime. But because of the lack of playing fields and the expense of even basic gymnasiums and equipment, sport struggled to become as central to working-class education as it was to public schools. Only with the passing of the 1902 Education Act was it officially recommended that physical education be included on each school's curriculum. By the Great War exercise – physical jerks in playgrounds – had become *de rigueur* in elementary schools, and many played football and basic games of cricket. Such activities capitalised on the new enthusiasm with which boys in particular followed sports. Their participation also served the nation's purpose in toughening up a generation that might have to fight a war.

VII

The range of leisure activities patronised by the working class were available to them thanks to the general availability of employment, and the gradual rise in real wages during the nineteenth century. However, working conditions remained arduous despite a succession of Factories Acts dating back to the youth of Lord Shaftesbury, and it became apparent to many workers that any improvement in them was likely to be secured only by the threat or reality of industrial action. Although the working class was now increasingly divided in its political affiliations between the Liberal party and the nascent Labour movement, it could unite behind the trades unions.

The Labour movement is often portrayed as having been made by men who had started off at the coalface (sometimes literally) of heavy industry and, with the assistance of working men's institutes and night school, had risen through the trades union movement to fight parliamentary seats. The radical wing of the Liberal party was their first home. However, those with socialist beliefs found the commitment to individualism that reconciled notable radicals such as Charles Bradlaugh to Liberalism incompatible with their doctrine. In time, socialist societies that encouraged debate and discussion on doctrine created an inexorable demand for a party that embraced, unequivocally, those beliefs. The final impetus came with the 1884 Reform Act, and a rash of militant industrial action later in the decade.

With his customary irony, Arnold Bennett reflected upon the working class's determination to assert itself against the forces of capital: 'Every effort had been made to explain by persuasion and by force to the working man that trade unions were inimical to his true welfare, and none had succeeded, so stupid was he.'[24] However, in the last quarter of the nineteenth century the real wages of certain working-class people – miners, steelworkers and engineers – rose sharply, as demand for their labour rose and their numbers did not keep pace with it. The economic lot of parts of the working class was far better than during the Industrial Revolution, though in an era of relatively cheap food agricultural labourers remained financially disadvantaged.

But one of the first manifestations of militancy came not from men, but women. Girls and women working in the Bryant and May match factory at Bow struck in July 1888 in protest at the sacking of a workmate. Conditions in the factory were poor, with food eaten at meal breaks being contaminated with white phosphorus used in the matches. This gave workers a form of bone cancer known as 'phossy jaw', which before inflicting death turned the side of the face afflicted green and then black. The owners – Theodore Bryant and Francis May, prominent Quakers and, in Bryant's case, a Liberal activist – were badly embarrassed by an article on the subject on 23 June by Annie Besant in her newspaper *The Link*. One of her allegations was that Bryant had stopped a shilling out of each of his operatives' wages to fund a statue of Gladstone; and that some women surrounded the statue and cut their arms and let them bleed over it, as they had paid for it with their blood.

The article – 'White Slavery in London' – described how the match-girls were paid twopence-farthing per gross of match-boxes, whereas the firm's shareholders had received a dividend of 23 per cent. Shares bought for £5 were now worth £18 7s 6d, and one dividend had been 38 per cent. Clementina Black, a radical feminist and close friend of Eleanor Marx, daughter of the prophet, had talked on female sweated labour at a Fabian Society meeting on 15 June, in which Bryant and May's iniquities figured prominently.

Those present at the meeting subsequently pledged 'not to use or purchase any matches made by this firm'.[25] Mrs Besant, who then went to Bow to interview some of the girls, described the dividends as 'monstrous'. She wrote that work began at 8 a.m. in winter and 6.30 a.m. in summer and continued until 6 p.m., with breaks for half-an-hour for breakfast and an hour for dinner. The work was done standing up and a sixteen-year-old girl, if diligent, could earn four shillings a week. However, the management levied disproportionate fines – such as threepence for leaving the bench untidy, or threepence for talking, or for going to the lavatory without permission; and the foreman would come round and hit girls 'when he is mad'.

Operatives were asked to sign a statement rubbishing the article, but refused. The following week Mrs Besant reported that 'the girls were being bullied to find out who had given me the information'.[26] She also said this 'cowardice' was instead of a libel action, which the management threatened but did not pursue. Three women were given little work to do and then dismissed, causing 1,400 others to walk out. Bryant and May offered to back down: but the workers were emboldened and demanded more concessions, notably regarding fines (which management had been warned about by a factory inspector), and being given a separate room in which to eat so as to avoid phosphorus poisoning (the use of white phosphorus in matches was banned after 1910). When these were refused the entire factory walked out.

Within a few days a strike fund was established, with radical newspapers collecting money and a Fabian committee, including Sidney Webb and Shaw, managing its distribution. A public meeting was called for 22 July with John Burns, a Londoner in his early thirties who had made a name for himself as an agitator for workers' rights in the preceding years, Mrs Besant and two radical MPs, Charles Conybeare and Robert Cunninghame Graham. Mrs Besant was invited to mediate between the women and management, and Bryant and May, distressed by the savage press they had received, gave in. A separate canteen was opened, fining was stopped and the women were assured they could have direct access to the management to air any grievances in the future. However, the company used white phosphorus until 1901; so General Booth had the Salvation Army start a model match factory nearby, where it used harmless red phosphorus and paid double the piece rates of Bryant and May, as part of Booth's campaign to expose the evils of sweated labour.

The relatively easy victory of these unskilled women sent a message to others who felt oppressed at the bottom of the industrial ladder: though women remained more poorly paid generally than men. Ben Tillett, who had in the 1880s worked a couple of miles south of the match factory in a warehouse in London's docks, took particular note. Tillett was a labourer's son from Bristol who, aged thirteen and after a childhood of little education and occasional menial work, joined the Navy. By sixteen he was in the merchant marine and in 1882 was married and living in Bethnal Green. Like many radicals he was a teetotal Nonconformist, his spare time devoted to reading as he educated himself. Tillett wanted to work in the docks, but the restrictive practices of the only extant dockers' union, the Stevedores, prevented his doing so, or even joining the union. When in 1887 the tea warehouse that employed him tried to cut the wages of its operatives, Tillett formed a union to represent them. It had no impact until the summer of 1889, when other unskilled workers in depots and warehouses flocked to it to voice their discontent at harsh conditions. Tillett, who hitherto had spoken for a handful of workers, found himself leading a movement: and one that, by paralysing the docks of the greatest city in the country, was threatening the prosperity on which the nation's power was founded.

Dockers lived in extreme poverty. The main demand of the strikers was 'the dockers' tanner': an assurance that they would be paid sixpence an hour. The *casus belli* was an argument over the unloading of a ship, the *Lady Armstrong*, at the West India Docks on 14 August 1889. A bonus, known as 'plus money' was usually paid for speedy unloading; but the East and West India Docks Company had lowered this rate to undercut other docks and attract business. The union was keen not to excite the prejudices of the middle and upper classes, and so took care to ensure its demonstrations were peaceful. This won them supporters in high places, notably Cardinal Manning, who mediated between workers and dock companies.

Coming the summer after the match-girls' victory, and days after workers in the new, but economically crucial, London gas industry had struck for an eight-hour day and had won, the dock strike confirmed the industrial power of a union of unskilled and casual workers, encouraging similar groups to form and agitate. John Burns, perhaps the most eloquent and forceful tribune of the people, assisted Tillett and organised marches through central London to display the workers' industrial muscle to the capitalist establishment. When the dockers were about to starve, money poured in from Australian trade unionists, and the owners were forced to talk: this was when Manning stepped in. Eleanor Marx did clerical work for the strikers, as she had for the gas workers earlier: 'She lived all her life in the atmosphere of social revolution', Tillett noted.[27] When the dockers got their tanner the boost to other unions was huge, and the Labour movement gathered strength that would, within twenty years, make it a feared opponent of government.

Another establishment figure to join in congratulating the dockers was Gladstone, in a speech at his Flintshire country house, Hawarden Castle, on 23 September 1889, when a deputation from the Hyde Reform Club presented an address on the occasion of his and Mrs Gladstone's golden wedding anniversary. To shouts of 'Hear, hear!' he said that the outcome of the strike indicated 'some turn in the balance in the favour of labour'.[28] He called the strike 'a real social advance' that had brought 'just relations' between labour and capital, the type of remark that made the Queen hate him.

Tillett launched a new, bigger and more powerful union, the Dock, Wharf, Riverside and General Labourers'. The contacts he had made during the strike brought him into the mainstream of the nascent Labour movement, and within a year or two he had become one of its leaders. In 1892 he was elected to the TUC's parliamentary committee, and joined the London County Council. He fought Bradford West as an independent Labour candidate that year, and in 1893 took part in the conference in the same city that culminated in the formation of the Independent Labour party. By then Tillett's sway was in decline. His union had set up provincial branches in the excitement that followed 1889, but a miscalculation of its strength in a strike at Hull in 1893 undermined it badly.

The Conservative government, however, took the unrest among organised labour very much to heart, and parliament passed a new Factory Act in 1891 to prevent underpayment of workers. A Fair Wages Resolution in February 1891 recommended wages for workers on government contracts comparable to those paid to similar tradesmen in the same area. In 1897 when the Tories were again in power they introduced the Workmen's Compensation Act, which imposed liability on employers for industrial accidents and diseases, and stopped the practice by which the victim had to prove that someone other than himself was responsible. Salisbury's administration after 1895 also attempted to ensure a negotiated way out of disputes by passing the 1896 Conciliation Act, which established a system of arbitration.

Like the Liberals, the Conservatives felt local authorities could be useful in providing work for the unemployed, a practice sanctioned in a circular issued by Chamberlain in 1886, and re-circulated in 1891. Under Balfour's administration between 1902 and 1905 London boroughs set up labour exchanges, something the Unemployed Workmen Act of 1905 enabled all over the country. It is ironic that the worst problems between government and labour in the quarter-century before the Great War should, as we shall see in Chapter 16, come late in that period, and under a Liberal government that claimed to be the worker's friend.

VIII

That the harsh conditions for the very poor Rowntree had discovered could prevail without provoking unrest might be considered remarkable. However, it was testament not only to the docility of the populace, but to the failure of the poorest to constitute a critical mass, thanks to higher living standards for others. However, the advent of the new century finally changed that. The perception of the rich becoming richer throughout its first decade, while the lot of the working man and his family remained hard, would eventually trigger the greatest wave of industrial unrest the Kingdom had ever witnessed.

That unrest stemmed not least from the organisation of a socialist movement designed to improve the conditions and political influence of the working classes. But in the 1880s, although the cohesion of the union movement became a considerable weapon against employers, and proved costly to them even when the workers lost because of loss of output and markets, there was no translation of this growing power into the political arena. There were radical Liberal MPs who identified explicitly with their working-class electorate – and would be until the party split and imploded at the end of the Great War. However, it soon became apparent that if the type of fundamental change that would improve the lot of working-class people were to be accomplished, it would require those people to have their own party dedicated to their struggle, and for it to become dominant in parliament.

The development of radicalism into socialism – which would, by the

1920s and with the help of faction-fighting, all but destroy the Liberal party – took more than a generation and a world war to accomplish. For socialism to have clout it needed to organise: not just as the trades unions, which would underpin the Labour party, had since the mid-nineteenth century, but as Tories and Liberals did, as political bodies that strove to win seats in parliament. Twin forces advanced socialism. Above, there were middle- and upper-middle-class activists and intellectuals for whom Liberalism was inadequate and who, often fuelled by class guilt, sought to break down the traditional order of society and rebuild it according to some measure of Marxist principle. Below, there were newly enfranchised working men and an army of increasingly angry and unfranchised working women, who felt divorced from the established political structures and sought their own leaders to take them forward.

By the 1880s socialism was emerging from a long dark age. The failure of Chartism after 1848 had robbed the working-class movement of impetus. The model of Christian socialism advocated by such men as Charles Kingsley and Frederick Denison Maurice was mild by comparison with what had been attempted before, and what would come later. There was occasional fresh blood from abroad, as with the arrival of French socialists after the fall of the Paris Commune in 1871: but even Marx himself, who had fled Germany and settled in London in 1849, was by the 1870s relatively quiet, writing pamphlets and books but not engaging directly in the political process in his adopted country; indeed, he never really mastered English, a handicap for anyone wishing to advance political ideas to the British public.

The 1867 Reform Act heightened working-class interest in politics. The process was slow, with working men firstly managing to secure election to school boards after 1870, then working their way on to local and municipal councils following the abolition, in 1878, of a property qualification (though by 1895 only four working men sat on Birmingham's corporation out of seventy-two councillors) and as guardians under the Poor Law. The working class needed more organisation if its voice were to be properly heard.

The Trades Union Congress – the collective body for individual unions – had been founded in 1868, but had its origins in earlier attempts from the 1830s to bring members of different trade bodies together. When the working class mobilised in the 1860s to demand repeal of the

Master and Servant Act, passed in 1823 to force employees to obey their employers or face criminal proceedings for breach of contract, it highlighted once more the need for a national organisation. A lock-out in Sheffield in the winter of 1866 prompted a local union organiser, William Dronfield, to invite representatives of other skilled trades to come to the city to discuss matters of common interest: 138, representing 200,000 workers, turned up, and the meeting is regarded as one of the founding moments in the union movement.[29] A further meeting was held in London in 1867. It was decided that Samuel Nicholson, the president of the Salford Trades Council, and William Wood, the secretary – both were 'journeymen compositors' – should plan a formal Congress for 1868, and that these congresses should become an annual event. A Royal Commission on Unions was deliberating, and it was clearly sensible to have an organised response.

The first annual meeting of the TUC took place in Manchester from 2 to 6 June 1868, with thirty-four delegates, only two of whom came from London. Wood presided, because Nicholson felt obliged to attend a meeting in Derby of the Order of Druids, of which he was the general secretary. The nascent movement was already split, with the London Trades Council, formed in 1860, deciding to boycott the event, which it saw as a threat to its own standing. Nonetheless, the Congress proceeded with a serious agenda – including extending the Factory Acts to protect women and children, technical education, use of apprentices, law reform and the importance of co-operation. The movement was lower-middle-class – skilled workers a cut above manual labourers, who were paid more and were more aspirational, and had in many cases just been given the vote.

Gladstone's administration had felt it better to work with unions rather than against them, not least because so many of their members were Liberals. Unions were formally legalised in 1871 after the Royal Commission reported, but certain activities – such as picketing and other forms of intimidation – were banned by the Criminal Law Amendment Act the same year. The TUC's first great campaign was against this statute, which it succeeded in having repealed by the Disraeli administration in 1875. It then petitioned for those injured at work to be compensated, prompting the 1880 Employers' Liability Act: though if the injury was in part caused by the negligence of a fellow worker the employer could escape responsibility, a loophole closed in 1897. Ministers saw it was in their interests to have regular contact with union officials, though prime ministers rarely met them, a notable exception being Gladstone on the occasion of the 1884 Reform Act. His administration had appointed a union leader to a factory sub-inspectorate in 1881 – a move the TUC called 'the entrance into the governmental system of the country of a *bona fide* workman'.[30]

In Gladstone's short third administration recognition went even further, with Henry Broadhurst, the Secretary of the TUC, appointed under-secretary at the Home Office. Broadhurst had trained under his father as a stonemason. Among his jobs had been the clock tower of the Palace of Westminster, before becoming a full-time official of the Stonemasons' Union. He was an unequivocal admirer of Gladstone, drawn to him by the Grand Old Man's stand against Disraeli for his foreign policy in the light of 'the devilish atrocities of the Unspeakable Turk in Bulgaria', when Gladstone's 'voice was heard in the land calling for vengeance upon the murdering and ravishing crew let loose by the black-hearted tyrant at Constantinople.'[31] At the 1880 election Broadhurst stood as a Liberal-Labour candidate in Stoke-on-Trent, and was elected. The unions paid his salary: the state did not pay MPs until 1911. Concerned that the ruling class monopolised justice, he devoted himself to ensuring working men could secure paid time off to be magistrates, something he achieved by 1885 in removing the property qualification for that office too. His effectiveness as a minister was limited: he admitted that 'my own opinions on large questions of policy were, I confess, never sought for by the chiefs of the party', though that was true of most of his ministerial rank, whatever their background.[32]

Broadhurst was appointed a special commissioner to look at labour conditions at first hand, and what he saw shocked him. Early one morning in Birmingham 'we found children of both sexes and of ages ranging from tender years to fifteen or sixteen, scantily clothed and badly fed, working together in one tiny smithy about the size of the ordinary cottage wash-house. They were barely instructed in the first elements of education.'[33] Elsewhere he found young girls doing heavy manual work in iron foundries. It was as though Shaftesbury and the Education Acts had not happened.

The behaviour of the establishment towards this first representative of the working man in parliament was instructive of its determination not to make the continental mistake of alienating organised labour and forcing it into a confrontation, but rather to embrace it in the interests of maintaining the social order. The Prince of Wales asked Broadhurst to Sandringham, an invitation accepted with delight – unlike others in the Labour movement, he was a devoted monarchist – but with the reservation that Broadhurst did not own dress clothes, and was therefore not prepared to dine in company. The Prince refused to allow this to stand in the way, and arranged for him to be served dinner in his room on each evening of his stay. Princely courtesy was abundant. 'I left Sandringham', Broadhurst recalled, 'with the feeling of one who had spent a week-end with an old chum of his own rank in society rather than one who had been entertained by the Heir-Apparent and his Princess.'[34] When appointed to office Broadhurst asked to be excused an audience of the Queen, for it would have meant his wearing Court dress in which he felt 'I could not fail to look supremely ridiculous . . . at least to my own eyes.'[35] His wish was granted.

Not all union men would have felt as comfortable in the Liberal ranks as Broadhurst did, not least because the Liberals were a party of capital, and newly-made capital at that for the most part. Broadhurst could manage deference: most trade unionists wanted their own sort in parliament so they did not have to ask favours of their betters. As it grew in reputation, the TUC sought to expand the reach of unionism. Its greatest challenge was among agricultural labourers, for the countryside remained feudal, and the agricultural depression that began in the 1870s and lasted for the rest of the century drove down living standards of farm workers. The TUC attempted, for the first time, to organise them politically, to the horror of the landed classes, who felt this to be an interference aimed at sowing dissent. The movement also sought to recruit the new cadre of teachers required to implement the 1870 and 1876 Education Acts, which provided a school place for everyone under the age of twelve, and in doing so made the point that the movement could embrace white-collar as well as manual workers. By 1900 organisations of clerical workers in the Post Office, railways and civil service had affiliated to the TUC.

As it secured more friends in parliament – mostly well-disposed Liberals rather than working men until the 1890s – so its political influence grew. Eventually, thanks to an intervention by Gladstone, some TUC officials were allowed in the lobby of the House of Commons. The TUC would speak out on industrial relations and practices, and because of the large number of union men enfranchised after 1884, the government of the day would usually at least take polite note of the TUC's views. The organisation would seek to help individual unions push through Bills aimed at improving working practices, whether across-the-board Factory Bills or Bills aimed at one specific industry. The longer this went on, the less the sense of deference felt by leaders such as Broadhurst towards the political class, and the more the TUC came to regard itself as a political player in its own right.

IX

Not everyone on the political left believed in the Fabians' gradualist approach to change. John Burns, who would become one of the great political figures of the years before the Great War, was born in Lambeth in 1858. He was his parents' sixteenth child. His father abandoned the family; his mother was forced to become a washerwoman and to house herself and her children in a basement. He left school at the age of ten. Burns was apprenticed to an engineer, but sought further education at night school. He started to read radical literature and by his late teens was politically active, deploying a combative personality that had manifested itself both in his interest in boxing and upon being sacked from his apprenticeship. He was arrested in 1878 for holding a political meeting on Clapham Common despite a police ban. He worked in west Africa for a year, an experience that set him against imperialism. Returning to England in 1881, he looked for a platform from which to expound his revolutionary beliefs.

He found one thanks to Henry Hyndman, who in every respect apart from his views was as unlike Burns as could be imagined. When Hyndman was at Trinity College, Cambridge, he played cricket for the university and, on coming down in 1865, for MCC and Sussex. He studied law but went into journalism, and toyed with politics: he fought some of the 1880 election as an independent, but withdrew before polling day. Shortly afterwards he read a life of Ferdinand Lassalle, the German socialist and friend of Marx: it was a short step from there to reading the *Communist Manifesto*. Although Hyndman did not buy all of Marx's doctrine he was drawn into socialism and founded a new party, the Democratic Federation. It held its first meeting on 7 June 1881, and Shaw was an early member (he claimed to be the only one who had actually read *Das Kapital*). Some socialists – notably Friedrich Engels and Marx – kept clear of it because they did not trust Hyndman; but he soon had a following, and his was the first effective socialist grouping in Britain.

One of his early recruits was Burns. He was soon on the executive committee, propelled there by his ability as a speaker – he had a stentorian voice, an invaluable asset in an age before amplification – and by his background, which contrasted usefully with that of Hyndman and his well-heeled friends who dominated the organisation. Hyndman wrote the first book about Marxist ideas in English, but upset Marx by not attributing the ideas to him. In 1883 he changed the party's name to the Social Democratic Federation and published a second book – *Socialism Made Plain* – outlining its programme. It too was broadly Marxist in its demands to nationalise the means of production and distribution, and it included a call for universal suffrage. This democratic urge was at odds with Hyndman's personality, which was profoundly anti-democratic. He resisted the impulses of others to modify the policies of the party with the result that, on 27 December 1884, he lost a vote of confidence in his leadership. He refused to resign, prompting many to leave the SDF.

Burns remained loyal to Hyndman, but among those who went were two of the most prominent members: William Morris and Eleanor Marx. 'We wish to make this a really international movement,' Miss Marx said. Hyndman, by contrast, 'endeavoured to set English workmen against "foreigners".'[36] One of the paradoxes about the birth of socialism as a doctrine in Britain is that few of its early apostles were working class, and many working men were happy with what the Liberal party (or even, in some cases, the Tories) offered them, until enlightened by their betters. There was an aspect of self-indulgence to the socialism of some early advocates, for whom it was a rejection of capitalism (hypocritically so in some cases, since some, including Morris, were in business to make money) and a harking back to the feudal times so beloved of Thomas Carlyle. Also Morris, unlike those for whom he professed to crusade, was an accomplished *bon vivant*. 'I am enjoying myself hugely,' he tells his daughter in a typical letter of 1885, written from the Sussex coast. 'Had oysters for supper last night, and all the delicacies of the season.'[37]

Morris, an Oxford-educated son of a city broker whose contribution to artistic culture is considered in Chapter 10, had come heavily under the influence of Marx in the 1870s. Like Broadhurst, he had been attracted to Gladstone over the Eastern Question, even to the point of writing a song to be sung before meetings of the Eastern Question Association, which he temporarily joined:

> Wake, London lads! Wake, bold and free!
> Arise and fall to work,
> Lest England's glory come to be
> Bond-servant to the Turk![38]

Unlike Broadhurst, Morris had a short-lived flirtation with the Liberals. By the 1880s he was a revolutionary socialist, disenchanted by Gladstone's experiments to coerce the Irish in order to bring the Home Rulers under control, and his failure to undo Britain's annexation of the Transvaal after the First Boer War of 1880–81. He found radicalism distressingly middle-class and said it would 'always be under the control of rich capitalists', but nonetheless in 1881 agreed to serve on the executive committee of the Radical Union, an umbrella organisation of working-class groups.[39] It was not long before Morris had become disillusioned with it.

He joined with Hyndman in January 1883 but, as during his time with the Liberals and the Radicals, had no desire to follow anyone else's lead in creating the socialist utopia, least of all that of Hyndman, whom he found personally offensive: so he founded the Socialist League in 1884, though even broke with that six years later, when comrades chose to embrace anarchism. Morris always struggled to be a team player, perhaps because he serially failed to make the right choice of team. Morris told his friend J. L. Joynes, on Christmas Day 1884, two days before the split that caused Morris and Miss Marx to leave the SDF, that:

> Hyndman can accept only one position in such a body as the SDF, that of master . . . [He] has been acting throughout . . . as a politician determined to push his own advantage . . . always on the look out for anything which could advertise the party he is supposed to lead: his aim has been to make the movement seem big; to frighten the powers that be with a turnip bogie . . . [A]ll that insane talk of immediate forcible revolution, when we know that the workers of England are not even touched by the movement.[40]

Before the break Morris travelled the country to deliver lectures on socialism. Polite society, having regarded him as a charming interior decorator, was shocked at this Mr Hyde emerging from Dr Jekyll. His lectures were met with torrents of abuse in the press. Having been asked to go to Oxford in November 1883 to lecture on 'Democracy and Art', he instead spoke on socialism, which caused a small scandal. In February 1884 he and other SDF members went to Lancashire to show solidarity with cotton workers during a long strike, and Morris lectured the strikers on the glories of socialism. He was co-author of the SDF's manifesto, *Socialism Made Plain*, which among other things called for widespread nationalisations (banks, land, the railways, agriculture and industry) and the abolition of the national debt, but had some policies familiar in the twentieth century: all children to have a compulsory state-funded education, free school meals, an eight-hour day and improved housing for the working classes.

Several SDF branches joined the League once it was launched in January 1885. Morris proudly announced to his daughter, May, on 20 February that 'the Leeds branch of the SDF has come over to us; not a big one but good to begin with.'[41] He added that 'the Labour Emancipation League has formally joined us now; they are in very good humour.' He and his comrades put out a statement addressed to all socialists that explained they had acted in the interests of promoting principle and eschewing opportunism. This was designed to rally more leftists to his flag, but was not entirely successful. He told May on 11 March that his home branch in London, in Hammersmith, was 'rather languishing', and urged her to become assistant secretary to lead its recovery.[42]

Morris launched a monthly (subsequently weekly) paper called *The Commonweal*, whose small circulation he subsidised, but the League grew slowly. It soon began to attract the anarchists who would eventually drive Morris out, and was constantly on the verge of insolvency, were it not for regular subventions from Morris. The League soon fragmented, and with Morris's departure late in 1890 became entirely the province of anarchists, many from Russia and Eastern Europe. He wrote 'fraternally' but in despair to the editor of *The Commonweal*, David Nicholl, on 12 July 1890 about an article he had published, rebuking him with the observation that 'I must say I think you are going too far: at any rate further than *I* can follow you.'[43] He continued: 'You really must put the curb upon Samuels' blatant folly, or you will *force* me to withdraw all support. I never bargained for this sort of thing when I gave up the editorship.' Thus did the romantic idealism of socialism hit the realities of revolutionary extremists.

The Labourers' League – a moderate body of unskilled London workmen – and Hyndman's SDF decided to hold rival meetings in Trafalgar Square on 8 February 1886, in the SDF's case to protest about unemployment. The Fair Trade League, whom the SDF regarded as capitalist stooges, supported the Labourers. *The Times*'s reporter wrote that the 'vast throng' that attended included 'many of the dangerous classes' who listened to rabble-rousing by those who would 'pose before the public as the exponents of working-class opinion'.[44] Trouble was expected, because the SDF had intimated it would seize the Labour League's platforms and stop them from speaking. Not since the Reform crisis twenty years earlier had there been a serious public order problem in London and the authorities were unprepared for one now: a small contingent of police turned up, and the light touch appeared justified when the meetings ended without serious incident – though the plain-clothes superintendent of police who melted into the crowd in the square managed to have his pocket picked.

Burns, whom *The Times* described as heading the SDF's presence, disobeyed a police injunction in order to climb on to the plinth supporting one of the lions at the bottom of Nelson's Column, the better to address some of the 15,000–20,000 people in the square. The police moved him on, only to find him and his friends returning, brandishing a red flag, and standing on the road in front of the National Gallery, where his harangue began again. 'Mr Burns had a stentorian voice, and it could be heard distinctly at a great distance,' *The Times* wrote. 'He declared that he and his friends of the Revolutionary Social Democratic League were not there to oppose the agitation of the unemployed, but were there to prevent people being made the tools of the paid agitators who were working in the interests of the Fair Trade League.' He then denounced the House of Commons as 'composed of capitalists who had fattened upon the labour of the working men' and 'no more likely to legislate in the interests of the working men than were the wolves to labour for the lambs.' To hang them, he added, 'would be to waste good rope'.

Burns was right that the working man's vote was useless if he could not vote for someone of a like mind to represent him. He added, menacingly, that his group wanted 'to settle affairs peaceably if they could; but if not, they would not shrink from revolution.' When speakers from the rival groups tried to speak, SDF supporters howled them down, with cries of 'we want work, not charity', and – when the subject of fair wages was raised – objections that the matter was not one of reductions of wages, but whether men could get wages at all. Leaguers claimed that argument would achieve more than force; and that the theories of the socialists were not remotely practicable and could not be put into execution. The meeting collapsed into disorder as the Leaguers denounced Hyndman, who was making a 'violent harangue', and what *The Times* described as 'roughs' went into the crowd to rob anyone who looked as though he might have something worth stealing.

However, as the meeting ended up to 2,000 people – described by *The Times*'s reporter as 'the vagabondage of London' and not all *bona fide* working men arguing for improved conditions – headed for Hyde Park to hold another one, and marched down Pall Mall, some carrying Burns aloft. This was where order broke down, with protesters breaking the windows of gentlemen's clubs as they walked past. The police reserve was called out: but the message was garbled and they went to the Mall, not Pall Mall, so the mayhem went unchecked. The windows of the Carlton Club were broken, and then Brooks's ('40 large panes of glass were smashed') and Boodle's.

As it continued up St James's Street and along Piccadilly the mob swelled to perhaps 5,000 and became a rabble, looting shops, robbing passers-by and holding up carriages: this was sheer criminality, for which 1866 offered no precedent. The mob forgot about the Hyde Park meeting but headed through Mayfair, wrecking jewellers' shops, a tailor's, a cigar shop, an upholsterer's, a poulterer's, a butcher's and a wine merchant's, and looting them. They smashed up the house of the saintly Baroness Burdett-Coutts among others, causing anyone remotely well-dressed to flee. They then headed for Oxford Street, smashed more windows and looted more shops. It was, said *The Times*, 'a work of disaster and shame such as London has not known within living memory.' The police response was pathetic; the shopkeepers of the West End exploded in united outrage at having been left to the mercy of a mob. 'Why', asked the manager of Thomas Goode, a china shop in South Audley Street, 'was not the telegraph put in operation to give notice either to police or military to prevent such havoc?'[45]

Burns and Hyndman were blamed. 'It was they who headed the mob in the march to Hyde Park,' *The Times* thundered. 'It was they who, before and after the march, delivered speeches directly inciting to violence.'[46] It branded Hyndman a 'fanatic', noting he had once said the life of a minister should be taken for every working man who starved, and called Burns 'as vehement, and his voice carries further,' alleging he had told the mob they had 'better die fighting than die starving'. It asked: 'We wish to know whether there is no law that can touch these men.'

An air of panic lingered in the smarter parts of London, as 'roughs' tried to organise marches from Trafalgar Square: this time, however, the police presence was heavy, and nothing happened. Rumours spread that, having pillaged the West End, the roughs were now heading for the inner suburbs: Peckham and New Cross were in particular ferment, because of the large numbers of unemployed there. The non-socialist union movement denounced the agitators, saying they did not represent the working man. Thieves and vandals were paraded before Bow Street Magistrates' Court for several days, many sent to a higher court for trial.

On 11 February there were rumours that Hyndman and Burns had been arrested, but Scotland Yard said it had had no such orders. It was then said that to charge SDF leaders with using seditious language would 'give the incident an importance it does not deserve', or so *The Times* was told.[47] The next day Hyndman, Burns and some associates went to Downing Street to seek an interview with Gladstone, which was declined. The men issued a statement asking 'whether the Government has decided to commence useful relief works in the different districts at living rates of wages, and to take other steps to meet the great and increasing distress among the unemployed workers and their families.'[48]

The next day, 13 February 1886, everything changed. After deliberations by the law officers, Burns, Hyndman and two other SDF members, Henry Hyde Champion, an artillery officer turned printer, and John Williams, a labourer, received summonses to appear at Bow Street Magistrates' Court. In splendidly medieval language, and in an almost interminable sentence, the summonses read:

> For that you, maliciously and seditiously contriving and intending the peace of our Lady the Queen and of this realm to disquiet and disturb, and the liege subjects of our Lady the Queen to incite and move to hatred and dislike of the Government established by law within this realm, and to incite and persuade great numbers of our

> liege subjects of the Queen to insurrections, riots, tumults, and breaches of the peace, and to prevent by force and arms the execution of the laws of this realm, and the preservation of public peace, on the 8th day of February in the year of our Lord 1886, within the Metropolitan Police District, in the presence and hearing of divers, to wit, 400 of our liege subjects of our said Lady the Queen then assembled together, in certain speeches and discourses by you then addressed to the said liege subjects as there assembled together as aforesaid, maliciously and seditiously did publish, utter, pronounce, and declare with a loud voice of and concerning the Government established by law within this realm and of and concerning the liege subjects of our said Lady the Queen, committing and being engaged in divers riots and breaches of the peace, certain seditious and inflammatory words and matter against the peace of our Lady the Queen, her Crown and dignity.[49]

Shaw recalled this time as 'when Mr Champion told a meeting in London Fields that if the whole propertied class had but one throat he would cut it without a second thought, if by doing so he could redress the injustices of our social system; and when Mr Hyndman was expelled from his club for declaring on the Thames Embankment that there would be some attention paid to cases of starvation if a rich man were immolated on every pauper's tomb.'[50]

Williams and Champion were represented in court; Burns and Hyndman defended themselves. Burns had apparently said, on several occasions, 'unless we get bread they must get lead'. He had also, it was alleged, said that the next time the SDF met it would sack the bakers' shops of the West End, and called himself 'a revolutionist'. It was said to have been he, brandishing a red flag, who had proposed the march. A reporter from *The Daily Telegraph* had recorded remarks by Burns near Hyde Park that had him saying, seeing the reporter present, 'I will ask this reporter to tell the Government and the people of London that unless they accede to our request there will be revolution in the streets of London.' The court was told that Williams, a working man, pleaded with the mob not to throw stones as that would invite an attack by 'armed soldiers'; and he had warned them too against attacking women and children – 'those who attack women in carriages are not fit to fight in a revolution.' Burns was reported as saying he expected himself and the other leaders 'to be in prison tomorrow', which was a good thing, since it would increase public outrage against the authorities, and make the movement strong enough for revolution: and he had supposedly asked: 'When we give you the signal, will you rise?' The mob had yelled: 'Yes', at which Burns had told them to 'go home quietly'. Williams had endorsed this, saying 'do not attempt a revolution when you are not organised for it.'

The arraignment of the four men, whose case was adjourned for further examination, energised the Labour movement, as Burns and Hyndman had predicted it would. On the Sunday after the Bow Street hearing thousands of supporters gathered at Hyde Park, ostensibly to protest against unemployment and in favour of fair wages and shorter working hours. Handbills had been distributed over preceding days saying that 'we call upon you to be present in thousands to make a vigorous demonstration in favour of the producing classes against those who rob and oppress them.'[51] The SDF told activists it was 'anxious to maintain order', but wanted them 'to uphold your right to live in comfort for the useful work which you are ready and eager to perform.' A 'social revolution' was now essential 'unless you wish your children to curse your memory for handing on to them yet worse slavery than that which you yourselves suffer from today.'

Burns, Hyndman, Williams and Champion, out on remand, were present, and Hyndman made a speech tracing the struggle back to Wat Tyler and John Ball in the Peasants' Revolt 500 years earlier. Around 5,000 people then marched to Westminster, quietly until 'roughs' broke windows in houses near Buckingham Palace as a prelude to what *The Times* called 'a riotous attack on the police and all who appeared to belong to the party of law and order.' The four were back in court that week, with the case against them already in trouble: although their matter was *sub judice*, *Punch* had published a cartoon of them being hanged, and the *Morning Post* had published a letter signed 'Naval Captain' that assumed their guilt and recommended they be flogged.[52] On 3 March, after further hearings, the men were sent for trial at the Old Bailey, starting on 6 April.

The proceedings – which the Newspaper of Record termed that 'very rare' event in the late nineteenth century of 'a true State Trial' – excited huge interest; there had been nothing like it since the trial of the Cato Street Conspirators in 1820. The Attorney-General, Sir Charles Russell,

QC, prosecuted; Hyndman and Champion defended themselves and Burns and Williams were represented. Among the witnesses was Chamberlain, whom Champion called in a clever attempt to prove that sentiments expressed in some of his radical speeches, particularly about land ownership, had been no more seditious than anything said in Trafalgar Square. Burns received the permission of the judge, Mr Justice Cave, to address the jury: Cave had already indicated dissatisfaction with the vagueness of the charges brought against the men.

Burns made a passionate defence of himself and his cause. He described his youth of poverty and how, since the age of eighteen, 'he had done everything that a workman could do in a peaceful and legitimate manner to call the attention of the authorities to the frightful poverty and degradation which existed among the poorer classes.'[53] He had foregone countless meals to afford the books and pamphlets through which he had educated himself. He had sought to educate other workmen. His only motivation had been to help the poor whose cause he had espoused. What he had said had not amounted to sedition, but had been the expression of 'an honest and virtuous indignation'. He claimed some of the words attributed to him had been shouted out by others in the crowd. He quoted a police superintendent who had said that Burns had done all he could to help keep order; and he said he had argued that only by parliamentary, and not extra-parliamentary, action would the movement prevail.

He himself had been 'boycotted' since fighting Nottingham for the SDF the previous year, and had no work. He did not feel his speeches were further-reaching than Gladstone's for Home Rule. He said the march out of the square had been orderly until it reached the Carlton Club, at the bottom of St James's Street, where some members of the club at its windows had exercised 'the stupid custom men in Pall Mall had of laughing at what some were pleased to term "the great unwashed".' Ridicule was more than the men could bear. He said his comrades were 'the true guardians of law and order', because they sought to remove the horrors that caused men to riot: and these were, he said, 'times of exceptional poverty'. He ended by saying that freedom of speech was in the jury's hands, and hoped their verdict would stigmatise 'as absurd, stupid, and frivolous the prosecution brought against the defendants by the Crown.'

Each man addressed the jury, though none so powerfully and

emotionally as Burns. In his summing-up, the Attorney-General, sensing things were going against him, tried to play down the gravity of the case. The jury retired for an hour and a quarter and returned verdicts of not guilty. They did note that Burns's and Champion's language had been not seditious but 'highly inflammatory and greatly to be condemned.'[54] They also claimed that, given the disturbances, the prosecutions were correct. The verdict was greeted with applause, and the men were cheered as they left court. The acquittal outraged the establishment, and, as the men had hoped, their near-martyrdom rallied the left: in the ensuing weeks and months, socialist groups were founded all over Britain.

There was no comparable challenge to the rule of law, however, for another eighteen months. When it came, it showed how the already factionalised socialist movement could be united, however temporarily, against the common enemy of the traditional ruling class and the forces of capital. On what became known as 'Bloody Sunday', 13 November 1887, several fronts in the unrest against Salisbury's administration coalesced in another massive protest in Trafalgar Square. The cause was the imprisonment of William O'Brien, the Parnellite MP, and new attempts to coerce Ireland. The Labour movement had taken up Ireland and Home Rule as a cause. But that was not the only reason why trade unionists, socialists from the SDF and the Socialist League, Marxists, Fabians and other leftists were in the square that afternoon: rising unemployment and working conditions were also at issue, the economy still experiencing low growth after the long depression that started in 1873 and continued until 1880. Even more alarming was how many of the demonstrators, perhaps having learned from February 1886, arrived armed with iron bars, knives and lengths of piping.

It was estimated that 30,000 spectators surrounded the square to watch 10,000 protesters marching from all directions. The stars of the socialist and radical movements were there: Morris, Burns, Annie Besant, and even the Fabian Shaw, who demanded the sacking of the Commissioner of the Metropolitan Police for trying to stop the meeting. The government deployed 2,000 police and 400 troops from before sunrise to prevent the meeting from taking place, and succeeded. Shaw attacked the 'cowardice' of the masses for not having taken on the police.[55] Burns and Robert Cunninghame Graham – a Liberal MP, Scottish Home Ruler, closet socialist and founder of the Scottish National party – were arrested for trying to lead a group to rush the square, and Mrs Besant asked to be;

but the police, smelling martyrdom, declined her offer. The infantry fixed bayonets but the cavalry did not draw their swords. The hooves of police horses caused most injuries.

Another demonstration occurred in the square a week later, and a protester run down by a police horse later died. His funeral was an occasion for Morris to call for 'holy war' to stop London being turned into a 'huge prison'. Charles Bradlaugh, the first MP to be a professed atheist (see Chapter 6), had been just one prominent public figure to declare the police prohibition illegal, and to demand that workmen come to the square and assert their right to hold a public meeting.

Burns and Graham appeared at Bow Street on 22 November, charged with disorderly conduct, and Graham also with assaulting police. Burns defended himself and a young lawyer who had won East Fife for the Liberals at the 1886 general election, Herbert Henry Asquith, defended Graham. The Crown tried to have the men charged with riotous and unlawful assembly, the defence arguing that the case against both rested on whether the authorities had the right to ban assemblies in the square. Bradlaugh was called as a witness, and testified to decades of convening meetings in the square without hindrance from the police. The magistrate nonetheless sent the two men for trial at the Old Bailey, where they appeared in January 1888. They were both convicted of taking part in an unlawful assembly, and sent to Pentonville for six weeks without hard labour.

X

London was emerging as the centre of intellectual socialism in Britain – as well as having a substantial Labour movement based on a wide range of skilled workers and, in the East End in particular, a large population of unskilled ones. But there was growing evidence of a Labour movement organising in the industrialised provinces. After 1884 the enfranchisement of miners improved the feasibility of a political party of the left, separate from the Liberals. The political muscle of these men was a factor in the foundation of the Ayrshire Miners' Union, under its secretary, James Keir Hardie. Hardie, a former miner himself, had attempted to organise miners in south-west Scotland since the late 1870s, working for them part-time, but it was not until 1886 that the funds and the political imperative needed to create a serious union existed.

Hardie was remarkable. He was the illegitimate son of a farm servant from Lanarkshire, born in 1856, who went down the pit at the age of eleven. He worked there for over a decade, while teaching himself shorthand. In 1877 he witnessed a pit disaster at Blantyre that killed 200 men; his knowledge of the strenuousness, harshness and danger of work underground gave him an authority in his political life, as well as the motivation to win better conditions for his fellow workers, whether miners or in any other trade. He went to night school and to supplement his studies embarked on a programme of autodidactic reading, notably of Carlyle. Meanwhile, his stepfather had become a drunk and was steering his family to destitution. When he reached his early twenties Hardie converted to evangelical Christianity and to the temperance movement, though he married the daughter of a publican.

Hardie offered himself as a union official in Hamilton. It was not a full-time job, and he supplemented his income with journalism. After a strike there in 1880 failed, he moved to Cumnock in Ayrshire, and began to build the organisation. As well as persisting with journalism, he worked as an insurance agent and for the Evangelical Union to make enough to support himself and his family. His experiences as a miner, and what he witnessed as a union official, radicalised him. Hardie, whose politics had been those of a Gladstonian Liberal, formed his own critique of capitalism that made him question Liberal economic doctrines, and to look for a different means of political expression. His radicalisation led him to found and edit a monthly newspaper, *The Miner*. His first flirtation with socialism came after 1884, when he started to read Hyndman's SDF newspaper *Justice*. By May 1887, after a strike in Ayrshire had been put down by force and the miners forced back to work without any concessions, Hardie's views had developed to the point where he would write in *The Miner*: 'The capitalist has done good service in the past by developing trade and commerce. His day is nearly done.'[56] He became a powerful advocate of the eight-hour day.

Hardie's Liberalism had not died by 1888, when he sought the party's nomination in a by-election in Lanark. When it chose a London barrister instead, he stood as an Independent Labour candidate. The Liberals were alarmed enough to try to bribe him with the promise of a safe seat at the next election. It failed; he lost, but gained 617 votes. The resulting momentum helped to found the Scottish Labour party, and he launched a monthly paper, *The Labour Leader*. He made the prophetic statement that 'the day would come when Liberalism would be dead and buried in Great Britain, and only the Labour Party existed.'[57]

Hardie's reputation in leftist politics was growing steadily. He was one of twenty British delegates (Morris was another) who attended the Second Socialist International in Paris in 1889, broadening his ideas and his range of contacts, and helping confirm him as a socialist. He became one of the left's leading propagandists through his journalism. He received an offer in 1890 from radicals in the West Ham Liberal party, which was badly split, to stand there at the next election. He did so as an Independent Labour candidate in an area heavily populated by unskilled workers. Instead of his hitherto main theme of the eight-hour day, he found himself championing the unemployed, of whom there were many in the docks of east London. He also called for a graduated income tax on those earning over £1,000 a year, to fund old age pensions.

He was returned to parliament in 1892, thanks to the support of radicals who had previously voted Liberal. Burns, who stood as a Liberal in Battersea, was also elected. Part of Burns's profound dislike of Hardie was rooted in his belief that the representatives of the working man should act within existing structures rather than set up new ones that could prove divisive. Nonetheless, Labour had made its breakthrough, and the working man had his own kind speaking for him in parliament. When Hardie took his seat on 3 August 1892 he was dressed in 'yellow tweed trousers, serge jacket and vest, and soft tweed cap.'[58] The cloth cap in a world of silk hats would become part of the Hardie myth, though his dress was not that of a Scottish working man, but of an artist.

XI

Hardie called a meeting in Bradford on 13 January 1893 that marked the birth of the Independent Labour party. Two years earlier there had been a nineteen-week strike at the city's Manningham Mills, owned by Samuel Cunliffe Lister and – with at its height 11,000 employees – one of the largest of its kind. The mill had twenty-seven acres of floor space and the fine Italianate chimney that rises from it is 255 feet high. The early 1890s were the beginning of the end of Britain's textile industry, as Lister and his fellow barons sought ways to cut costs. Strong foreign competition and tariffs in the American market had effectively closed it to British imports. In December 1890 Lister told 1,100 of his workers they would have to accept a wages cut of 25 per cent; if they did not he would close the factory until they changed their minds.

The mills, which had a near-monopoly of the country's plush and velvet production, were not heavily unionised, but workers called in the Weavers' and Textile Workers' Association to negotiate for them: they failed, despite pointing out that the mills had earned Lister £138,000 of profit the previous year, whereas the proposed wage reduction would save just £7,000. Against union advice the workers – mainly women – struck, despite there being no strike fund to support them. In April 1893 Bradford Corporation, controlled by Liberal councillors, banned marches the strikers held at weekends, which caused a protest by 90,000 people that the authorities could do nothing to prevent. However, the limited strike fund that was eventually set up ran out, and Lister (who had started to move machinery out of his mill to other sites where work could continue) refused to compromise.

There was a slow drift back to work – by Saturday 11 April the mills said that 400 hands were working in their plush department, but that still left 4,500 others out. Strike-breakers became subject to violence – as *The Times* put it, 'assaults have been committed and stone-throwing has been indulged in'.[59] Tillett, still the cynosure of the movement, went to Bradford to address a public meeting. The police banned an outdoor gathering for the overflow and sent 200 men to stop it. There was disorder after the main meeting – which 5,000 had attended – and the crowd formed their own outdoor meeting. There was much 'hooting and shouting' but only a few arrests.

The confrontation was merely postponed. The next afternoon 'some persons calling themselves Social Democrats, from Leeds' occupied the square where the overflow meeting would have occurred.[60] There were arrests, and the crisis appeared to have passed: but that evening widespread disturbances broke out. The mob attacked a small contingent of police, and broke shop windows. The mayor, flanked by the chief constable and other worthies, read the Riot Act; when the crowd did not disperse the Durham Light Infantry charged them, with bayonets fixed. This seems to have inflamed rather than cowed the mob, so the police mounted a baton charge. The chief constable was injured, knives were thrown at the police and a police horse was stabbed.

By late April the whole workforce returned, defeated. Textile workers were determined not to be in such a position of weakness again, and particularly blamed the Liberal party – whose MPs dominated the area – for their lack of support. This confirmation that the Liberals were the party of capital and not of labour caused the Bradford Labour Union to be founded, to provide a separate organisation with workers' interests paramount. Bradford's pioneering work in establishing a socialist group made it the ideal choice when Hardie sought to stage the conference to found the ILP.

A week before that meeting the Scottish Labour party – of which Hardie was secretary – became the Independent Labour party (Scottish Branch), and prepared to federate on equal terms with an English party. The SLP voted that no one could hold office if a member of another political party, severing the link between the organised working class and the Liberals. At the Bradford meeting there were 115 delegates, including eleven Fabians (among them Shaw), but most from what would become ILP branches. Hardie was elected president. The name was discussed, and 'the Socialist Labour party' was rejected. The embryonic movement was innately conservative, and wished to avoid association with the revolutionary socialism of middle-class dreamers such as Morris.

Tillett 'said he could not understand why their friends should apply the term Socialism to their party'.[61] He felt no need to identify the British party with its continental brethren who used such names. The report of his speech continues: 'He was glad to say that if there were 50 red revolutionist parties in Germany he would rather have the solid, progressive, matter-of-fact, fighting trade unionist of England, and for that reason he desired that they should keep away from their name any term of socialism.' And, in a shaft at Morris and the Webbs, he added: 'He preferred a man who had spent his life in the labour movement to those chattering mags [Australian slang for a gossip] who had neither the courage of their convictions nor the capacity to deal with details of their opinions.' For good measure, he added that 'there was not a Socialist party in the world who could show the effective organisation of those men and women [in trades unions] in Lancashire.' Thus the ILP was born a coalition, and the factions within it and its successor party would strain against each other for more than a century to come.

The manifesto offered at Bradford embraced much familiar from the programme of radical MPs who sat as Liberals, but also much that pushed the interests of the working man or woman further than ever before and that was – whatever Tillett might claim – socialist. It demanded the abolition of overtime, piece rates and child labour, a legally enforced forty-eight-hour week (this was amended to an eight-hour day), benefits for the aged, sick, disabled, widowed and orphaned, free and unsectarian education, collectivisation of land 'and of all means of production and distribution'. It wanted adult suffrage, short parliaments, publicly-funded election expenses, salaried MPs, and the abolition of the monarchy and the House of Lords. It also wanted to abolish indirect taxation and instead to tax unearned income 'to extinction'.

At its Congress the next year the TUC, until then traditionally a haven of labour-minded Liberals such as Broadhurst, also voted for public ownership of the means of production, distribution and exchange: its first major socialist act, and a key moment in uniting the Labour movement behind one political party. Once Broadhurst's generation had passed, there was no obstacle to the TUC committing itself to the ILP and, once it did, beginning the process of supplanting the Liberal party altogether.

Despite Hardie's belief, expressed in Bradford, that the party could hold the balance of political power, it failed at the 1895 general election, with Hardie losing his seat, but it quickly established itself in mining areas, notably the West Riding, Lancashire and South Wales. Until the Great War there would be a battle between Hardie and Burns and their followers for the backing of the working man. Hardie's defeat was partly down to the notoriety he acquired by attacking the Royal family in the Commons in 1894, during a debate to congratulate the Duchess of York on the birth of her son, the future Edward VIII. Even some of his supporters in West Ham were appalled that he should say of the infant Prince that 'from his childhood onwards, this boy will be surrounded by sycophants and flatterers by the score.'[62] He also said that the boy's grandfather, the Prince of Wales, owned some of London's 'vilest slums' and that aspects of his private life it 'would be better to keep covered'.

Hardie determined to unite leftism, linking up socialist societies with the working-class movement. In 1899 the TUC was asked to endorse a proposal to form a Labour Representation Committee along the lines Hardie had suggested, and narrowly voted to do so. Hardie chaired this committee when it first met on 27 February 1900, and Ramsay MacDonald (like Hardie a Scot, the illegitimate son of a farm servant, a formidable autodidact and a jobbing journalist) became its first secretary. It comprised seven trade unionists, two ILP delegates, two Marxist Socialists (who, dissatisfied with the company they were keeping, soon left) and a Fabian. It won two seats in the Khaki election of that year, on 24 October – one of whom was Hardie, returned for Merthyr Tydfil – and in 1906 the LRC changed its name to the Labour party.

Wells, writing of this period, said the urge of the politically motivated was to 'build the state' as a provider of social services, to intervene and redistribute wealth to alleviate poverty.[63] Private ownership would become outmoded: 'The man who owns property is a public official and has to behave as such. That's the gist of socialism as I understand it,' says a character in *The New Machiavelli*.[64] Wells believed Labour should be 'a class party . . . whose immediate interest is to raise wages, shorten hours of labour, increase employment and make better terms for the working-man tenant and the working-man purchaser.'[65] He said it should stand 'for the expropriated multitude, whose whole situation and difficulty arise from its individual lack of initiative and organising power.' He admitted the mass movement failed to grasp difficulties attendant on nationalisations of land and capital; and therefore doubted that a separate, long-lived Labour party would emerge from 'the huge hospitable caravanserai of Liberalism'. He feared Labour would articulate socialism 'in the entirely one-sided form of an irresponsible and non-constructive attack on property', a form he felt was 'mutilated'.[66] Unfortunately for Wells, the future of the working-class movement had been taken out of the hands of middle-class intellectuals.

PART II

COMING STORMS

CHAPTER 4

IMPERIAL TENSIONS

I

In the mid-Victorian period historians such as James Anthony Froude had supplied a Tory view of Britain's past that legitimised its institutions, arguing for continuity with the past and support of the constitutional settlement, while J. R. Green's Whiggish and hugely influential *A Short History of the English People* charted a nation's moral and social progress. By the end of the century, however, Britain was no longer simply a nation: it was an empire. Indeed the decades before the Great War would mark the zenith of the British Empire in power and influence (though not in extent – that followed the Treaty of Versailles in 1919, when Britain gained German territories in Africa). Historians therefore felt that they now had to justify Britain's role in the world; and its intellectuals had not only to legitimise Britain's conquest of other nations, but to outline the rules for the conduct of imperial policy. They did this largely through the adoption of high-minded theories of civilising backward peoples and of extending Christianity to savages.

In reality, of course, the imperial venture was both less selfless and more complicated. It was driven by the pursuit of profit, and it took the form of a patchwork of different relationships. The white colonies (Canada, Australia and New Zealand) were self-governing (the Australian ones united to form the Commonwealth of Australia in 1901). India and colonies peopled by those of non-European descent, on the other hand, were run by the British. Empire offered Britain many advantages: additional manpower for the Armed Forces that would prove vital in the twentieth century's world wars; job opportunities for civil servants, soldiers and policemen as well as buccaneers; chances for Oxbridge-educated aesthetes as well as hucksters and barrow-boys. It also brought new words into the language, notably from the sub-continent, with its bungalows and gymkhanas. At the same time, however, it created tensions between Britain and other European powers, notably in Africa. It also had a markedly racial undertone, especially in Africa, and in India according to class and caste. And the desire to secure territory and exercise hegemony would cause the disaster in the Sudan that helped bring down Gladstone in 1885; while the lure of huge riches, and a measure of imperialist arrogance, would provoke the Second Boer War of 1899 to 1902, in which a pyrrhic victory for the British proved a negative turning point for national self-confidence.

Not surprisingly, politicians were ambivalent about imperialism. Disraeli had gloried in it; Gladstone found it offensive to his idea of liberalism; Salisbury tolerated it with reluctance; Joseph Chamberlain saw it as Britain's magnificent destiny – with him at the heart of it. He said, in 1902 while Colonial Secretary, 'the days are for great Empires and not for little States': and Britain's was, when he said that, the greatest of all.[1] Britain never had more self-belief than in the late nineteenth century, and imperialism profoundly affected the culture and attitudes of the mother country, broadening horizons and encouraging emigration. Children were schooled to run an empire, not a nation. Yet, the challenges and setbacks of Britain's imperial adventure also led to periods of national self-doubt and political turmoil, and raised profound questions – both about Britain's relationship with its colonies and its place in the world – that the Edwardians and their successors struggled to answer.

II

No history written in this period would influence policy so much as *The Expansion of England*, by J. R. Seeley, Regius Professor of History at Cambridge. Published in 1883, it was a development of two courses of lectures Seeley had given the previous year on the history of empire, whether British or those of former powers. Its author saw history as a study designed not so much to understand the past, as to discover possibilities for the future. It was a study that 'ought to exhibit the general tendency of English affairs in such a way as to set us thinking about the future and divining the destiny which is reserved for us.'[2] Men such as Rosebery, before he became either Foreign Secretary or Prime Minister, and Chamberlain, who would not only be Colonial Secretary in the Salisbury administration after 1895 but would in many respects be the key figure in that ministry, would claim to be deeply influenced by Seeley.

His assumptions were the imperialists': that 'the part played by our country in the world certainly does not grow less prominent as history advances', whereas other nations – he named Holland and Sweden – 'might pardonably regard their history as in a manner wound up'. There, the study of history could be only scientific or sentimental: but Britain's greatness was in the future as well as the past, so the past merited detailed study. 'The prodigious greatness to which it has attained makes the question of its future infinitely important and at the same time most anxious,' he wrote, 'because it is evident that the great colonial extension of our state exposes it to new dangers from which in its ancient insular insignificance it was free.'[3]

Seeley's value to statesmen was that he delineated anxieties and, by warning of potential difficulties, suggested how they could be averted. He distinguished between the vast population of India under British rule, and the 10 million or so 'Englishmen' who lived outside the British Isles, either in colonies with majority white settlements, or in others where the 'Englishmen' were not so greatly outnumbered as on the subcontinent. 'The latter are of our own blood, and therefore united to us by the strongest tie. The former are of alien race and religion, and are bound to us only by the tie of conquest,' he observed.[4] He doubted the Indian Empire added to British power or security, but felt it greatly increased the mother country's 'dangers and responsibilities'.

His doctrine therefore distinguished between the Indian and colonial empires. The latter was an astonishing prospect, not just for its geographical spread, but because of how colonists of British stock would multiply. 'In not much more than half a century the Englishmen beyond the sea – supposing the Empire to hold together – will be equal in number to the Englishmen at home, and the total will be much more than a hundred millions.'[5] He called this 'the great fact of modern English history' and stated that 'the growth of Greater Britain is an event of enormous magnitude' with 'moral and intellectual consequences' as well as material ones.[6] He added: 'Evidently, as regards the future, it is the greatest event.' He admitted that losing the American colonies, a century earlier, had left 'a doubt, a misgiving, which affects our whole forecast of the future of England.'[7] He continued: 'The greatest English question of the future must be what is to become of our second Empire, and whether or no it may be expected to go the way of the first.' He detected a 'tendency to expansion' among the English, which had to be understood before deciding how the future would develop.[8]

Seeley knew competitiveness with other expanding nations had caused this tendency. Canada had been acquired in the eighteenth century in competition with France; and England had checked France's progress towards India. He wrote at the start of the 'scramble for Africa', provoked by competition with France and other European powers. Politicians could doubtless have worked out the dynamic of imperialism for themselves, but it helped to have it reinforced by so distinguished an intellectual. Several time Seeley quotes an apophthegm of Turgot, the eighteenth-century French statesman and economist, who gave what hindsight proves to be the best advice for those seeking to predict the future: 'Colonies are like fruits which only cling till they ripen.'[9]

The need for empire grew, Seeley said, because the population had doubled in seventy years and was doubling again; Britain was of limited size, but 'the territory governed by the Queen is of almost boundless extent.'[10] Seeley advised his readers to regard emigrants to Canada or Australia as simply a different sort of Briton from those living in Kent or Cornwall; and he deplored thinking of colonies as 'possessions': 'In what sense can one population be spoken of as the possession of another population? The expression almost seems to imply slavery,' he wrote.[11] If such terminology implied a place to be 'worked' for the benefit of the mother country, that was 'essentially barbaric': he was clear that any gains from the colonies had to be returned in services or benefits, such as defence, provided by Britain.[12] Countries such as India, held by right of conquest, could not be exploited by a conquering nation that wished to consider itself civilised.

British imperialists seized on insights relevant to their own aims, as they plotted policy. 'Greater Britain is an extension of the English State and not merely of the English nationality . . . when a nationality is extended without any extension of the State, as in the case of the Greek colonies, there may be an increase of moral and intellectual influence, but there is no increase of political power.'[13] For men such as Chamberlain, and for another of Seeley's readers, Cecil Rhodes, the buccaneering future prime minister of Cape Colony, the increase in British power was essential to the Anglocentric, capitalist empire they wanted, and for which they would campaign. But Seeley feared India was 'precarious' because the state had advanced beyond the limits of nationality – it had imposed itself on people to whom its ways were not natural, restricting their ability to participate in their own polities. Of most interest to Seeley's devotees was his question about the risks of expansion: whether 'Greater Britain . . . can modify her defective constitution in such a way as to escape them for the future.'[14]

The Expansion of England is a rulebook for 'decent' imperialism, an imperialism that sincerely believed it was improving the government and lives of its conquered peoples: that too made it invaluable to governors of the great imperial nation in an increasingly democratic age. It was a roadmap for a future that assumed more expansion and growing power. But in imparting the lessons of history – particularly about the American revolution – it showed what to avoid if the second British Empire was to be held. Seeley pronounced 'that politics and history are only different aspects of the same study . . . politics are vulgar when they are not liberalised by history, and history fades into mere literature when it loses sight of its relation to practical politics.'[15] The subject of 'Greater Britain', he said, 'belongs most evidently to history and politics at once': successful imperial government could be achieved only by the closest study of history. It showed that 'we are not really conquerors of India, and we cannot rule her as conquerors.'[16] Given the apparent certainty of an imperial future, Seeley successfully imparted the message that that future could be embarked upon only after the closest possible study of the past.

III

The moral crusade of the Midlothian campaign before the 1880 election, when Gladstone returned to politics after a four-year hiatus in a detailed series of attacks on Tory foreign and economic policy, left no one in doubt that the Grand Old Man's first priority was to eradicate 'Beaconsfieldism' from British politics. He disliked the obsession with imperialism and the self-aggrandisement brought upon the nation by trying to broker the international relationships of others, both traits of the late prime minister, and viewed with as much suspicion by his successor: Salisbury, architect of 'splendid isolation'.

Gladstone knew the importance to national morale and prosperity of having an empire. Yet he seems to have taken the view of the Romans in the early centuries of their own that one became involved in expansionism purely to secure one's own frontiers rather than gratuitously. Popular freelance acts of conquest were an affront to his idea of liberalism. He pointed his party firmly towards the centre-left's later anti-imperialism, resolving to manage the Empire as humanely as possible so long as he was required to do so. He was conscious of the strategic and commercial importance of India, not least given its proximity to Russia and China and as a staging-post for territories further east and in Australasia. However, some leading Liberals would choose not to take Gladstone's view, and a group of Liberal imperialists emerged – led by his successor, Rosebery, but including a younger generation who would lead Liberalism in the run-up to the Great War: H. H. Asquith, R. B. Haldane and Sir Edward Grey. The two factions in the party would experience great tensions, not least during the years of opposition from 1895 to 1905, which covered a period of confrontation and then of war in southern Africa.

Although painted as a triumph for Beaconsfield, the 1878 Congress of Berlin left a legacy for Gladstone of maintaining the concert of Europe against a constantly provocative Turkey, even more bent on destabilising south-eastern Europe following its defeat in the Russo-Turkish War of 1877–8 and the Congress's dismemberment of much of the Ottoman Empire. It was an additional burden that the man who had railed against the Bulgarian atrocities, when in April 1876 Ottoman soldiers massacred up to 30,000 Orthodox Christian Bulgars in fifty-eight villages, could have done without. Paradoxically, a prime minister who saw imperial expansion as something done out of necessity rather than because it was possible – the view of most Tory and even some Liberal imperialists – would hold office during the 'scramble for Africa', which began with British intervention in Egypt and spread south until it reached existing possessions on the Cape. In the 1880s much of Africa was colonised, with the French, Spanish, Belgians, Portuguese and Germans planting their flags all over the continent: but the Union flag was planted more frequently than any other, and the range of possessions on all continents and in most of the great oceans was augmented. Britain's industrial output might be declining relative to Germany and

America, but in territorial expansion she led the world, and was evaluated on that basis.

Gladstone's first imperial problem was in southern Africa, where a year earlier British soldiers had been massacred at Isandlwana, and where the Dutch-descended Afrikaners in the Transvaal were determined to resist British rule. Gladstone had sought a confederation of the colonies in South Africa (to include Orange Free State, Cape Colony and Natal as well), and stated this policy to the agreement of his colleagues at a cabinet meeting a fortnight after taking office.[17] War between the Boers and the British lasted until the spring of 1881, when Gladstone ordered a truce, not least to save public money. For the war to be resolved decisively huge, and expensive, reinforcements would have to be sent. With other problems nearer home – notably Ireland – Gladstone persuaded his colleagues and parliament that Britain did not need the distraction of an imperial war in another hemisphere. So it was agreed that in the Transvaal the Boers would have self-rule, though Britain would still control their foreign policy. This compromise bought time, but nothing more: the remaining discontents would eventually be resolved, but not until after the Second Boer War of 1899–1902. What had changed by 1899 was the discovery of large deposits of gold south of Pretoria, the Boers' seat of power: mineral wealth that in the view of ardent British imperialists justified the loss of blood and treasure on both sides that that war entailed, and which made the Boers all the more determined to resist.

Gladstone had managed to calm matters in southern Africa for the time being, but was less successful in dealing with a region of north Africa that now became crucial to British imperial policy. Access to India, the most precious imperial possession, had been facilitated by the Suez Canal, opened in 1869, and it had soon become clear that control of the canal could not be allowed to fall into the hands of any power hostile to Britain. Egypt, through whose territory it had been cut, was in the early 1880s alarmingly unstable. The Khedive Ismail, who was financially incontinent, ruled under Ottoman authority. When in the early 1870s the Egyptian economy imploded, partly because of the Khedive's extravagance but also because of the collapse of the international cotton market, Disraeli offered that Britain would pay his debts in return for a controlling share in the canal. Shortly afterwards an Anglo-French commission, representing Egypt's two main creditors, took over management of the economy, and in 1877 these two powers persuaded the Khedive to abdicate in favour of his son, Tewfik.

Bonaparte had said in 1798 that whichever European power controlled Egypt would control India, and the maxim held good. Egypt had in turn been controlling the Sudan to its south, not least to secure its southern border against an insurgency by what the twenty-first century calls Muslim fundamentalists. In 1873 Ismail had sent a British soldier with a reputation for heroism won in China, Colonel (later General) Charles 'Chinese' Gordon, to govern it. Gordon found himself embarking upon a long war in Darfur, and by the time Tewfik succeeded his father he was exhausted, his soldiery depleted by death and disease, and in desperate need of reinforcement. Tewfik had little interest in the Sudan and sent no help: Gladstone's administration wanted nothing to do with it either, feeling it had no strategic relevance.

Gordon resigned and went, briefly, to India, leaving the substantial Muslim minority in the Sudan aggrieved and restive. The Turks who controlled the country were increasingly secular, which offended orthodox Muslims. One of their leaders, Muhammad Ahmed, started a holy war against the perceived enemies of his faith, and travelled through the Sudan in 1881–3 recruiting followers and effecting an uprising whose size alarmed the Egyptian authorities, including the hitherto detached British. Ahmed proclaimed himself the Mahdi, or 'the Expected One', in 1881. He and his followers massacred a sizeable Egyptian force in June 1883, an event terrible not just for the slaughter but for the opportunity it gave the Mahdists to loot arms, ammunition and matériel from the army it had annihilated. Britain feared any further military losses would fatally weaken Egypt, and became especially concerned about the substantial Egyptian garrison surrounded by Mahdist fighters in Khartoum.

By late 1883 it was apparent that if the Sudan were to be evacuated and Egypt shored up, Britain would have to do it. British forces had helped put down a rebellion in Egypt in 1882, and now militarily underwrote its government. Between 3 and 5 November 1883 around 40,000 Mahdists crushed an army of largely disaffected Egyptian soldiers, reckoned to be 10,000 strong and under the command of a retired Indian Army officer, Colonel Billy Hicks, at El Obeid, 200 miles south-west of Khartoum. Ten thousand Remington rifles, 5 million rounds of ammunition and five artillery batteries were lost, which with the fanaticism of the Mahdi's fighters made the holy warriors a lethal enemy. Around 500 Egyptian soldiers returned to Khartoum: almost all the Europeans, including the officer class and some journalists, were killed. The victory boosted the Mahdists further, encouraging another tribe, the Hadendo from the coast of the Red Sea, to join them: British soldiers called these tribesmen 'fuzzy-wuzzies'.

On 20 November, before the news of the massacre of Hicks's army reached London, Gladstone told the cabinet there was no question of sending either British or Indian Army troops to Egypt. He also noted: 'Do not encourage British officers to serve.'[18] Two days later, with the scale of the rout clear, he asked Sir Evelyn Baring, the consul-general in Cairo, 'to *tender* advice about retirement from Soudan.'[19] Baring replied that the Egyptian forces could not hold Khartoum against the Mahdists. For a time the government considered asking the Turks, to whom the Khedive owed allegiance, to intervene: but Gladstone feared an Ottoman intervention might challenge British influence. So Britain had to act, but the chosen method was diplomacy and leadership through Baring rather than committing troops. It was of no interest to Gladstone who controlled the Sudan, and if the Turks wanted to go there – as opposed to Egypt – he was happy for them to do so, provided they did not expect Britain to foot the bill.

As in the First Boer War, Gladstone decided that cutting Britain's losses was the most responsible course. The Egyptians could not afford, financially or militarily, to be in the Sudan. So the Khedive, whose mind the British helped make up, resolved to evacuate all Egyptians and leave the Sudan to its own devices, even if that meant the Mahdi controlled it. The evacuation risked turning into a massacre unless conducted in a properly protected fashion: so the Egyptians asked for a senior British officer to plan and oversee the exercise. They also reasoned that the Mahdists would not dare to attack a force led by a European Christian for fear of reprisals.

The man Tewfik wanted was Charles Gordon. In England, Gordon was a celebrity soldier with traits of the Renaissance man – he had recently undertaken studies that convinced him the Garden of Eden was in the Seychelles, and had spent 1883 in Palestine seeking to determine where Christ had been crucified and buried. The government eventually sent him in January 1884; but many who knew Gordon regarded the appointment as more likely to inflame the problem than defuse it, because many who knew Gordon thought him mad. Gladstone noted on

22 January that, in his view, Gordon's was 'a mission to report', and he would be placed in authority under Baring.[20] That, fatally, would not be how Gordon would see it.

He was fifty when he left for Africa. His life had embraced fame and a degree of notoriety. He had been in trouble at the Royal Military Academy at Woolwich for hitting other cadets on the head with a broomstick or a hairbrush: he had been put on a charge for bullying. He had joined the Royal Engineers rather than follow his father into the Royal Artillery, and while serving as assistant garrison engineer at Pembroke Dock during 1854 had come under the influence of a zealous Irish Protestant officer, who had begun his conversion into a religious fanatic. The process had been accelerated by Gordon's illness with smallpox in 1862, which had made him believe his fate was entirely in God's hands. He had started obsessively to read the Bible, religious commentaries and tracts. He felt he was constantly in the presence of God, once telling the future Lord Esher that 'as I came to your house He walked with me arm in arm up South Audley Street'.[21]

He had served with distinction in the Crimea, and then had become one of the Army's most gifted map-makers in detailing the borders between the Russian and Ottoman Empires. He had also proved to be a gifted photographer. He had sealed his reputation in China, where between 1862 and 1864 he had mobilised an otherwise untrained and ineffective army to put down an insurgency and protect Shanghai. Success had gone to his head, however, and he had started to behave insubordinately, creating his reputation for being difficult. His leadership qualities were magnificent when in charge of Chinese or, later, Egyptians: the English soldiery was less impressed. Back in England he had been posted to Gravesend where, out of Christian duty but also because he enjoyed it, he had housed street-urchins in his quarters where he treated them as if they were his own children, even to the lengths of bathing them.

Some stories about him on his first posting to Khartoum reached home and coloured opinions of him: a demand to have his salary halved, his refusal to take credit for discoveries made in the course of explorations in the Upper Nile, in case it led to him being *fêted*, and his occasional habit of embracing his enemies as brothers in Christ – even though they were usually Muslims. Nonetheless, he had eliminated the slave trade in parts of the Sudan, and had begun to root out corruption. Back in London in January 1880 he had given the impression to Foreign Office officials of being mildly unhinged, which one, Sir Thomas Wade, attributed to his 'long life of isolation'.[22] Wade had noted his religious mania, and had recorded that 'his very devoutness is dangerous'. Gordon now disregarded what his notional superiors told him and followed only his own instincts, which he had convinced himself were akin to divine inspiration and instruction.

He had a death wish, not least because death was his route to eternal salvation. He also believed in reincarnation. This was not a helpful cast of mind for a senior officer to have. He turned into an ascetic, hence demanding his salary be reduced when he received new appointments, and regarding comfort and luxury as effeminate. He sought to subjugate himself entirely to God, disdaining earthly rank and pretensions to it. He was celibate, a trait that led the Arab world to view him with awe. No proof exists of the homosexuality of which he has been accused, despite his enjoyment of the company of boys. His main recorded vice was chain-smoking, ideal for one with a death wish, and it gave him angina. Rumours of his being a secret drunk are unsubstantiated.

He could not settle down in a job, partly because of his psychological problems, partly because of his natural talent for insubordination. He had gone to India in June 1880 as private secretary to the Marquess of Ripon, the Viceroy; his resignation within a week confirmed the official view that he was unreliable and unstable. Later that year he had gone to Peking at the invitation of Sir Robert Hart, the Inspector-General of customs, then back to Britain and to Mauritius in April 1881. He had served there as Commanding Royal Engineer for almost a year, being promoted to major-general. He had been sent to restore order in Basutoland, then returned briefly to England before his year in Palestine. This excursion had produced his book *Reflections in Palestine*, in which he advanced his theory about the place of the Crucifixion. On his return King Leopold of the Belgians had asked him to govern the Congo, where Henry Morton Stanley had laid the foundations of a state. On 19 October 1883 Gordon had accepted the offer, believing he would die there, and had prepared to resign his commission. He had sought permission from the War Office to go, and it was granted; but then Granville, as Foreign Secretary, had rescinded it, on the grounds that he thought Leopold would cut off the money needed to keep the enterprise afloat. However, a telegraphist had mistranscribed 'declines' to give permission as 'decides', so Gordon had pressed on.[23]

In Brussels on 2 January 1884 he met the King, and agreed to go to the Congo in February. However while there he received a letter from his close friend Lord Wolseley, Adjutant-General of the Army and its second most senior soldier after the commander-in-chief, the Duke of Cambridge, the Queen's cousin. Wolseley could not tell Gordon that he had featured prominently in discussions in London about the Sudan, though said he would like to talk to him about them as 'things can't go on'.[24] He also said he did not want Leopold to take 'our best man from the English Army', and tried to talk him out of the mission. 'The world does not seem bounded with the clear horizon that would warrant – if I may venture to say to an old friend – our very best man burying himself amongst niggers on the Equator.'[25] Gordon believed London had underestimated the Mahdist threat, and believed a civil commissioner should talk to the Mahdi about his terms for a Sudan free from Egyptian control. This did not chime with the Khedive's view. He wished to keep it under his control, so Hicks was sent with inadequate troops to his and their deaths.

A Royal Engineer colonel, Bevan Edwards (later a lieutenant-general), had put the idea of sending Gordon in a letter to General Sir Andrew Clarke, commander of the regiment. Edwards had served under Gordon in China and felt he could transform the Sudan. However, he entered a proviso that, once Gordon was sent, was not followed: that to reinforce his authority as Governor-General a division should be sent from India. Edwards added that southern Sudan could be abandoned but Khartoum and the north held as a buffer between the Mahdists and Egypt.

Clarke agreed, and sent the letter on to Childers, the Chancellor of the Exchequer. Childers passed it to Granville, who understood that an appointment was a matter for the Khedive; but on consulting Baring was told the Khedive's prime minister had reservations about Gordon because he was a Christian. In fact, Gordon had great sympathy with the Mahdists. Writing to a friend from Brussels on 3 January 1884, he said: 'I feel for the rebels and am proud of their prowess.'[26] Meanwhile, on 1 January, the debate about Gordon had broken out in public, with his predecessor as Governor-General of the Sudan, Sir Samuel White Baker, writing to *The Times* to demand he be sent.

Before the government could ask Gordon he gave an ill-advised two-hour interview to *The Pall Mall Gazette*, in the person of its lively editor W. T. Stead, in which he revealed his opinions about the Sudan crisis –

arguing that Khartoum should be held at all costs as a base from which to take the fight to the Mahdists. Stead had heard the rumours that Gordon might be considered for the mission and was determined to get in first: Gordon had found a message from Stead awaiting him when he docked at Southampton from Brussels, but 'with characteristic modesty' had declined the request.[27] Stead was not a man to let a refusal impede him and headed for Southampton, where he tracked Gordon to his sister's house outside the town. The general continued to show 'considerable disinclination' to talk, but Stead persisted, flattering his vanity by telling him no one in England could rival his knowledge of the Sudan, and urging him to share his wisdom.

The interview broke new ground for British journalism because of its direct approach to a public figure, and having that figure outline such controversial views in the press. Stead, as we shall see, made a habit of engaging in very twentieth-century practices. 'As soon as he [Gordon] had broken the ice', he wrote, 'he went on with the greatest animation, and even vehemence'. Stead did not take a shorthand note, but wrote the meeting up from memory, an astonishing feat and one to which few modern journalists would feel equal. It raises questions of accuracy: but there was also present Gordon's friend Captain John Brocklehurst (later General Lord Ranksborough), who checked the proofs and confirmed their veracity.

Gordon set out why it was crucial to Egypt to hold eastern Sudan and Khartoum. It was not that the Mahdists would head north, but 'the influence which the spectacle of a conquering Mahomedan Power, established close to your frontiers, will exercise upon the population which you govern.' He stressed the weakness was in Cairo, and had caused the massacre of Hicks and his men. He sympathised with the Mahdists because of what they endured under, ultimately, Turkish rule; anyone who had been in a Turkish province and seen their style of governance would understand how oppressive it was. Rebellion was the only answer: 'The movement is not religious, but an outbreak of despair.' Gordon asserted that when he had been in the Sudan 'I had taught them something of the meaning of liberty and justice, and accustomed them to a higher ideal of government than that with which they had previously been acquainted.' Once he had gone the oppression resumed. 'They are a good people, the poor Soudanese, and if I can do anything for them I shall be only too glad.'

Stead wrote an editorial extolling Gordon that stirred up mischief between the government and the general. It said Gordon's views on the 'impolicy' of evacuating the Sudan – which Baring recommended – were shared by 'every authority who looks at the matter from a purely Egyptian standpoint.'[28] Stead continued: 'We cannot send a regiment to Khartoum, but we can send a man who on more than one occasion has proved himself more valuable in similar circumstances than an entire army. Why not send Chinese GORDON with full powers to Khartoum, to assume absolute control of the territory, to treat with the Mahdi, to relieve the garrisons, and do what can be done to save what can be saved from the wreck of the Soudan?'

Although it was unclear how one man, however talented, could relieve garrisons without an army was not explained: but Stead was not one to let practicalities interfere with rhetoric. His tactics worked, and other papers took up the cry: *The Times* demanded that Gordon be approached; people in the streets shouted 'Gordon must go'. Thus was an unreasonable expectation created of what he could accomplish in the Sudan if he went there, with regrettable results for the government. Gordon, a monument to personal vanity, did nothing to talk down his miraculousness. The government followed public opinion, though it was far from clear as Gordon left what he would do when he reached Africa. Baring, their man in Cairo, was far from happy at having one of his critics sent out to handle the Sudan, and agreed to the mission only if Gordon was instructed what the policy would be.

Wolseley summoned Gordon to London on 15 January, and asked him to go to the Sudan. This seems to have been a shock to Gordon, who was still assembling equipment for the Congo. He agreed to go, but told Wolseley he could not countenance surrendering the Sudan unless he was ordered to reconquer the country on behalf of the Turkish-controlled Egyptians: for he felt that would be even worse for the Sudanese. Wolseley, aware of Baring's reservations, briefed Gordon on what was expected. Being the end of the parliamentary recess the cabinet had not met for weeks, and Gladstone was at Hawarden. Four members of the cabinet, led by Hartington, saw Gordon at the War Office. Hartington, as War Secretary, told Gordon his job was to evacuate the garrisons; Granville told him to write a report on the situation, and to act on Baring's instructions to do whatever the Khedive's government wished. There was sufficient vagueness in that to cause problems, which would be compounded by the extreme difficulty of communication between Khartoum and Cairo.

That evening Gordon – having telegraphed the King of the Belgians to say the Congo would have to wait – left from Charing Cross, seen off by Hartington, Granville and the Duke of Cambridge, the Commander-in-Chief. Granville bought Gordon's ticket; Wolseley, ascertaining Gordon had no cash, gave him his gold watch to sell to raise funds. The nation was relieved, but widely believed it was too late: none more so than the Queen, who added it to her charge-sheet against Gladstone. 'The Queen trembles for General Gordon's safety,' she told her prime minister on 9 February. 'If anything befalls him, the result will be awful.'[29]

IV

There was not merely a demoralised, poorly-trained and under-equipped Egyptian army to evacuate, but also European civilians and children. Baring gave Gordon further instructions about how to accomplish the latter when, accompanied by Lieutenant Colonel J. D. H. Stewart of the 11th Hussars, he reached Cairo late in January 1884. The moment Gordon set foot in Egypt and began firing cables back to London, it became clear he had no intention of engaging in a 'reporting mission'. Instead he proposed to go south of Khartoum with Egyptian troops and seize the Sudan's equatorial provinces, handing them over to his erstwhile patron the King of the Belgians. Word was sent to Baring to tell Gordon not to do this, a course Baring himself had recommended to London. The government had, however, encouraged Gordon to offer his opinions whenever relevant. But as Wolseley informed Hartington, he had told Gordon before leaving London that 'the employment of an English Brigade will not enter into his calculations as a *possible* operation.'[30] Baring, acting on his own authority, instructed him to act as Governor-General once he reached the Sudan, and to set up a government to replace Egyptian rule. This dramatically changed the terms of trade settled in London. Before heading south Gordon had an audience of Tewfik, and apologised for having called him a 'snake' in the interview with Stead. Gordon knew that of which he spoke.

In London, the Conservative opposition made political capital out of events in Africa. On 12 February Northcote, who led the opposition in the Commons, moved a vote of censure on the government, arguing that Egypt was being destablised by events in the Sudan, the Mahdi was making a mockery of British imperial power and the government was operating a 'vacillating and inconsistent policy'. This mockery had assumed the practical form of the slaughtering of Hicks's army the previous November, while parliament had been in recess. Northcote told the Commons Hicks had been sacrificed because of the government's lack of grip. Indeed, when Hicks had asked for reinforcements Baring had told him it was impossible, not least 'because the Government contemplated the immediate withdrawal of the troops of Her Majesty from Egypt.'[31] This, Northcote said, had demoralised the whole Army. He then made a point that would plague Gladstone:

> There is one on which, of course, all our minds are fixed – namely, the mission of General Gordon. But on that point I am anxious, on the present occasion, to say little or nothing; and for this reason – General Gordon is now engaged in an attempt of the most gallant and daring character. No one can speak with too much admiration of his courage and self-devotion; no one in this country can fail to sympathise with him and earnestly desire his safety. It would be the greatest possible misfortune if by any words accidentally or carelessly dropped, here or elsewhere, anything were done that could in the slightest degree imperil or destroy the success of his mission. All I will say is, that I trust that the Government are not proceeding in the case of General Gordon as they have done in too many instances; that they are not throwing all the responsibility upon him and leaving none on themselves; that they are not confusing his position and leaving him uncertain as to whose servant he is and to whom he is responsible.[32]

Gladstone said the policy had been consistent: he did not want to commit British troops to a holy war in Egypt, and never had. The responsibilities in Egypt were inherited from Beaconsfield: and he wished to do the minimum required to discharge those obligations as a shareholder in the Suez Canal and a creditor of Egypt. But he repudiated the notion that it was up to Britain to defend Egypt, which had an army of its own, and certainly not to commit to the reconquest of the Sudan. Hicks had worked for the Khedive, and the Khedive's government had directed the war: Gladstone stressed that he could not have taken over that direction without becoming responsible for it, with all that would entail. However, Baring had reported to him that the Egyptian Army was 'mutinous', prompting Gladstone to put on standby two battalions in Gibraltar and Malta.

The government won the vote of censure after several days' tedious debate, but Salisbury kept up the pressure. Meanwhile, Gordon had left Cairo in thrall to his death wish: he dined on his last night there with Sir Evelyn and Lady Wood, and gave their butler his evening tailcoat and waistcoat, saying he would never need them again. When he reached Khartoum on 18 February – to a hero's welcome – after a journey by train and steamer, he immediately sent to Egypt sick and wounded soldiers and women and children, evacuating 2,600 before the Mahdists besieged the city on 18 March. He told Cairo he needed more troops. He ordered a public bonfire in which were burned the stocks and some whips, showing that the oppression by the former rulers was over. Once the inevitable siege started Gordon determined to stay; but London confirmed its reluctance to send a relief force, fearing it would be slaughtered. Baring had made £100,000 available to fund Gordon's mission, but the money was embezzled before it reached Khartoum, causing Gordon to issue his own currency.

Baring told London on 27 March he advocated a relief expedition, 'or at any rate the promise of one', according to the diary of Eddy Hamilton, Gladstone's private secretary.[34] The Queen sent a telegram 'strongly in favour' of Baring's views. Hamilton noted that such an expedition 'could not be contemplated'. The Tories made Gordon's position the key weapon in their assault. On 3 April Northcote harried Gladstone on whether he would abandon Gordon, quoting the local Consular Agent in the city, who was professing that 'we cannot bring ourselves to believe that we are to be abandoned by England.'[35] Northcote did not know whom Gordon was serving: the Queen or the Khedive. Gladstone accused him of simply causing trouble: it was the seventeenth time in two months that the House had debated Egypt. This bluster disguised – and not well – the fact that Gladstone did not know what was happening in the Sudan, and was increasingly anxious about having to send a rescue mission.

The next day – 4 April – Gordon wrote: 'No human power can deliver us now, we are surrounded, and unless God causes the savage Arab tribes to disperse no English troops will do so until they have racked Khartoum and massacred the inhabitants.'[36] He thus outlined Gladstone's best defence when public outrage erupted after the fall of Khartoum: once the siege was laid, the inhabitants would be slaughtered irrespective of when a relief force was sent – though Gordon still hoped such an expedition would be sent, just in case it got through in time. Having decided to have no army accompany him, the government had decreed he was a dead man. Gladstone's misjudgment was not to have paid more attention to Gordon's mission when he sent him: ensconced at Hawarden, he had not even mentioned it in his diary. It was not that Hartington and Granville had inadequately briefed Gordon, who then had contradictory orders from Baring on his arrival at Cairo. It was that the mission was flawed from its inception.

Word in the press and from travellers in Africa that Khartoum was daily expecting British soldiers to protect it from the Mahdists embarrassed Gladstone and his colleagues, and began to cause a serious division between him and Hartington, who wanted a force sent without delay. Baring's dispatch on 18 April included the observation 'Gordon evidently thinks he is to be abandoned and is very indignant', which exacerbated matters. In private conversation with Hamilton on 26 April Gladstone admitted his responsibility towards Gordon, but protested he felt none towards Egypt. 'It is madness', Hamilton recorded him saying, 'to suppose that we can undertake the Government of Egypt – Egypt, which is a Mahometan country, in the heart of the Mahometan world, with a population antagonistic to Europeans.'[37] In another vote of censure on 12 May Gladstone defended the government's reluctance to intervene, but admitted to his diary that he had done 'the best I could, though far from good.'[38] It was exceptionally uncomfortable for him that Hicks Beach, the Tory former Colonial Secretary, quoted back at him words he had uttered the previous February that 'General Gordon is no common man . . . it is no exaggeration to say that he is a hero. It is no exaggeration to say that he is a Christian hero.'[39]

Hicks Beach warned Gladstone that the government had to 'leave no stone unturned to avert from this country the intolerable stain which would be left upon her honour by any injury inflicted on General Gordon.'[40] The Tories weakened their case by claiming Gordon had had no wish to serve the Egyptian government, when that was exactly what he did have. Gladstone specified the mission the British government had sent him on: it was to report on the evacuation of the Sudan, and nothing else.

Gladstone was sure Gordon was acting as a freelance and ignoring the orders, reinforced via Baring, not to hold the Sudan. However, he saw that far more outrage would be caused, and his own position would become far more precarious, if Gordon were not relieved. Public opinion demanded a force be sent. Cynically, the Tories fed this clamour. Gladstone started to consider that a relief expedition might, after all, have to rescue Gordon, even though Tory agitation for the moment redoubled his determination not to act. Nonetheless, he also studied plans of different means by which a relief force could be delivered – a combination of rail, then camel, then sailing up the Nile. A promising young officer, Major Herbert Kitchener, was in Egypt helping restructure the Egyptian Army, but was also reconnoitring, and the government waited upon his reports.

In Khartoum, the Mahdist strategy was to starve the garrison into submission. It failed: the garrison could still fight, and did so successfully several times in the summer of 1884, capturing supplies. On 5 July the cabinet discussed the prospect of sending an expedition. 'Much difficulty felt,' Gladstone noted.[41] Eleven days later he discerned growing clamour in the cabinet, led by Hartington but ably assisted by Childers, who had been briefed by General Clarke, for an expedition. He expressed himself 'disappointed' with them.[42] The key pressure came from Selborne, the Lord Chancellor, who on 29 July sent Gladstone a long memorandum demanding an intervention. Gladstone told him he thought a massacre at Khartoum 'improbable': a fatally complacent belief, as it turned out.[43] Gladstone admitted there was 'insufficient and unsatisfactory' evidence of how things were; but saw far stronger arguments against intervening. He told Selborne his main reservation was that sending an army 'would wholly alter the character of the situation, involving us as is probable in a religious war' – and, worse, 'a permanent establishment in, and responsibility for the Soudan.' There would also, he was sure, be serious loss of life.

The next day Gladstone was 'alarmed' by a letter from Hartington to Granville, in which the former threatened to resign if no expedition were sent. It was a tense time: the Franchise Bill argument was at its height, and the Khedive was complaining about lack of funds. On 2 August Gladstone accepted the cabinet's view that £300,000 should be voted for an expedition, and preparations made in case it were needed. A week later the cabinet agreed a force should go to Wadi Halfa, 550 miles north of Khartoum. Still Gordon sent no word, which gave Gladstone a further excuse not to act, and Hartington an excuse to press him. He wrote to Hartington on 19 August to remind him that 'a movement of British troops . . . would be a step of great political importance, and clearly could not be decided on without reference to the members of the Cabinet.'[44] It was hardly likely to appease Hartington to add that assembling their colleagues would be 'inconvenient'. However, Gladstone's mind was opening to the possibility of an expedition. He asked Hartington how quickly that might be feasible, and what it would be designed to achieve.

Gordon now sent word that he needed reinforcements, mentioning tartly that he had asked for them on his arrival six months earlier but nothing had happened. On 23 August he asked Cairo for troops, and the message was sent on to England. 'Is it right', he asked, 'that I should have been sent here with only seven followers and no attention paid to me?'[45] The Queen saw this message and raged, even though by the time it reached London a relief force had been sent. Wolseley, who felt a heavy moral responsibility for the situation, told the general's brother that Gordon was 'the only man I have ever known who comes up to my notions of what a real hero is and should be.'

Gladstone, though, was becoming infuriated with him. He told Hartington that evidence Gordon was communicating with others but not with London seemed 'to strengthen the presumption that he purposely refrains from communicating with us. I nearly, though not quite, adopt words received today from Granville. It is clear, I think, that Gordon has our messages, and does not choose to answer them.' Gladstone wanted Gordon to leave Khartoum and move to Dongola, 300 miles to the north on the Nile, where he could be more easily relieved: but Gordon showed no desire to leave. Gladstone pressed on Hartington his fear that the arrival of a British force in Khartoum would provoke 'the very serious danger of stirring a religious war.' In his own journal, published shortly after his death, Gordon admitted that: 'I own to have been very insubordinate to Her Majesty's Government and its officials, but it is my nature and I cannot help it . . . I know if I was chief I would never employ myself, for I am incorrigible.'[46]

Although Gladstone let Hartington send a small separate force to Dongola, the prime minister and his allies still believed Gordon had exaggerated his plight: 'He is not, and apparently never has been, in the straits which he and his friends in this country have tried to make out,' Eddy Hamilton noted on 21 September.[47] Wolseley took a force to Egypt, arriving in Cairo on 9 September, but not until November were they ready to move to the Sudan. By then Gordon had sent his second-in-command and last British officer, Colonel John Stewart, down the Nile on a steamer with the remaining Europeans, but they were captured and massacred. Before he knew of Stewart's fate Gordon told London: 'The reason why I have now sent Colonel Stewart is because you have been silent all this while and neglected us, and lost time without doing any good.'[48] Stewart's death was particularly outrageous: his party were asked to a meal by a local sheikh, who murdered them.

Letters from Gordon started to come through; rumours and accounts of varying degrees of veracity appeared in the press, whipping up public sentiment; but the government was misled about events in Khartoum. As an under-secretary, Lord Edmond Fitzmaurice, told the Commons on 2 December, intelligence had it that 'the Mahdi's troops were suffering from disease, that food was very dear, and that the Arabs were deserting him'.[49] In fact the Mahdi's followers were multiplying, and were closing in on Khartoum. Throughout the autumn skirmishing continued: the garrison was, at least, still heavily armed. However, on 14 December – the 277th day of the siege – Gordon sent a letter to a friend in which he stated, simply: 'I think the game is up'.[50] The same day, however, he sent a message to Wolseley – which he received on 2 January – that read only 'Kartoum [sic] all right'.[51]

Wolseley went south, slowly. He telegraphed Hartington on 8 January to say that 'I am strong enough to relieve Khartoum', which soothed feelings in London.[52] He wanted some ships sent to the Nile as a show of strength. An advance column on two Nile steamers reached Khartoum on 28 January, only to find that 40,000 Mahdists had captured it two days earlier, minefields around it failing to stop them. Gordon had been killed at the Governor-General's palace, by a spear in the chest according to an alleged eye-witness, despite orders from the Mahdi to spare him.[53] Gordon's personal servant found his master's body decapitated, the head taken as a trophy to the Mahdi. In the mêlée Gordon's corpse disappeared – it may have been thrown down a well – and was never subsequently found. The carnage continued for hours after Gordon died, with an estimated 10,000 dead before the Mahdi called off his troops.

Gladstone – who was staying with Hartington at his house at Holker in north Lancashire – heard the news of the fall of Khartoum, telegraphed from Wolseley via Baring, just after 11 a.m. on the morning of 5 February

1885. Had he been in London he would have read it in *The Daily Telegraph*, to which the news had leaked in the early hours (the Foreign Office had had the telegram just after midnight) and which had printed a special late edition at 8 a.m. to announce it. 'Khartoum fell on the 26th. Sir C Wilson [Major-General Sir Charles Wilson, leading the advance relief force] arrived at Khartoum on the 28th, and found the place in the hands of the enemy . . . The fate of General Gordon is uncertain.'[54] Wilson had arrived by Nile steamer, but had not been able to land, and he and his force had had to be rescued from an island in the river. Wolseley surmised that Gordon was 'most probably a prisoner'.[55] With an odd sense of perspective, Gladstone said that 'the circumstances are sad & trying: it is one of the least points about them, that they may put an end to this Govt.'[56] He wrote to the Queen, who in her rage – and in her glee at having her prime minister, whom she detested, so embarrassed – rebuked him by uncoded telegram and, in case her wrath was insufficiently apparent, wired Hartington and Granville *en clair* too. Hamilton recorded that Gladstone 'resented not a little' this humiliation, 'a strong message to send through the hands of innumerable telegraphists'.[57] The telegram reached him at Cartmel railway station as he hastened back to London, being read by Post Office staff *en route*. 'The Government alone is to blame,' she wrote in her journal, 'by refusing to send the expedition till it was too late.'[58] Whatever her feelings, Ponsonby, her private secretary, had the measure of Gordon: he had noted the previous autumn that 'I don't believe the Christian lunatic has the slightest intention of coming back again.'[59]

Gladstone's reply to her was a masterpiece, starting by observing that he had 'had the honour this day to receive your Majesty's telegram *en clair*' telling him Khartoum could have been saved by earlier action, and continuing: 'Mr Gladstone does not presume to estimate the means of judgment possessed by your Majesty, but so far as his information and his recollection at the moment go, he is not altogether able to follow the conclusion which your Majesty has been pleased thus to announce.'[60] He argued that the diversion of much of Wolseley's force at Gordon's request to travel 'by a circuitous route along the river . . . to occupy Berber' had been the problem. When Hamilton complained to Ponsonby about the rebuke being sent *en clair*, Ponsonby simply replied that the Queen had 'with difficulty abstained from writing more strongly than she did.'[61]

On 7 February Gladstone told Hartington that while Gordon might have been holding out in some corner of Khartoum it was probably unlikely; if it could he ascertained that he was, then Gladstone agreed Wolseley should advance as soon as possible. Gordon had been dead for twelve days by then, and the blissful ignorance of this in London would soon end. Even before that news reached London, the fall of Khartoum had, as *The Times* put it, 'occasioned a shock which few will ever forget.'[62] The last word the nation had had of him was 'All right – could hold out for years', in a letter sent to Wolseley on 29 December: a strange thing for Gordon to have said given the pessimistic tone of his journals. Around Britain demands were made, from the Queen downwards, for swift, harsh retributive action to show the Dervishes who was in charge. Unfortunately for British public opinion, the Dervishes were.

The Times, in its leading article after news of Khartoum's fall reached London, described 'the mingled feelings of dismay, consternation, and indignant disgust universally evoked by this lamentable result of a long course of disregard of the elementary maxims of statesmanship.'[63] It had been 'a long series of blunders illuminated by the lightning flash of failure' and 'everything had been done that could add to the risks of defeat.' Since the appetite to extend the British Empire was keen – the scramble for Africa was in full swing – what had happened had a wider significance: 'It is the *reductio ad absurdum* of a whole policy, a disaster not only pregnant with instant dangers to our scattered troops, but carrying with it dangerous possibilities of disturbance in the remotest corners of the Empire. We have heard many comfortable sayings about the moral effects of our victories, but we shall now have to face the moral effect of a defeat that will efface them all.' The idea that Gladstone had not just sacrificed brave soldiers, but had by 'the long and deliberate abandonment' of Gordon suggested to the subject peoples of the Empire that they, too, could rise up and overthrow European rule, was deeply corrosive. The usually parsimonious, anti-imperialist prime minister persuaded the cabinet on 9 February to spend £2,750,000 on reinforcing Wolseley, so stricken was he.

The London newspapers reported Gordon's death on 11 February, following Wilson's arrival at Korti, north of Khartoum. A messenger said that a traitorous Egyptian pasha had led the garrison to the opposite side of the city from the one the Mahdists were approaching, while another traitor had opened the gates and let the invaders in. Gordon, he reported, had been stabbed. The country was put on a war footing: the garrison at Aldershot was told to stand by for departure overseas, and ships were made ready at Portsmouth; Gladstone weighed up whether to send Wolseley to re-capture Khartoum and have a holy war against the Mahdi.

The prime minister was seventy-five, and the stress affected his health. He was execrated for taking Lady Dalhousie to the theatre on the night of the 11th, one newspaper accusing him of being 'heartless'.[64] He stayed in bed on 12 February, laid low by an 'overaction of the bowels'.[65] The Queen went into a state of collapse too, and took to her bed for several days. 'Mr Gladstone and the Government have – the Queen *feels it dreadfully* – Gordon's innocent, noble, heroic blood on their consciences,' she told Ponsonby. 'May they *feel* it, and may they be *made to do so*!'[66] By now, the only function of an expedition to Khartoum could be punishment, given Gladstone did not want to conquer the Sudan; yet he realised Gordon must be avenged. He told the Commons on 19 February that Wolseley would move on Khartoum and engage with the Mahdists. Even the loyal Hamilton felt the tone 'bad form' since 'he paid no tribute of praise to Gordon; he said nothing of the valour of our troops'.[67] Two other senior officers died in the Sudan in battles involving Wolseley's expedition, Major-General Sir Herbert Stewart (who was succeeded by Wilson) and Major-General William Earle.

That Gladstone was riddled with guilt is beyond doubt. He wrote to Gordon's brother on 22 February telling him 'there are & will be many who will strive to learn lessons, in their several places, from this noble example of Christian heroism.'[68] He also proposed civil list pensions for Gordon's sisters. He then had to defend his actions in a four-day censure debate. The motion was not merely a rebuke for the loss of Gordon, Stewart and others, but a demand to ensure the security of Egypt and those parts of the Sudan necessary for the security of Egypt. The Liberals themselves were divided over whether to leave the Sudan to its own devices, a fact Northcote used to taunt Gladstone when not blaming him for Gordon's death.

Gladstone heaped praise on Gordon's memory – 'a hero among heroes' – but that did little to placate public feeling.[69] He defended the government by saying the policies Gordon had followed were his own initiative and not imposed upon him by the government. He doubted whether a force sent in the appalling heat of the previous summer would have made Gordon's position easier, or would simply have brought more losses and humiliation on the British Army and nation. He cited an account by a messenger who had left Khartoum on 28 December that described Gordon as in good health, happy, and with boats coming down the Nile stocked with food. And he said that even if a relief expedition had been sent a month earlier the Mahdi's forces, sitting near the city, would have heard of its imminent arrival and moved to kill Gordon and seize Khartoum whenever it was on its way: Gordon had gone to an inevitable death when he left England. The prime minister outlined the core of his imperial policy: 'We shall endeavour . . . to maintain the honour of the British name, to fulfil every engagement into which we have entered directly or constructively, and to discharge every duty, onerous though it may be, which is inseparable at a crisis of this kind from the possession of a great and a worldwide Empire.'[70]

Nothing Gladstone said could moderate the anger of many MPs. One, Colonel Dawnay, said that the prime minister, 'deaf to every warning and every entreaty, had deliberately abandoned to his fate the hero who for 11 months, alone and unaided, had upheld the cause of civilisation and the honour of England against Arab fanaticism.' Dawnay concluded, militantly, with a reference not just to the *débâcle* in the Sudan, but the record of unrest in Ireland: 'The sands of the existence of the present Parliament are running out. Its record is an unbroken one of evil, a record of triumphant sedition at home and needless and useless bloodshed abroad.'[71] Hicks Beach put it more succinctly: 'General Gordon has perished and Khartoum been lost simply because the Government would not make up their minds to act in time.'[72]

The public's reaction was of horror, grief and anger, with rage directed at the government. The censure debate was won by just fourteen votes, with the Irish voting against the government. Gladstone had not fallen, and indeed turned to his front bench when the vote was counted and uttered, 'That will do'.[73] But his administration was badly damaged, and his personal credibility received the worst blow of his career. *The Times* described the outcome as 'a severe defeat and a crushing blow to authority already reduced to the lowest point.'[74] The cabinet discussed whether the government should resign, but decided to stay until the Redistribution Bill had passed. John Bright dined with Gladstone after the debate, and was told that sending Gordon had been 'a great mistake' and he had been 'a man totally unsuited for the work he undertook'.[75] Gladstone also regretted he had not seen Gordon before he left London, so he had never had an authoritative briefing on what he should do. In

April, after intensive discussions in cabinet, Gladstone proposed to end military action in the Sudan and to evacuate it. The Queen, who felt Britain had endured enough humiliation, told him she was entirely opposed to the idea, even though Baring strongly argued for it.

A memorial service for Gordon was held in St Paul's on 13 March, as services were held in Westminster Abbey and in cathedrals all over England, on the request of the Archbishop of Canterbury, to mourn him and all those who had died in the Sudan. Parliament voted £20,000 to the Gordon family. A call went up for a national monument to the dead hero. Statues and memorials were raised to him around the country, notably in Trafalgar Square (it was moved in 1953 to the Embankment), and around the Empire. Gladstone resigned in June after a defeat on a Budget amendment, declined the Queen's offer of an earldom, and Salisbury took office without a dissolution. An election in December 1885 returned Gladstone to power in January, to the Queen's horror. Irish Home Rule, not Muslim fanaticism, brought him down within months. But the Grand Old Man had become the Murderer of Gordon.

V

Gladstone's indifference towards empire was not in tune with the spirit of the age, nor with the views of some of the most charismatic politicians of both parties. As noted, enthusiastic imperialists such as Rosebery and Chamberlain were influenced by *The Expansion of England*, believing the British had a peculiar responsibility and ability to civilise much of the world by bringing Christianity and British-style political institutions to them; yet it was Seeley who also wrote that the British seemed 'to have conquered and peopled half the world in a fit of absence of mind,' as if some of the consequences of the actions of buccaneers, explorers and soldiers had yet to sink in.[76] The economic considerations Seeley touched upon – the demand for raw materials and minerals, and the reservoir of cheap labour in the colonised areas – motivated the scramble for Africa: though it is hard to find evidence that the mother country made an overall profit. Economic motives were matched with a mission to civilise and take Christianity to heathen lands: the Church Missionary Society, and similar groups, had been in Africa in particular since the early nineteenth century.

Empire was viewed as a means to avert, staunch or reverse decay. It prized adventure, pioneering, sacrifice and leadership. It became an engine for patriotism, encouraging pride in Britain and preservation of the Empire and its supposedly civilising mission. It became a key purpose of the public schools to train young men for imperial life. But empire also fostered ideas of racial superiority, and tried to forge a national identity in which Englishness became synonymous with Britishness, leaving the Scots, Welsh and Irish marginalised – the Scots, great builders of empire, apparently willingly so.

Yet not everyone applauded the advance of Britannia, and there was a profound vein of anti-imperialism on the left, then in the ascendant. 'I have heard', Wells wrote in *The New Machiavelli* in 1910, 'of that apocryphal native ruler in the north-west, who, when asked what would happen if we left India, replied that in a week his men would be in the saddle, and in six months not a rupee nor a virgin would be left in Lower Bengal.' He said such stories were given as 'conclusive justification' of Britain's civilising force: stopping the savages – as many considered the populations of those lands – from being savage. 'But is it our business to preserve the rupees and virgins of Lower Bengal in a sort of magic inconclusiveness?' he asked. The Union Flag was simply 'a vast preventive', and Wells appears satirical in proclaiming 'better plunder than paralysis, better fire and sword than futility.'[77] This minority view of anti-imperialism flourished in Liberal, radical and socialist circles, especially after the Boer War, in which British conduct was far from civilised.

No one drove imperialism more than Chamberlain, whom Salisbury invited to be Colonial Secretary (as Chamberlain had desired) when forming the Unionist government in June 1895. Shortly before his appointment Joe's former *inamorata*, Beatrice Webb, had told her diary that history would judge him 'a pre-eminent parliamentarian, ill-equipped with knowledge, and damaged by an irretrievable vulgarity of method and ideals'.[78] Chamberlain foreswore vulgar ambition to Salisbury, saying he wanted the colonies 'in the hope of furthering closer union between them and the United Kingdom.'[79] He seemed to conceive of empire almost as one country of self-governing parts, loyal to the common head of state and pursuing a common policy. Many thought like him. Empire Day was established in Britain in 1904, to be observed on Queen Victoria's birthday, 24 May: the idea had started in Canada six years earlier thanks to Clementina Fessenden, a clergyman's wife who developed an obsession with the Queen, dressing herself permanently in black, like the Sovereign, when her own husband died in 1896. Empire Day was her means of strengthening links with Britain and with other parts of empire, and it quickly took off.

In May 1912 *The Times* reported: 'Empire Day was celebrated throughout the United Kingdom and in the Dominions yesterday. In most cases large gatherings of school children saluted the Union Jack and sang patriotic songs.'[80] The press and the music halls, sharing the common aim of making their customers feel better about themselves and their country, led the cheerleading for the imperial project, all the more so after the shock to morale dealt by the Second Boer War.

The day before Empire Day *The Times* published a dense forty-eight-page supplement about the wonders of empire and the imperial family. At the Guildhall 11,000 London elementary schoolchildren heard the Lord Mayor tell them that 'they were born and grew up to that grand inheritance which had been built up by successive generations who had set to work as English men and women to create new spheres and new countries.'[81] He continued: 'They had before them an opportunity of staying with the parent country or of going out to a wider field, where there might be even more room for their activity, intelligence and labour.' That was the new mission of every young Briton, offering a future radically different from their parents' or grandparents'.

When the Duke of Cornwall – the future Prince of Wales and, subsequently, George V – was about to visit Australia in 1901, a fortnight after the Queen's death, and just a month after the separate colonies had been united into a Commonwealth, the new King raised objections to his son leaving Britain at such a time. Balfour, putting the government's viewpoint, said he saw the King's point: but added that 'the King is no longer merely King of Great Britain and Ireland, and of a few dependencies whose whole value consisted in ministering to the wealth and security of Great Britain and Ireland. He is now the great constitutional bond uniting together in a single Empire communities of freemen separated by half the circumference of the globe All the patriotic sentiment which makes such an Empire possible centres in him, or chiefly in him: and everything which emphasises his personality to our kinsmen across the sea must be a gain both to the monarchy and the Empire.'[82]

The King agreed 'reluctantly' to the visit. Knollys, his private secretary, told Balfour he hoped ministers would remember that 'he is parting with his only son for several months at a time when he would most wish him to be by his side.'[83] But the King and his family were now not just the Royal family, but the Imperial family: Chamberlain had said in 1895 that 'the Crown constitutes the visible link between all portions of the British Empire.'[84] The head of the Duke of Cornwall's father appeared on the charmingly coloured postage stamps the Duke himself so avidly collected from around the Empire, and on its coins too. When he succeeded as King he left Britain once more, going to India to the Durbar at Delhi in 1911, to exhibit his imperial standing and British imperial power. He did so with Britain mired in constitutional and industrial crisis, for his duty, as his father had been made to understand in 1901, was now to a much wider realm than that girdled by the seas around the British Isles.

VI

In 1895, when Chamberlain took office, 11,000,000 white British subjects held 7,000,000 square miles of territory in the name of the Crown.[85] Canada was the only self-governing Dominion, and its foreign policy was run from London; Australia would federate in 1901 and New Zealand would become a Dominion in 1907. India was an empire of its own, also run from London from the India Office. The maintenance of this vast empire and associated colonies required a vast army and navy. There were imperial garrisons around the world, and British dockyards on five continents. The 1891 census showed 249,000 men in the Armed Forces; by 1901, because of the Boer War, there were 422,700; by 1911, even though no war was being fought, but because of an arms race stimulated by the growth of German power, the figure had fallen back only to 342,800.[86] The Empire put military culture at the heart of British society in a way it had never been in the country's history, even before the outbreak of the Great War brought it into almost every family.

The growth of empire made it more important that Britain should have command of the seas. In May 1889 parliament passed the Naval Defence Act, which enshrined the two-power standard in British naval policy. Thus Britain was compelled by law to have a Navy at least as strong as the next two largest navies put together – which, in the late 1880s, were France's and Russia's. The Act came after years of reluctance to increase defence spending, the *volte-face* provoked by inquiries into the Navy concluding it was underpowered. The Salisbury administration, under public pressure, agreed to spend £21.5 million over five years to expand the fleet. This provided ten new battleships, thirty-eight cruisers – vital for protecting imperial supply lines – eighteen torpedo boats and four gunboats by 1894. However, far from deterring others from expanding their navies, the formal adoption of a two-power standard encouraged them. When Britain had built its ten battleships, France and Russia had built twelve, and the United States and Germany – Britain's two main economic rivals – were entering the race. Naval expenditure continued to increase, but to uncertain effect. The strength of the Royal Navy would, though, prove essential in the scramble for Africa. The European powers had carved up much of Africa, notably the unconquered regions of the west and the north, in the 1880s at the Berlin Conference of 1885, presided over by Bismarck.

Britain's place in Egypt remained secure – a place ever more vital since the opening of the Suez Canal in 1869 – but a threat was posed by a French expedition in 1898 to take control of Fashoda on the White Nile. The French were trying to form a transcontinental trading route from the Atlantic to French Somaliland on the Red Sea, along the southern edge of the Sahara and through an area of northern-central Africa designated at Berlin as their sphere of influence.

However, had they taken control of Fashoda they would have crossed the route imperialists such as Chamberlain and Cecil Rhodes had earmarked to link Cairo to the Cape, and would potentially have excluded Britain from the Sudan; and at that very moment, a British-led force under the command of General Sir Herbert Horatio Kitchener was securing the Sudan for the Queen Empress. Fashoda itself was worth little: Britain's determination to stop France having it was partly about imperial *amour propre*, with European rivalries having to be played out on another continent, and partly indicative of the spirit of acquisitiveness and materialism that had come to feed the imperial dream.

For thirteen years since Gordon's death there had been unfinished business in the Sudan, and on 2 September Kitchener's combined British, Egyptian and Sudanese force of 25,000 men confronted the 50,000-strong army of Dervishes loyal to Abdullah al-Taashi, the *soi-disant* successor to the Mahdi, just north of the Mahdist capital of Omdurman, a village in what are now the suburbs of Khartoum. Although the Dervishes used guns as well as spears, Kitchener's forces had artillery, which bombarded them from a distance of over a mile and a half, and Maxim guns and rifles to deal with any who continued to advance. Seeking to cut off the Dervishes' retreat, Kitchener deployed the 21st Lancers in a cavalry charge. No one knew there were 2,500 Dervish infantry hidden in a dip in the landscape, but the 400 cavalrymen – one of whom was Winston Churchill, a young subaltern – nonetheless drove them back, winning three Victoria Crosses in the process but sustaining seventy casualties and losing 119 horses. Each Dervish attack brought another wave of slaughter by British arms. The result was an overwhelming victory, though Abdullah escaped, to be killed the following year.

An estimated 10,000 Dervishes were killed, 13,000 wounded and 5,000 captured. Kitchener lost forty-seven men with a further 382 wounded. Not for the last time he attracted criticism for the number of wounded he allowed to be killed after the battle. Ernest Bennett, present as a journalist, wrote in the *Contemporary Review* of the conqueror's inhuman methods against the vanquished. Churchill made a similar criticism in his book on Omdurman published the following year. Conscious of his political ambitions, he toned it down in later editions.

Britain lauded Kitchener as a hero; he was ennobled as Lord Kitchener of Khartoum; and all over Britain streets in the housing boom were named after Omdurman. His celebrity showed how far the idea of British expansionism sustained contemporary heroism; so much so that the government, beyond bestowing a peerage on Kitchener, awarded him the huge sum of £30,000 from public funds as 'some signal mark of her [the Queen's] favour upon him'.[87] Empire was more than ever about boosting Britain in the world, and those who contributed could expect the highest rewards.

Kitchener was then dispatched to deal with the French. On 18 September he arrived at Fashoda with gunboats, having sailed up the Nile, presented his compliments to the commander of the small French force and agreed with him to await instructions from their respective governments. France backed down, not because of having any less right to engage in rampant expansionism than the British, but because had they chosen to fight over Fashoda the Royal Navy would have humiliated them. Also, in the list of French fears, Germany ranked higher than Britain, and Britain could, as the French saw it even six years before the Entente Cordiale, be the most useful ally were Germany to become a threat again.

Fashoda was not the only European tussle. As Africa's wealth became more apparent, and as rival European powers began to build power bases on the continent, British imperial priorities changed. This was apparent from 1890, when Britain challenged a Portuguese claim to land that became northern and southern Rhodesia and Nyasaland, on the grounds that British commercial interests effectively occupied it. If Portugal's claim had succeeded it would have controlled a band of Africa from the Atlantic Coast to the Indian Ocean; and would have thwarted the British South Africa Company, controlled by Cecil Rhodes, which had started to exploit the land in 1888.

The BSAC solicited London to object to Portugal's claim, even though that nation had been the first to explore Africa and had long-held claims to parts of the continent. Local consular officials declared British protectorates in parts of Nyasaland, Mashonaland and Matabeleland – the future Rhodesia – where for the preceding year or so Portugal had had a form of protectorate, before its influence could become entrenched. The Foreign Office, under pressure from Rhodes, confirmed British support for these. In dealing with Portugal, as with France at Fashoda eight years later, might would be right. On 11 January 1890 Britain issued an ultimatum to Portugal to withdraw troops from the disputed region or else Britain would withdraw its minister from Lisbon. Given the relative military strength of the two countries, and knowing it could not force the issue, Portugal quickly agreed. It was viewed as a national humiliation and brought down the Portuguese government: and also showed the ruthlessness with which Britain was prepared to prosecute its commercial interests, and expansionism.

Portugal's renewed interest came only after the explorations of David Livingstone had opened up Nyasaland, and after trading operations on Christian principles – notably anti-slavery, and underpinned by the teachings of Presbyterian missionaries – had begun there. When imperialists talked of projecting British or 'civilised' values, this was what they meant. But Portugal's attempt to expand beyond its colonies in Angola and Mozambique, and to link the two across a continent, was thwarted by its lack of force. As the jingoes often said, they had the guns, the men and the money, and were prepared to use them.

Throughout the 1890s the British secured as much of east Africa as they could, as well as consolidating in the west – in May 1892, for example, the Royal Niger Company had moved into the Nigerian interior, which was rich in minerals, and in 1901 the country would formally become a protectorate. Similar processes had been followed in east Africa – commercial pioneers, having established the potential of the lands they sought to exploit, were happy to hand over their governance to the Colonial Office in London in return for the British government and Armed Forces protecting their investments. Commercial gain was a main driver of imperialism, but not the only one: there were also humanitarian considerations, and the ideal of improving local governance. Part of what would become Nigeria was the city of Benin on the southern coast, which had acquired a new commercial importance in the nineteenth century because of its trade in textiles and in palm oil. This trade was attractive to Britain, as were local rubber plantations. After thirty years of resisting overtures to become a protectorate, Benin allegedly signed a treaty in 1892 in which it promised to do two non-commercial things that would help appease British sensibilities: to abolish the slave trade and end human sacrifice. It also apparently agreed to accept British jurisdiction and effectively become a colony. However, there was an immediate dispute over whether Benin's ruler, the Oba, had actually agreed to much that was in the treaty, or had been bamboozled into signing it, or indeed had signed it himself at all. Certainly H. L. Gallwey, the vice-consul who had proposed the treaty, was unable to give a clear account of what had or had not been agreed.

Tensions simmered until late 1896. The Oba showed what he thought of the British by continuing slavery and human sacrifice. The acting consul-general of the Niger Coast Protectorate, James Phillips, proposed to take a force into Benin that December disguised as a trading mission, with weapons hidden in their baggage. He asked London for permission but acted on his own initiative before having a reply. On 4 January 1897 his force was intercepted and massacred, with only two officers surviving. One precept of the imperial attitude was that small countries could not be allowed to behave in this way towards British subjects, even those acting without authority, and so what was termed the Benin Punitive Expedition was sent to avenge the massacre, and settle Benin's future.

Rear-Admiral Sir Harry Rawson, commander of the Cape of Good Hope Station, sailed up to Benin with 1,200 men, arriving on 9 February. The previous year Rawson had fought supposedly the shortest war in history, the Anglo-Zanzibar War, which lasted thirty-eight minutes (from 9.02 a.m. until 9.40 a.m. on 27 August 1896, as long as it took to wreck the Sultan's palace and force a surrender). He was similarly businesslike in Benin. His orders to his force, mainly composed of Royal Marines but also of naval ratings and men of the Niger Coast Protectorate Forces, were to burn down everything in sight, bring back what loot they could (to cover the costs of the expedition) and to hang the Oba if they found him. Many cultural artefacts were thus saved, and auctioned the following summer: the Oba was sent into exile rather than hanged. Benin, or what was left of it, became British.

The torching of Benin shows how British policy had developed since the 1870s, when the main concern was to hold Egypt to secure the Suez Canal, and to hold the Cape to command the Cape route. The recognition that Africa was rich in minerals, not least gold and diamonds, turned the focus away from the coasts, and attracted the interest of entrepreneurs and buccaneers. The Tory government that held office for most of the period from 1886 to 1905 supported and endorsed this expansionism, and, most important, made the Armed Forces available to secure and hold these territories in the name of the Queen and thereby establish British hegemony and greater influence, relative to Britain's continental neighbours. In one of the three years in that period when there was no Tory government the country was run by Rosebery, the great Liberal imperialist. Then, in 1892, Rhodes proposed linking Cairo and the Cape by rail, not just by a telegraph wire. A British protectorate in Uganda after 1894, and the establishment of protectorates further south by the BSAC, made this more feasible: but there was a missing link, Tanganyika, controlled by the Germans until they lost it at Versailles. Britain had not just a slice of Africa, but a slice with the richest mineral deposits both in east and west Africa, it controlled the main trade routes, and above all its military power ensured it called the tune.

Although the commercial imperative for imperialism was obvious – especially to those profiting from it – the idea that a higher civilisation was being exported to hitherto primitive peoples held fast among those seeking a moral justification for conquest. Kipling articulated it most tellingly and, in retrospect, notoriously in 1899, eight months before the Second Boer War broke out:

> Take up the White Man's burden, Send forth the best ye breed –
> Go bind your sons to exile, To serve your captives' need;
> To wait, in heavy harness, On fluttered folk and wild –
> Your new-caught sullen peoples, Half devil and half child.[88]

The 'burden' included fighting 'savage wars of peace' and incurring 'the blame of those ye better, The hate of those ye guard'. When Kipling is accused of racism, these lines are usually invoked. He cannot be judged by twenty-first-century standards: he sincerely believed in the civilising mission.

VII

Britain fought the Second Boer War, between 1899 and 1902, for hegemony in southern Africa, and to secure control over its enormous mineral wealth – not least gold and diamonds. Troops from all over the Empire – not just British, but Australians, Canadians, New Zealanders, Indians and South Africans loyal to the Crown – fought, confirming Seeley's theory about the oneness of British identity wherever it was found in the Empire. This imperial unity did not end the war quickly, but it did show a coherence among the British diaspora that would become vital in the Great War. It confirmed the extent of British imperial power and, to its rivals, the power of the United Kingdom. However, it bore little resemblance to Kipling's ideal of the civilising mission.

The two Boer Wars – one lasting just three months from December 1880 to March 1881, the other two and a half years from October 1899 to May 1902 – illustrate precisely the type of problem Seeley had not foreseen. In them, challenges came not from a conquered indigenous African population, but from white settlers not of British descent. When this problem came to a head – the issue forced by the British – not only did it expose the weaknesses of the imperial power, but also shook the faith of millions of Britons in an imperial project that had, up until that point, been predominantly a source of glory and national pride.

Britain had acquired the Cape Colony in 1814, after defeating the Dutch (who had been there since 1652) in a battle in 1806. They rapidly populated it and marginalised the Dutch there. The last straw for the Dutch was Britain's abolition of slavery in 1834, which caused a mass migration from the Cape – the Great Trek – to Natal. Britain colonised that in 1843, which drove the Boers to the interior where they founded the two Boer republics: in the Transvaal in 1852, and the Orange Free State two years later. Britain's attempt to annex the Transvaal in 1877 led to the First Boer War three years later. Britain lost after the Boers' largely amateur army won the Battle of Majuba Hill on 27 February 1881, killing the general in command, Sir George Colley, two other officers and eighty-two men. Another 131 officers and men were wounded and fifty-seven taken prisoner, with an indeterminate number missing, out of a force of 723. The news was in London within hours. It was a terrible blow to Britain's reputation and to Gladstone's administration at a time when it was focused upon problems in Ireland, and the damage they were doing.

Hugh Childers, the War Secretary, admitted on 1 March that he knew only what was in the newspapers: the immediacy of news made this a new sort of war. Childers asked the press to show restraint, because if troop movements became known to the Boers this 'cannot but be injurious to the public interests.'[89] Three divisions were sent as reinforcements, and General Sir Frederick Roberts went to command the forces in Natal, assisted by Acting Brigadier-General Sir Evelyn Wood, who had been second-in-command to Colley. Wood began negotiations with the Boers at once. A truce followed on 6 March, and a peace was settled within weeks that confirmed British recognition of the two republics. But such was the desire for revenge among a section of the British public who wished to reverse this humiliation, not to mention Britain's growing entrepreneurial and mercantile ambition, that it became apparent further challenges would be issued. It was also clear that the shocking nature of the defeat should prevent Britain underestimating the Boers again.

Once gold was discovered in the Transvaal in 1886 the area became of intense interest to British buccaneers. Sparsely populated, the republic needed substantial immigration to exploit its potential; so that by the mid-1890s immigrants outnumbered the Boers who had settled the area. One recent arrival from Britain, Cecil Rhodes, had from 1871 (when just eighteen) managed to buy most of the diamond mines around Kimberley, helped initially with funding from Rothschild's. Once diamonds had been discovered in the Orange Free State the land was successfully annexed by the British-controlled Cape Colony. A similar move on the goldfields of the Transvaal would not be so easy.

Rhodes, a grammar-school boy from Bishop's Stortford, would become a high priest of British imperialism, and the greatest exponent of expansionism. He persuaded Britain to threaten force in throwing Portugal out of Nyasaland, Mashonaland and Matabeleland. His first step in politics was to become a member of the Cape Colony parliament, in 1880. Within a decade he was prime minister, running a legislative programme that assisted the exploitation of the mineral wealth of the area and reduced the influence of the black population. His business interests encircled and penetrated the Boer republics.

By the mid-1890s Boer policies towards the foreigners, or *uitlanders*, who had come to the Transvaal to exploit its mineral wealth were irritating Rhodes. They not only taxed *uitlanders* heavily, but restricted their right to vote. The main city, Johannesburg, became a cauldron of dissent, with many of its more prominent citizens demanding secession. Rhodes's British South Africa Company had colonised a substantial territory to the north of the Transvaal, occupied by the Matabele tribe, which from 1898 would be known as Rhodesia. Justifying an intervention as good for the Empire, as it would secure this wealth and with it the whole of southern Africa, Rhodes planned an incursion from Rhodesia that would support a rebellion in the republic.

The *casus belli* for this incursion, or raid, was a dispute in late 1895 over the price the Transvaal government sought to charge Cape Colony for access to the railway through its territory to Johannesburg. The colonists sent goods by wagon train instead, using fords, or drifts, on the Vaal river. When Paul Kruger, the president of the Transvaal Republic, decided to close them, war seemed inevitable. Kruger backed down because of the harm this blockade did to the republic's economy; but the *uitlanders* knew they needed to prevent such a situation again, and that was best achieved by controlling the Boer republics. Rhodes and Chamberlain, who had a history of mutual suspicion founded partly on Rhodes's having given Parnell £10,000, were in close contact about this; and evidence eventually emerged that Chamberlain colluded in the raid. He knew the rights of the *uitlanders* had to be secured, and that the Boers had ordered huge amounts of arms. On 1 November 1895, back from a seven-week holiday in Spain, Chamberlain sent a message to the High Commissioner at the Cape about the closure of the drifts, saying Britain would fight if necessary to rectify the situation. The message was sent straight on to Kruger, warning him about his 'act of hostility'.[90]

Seven weeks before the raid, in November 1895 at a dinner in honour of the new Governor of Western Australia – Australian unification was a high priority for the Colonial Secretary – Chamberlain had spoken sincerely of 'that imperial unity which we cherish as the ideal future of the British race.'[91] His vision was deeply patriotic: he saw empire enabling 'this old country of ours to extend its fame and its history in the greatness of its children across the sea.' He outlined his qualifications for being Colonial Secretary: 'In the first place I believe in the British Empire, and in the second place I believe in the British race. I believe that the British race is the greatest of governing races that the world has ever seen . . . I believe there are no limits accordingly to its future.'

The Chartered Company for Matabeleland, of which Rhodes was chairman, told Chamberlain that the moment was ripe for an uprising in the Transvaal. They did not tell him – according to a memorandum he wrote after the event – that Rhodes had ordered a force to be ready at the Transvaal border to invade the republic. However, Chamberlain did permit the Chartered Company to recruit members of the Bechuanaland Border Police, which was about to be disbanded, and was at ease with the idea of a rebellion that would allow London to force the issue. J. L. Garvin, Chamberlain's friend and biographer, denies in his *Life* that any private meetings happened before the raid between the Colonial Secretary and Rutherfoord Harris, Rhodes's 'factotum' in London.[92]

Dr Leander Starr Jameson, administrator of the Chartered Company, would lead the raid. Jameson, a forty-two-year-old Scot, was a doctor of some repute. His health failed and he moved to Kimberley for the climate, setting up a prominent medical practice. He soon showed other executive abilities and one of his patients, Rhodes, made use of them in developing Rhodesia. Most who knew Jameson regarded him with awe and devotion, and Kipling admitted he inspired his poem 'If'.[93] Circumstances would require Jameson to keep his head while all around him lost theirs. Around 600 men, 400 of whom were Matabele mounted police, formed his raiding party. They were armed with rifles, but also had some machine guns and light artillery. The idea was that when the *uitlanders* rebelled in Johannesburg and captured key strategic targets – such as the Boers' armoury – Jameson would invade to impose a ceasefire that left the *uitlanders* in control.

When Chamberlain was told in mid-December that the uprising might not happen soon he was worried: the longer it was postponed, the more chance of foreign intervention on the Boers' side. The Germans had made threatening noises. He was relieved when information suggested, on 19 December, that a rebellion might blow up within 'about ten days'.[94] On Boxing Day he wrote to Salisbury that 'I have received private information that a rising in Johannesburg is imminent'. He mentioned that, following discussions with the War Office, two troopships would put in at the Cape in early January, the men to be available if needed. 'If the rising is successful it ought to turn to our advantage', he added.[95]

The raid was a shambles. There was a split among the *uitlanders* about what should happen next – 'the capitalists financing the movement made the hoisting of the British Flag a *sine qua non*. This the National Union rejected', Sir Hercules Robinson, the High Commissioner, reported – and they advised Jameson to stay his hand.[96] Chamberlain was informed, and passed the news of the non-event to Salisbury at once, predicting that the uprising 'is going to fizzle out'.[97] However, another report reached him that a raid was being prepared despite the absence of a rebellion: and he at once sent a 'strictly personal and confidential' word to Robinson to tell Rhodes that the government could not possibly support such an action; what had happened was 'a fiasco . . . owing probably to Rhodes having misjudged the balance of opinion'.[98] The message arrived after Jameson had left, having decided to force the issue, on 30 December 1895. The next day, having heard from Robinson, Chamberlain told Salisbury that 'Dr Jameson . . . has crossed the border with Transvaal with 800 armed police. This is a flagrant piece of filibustering for which there is no justification'.[99] The British Agent in the Transvaal had told Kruger he could not believe British troops were involved; Robinson 'repudiated the act and ordered force to return immediately'.[100]

The raiders, thinking they were cutting the telegraph wire to Pretoria, cut a fence instead: thus the Boers were still able to be informed of their every move. Chamberlain saw how disastrously this could be represented. He told Salisbury the raid could not be supported without confirming German suspicions of the ruthless nature of British imperialism. It was the night of the servants' ball at Chamberlain's house, Highbury, but he realised he could not attend. He told some of his children what had happened, and said: 'If this succeeds, it will ruin me. I am going up to London to crush it.'[101] He telegraphed Robinson to 'leave no stone unturned to prevent mischief', and had Rhodes warned that his company could lose its charter if it transpired he had been involved. 'Represent to Rhodes', he told Robinson, 'the true character of Jameson in breaking into a foreign state in friendly treaty relations with Her Majesty at a time of peace.'[102]

Chamberlain sent a telegram *en clair* to Kruger regretting Jameson's action, confirming that messengers had been sent to call him back and asking: 'Can I co-operate with you further in this emergency in endeavouring to bring about a peaceful arrangement which is essential to all interests in South Africa?'[103] Rhodes repudiated the raiders immediately. The Boers ran rings around them – they had between them just six Maxim guns and four cannons – killed several and made the rest surrender. They were taken to Pretoria and thrown in jail. The prisoners were turned over to the British, and the ringleaders tried in London. Rhodes managed to avoid trial; but Jameson, who would in 1904 become prime minister of Cape Colony, and be rewarded with a baronetcy for his part in forming the Union of South Africa in 1910, served fifteen months in Holloway. He became a national hero thanks to the Germans, however. Kaiser Wilhelm II, in what would not be his last amateur excursion into diplomacy, congratulated Kruger for having seen the raiders off. This caused outrage among a public bristling with anti-German feeling, and who knew Germany was now both economically and militarily Britain's main rival.

The BSAC paid the Transvaal £1 million in reparations, and Rhodes was forced to resign as prime minister of Cape Colony. He and Chamberlain agreed to protect each other, and their ploy worked, thanks not least to seven telegrams going missing. Years later they emerged: one, dated 13 August 1895, said that 'Chamberlain will do anything to assist . . . provided he officially does not know of your plan.'[104] The *uitlanders* who had plotted the rebellion were tried for treason and the ringleaders sentenced to death: one was Rhodes's brother Frank, a colonel in the British Army. The sentences were commuted to fifteen years in prison, but the ringleaders were released in June 1896 on paying huge fines. A vacuum had been created in Matabeleland; and the Ndebele, soon joined by the Shona, revolted against white settlers in what became the Second Matabele War. It took until October 1897 for British troops to prevail.

That, though, was not the raid's only consequence. The Transvaal concluded a formal alliance with the Orange Free State and began to import huge quantities of arms. Chamberlain's political position was precarious, but the establishment closed ranks to keep secret the extent to which he, and Robinson, knew of the raid. As Jameson's subsequent rise would prove, not only did successful imperialism require ruthlessness, risk-taking and buccaneering, but the establishment would overlook such vulgar conduct if it had the right result.

A colonial secretary could not, however, be party to this, and the very public way in which Chamberlain repudiated the raid had, for him, the desired result. In February 1896, when Parliament reassembled, Harcourt, as leader of the opposition, intoned: 'I think we ought all to express our complete approval of the conduct of the Colonial Secretary [Cheers] and of the statesmanlike courage, promptitude, and decision with which he has disengaged all responsibility on the part of the British Government for this deplorable attack made upon a friendly State by men for whose actions we are *prima facie* responsible. [Hear, hear!]'[105]

Sir Graham Bower, Robinson's private secretary, was scapegoated for British complicity, and packed off to Mauritius. British honour and face were saved. Rhodes could have destroyed Chamberlain by revealing details of his personal complicity, and of his hope that if a raid happened it was sooner rather than later. Instead the select committee – chaired by Harcourt, with Chamberlain part of it – charged with investigating the raid acquitted Chamberlain entirely, taking his word as a gentleman that he had known nothing. He survived, to wreak havoc among Unionists as he had done among Liberals.

VIII

The raid's main consequence was the Second Boer War. It was fought in a mood of jingoism bred not just by Kruger's policies but by the Diamond Jubilee of 1897. The Jubilee did not just reinforce an idea of Britain as the world's superpower; it also bred a sentimental patriotism that left the ethics of imperialism largely unquestioned. For Edwin Clayhanger 'whenever he thought of it, his fancy saw pennons and corslets and chargers winding their way through stupendous streets, and somewhere in the midst, the majesty of England in the frail body of a little old lady, who had had many children and one supreme misfortune.'[106]

However mighty Britain might be, the rights of *uitlanders* to participate in the governments of the Transvaal and the Orange Free State remained limited. The Boers resisted equal suffrage for those of British descent because they feared they would dominate the Boer republics and, therefore, the whole of southern Africa. However, by early 1899 these disabilities had become the subject of intense negotiation between the British and the Boers. In May 1897 Chamberlain had chosen Sir Alfred Milner, chairman of the Board of the Inland Revenue, to be Governor of the Cape Colony and High Commissioner for Southern Africa. His mission was to bring about a South Africa unified under the Crown: a tall order while Britain guaranteed the independence of the Boer republics. Milner, of mixed Anglo-German descent, was only forty-three and had had a meteoric and brilliant career. A first from Balliol had been briefly followed by a fellowship at New College, brief because of Milner's innate restlessness. This also led to his being called to the bar, but he never practised, instead going to *The Pall Mall Gazette* as an assistant to John Morley, and then to Stead. He was attracted to politics and fought and lost the 1885 general election as a Liberal. Goschen took him up; and when he became Chancellor in 1887 used his patronage to make Milner under-secretary of finance in Egypt.

Such was Milner's success in managing Egypt's money – he staved off the country's bankruptcy and introduced wide-ranging structural reforms that improved the long-term soundness of the economy – that he earned his place at the Inland Revenue and, aged just forty-one, his knighthood. The opposition as well as the government warmly endorsed his mission to southern Africa, with Asquith presiding over a grand dinner for him on his departure. The mission was clear, though not straightforward: it was to lead discussions with the Transvaal and the Orange Free State to grant equal rights to *uitlanders*. There was, though, another agenda, unspoken by the British government, which was the desire to control a route from Cairo to the Cape; and the knowledge that whoever controlled the gold and diamond reserves of the Boer republics controlled southern Africa.

Milner, an avowed imperialist, was determined to control the republics, ostensibly to prevent Britain's retreat from southern Africa. It has also been alleged that he was closely associated to a network of businessmen led by Alfred Beit, the leading player in the international gold markets and a crony of Rhodes, and had a secret agenda to further Beit's and his business's prospects. However, the furtherance of Beit's prospects also furthered Britain's, and the accusation of complicity with Milner ties in with anti-Semites of the time blaming the Boer War on a Jewish conspiracy; Beit's other big partner was another Jewish businessman based in London, Lionel Phillips. Together they controlled the main mining syndicate in southern Africa, H. Eckstein and Company.

The difficulty was squaring the treaty signed after the First Boer War to safeguard the existence of the republics along with naked expansionism. The Transvaal overwhelmingly re-elected Kruger as President in 1898, further entrenching the Boers' position. Milner decided to ramp up the pressure: he chose to deliver a speech in a Boer enclave in Cape Colony on 3 March 1898, advocating equality for Britons in the Transvaal and urging Boers to join his campaign for these fundamental liberties. Given his wish to have Britain control the republics, this was disingenuous to say the least.

Milner's idea backfired. Exercising a right denied to the British minority in the republics, Boers in the Cape Colony mobilised to elect one of their own, William Philip Schreiner, as prime minister in October 1898. The next month Milner, fearing Britain's grip on southern Africa was about to be loosened, visited England for talks with Chamberlain. He was back in the Cape by February 1899, with full backing to pursue *uitlanders'* rights. He sent a dispatch to the Colonial Office on 4 May, for public consumption, recommending intervention and describing the subjection of Britons in the republics as damaging to British imperial prestige and credibility. Milner ensured that the leading Cape Dutch knew of the contents of his dispatch, and the most prominent, Jan Hendrik Hofmeyr, a moderate, urged at once that Milner and Kruger sit down and talk. Hofmeyr warned Kruger to make concessions, and of the likely consequences if he did not: he knew Milner would force this to a fight, and doubted that in the next Boer War the Dutch would win.

The two met at Bloemfontein between 31 May and 5 June. Milner set out his demands, which he knew Kruger would reject. The first was to give *uitlanders* of over five years' residence the vote at once; the second was to conduct business in the Transvaal parliament in English; and the third was that London had to rubber-stamp laws the parliament passed. Kruger realised he had been forced into a corner. He offered the vote in two years' time for those resident since before 1890, and the vote for others seven years hence. Reputedly, he left the conference in tears. Milner was delighted by the outcome. A master of public relations, he used the press and the speed of modern communications to get his version of events out first: newspaper readers learned the Milner version days before parliament was formally told of the breakdown of talks. Lord Selborne, under-secretary for the colonies, said this news was 'unfortunately true', but Chamberlain saw nothing unfortunate about the truth at all.[107]

After an interval to allow Kruger to relent, and after a cabinet meeting on 8 September at which Boer intransigence and the dispatch of 10,000 troops to Natal were discussed, Chamberlain called for voting rights for *uitlanders*. Britain talked up the prospect of Boers invading Cape Colony, and evacuations of women and children began from border towns. Chamberlain and Milner reiterated in early October that they merely sought the same privileges for Britons in the Boer republics that Boers enjoyed in Cape Colony. Confident these would not be granted, the government had from June onwards sent troops from Britain to Durban, whence they entrained for Ladysmith. They were sent ostensibly to defend Britons and British property, and not yet in numbers sufficient to wage war.

This irritated Wolseley, the commander-in-chief, until permission to send troops came after 8 September: the government had until then feared that a large force would provoke war, not prevent one. Wolseley had already sent an unofficial force under a trusted officer, Colonel Robert Baden-Powell. He was forty-two, a veteran of the Zulu and Second Matabele Wars and son of a clergyman and Oxford geometry professor. His background was in intelligence, which he gathered by posing as a butterfly-collector. He had orders to raise a corps of Volunteers, and to acquire stores and supplies discreetly. He made his headquarters at Mafeking, in northern Cape Colony near Bechuanaland, just across the Transvaal border. He told journalists who had followed him there that his garrison was prepared for any Boer attack.

On 7 October the Army reserve was called up. This meant 25,000 of the 62,000 men on the reserve list being liable for service in southern Africa. There then followed a shock to British sensibilities; more than 40 per cent of recruits, whether from the reserve or from the adventurous young men who volunteered, were unfit for service, mostly because they were suffering from rickets. The crisis had exposed the real condition of the working classes in a supposed land of plenty.

Kruger, in a press interview on 9 October, pronounced the situation 'very grave'.[108] Liberal politicians, including Morley and Harcourt, began vociferously to condemn the government's bellicose tactics. Beatrice Webb called the activities of the British on the Cape 'underbred'.[109] Wider public opinion, however, had it that the Boers, not the British, had breached the convention guaranteeing the independence of the republics, in denying equal rights to *uitlanders*; and therefore war was permissible. Everything had been entirely predictable since Milner's dispatch and Chamberlain's speech.

The press reported Boer outrages on women and children fleeing the republics to the Cape Colony or to Lourenço Marques in Portuguese East Africa, which only stoked up jingoism. Then Kruger, on 9 October, issued an ultimatum: British forces on his borders had to go within forty-eight hours, in accordance with his government's interpretation of the 1884 convention. All reinforcements sent to Africa since 1 June 1899 had to leave Africa, and none in transit could be landed at any southern African port, or the Transvaal and the Orange Free State would declare war on Britain.

Britain rejected the ultimatum, the delivery of which *The Times* described as 'an infatuated step' and a 'wanton action'.[110] The newspaper, whose editor, Henry Buckle, was close to Balfour, said that had a great power issued such a document it must have led to war; for a 'petty Republic' to have done so was an act of 'studied and insolent defiance'. It said the Boers were 'bent upon deciding their controversy with us by the sword, and by the sword it must now be decided.' Milner and Chamberlain had wanted this for years; the ultimatum was the excuse for the war they, and much of the British public, wanted. 'They have declared war upon the British Empire,' *The Times* intoned. 'They must feel her arm and pay the penalty of their aggression . . . Napoleon in his palmiest days could not have made more insolent demands on England than these.' This was the zenith of empire, and of British self-assurance and self-righteousness. *The Times's* leader concluded: 'The sons of CROMWELL and of BLAKE will cry, "Strike, England, and strike home." It is the old cause.'

It was assumed the war would last weeks or months, not years; an estimation so wrong it makes it all the more surprising that similar sentiments were uttered in 1914. The Boers entered Cape Colony and Natal immediately, their fighting men mainly volunteer farmers in their work clothes. Within a week these militias numbered between 30,000 and 40,000 men. They made for British garrisons at Mafeking, Ladysmith and Kimberley: so when General Sir Redvers Buller arrived with reinforcements to lead an anti-Boer offensive, they instead had to be divided up and used to try to end the sieges.

Ladysmith, in Natal, under the command of Sir George Stuart White, was the first garrison the Boers attacked. It had been reinforced the previous June with 15,000 troops from India and the Mediterranean. White took the fight to the Boers by assaulting their artillery positions, hoping to knock out their siege guns. This attack was ineffectual and a catastrophe for the Ladysmith garrison, 140 of whose men were killed and another 1,000 taken prisoner. From 2 November 1899 until 28 February 1900 the Boers besieged it, cutting the railway line to Durban. On the last train out were two officers whose names would recur in British military history, Major-General John French and his chief of staff, Major Douglas Haig. Ironically, French had lost a fortune dabbling in South African mining shares, and had been saved from bankruptcy by a £2,500 loan from Haig.

White communicated by heliograph, using the sun to flash Morse code signals. He was confident of early relief, but the first column of reinforcements under Buller himself was defeated at the Battle of Colenso on 15 December. Buller urged White either to try to break out or to surrender; White refused to try to get out as his horses were in poor condition for want of proper feed, and would not hear of surrendering. In early January 1900 the Boers tried to storm the town again, but failed after a bloodbath in which the British came off worse, with 175 dead against fifty-two Boers. By this time the garrison was on its last legs, its water supply cut off, disease rife, and horses and oxen being eaten.

White held out, however, until 28 February, when Buller broke the siege, the Boers too by then suffering from want of supplies and horses. In the relief column were two other officers who would leave a mark on history: Major Hubert Gough, who led the first party in, would in March 1914 be central to the greatest military crisis in the United Kingdom of the twentieth century (see Chapter 18); and Lieutenant Winston Churchill. When news of the relief of Ladysmith reached Britain it was rapturously celebrated, transforming the mood of a public whose initial enthusiasm for the war had evaporated once they realised it would not be the walkover they expected.

However, other sieges were in progress, the tactic being central to Boer strategy. One was at Kimberley, a town more of economic than military heft, where Lieutenant Colonel Robert Kekewich commanded the garrison and where Rhodes was present. There were 40,000 people there, only 5,000 of whom were fighting men, but unlike at Ladysmith there was ample food; it was only a matter of time before the Boers were routed. Lord Methuen led the division that lifted the siege. He moved on to Mafeking, besieged since 13 October 1899 and where Baden-Powell commanded the garrison. Matters there were more difficult, and the inhabitants were soon driven to eat the horses.

Baden-Powell repulsed an initial attack by 6,000 Boers, who then decided to starve him out. He had chosen Mafeking because it had good stocks of food and was on the railway from Bulawayo in Rhodesia to Kimberley. He had quietly recruited 500 men into his Protectorate Regiment, and 600 others, half from the Cape Police and Bechuanaland Rifles, the other half Volunteers from the town, supplemented them. Baden-Powell made two other key innovations. He armed 300 black men with rifles to help the defence; and formed a cadet corps of boys aged between twelve and fifteen to take on non-combatant roles to support the fighting men. He also built a network of communication trenches and fortifications, and even issued banknotes so normal commercial life could continue.

Such resourcefulness allowed Mafeking to hold out for 217 days, but was only part of what Baden-Powell did. He moved guns and searchlights around to create a false idea of the garrison size; he had imitation landmines placed around the town's perimeter. He even had soldiers dress as women and undertake household chores in sight of the enemy. The town was sporadically shelled: but this was a war from another age, and Baden-Powell negotiated Sunday truces to maintain the morale of his men and of the civilians. His Boer counterpart was outraged when these truces were used not to praise God, but to play cricket.

In November half the Boer force besieging the town, which had swollen to 8,000 men, had been redeployed elsewhere. By May it was clear Baden-Powell would not surrender, and on 12 May a force of 240 Boers tried to storm the town. Despite capturing the police barracks they were beaten off and heavily defeated, with sixty killed and more than a hundred being taken prisoner. The British prevailed not least because of the communications systems Baden-Powell had established, which kept him a step ahead of the enemy. Five days later a column under Colonel Bryan Mahon, from the advancing army of Lord Roberts, fought its way into the town and lifted the siege. Baden-Powell's leadership and ingenuity were rewarded by his being promoted to be the youngest major-general in the Army: in the wild celebrations that marked the arrival of the news in Britain, he was also elevated to the status of national hero.

The Boers not only had in many cases superior weapons, supplied from the German factories of Krupp and Mauser, but used methods such as trench warfare developed in the American Civil War: the British had not moved on from the Crimea. There had been a disastrous passage in December 1899 – known as Black Week – where the Army lost three separate engagements: General Gatacre's force at Stormberg on 10 December, Methuen's at Magersfontein the next day, holding up the reliefs of Kimberley and Mafeking, and capped by Buller's failure at Colenso on the 15th. It was after this that the Queen, in one of her most renowned utterances, told Balfour: 'Please understand that there is no one depressed in this house; we are not interested in the possibilities of defeat; they do not exist.'[111]

Defeats forced Britain to send more troops, and to call for Volunteers from Britain and the colonies. A nation reared on the myth of British invincibility was shocked – especially that an army of farmers could defeat it. It was a sign of the decadence of the imperial masters. Campbell-Bannerman lambasted a policy that 'presumed an early collapse of the Boers'.[112] On 14 January Earl Spencer, to whom he made that remark, called the position 'lamentable', the country being forced 'to have recourse to Scottish gillies and hunting men to fight our battles. One admires the pluck and patriotism of those who respond, regardless of other home duties, to the call of Government, but one must stand aghast at the revelation which the War has made of our helplessness.'

By January 1900 Britain had 180,000 men in southern Africa, the largest army it had ever sent abroad. Buller, sent to the Cape with a high reputation, on 24 January presided over the *débâcle* at Spion Kop, a hill captured after crossing the Tugela river. Poor generalship led to contrary orders at different levels of command, and 350 men being killed and 1,000 wounded during the retreat across the river. Lord Roberts, who brought Kitchener from the Sudan as chief of staff, soon replaced Buller, the government in London having decided to blame him for the defeats. However, like Buller, Roberts still faced the problem of lifting the sieges before the long-awaited offensive.

French lifted the siege at Kimberley on 15 February, after 124 days. Between then and the relief of Mafeking on 16–17 May the Boers suffered a succession of defeats, though at heavy cost to the British not just from the fighting but from outbreaks of typhoid after drinking contaminated water. Boer morale collapsed. On 28 May the British annexed the Orange Free State, and turned their forces against the Transvaal. Roberts captured Johannesburg on 31 May and a New South Wales force took Pretoria on 5 June. He declared the war was over and on 3 September the Transvaal was annexed.

However, the Boers had started a guerrilla war in March and did not intend to end it simply because their republics were annexed. General Louis Botha led this new form of warfare. Kruger was spirited out of Portuguese East Africa on a Dutch ship, sent by Queen Wilhelmina of the Netherlands, and would die in exile in Switzerland in 1904. More than 26,000 prisoners of war were also expatriated, many to St Helena. The guerrilla war continued until May 1902. The British (who soon numbered a quarter of a million) were initially unable to pursue the disparate bands through so large a territory.

When the British realised Roberts had spoken too soon they pursued ever more ruthless policies. Kitchener replaced him as commander-in-chief and launched a campaign of attrition. A system of 8,000 blockhouses was built across southern Africa to protect key strategic points such as bridges, and to provide bases from which sweeps of the surrounding countryside could be made. These proved highly effective, but drained manpower: it took 50,000 troops to man them and keep at bay 30,000 guerrillas.

The British Army introduced mounted columns, including heavy contingents of armed black Africans, that implemented a scorched earth policy. This caused outrage in Europe, where pro-Boer sympathy was high, but also deep dissension at home. It included burning houses and farms and interning the inhabitants in concentration camps, which developed from refugee camps set up under the Roberts regime. Goschen, as First Lord of the Admiralty in 1896, had, quoting the Canadian Finance Minister George Eulas Foster, spoken to a Unionist meeting at Lewes approvingly of Britain standing 'alone in that which is called isolation – our splendid isolation, as one of our colonial friends was wont to call it', rejoicing that Britain was so strong, and to such an extent master of its own empire and destiny, that while it sought good relations with other powers it needed no entanglements with or obligations to anyone else. Now that aloofness brought serious difficulties. In some quarters Britain became a pariah.

Kitchener intended to depopulate entire areas, and drove women and children into his network of sixty-four tented camps. His administrative system could not, however, cope with the numbers interned. There was no deliberate policy of starvation, but it proved impossible to get adequate food into the camps, not least because of Boer raids on supply lines. As well as malnutrition, diseases such as typhoid felled the inmates.

In all, 26,400 women and children died, 24,000 of them under the age of sixteen, and conditions were even worse but less well documented in the camps for black internees. The British Army also destroyed crops, massacred livestock and poisoned wells.

Although the 1895 parliament could run until 1902, Salisbury called a Khaki election in September 1900 that, in the euphoria after Mafeking and other perceived British triumphs, led to a Unionist majority of 130. Tories were returned uncontested in 163 seats. Chamberlain led the campaign, and the result greatly enhanced his standing: Salisbury was ill and did not speak, and Balfour, the First Lord of the Treasury, was entirely eclipsed. The war would never be so popular again.

As word reached home early in 1901 about the camps, a public outcry began. Activist women were outraged by what was being done to their Boer sisters. The foremost was Emily Hobhouse, a Cornish clergyman's daughter and the elder sister of Leonard Hobhouse, the father of social liberalism. She had first heard of the camps in the summer of 1900. She founded the Distress Fund for South African Women and Children, and in December 1900 went to the Cape to oversee relief efforts.

Through a family connection she had an introduction to Milner and Kitchener, who allowed her two railway wagons to take supplies to Bloemfontein in the Orange Free State. What she found in the camps horrified her, with as many as fifty children dying daily and twelve people crammed into tents made for three. She saw people reduced to skeletons, much like Nazi camps in the 1940s. Hygiene was non-existent; flies swarmed in the heat of high summer around the tents and their inmates. When she came home in February and related what she had seen she was denounced for succouring the enemy; but some Liberal politicians – the party was split between imperialists and anti-imperialists – took up her cause, as she set about writing a formal report to send to the government.

A sulphurous debate on the war – now costing £2.5 million a month – was held in the Commons in February 1901, during the debate on the Queen's Speech.[113] David Lloyd George, a young radical Liberal MP, said the government had 'made every possible blunder [it] could make from any and every point of view.'[114] From having sought to redress a legitimate grievance, ministers 'have so conducted the controversy as to have ranged against them every friend of freedom throughout the world, outside Great Britain.' Further evidence of incompetence was that 'though they have the resources of the wealthiest Empire which the world has ever seen to draw upon, they have so directed their operations that their own soldiers have been half-starved, stricken by disease, and have died by thousands from the sheer lack of the simplest appliances.'

He read out a proclamation by Roberts promising that the homes and farms near any part of a railway or public works that were damaged would be 'destroyed', and asked whether his fellow MPs approved of that.[115] He called the burning of homesteads 'the first touch of Kitchener's iron hand', casting women and children into the wilderness, and said 'really brave men are revolted by this.'[116] He called General Bruce Hamilton, on whose orders Ventersburg had been razed, 'a brute, and a disgrace to the uniform he wears', and accused him of leaving the women and children of the village to starve.[117]

Chamberlain and other Unionists accused Lloyd George and his allies of being 'pro-Boer', and of ignoring Boer atrocities. They hoped this would close the argument down: it did not. George Cadbury, true to his Quaker roots and at the behest of Lloyd George, put up the money to buy the *Daily News*, which became an organ of criticism of the government in its conduct of the war. On 26 February the War Secretary, St John Brodrick, had admitted to the Commons that the women and children of men who were not fighting were being given larger rations than those 'whose relations are still in the field', a point he had appeared to deny when Lloyd George had raised it in his speech.[118] Miss Hobhouse had not yet broadcast her testimony, but the ubiquity of war correspondents on the Veldt meant the newspapers were full of eye-witness reports of the suffering. The debate opened with John Dillon, the Irish Nationalist MP, proclaiming that 'since the fall of the Roman Empire I have never heard that any civilised nation has ever reverted to so barbarous a practice as capturing women and children by the thousand and detaining them as prisoners of war.'[119]

Dillon accused Kitchener of having done what he did before Omdurman, and ordering his men to take no prisoners. A soldier had been reported in a Liverpool newspaper as saying that he had received such orders. Another soldier had said something similar to the Wolverhampton *Express and Star*: 'We take no prisoners now . . . there happened to be a few wounded Boers left. We put them through the mill. Every one was killed.'[120] Irish Nationalists had reasons to expose British imperial iniquity, but the catalogue of outrages Dillon recited was intensely damaging, not just to the government and the Army, but to Kitchener in particular, who was presented as the author of this savagery.

Sir Henry Campbell-Bannerman, who had succeeded Harcourt as Liberal leader in 1899, had exercised great caution in attacking the government for its conduct of the war. He did not wish, as leader of the opposition, to be thought unpatriotic or unsupportive of British forces in the field; and his party was split between imperialists and anti-imperialists, though he was in neither camp. While his front-bench imperialists remained tactful, those freed from the cares of office or shadow office showed no such restraint; notably Rosebery, whose long sulking retirement after losing the 1895 election would see him, by the time of the Asquith government, in bitter but ineffectual opposition to his own party. He openly attacked Campbell-Bannerman for being insufficiently imperialist, as he would later attack his former acolyte Asquith over Irish Home Rule. Partly because of the hostility of the imperialists, but also after meeting Emily Hobhouse, Campbell-Bannerman realised he could remain silent no longer: on 14 June 1901, at a dinner the National Reform Union gave in his honour in the Holborn Restaurant in London, he made the speech of his life, provoking outrage among the jingoes.

Supported by two senior anti-imperialists, Harcourt and Morley, Campbell-Bannerman apologised for spoiling a 'festive occasion' by raising 'the spectre of this terrible war'.[121] He said he did not believe the horror of the camps was the 'deliberate and intentional policy of His Majesty's Government': but it was happening at that very moment 'in the name and by the authority of this most humane and Christian nation.' Were any other nation to have done this it would have been denounced: as, indeed, Britain had denounced Spain for such behaviour in Cuba in 1898. He accused Unionists – he named Balfour – of shrugging their shoulders and saying that 'war is war'. 'When is a war not a war?' he asked, occasioning laughter. The tone changed: 'When it is carried on by methods of barbarism in South Africa.' He called for civil government to take over, if Kitchener was 'too busy' to clean up the mess. He also noted that 'the insane policy of subjugation and obliteration' was being pursued against future British subjects, given the inevitable outcome of the war. Like others in the Empire – he did not say, but he meant, other white subjects – they had to be treated as equals if their long-term loyalty were to be assured.

The Times spoke for the patriotic populace who, after the shocks of 1899–1900 had rejoiced at the relief of Mafeking – in voicing outrage at the phrase 'methods of barbarism'. 'Until some semblance of proof is forthcoming that Lord Kitchener and the British soldiers under his command have been guilty of the acts which Boers and Pro-Boers have charged against them, there can be no justification for crippling the conduct of men with a most difficult and responsible task to carry out by subjecting every one of their actions in the field and in territory held by armed force to a fishing expedition,' it roared.[122] The heat of war allowed no room for subtlety; anyone expressing concern at the damage done to Britain's reputation by killing thousands of women and children was automatically a 'pro-Boer'. The newspaper attacked Harcourt (who had mocked Chamberlain for hypocrisy) as 'histrionic', and indicated the problem Campbell-Bannerman had – citing the approval of Sir Edward Grey, an elevated Liberal imperialist, for the government's policy, as recently outlined in the refined setting of a luncheon at Claridge's by Milner, on a visit to London.

Campbell-Bannerman's speech had aggrieved some colleagues – notably Asquith – who wanted a harder line on the Boers. He annoyed them further on 17 June by supporting a call by Lloyd George to debate the Hobhouse report. Lloyd George said the death rate in the camps was now 120 per 1,000 inmates and rising month on month: 'For the sake of the credit and good name of this country something should be done,' he said.[123] He complained that Joseph Rowntree had tried to get to Bloemfontein but had been prevented, on Milner's orders, from leaving the Cape, to avoid repeating the Hobhouse *débâcle*. 'No doubt what has happened since in these camps and elsewhere has entitled him to his peerage,' he observed of Milner's recent elevation. He had worked out that the food allowed per person was less than that given to criminals on hard labour: and most of the food was, as Miss Hobhouse had testified, infested with vermin and unfit for human consumption. 'When children are being treated in this way and dying,' he added, 'we are simply ranging the deepest passions of the human heart against British rule in Africa.'[124]

When Miss Hobhouse's report was published on 18 June *The Times* gave it the shortest possible shrift, highlighting the few positive things she said about her visit to southern Africa, and declaring that, in her accounts of the suffering of the Boer women and children, 'it would not appear that the narrators were subjected to any searching cross-examination by

Miss Hobhouse.'[125] The cover-up could not, however, last much longer. Brodrick was forced to admit the truth, and set up relief committees of Dutch and British representatives. He blamed the Boers for forcing the policy upon Britain, and said the camps were preferable to the women and children having no shelter at all. Campbell-Bannerman asked why Boers were removed from their homes without any provision being made to house them elsewhere. Fifty Liberal MPs abstained rather than follow Campbell-Bannerman, and on 20 June, at another political dinner, Asquith said his leader did not, on this matter, speak for the whole party. This was too much for Campbell-Bannerman, who demanded his party back him or sack him. Chastened, it re-elected him unanimously on 9 July.

Damaged and deeply embarrassed, the government appointed a commission to investigate the camps under the leadership of Millicent Fawcett. It was composed entirely of women, including doctors and a factories inspector. Its report corroborated everything Miss Hobhouse had found. However, when she tried to return to the Cape in October 1901 she was forbidden to land and, after five days, was deported. Nothing could better have indicated the government's embarrassment and shame. As a result of the scandal Milner put the camps under civilian administration, and Kitchener told his officers to stop rounding up women and children.

Kitchener's policies severely limited what the Boers could do but did not stop them entirely. From late 1901 to early 1902 the guerrillas stepped up their attacks. One on a column Methuen was leading at Tweebosch in the Western Transvaal on 7 March 1902 ended in a rout and the General's capture after he was wounded. The British poured in reinforcements and on 11 April an attack on a force led by Colonel Robert Kekewich led to a severe Boer defeat, precipitating the end of the war; in the Eastern Transvaal Botha's guerrillas were driven into Swaziland, and the Orange Free State had been cleared. The British feared a Boer uprising in the Cape Colony, but it never happened. There were, however, occasional attacks led by Jan Smuts, who less than a decade earlier had graduated with a double first in law from Cambridge and would be one of the twentieth century's greatest statesmen.

In March 1901 the British had offered Botha peace terms but they were rejected. A year later the Boer army was hungry, demoralised and, in a self-inflicted wound, antagonised the Zulus who started to attack them. By May 1902 they sued for peace, concluded under the Treaty of

Vereeniging on 31 May. The two former self-governments had a degree of autonomy within the British Empire, and were incorporated into the Union of South Africa in 1910. This was forged by members of the British Colonial Service, under instructions from Milner until he returned to England in 1905 – a group of young, highly trained men known as his 'Kindergarten'. The Treasury gave the Boers £3 million to rebuild their farms and restore their lands, and the authorities worked to establish among them a new identity as South Africans. Many Boers went to work as labourers in the mining industry, fundamentally changing the nature of white European society in South Africa.

There was a lengthy inquiry into what reforms might be needed in the British Army to make it more effective.[126] The debate about the ethics of the conduct of the war by the British continues over a century later. There is still no evidence that Kitchener intended to kill around half the population of Boer children, a couple of thousand of their mothers and grandmothers and perhaps 15,000 black labourers. But there was no serious thought given to the consequences of putting 154,000 people in the camps, and little effort spared to improve their lives once there, until the government was embarrassed into doing so. Kitchener seems to have been recklessly callous, and the government incapable of controlling him.

The war boosted British anti-imperialism. It reduced the influence of the Liberal imperialists, though Rosebery would continue to rattle his chains for years to come. The Labour movement was anti-imperialist almost to a man. There was an arrogance and certainty about the rightness of Britain's conduct in undeveloped lands that would not survive the Great War; but the Second Boer War knocked the first nails into the coffin of British imperial power, because of the methods Britain used to reinforce that power. Even a committed imperialist such as Kipling was repelled. Now using his poetry mainly as political propaganda, he gave *The Times* his poem 'The Islanders' to publish in January 1902. Even the archaic and self-conscious diction cannot mute the rage of certain passages:

And ye vaunted your fathomless power, and ye flaunted your iron pride
Ere – ye fawned on the Younger Nations for the men who could shoot and ride!

> Then ye returned to your trinkets; then ye contented your souls
> With the flannelled fools at the wicket or the muddied oafs at the goals.[127]

Wells, looking back in 1910, said the war's conception had been 'clumsy and puerile'.[128] Lloyd George told Frances Stevenson, his mistress, in 1915 that Britain had in fact lost the war. 'The Boers – the Dutch – are the rulers in South Africa,' he said, referring to how a Boer prime minister, Louis Botha, ran the Union. Afrikaners dominated it until the end of white rule.[129] The beginning of the end of British imperial power was down to incompetence, not deliberate evil, the result of the highly educated colonial civil servants' failure to control commanders in the field thousands of miles from home.

However, among the less philosophical majority, particularly buccaneers who had done well out of empire, the idealism remained intense. The native populations they had subjugated and plundered had never exploited or developed the wealth of their lands; so it was only right, in their view, that someone else should do so, and should import British values – those preached by Christian missionaries in Africa for decades – with them. It is hard to imagine Livingstone sanctioning Kitchener's policies towards Boer civilians, however.

When Rhodes died in April 1902, just before the end of the war he had wanted so much, he was just forty-eight. He had endured a lifetime of ill health caused by a weak heart and lungs. Stead wrote that his death took away 'the most conspicuous figure left in the English-speaking race since the death of Queen Victoria'.[130] Rhodes's view of the imperial project was, like Chamberlain's, essentially racial, and he was not unusual in that. In his *Last Will and Testament*, edited by Stead, he contended: 'We are the first race in the world, and that the more of the world we inhabit the better it is for the human race'.[131] World domination was economically desirable, for the British were better equipped than any other people to develop a country, as he had shown in southern Africa.

Rhodes believed, too, in the comity of the British nations, and wanted the British parliament to adapt to the nation as an imperial power. He wanted representatives of those nations controlled by those of British stock to sit at Westminster in a truly 'imperial' parliament. Rhodes is easily portrayed as a villain, and an incarnation of the most exploitative brand of capitalism, but he had a vision of democracy and enlightenment – shown by the scholarships founded in his name – that mark him out as a liberal whose reputation has been lost to the world. His vision would never be achieved, and not least because of the damage the war did to perceptions of empire among Britons everywhere.

For Britain, the Second Boer War proved that empire was not a cost-free enterprise, and further that all was not well in the mother country. It began to sow doubts about the viability of empire; it confirmed the desire for self-determination that would eventually be the British Empire's downfall; it revealed the terrible levels of health and fitness among the citizenry of the imperial power; and it provided another cause of division in British politics. Empire had been conceived as a source of wealth and glory, but maintaining it had become an ever-expanding challenge.

CHAPTER 5

IRELAND

I

Gladstone's second ministry had begun amidst heightened consciousness in Ireland about self-determination. Britain's empire was expanding, and Britons viewed any possible erosion of the United Kingdom with horror. However, as noted in the previous chapter, the desire to assert self-determination against the will of a perceived conqueror from overseas would eventually prove incompatible with empire. Although Ireland was part of the Kingdom, it was accorded (particularly by Tories) the sort of treatment and attitudes usually reserved for a colony. This contradiction was a further handicap for policy, exacerbated by the existence of two disparate groups on the island of Ireland: those, almost all Protestant, who felt British and wished to be ruled from London in perpetuity; and those, almost all Roman Catholic, who felt Irish and wished to rule themselves. The former were, as in most British possessions overseas, in a minority, yet possessed most of the wealth and much of the power. Among the Catholics there was a further split: between those who, wanting Home Rule, wished to remain part of a United Kingdom, and those extreme Nationalists who sought complete independence.

Many British politicians – including some Liberals – worried that if Ireland could not be held, would secession of part of the mother country precipitate the loss of empire and international prestige? Ireland had had an immense impact on British politics since the Union of 1801 (a security measure designed by Pitt the Younger to help protect Britain against France, after French involvement in the United Irishmen's rebellion of 1798). The potato famine of the 1840s had promoted repeal of the Corn

Laws, and free trade. Now, Ireland would split the Liberal party, creating a group of Liberal Unionists under Hartington and Chamberlain distinct from the majority of the party, who followed Gladstone's policy on Home Rule. It changed the nature, and the name, of the Conservative – or Unionist – party.

British bigotry against Roman Catholicism, and the almost racist view many Britons had of the Irish as crude, uncivilised and uneducated peasants, caused many politicians to believe Ireland was simply incapable of ruling itself. Land, however, was the practical obstacle to Irish sovereignty. In 1870 landlords, often domiciled in England, owned about 97 per cent of Ireland, which helps explain its treatment as a colony and not as a country in its own right.[1] About 1.5 per cent of proprietors – 302 people – owned one-third of the land. Irish landowners were caricatured as absentees; but ownership in Ireland was little different from that in large tracts of Britain, notably in Scotland and northern England. In mid-nineteenth-century Lincolnshire only 7 per cent of parishes had a resident landowner, whereas local people owned half of Ireland. The main problem there was lack of security of tenure, and the ease with which some (but not all) landlords could evict tenants in arrears. The system of poor relief, introduced in 1838, made landlords financially responsible for their paupers. Eviction ended that problem.

Despite a slow improvement in conditions since the famine – not just food supply, but also fewer people having to subsist in mud cottages with earth floors – lack of security of tenure gave tenants no incentive to improve their property. A few landlords, such as the Marquess of Rockingham in the eighteenth century, attempted to look after their people; others sought to exploit them, charging excessive rents that land productivity could never justify. In the nineteenth century landlords became harsher, even those renowned in England for promoting good conditions, such as the Marquess of Lansdowne, who had his agents evict as ruthlessly as anyone. Lansdowne was no great absentee: he spent at least a quarter of the year in County Kerry.

Mass emigration had followed the famine. This altered the balance of the population in the United Kingdom and fed anti-British hostility among those who remained, because of Britain's failure to act sooner and thus prevent the breaking up of families and the depopulation and weakening of Ireland within the Kingdom. At the 1841 census England had 56.2 per cent of the national population.[2] Irish emigration, rising birth rates and declining infant mortality rates in Britain between the 1840s and the 1870 meant that by 1881 England accounted for 70.6 per cent of the UK population. The more dominant England became, the more Ireland sought self-determination, and the more control of Irish land became paramount. A section of Irish opinion was increasingly militant, and potentially violent. The Fenian Brotherhood had been founded among immigrants to the United States in 1858, and its associates in the Irish Republican Brotherhood (IRB) mobilised in England in the 1860s. They plotted an uprising, whose leaders were arrested in Manchester in September 1867. Others tried to blow up part of Clerkenwell prison that December to liberate a comrade.

Gladstone knew the Irish had been dealt a bad hand. On becoming prime minister in December 1868 he had said, while felling a tree at Hawarden, 'my mission is to pacify Ireland': to reconcile Irish Nationalism with a United Kingdom.[3] He sought to meet Irish aspirations, notably by disestablishing the Church of Ireland. However, on Forster's becoming Chief Secretary for Ireland in May 1880, Gladstone wrote to him: 'Ireland has been illegitimately paid for unjust inequalities by an unjust preference in much lavish public expenditure . . . I do not recollect ever, during nearly 10 years for which I have been Finance Minister, to have received from a Secretary for Ireland . . . a *single suggestion* for the reduction of any expense whatever.'[4] Most of Ireland, with the exception of predominantly Protestant Belfast, had been bypassed in the Industrial Revolution; and the contribution to the Exchequer that its long-depressed agricultural economy had made during the mid-nineteenth century had not matched even the modest spending made on infrastructure in that period, and the costs of poor relief and garrisoning the island against possible rebellion. The economist in Gladstone had reason to see a powerful case for Home Rule, and for Ireland to have to raise much of its own funding. That, however, was not what motivated the Irish people in their desire to shake off British domination.

II

Charles Stewart Parnell was the son of an Anglo-Irish landlord in County Wicklow. His mother was American. He was related to many leading families of Ireland and England, and through those to the political establishment. Several kinsmen had sat in the old Irish parliament. He inherited his father's estate, Avondale, in 1859 aged thirteen, and completed his education at Magdalene College, Cambridge. Determined to improve his estate, he missed much of his time at university and never took a degree. He took a direct interest in the welfare of his tenants, and this concern for them prompted a belief that they would be better treated if governed by their own people rather than by the British.

Parnell's own view gained ground generally throughout his youth and early manhood, and the political structures whose leadership he would inherit, and through which he would exercise his influence, were put in place in that period. In 1873 Isaac Butt, a barrister and son of a Church of Ireland clergyman from County Donegal, formed the Home Rule League. It succeeded the Irish Home Government Association, which Butt had founded in 1870 to advance his view of a federal United Kingdom. It comprised mainly people such as Butt: well-to-do Protestants who supported the Liberal party. Butt had been an Orangeman, but the famine convinced him of the need for land reform and self-government, and he and other Protestants saw concessions to Nationalist feeling as a means of preserving Ireland's links with Britain rather than severing them altogether. He even defended Fenians; at public meetings women occasionally heckled him, claiming he had fathered children on them, in order to discredit him and his views. Parnell was attracted to the Butt doctrine. In 1874 he tried to stand for Wicklow as a Home Rule candidate but was disqualified because he was already High Sheriff of the county. He failed to be elected when standing for Dublin. Butt had fifty-nine supporters elected, however, sending a clear message to Disraeli that the educated and enfranchised Irish wanted self-government. Disraeli, having bigger fish to fry, chose to ignore them.

Parnell had a short wait for his place in parliament, being elected for County Meath at a by-election in 1875. Butt – by then MP for Limerick – and his friends had three demands: the release of Fenian prisoners, security of tenure and a measure of Home Rule. However, as the Conservative government carried on as though nothing had changed in Ireland, Butt was pressed to use militant tactics, notably obstructionism. There was no limit on how long an MP could speak in the Commons: so some, led by Joe Biggar, the MP for Cavan, spoke for hours. An Ulster Presbyterian, Biggar joined the Irish Republican Brotherhood in 1874 and converted to Catholicism in sympathy with his Nationalist friends. His use of the filibuster caught on, and badly disrupted business.

Butt had created a beast, in the shape of the League, that he could not control.

Biggar and his associates started by obstructing Irish legislation, but then held up anything that would aggrieve the government. After 1880 the House introduced a closure restricting this power. The Irish, however, would not be trifled with. Parnell and Biggar made common cause. Although in the terrorist IRB, Biggar opposed violence; abuse of parliamentary procedure was an ideal alternative weapon. He also hoped, vainly, to persuade the IRB to use constitutional methods. Home Rulers advocated what they considered the limit of the politically possible. Home Rule implied control of domestic policies moving from Westminster to Dublin, while defence and foreign policy and most financial arrangements remained in what the Irish termed 'the imperial parliament'. This would have given an Irish parliament control of land policy, resolving a main point of conflict. It was too little for the republicans, who wanted complete independence. In 1877 the IRB expelled Biggar and others who refused to abjure the Home Rule movement.

The IRB courted Parnell; and, like Biggar, he worked to win their support, possibly (there is no proof) including his taking the IRB oath. He visited America to cultivate members of Clan na Gael, a republican group. After months of talks with Fenian leaders there, in Paris, in London and in Ireland, Parnell was offered a 'new departure': in return for abandoning federalism but pursuing separatism, strongly resisting coercion and advocating land reform, the IRB would drop militancy and make common cause with the Home Rulers. Parnell was cautious.

Butt failed to see that many Irish no longer believed in a United Kingdom, or that some never had. He was at odds over this with Parnell, whose charm, intelligence and wealth propelled him to eminence. Butt died in May 1879; his successor, William Shaw, lasted a year before Parnell defeated him for the chairmanship after the 1880 general election. Shaw sat on the Liberal benches in the Commons: Parnell and his friends wished to be separate from the Liberals, not least now they were in government, and Shaw was defeated. The Home Rule League had been a coalition of interest. Parnell now set about transforming it into the Irish party.

In 1879, having addressed meetings of aggrieved tenants, Parnell grasped the potential of the land reform movement. He was introduced to it by Michael Davitt, recently released from prison in England following a conviction for treason felony, the non-capital, second-degree version of treason: Davitt had helped organise the IRB in England and had tried to raise money and arms for the planned uprising in 1867. His family left County Mayo after the famine and settled in Lancashire. As an eleven-year old in a cotton mill he caught his arm in machinery and it had been amputated. However, a local philanthropist paid for him to go to school, and despite his disability he became a typesetter.

Davitt believed Irish self-determination would come when those who cultivated land owned it. After his release on a ticket-of-leave in December 1877, Davitt persuaded fellow Fenians of the justice of this idea; and in January 1879, after touring America, returned to Mayo to implement it. The west of Ireland was nearing famine after a third successive failure of the potato crop; 1878 had been one of the wettest years in memory. Agricultural prices had fallen since 1874 across Europe, but rents had not. Davitt's ticket-of-leave meant any criminal act could return him to Dartmoor, so while he organised meetings of thousands of tenants in Mayo demanding rent reductions, he avoided attending them. The local landlord was a Catholic priest, Ulick Burke. A campaign of non-payment made Burke cut his rents and his evictions. The Land War had begun, with first blood to the tenants.

On 16 August 1879, supported by Parnell, the Land League of Mayo was formed. Within nine weeks the Irish National Land League began in Castlebar, Mayo. It elected Parnell as President – sparking a conflict with Shaw and the moderates of the Home Rule League – and Davitt became secretary. The League sought reduced rents and security through ownership; it opposed criminal action, and promised to support members threatened with eviction. Its aims evolved into those developed by the Tenant Right League thirty years earlier, known as 'the three Fs': Fair Rent, Fixity of Tenure and Free Sale. Inevitably, with other tenants turning up at evictions, disorder broke out. Parnell tried to make common cause with the IRB, even though he could not condone their methods: he knew he needed decent relations with potential allies at Westminster, but seemed not to realise how some of the actions he supported could lead to violence. Exploited tenants resisting eviction was one thing he and the IRB believed in that he could justify morally to constitutional politicians; the rest of the IRB's strategy he could not. He and the IRB did not even agree on land reform: he wanted tenants to have long leaseholds, the IRB took an agrarian Marxist view that land should be common property. Parnell had chosen problematical bedfellows.

However, his presidency of the Land League was the making of him. In the winter of 1879–80 he toured America and Canada, raising £70,000. He met President Hayes, addressed the House of Representatives and spoke in sixty-two cities. The 1880 general election brought him back to Ireland where he contested three seats – Mayo, Meath and Cork City. He chose to sit for the last, which he held until his death. There were sixty-three Home Rulers elected, including twenty-seven of his supporters. His immediate replacement of Shaw as chairman of the Home Rule League concentrated the leadership of Irish politics in his hands. He led his party like an autocrat, and the autocracy became more absolute the longer it lasted. He supposedly once said to his mistress, Katharine O'Shea: 'I can never keep my rabble together if I were not above the human weakness of apology. Never explain. Never apologise.'[5] His colleagues knew their place, and kept to it.

The agrarian situation worsened. Evictions rocketed in 1880, with 2,110 compared with 1,238 in 1879. Violent incidents trebled, from 863 to 2,590. To retain the sympathy of Gladstone and the government, Parnell argued for peaceful protest. This included mass meetings, which intimidated the authorities, and the boycott. This term entered the language in 1880 following widespread coverage of the activities of tenants on the Mayo estates around Lough Mask of the 3rd Earl Erne, an elderly Tory whose main Irish base was three counties away in Fermanagh, where he was Lord Lieutenant. Erne offered to cut rents by 10 per cent, but in 1880 his tenants demanded a 25 per cent reduction. Erne refused, and his agent, Captain Charles Boycott, set about evicting those in arrears. Boycott was the son of a Norfolk clergyman. His family had bought him a commission in the 39th Foot Regiment after he failed his exams at the Woolwich Royal Military Academy. His army career was undistinguished, but he served in Ireland and married an Irishwoman. He became a minor landlord, using inheritances. He was never popular with his tenants. Having become Erne's agent for 1,500 acres of the 2,200 he owned, Boycott aggrieved the tenantry, imposing petty restrictions and fining malefactors.

He undertook eleven evictions just as Parnell spoke in Ennis, Co. Clare, on 19 September 1880. He asked: 'What do you do with a tenant who bids for a farm from which his neighbour has been evicted?' Someone shouted: 'Kill him!' Parnell retorted there was 'a very much better way – a more Christian and charitable way . . . When a man takes a farm from which another has been evicted, you must shun him on the roadside when you meet him – you must shun him in the streets of the town – you must shun him in the shop – you must shun him on the fair green and in the market place, and even in the place of worship, by leaving him alone, by putting him in moral Coventry, by isolating him from the rest of the country, as if he were the leper of old – you must show him your detestation of the crime he committed.'[6]

Boycott occupied no one's farm: but he was the first and most famous target of the policy. On 22 September a process server and seventeen policemen attempted to serve Boycott's eviction notices. Three were served before news reached other tenants, and the eviction party was repulsed. Another failed attempt occurred the next day. Land Leaguers told Boycott's staff and labourers to leave his employment. Eventually, under the threat of violence and reprisals, they all went, leaving Boycott with a farm he could not run. Within days the community had isolated him: the postman would not deliver his mail, the blacksmith would not shoe his horses and no one would do his laundry. When his nephew offered to deliver the post he was warned he was in danger. The local shops stopped selling Boycott provisions, which had to be shipped in instead.

Threats of violence were taken seriously: 'An armed party of men, their faces blackened' had shot dead Charles Boyd, son of a land agent near Wexford, in August.[7] Lord Mountmorres, another Mayo landowner, was murdered on 25 September as he drove from a magistrates' meeting in Clonbar, shot six times at close range. He had refused a rent reduction but had evicted no one: Davitt accused him of spying for Dublin Castle. No one was convicted of his murder, despite the offer of a £1,000 reward. On 18 September 'a gentleman named Walsh' was shot at and hit with bludgeons near Boycott's estate, until the attackers were called off with the cry 'he is not the man we want': he had been mistaken for Boycott.[8] On 1 October Boycott's herdsmen's house was surrounded and they were ordered 'on pain of death' to leave work.

The violence shocked Forster and Gladstone, who consulted his law officers about remedies. The choice was between prosecutions or legislation. Gladstone told Forster: 'We are . . . inquiring whether the law allows under certain circumstances of combinations to prevent the performance of certain duties, and the enjoyment of certain rights.' If it did not, he hoped it could 'be brought up to the proper point by an

Amending Act.'[9] Meanwhile, Boycott did what a man in his position must inevitably do: he wrote to *The Times*. He spoke of the 'howling mob' that had surrounded the process-server and policemen, and how on 23 September 'the people collected in crowds upon my farm, and some hundred or so came up to my house and ordered off, under threats of ulterior consequences, all my farm labourers, workmen and stablemen, commanding them never to work for me again.'[10] The blacksmith and herdsmen had been threatened with murder, his crops trampled and his locks smashed. 'I say nothing about the danger to my own life, which is apparent to anybody that knows the country.' Boycott did not talk of 'terrorism', but the tactics had a psychopathic dimension.

His cry forced the establishment into action. The Queen harried Gladstone to stop the 'very treasonable' actions of 'this monstrous Land League': or the government would be 'held responsible for loss of life'.[11] A threat to prosecute leaders of the League caused the dogs, for a while, to be called off. Parnell was careful: *The Times* on 18 October – the day of Boycott's letter – described his latest speeches as 'defiant in generals, but cautious in particulars'.[12] Parnell knew his political influence could evaporate if he condoned criminality. Gladstone and Forster wished to avoid new laws that would be depicted as restraining Irish liberties: the Liberal ethos was to govern in Ireland as in Britain.

Throughout 1880–81 the Land War raged. Davitt raised money, mostly from America, funding a big organisation that became a threatening extra-parliamentary force. The number of armed agitators began to cause serious alarm. There were calls to prosecute and punish severely anyone carrying an unlicensed weapon. *The Times* reported on 1 November that 'at present there is practically no restriction, and arms of all kinds are openly carried about, and the crack of rifles and revolvers is heard on every side by day and night. The owners are becoming marksmen by frequent practice, and no one interferes with them.'[13] The agitation stirred up Orangemen in Ulster, who in Belfast on 31 October protested that any attempt to introduce the League's methods into their province would be resisted by equally violent and resolute means. Six months into his second ministry, Gladstone realised Ireland could erupt. The remedies for its problems his liberalism dictated seemed unfeasible; and treating Ireland as though it were England seemed either impossible or futile.

Forster had no such illusions. To him this was an imperial, not a domestic, problem. He wanted to act accordingly. He called for the suspension of Habeas Corpus. Gladstone disagreed, not merely for fear of affronting liberty: he also feared it would fail. The difficulty was that Parnell and his friends 'not only are not suspected of intending to commit crime, but . . . have no idea of committing it, and who only think of intimidating landlords with a possible crime now and then to back the intimidation.'[14] This letter to Forster is of great significance, for it contains – if only to disavow it – the first germ of what would become Gladstone's policy on Ireland. 'Do not suppose I dream of reviving the Irish Parliament; but I have been reading Union speeches and debates [from 1800], and I am surprised at the narrowness of the case upon which that Parliament was condemned.'

The Irish Protestant, and British, public flocked to Boycott's aid. Funds were raised in Belfast to send, effectively, mercenaries to harvest his potatoes and turnips. Parnell went to Tipperary to urge formation of a branch of the League there to take the fight to the landowners. This was not because of an outbreak of rampant landlordism there, but because Tipperary had sent police to Mayo, and Parnell wanted to keep them busy enough at home to stop their becoming reinforcements to protect Boycott. On 3 November, after much ministerial debate, Parnell and four associates were summonsed to appear in court in Dublin on charges of conspiracy, 'being evil-disposed persons, and unlawfully and wickedly devising, contriving and intending to impoverish and injure divers large numbers of the liege subjects of our said Lady the Queen'.[15] There was also the matter of inciting people not to pay rents, and the widespread intimidation.

Boycott was soon under further attack. In another letter to *The Times* he told how in his town of Ballinrobe 'I was suddenly surrounded by a yelling, hooting mob of fully 500 persons. Had it not been for the prompt manner in which the constabulary on hearing the noise forced their way through the crowd, and closed round me, I should infallibly have been torn in pieces by the infuriated mob.'[16] The police could not cope. 'A requisition was sent from the resident magistrate to the officer in command of the 76th for thirty men, and it was not until they arrived at the constabulary barracks, where they were actually forced to fix bayonets to assist the twenty-eight police, that my man was able to bring my dog-cart to the infantry barracks, where I had been detained for three hours, and I was able to proceed on my journey.' This time Boycott spoke bluntly: 'The spirit of terrorism towards me is decidedly on the increase, and the determination to hunt me out of the country more openly expressed.'

The news of prosecutions did not excite the outburst the League desired. Meetings were planned to raise money for the defence fund. Subscriptions were closed for the fund to help Boycott, and plans made to mount what *The Times* called the 'relief expedition' to Lough Mask.[17] Rumours began that 'a large body of Orangemen' would march from Ulster, but the organisers proposed that to keep the provocation to a minimum numbers should be limited to 100.[18] They planned to travel by train, but the railway, fearing reprisals, refused to carry them. Forster sent reinforcements to Ballinrobe, and banned the march. The gentry did little to help their own cause. An agent called Allan from Tipperary was told that if he went to Galway and Roscommon to collect rents for his employer, a Mr French, he would be shot: this was shortly after Allan had evicted a widow from a house where she and her children had been lying sick.

The government let fifty men go to Boycott's estate to undertake his harvest, the state providing a guard. 'The country swarms with police', *The Times* reported on 10 November, noting there were now 700 soldiers at Ballinrobe, with the 10th Hussars and 400 men of the 84th Regiment on their way.[19] These were not so much to protect Boycott and those working for him as to keep at bay columns of Orangemen rumoured to be *en route* to Mayo: the government feared civil war. Outnumbered, the Land League said it had no objection to men harvesting the crops, provided they left afterwards. There was no violence, though there were protests, and not all tenants obeyed the League. Boycott's continued tenure was, however, impossible. On 27 November he and his family left Lough Mask, escorted by Hussars. No one would drive their carriage, so they left in an army ambulance. They planned a week's holiday in Dublin, but were met with protests and their hotel was threatened with a boycott if they did not leave. On 1 December they boarded the Holyhead mail.

The military operation cost £10,000. It was a conspicuous victory for the League, but also for terrorism: it is true that Boycott was high-handed, but at the same time Erne had offered to cut rents, and the result was that sheer force prevailed over the rule of law. The government rescue operation could not be repeated everywhere, so boycotting spread. Boycott let it be known he had lost £6,000 on his estate, leased from Erne, showing the risks of farming in Ireland. He and his family stayed with a Tory MP, Major-General Edwyn Burnaby, in Leicestershire, where some of Burnaby's friends offered to fund a mission to liberate Boycott's furniture from Lough Mask House. He declined: it would be dangerous as well as costly. Intimidation had altered the balance of power in Ireland, and at Westminster politics had to bend to force.

III

By December 1880 Ireland was in deep crisis. Thousands of tenants had joined the League and widely refused to pay rents. By creating a militant Irish identity, the League had made Ireland effectively a problem of imperial management and taken it out of the normal run of domestic politics. Gladstone, who had witnessed Chartism at first hand and seen how close it came to causing a breakdown of civil order in the early 1840s, realised Ireland could be threatened by what amounted to an uprising. The Queen, who felt unable to communicate directly with her prime minister, pleaded with Hartington 'in the *very strongest manner possible* to use *all his* influence' with Gladstone to squash the League.[20] 'The law is *openly defied, disobeyed*, and such an example may spread to England, if it prove successful in Ireland,' she wrote on 12 December. If ministers such as Bright and Chamberlain were opposed to coercion – 'boldness and firmness', as she put it – then the government should '*let* them *go*'.

Gladstone appointed a Land Commission under the Earl of Bessborough to advise how to restore order. Bessborough had practised as a lawyer without great distinction; his main success had been as a considerable cricketer who was a co-founder both of the Surrey county club and of the elite I Zingari. After taking evidence from 500 tenants, eighty landlords and seventy agents, the Commission recommended the three Fs: fair rent, free sale and fixity of tenure. The process bought Gladstone time against Forster's demands (echoed also by the Viceroy, Lord Cowper) to suspend Habeas Corpus, as did more moderate comments by Parnell – whose demeanour seemed to have changed since he faced prosecution – about the League working within the law and the constitution. Gladstone argued to colleagues that it would prejudice the trial of Parnell and the others if Habeas Corpus were suspended before its conclusion. Chamberlain wrote to Gladstone on 17 November threatening to resign if more coercive measures were taken, a letter Gladstone received 'with much anxiety'.[21]

Forster, hearing Bessborough's recommendations, told Gladstone he thought an announcement of the 'three Fs' would end the agitation. Gladstone, ever alert to the complexities of apparently simple concepts, discussed with Forster the interpretation of each of the Fs, and the possibility of causing cabinet divisions. He feared the Commission exceeded its remit in suggesting the state should compensate landlords forced to make financial concessions to tenants. Gladstone's liberalism meant he wanted change with as little interference as possible between landlord and tenant. This clashed with the Marxism – the word was not used until 1887 – of the more extreme members of the League.

However on 15 December he proposed a Land Bill to adjust rents, allow free sale by a tenant of his interest in a property without the right of a landlord's veto, stop arbitrary and frequent changes in future rents, and promote 'peasant proprietorship'.[22] This shocked Hartington, who warned Gladstone he disagreed with almost every aspect of the policy except prosecuting the League, which he thought had taken too long to effect. Hartington's father, the Duke of Devonshire, had extensive Irish estates experiencing agitation. Hartington was still being wound up by the Queen, who appealed to his 'loyalty and straightforwardness . . . firmness and determination' to ensure her delinquent prime minister became tougher.[23] She also directly rebuked Forster for the policy – she was sufficiently agitated to write to him on Christmas Day 1880 saying the Land Bill was 'a great mistake' and Forster's language had done 'great harm'.[24] She told him it was his 'duty to *insist* on the *immediate* suspension of the Habeas Corpus Act' and to 'threaten to resign *unless* it *is complied with*. Nothing *else* will do *now*.'[25]

Gladstone stood firm, but governing was becoming harder. On his seventy-first birthday, 29 December, he noted the 'anxieties' Ireland caused him, but that 'the rich and holy words of Scripture are still abundantly ministered to me for support.'[26] Parliament would return in early January, a month earlier than usual, because of the crisis. The debate on coercive measures would start during what the newspapers called 'The State Trial', which began on 28 December 1880. Parnell and his comrades faced nineteen counts of conspiracy. Heard in the Four Courts in Dublin, the Lord Chief Justice of Ireland, George May, and two High Court judges presided. However, May was accused of inadvertently passing comment on the case and thus prejudicing it, and appeared solely to announce he would not be sitting. It continued under the other two judges. In the galleries were Davitt, the Lord Mayor of Dublin, the High Sheriff, Lord Randolph Churchill and at least seventeen Irish MPs (to add to the four on trial with Parnell) including Timothy Healy and T. P. O'Connor, names synonymous with the Home Rule fight. By the fourth day of the trial interest had evaporated, and the galleries were half empty.

The Times noted the jury 'consists of eight Catholics, three Protestants and one Quaker.'[27] It also observed that 'beyond the gathering of a couple of hundred of the lowest classes on the quay in the vicinity of the Four Courts' there had not been 'the slightest manifestation of public feeling' in the capital in support of the League. By contrast, 700 people – Lords Lieutenant, deputy lieutenants and magistrates mainly – had written on 23 December to Gladstone to inform him that 'the state of lawlessness and intimidation at present existing in this country is such that the law is utterly unable to cope with it'. The Attorney-General for Ireland, leading the prosecution, said Parnell's aims had gone far beyond the fair rents and fixity of tenure: the Land League wanted 'one fell swoop on the landlords, driving them out of the country'.[28] He added that 'the landlords were branded as a class, and as a class described as robbers, thieves, aye, and murderers, and were held up to the odium and execration of the Irish people as men who by force or fraud had possessed themselves of the property of others.'[29]

The hearing lasted twenty-one days, during which Gladstone and his colleagues discussed legislation to bring an apparent insurrection under control, and troops were sent to the areas of greatest agitation in the west and north to prove the authorities' determination to keep order. Simultaneously, boycotting moved outside the agrarian world, with firms of solicitors representing landlords whom the League regarded as undesirable being asked to contribute to League funds or lose business. Worse, it became clear that any juror in a case – such as that of the conspirators – who assisted in a conviction would find himself in trouble with the League.

The newspapers published the names and addresses of the twelve jurors in the conspirators' trial the day after it started. It was no surprise they failed to reach a unanimous verdict, and were discharged. The defence case had relied on the assertion that there was no evidence of a conspiracy, and no proof that any violence was perpetrated as a consequence of any action or statement by anyone in the dock. The judge, summing up, noted that the atmosphere had been greatly soured by the 1,000 evictions in the first four months of 1880, but this was a result not of vicious landlordism but of the League's telling tenants to withhold their rent. However, it would not be force of argument that decided the trial.

The public flocked to the court and the quay outside as the verdict was expected. 'During the night tar barrels were burnt in some of the leading thoroughfares, bands played boisterously, crowds marched through the streets for some hours,' *The Times* reported.[30] However, it also noted that a postcard for Parnell, addressed to the offices of the League, had arrived bearing the message: 'Twelve of us will shoot you tonight, CSP, you rogue, if you are acquitted. If you escape we will shoot you. God save the Queen.' Parnell and his friends were acquitted, but he remained unshot.

Parnell regarded the outcome as a victory, and valued the publicity. Gladstone and Forster, having seen the effects of terrorism and now defeated by the law, realised there would have to be a political accommodation. The 1880 election had shown a choice not between Fenianism and constitutionalism, but between Fenianism and the Home Rule movement, which meant freezing British parties out of the argument. Once the two countries stopped sharing common parties, the argument for separation became increasingly unanswerable.

A law implementing Bessborough's recommendations would represent an unthinkable (for most Liberals) interference in private property and the bargain between landlord and tenant. Forster therefore convinced Gladstone this could only be considered if preceded by a Coercion Bill, to punish anyone disrupting the new settlement. The Land Bill would not be introduced until April 1881, but Forster brought in the Protection of Persons and Property Bill, to the outrage of Irish MPs, on 24 January. Its harshest measure would allow imprisonment without trial for up to eighteen months of those 'reasonably suspected' of crime and conspiracy. Since the government had shown the will to get tough the number of outrages had decreased: and he felt this law would have a more salutary effect still. The Irish argued that those lacking other remedies had caused the outrages, and that if remedial measures preceded coercive ones coercion would be unnecessary. They were drowned out. The main Tory opposition, representing as it did the landlords, saw no need for half-measures.

Forster said a 35 per cent rise in agrarian outrages in 1880 made the case for the Bill. He contended that freedom no longer existed in parts of rural Ireland because of the League. As well as people being attacked or threatened by trigger-happy Leaguers, livestock was being killed, with sheep being pierced between the eyes to damage their brain. Evictions had effectively ended, because no process-server would dare. Fenians had exploited genuine concerns; and he wished to use the proposed measures very sparingly, and only when the situation could be resolved in no other way. He said he acted 'with the very greatest reluctance' and understood the 'bad example' of setting a precedent.[31] He knew the Irish termed this coercion, but he preferred to call it protection.

A debate over five days provoked a definitive act of Irish filibustering; and an unprecedented announcement by the Speaker, Henry Brand, early on 2 February, to close the sitting, after forty-one and a half hours of debate and 'discussions upon repeated dilatory motions for Adjournment'.[32] The closure followed days of talks between the British parties about handling obstructionism. Brand said that 'the usual rules have proved powerless to ensure orderly and effective debate' on 'an important measure' causing the House's will to be frustrated by 'an inconsiderable minority'. As a result, 'the dignity, the credit, the authority of this House are seriously threatened.' He warned the House that it would have to change its rules, or vest more power in him to close debates where obstruction was happening. Gladstone, according to Eddy Hamilton, was 'ecstatic'.[33]

The Bill excited more protest. Davitt was arrested in Dublin for the use in speeches of 'inflammatory and scurrilous language' about the Bill and about Forster.[34] His technical offence was to have violated the terms of his ticket-of-leave. He was brought to England and locked up in Portland jail. Gladstone asked Sir William Harcourt, the Home Secretary, to ensure Davitt had 'treatment as mild and with as much comfort as can be fairly given', to give him nothing else to complain about.[35] The day Davitt was arrested the Commons debated restricting the filibuster: Hansard prefaces its report with: 'It is to be understood that throughout the subsequent proceedings the greatest excitement and confusion prevailed.'[36] First the Speaker named and expelled John Dillon, then Parnell, then thirty-three other members of Parnell's party, for defying the authority of the Chair. The next day the Protection Bill began its second reading, passed four days later by 359 votes to fifty-six. It was considered clause by clause in a committee of the whole House, which the Irish tried to obstruct; but after several days the House voted by a majority of 352 to end discussion on it, and the Bill went to the Lords.

A Peace Preservation Bill was debated on 2 March, allowing suspension of Habeas Corpus. Gladstone and Forster drew up a blueprint for the new Land Bill, aware the time had come for the carrot after the stick. On the Peace Preservation Bill's third reading on 11 March, Parnell accused the government of abandoning the principles of liberalism that supposedly underpinned it, and to have become instead 'the tools of the landlord interest in Ireland'.[37] He warned Gladstone that 'it was impossible, in the present times of the electric telegraph and steam communication, to coerce the public opinion of a whole country'; and that America, too, was watching closely. He said the main result of this new coercion would be to drive more people, especially the young, into the arms of the Fenians. His unfavourable comparison with America prompted a Liberal MP, Charles Newdegate, to remind him how less than twenty years earlier America had dealt with an internal rebellion: and he asked whether Parnell would prefer such methods in the United Kingdom. The Bill passed by a majority of 210.

The Land Law (Ireland) Bill was launched on 7 April. Its proposals had already damaged the government. The Duke of Argyll, the Lord Privy Seal and a substantial landowner, resigned on 31 March over the notion that tenants could sell their interest in a farm without the landlord having the right of veto. Gladstone, who tried to persuade him to stay and who also feared losing Hartington, told him he had studied the matter and that the case for change was 'overwhelming'.[38] Gladstone introduced the Bill in a speech of over an hour and a half that had even Northcote expressing admiration. Those seeking a demonstration of the range and power of Gladstone's titanic intellect should read it in full. He said it was 'the most difficult and complex question with which in the course of my public life I have ever had to deal' but promised the legislation would be 'of an improving and reforming character.'[39] It was certainly that. Dillon noted on 13 April: 'I very much fear that this Act was drawn by a man who was set to study the whole history of our organisation and was told to draw an Act that would kill the Land League.'[40]

It would establish a system of Land Courts that fixed rents for a period of fifteen years; or set for fifteen years rents agreed privately between landlord and tenant. The state would also advance money to buy land at up to three-quarters of its value, repayable over thirty-five years. The constraints upon landlords turned out to be such that they welcomed the chance to sell their land, though most tenants did not want to buy. It is thought that only around 400 farms were bought under the provisions of the Act. Gladstone said that reference of a problem to the court would be voluntary, because landlord-tenant relations were not inevitably the same from case to case. Where necessary the court would set a 'judicial' or 'fair' rent.[41] After a mass of detail, he summed up what this would mean:

> On the morning that this Bill passes every landlord and tenant will be subject to certain new provisions of the law of great importance. In the first place, an increase of rent will be restrained by certain rules. In the second place, the compensation for disturbance will be regulated according to different rates. And in the third place – more important probably than any – the right to sell the tenant's interest will be universally established. These are some of the means outside the Court which we propose; but there will also remain to the tenant the full power of going to the Court to fix a judicial rent, which may be followed by judicial tenant right.[42]

Parnell asked only whether the Bill would be retrospective, to help those already evicted; and whether the government would buy land on which to settle Irish labourers with no hope of employment. Otherwise he reserved judgment.

At the second reading on 25 April the former Tory Attorney-General for Ireland, Edward Gibson, denounced what he felt to be the confiscatory nature of the Bill, which he regarded as 'neither direct nor intelligible'.[43] However the genius of what Gladstone and Forster had devised was such that another Tory, the Armagh MP James Richardson, said approvingly that his colleague had merely 'made the discovery that this was a strong and a drastic Bill; and that a British ministry had at last, after centuries, determined to bring in a measure which was more in the interests of the tenant than of the landlord.' However Lord Elcho, who saw himself as one of the last remaining Whigs, unsuccessfully proposed an amendment, describing the proposals as 'economically unsound, unjust and impolitic.' He said the 'Parnellism' to which the government had surrendered was 'if not communism practically the same thing', and that Gladstone was giving 'effect to the carrying out of the Communistic principle . . . the expropriation of the few for the benefit of the many.'[44] A. J. Balfour, who would later be Chief Secretary for Ireland, felt the Bill 'socialistic in its character'. Other Tories objected that areas of agricultural distress in England were not being given state money in the way that Ireland would be.[45] Such was Elcho's concern at the spread of socialism in his own party that the following year he founded the Liberty and Property Defence League, a campaigning organisation devoted to resisting the communistic principle.

For all Elcho's colourful language he was right: the balance had shifted, and the party of liberal principles was now challenging them. It was indicative of the change in Ireland that Gladstone, to fulfil his mission of pacification, knew he must effect, whatever the other considerations. Bright observed that the Bill was one 'on which depends, to a large extent, the social interests of Ireland, and, I believe, also on which depends, to a large extent, the political interests of the United Kingdom.'[46] The Bill distressed many Irish MPs, not least because, as Dillon said, it undermined the League so thoroughly (Dillon was arrested under the Coercion Act during the debate). Also, some Land Leaguers did not want peace between landlords and tenants: they wanted a Marxist-style confrontation. O'Connor said this on the seventh night of the debate, speaking of 'this grim reality, that either the landlords or the tenants must go down.'[47] He added that 'both could not survive the struggle' and that he was 'an advocate of the eviction of landlords'. That was 'the final solution of this question, and he was not going to vote for a Bill which impeded rather than accelerated the final solution'.

Parnell, on the eighth and last night of the debate, announced that he would abstain: he had no desire to have 'Irish landlords and the Irish tenants continually to live in opposing camps', thereby rejecting the proto-Marxist doctrine. The League was about more than tenants' rights: it was a movement for self-determination, and in everything Parnell, as its leader, did he had to note the prejudices of its radical wing: hence his abstention. The Bill passed its second reading by 176 votes. The Land Leaguers expected the Lords to vote the measure down, and therefore give them even greater cause for protest, but were disappointed: it became law in August 1881. 'We have now come to a very critical moment, that of the real battle between the Land League and the Land Act,' Gladstone told Cowper, the Viceroy, on 22 August.[48] Parnell tried to steer a middle way between militants and those Leaguers who liked the widespread rent reductions of around 20 per cent and a rapid end to landlordism. In its first year of operation there was a total reduction in rents of £115,494, and eighty-one tenants were advanced money to buy their land.[49]

In September the Liberals won a by-election in Tyrone, which Gladstone saw as a stunning defeat for Parnellism, his candidate coming a distant third.[50] It put him on the front foot against Parnell who, despite acceptance of the Land Act among members of the League, called for its rejection on the grounds that the mechanism for revising rents every fifteen years would provoke further disunity, by continuing to set landlord against tenant. The government scrutinised Parnell's remarks closely. A huge League demonstration in his honour in Dublin on 25 September unnerved ministers, who smelled an attempt to whip up rebellion just as the harvest was being brought in. Parnell spoke at Maryborough the next day, and the tone of what he said alarmed Forster: 'It has been our principle', he told the rally, 'that the resources of Ireland should be for the benefit of those who work in this country . . . we desire to test this Land Act, but we do not desire the tenant farmers of Ireland to use it until it has been tested.'[51] He instructed tenants not to use the Land Courts, 'to avoid the demoralisation of the ranks of the Land League'. He said the courts would buy off individual tenants and establish a principle of divide and rule and, except in League-approved test cases, should be shunned.

Forster asked Gladstone whether he would agree to Parnell's arrest under the Coercion Act. Gladstone replied on 27 September that 'if you are deliberately advised by your lawyers that Parnell has by his speech been guilty of treasonable practices . . . he should be arrested.'[52] Parnell also, injudiciously, told the Land League in America that tenants had been advised to 'rely on the old methods to reach justice'.[53] Gladstone took this as a challenge, telling Bright he would go to Leeds on 7 October and 'denounce outright Parnell (not the Irish party, nor even the Land League) and his works and ways'.[54] Before he could Forster told him the central and local leaders of the League should be arrested, to prevent the sabotage of the Act: 'Unless we can strike down the boycotting weapon, Parnell will beat us; for men, rather than let themselves be ruined, will obey him and disobey the law.'[55] Gladstone told him that if legal advice were forthcoming in support of this, he would back the plan.

At Leeds Gladstone called Parnell 'a man of considerable ability'.[56] But he claimed that, after the Land Act, Parnell was 'afraid lest the people of England, by their long-continued efforts, should win the hearts of the whole of the Irish nation' and therefore had 'an enlarged gospel of plunder to proclaim.' He mocked Parnell's adulation of America, a nation with 'a knot of Irishmen who are not ashamed to point out in the press which they maintain how the ships of Her Majesty's Navy ought to be blown into the air to destroy the power of England by secret treachery, and how individuals they are pleased to select ought to be made the object of the knife of the assassin and deprived of life because they do not conform to the new Irish gospel.' He strongly endorsed Forster – the League was spreading the rumour that Gladstone disapproved of Forster's hard line – and ended with a threat: 'The resources of civilisation are not yet exhausted.'

Between eight and nine o'clock on the morning of 13 October Superintendent Mallon of the Dublin Metropolitan Police arrived at Morrison's Hotel in Dawson Street with four other officers to arrest Parnell, staying there while travelling from his house in Wicklow to a League meeting in Naas. Mallon had two warrants signed by Forster, who had arrived that morning from Holyhead having secured the cabinet's agreement the previous day. One warrant charged Parnell with inciting others to intimidate tenants into withholding just rents; the other with intimidating people not to take benefits under the Land Act. 'Mr Parnell appeared greatly surprised,' *The Times* reported, 'but asked for some little time in which to dress and have his breakfast.'[57] The request was granted, and Parnell wrote a quick letter to Mrs O'Shea that Mallon let him post in the pillar-box outside Kilmainham jail, where he would spend the next six and a half months. An emergency meeting of the League's executive interpreted his arrest as a fulfilment of the threat Gladstone had issued at Leeds.

In his letter to Mrs O'Shea Parnell predicted all would be quiet within months, and he would be released. Gladstone, enjoying a rare moment of Royal approval – the Queen telegraphed him to say 'Parnell's arrest a great thing' – hoped things would be quiet too: the disturbances that summer had led to the imprisonment of around 1,300 people.[58] He hoped the Land Act would create a middle class who would want to work with, rather than against, the system: 'A more intelligent and less impassioned body,' he told Forster the day Parnell was arrested, adding that 'it is on this body, its precepts and examples, that our hopes depend, for if we are at war with a nation we cannot win.'[59] The League responded to the arrests on 19 October, the day before the Land Court opened, by demanding a national rent strike, with a statement issued from Kilmainham signed by Parnell and some of his fellow inmates. Forster immediately took legal advice and the next day the League was proscribed, and it abandoned its meetings. 'The Leaguers are showing no open fight,' he told Gladstone.[60]

The government tried to calm the situation, and give the Land Act a chance: but the League, driven underground, convened secret courts where those believed to be collaborating were marked down for punishment, being beaten or shot by gangs known as 'moonlighters'. Murders became so frequent that on 20 November Forster demanded more soldiers and more arrests under the Protection Act. He also told Gladstone that 'while we are fighting for law and order, I cannot desert my post; but this battle over, and the Land Act well at work, I am quite sure that the best course for Ireland, as well as for myself, would be my replacement by someone not tarred by the coercion brush.'[61] Landlords formed an Irish Land Committee and on 9 November urged their brethren in England to help fund their legal representation in cases brought against them in the Land Court. The Marquesses of Drogheda and Waterford endorsed the appeal because 'several landlords of limited income are totally unable, from non-receipt of rents, to take effective steps to defend their rights.'[62]

Nationalists and their supporters in the press – Tories (including Salisbury, who rejected the idea of detention without trial) and English landlords – attacked Forster: his desire to leave office intensified. The cabinet thwarted an attempt to bring him before a select committee to answer for the workings of an Act that had hardly been allowed to work. So too did the Commons, who detected a Tory stunt to damage the government. A portent came when the police intercepted crude letter-bombs addressed to Forster's office; but when the Queen escaped an assassination attempt in early March a lunatic, not an Irishman, was responsible.

Parnell had contact with Chamberlain through Captain William O'Shea, MP, the husband of his mistress. The O'Sheas became so reliable a 'usual channel' for the government to deal with Parnell that even Gladstone would use it. Through it Forster was persuaded to grant Parnell parole in April 1882 to attend the funeral of his sister's only son. He also visited Mrs O'Shea, who had in February given birth to his daughter, who was dying. Parnell was unmarried: Mrs O'Shea felt her husband had, *de facto*, ended their marriage years earlier. Parnell attempted to come to an accommodation with the government. O'Shea wrote to Gladstone on 15 April 1882 outlining terms Parnell would be prepared to offer in return for his release. The offer was this: if the government helped settle the question of arrears of tenants who had refused to pay rents, and for the release of leading Leaguers in the west of Ireland who he promised would help calm feelings there, he would use his influence to argue against further agrarian outrages.

Gladstone replied that 'no resentment, or personal prejudice . . . will prevent the Government from treading whatever path may most safely and shortly lead to the pacification of Ireland.'[63] Later, on 28 April, Parnell amplified the main points in a letter to O'Shea; adding that if amendments were made to the Land Act to improve leaseholders' rights he would 'co-operate cordially for the future with the Liberal Party in forwarding Liberal principles and measures of general reform.'[64] The offer bore a striking resemblance to proposals set out on 3 April by John Morley in the paper he edited, *The Pall Mall Gazette*: though he had added another proposition, the resignation of Forster. The Chief Secretary shrugged this off: police intelligence had told him he was being shadowed by Fenian extremists known as the Invincibles, who wanted to murder him. Forster seemed determined to help by demanding his police escort be discontinued.

Parnell's offer – which became known as 'the Kilmainham Treaty' – would have far-reaching consequences, mostly unintended. Gladstone forwarded O'Shea's letter of 15 April to Forster, who rejected the terms and hinted at resignation.[65] On 19 April – when the Invincibles would have murdered Forster at a railway station in Dublin had he not decided to catch an earlier train – Chamberlain was brought into the negotiations. At cabinet on 22 April it was agreed he should be the link man with O'Shea. He had told O'Shea on 17 April that 'there appears to me nothing in your proposals which does not deserve consideration.'[66] There were limits to Joe's radicalism, however, and he warned O'Shea that while he felt it important for the government to note the opinion of all classes of

Irishmen, he made the proviso that 'they are animated by a desire for good government and not by a blind hatred of all government whatsoever.' He also wanted a *quid pro quo*: the Irish party must show consideration for the Liberals and 'pay some attention to public opinion in England and Scotland. Since the present Government have been in office they have had not the slightest assistance in this direction. On the contrary, some Irish members have acted as if their object were to embitter and prejudice all English opinion.'[67]

Forster told Gladstone on 29 April that unless Parnell made a 'public declaration' of his support for the Land Act he could not be 'a party to his release'. When Gladstone received Parnell's letter to O'Shea he described it to Forster as 'the most extraordinary I have ever read'.[68] The offer of co-operation with the Liberal party especially struck Gladstone: he called it 'a *hors d'oeuvre* which we had no right to expect, and, I think, have at present no right to accept.'

Chamberlain asked O'Shea about a public assurance from Parnell, and on 1 May reported he would only give a private one. Gladstone concluded what he described as 'a most anxious day' with a late-night talk with Forster, who told him he had decided to go.[69] When Gladstone accepted Parnell's terms, to allow the Land Act to work, Forster resigned, propelled also by a cabinet refusal to proceed with a new Crimes Bill, which Forster sought as a condition of Parnell's release. He thought Gladstone's action 'a disgraceful compromise'.[70] Gladstone received his resignation 'with much grief' but said: 'I have no choice; followed or not followed, I must go on.'[71] He felt 'the moment is golden', and on the verge of a transformation of Irish affairs.[72] The Tories disagreed, with Balfour observing that if the new policy was right, the old one – and therefore the decision to imprison Parnell and his associates – had been wrong. Indeed, events were about to prove to Gladstone that if the moment seemed golden, the lustre would quickly tarnish.

IV

Gladstone had retired Cowper, the Viceroy, on 26 April, deciding he needed a man of cabinet rank in Dublin. He also knew Cowper would not approve the new policy. One of Cowper's last duties, on 2 May, was (with great reluctance) to order the release of Parnell and two other MPs, Dillon and O'Kelly. Gladstone advised the Queen of the new policy. She 'gave a very reluctant assent'.[73] She felt it 'hazardous' and 'a triumph to Home Rule'.[74] Later, she was horrified when hearing it had been decided to release Davitt, 'one of the worst of the treasonable agitators'.[75] Gladstone, led by Chamberlain's view that to signal the new direction the post should be given to an Irishman, asked Andrew Marshall Porter, solicitor-general for Ireland, to succeed Forster. Porter refused, on personal grounds, and so Gladstone appointed Hartington's younger brother, Lord Frederick Cavendish, Financial Secretary to the Treasury and husband of a niece of Mrs Gladstone, as Chief Secretary.

The Times was dismissive, as were most of the press and the political class, saying there were half-a-dozen men better suited, and interpreting the move as proof Gladstone would run Irish policy himself. Alluding to Cavendish's rank, the paper noted that 'he has, at all events, the advantage of occupying a station which raises him above the ordinary flights of envy; he is not exposed to the adverse influences which tell against a statesman who attains to such a position by mere merit.'[76] On 5 May Cavendish left London for Dublin with Earl Spencer – known because of his big red beard, and not because of his politics, as the Red Earl – who became Viceroy. Spencer went with great reluctance – he had been in Ireland before, during Gladstone's last administration – but Gladstone relied on him as a guiding hand over an inexperienced Chief Secretary. Spencer had told Hartington on 12 April that 'it is everyone's duty to give his help where it is wanted, and I should be a coward to refuse if I am told to do this.'[77] He had also believed he would be working with Forster, so had to adjust his expectations.

On the morning of Saturday 6 May Cavendish was sworn in, and spent the day in Dublin Castle reading himself in. That evening he walked through Phoenix Park towards the viceregal lodge with Thomas Henry Burke, his permanent under-secretary and Ireland's leading civil servant. At 7.17 p.m. some Invincibles attacked them with knives, and murdered them. Cavendish was stabbed in the chest, puncturing his right lung; Burke was stabbed in the heart and his throat cut. It subsequently became known that Burke, an Irishman, was the target of the attack: Cavendish was in the wrong place at the wrong time.

The Gladstones had been dining with the Austrian Ambassador, and walked back to Downing Street to be 'met by the frightful news from Dublin of the assassination of dear F Cavendish and Burke'.[78] The telegram with the news had been handed to Harcourt, who was at the same dinner. He did not tell Gladstone, but took the message to Eddy Hamilton and told him 'you must break the news to them on their return. I must go in search of Hartington.'[79] Lady Frederick was still in London, and Gladstone went immediately to see her – 'it was an awful scene but enlightened by her faith and love'. Gladstone, who could appear emotionally desiccated, was stricken. The Queen immediately blamed him and 'his violent Radical advisers'.[80] Hamilton recorded that the Gladstones 'threw themselves on their knees' when hearing the news. In Dublin, Spencer wrote to his wife that 'I dare not dwell on the horror for I feel I must be unmanned.'[81]

Gladstone wrote the next day that 'this grief lay heavy and stunning upon us'.[82] He told Brand, the Speaker, that 'even in this black crime and terrible calamity, there may I hope be a seed of good . . . the pure and noble life may be a great peace-offering'.[83] He heard of the shock with which Parnell had received the news, and that even Davitt had written a circular (signed also by Parnell and Dillon) denouncing the assassins and urging their fellow countrymen to give them up. Parnell was indeed mortified. O'Shea told Gladstone Parnell had offered to resign his seat if that would help matters. Gladstone rejected this, telling O'Shea: 'I am deeply sensible of the honourable motives by which it has been prompted.'[84] Parnell took to carrying a pistol, against attacks by Fenians who thought he had sold out.

Parliament was adjourned on the Monday after the assassinations as a mark of respect. In a short debate Parnell expressed his 'most unqualified detestation of the horrible crime', and said the perpetrators 'absolutely detest the cause with which I have been associated.'[85] Britain reacted with shock, anger and outrage. *The Times* described the atmosphere among the Irish public as 'a feeling of universal horror' and 'immense and universal execration'.[86] In Cork a meeting to celebrate Parnell's release, attended by Leaguers and Nationalists, resolved to 'denounce it as a crime that calls to Heaven for vengeance' and 'to repudiate its authors . . . with disgust and abhorrence as men with whom the Irish nation has no community of feeling.'

Gladstone offered Cavendish's post to Dilke, who declined as it would be outside the cabinet, something Gladstone considered 'very wrong indeed . . . The notions of rights, as between party and person, have greatly changed since I was young.'[87] Dilke was fortified by his friend the Prince of Wales, whose secretary, Francis Knollys, told Dilke that 'if you had accepted the post without a seat in the Cabinet your position . . . would be a very unsatisfactory one – if the policy, whatever it is, proved a success I doubt whether you would have obtained much credit for it, and if it turned out a failure you may be quite sure that a great deal of the blame would fall upon you'.[88] This was ironic: the main reason Gladstone had not offered Dilke cabinet rank was because 'it would have been perfectly useless to submit such a proposal to the Queen.'[89]

The post went instead to George Otto Trevelyan, whom Spencer had wanted. The outrage in Ireland at the murders was nothing compared with that in England, and Gladstone considered the latter deeply unhelpful. He described *The Times* as 'little less than diabolical' for trying to blame the whole Irish nation for the crime.[90] The paper had described the murders as 'deliberately planned with the object of showing the British Government the futility of attempting to arrange a compromise with Irish Nationalism'.[91] What it called 'the disloyal section of the Irish people' were determined to use 'atrocity' to continue their 'implacable warfare' against the English. It goaded Gladstone by recalling that Forster had resigned because he thought the relaxation of coercion would cause more crime, and he had been proved right, since the joint policy of Gladstone and Parnell in trying to pacify Ireland had lasted just four days. This inculpation of Gladstone in the murder of Cavendish was a brutal twist, heartily endorsed by many Tories, who saw an opportunity to inflict possibly fatal damage on Gladstone too. The Queen told the Prince of Wales that 'this dreadfully Radical Government which contains many thinly-veiled *Republicans*' had not only 'truckled to the Home Rulers' but had shown an 'utter disregard of all my opinions which after forty-five years of experience ought to be considered'.[92] This had left her 'very miserable' and filled with 'disgust', and she asked the Prince to try to knock some sense into Hartington. 'The mischief Mr Gladstone does is *incalculable*.'

An estimated 30,000–40,000 people surrounded the church at Edensor, on the Duke of Devonshire's estate at Chatsworth, on 11 May for Lord Frederick's funeral. A special train brought 250 MPs from St Pancras. Gladstone, the Lord Chancellor, the Speaker and many ministers attended. The Queen sent a wreath. Lady Frederick wrote to Spencer, to whom she was also related, to say that 'I would never grudge the sacrifice of my darling's life if only it leads to the pulling down of the frightful spirit of evil in the land . . . let those noble Christian principles be our guide at this moment of trial and anxiety.'[93] The Dublin police rounded up Fenian activists and questioned them, but it was not until 13 January 1883 that they had a breakthrough. Arresting James Carey, an Invincible, with sixteen others who were all charged with conspiracy to murder, the police managed to turn some of the men against the others. Carey, who had been in Phoenix Park and had pointed out Burke to the assassins, turned Queen's evidence.

Five men were convicted, and hanged in May and June 1883 in Kilmainham. Carey and his family were sent to South Africa for their own safety, but an Irishman there discovered his identity and shot him dead: he too was hanged. Despite the turmoil, the government kept its word to legislate on arrears of rent; and Parnell kept his side of the bargain, seeking to calm the atmosphere and replacing the banned Land League with the more moderate Irish National League (INL) in October 1882. However, the assassinations prompted a new Coercion Bill – the Prevention of Crime (Ireland) Bill – that included suspension of trial by jury in certain circumstances, and the right to detain witnesses.

The Fenians, outraged at Parnell's accommodation with Gladstone, continued to mount attacks on the mainland: having tried to bomb the Mansion House in May 1882, six days after the Phoenix Park murders, they blew up targets in Glasgow in January 1883, exploded devices in Whitehall and at the offices of *The Times* in March that year, and injured seventy people in a blast at Paddington underground station the following October. More London railway stations were attacked in February 1884, Scotland Yard and the Carlton Club in May (a bomb under Nelson's Column failed to go off), and London Bridge in December, when three men planting the device were blown up. The most audacious attempts were in January 1885, when Fenians tried to blow up the House of Commons, Westminster Hall and the Tower of London.

The INL, committed to securing change by constitutional means and endorsed by the Catholic church, became a powerful force for Home Rule. However, it did not change Irish politics so much as the 1884 Reform Act, which added many more working-class men to the electoral roll, and boosted the numbers in the Irish electorate in favour of Home Rule. This confirmed the shift in Irish politics from the question of who owned the land to that of who governed the Irish nation, and placed a coherent third party in parliament.

Also in 1882 Parnell changed his party's name to the Irish Parliamentary party (IPP); and at the 1885 election its representation increased from sixty-three to eighty-six of the 103 Irish seats, its MPs predominantly from the Catholic middle class and marginalising the Protestant or Anglo-Irish Ascendancy interests within Irish politics; the Tory party was almost entirely eliminated while the IPP, true to Parnell's word, co-operated often, but not always, with the Liberals. Once a Liberal government resumed office in February 1886 the Home Rule debate, because of the overwhelming vote in Ireland, was wide open, and the cause was fortunate enough to have a prime minister as open-minded and visionary as Gladstone to seek to embrace it.

V

Chamberlain was not a Home Ruler; but was, as Parnell's friend, keen to propose concessions to counter arguments for Home Rule. In the spring of 1885 he set out a plan for county administrations in Ireland and a 'central board' of elected politicians able to legislate on domestic matters such as education, land and infrastructure. However, nothing it decreed could happen until Westminster agreed. Chamberlain, misled by O'Shea (who continued to act as intermediary), hoped Parnell would jump at his ideas: but Parnell had moved beyond them. In January 1885, in his Cork constituency, he had asked for the re-establishment of an Irish parliament, saying that 'no man has the right to fix the boundary to the march of a nation'.[94] In the same speech he predicted a massive response to the programme of the Irish Parliamentary party, which was not least 'to gain for our country those rights that have been stolen from us.' It was precisely because he and other anti-Home Rule Liberals feared this outcome that Chamberlain advanced his proposals: but it was too late.

Not only was the Irish Parliamentary party lukewarm about them, so too were Chamberlain's colleagues. The plan, which Gladstone supported, was defeated in cabinet on 9 May 1885 thanks to the opposition of all but one of the peers, and Hartington. Gladstone, who knew the Irish had to have some measure of responsibility for themselves, told a colleague that 'within six years, if it please God to spare their [his cabinet opponents'] lives, they will be repenting in sackcloth and ashes'.[95] He told Spencer the subject was 'dead as mutton' for the time being, but he believed it would 'rise again . . . perhaps in larger dimensions.'[96]

Partly because of disagreements with Chamberlain and Dilke on Irish policy, but also because of the battering since Gordon's death in January, the government and the Liberal party were fractious: and matters came to a head in the early hours of 9 June, when the government lost by 264 to 252 an amendment to the Budget. Many Irish voted with the Tories because of their anger at the coercion measures. The government decided to resign. Gladstone did not seek a dissolution: there needed to be no election for nearly two years. Salisbury went to Balmoral and, on 23 June, and after much deliberation and seeking undertakings from Gladstone to support him on supply – ensuring a parliamentary majority to vote the government funds when needed – accepted the Queen's commission to form a government.

The Tories decided not to pursue coercion, explicitly criticising Gladstone's Irish policy. Churchill, who had just become Secretary of State for India, set the tone, announcing on 17 July 1885 that 'it is only by divesting ourselves of all responsibility for the acts of the late government that we can hope to arrive at a successful issue in the task on which we have entered.'[97] This caused one of the few surviving Tory MPs in Ireland – Charles Lewis, the MP for Londonderry – to rebuke him for forgetting that Spencer 'had upheld respect for the law at the risk of his life from day to day'. He said he would not be 'dragged into any implied, however slight, condemnation of Earl Spencer's conduct as Viceroy of Ireland, because it happened to suit the exigencies of party warfare.'[98] The Tory party had no clear idea what their policy in Ireland was to be, other than that it was not to be like the Liberals'.

Gladstone had noticed the shifting of the Irish position. He told Derby on 17 July that 'it is now said that a central board will not suffice, and that there must be a parliament. This I suppose may mean the repeal of the Act of Union, or may mean an Austro-Hungarian scheme, or may mean that Ireland is to be like a great colony such as Canada.'[99] He saw this as 'an entirely new point of departure'. In a letter to Granville on 6 August, looking forward to the election Salisbury would call for the autumn, he said that if it 'gives a return of a decisive character, the sooner the subject is dealt with, the better'. His mind was turning to the inevitability of Home Rule: he did not know that on 1 August Parnell had met Lord Carnarvon, the new Viceroy, and outlined proposals for working with the new government. Salisbury was entirely opposed to Parnell's idea of Irish self-government 'not quite equal to that enjoyed by a State in the US Union'; but, as a ruthless party politician, hoped Gladstone would learn of the meeting, and offer Parnell even more than the Tories could, thereby splitting the Liberals.[100] Gladstone was happy for the nationalists to try to get the Conservatives onside: his main priority was to solve the problem as speedily as possible.

Carnarvon was believed to be sympathetic to Home Rule, and he and Parnell hit it off at a meeting of which no formal note was taken. Parnell, more realist than fanatic, indicated that a small measure of devolution would be acceptable, with more when the Irish had proved able to take responsibility for themselves. He understood that because the Tories controlled the House of Lords it was only they, and not the Liberals, who could guarantee him anything, and so would take what he could get. However, Salisbury would not countenance even a small measure of self-rule, because of the vulnerability of the Ascendancy.

Some politicians regarded the Irish as little more than savages. Gladstone, however, told Hartington on 7 August that 'I cannot treat the people of Ireland as foes or aliens, or advise that less shd be done for them than wd in like circumstances be done for the inhabitants of any other portion of the UK.'[101] For Gladstone it had become a moral issue to give the Irish some independence and, like other matters he regarded in that light, he would not rest until he had discharged his moral obligation towards Ireland: an obligation that would become more pressing after the general election, which returned eighty-five Parnellite MPs out of 103 seats, and an eighty-sixth for a seat in Liverpool.

Gladstone urged Parnell to set out thoughts on a constitution for Ireland, bearing in mind the last cabinet's rejection of a central board. As he cruised the Norwegian fjords in August he reflected on his position, and how much life had changed since 1880. He read widely about Norway and its status as a self-governing nation under the Swedish crown. This gave him an idea about Ireland. At home, Chamberlain was embarking upon what his biographer called 'an open crusade against coercion and Dublin Castle and for drastic Irish reform.'[102]

'Radical Joe' was, however, about to have one of the many ideological turns that punctuated his career. He had said in a speech at Holloway on 17 June 1885 that 'the pacification of Ireland at this moment depends, I believe, on the concession to Ireland of the right to govern itself in the matter of purely domestic business.'[103] Gladstone had taken this as an unwarranted attack on Spencer's viceroyalty. Now, he prepared to do exactly what Chamberlain had wanted, only to find Joe had changed his mind, and cooled towards the Nationalists. He had fallen out with Parnell – with whom he in any case had little direct contact – because of a series of attacks on him by the Irish Nationalist newspaper, *United Ireland*, which accused him of using Ireland to further the radical agenda rather than seeking to improve things for their own sake. Parnell claimed not to influence *United Ireland*; Chamberlain did not believe him. Despite efforts by O'Shea to mediate, his break with Parnell was final.

Parnell spoke in Dublin on 1 September and challenged the government either to bestow Home Rule on Ireland, or govern it as a Crown Colony without any parliamentary representation. In that case, he added, it would expect to be treated in the manner of the larger and more advanced colonies – Canada, New Zealand or the colonies in the as yet unfederated Australia – and given a measure of self-government. Gladstone found this 'a very remarkable and rather formidable speech, much what I expected.'[104] Hartington took issue with Parnell, presaging the split in the Liberal party that Home Rule would bring, and causing Gladstone to feel compromised. However, Gladstone had changed his tune within twenty-four hours, telling Hartington he now found the speech 'as bad as bad can be' because of its demands on England and its 'monstrous' promises to the Irish.[105] He knew that because of the Reform Act the Home Rule party would dominate Ireland at the election: and he warned Hartington, whose family were big landowners in Ireland, that the old responses would not work in such a situation.

Hartington feared Gladstone's change of tone, and suggested a meeting of the former cabinet to see whether 'the various sections of the party can acquiesce in the policy you propose to adopt'.[106] On 9 September Gladstone warned Chamberlain that unity was essential because 'only the Liberal party can (if it can) cope with the great Irish question which may arise three months hence.'[107] Chamberlain was no keener on Home Rule than Hartington was, because he remained wedded to the 'central board' idea and had fallen out with Parnell, whom he no longer aspired to bring round to his own way of thinking. Two days later Gladstone told Rosebery that 'what I do think of is the Irish nation, and the fame, duty and peace of my country.'[108] On 19 September he wrote: 'I have long suspected the Union of 1800. There was a case for doing something; but this was like Pitt's Revolutionary war, a gigantic though excusable mistake.'[109]

In late October Parnell sent Gladstone, via Mrs O'Shea, his outline for an Irish constitution. Gladstone, again through Mrs O'Shea, urged Parnell to press the government, saying Tory administrations had passed Catholic emancipation and the second Reform Act, and might accept Home Rule. He noted that Parnell had made no allowances, post independence, for 'the Irish share in the National Debt, in Naval Defence, or in Royal Charges. This is only by the way.'[110] By 14 November Gladstone was drawing up plans for how Home Rule might work: an Irish chamber in Dublin to consider Irish affairs; the Crown to have the same prerogatives in Ireland and to command the same oath of allegiance; the protection of minority – Protestant – rights; the Irish government would have first call on Irish revenues and receive a share of 'imperial' revenues; the authority of the 'imperial' or Westminster government would be suspended in Ireland except in matters of defence; and Irish MPs would sit in the imperial parliament, but only vote and speak on matters of 'imperial' relevance – those covering all of Great Britain and Ireland. The Irish chamber would be two-thirds composed of MPs elected to Westminster and one-third composed of nominees.

In order to make Home Rule more likely, the Nationalists no longer demanded repeal of the Union, but wanted a chamber under the authority of Westminster. Gladstone used this concession to try to bring Hartington round, promising also to make Parnell consider proper protection for landlords; but he dismissed special protection for Ulster's Protestants. So successful had Carnarvon's wooing of Parnell been that on 21 November he suggested that Irish voters in Britain should vote Tory. In the election, which lasted from late November to early December, many Parnellites in Ulster voted Tory too, while Ulster Liberals made clear their fierce resistance to Home Rule, saying they would consider no devolution of power beyond, effectively, county councils.

The election results realised Gladstone's expectation of a Parnellite landslide in Ireland. The party that would form the government would need Parnell's support, as of the 670 seats in the Commons the Liberals had 319, the Tories 247 and the Irish Parliamentary party eighty-six. Salisbury, counting on Parnell's support, decided not to resign. Gladstone believed in mid-December that to keep Parnell onside Salisbury, Carnarvon and Churchill were all plotting to offer some measure of Home Rule to the Irish. This contradicted what Salisbury had said at the Mansion House on 9 November, which was that his party would stick to its traditional view of Ireland as to all imperial considerations, and that 'the integrity of the Empire is more precious to us than any other possession.'[111] Gladstone told Hartington on 15 December that 'the urgency and bigness of the Irish question are opening to men's minds from day to day.'[112] Hartington had already learned from Granville, who had been to Hawarden, that Gladstone was minded to award 'some large concession of self government' to the Irish if returned to office, and had written to him to ask for clarification.[113] Gladstone had not mentioned Ireland in his election address, so had given no indication of his thinking; and now, to the annoyance of his senior colleagues, he went silent.

His son Herbert, also a Liberal MP, shared with his father the belief that Chamberlain and Dilke wanted to keep the Conservatives in power. This was because of their fear that what they presumed to be Gladstone's ideas would split the Liberal party: the so-called radicals were far more conservative than the prime minister. Herbert then embarked on what the press called 'flying the Hawarden kite'. It was prompted by an exchange of letters with a Flintshire neighbour, a Mr Frank Miles, who was permitted to send it to the newspapers. Herbert said that 'nothing could induce me to countenance separation; but if five-sixths of the Irish people wish to have a Parliament in Dublin, for the management of their own local affairs, I say, in the name of justice and wisdom, let them have it.' Herbert was thirty-one and had been an MP for five years: he was clearly speaking for himself but, equally, it was assumed his father did not dissent from the views he expressed, and wanted them brought into the public sphere.

Herbert then gave what he thought was a confidential briefing to a journalist called Dawson Rogers, of the National Press Agency, on 16 December 1885 on his father's ideas for Home Rule. Herbert hoped to calm things down, but had the opposite effect. In what, reflecting his naïvete, Herbert described as 'a gross breach of confidence', the NPA sent the story to provincial newspapers. Only two picked it up, it being the morning of the 18th before the establishment broadsheet, *The Times*, carried the story.[114] Gladstone, with complete honesty, denied all knowledge, but did not deny its substance: the kite was flying.

The timing of the kite-flying was unfortunate, because Hartington heard the story before a letter, written on 17 December, reached him from Gladstone outlining the plan. There was a nuance in the letter that was lost in the leak: he told Hartington that 'I have more or less of opinions and ideas, but no intentions or negotiations.'[115] He continued: 'I consider that Ireland has now spoken; and that an effort ought to be made by the Government without delay to meet her demands for the management by an Irish legislative body of Irish as distinct from Imperial affairs.' Knowing Hartington's fear that empowering Ireland would undermine the British Empire and sell out landowners such as the Cavendishes, he prefaced the outline of the plan he made to him with the statement that 'union of Empire and due supremacy of Parliament' were the foundations upon which the plan would proceed. He also stressed that consideration would be given to the 'protection' of Protestants and to ensuring Ireland paid its share towards 'Imperial charges'. Hartington was not appeased, and wrote to the chairman of his own Liberal association to say that his views on Ireland had not changed. He would not be the only one. Chamberlain too had been wrong-footed, and decided to stall while considering his position. No longer friends with Parnell, and his central board plan having failed to win support, he found himself moving away from a radical position on Ireland. Having apparently embraced Home Rule six months earlier, he now advocated Unity of Empire.

Over Christmas Gladstone cut himself off from his colleagues and said nothing. He did, however, confide in a few he knew shared his view on Ireland – Morley, Rosebery and Spencer, the last of whom had converted to Home Rule. 'You and I will be looked upon by ex-colleagues as co-conspirators in aiding and abetting the GOM in his wickedness,' Spencer told Rosebery on 30 December.[116] 'The GOM is sulking in his tent. No one can get a word from him,' Chamberlain told Labouchere on Boxing Day.[117] Rosebery described the ex-cabinet as in 'open revolt' because of Gladstone's refusal to communicate.[118] As for the Tories, Hicks Beach wrote to Churchill on Christmas Day to say his holiday would have been improved 'if we had any certain prospect of the pleasure of Opposition!'[119]

The Grand Old Man resisted calls for a meeting of the late cabinet until the day of the Queen's Speech to open the new parliament, on 21 January. There was more accord than expected – mainly because the speech was pusillanimous on Ireland – with only Hartington staying 'stiff' in his manner because of his fear that Gladstone was about to embrace Home Rule.[120] Gladstone, too, hoped the Tories would remain in power and undertake this mission, because he knew they could do it with Liberal support whereas a Liberal administration would struggle to achieve Home Rule because of the likely paucity of Tory support: he waited to see how matters developed between the Tories and the IPP. What he did not know was that because of more agrarian disturbances during the autumn of 1885, Salisbury had decided that a measure of coercion would be necessary. Carnarvon said he would resign, though this was not known until mid-January. Those Irish opposed to Home Rule – mainly but not exclusively in Ulster and around Dublin – suddenly realised the Commons could sanction such a measure with ease; as a result the Liberal Unionist party was formed on 20 January 1886.

Parnell switched support to the Liberals, giving the two parties a big majority in the Commons. He did this only after confirming the administration would probably be led by Gladstone: he would not lend his party's support to a Hartington-Chamberlain ministry, about which Chamberlain had sounded him out via O'Shea on 22 January, with Chamberlain arguing that 'I am not at all clear that it is desirable to turn out the Government at this moment.'[121] However, the government was defeated on the Queen's Speech on 26 January, having just announced an imminent Coercion Bill. Salisbury and his ministry resigned on the 28th. Gladstone had changed his mind and assisted the defeat because 'it was now plain Ireland had no hope from the Tories'.[122] He was appalled that the Tories' response to a democratic expression of feeling by the Irish should have been to coerce them rather than respect their views. When preparing to vote down the government Harcourt, the former Home Secretary, asked him with incredulity 'are you prepared to go forward without either Hartington or Chamberlain?' Gladstone noted that 'I was prepared to go forward without anybody. That is to say without any known and positive assurance of support. This was one of the great imperial occasions which call for such resolutions.'

The Queen wanted anyone but Gladstone to form her government, and in desperation asked George Goschen. He was an anti-radical who found Chamberlain shocking and had been a minister in Gladstone's first administration. He shared Hartington's mind on Ireland, and the Queen now asked whether he could find like-minded men to form a ministry. Goschen was a formidable intellect, a successful banker and diplomat, and had already declined offers of serving in Gladstone's second ministry, a GCB, the viceroyalty of India and the Speakership of the House of Commons. Now he declined to support the Queen in her attempt to keep Gladstone out of office – 'I would earnestly entreat your

Majesty to send for Mr Gladstone,' he said.[123] At a quarter past midnight on Saturday 30 January 1886 Sir Henry Ponsonby, the Queen's private secretary, arrived at Gladstone's house to convey Her Majesty's invitation to form a government, couching it in terms that made it clear the Queen would not mind if, given his often-expressed wish to retire, he declined the offer. He accepted without hesitation, and began writing a memorandum to the Queen alerting her that he intended to try to find a way to meet the democratically expressed wishes of the people of Ireland. When Ponsonby told the Queen that Gladstone would serve, her response was 'alas!'[124]

Hartington, who with Goschen and eighteen other Liberals had voted with the Tories on 26 January, refused to serve: to them, as to many who stayed in the Liberal ranks, there was a whiff of autocracy about the way Gladstone conducted Irish policy. This failure to bring his party and the country with him would have serious consequences. Gladstone saw Hartington's defection as signalling the beginning of the end of the Whiggish element in their party. Chamberlain agreed to become President of the Local Government Board, after declining Gladstone's offer of the Admiralty. Gladstone had refused his request for the Colonial Office.

The appointment of Morley, one of the party's leading intellectuals and an avowed Home Ruler, as Chief Secretary for Ireland, panicked Harcourt. He felt it circumscribed discussion in cabinet on Ireland. Gladstone, casuistically, rejected this, saying no one by joining the cabinet committed himself to support an Irish parliament. Trevelyan, highly sceptical about Home Rule, took the Scottish Office, but Goschen, Derby and Bright all declined to serve. On 1 February Gladstone set off for Osborne to see the Queen, and to hand her his memorandum. 'I kissed hands and am thereby Prime Minister for the third time. But as I trust for a brief tenure only.' That prediction would be all too accurate.[125]

VI

In Arnold Bennett's novel *Clayhanger*, the Home Rule Bill throws the Liberal Club in Bursley into chaos. 'The epidemic of resignations had already set in, and there had been talk of a Liberal-Unionist Club. The steward saw that the grand folly of a senile statesman was threatening his own future prospects.'[126] The imaginary Potteries Liberal Club reflected the effect of Gladstone's intentions on the party at Westminster and through the country. Morley was instinctively more radical even than Gladstone, but understood the necessity of keeping in step with him. He also saw the need to propitiate the many Liberals who were uncertain, and told Gladstone of the importance of re-addressing the land question to 'prevent the tenants from confiscating the property of the landlords'.[127] The Queen showed surprising equanimity, not least because Salisbury (with whom she continued to plot) had assured her the measure would not pass. When Gladstone kissed hands she had told him that 'I feared his proposal of a Central Legislative Assembly in Dublin would never succeed', and she spoke with conviction.[128] She also warned him there would be a civil war, a prediction that in time came true. 'He answered, he might fail, it was 49 to 1 that he would, but he intended to try.'

There was some delay in framing the Bill, because of the complexities of the financial, administrative and political questions, and because of Gladstone's insistence of doing it almost all on his own. This led to press speculation and restlessness among the opposition. On 23 February Churchill made a speech in Belfast with which he hoped to destabilise the government. His visit caused such controversy that 350 extra policemen were drafted in from all over Ulster. He addressed 7,000 people in the Ulster Hall, endowing that building with a significance for Unionists that persists today. After attacking Gladstone he said: 'I think at the present crisis that I have a right to appeal to the Loyalists of Ireland to come forward and declare themselves openly . . . and I appeal to the loyal Catholics in Ireland to show which side they are on.'[129] But he turned to the Protestants who formed the near-entirety of his audience. 'For nearly 200 years your motto, your password, your watchword, and your cry has been "No surrender",' he roared, and they cheered. Gladstone was about to plunge 'the knife into the heart of the British Empire'. It was allegedly on this occasion that he uttered, 'Ulster will fight, and Ulster will be right,' but reports of his speech make no mention of it. A quarter of a century later Unionists would exploit the Orangemen and their fears even more ruthlessly; Churchill paved the way with what became known as 'playing the Orange card'.

The cabinet discussed Home Rule on 13 March and Chamberlain – who had told his brother he would resign 'if Mr G's scheme goes too far' – expressed his hostility to the policy and to a scheme of land purchase to help aggrieved landlords.[130] He balked at buying out landlords for £120 million, the equivalent of twenty years' purchase of their existing rents, amazed that the normally parsimonious Gladstone could consider it. The Queen could not understand why a radical such as Chamberlain was against Home Rule; Goschen told her it was because he 'disliked disorder and was very dictatorial'.[131] 'This I knew,' she noted.

On 14 March Gladstone told the cabinet that, as parliamentary draftsmen worked on the Bill, 'I cannot see my own way to any satisfactory measure except it be one which shall constitute a Statutory Legislative Chamber in Dublin.'[132] Chamberlain threatened resignation, but only after the proposals had been fully discussed in cabinet: he was burdened by his vanity, a self-regard that would have deep consequences for himself, Gladstone, his party and the Irish question. Trevelyan also threatened to resign. The ring was held until 26 March, with Gladstone proposing a separate measure to guarantee the rights of landlords that would precede the Government of Ireland Bill, as the measure would formally be known. That day Trevelyan said he could not face law and order being handed over to the Irish, which he felt would necessitate buying out Irish landlords.

Chamberlain – in close touch about tactics and strategy with Churchill – objected to giving the Irish the right of taxation and of appointing judges and magistrates. He wanted a specific and narrow expression of such powers as might be delegated to Ireland – rather like his own, stillborn scheme for a central board; and he suggested the only acceptable constitutional change was an American-style federation. Both he and Trevelyan resigned, walking out of the meeting, as Gladstone was adamant that things had to be done his way. In his diary he confided that 'the burden on mind and nerve becomes exceeding heavy: heavier than ever I felt it,' unsurprising given he was in his seventy-seventh year, and his eyesight and voice were both failing.[133] When he told the Queen of the resignations, she happily reminded him that his policy was doomed.

In early April Parnell and Morley discussed the detail of the Bill: Parnell met Gladstone only once, to discuss financial arrangements, with which the Irish leader never, in the end, felt happy. Had the Bill not fallen for other reasons, this might have caused the Irish to withdraw support. The government diluted the idea of complete taxation rights once Chamberlain had resigned, proving his impetuousness. It was

Admiralty Arch: a temple of the Edwardian Baroque.

The Edward VII 5d dull purple and ultramarine, reflecting the glory of the nation.

Sir Edward Elgar, the composer of swagger.

Gertrude Elizabeth Blood, Lady Colin Campbell, proving the value of the corsage, by Boldini, 1897.

Thomas Lister, 4th Baron Ribblesdale, in everyday pose, by Sargent in his bravura style, 1902.

Off to the seaside for a spot of lunch in the Daimler, 1907.

Robert Gascoyne-Cecil, 3rd Marquess of Salisbury, a landmark of Tory pessimism and proprietor of the Hotel Cecil, painted by Millais, 1883.

Arthur James Balfour, a long-term resident of the hotel, and defender of philosophic doubt, by Sargent, 1908.

Low behaviour in high society: the ill-fated house party at Tranby Croft, 1890. The Prince of Wales is third from the right in the front row; Lt-Col Sir William Gordon-Cumming is to the Prince's right.

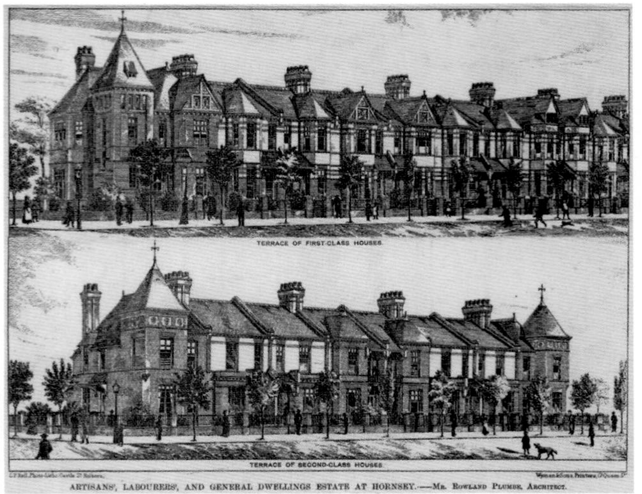

Homes for the growing middle classes: new build at Hornsey as London expands, 1883.

Blythe (Kent) bowling to Tyldesley (Lancashire) at Canterbury, 10 August 1906, by Albert Chevallier Tayler. Kent won by an innings and 195 runs.

Mr Selfridge's baroque palace: *de luxe* department store shopping comes to London's Oxford Street, 1909.

The power couple of middle-class radicalism: Beatrice Webb, beloved of Joe Chamberlain and mocked by H. G. Wells, and Sidney Webb: 'his tiny tadpole body, unhealthy skin, lack of manner, Cockney pronunciation, poverty are all against him'.

Alfred Harmsworth, 1st Viscount Northcliffe, who built his fortune on never overestimating the taste of the aspirant reading public.

THE BOY'S OWN PAPER

No. 639.—Vol. XIII. SATURDAY, APRIL 11, 1891. Price One Penny. [ALL RIGHTS RESERVED.]

THE COCK HOUSE AT FELLSGARTH.

A PUBLIC SCHOOL STORY.

By Talbot Baines Reed,

CHAPTER XIV.—THE SHOP OPENS.

ROBERT—no one knew his surname—was a regular institution at Fellsgarth. Pluralist and jack-of-all trades as he was, he seemed unable to make much of a hand at anything he took up. He was school porter, owner of the school shop, keeper of the club properties, and occasional school policeman; and he dis-

"He brought D'Arcy to hang on to the end."

The Boy's Own Paper, morally equipping the future rulers of the Empire.

The newly monied working-class at play: the Edwardians did love to be beside the seaside, appropriately dressed.

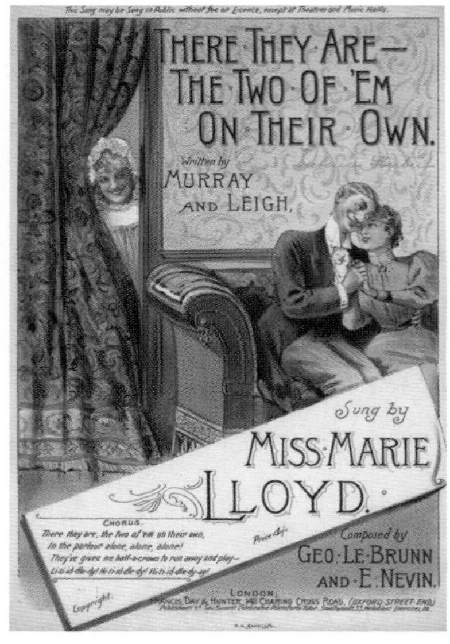

A poster for Marie Lloyd, enemy of the Social Purity Movement: she'd never had her ticket punched before.

The happiest days of their lives: Edwardian children at the St James's Road Council School, Northampton – one of those established after the 1902 Education Act.

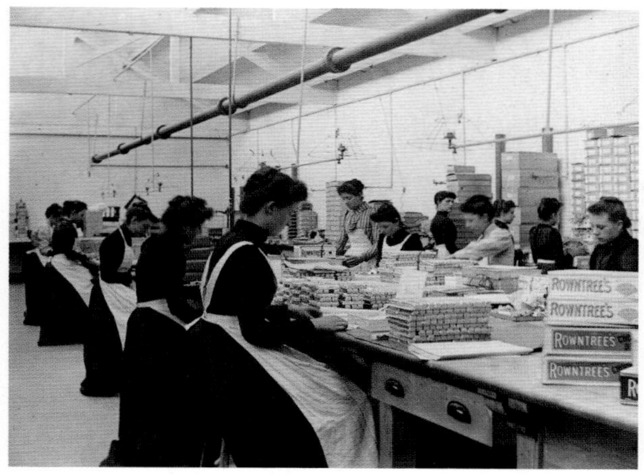

Women workers in Mr Rowntree's splendid new chocolate factory, 1910.

John Burns, a thoughtful working-class rebel who became a Liberal statesman.

James Keir Hardie, in the age before amplification, addresses the faithful in Trafalgar Square, 1913.

A. E. Housman ponders a blue remembered hill, and almost certainly premature death.

Cecil Sharp (left) captures another folk song from Edwin Clay, at Brailes in Warwickshire, c. 1905.

The plan for C. F. A. Voysey's house for J. W. Buckley Esq. at Windermere, 1899: the apotheosis of Arts and Crafts.

decided to list what the Irish parliament might not do; and to exclude Irish members from Westminster, to stop them influencing British matters. It was unclear how they would continue to influence imperial affairs such as defence, foreign policy or the Crown.

Gladstone introduced the Bill on 8 April 1886, in a titanic speech of three and a half hours. His intention, he began, was 'to establish good and harmonious relations between Great Britain and Ireland on the footing of those free institutions to which Englishmen, Scotchmen, and Irishmen are alike unalterably attached.'[134] He argued that Ireland could now govern itself: agrarian crimes had fallen by three-quarters since 1881. Since 1832 the murder rate too had dropped by three-quarters, and the total number of criminal offences by 80 per cent; but the great emigration had reduced the population from 7.67 million in 1831 to 5.17 million in 1881. With America increasing in its allure the population would continue to fall until the 1930s. However, Gladstone pointed out that the drop in disorder was far greater than the proportionate drop in the population.

He argued that a separate parliament in Dublin would not affect the unity of the Empire, any more than its unity had been compromised before 1801. He promised to protect the traditions of Ulster – the factor that would bedevil Anglo-Irish relations for the next century and beyond – but argued Ulster could not have the right of veto over a policy endorsed by five-sixths of Ireland's electorate. He referred to partition only to dismiss it as unpractical. None of the various ideas advanced to set Ulster apart had been sufficiently credible to be included in the Bill. However, he agreed that if during the deliberations a workable scheme emerged to safeguard Ulster's way of life, he would consider it.

He claimed an earlier attempt to effect a settlement in Ireland, in 1782, had failed because it had taken too much into account 'the pernicious voice and claims of ascendancy'.[135] The new constitution of that year had allowed Catholics the same property rights as Protestants and to open schools in which they could educate their children as Catholics: but it had been still too heavily weighted in favour of the Ascendancy to give anything except short-term relief, and to do nothing to stop the gerrymandering of the Irish parliament – which itself had fewer than twenty years to run – in the interests of the Protestants.

He admitted it was too difficult to distinguish imperial from domestic affairs sufficiently to allow Irish representatives to attend either House of Parliament for United Kingdom questions: a profound weakness, for it meant that Ireland forfeited a say in matters such as defence and foreign policy. He accepted, as a government in 1997 would not in relation to Scotland and England, the impossibility of Irish MPs influencing British affairs. He preferred to recommend their exclusion altogether. Ireland's compensation, however, would be strong powers of taxation: 'Great Britain will never force upon Ireland taxation without representation.'[136] To safeguard against the idea that the Westminster parliament, without any Irish representation, might revoke the privileges the Bill would confer on Ireland, Gladstone announced that only the Irish parliament itself might petition Westminster to do such a thing, or it could happen only after Irish representation had been restored, to give the Irish the same means of defending their constitutional rights as before Home Rule.

Gladstone then outlined what the proposed legislative body would not be able to influence. As well as defence and foreign policy, and anything affecting the prerogatives of and succession to the Crown, he announced that no single religion would become established in Ireland, to protect Protestants from living in a formally Catholic state; and Ireland would continue to enjoy the protection of the United Kingdom law of trade and navigation. Other institutions, such as the Post Office, the census and the quarantine laws, he felt Ireland would benefit from under British control, but he would surrender them if the Irish thought otherwise.

The most complex proposal was about the new legislative assembly. A unicameral parliament in which the 103 MPs who currently sat at Westminster simply transferred to a chamber in Dublin would, he saw, give insufficient protection to minorities – by which he meant the landed interest, notably in Ulster. So he proposed two chambers – he called them orders – the second of which would be the 103 MPs plus another 103 representatives from the same constituencies, and the first of which would be the twenty-eight Irish representative peers in the House of Lords (to be replaced by Crown nominees when they died) and seventy-five elected members, for whom a high-value property qualification would be imposed, both in order to stand and for the franchise. The members of this upper house would sit for ten years, and neither house would have a right of veto lasting longer than three years. The Viceroy would remain, but would not be a political appointee, or leave his post with a change of government at Westminster. He would become something akin to a constitutional monarch, ensuring continuity. Gladstone outlined transitional arrangements to bring the police (which Britain would, if necessary, subsidise), the judiciary and the civil service under Irish control. He explained how taxation would change and what contributions Ireland would make to the imperial Budget and the national debt.

The present rule was unpopular with the Irish, wasteful of money and demoralising. 'I ask that we should apply to Ireland that happy experience which we have gained in England and in Scotland . . . that the best and surest foundation we can find to build upon is the foundation afforded by the affections, the convictions, and the will of the nation; and it is thus, by the decree of the Almighty, that we may be enabled to secure at once the social peace, the fame, the power, and the permanence of the Empire.'[137]

Colonel Thomas Waring, Conservative MP for North Down, praised Gladstone's 'wonderful and unparalleled piece of oratory'. However, he predicted that 'when the glamour and the eloquence of the oratory had passed away it would be found that the measure itself was not one which would be accepted by the House or by the country': and this was because of the Parnellite influence on it, which had caused the Bill to acquire 'an odour and flavour which all the spices of the East could not remove – an odour left by hands steeped in treason.'[138] He thought the arguments could be applied to Ulster, which would then petition the new Irish assembly to have Home Rule of its own. His cry to rule Ireland with the same hand that ruled England and Scotland would reverberate down the decades: the resistance of Ulster, largely discounted hitherto, would grow as a consideration until, on the eve of the Great War, it reached the point where what Waring called 'the West Britons of Ireland' were prepared to mutiny.[139]

His views were echoed not just by Ulster MPs but also by MPs from the mainland: and by Liberals as well as Tories. Trevelyan pronounced himself awestruck by Gladstone's 'remarkable . . . energy and diction' in a speech that had 'actually benumbed the faculties of all who heard it'.[140] He said he had hoped the matter would be knocked around in cabinet and modified, but implied that Gladstone's rigidity had left him with no choice but to resign. He believed the level of violence in Ireland made it unwise to hand control of law and order to the Irish: he did not trust the sincerity or the motives of Parnell and his party, or the attempts to shape Ireland using American money. Parnell then endorsed the Bill as settling the quarrel between England and Ireland, and took issue with much of the detail of Trevelyan's speech. Divisions were deep.

Chamberlain and Gladstone argued about why he had resigned, and his objections to the land purchase scheme. Chamberlain identified the Achilles heel of Gladstone's scheme – the lack of Irish representation at Westminster, and that the Irish contribution would not rise during a national emergency, such as war, which he said made a mockery of the unity and integrity of the British Empire. For Chamberlain it was all or nothing: he felt Home Rule in this form was not merely unsatisfactory, but would encourage demands for more autonomy. He saw the point that would bedevil the Irish question for decades: 'Ireland is not a homogeneous community . . . it consists of two nations [cries of 'No! No!'] – that it is a nation which comprises two races and two religions.'[141] He made a nakedly sectarian argument. A disproportionate amount of Irish industrial wealth was held by Protestants in Ulster: and wherever Protestants were found in the other three provinces 'they are the nucleus of industry and enterprise'.[142] They would resist Irish rule: would they be coerced for the crime of loyalty to Britain, while the disloyal did as they liked? The speech, and the resignation that preceded it, earned Chamberlain respect. Beatrice Webb, no admirer, watched him from the Ladies' Gallery and admitted he appeared 'in a new light'.[143]

Then Hartington, without accusing Gladstone of bad faith, complained there had been no warning of the 'magnitude and vastness' of the proposals before the election: parliament had 'morally not the right' to take such a step without a mandate.[144] He asked how the will of the imperial parliament would be enforced in Ireland, if Ireland chose not to comply: he presumed martial law. (The Queen sent him a note of congratulation, 'this being no party question'.[145]) Churchill, who had just described Gladstone as 'an old man in a hurry' for driving the Bill through with so little consultation, and who regarded 'playing the Orange card' as the way to derail it – echoed the sentiments of the three former ministers, believing the Bill was 'unconstitutionally sprung' on the House.[146] He spoke for his party.

Until the second reading debate began, Gladstone remained intensely secretive about the Bill's contents. The Irish found the measure flawed, but once Parnell agreed to vote for it, disbelief was suspended. There was a widespread suspicion among opponents that the Irish, in any case, would take what they could get, and use it as the thin end of the wedge.

The debate ran from 10 May until 7 June, with twelve nights set aside to discuss detail. Gladstone proposed a joint committee of members of both parliaments to allow an Irish input on 'Imperial' questions, and to give the Irish parliament 'the right by address to claim representation upon any question of Imperial policy.'[147] The cabinet remained fractious; the press teased him about what exactly the House was being asked to vote for. Gladstone became more combative as the atmosphere became more negative. 'The Tory Party have announced their policy,' he said in his second reading speech. 'Repression.'[148]

The press had been energetic in drawing comparisons between the success of the National League and the funding it had drawn from America – akin to an interference in United Kingdom politics by a foreign power. The opponents of the Bill became more aggressive against Parnell, Lord Ebrington, the Tory member for Tavistock, mocking him with his nickname 'the uncrowned king of Ireland' and saying it was proposed to put in charge of Ireland 'men whose influence would disappear if they ceased to be disloyal'.[149] The atmosphere had become intensely febrile, with Liberal unity shattered, and Gladstone, rather like Disraeli during the passage of the 1867 Reform Bill, prepared to take almost any step to secure Home Rule. 'Many private friendships have gone into the deep,' Regy Brett, the future Lord Esher, noted in his diary on 20 May.[150] 'All the argument, all the authority, all the social influence are against Mr Gladstone. This only drives him to fight the harder; and among a despondent host, he, with his seventy-six years of conflict behind him, alone is full of confidence and indomitable pluck.'

The idea of halting the Bill if it passed its second reading, and framing a new one with wider support, was discussed and, on 28 May, settled upon by Gladstone. When he heard that Unionists had asked the press to investigate his work with prostitutes, which he (and Mrs Gladstone) had conducted since the 1840s, he stopped it, a massive blow for him since he believed in it profoundly, but a sign of his determination to enact the Bill. On the twelfth and final day of the debate Goschen and Gladstone argued over the promise to reframe the Bill. Goschen goaded him: MPs supporting the second reading would not know what they were voting for, and that any Act would cause conflicts between the two parliaments. Parnell, speaking shortly before the debate ended, rejected partition, saying an independent Ireland would need all the talent it could get: and in any case the Protestants were, as everyone knew, not just in Ulster.

Sir Michael Hicks Beach – who would soon be Chief Secretary for Ireland – argued that he and his colleagues sought means to bind the constituent parts of empire more firmly rather than loosen them. Ireland was going against the grain of the imperial expansion of the 1880s, but then unlike the new African colonies it had been linked to the Crown for centuries. Just before the vote Gladstone implored MPs to think not for the moment, but for the years ahead. 'Go into the length and breadth of the world,' he told them, 'ransack the literature of all countries, find, if you can, a single voice, a single book, find, I would almost say, as much as a single newspaper article, unless the product of the day, in which the conduct of England towards Ireland is anywhere treated except with profound and bitter condemnation. Are these the traditions by which we are exhorted to stand? No; they are a sad exception to the glory of our country. They are a broad and black blot upon the pages of its history.'[151]

He lost by 341 to 311. He considered a dissolution of parliament, and therefore a fresh election, or merely resigning to let Salisbury see what he could do: the cabinet the next morning was unanimous for a dissolution. He was beaten but not demoralised: 'Upon the whole we have more ground to be satisfied with the progress made, than to be disappointed at the failure.'[152] It was true that, without a mandate, 311 MPs had backed Home Rule: but ninety-three Liberals had voted against. Two years later Oscar Wilde, born in Dublin, would tell Gladstone he was 'the one English statesman who has understood us, who has sympathised with us, whom we claim now as our leader, and who, we know well, will lead us to the grandest and justest political victory of this age.'[153]

The dissolution was granted, the Queen having been advised to do so by both Salisbury and Goschen. The election was held from 1 to 17 July: 317 Tories and seventy-seven Liberal Unionists were elected. Hartington and Chamberlain, leading the dissident faction, did not coalesce with the Conservatives, but offered support: they would serve in Salisbury's third administration after a formal coalition in 1895. Chamberlain had sought to keep channels open with the Conservatives. In November 1884, when at odds over reform and redistribution, he had written to Churchill: 'I am sorry that we have been forced into public conflict. I should be still more sorry if political opposition degenerated into a private quarrel.'[154] During the winter of 1885–6 the two men dined together on several occasions, perhaps paving the way for Chamberlain's move, but also so

Churchill could gather intelligence to pass on to Salisbury. He himself had been sceptical about the Liberals' boldness: 'I suspect they will force Gladstone to hold back,' he wrote to Churchill days before his own administration resigned.[155]

Goschen would join Salisbury's second one. First, though, he would have to find a seat, for he had been defeated in Edinburgh as a Liberal Unionist: 'A disgrace to Edinburgh and Scotland' was how the Queen consoled him: they had done it to support 'that really half deluded old man.'[156] The Liberals, with 191 seats, were greatly reduced, and it appeared as though Gladstone's career might be over. 'I cannot help feeling very thankful,' the Queen noted.[157] He, though, sought to reunite the Liberal party: and would not give up on Ireland.

VII

The Conservative and Unionists' victory was not just a defeat for Gladstone and the Liberals, but for the idea of Irish self-government. There were growing agrarian tensions in Ireland after two bad harvests in 1885 and 1886. Restive elements considered criminality and anti-constitutional behaviour to be the only means of achieving their aims. Timothy Healy and colleagues in the National League devised a plan – the Plan of Campaign – whereby tenants who could not afford to pay their rents would offer a lower figure to the landlord. In many cases the landlord accepted; but where he did not the tenants, backed by the League, would refuse to pay any rent at all, until the landlord caved in and cut the rent.

There were ugly confrontations, mainly on big estates with absentee landlords, notably the Marquess of Clanricarde's 52,000-acre landholding in Co. Galway. Clanricarde, whose landed income was around £25,000 a year, refused a 25 per cent rent reduction. Instead of paying their rents, his tenants paid the money to the League, who banked it for them. It told Clanricarde he would not get a penny until he reduced the rent as requested. This presented another difficulty for Parnell, who was not only trying to convince the English to accept Home Rule – he had canvassed exclusively in England during the election on behalf of sympathetic candidates – but also wished to keep Irish landlords on his side by showing the moderation of a self-governing Ireland. He distanced himself from the Plan of Campaign, which he saw would alienate those he wished to convince about Ireland's willingness to work within the constitution. Parnell's caution was justified, because in December 1886 Salisbury's administration declared the Plan of Campaign to be an unlawful and criminal conspiracy.

Matters then became even worse for the Irish. Churchill – whom Salisbury had appointed to the Exchequer in August and with whom he had bickered ever since, lately over defence spending – resigned just before Christmas, confident his resignation would be refused. Churchill told Brett that when he outlined his Budget plans to the cabinet, Salisbury had been 'very satirical and carping . . . the incarnation of pessimism'.[158] But, as Churchill famously said, he had forgotten Goschen: the Liberal Unionist who accepted Salisbury's offer to succeed him. In the ensuing reshuffle Salisbury appointed his nephew, A. J. Balfour, to replace Hicks Beach (who thought, wrongly, that he was going blind) as Chief Secretary. He was the tenth incumbent in as many years. Hartington, who had reservations about Salisbury, declined to serve.

Churchill's great career, which had seen a meteoric rise to high office, was not just derailed, but finished. He died in 1895, just before his forty-sixth birthday, after a long decline that may have been caused by syphilis: indeed the mood swings caused in the earlier stages of the disease may have led to his fatal decision to challenge Salisbury. Rosebery, in a short memoir of great literary merit, wrote that Churchill 'will be pathetically memorable, too, for the dark cloud which gradually enveloped him, and in which he passed away. He was the chief mourner at his own protracted funeral, a public pageant of gloomy years.'[159] Worse still, 'there was no curtain, no retirement, he died by inches in public.'[160]

Balfour, a philosopher by training, acclaimed for his book *A Defence of Philosophic Doubt*, moved firmly against the Irish troublemakers. He exhibited a ruthlessness that would desert him, fifteen years later, when he became a near-disastrous prime minister in succession to his uncle. He was sensitive to the accusation of nepotism: the phrase 'Bob's your uncle' originated at this juncture, and the branding of Salisbury's administrations as 'the Hotel Cecil' came later. Determined to prove he was not deficient, he discharged his duties with an almost reckless determination to show a leadership of force, surprising everyone. His nickname, 'Nancy', reflected a wide perception of him as fey, or even effeminate; though he conducted a long affair with Lady Elcho, the wife of one of his friends. As the Nationalists would find, appearances can be deceiving.

Gladstone branded the Tory party's policy as repression, and Balfour took him at his word. There was no Dublin-based Viceroy in the Cabinet to exert an influence over the Chief Secretary, as had been the case in earlier ministries. The Viceroy now had the status in Ireland of a constitutional monarch (something suggested by the Home Rule Bill), and the one who swore Balfour in, the Marquess of Londonderry, had been his fag at Eton. Salisbury backed Balfour's hard line, noting that, in dealing with the Irish, there might be a place for conciliation, but 'severity must come first'.[161]

The anti-Home Rule majority in the Commons saw through the Irish Crimes Bill in 1887, which addressed the breakdown in order that caused over 900 people in Ireland – almost 500 in Munster alone – to require expensive police protection. It forbade unlawful conspiracies against payment of rents, as well as punishing boycotting, unlawful assembly and intimidation: and, to make it easier to enforce the law, trial by jury was suspended. Unlike earlier such Acts this did not require annual renewal. Its draconian provisions led to hundreds of arrests, including of people who had helped evict tenants. Balfour made a point of using the Act against MPs, who behaved respectably at Westminster but went to Ireland to incite trouble. If imprisoned, they would be treated like ordinary convicts.

He had the National League proscribed, used soldiers to evict tenants and ordered the breaking down of farmstead doors with battering rams if the inhabitants would not leave. On 9 September 1887 a Parnellite MP, William O'Brien, was put on trial in Mitchelstown, Co. Cork, together with a farmer called John Mandeville, for organising a rent strike on Lady Kingston's estate, contrary to the Crimes Act. John Dillon, another MP, made a speech outside the courthouse attacking Balfour: the police were pelted with stones and opened fire, killing three men. There was shock not just in Britain but in America and around the world: the event became known as the Mitchelstown Massacre.

When, in the Commons the next day, the Chief Secretary was asked to justify the police's conduct, he was wrong-footed by inadequate information, based on an outline of events sent by telegraph. The Irish MPs who questioned him had their own detailed account, which Balfour could neither confirm nor deny. He asserted, however, that there had been 'an assault upon the police, utterly unprovoked and of the most violent and brutal character.'[162] He repeated this formula later, to the growing anger of Irish members, adding that the police had acted in self-defence. Edward Carson, one of the most prominent actors in the Home Rule crisis of 1911–14, prosecuted O'Brien for the Crown. He told Balfour that when he approached Mitchelstown 'all the persons going into the town were armed with heavy sticks. I also observed a great number of persons on horseback, also armed with sticks'.[163] Carson also witnessed the mob dispersing once shots were fired: 'a good many with signs of having been severely handled by the police'. The police themselves presented 'a very battered appearance'.[164]

Unfortunately for Balfour the press almost unanimously carried a version of events that blamed the authorities for accelerating the violence, and which reflected disgust in England at this most un-English behaviour. When Balfour spoke of 'self-defence', Hansard recorded an unnamed Parnellite crying out 'retribution'.[165] The mood against Balfour was ugly, and his party did not run to his support. There was a sense that freedom of speech had been attacked, not the police. John Gibson, the Attorney-General for Ireland, tried to help Balfour: he claimed a mob of between 3,000 and 4,000 had confronted a force of between fifty and sixty police, and had entered the town determined to disrupt the trial and hijack justice. This inflamed the House, and not just Irish MPs, further.

Two days later the Irish policy was debated under a fierce spotlight. Harcourt said the *débâcle* had been 'the usual and necessary results of a violent and unconstitutional action on the part of the responsible Government of the Crown', a policy of coercion that was the fruit of voting down Home Rule.[166] He said the Liberals would not stand for Balfour hiding behind a veil of secrecy about the orders given to the police, not least because he went public on such things when it suited his propaganda purposes: Harcourt reminded the House that the first such disclosure had been Balfour's advice to the police in an open telegram – 'do not hesitate to shoot'.[167] This made a mockery of what Conservative, and Liberal Unionist, candidates had said at the election: that they wished Ireland to be treated in exactly the same way as England. The police in England seldom interfered in public meetings; Harcourt said that if, a century earlier, the authorities had felt no need to suppress meetings in support of John Wilkes, or those who took the part of the American rebels, why were they now suppressing meetings in Ireland by such violent means?

Harcourt raged that 'the object of your policy, as we always affirmed it was intended to be, is to stifle opinion, to crush the sympathies and the sentiments of the Irish nation, which you govern against its will.'[168] Balfour called this an 'astonishing speech' marked by 'the total absence of the ordinary good taste which distinguishes ministerial speeches in this House'.[169] Heckled by Irish MPs, Balfour defended his policy by reference to the agrarian outrages. The crowd around the courthouse that day represented a serious threat to public order; but the almost universal perception was that the police had lit the touchpaper. Balfour implied they had faced an almost paramilitary threat, with farmers on horseback compared to a cavalry, and had responded accordingly. However, he could not alter what Gladstone called the 'sentiment of horror and disgust throughout Great Britain' at what had happened.[170] Churchill, from the back benches, condemned the credulity of Gladstone and his colleagues in accepting as fact every claim the Irish made about the event. Churchill preferred to believe every word said by Balfour, who had not been present at the riot, in preference to believing Dillon, an eye-witness to the proceedings.

On Sunday 13 November 30,000 people rallied in Trafalgar Square to call for O'Brien's release. The main organisers were the National League but also Henry Hyndman's Social Democratic Federation. Around 2,000 police with truncheons drawn stood four deep around the square to stop the meeting taking place. Another 300 were in reserve in a side street and there were 100 mounted police, who charged groups attempting to enter the Square. The rally turned violent, the police could not cope, and mounted troops – including Lifeguards in scarlet uniforms and polished breastplates and helmets – were called up from Horseguards. Infantry came with bayonets fixed, but no order was given to engage. A policeman was stabbed and some horses were attacked with knives; demonstrators were hit with truncheons or trampled by police horses.

It would not be the last such day to be christened 'Bloody Sunday', which the press immediately did. One speaker, John Burns, who would become a Liberal cabinet minister and resign on principle against Britain's decision to enter the Great War in 1914, was given six weeks in prison for inciting a riot. It was the first of the series of demonstrations partly about Ireland and partly about the working class in general that occurred in London in the winter of 1887–8. Their immediate effect was to harden the government's resolve and, as Gladstone himself appreciated, damage the cause of Home Rule by creating 'disastrous prejudice' against it through its adherents.[171] After Mitchelstown and Trafalgar Square the Irish Secretary earned the nickname 'Bloody Balfour', a more pleasing sobriquet than 'Nancy'. He revelled in it, writing (in red ink) to Lady Elcho on Christmas Eve 1887: 'Greetings from Bl—dy B-lf—r. I write to you in a hue appropriate to my sanguinary character.'[172]

Balfour did, however, believe that, following severity, there should be an attempt to make things better; and until he left the Chief Secretaryship in October 1891 that was what he did. The policy became known as 'killing Home Rule with kindness'.[173] He hoped to extend to Ireland the civilising, and modern, aspects of enlightenment that had changed England greatly since the 1840s, to further peaceful co-existence. He would introduce social legislation, but – surprisingly for one of such intellect – never grasped how far the tide of Irish Nationalism had advanced. He believed that improving the economic condition of the peasantry was the key to making them love Britain and wish to remain in the Union: he could not see the Irish determination to govern themselves, irrespective of the economic consequences. His strategy was underpinned by land reform – ironically inspired by Gladstone's ideas – with the state underwriting loans to help tenants become proprietors, with a stake in the country courtesy of the British taxpayer. A Land Act of 1887 followed the Crimes Act to sweeten the pill by enabling such reforms. A second Land Act came in 1891, expanding the funds available for underwriting purchases to £33 million. In an act of Keynesianism before Keynes invented it, Balfour also launched infrastructure projects, including the building of 300 miles of light railway. This not only provided work for labourers struggling to find any in the agricultural depression, but by allowing the better movement of goods and people helped boost the economy as in England in the 1840s and 1850s. There was no doubt that the Tories were determined to invest in Ireland, in the hope of persuading the Irish they were better off in the Union.

Balfour also set up the Congested Districts Board, which channelled state money and advice on agricultural and industrial matters to areas with many tenancies whose landholdings were too small to be sustainable: these were mainly on the west coast, from Donegal in the north to Kerry in the south. By targeting these areas poverty was more effectively relieved in times of crop failure, and education was improved so people were better equipped to look after themselves. An idea, pushed by prominent Catholic Unionists such as the Duke of Norfolk, to have the state fund a Catholic university in Ireland did not come to fruition, largely because of Protestant objections to the amount of influence the Catholic prelacy wished to have over such an institution.

The effectiveness of the Parnellites against such seductive policies was handicapped. *The Times* – whose tone on Ireland, even in its supposedly objective news coverage, was toadying to the government and dismissive of Irish aspirations – published articles in March and April 1887 entitled *Parnellism and Crime*. Its main allegation was that Parnell had written a letter on 15 May 1882, nine days after the Phoenix Park murders, in which he said that while regretting Cavendish's death, Burke had had 'no more than his deserts.'[174] The letter was a crude forgery by an unsavoury, financially embarrassed Irish journalist called Richard Pigott, a long-standing critic of Parnell. The paper recklessly published several others accusing Parnell of various offences. Parnell chose not to sue, but requested a select committee examine the letters. Salisbury, trying to bolster *The Times*, instead appointed a Commission of Inquiry to look at the allegations *in toto*. It held 128 sessions over two years. At one, when Pigott was cross-examined over how he had acquired the letters and passed them to *The Times*, he broke down and admitted forging them, betrayed by his spelling mistakes – 'spelling is not my strong point'.[175] Before this, however, the Tories had sought to make great capital out of the letters, with even Salisbury himself, on 20 April 1887, accusing Gladstone of having an ally 'tainted with the strong presumption of conniving at assassination.'[176] Churchill, his career wrecked by his precipitate resignation, did himself further harm by using the forgeries to attack Gladstone. The Tories were not the architects of the forgeries, but they jumped on the bandwagon, and the episode damaged them badly.

Once Pigott was exposed Parnell – disappointed the forger was not O'Shea, whom he had suspected – did sue *The Times*. The paper settled out of court for £5,000, its reputation badly harmed. (The editor, George Earle Buckle, a relatively inexperienced man of thirty-two when he published the story, offered his resignation to his proprietor, John Walter: it was refused.) Pigott fled to Madrid and killed himself. Gladstone led an ovation when Parnell entered the Commons on 1 March 1890 after his exoneration, but the inquiry (whose report comprised thirty-five volumes) was not all good news. It had found links between the IPP and extremist groups routinely engaging in criminal activity. However, because of the closeness of *The Times* to the Conservatives, and the perception that publication had been politically motivated, the government was damaged too.

Yet all was not well for Parnell, despite his exoneration. Just before Christmas 1889 O'Shea had cited him as co-respondent in his divorce. The O'Sheas had been separated for a decade, and O'Shea had known of his wife's affair with Parnell, by whom she had had three children. He had not divorced her before because he had hoped to enjoy a big legacy she expected from an aunt. When the aunt died and the inheritance was left in trust so O'Shea could not get to it, he saw no reason to stay his hand. The more tasteless of Parnell's opponents rejoiced, Hartington (himself an accomplished philanderer) writing to the Queen that he 'never thought anything in politics could give me as much pleasure as this'.[177]

Parnell had acted unwisely in respect of Mrs O'Shea, having moved in with her in a house on Eltham in 1886. O'Shea had been MP for Clare from 1880 to 1885, when the constituency was abolished, and wished to re-enter parliament. Sensing the problems O'Shea could pose, Parnell sought in November 1885 to persuade him to fight the Mid-Armagh seat, claiming a high proportion of Protestant voters there would support him. O'Shea made enquiries and found the seat was dominated by Catholics, and wrote to Parnell in a threatening tone. 'Several very important personages who have had the best opportunities of appreciating what I have done for you are of opinion that, as a gentleman, you are under the clearest obligation to declare to your friends that you insist on my being returned to Parliament *quand même*, and that if the necessary steps are not taken for this purpose you will resign the leadership of your party. You will, I am sure, not fail to answer this letter without delay.'[178]

The price of his silence was the candidature at a by-election in Galway in February 1886. Parnell's main associates did not want O'Shea to have the seat and could not understand why Parnell was forcing him upon them. It was hardly worth the effort, as he was not readopted for the election held just five months later. However, when Parnell was cited in the divorce his motives for pushing O'Shea's candidacy began to look questionable. He assured his confederates that he would be exonerated, which was like signing his political death-warrant.

When the extent of his involvement with Mrs O'Shea became widely known it caused one of the great scandals of the nineteenth century. For a man in public life at a time of extreme puritanism – albeit mostly hypocritical – and representing people who, as Roman Catholics, were paradoxically among the most puritanical to be found, his conduct seems almost unhinged. Having said he would be exonerated, he then proceeded not to contest the divorce case when it came to court in November 1890. He wanted the decree granted so that he could marry Mrs O'Shea; a remarriage explicitly banned by the Catholic church, though Mr and the new Mrs Parnell were both Protestants.

The scandal threatened to derail a policy Gladstone had been developing with Parnell during his years as leader of the opposition. The two men had met twice, for ninety minutes on 8 March 1888 and a more extensive meeting on 18 December 1889, when Parnell went to stay at Hawarden, five days before O'Shea cited him in his divorce. At the first meeting Gladstone found Parnell looking 'not ill, but far from strong.'[179] He confessed he had no hopes of securing concessions from the Tories and, while appearing 'extremely moderate and reasonable', felt he could accept nothing short of a parliament in Dublin, even if its powers were restricted, for it would give him a basis from which to secure more powers. Gladstone's concession to Parnell was over money, since Parnell regarded the financial settlement mooted in the 1886 Bill as unsatisfactory. Gladstone agreed this required 'further investigation'.

The Hawarden meeting twenty-one months later also went, in Gladstone's view, well. The discussion was largely about which elements of the 1886 Bill were still acceptable, and which needed revision: the key issues on which Gladstone was prepared to move were continued Irish representation at Westminster to discuss 'imperial' questions and, as he had earlier intimated, money. The talks were held over two days, and at their end Gladstone pronounced Parnell 'certainly one of the very best people to deal with I have ever known'.[180] In a later note he said that 'nothing could be more satisfactory than his conversation; full as I thought it of good sense from beginning to end.'[181] In the event of a Liberal administration there was a basis on which it and the IPP could proceed jointly. 'So far as I could judge, nothing like a crotchet, or an irrational demand, from his side, was likely to interfere with the proper freedom of our deliberations when the proper time comes for practical steps.' The question of representation was the only one on which the two men still had work to do.

Gladstone met members of the former cabinet on 8 February 1890 to discuss his meeting with Parnell, and realised few of his colleagues shared his enthusiasm. According to Morley, Harcourt was the main problem – the most he wanted was 'a big county council'.[182] Morley reckoned half the ex-cabinet wanted to shelve Home Rule altogether 'and are only occupied in finding how to do it without discrediting the party': they would have embraced Chamberlain's central board idea, were it not that this would mark them out as 'Joe-ites'. A few, including Morley, were with Gladstone; but Rosebery and Campbell-Bannerman, the next two Liberal prime ministers, wanted a third option, akin to federation. Since there was no immediate prospect of the Liberals being in office, the matter of whether to continue with a Home Rule policy was not pressing.

After many months of reflection Gladstone, as ever when he faced a political problem, wrote himself a memorandum on 21 November 1890, in the light of the scandal. He seemed unsurprised by Parnell's irregular private life, but stated that 'it is no part of my duty, as the leader of a party in Parliament, to form a personal judgment on the moral conduct of any other leader or fellow-member.'[183] This may have been disingenuous, for he admitted a duty to estimate the results of Parnell's behaviour, and could do so only on the basis of facts proved in the court case. The key question was whether Parnell could maintain the respect of other MPs in order to secure the argument for Home Rule. Gladstone felt that Parnell's 'weight or moral force' would be 'impaired' after what had happened. There was an 'uncontradicted assertion of deception and untruth'. As such, Gladstone concluded, 'with deep pain but without any doubt, I judge that those interests [of securing Home Rule] require his retirement at the present time from his leadership.' Within two days Harcourt reported the feelings of the National Liberal Federation, whose meeting at Sheffield he had just attended: 'Opinion was absolutely unanimous and extremely strong that if Parnell is allowed to remain as the leader of the Irish Party all further co-operation between them and the English Liberals must be at an end. You know that the Nonconformists are the backbone of our Party, and their judgment on this matter is unhesitating and decisive.'[184]

Gladstone knew that by not contesting the suit Parnell had effectively admitted causing the divorce; and that this *de facto* admission of immorality would split his party, and deter many Liberals from supporting him. He warned Justin McCarthy, a former Liberal and now Parnellite MP acting as intermediary, of his views, but McCarthy did not pass them on. Gladstone nonetheless put his warning in a letter to Morley, which Morley was supposed to show Parnell. He ended his letter 'as respects the manner of conveying what my public duty has made it an obligation to say, I rely entirely on your good feeling, tact and judgment.' Morley exercised these last three qualities by leaking the letter to *The Times* when he learned that, before he could get to Parnell himself, the IPP had re-elected him leader. He had been reluctant to do this, but Gladstone, whose restraint had by now become cosmetic, agreed with great enthusiasm.

The IPP were alarmed, and convened a new meeting. Parnell refused to retire, saying he would allow neither Gladstone nor the Catholic church to dictate terms. The party deliberated for five days, at which point a majority faction (forty-five against twenty-eight of those present) led by McCarthy walked out: Gladstone's prediction of a split was realised. Two days later, in a statement that smacked of the middle ages and reinforced the fears many Protestants held of an Ireland under Home Rule, the Irish Catholic hierarchy told their co-religionists to spurn Parnell. The two factions evolved into the Irish National League, under John Redmond, a scion of Catholic gentry from Wexford who, over the next twenty years, would become the key figure in Irish politics; and the Irish National Federation, a more militant organisation, led by Dillon and including Parnell's former associates O'Brien, Healy and Davitt. Redmond was a constitutional politician in the mould of Parnell, whose work the INL sought to continue; the INF took a more flexible view of constitutional propriety. The factions embodied the split personality of Parnell himself, longing for respectability but prepared to flirt with danger if he thought it might keep the movement together.

Parnell, robbed of a party to lead, toured Ireland in early 1891 to rebuild support: but the Catholic church, which became closely associated with the INF, turned many of his former followers against him on the moral question. In by-elections his candidates lost. On 2 December 1890 Brett had noted in his diary that 'it is impossible not to respect the courage and skill which Parnell exhibits in his tremendous struggle. A man who can fight thus in a tight place deserves to lead his countrymen in spite of his breach of the seventh commandment.'[185] When Parnell married Mrs O'Shea, on 25 June 1891 in a Sussex register office – he had, with his now-customary obliviousness of reality, unsuccessfully sought a church wedding – the Bishops of the Irish Catholic church condemned him as unfit for leadership: this would have been unanimous but for the Bishop of Limerick, Edward O'Dwyer, refusing to cast the first stone, and was aimed at instructing parish priests not to support Parnellites.

His marriage, like his life, was doomed to be short. Parnell had kidney disease, aggravated by a relentless speaking tour throughout the summer and autumn of 1891. He divided opinion profoundly: at one meeting in Co. Kilkenny quicklime was thrown in his face, and he needed medical attention. He left Dublin on 30 September 1891 suffering from a chill, returned to his new family home in Hove, and died there of a heart attack on 6 October. He was just forty-five. More than 200,000 people attended his funeral in Glasnevin cemetery. He lies near Daniel O'Connell, his great predecessor in the cause of Irish Nationalism, and Michael Collins, one of his great successors. By the time his gravestone, a huge rock of Wicklow granite, was raised in 1940 it needed to bear just one word – Parnell – such was his fame, and so far had bygones become bygones.

His death opened a new chapter in Irish politics. It came as Balfour was leaving Ireland, to become the last First Lord of the Treasury not to be prime minister, and Leader of the House of Commons – his uncle, the prime minister, sitting in the Lords. Salisbury called an election in July 1892 and the Conservatives won the largest number of seats, including a depleted number of Liberal Unionists; but with 313 out of 670, they did not command a majority. Salisbury refused to resign, but the government was defeated on 11 August in a vote of confidence by the combined forces of the Liberals and the divided Irish Parliamentary party, which still had eighty-one seats.

Gladstone, supported by the Irish, formed a minority administration and became prime minister for the fourth time, once more resisting a suggestion from the Queen that he should take an earldom (she was 'cautiously polite' but 'in nothing helpful . . . not one sympathetic word on any question however detached').[186] Drenched in self-pity, the Queen was pleased that Gladstone's first move, because of his dependence on the Irish, would be another Home Rule Bill 'as that is sure to bring him into great difficulties.'[187] She was also relieved that Rosebery, after much indecision and persuasion by, among others, the Prince of Wales and the ubiquitous Brett (who as Lord Esher would be a strong influence on

Edward VII), had agreed to be Foreign Secretary. She squared up for more attrition with her aged prime minister: 'Mr Gladstone has brought so much personal violence into the contest, and used such insolent language, that the Queen is quite shocked and ashamed,' she told Ponsonby.

VIII

On losing office Salisbury declined for the second time – the first had been in 1886 – the Queen's offer of a dukedom, saying, as before, that he could not afford to maintain the establishment expected of that rank. He wrote a clever article for the *National Review*, published that November, rejecting the idea that Gladstone had a mandate for Home Rule, because it lacked a majority in both England and Scotland; and if there were to be no plebiscite, it would fall to the House of Lords to provide the consultative services needed to evaluate the nation's true view on the question. This was sophistry in the extreme, since no one had ever voted for the House of Lords, giving it even less of a mandate than the government. It did, however, have an entrenched Tory majority, which Salisbury correctly surmised would be an adequate defence against a Home Rule Bill now that the Liberal Unionists could no longer defeat Gladstone in the Commons.

Gladstone did not wish to anger his party by letting the issue swamp the parliamentary agenda, leaving Liberals struggling to do anything else to propitiate the electorate. He hoped to achieve universal manhood suffrage, to reform county councils and empower them more, and to restrict working hours in mines, among other things. In July his Irish priorities were to abolish the Coercion Act, facilitate the readmission of evicted tenants and pass a resolution on Home Rule. However by 1 August, when it became apparent the Salisbury administration would fall, a Bill for the Government of Ireland was written in at the top of the list of priorities, above the County Councils Bill, the Budget and 'one man one vote'.[188]

Gladstone asked Alfred Milner, who had been running finance in Egypt, to lead an inquiry into the financial relations of Britain and Ireland. To show the administration's *bona fides*, Morley began directing the rehousing of evicted tenants. John Redmond put himself up as the leader of Nationalist opinion, an idea Gladstone treated with disdain since he doubted Redmond genuinely spoke for Ireland, the divisions after Parnell's death remaining deep. Late in October, in a lengthy memorandum, Gladstone sought to soften up the Queen on Home Rule, saying it was 'a proposal eminently Conservative in the highest sense of the term, as tending to the union of the three countries (whose moral union must surely be allowed to be at the least very imperfect), and to the stability of the Imperial throne and institutions.'[189]

One lesson he had not learned from 1886 was to consult widely on the Bill. Asquith, Home Secretary in Gladstone's last ministry, wrote of him that 'no one outside the Cabinet could form any trustworthy forecast of what he was going to say.'[190] Sometimes few in the cabinet could, either. He presented an outline of the Bill to the cabinet on 11 November 1892. It had similarities to the 1886 measure, but stated Ireland would retain all taxes it collected apart from customs and excise, from which the Irish contribution to the imperial exchequer would be deducted. All affairs 'distinctively Irish' would be handed over to Dublin, and the Viceroy would exercise a veto on behalf of the Crown 'in the same sense and spirit as under the Canada Dominion Act', by which he meant the Constitution Act of 1867 that established self-government in that Dominion.[191] There would be a transitional period before full powers to appoint judges and recruit police were transferred.

Gladstone had not specified whether there would be a unicameral or bicameral legislature; he did assume the Irish would be represented at Westminster, but wanted to discuss whether it should be by members of the Irish parliament, or by Irishmen elected specifically for that purpose. There was then a debate about how many representatives; Gladstone felt the number should be reduced, not least so as not to denude a Dublin parliament of men with legislative experience.

A cabinet committee discussed the detail for several days, suggesting a House of Commons in Dublin and a senate of fifty-four members, a third of whom would be Crown appointees, another third elected from Irish peers and the last third elected from constituencies but requiring a property qualification: this was to protect the landed interests and the Ulster minority. Gladstone had to accept Redmond spoke for a substantial proportion of Irish opinion, and so forced himself to read an article Redmond had written in the October number of *The Nineteenth Century*, in which he had mocked Gladstone for saying nothing on Home Rule and had, therefore, set out his own prescription. Redmond believed Irish MPs would still sit at Westminster: and this fundamental change would 'naturally affect every other provision in the Bill.'[192]

He was angry that, as in 1886, the Irish were not consulted, and would be presented with 'a cut-and-dried scheme' that 'must be accepted or rejected as it stands'.[193] He quoted Sir Charles Gavan Duffy, who had said that 'the convict population of Van Diemen's Land, equally with the intelligent and aspiring citizens of Canada and Australia, picked and chose for themselves' when it came to designing a constitution; so why should not the Irish? Redmond had no objection to Westminster retaining the right to legislate for Ireland, provided it was never used, as in other Dominions. He was happy with the provisions of the 1886 Bill towards the judiciary, but wanted British control of the police ended. He felt Westminster incapable of settling the land question, and wanted 'a complete system of federalism'.[194] 'We are not now asking for a repeal of the Union,' he protested. 'We ask for a readjustment.' Gladstone told Morley these demands 'were such as might more reasonably be made by some inhabitant of another planet', and called Redmond 'a statesman of Patagonian stature.'[195]

Even beyond the opening of parliament in late January 1893 arguments persisted in the cabinet about how a Home Rule Ireland would be financed. Gladstone, in a speech of two and a quarter hours, asked on 13 February for leave to bring in the Government of Ireland Bill. He argued that under permanent repression there could be 'no true political stability, and no true social civilisation'.[196] He admitted that the 1886 election had shown a large majority of English MPs in favour of the status quo; but that majority had fallen by two-thirds, and he saw no guarantee of the other third holding on: public opinion was, he believed, changing. For Gladstone, in his eighty-fourth year, this was a moment of destiny, and he said as much in his peroration: 'I never will, and I never can, be a party to bequeathing to my country the continuance of this heritage of discord which has been handed down from generation to generation, with scarcely a momentary interruption, through seven centuries – this heritage of discord, with all the evils that follow in its train.'[197]

Unlike in 1886 there was no Liberal split. However, the Tories taunted Gladstone for changing his mind on Irish representation at Westminster.

One Ulster member, Richard Dane, described the proposal as 'insane' and aimed at creating a legislature whose members 'would be mere puppets of the priests.'[198] The upper chamber, despite its safeguards, would be 'manned by agents of the clerical party', the Royal Irish Constabulary would be abolished and, three years after Home Rule, the parliament would be 'let loose on the Land Question'.[199] He predicted the expulsion of Protestant landlords, and then Protestant tenants. Balfour tried to pick holes in the detail, claiming Gladstone could create the confusion of giving the Sovereign two sets of advisers: Gladstone interrupted him to say that 'there are twenty sets of advisers in the Colonies.'[200] Balfour was on firmer ground when he asked what would happen if – as was presently the case – an English government became dependent for its majority on Irish members, perhaps ones who were allowed to vote only on certain issues.

Redmond pledged support, but raised tensions by illustrating how unsatisfactory the Bill was, and how his party would strive to change it in committee. He said the parliament it would set up would be the start, and not the end, of an evolutionary process. The Ulster contingent, who feared being thrown to the wolves, took such statements as proof; and Chamberlain, in a detailed assault, warned the House: 'This is a Bill to give relief to parliament. On the first occasion of the assertion of the supremacy of the Imperial Parliament over Irish affairs you may bid good-bye to the relief of Parliament.'[201] He suggested five parliaments: one for each of the home countries and one for the United Kingdom. Otherwise there would be chaos, the commission of a 'national crime': 'Never in the history of the world has a risk so tremendous been encountered with such a light-hearted indifference to its possible results.'[202]

During this four-day debate Morley had secret meetings with two leading Irish MPs to consult them on the wording of the Bill, so as to avoid difficulties when it came to the second reading. Harcourt, as Chancellor of the Exchequer, raised last-minute quibbles about the financial provisions, but Gladstone told him it was too late to change anything without upsetting the Irish and wrecking the whole process: Gladstone was trying the patience of his colleagues. There was a lull before the second reading so the government could proceed with other business; but in that period, on 9 March, Morley warned the cabinet that 'ferment' was increasing in Belfast and expressed the 'fear that the

Orange leaders may be unable as the Bill proceeds to restrain their followers'.[203]

As in 1886 the Bill was debated for twelve days; only this time it won a second reading by 347 to 304. Soon after, members of the Stock Exchange burned a copy of it outside the Guildhall, where Chamberlain was speaking. On 8 May it went into committee on the floor of the Commons, where it was discussed clause by clause, with increasing impatience and bad feeling, over three months in a total of forty-seven sessions. 'I have never known such an opposition, one so detached from the merits and from rule', Gladstone wrote on the first day.[204] Chamberlain showed himself formidable in the legalistic discussion of individual points and rang rings round Redmond, who seemed to justify Gladstone's lack of faith in him as an ally. Progress was painfully slow.

Tempers finally snapped late on 27 July, the final night of discussion, when T. P. O'Connor, the MP for Liverpool Scotland, called Chamberlain 'Judas' after he had branded Gladstone a dictator and compared him with King Herod.[205] The deputy speaker, John Mellor, claimed not to have heard the word: almost everyone else had. Fighting broke out among about forty MPs. Harcourt recorded that 'a sort of general free fight took place at the top of the gangway between the Tories and the Irish', but that was not the only scuffle.[206] The Speaker was summoned and took the chair, ordering O'Connor to apologise: he claimed Unionist MPs had physically assaulted two of his colleagues during the chaos. He apologised, but then an Ulster Unionist MP, Colonel Edward Saunderson, claimed to have been smacked on the head by a Nationalist; at which point another Nationalist said he had seen Saunderson smack several Nationalists. The House, unusually, voted to have details of the fracas recorded in Hansard, in the hope of preventing further such shameful exhibitions. The Queen told Gladstone the 'unseemly violence' was effectively his fault because of the 'excitement and irritation' his proposals had caused.[207]

The House spent ten days in August considering the committee's report: whatever else was wrong with the Bill, lack of scrutiny was not a problem. The three days allotted to the third reading debate, when the Bill finally completed its Commons stages on 1 September, made a total of eighty days' discussion. Arguments continued about Irish finances (Milner had not done a good job, miscalculating the revenues from excise duties). It was sent to the Lords with a Gladstonian flourish by Morley:

> We have had during these seven years long, toilsome, and harassing marches under skies that were sometimes starless. We have had many dark moments, which were not only dark but tragic. But we have had an indomitable and unfaltering captain . . . Whatever may happen, there is a Party in Great Britain who have made up their minds that Ireland shall no longer be the sport of an aimless destiny; that she shall no longer be the cockpit in which English factions choose to fight out their battles. Let us for tonight – we at least on this side of the House, aye, and even gentlemen opposite – let us raise ourselves above the mire and the confusion of ephemeral faction . . . wherever the Irish race toils, and hopes, and yearns, wherever Englishmen and Scotchmen are weary of the inveterate stain on the fame and honour of their country – it will be felt that we at least have taken a decisive step towards the true incorporation of Ireland in a United Kingdom.[208]

The vote passed by 301 to 267, and four days later the Lords began its debate. Spencer, who unlike most old Whigs had converted enthusiastically to Home Rule in 1886, led for the government: Gladstone had consulted him extensively while framing the Bill. He was First Lord of the Admiralty, but had told Harcourt that Home Rule was the measure 'for which alone some of us continue in politics'.[209] Hartington had succeeded his father as Duke of Devonshire in 1891 and led for the opposition, arguing that the 'justice' the government proposed to bestow on Ireland 'has been learned in the Courts of the Land League.'[210]

If some in the Lords, such as Devonshire, had estates in Ireland and therefore a direct interest, others instinctively identified with the landlord class. They queued up to denounce the Bill, and the Irish, over five days of debate. One or two, such as Lord Ribblesdale, said the problem would not go away just because the Lords threw the Bill out. But other arguments – that the Commons majority was small, that the committee stage had been guillotined, that it would revolutionise the constitution and that most British MPs were against it – were arguments that told. Having heard from Salisbury that the Bill was 'atrocious', 'mean' and 'treacherous', the Lords voted it down by 419 votes to forty-one, the largest turnout in the House's history.[211] They spoke for Britain, but not for Ireland.

Gladstone's career survived the killing of the Home Rule Bill by six months. This time, despite his instincts, there would be no election: the time to hold the Upper House to account for defying the will of the Commons was still nearly two decades away. The denouement came for other reasons. His cabinet colleagues, led by Spencer, wanted expansion of the Navy, and he refused to contemplate the extra expenditure this would entail: and he strongly objected to Harcourt's plan to impose graduated death duties to pay for more ships. 'Liberalism cannot put on the garb of Jingoism without suffering for it,' he said.[212] By early January 1894 he noted in his diary the likelihood of the irreconcilability of his opinions with those of his colleagues. In his eighty-fifth year, his eyesight failing, he felt his energy no longer equal to the fight. By 20 January, resting in Biarritz and writing an essay on Horace's *Odes*, he realised he was awaiting the right moment to go. By early February rumours he would resign were circulating and, understandably, raising the interest of the Queen.

On 8 February he told the chairman of his Liberal association in Midlothian that it was untrue, as *The Pall Mall Gazette* had reported, that he had decided to leave office. No decision had been taken, but his deteriorating sight and hearing made work, especially reading, difficult. 'The choice is not made, but the time *may* be very near,' he wrote, in a phrase hardly intended to dampen speculation.[213] Two days later he talked over the matter with his family. By 21 February he asked to see the Queen's private secretary, Sir Henry Ponsonby, to say he might warn the Queen he was going to resign, but only if she would keep the information to herself until the right moment. When he met Ponsonby, on 24 February, the courtier said he saw no impediment, only to write to Gladstone that evening to say that the Queen refused to promise secrecy on a matter that he would not specify. The absurdity of the relationship with her prime minister would be maintained right to the end.

Gladstone warned Harcourt and Rosebery of his impending departure, which caused an outpouring of emotion from the former and a handsome tribute from the latter, in letters sent at once. He wrote to the Queen on 27 February saying he would resign 'on physical grounds' at the end of a session unnaturally prolonged by the Home Rule Bill, which the cabinet had decided would come the following week. He saw her the next day at Buckingham Palace. 'She was at the highest point of her cheerfulness,' he recorded, noting that she expressed sorrow 'for the cause' of his resignation rather than for the resignation itself.[214] 'She does not even consider it a trouble, but regards it as the immediate precursor of an arrangement more agreeable,' he added. Having twice declined an earldom he was not offered one a third time, though he was later, and declined again. He also advised his wife to refuse a peerage, which she did. The Queen did not ask him for whom she should send – he would have said Spencer, whom the Queen had distrusted since his conversion to Home Rule – but on her own initiative invited Rosebery to take over, despite Ponsonby's advice that there was growing feeling against having a prime minister in the Lords.

For all the Queen's lack of appreciation of him, Gladstone had the consolation of an inundation of gratitude from colleagues, some of whom (including Morley, who found the scene 'painful' and 'nauseous') cried at his last Cabinet meeting when Harcourt, himself in tears, read out his letter of tribute.[215] Morley said that there 'never, never was such an exhibition of bad taste and want of tact and decency and sense of the fitness of things'.[216] Had Harcourt not been 'the bane and torment of Mr G's life' Morley might have borne it better. The Grand Old Man wrote an *aide-mémoire* in March 1894 to describe his resignation and his relations with the Queen:

> Let me now make in few words a clean breast of it.
>
> I am as I hope loyal to the throne.
>
> I admire in the Queen many fine qualities which she possesses . . .
>
> Further I am grateful to the Queen as I have confirmed it in my letters for many kindnesses received at various periods of my service under her.
>
> And I have a new source of gratitude to HM in her having on this last occasion admitted my wife anew on a footing of confidence and freedom. She had too long, I think, been suffering on my behalf. I am delighted this chapter is well closed. God Save the Queen!
>
> Everyone knows her attitude towards Liberalism. But taking relations to me since 1844, as a whole, there is in them something of a mystery, which I have not been able to fathom, and probably never shall.
>
> I hope my duty to her and her family has never in fact, as it has never in intuition, fallen short.[217]

Gladstone lived four more years in increasing decline, but on his death from cancer of the mouth in May 1898, aged eighty-eight, was given a state funeral, with two future kings – Edward VII and George V, much to the Queen's dismay, as pall-bearers. There was no greater public life in the nineteenth century.

'What fools we were not to have accepted Gladstone's Home Rule Bill,' King George V told Ramsay MacDonald, his prime minister, in 1930. 'The Empire would not have had the Irish Free State giving us so much trouble and pulling us to pieces.'[218] It was in fact doomed to tensions whatever happened in Ireland, and doomed to decline after the upheavals of the Great War, when both financial stringency and the growth of American power applied the squeeze. However, the failure to pass either of Gladstone's Bills, or to implement the measure Asquith's administration would enact, forced a confrontation the British state could not win. The playing of the Orange card would, by the time of the third Home Rule Bill, become Tory party policy, as Lord Randolph Churchill would have wished: and only the outbreak of the Great War would stop Ireland having its own civil war in 1914. The eventual establishment of the Free State in 1922 signalled to others under the British flag the start of a long retreat. The opponents in 1886 and 1893, not that they realised it, triggered a profound failure of policy that would assist the collapse of British power.

CHAPTER 6

THE DEATH OF GOD

I

The decline of faith and the rise of secularism characterised the nineteenth century, not merely in Britain, but also across northern, Protestant Europe; in 1882, in *Die fröhliche Wissenschaft*, Friedrich Nietzsche had, after all, pronounced that God was dead. The process of urbanisation had broken up traditional communities and loosened the grip of the established Church upon them, and 1851 had marked the moment when the census showed more people in the Kingdom living in urban areas than in rural ones. The decline of faith was matched by a decline in religion, as the greatly changed society of the nineteenth century ceased to regard organised religion as an integral part of its social organisation – as was clear in the new communities that grew up as a result of the Industrial Revolution. The growing secularisation of society provided a new challenge to all who lived in it. It raised questions about its purpose and its cohesion around a set of common values, and the threat of a society consumed by materialism. And, as earlier in the century, the questioning of religion itself caused debates within the Church about how it should carry on its practices.

During the 1880s a final bastion of religious conformity – parliament – fell to the determined assault of a principled atheist, and the Church of England came under attack for its doctrinal inflexibility. The democratisation of politics led the assault on faith. In the mid-Victorian era the Liberal party had broadened into a coalition of Whigs, Christian socialists, trade unionists and radicals whose common enemy was Toryism. Underpinning it was a culture of free thought and speech that, when asserted, would challenge established values. The fight by a Member of Parliament, Charles Bradlaugh, to sit in the Commons without swearing a religious oath, personified this. His eventual victory represented a triumph of secularism, a turning point in relations between church and state, and a new moral and intellectual settlement in Britain.

II

On 3 May 1880, as the Commons assembled after Gladstone's election victory, one new member refused to follow the procedure for taking his seat: swearing the oath. Hansard reported that 'Mr Bradlaugh, returned as one of the Members for the Borough of Northampton, came to the Table and delivered the following Statement in writing to the Clerk: "To the Right Honourable The Speaker of the House of Commons. I, the undersigned Charles Bradlaugh, beg respectfully to claim to be allowed to affirm as a person for the time being by Law permitted to make a solemn Affirmation or Declaration instead of taking an Oath." And being asked by the Clerk upon what grounds he claimed to make an Affirmation, he answered, by virtue of the Evidence Amendment Acts 1869 and 1870.'[1]

Bradlaugh told the Speaker, Henry Brand: 'I have only now to submit that the Parliamentary Oaths Act, 1866, gives the right to affirm to every person for the time being permitted by law to make affirmation. I am such a person; and under the Evidence Further Amendment Act, 1869, and the Evidence Amendment Act, 1870, I have repeatedly for nine years past affirmed in the highest Courts of Jurisdiction in this Realm. I am ready to make the Declaration or Affirmation of Allegiance.' The quibble was about four words at the end of the oath of allegiance, which the juror promised to maintain 'so help me God'.

Bradlaugh was forty-six, the son of a solicitor's clerk from east London. He had been a Sunday school teacher, but had fretted over contradictions between the Thirty-nine Articles and the Bible. The Anglican clergyman who ran his Sunday school expelled him, accusing him of atheism. If Bradlaugh was not a fully formed atheist then, this incident, coupled with his family's disgust, accelerated and completed the process. He joined the Army at seventeen, but bought himself out with a legacy at twenty. He followed in his estranged father's footsteps as a solicitor's clerk, but joined radical societies and by the late 1860s was renowned not merely as luminary of the Reform League but as a secularist and pamphleteer.

With one exception, if there was a radical cause to espouse, Bradlaugh espoused it. He was a strong supporter of trades unions. He was a committed republican, something more common in the 1860s and 1870s than in the later decades of the century. He co-founded, with Annie Besant (who may or may not have been his mistress), the National Secularist Society, and edited its newspaper *The National Reformer*. In 1877 he and Mrs Besant published Charles Knowlton's *The Fruits of Philosophy*, a pamphlet advocating contraception, and were prosecuted for obscenity (see Chapter 8). They were convicted, fined and sentenced to six months in prison, but their convictions were overturned. He supported Home Rule. He would not embrace socialism, such was his commitment, as a liberal, to the pre-eminence of the individual.

His election came at the fourth attempt. Northampton had been a hopeless cause for radicals until the Second Reform Act, which coincided with a growth of the town's manufacturers. The number of freeholders – who qualified for a vote by dint of owning property of sufficient value – rose steadily through the 1870s as the shoe trade grew. The Tories, who had held the seat for decades, came under threat, as did mainstream Liberals. Bradlaugh, a local orator and personality, built up his base relentlessly, and was unstoppable by 1880. However, even before he reached Westminster, he was described in the *Sheffield Telegraph* as 'the bellowing blasphemer of Northampton', a portent of grief to come.[2]

Speaker Brand's mistake was to fail to rule on the question. He had been Speaker since 1872 and had the experience to do so. This amoebic reaction would cost him, and the credibility of parliament, dear. Apparently clueless, and fearful of turning MPs against him, he told Bradlaugh to withdraw while the House discussed his case. It was settled that a select committee be appointed to consider whether the Acts cited could apply to parliamentary oath-taking. The committee, which refused to call witnesses or hear evidence, rejected allowing Bradlaugh to affirm, despite Sir Henry James, the Attorney-General, advising that he should, just as he could – and had – in courts of law. The vote was tied at eight all: all seven Conservatives opposed the idea, and were joined by one Liberal. Eight Liberals voted for the Attorney's position, but, following custom, the chairman, former Conservative Home Secretary Spencer Walpole, supported the amendment, which his party had moved.

On 21 May, Bradlaugh (having notified the Speaker) tried to take the oath, going through what he regarded as a formality that meant nothing to him. Gladstone told the Queen (in whom Bradlaugh believed no more than he did in God) this would 'relieve the House' of further complications.[3] However, never content to avoid confrontation, Bradlaugh had set out his philosophy in a letter to *The Times* that morning. He said he had done 'nothing more than put in the fewest possible words my contention that the Parliamentary Oaths Act, 1866, gave the right to affirm in Parliament to every person for the time being by law permitted to make an affirmation in lieu of taking an oath, and that I was such a person, and therefore claimed to affirm.'[4] He said many other members felt as he did, but had been afraid to make a stand out of 'habit and the fear of exciting prejudice'. He would take the oath and 'regard myself as bound, not by the letter of its words, but by the spirit which the affirmation would have conveyed had I been permitted to use it.'

This caused Sir Henry Drummond Wolff, a Tory who from Bradlaugh's election had announced his resolve to stop him being admitted, to object to the House being trifled with in this way. The Speaker – who should not have allowed the interruption, and therefore made another error whose consequences would resonate for years – asked Bradlaugh to withdraw, before asking Wolff to explain himself. Wolff protested: 'Under the Act of 1866, any Member taking his seat in this House, and not belonging to certain sects or denominations, is liable to penalties recoverable in the Court of Westminster, and his seat is to be declared vacant. That cannot be set aside by any Resolution of this House.' He said Bradlaugh was 'a professed Atheist' and 'by the Common Law of England an Atheist is not entitled to take an oath.' He had 'a pamphlet entitled, *A Plea for Atheism*, written by the hon Gentleman, and advertised and sold under his name. At the beginning of the pamphlet are these words – "It is as a propagandist of Atheism that I pen this essay."'[5] Wolff argued that an atheist could not fear the wrath of God and the certainty of divine punishment; there was no sense of 'moral and religious accountability to a Supreme Being'.

Wolff's motives were cynical. He and three younger Tory MPs – Churchill, Balfour and John Gorst – had formed a clique to keep the leadership on its toes. Known as 'The Fourth Party', it looked for divisions among Liberals and worked to exploit them. Bradlaugh's stand was a great opportunity, given Gladstone's religiosity. The group also hoped to propitiate Catholic Irish MPs, who would be outraged by this godlessness. But shock at Bradlaugh's stance went far beyond the Irish. Robert Fowler, MP for the City of London, presented a petition from merchants and businessmen arguing 'that no step be taken to allow any alteration of the law and custom of this Realm for the purpose of enabling one who denies the existence of a God to sit in Parliament.'[6] Fowler and his constituents – to give them the benefit of the doubt – did at least appear to be protesting against the possible social consequences of undermining this act of deference to organised religion, unlike the Fourth Party.

Gladstone later told Brand he had not expected such capital to be made by other MPs 'out of Bradlaugh's loathsome and revolting opinions.'[7] He said the oath was not the parallel of that in a court of law; and a further complication was that Jews and Quakers could take an oath of sorts and their seats. The Commons had allowed an amendment to the oath to satisfy the conscience or beliefs of the juror, and Gladstone felt Bradlaugh sought to do the same. Another MP, Edward Gibson, took great delight in reminding Gladstone that, as Chancellor in 1854, he had said: 'I revere the principle of the oath. I think it tends to maintain that serious, reverential temper with which men ought to address themselves to solemn duties', and he was keen to know what had changed in the intervening years.[8] All Bradlaugh sought, Gibson and those who thought like him – on both sides – maintained, was to outrage the conscience of the Commons by taking God's name in vain. John Bright, the veteran radical, predicted the House would 'stand badly with the nation and with history' if it chose to exclude Bradlaugh, and warned it against repeating its mistake with John Wilkes more than a century earlier.[9]

Churchill dissented, and despite Gladstone's legendary piety chose to paint the Liberal party as an engine of godlessness. 'Hon. Members opposite', he said, 'were not returned in such numbers in order that the House of Commons might become a place where the solemn forms and practices of the Christian religion might be safely derided, and the existence of a God publicly and with scorn denied.'[10] Churchill claimed to see Bradlaugh not so much as an atheist as an anarchist, whose purpose was not to have freedom of conscience but to deride the Commons and the true religion. This provoked the radical John Robertson to observe that 'there are many points in the story of this struggle at which it is hardly possible to abstain from imputing wilful falsehood to some of the actors.'[11] He noted that some Tories most militantly opposing the tide of secularism had 'committed bribery [or were] unscrupulous stock-jobbers and company promoters, men about town, topers, libellers and liars.'[12] It remains uncertain whether Churchill himself succumbed to a brain tumour, or to tertiary syphilis as a consequence of familiarity with prostitutes.

Gladstone was sufficiently liberal-minded to believe Bradlaugh had a right to his views, and that they should not prevent his sitting in a legislature that no longer pretended to be exclusively Christian. He knew times had changed, and would not be changing back. Yet he had to tread carefully: Ponsonby wrote to him on 24 May to say how anxious the Queen was that 'care will be taken to prevent its being supposed (erroneously of course) that the Government sympathise with the opinions Mr Bradlaugh is stated to hold.'[13] Gladstone proposed a second select committee to discuss whether the House had the right to prevent a member from taking the oath, and it convened on 4 June 1880.

A key exchange had happened before the committee met. The prime minister told the Speaker that he believed, having studied the small print of the Parliamentary Oaths Act, that 'the jurisdiction which so many take for granted as belonging to the House' did not in fact exist in this regard.[14] However Brand, who had nothing like Gladstone's intellect or understanding of the constitution, did not move, telling Gladstone it remained his view that the House had the discretion to receive or not to receive Bradlaugh without infringing the Act.[15] Legal wrangling would continue on this point for the following five years.

The controversy seized the public imagination. Recalling the period, Arnold Bennett referred ironically to Bradlaugh as 'the shameless free-thinker'.[16] In the same tone he referred to 1880 as the year when, recalling how the military had been summoned to put down a riot by Bradlaugh's supporters, 'the British Army had been employed to put reason into the noddle of a town called Northampton which was furious because an atheist had not been elected to parliament.'[17] Bennett described the effect on British life: 'Than this complication of theology and politics nothing could have been better devised to impassion an electorate which had but two genuine interests – theology and politics. The rumour of the feverish affair had spread to the most isolated communities . . . In loquacious families Bradlaugh caused dissension and division, more real perhaps than apparent, for not all Bradlaugh's supporters had the courage to avow themselves such.'[18]

This time the select committee considered evidence and saw witnesses, one of whom was the Clerk of the Commons and expert on its procedure, Sir Thomas Erskine May. Erskine May said there was simply no precedent for a man wishing to take the oath (however insincerely) being told by the House that, because of what they considered his insincerity, he could not. The committee further stressed that 'no instance has been brought to the attention of your committee in which any inquiry has been made into the moral, religious or political opinions of the person who was desirous to make any promissory oath, or of any objection being made to his making such an oath.'[19] It warned that 'it would be impossible to foresee the evils which might arise if a contrary practice were sanctioned.' However, if – as Bradlaugh had done – the person about to swear made it clear he was simply doing so for the sake of form, then it was inevitable MPs would feel inclined to consider such a protest.

The committee concluded that the Commons had the right to prevent his taking the oath. However, it urged that he be allowed to seek redress in the High Court, and that the Commons do nothing to stop him: and thus it recommended that if he sought to affirm again, he should be allowed to do so, that action being open to legal challenge. Erskine May noted the precedent set by Francis Bacon, the Jacobean statesman and jurist, when taking the oath despite being disqualified, as a barrister, from sitting – 'their oath their own conscience to look into, not we to examine it'.[20]

On 21 June a petition was presented to the Commons from electors in Northampton demanding that no 'person of atheistical opinions' be admitted.[21] However, a further petition, presented by Henry Labouchere, also from electors in Northampton (he was the other of the constituency's two MPs), prayed (to use the technical parliamentary term) that Bradlaugh be allowed to affirm. Labouchere then introduced a motion, which the cabinet had decided to support, asking that Bradlaugh be allowed to take the oath.[22] A bad-tempered debate ensued over two days.

Labouchere himself was one of the more controversial MPs. He had a long history of causing outrage, propelled by a lethal combination of a titanic natural arrogance and a large private income. His uncle, Lord Taunton, left him his fortune, which Labouchere augmented in the 1870s by becoming a theatre and newspaper proprietor. His newspaper, *Truth*, was a vehicle for lambasting those of whom Labouchere disapproved and for propounding his beliefs: misogyny (he despised the women's suffrage movement) and anti-Semitism chief among them. Long before then he had been thrown out of Trinity College, Cambridge for cheating in examinations, thrown out of the Foreign Office for refusing to accept a posting to Buenos Aires unless its duties could be discharged from Baden-Baden, and thrown out of the Commons after a petition against him for electoral malpractice was upheld. He also lived with an exotic woman who was not his wife, but whom he eventually married, and (unlike Bradlaugh) had insufficient integrity to make a public statement about his lack of religious belief.

Labouchere argued that laws permitting minorities such as Quakers, Shakers and Moravians to affirm in court should apply to Bradlaugh. His opponents put a fundamental counter-argument: that though a person might give evidence in a court of law while not believing in God, he would certainly be unfit to sit in the legislature. One of the most vocal opponents of Bradlaugh, Robert Fowler, said that 'if I could assent to the proposal of the hon Gentleman opposite, I should be recreant to my country, my Sovereign and my God.'[23] Emotionalism overrode the idea that denying a man his elected right to sit in Parliament because of his opinions was an outrage in modern Britain.

Bright doubted that the British people, whether working class or from the aristocracy, were so burdened by religious dogma that they could care less about Bradlaugh affirming.[24] Gladstone said that an inability to believe in a 'Supreme Being' was 'the greatest of misfortunes', but the question before the House was not whether an atheist could sit there: it was how to interpret the existing law.[25] Aware of the effect this argument was having on the country, he said he wished above all 'to avoid whatever can stir feeling'. He described atheism as a 'rare form of unbelief in this country', and could not understand why it should be singled out as a form of disability when 'Positivism, Agnosticism, Materialism and Pantheism' did not appear to elicit such disapproval.[26]

He mocked those opposed to Bradlaugh for the lack of logic behind their ideals. 'In accordance with your principles, if I understand them, you would allow a Mahomedan to sit in this House without question; you would probably allow a Parsee to sit in this House; but you could not, with any consistency, allow a Buddhist to do so,' presumably because Buddhists do not believe in God.[27] He recalled that in the early days of the Hanoverians the House had allowed men to swear the oath of loyalty to George I even though everyone knew some were avowed Jacobites: so it seemed odd to prevent an avowed atheist from taking the oath now. Bolingbroke, 'without any religious belief at all', had managed to join and prosper in the House when it was intimately bound to the Church of England.[28]

The speech was one of Gladstone's most brilliant, and a model of parliamentary rhetoric: but it had little effect on those whose minds were made up. In the end the vote was against Bradlaugh affirming, by 275 to 230. While the atheist had the support of 219 Liberals, one Conservative and ten Home Rulers (including Parnell), over 200 Tories, sixty-five of his own party and some Home Rulers, under pressure from the Catholic church, voted against his right to enter the House. Parnell, a Protestant, would come under severe attack for his support, and soon modified his position, intensifying Bradlaugh's disappointment after all his support for Irish Home Rule. Bradlaugh announced he would attend the House in any case at noon the next day, to ask to take the oath again.

Amid roars of 'Withdraw!' from the Tory benches, he presented himself at the table and asked to swear, but was told by Erskine May, as Clerk, that a resolution had been passed preventing his doing so. Bradlaugh disputed that May had any right not to tender him the oath, and May sought support from the Speaker. Brand then told Bradlaugh he could not take the oath; Bradlaugh's response was to demand the right to be heard in his own defence, which only caused the Speaker more pain. Yet again unwilling to decide, Brand had Bradlaugh withdraw while the House discussed whether to hear him.

It decided swiftly, on a motion of Labouchere, to let him speak, but from the Bar of the House – the line on the carpet just inside the doors from the Members' Lobby, beyond which no non-member except the clerks is supposed to stray when the House sits. Bradlaugh said, pointedly but with a dignity that never deserted him, that he was in 'a position unexampled in the history of this House', and that 'the traditions of the House' argued against the resolution passed the previous day being enforced.[29] He said he sought not a favour, but justice; he attacked the Tory benches for intolerance; above all, he said, with defiance, that he was unashamed of his opinions. He admitted that 'I had tried to gain a feigned entrance here by pretending to be what I am not'; which he felt was all the more reason why the House should relent and let him affirm.[30]

He argued that his electors would be left disfranchised; and that if the House tried to declare the seat vacant it would be exceeding its authority. He told Brand he had the power to admit an atheist. 'Do you mean that I am to go back to Northampton as to a Court, to appeal against you?' he asked.[31] 'Do you mean that I am to tell my constituency to array themselves against this House? I hope not; but if it is to be, it must be. If this House arrays itself against an isolated man – if it be its huge powers against one citizen that you are thinking to use – if it must be that, then the battle must be, too. But it is not with the constituency of Northampton alone – hon Members need be under no mistake – that you will come into conflict.' He warned Brand that the House 'cannot supersede the rights of the people of this country'. The court to which he would appeal, he announced, would be 'the court of public opinion'.[32]

Brand asked whether the House wanted Bradlaugh – who had left the chamber – called back in to be told that it had not changed its mind; and he was then turned on by other MPs who argued that the House's view had, or had not, changed. He capitulated under this assault and invited Labouchere to speak. Labouchere simply wanted to clarify what Brand would say to Bradlaugh if he called him back in – would he tell him that he could neither affirm nor take the oath? He cited Gladstone in his support, on which point the prime minister chose to remain silent. After an interlude of procedural chaos it was agreed nothing had changed, and Bradlaugh was recalled.

He had stressed his respect for Parliament, but would not take this quietly. When Brand told him his fate, and asked him to withdraw, Bradlaugh told him: 'I beg respectfully to insist upon my right as a duly elected Member for Northampton: and I ask you to have the oath administered to me that I may take my seat. I respectfully refuse to withdraw.'[33] Brand asked again, more firmly. Bradlaugh was, metaphorically at least, immovable. 'With great respect, Sir, I refuse to obey the orders of the House, which are against the law.'[34] Brand, realising confrontation was inevitable, asked the House to support the execution of the order. Northcote moved a motion to have the atheist forcibly removed. The House voted by a majority of 288 to do so, with many Liberals abstaining. Bradlaugh refused again to obey: the Serjeant-at-Arms tapped him on the shoulder, and he went without a struggle. He did, however, promise that 'I shall immediately return'.[35] He did, indeed: having turned to leave the House, he turned right back, and amid a scene of uproar walked up to the Bar again and announced that 'I admit no right on the part of the House to exclude me, and I refuse to be excluded'. Bradlaugh had plotted every move carefully, 'determined to force the House to further steps, and to make its path a *cul de sac*.'[36]

Brand realised this was a temporary respite, and that his authority was under threat; and that the image of the elected chamber refusing to admit someone entitled to be there, because they knew he would swear the oath insincerely if allowed to do so, would fuel intense controversy. Again, he pleaded for guidance. Gladstone, who shared Bradlaugh's view if not about the illegality of what had happened then about its profound unwisdom, was compromised. Northcote, posing as the loyal servant of procedure but also milking the episode for all the political advantage he could, stated that the authority of the chair had to be upheld, and therefore proposed – 'not in any spirit of vindictiveness, but simply for the purpose of asserting the authority of the House and the Chair' – that Bradlaugh be taken into custody: which meant the Serjeant-at-Arms locking him in the cells under the clock tower. Gladstone had to agree the House had no choice, if determined to exclude Bradlaugh. Even Labouchere understood this, though he said it was 'a somewhat strange thing that a citizen of this country should be sent to prison for doing what eminent legal Gentlemen on this side, and an eminent legal Gentleman on that side of the House say he has a perfect right to do so.'[37] He mocked the House's authority too, warning MPs that sending Bradlaugh down would be the first step to recognition of his legitimacy as a Member. Bradlaugh tried to speak again, but was told he had no right.

An angry debate followed, with suggestions that Bradlaugh might be able to seek a writ of Habeas Corpus to challenge the legality of his exclusion. Parnell warned comrades who might think of supporting Bradlaugh's imprisonment that they would, by taking the side of British authority against liberty, offend most of their constituents in all places apart from Ulster. 'He did not believe the Irish constituencies would wish even an atheist to be imprisoned.'[38] He was attacked, however, by two Irish members for implying Bradlaugh was being imprisoned for his views on religion, not for his views on the authority of the Commons.

The House voted by 274 votes to seven, again with many Liberal abstentions, for the Serjeant-at-Arms to take Bradlaugh into custody, and – once a warrant was made out, during which time he enjoyed the hospitality of the Serjeant-at-Arms in his private room – he was locked up. It was not too much of a hardship for Bradlaugh. He could telegraph his friends to come to visit him, the first of whom was Parnell with a group of his as yet unintimidated colleagues. That evening Bradlaugh entertained his daughter and Mrs Besant to dinner. *The Times* reported that 'he spoke in warm terms of the courtesy and consideration of the Speaker and the Serjeant-at-Arms', but 'complained bitterly' of attacks made on him by some of his less charitable opponents.[39] He felt especially betrayed by the Irish. He offered a menacing thought, however: that 'if he is kept in the Clock Tower for any length of time the people will come to fetch him.'

The next day Northcote – under pressure from Beaconsfield, who considered the architects of the persecution 'fools' – proposed that Bradlaugh, who he assumed had learned his lesson, should be released.[40] Beaconsfield had been alarmed by the groundswell of feeling in Bradlaugh's favour: in the week after his imprisonment 200 meetings in his support were held around the country. Some of Northcote's younger colleagues, notably Churchill, felt there was still plenty of mileage in exploiting the godlessness of this Liberal. They were helped by the vocal support of the Archbishop of Canterbury, who put himself at odds with Gladstone. Bradlaugh had not learned his lesson, and proposed to return and demand his legal right to sit in the Commons once released. Hartington had talked to Labouchere about keeping Bradlaugh quiet until progress could be made. When Labouchere, on 25 June, requested a new debate to have the resolution rescinded, Churchill asked him whether it was Bradlaugh's intention 'to continue his attempts to disturb the peace of the House'.[41] That was not Bradlaugh's point at all, as Churchill well knew, and he was shouted down for saying so. Eddy Hamilton, Gladstone's private secretary, described the Tories' behaviour as an example of their 'parading their religious fanaticism and of embarrassing the Government.'[42]

III

The argument was only just beginning. Such was Gladstone's and the cabinet's discomfort that he moved a motion on 1 July allowing members to affirm, but (as the select committee had suggested) at their legal peril: that is, if anyone wished to challenge their legitimacy in court, he could do so. The motion was carried by 303 votes to 249, and Bradlaugh attended the next day to affirm. However, the moment he cast his first vote he was served with a writ claiming he had done so illegally. It later became known that one of the more reactionary Tory MPs, Charles Newdegate, was funding the suit against him. To rub matters in, Sir Eardley Wilmot, an elderly Tory and an authority on the law, foxhunting and hydropathy, sought to introduce a Bill disqualifying anyone who had expressed atheist opinions from sitting in parliament. The debate now was whether Bradlaugh had proclaimed his atheism or whether it had been prised out of him. Gladstone wrote on 27 June that 'it seems now that Bradlaugh did *not* volunteer a confession of his unbelief, but that it was drawn from him by inquiries'.[43] This notion – that Bradlaugh had not sought to be offensive or provocative at a time when the profession of atheism was highly likely to offend or provoke – was key to Gladstone's willingness to support him.

In March 1881 the High Court decreed it had been illegal for him to take his seat after affirming. He appealed, unsuccessfully. A writ was moved for a by-election: he was deemed to have vacated his seat by voting unsworn. This was a criminal offence, but Bradlaugh – in several court cases in which he was prosecuted for his behaviour – always successfully defended himself, despite the big guns of the Bar opposing him. On 26 April 1881, having fought the by-election and been re-elected, he tried to take the oath again, and Brand tried to let him, pausing when Northcote (whom Bradlaugh had warned of his plans) rose to protest that as the resolution passed the previous year was unrescinded, Bradlaugh could not take the oath. He added the extra element of self-righteousness the Tories felt was necessary to justify their obstruction of democracy and their exploitation of it as a party political issue, by saying that for Bradlaugh to take the oath would be 'a profanation of a sacred form'.[44]

Supporters of Bradlaugh argued that the House should not exploit what it happened to know about Bradlaugh to impede his taking of the oath. Labouchere had found a statement by Lord John Russell, from 1842, in which he had declared that a resolution was binding for one session of parliament only. Labouchere felt Northcote was demanding a 'recantation' from Bradlaugh as a condition of his taking his seat, an idea Labouchere dismissed as 'utterly absurd'.[45] The spectacle of a professed atheist swearing the oath was the fault of the House for not allowing him to affirm. Bright said the matter was not one of law so much as of 'religious disability'; a disability that should be lifted, as that on Roman Catholics had been in 1829.[46] To try to invent a new disability was, he proclaimed, 'an act of bigotry' and 'nothing consonant with Christianity in its highest principles'.[47]

The House agreed to hear Bradlaugh, from below the Bar. 'You have force,' he told the Commons. 'On my side is the law.'[48] He maintained that the Tories had turned the argument into a party political one. He protested that the resolution of the previous year could not bind the House any longer. He warned them that 'the force that you invoke against the law today may tomorrow be used against you.'[49] This raised the already considerable level of discomfort, as did his later point that he was being excluded purely because his opinions were 'obnoxious'.[50] His peroration was cutting:

> I ask you now, do not plunge with me into a struggle I would shun. The law gives me no remedy if the House decides against me. Do not mock at the constituencies. If you place yourselves above the law, you leave me no course save lawless agitation, instead of reasonable pleading. It is easy to begin such a strife, but none knows how it would end. I have no Court, no tribunal to appeal to; you have the strength of your votes at the moment. You think I am an obnoxious man, and that I have no one on my side. If that be so, then the more reason that this House, grand in the strength of its centuries of liberty, should have now that generosity in dealing with one who tomorrow may be forced into a struggle for public opinion against it.[51]

There were rowdy and ill-tempered scenes during the debate. Gladstone said that the finest legal minds agreed Bradlaugh should be admitted. He believed Bradlaugh ought 'to be credited with the best and highest motives': it was none of the House's business if he took an oath he could not reconcile with his conscience.[52] He also agreed that the resolution could not be held over Bradlaugh. He warned the opposition that Bradlaugh was right to say that if it could not find legal means to bar him it would find illegal ones; and that there would be consequences for its reputation. Gladstone was shocked by the tone of the debate, describing the occasion as 'a bad night: bad acrid intolerant feeling and unseemly squabbles.'[53] Not normally one to allow his calm to be violated by such things, he admitted to his diary that he was then 'quite upset in the night for once.' Hamilton found him 'greatly worried and distressed'.[54]

Once again the House voted to stop Bradlaugh taking the oath, by 208 votes to 175. Once again he tried, was told he could not, and told the Speaker it was illegal to prevent him. Brand once more asked the House to agree to have Bradlaugh forcibly removed; Labouchere warned him that if it did Bradlaugh would have to be locked up for the duration of the parliament. He taunted Northcote for having had to ask the House to release Bradlaugh the previous year, such was the ferocity of opinion in the country against the Tories for their exploitation of the issue. 'I tell the Rt hon Gentleman,' Labouchere added, 'that when he tries to set himself against the whole constituencies of the country, though he may have a subservient majority behind him, he may find that he is not the first man who has set himself against the nation.'[55]

Bradlaugh was taken to the Bar, and promptly walked back again to the table to demand to take the oath. Northcote having learned his lesson the previous year, he did not move that Bradlaugh be taken into custody; but the rowdy scenes in the chamber, with Brand's authority draining away, instead caused the adjournment of the House. *The Times* reported that 'the messengers [usually former soldiers] were called in, and, surrounding Mr Bradlaugh, forced him back to the Bar, the hon member protesting all the time against the employment of physical force'.[56] The next day Bradlaugh was back, trying to take the oath, and Brand was back telling him he could not. The Serjeant-at-Arms removed Bradlaugh again to below the Bar, though not to the cells.

Strong feeling in the country rose again in favour of Bradlaugh: but there was also organised opposition to him, in which clergy of all brands played a significant part. As well as vocal complaints from the established Church there were representations against him by the President of the Wesleyan Conference, who instructed his brethren to mobilise against this blasphemy. As John Robertson put it: 'Protestants vied with Catholics in the foulness of their abuse, the ferocity of their enmity.'[57] At least one Wesleyan minister, J. F. Duncan of Nottingham, was forced to apologise and retract remarks about Bradlaugh's evil, under the promise of legal action. However, some clergy were sufficiently enlightened to defend Bradlaugh's right to freedom of thought, just as some devout Christians in parliament had.

Labouchere asked the government to support a Bill to change the oath. Gladstone was sympathetic, but such an act would require postponing the Irish Land Bill, with consequences even more severe than interfering with Bradlaugh's stand.[58] However, when it became clear that the turbulence would not otherwise end, the government agreed to such a Bill, much to the delight of Churchill and the Fourth Party. They saw it as an opportunity to paint the Liberals as blasphemous and irreligious, and to exploit divisions among the Irish nationalists. Also, since Bradlaugh had made no secret of his republican opinions any more than of his atheistic ones, Tories asked how he could make an affirmation that professed allegiance to the Queen. To allow him to affirm, Churchill observed with his customary moderation, would be 'imperious and arbitrary' and would provide 'facilities for placing in the House of Commons brazen Atheism and rampant disloyalty.'[59]

Bradlaugh agreed to keep away pending discussion of the Bill. James, as Attorney-General, tried to introduce it on 2 May 1881. However, repeated adjournments, engineered by Tories and secured by the failure of some Liberals to vote to have the Bill read, forced the government to abandon plans for a special morning sitting to discuss the matter when Irish business was overwhelming. This failure brought Bradlaugh back to the Bar on 10 May to demand his rights. The patience of the House was wearing thin, and this time Bradlaugh was forcibly removed from the precincts but not imprisoned. He wrote a letter of protest, not just about his removal but also because the courts decided that what the House had done was not justiciable by them: so Bradlaugh was checkmated.

Gladstone became increasingly hard-line in his defence of Bradlaugh the more the Tories sought to exploit the difficulty. He told John Hubbard, a Tory MP, High Churchman and obsessive income-tax reformer, that Bradlaugh had 'committed a gross error by presenting himself to take the oath.'[60] The problem was that 'he has no moral right to bisect it into a significant and an unmeaning part'. However, he compared what Bradlaugh had done with the much-derided marriage, recently contracted, between Baroness Burdett-Coutts and her much younger American secretary, which had not only made her a laughing stock but had caused her, under the terms of her inheritance, to forfeit her fortune: 'But *I* could not on that account interfere to prevent it, nor can I deny her legal right to do this deplorable moral wrong.' He told

Hubbard that the Commons 'has acted, in my view, beyond its powers: has acted, as I should say in ignorant and lay phraseology, illegally. Can any good come of this?'

The Irish Land Bill derailed any further attempts to reform the oath. Gladstone told Bradlaugh of this on 2 July. Thus thwarted, he took legal advice, and wrote to Brand to say he would try to take the oath again, as his removal by the Serjeant-at-Arms was also, he believed, illegal. Gladstone was deeply unsettled by this, telling James that 'if B resorts to physical force, and mischief results, it will be very difficult to carry on the resistance to him by physical force only.'[61] He lamented that the matter was not considered justiciable. 'I wish it were possible for him to get an appeal in a court of Law.' Bradlaugh was however already heavily in debt because of legal fees; there was a serious risk that even if he obtained the right to be administered the oath, he would be bankrupt and thus under parliamentary convention unable to take his seat. On 3 August, after addressing a rally of supporters in Trafalgar Square, he attempted to go to the Bar again: but was removed by Commons officials – it took four messengers and ten policemen – before he could even enter the lobby. This allowed the House to proceed uninterrupted: and although Labouchere complained, that was how matters stayed. With Ireland derailing the parliamentary timetable, and Gladstone's plans for his second administration unravelling, Bradlaugh's needs were just another casualty.

In 1882 he returned at the beginning of the session, proclaiming after another act of defiance that 'the grave alone shall make me yield'.[62] Labouchere then tried to move a writ for another by-election, so Bradlaugh could stand and win again. Sensing a stunt, the Conservatives threw the motion out. 'Then followed', *The Times* reported, 'a grossly indecorous act on the part of Mr Bradlaugh' who 'advanced from the Bar to the table, produced from his pocket a sheet of paper and a book, and read from the paper what were supposed to be the words of the oath. When he had finished reading he kissed the book and signed the manuscript. He then tendered it to the Clerk as the oath taken according to law.'[63] The book was a New Testament. Bradlaugh, to general astonishment, then sat on the Liberal benches. Now it was the Tories' turn – in the person of a gleeful Churchill – to call for a by-election writ to be moved, Bradlaugh having disqualified himself by being seated without taking the oath. This was not strictly true, since the disqualification only applied if someone sat during a debate (and the House had not yet moved on to that business) or voted.

However, the next day Churchill had his wish: Bradlaugh was expelled, with most Liberals abstaining so as not to challenge Brand's diminished authority. Bradlaugh had appealed to Gladstone for help, but Gladstone replied that, given the House's determination to exceed what he considered to be its jurisdiction, he had run out of ideas. He came under sustained attack from others who, like him, were devout: but, as he told one of them, his old friend and fellow Peelite Sir Thomas Dyke Acland, a Church Commissioner, '*we do not say Bradlaugh ought to sit*; but simply that his right or non-right to sit should be determined by law; by a dispassionate Court of Law, instead of by a House of Commons, of which the majority have in dealing with this question exhibited a degree of unfavourable excitement rare even in the struggles of party.'[64]

Petitions poured in from all over Britain. The radical movement mobilised, arranging public meetings that Bradlaugh addressed, and organising an extensive canvass of Northampton to help ensure he won the by-election. On 4 March he won again, and turned up at the Commons. This time Northcote's motion to prevent his taking the oath was passed by just 259 votes to 244. On Sunday 14 May between 70,000 and 80,000 supporters attended a mass meeting in Hyde Park, four days after a smaller one in Trafalgar Square. The Liberal press, led by *The Pall Mall Gazette*, called for urgent legislation to allow affirmation, and taunted the government for a lack of courage. The Duke of Argyll, the Lord Privy Seal, eventually tried, and failed, to introduce an Affirmation Bill that July.

Bradlaugh led a relentless campaign of agitation in the constituencies, and encountered increased vilification from politicians and clergy. Cardinal Manning, the Archbishop of Westminster, had visited Northampton to stir up Irish Catholic voters against supporting an atheist. He wrote articles in *The Nineteenth Century*, to which the magazine's editor graciously denied Bradlaugh the right of reply. To retaliate he published a pamphlet savaging Manning as one who owed allegiance to the Pope in Rome rather than to the Queen (rich coming from a republican, but needs must), and told the Cardinal that 'you only reside here without police challenge by the merciful forbearance of the community.'[65]

In April 1883 the government introduced its own Bill, which it stressed would not be retrospective – Bradlaugh would need to be re-elected –

and for the benefit of constituents, who would not be deprived of representation by the Commons' preventing their MP from being sworn. An Archdeacon, R. W. Browne, wrote to Gladstone, apparently (his letter is untraced, but we have Gladstone's reply) asserting that the Bill would legitimise or encourage immorality. 'To take cognizance of moral conduct in any Law regulating admission to Parliament would be mischievous even if it were not impossible,' Gladstone replied. 'To allege immorality in connection with atheism and as its fruit would be open to the answer that there are many atheists of irreproachable life.'[66]

A naked dislike of Bradlaugh was revealed: such as William Sullivan, the Irish National MP for Limerick, saying he was 'astonished that a pious, good Christian like the Prime Minister, at a time when infidelity was spreading in the land, should bring in a Bill to facilitate the admission to the House of a man who denied the existence of a Supreme Being.'[67] Lord Elcho said if Scotland were to be considered bigoted for a dislike of professional atheism, then he was 'proud to believe that Scotland was bigoted'.[68] If the House passed the Bill it would be purely in response to threats from Bradlaugh and from his 'impresario' Labouchere.[69] Fowler said the Bill would be tantamount to 'a national insult to the God who has made us great', a 'disgrace to the country' and a demand 'at the bidding of Mr Bradlaugh to renounce the Christian religion of this country'.[70]

Gladstone, in a long, erudite speech of constitutional, theological and classical learning, concluded by lamenting the damage done by a controversy that had lasted three years. 'Great mischief has been done in many minds through the resistance offered to the man elected by the constituency of Northampton, which a portion of the community believe to be unjust. When they see the profession of religion and the interests of religion ostensibly associated with what they are deeply convinced is injustice, they are led to questions about religion itself, which they see to be associated with injustice. Unbelief attracts a sympathy which it would not otherwise enjoy; and the upshot is to impair those convictions and that religious faith, the loss of which I believe to be the most inexpressible calamity which can fall either upon a man or upon a nation.'[71] Gladstone disingenuously claimed Bradlaugh was nothing to do with the decision to have a Bill, provoking Lord Lewisham to ask why in that case the Liberals had not introduced such a measure before.

The debate ran over five nights. Visceral, not to say atavistic, sentiments seeped through. Alexander Beresford-Hope, MP for Cambridge University, mocked the notion that allowing an avowed atheist to sit was no different from admitting a Jew or a Roman Catholic. 'The Atheist is morally an unsafe man. There is no possibility of binding him to his obligation. The word "God" has no meaning to him, while, for the extent to which it needs a meaning in the Oath, it has the same meaning for Christian, for Jew, and for all who recognise a supernatural moral government of the Universe.'[72] On 3 May 1883 the Bill fell by 295 votes to 292; the Irish largely voting with the Tories to appease their devout and predominantly Catholic constituents, and some Liberals from strong Non-conformist backgrounds placating their deeply religious voters. The government's plea to recognise liberty of conscience, the clarion call of the Marquess of Hartington's winding-up speech, was ignored.

The House agreed Bradlaugh could be heard at the Bar again. He had now been elected three times in three years; he joked that even if he was as vile as some said, vileness itself was no disqualification. Again he was refused leave to swear the oath. He threatened two months later to come again, but a vote was carried, with most Liberals abstaining, to exclude him. In February 1884, for the second time, he administered the oath to himself. This provoked Northcote to move his expulsion, which occasioned a third by-election. Bradlaugh won again, and so for the avoidance of doubt Northcote moved that he be excluded from the precincts. That motion was carried, and an attempt by Bradlaugh to get the courts to support his self-administration of the oath also failed.

Although he had fierce critics in the country, who despised his free-thinking and saw him as subversive, Bradlaugh won the widespread support and respect of the public. There was a perceived correlation between intellectual enlightenment and defence of his position: which might explain why Churchill, an unoriginal mind and one whose position in politics was earned by his social status and charisma more than by talent, continued his persecution. The argument stretched into the next administration: when Salisbury formed his new ministry, in July 1885, Bradlaugh attempted to swear again and was excluded again. At the election held that November, Bradlaugh and Labouchere were once more returned as members for Northampton.

Brand's health had been poor, and he went to the Lords as Viscount Hampden in 1884. His successor, Arthur Peel, waited until the new parliament was elected; but when Bradlaugh came to take the oath on 13

January 1886, Peel did what Brand should have done, and directed that the House had no right to prevent him. Hicks Beach, who now led the Conservatives in the Commons, tried to pressurise Peel into maintaining the stand against Bradlaugh. He wrote Peel a mildly menacing letter instructing him that a precedent had been set. Two other senior Tory MPs signed a similarly insolent communication. All had misjudged their man. Labouchere had been in private communication with Churchill over the preceding weeks, and the former scourge of atheism now resolved to keep quiet. 'A wilful man', Labouchere told Churchill, 'must have his way.'[73]

Peel was having none of the Tory protest. 'I know nothing of the Resolutions of the past. They have lapsed, they are void, they are of no effect in reference to this case.'[74] He took Bradlaugh's view exactly: 'It is the right, the legal statutable obligation, of Members when returned to this House, to come to this Table, and take the Oath prescribed by Statute. I have no authority, I have no right, original or delegated, to interfere between an honourable Member and his taking of the Oath.' As for Bradlaugh's supposedly toxic opinions – published again in the press a few days earlier, and helpfully drawn to Peel's attention by Hicks Beach, the Speaker was equally firm. 'It is not for me, I respectfully say it is not for the House, to enter into any inquisition as to what may be the opinions of a Member when he comes to the Table to take the Oath.'

Bradlaugh took his rightful place on the Liberal benches of the House of Commons. Churchill – briefly, after the failure of the first Home Rule Bill in 1886, Leader of the Commons – sought to placate him and confirmed there would be no further Tory opposition. Some of his colleagues sensed that the persecution of Bradlaugh, and the ruthless way men such as Churchill had exploited it, had damaged their party. It helped force a change in the tone of Conservatism under Salisbury from 1886 to 1892, marking out the reactionary elements as a force of self-interest rather than of public interest. In 1888 Bradlaugh succeeded in getting an Affirmation Bill on the statute book, thus effectively secularising the Commons and making a vital extension of the right of freedom of thought. And in January 1891, as he lay dying, the Commons belatedly admitted its shameful conduct, and passed a motion expunging from the record the resolutions it had, in a prolonged fit of self-righteous hysteria, passed against him a decade earlier.

IV

Bradlaugh had effectively secularised parliament, though prayers continued to be held there daily (and continue to be held to this day, for those who wish to participate). With the upper classes increasingly paying only lip service to religion (except when it suited their political purposes), and the working classes less observant in the decades since urbanisation, Christianity in Britain was increasingly upheld by the middle classes. The inculcation of the Christian ethos in the new minor public schools and grammar schools was systematic and on Arnoldian lines, though had evolved into 'muscular Christianity', with an emphasis on games and physical strength. This was not merely, as is usually reported, to take the minds of testosterone-laden boys off sexual matters, but to equip them to run and if necessary defend an empire and to advance the idea of 'manliness'. Many of its products are recorded on countless school war memorials around Britain.

Not least by these means the Anglican hold on society remained strong. Bennett observed, writing of this era in *Clayhanger*, that 'in spite of numerous attempts, nobody had contrived to make England see that its very existence would not be threatened if museums were opened on Sunday, or that Non-conformists might be buried according to their own rites without endangering the Constitution.'[75] In the midlands and the north Non-conformity was strong, with membership of a dissenting congregation routinely seen as a mark of respectability for the aspirant tradesman and his family. Such societies could be, and often were, stifling, and helped define the idea of provincialism among the London *beau monde* and those, such as Bennett, who managed to escape the provinces – though the snobbery of Virginia Woolf towards Bennett showed that in late-Victorian and Edwardian Britain one could physically separate oneself from one's upbringing, but never entirely metaphysically. In 1900 33 per cent of the population of the United Kingdom were members of a church: the proportion declined steadily throughout the following century.[76] Throughout the Kingdom at the turn of the century Sundays were predominantly days of rest; businesses did not open, no professional sport was played, and amateur sports were kept until the afternoon, when morning worship was over. In many observant Non-conformist households Sundays remained days of contemplation when recreation of any description was frowned upon.

Woolf was an Olympian in the snob stakes, but even Galsworthy, who was not, could find the provincial middle class tedious, with their unquestioning acceptance of conventional religious teaching and observances. Replying in 1913 to William Archer, the critic, who said Bennett 'bored him stiff', Galsworthy admitted 'me too, a bit'.[77] However Bennett, whose view of religion was warped by the strict Wesleyan Methodism of his parents in Hanley (now Stoke-on-Trent) in the 1870s, shows some characters in his novels suffering religious oppression by their families and communities, notably Anna Tellwright in *Anna of the Five Towns*.

It remained one of the marks of Anglican devotion in the late nineteenth century to be resolutely anti-Catholic, with a rigorous interpretation of the Thirty-seventh Article: that the Bishop of Rome 'hath no jurisdiction in this realm of England.' It was not merely the prospect of popish interference that upset many of the Protestant English: they also regarded Roman Catholic countries as inherently backward and superstitious. When Edward VII prepared for his Coronation in 1902, he was so stunned by the anti-Catholic bigotry of the oath his mother had taken in 1838 that he demanded it be changed.[78] The religious disputes of the previous generation – a determination by intellectual theologians to reintroduce elements of pre-Reformation doctrine into Anglican worship, and an equal determination by committed Protestants of all classes to keep Roman Catholicism on the margins of society – still raged within the Church of England, despite Disraeli's attempt in 1874 to kill the Oxford Movement by having parliament pass the Public Worship Regulation Act. Put through at the urging of the Archbishop of Canterbury, Archibald Campbell Tait, the Act sought to end the Roman Catholic-style ritualism creeping into acts of worship in the established Church and to reinforce the supremacy of Protestantism. Anti-Catholic bigotry was a staple of the rising middle class, particularly but not exclusively in the Church of England, and Disraeli saw political advantage to the Conservative party in doing Tait's bidding.

Although Gladstone, as a High Churchman himself, was appalled by the Act, he let it rest on returning to office in 1880, even though three of the five clergymen imprisoned under it were sentenced during his rule.

One, Father Richard Enraght, refused to attend his trial for adoration of the sacrament, wearing a chasuble and an alb and using lighted candles in his church near Birmingham. He was sentenced *in absentia* and sent to Warwick jail in December 1880. The case embarrassed the Church, and attracted international attention. The absurdity of the Act rapidly became apparent: it encouraged a group of militant middle-class Protestants, the Church Association, to infiltrate parishes and inform on priests. Edward Pusey, who with John Henry Newman and John Keble had been one of the leaders nearly half a century earlier of the Anglo-Catholic Oxford Movement, wrote to *The Times* to defend himself from the assertion by an unnamed diocesan chancellor that he was among 'the advocates of ecclesiastical anarchy and the right of parsons to persecute the laity of the Church of England', but also to defend Enraght and others like him, opening up old wounds from the early days of the Movement more than forty years previously.[79] He proclaimed: 'I think that posterity will think that these vehement measures . . . are very like straining at a gnat and swallowing a camel.'

Pusey wrote again on 14 January 1881 to say Enraght and another clergyman who had been prosecuted, Alexander Mackonochie, 'have not been struggling for themselves, but for their people.'[80] He concluded that 'the Ritualists do not ask to interfere with the devotions of others – only to be allowed, in their worship of God, to use a Ritual which a few years ago no one disputed, and that only when their congregations wish it.' Enraght was released on a technicality after forty-nine days. His case led to a Royal Commission that drew attention to weaknesses in the Act, an argument so convincing that even Tait changed tack: it was starting to smell a little too much of the sixteenth century.

Another martyr to it, the Reverend Sidney Faithorn Green, who had a parish in Manchester, was a serial offender both before and after the Act, having been reproached by the Bishop of Manchester, James Fraser, in 1871 for mixing water with wine at Holy Communion. By 1877 matters had become even worse. Green was using lighted candles and unlawful vestments, and performing such outrages as using the sign of the cross towards the congregation, kneeling during the prayer of consecration, and unlawfully and ceremoniously raising the chalice. Green was tried for contumacy – downright disobedience – but refused to accept the verdict, and was thrown into Lancaster Castle for contempt in March 1881, languishing there until November 1882: when, having been deprived of his living and bailiffs having extracted the costs of his prosecution, he was released.

Gladstone had tried to have Green released sooner, telling Harcourt, the Home Secretary, in September 1881: 'I am under the impression that Mr Green's imprisonment grows out of disobedience to a judgment of the Privy Council touching clerical vestments. But unless I am grossly mistaken, that same judgment is disobeyed systematically and with impunity every day in the year by every Clergyman who wears what is called a stole, that is I imagine by ninety-nine in every hundred of the whole Clergy of the country.'[81] Harcourt said that as Green was inside for contempt, and his health was good, there was no 'decent excuse' to release him.[82] Gladstone then subtly pressed Harcourt to alert the prison doctor to 'the state of his [Green's] mind', but that made no difference: Green was keen on martyrdom.[83] Gladstone opened a long and fruitless discussion with Harcourt about the severity of the contempt laws.

However, just when common sense appeared to have prevailed – though the law would not be changed until the 1960s – the highest-profile case yet occurred. Edward King was a senior Oxford theologian known and admired by Gladstone, who offered him the Bishopric of Lincoln in 1885. In June 1888 Edward Benson, Tait's successor, was petitioned by some aggrieved parishioners in Lincoln about changes of ritual King had effected. Benson doubted he could try King in an ecclesiastical court, but a commission of five judges and five bishops decided in August 1888 that he could. Such an accusation against a prelate was without recent precedent: someone so senior had last been referred to an Archbishop in the 1690s, when Archbishop Tenison had had Bishop Watson of St David's excommunicated for simony, the selling of preferment in the Church.

Benson read the copious records of the proceedings against Watson – 3,000 folio pages in all – to ensure the case was not lost because of a departure from precedent. The decision would be his and his alone: the five bishops sat with him for consultative purposes, with legal advice from the vicar-general, Sir James Parker Deane, QC. King hired two QCs. The hearing began on 12 February 1889 at Lambeth Palace, to be adjourned immediately. The case dragged on into 1890, with attempts by the High Church party to prove Benson had no authority to try the case; and to argue that even if King were found guilty it would be personal guilt, applying to him alone – any other clergy who committed such offences would have to be tried separately for them.

The specific charge was that on 4 December 1887, while celebrating Holy Communion in a Lincoln church called St Peter at Gowts, King had placed lighted candles on the communion table, mixed the sacramental wine with water, and had his back to the congregation so they could not see him break the bread and take the cup into his hands. Part of the service had been sung and King, 'while pronouncing the absolution, conspicuously and ceremoniously having both his hands elevated and looking towards the congregation, made with his hand the sign of the cross'.[84] He had then, allegedly, repeated these offences in the cathedral a fortnight later. When he appeared before Benson and his court he said he did so out of deference to the Archbishop and in keeping with the oath he had taken to obey him: 'But I appear under protest, desiring, with all respect, to question the jurisdiction which Your Grace proposes to exercise.' It was a put-up job: the chief complainant was an auctioneer from Cleethorpes, Ernest de Lacey Read, a churchwarden who had earlier tried to make trouble about his own rector's practices. When the Lincoln diocese had exonerated the rector, Read and some of his supporters decided to look for other irregularities in the diocese and refer the next example not to Lincoln, but to Lambeth Palace. King's protest caused an immediate adjournment while the legitimacy of the hearing was discussed further.

For a month the vicar-general, in his chambers at the Law Courts, heard petitions from both sides about whether or not the case should, or could, proceed. The argument then returned to Lambeth Palace, where the Archbishop engaged in the discussion, conducted in one or two sessions a week. Thus the Church made a spectacle of itself over weeks and months, not arguing about ritualism, but arguing about whether those accused of it had committed an offence susceptible to trial in an ecclesiastical court. Dickens could have made it up: the damage to the Church was considerable, and the case assisted the march towards a secular society. It was not until mid-May that Benson declared that he had jurisdiction, a decision that was promptly appealed against.

Not until February 1890 – a year after the case had begun, and more than two after the alleged events – did the court discuss the facts and the theology. The comedy continued, as counsel for the defence announced that 'he did not require evidence that the Bishop was the Bishop of Lincoln', only for a prosecution QC to say precedent seemed to require that anyone accused of a misdemeanour had to prove he had been 'properly instituted'.[85]

Benson, his patience wearing thin, said that if it did have to be proved that the bishop was actually the bishop, it could be done afterwards. The facts were stated and proved by late February, at which point Benson announced he would require time to consider his judgment.

He delivered it on 21 November 1890 in the Library at Lambeth Palace, 'densely crowded' for the occasion.[86] He and his fellow bishops had spent the intervening months steeping themselves in the history of theological practice, and he ruled, first, that there was no basis for the mixing of water with wine; second, paradoxically, 'the consecration of a mixed cup, however, is . . . a primitive, continuous, and all but universal practice in the Church', and therefore even though the mixing was an ecclesiastical offence, the consecration of a mixed cup was not; third, that the bishop's pouring wine and water into a paten and chalice and drinking it himself was not an offence; that engaging in the 'popish superstition' of facing east could not be proved to be an offence; that the breaking of bread and other 'manual acts' should be done in sight of the congregation; that the choir singing an anthem was 'not an illegal addition to the service'; that the law had not been broken by lighting candles; that making the sign of the cross in giving absolution 'is an innovation which must be discontinued', and making it in giving the benediction was a ceremony 'additional to the ceremonies of the Church' and 'must be discontinued'.

Benson knew King had been set up, and having delivered a judgment over three hours, reserved some words for the bishop's persecutors: 'It is not decent for religious persons to hire witnesses to intrude on the worship of others for purposes of espial.'[87] He regretted that 'time and attention' had been 'diverted . . . from the Church's real contest with evil' and 'the fraternal union of mankind'. If this was designed to shut up the Church Association it failed, since it immediately appealed to the Judicial Committee of the Privy Council, who threw it out. King dropped the practices Benson had criticised; Benson's successor, Frederick Temple, prosecuted two priests for using incense and candles, but otherwise the Church of England's persecution of Anglo-Catholic priests came to an end. By 1914 many of King's practices were widespread, and have remained so, a Royal Commission in 1906 having recognised the legitimacy of ritualism and confirmed the idea of the 'broad church'. This new permissiveness and flexibility set the tone of the Church of England, and of the wider approach to Christianity, in the twentieth century and beyond.

CHAPTER 7

THE CIVILISING MISSION

I

When Gladstone came to power in 1868, at the time of his first administration, his clear priority was to improve the lot of the people, specifically in enhancing social mobility, living conditions and allowing in to their lives what his friend Matthew Arnold called 'sweetness and light'. All this was of lesser importance to him when he returned to office in 1880, troubled as he was by Ireland, sensing the need for further parliamentary reform, and increasingly weighed down by party political concerns. There was a glaring absence of visionary domestic legislation that might have addressed the need to improve living conditions for the masses, alleviate their poverty, increase their educational opportunities or facilitate their social mobility. Instead, the immediate domestic agenda included such marginal matters as passing the Burials Act of 1880, which (provided a representative of the deceased gave forty-eight hours' notice to the incumbent of the deceased's parish) allowed interments without the rites of the Church of England, but also to use the rites of the Church to bury someone in unconsecrated ground. It was another recognition by the deeply religious Gladstone of the secularisation of society, and of the departure from accepted practices provoked by the rise of free thought. These provisions would also apply to paupers, previously denied any choice about the disposal of their remains. In case anyone wished to object, the Act made it an offence to engage in riotous, violent or indecent behaviour at a burial. However, it was at best a meagre improvement in the lives of the people.

Another measure, at a time of continued agricultural depression, was the Ground Game Act, which gave tenant farmers the inalienable right to shoot hares and rabbits on their farms to restrict damage to their crops. Hitherto, these had been the property of their landlord. The Queen regarded this Act as 'most injudicious' since it would cause 'people' – by which she meant the landed elite and not the general public – to 'become alarmed and lose confidence' at the idea that tenant farmers could with impunity shoot (and perhaps even eat) other men's animals.[1] It was symbolic of the loss of landowners' power.

Other new measures altered society and chipped away at the influence of the old ruling class: the Married Women's Property Act of 1882, notably, considered in the next chapter; and the Elementary Education Act of 1880, which enforced compulsory attendance at school up to the age of ten. In 1883 parliament passed 'an Act for the better prevention of Corrupt and Illegal Practices at Parliamentary Elections', which (eleven years after the 1872 Ballot Act had introduced the secret ballot) helped clean up British politics, and stop bribery and intimidation. Candidates were forced to publish election expenses, which were not to exceed £710 for the first 2,000 voters in their constituency and a further £40 for each additional 1,000. This helped poorer men stand for parliament, because rich men could no longer vastly outspend them.

As Gladstone told Tait, the Archbishop of Canterbury: 'It is certainly the business and duty of the politician, by his measures, to labour towards the union of classes.'[2] The Queen strongly disagreed, telling Earl Granville, the Foreign Secretary and a Whig palatable to her, that too many MPs asked insolent questions of her ministers, that the Commons was interfering too much in the government of the nation, and that 'it would be grievous indeed and very serious if this democratic tendency were not checked'.[3] Her prime minister, whom Granville alerted, disagreed, and politely told the Queen so, further damaging relations.

She was not interested in reason, but sought the treacle-like sycophancy Lord Beaconsfield had dispensed. She was also oblivious to the notion that reform was essential to maintain the peace, convinced it was simply done 'for the sake of alteration'.[4] She had as a house-guest at Osborne the deposed Empress Eugénie of France, widow of Napoleon III, unseated in 1871 by 'communistic' public opinion, a living example of what went wrong when radicals rocked constitutional monarchy.[5] Gladstone, on the other hand, supported the 'democratic tendency'. He saw the need for parliament to champion further constitutional reform: but it was inherent in his idea of Liberalism that it was not the place of the state to legislate to improve every aspect of individuals' lives. He felt the task lay with well-motivated Christian individuals, who he hoped would with the support and encouragement of the state provide the leadership necessary to ensure that society progressed and the condition of the people was improved.

II

Gladstone's vision of private philanthropy still had great traction in the late nineteenth century. In the 1850s the woollen manufacturer Titus Salt built a model village for his workers just outside Bradford, providing all grades of employees with homes built to a specification most could hardly otherwise have imagined.[6] Salt was aggressively paternalistic – he even issued recommendations about how often workers should wash – but did understand that a higher standard of living translated into better productivity. He also created a sense of aspiration; his paternalism taught his workers to emulate the habits of the middle class. Other employers sought to support their workers in less comprehensive ways – such as coal owners providing social clubs or playing fields. In time, however, other industrialists undertook major acts of philanthropy that emulated Salt's and helped expand the middle class.

William Lever was a soap manufacturer from Bolton who in 1872, aged twenty-one, became a partner in his family's grocery business. In 1886 he and his brother James began a soap-manufacturing company, using vegetable oils to make their product. It was immediately successful and quickly expanded. The Levers bought a site on the Wirral where they built not only a factory but also, from 1888, a model village, Port Sunlight (named after their soap brand), for their workers. The Levers were rigidly paternalistic both in their motivations and policies. William saw Port Sunlight as a form of profit-sharing: only instead of giving his workers cash that they might spend in ways of which he did not approve – such as on drink or gluttony – he gave them fine homes at a low rental and built other facilities in the village, as Salt had in Saltaire.

These included a cottage hospital, schools, a church, a lido, a concert hall and, ultimately, an art gallery. The quality of the houses was such that 900 are now listed buildings, many in the Arts and Crafts style – in vogue at the time among patrons who wished to recreate an idea of an idyllic past (see Chapter 10). Lever wanted an environment in which relations between men were like a brotherhood, as in the days before industrialisation. In also providing musical, dramatic and sporting societies that workers were strongly encouraged to join, he allowed workers access to a particularly middle-class way of life; but unlike the middle class they lived in tied housing from which they would be evicted if they lost their jobs, and were otherwise governed at work and at home with a degree of paternalism inimical to the self-reliance that accompanied the aspirant middle-class lifestyle.

George Cadbury, whose father John had started a hot drinks business in Birmingham in 1824, did something similar. Cadbury and his brother succeeded their father in 1861 when the business was almost ruined; they turned it round within three years, helped by new methods of processing cocoa beans and by concentrating on chocolate products alone. By 1878 it was so successful that they bought a site outside Birmingham, at Bournbrook, to build a new and bigger factory where in the 1880s they would seal their success by moving into confectionery. It was an early experiment at manufacturing in what was then countryside, but the site – which the Cadburys named Bournville, distinguishing it from Bournbrook to the north – was chosen because it was on both the Worcester and Birmingham Canal (along which milk could be brought in) and the new Birmingham West Suburban Railway (which could bring almost to the factory door cocoa beans from docks in Southampton and London).

The Cadburys wished to avoid replicating industrial England in building their factory. It was surrounded by grassy banks, shrubs and flower-beds, and ivy and other creepers were trained along its walls. The brothers said that 'we consider that our people spend the greater part of their lives at their work, and we wish to make it less irksome by environing them with pleasant and wholesome sights, sounds and conditions.'[7] They paid staff well by industrial standards and provided them with pensions and medical care.

The huge success of the business in the 1880s, as rising real wages left Britons more money for treats, allowed the Cadburys to buy, eventually, 330 acres of land near their factory and for George, appalled at how workers lived in the slums of Birmingham, to follow Lever's example and build a model village. A deeply religious Quaker, Cadbury had in the 1870s volunteered in Adult Schools in Birmingham. He said that had he not 'found from visiting the poor how difficult it was to lead a good life in a back street, I should probably never have built Bournville Village.'[8] He felt 'that it is impossible to raise a nation, morally, physically and spiritually in such surroundings, and that the only effective way is to bring men out of the cities into the country and to give every man his garden where he can touch with nature and thus know more of nature's God.' His first idea – that the village would be a Quaker settlement – was overtaken by the scale of the problem, with most of those he wished to help from outside that sect.

Work started in 1893 and by 1900 the firm had built 313 houses, again in the Arts and Crafts style and mostly designed by the firm's young resident architect, William Alexander Harvey. C. F. A. Voysey, whose work is discussed in Chapter 10, was his main influence. As in Saltaire, the higher the worker's rank, the finer his house: the first grade went to foremen, with the overall foreman having the best house of all. The building programme carried on into the twentieth century: the factory had begun with 230 workers, but there were 1,200 within twenty years and 2,700 shortly before the Great War. Cadbury insisted that, unlike in Birmingham, light and space should prevail. Every house had a decent-sized garden, and playing fields were laid out. To ensure quality, no house would cost less than £150 to build. There was no pub: as Quakers the Cadburys were opposed to drinking. Investment was maintained thanks to the continuing success of the company, which purchased more land and built more houses throughout the twentieth century. It introduced its Dairy Milk brand (so called because it contained more milk than its competitors' chocolate) in 1905, which was an instant success. It was also the first mass-produced chocolate, and the economies of scale boosted profits.

Cadbury, like Lever, wanted a healthy and happy workforce for commercial as well as for philanthropic reasons. Like Lever, he built sports clubs, schools and a lido, and a hospital and a museum; and in deference to his own beliefs, a Quaker meeting hall. Unlike Lever he allowed this relatively low-cost, high-specification housing to be rented by non-employees; which extended a middle-class life to many other workers. Other Birmingham industrialists failed to follow his example: the city's housing inquiry – on which sat both Cadbury's son George and Joe Chamberlain's son Neville – in 1914 found that 40,020 houses in the city had no water supply and 55,028 lacked a lavatory, and its report said that 'a large proportion of the poor in Birmingham are living under conditions which are detrimental both to their health and morals'.[9]

Cadbury's fellow Quaker and confectionery magnate Joseph Rowntree followed his example. Like Lever and Cadbury, he had witnessed the slum conditions in which many workers lived – in his case in York. Rowntree set up the Joseph Rowntree Village Trust in 1904 to manage a garden village at New Earswick, just outside York, that he had started to build two years earlier. His father, who founded the family grocery business, had taken him in 1850 as a fourteen-year old to Ireland, where young Joseph saw the devastation and suffering caused by the potato famine. It had a profound effect on his social and political philosophy, of which New Earswick was a result: the decision to build it came after the 1901 report of Rowntree's cousin Seebohm into the appalling squalor of parts of York. Joseph's brother Henry had started the confectionery business, which Joseph inherited in 1883, and which he used to fund his social philosophy. Like both Cadbury and Lever, this included establishing a staff pension scheme, and culminated in a newly-founded community.

Rowntree could not wait to give his money away – he wrote to David Lloyd George, the Chancellor of the Exchequer, in 1914 to say that 'there is hardly any cheque which I sign in the year with greater satisfaction than that for the Super Tax'.[10] However, he did not want his village to be a charitable undertaking, but one that encouraged tenants to look after themselves with the support of his Village Trust. He enlisted Raymond Unwin, who would be asked to build Letchworth Garden City, as his architect, and Unwin put up twenty-eight houses in the first two years. The Trust then expanded the village, which, like Bournville, avoided rigid paternalism except in allowing no public house. A school and an Anglican church were built before the Great War. The Trust allowed any working people to live there whether Rowntree employees or not, and rents were low by comparison with similar properties. The village included well-planted open spaces, and each house came with two fruit trees in the garden. Like Lever and Cadbury, Rowntree had given a small part of the working class an opportunity to aspire to something better.

III

Despite these local good works, it was glaringly apparent that philanthropy alone was insufficient to deal with the problem of poverty, bad housing conditions and limited opportunity on a national scale that affected the unskilled working class and their families. The economic downturn after 1873 had worsened living standards generally, and for this group especially. Under the Disraeli government from 1874 to 1880 Tory paternalism had tried to improve matters, partly because of its collective social conscience, but also to try and garner the votes of the recently enfranchised working class. In 1883, with Beaconsfield dead, his party in opposition and the Liberal government more immersed than ever in Ireland and reform, Salisbury showed he shared the same motivations. He wrote an article in the November's *National Review* demanding improvements to the housing conditions of the working class and, if necessary, state intervention to achieve them. He depicted a squalid and indecent life among the poor, with families living and sleeping together in one room, vulnerable not just to disease but to moral degradation. This embarrassed a prosperous nation. He blamed parliament partly for the problem, by having sanctioned infrastructure improvements since the 1840s – such as street widening, railway building and embanking the Thames, which had reduced the housing stock. It was now up to politicians to put matters right.

The Times agreed the 'rookeries and the slums of the East end' had to be dealt with, but not by the means Salisbury advocated, which some leader-writers likened to state socialism.[11] It said there were already enough laws against 'speculative jerry-builders and rack-renting house-farmers' that could force them to close or improve their properties – it cited the Public Health Act of 1875, passed by a government of which Salisbury was a member – but maintained these were inadequately known and used. Local authorities, before Britain had an ordered structure of local government, were feeble. The Lodging Houses Act of 1851 empowered localities to build accommodation for the poor and to borrow against the rates to do so, but this measure was little used. Laws put the onus on the landlord, not the state, to rectify problems: and that was where *The Times* and other newspapers felt it should stay.

However, Salisbury had struck a nerve. Gladstone – whose private secretary, Eddy Hamilton, thought Salisbury had voiced 'the very essence of socialist principles' – ordered a Royal Commission to investigate the problem, and put Dilke in charge.[12] It had a distinguished membership. Salisbury served; others included Goschen, Cardinal Manning, Sir Richard Cross, architect of the Artisans' Dwellings Act, the Bishop of Bedford, Henry Broadhurst and Jesse Collings, who had succeeded Chamberlain as Mayor of Birmingham. Dilke also wanted Octavia Hill, who had run housing projects for artisans in London with support from John Ruskin, to be invited, but Gladstone refused.[13]

Also invited was a yet more elevated personage. A concern of prime ministers after the 1860s was how to occupy the Prince of Wales. Gladstone, who could see the good in anyone, had suggested various occupations, all of which the Queen vetoed: because Prince Albert's last opinion of his son (barely twenty when Albert died) was that he was incapable, and because of her contempt for Gladstone's judgment. Disraeli, recognising in the Prince a fellow *flâneur*, did not push the issue; but once Gladstone returned the search began again. Dilke sounded out Ponsonby about the Prince's suitability for the Royal Commission. Remarkably – since one of the few people the Queen despised more than Gladstone was Dilke – she agreed with Ponsonby that it was an 'excellent' plan: so the Prince was invited to join.[14] His presence not merely underlined the importance of the inquiry, but also its non-partisan nature: and he too called, unsuccessfully, for Miss Hill to join. He owned, as Duke of Cornwall, land in south London with slums that he was anxious to improve, and had pulled down what his agent, giving evidence to the Commission, described as some 'miserable hovels' at Sandringham.[15]

The Lords debated the Commission's role on 22 February 1884. Salisbury spoke frankly about inadequate sewerage arrangements and the poor supply of 'privies, water-closets, etc.': but, laying down what he clearly hoped would be the priorities for the forthcoming discussions, stressed that pulling down bad housing in the hope that good would replace it was a 'cruel' way to proceed, since it would leave many poor people without any home at all.[16] He said the agricultural depression had driven people to the towns in search of work, aggravating the problem. He admitted that 'I may have to defend myself against the charge of socialism . . . I do not favour any wild schemes of state interference.'[17] Yet he believed the 'evils' were so widespread that it would be 'political cowardice' to avoid a solution dictated by 'common sense'. The Prince spoke too, saying he had just visited slums in Holborn and St Pancras, which he had found 'perfectly disgraceful'.[18] Lord Shaftesbury reminded peers he had studied this issue for forty years, and he had been talking to a young woman who had told him: 'Every night scores of rats come into the room, and I have to sit up all one night, and my husband has to sit up all the next, to prevent the rats from eating the baby.'[19] Shaftesbury could not fathom how, given the price of land in London, people with little money could ever afford decent housing. Some form of state subsidy would be essential, he felt.

The Royal Commission met thirty-eight times. It visited slums, and heard evidence from scores of people – clergy, Poor Law officials, police, sanitary officers, medical staff and social workers – who had to deal with the effects of slum housing. Its report described sanitary failings caused by poor building and infrastructure, notably bad drainage, and sheer overcrowding. Salisbury wrote a minority report, advocating government loans and subsidies. He was uneasy about how far Dilke had incorporated Chamberlain's philosophy into recommendations to increase drastically the powers of local government.

Its proposals included removing restrictions on building working-class dwellings on land in central London, which had the worst housing problem in the country. However, such land was increasingly in demand for purposes that gave the landlord a far better return on capital: as shops, offices or substantial houses for the newly prosperous. The Royal Commission failed to take into account that, increasingly, houses built for one large well-to-do family were divided up for several poorer ones; and smaller, more crudely built and often insanitary ones often hemmed them in. Many infrastructure projects made the overcrowding even worse.

The Royal Commission reported too late for the government to do anything with its findings. However, days after the short-lived first Salisbury administration took office in July 1885, he himself introduced the Housing of the Working Classes Bill in the Lords: not, he stressed, because he had sat on the Commission but because as prime minister he supported the measure. It had, he said somewhat inaccurately, been drawn up with the 'unanimous consent' of the Commission's members.[20] He dismissed the idea that there was 'any magic formula' to rectify the problem, but said there would be 'slow and gradual steps'.[21] Perhaps because he wished not to cause alarm at the prospect of the radical steps the Bill would propose he deliberately understated its scope.

Salisbury highlighted a paradox: 'The more prosperity increases the more sanitary evils will vanish; but the more our prosperity increases, the more there is the danger that unless remedial measures are taken the evils of overcrowding will also increase.'[22] So the Bill would give the local sanitary authorities the right of supervision over tenements, with the right to inspect them. He admitted the limitations of the Artisans' Dwellings Act, which had empowered local authorities to clear slums, but had not predicted the resistance of local landowners and, therefore, the reluctance of local corporations to take them on. This Bill would give Local Government Board inspectors the power to declare a building unfit for human habitation and to order the local authority to pull it down. And because of the incidence of typhoid in rented houses, *rentiers* would be liable for any death or illness as a result of failure to ensure the drains were adequate. Also, county districts could apply for Treasury loans to undertake improvements.

One of the main reasons to improve housing conditions remained the goal of improving working-class health. Even after the Bill was enacted the problem persisted: in the Boundary Street area of Shoreditch 5,179 people lived on fourteen acres in 1890 and the annual death rate was forty per 1,000. In London as a whole it was 18.4.[23] Boundary Street was replaced by a radial plan of council housing, built by the LCC, called Arnold Circus, inspired by the Peabody housing of the previous decades.[24] Such new estates grew up all over inner London in the 1890s and 1900s: many still stand, notably in Drury Lane, where the slums north of Aldwych were cleared. In the outer suburbs – such as Tottenham and Tooting – estates of two-storey cottages were developed, based on those built in the new Garden City at Letchworth in Hertfordshire, described in Chapter 10.

One consideration behind the 1885 Act was the speed with which what Salisbury called 'the small houses, which are run up in the suburbs at a cheap rate, and the building of which has often been exceedingly disgraceful' were multiplying.[25] The thought that the slums of central London, which the government was desperate to eliminate, should be constructed anew in the suburbs, was a shocking prospect. Yet Salisbury remained averse to a too centralised or statist approach to jerry-building: he hoped there was a 'stirring up of public opinion' after the Royal Commission that would cause builders, owners and occupiers to reject low standards, and that market forces would end the building of shoddy, insanitary properties that bred disease.

Dealing with overcrowding was another matter. Outside London there was still scope to build cottages on the outskirts of towns. In the capital, however, Salisbury felt – despite the spread of railways that had created the commuter – that to build on the edge of the metropolis would result in houses too far out to be viable. In 1885 the Underground was still in its infancy. The Metropolitan line went out to Harrow – mainly overground – by 1880; the Circle line, joining the main London termini, had started in October 1884. However, it would be years before the railway network spread further and made more distant developments feasible. The Central line opened from Shepherd's Bush to Bank in 1900;

the District line went to Upminster in 1902; the Bakerloo, from Baker Street to Elephant and Castle, followed in 1906, as did the tube from Hammersmith to Finsbury Park (now part of the Piccadilly line). In 1907 the Northern line opened from Charing Cross to Archway and from Euston to Clapham Common; little further progress was made before the war.

However, sites of former public buildings in London, such as the prison at Coldbath Fields and the Millbank Penitentiary, would be cleared, and sold to the Metropolitan Board of Works (MBW), which would let them to trusts such as the Peabody 'solely to the purpose of erecting dwellings for the working classes'.[26] Salisbury lamented, though, that some Peabody flats were now, because of their quality and location, let at rents beyond many working men's reach; the move of the artisan class into the middle class had begun. The MBW's inability to grasp the problem as the prime minister would have wanted was one of the factors in the decision three years later to form the London County Council, which took over its powers and had much greater clout to use them.

The new powers proved controversial, despite the cross-party nature of the Royal Commission advocating them. Lord Wemyss, chairman of the pro-*laissez-faire* Liberty and Property Defence League, speaking from the cross benches of the Lords during the Bill's committee stage, called some of its provisions 'objectionable': notably allowing the sale of public land in London for a price below market value for the 'special purpose' of building affordable housing for the poor.[27] This amounted to a 'state subsidy' that Wemyss and others who felt like him thought 'dangerous'.[28] He feared this plan threatened to undermine the whole idea of private enterprise upon which the greatness of the nation had been built. In Edinburgh – Wemyss spoke as a Scotsman – the local trade council, on behalf of the working men, had 'repudiated . . . the notion that the State or Municipality should supply them with houses.'[29] Salisbury noted there was not the overcrowding problem in Edinburgh that there was in London. Before long, many counterparts of the working men of Edinburgh would happily accept the idea of council housing. The Tory reverence for property ownership did not at that stage apply to the lower classes, and was overtaken by the need to avert the social unrest Salisbury and others feared would be the consequence of allowing squalor to persist.

Lord Bramwell said 'he did not see why the State should provide houses any more than it provided food and clothing for the working classes.'[30] Other peers deplored the order for insanitary buildings to be demolished. Nonetheless, the Bill passed in the Lords without a vote, before the Commons ripped into it. Lyulph Stanley, a Liberal who had sat on the Royal Commission, accused the Tories of 'State Socialism'.[31] It was the thin end of a wedge: not only would every interest group cry 'Give, give', but it would lead to 'a far more democratic Parliament than the present one'. Private enterprise would be 'paralysed'. But piloted through the Commons by Cross, Home Secretary again, who was helped by Dilke, the Bill became law in mid-August 1885.

Some new housing went up in inner London; but the real impetus would come with the LCC in 1889, with an electoral mandate behind it. Once the Millbank site was cleared flats were built to house 4,430 people by 1902 – but that was merely a pinprick. The distinctive Edwardian outer suburbs spread out along Underground lines as they opened in the years before the Great War, just as great Victorian suburbs such as Clapham, Hornsey, Peckham and Hackney had spread out around the railways between the 1860s and 1890s.

This provision, coupled with growing prosperity especially around the metropolis, pushed up standards for those rising from the skilled working class into the new lower-middle class. In time, many whose lives were transformed by moving from slum housing into decent, less crowded, sanitary homes formed the basis of that expanding class. Such homes provided the model for housing in London's outer suburbs and in many other cities where the arrival of trams and motor buses shortly before Great War allowed more spacious developments away from the centre.

Workmen's trains reduced the price of commuting and expanded the area for suburban development. Ilford, an Essex village on the railway between London and Colchester opened in 1843, had a population of 11,000 by 1891. Just seven miles from the Liverpool Street terminus, Ilford nearly quadrupled in population by 1901, with over 41,000 people recorded at the census. By 1911 it was 80,000. Builders acquired huge amounts of land for private housing: a simple four-room house on a new estate in Ilford was £260 in 1906, a four-bedroom one £375 and a five-bedroom one £450. In a period in which child mortality had been reduced but contraception not yet properly developed, families with six, eight or ten children were usual. But Ilford, like many such suburbs, expanded not because of state intervention in the planning process, but because of cheap public transport. Such infrastructure also helped aspiration, allowing people a wider choice of occupation and a far better standard of housing.

The Salisbury administration passed another Housing of the Working Classes Act in 1890, giving councils wider powers to build council housing. However, many still felt it wrong for the state or agents of the state to become landlords, so progressive politicians in the Labour movement and among radical Liberals became frustrated at the continued lack of housing for the poor in certain areas. A Housing and Town Planning Bill in 1908 took matters further. As well as making it easier for municipalities to acquire land and build sanitary housing, it required them to provide council housing, and plan the development of their towns rather than allow them to proceed haphazardly. It also banned the building of cellar and back-to-back housing, statistically identified as a leading cause of early death, and encouraged the provision of parks and open spaces to allay fears that areas would be built over in their entirety.

John Burns, the union militant turned Liberal minister who introduced the Bill, said £300,000 was available for parks and open spaces, and that 'to suggest that we want to filch commons and run away with parks and open spaces is absurd'.[32] To ensure continued improvements in sanitation, every county council would have a full-time medical officer. Burns said the Bill's aim was 'to provide a domestic condition for the people in which their physical health, their morals, their character, and their whole social condition can be improved'.[33] He wished to secure 'the home healthy, the house beautiful, the city dignified and the suburb salubrious', and not just to improve health: the project 'was so that the character of a great people in towns and cities and in villages can be still further improved and strengthened by the conditions under which they live.' This was a moral campaign too.

This state interference in planning and land use caused the Bill to be postponed for a year: it was torn apart in committee and Asquith, the prime minister, resolved to reintroduce it the following year. Burns told the Commons in April 1909 that councils could acquire land to build for the working classes and pay for it with loans of up to eighty years' duration at the lowest possible rate of interest. He said the planning provisions would ensure that streets of houses were built where they would get sun and air. He was also alert to the effect poor road planning was having on the economy, and roads would now be planned according to the flow of traffic, something increasingly more important as motor-vehicles became less of a rarity.

There were still some strong Tory objections, about unacceptable burdens and financial losses for landowners. Some attacked compulsory purchase; others wondered why the state should build where private enterprise would not, and what burdens this placed on taxpayers and ratepayers; and there were objections to the idea that the Local Government Board could override the wishes of communities that did not want public housing. The very idea of town planning could only be implemented by ignoring the rights of individual property owners. There were prolonged arguments about compensation. But one Tory – the eighty-six-year-old Richard Cross, now Viscount Cross – recalled his work thirty-four years earlier on the Artisans' Dwellings Act, predicting 'a great calamity' if the new Bill were not brought into law, whatever the doctrinal considerations.[34]

With this Act as with that of 1885, improvements made for the working class had a knock-on effect for the middle classes. There was an explosion in their housing too, again helped by better transport and infrastructure; changes that, in London and southern England especially, would be accelerated between the wars, but whose roots lay in the ambition of the late Victorians and Edwardians. As well as villas spreading out through the newly connected suburbs, the middle classes colonised more of inner London, and with space being at a premium did so through the medium of the mansion flat, a continental idea also familiar from Edinburgh and Glasgow: though there it had been deployed for the working classes, and in some cases would degenerate into slums. As described in Chapter 2, in these new middle-class suburbs an ordered and domesticated existence sprang up, the occupants using their disposable incomes and leisure time to tend the gardens that came with their houses, and to beautify and improve the home, often acquiring a piano as a hub of entertainment.

In London mansion flats provided living accommodation for the middle classes in affluent areas such as Chelsea, Kensington and Mayfair, and where slums were being cleared and the middle classes moving in, such as Westminster and Victoria, and in other areas that had not hitherto been predominantly residential, such as Whitehall and St James's: in this respect late-Victorian London imitated Paris. Then the idea moved out to the more salubrious suburbs, such as Maida Vale, St John's Wood, Hampstead and, further afield, Turnham Green, next to the Bedford Park development. The exclusivity of some of these was emphasised by Norman Shaw, when he built Albert Hall Mansions in Kensington, adding a separate servants' wing.

IV

Salisbury's attempts to improve working-class conditions through his housing and health reforms, and his local government reforms of 1888–9 that provided a booming population with better public services, signalled the ideological shift of the state towards taking a direct interest in public welfare. The local government measures – which established county councils and, in large cities and densely populated urban areas, county borough councils – were a price the Liberal Unionists exacted for their support of Salisbury's Conservatives after Gladstone's administration fell in 1886. The Liberals' ancestors designed the 1835 Municipal Corporations Act, which introduced an element of democracy to 178 towns across England and Wales previously run by self-perpetuating oligarchies, often against the interests of their citizens. The reform of county government would pursue the same principles. Although it seemed merely to regularise the provision of the limited services for which counties were responsible, the effect of creating a body of elected councillors was to give new impetus to expanding the role of local government in raising living standards.

Counties were, until 1889, run by magistrates through the quarter sessions. These were courts presided over by three magistrates (usually not legally qualified) who with a jury tried all but the most serious crimes. Despite a reputation for dispensing cack-handed justice they survived in parts of Britain until 1972. The quarter sessions also used ratepayers' money (which they raised) to maintain infrastructure such as roads and bridges, to raise a county militia and police force, to license public houses and run prisons and lunatic asylums.

Now each historic county of England and Wales would have its own council: Yorkshire would have three, one for each riding, and Lincolnshire three also, one for each of its parts. Sussex and Suffolk would be split in two, Cambridgeshire and the Isle of Ely were separated, as were Northamptonshire and the Soke of Peterborough. The London County Council governed the area run by the Metropolitan Board of Works. Rosebery had been persuaded to stand for election in London, to encourage people to take the new council seriously: once elected, he found himself, for the same reason, coerced into being its first chairman. Brett, acting on behalf of various friends in the Liberal party, had written to him – the two had known each other since Eton – to say that 'having assumed the lesser responsibility by becoming a member of the Council, you cannot properly or rightly shirk the greater.'[35] He strove to keep party politics out of local government, with some success.

Sanitary districts, responsible for sewerage and other public-health matters, were placed within counties; in 1894 a further reform would merge them into urban and rural district councils. This not only set a framework for local government that has existed, with some changes, ever since: it also created an accountable local bureaucracy to allow the state to provide all the services a more prosperous and civilised society required. And as well as superseding quarter sessions and establishing a bureaucracy, the counties took over responsibility for reformatories and industrial schools from charities and religious organisations. The councils took control of asylums for mentally ill paupers, though their treatment was still unsatisfactory: epileptics, for example, were as liable to be consigned to these institutions as the certifiably insane. At last, the haphazard and largely medieval business of administering England and Wales was formalised and made democratically accountable.

Once this framework of responsible local authorities was in place it could, and did, assume other powers, notably for education. The 1870 Education Act had set up 2,568 school boards, making central control almost impossible. A third of children went to church schools, mostly run by the Church of England, but with a minority run by the Roman Catholic church, and which received no state funding. Another pillar of those values was education. Until the state took over education in 1902 the Church of England was the most significant force in schooling; not just because of its role in elementary schools but also in its ragged and Sunday schools.

Although there was a state contribution, charitable giving was essential to keeping these schools going and, indeed, in many cases their pupils. In Lord Randolph Churchill's papers are two letters dated March 1886 from a Peckham Sunday school teacher, Beatrice E. Parsons, sent on behalf of a boy, Henry Randolph Greenland. The first tells how young Henry, 'six years old and a fine, manly little fellow', had until recently, 'like his many brothers and sisters . . . regularly attended Sunday school and Church; but now he has no boots, and cannot go out. Five or six shillings would buy him a pair. My Lord, is it not a pity that the possessor of such an illustrious name – a name which there is every reason to expect will shine in English history as the names of Chatham, Russell and Beaconsfield shine – is it not a pity that he should go barefoot?'[36] A well-executed drawing of the little boy sitting barefoot on a stool adorns the letter. Churchill sent five shillings at once. Miss Parsons replied: 'You could not possibly have spent five shillings in any other way which would have given so much real pleasure to so many people', and said that Lord Randolph was included in his namesake's nightly prayers. She also told him the boy's family 'are Conservatives'. This time, the drawing illustrating the letter is of the same boy, but standing in his fine new boots.

The 1902 Education Act ended the distinction between voluntary and board schools, putting them all under local education authorities in the counties and county boroughs. These employed teachers, though the churches continued to own and maintain the buildings. All schools used ratepayers' money to supply textbooks and other equipment.

Elementary schools varied from the enlightened to the brutal. The best had their own libraries and teachers with a profound vocation, who encouraged intellectual curiosity and self-improvement. The educational historian H. C. Dent, at elementary school from 1900 to 1904, had a different experience. 'With relatively rare exceptions . . . teachers and taught were sworn enemies. The latter resisted by every means known to them (and some of them were extremely unpleasant) the desiccated diet of irrelevant facts the former insisted on pressing upon them; teachers retaliated with incessant applications of corporal punishment, impartially inflicted for crime, misdemeanour or mistake.'[37] Although Dent's account reflects the stereotypical view of school at the turn of the twentieth century, it was far from universal, and the social mobility of that time reflects schools that did their job, for the most part, highly effectively, and waged a largely successful war against ignorance – much to the nation's benefit. As for the thrashings, surveys showed that children and parents approved of them, in the interests of discipline.[38]

Local supervision raised standards. Teachers' qualifications were studied rigorously. Councils established schools, increasingly to provide secondary education when the country needed more skilled workers and, for the growing service industries, more clerical staff. By 1914, 1,000 new secondary schools had opened in England and Wales, 349 of these for girls. This was a golden age for the expansion of girls' education; in the private sector the Girls' Public Day School Company set up thirty-seven schools between 1872 and 1905, when it changed its name to the Girls' Public Day School Trust. The schools were largely funded by share capital raised from local people in areas with a high demand for such establishments, and specialised in training young women teachers under the pupil teacher system.

But there was a political price for the 1902 Act: state funding of Anglican and Catholic schools, an issue when Forster's Bill went through in 1870, incensed the Liberals, whose base was Non-conformist. Such people objected to being asked to pay rates to support schools whose religious teachings were not theirs. The measure divided the government when Chamberlain, leader of the Liberal Unionists, warned it would alienate that important faction's Non-conformist supporters. The Act was good for children's education and prospects, but helped destabilise the Tory party and contributed towards its heavy defeat at the 1906 general election. One of the organised forces that campaigned against Tories in that election was the Passive Resistance Movement, led by John Clifford, a London Baptist minister who had achieved celebrity as head of the Stop the War committee during the Second Boer War. The movement told Non-conformists to refuse to pay their rates. Many, including Clifford, had goods taken by bailiffs in lieu, and 170 went to jail. In 1906 the Liberals tried to reverse the measure, but the House of Lords blocked their Bill.

The Act also encouraged milder regimes in schools, some of which – notably in rougher urban areas – resembled reformatories. Its instructions on corporal punishment 'urged that no punishment which excites the emotion of terror should ever be employed; that in infant schools no punishment should be inflicted which causes bodily pain; that in schools for older children corporal punishment should be discouraged as an ordinary expedient in a boys' school and altogether in a girls' school'.[39] When a backbencher, in 1908, asked how far these guidelines were followed, Reginald McKenna, the President of the Board of Education, said it was a matter for local education authorities, and his department would intervene only in a case of excessive punishment. So, despite the rhetoric since the 1880s about protecting children, and the intentions of the 1902 Act, schoolteachers could still beat pupils black and blue, and frequently did. In one division of the London Education Committee, East Lambeth, in 1906–7 there were 39,505 cases of corporal punishment upon boys, 9,723 upon girls and 6,069 on infants (those aged seven and under). In West Lambeth that year there were 49,979 cases upon boys, 7,623 on girls and 5,567 on infants.[40] Teachers must have been so busy with acts of violence against pupils that it is remarkable anything was actually taught.

Further state intervention came with the Campbell-Bannerman

ministry's Education (Provision of Meals) Act 1906, which gave local authorities a grant to cover 50 per cent of the cost of school meals. This was a legacy of the national shame during the Boer War, when so many Volunteers were, often because of malnutrition, unfit for service. This had also prompted the formation in 1904 of a Physical Deterioration Committee to examine the causes behind the weakness of so many young men; this prompted the anti-smoking measures in the 1908 Children's Act.

Similarly, the Education (Administrative Provisions) Act 1907 allowed local authorities to run school medical services, and allowed school boards to act against parents whose children were in a 'verminous condition'. Free medical treatment for schoolchildren after 1912 reinforced the programme. By the Great War children were better educated, treated, fed and protected than probably at any time in history; and the nation was equipping the next generation for a world of rapid progress and advancement as well as giving working-class children of both genders a better chance to compete with their social superiors.

V

Whatever steps were taken to improve housing, sanitation and education, one scandalous problem persisted in late-Victorian society: too many children were still victims of abuse and neglect by their parents. It was a short step from this to crime or other delinquencies. Since 1857 industrial schools had existed to which magistrates could send vagrant children between the ages of seven and fourteen, to be taught basic skills or a trade and be made subject to strict discipline. Children found begging or in receipt of alms could also be sent to them, as could those found in the company of criminals, to remove them from destructive influences. A child of twelve or under convicted of a crime, or a child under fourteen whose parents claimed he or she was out of control, could also be sent there. The schools were residential, though an Act of 1876 established day schools. They catered mainly for boys but also for girls, who were taught domestic skills. Most began as private charitable institutions, often run by religious groups: one, run at Whitwick in Leicestershire by the monks of St Bernard's Abbey there, was described as an 'agricultural colony', to which errant Catholic boys were sent to learn the rudiments of farming. It was closed in 1881 after a riot and mass absconding by sixty boys.

Industrial schools had been preceded in the early 1850s by reformatories, whose inmates were convicted criminals and usually older children. These were deeply unpleasant places. By 1885 there were sixty-one reformatories in England and Wales, 136 industrial schools and thirteen day industrial schools. There were also three notoriously spartan training ships, classed as reformatories: the *Clarence* and the *Akbar* on the Mersey (the *Clarence* was for Roman Catholics and the *Akbar* for Protestants) and the *Cornwall* on the Thames at Purfleet, near Tilbury. A Royal Commission on these institutions had reported in 1883, concluding that they had been useful for reforming delinquents and for preventing some from drifting into crime: but they needed tighter control and reform themselves.

In 1888 the plight of young offenders, or those susceptible to criminality, prompted MPs and peers to propose three separate Bills to tackle what they perceived as a growing social problem. One, promoted by the government, allowed young offenders to be sent to reformatories even if they had not committed a custodial offence: the institutions were deemed so salutary that any youth who might contemplate a life of crime would be deterred by the experience, and Salisbury and his colleagues sincerely believed the outcome would be profitable for the children concerned. The Bill also told magistrates not to send offenders to a reformatory unless they knew there were places for them. Another Bill, proposed by backbenchers, sought to reduce admissions to reformatories by substituting a sentence of birching, which was regarded as more humane in that it did not expose the offender to the malign influences he would meet in a reformatory. It also aimed to make parents take more responsibility for their children by making them culpable for their offences, forcing them to pay compensation for any damage.

The third Bill, introduced by Lord Norton, President of the Board of Trade under Disraeli, sought to separate children's penal treatment from their education. However, because of the passage of the Local Government Bill in 1888 many other measures were not completed, and these were among them. In April 1889 a Bill was finally introduced in the Lords, the under-secretary of state, Earl Brownlow, defining the point of reformatories – 'to place young criminals of both sexes under such careful educational restraint as may tend to wean them from the vicious courses into which they have fallen upon the very threshold of life, very often not by their own fault, but through the neglect and carelessness of their parents and guardians.'[41] The government was vague about whether educational standards in these institutions should be raised – it would not agree to have the Board of Education inspect reformatories – and about whether or not reformatories were part of the punishment, or something that followed it. Given the social pressure not to imprison young people, the Bill proposed other sanctions: birching for youths, an undertaking from parents to punish the child, or a fine and/or compensation order levied on the parents. Parents would also be asked to contribute towards the keep of a child in a reformatory.

The Bill stated no one under fourteen should be sent to a reformatory. There would be a two-year probationary period after discharge that allowed for the former inmate to be returned there for up to two years if he offended again, plus any other punishment that might be meted out. There was a consensus that the fewer young people in reformatories the better, and that it was better to send them to an industrial school before they committed crime; reformatories should be solely for those of 'hardened character'.[42] The Earl of Meath demanded the Bill be amended to allow delinquent girls to be whipped as well, on the grounds of fairness. He cited the late Dr Arnold and various female authorities to support his view, claiming opposition to this particular piece of equality legislation was for fear of a 'sentimental outcry'.[43] The government rejected his suggestion.

However, a Bill later that year raised the age up to which youths could be birched from fourteen to sixteen, since public opinion was so opposed to fifteen-year olds being jailed, and because any fine imposed effectively fell on their parents, rendering such an offender practically unpunished. The Bill also sought more corporal punishment of adults, for armed robbery and offences against women. The proposer, Thomas Milvain, a Tory MP, was unequivocal. 'As to the argument about the punishment being brutalising, in my opinion you cannot brutalise a person who has already brutalised himself by the commission of any of these offences. I cannot help thinking that the class who commit the kind of offences which I incorporate in this Bill, are entirely lost to all moral sense, and I maintain that the only way to get at them is by appealing to their animal feelings.'[44] Milvain called his measure 'an act of mercy to defenceless women and children'.[45] His view was widely, but not universally, shared: he was bitterly opposed by Bradlaugh and by Jacob Bright, the former arguing that the punishment was brutalising, the latter that it did not deter. Other MPs argued that of all European powers England was retrograde, not just in continuing flogging but in extending its scope. These pleas, and indeed the equivocation of Henry Matthews, as Home Secretary, who felt flogging contrary to progress, were ignored; the Bill had its second reading.

There was a growing recognition at this time in society and by MPs that children were not simply miniature adults, but required a different sort of treatment. However, there was no diminution in the belief that malefactors of any age had to be punished, though what would start to moderate in the succeeding decades were ideas about what form such punishment would take. Most MPs in the late nineteenth century seemed determined to have children thrashed for their own good; but some public figures identified a scandal of cruelty towards the young and felt it needed to be tackled. The Americans were ahead of Britain in this respect, and since 1874 New York had had a flourishing Society for the Prevention of Cruelty to Children. Thomas Agnew, a Liverpool businessman, visited the society in 1881 and was so impressed that on his return he set up a counterpart in Liverpool. Benjamin Waugh, a Congregationalist minister whose work in the slums of Greenwich had made him acutely aware of children's suffering there, set up a society in London, where the problems for children and the numbers at risk were significantly worse. Waugh's aim was not merely to raise funds to protect such children, but to raise political consciousness and have laws passed to ensure their rights.

Waugh was an early advocate both of juvenile courts and of separate institutions for child offenders, to help deter them from lives of crime. He joined those criticising the workhouse system for its treatment of children and encouragement of crime. In 1884, under the patronage of none other than Lord Shaftesbury, he established the London Society for the Prevention of Cruelty to Children. The society touched a public nerve, not least in shaming parliament into legislating to protect children: with so many destitute families in the capital, it had its work cut out. Branches sprang up all over Britain; the London society evolved into the National Society for the Prevention of Cruelty to Children in 1889. Six years later it received a Royal Charter and, with Shaftesbury dead, the Queen became its patron. By the time the NSPCC received its charter the Royal Society for the Prevention of Cruelty to Animals had existed for over seventy years, a point not lost on Victorian reformers.

In 1886 parliament passed the Intoxicating Liquors (Sale to Children) Act, which stopped those under thirteen from buying alcohol; the age limit would be raised gradually over succeeding decades. It was a belated signal that the law, which had long distinguished between adults and children in conditions of work, should now intervene in other aspects of a child's life. The great achievement of Waugh's campaign was, however, the Prevention of Cruelty to Children Act 1889, the direct result of evidence collected by the LSPCC since its foundation. This made it, for the first time, a punishable offence to ill-treat or to neglect a child: or, as Lord Herschell, a former Lord Chancellor, put it, 'to extend . . . to children that protection that has long been afforded to animals.'[46] The courts were full of people who had overworked or tortured their horses, but they could ill-treat a child with impunity. However, there were also the cases where a parent or guardian had a pecuniary interest in the death of a child – perhaps because the abuser stood to inherit property if the child died, or because its life was insured. As will be discussed in the next chapter in relation to baby-farmers, such people usually caused the child's health to deteriorate until it died. Not only was this now punishable, but if a pecuniary motive could be proved the penalty could be far more severe.

The Bill also allowed for the punishment of adults who sent children out begging, and also prohibited children from working at night as entertainers or in public houses, or as hawkers, bringing these trades into line with the provisions of the Factories Acts and those for agricultural work. There was extensive argument in the Lords in August 1889 about banning children from working in theatres, which would make some plays impossible to stage. Lord Clifford of Chudleigh asked the Earl of Dunraven, who raised the objection, why *A Midsummer Night's Dream* could not be played without very young children. 'There must be small fairies,' Dunraven replied.[47] Eventually, a compromise was reached to allow local authorisation for certain entertainments.

The Poor Law Acts of 1889 and 1899 gave local guardians rights over abused or deserted children. Rosebery's administration passed another Cruelty to Children Prevention Act in 1894, which reinforced the first measure. The ensuing five years, according to Herschell, again Lord Chancellor, had 'brought to light an amount of cruelty towards young children which is perfectly appalling.'[48] Between 1889 and 1894 there had been 5,792 prosecutions, with convictions in 5,460 of them – a success rate of 94.27 per cent. There had however been 47,000 investigations, and in 28,895 of them warnings were issued to the adults involved. Herschell reported that nearly 7,000 of the 7,398 people charged with cruelty were living with their children 'under happier circumstances' than before the law intervened. The new Act raised from fourteen to sixteen the age up to which a boy could be protected, and it broadened the definition of 'ill-treatment'. It also increased the penalties for those found guilty of cruelty, and made further arrangements for the boarding out to private homes of children who would otherwise, to escape from their parents, be in industrial schools or workhouses as inmates.

The allegedly Christian Victorians believed in redemption for those who had sinned, such as criminals, but the road back had to be harsh. Gradually, a more humane view was taken of young offenders, combining punishment with work in such a way as to give the offender a skill useful after release, and improve his character while in custody. A main proponent of this was Evelyn Ruggles-Brise, a senior civil servant in the Home Office. He came from an Essex landed family, and had been a brilliant scholar at Eton and Oxford. He came sixth in the civil service exam in 1879 and joined the Home Office the following year. His talent was immediately recognised and he served as principal private secretary to four successive home secretaries – Sir William Harcourt, Richard Cross, Hugh Childers and Henry Matthews.

Matthews appointed him a Prisons Commissioner in 1892, and Asquith, when Home Secretary, made him chairman of the Prisons Commission in 1895, when he was just thirty-seven; he held the post until 1921. His appointment came after fierce criticism of the incumbent chairman, Sir Edmund du Cane, who ordained prisons as places of silence, hard labour and state retribution. Ruggles-Brise sought to alter all this, abolishing the treadwheel and the crank in 1898. He decided to focus his efforts on those who he felt were not necessarily beyond help, and with this in mind he went to America in 1897 to examine their reformatory system. As a result, he created the first separate section for youths at Bedford jail in 1900. The first such separate institution was opened in the village of Borstal in Kent on 16 October 1902, the year Ruggles-Brise was knighted. It accommodated young men under twenty-one, with an emphasis on education, physical exercise and training rather than on punishment. The regime was highly structured and military in tone, but with the aim of producing reformed characters. There was none of the arbitrary corporal punishment familiar from reformatories: male trainees (as they were known) could be birched for mutiny or assault on a warder, but only with the approval of the visiting magistrates. For all his liberal tendencies, Ruggles-Brise refused to abolish the birch altogether.

Released inmates also had a mentoring service staffed by well-to-do volunteers, many of whom were friends of Ruggles-Brise. This, together with the approach taken at Borstal, helped dramatically reduce reoffending. Once the success of Borstal had been proved other such institutions were set up around Britain. The Prevention of Crime Act 1908 recognised them as a formal part of the criminal justice system, and the preferred destination for all but the most serious young offenders. The youth prisons took their name from the Kent village where the first had been founded; and reform and rehabilitation became as significant in the treatment of young criminals as retribution and deterrence.

Eventually, parliament concentrated on the most effective methods of sparing children from influences that might make them degenerates rather than on the most savage means of punishing them once they were. The Employment of Children Act 1903 had imposed restrictions on child labour in all trades not covered by the Factories Acts. The greatest advance, however, was the 1908 Children Act. It encompassed and expanded the 1894 Act and recognised the role of the NSPCC and other child protection organisations; it took over the provisions of the 1897 Infant Life Protection Act, which had sought to eliminate baby-farming. It made negligence, as opposed to deliberate cruelty, a crime: around 1,600 infants a year died because their parents lay on top of them in the same bed, often when the parent was drunk, and around the same number died from burns or scalds from falling on unguarded fires.[49]

It introduced juvenile courts, and places of detention for children awaiting trial who could not be bailed. It demanded parents take responsibility for delinquent children, by accompanying them to court and paying fines levied on them. A father 'cannot be allowed to neglect the upbringing of his children, and having committed the grave offence of throwing on society a child criminal, wash his hands of the consequences and escape scot free,' the under-secretary at the Home Office, Herbert Samuel, told the Commons on 10 February 1908.[50] It stopped those under fourteen being imprisoned and barred those under sixteen from being hanged: though people so young had not been hanged for decades. A separate measure raised the age of admission to reformatories to above sixteen, to keep younger offenders away from older ones. It banned the sale of cigarettes and alcohol to those under sixteen (the eighteen age limit would not come until 1923), and it became an offence for a child under sixteen to smoke in public. It also forbade children under fourteen from being on licensed premises. In the hope of providing high-quality quasi-parental support to children whose families had failed them, it introduced local authority registration for foster parents. The Secretary of State could also send inspectors into any children's home run as a charity, and check the money was being spent on the children and not the staff.

This series of interventions in the hitherto sacrosanct area of family life marked a profound ideological departure. Balfour's Home Secretary, Aretas Akers-Douglas, had said as recently as February 1905 that the government was reluctant to legislate on tobacco sales – a matter then widely discussed in the press because of the growing belief that the habit adversely affected children's health and particularly their growth – because 'the public attention that has been called to the evils of juvenile smoking is likely, I think, to do good, by arousing parents to exercise more control over their children in this respect.'[51]

The 1908 Act maintained the distinction between reformatories and industrial schools, but allowed children to be transferred between the two. It also introduced probation officers to supervise young people rather than have them admitted to an industrial school. But while the Act had introduced all manner of protection for children who lived with parents or guardians, it did nothing to change the often ferocious regimes in reformatories. Superintendents could birch miscreant boys, a punishment that in February 1908 Herbert Gladstone, the Home Secretary, admitted could be used in girls' reformatories 'in exceptional cases as a last resort, after due consideration by managers.'[52] The courts could order the birching of juvenile male offenders for a wide variety of offences under the 1861 Larceny Act, the 1861 Offences Against the Person Act, and the 1885 Criminal Law Amendment Act, and by order of a court of summary jurisdiction on conviction of any indictable offence. In some years over 3,000 such sentences were passed in the United Kingdom, and there was widespread public support for them in preference to putting youths in prison or reformatories where they would have opportunities to learn more about crime.

The magazine *John Bull* published on 22 October 1910 details of life on the training ship *Akbar* under the headline 'Reformatory School Horrors – How Boys at the Akbar School are Tortured – Several Deaths.'[53] The school, relocated to dry land in 1909 because of the unseaworthy nature of the ship from which it took its name, was one of four institutions run by the Liverpool Reformatory Association, a voluntary body, under Home Office surveillance. Severe corporal punishment was routine.

Those reporting sick were caned as malingerers. As an alternative, boys had cold water thrown over them, or were forced to stand up all night. This was far from the official regulations on discipline, which stated with remarkable vagueness that 'moderate personal correction' was permitted.[54] The paper's informants were a Mr and Mrs Adams: he was the former deputy superintendent, she the former matron. Adams had told his story to the Home Office's chief inspector, T. D. Robertson, who had dismissed the allegations: he would be sacked in 1911.

Immediately *John Bull* had published the charges, Winston Churchill, the Home Secretary, asked Charles Masterman, his under-secretary, to hold a formal inquiry, a peculiar choice given Masterman also held ministerial responsibility for the training ship. Captain Edward Beuttler, the superintendent, and his staff were not suspended from duty. On 7 January 1911 *John Bull* reported that two boys due to give evidence had absconded from *Akbar* and had pleaded with magistrates to put them in prison for their own protection. Masterman appears to have ignored this, and evidence that one boy, after frequent birchings, had tried to cut his own throat. He reported in March 1911 that while there had been irregular punishments, the regime was not brutal.

Even before his report MPs feared Masterman and his inquiry were taking the allegations too lightly; once the report was out a debate was forced in the Commons on 23 February. Llewellyn Atherley-Jones, the Liberal MP for Durham, a QC and a radical – his father had been a prominent Chartist – said the medical officer from Wormwood Scrubs had inspected boys on the ship: twenty-seven of the eighty-eight examined had been scarred by their beatings, some inflicted with a cane he adjudged as far heavier than one permitted under Home Office Regulations. Beuttler, according to witnesses, had stuffed blankets into his victims' mouths to muffle their yells. When public attention was drawn to the alleged abuses on *Akbar* the number of canings dropped dramatically – from 160 in 1909 to seventy-two in 1910.[55]

Atherley-Jones said boys had been underfed, and made as a punishment to stand up from 10 p.m. until 5 a.m. by their hammock, alternately fifteen minutes to attention and fifteen minutes at ease. It was not clear what 'offence' a boy had to commit to receive this punishment. Another boy had fifteen pails of cold water thrown over him on a freezing November night. That outrage alone, he said, should have had Beuttler sacked: but he remained in his post until 1913. Worst of all, a doctor had, in February 1909, diagnosed a boy called Brooks with a lung disease. However, the same doctor had, in what the MP described as an 'unaccountable' way, decided he was fit for work.[56] When he did not work hard enough, Beuttler ordered him to be caned. Mr Adams intervened and Beuttler changed his mind; later that day Brooks died. As Atherley-Jones said, if such mismanagement did not suggest something was 'radically wrong', what would?

Boys were hit with the ends of ropes almost randomly, and smacked around the head. Those in authority swore at them and used 'coarse and brutal language'. Another Liberal MP, Watson Rutherford, branded the punishments 'excessive and inhuman' and detailed three other deaths.[57] Two months after Brooks's demise a boy called Mills died of heart failure. In December 1909 a boy named Yeadon died, and a third boy, Brown, died after being drenched with water.

Masterman's defence of Beuttler and, indirectly, of himself was remarkable: it was that much of the severe punishment had been meted out to bring under control a homosexual ring – what, with the usual eye to euphemism, he called 'organised immorality in which a large number of small boys were involved, and which was a corrupting influence to the whole school.'[58] In a public school, he argued, boys guilty of 'such corruption' could be expelled. They could not be expelled from *Akbar*, so had instead to be thrashed until they stopped. He agreed, though, there was no justification for throwing water over a boy – who had been heard swearing – and said he had severely reprimanded Beuttler for sanctioning it. Masterman regarded that as the end of the matter: 'I saw the boy myself, and he had received no harm.' The boy made to stand all night had received that punishment because Beuttler was tired of thrashing him.

The local reformatory inspector described Beuttler's conduct of the school as 'by far the most wonderful thing he had ever seen in a reformatory'.[59] He would escape unscathed, the government sympathising with him for having to deal with the uncooperative and often unpleasant boys in his care. Masterman cited local residents who were impressed by the behaviour of *Akbar* boys when they were allowed out; he cited the chaplain who commended the transformation in the boys' character during their spell in the reformatory; and cited boys who had left *Akbar* and taken up useful employment. The Home Office felt Beuttler was doing a remarkable job, and could be forgiven the odd mistake. Masterman's one concession to criticism was that some of the boys were physical weaklings who would be better off in a less bracing part of the country than the Mersey estuary, and would perhaps thrive in one of the new Borstals.

John Bull was outraged and called the inquiry a whitewash. Public opinion agreed: on 14 May 7,000 people protested against the results. Horatio Bottomley, in his first parliament, accused Masterman of being neither 'competent' nor 'impartial', and he had a point.[60] He made Churchill squirm by forcing him to deny that 'loyal' staff on the *Akbar* had received a month's extra pay for refusing to criticise Beuttler.[61] But no one in authority paid any price for the brutalities on *Akbar*.

The government's complacency contradicted its professed desire to protect young people from the occasionally monstrous and capricious cruelty of adults. Yet Churchill, shortly after becoming Home Secretary the previous year, had begun to reform the penal system, and to end what he called 'the great disaster' that 'six or seven thousand lads are sent to prison every year under these stupid, entirely non-curative, short sentences for offences which are not criminal but merely mischievous.'[62] He advocated a 'disciplinary probation', including physical training, which would be 'highly salutary and extremely disagreeable'. It would take a world war before the ideals of liberalism penetrated this area of penology.

By the end of the nineteenth century much practical progress had been made, both in the material sense of improving housing and living conditions and in the practical one of treating children and youths in a way less likely to make criminals and delinquents out of them. There had also been an ideological shift, in the general acceptance that if the country were to become more humane and civilised in its alleviation of poverty, then more state intervention would be necessary. Central and local government now took a role in social welfare that would have been unthinkable half a century earlier. However, as the Edwardian era began, challenges to the relief of poverty still remained, and would fuel the ambitions of the Liberal party that came into government at the end of 1905. The rise in real wages of the working classes during the first decade of the twentieth century would not match the rise in the level of dividends taken by those who employed them. For the unemployed, the elderly or the long-term sick with no savings or extended family to rescue them, the workhouse with all its stringencies was the inevitable destination. These challenges would continue to vex the Edwardians, and the Liberal government, amidst massive controversy, would seek to address them.

CHAPTER 8

PROTECTING WOMEN

I

The poverty afflicting millions in the late nineteenth century was especially hard on women. Those in the working classes frequently toiled long hours in factories and sweatshops as well as running homes. A gradually falling birth rate reduced some of the pressures that motherhood involved (in 1871 there had been 295.5 legitimate live births per 1,000 women aged between fifteen and forty-four; by 1911 the number had fallen to 173.5).[1] Rearing a small child nevertheless remained fraught with danger. Childbirth occurred in the home, with a midwife and without drugs; and it killed a distressing proportion of women. The figures yo-yoed in the late nineteenth century, suggesting doctors relied on chance rather than science to solve the problem. In 1875 there were around seventy deaths of mothers per 1,000 confinements, but thirty-seven per 1,000 by 1880. The figure rose again to fifty per 1,000 in 1882, fell to forty by 1891 and then shot up to sixty-five within two years. It fell again to below forty, where it stayed until the Second World War, after which it fell until becoming almost negligible by 1970.[2] The constant round of giving birth, raising children, running the home (most working-class – and middle-class – husbands still expected their wives to take charge of domestic matters), and often having to take on paid work, too, took its toll. The average life expectancy for women in 1881, though a little higher than for men, was still only 47.2 years (for men it was 43.7 years). By 1911 it had increased to 55.4 and 51.5 years respectively.[3]

Enlightened ideas about the condition of women and the rights and protection that the law should offer them had gradually infused legislation and social attitudes since the 1830s. Women had no vote, but until the turn of the century their suffrage was rarely discussed, with many women seeming unconcerned about the denial of their right to take part in politics – though when local government was reformed after 1888 women could participate as voters and councillors. Having no voice in the councils of the nation, they were unable to influence the laws that affected them. For example, although divorce had been feasible since 1857, it remained easier for a man to divorce his wife than vice versa. An attempt in 1902 by Earl Russell to equalise the law, and have cases heard in county courts to make them cheaper so the working classes could afford to divorce, was thrown out. The Lord Chancellor, Halsbury, reviled the notion that such a Bill could even be discussed, claiming 'this Bill is one for the abolition of the institution of marriage'.[4]

Women at last took a measure of control of their reproductive capabilities as contraception became more widely available, and education about it improved. Not all working-class women had access to contraception, and so illegitimacy was not uncommon. In 1871 there were 15.1 illegitimate births per 1,000 women aged between fifteen and forty-four, the number falling to 8.1 by 1911.[5]

Illegitimacy carried a heavy social stigma; women without a family to support them would be consigned to workhouse hospitals to give birth. Infanticide was therefore common. In some cases women murdered their children, often while depressed and when incapable of coping because of a shortage of help. In other cases they would entrust their babies to a baby-farmer, a woman who for a few pounds would take the child and farm it out to working-class families; or if they could not, would allow the infant to die of neglect, or would drug or starve it to death and then dispose of the body. The Infant Life Protection Act of 1872, prompted largely by the case in 1870 of the Brixton baby-farmer Margaret Waters, was supposed to have ended the practice but merely sent it further underground. Waters was hanged, but the deterrent effect was insufficient. The chances of an illegitimate child reaching adulthood seem to have been small: one estimate suggested that 90 per cent of them died before their first birthday.[6] Of the 5,722 homicides recorded between 1878 and 1892, 20 per cent were thought to be of children under a year old.[7]

One of the most notorious baby-farmers, Amelia Dyer, was hanged in Newgate in June 1896. She had trained as a nurse, but soon learned of more profitable employment. She offered rooms to unmarried expectant mothers where they could stay hidden, and offered to take their babies once they arrived. She used a concoction called Godfrey's Cordial to kill those she could not farm out. The cordial was a pacifier – it contained opium – but an overdose could, and did, kill. Dyer murdered a baby in March 1896, and threw the body in the Thames near Reading. However, it was insufficiently weighted: a bargee found it in a brown paper parcel shortly afterwards. Forensic evidence – including pawn tickets for baby clothes, since Dyer wished to maximise profits – led to her, and she was arrested within days.

The river was dragged and six more corpses found. One was identified from clothing by a Bristol barmaid who had paid Dyer £10 to put her baby girl out for adoption, having seen a newspaper advertisement offering a home to a child. In most cases death was by strangulation: Dyer had become too impatient to wait for her charges to starve to death. It is thought she murdered 400 babies. Dyer wrote to the magistrates from Reading Gaol on 16 April to confess. 'I must relieve my mind . . . I feel my days are numbered . . . I do know I shall have to answer before my Maker in heaven for the awful crimes I have committed'.[8] She pleaded insanity – she had had several spells in lunatic asylums and the court was told she had attempted suicide – but medical experts called this a ploy. The jury took five minutes to convict her. The judge, Mr Justice Hawkins, denounced her 'cruelty and wickedness', saying he was 'sorely afraid that she had carried out a cruel and wicked system of crime for a long time past.'[9]

The Times noted – as was mentioned in the last chapter – that it was not just the likes of Dyer who posed a threat to children. There were also parents who took out insurance polices against their children's lives, and murdered them for profit. It called for legislation, but accepted the difficulty of protecting children from all manner of people who saw a financial benefit in killing them.

Although contraception was, even in the late-Victorian period and before Marie Stopes, available – popular magazines often had tactfully worded advertisements for it – abortion, sometimes resulting in the death or sterilisation of the woman, was also commonplace. One method was the ingestion of lead plaster. A survey found that by 1914 abortion was common in twenty-six out of 104 registration districts north of the Humber – in other words in the main industrial areas of England.[10] The cheap press advertised pills for 'female ailments', including 'the most obstinate obstructions', but these were generally quack remedies. The temptation for the poor to engage in infanticide increased, paradoxically, with improvements to society. Once it became compulsory to send a child to school the expense of having a large family greatly increased, as there was a longer wait before the child could contribute to household income. This drain on family resources would frequently be a struggle, even though in the long term the educated child would be equipped for a more highly skilled trade, and therefore earn higher wages than his or her parents' generation. Although family sizes fell, which also removed some of the financial strain for individual households, the population grew: partly as a legacy of the larger families of the preceding generations, partly as a result of the decline in infant mortality.

II

Female poverty and vulnerability in the late nineteenth century were seldom displayed so starkly as in the high incidence of women engaging in prostitution. There are no reliable figures – it suited charitable societies to exaggerate the numbers – but in 1857 the Metropolitan Police gave the reformer William Acton statistics that suggested they knew of 2,825 brothels within their district and 8,600 full-time prostitutes. The national figure was claimed to be 80,000[11]. For some (often married) women, prostitution was a short-term means to meet an immediate financial problem, so the number of part-timers will have inflated the figures considerably. It was notably rife among very young women, many little more than children. The natural Victorian tendency was to ignore the problem, a hypocritical stance born mainly of prudishness about sexual matters: some of the unfortunate girls' best customers were men of the class that supposedly set the moral tone, and made the laws, for everyone else. By the 1880s, however, it was clear to many in public life that the problem was multiplying, thanks to the inequalities inherent in the country's growing prosperity, and could no longer be ignored.

In 1881 a select committee was established 'to inquire into the state of the law relative to the protection of young girls from artifices to induce them to lead a corrupt life'.[12] It examined fifteen witnesses, and found that juvenile prostitution in London had over the previous three or four years increased 'with alarming rapidity', resulting in a flourishing traffic in young girls. The committee sought to question more witnesses before making recommendations, and was reappointed for the 1882 session. It included Salisbury and the aged Shaftesbury, as well as the Bishop of London and the former Lord Chancellor, Lord Cairns.

What ultimately prompted the government to act, however, was not the deliberations of the committee, but the single-handed efforts of a journalist: W. T. Stead, editor of *The Pall Mall Gazette* and scourge of the depraved. The man, who as we have seen went to such lengths to persecute Dilke (see Chapter 1), proved equally assiduous in exposing the scandal of juvenile prostitution.

Stead was born in 1849, son of a Congregationalist minister from Northumberland. At fifteen he became a clerk in Newcastle docks, but was soon contributing to the *Northern Echo*, based in Darlington. His talent was noted, and at the age of twenty-two he became editor. Stead was motivated by moral considerations; but he also recognised the power of the popular press in a newly literate society. He had whipped up public feeling in Gladstone's campaign on the Bulgarian atrocities in 1876, the same year he launched a campaign to repeal the Contagious Diseases Acts. Gladstone's victory in 1880 was perhaps the first that owed much to the power of the press, and in that sense it was partly Stead's triumph, and the eventual repeal of the Act would be but one of his other victories.

He acquired a national platform in 1880 when he came to London as assistant editor of *The Pall Mall Gazette*, a popular evening newspaper. That year it came under new ownership and transferred allegiance from the Conservatives to the Liberals, under the editorship of John Morley. When Morley won a by-election in Newcastle in 1883, Stead succeeded him as editor. Morley had begun to make the paper more populist, but Stead went further – not just in his tone and choice of subject matter, but in terms of design, layout, the use of illustrations and the blurring of the lines between facts and opinions – Stead's opinions. He also invented the interview as we understand it, that with Gordon in 1884 having, as we have seen, great political and historical consequences. He ran an emotive series on London's slums, which provoked government action to improve the housing stock. He also highlighted what he considered the weakness of the Navy. But it was a series about child prostitution that catapulted him to fame.

The age of consent had been raised from twelve to thirteen in 1875, triggering a campaign led by Josephine Butler, the proto-feminist and friend of Stead, to have it raised to sixteen. This campaign prompted the House of Lords committee. After sitting for the 1881 and 1882 sessions it proposed an amending Bill, introduced in May 1883. It had found that young girls were being abducted and sold into prostitution. However, the Bill failed because of dissatisfaction with its composition, and a feeling that it would not protect innocent young females because of the difficulties of enforcement. There were also fears that it would encourage unscrupulous prostitutes to make false accusations against innocent men.

It was this failure to legislate despite what he considered overwhelming evidence of the need to do so that pushed Stead into his most sensational campaign. In May 1885, with the Criminal Law Amendment Bill seeming about to founder again because of the Liberal government's resignation, Benjamin Scott, Chamberlain of the City of London and a leading campaigner for the protection of girls, took further evidence to Stead about young women forced into prostitution and abducted to work in continental brothels. With Josephine Butler and Bramwell Booth, son of the founder of the Salvation Army, Stead resolved to find definitive evidence of such trafficking that would shame parliament into action. He established with Mrs Butler and Booth 'a Special and Secret Committee of Inquiry', and was joined by representatives of the snappily named London Committee for the Suppression of the Traffic in British Girls for the Purposes of Continental Prostitution, which he also chaired.

As part of their inquiries two young women, one an employee of *The Pall Mall Gazette* and the other a Salvation Army volunteer, went undercover as prostitutes, though they managed to escape from the brothels where they did their research before being made to participate in sexual acts. Mrs Butler and her son walked the streets of London for ten days pretending to be a brothel-keeper and her ponce, and for an outlay of £100 acquired several children from brothels they visited. Stead's research included the police, all manner of prostitutes, and some clergy. When he decided to push his research to the limit, matters became sensational.

Stead decided to buy a girl. At his behest Rebecca Jarrett, a reformed prostitute who assisted Mrs Butler, met an old friend called Nancy Broughton, who knew of a thirteen-year-old girl, Eliza Armstrong, whose alcoholic mother was destitute and whose chimney-sweep father was not in evidence. The mother agreed to sell Eliza for £5, under the pretence that she would be the maid to an elderly gentleman. This Eliza lived in Lisson Grove (as did Eliza Doolittle, Shaw's creation in *Pygmalion* whose genesis owed something to this case). Having bought the girl, Jarrett took her to an abortionist, Louise Mourez, who certified she was a virgin, and sold Jarrett some chloroform, with which the girl was drugged before being taken to a brothel.

Then Stead arrived, posing as a degenerate: so deeply did he go into character that he had drunk a pint of champagne, even though a teetotaller. He waited in Eliza's room for her to come round. When she did she screamed, which was Stead's cue to leave, the rest of the house inferring from the scream that she had been raped. Jarrett then took the unharmed girl to Booth, who had her moved to France and put into the care of a Salvation Army family.

The combination of Stead's nose for publicity with his lubricious subject created the greatest journalistic coup of the age, on which rests his deserved reputation as the father of what we now call tabloid journalism. On 4 July 1885 he published a 'Notice to our Readers: A Frank Warning'.[13] He began by lamenting the failure of parliament to legislate to protect young girls, and regretting too the latest reason adduced for it – that the public simply didn't care enough. It was, therefore, 'necessary to open the eyes of the public, in order that a measure the urgency of which has been repeatedly admitted may pass into law this session.' So he would be publishing the report of his own committee of inquiry, dealing with 'sexual criminality'. 'Nothing', he continued, 'but the most imperious sense of public duty would justify its publication.' With the Criminal Law Amendment Bill about to be dumped for a third time, *The Pall Mall Gazette* simply had to act.

Serialisation, under the title *The Maiden Tribute of Modern Babylon* – a reference to virgins who in classical mythology were devoured by the minotaur – would start two days later, on Monday 6 July, and would continue 'until the whole infernal narrative is complete'; this he would do 'in the public interest'. No one has ever proved the value of a free press so much as Stead. He warned his readers of the shocking content of the 'report' – 'we have no desire to inflict upon unwilling eyes the ghastly story of the criminal developments of modern vice,' he wrote. So he told them, 'quite frankly':

> . . . all those who are squeamish, and all those who are prudish, and all those who prefer to live in a fool's paradise of imaginary innocence and purity, selfishly oblivious to the horrible realities which torment those whose lives are passed in the London Inferno, will do well not to read *The Pall Mall Gazette* of Monday and the three following days. The story of an actual pilgrimage into a real hell is not pleasant reading, and is not meant to be. It is, however, an authentic record of unimpeachable facts, 'abominable, unutterable, and worse than fables yet have feigned or fear conceived.' But it is true, and its publication is necessary.

Nothing else was required to make the paper an instant sell-out when it appeared on 6 July, even though W. H. Smith refused to stock it: volunteers (many from the Salvation Army) took to the streets to offer it for sale instead. Such was the demand for subsequent issues that Stead's suppliers ran out of paper, and his offices were besieged: used copies of the penny newspaper changed hands for a shilling. Stead disguised Eliza as 'Lily' and kept one fact of the case quiet: that he had purchased her. Otherwise, all the salacious details were there, and the nation was, as he had intended, outraged.

'London's lust annually uses up thousands of women, who are literally killed and made away with – living sacrifices slain in the service of vice,' the first instalment proclaimed.[14] It listed five crimes of 'the most ruthless and abominable description' rampant in London – 'the sale and purchase and violation of children', 'the procuration of virgins', 'the entrapping and ruin of women', 'the international slave trade in girls' and 'atrocities, brutalities and unnatural crimes.' Fabulously overwritten, laced with biblical references and teetering on the verge of hysteria, *The Maiden Tribute* went into graphic detail about the violation of screaming virgins, the confessions of brothel-keepers, sado-masochism and the workings of 'the London slave market'.

One extract must suffice:

> To oblige a wealthy customer who by riot and excess had impaired his vitality to such an extent that nothing could minister to his jaded senses but very young maidens, an eminently respectable lady undertook that whenever the girl was fourteen or fifteen years of age she should be strapped down hand and foot to the four posts

> of the bedstead, so that all resistance save that of unavailing screaming would be impossible. Before the strapping down was finally agreed upon the lady of the house, a stalwart woman and experienced in the trade, had volunteered her services to hold the virgin down by force while her wealthy patron effected his purpose. That was too much even for him, and the alternative of fastening with straps padded on the under side was then agreed upon. Strapping down for violation used to be a common occurrence in Half-moon-street and in Anna Rosenberg's brothel at Liverpool. Anything can be done for money, if you only know where to take it.

The first instalment concluded with details of the purchase of Eliza Armstrong, though did not specify by whom. The other three piled on the evidence from one brothel after another.

Sir Richard Cross, the Home Secretary, urged Stead to stop publishing for fear of public order breaking down, such was the outrage his story had caused. Stead demanded immediate legislation, but when Cross could not oblige he carried on printing. There were no riots, but mass protests erupted all over England, including armies of virgins dressed in white. The Salvation Army escorted to Westminster a petition signed by 400,000 people. Suddenly, MPs realised the moral climate, dictated by the middle class and an aspirational working class heavily influenced by popular journalism, had changed. Parliament saw it had no choice but to legislate.

On 7 July, after the first revelations, the reaction of the political class was of outrage against Stead. George Cavendish-Bentinck, a Tory MP, complained of the 'objectionable subjects' in the paper, and asked whether 'any means exist of subjecting the authors and publishers . . . to criminal proceedings.'[15] Cross told the complainants that publishing obscene material was a misdemeanour, but showed no enthusiasm for causing greater outrage by prosecuting Stead. On 9 July, shocked by the impact of the reports, the new government resumed progress on the Criminal Law Amendment Bill in the Commons. As Salisbury had taken office on Gladstone's resignation without a dissolution, no new session had started and the existing Bill could continue through parliament.

Cross claimed the Tories wanted the law passed as much as the Liberals had. (He was as good as his word, because it was on the statute book in little over a month.) Despite Stead's campaign opposition remained: Charles Hopwood, a Liberal MP, called the legislation 'repressive' and the Bill 'most objectionable', as girls of thirteen were quite capable of looking after themselves. He reminded Cross that as Home Secretary under Disraeli he had objected to the age of consent being raised to fourteen.[16] Hopwood felt the proposed law was no substitute for 'the elevation of the population . . . by providing them with employment'; and said it would corrupt the police, having them pursue teenage girls suspected of being engaged in prostitution. The law would hurt prostitutes rather than those who exploited them, he argued; and young men deserved protection as much as girls, a thought already fermenting elsewhere on the Liberal benches.

The clamour to have Stead prosecuted for publishing 'abominations' grew as more appeared: this hypocritical determination to suppress facts highlighted society's disregard of the vulnerable.[17] However, by 16 July the tone had changed, with a demand for a Royal Commission to investigate the claims and – if they were proved true – to bring the guilty parties to justice: Cross had no hesitation in affirming that 'every endeavour' would be used to do that.[18]

Yet when the Bill reached its committee stage on 30 July there were still pockets of hostility, Hopwood denouncing 'sensational statements of a filthy nature in a public journal, many of them being untrue'.[19] He goaded Cross for having previously 'acquiesced in a state of things he was now so anxious to amend' and mocked 'all talk about the purity of homes and the inviolable sanctity of the family' as 'inflammatory'.[20] He did not see how a new, essentially middle-class sense of Christian propriety was abroad, and would set the moral tone for decades ahead. The National Vigilance Association embodied this. It was set up once the law against child prostitution was passed, and included on its council such luminaries as Stead, Mrs Butler and Millicent Fawcett, who would lead the suffragist movement. It devoted itself to ensuring the law was enforced, campaigning against prostitution, and elevating public morality.

Stead and his activist, religious, middle-class associates held views that would permeate millions of the respectable working-class and middle-class homes throughout the suburbs of London and all major towns and cities in the Kingdom. More radical views of human sexuality, such as those espoused by Henry Havelock Ellis, the sexologist and eugenicist, or his friend Edward Carpenter, would take decades to pass beyond a small group of intellectuals. Yet Hopwood, a barrister, predicted that girls 'steeped in depravity' would now blackmail boys and young men, and that such unfortunate youths would end up in the dock facing charges based on false accusations.[21] He predicted that even the parents of such girls would use the law as a means of extortion.

Another MP, Charles Warton, dismissed Stead's report as 'invented', and the Bill's promoters as 'ill-conditioned Democrats and Salvationist sentimentalists' who wished 'to set class against class'.[22] He adduced as proof that it was 'scandalously alleged that the daughters of working men were to be the victims and slaves of those above them in rank; for there was nothing more congenial to the ill-conditioned Democrat than to cast foul slanders and aspersions on the higher orders of society.' Harcourt, for the Liberals, said he respected Hopwood's objections: but the measure would nonetheless have the full support of the opposition.

The age of consent rose to sixteen; consent between sixteen and eighteen was subject to parental approval. It became illegal to detain a girl over eighteen for immoral purposes, to procure females under twenty-one as prostitutes, or to allow them to enter a brothel, the purpose of these measures being to stop a girl taking the first step to a life of immorality. It would also be an offence to procure a girl for export. Men and youths could be flogged, in addition to a prison sentence, if convicted under the Act. Judicial corporal punishment had been increasingly questioned for its effectiveness and suitability in a supposedly advanced society; that Cross supported its application for these offences shows the moral panic Stead had provoked. Nonetheless, backbenchers tried to amend the Bill to allow prosecution of publications such as *The Pall Mall Gazette* for printing what they considered obscene material.

There was a further, unintended consequence. Labouchere, whose moral fervour could match Stead's, proposed an amendment on 6 August making any homosexual act – which the law would term 'an act of gross indecency' – a crime, punishable by up to two years with hard labour. Homosexual acts between men had been illegal since 1533. Until 1861 sodomy could be punished by death. Prosecutions were rare because of the difficulty of obtaining evidence. However, the Labouchere amendment required no evidence to prosecute, and all acts in addition to sodomy were criminalised. This would be Wilde's eventual undoing. Nor did it define 'gross indecency'.

Labouchere said his amendment criminalised men who made 'an assault' on any other male; hitherto the 'assault' was criminal only if on a boy under thirteen. Hansard reported: 'He did not think it necessary to discuss the proposal at any length, as he understood Her Majesty's Government were willing to accept it.'[23] Indeed, the only comment came from the ex-Attorney-General Sir Henry James, who felt the suggested punishment for gross indecency – a year's imprisonment – was inadequate, and proposed it be doubled. It was. The entire debate took four minutes. Homosexual acts remained criminalised until 1967.

This was not the end for Stead. His rivals sought 'Lily', and when the girl's real name emerged her dissolute mother said she had thought her daughter was going into domestic service, not vice. For the girl to be removed technically required her father's approval, which had not been obtained. Therefore – even though Salvationists were caring for her – Stead had financed her abduction. He, Jarrett, Booth, Mourez and two others were charged with assault and abduction on 2 September; the trial began on 23 October.

Stead's public profile and personality complicated matters. There was undoubtedly a political element to his prosecution; some politicians resented having been forced to pass the Bill because of his rabble-rousing. Sir Richard Webster, the Attorney-General, led for the prosecution. He told of the alleged respectability of the girl's father, a former soldier, and how Jarrett had duped Mrs Armstrong by saying Eliza would become a maid in Wimbledon or Croydon. Webster conceded that when Eliza had been 'bought' by Stead and consigned to the Salvation Army in Paris, 'she was treated kindly, and nothing improper was done to her there.'[24]

However, he then veered from the abduction into journalism, without any objection from the judge, Mr Justice Lopes. *The Pall Mall Gazette* had published an article 'of a most disgraceful character, for, whatever the motive might be, there could be no question that the language was disgraceful.' The barometer of offence was calibrated so that talking about a girl of thirteen being raped was more offensive than the rape itself, which was best not discussed. That explained the Labouchere amendment, scuttled through in the blink of an eye. Stead was prosecuted for abduction because it was easier than prosecuting him for discussing things in print that polite society would rather pretend did not exist.

Webster was milder to Booth – not a journalist, nor a reformed common prostitute or abortionist – commenting how surprising it was that a 'man of religious feeling' could have associated with the likes of Stead or Jarrett. The judge ruled that 'no motives, however philanthropic, justified the taking away of a child from parents without their consent, and any consent obtained by fraud was no consent at all.' From then, early in the trial, Stead had had it. Worse, he conducted his own defence, and Lopes rebuked him over his lines of questioning. He reduced Eliza's mother to a fit of theatrical sobbing under cross-examination, which played badly.

In the witness box, Stead pursued martyrdom. He said he was prepared to submit to 'any punishment', having achieved his aim of having the Criminal Law Amendment Bill passed. He had proved London was a city where a girl could be bought and sold, and where there were women who in return for a sovereign or two would certify such girls as virgins. His next aim was to secure repeal of the Contagious Diseases Act. He contended Jarrett had told him the child had been offered for sale, and neither Jarrett nor he had had to induce the parents to perpetrate what Lopes called 'one of the most terrible crimes they could commit.'[25] He continued: 'I have stated that I desired to purchase only girls who were in the market, and who would be ruined if I did not buy them. Many mothers sell their children as soon as they come to a seducible age.' Asked by Lopes whether he meant to suggest that Eliza had been 'in the market', Stead replied: 'That is the essence of my case.'

He tried to call the Archbishop of Canterbury, who attended court, to testify to the decency of his motives: but Lopes refused to let him unless Archbishop Benson could give evidence that Stead had not been instrumental in Eliza's abduction. He could not: as Lopes said, no one was questioning Stead's motives, only the legality of his actions. Nearly forty other potential witnesses were barred for the same reason. Lopes constantly told Stead of his shortcomings in understanding the law. When Stead summed up he said it was 'the supreme moment of his life'; he spoke 'with a very full heart, with very full convictions'.[26] Playing to the gallery, he spoke of the '10,000 little girls in this country living in a condition of prostitution', and the one in ten violators who had been punished. 'When he thought of those 10,000 little girls, he knew that our civilisation was a ghastly farce and our laws even more ghastly. When he walked through London streets and heard the Church bells ringing calling Christians to prayer, and when he thought of the poor children who were being nightly ensnared and entrapped to their ruin, he seemed to see written over the doors of the brothels the ghastly parody of our Saviour's words, "Suffer little children to enter here, for such is the Kingdom of Hell".' He emphatically denied being motivated by pecuniary considerations: which was true. It did not, however, alter the law.

When he finished his summing-up – 'delivered with great animation and force', according to *The Times* – there was a loud burst of applause. Lopes, in his summing-up, distinguished between Stead's involvement and Booth's, in that Booth had no prior knowledge of the abduction: which seemed like a direction to acquit. He also ruled it was no defence that Mrs Armstrong had been told the girl would have a position in service, and had been found one: it did not undo the fact that her father had not given permission. Lopes congratulated Stead on his summing-up – 'a speech more impressive I think few of us have ever heard'.[27] However, the 'filthy and disgusting' articles had 'suggested to the minds of innocent women and children the existence of vice and wickedness which had never occurred to their minds before' – and that seemed the greatest offence of all.

The jury retired for three hours, and found Stead and Jarrett guilty. They agreed Stead had been driven by 'the highest motives', a recommendation to mercy. The possibility of a conspiracy charge was dropped. Stead was given three months without hard labour; a colleague, Sampson Jacques, was given one month. Jarrett, whose role was that of a victim of circumstance, received six months; Mourez, the abortionist, six months with hard labour.

Stead was taken to prison at Coldbath Fields, where he spent just three days: he passed the rest of his three months at Holloway where, as a first-class prisoner, he had a comparatively comfortable cell, could have traffic with the outside world and wear his own clothes. He continued to edit his newspaper from jail; he wrote a pamphlet about his martyrdom when he came out; and on 10 November each year, the anniversary of his conviction, would wear his prison uniform to remind others of his personal Calvary. He had worn that uniform for just three days, but cunningly asked the governor whether he might keep it, enabling a lifetime of self-publicity. On 15 April 1912 he would become one of the most notable casualties of the sinking of the *Titanic*. He was last spotted clinging to a life raft in the sea with John Jacob Astor IV – both men drowned after, it is presumed, succumbing to hypothermia in a near-freezing sea.

III

The year after his conviction Stead had another wish granted: the Contagious Diseases Acts of 1866 and 1869 were repealed.[28] It was not Stead's cause alone. It had affronted feminists from Josephine Butler downwards, and between 1870 and 1885 17,365 petitions calling for repeal had been presented to parliament, with 2,606,429 signatures.[29] The double standard – of men seeking prostitutes, but prostitutes having to endure the humiliation resulting from that – was at last challenged, and another element of Victorian hypocrisy held up to scrutiny. Two groups had co-ordinated the fight against the Acts since the late 1860s: the National Association for the Repeal of the Contagious Diseases Act and the Ladies' National Association, founded by Mrs Butler.

A Bill for repeal was first read on 22 January 1886, but the change of government derailed the process. On 16 March, during Gladstone's short-lived administration, James Stansfield, the Liberal MP for Halifax and a former minister, proposed a resolution to repeal the Acts. As with the Labouchere amendment, the Victorian reluctance to discuss sexual matters had compounded the problem. Stansfield argued that Gladstone had said, in 1883, that 'most unfortunately, though from the best of motives – from the desire to prevent public discussion on a subject not fit for proper discussion – these Acts were passed almost without the knowledge of anyone.'[30]

That had been a remarkable statement; the first Act had been passed when Gladstone led his party in the Commons, and in 1869 he had been prime minister. It showed how civil service influence pertained even in a well-run government – War Office officials had driven the Acts, to limit prostitutes with venereal disease infecting servicemen – and the prim reluctance even among educated men to discuss this frankly led to the Acts being 'smuggled through Parliament', in Stansfield's phrase. Otherwise they would never have been passed, 'so strong would have been the public indignation at their provisions'.[31]

Stansfield said that if the Army and Navy wanted to protect their men, they needed to find a way that did not 'sin against the principle of liberty and law'.[32] He felt the Criminal Law Amendment Act's regulation of prostitution made the Contagious Diseases Acts redundant. Henry Campbell-Bannerman, the Secretary of State for War, agreed.

The priority was to ensure that hospital treatment for diseased women, given under the Act, was continued; Campbell-Bannerman promised it would be. The House resolved to repeal the Acts, but there were still those who wished to keep them. George Cavendish-Bentinck, a junior law officer in Disraeli's second administration, claimed that since the *de facto* end of compulsory examinations venereal disease had increased by 80 per cent in the Army and by 80–100 per cent in the Navy.[33]

He claimed a great increase in women voluntarily presenting themselves for treatment: not only were more women contracting venereal diseases but a higher proportion of them were younger. He read out a letter from a clergyman in Chatham about a twelve-year-old girl who had recently 'sinned' with four men, and how nearly half the females who had sought treatment for venereal diseases that year had been teenagers. Those reporting with syphilis – 'physical disease in the worst form' – rather than gonorrhea had increased.[34] Others who represented garrison and dockyard towns suggested that depravity on an epic scale would be unleashed if the Acts went. Nonetheless, the second reading of the Repeal Bill was unopposed. When the Royal Assent was given on 16 May a notable battle against the Victorian double standard had been won.

The moral panic forced legislation, but it did not inhibit sex crime. Prostitution, sodomy and incest increased, and what one MP called 'painted boys' had appeared on the streets of London.[35] The 1885 Act inadvertently encouraged pimping, with up to 1,000 prosecutions a year of prostitutes running small brothels. Another Act in 1898 made pimping an offence, with prison and flogging for the culprits. This, too, tested the ingenuity of the pimp, and during the Edwardian age substantial vice and prostitution rings of a sophistication that made them intractable under existing laws became apparent. The trafficking of girls into London, mainly but not exclusively from other parts of Britain, became commonplace. A horrified nation even devised a new term for this abomination – white slavery – and the white slave trade became the target of a new law in 1912, driven by outraged male legislators, and ironically with a Liberal government providing yet more scope for draconian punishment.

The 1912 Act was a direct result of a wave of posthumous regard for Stead after he went down with the *Titanic*, and was designed to complete his work. A Tory backbencher, Colonel Arthur Lee – remembered for having given Chequers to the nation – introduced a Bill aimed at ending the white slave traffic; and on 17 May a 'Pass the Bill Committee', led by various aristocratic women and, notably, the Dowager Duchess of Bedford, was formed to lobby for this to be enacted, after the 'irreparable loss of Mr Stead.'[36] The following week the Reverend Dr J. Scott Lidgett presided at a meeting of the Ladies' National Association for the Abolition of State Regulation of Vice and for the Promotion of Social Purity at Caxton Hall, Westminster, where the traffic was the sole topic of discussion. It too passed a resolution hoping Lee's Bill would be enacted as a 'monument' to Stead: eighty-five other societies had passed similar resolutions.[37] Not to be outdone, some professional men, led by Harley Street doctors, formed a committee to demand not just the enactment of Lee's Bill, but for its sanctions to be drastic.

This outburst persuaded MPs from all parties to send Asquith, the prime minister, a letter urging him to support the Bill. Within days the government adopted it. It had its second reading on 10 June without a division. The government's decision to sponsor it excited more public support. While many agitators simply wanted the most brutal possible punishment for traffickers, an enlightened minority – led by Mrs Philip Snowden, wife of a Labour MP – issued the reminder that 'the problem of prostitution would not be touched until they had gone a long way towards solving the poverty problem and brought about a reform of our educational system.'[38]

A committee of MPs scrutinised Lee's Bill. It resolved not only to include flogging as a punishment for traffickers, but to put no statutory limit on the number of strokes administered. Lee told the committee that the sort of men who would be affected were 'the greatest cowards on earth' and would flee Britain at the very thought of the cat o' nine tails.[39] A Home Office official said the government agreed. No woman had been flogged since 1820, and procuresses would not suffer it now: the following week, on 23 July, Madeline Lancashire, a thirty-six-year-old woman, appeared at the Old Bailey and pleaded guilty to a charge of trying to procure her eighteen-year-old niece 'for an improper purpose'.[40] The Recorder gave her eighteen months with hard labour.

Reginald McKenna, the Home Secretary, endorsed severity. 'In my opinion, flogging is right; it is quite idle to say . . . that it is not a deterrent,' he said on 12 November 1912. 'I have endeavoured to discover in what number of cases the same person has been flogged twice. I do not say there are no such cases; but I do say this: that my most competent adviser on this particular point only recollects one case. There may be more; but it is certainly true to say that it is the rarest possible thing for any man who has once been flogged to commit another offence for which flogging may be administered.'[41]

In the Lords Randall Davidson, the Archbishop of Canterbury, agreed, as did Lord Alverstone, Salisbury's Attorney-General, who had for years sat as a judge. He had, he said, never sentenced a man to a flogging, but could see this class of criminal richly deserved it. Lord Lytton seemed to strike a humanitarian note in opposing flogging, proposing instead to brand pimps on their foreheads. The archiepiscopal view shocked the Penal Reform League, whose secretary wrote to *The Times* condemning 'hasty and crude methods of retribution for the individual symptoms of our collective wickedness.'[42] His was not a widespread opinion. Davidson was unmoved, telling a meeting at the Opera House in Covent Garden on 12 November of his contempt for those who said 'they must not use the lash, lest they degraded the criminal or the man who flogged him. He defied them to degrade the villain who had sunk to cowardly devilry to obtain the carefully-contrived ruin of innocent girls.'[43] The flagellator, he surmised, would be only too delighted to save such girls.

In the Commons a number of Sir Galahads took the opportunity to jump to the defence of their womenfolk in the most violently retributive fashion. Lee said that 'you are dealing with a class of professional specialists engaged in a cold, calculating, sordid business for the ruin and subsequent financial exploitation of human bodies and souls. The circumstances are entirely exceptional. These men . . . constitute the very worst feature of commercialised vice. If you succeed in repressing them, you will relieve these unfortunate women from the most intolerable oppression to which they are now subjected.'[44]

Lee believed aliens had introduced this contamination. He continued: 'These people are numbered not by hundreds but by thousands in London alone. A very large proportion of them, I am glad to say, are not Englishmen. I regret that some are, but if hon. Members could see not merely foreigners, not merely debased Englishmen, but dozens of negroes in the West End of London running white English girls on the streets they would see the people at whom we wish to get . . . it has been proved that the existing methods of punishment are powerless to act as a sufficient deterrent.'

Colonel Charles Burn, Unionist MP for Torquay and an old India hand, reinforced Lee:

> Our mission . . . is not to reclaim girls who have gone astray; but it is our mission and our duty to protect the womanhood and girlhood of this country. Never was there a time in the history of a nation when the protection of the House of Commons was more needed for these girls. Those men who ply this trade are certainly what I should call the dregs of humanity. They are debased and debauched, and when they get these wretched girls into their clutches and live on their earnings, they deserve no pity from anyone.

His peroration was sonorous:

> I say the only punishment that fits the crime is a good, sound flogging. I claim this because it is proved up to the hilt that nothing else will stamp it out in this country. Let us show the people of this country that we mean business and that we intend that men who live upon the earnings of these girls should meet the punishment they deserve.[45]

Sophia Lonsdale, a prominent suffragist and social reformer, wrote to *The Times* on 23 November 'at the request of many women actively engaged in various forms of social work' to describe the 'increased boldness' of the white slavers 'trying to make hay while the sun shines', before the passage of the Bill.[46] The traffickers were going around trying 'to entrap the innocent and unwary . . . We wish through you, Sir, to warn all persons who are responsible for girls from the age of thirteen to twenty-four in any rank of life, and to urge them to impress carefully on their charges that they should on no account or pretext accompany anyone not personally known to them'. Girls should especially 'be warned against women in nurse's uniform and persons apparently suddenly taken ill who appeal to them for help in the streets, the public parks, underground railways, stores and shops.' No young woman was safe: England was convulsed by panic: the new law and its savage punishments were needed urgently.

One MP looked more deeply into the question. J. H. Thomas, who would be a cabinet minister in the first two Labour governments, echoed

Mrs Snowden in saying: 'This Bill does not touch the real root of the question. The real root of this question is an economic one. While vice is more amply rewarded than virtue, while young girls in factories and workshops in every town in this country are paid sweated wages, these girls are driven invariably to prostitution . . . housing conditions, low wages, slum landlords and sweaters are equally responsible'.[47] It was the point Shaw had made in *Mrs Warren's Profession*, highlighting the social conditions that encouraged girls into vice, and which the Lord Chamberlain refused until 1925 to license for public performance. Shaw had tried to write a play that would not aggrieve the censor, and his failure made him, as we shall see, a ferocious opponent of censorship.

The Bill was enacted on 13 December. Scotland Yard formed a special squad to round up traffickers, although it was reported that 'many miscreants of foreign nationality have already left London for the Continent,' which seemed to prove that flogging and jail really did deter.[48] The first man sentenced under the Act was one Timothy Patrick O'Connor, who three weeks after their marriage had persuaded his wife to engage in prostitution to provide for them until he could find work. Mr Justice Darling ordered him thirty strokes of the cat o' nine tails and eighteen months' hard labour.[49] Soliciting and importuning by men also became a crime, and women running brothels or living off immoral earnings faced long sentences. Those who ran refuges for victims of the trade opened their doors more widely – such as the London Female Guardian Society, whose president, Lord Kinnaird, announced that the institution offered 'love and sympathy combined with useful domestic training' and not 'the severe lines of the old reformatory system'.[50] In that respect, at least, the compassionate society had arrived.

IV

Parallel with the greater protection afforded to vulnerable females, parliament also sought to rectify inequalities in women's financial status. Historically, it had been the case that an unmarried wealthy woman could spend as she liked. However, the moment she acquired a husband she had lost that right without, presumably, losing the financial acumen and judgment exercised without him. This notion, called coverture, had existed in English law since the thirteenth century. It specified that a married woman was under the protection, and also the influence, of her husband.

The only exception was a queen – regnant or consort. The movement to allow married women to own property had, in the Anglo-Saxon world, begun in America, when Mississippi legalised it in 1839. By 1865 twenty-nine American states had such laws. This gave great momentum to the movement to empower women economically in England.

By the 1860s women were seeking a legal identity distinct from their husbands'. The main impetus behind the lobbying for this right had started with Emily Davies, a feminist who would become co-founder and mistress of Girton College, Cambridge.[51] In 1865–6 she formed the Kensington Society, a group of like-minded women who met in that London suburb, and would become strong advocates of women's suffrage. Having a legal identity of their own did not just mean women could own property. It also meant they could make their own wills and dispose of their own chattels; but also that they were liable for their own debts, and could sue or be sued. In 1870 an Act of Gladstone's first ministry, which acted in response to submissions from the Kensington Society, allowed a woman to keep any money she earned (hitherto it had automatically become her husband's) and to keep any property she acquired using those earnings. Also, the 1870 Act stopped a man's creditors from taking his wife's property to settle his debts. A Bill of 1882 proposed to allow her the right to all her property, however acquired: because of the limited number of women in well-paid employment, acquisition had usually been by inheritance. It also specified that she could go bankrupt separately from her husband, and allowed her the right to enter into her own contracts. This was not that revolutionary: the Commons had passed a similar measure the previous year that solely affected Scotland.

A Commons select committee deliberated during 1881; and in February 1882 the House of Lords brought in the Bill. Because of the turbulence in Ireland the legislation passed almost unnoticed in the press. When it came before the Commons in committee on 11 August one MP, Sir George Campbell, announced he was determined, at last, that the Bill should be properly discussed. 'It created a social revolution that affected almost every family in this country,' he said, 'and was being passed through the House without one man or woman in a million having any idea what was being done.'[52] There was little sympathy for his view that women were riding roughshod over men, or for his assertion that 'the case of the poor married man was hopeless.' The Bill was quickly passed into law: and if, as Campbell said, few understood its provisions before enactment, plenty understood when it was in force. At last, a married woman could have not just her own legal identity, but her own property.

George Gissing, a few years later, felt the Act of sufficient significance that he could mention it in his novel *New Grub Street*:

> 'But is it her own?' asked Mrs Yule. 'Is it for her separate use?'
>
> 'Of course it is. She gets the benefit of last year's Married Woman's Property Act . . .'
>
> 'What a splendid Act of Parliament that is!' cried Amy. 'The only one worth anything that I ever heard of.'[53]

There was further legislation in the late nineteenth century that expanded women's rights. They were allowed custody of children under sixteen by an Act of 1873; after 1886 a woman could be her children's guardian without her husband's consent, or could appoint other guardians; and courts could take children from a father's custody if that would be better for them. Most significant, after 1895 a woman could seek a judicial separation and maintenance if her husband assaulted her: though the assumption of the Divorce Law of 1857, which held it that an adulterous woman had engaged in a premeditated act whereas a man had committed it accidentally, stayed unchallenged. The achievement of true equality was still some way off.

V

It was, inevitably, middle- and upper-class women who benefited most from the social reforms of the late nineteenth century. Now they could enjoy greater control of their own money, greater control over the welfare of their children and – in extremis – greater control of their marriages. Perhaps most crucially, many girls' schools were also founded in this period, laying the foundation of greater female participation in higher education, public life and the professions in the twentieth century, and forcing society to recognise that a female had as much right to be educated and to have her mind trained as did a man. Initially, the main beneficiaries of these schools were middle- and lower-middle-class girls, but in the twentieth century their legacy would be to accommodate in secondary education girls from other backgrounds and to act, as boys' grammar schools long had, as engines of social mobility.

Women also benefited from more general changes in society, in particular the gradually falling size of families. Until the mid-nineteenth century nature had been an effective contraceptive, the prevalence of smallpox, cholera and other diseases often ensuring that several children in each family died before maturity. The perilous nature of childbirth had also had a devastating impact on survival rates. Even so, large families had tended to be the rule. Queen Victoria, for example, bore nine children, all of whom reached adulthood. In the fifty years before the Great War, however, the birth rate fell. Marriages in the late 1860s that had lasted twenty years or more produced 6.16 children. By 1915 this had fallen to 2.43.[54] At the same time, the spread of birth control had a marked impact. Condoms had been used since the early seventeenth century, the earliest devices being made either from linen or animal intestines; but the discovery by Thomas Hancock and, simultaneously in America, Charles Goodyear of how to vulcanise rubber (both took out their respective patents in 1844) allowed the development of condoms from the material. These were produced from 1855.

Various forces militated against their immediate and widespread adoption. The Church and the medical profession both publicly deplored contraception. As with the campaigns to tackle child prostitution or to repeal the Contagious Diseases Acts, there was a cultural determination to brush sexual questions under the carpet. Any attempt to air such matters could provoke a trial for obscenity. The dissemination of information about birth control was therefore inevitably restricted. Nevertheless, when Charles Bradlaugh and Annie Besant were prosecuted for publishing Charles Knowlton's *The Fruits of Philosophy, or the Private Companion of Young Married People* in 1877, George Drysdale, a utilitarian, and his brother, Dr Charles Drysdale, founded the Malthusian League to promote the limitation of the size of families. The League took its name from the eighteenth-century cleric Thomas 'Misery' Malthus, who predicted that a rise in the population, unless checked, would result in too little food to feed everyone. It called for a programme of education about birth control, and also sought to decriminalise advocating it and providing information about it. It had become clear during Bradlaugh's and Mrs Besant's trial that there was huge public interest in the subject, not out of prurience but out of a desperate desire to stop repeated pregnancies.

The League had one major flaw: the problem it sought to address was prevalent mostly among the poorer classes, but it alienated them by a doctrinaire opposition to socialism. It contradicted socialist ideas that poverty was the result of exploitation by the forces of capital, arguing instead that it was caused solely by overpopulation. It therefore lost the sympathy of the working classes, remaining little more than a middle-class discussion group. Not until after the Great War, in the age of Marie Stopes, would clinics for birth control open in the working-class areas where they were most needed; the prejudice against them was overwhelming. Gladstone called it the 'saddest and most sickening of subjects'.[55]

In November 1887 H. Arthur Allbutt, a Leeds doctor and member of the Malthusian League, who had tried since the 1850s to advocate contraception, was struck off the Medical Register for publishing a cheap edition of *The Wife's Handbook*. He was pursued after the *British Medical Journal* had attacked him, saying 'he might have ventilated his views without let or hindrance from professional authority had he been content to address them to medical men instead of the public.'[56] Their main objection to the book – which outlined the main methods of contraception – was that it was so cheap and therefore readily available to the poor. If one searched for an epitome of Victorian hypocrisy, one would struggle to find one more impressive than this. Allbutt's book went through forty-five editions by 1913, so the attempt to muzzle him failed spectacularly. Its impressive sales, and the evidence of the shrinking size of middle-class families, may well suggest that whatever access to contraception the working class had, among their immediate betters it was becoming widely adopted.

Among these classes there was, however, no decline in enthusiasm for the institution of marriage. Wells was distinctly in a minority when he wrote in 1902 that 'the institution of permanent monogamous marriage . . . is sustained at present entirely by the inertia of custom, and by a number of sentimental and practical considerations'.[57] This too was breathtakingly hypocritical, given that he himself was married – indeed, he enjoyed marriage so much that when he wrote this he was on his second wife. His dislike of the institution seems to have had more to do with the inconvenience it caused him as a philanderer. For the wider middle class, marriage remained part of the bedrock of society and of the national culture, and a cornerstone of those values that defined conventional morality.

Although male bigotry closed off many trades and professions to Victorian and Edwardian women, their role as mothers, became, if anything, enhanced. Indeed the drive towards middle-class values, based on Christian principles and the regularity of family life, entrenched what became understood as Victorian morality, and vice versa. It was in this climate of propriety that, in 1876, Mary Sumner, the wife of a Hampshire clergyman, founded the Mothers' Union. At the start the activities of this overtly Christian organisation were confined to the diocese of Winchester, where it brought together women of all classes to provide advice on bringing up families. Inevitably, given the leadership of the organisation, the values imparted to working-class women grateful for the help and support of the Union were middle-class ones. Mrs Sumner addressed churchwomen at Portsmouth in 1885 about how the mothers of Britain could help the nation. Her speech caused a sensation, with many women returning home and setting up branches of what soon became a national, and international, Christian organisation. By 1900 there were almost 170,000 members, and the Queen became patron on her Diamond Jubilee in 1897. When women had no political voice, and men were the main breadwinners, the Mothers' Union became an important means not merely of supporting motherhood, but of developing it on a middle-class model. That included the representation of childhood as a state of innocence, braced by the teachings of Christianity.

By the first decade of the new century the lot of women of all classes had improved, thanks not merely to the philanthropic action of women such as Mrs Sumner towards the less fortunate of their sisters, but also to the greater protection the law provided them, the greater opportunities for education and white-collar employment, and the right of women entitled to property to have it in their own names. They had also proved their fitness to participate in politics by their growing and successful role in local government, as voters and as councillors. But men still denied them the parliamentary franchise, and the growing indefensibility of this position would create one of the most profound and destructive tensions of the years before the Great War. It was not solely in the matter of the vote that equality was elusive. However, more women were realising that the attainment of all their rights – such as to work and be paid on the same basis as men, and in the same trades and professions – would never happen until members of their sex sat in parliament and helped make the laws. That was the next great battle, and it would shortly be joined with a ferocity that shocked the nation.

PART III

PUBLIC DEBATES, PUBLIC DOUBTS

CHAPTER 9

THE FUTURE

I

The third Salisbury administration, elected as Unionists in the summer of 1895, would be marked by tensions between those wishing to conserve the past and those wanting controlled change. Even the latter were divided about how to confront the future. Chamberlain, the new Colonial Secretary, was radical in a way another progressive, Balfour, Salisbury's nephew and Unionist leader in the Commons, was not. Chamberlain would come to advocate protectionism in trade on a scale not seen since before the repeal of the Corn Laws; Balfour's progressiveness was more paternalistic – as he had shown in Ireland – and he was, unlike Chamberlain, a man of innate caution. Salisbury himself, whose political creed had been set out before the public since his time as a regular writer for reviews in the 1860s, was a man imbued with a traditional Tory pessimism that saw barbarians at the gates, and his job as being to keep them at bay as best he could. His experience of his seven years in office – he departed at the time of Edward VII's Coronation in 1902 – would only confirm in his own mind that he was right, for he was a man who felt ever more profoundly ill at ease with the modern world that was developing, and one for whom, like many other politicians, the unforeseen difficulties of the Boer War seemed to be a portent of even graver challenges to come.

The Liberals entered opposition in 1895 subdued by a mixture of boredom and exhaustion: in the ten years they would spend there they would begin to undergo an ideological shift, from a party that prized the freedom of the individual above all to one that increasingly believed in the need for the state to intervene, to bring about a better society. Although Liberals claimed to be more concerned about social justice, and about having the country's growing prosperity shared more equally, they would continue to diverge from the burgeoning Labour movement, leaving the support of the working class more and more to the leadership of men such as Hardie and MacDonald.

'I suppose the scattered remnants of our routed army will have to put in an appearance next week,' Harcourt wrote to Spencer on 6 August 1895.[1] In contemplating 'the line of action', the Liberal leader in the Commons observed that it 'should be as nearly *in*-action as possible.' Before the Liberals could properly focus on the future, they would require a new sort of leadership – one that neither Rosebery, who would stand down the following year, nor Harcourt, who would succeed him for three futile years, would be able to provide. Elements of the Liberal party were also susceptible to some of the new academic thinking on the development of their political creed: notably from men such as Leonard Hobhouse, an Oxford classicist turned sociologist who propounded a corpus of ideas that became known as social liberalism. These ideas attracted Hobhouse's sister Emily, whose campaign to improve conditions for women and children in concentration camps during the Second Boer War had shamed the British government, but would also later on appeal to Asquith and Lloyd George, and lead to the development of basic welfare provision by the Liberals after 1906.

But if the governing classes were determined to stay in their privileged bubble, the people they ruled, by now predominantly literate and eagerly devouring newspapers, periodicals and cheap fiction, were fascinated by ideas of progress and change. The future was of immense concern to late Victorians and Edwardians. Politically, it offered huge opportunities (and responsibilities) because of the scope of British power and the extent of the Empire. Ideas of how Britain might change had also to take into account how to rule a large area of the world, with disparate peoples, not all of whom were willing participants in the imperial project. Technological advances – notably in electronics and communications, but also in motive power and the greater ease of travel this caused – stimulated the public imagination. The speed of change in the late nineteenth century left young people agog at the prospect of what might happen in their lifetime. Also, the population continued to boom: at the 1901 census there were 41,500,000 people in the United Kingdom, rising to 45,200,000 a decade later, and that in an age of emigration to the colonies and the predominantly white parts of the Empire.

The new century provoked great interest in futurology, with a sense of fear and hope about scientific developments, notably exploited in the fiction and essays of H. G. Wells. Concern for the future provoked interest in eugenics, and the idea that human perfection could be achieved by scientific means. And there were other speculations about things to come: the newly popular genre of science fiction imagined aliens arriving from another planet; the influx of foreigners from Europe, including Jewish victims of pogroms in Russia and political dissidents from other parts of the continent, created a more cosmopolitan London; and the idea developed of a German threat to Britain, potent among a nation more aware of its possible vulnerability after the less than straightforward success of the Second Boer War.

II

In *Anticipations*, his 1901 book of essays, H. G. Wells predicted the future. He had received a good scientific education, under T. H. Huxley at the Normal School of Science in Kensington, and by the late 1880s, in his mid-twenties, was teaching science at further education colleges. In the seven years before *Anticipations* he had published five hugely successful science-fiction novels, aimed at the newly-literate, lower-middle class whose origins were similar to his. Through those novels – *The Time Machine*, *The Island of Dr Moreau*, *The Invisible Man*, *The War of the Worlds* and *The First Men in the Moon* – he did more than any writer since Dickens – indeed, more than Dickens – to stimulate and mobilise the British public's imagination. These books had a profound effect on the literary world: Ford Madox Hueffer (later Ford) recalled that 'it did not take us long to recognise that here was genius', and Shaw called Wells 'a giant among pygmies'.[2] It was only natural that this titan should move from fiction to informed speculation and set himself up as a prophet. His huge and devoted public eagerly awaited his views.

Wells knew railways and roads would cause cities to expand, and that businesses based in London would, because of better communications, move to the provinces. Nonetheless, he foresaw a London of 20 million people within a century, plus a city covering much of east Lancashire and west Yorkshire, and a conurbation from Glasgow to Edinburgh. He envisaged the 'motor truck' transporting goods, penetrating areas where even the late-Victorian railway system did not run.[3] The 'hired or privately owned motor carriage' would move people, adding 'a fine sense of personal independence to all the small conveniences of first-class railway travel', eventually capable of a day's journey 'of three hundred miles or more'.[4] Wells imagined relays of men chauffeuring the passengers – a plentiful supply of domestic servants was assumed – and people, in time, sleeping on board their cars as on trains or boats.

He foresaw a private network of roads, because motor-omnibuses would be too slowed down by the horse-drawn traffic he imagined would continue. He did not predict planning regulations or the green belt, but otherwise foresaw much of what progress would bring: 'And dotted at every convenient position along the new roads, availing themselves no doubt whenever possible of the picturesque inns that the old coaching days have left us, will be wayside restaurants and tea houses, and motor and cycle stores and repair places.'[5] He deplored restrictive practices that tied telephone companies to the Post Office, realising how a cheap telephone service would help business boom. Many of Wells's predictions were right; but his idea that a network of tubes would carpet the country, down which parcels would travel at high speed, awaits building.

He envisaged changes in family life, too: more working women would mean fewer children, with many more marriages childless. Religious observance would wane, leading to a change in moral values. 'In the case of the unmarried mother who may be helped to hold her own, or may be holding her own in the world, where will the moral censor of the year 1950 find his congenial following to gather stones?'[6] He believed – with, as we shall see, much self-interest – that 'there must be a movement towards the relaxation of the marriage law and of divorce that will complicate status very confusingly.' Different laws would apply in different countries, a man being a bigamist in one jurisdiction but not in another. 'But this impending dissolution of a common standard of morals does not mean universal depravity,' he said. 'Each human being will, in the face of circumstances, work out his or her particular early training as his or her character determines.'[7]

Wells's speciality in his science fiction was imagining technological advances. One of the more remarkable passages in *Anticipations* seems to foresee the internet. He talks of a constantly updated global newspaper, the only limits upon which were the cost of typesetting down telegraphic lines. He also imagines that pictures will be transmitted by telegraph. By the late twentieth century that was routine; constant updating came with the digital revolution. He also had a sense that turbulence and conflict would come in the century ahead. 'I know', he wrote, 'of no case for the elective democratic government of modern States that cannot be knocked to pieces in five minutes.'[8] He felt the 'new democracy' after widespread manhood suffrage would cause a great war in which the opening stages would be 'a disorder of conflict between more or less equally matched masses of stupefied, scared and infuriated people'.[9]

He commented that: 'I have said nothing . . . of the coming invention of flying' – this was written nearly two years before the breakthrough by the Wright brothers.[10] 'I do not think it at all probable that aeronautics will ever come into play as a serious modification of transport and communication'. He predicted far more precise automatic weaponry, long-range shells, submarines and 'dirigible aerial devices that can fight'. He added: 'Long before the year AD 2000, and very probably before 1950, a successful aeroplane will have soared and come home safe and sound.'[11] He saw this would change warfare: 'Once the command of the air is obtained by one of the contending armies, the war must become a conflict between a seeing host and one that is blind.'[12] Wells, who disliked the class system, relished the growing technological sophistication of warfare, predicting it would end the traditional British officer class – 'the well-bred young gentlemen of means who are privileged to officer the British Army nowadays will be no more good at this sort of thing than they are at controversial theology or electrical engineering or anything else that demands a well-exercised brain'. When such people were dying in vast numbers in battle just over a decade later, Wells was more reticent.

In these writings he is excited by the future, but there is always a tension between optimism and fear. He has a schoolboy's excitement about technological progress, but worries about the growth in population already discernible after recent improvements to sanitation, higher disposable income and improved infant mortality figures. In another of his futurological works, *A Modern Utopia*, written in 1905, he refers with approval to Malthus's doctrine that 'a State whose population continues to increase in obedience to unchecked instinct, can progress only from bad to worse.'[13] Wells had his own struggles with unchecked instincts, as we shall see, and played his part in ensuring the population boom did not diminish. Yet he continued: 'From the view of human comfort and happiness, the increase in population that occurs at each advance in human security is the greatest evil of life.' He noted, in a tone that seems only to reflect ambivalence, that 'the way of Nature is for every species to increase nearly to its possible maximum of numbers, and then to improve through the pressure of that maximum against its limiting conditions by the crushing and killing of all the feebler individuals.'

One who read *Anticipations* with fascination was Winston Churchill, then a twenty-seven-year-old Unionist MP and already deeply concerned about changes in British society. He wrote to Wells, complaining only that the pace of change he predicted was unrealistic. Wells replied, on 19 November 1901, that Churchill's view was 'simply due to the difference in our social circumstances'.[14] He said if Churchill could go back to Blenheim in 1800 he would quickly feel at home; but if Wells went back to meet his four grandparents at the same time 'it's highly probable two could not read & that any of them would find me and that I would find them as alien as contemporary Chinese. I really do not think that your people who gather in great country houses realise the pace of change.'

In all Wells's futuristic writings there is a sense of ambivalence, not least because his optimism about the advances of the future clashes with his pessimism about the degenerative nature of what his generation called 'the race' or 'British stock' – something that had become apparent when so many young men were rejected as recruits for the Boer War. Churchill shared this fear, as to an extent did Shaw, from whom Wells was in other respects undergoing a divergence of opinion. For imperialists such as Churchill especially, it was clear that Britain could not remain an imperial power if the indigenous population was in such steep mental and physical decline that it was held in contempt by those over whom it professed to rule, and if it declined relative to its European rivals. However, a new scientific movement that would have unspeakable and far-reaching consequences was growing up to address their concerns.

III

Francis Galton coined the term 'eugenics' in 1883, in his book *Inquiries into Human Faculty and Its Development*. Its etymology includes the Greek words for 'good' and 'heredity'. Galton, a cousin of Charles Darwin, whose scientific training included the ignominy of leaving Cambridge in

1844 with the lowest rank of degree conferred after what seems to have been a nervous breakdown, would make invaluable contributions to scientific knowledge and establish himself as one of the nineteenth century's most gifted polymaths. After a successful period in the early 1850s as a tropical explorer in what is now Namibia, he helped to map that part of Africa. He also devised the first weather map, published in *The Times* in 1875, and his fascination with meteorology led to his discovering the workings of the anticyclone. In 1888 he provided the scientific rationale for fingerprinting as a means of definitively identifying suspects in criminal cases.

Before exploring eugenics he had collected statistics on his fellow human beings for decades, seeking evidence that genius was inherited: he published the first work on the subject, *Hereditary Genius*, in 1869. Darwin's *The Origin of Species*, published in 1859, set him on this course: a chapter in the book deals with breeding domestic animals, a field Galton developed obsessively over the next fifty years. Galton (and Darwin) had forebears among the 'Lunar Men' of Birmingham – the eighteenth-century society of intellectuals that included James Watt, Josiah Wedgwood and Joseph Priestley – and he believed such talents were passed down the generations. His research methods ranged from writing to the headmasters of public schools to ask for data about the age, height and weight of their pupils to making a note as he walked through London of what proportion of women he saw that struck him as attractive. Thanks to a huge inheritance from his banker father he could pursue his studies untroubled by financial concerns and, indeed, once he had led the development of eugenics to the point where it was a serious scientific concern, he was able to use part of his fortune to further the study. He founded the journal *Biometrika* in 1902, set up a Laboratory for National Eugenics and endowed a chair in eugenics at University College London.

For Galton the study became a political project as well as a scientific one. Eugenics would 'give the more suitable races or strains of blood a better chance of prevailing speedily over the less suitable'.[15] In that statement, though he was too naïve to see it, lay the seeds of controversy and, later, of something far more sinister. Galton's supporters say, with justification, that he took a positive view of eugenics, seeking to improve the human race. He chose scientifically rational means, such as funding research into the elimination of hereditary diseases; but also advocated some in questionable taste, such as offering tax incentives for intelligent men and women to marry one another and breed prodigiously (Galton, a descendant of Erasmus Darwin, and his wife Louisa, daughter of George Butler, the headmaster of Harrow, managed to have no children).

However, some of Galton's adherents took eugenics to its nadir under Nazism thirty years after his death in 1911: in their most appalling incarnation these ideas caused the murder of the mentally and physically handicapped to eliminate them from the breeding stock, and the idea of a 'master race' that would promote genocide. Some – including, as we shall see, people eminent in public life – called for the government to sterilise the weak and feeble-minded, to stop them from reproducing. Many eugenicists, without support from Galton, took the same attitude to the breeding of humans as the Kennel Club takes to the breeding of dogs: though the Kennel Club does not demand the extermination of mongrels. Fears were fed by the 1901 census that, partly it is thought because of the question's phrasing, found a 21.44 per cent increase in mental defectives in Britain since 1891. The question simply asked the householder to state whether a specified member of the household was '(1) Deaf and dumb (2) Blind (3) Lunatic or (4) Imbecile, feeble minded.' One can just imagine how many acts of domestic retribution were contained within those answers. In the previous decade the number had risen by just 3.23 per cent: even allowing for some mischief, the decline of the race seemed unstoppable.[16]

Even Galton could stray into territory exploited by fascists in the twentieth century. On 5 June 1873 *The Times* had published a letter from him, based as much on his experience as an explorer as on his study of heredity, in which he argued that the Chinese should be encouraged to emigrate *en masse* to Africa, because the 'industrious, order-loving Chinese' would 'multiply and their descendants supplant the inferior negro race'.[17] The latter he characterised as 'lazy, palavering savages', despite 'notorious instances of negroes possessing high intelligence and culture, some of whom acquire large fortunes in commerce, and others become considerable men in other walks of life.' However, such paragons were 'much more exceptional in the negro than in the Anglo-Saxon race', and 'average negroes possess too little intellect, self-reliance and self-control to make it possible for them to sustain the burden of any respectable form of civilisation without a large measure of external guidance and support.' Yet he felt 'the Chinaman' was enduring a 'temporary dark age', with individuals 'cowed' by an 'effete' education system, but had proved wherever he went their capacity to compete and thrive. Best of all, 'they give no trouble to their rulers so long as they are allowed to manage [internal government] by themselves.'

Galton used his admiration for the 'Chinaman' to compare him with other races. 'The Hindoo . . . is inferior to him in strength, industry, aptitude for saving, business habits and prolific power', he wrote. As for the Arab, he was 'little more than an eater-up of other men's produce . . . a destroyer rather than a creator'. Inevitably, Galton's plans were attacked, though the main line of opposition was not to discount his racial theories but to point out that the Chinese government opposed such foreign adventures.

The Eugenics Education Society was founded in 1907, with Galton as honorary president. Its aims included lobbying for a campaign of sterilisation and restrictions on marriage among the weak, to prevent their reproducing. The following year Sir James Crichton-Browne, an eminent psychiatrist who rejoiced in the title of the Lord Chancellor's Visitor in Lunacy (it was his job to examine those of doubtful sanity who came before the Chancery Courts), gave evidence to the Royal Commission on the Care and Control of the Feeble-Minded, and recommended compulsory sterilisation of the mentally ill and the hard of understanding. He termed them 'social rubbish' who should be 'swept up and garnered and utilised as far as possible.'[18]

From 1909 the Eugenics Education Society published the *Eugenics Review*; and in July 1912 under its auspices the First International Congress of Eugenics was held in London. One of the star turns was Major Leonard Darwin, son of the evolutionist, who would lobby the government to establish a force of scientists to comb Britain looking for the unfit: those so identified should then be segregated into colonies with others like them, or sterilised. Winston Churchill, then First Lord of the Admiralty, was among the 400 who attended, as was Balfour. Two years earlier Churchill had sent a memorandum to Asquith in which he had warned 'the multiplication of the unfit is a very terrible danger to the race.'[19] Sidney Webb, Shaw and Wells were among others to embrace eugenics before 1914; G. K. Chesterton was an early opponent, though his own denunciation of the science, *Eugenics and Other Evils*, did not appear until 1917. It was not until 1930 that the Catholic church, in Pius XI's encyclical *Casti Connubii*, condemned laws passed by various countries to enforce eugenic practices.

In 1912 a private member's Bill on 'control of the feeble-minded' was introduced in the House of Commons, inspired directly by the work of the eugenics movement and by the findings of the Royal Commission, which had a strong eugenicist tinge to them. Although opposing sterilisation, the Bill did call for segregation of 'mental defectives', their compulsory registration and restrictions on their marrying, which led to its being attacked from the outset by Roman Catholics, notably Chesterton. The Bill was withdrawn and replaced by a government measure that became the 1913 Mental Deficiency Act, which allowed for the institutionalisation of tens of thousands whom the law deemed either a danger to themselves or others.

Marie Stopes, like Hitler another early convert, would soon win the antipathy of more than just the Catholic establishment for her eugenics-inspired campaign for birth control. Havelock Ellis, a doctor who had in 1897 published the first serious study of homosexuality (which, inevitably, violated the obscenity laws), and had married a lesbian, was among supporters of eugenics who openly called for sterilisation of the unfit, notably in his 1912 work *The Task of Social Hygiene*. The ethnologist Augustus Keane – a Roman Catholic – developed ideas of racial differences whose first impact was to encourage racial segregation in southern Africa. The consequences of eugenics would scar the twentieth century beyond the horrors perpetrated by the Nazis.[20]

So distressed was the government by the experience of recruiting (or, rather, failing to recruit) for the Boer War that in 1903 it set up an Inter-Departmental Committee on Physical Deterioration, which reported the following year. What they found seemed to justify the interest in eugenics as a means of improving the stock of humanity. In private schools boys aged eleven were on average five inches taller than boys in industrial schools – four feet seven inches against four feet two. Adults with the same background had an average height differential of three and a half inches.[21] The committee accepted that standards of living for the very poorest would have to be raised if their physical characteristics were to improve: this was further proof to social liberals of the sort who waited to take power when Balfour's administration fell, that state intervention and the application of welfarism were not just desirable, but essential.

The committee itself recommended intervention, at least through establishing a central office to accumulate data on the question, with teams of inspectors sent out on surprise visits to schools to check how the British race was, or was not, developing. It wanted a national 'anthropometric survey', whose findings would inform a new advisory council whose role would be 'to advise the Government on all legislative and administrative points in respect of which State interference in these matters was expedient.'[22] The committee certainly found areas in which only the interference of the state would be likely to make any difference: the overcrowding of people in insanitary conditions in industrial towns, for example, which the committee noted had been identified as a problem in London as long ago as 1598, when the suggestion had been made to punish slum landlords for renting out bad properties. While using different language the committee saw the continuity of the problem, and quoted the reformer Charles Booth in saying that 'crowding [is] the main cause of drink and vice.'[23]

The committee found that urbanisation, and the insanitary overcrowding that because of its unregulated state often came with it, also seemed to shorten life expectancy. In Finsbury, where 14,526 people lived in one-roomed tenements, the death rate in 1903 was 38.9 per 1,000, yet among those who lived in four-roomed tenements it was 5.6 per 1,000. Life expectancy in Hampstead at birth was 50.8 years against 36.5 years in Southwark. In the seven most overcrowded districts in recent years the infant mortality rate had risen from 142 per 1,000, which had been bad enough, to 223 per 1,000, though the committee felt this had much to do with the decline in breastfeeding as well as with women doing heavy work in the late stages of pregnancy – not least because they had either been deserted by their husbands, or their husbands had died or were unfit for work.[24] The report called the housing conditions 'a grave menace to the community' and said the time had come for 'dealing drastically' with it, by local authorities closing down tenements that were deemed particularly insanitary. Parental ignorance and neglect were rife, however, and there was still much evidence of the adulteration of food and the toxic nature of milk, which also contributed to infant mortality.

A factories inspector noted that 'the poorest specimens of humanity I have ever seen, both men and women, are working in the preparing and spinning departments of certain Dundee jute mills', specimens who lived mainly in one- or two-roomed tenements and shared a single lavatory with dozens of other families.[25] In Edinburgh numerous families with seven, eight or nine children lived in one or two rooms each; in

Sheffield unpaved courts around tenements were 'saturated with filth' thanks to inadequate sewers, and 'the number of deformed people is something terrible'. In what will have struck a worrying chord with many at the time, the committee noted how much better things were done in Germany, and indeed how even the French had a superior law on public health. However, so long as pre-pubescent children, boys especially, were sent to work in strenuous occupations, in dusty, overheated factories, there would be lasting effects: 'the stunted child elongates slightly in time, but remains very thin, loses colour, the muscles remain small, especially those of the upper limbs, the legs are inclined to become bowed, more particularly if heavy weights have to be habitually carried, the arch of the foot flattens and the teeth decay rapidly.'[26]

Among its many recommendations, the committee suggested a network of crèches in which mothers could be properly educated about how to feed and bring up their children. It also advocated a system of health visitors. It recommended more games and physical education in schools, schooltime being the only opportunity the state had to police fully the lives of its children. It wanted girls taught cookery, hygiene and domestic science at school, the better to feed and care for their children later in life; and it wanted children fed at school to ensure they had a better diet. It was also from this report that the decision to restrict the sale of cigarettes and alcohol to children stemmed. The report discovered that syphilis was far more prevalent than had been imagined, and that far more systematic treatment of the disease was essential. The number of certified lunatics was also rising, which the committee believed to be partly attributable to the ubiquity of cheap alcohol. Given Britain's status as a pre-eminent economic power, such findings and recommendations were not merely embarrassing but humiliating: they intensified rather than alleviated the feeling of pessimism brought on by the end of the Boer War; and provoked the demands of reforming politicians, and the whole Labour movement, for change.

Such findings gave enormous ammunition to politicians and the politically active, especially those who saw the underclass and the poor as their main constituency. It was clear there were two options: either the state provided the impetus, through physical education in schools, economic reforms that helped improve nutrition and a form of health service that monitored the poorer classes, to encourage a healthier lifestyle and upbringing for the masses; or it took the illiberal steps some eugenicists were advocating, including sterilisation and segregation of the 'feeble-minded' so they could not breed. Most, but not all, leftist opinion took the former view.

The pessimism that seeped into British attitudes in the early twentieth century, not least after the near-disaster of the Boer War, caused some to advocate extreme solutions: but more Whiggish, or liberal, elements sought to provide for a future of greater enlightenment and opportunity. Wells too, in his fiction and his essays, advocates greater equality. But, despite his huge readership, his campaigns were a shadow of those launched by Shaw, his senior by ten years and his superior in literary expression if not in imagination. For Shaw, being a controversialist would sometimes trump ethical considerations. He also had a more practical understanding of how the constituency that mattered to them could best be helped and improved. As well as campaigning for his broadly socialist doctrine in his plays – at a time when hardly any socialists sat in parliament – Shaw wanted institutions to advance people outside existing elites by reform not revolution, in accordance with Fabian doctrine: hence his part in founding the London School of Economics. He did, however, appear to harbour some extreme, and unpalatable, views, a few of which may not have been entirely satirical.

Shaw's interest in eugenics was not for the purposes of scientific advancement, but explicitly because his vision of a socialist utopia could best, he thought, be obtained by eliminating the weak. Eugenicist doctrine, developed direct from Nietzsche rather than from Galton, partly underpins *Man and Superman*, first performed in 1903: and in the play, based loosely on the Don Juan myth, it suggests that the real power in humankind is the woman, who in Shaw's view finds an acceptable mate and forces him to marry her. It was regrettable, however, for Shaw's reputation that he should deploy irony in March 1910 when addressing the Eugenics Education Society. He said that to rid the world of those unfit to live, a 'lethal chamber' might need to be developed for their rapid dispatch; and that it would be as well to develop a 'humane' lethal gas for the efficient removal of these unfortunate people.

These shocking sentiments were meant as a rebuke to the Social Purity movement that had developed alongside the eugenicists, and at those eugenicists who wished to take the science to an extreme; sadly for Shaw, seen out of context and in cold print they do not transmit the savage wit he intended. He also teased this movement with plays such as *Mrs Warren's Profession*, whose subtext was that until women were paid properly and given equal opportunities with men they might as well become whores, and defied it by his own loose regard for sexual morality: his wife had refused to consummate their marriage, and Shaw, forty-one at the time, looked elsewhere for consolation.

But he was serious about eliminating 'bad breeding', and linked this to the accomplishment of the socialist future. In his *Revolutionist's Handbook*, an appendix to his preface to *Man and Superman* in 1903, Shaw says that 'equality is essential to good breeding; and equality, as all economists know, is incompatible with property.'[27] He also asserts that the mentally and physically defective should be encouraged to marry each other – 'Are we to try to correct our diseased stocks by infecting our healthy stocks with them? Clearly the attraction which disease has for diseased people is beneficial to the race. If two really unhealthy people get married they will, as likely as not, have a great number of children who will all die before they reach maturity. This is a far more satisfactory arrangement than the tragedy of a union between a healthy and an unhealthy person.'

Nearly 200 years earlier Dean Swift had suggested, in *A Modest Proposal*, that the Irish poor sell their children to the rich as food, to satirise Britain's treatment of Ireland and the attitudes of the rich towards the poor generally. If Shaw was not writing in the same vein – and we must presume he was – then he was advocating authoritarian barbarism. Yet it must be noted that when, in 1922, he wrote the preface to a book on prisons by the Webbs, he asked what the point was of imprisoning habitual criminals. 'Releasing them is like releasing the tigers from the Zoo to find their next meal in the nearest children's playing ground. The most obvious course is to kill them.'[28] He sets out the arguments against this, culminating with 'who is to be trusted with the appalling responsibility of deciding whether a man is to live or die?' and whether a government would not abuse the power by killing 'its enemies under the pretence that they are the enemies of society', only to answer: 'Such responsibilities must be taken, whether we are fit for them or not, if civilised society is to be organised.'[29] A terrible war had intervened by the time he wrote those words: but even before it, the sense of a nation falling behind socially and economically was all too pervasive.

IV

If the Boer War had shown the precariousness of Britain's imperial project, the economic realities at the turn of the century showed how increasingly unfit it was to maintain its place among the most powerful nations in Europe and the world. Britain was weak in the new industries – such as cars, chemicals, electrical goods and telecommunications – and so by 1900 was struggling to match the output of the United States and Germany. As well as being a nation of old staple industries, Britain had a productivity problem, because of a failure to invest in research and development and to train its workforce properly – criticisms that would echo throughout the twentieth century. Simple figures show the extent of the decline: between 1880 and 1910 pig iron production in Britain rose from 7.8 million to 10.1 million tons. In Germany it rose from 2.5 million to 13 million tons. Consumption displaced investment, with the well-to-do spending more of their dividends on themselves instead of on their businesses, when real incomes for their workers remained static. As we shall see, this led to disastrous industrial relations well before 1914; but it was also indicative of a decadence that bred complacency about Britain's future, and its place in the world. It also had a bad effect on productivity, which fell steadily behind Germany's because of greater German investment in plant and new processes. The growing might of Germany worried the public; it was also reflected in the toxic personal relations between Edward VII and his nephew, Kaiser Wilhelm II, which became especially bad once Queen Victoria was no longer around to referee their squabbles.

Wells led the vogue for predicting an aggressive, threatening Germany, its powerhouse as much 'the most efficient middle class in the world' as its militaristic culture and the 'martinet methods of the Prussian monarchy'.[30] He added that 'the habits and traditions of victory . . . may prove in the end a very doubtful blessing to Europe as a whole'. He feared the Kaiser's near-autocracy, whose oppressive nature 'must finally be bad for the intellectual atmosphere which is Germany's strength'.[31] He regretted that 'His Imperial Majesty's disposition to regard criticism as hostility stifles the public thought of Germany', and was nearer the mark when reflecting that 'a very easily imagined series of accidents may place the destinies of Germany in such lazy tongs again.'[32]

He believed the future of Europe would be dominated by the desire for 'a greater Germany', writing that 'before Germany can unify to the East she must fight the Russian, and to unify to the West she must fight the French and perhaps the English, and she may have to fight a combination of these powers'.[33] This was two years before the Entente Cordiale and six before the Triple Entente between Britain, France and Russia that caused the Kaiser to complain of encirclement.[34] The threat to peace would, Wells felt, be removed if French were the common language of Europe, and English the common tongue of the rest of the world. That achieved, the world would before long become 'a Republic that must ultimately become a World State of capable rational men'.[35] And although Wells did not use the phrase, his world state would be a welfare state in which 'the State will . . . be the reserve guardian of all children'.[36] He specified: 'If they are being undernourished, if their education is being neglected, the State will step in, take over the responsibility of their management, and enforce their charge upon the parents.'

Ernest Williams, like Wells a Fabian, had drawn attention to the way in which Germany was pulling ahead of Britain in his book *Made in Germany*, published in 1896, and a collection of articles he had written for the *New Review*. Unfashionably, Williams had argued for protectionism, and an imperial tariff union of the sort that would be championed by Joe Chamberlain: he had also pointed out that Germany was forging ahead in iron, steel, shipbuilding, textiles, and chemicals, rendering British industrial supremacy 'a myth'.[37] He pointed out to his readers the saturation of their lives by German products:

> You will find that the material of some of your own clothes was probably woven in Germany. Still more probable is it that some of your wife's garments are German importations; while it is practically beyond a doubt that the magnificent mantles and jackets wherein her maids array themselves on their Sundays out are German-made and German-sold, for only so could they be done at the figure. Your governess's fiancé is a clerk in the City; but he also was made in Germany. The toys, and the dolls, and the fairy books which your children maltreat in the nursery are made in Germany: nay, the material of your favourite (patriotic) newspaper had the same birthplace as like as not. Roam the house over, and the fateful

> mark will greet you at every turn, from the piano in your drawing-room to the mug on your kitchen dresser, blazoned though it be with the legend, *A Present from Margate* . . . At midnight your wife comes home from an opera which was made in Germany, has been here enacted by singers and conductor and players made in Germany, with the aid of instruments and sheets of music made in Germany. You go to bed, and glare wrathfully at a text on the wall; it is illuminated with an English village church, and it was 'Printed in Germany'.[38]

British politicians understood that German economic expansion would lead to more armaments, and an increased threat to British supremacy. With this in view, one of the dying acts of the Balfour government, on 2 October 1905, was to lay down HMS *Dreadnought*, the first of a class of battleship that would help Britain maintain command of the ocean. It was launched on 10 February 1906, and commissioned on 2 December that year. When Balfour had the comparative leisure of opposition he returned to writing philosophy, including delivering the Henry Sidgwick Memorial Lecture at Cambridge in January 1908 on the subject 'Decadence'. In common with other classically-educated politicians and intellectuals of the time, Balfour understood how decadence had destroyed Roman power, and mused on whether it was an inevitable stage in the evolution of the British state.

'The decadence respecting which I wish to put questions', he said, 'is not literary or artistic, it is political and national. It is the decadence which attacks, or is alleged to attack, great communities and historic civilisations: which is to societies of men what senility is to man, and is often, like senility, the precursor and the cause of final dissolution.'[39] Balfour, seeing both sides of the story as always – one of his great failings as a political leader – professed optimism, after much discussion, that this would not happen to Britain, and that civilisation showed 'no symptoms either of pause or of regression in the onward movement which for more than a thousand years has been characteristic of Western civilisation.'[40] Less rational beings were not so sure.

The new super-powerful fleet of Dreadnoughts calmed the anxieties of a public that was constantly told how Germany would overrun Britain and sequester its empire. Rudyard Kipling, at the height of his fame, had used his poem of 1902 'The Rowers' to insult the Kaiser and the Germans as 'Huns', after a speech Wilhelm II had made in 1900 about how he hoped German soldiers would deal with Chinese recalcitrants in the Boxer Rebellion. Later, Kipling told *Le Figaro* that Britain and France must ally against the German menace. In Edwardian Britain both cultural and political forces allied to stoke British suspicions of Germany, helping create a climate of opinion that made Britain's entry into the war in August 1914 that much easier.

Erskine Childers, a Boer War veteran, stoked fears in 1903 in his hugely popular spy novel *The Riddle of the Sands*. In it, a minor Foreign Office official sailing in the Frisian Islands rumbles a German plot to move a massive army by stealth to the east coast of England. The plot is thwarted: but the sensation the novel caused triggered a debate on British preparedness for a German attack, feeding a public outcry that forced the expansion of the Navy, the building of more naval bases on the east coast, and the development of the Dreadnought.

In the House of Lords in 1906 Field Marshal Earl Roberts caused widespread alarm when he condemned under-investment in the Armed Forces. Roberts, a great popular hero of the day, had been advanced to his earldom and given a grant of £100,000 in 1900, having offered his services at a bad stage in the Boer War and helped turn the tide in South Africa. He also became commander-in-chief of the Army and president of the National Service League, a notably Tory body that wanted compulsory military training and which, from 1906, goaded the Liberal government about its lack of seriousness in defending the nation.

The field marshal told the Lords on 10 July of that year of the 'unpreparedness of the nation for war' and that 'no military system could be considered satisfactory which did not contain powers of expansion outside the limit of the regular forces of the Crown, whatever that limit might be.'[41] This required a proper Army reserve, a body of trained men able to move into the front line at a moment's notice. He referred to the policy, prevailing since the early 1880s, that the Royal Navy could hold the Empire, which was why the service had expanded: Roberts told the House that 'our sea power was not won altogether upon the sea, and . . . it cannot be maintained solely by the Navy.' Roberts also argued that in the last great continental struggle, against Napoleon, Britain won only because of help from its allies: and such militarily powerful allies were scarce ninety years on. Nor could he see why, when the population of Britain had almost trebled since the Napoleonic era, the number of men under arms was nearly the same as it was then: 600,000.

He identified Germany – the great ally in 1815 – as the potential enemy, and one that enjoyed a military preponderance. And Germany was now such a commercial rival that it could help Britain against a third party only by diluting its own competitive position. Roberts was right that 'history tells us in the plainest terms that an Empire which cannot defend its own possession must inevitably perish.'[42] His economics, though, were askew. As the Great War would show, Germany's hard-won economic supremacy would end if it took on an adversary – and an investor – so powerful as Britain. But in the spy mania of mid-Edwardian Britain, such details were lost as every propaganda tool was used to press politicians to rebuild the Army. If the effect was to create suspicion, fear or downright loathing of the Germans, so be it.

However, the government erred in having the under-secretary for war, Lord Portsmouth, belittle Roberts's arguments. He claimed Roberts had withdrawn a condemnation of the Army made the previous year – which Roberts, to Portsmouth's astonishment, said he had not. He professed not to know what would constitute a national emergency, which was simply hair-splitting; and said Britain could not afford £1,275,000 for 8,500 men of warrant-officer rank to train the 340,000 medically fit youths who attained the age of twenty each year. It was just that cheese-paring attitude to national defence that boosted the arguments of Roberts and his associates. Portsmouth was on stronger ground when he spoke of Liberal opposition to conscription: especially since the threat to Britain and her empire was then largely in the financially inspired imaginations of men such as Lord Northcliffe, the Teuton-loathing proprietor of the *Daily Mail*, who had spotted a means of allying his commercial imperatives with his hatred of Germans.

Fantasies about a German invasion were part of the debate about spending priorities under the Balfour and Campbell-Bannerman governments. The most foaming, William Le Queux's novel *The Invasion of 1910*, was written in 1906 and serialised in the *Daily Mail*: Le Queux was a lackey of Northcliffe. In the novel, the result of inadequate defences, notably at sea, is that the Germans land one early September night at Great Yarmouth and Lowestoft. They set up a headquarters at Beccles (many towns were named in their advance, the order having gone out from Northcliffe that the fictional forces should 'not keep to remote one-eyed country villages where there was no possibility of large *Daily Mail* sales') and move south and west and eventually besiege London.'[43]

In Le Queux's book the Germans invade because the Navy is surprised, and the want of a decent army is most keenly felt.[44] Roberts, foolish enough to assist a sensationalist such as Le Queux, helped him plan his novel and allowed his name and his speeches to be cited in the book. Le Queux had worked for the Harmsworth press from its earliest incarnation. He was a fantasist and self-publicist who claimed to have had an exotic private education and to have been urged by Emile Zola to write novels. In the 1890s he had written bodice-rippers and pot-boilers. In 1897 he had, at Harmsworth's bidding, written a novel about the French invading England; to order, the invader had changed. Three years after *The Invasion of 1910* he wrote a spy story about the Germans that had readers sending him details of spies they thought operated near them. Le Queux passed the letters to the government, whose response was to found the Secret Service Bureau, which became MI5 and MI6.

Le Queux enlisted Herbert Wrigley Wilson, a naval expert, to write passages in *The Invasion of 1910* about naval warfare; and Wilson, having described a humiliation for the fleet in the Firth of Forth, thundered: 'The real criminals were the British ministers, who neglected precautions, permitted the British fleet to be surprised, and compelled the British Admiral to play the most hazardous of games while they had left the coast without torpedo stations, and without any military force capable of resisting an invading army.'[45]

However, the book blames democracy for the shortcomings of national defence. 'It was the cry of the people and the politicians for all manner of "reforms" at the expense of national security; the demand for old-age pensions, for feeding children, for State work at preposterous wages for the work-shy; the general selfishness asked everything of the State and refused to make the smallest sacrifice for it.'

The thesis chimed with Northcliffe's belief in the evil intentions of the Germans. The serialisation, and the book, were immensely popular; yet Northcliffe would, with a straight face, tell Churchill in 1911 that 'my newspapers have never been provocative about Germany. Germany resents my printing the facts about her forces and intentions.'[46]

Churchill had met the Kaiser a few weeks earlier. He told his wife that 'he did not think France would ever fight him unless egged on and supported by us and our press. He particularly mentioned Harmsworth and the *Daily Mail* . . . as being most hostile to Germany and doing much harm.'[47] The book the *Mail* serialised did not, however, spare Northcliffe's trade in apportioning blame for the decadent approach to national security: it savaged 'the degenerate slackness of the Public and the Press, who refused to concern themselves with these tremendous interests, and riveted all their attention upon the trivialities of the football and cricket field'. Britain, with its hero-worship of Jack Hobbs and C. B. Fry, was portrayed as no longer a serious nation.

In the end, Le Queux has the Germans massacred after bombarding London, and driven back across the North Sea: but the victory is pyrrhic. Britain is almost bankrupted; the nation rises up and almost literally throws the Germans out, prevailing without an organised and trained army. The Germans, as part of their expansionism, occupy and annex Denmark and Holland (which would not happen in 1914, but would in 1940). They have left the British Empire intact only in name; the mother country's weakness has been proved. Le Queux sermonises that 'socialism, with its creed of "Thou shalt have no other god but Thyself", and its doctrine "Let us eat and drink, for tomorrow we die" had replaced the religious beliefs of a generation of Englishmen taught to suffer and to die sooner than surrender to wrong.'[48]

Such want of subtlety prevented the more intelligent reader from taking such work seriously. The rash of invasion novels continued until war came as if from nowhere. Wells, recalling his speculations in *Anticipations*, had the Germans as invaders in his 1908 novel *The War in the Air*. He too showed a Britain ill-equipped to fight and peopled by weaklings. As futurology it was off-beam, though, since the war it described, fought largely by aircraft, was more like Hitler's war than the Kaiser's. P. G. Wodehouse also jumped on the bandwagon with *The Swoop! Or How Clarence Saved England*, which allowed him in 1909 not only to satirise invasion novels but also the Boy Scout movement: Clarence, who saves the nation single-handedly, is, inevitably, a fourteen-year-old scout.

Saki's 1913 novella *When William Came*, subtitled *A Story of London under the Hohenzollerns*, was a far more sophisticated exercise. The action begins after Germany has annexed Britain, following a short war triggered by a border dispute in east Africa. The scene is a West End drawing room, where caviar and crab are being served for lunch. A character lists the reasons for defeat, reasons that had echoed through Commons debates for the preceding decade. 'Our ships were not able to cope with their ships plus their superiority in aircraft . . . our half-trained men and our untrained men could not master the science of war at a moment's notice, and a moment's notice was all they got. The enemy were a nation apprenticed in arms, we were not even the idle apprentice: we had not deemed apprenticeship worth our while.'[49]

Saki was the *nom de guerre* of Hector Munro, who would enlist over-age in the ranks and die in November 1916 on the Somme, just before his forty-sixth birthday. A visceral Tory, he makes a political point in the book ('the Liberals naturally are under the blackest of clouds', and the socialists' attempt to establish 'universal brotherhood . . . did not blunt a single Teuton bayonet'), but is also careful to emphasise that 'in a democracy such as ours the Government of the day must more or less reflect the ideas and temperament of the nation in all vital matters, and the British nation in those days could not have been persuaded of the urgent need for military apprenticeship or of the deadly nature of its danger.'[50]

A future under German rule was hopeless: 'The conquerors have to count on time and tact to weaken and finally obliterate the old feelings of nationality; the middle-aged of today will grow old and acquiescent in the changed state of things; the young generations will grow up never having known anything different.'[51] At the very end there is a hint that the young of Britain refuse to accept their fate; but there is plenty of evidence that even those opposed to German rule had learned to stomach the conqueror, while those for whom it was unbearable had gone to the colonies. However, with Britain humbled, it is far from certain how long the imperial future envisaged by Seeley and his pupils would last, and how long it would be before other vultures picked at the corpse.

Saki is vicious towards his own class, not only for their having fostered the decadence that brought Britain down, but for their refusal to mobilise, to lead the country against the Germans. The parties, balls and entertainments that continue regardless, and the willingness with which the ruling class have fled abroad, taking their money with them, signify the inertia. His vision of the future is unpleasantly laced with snobbery ('Tony Luton was a young man who had sprung from the people, and had taken care that there should be no recoil') and anti-Semitism, also a staple of Munro's cousin Dornford Yates.[52] 'London', one of the characters says, 'has taken on some of the aspects of a No-Man's-Land, and the Jew, if he likes, may almost consider himself as of the dominant race; at any rate he is ubiquitous.'[53]

Upper-class decadence alone is not to blame for Britain's plight. The enfranchised lower orders 'had to choose between the vote-mongers and the so-called "scare-mongers", and their verdict was ' "for the vote-mongers all the time".'[54] This over-simplifies the spending battle between a proto-welfare state and a properly defended state that happened before 1914, but reflects attitudes towards Lloyd George's 'People's Budget' of 1909 (discussed in Chapter 15). Saki sees collaboration as coming naturally to an idle upper class whose only concern is their personal comfort; and to those whose origins were in 'the Jordan Valley', whose loyalty he sees as easily transferrable, and who will miss no opportunity for social advancement.[55] Clubland is now the province of 'Hebraic-looking gentlemen, wearing tartan waistcoats of the clans of their adoption.'[56]

Saki's future view is not merely one where failure to spend on defence brings down a nation; it is one in which that fall demoralises the masses and allows cynical groups nearer the top to advance through collaboration, something impossible under the old order. His innate, pessimistic Toryism dominates this work as it does all his writings; its biliousness may be fed by various prejudices, but was motivated by his sense of a Britain asleep, which would by invasion be finally emasculated. While those with a vivid imagination such as Wells, or with a utopian vision such as Shaw, argued for a future constructed to their blueprints, those across the political divide became more like Saki, and in the increasing depths of their pessimism doubted there would be any independent future at all. The pessimism was overdone, but it would better reflect the true temper of the mythically golden years before the Great War.

CHAPTER 10

NOSTALGIA

I

Change and its possibilities excited the Victorians: but it came so fast that it also caused uncertainty, and, among many, a desire to cling to a vanishing past. The railway brought ease of travel; suburbia brought better housing; the penny post and the telephone improved communication; the steel-framed building enabled construction on a larger scale; free trade had brought greater and broader prosperity; school places had encouraged aspiration and improved Britain's ability to compete through a more skilled workforce. However, by the mid-1890s the speed of such radical change was perplexing and, to many, unsettling: and there was a new longing for the comfort of the familiar; and it was exacerbated after the Boer War had shaken the national sense of self-confidence. Nor was change confined to the material. Manners and human relations were different from a generation earlier, notably between the sexes, but also in challenges by the working class to landlords and employers. Technological change was alarming to some: by 1900 motor-cars were a familiar sight on the expanding network of metalled roads, shocking pedestrians and the horse-drawn traffic.

Among designers, writers and thinkers a wave of nostalgia, the inevitable response to seismic change in a country that had evolved slowly for centuries, became prevalent and, in some quarters, even an obsession. At this time the word itself – coined in the eighteenth century to describe a medical condition akin to homesickness – started to be used in the sense the *Oxford English Dictionary* defines as 'sentimental longing for or regretful memory of a period of the past, especially in one's own lifetime; [also] sentimental imagining or evocation of the past.' An overriding determination grew up to record what might disappear, if it were impossible to prevent its disappearance. However, the late Victorians and Edwardians also tried to entrench the past wherever possible, to cling on to a vanishing world.

The national past and its culture were institutionalised to capture the essence of British life and celebrate its achievements in a way that would survive change and the passage of time. This was the era of the compilation of the *New English Dictionary*, which became the *Oxford English Dictionary*; and of attempts to settle English grammar by scholars such as the Fowler brothers and Charles Talbot Onions, all of whom were involved with the dictionary project. Great British lives were recorded in the *Dictionary of National Biography*, behind which the initial driving force was Leslie Stephen, father of Virginia Woolf. The *Cambridge History* appeared between 1897 and 1911, and popular children's fiction of the time, whether in *The Boy's Own Paper* or Henty's novels, took tales of English historical glory as a main theme. In 1897 the National Gallery of British Art, later named after its main patron Sir Henry Tate, the sugar magnate, opened in London, with Sir Henry's collection of British Victorian art forming its kernel. Britain's culture was now widely recognised as demanding preservation, in keeping with the country's new idea of itself; and two years later Queen Victoria made her final public appearance to lay the foundation stone of a magnificent new building constructed to house what had been the South Kensington Museum but which, on that day, was renamed the Victoria and Albert, which would showcase British design and artefacts from previous centuries. Britain had always taken the classical past seriously, as shown in the galleries of the British Museum: now it was taking its own seriously too.

II

Cities were changing out of recognition, and larger towns too. Around 700,000 people moved into the new suburbs of London between the 1901 and 1911 censuses. When in the early 1880s Hilda Lessways, heroine of Bennett's *Clayhanger* novels, visits Hornsey in north London, she sees 'the longest street that she had ever seen. On her left were ten thousand small new houses, all alike. On her right were broken patches of similar houses, interspersed with fragments of green field and views of the arches of the railway.'[1] Bennett wrote that 'even in 1880 the descent upon London from the suburbs was a formidable phenomenon'. At a suburban station 'a dark torrent of human beings, chiefly men, gathered out of all the streets of the vicinity, had dashed unceasingly into the enclosure and covered the long platforms with tramping feet. Every few minutes a train rolled in, as if from some inexhaustible magazine of trains beyond the horizon, and, sucking itself into a multitude and departing again, left one platform for one moment empty, – and the next moment the platform was once more filled by the quenchless stream . . .'[2] According to *The Buildings of England*, in Hornsey, 'until the mid C19 there was only a small village centre along the High Street, a hamlet at Crouch End to its SW, scattered farms and villas, a few large houses'.[3] In 1850 the railways came and the building started: first houses, then shops, pubs, schools and churches. Of the medieval church only the tower survived, and of the old big houses none survives. Sold for development in the 1860s, their grounds soon housed vast Victorian terraces built by developers such as the British Land Company and the Birkbeck Freehold Land Company.

Wells, writing in 1910, recalled in his semi-autobiographical novel *The New Machiavelli* how the relentless march of London's suburbia had consumed the countryside of north-west Kent he had known as a boy. The process had started around 1750, thanks to 'machinery, and a vague energetic disposition to improve material things'.[4] Unencumbered by laws on planning, villas for the well-to-do sprang up in fields. Slate replaced thatch. The railway came, bringing mass construction. 'This enterprising person and then that began to "run up" houses, irrespective of every other enterprising person who was doing the same thing . . . Weekly properties, that is to say small houses built by small property owners and let by the week, sprang up.'[5] Villages joined with their neighbours; land was annexed not merely for houses, but for cemeteries and sewage works. Recalling the water meadow in which he had played as a boy, Wells noted that 'after I was eleven . . . all the delight and beauty of it was destroyed.'[6] That, though, was only the beginning.

'Hard upon that came the pegs, the planks and carts of devastation. Roper's meadows, being no longer in fear of floods, were now to be slashed out into parallelograms of untidy road, and built upon with rows of working-class cottages. The roads came – horribly; the houses followed. They seemed to rise in the night. People moved into them as soon as the roofs were on, mostly workmen and their young wives, and already in a year some of these raw houses stood empty again from defaulting tenants.'[7] Also, 'the serene rhythms of old-established agriculture' were replaced by dislocation, despoilment and disorder. Although this was 'the replacement of an ancient tranquillity, or at least an ancient balance, by a new order', Wells saw 'manifestly no order at all'.[8] The thirty years before the Great War brought 'a multitude of incoordinated [sic] fresh starts, each more sweeping and destructive than the last . . . it was change out of hand, and going at an unprecedented pace nowhere in particular.'

Wells's damning judgment was that 'the Victorian epoch was not the dawn of a new era; it was a hasty, trial experiment, a gigantic experiment of the most slovenly and wasteful kind.' The fields where he had played as a child were 'now frankly a slum', his former village 'a dull useless boiling-up of human activities, an immense clustering of futilities.' It is another reflection of the ambivalence about change and modernity found elsewhere in his writings. Wells was read widely by the newly-literate classes, by first-generation voters, by boys who would shape the world after the Great War, if they survived. But even before he influenced his mass readership with such views, many of his contemporaries shared them. As mentioned earlier, this stimulated a harking back to the past, a longing for the certainties of the world of yesterday, and a determined search for whatever was left of them.

As Aunt Juley makes her journey to Howards End at the opening of Forster's novel, published in 1910 and set in the years immediately preceding, she travels on the railway parallel with 'the Great North Road . . . awakening, after a nap of a hundred years, to such life as is conferred by the stench of motor-cars, and to such culture as is implied by the advertisements of antibilious pills.'[9] When she reaches Hilton, the station for Howards End, she sees its 'long High Street had budded out right and left into residential estates', and the station is at a point where one must choose 'England or suburbia'; yet from the railway one can see 'six Danish tumuli that stood shoulder to shoulder along the highroad, tombs of soldiers'. England is an old country, but its antiquity is threatened and suffocated all around. Aunt Juley divines from her first sight of Mrs Wilcox that 'she worshipped the past, and that instinctive wisdom the past can alone bestow . . . she cared about her ancestors, and let them help her.'[10]

The speed of change was frightening. London 'rose and fell in a continual flux, while her shallows washed more widely against the hills of Surrey and over the fields of Hertfordshire. This famous building had arisen, that was doomed. Today Whitehall had been transformed: it would be the turn of Regent Street tomorrow. And month by month the roads smelt more strongly of petrol, and were more difficult to cross, and human beings heard each other speak with greater difficulty, breathed less of the air, and saw less of the sky. Nature withdrew; the leaves were falling by midsummer; the sun shone through dirt with an admired obscurity.'[11]

Until the 1880s a landowner could with impunity raze a medieval cottage, for example, for a housing development. The spectacle of so many buildings being 'doomed' propelled ministers to prevent this wrecking of what the twentieth century would call 'heritage'. There had been attempts to introduce Bills to protect ancient buildings but these had failed because the drafts included a 'compulsory power of interference with ancient monuments'. However, there was some success with the Ancient Monuments Protection Act in 1882, which enabled state intervention to protect historical monuments. It allowed owners to put such ancient sites 'under the public guardianship of the Commissioners of Works'.[12] It also provided funds to the commissioners to buy endangered buildings: but if the owners would not sell, they might fall into ruin.

The Act appointed an inspector to report on buildings at risk and it drew up a register of some meriting protection. However, it was nowhere near complete, and antiquaries began to lobby for a comprehensive list to enable the principle to be enforced. All the listed sites were prehistoric, and there were just sixty-eight of them, only twenty-six in England – seven, including Stonehenge and Silbury Hill, in Wiltshire.

While going through the Commons even this mild Bill had its critics. Charles Warton, MP for Bridport, 'protested against the invasion of the rights of property which was to be carried out under the Bill in order to gratify the antiquarian tastes of a few at the public expense', not the last time an anti-elitism argument was deployed to derail culture.[13] Sir John Lubbock, MP for the University of London, who had led the movement to have ancient buildings protected by statute, urged successfully that buildings could be deemed needful of inspection by Order in Council, if not covered by the proposed Act; but the Commons would not accept Lubbock's idea, behind earlier attempts at legislation, to allow compulsory purchase.

The 1900 Ancient Monuments Protection Act tried to tighten up the regulations and expand the types of property that could be protected. It broadened the idea of the public interest, including artistic merit as a reason to preserve a monument: and it allowed county councils to buy any vulnerable site of interest, or to contribute funds to their upkeep. In return for such support the public could gain access to the sites concerned. Then in 1905 Gerald Baldwin Brown, Professor of Fine Art at Edinburgh University, published a study of the legislation preserving buildings in other European jurisdictions, *The Care of Ancient Monuments*, finding that Britain was failing in comparison with its neighbours.

John Sinclair, who in December 1905 became Scottish Secretary in Campbell-Bannerman's government, read Baldwin Brown's book with interest. He drew its criticisms to Campbell-Bannerman's and to other colleagues' attention: notably that no law could be effective without a specific list of buildings and monuments to be protected. Baldwin Brown referred to the Royal Commission on Historical Manuscripts, established in 1869, as a model for dealing with buildings: the Royal Commission had ensured the preservation of valuable archives and papers in private hands. In establishing the Royal Commission on Historical Monuments (RCHM), under the Home Office, in October 1908, the King's Warrant proclaimed that 'we have deemed it expedient that a Commission should forthwith issue to make an inventory of the Ancient and Historical Monuments and Constructions connected with or illustrative of the contemporary culture, civilisation and conditions of life of the people in England, excluding Monmouthshire, from the earliest times to the year 1700, and to specify those which seem most worthy of preservation.'[14] In November 1913 the remit was extended to 1714, the end of Queen Anne's reign.

The government followed the example of the London County Council. Less than a decade into its existence, it commissioned a work that is still, after forty-four volumes and 120 years, in progress: *The Survey of London*. On 21 January 1896 the council passed a motion proposed by Lubbock that its General Purposes Committee should 'consider and report in the case of contemplated destruction of any building of historic or architectural interest, what course of action the Council should adopt'.[15] This idea of an arm of the state interfering in private property was novel and, to some, outrageous. A year later the council, having consulted representatives of the capital's antiquarian, architectural and archaeological societies and institutes, decided to publish 'a list' of the buildings of interest in London, parish by parish. Sir Robert Hunter, a pillar of the National Trust, formed in 1895, raised that idea during the consultation.

But the LCC had not simply compiled a list, or register, of buildings its experts regarded as important – something for which in 1897 it voted funds. It also obtained an Act of Parliament in 1898 that stated: 'It shall be lawful for the Council if they think fit to purchase by agreement buildings and places of historical interest or works of art, or to undertake or contribute towards the cost of preserving, maintaining and managing any such buildings or places, and to erect and maintain or contribute towards the provision, erection and maintenance of works of art in London.'[16] The LCC also obtained the statutory right to acquire all objects of archaeological interest found during excavations in the county by railway companies. The council's Statistical Officer, G. L. Gomme, reported that 'the Council has by these acts taken all possible steps to do what is necessary in the preservation and recording of places of historic interest in the county. It has been the pioneer among the local authorities of the country in the matter, and the statutory power which it obtained in 1898, or something equivalent, is now likely to be extended to all the county councils of the kingdom, with the result that places of beauty and historic interest may not be swept out of existence without good cause being shown.'[17] The first volume of the *Survey of London*, covering Bromley-by-Bow, was published in 1900.

The RCHM did not just concern itself with buildings liable to obliteration. The depopulation of villages in the nineteenth century caused by industrialisation and the agricultural depression had caused some old cottage dwellings to fall into ruin, and some medieval churches too. The RCHM was also charged with preserving relics of more distant ages: prehistoric earthworks and hill forts, Roman remains including the course of their roads, Saxon burial mounds and ancient barns. The commission's first chairman was Lord Burghclere, President of the Board of Agriculture in Gladstone's last government and under Rosebery, and an Ecclesiastical Commissioner. It included some leading antiquaries of the day: such as Sir Henry Howorth, President of the Royal Archaeological Institute, John Clift, secretary of the British Archaeological Association, Francis Haverfield, Camden Professor of Ancient History at Oxford and expert on the archaeology of Roman Britain, and Leonard Stokes, vice-president of the Royal Institute of British Architects and a leading builder of Gothic Roman Catholic churches and, because of his marriage to the daughter of the general manager of the National Telephone Company, telephone exchanges. There were also sub-committees of learned experts in all the fields within the competence of the RCHM.

This force of antiquaries set about cataloguing England county by county, with some requiring several volumes. The books were remarkable for their time, lavishly illustrated in the manner of *Country Life* (itself launched only in 1897 partly to present the beauties of rural England to its readers, but partly to tap into the wave of appreciation for the past), containing plans of churches and other notable buildings, and arranged by parishes. It was an astonishing work of state-sponsored scholarship that laid the foundations for other studies during the twentieth century, and created a mood to stop the demolition of ancient buildings.

The preservation of architectural heritage is now most closely associated with the National Trust, founded in 1895. But the impetus for the creation of the Trust was an earlier group, the Kyrle Society, formed in 1876 to help preserve heathland in urban areas, notably London. As well as defending open spaces for their own sake, there was among some preservationists an overtly political motivation to maintain areas for the recreation of the working class. The driving force of the Kyrle – named after a seventeenth-century philanthropist, John Kyrle, who built public parks and other amenities in his home town of Ross-on-Wye – was Miranda Hill who, like her sister Octavia, was a housing reformer.[18] The Kyrle Society's aim was to make things of beauty that were formerly exclusively the preserve of the upper and middle classes accessible and available to the poor. Using a network of branches around England, the Kyrle sought to bring a degree of artistic decoration into buildings used by the poor, such as schools, hospitals and working men's clubs, and also to set up a library service for them: a prominent supporter was William Morris, and the Arts and Crafts movement had a strong link with the Kyrle. The society also fought in the 1870s and 1880s to preserve public spaces and commons around central London. Hampstead Heath was a notable triumph for them, when in 1885 they joined with other bodies to campaign to protect the heath from further incursions by speculative builders.

Although the Kyrle did useful work the task, as cities expanded, required a bigger organisation with, ideally, official support. In the early 1890s interest in ancient buildings was a rarefied pursuit. It would be another decade before there was any serious state support for it. The agricultural depression, then entering its third decade, had left many rural ancient buildings in serious dilapidation, while those in the way of urban expansion were usually swept aside without a thought. The National Trust could not alter the pace of change, but it could protect some of the landscapes and buildings that might otherwise have been destroyed.

The driving force behind the Trust was Octavia Hill, together with two other veterans of the fight to preserve open spaces: Sir Robert Hunter, a senior civil servant who had advised her sister over Hampstead Heath, and Canon Hardwicke Rawnsley, a clergyman who had run successful campaigns to spare parts of the Lake District from railways, roads and coal mines. Ruskin inspired Rawnsley and Hunter, who had collaborated in the Lakeland battles, to set up a trust to raise funds to buy vulnerable landscapes and buildings, and through that ownership to make them inviolable in perpetuity; Ruskin had also been a mentor of Hill.

The urgent need was proved in 1884, when W. J. Evelyn, a descendant of John Evelyn, offered the nation Sayes Court, an estate in Deptford where the diarist had lived and designed sumptuous gardens in the late seventeenth century. His successor had turned the gardens into a ten-acre public open space, with bandstands and a former dockmaster's house that could have housed a museum. He now wanted them taken into national ownership and protected. However, no body existed to accept ownership on the donor's terms, which caused Hunter, when consulted, to suggest a land company should be established to protect the public interest in such cases. Octavia Hill suggested calling it the Commons and Gardens Trust; Hunter suggested the National Trust. However, settling the name was easier than establishing the company, and before it could happen the chance to buy Sayes Court had passed. Instead, a one-and-a-half-acre plot was entrusted to the Kyrle Society, a park that still exists in a rundown state in a grim urban area; the once-popular public gardens have vanished and part of the surroundings are derelict, the historical associations with Evelyn almost invisible.

In November 1893 Hill, Hunter and Rawnsley set up the formal framework of a trust, to raise money to buy vulnerable land and buildings. Its full title would be the National Trust for Places of Historic Interest or Natural Beauty. The Duke of Westminster became president, and the institution was inaugurated as an 'association not for profit' in July 1894. It opened for business on 12 January 1895. As well as helping Hill secure Hampstead Heath, Hunter – chief solicitor to the Post Office, and a considerable legal brain – had stopped building on Wimbledon, Tooting and Plumstead Commons, having written a definitive essay setting out the public interest in such cases. His expertise also helped secure 3,000 acres of Epping Forest on behalf of the Corporation of London against potential developers in a three-year legal action. When the Corporation won in 1882, Hunter's achievement was crowned by a formal visit to the Forest by the Queen, who declared it 'available for her people's enjoyment.'[19]

Hunter was knighted for services to conservation as the Trust was inaugurated, a sign of government commitment to his ideals. He stated at its first meeting, however, that the Trust needed formal underpinning and permanent powers: either a Royal Charter or an Act of Parliament. The Liberal government in 1907 at last found parliamentary time, and parliament debated a Bill Hunter had drafted to give the National Trust the status of a statutory corporation. By the time of the 1907 Act the Trust had twenty-five properties. Its first was a fourteenth-century Wealden hall house at Alfriston in Sussex, a farmhouse used as a clergyman's house, bought for £10 in 1896. In 1899 the Trust acquired its first nature reserve, Wicken Fen in Cambridgeshire, the land donated by Charles Rothschild, a banker who was also a keen amateur entomologist. In 1909 it bought, via public subscription, its first archaeological site, White Barrow on Salisbury Plain, a prehistoric burial chamber thought to date from 4000 BC. The White Barrow acquisition exemplified the importance of the Trust: the War Office was buying large parts of Salisbury Plain to accommodate on manoeuvres an army that was expanding because of the national preoccupation with a German invasion.

Hunter, speaking at Manchester University in 1907, explained the rationale of the National Trust in the context of the Edwardian desire to connect with, and understand, the past. The New Forest, he said, had been preserved not just because it was a place of beauty but as a 'perpetuation of the economic history of the land, as visible evidence of the habits of the people from century to century.'[20] But the plunder of England's past continued: 'There are old Roman and British camps which at the present are being mutilated out of recognition merely to supply gravel and stone for public roads. Many abandoned castles and abbeys have been robbed of their stone to build cottages, even pig sties, for the peasants of the district.' Hunter added to this the ruination of landscapes for quarrying, and regretted the state could not compel preservation of an ancient monument in private ownership: but he noticed the *Zeitgeist*, the 'growing desire to preserve the material evidence of the history of each people, and the charms of the country it occupies.'

Preservationists had asked local authorities to care for historic landmarks – Hunter noted how Northamptonshire County Council had taken over the Eleanor Cross outside the county town – but more awareness was needed. What scandalised him most was that the owner of England's foremost prehistoric monument, Stonehenge, had enclosed it with barbed wire and was charging for admission: an assertion of ownership that also, in theory, allowed him to 'cart away every stone in the place'. 'To the minds of most persons there is something absurd in the idea that a national possession like Stonehenge should be at the mercy of a private person!' He demanded a national register be made of such sites and landscapes, of historical or scientific importance. A private member's Bill to do this had been attempted several times, but had fallen victim to party warfare. Eventually the British would stop despoiling ancient monuments and buildings; people such as Hill, Hunter and Rawnsley started the process.

III

The greatest and most visible change of all in the nineteenth century was to the landscape, as the suburban sprawl devouring the countryside around London was replicated in other towns and cities while their populations grew. Throughout the century architecture had often tried to evoke the past that the National Trust now sought to preserve. The Gothic Revival was visible in every British city, in the churches built for the new industrial working class, and in many secular buildings. But Gothic, for whom the great evangelist was John Ruskin, had peaked by the time of the death of perhaps its greatest practitioner, George Gilbert

Scott, in 1878. That same year Ruskin had the first of a series of mental breakdowns that gradually disabled him until, between August 1889 and August 1890, he had such a long attack of madness – possibly paranoid schizophrenia – that his creative and public life came to an end. The decade until his death in 1900 was spent in seclusion and, increasingly, silence.

The great Gothic design, by Giles Gilbert Scott, grandson of Sir George, that won the competition for the Anglican cathedral in Liverpool in 1903, showed the revival was not quite over. G. F. Bodley and Richard Norman Shaw were the assessors, and all five shortlisted designs of the 103 submitted were Gothic. Scott's design – termed by Pevsner 'the final flowering of the Gothic Revival as a vital, creative movement, and one of the great buildings of the twentieth century', won easily. As he was only twenty-two at the time Scott's work was overseen by Bodley for the first three years, until the latter's death in 1907.[21] Scott redrew his plans in 1909–10, wishing to replace the original two-tower plan with the great, brooding single tower that adorns the finished building. This resulted in much more redesigning below, but the Gothic ideal remained intact. Two world wars and Liverpool's economic decline further held up construction: Scott made alterations until he died in 1960, but the building was not finished until 1978.

In domestic building architects strove to bring out the inner peasant in every Englishman, to reconnect him with an imaginary rural idyll where he could escape the modern world. This, albeit from a religious motivation, was what George Cadbury had sought to achieve in Bournville. However, the rusticated architecture that would symbolise the best late-Victorian and Edwardian building was far beyond the pocket of any peasant or artisan. It was ideal for the well-to-do middle class who aspired to gracious country living on a scale beneath the great landed estates, and could have it thanks to the spread of the railways. As the style developed it became more concerned with providing an ersatz Olde English cocoon in which its inhabitants could insulate themselves from the twentieth century.

In the 1850s Ruskin had deeply influenced William Morris, then an Oxford undergraduate and part of the Pre-Raphaelite Brotherhood. Ruskin's political views more than his aesthetic underpinned his doctrine: he rejected factory-made objects as examples of servility, believing that only the true craftsman, working for himself and using his skill to make something of beauty, could feel the dignity of the human spirit. Morris shared Ruskin's view that Gothic was the uniquely moral style; he also shared Ruskin's utopian idea of a romanticised, distant past, which Ruskin had imbibed from Carlyle. Morris spent two years in George Edmund Street's firm training as an architect, but never practised. His forte would be design, and he insisted (again following a Ruskinian doctrine) on learning how to make objects he had designed. The satisfaction gained from the labour of creation played an important part in making Morris a socialist.

Upon his marriage in 1860, Morris collaborated with the architect Philip Webb to build Red House at Upton, now part of Bexleyheath in Kent, a showpiece of the incorporation of medieval principles into modern domestic architecture. It proved unpractical for Morris to live there, and he and his family moved out after only five years. It nevertheless became a template for the Arts and Crafts movement – the term was coined by the artist and bookbinder Thomas Cobden-Sanderson in 1887 – and Morris would be seen as its progenitor.

His great period as a designer of wallpaper and fabrics – not to mention furniture and stained glass – came after 1871, when the Morrises decided to share Kelmscott Manor in Oxfordshire with Dante Gabriel Rossetti. Kelmscott was a sixteenth-century house and it, rather than medieval structures, became Morris's ideal of the English past. The local flora inspired his designs. The neighbouring Cotswold villages, untouched by the Industrial Revolution, had a huge influence on him: he called Bibury 'surely the most beautiful village in England.'[22] Again, the elaborateness of what he and his school would produce ensured an almost exclusively upper-middle-class clientele. His aesthetic would grow in influence after his death in 1896, not least through its effect on a leading architect of late-Victorian and Edwardian England, Charles Francis Annesley Voysey.

Born in 1857, Voysey made his living from fabric and wallpaper designs until the 1890s. He had been a pupil of Arthur Heygate Mackmurdo – another devotee of Ruskin, who had set up a design partnership with other artists – and Voysey's early ideas owed more to him than to Morris. Pugin also influenced Voysey, but once his architectural practice took off Morris's influence became evident, not least in the details in which Voysey delighted, and which evoked the bucolic craftsmanship of a distant and idealised past that would enchant his patrons; Edwin Lutyens followed the same template. His medium was the small country house, a romanticised aggrandisement of the cottage. These were often long, low buildings of stone with heavy corner buttresses, with leaded windows and steep-pitched slate roofs: roomier versions of cottages seen all over Olde England. Such building both reflected and fed a change in the intellectual climate.

The architect explained to an interviewer in 1897 that the buttresses were an economy measure, designed to eliminate the need for thicker walls, and not, God forbid, mere ornament: 'Mr Voysey would no more dream of adding a superfluous buttress than he would add an unnecessary panel of cheap ornament.'[23] Also for reasons of economy he used roughcast on his walls rather than neat bricks and mortar. His trademark, though, was in the ironwork: his long door-handles, and long, medieval-style hinges that ended in the motif of a heart or, sometimes, of the profile of the client for whom he was building. All this fulfilled the Arts and Crafts doctrine that ornament should be produced for the satisfaction of the craftsman first and foremost and not simply for profit. Among his patrons before the Great War was Wells, for whom he built Spade House at Sandgate in Kent. Wells described Voysey as 'that pioneer in the escape from the small snobbish villa residence to the bright and comfortable pseudo-cottage'.[24] Voysey, Wells recalled, 'wanted to put a large heart-shaped letter plate on my front door, but I protested at wearing my heart so conspicuously outside and we compromised on a spade': hence the name. Voysey spawned many imitators, including Harvey at Bournville.

Several of the leading designers in the movement, such as Morris, Mackmurdo and (though he later specialised in architecture) Voysey, trained as architects. For architecture to be liberated from the mass-produced style ubiquitous in the new suburbs, craftsmanship had to be put back into building. Somers Clarke, an Arts and Crafts architect, wrote in 1893: 'Until the craftsman in stone and wood is more of an architect, and the architect more of a craftsman, we cannot hope for improvement.'[25] Such architects learned to be craftsmen: the results of their labour are all over the home counties, wherever the railway would take their clients home from the City, but notably in Middlesex, southern Hertfordshire, Surrey and north-west Kent. Some work is found further afield: William Lethaby, a great precursor of the Early Modern movement, who had begun as a clerk to Norman Shaw, built an Arts and Crafts church at Brockhampton in Herefordshire in 1901–2, and offered, with Henry Wilson and others, a design for Liverpool Cathedral. Edward

Prior, in 1885, built an Arts and Crafts terrace at Bridport; and a church at Roker in County Durham between 1904 and 1907.

While the diocese of Liverpool lacked the courage to commission Lethaby to build their new cathedral, other institutional patrons were more daring in patronising Arts and Crafts architects to design significant public buildings. In 1896 Charles Harrison Townsend was commissioned to build the Horniman Museum in south-east London and in 1899 the Whitechapel Art Gallery a few miles north of it. Both feature towers and Romanesque arches, the latter a bold innovation in medieval revivalism. The great mosaic at the Horniman was to have had a counterpart at the gallery, but money ran out: the great panel to accommodate it on the front elevation is blank to this day.

Most of the surviving fine architecture from this period is, however, domestic, and, as with Voysey, often looks back to a romanticised rural vernacular. A dozen years younger than Voysey, Lutyens developed such a style in the 1890s. His immediate mentor was Gertrude Jekyll, the garden designer, whom he had met in 1889. In 1895, aged twenty-six, he designed a house for Jekyll at Munstead Wood near Godalming that relied heavily on her knowledge of the pattern of building in Surrey and the nature of the crafts there. Its materials were from antiquity – stone and oak – and the look of Lutyens's houses owed much to rural buildings of earlier centuries, not just domestic but also agricultural. Thanks partly to Jekyll's own clientele Lutyens's practice took off, and was greatly boosted after 1897 by *Country Life*, created to reflect an idealised rural past preserved or recreated in the present. Its founder, Edward Hudson, became one of Lutyens's clients. His style would move from the vernacular to the baroque: but however he built, his clients wanted a style from the past that evoked what nostalgists presented as a happier, less divided and stressful Britain.

The Arts and Crafts style was not merely apparent in individually commissioned country or suburban houses, but also in whole housing developments. From the late 1880s over 350 properties at Bedford Park in Chiswick were built in the style. These included houses by Voysey, E. W. Godwin and Norman Shaw, now best remembered for Scotland Yard on the Victoria Embankment that for seventy years housed the Metropolitan Police. Bedford Park originated in the work of a speculative builder, Jonathan Thomas Carr, who built his first house there in 1876 in the Queen Anne Revival style: but it became an Arts and Crafts 'garden suburb' a decade later, as it attracted the attention of the style's leading architects. In 1960 John Betjeman called it 'the most significant suburb built in the last century, probably in the western world.'[26]

Bedford Park was a social as well as an architectural project. This had happened before: at Saltaire and, as noted, Bournville. But Bedford Park was no paternalist enterprise for workers, more a self-selecting mission for the middle classes. There was a conscious attempt to fashion a community, with a church, shops, a social club with a library, communal tennis courts, a school (in which there was no religious instruction) and – unlike Saltaire and Bournville – a pub. The houses in Bedford Park were designed for people with incomes of between £300 and £1,500 a year, and this was an enterprise from which builders intended to make money. Individual houses were essays in architectural expression, with ample gardens as part of the overall aesthetic. The estate's layout was designed to avoid the row-on-row monotony of the lower-middle-class suburbs. The community attracted artists and writers, including Pinero, the young W. B. Yeats, and members of the Chiswick School of Art: at the social club (subscription two guineas a year, ladies half a guinea) the 'advanced' discussions were about aesthetics and women's rights.

The ideology and aesthetic of Bedford Park inspired the Garden City movement. This initiative would be the ultimate repudiation of modern, mass-produced, industrial life, and the apotheosis of the Arts and Crafts movement. Politics and art met, fulfilling an ideal expressed in 1893 by the artist and illustrator Walter Crane in *Arts and Crafts Essays*, written by him and other members of the Arts and Crafts Exhibition Society. Crane, a committed socialist and friend of Morris, wrote that the movement 'represents in some sense a revolt against the hard mechanical conventional life and its insensibility to beauty . . . It is a protest against that so-called industrial progress which produces shoddy wares, the cheapness of which is paid for by the lives of their producers and the degradation of their users.'[27] All this was 'darkened by the hurried life of modern towns in which huge aggregations of humanity exist, equally removed from both art and nature and their kindly refining influences.'[28] It was a liberation movement, protesting against 'the cheapening of human life and labour'.[29]

Ebenezer Howard, a social reformer who ran a shorthand transcription business and was an expert on typewriters, pioneered the Garden City movement at Letchworth, in Hertfordshire, in 1903. He sought to incorporate such refining influences in his avowedly utopian idea of a garden city, a post-industrial place where man and nature could learn again to co-exist. The notion had come to him in the 1870s, visiting Chicago while public parks were being laid out in its suburbs: these parks were called 'garden cities'. In 1898 he wrote a pamphlet called *Tomorrow: A Peaceful Path to Real Reform* in which he advocated building new towns under collective ownership to alleviate the squalor of existing ones caused by the urban population boom. But Howard's idea of a new town combined urban amenities with the space, peace, light and healthiness of rural life. Homes and factories would be encouraged to use gas or electricity rather than coal. The houses would have gardens, and the towns would be surrounded by enough agricultural land to grow food for the inhabitants: hence the term 'garden city'.

Howard hoped to start a reverse migration, not least that the unemployed would again find work on the land: this had been a theme of the left's in the 1890s. Howard revered the countryside, and saw it in entirely spiritual terms. Looking to an earlier age was not merely, as with Carlyle and his followers, to find work for men, but to reconnect with God. 'The country is the symbol of God's love and care for man,' he wrote.[30] 'Town and country must be married, and out of the joyous union will spring a new hope, a new life, a new civilisation.'[31] His perfect city would cover 6,000 acres, house 32,000 people, and be laid out in concentric circles with radial boulevards interrupted by open spaces. When it filled up another would start nearby. Eventually there would be several cities all linked to each other, called 'the social city'.

Howard was a practical man, and much of his pamphlet is devoted to the economics of his idea, and how it could be financially viable. A revision of his original pamphlet, *Garden Cities of Tomorrow*, published in 1902, reviewed progress. The idea had had widespread support, but among some sceptics had also provoked ridicule of Howard as a crank: but Letchworth would succeed, and Howard would eventually be knighted, so he had the last laugh. The Garden City Association had been founded since his original pamphlet appeared, with the three great philanthropists of the age, Lever, Cadbury and Rowntree, as directors. Howard signed off the revision with the exhortation: 'I trust we shall meet in Garden City'.[32] Vice-presidents included the Countess of Warwick and Lord Carrington, several bishops and other senior clergy, numerous

MPs and such luminaries as Marie Corelli, Walter Crane and H. G. Wells.

The list also included several architects. The Arts and Crafts movement recognised the garden city idea as the perfect canvas for their philosophy and aesthetic. Morris had defined 'decency of surroundings' as including 'good lodging, ample space, general order and beauty', which was what the architects and planners in Letchworth sought to follow.[33] Howard's supporters set up a joint stock company in 1903. After looking at potential sites in Staffordshire, Essex, Oxfordshire and Worcestershire, they bought 3,826 acres of north Hertfordshire around three villages, Letchworth, Willian and Norton, the garden city taking the name of the first, whose population at the 1901 census was ninety-six. Hertfordshire was chosen because it seemed best located to attract the industry to provide employment. Quakers who had hoped to form their own community had originally bought the land. The development was aided by an amendment in 1900 to the 1890 Housing of the Working Classes Act, which empowered local authorities to relieve town and city centres by acquiring, or allowing the development of, outlying land.

Letchworth was the work of two unexceptional architects, cousins and socialist teetotallers, Barry Parker and Raymond Unwin (Unwin was married to Parker's sister). Unwin was a disciple of Morris and the more committed socialist, Parker the more driven artistically; Unwin had heard Ruskin's lectures in Oxford in the 1880s, just before the critic went mad. He had addressed the first Garden City Association Conference at Bournville – chaired by George Cadbury – in September 1901, where he had set out his vision. Parker, like Voysey, had begun as a designer of wallpaper, furniture and textiles. Their first big collaboration was Rowntree's model village at New Earswick, where the two men strove to avoid the back-to-back rows of houses that had become the standard for the working class.

That venture helped win them the competition to build Letchworth. Far more inspiring partnerships, notably Halsey Ricardo and William Lethaby, and Geoffrey Lucas and Sydney Cranfield, were not chosen. Ricardo's masterpiece would be the house he built off Holland Park in London for Ernest Debenham, the department store magnate, its Arts and Crafts interior concealed within a polychromatic exterior; Lucas would build high-specification houses in Hampstead Garden Suburb, which also featured work by Lutyens (and by Unwin and Parker) and in the less-well-known Romford Garden Suburb, Gidea Park, in Essex. Letchworth was a more earnest and democratic project, and ended up with earnest and unimaginative architecture.

Unwin laid out the town, starting in 1904. Among his achievements was planning Britain's first roundabout, opened in 1909. In accordance with Howard's strict principles, industrial areas were separated from residential ones. The green belt around the town – the first of its kind – was respected, and in the first phase of the plan only one tree was cut down. However, Howard's concentric layout was ignored. The houses followed elements of the Arts and Crafts ideal, with Parker heavily influenced by Voysey, but because the city was designed to attract the working and lower-middle classes compromises had to be made, which deeply aggrieved Unwin and Parker. Miss Elizabeth Revill moved into the first house – number 1 Alpha Cottages – on 7 July 1904.

One compromise was that the town pioneered pre-fabrication and, unthinkable in true Arts and Crafts buildings, relied on non-traditional mass-produced building materials. Northcliffe's *Daily Mail* sponsored two Cheap Cottages Exhibitions ('cheap' defined as costing £150 to build a house of three bedrooms, a scullery and living room) there in 1905 and 1907, the forerunner of the Ideal Homes Exhibition.[34] With market gardening a main occupation, and an agricultural labourer's wages at around fifteen shillings a week, there was no scope for extravagance. The Letchworth-style house, or a bastardisation of it, would influence suburban building for decades, as the desire to escape modern life for an idealised, imaginary past gripped the British public. The Housing and Town Planning Act of 1909 conferred powers on towns and cities to plan new suburbs; and that year Unwin published *Town Planning in Practice: An Introduction to the Art of Designing Cities and Suburbs*, a book devoured by all those building suburbs, and whose influence would lead to the mass-produced elements of Letchworth being replicated all over Britain until 1939.

What would most have offended Morris was that the railway – always envisaged in Howard's proposals – came to Letchworth once building started. The town became a destination for day-trippers, rather as they might have gone to a zoo. There was less there than they might have hoped for, since the town's pub – the Skittles, opened in 1907 – sold no alcohol. But industry soon came to Letchworth – a corset manufacturer, Spirella, was the first manufacturer there in 1912 – and its future was assured. However, Howard's principle that the land should be held for the common good – all tenants of the company were effectively shareholders, and all profits were reinvested in the town – held good indefinitely. A trust still owns Letchworth and a foundation administers it. For a time, communal kitchens served apartments built round a courtyard, and there were communities of progressive thinkers who believed in 'arcadianism', a classless society, and wore smocks and sandals. Such utopian dreams did not survive the Great War.

The popularity of the garden city ideal led to the mass production the Arts and Crafts movement existed to repudiate. Lutyens wrote to his fellow architect Herbert Baker in 1909 that 'there is a boom coming for Garden Cities. I am in the train for Tavistock to lay out a building estate for the Duke of Bedford. I have an estate to lay out at Romford . . . and then there is the Central Square at Hampstead.'[35] The Great War ended the Arts and Crafts movement; the garden cities that came afterwards would adapt the ideal. Unwin was in 1905 appointed chief planner for Hampstead Garden Suburb – whose main square Lutyens laid out. Here, unlike in Letchworth, there was plenty of money, and what one critic has called 'a complete Arts and Crafts village' emerged.[36] The affluence and consequent exclusivity contradicted Unwin's ideology, but only where money abounded could the vision be achieved. But then most nostalgia is a distortion of memory, and the reality of the old countryside to which the idealists looked back was far distant from that of their imaginations.

IV

If one had the money one could live in an incarnation of the past, but the vogue for nostalgia also provided intellectual refreshment in keeping with that spirit. Literature – fiction, non-fiction and poetry – helped fetishise a national mood of cherishing the past, and emphasising a continuity of national culture and life. In non-fiction the favoured genre was topography: rhapsodising about the landscape, its buildings, those who dwelt in it (painted, inevitably, in the most romanticised form), its trees and hedgerows and its very soil. This appreciation of natural and man-made beauty, coupled with an awareness of their history, helped build the sense of a British identity. The countryside's features were further sources of pride, and the way in which they were preserved and celebrated became further cause for self-congratulation. Hilaire Belloc spoke of 'the fascination of antiquity' in *The Old Road*, his account, published in 1904, of a walk along the Pilgrim's Way, between Winchester and Canterbury, through a landscape little changed since either cathedral was built.[37] He wrote a doctrine for Edwardian nostalgics: 'By the recovery of the Past, stuff and being are added to us; our lives which, lived in the present only, are a film or surface, take on body – are lifted into one dimension more. The soul is fed. Reverence and knowledge and security and the love of a good land – all these are increased or given by the pursuit of this kind of learning.'[38]

Belloc believed an understanding of the topography of the country was essential if one was to understand its people. The south-west of England, he felt, was 'one in spirit with Brittany, with Ireland, and with Wales; nor is it by any means certain that this racial sympathy was the product of the Saxon invasions alone.'[39] Kent was full of 'slower and heavier men before Caesar landed', and 'it is certain that the sheltered vales and the high tors would nourish men very different from those of the East Anglian flats or the Weald.'

Edward Thomas was an even more adept practitioner, paving the way for the boom in topographical writing between the wars. The Wiltshire naturalist Richard Jefferies, of whom Thomas wrote a biography, heavily influenced him: Thomas wrote poetic prose about English and Welsh landscapes. He walks into the countryside from London in most of his writings – though there is a concession to modernity in his use of a bicycle – and he writes of ploughmen, tramps (he was responsible for promoting the career of W. H. Davies, author of *Autobiography of a Supertramp*), farmers, fields, hills, footpaths, streams, woods, churches, inns, cottages, cottage gardens, stables, ricks, oaks, elms, limes, marigolds, blossom, and all manner of birds, evoking an ancient England whose serene continuity has yet to be wrecked; and when modernity intrudes he reviles it – he writes, for instance, of an 'addle-faced motorist'.[40] His writing can be seen either as a hymn to atavism, or a supreme example of the pornography of nostalgia.

There was a melancholy in this recall of a vanishing culture, even among those who knew how hard life had been. Thomas Hardy, who had (because of adverse criticism of *Jude the Obscure*, published in 1896) stopped writing novels that idealised and criticised the life of the rural poor, was by the Edwardian era expressing himself almost exclusively in verse. Although he dealt with subjects so diverse as the Boer War and romantic love, his poetry became increasingly reflective of the past. Before the memory of his wife came to dominate his poetry – she died in 1912 – it concentrated in part on what his fellow nostalgic A. E. Housman would call a 'land of lost content', and also of the effect of the past on the present, notably the repercussions of the Napoleonic Wars on the whole of the nineteenth century.

His third volume of verse, *Time's Laughingstocks*, published in 1909, is steeped in memories of yesterday and, like his novels, captures a countryside disappearing from view or – because some of the poems were written as far back as the 1860s – that has already gone. He views one set of village memories in 'The Dead Quire' from 'the Mead of Memories', acknowledging the power of landscape to hold and reflect the past.[41] In 'The House of Hospitalities' he notes that:

> Time has tired me since we met here
>   When the folk now dead were young . . .
> Yet at midnight if here walking,
>   When the moon sheets wall and tree,
> I see forms of old time talking,
>   Who smile on me.[42]

The conceit of the ghosts of the long-dead inhabiting a sacred landscape and linking its history with the present recurs in these poems. At the end of 'Casterbridge Fair', written in 1902, he says:

> And midnight clears High Street of all but the ghosts
>   Of its buried burghees,
> From the latest far back to those old Roman hosts
>   Whose remains one yet sees,
> Who loved, laughed and fought, hailed their friends, drank their
>   toasts
>   At their meeting-times here, just as these![43]

In one of his greatest poems, 'Before Life and After', Hardy strives not just for a past within memory, but for an 'ancient' one – it is one of his favourite adjectives – long before modernity and the sensibilities it brought with it, and long before 'the disease of feeling germed':

A time there was – as one may guess
And as, indeed, earth's testimonies tell –
Before the birth of consciousness,
When all went well.[44]

In this era not merely were cities, towns and rural landscapes changing: so too was society, with the lives of individuals transformed by time, chance and social mobility. Hardy was but one of the poets this rapid upheaval affected deeply.

In October 1877 Alfred Edward Housman went up to St John's College, Oxford, to read classics. He had grown up in a happy middle-class family in Worcestershire – his father was a solicitor – and throughout his childhood and youth the hills of Shropshire were his western horizon, betokening a land of dreams that lay, unknown, beyond it. At Oxford a fellow undergraduate, Moses Jackson, whose interests were sporting rather than intellectual, captivated him. Jackson does not seem to have returned these feelings, which Housman would harbour for life and which would dominate him emotionally. The obsession with Jackson, with whom he shared lodgings in his last year at Oxford, distracted Housman from his studies. To everyone's shock he failed his final examinations, though retook and passed them a year later. He went to work in the Patent Office as a clerk, not least because Jackson worked there. From 1883 the two shared lodgings in Bayswater with Jackson's younger brother Adalbert, on whom – to complicate matters further – Housman also developed a crush.

There may have been more to the relationship than that. Towards the end of 1885 Housman left the *ménage* suddenly, never to return, and went missing for a week: the reasons are unclear, but may have been connected with an inner turmoil in his private life. His life was intense: when he left work – which he likened to a form of penal servitude – each evening he would undertake classical research in the British Museum library, writing and publishing learned papers. By 1892, despite having failed at Oxford, he had sufficient clout in the academic world to apply for, and be awarded, the chair in Latin at University College London.

Once in his post, and despite its heavy demands, Housman poured out his feelings about the past in the work that made him famous, *A Shropshire Lad*. Jackson had gone to teach in India, and he and Housman hardly ever met again; Adalbert died of typhoid in 1892. To colleagues and pupils Housman was a reticent, ascetic, desiccated man; the tone of his collection of short lyrics amazed acquaintances who had not thought these depths existed in him. The land of dreams is the setting for the poems; the subject matter not merely the beauty of a timeless landscape untouched by the nineteenth century, but of 'the lads' whose promise was snuffed out when they died young: usually in some foreign war. The metaphor reflects Housman's lack of fulfilment, his imagination of a place and a time when (as Hardy would put it) 'all went well', seen from a time of loss and aridity.

Housman wrote the verses in an intense burst of poeticism in the first five months of 1895, when he was thirty-six. One of his biographers, Norman Page, has drawn attention to Wilde's trial, happening during the same period, and implied Housman might have been affected by the plight of a fellow homosexual: all that is lacking to support that contention is hard evidence. Housman could not find a publisher and had to pay to publish the collection himself; it sold slowly but steadily. However, as men began to suffer the fate of Housman's 'lads' in the Second Boer War, dying young in distant battles for Queen and country, far removed from the rural idyll of England, sales took off. As the vogue for nostalgia developed, and people craved touchstones of Englishness in a period of change, the poems became ever more popular. The seismic events of 1914–18 and their aftermath supercharged their, and Housman's, fame.

In the poems, death – sudden death – is an ever-present threat, as are its cousins disappointment, lack of fulfilment, loss and longing. Their counterpoint is 'the land of lost content', possibly a reference to his loss of Moses Jackson – 'The happy highways where I went/And cannot come again.'[45] He extols and luxuriates in the English landscape, which he paints in the most gorgeous of colours and the most sumptuous of lights, and which, as in Hardy, is that agent of continuity that links the present generation with their shared past, and is rich in memory. In 'Bredon Hill' he writes that:

Here of a Sunday morning
  My love and I would lie,
And see the coloured counties,
  And hear the larks so high
  About us in the sky.[46]

Housman takes obsession with the past to an extreme: the present cannot provide joy, which is to be found only in a time that is irrecoverable: 'With rue my heart is laden/For golden friends I had.'[47] He writes of a rural life unchanged from the eighteenth century, and when he describes men hanged on public gibbets he is being self-consciously anachronistic, or visiting a world gone for half a century.

The poetry of nostalgia deals not just with a world lost through change or death, but with a landscape and sense of place that are eternal while life comes and goes. It is a view of an England that is hallowed ground, the holy soil linked to a rarefied people and way of life honoured by time. A minor poet of the 1880s and 1890s, William Ernest Henley, writing about sailing upriver from Richmond to Kew, called this idea of England 'the enchanted long ago'.[48]

Not normally prey to nostalgic sentiment – he was too engaged in the stereotypically decadent life of the Edwardian *jeunesse dorée* – Rupert Brooke wrote one of the definitive poems of this genre. Brooke flirted with the Bloomsbury Group: but his restless travelling and passion for the countryside meant more to him. When not abroad he was usually holed up in lodgings at Grantchester, a pretty village two miles' walk along the river from Cambridge, working on dissertations on John Webster and the influence of Puritanism on seventeenth-century drama. He hoped to be elected a fellow of King's, where he had been an undergraduate.

In early 1912, in his twenty-fifth year, Brooke had a nervous breakdown, the result of self-inflicted wounds in his private life. After various homosexual experiments he had decided mainly to pursue women, doing so with an emotional incontinence forgivable only in a poet. They ranged from Noel Olivier, a fourteen-year-old girl when he met her, to Katherine Baird Cox, a rather masculine woman from Newnham whom he met through the Fabian Society, and who his mother thought looked like a bear. The inevitable collisions of such a life undermined Brooke's mental and physical health, and he went to Berlin in April 1912 to stay with his friend Duncan Grant. He would sit in the window of the Café des Westens near Grant's apartment in Charlottenburg, by the busy Zoo *U-Bahn* station, and watch the world go by. The mental turmoil of his private life was accelerated by a homesickness that presented itself in a longing for an England of familiar values and landscape: and he captured it in his poem 'The Old Vicarage, Grantchester', named after his lodgings in the village.

What the poem lacks in profundity it makes up for in its scene-painting and evocation of an immortal England, home and beauty:

Oh! there the chestnuts, summer through
Beside the river make for you
A tunnel of green gloom, and sleep
Deeply above; and green and deep
The stream mysterious glides beneath,
Green as a dream and deep as death.
Oh, damn! I know it! and I know
How the May fields all golden show,
And when the day is young and sweet,
Gild gloriously the bare feet
That run to bathe . . . [49]

Anticipating T. S. Eliot, Brooke sees his rural paradise as a place where time past is in time present and quite possibly in time future:

I only know that you may lie
Day long and watch the Cambridge sky,
And, flower-lulled in sleepy grass,
Hear the cool lapse of hours pass,
Until the centuries blend and blur
In Grantchester, in Grantchester . . . [50]

There is a moral grandeur about Brooke's country – 'For England's the one land I know/Where men with splendid hearts may go'. Although his religion was tenuous to say the least, the England he loves is invested with a holy or spiritual dimension that distinguishes it from other nations: there is a bond between itself and his soul, as there should be between it and the souls of all other Englishmen. Grantchester is a place of 'peace and holy quiet' that has:

Great clouds along pacific skies,
And men and women with straight eyes,
Lithe children lovelier than a dream,
A bosky wood, a slumbrous stream,

And little kindly winds that creep
Round twilight corners, half asleep.[51]

The very smell of the place is 'unforgettable, unforgotten', its landscape intrinsic to its godly aura:

Say, do the elm-clumps greatly stand
Still guardians of that holy land?
The chestnuts shade, in reverend dream,
The yet unacademic stream?
Is dawn a secret shy and cold
Anadyomene, silver-gold?
And sunset still a golden sea
From Haslingfield to Madingley?[52]

This is not merely a nostalgia for a pre-industrial, feudal England: it is one that, at the beginning and end of the poem, is rooted in the cosy domesticity of the English hearth and home, the flower-strewn cottage that would become the cliché of the English rural idyll in the twentieth century. Having opened with:

Just now the lilac is in bloom,
All before my little room;
And in my flower-beds, I think,
Smile the carnation and the pink . . . [53]

the poem ends:

Say, is there Beauty yet to find?
And Certainty? And Quiet kind?
Deep meadows yet, for to forget
The lies, and truths, and pain? . . . oh, yet
Stands the Church clock at ten to three?
And is there honey still for tea?[54]

Kipling echoed this view of England as hallowed ground in his historical fantasy of 1906 *Puck of Pook's Hill*. One of the great children's books of the era, Kenneth Grahame's *The Wind in the Willows*, published in 1908, treated England similarly, its chapter 'The Piper at the Gates of Dawn' using nostalgia as mysticism, going far over the heads of its intended readership, but which, in common with so much literature of the time, turns the English countryside into a poem in prose.

Other nostalgics invested huge quantities of emotion in the everyday. Francis Thompson, the opium-addicted Lancashire poet, was so affected by the memory of a cricket match he watched when he was nineteen, when Lancashire played Gloucestershire at Old Trafford in 1878, that years later, when invited to Lord's to watch Middlesex play Lancashire just before his death from tuberculosis in 1907, he was too overcome to go. Instead, he stayed at home and wrote cricket's most celebrated poem, imagining himself at Lord's consumed with nostalgia; and recalling the Lancashire opening partnership of 'Monkey' Hornby and Dick Barlow:

> For the field is full of shades as I near the shadowy coast,
> And a ghostly batsman plays to the bowling of a ghost,
> And I look through my tears on a soundless-clapping host
> As the run-stealers flicker to and fro,
> To and fro:
> O my Hornby and my Barlow long ago![55]

V

Perhaps nothing in the culture of nostalgia played on the emotions so directly, or potently, as music, the vogue for nostalgia coinciding exactly with the English Musical Renaissance, and with the determination of young composers to construct a musical idiom that was explicitly English. Cecil Sharp, son of a slate merchant from south London, left Cambridge in 1882 with a third-class degree in mathematics, this poor outcome the result of an undergraduate life devoted to music. He spent most of the next decade in Australia, returning to London in 1892 determined to become a composer. He struggled: he taught at a prep school until 1910 and directed the Hampstead Conservatoire. But Sharp's intellectual life during these years was far wider-ranging, indicative of some prevailing currents of the time, and of the greatest cultural significance. Sharp had attended a lecture by William Morris that had converted him to socialism; his wife was a Fabian, which further influenced his politics; he studied Christian Science, and dabbled in spiritualism, a craze whose popularity grew before the Great War but rose exponentially after it.

Sharp's cultural importance derived from an event on Boxing Day 1899, while he was staying with his wife's family. Nine men arrived at the house, and one, William Kimber, played folk tunes on a concertina while the others danced. Sharp invited Kimber to return the next day, and noted down the tunes: and the experience caused him to reflect that England, without a national music since Purcell died, had had one all along in the folk songs of its rural working class. Parry, Stanford and Elgar had come to prominence by the early twentieth century, but each was heavily influenced by the German tradition. Sharp realised he had found a national music for England, and would pursue it.

This enthusiasm, as in Morris's conception of visual art, looked back to an idealised, pre-industrial past. The Victorians were obsessed with tradition, and it was tiresome to lack a musical one to match its literature or architecture. Sharp set out to establish it. His first exercise was *A Book of British Song for Home and School*, published in 1902, assembled from nineteenth-century collections by such men as John Broadwood, a Worthing clergyman. He had assembled them from Surrey and Sussex in a book of 1843 that began the slow process of stimulating interest in folk song. Other nineteenth-century clerics, such as the Reverend Sabine Baring-Gould, took up the pursuit, and in 1898 the Folk-Song Society was founded. But celebrating these songs was one thing: finding them quite another. Sharp knew numerous songs were uncollected, and sensed the advance of urban society and the end of traditional village life might kill them. Saving them for posterity became his next task.

He started in Somerset in 1903. He had written to a clergyman friend, Charles Latimer Marson, who lived there to ask if he knew of a local folk-song culture. Marson asked him down, and on 22 August his gardener, the appropriately named John England, sang Sharp 'The Seeds of Love' in return for a pipeful of tobacco. During a tour around Somerset, he collected forty-two songs, and on 26 November lectured at the Hampstead Conservatoire about them. Over the next four years he would collect 1,500 songs; then, at the prompting of Mary Neal, a social worker, collected folk dances from morris men. Neal arranged for these to be taught in Esperance Girls' Clubs around England. Sharp argued in his writings for the fundamental place of the folk song in the national culture. Such was the esteem in which this placed him that he became music tutor to Prince Edward and Prince Albert – the future Edward VIII and George VI – in 1904.

Another young composer had grown up on Broadwood's folk songs and had, in the late 1890s, started to study them and see them as the foundation of an English musical tradition: Ralph Vaughan Williams. He was a parson's son and descended from, among others, the Darwins and the Wedgwoods, so part of the intellectual aristocracy of England. He spent much of 1903 touring England, lecturing on the English folk song. On 3 December – a week after Sharp's Hampstead lecture – the vicar of Ingrave, a village near Brentwood in Essex that was then in deep countryside, invited Vaughan Williams to a tea party for the parish elderly. There the composer met an old labourer called Charles Pottipher, who said he knew a folk song; he would not sing it at the party but if Vaughan Williams saw him separately, he would. The following day he returned to Ingrave and Pottipher sang him 'Bushes and Briars': and when Vaughan Williams heard it, according to his widow's account, 'he felt it was something he had known all his life.'[56] As with Sharp, the collecting bug struck hard. Vaughan Williams spent Christmas at his family home in the Surrey hills and took his bicycle around nearby villages searching for songs; in early 1904 he returned to Ingrave and took down more from Pottipher.

He spent much of 1904 and 1905 in this pursuit, notably in the eastern counties, working from Essex to Norfolk. He also went into Wiltshire, noting down songs from elderly people in the Salisbury workhouse and from the surrounding villages. Writing to the *Morning Post* that autumn, after an Essex reader had said how scarce songs were there, Vaughan Williams told of his experience in Ingrave, saying he did not imagine it was an 'exceptional village': 'I imagine if every village, not only in Essex, but all over England, were investigated, an equally rich store of traditional songs will be found.'[57] He agreed it required 'some trouble', that younger people tended not to know the 'ballads' and the older ones had to be persuaded they would not be 'laughed at'. He added that the music was founded on the old 'Church modes' and its roots were ancient: 'I believe that we are only now beginning to realise what a store of beautiful melody has existed in our country,' he added, referring to Sharp's work. They had begun to collaborate in the Folk-Song Society, whose secretary was Lucy Broadwood, niece of John.[58]

In common with those seeking to preserve buildings, or landscapes, before they disappeared, Vaughan Williams saw the urgency of the task as Sharp had. 'Whatever is done in the way of preserving traditional music must be done quickly; it must be remembered that the tunes, at all events, of true folk songs exist only by oral tradition, so that if they are not soon noted down and preserved they will be lost forever.' The cultural effect of these two men and their supporters would be enormous. In 1909 Sharp persuaded the chief inspector of elementary schools, E. G. A. Holmes, to have folk songs taught in schools; the previous year he had become editor of the Novello series *Folk Songs for Schools*, a work that would by the 1920s be in thousands of British schools.

The effect on Vaughan Williams's development as a composer was even more profound. He incorporated folk song and its influence in early orchestral works, such as the *Norfolk Rhapsodies* and *In the Fen Country*. When he edited *The English Hymnal* – a commission granted at Sharp's suggestion – between 1904 and 1906, he laced it with folk tunes he had collected: the carol 'O, Little Town of Bethlehem', for example, has the Sussex tune from 'The Ploughboy's Dream', and 'Fight the Good Fight' was originally 'Tarry Trowsers'. Vaughan Williams's Second Symphony, the *London*, of 1914, includes echoes of street cries from lavender sellers and sea songs heard in the docklands. And the earliest of his masterpieces, the *Fantasia on a Theme by Thomas Tallis*, first performed in 1910, exhibits another influence of the English past on his music in evoking the medieval 'church modes' and Tudor polyphony. It established as the dominant force in the present the influence of the music of the English past. He also influenced composers such as Gustav von Holst, his close friend and contemporary at the Royal College of Music, and George Butterworth, to collect folk songs and use them in their music. (Holst would journey further, into Arab and Indian music, and also Japanese.) English music had found a voice whose roots were at home, and advanced clinging to those roots: much of Vaughan Williams's music evoked pre-industrial England, and after a period of neglect following his death in 1958 his reputation rose until he became the composer most closely identified with England. His is partly a music of nostalgia.

Sharp proved more controversial, in life and in death. Instrumental in the formation of the English Folk Dance Society in 1911, his interpretations of the morris tradition, however, conflicted with those of Mary Neal and her followers; though after much rather ridiculous acrimony Sharp's view prevailed. Long after his death far-left historians accused him of expropriating songs of the urban working class – 'broadsides' – and passing them off as the products of rural society. As well as being tendentious the criticism was ironic, given Sharp's political motivations and his determination to record working-class culture. What is certain is that he and Vaughan Williams between them captured a genre of the indigenous musical culture before it vanished, and its influence bore heavily on British music for decades afterwards.

CHAPTER II

IMPERIAL CONSEQUENCES

I

The British crisis of confidence after the Boer War caused many to question not whether empire was feasible or desirable (though some did), but how Britain could better manage it without risking another humiliation, and how it could become more cohesive. Imperialism had seeped into the culture of the nation and altered the outlook of its people. It affected the way late-Victorian and Edwardian children were brought up, whether in what they were taught in school, or for what sort of future they were trained. By the time of the outbreak of the Great War no Briton was untouched by the country's imperialism, its propaganda, its reach, its sheer ubiquity, whether literally or metaphorically. To most Britons empire was the basis of the nation's ranking as a great world power, if not the greatest.

The difficulties in securing victory in South Africa prompted not only Lord Esher's detailed inquiry into the functioning of the Army, but debates on a range of issues, from national efficiency and the standard of living, health and education, to the value of eugenics. It created a tension about the extent to which co-operation was possible with the subject peoples, or how far they had to be treated as objects of conquest – this was especially true in India, but also in South Africa. However, the man who was notionally in charge of the Empire when the war ended – Joe Chamberlain, the Colonial Secretary – had more straightforward ideas about how to improve Britain. These were economic in origin, and comprised his plans for a system of protectionism in trade that would strengthen imperial bonds but also fund the new or improved public services that would turn out stronger, fitter and better-educated people to run the Empire in the next generation. As with many of Radical Joe's plans, all that was required was the highly elusive agreement of colleagues and parliament.

II

Having won the Second Boer War – eventually – Britain now had to unify the country that would, in 1910, become the Union of South Africa. Chamberlain took his wife there from Boxing Day 1902 until 25 February 1903, touring twenty-nine cities and making over sixty speeches. He strove to reconcile former enemies and to make Boers feel welcome under the Crown. But while abroad he brooded on a great question that had troubled him for years: in order to boost the Empire, should Britain impose tariffs on imports from outside it, making them more expensive than those produced within the Empire? This doctrine – Imperial Preference – was the next step in Chamberlain's imperial vision. Having split the Liberals over Ireland, his ideas would now split the Unionists over free trade and leave them no chance of winning a general election.

Despite his Liberal origins, Chamberlain saw free trade as less important than imperial unity and economic strength. He saw an imperial trading bloc, whose terms of trade favoured its members against all others, as the means to both those ends. It would shore up the British world against America and Germany. Moreover, he wanted revenues from tariffs to fund old age pensions, so that Britain did not have to consign its indigent elderly to the workhouse, and to help pay for other improvements. This is the paradox of his Liberal imperialism: his Liberalism compelled him to advocate state support for the elderly, but his self-definition as the champion of empire meant that the doctrine of free trade that had underpinned his old party since its inception was dispensable.

And there was further paradox: if it did not occur to Radical Joe that the boom that made Birmingham the workshop of the world, and Britain its leading economic power, came in the wake of the repeal of the Corn Laws and the torrent of free trade in other commodities that ensued, then the irony was not lost on some Unionist colleagues, not least the Chancellor of the Exchequer, Charles Ritchie, who supported free trade. A Colonial Conference in the summer of 1902 had endorsed Imperial Preference; and before Chamberlain left for the Cape he had argued his case in cabinet, and managed to convince his colleagues to create a preferential tariff on corn for the self-governing colonies. Ritchie, however, was determined to reverse that, and throughout Chamberlain's absence set about doing so. Nor was it just free-trading economic liberals who were opposed: Wells wrote that Chamberlain's ideas were 'calculated to combine the financial adventurers of the Empire in one vast conspiracy against the consumer.'[1]

Chamberlain returned to England after his South African odyssey on 14 March 1903. At a cabinet meeting three days later he found his colleagues sharing Ritchie's view. To Chamberlain's intense annoyance, Balfour refused to take sides, largely for fear of losing Ritchie so close to a Budget. This lack of leadership – as mentioned earlier, one of Balfour's books was entitled *A Defence of Philosophic Doubt* – was the beginning of the end of the Unionist government, and of his personal authority. Chamberlain grasped the importance of not losing Ritchie and did not force the issue. But on 15 May, three weeks after a free-trading Budget, he made a speech in Birmingham asserting that the time was right for Imperial Preference; and that it should be discussed at the next election. Balfour, who had at last said the time had not come to introduce tariffs, was horrified. Some of his MPs, notably Churchill, a committed free-trader, demanded a strong lead one way or the other: Balfour felt unable to give it.

Chamberlain repeated his view in the Commons on 28 May, with support from some Unionist colleagues. Empire had far-reaching consequences for the mother country, as has already been made clear: the management of Gordon's expedition helped bring down Gladstone; the Boer War shook national self-confidence. Chamberlain, who had already split one party over Ireland, was now proceeding to split another over free trade. The Liberals goaded Balfour for his indecision; his response was to ask the Board of Trade to compile data on the question. Meanwhile, pro-imperialists who disagreed with tariffs started to coalesce, furious that Chamberlain was implying that his opponents were against the Empire. St Loe Strachey, editor of *The Spectator*, told Churchill that 'we oppose him [Chamberlain] because we are determined that the Empire shall not be smashed by the reversal of the policy which has made it great.'[2] On 13 August the cabinet discussed the issue, failed to agree, and postponed debate for another month. Balfour sought a compromise; but on 9 September Chamberlain sent Balfour a letter of resignation, saying he wished the freedom to campaign for Imperial Preference. This was kept secret; but an hour before the cabinet met on 14 September Chamberlain agreed with Balfour that he would resign only if the cabinet refused to accept the policy.

He did resign. Balfour, oddly, declined to tell his colleagues about the letter, claiming he did not think Chamberlain was serious – even though he knew he was. Balfour saw no future for hard-line free-traders in his cabinet, and made it clear to Ritchie and Lord George Hamilton, the Secretary of State for India, that their opposition to tariff reform was incompatible with government policy. They resigned; as did the Scottish Secretary, Lord Balfour of Burleigh, and the Duke of Devonshire, Leader of the Lords and, after Chamberlain, the only other prominent Liberal Unionist. This removed more than a quarter of the cabinet, undermining the whole ministry: confidence in Balfour was shattered when his deception over Chamberlain's letter of resignation was revealed. The issue had been handled disastrously.

Chamberlain had told Churchill, who he knew was an ardent free-trader, on 15 August: 'I do not think there is much room in politics for a dissentient Tory, but heaven knows the other side stands much in need of new talent, and I expect you will drift there before very long.'[3] A month later Churchill's Unionist chairman in his Oldham constituency told him that if he was going to oppose Chamberlain 'the sooner you say so the better. There is a strong Pro Chamberlain feeling in the Constituency and I am afraid it is growing and it will have to be dealt with very tactfully.'[4] Churchill was lobbying Rosebery to leave the sulk in which he had sunk himself since 1895 and lead moderate Liberal free-traders: Rosebery announced his opposition to tariffs, but sought no return to the front line. Churchill told his constituents that Balfour's approach – which he feared, privately, was an exercise in procrastination – had only his qualified support: they told him that unless he was prepared 'blindly to follow' Balfour's policy they would not support him at the next election.[5] Oldham's Unionists believed rumours that Churchill was thinking of joining the Liberals. They were right: he feared that the Unionists were about to embrace protectionism, leaving him with no choice but to defect. He started looking for a Liberal candidacy, and Herbert Gladstone, the Liberal chief whip, did all he could to help. The Oldham association passed a vote of no confidence in Churchill in January 1904; the Unionist whip was withdrawn, until he complained to

Balfour and it was reinstated. Yet in late April he agreed to fight a Manchester seat as a free-trader, and on 31 May walked into the Commons and sat on the Liberal benches, next to David Lloyd George.

For another eighteen months the Unionist government hobbled along, riven by dissent, until Balfour resigned and Campbell-Bannerman took office, calling a general election. The crushing Liberal landslide of January 1906 buried Imperial Preference for decades. Chamberlain, with the fervour of a zealot, established the Tariff Reform League, its posters adorned with the noble image of Radical Joe, monocle screwed into his right eye and orchid in the buttonhole of his frock coat. Most of his party and the press backed him, and the prospect of defeat appears not to have occurred to him. His son Austen had replaced Ritchie as Chancellor, so the voice of Chamberlainism remained strong in cabinet. It seemed a temporary fix while Joe was away, crossing the nation giving great public speeches, until he returned to assume his rightful place as leader of the protectionist Unionist cause, possibly as prime minister. Beatrice Webb had in 1888 written what she called an 'epitaph' on him: 'Courage: masculine strength: ability to execute and manipulate: intense egotism, showing itself on one side by a strong desire for personal power, on the other by a love of ease, luxury and splendour. Bitterly resentful of personal slight or personal injury.'[6]

As he barnstormed, promising to save British industries from ruin by protecting their markets against cheap imports and demanding support from the working class, two things happened. His health began to fail – he was sixty-seven – and Asquith led a contrary, and increasingly successful, campaign for the Liberals. In 1905 Chamberlain increased the attacks, but the main victim was the unity of his party, which was in ruins. Balfour surrendered on 4 December, and on losing his seat in the election Chamberlain replaced him as acting leader of the opposition. While Balfour found a seat, his temporary successor identified their party with Imperial Preference, but it would not rule alone again until 1922. Chamberlain had noted in May 1905 that 'unless I have the support of the working people, clearly my movement is already condemned and utterly a failure.'[7] Thanks in part to the rise of Labour, and public fear of more expensive food, he was thwarted.

In early July 1906 Birmingham celebrated Chamberlain's seventieth birthday. On 10 July he addressed a vast audience about his two passions: radicalism and imperialism. Three days later he keeled over while dressing for dinner, having suffered a massive stroke. He made a partial recovery, and his family sought to conceal how debilitated he was; he could walk only a few steps, his speech was impaired, and his sight was damaged. His interest in politics did not fade, but his participation was limited to the issue of proclamations from Highbury. He was re-elected twice in 1910 but could not attend the Commons. He died of a heart attack on 2 July 1914, weeks before the catastrophe that undid his beloved empire forever.

III

Imperial Preference would crop up for decades to come – notably at the 1932 Ottawa Imperial Conference, when in response to the Great Depression it was adopted for five years. In the Edwardian era Britons sought other means to make their empire more cohesive, but realised that different methods had to be used in different places. In African colonies of relatively recent acquisition a straightforward master and servant policy was adopted, since the Colonial Office assumed that the indigenous populations there would have no idea how to rule according to British standards. In the white empire – future dominions such as Australia, Canada and New Zealand – it was assumed, equally, that those of British descent would rule in an appropriately British fashion. The difficulties came with India, the most prized imperial possession, where highly educated and civilised people who were not of British descent could not begin to see why they should not rule themselves, and which embraced highly advanced cultures: some more so than those of the white ruler.

The 1881 census of India found the country had 255 million people, whom the Crown ruled in eight provinces, under lieutenant-governors or commissioners, that formed a single polity, or Raj, whose capital was Calcutta. There were also nearly 600 Princely States, governed by Indian rulers under the Crown, but who contracted out many functions of government to the British. The Viceroy represented the Crown. India had its own Secretary of State in the cabinet, his department distinct from both the Foreign Office (in whose building the India Office was accommodated) and the Colonial Office; the Viceroy was accountable to parliament via the Secretary of State. This had been so since 1858 when, after the Mutiny of the previous year, the Crown took responsibility for India from the East India Company.

The Mutiny had shown Britain the futility and danger of trying to use authoritarian methods on the sub-continent. The lesson had been widely learned. The Princely States had however mostly not mutinied, which was why they were preserved by treaty after it, as bastions of loyalty in a country too large to be governed without help from the indigenous population. The Princely States provided the bulk of the Indian Army, which at the end of the nineteenth century was over half a million strong, an eighth of it European. More enlightened viceroys and their staffs sought to co-operate with Indians from outside the Princely States and involve them in the running of the country and in improving the conditions of the Indian people.

Although some Hindus and Muslims populated the middle ranks of the civil service, almost all the most senior positions were reserved for the white British. There was recruitment by competitive examination, but by 1900 only thirty-three Indians were employed in a civil service of 1,021 people.[8] In the wider government service in 1887 there were 21,466 positions paying at least seventy-five rupees a month (enough of an income to live respectably), 45 per cent of which were held by Hindus; Muslims held 7 per cent, Eurasians 19 per cent and Europeans 29 per cent.[9] The nation's schools and colleges were mainly the legacy of Thomas Babington Macaulay, who served on the Supreme Council of India in the 1830s. Universities had been opened in Calcutta, Bombay and Madras in 1857, many of whose graduates entered the lower ranks of the government service. Macaulay had also insisted on making English an official language. Knowledge of it would expand the intellectual horizons of young Indians because of the greater availability of historical and scientific literature in English.

India's gross domestic product as a proportion of the world's output fell after 1858; Nationalists blamed British mismanagement but growth elsewhere, notably in the US, Germany and in Britain itself, was responsible for the shrinking size of its slice of the global cake. Britain invested heavily in irrigation systems to help improve Indian farming; and it developed railways and a telegraph system, though for strategic as well as economic and philanthropic reasons. Paradoxically, despite all these improvements, it was at the Raj-funded new seats of Indian learning that the Nationalist movement took off, with the foundation in 1885 of the Indian National Congress.

One of the more enlightened rulers of India was George Nathaniel Curzon, Viceroy from 1899 to 1905. He understood the need to improve

India and the lives of Indians if Britain were to justify its rule there. For him, that rule was vital to British geopolitical supremacy: in 1900 he told Alfred Lyttelton, who would succeed Chamberlain as Colonial Secretary, that 'the mastery of the world' was 'in the possession of the British people' if they had 'the Empire of Hindustan'.[10] Curzon saw the importance of Indians governing themselves as far as possible, rather than having London's rule imposed upon them. He was the embodiment of the English aristocracy. He came from one of the oldest families in Britain – his father, Lord Scarsdale, had as his seat the palatial Kedleston Hall in Derbyshire, where the family had lived since the twelfth century – and Curzon was often mocked for his apparent grandeur, though his hauteur was at least partly caused by the corset he had worn since childhood because of a spinal injury. At Oxford in the early 1880s, where he was a brilliant scholar and ended up a Prize Fellow of All Souls, he was the subject of a Balliol rhyme:

> My name is George Nathaniel Curzon,
> I am a most superior person,
> My cheek is pink, my hair is sleek,
> I dine at Blenheim once a week.[11]

What was perceived, perhaps unfairly, as his crushing arrogance meant he divided opinion not just at Oxford, but at Eton before it and in the Commons afterwards when elected an MP in 1886, aged just twenty-seven. He intended to be prime minister and dreaded his father's death, not through filial devotion but because he saw, even in the 1890s, the unlikelihood of any prime minister sitting in the Lords again. When it was insisted he take a peerage on becoming Viceroy he took an Irish one, becoming Lord Curzon, but not being eligible to sit in the Lords. His viceroyalty was, in his eyes, a training for eventual leadership of his country, not a substitute for it. He was a committed imperialist in the sense of Britain doing good in the world, rather than conquering, and his personal style was central to his exercising a dignified and civilised rule over India. He had in common with Lord Cromer, Consul-General in Egypt from 1882 to 1907, a gift for administration.

He sought to project the image of a beneficent empire after the damage done to the imperial project during the Boer War. Consequently, he attempted a prodigious programme of reform in India. Most fundamentally, he put the currency on the gold standard to stabilise it. He introduced measures to improve agriculture, encourage commerce, industry and trade, reform the police, manage famines better, lower taxes, improve communications, tackle pollution, advance the railways, alleviate debt, streamline the civil service, improve universities and enhance the role of the Princely States. Also, being highly attuned to Indian cultures, he founded an Imperial Library, sponsored archaeological research and established a framework to preserve antiquities. He also wanted a national tree-planting programme, a nursing service, a sanitary commissioner, better inland navigation, technical education, and inspectorates of mines and agriculture. This epic programme required application and resources, and a huge personality to see it through. This massive expansion of the role of the state inevitably brought Curzon into conflict with his masters in London, and with colleagues in India. Crucially, though, he wanted Indians to 'share in the glory' of the project.[12]

His most controversial decision was to partition Bengal. In October 1905 the province was divided into the Hindu-dominated west and the Muslim-dominated east. Curzon advocated it on administrative grounds, separating distinct cultural and linguistic areas and helping ensure more official attention was paid to the new eastern province, where modernisation could be effected. However, he also felt it would set back the growing Nationalist movement by separating different religious groups of Indians and breaking an idea of unity. The result went contrary to his expectations. Muslims welcomed the idea; the Hindus deplored it, and increased their demands for political power precisely because it reduced the Bengali power base of the Congress Party. Several years of intense protest caused the partition to be reversed in 1911.

The Bengal partition crowned a series of controversial actions that had left Curzon's relations with his government colleagues badly strained. He should have come home in 1904, but early in 1903 demanded to be allowed to stay a further two or three years, to see his reforms through. At that very time Curzon's friends at home were begging him to return and replace Balfour – who had been prime minister for barely six months – because of his failings, and because of how Chamberlain was dictating economic policy. Balfour knew Curzon should come home, but equally knew he would be less of a threat where he was: so he agreed to keep him in Calcutta, despite Curzon's demands becoming ever more exhaustive – he now wanted a four-month holiday in England, despite the King and Balfour both believing a viceroy could not be absent that long. In May 1903 Balfour told Knollys, the King's private secretary, that 'in spite of Curzon's extraordinary behaviour and still more extraordinary letters, I am disposed to recommend his plan should in substance be accepted'.[13]

Curzon was not always a good colleague, not least because he saw his critics as incipiently stupid. His methods brought him into conflict with Kitchener, whom Balfour had sent as commander-in-chief of the Army there. Their quarrel over the governance of India, which broke out as Balfour was trying to hold his and Curzon's party together over Imperial Preference, undermined British rule there in the long term, and had a profound impact on Curzon's place in domestic politics. When Kitchener took up his post after the Boer War, Curzon supported him. Within months, however, the two were at odds over whether there should be a separate 'military member' of the Viceroy's council, with important responsibilities for supply and transport, or whether the commander-in-chief should do the job. Kitchener wanted no rivals and would use the press and go behind Curzon's back – using Balfour's cousin-by-marriage, Lady Salisbury, to lobby the prime minister – to get what he wanted. He tried to resign in September 1904 while apparently failing to get his way, but an inquiry into army administration soothed him. Constitutionally, the decision was the Viceroy's, and London would force his removal by overriding him.

The Viceroy eventually lost the argument because he lacked Kitchener's skills as an intriguer who was adroit in manipulating public and political opinion on to his side. Curzon also had dismal relations with his former close friend St John Brodrick, who had in late 1903 become India Secretary. Brodrick eventually appointed a heavily-biased committee to advise him what to do, and chaired it himself. It decided to leave a military member on the Viceroy's council, but with little or no power, that having been transferred to the commander-in-chief. Curzon considered resigning but instead rejected the proposals, complained about their insulting nature and the behaviour of Brodrick, and, what is more, used his superior powers of reasoning to persuade Kitchener to reject them too, which he did.

Curzon told the King on 6 July 1905, writing from Simla, that:

> [I]t seems certain that the government at home can never have contemplated that they would bring about such a commotion in

India, or that their action would be so universally and unanimously condemned by public opinion here. There is scarcely a dissentient voice, and what has made the public here particularly angry has been the tone in which the Government of India have been publicly addressed, not for the first time, by the present Secretary of State. The instruments of your Majesty's rule in India cannot be openly humiliated without weakening the foundations of the rule itself.[14]

He demanded that General Sir Edmund Barrow, who he believed was the best soldier in India, should become what was now designated the Military Supply Member on the Viceroy's council. Kitchener, who regarded Barrow as too able and too loyal to Curzon, disagreed, and protested to London. Curzon told Brodrick he would resign unless Barrow was appointed. Brodrick refused: and to his and Balfour's delight, but to the dismay of Lord Lansdowne, the Foreign Secretary, Curzon resigned.

The King felt Curzon had been poorly treated. On 1 September Knollys cabled Balfour to say that 'the King desires me to inform you that he thinks Viceroy of India should be offered an Earldom, and at once. He hopes that considering Viceroy of India's character, such an offer made immediately might soothe his feelings.'[15] When Balfour refused, Knollys admitted that 'there is something to be said on the other side'.[16] However, he said the government had stuck with Curzon knowing he disagreed with its policies; he had resigned, and not been recalled though he had rendered 'brilliant services' for most of his rule.

By 7 October Balfour agreed to recommend Curzon for a 'fitting honour'.[17] But he did not wish to honour him in a way that made it seem he had been right and Brodrick and Kitchener wrong: and there was also the danger that 'George on his return home may think it right, in his own or the public interest, to continue the late unhappy controversy in the press or on the platform. He may cross swords with Kitchener or denounce Brodrick and the Government.'[18] How, in such circumstances, could he have an earldom? 'A further embarrassment', Balfour added, 'arises out of the fact that I cannot explain to George himself how matters stand. To do so would lay me open to the interpretation that I sought to close his mouth by the offer of a peerage, and conceived him to be the kind of man to whom such a transaction would not be offensive.'[19] The King wanted no fight. He told Knollys to tell Balfour the best course was to 'do nothing', avoiding further controversy in the 'interests of the British Empire'.[20] The government then fell with the matter still unresolved; when Campbell-Bannerman came in he tactlessly told Curzon that Balfour was against his being honoured – which caused Balfour to protest 'George Curzon's services as Indian Viceroy deserved a Peerage' and that he had not expected 'any prolonged delay' in its award.[21]

Curzon had to wait for his earldom until the Coronation Honours of 1911. The Liberal India Secretary, John Morley, however, embraced his doctrine that Indians should be more involved in running their country. He collaborated with Curzon's successor, the Earl of Minto, to bring in the 1909 Indian Councils Act. Known as the Morley-Minto reforms, these measures allowed Indians to be admitted to the Viceroy's and Governor's councils, and more to be elected to provincial legislative bodies. Curzon feared the measures because he thought they would lead to an Indian parliament, something he could not countenance: but Morley saw them as essential to improving morale among the highest class of Indians, on whom the Raj relied. Although the Act limited Indian representation, it allowed dedicated seats for Muslims, to avoid their being outnumbered by Hindus.

Aware of the difficulties when the government in London went out of step with the Viceroy, Morley consulted Minto at every step. It was the first of many reforms over the ensuing decades; but none would prevent the drive towards independence that became inevitable in an educated, economically developing India. In 1911, when Lord Crewe succeeded Morley, he accepted the advice of Sir Charles Hardinge, Viceroy from 1910, to move the capital from Calcutta to Delhi and to give more self-government to the provinces until they were autonomous. That also angered Curzon, whose reforms had depended upon strong central authority, but India was on the inevitable path to self-rule.

As in Britain, wider education created a political challenge from the newly educated; in India's case, by 1900 it had led to mounting Indian Nationalism, which the rulers attempted to meet after 1892 by allowing more Indians to serve in local legislatures and by making it easier for them to enter the civil service. The highly-educated and politicised men who did so were an elite within an elite, unrepresentative of the ordinary Indian; but they argued consistently in the ensuing decades that Britain exploited India, extracting wealth that should have been invested to make the country grow. They also lobbied the government, with some success, for a bigger role for Indians in shaping society. The more this new Indian middle class grew, and the greater their involvement with governance, the harder it was for the British, who faced no such challenges in Africa or their Caribbean possessions from non-white subjects. The seeds of Nationalism were sown, and their growth would eventually help bring about the end of British rule in 1947. And when that came, it hastened the end of Britain's empire around the globe, feeding the appetite for independence in territories from the West Indies to the Pacific via Africa, the Mediterranean and the Far East.

IV

In its Edwardian heyday empire was a force that could make or break careers and reputations. It allowed opportunities for the sort of men that F. E. Smith had in mind when he talked of the 'glittering prizes' awaiting those who had 'stout hearts and sharp swords'.[22] It also served as an inspiration to the young, who learned about heroes whom they could emulate, or territories where they could help and civilise the people. This was a job not just for soldiers, but for thinkers and administrators. For example, although the embarrassments of the Boer War ruined many reputations, Sir Alfred Milner, the former High Commissioner, came out of the wreckage with his standing enhanced. Elevated to the peerage in 1901, he became the ultimate proconsul. Having steered South Africa towards Union he returned to England in 1905. The following year, shortly after his delayed maiden speech in the Lords, that House honoured him by debating his services for a day, and gave him an overwhelming vote of appreciation. The Archbishop of Canterbury, Randall Davidson, no party man, professed that Milner had 'proved himself to be one of the most illustrious of an illustrious line' of public servants.[23] Imperial service was, morally, fine service: it was about bringing British standards of constitutional government, justice, fair play and – for the most part – Christianity to large areas of the world that had hitherto remained unblessed by it.

Yet if the establishment was more imperialist than ever by the end of Edward VII's reign, there were signs elsewhere the zenith had been reached. Cracks were beginning to show in the great edifice of the imperial project, and of the support of opinion-formers for it. There was a new uncertainty about the future, and continued dominance, of British power. This caused a sort of schizophrenia in the national psyche, between ardent supporters of the imperial destiny, and those who feared the project could not be sustained.

The imperialists were determined to put up a strong defence, however. The shock of how physically unfit so many recruits had been when the Second Boer War broke out reverberated through the inquiry into the Army's performance in the war, led by Lord Esher, and worried the public: many feared the Germans might come and have to be fought, and Britain would be too weak to do so. There were constant initiatives to propagate the cult of manliness deemed essential to maintain imperial power; all too often, exhibiting manliness required taking a hard line against people with the misfortune not to have been born British.

C. B. Fry, a leading amateur cricketer of the day, started a magazine for boys dedicated largely to building manliness, and in 1908 became superintendent of a boys' naval training ship. *The Boy's Own Paper* had aspirations to heroism as its staple, as did the hugely popular historical adventure novels of G. A. Henty that appeared throughout the 1880s and 1890s, with their subtext of British racial superiority. The most significant consequence of the Boer War for the young, however, was Robert Baden-Powell's founding of the Boy Scout movement. An interesting aspect of the imperial cult of manliness was how so many of its greatest advocates either never married, or married late. Kitchener and Rhodes were among the former; Baden-Powell married at fifty-five and Milner at sixty-seven.

As has been noted, Baden-Powell had seen at Mafeking how adolescent energies could be channelled into something constructive and public-spirited. He realised boys could valuably and – most important – enjoyably learn some of the principles of military scouting, notably reconnaissance and survival techniques. Although this was not Baden-Powell's purpose, the idea furthered the subtle militarisation Britain would need to preserve its power and its empire: and Baden-Powell was a committed imperialist, determined to do all he could to defend and further the project. The subtitle of the biblical text of his movement, *Scouting for Boys*, published in 1908, is 'A Handbook for Instruction in Good Citizenship': and citizenship of Britain was, for Baden-Powell, synonymous with that of empire. *Scouting for Boys* is an almost random assembly of Baden-Powell's gems of wisdom and experience, expounded directly to boys – the pronoun 'you' is ubiquitous. He had kept a commonplace book and written manuals for soldiers, and distilled all that and more into what was not merely a manual for scouting, but a manual for life and 'citizenship' in Britain's empire.

As he wrote it during 1906 and 1907, Baden-Powell consulted others with experience in scouting, notably Frederick Russell Burnham, an American who became Chief of Scouts for the British Army in Africa, and in organising boys in movements such as the Boys' Brigade, which William Alexander Smith, a Scot, had founded in Glasgow in 1883 with the avowed aim of developing 'Christian manliness'. Although the scouts would have this spiritual dimension too it took second place to encouraging adventure, self-reliance and self-discipline – in other words, 'manliness'. It was also about having fun, liberating boys from the strict, seen-and-not-heard rote-learning that had hitherto dominated their lives. It was explicitly classless, though relied on extending the sporting ethos of the post-Arnoldian public school throughout the social system. It also touched a nerve with parents, who had been told that the nation's young were physically weak and morally inadequate.

Baden-Powell did not envisage a separate movement, but hoped to have existing organisations, such as the Boys' Brigade, adopt his ideas alongside their own. From 1 to 9 August 1907 he organised the first Scout Camp, for twenty boys from schools in London and around Bournemouth, on Brownsea Island off the Dorset coast, to test his ideas. The boys, who slept in tents, were woken each morning by Baden-Powell's blowing a kudu horn, an instrument sounded by the Ndebele as they went into battle. At the end of the camp he suspected he had a success on his hands; and so did his publisher, C. Arthur Pearson, proprietor of the *Daily Express* and a man with an eye to making money, who urged him to get the book out, preceded by a six-part fortnightly magazine from January 1908.

It was an instant success. Boys, many of whom led dull lives in the new suburbs spreading across Britain, formed scout patrols and connected to an exciting, outdoor, 'backwoods' way of life that had otherwise seemed lost. Kipling may have been *passé*, but Baden-Powell used principles from *The Jungle Book* and *Kim* (cited in detail early in the book, with Kim praised for being 'strong-minded') to set out rules for scouting – notably the idea of the group, or patrol, following the instructions of a leader: but these Kipling had copied from what he knew of military practice, and were second nature to Baden-Powell.[24]

The Scouts were explicitly patriotic: the 'instructors' organising the boys were told that each parade (the military term, too, is notable) would begin with hoisting and saluting the Union flag (there was advice on flying it the right way up). Pursuing the military theme, there were also to be 'physical exercises' and 'drill'.[25] The Scout Oath was to be loyal to God and the King but also 'to help other people at all times' and to obey Scout law.[26] Having taken the oath, boys learned secret signs and signals, to foster brotherhood and group loyalty. The right spirit was also inculcated through a series of 'camp-fire yarns', the first of which, appropriately enough, was about the boys of Mafeking.

The basics of scouting were outlined as woodcraft – learning to identify animals, to kill them if needed for food or if they were harmful, but not otherwise; campaigning – learning to live in the open, make camp fires and cook their food, but also how to tie knots and to use logs to make bridges and rafts; chivalry ('in the old days the knights were the scouts of Britain . . . they would not do a dishonourable thing, such as telling a lie or stealing'[27]), which also included doing a good turn every day; saving life ('remember the case at the Hampstead Ponds last year when a woman drowned herself in shallow water before a whole lot of men, who were too frightened to do anything but shout at her. It was a disgrace to our nation that there was not a real man among them'[28]); endurance ('sleep with your windows open, summer and winter, and you will never catch cold . . . Scouts breathe through the nose, not the mouth . . . alcohol is a mere poison when a man takes too much of it . . . no boy ever began smoking because he liked it, but because he thought it made him look like a grown-up man. As a matter of fact it generally makes him look a little ass'[29]); and, of course, patriotism ('this vast empire . . . was made by your forefathers by dint of hard work and hard fighting, at the sacrifice of their lives – that is, by their hearty patriotism'). 'Country first, and self second, should be your motto.'[30]

The yarns showed these virtues, notably 'pluck', in action, and how the alert, well-trained scout could stop all sorts of evils. 'Scout's honour' became a national cliché. Baden-Powell wanted the nation to cohere, through scouting, against common enemies. This required the elimination of social divisions ('A scout must never be a SNOB') and cast-iron loyalty to the King 'and his officers'.[31] Scouts were instructed not to whine when faced with hardship, and not to swear: the punishment for bad language was decreed as a mug of cold water poured down the offender's sleeve. There was also a strong emphasis on physical exercise, and scouts were taught to track animals, and men, and to be able to hide themselves, to deal with mad dogs, and to navigate by the sun and the stars. 'Scouts should also know how to kill and cut up their cattle', he wrote, though it is to be doubted that many suburban patrols actually engaged in the work of the abattoir. 'Cattle are generally poleaxed,' he wrote, helpfully, before describing how best to cut the throat of a sheep.[32]

Scouting was also about intellectual and personal growth. The Founder envisaged winter evenings devoted to debates and discussions; and, as a keen amateur thespian himself, to plays and acting. All this was designed to breed confidence, and to keep the troops cheerful in adversity. The scout was trained to be an observer, notably of people, to discern their characters, and to be able to give a description to the police if necessary. The rich could be discerned from the poor by their boots. The book's tone was strongly reminiscent of Samuel Smiles's *vade mecum* for the Victorian lower-middle class, *Self Help*, promoting self-improvement, but without using the term.[33] Baden-Powell's 'chivalry' was about teaching boys to be gentlemen, especially in practising kindness and courtesy to women. They were urged to 'get on', to aim to join the forces or the professions; also to watch their health – bad teeth would stop them eating the hard biscuits and tough meat encountered on campaign, and smoking would mask their vital sense of smell. The chapter he wished to include on the unspeakable evils of masturbation was dropped at Pearson's insistence.

Ultimately, however, *Scouting for Boys* is about empire, and how the moral qualities instilled in the scout could secure it. Quoting George Wyndham, a Unionist minister under Balfour, Baden-Powell warns his readers that 'the same causes which brought about the fall of the great Roman Empire are working today in Great Britain.'[34] The scouts would be a rearguard action against decadence. The chapter on patriotism begins with a yarn on 'Our Empire: How it grew – How it must be held.'[35] Perhaps only a man who had seen at close quarters the 'victory' of the Boer War could understand the febrility of British power; and *Scouting for Boys* subtly addresses the need to develop the right 'stock' for continuing an empire without which, Baden-Powell feared, Britain would be a nullity. But the Empire must be held honourably: Baden-Powell more than once utters Newbolt's imprecation to 'play the game'.

He had founded a movement whether he had wanted to or not. In 1909 the first Scout Rally was held at Crystal Palace, with 11,000 scouts attending. By 1910 there were 100,000 boys in the movement, and it spread throughout the Empire – first Gibraltar, then Malta, then Canada, then Australasia and Africa – and to countries outside the British-dominated world. Baden-Powell became Chief Scout and, because of the mushrooming nature of the organisation, set up training camps for potential scoutmasters to help supervise patrols.

Girls went to scout rallies disguised as boys because they were desperate to join, and in 1910 Baden-Powell's sister Agnes was enlisted to form the Girl Guides. The initial appeal to girls was also couched in the rhetoric of enlisting the young to fight against decadence, because 'decadence is threatening the nation'.[36] In 1912 the Baden-Powells published *The Handbook for Girl Guides: How Girls Can Help to Build Up the Empire*, a reworking of *Scouting for Boys*, even counselling avoiding the solitary vice: 'All secret bad habits are evil and dangerous, lead to hysteria and lunatic asylums, and serious illness is the result . . . blindness, paralysis and loss of memory.'[37]

Wells noted the effect on British youth of Baden-Powell's great initiative. 'There suddenly appeared . . . a new sort of little boy, a most agreeable development of the slouching, cunning, cigarette-smoking, town-bred youngster, a small boy in a khaki hat, and with bare knees and athletic bearing, earnestly engaged in wholesome and invigorating games up to and occasionally a little beyond his strength – the Boy Scout.'[38] He also lamented that 'Liberalism hadn't been able to produce, and had indeed never attempted to produce, anything of this kind.'

However Wells – who was certainly not in Baden-Powell's camp, but one whose scepticism about empire was profound – was sure he identified in imperialism a creed in decline, despite the efforts of the Chief Scout and his allies. In 1910 in *The New Machiavelli* he wrote of the influence of 'Kiplingism' at the turn of the century, and how young, intelligent people were 'very distinctly imperialists' with 'a vivid sense of the White Man's Burden'.[39] He said Kipling had, however, gone out of favour, 'mercilessly and exhaustively mocked, criticised and torn to shreds'. In the 1890s people had relished 'boyish enthusiasm for effective force' and 'the very odours of empire', with Kipling mastering the 'poetic dialect' of the empire-builder. Wells saluted him for his 'haunting quotations', and saw 'Recessional' as the poet's 'climax'. But it was the 'exasperating and humiliating struggle' of the Second Boer War that had changed these perceptions, and caused Kipling to appear as one sounding a wrong note.[40] It should be remembered, however, that when Kipling wrote in 1899 – just before the Second Boer War broke out – about 'the White Man's burden', he was referring to the war between America and the Philippines, not directly to the perceived duties of the British imperialist.

As the popular perception grew that the ideals of empire were in decline, another of its poets, Henry Newbolt, suffered a similar fate. Much of his poetry was about the main love of his life, Clifton School, which he had attended in the 1870s: but it is the school life and its preparation for empire that informed his most celebrated poem, '*Vitai Lampada*', one every bit as well known as 'If'. Parodied to exhaustion, the poem captured the predominantly uncynical mood about empire, and the heroism of the endeavour, in 1892 when it was written and in 1897 when it was published.

The poem extols the virtues of muscular Christianity fundamental to the establishment of empire. In the second stanza, Newbolt alludes to the Battle of Abu Klea in 1885, fought during the failed expedition to rescue Gordon, when Colonel Fred Burnaby was killed and a machine gun – a Gardner rather than a Gatling – seized up:

The sand of the desert is sodden red,
  —Red with the wreck of a square that broke;
  —The Gatling's jammed and the Colonel dead,
And the regiment blind with dust and smoke.
The river of death has brimmed his banks,
And England's far, and Honour a name,
But the voice of a schoolboy rallies the ranks:
'Play up! play up! and play the game!'[41]

Newbolt wrote much more verse about imperial glory, notably *The Island Race*, written before the Boer War, and *Songs of the Sea* and *Songs of the Fleet*, written after it. But the war had tarnished the idea that imperialism was romantic; the Great War would render schoolboy virtue under fire and the inevitability of glory somewhat tasteless. Newbolt himself prospered: the government recruited him in 1914 to assist with propaganda, at which he so excelled that he was knighted in 1915 and made a Companion of Honour in 1922. But by that stage his earlier work was no more than a period piece, and his poetic reputation shot.

Sometimes the poets of empire themselves fell victim to doubt. A. C. Benson, an Eton master who became a Cambridge don, wrote the words to the part of Elgar's *Coronation Ode* of 1902 that used the tune from the first *Pomp and Circumstance* march of the previous year:

> Land of Hope and Glory, Mother of the Free,
> How shall we extol thee, who are born of thee?
> Wider still and wider, shall thy bounds be set;
> God who made thee mighty, make thee mightier yet.

As a result of this Benson was invited, and inevitably refused, to make speeches on Empire Day. He explained his diffidence in 1917: 'The "Empire" . . . leaves me cold . . . How can little limited minds think about the colonies, & India, & the world at large, and all that it means? . . . nor can I back our race against all races. I believe in our race, but I don't disbelieve in theirs.'[42]

V

For all the moral dubiety and mixed results of the Boer War, the bullying of other European nations in the cause of profit, and the racialist treatment of conquered and colonised peoples, millions saw empire as a noble ideal, the least of many other potential evils, a benign form of international paternalism. The intelligentsia may have been angered and disillusioned by what had happened in South Africa, but the enthusiasm of the masses for the project remained constant, at least until the Great War. The ideal they admired also offered challenges to take the Union flag, and therefore what many Britons believed to be the highest form of civilisation, to the farthest reaches of the globe.

What inspired the small boys – and indeed the small girls – of Britain was the heroism of those who fought to achieve this expansion, and (as they were told in their schools, in church and by their parents) to extend Christianity and British values among savage races. Imperial endeavour was the stuff of *The Boy's Own Paper*, which illustrated the nobility of the aim of all young Britons to participate in it. It was romanticised (albeit with an increasing degree of cynicism) by Kipling in his stories and poetry. Empire also acted as an inspiration to millions of Britons about what was possible in their own lives: lives that could now be played out on a far vaster canvas than just Britain alone. And attitudes to what might best be described as glorious failures shifted in the quarter-century after Gordon: whereas the nation beat its breast about the *débâcle* of his last expedition, that of Captain Scott in 1912 was presented as a triumph of the pioneering spirit and British phlegm.

No act of imperial flag-planting has lodged in the British historical imagination in quite the same way as Robert Falcon Scott's ill-fated expedition to the South Pole has. It also, more than any event from the years before the Great War, symbolised the tensions within, and the ultimate fate of, the great imperial adventure. In many ways the *ne plus ultra* of heroic failures, the very celebration of it fits in appropriately with the values of an age of decadence. It ended in defeat and death, yet children were instructed to admire it: and, in truth, there were elements in it that were entirely admirable, and heroic. It left in the summer of 1910, Scott joining the ship *Terra Nova* in South Africa. He reached Australia in October to hear that the Norwegian explorer Roald Amundsen was *en route* too, and that he faced a race to the pole. Scott, a naval officer of rigid self-discipline, iron will and bloody mind, had already, on the Discovery Expedition of 1901–4, gone with Ernest Shackleton and Edward Wilson further south than any other men in history, a feat that established him as a popular hero. He had discovered the Polar Plateau, where the South Pole is situated, and determined to go back and complete the job, an additional trek of 530 miles. He was like the great explorers who had defied death, disease and the elements in opening up central Africa in the 1850s and 1860s. But unlike them he was doing it not to take Christianity to heathens, or for commercial reasons, but because it was there to be done, and Britain would do it, further embellishing her imperial glory.

The expedition was dogged by misfortune. While sailing to Antarctica from New Zealand the *Terra Nova* was trapped in ice for three weeks, and the delay affected the preparations for the trek. The ponies Scott had taken with them succumbed to the cold and either died or had to be shot. Eventually, five men reached the Pole on 17 January 1912, to find Amundsen had been there five weeks earlier. Scott recorded his despair in his diaries: 'The worst has happened . . . Great God this is an awful place.'[43]

After two days' rest they began the 800-mile trek back to their ship, but the advance of the long Antarctic night and winter slowed them down and magnified their exhaustion. Scott recorded the privations in his journal, but also the nobility of his comrades and, unwittingly, of himself as they neared their deaths. For all the futility of his expedition, and the loss of their lives, there emerges from the journals one of the greatest tales of heroism in Britain's history, which inspired and humbled a nation when it was told.

Edgar Evans, a Royal Navy petty officer and veteran of the earlier expedition, died on 17 February. Scott had hoped to meet up with dog teams sent from *Terra Nova* with new supplies, but they could not find him. On 16 March, 400 miles from base, Captain Lawrence 'Titus' Oates, a cavalry officer and Boer War veteran, suffering from frostbitten toes and gangrene, told his comrades: 'I am just going outside and I may be some time.'[44] Scott too had frostbitten feet, but he and his two surviving colleagues – Wilson, a doctor and the chief scientific officer of the expedition, and Henry Bowers, a naval lieutenant – managed to walk twenty miles in a raging blizzard before making their final camp. They were still eleven miles from a depot, and almost out of supplies, but the weather was too bad, and they were too weak.

Scott realised there was no hope of going on. He settled down with his comrades to write their last letters home and, in Scott's case, his final journal entries. The last is dated 29 March, which is presumed to be the day he died. It ended with a reminder that this had been a British enterprise on behalf of the British Empire, and the family were all in it together, and would now be expected to rally round: 'For God's sake look after our people.'[45] The men's bodies were found on 12 November, and news of their fate reached London on 10 February 1913, hours after *Terra Nova* reached New Zealand. Asquith, the prime minister, made a statement about the expedition in the Commons the next day, in response to a request from Austen Chamberlain echoing Scott's plea for the men's families to be looked after by the state. He called Scott's last message 'one of the most moving and pathetic utterances in the annals of discovery of a brave and enduring man face to face with a tragic but noble end to a career of self-devoting service. I can only say that his appeal will not fall on deaf ears.'[46] The country did rally round: more than £75,000 was raised, and Mrs Scott was given the rank and precedence of the wife of a Knight Commander of the Order of the Bath.

In the Lords Lord Lamington mused: 'I do not suppose that in the annals of human self-sacrifice there was ever anything finer than the passing of Captain Oates into the blizzard.'[47] Lord Emmott, under-secretary of state for the colonies, announced that 'the splendid example which these men have set will be, I am sure, an inspiration to Englishmen for all time. Their last thoughts were for others, and not for themselves.' Both men called the explorers 'heroes'. Scott had helped define empire as about setting an example to a nation and to the world, of moral as well as physical growth. Baden-Powell, who knew something about heroic endurance, remarked: 'Are Britons going downhill? No! There is plenty of pluck and spirit left in the British after all.'[48] On the day of the memorial service at St Paul's – 14 February – the heroic story of Scott and his companions was read to schoolchildren throughout the land.

Also found with Scott's and his comrades' bodies was a final 'Message to the Public', in which Scott – a master of public relations, who saw the need to design and bequeath his own legend – justified the expedition, despite its outcome. Eventually his heroism was derided and parodied, partly because it was out of tune with the later twentieth century, partly because Scott presided over a heroic failure, and one for which his own misjudgments were largely responsible. But he never sought to evade culpability; indeed, his willing acceptance of it redoubles his moral stature. The most famous passage of the Message exemplified the heroic attitude not just of him and his comrades, but of other pioneer imperialists, at once adventurous and devoid of self-pity, and was intended as an example to the nation and people Scott left behind. The words incarnate his view of the national spirit of a grand imperial power, and a spirit of greatness at that:

> We took risks, we knew we took them; things have come out against us, and therefore we have no cause for complaint, but bow to the will of Providence, determined still to do our best to the last.[49]

CHAPTER 12

ART AND LIFE

I

To many minds no one symbolised the decadence of the Belle Époque more perfectly, and indeed more unfortunately, than Oscar Wilde. His homosexuality would alienate him from the vast majority of contemporary opinion, and render his name literally unspeakable in most society. His hedonism, too, would have him marked out to most contemporaries as an obvious degenerate entirely at odds with the contemporary cult of manliness.

That Wilde's case has become so indicative of the Belle Époque owes more to the flamboyant celebrity of its victim, by the mid-1890s a leading wit, critic, dramatist and aesthete, than to his offence, a practice to which students of depravity were inured after Cleveland Street. Wilde had referred to that scandal in his 1890 novel *The Picture of Dorian Gray*, some of whose homoerotic passages he toned down for a second edition the following year, and which was in part inspired and influenced by the novels of the French decadents of which English opinion so heartily disapproved. The year after its publication he met Lord Alfred Douglas, a younger son of the Marquess of Queensberry – whose own contribution to the cult of manliness had been to codify the rules for boxing, a sport in which Lord Alfred appears to have shown not the slightest interest. According to Wilde's account of their friendship, written in Reading Gaol in 1897 and published posthumously as *De Profundis*, he allowed himself to be exploited, emotionally and financially, by his much younger friend, bankrupting himself as a result.

It was not just the endless suppers of champagne and delicacies that did this, but having to pay Queensberry's court costs when Wilde, who had at Douglas's insistence sued the thuggish and semi-literate peer for criminal libel when he accused Wilde of being a 'somdomite', lost the case: and in doing so invited a prosecution under the Labouchere amendment. Queensberry, whom Wilde ridiculed as 'the Scarlet Marquis', had turned up on 14 February 1895 at the first night of *The Importance of Being Earnest* with a prize-fighter in tow, determined to address the audience.[1] Wilde was tipped off and a police guard was posted. Queensberry, denied entry, 'prowled about for three hours, then left chattering like a monstrous ape.' He left Wilde 'a grotesque bouquet of vegetables', suggesting, yet again, that he was not entirely sane.

The forty-one-year-old Edward Carson, one of the most fearsome QCs at the criminal bar and an exact contemporary of Wilde from Trinity College Dublin, appeared for Queensberry. 'No doubt', Wilde could not resist observing, 'he will pursue the case with all the added bitterness of an old friend.'[2] Carson did not deploy bitterness, but he did, in keeping with his duty to make the best possible case for his client, make the most brutally comprehensive one against Wilde. No aspect of his friendships, private life or published works went unexamined or unexploited for the proof they provided of his degeneracy and corruption – notably his romantic attachments to young men, on whom he showered gifts and much of his time. When Carson said he intended to call male prostitutes who would speak of their escapades with Wilde, he surrendered.

In Victorian homosexual slang a term used to describe a homosexual man was 'earnest'. So the title of Wilde's most celebrated play, which enjoyed a brilliant success on its debut, just seven weeks before his arrest on 6 April, was more than just a *double entendre*; though those who knew enough to get the joke in all three dimensions were probably looking over their shoulders as they laughed. Innuendo about Wilde's sexuality was rife. When *The Picture of Dorian Gray* was published in July 1890 a reviewer in *The Scots Observer*, edited by W. E. Henley, praised Wilde's wit and style, but added, in a reference to Cleveland Street, 'but if he can write for none but outlawed noblemen and perverted telegraph boys, the sooner he takes to tailoring (or some other decent trade) the better for his own reputation and the public morals.'[3]

Douglas's worst favour to Wilde was to introduce him to the homosexual underworld, linking him to several rent boys who were later prepared to give evidence against him. Wilde, who was then forty compared with

Douglas's twenty-three, behaved foolishly, flaunting their relationship all over fashionable London. His letters to him left little to the imagination: writing to his 'Dearest of all boys' from the Savoy in March 1893, Wilde described 'Bosie' as 'so Greek and gracious' and added 'I must see you soon – you are the divine thing I want . . . why are you not here, my dear, my wonderful boy?'[4] In July 1894 Wilde wrote to him: 'Write me a line, and take all my love – now and for ever . . . I have no words for how I love you.'[5]

Even while in Holloway awaiting trial, on 29 April 1895, after losing the libel case, Wilde wrote recklessly to Douglas 'to assure you of my immortal, my eternal love for you . . . our love was always beautiful and noble . . . Dearest boy, sweetest of all young men, most loved and most loveable.'[6] The trial ended in a hung jury; a second convicted Wilde on 25 May 1895 of gross indecency. A cry of 'Shame!' went up when the verdict was announced.[7] The jury asked the judge, Mr Justice Wills, whether if Wilde were guilty, Douglas were not guilty too: Wills said that was nothing to do with them. *The Times* reported that, passing sentence, the judge said that 'one had to put stern constraint upon oneself to prevent oneself from describing in language which he would rather not use the sentiments which must rise in the breast of every man who had any spark of decent feeling in him'. The severest sentence he could pass – two years' hard labour – was 'totally inadequate to such a case as this'. This provoked further cries of 'Shame!'

Wilde wrote *De Profundis* towards the end of his incarceration, after nearly two years in which his health, mental and physical, had suffered greatly. He may thus be forgiven the self-obsession, the boasting and the epic self-pity that permeate the work, which is largely an attack on Douglas's parasitism, vanity and ignorance. But it contains insights into the time as well as into the mind of the author. In one of his most richly metaphorical phrases he wrote:

> People thought it dreadful of me to have entertained at dinner the evil things of life, and to have found pleasure in their company. But they, from the point of view through which I, as an artist in life, approached them, were delightfully suggestive and stimulating. It was like feasting with panthers. The danger was half the excitement.[8]

Wilde's hedonism fed his creative temperament; he would not be the last artist to make that excuse.

He paints himself as a productive genius, creating art by hard work. This is the opposite of decadence, the pursuit of pleasure preferably funded by someone else – in Douglas's case Wilde – with no regard to how the income to live such a life is to be obtained, and with no sense of creating anything lasting or useful. Wilde admits to massive self-indulgence too but has the capacity to regret it, whereas his catamite does not. He also admits: 'I used to live entirely for pleasure. I shunned sorrow and suffering of every kind. I hated both.'[9] Eventually, he saw it was rather 'pleasure for the beautiful body' but 'pain for the beautiful soul'.[10]

Wilde's flamboyance alone would have made him an object of suspicion to more conventional souls. The charge of gross indecency made him a pariah. What sealed the matter in the eyes of the narrow-minded was his love of continental culture. He was a frequent visitor to Paris in the fifteen years before his arrest, and took refuge there after his release from prison. He was an avid reader of contemporary French literature: the notorious 1884 novel *À rebours* by J. K. Huysmans, about a decadent aesthete, among them. He wrote freely about his consumption of absinthe and how it aided his creative processes; he even dared to write a play, *Salomé*, in French. Such things shocked respectable English society, a tribe in which any expression of individuality or originality was viewed with horror.

Yet, paradoxically, his love of all things French (something he shared, ironically, with the Prince of Wales, whose interests were more carnal and less cultural) also shows how relatively conventional he was in artistic matters. *Salomé* is, admittedly, a daring play for the period, but the works for which Wilde is now celebrated – the plays, the children's stories, *The Picture of Dorian Gray* – all betray a fundamentally English middle-class outlook: Dorian Gray, for example, for all his largely unspecified waywardness, is ultimately punished for his decadence as contemporary attitudes would demand. Nothing in Wilde's output compares with the tone of some of the French writers he so admired. There is little in his work that would have upset audiences abroad.

In the decades before the Great War, the arts of continental Europe tended to be far more experimental and daring than those in Britain. In 1890, when Wilde was writing *Dorian Gray*, Henrik Ibsen's *Hedda Gabler* was being premiered. In 1893, when Aubrey Beardsley was producing his first drawings, Edvard Munch was painting *The Scream*. Late works by Paul Cézanne and Paul Gauguin featured the use or suggestion of three-dimensional images, which were to inspire Pablo Picasso and Georges Braque to develop the abstract style of painting that became known as Cubism, in which multiple angles are offered to the viewer simultaneously: but this phenomenon, centred on Paris, barely penetrated Britain before 1914. It would not be until after the Great War that Cubist ideas would influence the writing of novelists such as Aldous Huxley and Virginia Woolf, looking as they often did at characters and events from different angles and perspectives in order to break up linear narratives.

Instead, Britain's arguably most celebrated and successful artist was Sir Lawrence Alma-Tadema, a Dutchman by origin, whose late Victorian and Edwardian paintings adorn galleries all over England. They usually have classical or biblical subjects, painted literally and elaborately: Ruskin hated him, and he came to embody the 'chocolate box' style of painting that made the late Victorians such a cliché for much of the twentieth century. His older contemporary William Holman Hunt had been a co-founder of the Pre-Raphaelite Brotherhood and his style never really moved on. Like Alma-Tadema he specialised in biblical scenes, but also depicted the popular poems of the era, usually written by his fellow cultural conservatives, such as his 1905 representation of Tennyson's *Lady of Shalott*. Hunt was a strong believer in taking art to the people, and having the widest possible appreciation for and understanding of it, a laudable aim that ruled out experimentalism, even had it been in his nature.

The same conservatism could be found in other spheres, British thought in most forms of cultural expression being resistant to radicalism because it was too often resistant to external influences. The steel frames that drove up the first skyscrapers in America – such as the Flatiron Building in New York – were used to support Edwardian baroque palaces in Britain. In America, jazz – in the form of ragtime – made an appearance before the Great War, showing how open the culture there was to the influence of the black minority while Britain still clung to cultural conservatism. Meanwhile in Europe the established musical cultures were becoming revolutionary too. Arnold Schoenberg, writing in Vienna, discarded traditional tonal structure to write in an atonal idiom, producing his Second String Quartet in 1908. In the same year in Britain, Elgar produced his serenely *nobilmente* First Symphony that owed everything to the nineteenth century. In 1913, Stravinsky horrified even the *avant-garde* of Paris with his violently rhythmic ballet *The Rite of*

Spring. In Britain, with little musical culture to speak of for two centuries, new composers used, as we have seen, either a form of German classicism that had its roots in eighteenth-century Vienna, or magnified the idiom of English folk song. For so industrialised a society, Britain's determination to use its music to reflect ideas of the past rather than the realities of a disturbed and changing present suggests a divorce from reality, or at least a reluctance to embrace it.

Poetry remained similarly insular. D. H. Lawrence's verse, for example, showed none of the continental intellectual influences that shaped his fiction: in that way, and that alone, he conformed with other British poets. In 1912 Edward Marsh, a civil servant and Winston Churchill's private secretary, edited a collection entitled *Georgian Poetry* that showcased a new, and short-lived, literary school that intervened between the rigidities of the Victorians and the radicalism of the modernists. There would be five volumes, the last of which was published in 1922, but the first introduced names that would resonate for decades afterwards, including Lawrence. Other poets represented included Rupert Brooke, whose literary executor Marsh became; Chesterton; Lascelles Abercrombie; Walter de la Mare; W. H. Davies; John Masefield; and James Elroy Flecker. Marsh and his contributors regarded their work as approaching an act of rebellion. In that it differed greatly from the high Victorians such as Browning or Tennyson, it was: but the Georgian poets' approach remained traditional, and would be swept away by the shock of the conflict to come. By 1922 such poems were an anachronism: this was the year of *The Waste Land*, and seven years after *The Love Song of J. Alfred Prufrock*. It had taken the seismic events of the Great War to shake British culture out of its suffocating conservatism.

For all their political espousal of Liberalism after 1905, the British remained a conservative people with a conservative culture, alert and hostile to any developments that might suggest decadence or portend radical change. Artistic – particularly literary – influences from abroad were regarded almost universally as degenerate, decadent or pornographic, and their study actively discouraged. In May 1888, Samuel Smith, a Liberal MP, publicly deplored 'the rapid spread of demoralising literature', and called for the strengthening of the law against obscene publications.[11] He singled out a Frenchman named Vizetelly as 'the chief culprit in the spread of this pernicious literature', who had 'boasted' to *The Pall Mall Gazette* that his firm had sold in England 'more than

1,000,000 copies of the worst class of French novels.' In fact Henry Vizetelly was an Englishman and a Francophile, a renowned expert on wine who had set up his own publishing house. To Smith's horror, Vizetelly (who would be successfully prosecuted for obscene libel for his translation of Zola's *La Terre*, further retarding the march of literature) was engaged in selling '1,000 copies of the writings of Zola.' Smith regarded these works as 'only fit for swine' because of their 'realism', of which Zola was the 'prophet'.[12] Smith saw realism as 'sheer beastliness; it means going out of the way to dig up foul expressions to embody filthy ideas . . . the laying bare of social sores in their most loathsome forms . . . In a word, it is dirt and horror pure and simple'. This would remain the majority view until 1914. As Smith also said, 'France today was rapidly approaching the condition of Rome in the time of the Caesars.'[13]

Henry Matthews, the Home Secretary, agreed entirely, adding to the list 'the penny dreadfuls, the quack advertisements, and the full reports of divorce cases which appeared in the public daily press.'[14] The same attitudes would rule out an Ibsen in Britain. The guardians of morality in parliament and elsewhere would make very sure that the time of the Caesars did not reach Britain. As Samuel Hynes argued in his masterful review *The Edwardian Turn of Mind*, for most people the splendid isolation praised by Unionist politicians created barriers against European cultural forces: and for many, even among the better-read middle classes, the idea of British superiority had as its opposite an assumption of foreign inferiority, giving rise almost to a fear that European culture in particular was striving to subvert that of Great Britain.[15]

An idea of establishment appreciation of the arts in the world before that war, and evidence of how the imposition of conservatism was a top-down affair, can be seen in a letter Balfour sent Knollys on 5 June 1905 after a request for advice about appointments to the Order of Merit. The Order was in the King's gift: the advice was not binding. 'If there is an attempt to reward pure Literature, you get on to the thinnest ice, and raise no end of jealousies. About Swinburne there are special difficulties': a riot of understatement about the elderly flagellomaniac. 'Kipling, Bernard Shaw, Hardy, are all no doubt men, in their respective ways, of originality and imagination.'[16] As for painters, Alma-Tadema's name was raised to be dismissed, as it was doubted he was 'sufficiently superior to his brother RAs' for his selection not to be 'invidious'.[17] The King was pointed towards Holman Hunt who, although old, 'has a very distinct place in the development of British Art during the last 40 years. And though opinion may well differ as to the merit of his work, its originality is undoubted.'

II

British art did not, however, remain wholly static in this period. Design, for example, became noticeably less Anglocentric. Art Nouveau arrived from the continent in the 1890s. Its few distinguished practitioners in Britain included Charles Rennie Mackintosh and a group of collaborators in Glasgow. Mackintosh's masterpiece, the Glasgow School of Art, was built between 1897 and 1909 – and severely damaged by fire in 2014 – but he also applied his variation of Art Nouveau to furniture, textiles, metalwork and ceramics: his work is now highly prized and representative of the most innovative streak in Edwardian art. His circle became known as the Glasgow School, and much of the work was done in collaboration with his wife, Margaret MacDonald, her sister Frances, and Herbert McNair, an architect who had befriended Mackintosh when they were students. It was rare for a provincial school to take such a cultural lead: London took some years to follow.

Readers of fiction, too, were exposed to some degree of innovation: it was perhaps the one art form where Britain was not so far behind the continent, and if it did not break boundaries it did, at least, push at them. Even in his earlier novels, such as *Far from the Madding Crowd* (1874), Thomas Hardy presents a harsh realism far beyond even that of his inspiration, Dickens. The later books were stronger meat still. *Tess of the d'Urbervilles*, in 1891, caused outrage because of how it challenged sexual morality: its initial publication, possible only after it was censored, was as a serial in *The Graphic*. Tillotson, Hardy's publisher, believed the subject matter was unsuitable and demanded major changes, which Hardy refused to make. He confronted his critics in the very subtitle of the novel – 'A Pure Woman' – attacking the hypocrisy of society's distinction between the sexual mores of men and women. The work was finally published in book form in 1892, more or less as Hardy wished it.

The last novel he finished, *Jude the Obscure* – he would devote the rest of his life to poetry – shocked polite society even more. It not only challenged conventional sexual morality – Jude and his married cousin, Sue Bridehead, live as man and wife even though unwed, and have two children – but questioned orthodox religion, dealt with divorce, murder, suicide, miscarriage and the class system: Jude's misery begins when, despite his interest in Latin and Greek, he cannot study at Oxford because he is an artisan. The book was branded obscene when published in 1895: it shows the nineteenth century had little to teach the early twentieth about realism and the depiction of the working of the mind.

Some contemporary writers were, like E. M. Forster, moving towards the narrative complexity that would be achieved in the streams of consciousness of James Joyce, Marcel Proust and Virginia Woolf and away from the (by comparison) straightforward storytelling of Bennett, Wells and Galsworthy, in which the psychological dimension of characters is present but less deeply explored or analysed. The great impresario of this movement was Edward Garnett, who as a publisher's reader and editor was nurturing some of the finest new talent in English letters. He had encouraged Galsworthy, who dedicated *The Man of Property* to him. He had brought on Joseph Conrad and Ford Madox Hueffer, who after the Great War would change his name to Ford Madox Ford. Garnett's greatest success, however, was D. H. Lawrence. Hueffer had discovered Lawrence, a miner's son and schoolteacher from Nottinghamshire who was plagued by ill health, and commissioned him to write for *The English Review*. Lawrence then met Garnett, who advised him about the composition of the manuscript that became *Sons and Lovers*.

That novel was realism as the British reading public had never encountered before: semi-autobiographical, it presents an unadorned view of the life of the industrial working classes of the East Midlands. Lawrence finished it in the autumn of 1912. By then it had been through four drafts, and he pronounced himself pleased with it. The period during which he wrote it had been turbulent for Lawrence. He ditched two long-term girlfriends, ran off with the wife of a professor, had a near-fatal attack of pneumonia, endured the death of his beloved mother, and left his job. The draft Garnett saw not only reflected these upheavals, but suffered from them. Lawrence had such faith in Garnett's judgement that he allowed him to cut a tenth of the manuscript. The novel shows a clear continental influence: Lawrence had read Sigmund Freud and understood what was coming to be known as the Oedipus complex. In the novel, the Oedipal bond between Mrs Morel and her son Paul is obvious, and Lawrence portrays a relationship reflecting that of himself with his mother, and his sense that she had thrown herself away in marrying his father, a miner who could not appreciate the subtleties of her mind. The book contains an intensity of observation and analysis of the relationship of a depth that would have been unfamiliar to readers of Bennett and Wells.

Garnett did remove some sexual references, but only enough to stop the book breaking the obscenity laws. He saw that this portrayal of working-class life was made without the sanitisation middle-class writers normally applied to it, and therefore had a realism, however shocking, that gave it exceptional literary and indeed documentary value. Lawrence recognised the role Garnett played as his literary midwife, and dedicated the book to him. His editor let Lawrence lead readers into his characters' minds and create a multifaceted point of view, which distanced the form of the book from much of the preceding English canon. The areas of the lives of his characters into which Lawrence went, notably in sexual matters, was also mould-breaking, and opened the way for some of Joyce's descriptions of sexual matters in *Ulysses*. The book's realism – whether in depicting working-class lives at home and at work, or in more intimate areas – was unprecedented.

III

Fiction in the years before the Great War may have begun to push at the boundaries of polite expression, but as the theatre grew in popularity it was the stage that proved the prime artistic means to deal with Edwardian Britain's burning social concerns. Galsworthy's *Strife* (1909), for example, dealt with the difficulties of industrial relations in a country where workers saw the gap widening between their standard of living and that of their employers; *Justice*, written the following year, was about the unfairness of the judicial and penal systems.

Shaw's career was an exercise in seeing how far he could go, such as in goading the censor by writing a play (*Mrs Warren's Profession*) about women who felt forced to choose a career in prostitution, or by agitating for the liberalisation of the divorce laws (*Getting Married*). Shaw was, though, a businessman first and a crusading man of letters second. In October 1909, for example, he gave G. K. Chesterton advice on how, and why, to proceed as a playwright. Even though the two were far apart politically, he had assured himself of Chesterton's abilities. 'A full length play should contain about 18,000 words (mine frequently contain two or three times that number). I do not know what your price per thousand is. I used to be considered grossly extortionate . . . for insisting on £3. 18,000 words at £3 per thousand is £54 . . . let us assume your work is worth twice as much as mine: this would make £108.'[18] Shaw, branching out as an impresario, offered £100 if Chesterton would supply him within three months with a 'stageable' drama about St Augustine revisiting England. This might seem a satirical offer, given the censor's opposition to depictions of religion on stage. However, within three years Shaw would have a success with *Androcles and the Lion*, which deals with Christians being persecuted in Rome, and exposes religious hypocrisy.

Works of fiction occasionally fell foul of the authorities, or, as with *Sons and Lovers*, were nervously censored by their publishers: Grant Richards, for example, fearing that sexual references and the use of the word 'bloody' in James Joyce's short-story collection *Dubliners* could get him into trouble, insisted on changes that the author indignantly fought. With dramatic works, grounds for censorship were more institutionalised, broader and more arbitrary. The responsibility for allowing performance *in* a public theatre rested with a single person: the Lord Chamberlain – or rather, since the Lord Chamberlain was preoccupied with running His Majesty's Royal Household, a man in his department called the Examiner of Plays.

The office had been established in 1737, when Walpole imposed censorship specifically to keep Henry Fielding's satires off the stage, but by Edwardian times had acquired a remit that extended well beyond politics and into the realms of making arbitrary judgments about what public taste would, or would not, countenance in the theatre. Given the determination of a number of Edwardian dramatists to explore contentious social issues, and the innate conservatism of the Examiner of Plays from 1895 to 1912 – a former bank manager named George Redford – confrontation became inevitable; and the very public dispute that followed showed how far English drama was moving away from Victorian theatre in the years before the Great War. It remained less experimental and provocative than the plays of Ibsen or Strindberg, but was nevertheless prepared to tackle themes and topics unthinkable a generation earlier.

While sophisticated playwrights struggled to put sophisticated ideas on the stage, the 'blue' joke developed nicely in the music hall, where the Lord Chamberlain had no control. To complicate matters, music halls could also stage plays, and, being free from the Lord Chamberlain's supervision, whatever plays they wished. However, this did not mean that complex and controversial subjects that could not be aired on the theatrical stage were put on the halls; but trivial ones in doubtful taste, the ancestors of the *Carry On* films from half a century later, most certainly were.

Claims by dramatists and their supporters to literary merit did not affect any judgment that Redford had to make: he retained a suburban bank manager's idea of what might offend, and anything that might offend was banned. This was, at least, consistent with the view of most of society: an unenquiring one that stopped English drama developing as, for example, European drama had through Ibsen and Chekhov. Sex and related matters were out: but so was religion, and anything that might annoy friendly foreign powers. Hack playwrights tended to be docile when asked to cut their works: more rarefied writers, such as Shaw or Harley Granville Barker, who as well as being a dramatist either produced, directed or acted in most of Shaw's new plays in the Edwardian period, found such interference outrageous. They argued that a modern, progressive society – which some of them believed could be created – should free dramatists of these shackles. A select committee had considered the question in 1892 after a refusal to license Shelley's *The Cenci*, with its theme of incest, but nothing had changed; by 1907 the temperature had risen again, and demands for censorship to be reconsidered rose with it.

Galsworthy, whose first play *The Silver Box* Barker had staged to great acclaim the previous year, led the opposition to censorship, suggesting in February 1907 to William Archer, who as well as being the leading critic was the translator of Ibsen into English, that 'a petition should be got up and presented in whatever may be the proper quarter, and circulated in the press'.[19] He added: 'I imagine that the whole theatrical profession – playwrights, critics, actor managers and actors would willingly sign . . . no playwright who had had a play censored should be asked to sign, to avoid suspicion of personal feeling; I should also suggest circulating the Petition amongst members of the Literary profession and Members of Parliament.' Galsworthy did not imagine censorship could end altogether. 'The great point to settle is what would best take the place of the existing ridiculous one horse system.' One suggestion was a committee of six, which he liked because a committee could fill vacancies by election rather than be appointed 'by a Court Official'.[20] There was one difficulty: 'How and by whom to get the first committee appointed?'

By July 1907, after consulting Shaw – who had been running a campaign against censorship – Wells, Gilbert Murray and Barker among others, Galsworthy proposed a 'League for the Defence of Moral Plays', whose main object was 'to secure the abolition of the Censorship.'[21] Campbell-Bannerman's private secretary had told Galsworthy that the prime minister himself was 'in favour of abolition'.[22] However, 'failing abolition, [they should] report all plays rejected by the Censor, and champion them by all means in the League's power, if found fit for championship.' Galsworthy wanted to broaden the ranks of supporters beyond dramatists, but also told Archer to be wary of 'names that would frighten supporters' – though he did not specify them.[23] On 29 October 1907 a squadron of the nation's leading writers signed a letter to *The Times*, drafted by Galsworthy, complaining that the office of censor was instituted 'for political, and not for the so-called moral ends to which it is perverted – an office autocratic in procedure, opposed to the spirit of the Constitution, contrary to common justice and to common sense'.[24]

The seventy-one signatories included Barker, J. M. Barrie, Laurence Binyon, Joseph Conrad, Galsworthy, Garnett, W. S. Gilbert, Hardy, Anthony Hope, Laurence Housman, E. W. Hornung, Roy Horniman, Ford Madox Hueffer, Henry James, John Masefield, A. E. W. Mason, Somerset Maugham, George Meredith, Gilbert Murray, Pinero, Shaw, A. C. Swinburne, J. M. Synge, Wells and W. B. Yeats. This was literary Britain, and Ireland, speaking with a united voice. They demanded a right of appeal against the censor's ability to destroy the reputation of 'any member of an honourable calling'; they said his existence served 'to relieve the public of the duty of moral judgment', and his decisions were 'arbitrary'. They asked to have their art 'placed on the same footing as every other art.'

Two acts of censorship provided the final provocation. Garnett's play *The Breaking Point* and Barker's *Waste* had both been refused licences. Frederick Harrison, manager of the Haymarket Theatre in London, had offered in December 1906 to stage Garnett's play. *The Breaking Point* – about a pregnant unmarried woman who commits suicide after her lover and father fight for control of her – was according to its author designed to 'claim the interest of those people who are striving to obtain an intellectual English drama – a drama that is a criticism of life.'[25]

Harrison told Garnett he wished to stage it for 'that section of the public which is alive to what the theatre might be.' As the public was unadventurous and uninterested in such plays it would not be a commercial success: but he wanted to put it on for the furtherance of art. Garnett's outrage when it was refused a licence was not least because he felt it was 'obviously a moral play – strongly moral, for it happens to inculcate moral lessons in several aspects.'[26] He also believed it was the censor's duty 'to prevent gross or prurient indecency on the public stage'; the censor had licensed 'many silly, inane, semi-indecent plays'. It was not his role 'to suppress works of art'.[27]

For Barker the artistic frustration was one thing, but the commercial damage was of another order altogether. He had had several successful seasons at the Court Theatre with his company, mainly staging Shaw; but now the company intended to move to the greater showcase of the Savoy Theatre, with *Waste* as its new production. Barker's subsequent assault on the censor was certainly in part motivated by what he considered to be the suppression of his artistic freedom, but also by rage at the effect this arbitrary decision had had on his career as a playwright and actor-manager.

Waste and *The Breaking Point* exemplify what was 'new' about the direction of Edwardian drama, and illustrate the desire to show the uglier side of life on the stage. *The Breaking Point* is set in a village in Devon, and tells the story of two unpleasant men, a woman's father and her lover, who demand ownership of her. She is pregnant, twenty-three and naïve, and eventually drowns herself. It is not a work of great literary merit: the characterisations are superficial and the dialogue stilted. Even the most enlightened audience would have struggled with its *longueurs* – and it is a relatively short play. Its value lies in its sympathy for the abused girl and the exposure it provides of her lack of free will and of the ease with which men manipulate her. The spectacle on stage of a young, unmarried, pregnant woman was enough to have Redford issue his ban.

Waste is of a different order of creativity. Archer considered it 'our greatest modern tragedy'.[28] Later critics felt that by writing only nine plays, most of them rarely performed, Barker lacked dedication to the art and could not be regarded as a front-rank playwright. But it is clear from *Waste* – as from his most successful play, *The Voysey Inheritance* – that he has a significance in dramatic history that extends beyond Edwardian London. Although Redford had complained to him about the way in which the play dealt with sexual matters and abortion, it also takes on the Church of England through the character of the protagonist, Henry Trebell, an avowed atheist, and portrays the political class as unprincipled, cynical, self-interested and self-serving.

Trebell wants to disestablish the Church of England, something not on the political agenda at the time. He wants to use its money to set up schools and colleges to spread education and enlightenment throughout England. He has sat in the Commons as an independent, but has promised to join the Tories. In return for his support – which will allow them to form a government – he is offered a cabinet post. He is promised that his disestablishment measure will become government policy. However, it becomes clear that he has impregnated another man's wife, and that she has died after an illegal abortion – or as Barker has Trebell put it, in an example of the uncompromising language he uses routinely, 'An unwelcome baby was arriving. She got some quack to kill her.'[29] The statement is all the more shocking for being addressed to Trebell's middle-aged maiden sister. Trebell then commits suicide. The play is at times dense and wordy –Barker re-wrote it in the 1920s before it eventually had a public performance in 1936 – but its characters are entirely credible, and the nature of its politicking entirely true to life. Barker was a Fabian with little interest in either of the established parties; but he uses the play to attack what he regards as Tory venality, and its utter lack of principle. Shaw claimed the play was banned because of 'the observation of an absurd rule forbidding dramatists to mention the subject of obstetric surgery.'[30]

With the cry that 'a serious artistic drama implies a free drama', Garnett published not just the text of *The Breaking Point* but also a letter to the censor in the autumn of 1907, shortly before a deputation of playwrights was due to see Campbell-Bannerman to lobby him over censorship.[31] He was too ill to meet them, and the Home Secretary, Herbert Gladstone, saw them instead, to no immediate avail. The letter Garnett published referred to an earlier one from Redford, in reply to an enquiry about why the play had been banned, that had refused to answer the question by referring to the fact that the censor had 'no cognisance' of authors.[32] Garnett told him: 'You claim the right to ignore my existence while destroying my property – for a play debarred the Stage is practically destroyed.' Garnett was furious to be denied a right of appeal, and with a system that meant Redford need justify his arbitrary decisions to no one. He knew Redford could not provide evidence of the play's indecency, because there was none. 'Could there be a more cutting commentary on the futility of your office and the unintelligence with which you administer it?' he asked the censor.[33]

Waste was performed privately – as legally it could be – to an *ad hoc* club, the Incorporated Stage Society, at the Imperial Theatre in London on four occasions between 24 November and 28 November 1907. *The Times* reviewed it; Barker himself played Trebell. The newspaper gave an extensive précis of the action, and called the play 'a work of extraordinary power, dealing with some of the most fundamental facts of human life with an unflinching truthfulness and at the same time blending these facts with certainly the most vivid and probably the most authentic presentation we have yet had on the English stage of great social and political questions that come home to all Englishmen's business and bosoms.'[34]

The reviewer – the paper's drama critic, A. B. Walkley – spoke of Barker's 'right to take a foremost place among English dramatists', and said the play went beyond 'the ordinary limitations of drama'. He noted Shaw's influence on *Waste*, but not as much as on *The Voysey Inheritance*. But there was, the critic continued, nothing 'to impair the strength and unity and veracity and total impressiveness of this fine play.' However, he added: 'We have no hesitation in approving the Censor's decision. The subject-matter of *Waste*, together with the sincere realism with which it is treated, makes it, in our judgment, wholly unfit for performance under ordinary circumstances before a miscellaneous public of various ages, moods, and standards of intelligence.' In other words, only a select few had the brains and experience to cope with such a play, and the rest of society could not be trusted with it.

Walkley warned Barker and his fellow authors 'clamouring just now for a "free" stage that questions of art are one thing and questions of public policy and expediency are another thing.' As he pompously told the joint select committee empanelled to investigate censorship two years later, 'there are two publics – the enlightened public, the public who are interested in advanced ideas, and the general public.'[35] He also observed that had he taken his daughter to the play he would not have been able to sit it out: but then one would have expected the drama critic of *The Times* to have known in advance that this was not the type of play to which to take someone who had led a sheltered life.

IV

On 23 June 1909 Asquith, the prime minister, announced it was time to review censorship of plays. Since the problems highlighted by the rejection of the plays by Garnett and Barker he, like Campbell-Bannerman before him, had been lobbied by authors and by Liberal MPs, who felt the existing system was anachronistic and harming the development of a national drama. He established a joint select committee of both Houses of Parliament. In response to this George Alexander, a famous actor-manager who ran the St James's Theatre in London, wrote to *The Times* to applaud the idea, though to commend the Lord Chamberlain's role in licensing theatres – it was in the suppliers' interests to keep supplies regulated. Alexander embraced the status quo. 'It is absolutely essential that the power of licensing plays by some high authority should be maintained,' he wrote.[36] 'It is wanted in the interests of the State to regulate and, if necessary, to prevent the public performance of plays dealing with political questions, whether at home or abroad. It is wanted in the interests of the public to deal with blasphemous or indecent plays.'

He had been regarded as one of the more adventurous of his breed, having put on not only *Lady Windermere's Fan* in 1892, but also *The Importance of Being Earnest* three years later, on the first night of which he had ensured that Queensberry was ejected from the theatre. He had also staged, and performed in, the first production of *The Second Mrs Tanqueray*, so was thought willing to have challenging questions aired on stage. He had enlisted contemporary artists such as Walter Crane to decorate his theatre, and Alma-Tadema to design some of his sets. However, he was not alone in believing that the public mind could not be trusted to cope with such questions – the working class, with their limited education, were thought especially in need of protection. If either blasphemy or obscenity were allowed on the stage the police would have to intervene, and Alexander wanted them kept out: the censor, as he preferred not to call him, was preferable. Also, Alexander was a public figure – he had been a London County Councillor for two years, and was perhaps keen not to rock the boat of dignified public service that would secure him his knighthood in 1911.

He understood why playwrights sought an end to licensing, but warned them this would lead to local authorities, many far less well-regulated and consistent, making the decisions instead. He was right that one authority's definition of obscenity or blasphemy might not be another's. But again, he put his commercial interest as an impresario before freedom of expression: the licensing system left local authorities without a right to intervene. If it went, he feared theatres would be scapegoated for any supposed offences, and would not have their licences renewed: the quiet life, free from intellectual adventure, seemed the better course.

This self-interested defence of censorship provoked Shaw. The next day *The Times* published a savage attack by him on Alexander's judgment and intelligence. Asking him to 'enlarge a little' on his letter, Shaw wrote:

> Why does he regard dramatic art as unfit to deal with serious questions, which are all political questions? Why does he believe that a court official, none of whose duties involve any higher qualifications than those of the acting manager of a box-office, is a better judge of a play than Sir Herbert Beerbohm Tree, Sir Arthur Pinero, or the British public? Why does he believe in the Spanish theory of the Inquisition rather than in the English theory of liberty?[37]

This was a front-line clash between the repressed attitudes of conservative middle-class Victorians, and progressives who sought to expand debate and experience. Shaw also reminded Alexander that just because a play was licensed did not mean that was the end of the matter. *The Mikado* was taken off-stage for six weeks in the summer of 1907, under pressure from the Lord Chamberlain, because of fears it would offend a visiting Japanese prince: even though W. S. Gilbert had used the foreign setting to satirise not Japanese politics, but British ones. 'In what sense', Shaw fulminated, 'can a licence which is at the mercy of a single virtually irresponsible individual be said to be safe?'

He mocked Alexander for having subscribed to a gift of silver on the retirement of the previous Examiner of Plays; he asserted that Alexander 'perforce confines himself at the St James's Theatre to the production of plays which are suited to Mr Redford's capacity' – a barbed reference to the undemanding drawing-room comedies that had become the staple of that theatre. And he asked of Alexander: 'Why does he make his entirely justifiable objection to censorship by the local authorities, which would at least be subject to the control of a representative body responsible to the public, a reason for supporting an infinitely more odious censorship which is responsible to no-one, and which classes him with the disorderly footmen and waiting-maids of a bygone period?' He awaited 'an answer to these unanswerable questions', advising Alexander and others who 'to their infinite shame . . . are satisfied with their present comfortable slavery' that they should prepare for an uncertain future if the system were changed. A world in which managers of theatres such as Alexander were responsible for productions was, he concluded, better than a system under which one could 'procure for two guineas, and compliance with a few transparent hypocrisies, a licence for practically anything that the lowest class of playgoer will stand.'

Reform of censorship – conducted under the Theatres Act of 1843, which said plays could be performed in public only on licensed premises and that all new plays must be submitted for inspection – would depend on the joint select committee of five peers and five MPs. It sat in the summer and autumn of 1909 and examined forty-nine witnesses, from the Speaker of the House of Commons to the clerk of the London County Council, including representatives of the Archbishop of Canterbury and the Archbishop of Westminster. Dramatists, critics, theatre and music-hall managers and actors also gave evidence: as did Redford himself.

The Bishop of Southwark observed that, while he favoured censorship, he felt it would be harmful if it impeded 'the treatment, quite free and bold, of what may be called moral questions'. This was certainly what had happened to *Waste*. It was a key moment of recognition: that the theatre, long considered a place of recreation, was also a forum in which, as the eventual report said, 'great ideas, of profound importance to human well-being, whether touching on relationships between the sexes or on other problems of human society, may be communicated by the thinkers to the citizens at large.'[38]

Redford was questioned early on. He said his relationships were with theatre managers, not writers; though he knew many writers, and was happy for any who wanted to see him to ask for an appointment. The illogicality of the system soon became clear. Redford said a 'religious' play was one based on stories from scripture, and was asked whether this meant he would refuse a licence to *Everyman*, the late-medieval morality play that dealt with the attainment of Christian salvation. 'I regarded that play as a play that came very much under the same head as the plays of Shakespeare,' he argued.[39] Having been around since before licensing, such plays were treated as though they were licensed.

He squirmed when asked whether *Everyman* would be given a licence if it were new. He said he would 'certainly not' have considered it a 'scriptural play', even though by all the criteria he applied it unquestionably was: later, indeed, he said that 'if a play was avowedly scriptural I would have said that it was ineligible for a licence.'[40] He suggested that in Shakespearean times the Master of the Revels would have approved plays, which was why he considered them licensed: but he knew no date when the old dispensation ended, and the new began. By the same token that Shakespeare and his contemporaries could be performed, so could Congreve and the Restoration playwrights.

However, foreign old plays were a different matter. Pigott, Redford's predecessor, had refused a licence to the Passion play from Oberammergau: Redford pronounced that 'religious feeling would be outraged at seeing the Crucifixion, for instance, enacted on a public stage in a theatre.' Yet the Deity was represented on stage in *Everyman*: Redford could merely say that he did not 'think it necessary' to license it because he did not think it 'desirable'.[41] Even he, it seems, had worked out the massive inconsistencies of his policies.

Religion was not his only problem. Herbert Samuel, chairman of the committee and a Liberal MP, asked him why political allusions in pantomimes were 'considered objectionable'. Redford replied that 'the stage is not a political arena'; which was precisely what men such as Shaw, Galsworthy and Barker thought it was. Redford was concerned about allusions to foreign powers, and causing a diplomatic incident. Evidence of his success in suppressing political expression was that he believed – or so he told the committee – that there had been more politics in plays when he began his job, but 'the influence of the censorship' had dealt with that. Samuel asked him: 'May it not be a healthy thing sometimes for politicians to be satirised on the stage?' With a predictable absence of self-doubt, Redford replied: 'Personally I do not think so.'

Some members of the committee were intent on exposing Redford's limitations. He proclaimed that no representation of a living person would be allowed: yet it was pointed out that Shaw himself had been mocked in a play called *Punch and Super Punch*. Redford, oblivious to the allusion to *Man and Superman*, said he could not have gathered that from the script. Might he, though, have gathered that a play called *The Orchid*, about a great statesman who ends up marrying his typewriter – as typists were then called – was about the nation's most famous orchid-wearer, Joe Chamberlain? 'Certainly I had no official knowledge of it,' Redford replied.[42] Under further examination, he admitted he had no qualifications for his job whatsoever, other than having been a friend of the previous incumbent, and had been subject to no enquiry about his background.

He exposed the workings of his office as capricious and arbitrary. He was required to give no reasons for not licensing a play, but would, unofficially, if asked. He would communicate with authors whom he knew: too bad for those he did not. The secrecy in which he liked to operate served to perpetuate the irregularities that had begun with his appointment. Matters took a comical turn when Redford was asked about foreign plays. Did he allow more latitude to a French play than to an English one? 'I think so,' he replied. 'It is a foreign language, you see.'[43] It did not help that he did not speak some of the languages in which plays were submitted; but, luckily, Mrs Redford was 'a German scholar', and read to him, in her translation, plays in that tongue.

The absurdities became a torrent: Dryden's version of Sophocles' *Oedipus Tyrannus* could be performed, because it always had been, whereas a licence had just been refused to a contemporary translation. He admitted that music halls, in which things happened that would never be licensed in a theatre, were a law unto themselves, even when they put on plays: 'The music halls ignore us, and we ignore them.'[44] Redford also admitted that if a new examiner were to replace him he would receive no written instructions about the job. Given how Redford did it, that might have been as well. He said he had refused a licence to *Mrs Warren's Profession* because a procuress could not be depicted on stage, and prostitution was not a proper subject for the theatre. He refused licences for religious plays because that was 'the custom': though he had no clue why.[45] Merit and propriety had nothing to do with it.

The next witness, William Archer, the leading critic, said a new drama had existed in England since about 1885: 'And from that time onwards I think the censorship has had a very distinctly and growingly depressing and repressing influence upon the development of the English drama,' he said.[46] 'It has prevented the development in the direction of serious drama – the serious treatment of life.' When parliament had last discussed the question, in 1892, no playwright would protest: now 'practically all' would. He denounced the religious ban as 'very repressive', and Redford for saying he would not read a play on that subject.[47]

Archer was opposed to all censorship, and attacked the theatrical managers for their craven behaviour. He agreed a check on obscenity was necessary, but the law covered that. Asked about 'the sexual problem', he was uncompromising: 'The relations of man and woman, which are probably the most important things in the world, should be treated upon the stage.'[48] That was certainly Shaw's view: he was examined next. He had submitted an 11,000-word deposition, which the committee refused to read because of its excessive length. 'The control that now exists', he said, 'is of the most tyrannical and impossible character.'[49] He said Redford had 'absolutely at his personal disposal my livelihood and my good name without any law to administer behind him. That, it appears to me, is a control past the very last pitch of despotism.'

Shaw poured contempt on Redford. 'At the present time a great many extremely immoral plays (and I am using the word now in the correct English sense; I had almost said in the sense in which it is *not* used from one end of the Bible to the other) are now passed and performed because the Censor (I do not know how to put this quite politely) is not sufficiently an expert in moral questions to know always when a play is moral and when it is immoral.' Therefore 'he has licensed a great many plays which he would not have licensed if he had understood them.' Shaken by this, Samuel asked Shaw whether the system should be improved. Shaw answered: 'The more you improve it, the more disastrous it will be, because the more effectually will it stop the immoral play, which from my point of view is the only play that is worth writing.'

He said the only control to which he would submit was the law, and that 'you must accept as a necessary thing that there are certain things which the community at large will not tolerate. Even with the strongest conviction that you must allow liberty of speech and liberty of conscience, there are certain things which would create an irresistible demand to have them prosecuted under the ordinary law dealing with obscenity or blasphemy.'[50] Lest that seem unduly conservative, Shaw added that these laws were 'far too stringent, especially the blasphemy laws, which would put us all in prison if carried out.'

Shaw had come to provoke, not least by mild hyperbole such as that, and was far from done. He declared: 'A very large percentage of the performances which take place at present on the English stage under the censorship licence have for their object the stimulation of sexual desire'; 'I am responsible to the law and not to Mr Redford or the Lord Chamberlain' followed later. He distinguished between incitement to sexual immorality and incitement to sexual vice. 'I think that the danger of crippling thought, the danger of obstructing the formation of the public mind by specially suppressing such representations is far greater than any real danger that there is from such representations.' Lest the committee think he advocated staging one outrage after another, he emphasised: 'It is an extremely difficult thing to put on the stage anything which runs contrary to a large body of people.'

Samuel asked Shaw whether he would agree that a play that might cause a riot should be banned; Shaw said: 'I put it on exactly the same footing as political meetings, which, in my experience, very often have ended in riot.'[51] Samuel tried to disagree, but Shaw told him: 'The same rights and liberties apply to both.' When he wrote *John Bull's Other Island*, in which he mocked a Liberal political figure, he had not been censored: but when he wrote *Press Cuttings*, in which he mocked a Conservative, he was. 'The objection is clearly to my politics and not to my personalities. The fact is that I have to ascertain what the Censor's politics are before I know whether the play will pass.'[52] Shaw referred to this as 'the chaos of the Censor's mind'.

Mrs Warren's Profession had almost caused a riot in New York. Shaw attributed this to the notoriety created by Redford's banning it. The entire company was arrested: but once the judge had read the play they were all acquitted, and he had said of Shaw that 'his attack on social evils is one which may result in effecting some reforms.' But because the English censor was less enlightened, Shaw said he had 'suffered severe pecuniary loss and a great deal of discredit'. He added: 'The great mass of the people naturally believe that if an officer of the King's household acts in that way there is some sort of reason for it, and that I am what such a decision implies.' Shaw said the implication was that he was 'an indecent and unconscientious author', and it 'will follow me to the very end of my career.'

Barker gave evidence, pronouncing himself 'absolutely opposed' to censorship, which he agreed had been injurious to the development of

English drama.[53] 'The moment that any original point of view, or unusual point of view, on any subject is put before the Censor he naturally stops to think about it, and the process of his thinking very often interferes with the licensing of the play,' he said. 'The result of that has been to narrow the field which drama covers in England'. It was one thing for Ibsen's plays to be performed uncensored in England – as, with the exception of *Ghosts*, they all had been – because the censor could assume the shocking events they included could only happen in Norway, and were impossible in England. But the censor's existence limited the chances of an Ibsen emerging here.

Barker had tried to produce Shaw's *Major Barbara*. Redford threatened to refuse a licence because 'the feelings of the Salvation Army would be outraged by its being put upon the stage.'[54] Barker told him he had asked the Salvation Army, who regarded it as 'an excellent advertisement' for their work: at which point Redford relented. The committee asked the playwright whether, when writing *Waste*, he had imagined it would be rejected. 'I have long ago,' he replied, 'given up trying to forecast what the judgment of the Examiner of Plays will be, because I have been unable, by studying his decisions, to arrive at any principle of his working, and, therefore, I have held that the best plan for a dramatist to pursue is merely to write the play which he wishes to write, and take his chance.'

Redford had told Barker he 'must be prepared to moderate and modify the extremely outspoken references to sexual relations'; Barker told him that if there were 'particular phrases' to which he objected, he would consider changing them. 'To that he paid no attention whatever,' Barker added. Redford had told him that the depiction of a 'criminal operation' – an abortion – in *Waste* was also a problem, and all references to it would have to go. This nonplussed Barker, who had just produced a licensed play, *Votes for Women*, by the American actress and suffragette Elizabeth Robins, that had also referred to abortion. The censor's caprice made it impossible for dramatists such as Barker to break new ground. Such a playwright 'must either write purely conventional plays, which he practically knows the Lord Chamberlain will not object to, or he must take to some other form of literary work, such as book-writing – the writing of fiction – where he is not hampered by any such dictation.'

Barker said he had, half-a-dozen times in the previous four or five years, had to tell a dramatist not to bother pursuing an idea because it would not get past the censor; he felt the existing laws governing public speaking and writing in England were sufficient to protect society against 'grossly improper' plays, and that theatres should be licensed only for reasons of public safety.[55] He had no qualms about managers being prosecuted for allowing obscenity or criminal libel on the stage, but had reservations about prosecuting them for blasphemy – 'the interpretation given to the Blasphemy laws quite lately has been so very peculiar that I hesitate to put that forward without some qualification.' As for the depiction of foreign powers, he was in favour of freedom of expression except where there was clearly a criminal libel.

He told Lord Willoughby de Broke, a Tory member of the committee whose main expertise was foxhunting, that Redford forbade things that 'custom and the common decency of the land' did not.[56] He did not think abortion had been 'treated in such a way as to be indecent or obscene'. When Willoughby de Broke asked whether 'a subject of that kind' should be allowed on the stage, Barker replied: 'I think that you have no right to represent vice upon the stage, unless you are prepared also to represent the consequences that vice entails.' He agreed that if a playwright depicted the 'illegal operation' in a way that was 'indecent or obscene' – which he had not – he should be liable to prosecution. When Lord Newton asked him whether the rejection of *Waste* had been a 'shock', Barker responded that 'it was a great disappointment.' Asked whether he was surprised he answered, wearily, that 'I am never surprised at the action of the Lord Chamberlain.'

Part of the grievance Barker and his fellow playwrights had was that Redford never had to explain his reasons, an unaccountability that gave free rein to his caprice and the indefensibility of his decisions. Barker, as a manager, did engage in a correspondence with him about *Waste*, and Redford told him that 'outspoken' references to sexual relations had to go. Barker had told him: 'I considered in such a play, sober, plain speaking to be the only honest course; that innuendo would be indecent.'

Barker and his colleagues were not merely up against Redford: they were up against spokesmen for conservative public opinion in parliament. Colonel Amelius Lockwood, a Unionist MP and retired Guards officer, asked Barker: 'Do you think . . . that it is a healthy thing for the public to be asked to judge of your advanced opinions in their individual capacity? Do you think that it is a wholesome thing for the drama that your advanced views should be put straight in front of the public without any further question?'[57] Barker replied: 'I think there is nothing to be gained by treating the public as children.'

When Colonel Sir Douglas Dawson, the Lord Chamberlain's Comptroller and the man to whom Redford directly answered, gave evidence, he was asked whether his 'experience of the world and the numerous dramas and pieces that you have seen, proper and improper, enable you to give a very good idea of what is that class of play that should be licensed in England?'[58] Dawson said he had lived abroad 'for a great many years', and had seen plays 'in most of the capitals of Europe'. 'And you have seen very doubtful plays?' he was asked; and his reply left no question that he had. 'I lived six years in Paris, and five years in Vienna.'

J. M. Barrie, author of (among many other works) *Quality Street*, *The Admirable Crichton* and *Peter Pan*, agreed the censor had an 'evil effect' on the English drama.[59] Barrie's works – including *Peter Pan* – all have a more profound social relevance than may at first be apparent: in *The Admirable Crichton*, notably, the family butler asserts his dominance on the desert island when washed up with his aristocratic family, not the utterly incompetent peer he serves; and there have been suggestions that Barrie's interest in small boys might not have been innocuous. He argued that censorship 'is a stigma on all who write plays'. He made one especially telling point: dramatists who wrote 'unconventional' works could not hope to make money out of them because they mocked public taste; they wrote, instead, out of integrity and conviction. 'Suppose that any such theory as Darwin's had been suggested to a Censor, he would have thought it a very dreadful thing, or anything so advanced. Similarly, all the other arts are allowed to present their case: the play alone can be condemned unheard. There is a restriction upon the playwright that lies on no other man in this country.'[60]

Galsworthy gave evidence on 12 August 1909. *A Man of Property*, published in 1906, contained a passage that would never have been allowed on the stage: that in which Soames Forsyte rapes his wife, Irene. Galsworthy had written three plays, all of which had been licensed 'without comment'.[61] Yet he found the 'arbitrary censorship' had 'certainly deterred me from attempting to dramatise a subject which I think should be dramatised'. He had asked other writers about this, and relayed their answers.[62] Hardy and James had agreed. Wells had said 'the wanton power of suppression' was why he did not write plays; Bennett had told him the censor's existence 'makes it impossible for me even to think of writing plays on the same plane of realism and *thoroughness* as my novels.' Certainly his novel of 1906, *Whom God Hath Joined*, with its references to sexual relations and depiction of adultery, would never have got past Redford. Bennett observed: 'The Censor's special timidity about sexual matters is an illusion. He is equally timid about all matters'. Joseph Conrad called censorship 'an outrage upon the dignity and honesty of the calling'.

Galsworthy argued that, apart from those authors who were trying to break the mould, there was no English dramatist of the previous century to rank with the authors, poets or men of letters the age had produced. Willoughby de Broke asked whether this was the censor's fault; Galsworthy claimed there was a 'fair presumption . . . that it has a very distinct influence in producing that state of affairs.'[63] Some managers – notably Sir Herbert Beerbohm Tree, who said 'some kind of censorship is absolutely necessary' – argued for the status quo in the interests of 'convenience'. He advocated a court of appeal for the censor's decisions, sharing this view with W. S. Gilbert, who felt it would have helped prevent *The Mikado* from being banned.[64] Sir Herbert Beerbohm Tree, freshly knighted, was also the leading Shakespearean actor of the day and knew something about morals, having a string of mistresses and even more illegitimate children. He feared the alternative to the 'benevolent autocracy' of Redford was something 'chaotic'.[65] Managers wanted to know they could proceed with productions without fear of prosecution.

The joint select committee concluded that, in 'the public interest . . . theatrical performances should be regulated by special laws' because the nature of drama and the 'human personality' of actors could make words that were not indecent, blasphemous or libellous seem so to an emotionally charged audience.[66] Worse, they might 'give occasion to demonstrations injurious to good relations between this country and foreign powers'. However, it also concluded that 'a Censorship with a power of veto before production is open to grave objection. Secret in its operation, subject to no effective control by public opinion, its effect can hardly fail to be to coerce into conformity with the conventional standards of the day dramatists who may be seeking to amend them. Those standards are not absolute . . . only through the toleration of that which one age thinks to be error can the next age progress further in the pursuit of truth.'[67] The report also acknowledged that a new breed of playwright, more sharply intellectual, was being drawn to the theatre to write 'sincere and serious dramas, critical of existing conventions.' Although Redford had vetoed only thirty plays out of 7,000 submitted since 1895, modifications took place all the time to please him, 'and we have been assured by playwrights that the fear of intervention seriously hampers their work.'

Therefore, in the interests of 'the development of thought and of art' it wished to remove the censor's power of veto, and to add an advisory committee composed of people who knew about drama. It would become optional to submit a play for licensing, and a play could be performed if a licence were refused. The committee accepted this would require safeguards, to prevent 'a drama of indecencies' becoming prevalent: the report warned its readers: 'There are few things more harmful to a community than the influence of a licentious stage.'[68] The committee imagined that in small towns with only one theatre it would cater for what constituted an average of public opinion; but in large cities some theatres 'might find it to their profit to cater for the minority, existing everywhere in varying proportions, which offers a market for indecency', and would become 'centres for the spread of demoralisation' that would bring 'the stage as a whole into disrepute'.

Instead of censorship, 'the public authority should be empowered by a summary process to suspend the performance of unlicensed plays which appear to be of an improper character', and their producers and the playwright should be liable to penalties. That 'public authority', it proposed, should in matters of indecency be the courts of law, and in all other matters a committee of the Privy Council; and the penalties could include banning further performances of the play in question for up to ten years, and closing down theatres that repeatedly offended. It also demanded the Lord Chamberlain be called upon to answer in the Lords for any decisions taken in his name, and that someone be appointed to answer for him in the Commons. The prohibition representing a biblical character should, it argued, be lifted, but a licence should be refused if damage could be done to the 'sentiment of reverence' through such a representation.[69]

Yet nothing happened: as we shall see, parliament after 1909 was preoccupied with the worst constitutional crisis in living memory, the worst industrial action in history, the militancy of suffragettes and the prospect of a civil war in Ireland. The right of dramatists to have their exact words spoken on the stage was a low priority. The dramatists did not give up, however: Shaw, in satirical mode, asked in February 1912 whether censorship ought not to be extended to actors, who could make 'the most harmless speech indecent by gesture'.[70] Censorship would remain, in increasingly dilute form, until 1968: in March 1912 the Lord Chamberlain, Lord Sandhurst, admitted the government had not even considered the 1909 report. Redford, having retarded the progress of English drama, was the ideal man to become the first film censor, and he did.

His successor, G. S. Street, took a literary view of drama, and in 1914 licensed a translation of Ibsen's *Ghosts*. The conservative hegemony had been broken. One of the exchanges in Shaw's great success *Pygmalion*, first staged in Britain at His Majesty's Theatre on 11 April 1914, showed how things had changed: as noted in Chapter 2, Doolittle, when accused of having no morals, replies that poverty means he cannot afford them.[71] Elsewhere Eliza utters the profanity 'not bloody likely', the first time such language had been heard on the English stage.[72] It caused public outrage, however much the world had moved on since Redford's departure.

In Edwardian Britain it was not only the Lord Chamberlain's examiner's ham-fisted censorship of plays that vexed creative types: groups campaigned for the withdrawal of books that the law did not consider obscene, such as Wells's *Ann Veronica*, from the circulating libraries that retailers such as Boots and W. H. Smith operated. The nascent British film industry chose to self-regulate, with uniform standards across the country, to remove the temptation for either the state or local authorities to censor it. The business was regulated under the 1909 Cinematograph Act, passed to require cinemas to be licensed by local authorities. This happened after a series of fires, caused by nitrate film combusting in cinemas converted from other uses. However, in 1910 the courts upheld the right of local authorities to refuse a licence for reasons unconnected with public safety, but because of disapproval of a film's content.

Cinema managers knew a national self-censorship could protect them against the whims of local authorities. They drew up plans during 1912 and on 1 January 1913 launched the British Board of Film Censors. Local councils retained the right to ban the exhibition of any film in their area: but those who formed the BBFC hoped its very existence and pre-emptive certification would deter such action. The cinema was, for a time at least, to be seen as a medium of wholesome entertainment, especially for those into whose lives relatively little light shone.

On 20 March 1913 the new Brixton Palladium Picture Play House opened in south London, seating 2,000 patrons. Two local MPs attended the opening ceremony, as did the Reverend A. J. Waldron, the vicar of Brixton. Proceeds from the first night were shared between the local nursing home, dispensary and orphanage. Waldron, acknowledging this act of charity, admitted being the chaplain of the local theatre and of the Empress Theatre of Varieties; now he would also be chaplain of the Brixton Palladium. He added: 'We must have enjoyment, and we want the best we can get. I am never ashamed to take my own boy to the picture palace. I am never ashamed to take him to the theatre or music-hall, if the play is clean . . . I shall come into this picture palace, and I hope that sometimes I shall be able to forget the worries of the parish and everything else.'[73]

V

In her *de haut en bas* sneer at 'Edwardian' novelists delivered to the Heretics at Cambridge in May 1924 – published as *Mr Bennett and Mrs Brown* – in which she distinguished Bennett, Galsworthy and Wells from 'Georgian' writers (a term deployed to signify those who had broken with the Victorian school of poetry and novel-writing) such as Forster, D. H. Lawrence, Lytton Strachey, James Joyce and T. S. Eliot, Virginia Woolf asserted that 'on or about December 1910 human character changed'.[74] Her allusion was to the exhibition in London, which her friend Roger Fry curated, entitled *Manet and the Post-Impressionists*. It ran from 8 November 1910 to 15 January 1911 and introduced contemporary French and French-based art to the English. It showed Matisse and Van Gogh in England for the first time. In the view of art historians over succeeding decades, the exhibition changed taste and brought new influences to bear on British artists. Before the war other exhibitions showed radical departures from the conventional: early in 1914 the Whitechapel Art Gallery staged an exhibition of twentieth-century art, and one exhibitor, David Bomberg, a twenty-three-year-old graduate of the Slade, had a one-man exhibition at the Chenil Gallery in Chelsea the following July that included his celebrated work *The Mud Bath*, a Cubist representation of humans as a collection of apparently three-dimensional, right-angled oblongs.

To Mrs Woolf, Fry's exhibition evoked a radical modernity she had occasionally detected in literature. She claimed to have noticed the start of this change in Samuel Butler's *The Way of All Flesh*, which he started to write in the early 1870s but which was not published until 1903, and to have seen it too in Shaw's plays. 'All human relations have shifted,' she continued. 'Those between masters and servants, husbands and wives, parents and children. And when human relations change there is at the same time a change in religion, conduct, politics, and literature.'[75] The change she identified as taking place in 1910, when, as discussed in Chapter 15, Britain was convulsed by a constitutional crisis created by the conflict between the forces of the past and those who were determined to be the forces of the future.

Virginia Woolf wrote about modernism in literature not merely to distinguish its characters, with their streams of consciousness and bare emotions, from what she considered the more two-dimensional and repressed creations of the Edwardians, but to obliterate them completely. Speaking against Bennett, Wells and Galsworthy (the last of whom would eight years later win the Nobel Prize in Literature), she said that 'it seems to me that to go to these men and ask them to teach you how to write a novel – how to create characters that are real – is precisely like going to a bootmaker and asking him to teach you how to make a watch.'[76] The Great War had torn up the map of society and scattered the accepted norms of culture: Mrs Woolf was simply underlining that fact.

She claimed the Edwardian novelists described a world – a real one in Bennett's case, a utopia in Wells's and a rarefied one in Galsworthy's – rather than those who lived in it. Just as, in 1882 with the first volume of his life of Carlyle, James Anthony Froude had invented the warts-and-all biography, so (she would argue) the Georgians had invented the warts-and-all novel. (This showed a complete disregard for the achievement of Thomas Hardy.)

Forster's *Howards End*, published in 1910, contained acute and 'modern' studies of character – notably female, unusual for a novel of the period written by a man. Lawrence's *Sons and Lovers* of 1913 had similar qualities, as did Compton Mackenzie's *Sinister Street*, a *Bildungsroman* that appeared in two volumes in 1913–14 and which was banned by libraries not least on account of its two protagonists, a brother and sister, being illegitimate (worse still, they were from the upper-middle classes), its allusions to homosexuality and its discussion of religion. On 1 September 1910 Pope Pius X issued an encyclical entitled *The Oath Against Modernism* in which he said: 'I am completely opposed to the error of the modernists who hold that there is nothing divine in the sacred tradition'.[77] Pius referred to modern, science-based interpretations of dogma; but the metaphor held good for what was happening across Western culture.

Most leading modernists dismissed religion, Pius's or otherwise: but they also, before war interrupted the progress of their movement, drew inspiration from fractures in society and its values caused by industrialisation, urbanisation and technological advances. Art in all forms – literature, painting, music, sculpture and architecture notably – became experimental. In Europe, this movement had gathered pace since the late 1890s, with the work of such artists as Picasso, Schoenberg, Stravinsky and Strindberg, and with the growing influence of radical philosophers such as Nietzsche and Bergson. Although conservative Britain as yet lacked a large bohemian or artistically radical class – the Bloomsbury Group was in its infancy, reaching its zenith in the 1920s – such influences inevitably began to cross the Channel, galvanising a society that, as we have seen, was ripe for ferment.

Bloomsbury would lead that cultural uprising. It was a collection of modernist aesthetes and radicals that in 1910 included Virginia Stephen (who married Leonard Woolf in 1912), Forster, Lytton Strachey, the artists Roger Fry and Duncan Grant, the art critic Clive Bell (who married Virginia's sister Vanessa in 1907), the economist John Maynard Keynes and the writers Desmond and Molly MacCarthy. Mrs MacCarthy coined the term 'Bloomsberries' to describe the Stephen siblings and their circle, the term being taken up widely and used mockingly. Many of the group had known each other in the Apostles at Cambridge – an intellectual society of undergraduates based at King's College but drawing members from several others – and formed another self-selecting group in London. The group as a whole kept an open mind towards continental influences. But it was an open mind blended with a snobbery and sense of exclusiveness that arrested any intention its members had of spreading appreciation of their discoveries and ideas. This was further fed by their contempt for those who did not meet their standards or share their vision. As a result, they created an idea of culture that was class-based – as culture often had been, but not in the deliberately and aggressively divisive way Bloomsbury would make it.

Although radical aesthetics underpinned the group's ethos, it also embraced decadence in identifying itself with the most progressive notions of modern behaviour and attitudes and seeing nothing wrong with a lack of self-discipline and self-control. As such, it rejected the middle-class values lingering from the nineteenth century, and spectacularly rejected the prevailing sexual morality. Ironically, it had that in common with the much-despised Wells. Above all the Bloomsbury Group was on an artistic crusade. Looking back in 1949, the *Times Literary Supplement* described Bloomsbury as, in its own eyes, standing 'for tolerance and intelligence, for seriousness about art and scepticism about the pretensions of the self-important, and it carried on a crusade about the conscious philistinism of the English upper classes.'[78]

The group's exclusivity was predictable from its origins. Thoby Stephen, Virginia's brother, had been at Trinity College, Cambridge, with Leonard Woolf, Clive Bell and Lytton Strachey. After Cambridge, the men attended soirées given by Vanessa and Virginia Stephen at a house in Gordon Square the Stephen children had taken after Sir Leslie's death in 1904; Vanessa would have a disastrous marriage with Bell before becoming Grant's mistress, and the evenings would survive Thoby's death from typhoid in 1906, though the venue moved to 29 Fitzroy Square, formerly occupied by Shaw but taken over by Adrian (the youngest sibling) and Virginia Stephen after Vanessa's marriage. Grant was also Strachey's cousin and, occasionally, his boyfriend. Vanessa Bell brought in Fry, who was fifteen years older than the others, in 1910, having an affair with him before moving on to Grant. The members denied they were a group but met in each other's houses around Bloomsbury, and the communicants formed a bond that included promoting each other's works. The group advanced the idea of modernism, though its success, like the group's, would come after the Great War.

Although Fry achieved some pre-war celebrity through his Post-Impressionist exhibition, the first Bloomsberry to become famous was Forster. He was a King's man, but came to the group through his membership of the Apostles. He shared the privileged existence of the others, having inherited £8,000 from a great-aunt in 1887 when he was eight, enough for him to live on comfortably while he made his name. His first novel, *Where Angels Fear to Tread*, was published in 1905, and *Howards End* was his fourth.

Howards End, published in 1910, has been described as the first modernist novel because of its descriptions and use of modern phenomena in the narrative – train journeys, motor-cars, housing developments and the advance of industrialisation. The eponymous house is in the part of Hertfordshire where Forster had grown up; the Schlegel sisters, personifying the bohemian *demi-monde*, resemble Vanessa and Virginia Stephen. Forster examined characters in a way of which Mrs Woolf approved: though whether he examined them more deeply than Bennett had Hilda Lessways in the *Clayhanger* novels, or Wells Dick Remington in *The New Machiavelli*, is a matter for debate. The characters in *Howards End* are certainly more varied and complex, with interests and ideas beyond anything known to Bennett's and Wells's creations, but Bennett and Wells unquestionably do explore such depths as are there in their less-educated, more provincial characters, and would have maintained with conviction that their characters' lives were just as intense.

Forster writes for a more select audience, and tailors his language and content accordingly. The book examines Britain's increasingly fissured class system, and is never quite free from the elevated snobbery that poisoned so much of the Bloomsbury experience. The Schlegels are well-to-do, cosmopolitan bohemians who have directed their resources and brains towards aesthetics; their friends the Wilcoxes have made a fortune in the City. The other main characters are a couple with whom the Schlegels become accidentally entangled, Leonard Bast and his former prostitute partner, whom the Schlegels patronise and the Wilcoxes frankly despise.

Bast is lower-middle class, of that breed of clerks that blossomed with the growth of the City and suburbia in the late nineteenth century. He is instinctively kindly and intellectually curious, and seeks self-improvement. The liberal-minded Schlegels adopt him, to an extent; but when Margaret Schlegel marries Henry Wilcox, his family's obsession with money and appearances drives Bast not just out of their lives, but to his death: Wilcox's son attacks Bast, who dies of heart failure, and his attacker is sent to prison for three years for manslaughter. That Bast dies as a result of a case full of books toppling on to him would seem to suggest that intellectual inquiry is best left to the well-to-do, and it seems to symbolise the solidarity of the superior, educated class against him. Wilcox's first wife left Howards End, her own house, to Margaret in an addition to her will when she died, but Henry burned the codicil before

Margaret could see it. In a redemptive fit, he leaves the house to her after all, but Bast and his type are seen as victims in this class struggle, showing that Forster's epigraph to his novel – 'Only connect' – should be taken only so far.

VI

It was, however, thanks to Bloomsbury that London eventually caught up with modern ideas of design, of the sort Mackintosh had been developing in Glasgow throughout the early years of the century. On 11 December 1912 Roger Fry wrote to Shaw, not a member of the group but, by then, a rich sympathiser with some of its ideas, to ask for a donation for a 'workshop for decorative and applied art'.[79] He assured Shaw that 'the Post-Impressionist movement is quite as definitely decorative in its methods as the Pre-Raphaelite, and its influence in general design is destined to be as marked.' Although Fry said he would be assisted by some French artists and influenced by them, 'I wish to develop a definitely English tradition.' He noted that 'since the complete decadence of the Morris movement nothing has been done in England but pastiche and more or less unscrupulous imitation of old work. There is no reason whatever why people should not return to the more normal custom of employing contemporary artists to design their furniture and hangings, if only the artists can produce vital and original work.' A group of young artists who had in 1911 decorated the Borough Polytechnic showed what could be done by artists working co-operatively, and Fry wished to extend that principle: but it would cost him £2,000 in capital 'to give the scheme a fair chance'.

He intended the workshop to be commercial, with its goods bearing a registered trademark, and had found a house in Fitzroy Square for the purpose. He proposed his co-operative would start with wall decorations and move on to painted furniture. He told Shaw that Leonard Woolf was advising him on the business aspects, that there should be a 5 per cent return, and he would establish a profit-share scheme for the workers, something guaranteed to appeal to Shaw's socialist principles. He would use some of his own money, but was soliciting contributions of 'quite small sums, the loss of which would not be seriously felt'.[80] Shaw sent £250 – an eighth share in the business – by return.

This helped the enterprise, called Omega and set up at 33 Fitzroy

Square, get off the ground, but by the following October members of the co-operative had started to fall out with each other. Fry was so perplexed when a group of what he called 'seceding artists' wrote to Shaw and other investors making complaints of what he called an 'imaginary nature' that he wrote to him on 11 November 1913 to put the record straight.[81] He said 'the defection is really fortunate as only one of these four artists has been of any real use', and plans were well advanced for an exhibition of the group's work at the Army and Navy Stores.

The four artists – Wyndham Lewis, Frederick Etchells, Cuthbert Hamilton and E. Wadsworth – had told Shaw certain 'discreditable facts' about the Omega.[82] The first was that 'the Direction' – in other words, Fry – had only managed to secure the decoration for the Post-Impressionist Room at the Ideal Home Exhibition by a 'shabby trick' – an agent of the *Daily Mail* had originally offered the contract to Lewis and an outside artist, Spencer Gore, but Fry had interceded and closed the deal for Omega, downgrading Lewis's role and freezing out Gore altogether. The secessionists also accused Fry of restraint of trade, forbidding individual artists from exhibiting elsewhere. They said this would have been acceptable had Fry secured work for them, but he had not: his exhibitions were 'badly organised, unfairly managed, closed to much good work for petty and personal reasons, and flooded with the work of well-intentioned friends of the Direction.'

Worse still, the Direction seemed to have reactionary tastes, not in keeping with the spirit of Post-Impressionism – 'the idol is still prettiness, with its mid-Victorian languish of the neck and its skin is greenery-yallery, despite the Post-What-Not fashionableness of its draperies.' As a result, 'this family party of strayed and Dissenting Aesthetes . . . were compelled to call in as much modern talent as they could find, to do the rough and masculine work without which they knew their efforts would not rise above the level of a pleasant tea-party, or command more attention.' They claimed Fry had boasted of his generosity to workers to secure support from men such as Shaw, but there was little sign of it within Omega. 'This enterprise seemed to promise, in the opportunities afforded it by support from the most intellectual quarters, emancipation from the middleman-shark. But a new form of fish in the troubled waters of Art has been revealed in the meantime, the Pecksniff-shark, a timid but voracious journalistic monster, unscrupulous, smooth-tongued and, owing chiefly to its weakness, mischievous.' That metaphor presumably amused Shaw.

Fry entreated him to visit the workshop to reassure himself, and Shaw did, declaring himself 'pleased'.[83] He felt the project was succeeding, causing the discerning to 'abandon their ridiculous worship of mechanical finish'. However, Fry had managed to raise only £1,400 and by November 1913 had exhausted it; he put in another £1,000 of his own, but told Shaw he could afford no more. 'I hardly like to ask you to help again but would be immensely relieved if you felt inclined to,' he wrote. He found it 'interesting and rather surprising' to note the 'intense hatred' his enterprise had aroused 'among the collector and art historian and generally over-cultured circles' – circles many outsiders might once have concluded that Fry himself belonged to. 'I hear that the Burlington Fine Art Club spends its time abusing me – the more kindly ones excusing me on the grounds of insanity – and yet not one of them has ever been to see what we are about.'[84] After the war, Fry offered to give Shaw back some of his money from Omega, or to use it for charitable purposes for some of 'the best of the younger men who used to rely on the Omega'.[85]

Although it did break new ground in some ways – Omega not the least of them – Bloomsbury was not nearly so *avant-garde* as it thought it was. Nothing Fry, for example, was doing either on his own account or through Omega, could match what was happening on the continent. The group had some way to run – it would decamp for the duration of the Great War and then return with even greater force in the 1920s – but in its early stages there are already signs of the narrow elitism, snobbery and jealousy of gifted outsiders that would distinguish it after the war: such as in Mrs Woolf's disdain for James Joyce, whose talent and originality far exceeded her own, and whose example, whether she liked it or not, influenced her. Bloomsbury set out to challenge cultural conservatism, but seemed to want to replace it with a self-satisfied and exclusive conservatism of its own.

CHAPTER 13

THE USES OF LITERACY

I

By 1900 Britain had unprecedented mass literacy. This led to the establishing of an industry devoted to slaking a thirst for reading material, both fiction and non-fiction, in books, periodicals and daily journalism. Businessmen realised that greater leisure time and more disposable income created millions of potential new customers for newspapers and magazines. Even the arrival of the gramophone and the cinema at the turn of the century did not alter the growing taste for reading, whether as entertainment, for self-improvement or to acquire information. Before about 1880 most publications, whether books or journals, were by tone and content aimed at a social or intellectual elite. A golden age of the popular press lay ahead, starting in the three decades before the Great War. Men such as Alfred Harmsworth, Lord Northcliffe, created papers, magazines and penny dreadfuls – cheap fiction in serial form with a peculiar appeal to the taste, or lack of it, of the newly literate – to entice people to spend their money. The extension of education to all by the 1902 Education Act, under state-funded local education authorities, abolished the distinction between voluntary and other schools. The estimated 1,000 secondary schools that local authorities opened by the Great War consolidated and continually expanded this newly-literate class.

However, as well as enabling people to read, education helped them to think for themselves and to be more receptive to the ideas of others. One of the uses of the new mass literacy – other than to line the pockets of speculative publishers – was to acquaint the general public better with the issues of the day, and by doing so to make them more politically aware and engaged. The success of the new mass-circulation newspapers and magazines profoundly affected political debate – politicians realised the propaganda potential of a popular press, and courted and honoured its owners. A proliferation of magazines for women from the 1880s onwards encouraged their independence and ambition, and its editorial content set out to support them as wives and mothers. These journals were enormously popular with advertisers, since women were usually responsible for apportioning much of a household's expenditure. In consequence, advertising became an industry in its own right, and the press's provision of a platform for advertising assisted the rise of mass-produced branded goods. But that would be just one of the huge cultural and social changes that the widespread ability to read, and the habit of reading, would bring in its wake.

II

Mass literacy gave birth to the popular novel, making celebrities out of writers such as Bennett, Arthur Conan Doyle and Wells. Wells's initial fame was as a science-fiction writer. His celebrity enhanced his self-belief not just as a prophet, but as a political commentator, giving vent to his progressive Fabian ideas. Public acceptance also encouraged him to try other forms of fiction, beginning with *Love and Mr Lewisham* in 1900. His narrative gifts lent themselves to the humour and travails of the lower-middle-class life he knew intimately, and made popular successes of novels such as *Kipps* (1905) and *The History of Mr Polly* (1910). His experience as a Fabian, and his encounters with activists such as the Webbs, inspired him to write political satire such as *Ann Veronica* and *The New Machiavelli*; and he was a fine observer of life around him, as seen in perhaps his finest pre-war novel, *Tono-Bungay*, a 1909 satire on Edwardian quackery, charlatanism, the power of greed and of advertising.

Wells's novels made him famous and made him money. Intellectuals would sneer at him, led after the war by Virginia Woolf. But he did much to establish the idea of a public eager to read material beyond the penny dreadful and the cheap newspaper. His popularity waned only when his more radical views, particularly on sex and marriage, had free rein: like some music-hall turns, he failed to see the prudery of the lower-middle and working classes.

His friend and contemporary Arnold Bennett – with whom he shared a literary agent – played to the same audience by writing about the extraordinary lives of ordinary people, but in a less obviously Dickensian way than Wells. The two men met in 1897 after Bennett read a short story Wells had set in the Potteries. Bennett wrote to him that 'you are the first man I have come across whom the Potteries has [sic] impressed, emotionally.'[1] Bennett was more cautious than Wells in expressing his philosophy in his novels, yet he had much less to be cautious about, given Wells's baroque private life. Bennett was the son of a pawnbroker-turned-solicitor from Hanley, one of the six towns that would become Stoke-on-Trent but which he romanticised as 'the Five Towns' in his novels. In 1888, aged twenty-one, Bennett fell out with his father, for whom he had worked, and went to London as a solicitor's clerk. The following year he won a *Tit-Bits* writing competition, and decided to become a journalist.

Bennett resembled his creation Denry Machin, the personification of Edwardian enterprise and hero of his 1911 novel *The Card*, not least in his facility for furthering 'the great cause of cheering us all up'. In *The Regent* – Bennett's 1913 sequel to *The Card* – the author even reveals that Machin was born in the Potteries on 27 May 1867, in the very same place and on the very same day as Bennett himself. Like Machin, Bennett could spot an opportunity. As assistant editor of *Woman* magazine in 1893, he noted how sub-standard its fiction was. He wrote a serial himself, which became a success, and then others: by 1897 he had become editor and was writing his first novel, *A Man from the North*. He gave up his executive duties in 1900 to write full-time. 'I am sick of editing *Woman*, & of being bound to go to a blasted office every day,' he had told a friend in January 1899.[2] 'I want to work when I feel inclined, and to travel more.'

Within a decade – spent mostly in Paris, where he imbibed the recent French literary tradition and sought to be recognised as a serious artist – novels such as *Anna of the Five Towns*, which took him six years to write from 1896, *The Old Wives' Tale* and *Clayhanger*, and a clutch of wittily written self-help manuals, had made him a household name.

There were perhaps two unwritten reasons why Mrs Woolf detested him. First, like Wells, he wrote for the most part about people in the lower-middle class from which he had come, and for an audience largely (but not exclusively) of those people, whom in her long career as a novelist, critic and letter-writer Mrs Woolf gave no hint of understanding or, indeed, being interested in. Second, he made a great deal of money by doing so, enough to run a yacht before the Great War (it was taken over by the Admiralty once hostilities commenced) and a new one with a crew of eight after it, at a time when most people of Mrs Woolf's class and above were having to make savings.

Her dismemberment of Bennett in *Mr Bennett and Mrs Brown* (discussed in Chapter 12) had him written off for much of the twentieth century by generations of university lecturers and critics, who confused snobbery with literary criticism. Yet for all the structural weaknesses of some of his novels – *Anna, The Price of Love* and *Whom God Hath Joined* all end hurriedly, as if he were bored with them – his power of observation and depth of humanity make him a valuable witness to life in late-Victorian and Edwardian England. Given he had read (among others) Hardy, Flaubert and Turgenev, his sensitivity as a writer should be no surprise. He damaged himself by admitting, early in his career, that he wrote to make money. He was sensitive about this, and in 1912 threatened to sue *Everyman* magazine for saying his 'scale of literary values is primarily so many pounds per thousand words'.[3] The editor was forced into a grovelling apology. However, as creations such as Hilda Lessways and Anna Tellwright – a woman who conveys the sense of being imprisoned in a world without happiness or normal human experience when anywhere near her oppressive father – make clear, Virginia Woolf's accusation that Bennett failed to understand the human mind is little more than an exercise in snobbery.

Much of the fiction the new reading public absorbed was in periodical form rather than in hardback novels of the sort produced by Wells and Bennett. Crime and detective stories had filled penny dreadfuls for decades, and writers such as Dickens and Wilkie Collins had elevated them to an art form. The man who transformed the genre was a Portsmouth doctor and former ship's surgeon, Arthur Conan Doyle. He wrote for a hobby, more so during the late 1880s when his practice was slow. He abandoned it in 1890 and retrained as an ophthalmologist, setting up off Harley Street. He had sold *A Study in Scarlet*, his first novel-length story featuring Sherlock Holmes – a cocaine-addicted detective who solved cases by deduction, with the aid of his friend Dr Watson – in 1886, but it did not appear until *Beeton's Christmas Annual* for 1887. The character was based on a lecturer who had taught Doyle at Edinburgh University, Dr Joseph Bell, who had emphasised the importance of close observation in making a diagnosis.

Doyle turned out to be the perfect author for the new age. He took the detective story and, with great imagination and ingenuity, popularised it for a mass readership without alienating those of more literary sensibilities. His work was ideal for serial publication, which brought him a vast audience and made him and his publishers a fortune. *Lippincott's Magazine* published the second Holmes full-length story, *The Sign of the Four*, in February 1890, but after that they appeared in *Strand Magazine*, Doyle being unhappy with the fees paid by his earlier publisher, Ward Lock. Doyle wanted to write historical novels, and became disenchanted with Holmes. To discourage commissions for detective stories he kept demanding more money, but such was Holmes's popularity that his creator's demands were met, making him probably the best-paid writer of the age. By 1893 he had had enough, and sent Holmes and his nemesis, Moriarty, to their deaths over the Reichenbach Falls in Switzerland. Pleas to resurrect him were persistent: he eventually reappeared in 1901 in *The Hound of the Baskervilles*, the implication being that the story was set before Holmes's death. From 1903 the first of another fifty or so short stories appeared, the last in 1927, three years before Doyle's death. In the first, 'The Adventure of the Empty House', it was explained Holmes had faked his death to throw other enemies off his scent.

The Sherlock Holmes stories, which coupled mystery and thrills with a literary tone, characterised the middle-brow writing for which there was a high demand from the aspirant classes. Another practitioner was Bram Stoker, who for twenty-seven years from 1879 managed Henry Irving's Lyceum theatre in London. He started writing novels around 1890, when a visit to Whitby in Yorkshire is said to have inspired his most famous work, *Dracula*, published in 1897.

Conan Doyle's and Stoker's audience was predominantly male, but other popular writers of the age appealed, either intentionally or otherwise, to the women's market. In the former category was Elinor Glyn, who started writing in 1900 to fill the economic gap left by her dissolute husband's slide into debt. Mrs Glyn had a series of affairs with society philanderers and used her thinly-veiled experiences as fodder for her romantic fiction. Although tame by today's standards, it was considered shocking in its time: all the more so because among those reading it were shop-girls and others deemed easily impressionable. In the years before Mrs Glyn arrived, the leading shocker – and greatest commercial success – was *Trilby*, published in 1894 by George du Maurier, a retired Punch cartoonist. Although designed as a depiction of bohemian Paris in the 1850s, the novel projected its eponymous heroine in a way that made her a role model for modern young women, and one of which there was widespread disapproval.

As well as wearing a new style of hat that would become enormously popular among men, Trilby also smoke and drank and behaved in a rather forward and liberated way that was far from the fashion of the times. This caused a wave of imitation of her style and attitudes by young women, which the press called 'Trilbymania'. It was a clear example of the profound cultural effect that mass literacy could have: as were the play that Sir Herbert Beerbohm Tree developed out of the novel, which opened in London in 1895, and the silent film of it that appeared in 1914. The other character in the book whose name has passed into everyday usage was Svengali, Trilby's Jewish mentor, who hypnotises her into an ability to sing opera. His treatment by du Maurier as a rogue eventually led George Orwell, and others, to attack the book as anti-Semitic: a way in which it reflected a more established feature of the age.

The drive for literacy for both men and women started at school, and publishers were keen to hook children into the reading habit early on, hoping it would stick for life. As discussed in Chapter 2, school stories featuring the upper-middle classes and adventure stories about the Empire would become a staple of boys' fiction, subtly indoctrinating support for the social order and British imperial power. The publishers were also in the market for big-name writers who would help them boost their revenues, sales and circulations. Writing for children helped make the names of several whose works still resonate today.

By common consent Kipling was, in addition to his other talents, the pre-eminent children's writer at the turn of the nineteenth century. *The Jungle Book* made this reputation in 1894; *Kim*, for adults and children, consolidated it in 1901, both books fruits of his years in India as a child and a young man. The *Just So Stories* followed in 1902. *Stalky and Co.*, his school stories of 1899 based on his education at the United Services College in Devon, have a far darker tone than any school story featured in *The Gem* or *The Magnet*. His literary abilities were superior to those of any other children's author of the period except Stevenson; his talent for telling stories possibly exceeded even Kipling's. Like Stevenson, Kipling's imagination was fired by extensive travel, which equipped him for his role as a man of letters of empire; and also like Stevenson, he wrote fiction and short stories for adults too.

His short stories too were highly praised and, in the late 1880s, made his name. During the 1890s his work featured extensively in fiction magazines, reaching a mass audience. His first novel, *The Light that Failed*, about a painter who is struck blind, was published to acclaim in 1891, when Kipling was only twenty-six. When he married a few months later Henry James, who thought him a genius, gave the bride away. With fame, however, came an urge to become a public figure, and to pronounce on politics. Kipling's poetic gifts were perhaps less than he imagined, his excursions into moral and political didacticism appearing portentous through lack of wit, mannered diction and trite metres. His earlier verse, about colonial officials and soldiers, strove to be comical and, though sometimes deliberately like doggerel, had a charm his other poetry lacked. It found an audience among millions of instinctive patriots, and he would be quoted in countless households, especially those of the class that supplied the non-commissioned officers about whom he wrote so lovingly. He won a popular acclaim as a writer accorded to few of his illustrious contemporaries, and a spectacular level of international recognition. He was only forty-one when he won the Nobel Prize in Literature in 1907, and on various occasions turned down other honours and the Poet Laureateship. There was not merely money for those who managed to excite the reading public, but the glittering prize of establishment recognition too.

III

The last years of the nineteenth century were not just a golden age for writers of fiction: the same force of mass literacy that drove their success also made this the golden age of the popular newspaper. Until that time daily national newspapers existed principally for the benefit of the middle and upper classes, and dealt exclusively with matters of interest to them, in the tone adopted by one educated person talking to another. The London evening paper *The Pall Mall Gazette*, which Stead ran from 1883 to 1889, augured a new era and style of journalism. It was local and was aimed at an evening audience, not least the mass of clerks on their way home from a long day at the office who sought stimulation and relaxation. But Stead, as explained in Chapter 8, pioneered investigative journalism, which led to his manufacturing news rather than just reporting it. He also hired Shaw to write for him, a gesture Shaw repaid by describing Stead as 'a complete ignoramus'.[4] Stead introduced a strong element of muck-raking into the press, giving it entertainment value as a result; but he usually raked muck in the public interest, and with a high mind, as in his exposé of child prostitution. The press was, however, changing, and high minds would not always prevail.

Newspaper readership doubled between 1896 and 1906, and doubled again by 1914. The *Daily Mail* dominated the market for the newly-literate, but was far from alone in targeting them. In the early 1900s the *Daily Express* and the *Daily Chronicle* both sold over 400,000 copies a day, and the *Daily News* just over 300,000: the combined sales of the three quality newspapers, *The Times*, *The Daily Telegraph* and the *Morning Post*, were less than 300,000, nearly two-thirds of that being attributable to the *Telegraph*. The hierarchy of the middle class was echoed by its choice of newspaper: the top half bought the quality press and the lower half the more sensationalist *Mail*, *Express* and *News*. The other great implication of this revolution, apart from making the general public better informed, was the challenge newspaper proprietors offered to the government in mobilising public opinion against them, or against specific policies: it spelt the beginning of the end of public deference towards politicians, and the challenging of the traditional ruling class's sense of entitlement.

The Times, published since 1785, was the self-proclaimed paper of record and of the (predominantly Tory) establishment. Its main rival – which by 1880 had overtaken it in circulation – was *The Daily Telegraph*, founded in 1855 and owned by the Levy family. Joseph Moses Levy ran it until 1885, three years before his death, when his son Edward Levy-Lawson (he had taken the second barrel in the 1870s after receiving a legacy from an uncle) took over. The paper had backed the Liberals until the mid-1870s but then shifted its allegiance to the Conservatives and Unionists. Despite Levy-Lawson's securing a baronetcy from Gladstone in 1892 it remained a Unionist paper, something consolidated by Balfour who made him Lord Burnham. Levy-Lawson introduced drama criticism to the paper (he had begun his own journalistic career as a critic) and an emphasis on the reporting of sport, to chime with an obsession of the times. His influence as proprietor was to make the *Telegraph* a more lively, less stuffy newspaper.

However, its tone and diction limited its appeal to the rising and populous lower-middle class. In 1899 97 per cent of recruits to the Army, who were predominantly working class, could read.[5] This new era of unsophisticated mass literacy had to be catered for, and provided an enormous commercial opportunity for anyone who did. No one capitalised on it more effectively than Alfred Harmsworth. He, more than anyone else, helped prove John Carey's contention that 'the difference between the nineteenth-century mob and the twentieth-century mass is literacy.'[6]

Harmsworth, later the first and last Lord Northcliffe, was not merely one of the most important influences on British popular culture before the Great War; he was also a prime example of how the Edwardian establishment had the flexibility to take to its bosom men from outside who offered something valuable to them, and promote them. The man who – with his younger brother and partner Harold, later the 1st Viscount Rothermere – was born to a downwardly mobile barrister, but through his own efforts and enterprise ended up a peer and a key figure in public life, exemplified rapid social mobility. He also proved how ability could reap massive financial rewards, which would open doors to those outside the old aristocracy and its offshoots.

Harmsworth's power consisted in his foundation of two newspapers that captured different parts of the public mind: the *Daily Mail*, set up in 1896, and *The Daily Mirror*, which began in 1903 as a journal designed to appeal to women. His newspapers and magazines – he made his fortune in the 1880s, when still in his early twenties, with the periodical *Answers to Correspondents*, which also helped launch Wells's writing career – were derided by the middle classes and above for sensationalism or lack of intellectualism. But his harnessing of the interest of the newly literate gave him enormous and unprecedented influence. When, in 1908, he achieved a lifetime's ambition and bought *The Times*, he became perhaps the most powerful man in Britain outside the cabinet, and arguably more powerful than some within it.

Although he was middle-class in origin, Harmsworth's early years were overshadowed by a troubled family life. This was attributable to his father's alcoholism. Alfred senior was a barrister in Dublin but moved the family to London in 1867, when young Alfred was two, and a year before Harold's birth. Alfred attended a school in Hampstead and edited the school magazine; but by 1880, with the family fortunes in disarray, he sought work as a journalist. Maybe it was as well he left the school,

Henley House, at fifteen: Wells later referred to him as 'a sample of the limitations of the English private school education – and indeed of English education generally.'[7] At sixteen he impregnated the family's parlour-maid: he was sent abroad while the girl gave birth in her home village on the Essex marshes, and forbidden to return to the family home afterwards.

He made his living writing for periodicals. He contributed to the highly-regarded local newspaper, the *Hampstead and Highgate Express*, but also to *Bicycling News*, which reflected one of the great crazes of the 1880s. This was also a time of rapid expansion in the weekly magazines published for boys and girls, and contributions by him appeared in a number of them. Alfred cultivated journalistic contacts and by the mid-1880s was selling work to the *Morning Post* and the *St James's Gazette*. By the age of nineteen he was editor of the magazine *Youth*, at a salary of £2 a week.

The great journalistic success story of the age was *Tit-Bits*, founded by George Newnes, a pharmacist, in 1880, and it had a huge influence on Harmsworth. Newnes had seen the untapped audience of hundreds of thousands of young people who enjoyed reading as a recreation but were put off by the stodgy content of most of the press. Harmsworth saw more scope to exploit this trend: the political possibilities of a mass audience would become apparent only later on, when politicians sought to make common cause with him. Harmsworth wrote a self-help book for Newnes, *One Thousand Ways to Earn a Living*, exploiting another trend in popular culture; and another that appealed to the public's desire to improve itself by education, *All About Railways*. Through his prodigious activity he had by 1887 acquired a little capital and some useful contacts who might act as potential investors.

He founded *Answers to Correspondents*, the first number appearing on 16 June 1888, when the proprietor was still a month short of his twenty-third birthday. Its success, like his books for Newnes, was built on the half-educated lower-middle-class desire to acquire more knowledge. It was of the same genre as *Tit-Bits*. 'Neither Newnes nor Harmsworth,' wrote Wells, 'when they launched these ventures, had the slightest idea of the scale of the new forces they were tapping.'[8] Much of the content of *Answers* ('Interesting – Extraordinary – Amusing', the masthead proclaimed) was rubbish, fed to readers in short paragraphs comprehensible even to the most doltish.[9] For the first few months the paper struggled: after an initial sale of 12,000 it dropped to 8,000, but slowly climbed to 20,000. Harmsworth feared it would go bust, so devised means to drive up the circulation: competitions, puzzles and sensationalism. A favourite form of the latter was to answer questions such as what it was like to be hanged, or (more than once) how long a severed head might retain consciousness. An executioner from Saigon was reported as saying: 'I found that the eyes followed me'.[10] Burning to death, burial alive, suffocation and falling under trains also featured, violent death seeming a great passion of Harmsworth: when he relinquished the editorial direction to concentrate on expanding his publishing interests, such stories ended. But by these means, as well as by printing 'confessions' by criminals, circulation rose to 48,000 within a year, and to over 200,000 by mid-1890. *Answers* was aimed at men: the money-making opportunities of journalism aimed at women would soon occur to Harmsworth too.

Before launching *Answers*, he had said to his family that he had a 'schemo magnifico' about building a publishing business. The second stage of this was marked by the appearance of *Comic Cuts* – 'Amusing Without Being Vulgar' – launched in 1890. Thanks to heavy publicity in *Answers* (cross-promotion would be a key business practice in the Harmsworth empire) its first issue sold 118,864 copies. It was directed at even less-educated adults than those who bought *Answers*, assuming a low level of literacy and using copious illustrations to aid comprehension.[11] Wells was caustic: 'Some rare spasm of decency seems to have prevented them calling this enormously profitable, nasty, taste-destroying appeal for the ha'pence of small boys *Komic Kuts*.' Wells's strictures extended to viewing the Harmsworth empire as proceeding 'with an entire disregard of good taste, good value, educational influence, social consequences or political responsibility.'

This was the moment of the 'awakening mind of the British masses', and Harmsworth was 'pouring millions of printed sheets of any sort of trash that sold' into it. An opportunity to coax that mind into greater rigour, discernment or discrimination was thrown away in the pursuit of money. Harmsworth's brother Harold came into the business and they founded the Amalgamated Press Company, which was soon earning profits of £50,000 a year, helped by its successful women's magazines *Forget-me-Not* and *Home Chat*. Harmsworth engaged the leading writers of the day, such as Arthur Conan Doyle (who was paid £5 per 1,000 words) and Rudyard Kipling.[12] Within weeks of *Comic Cuts*'s launch it was selling 300,000 copies a week; by July 1894 there were nine publications in the stable including such novelties as *Chips*, *Home Sweet Home* and the *Sunday Companion*, with a combined weekly sale of 1.75 million.

In George Gissing's depressing masterpiece about writers and hack journalists, *New Grub Street*, published in 1891, Whelpdale, a character who resembles Harmsworth, unveils his plan (ultimately successful) to become rich. He wishes to acquire a periodical called *Chat* and re-name it *Chit-Chat*. He decrees: 'No article in the paper is to measure more than two inches in length, and every inch must be broken into at least two paragraphs.'[13] His reasoning is simple:

> I would have the paper address itself to the quarter-educated; that is to say, the great new generation that is being turned out by the Board Schools, the young men and women who can just read, but are incapable of sustained attention. People of this kind want something to occupy them in trains and on 'buses and trams. As a rule they care for no newspapers except the Sunday ones; what they want is the lightest and frothiest of chit-chatty information – bits of stories, bits of description, bits of scandal, bits of jokes, bits of statistics, bits of foolery . . . Even chat is too solid for them: they want chit-chat.

It works.

> From the first number, the success of the enterprise was beyond doubt; in a month's time all England was ringing with the fame of this noble new development of journalism; the proprietor saw his way to a solid fortune, and other men who had money to embark began to scheme imitative publications. It was clear that the quarter-educated would soon be abundantly provided with literature to their taste.[14]

Gissing, of whom the doomed and idealistic hero of the novel, Edward Reardon, is an incarnation, laments the effect on culture and literature that a press for the masses must have. But Reardon's world no longer exists, the consequence of measures to extend education starting with Forster's Education Act of 1870. However, in the real world these masses created the sound commercial basis that enabled the Harmsworths to change the face of the press.

They bought the London *Evening News* in 1894 for £25,000, which brought them into the newspaper market. By increasing the sensationalist content of the paper – crimes, particularly murders, played well – the circulation and profits rose. Advertising poured in as sales increased. A model had been established, and from there it was an inevitable step to have a national daily newspaper. Money was plentiful elsewhere in the business: by mid-1894 *Comic Cuts* alone was selling 425,000 copies a week.[15]

The potential mass readership of the lower-middle and upper-working classes provided the Harmsworths' opportunity to magnify and consolidate their publishing fortunes, and they seized it with the *Daily Mail*. The title was an act of plagiarism by Harmsworth's brother Leicester, who had heard a newsboy in Birmingham shouting out *Mail* – the name of a local paper – and thought it had resonance. Harmsworth seconded staff from the *Evening News* and bought in journalists from all over Fleet Street for the launch. There was a huge advertising campaign, not least in the Harmsworth press; it concentrated on how different the *Mail* would be from other newspapers: no pages of reported speeches, no columns upon columns of leading articles. It would shape and form opinion, but not by extensive reasoned argument. Harmsworth's instructions to his staff were as simple as the prose he wanted from them: 'Explain, simplify, clarify!'[16]

Harmsworth's diary for Sunday 3 May 1896 describes how he spent the day in the *Mail* office – where he had been for most of the preceding weeks, making plans, producing dummy editions and testing machinery, such as the new, ultra-efficient linotype setting machines – and then 'after some struggle got the papers to press with many misgivings at 1.20am.' The entry for 4 May, launch day, reads simply: 'A big success, I think, bigger than we anticipated. Sold 397,000. Letters and telegrams of congratulation pouring in on the debut of "The Daily Mail".'[17] He soon remarked: 'We've struck a gold-mine.'[18] As well as using a variety of short, snappy news stories, the paper aimed to hook readers by including a serial, and a part of the paper was set aside for what the proprietor regarded as women's matters.

As Whelpdale would have seen it, an easily digestible newspaper to read on public transport, to pass the journey to a day's hard work, was perfect for such people. The key to its success lay in avoiding the stodge of the broadsheets, whose tombstone-like pages of type recorded events in parliament, speeches by prominent politicians or analyses of events in Berlin, St Petersburg or the Sublime Porte, and instead to run stories it would never occur to *The Times* or the *Morning Post* to include: accounts of murders, divorces, missing children, crimes and so on. These human interest stories became the great differentiator between the middle-market and the up-scale broadsheets; and the tabloids, of which the *Mirror* would be the first, further differentiated themselves from the middle market by copious use of illustrations and, early on, a blatant appeal to women of the servant class. Above all, the *Mail* was a paper for those, such as Harmsworth himself, who were largely self-educated and aspirational.

Lord Salisbury dismissed the *Mail* as 'a newspaper run by office boys for office boys', although he (like another vulgarian, Gladstone) sent Harmsworth a congratulatory telegram on the day of its first publication.[19] However, an enormous number of people – the army of clerks and other white-collar workers who filled the newly-expanded suburbs and the commuter trains and trams in and out of the cities – wanted such a newspaper. Indeed, Salisbury himself, who had been a writer of some note, had written to Harmsworth in November 1894 about the *Evening News*, congratulating him on its prospects and noting: 'I believe that such organs of opinion may be of great value if they can be made financially to succeed.'[20] When in 1901 the *Mail*'s circulation passed a million, Salisbury observed that Harmsworth had 'invented a paper for those who could read but not think'.[21]

For all his uncle Salisbury's dismissal of the *Mail*, Balfour, as First Lord of the Treasury the second most senior member of the government, grasped its potential influence. He wrote to Harmsworth on 7 May 1896 to observe that 'though it is impossible for me, for obvious reasons, to appear among the list of those who publish congratulatory comments in the columns of the "Daily Mail", perhaps you will allow me privately to express my high appreciation of your new undertaking.'[22] He added: 'If it succeeds, it will greatly conduce to the wide dissemination of sound political principles . . . and I cannot doubt that it will succeed, knowing the skill, the energy, the resource with which it is conducted.' Balfour was writing to a fellow Tory: 'You have taken the lead in newspaper enterprise, and both you and the Party are to be heartily congratulated.' The *Mail* had an instant appeal to a readership beyond politicians too.

During a midnight rehearsal of *Henry IV*, Herbert Beerbohm Tree wrote to Harmsworth on 4 May to say he was reading the paper 'by limelight' at the Haymarket Theatre and 'it seems indeed a wonderful production – your paper, I mean, not *Henry IV*.'[23]

Harmsworth too saw the potential for the *Mail* as a political weapon. He had deployed the *Evening News* as one after the Jameson Raid, and relished his power to influence politics: it underpinned the decision to launch the *Mail* a few months later. He was politically motivated, having stood unsuccessfully as a Unionist candidate in Portsmouth at the 1895 general election. The link became stronger, and one can see how he was destined to end up on the Unionist benches in the Lords. On 18 July 1899 Balfour sent him 'a word of hearty thanks for the admirable service done to the Party by the "Daily Mail" during the recent St Pancras election.'[24] Balfour had a philosopher's grasp of how public opinion was shaped, referring in his letter to 'places where the amount of justice to be rendered to Englishmen is meted out on a scale strictly determined by the opinions held and to the strength and resolution of the English Government'. It was in reaching these places, and conveying those opinions and that resolution, that the *Mail* became indispensable. As early as December 1896 Bennett said it occupied 'the position of first *newspaper* pure & simple in this great country.'[25]

At the Diamond Jubilee the Harmsworths gave a party in Berkeley Square in honour of visiting colonial premiers and shaped the masses' appreciation of the Sovereign by publishing their ten-part series *Sixty Years a Queen*. In 1900 they had a new competitor, the *Daily Express*, founded by Arthur Pearson, a rector's son and Wykehamist, who had learned the newspaper business as Newnes's assistant at *Tit-Bits*. Pearson had bought the ailing *Morning Herald* in 1898 and now merged it with his new paper. The *Express*'s cover price was a halfpenny, and it lured readers by filling its front page with news stories, not advertisements. A circulation war ensued that helped both papers, as their owners and editors innovated and more interesting products attracted new readers into this marketplace. Unlike the Harmsworths, Pearson was not a long-term player in journalism: he began to go blind in 1908, and in 1916 the *Express* was sold to Sir Max Aitken, the Canadian magnate who became Lord Beaverbrook.

The incompetence with which the Second Boer War was prosecuted not only allowed Harmsworth to build circulation by reflecting public feeling that their soldiers were poorly equipped and even more poorly led; it also allowed him to show the political class, who found themselves forced to notice his strictures, just what power a newspaper proprietor could have. He shared his concerns with Balfour; the First Lord reassured him the government would regain command of the situation and not allow anyone to 'threaten the very existence of our empire', a sentiment Balfour promised to express 'in quite clear language'.[26]

In 1902 the Harmsworths opened a branch in Manchester and established new offices and printing works at Carmelite House, just off Fleet Street in London. Alfred installed the latest presses, cutting costs by 35 per cent, allowing him to undercut his competitors and boost profits. A strong enthusiast for cars and aviation, he had by 1906 motorised the distribution of both the *Mail* and the *Evening News*, once more beating his competitors. He was also quick to capitalise on the potential of a female readership. The *Mail* had a dedicated women's page, and *The Daily Mirror,* on 2 November 1903, was designed for women: indeed, its editorial staff were – to start with – all female, a bold move by Harmsworth and a sign of how a successful businessman does not allow social conventions or prejudices to prevent him from making money.

His diary for 1 November records that 'after the usual pangs of childbirth' the first copy of the *Mirror* rolled off the press at 9.50 p.m.[27] 'It looks a promising child, but time will show whether we are on a winner or not.' Telegrams and letters of congratulation poured in, and 276,000 copies of the first number were sold. However, pagination was soon cut from twenty to sixteen and the *Mirror* floundered. Within weeks Harmsworth tore up the blueprint and started again, emphasising illustration and a bent towards women, but putting men in charge: this time it worked. It was the first newspaper to make extensive use of photographs.

Harmsworth invented the template for the twentieth-century press baron, literally in his case as he became Baron Northcliffe of the Isle of Thanet in December 1905, just as Balfour was limping out of office; he had become a baronet the previous year, three weeks before his thirty-ninth birthday, news Balfour had conveyed to him 'with great pleasure'.[28] The barony was conferred with 'much pleasure'.[29] In the benighted years of Liberal government that followed, Northcliffe kept in regular contact with Balfour, searching for ways to extend Tory influence, notably by enlisting him to encourage other Tory magnates to buy local newspapers that might otherwise fall into enemy hands and spread the wrong sort of propaganda. Northcliffe also acquired other trappings of the tycoon, about which he was more discreet, such as a mistress (one of several) who bore him three illegitimate children.

Northcliffe had by now become the embodiment of the press's power to move public opinion, which is why Tory politicians (and some Liberal ones) courted him so. In the great internal battle in the party over free trade, he advocated Imperial Preference. The *Mail*'s chief leader writer, Herbert Wrigley Wilson, a refined Oxford man, sold him the idea. Wilson was a naval historian and close associate of Chamberlain, and acted as Harmsworth's director of studies on the historical questions that fascinated him. In Northcliffe's papers, for example, is a long annotated list of books on Napoleon, all in French, that Wilson recommended for his master's edification.[30] Harmsworth was obsessed with Bonaparte, and rejoiced in his nickname of 'the Napoleon of Fleet Street'. In a memorandum to his proprietor on 1 October 1903 Wilson argued that 'Joseph can promise employment for 130,000 men at good wages', because reciprocal preferential tariffs for British goods entering countries such as Canada had boosted British exports and, therefore, British jobs.[31] 'Joseph' had resigned a fortnight earlier, and the fight for the soul of the Conservative party over free trade, which would weaken it fatally and cause its defeat two years later, was in full swing. Chamberlain also had the support of Pearson at the *Express*.

Wilson told Harmsworth that 'Joseph continues very anxious to meet your views, and he will, I think, do so, by making it perfectly clear that by the aid of the tax on foreign manufactures much more taxation on food can be remitted than is going to be imposed.' Harmsworth had told Wilson that he resisted supporting Chamberlain because he feared tariffs would harm the cost of living. Wilson (who had told Chamberlain about Harmsworth's 'regard for the poor') felt he could prove there would be no such effect. He added that Chamberlain would carry much of the country with him – not just his fellow imperialists, but 'a large part of the middle class, sick with weak govt; a large part of the business class, which knows he is the only man capable of carrying protection; those who are attracted by a strong personality; a great many of the workers, when they hear what preference can do.' These were all readers or potential readers; and the Harmsworth press would want little truck with the groups Wilson identified as against preference, notably 'Little Englanders and Unprogressives, the Free Fooders and part of the Labour party. But the Free Fooders' guns will be spiked when they find that he is not going to raise the price of food.'

Attached to the memorandum was a draft of a leading article Wilson had written on the subject, which he sent for proprietorial approval. Harmsworth was so taken by the argument, and so strong was his conviction that the rest of the world with its tariffs was a conspiracy against British industrial might, that he published arguments for Imperial Preference under his own name in the *Mail* of 7 October 1903, dealing a further blow to the Unionists and whipping up the support of all who believed British businesses hard done by. Chamberlain was overjoyed and sought to meet him: Wilson attempted to arrange a meeting, but was thwarted by Harmsworth's falling ill.

On 4 November, just after the launch of the *Mirror*, Chamberlain spoke in Birmingham on tariff reform. Harmsworth could not attend, but technology came to his aid – 'Came to *Mail* office in the evening and listened to Chamberlain speech at Birmingham through the electrophone. Wonderful success,' he told his diary, the last remark referring either to the speech or the process.[32] 'Heard the great man distinctly – distance 113 miles. *Evening News* brought out a verbatim report of speech within half an hour of the finish.' Chamberlain wrote on 27 November to a common friend, Leo Maxse, that 'I am really most desirous of making the acquaintance of Mr Alfred Harmsworth.'[33] The two men met on 9 December in London. Thereafter they collaborated closely.

Northcliffe, not least under the influence of Wilson, believed the Germans were determined to attack England and destroy the British Empire, a theme first aired in his papers in 1897 but which took on great importance under the Liberal government after 1906. Wilson told him in 1905 that 'I have always held that war between England and Germany would be terrible, and I am very doubtful of the probability of our success in it. Even with France on our side I would not lay much money upon a British victory. The German Navy is being steadily increased and another large Navy Bill is to be introduced this winter.'[34] Wilson had little time for France ('she has constantly given way to German susceptibilities, and changed her cabinets to suit Germany') and quoted an Austrian view of the Entente Cordiale as 'two rotten nations leaning against each other and in mortal terror of Germany.' Before 1914 Wilson ensured his naval contacts had regular audiences of Northcliffe, to brief him on the precarious state of British sea power.

Northcliffe's political voice became even louder when he bought the oldest surviving Sunday newspaper, *The Observer*, in 1905, saving it from financial ruin. It was only after his appointment to the editorship in 1908 of J. L. Garvin, a former *Daily Telegraph* leader writer whose political journalism had made him famous, that the paper was transformed. Garvin used it for political purposes in a way the quality press had not been deployed before, making a new template for the heavyweight Sunday newspaper. Urging the Lords to reject Lloyd George's Budget in 1909 was perhaps his most audacious campaign. However in 1911 Garvin – who would later write, but not live to complete, an epic biography of Chamberlain – fell out with Northcliffe over tariff reform, and Northcliffe sold the paper to William Waldorf Astor. It is a measure of Garvin's power that Northcliffe did not simply sack him, as most proprietors would have done.

On buying *The Times* for £320,000 in 1908 from the Walter family, having outflanked Pearson, Northcliffe extended his influence even further. Politicians knew they could address the middle and lower-middle classes through the *Mail* and the *Mirror*: now Northcliffe could enable them to address their own class and, indeed, each other through print. G. E. Buckle, the editor Northcliffe inherited, praised his new proprietor, telling him on 23 June 1908 that 'the new arrangements and your vigorous personality have infused hopefulness and buoyancy into us all.'[35] Buckle was a man of substance – he would complete W. F. Monypenny's six-volume life of Disraeli – and of principle: he declined a baronetcy in Balfour's resignation honours as he thought acceptance would compromise the integrity of *The Times*. He was also angry that Arthur Walter, of whom he had been 'a friend of nearly thirty years' standing', had not consulted him about selling the paper.[36]

His relationship with Northcliffe, who despite Buckle's beliefs to the contrary was cut from a different cloth, would be difficult. This became clear within a fortnight as Northcliffe ordered the sacking of thirty *Times* staff members, including the head printer and the head reader. When he complained to Buckle about a report of the massacre in the *Daily Chronicle*, informed by word from inside the print room, Buckle advised him not to be surprised as 'they are, I imagine, rather sore.'[37] Buckle went off on holiday in early August with nervous exhaustion, revealing the effect the Northcliffe dynamo could have when attached to a more sedate engine, though Northcliffe did insist that he take two months off, recognising the intensity of his work. Buckle told Balfour in March 1909 that 'there is to be no change of any kind, save in the way of improvement on the old lines, in the conduct of the Paper.'[38]

The next few years would be dogged by difficulties over how much money the low-circulation, high-prestige paper lost: in December 1909 Northcliffe feared it was heading towards 'a financial Niagara'.[39] A tense stand-off was developing between Northcliffe and Buckle, not least because Northcliffe was sending in trusties from his other papers to work on the editorial and commercial teams, altering the paper's ethos and atmosphere. Northcliffe told his editor on 23 December 1909 that 'so long as we squabble and misunderstand each other, the exercise of initiative is impossible': and he piled on pressure by telling Buckle he had transferred high-performing staff to try to rescue *The Times* at the cost of his other businesses.[40]

Once Northcliffe acquired *The Times* he acquired too the counsel of its Military Correspondent, Lieutenant-Colonel Charles à Court Repington. Repington was one of the best-informed men on the British and rival armies, their strengths, capabilities, weaponry, and the quality of their generalship. He had left the service under a cloud, after irregularities with the wife of a British official in Cairo. He had helped Kitchener in his press campaign against Curzon; and many thought him, with justification, utterly unscrupulous. In the years before the Great War Repington stoked Northcliffe's disenchantment with the government's handling of national security with reports highlighting deficiencies against Germany affecting not only the Army, but also the surface fleet, submarines and airships. He used the *Mail* and *The Times* to campaign against the government's policy.

Repington's position became more controversial when as well as working for Northcliffe he also, from the summer of 1911, worked for the government, in the War Office, editing the *Army Review*; when Northcliffe raised an eyebrow at this, Repington bluntly told him that *The Times* had reduced his pay and expenses by £500 a year in 1909, and he had taken on the *Army Review* work to compensate – 'it is simply a question of money.'[41] Northcliffe expressed displeasure to Buckle that permission had ever been given for Repington to do both jobs, leading to 'unpleasant gossip'.[42] He suggested the paper seek a new military adviser. 'It is quite impossible for Colonel Repington to criticise the War Office and take this payment from them,' he told Buckle.

However, Northcliffe realised that so long as Repington had a foot in both camps – which lasted until the summer of 1912, when he fell out with the War Office – the flow of information would benefit both him and *The Times*. The information the press baron received was certainly high class: on 20 May 1912 Repington sent him a paper about a naval war with Germany, asking him to return it. On 1 June Repington had to ask for it back as 'it is desired to show it to the King, and I have no other copy quite complete.'[43] Repington also mentioned that an article in *The Times* about the Mediterranean situation gave him 'great concern', and when Northcliffe returned the paper he assured his confidant he agreed and 'nothing more of that kind will appear in the paper'.[44]

Liberal politicians were not Northcliffe's normal bedfellows, but he wrote to Lloyd George in April 1908, on the creation of the Asquith administration, to warn him Britain was 'suspect by the French for pro-German tendencies.'[45] Lloyd George helpfully replied that 'the only real pro-German whom I know of on the Liberal side of politics is Rosebery, and I sometimes wonder whether he is even a Liberal at all.' Haldane, the Secretary of State for War; who would be tarred with the pro-German brush up to and beyond the Great War, was acquitted of having anything more than an 'intellectual bent' towards the Teutons.

There was, with all politicians, a master and servant relationship in which Northcliffe was very much the master. When Lloyd George, the Chancellor of the Exchequer, complained to him, in September 1908, that a speech in Wales he regarded as important had hardly been reported, Northcliffe told him that 'newspapers – much as they desire to print your speeches – can hardly be expected to look for important utterances at Sectarian Meetings.'[46] For good measure, he added that Churchill had complained about a 'lack of system' in reporting. 'I admit this,' Northcliffe observed, 'but there is also lack of system in the way speeches are delivered . . . I am very desirous that reporting should be improved. That can only be done by co-operation between Statesmen and newspapers.'

If the effect he was having on politics and politicians was making Northcliffe feel like some kind of supreme being – and his increasingly unhinged behaviour later in life suggested it was – in other spheres he had found he could not do as he pleased. The *Mail* had had a lesson in the limits of its power the previous year, when William Lever, MP, the industrialist whose fortune was built on Sunlight soap and who had built Port Sunlight, sued the paper for libel. It and its sister titles – *The Daily Mirror* and the *Evening Standard* – had accused Lever of reducing the size of his soap tablets while raising the price and negotiating with competitors to establish a monopoly to the customer's disadvantage. The *Mail* ran story after story about 'the soap trust', encouraging grocers to boycott Lever's products and those of his accomplices, damaging their businesses as best it could. It also accused Lever of using sweated labour, and perpetrating bribery and fraud.

The *Mail* had an ulterior motive. Lever had begun a process of amalgamation with business rivals by exchanges of shares, which the *Mail* realised would, if continued, reduce substantially the amount of advertising revenue from the lucrative soap market. So, far from protecting the housewife and the washerwoman, it was protecting itself. Its reporters were pressed into writing stories, not all factual, about the hardship caused by the rise in the price of soap. Lever struck back by cancelling his firm's advertising with Northcliffe's papers: the reporting became more hostile and more biased. Lever's ruthlessness, the *Mail* announced, would cause 'hunger and poverty . . . It goes straight at the throat of people living on the verge of starvation.'[47]

Fatally for the *Mail*, the paper chose not to let Lever give his side of the story, savaging him as though he had committed a criminal offence, which he had not. He consulted F. E. Smith, the distinguished barrister and Unionist MP, who told Lever: 'There is no answer to this action for libel, and the damages must be enormous.'[48] In his testimony during the hearing in July 1907 Lever pleaded and proved substantial damage, not just to his trade but to the value of his shareholding. He also stated that in 1906 the price of raw materials had risen: he had pioneered the manufacture of soap from vegetable oil instead of from tallow, and the growth in demand for margarine had driven up the price of the oil. Although he had reduced a bar of soap from sixteen to fifteen ounces, he had advertised this and had done it in lieu of increasing the price.

The paper retained Rufus Isaacs, who would become Lord Chancellor, but as soon as he heard Lever's evidence he realised the game was up, and withdrew the *Mail*'s defence of justification. He made no attempt to contradict Lever's statement that much of what the *Mail* had written had been lies. This surrender, which the judge praised as honourable, did nothing to mitigate the damages Lever sought. The two parties agreed £50,000 for the *Mail*'s libels alone, far exceeding the previous record award of £12,000. Isaacs – who had begun by offering £10,000 – feared if the sum were left to a jury to decide it would have been even higher. He and Sir Edward Carson, who appeared for Lever, each had 1,000-guinea briefs, with refreshers of 250 guineas a day. A huge amount of costs – now all to be borne by the paper – had been run up in preliminary hearings.

Lever received £141,000 from all Northcliffe's papers. He used the money to endow schools of tropical medicine and town planning at Liverpool University. The settlement was a warning to the 'new journalism' to know its place. The fault was Northcliffe's, who through overweening arrogance that perhaps portended his later madness wrote much of the copy himself, and gave orders that no word of it be changed. Harold Harmsworth, showing more acumen, bought shares in Lever's company in correct anticipation of the outcome of the case. Northcliffe paid much of the costs out of his own pocket, to avoid punishing his employees, who were part of a profit-sharing scheme. The *Mail*'s editor, Thomas Marlowe, gave discreet instructions that any story furnished by the proprietor had to be thoroughly checked before it was printed. The new journalism had learned its place, but at a hefty price.

IV

Northcliffe was not alone in seeking to use newspapers to influence the public mind. It was why George Cadbury bought the *Daily News* in 1901 to act as an anti-Boer War and pro-pensions newspaper. It would also campaign against sweated labour and took up the cause of suffragists, though turned up its nose at suffragettes. When it supported their force-feeding in 1909, two renowned writers, H. N. Brailsford and H. W. Nevinson, resigned. By then the corrosive effect newspapers had on public deference towards politicians was obvious. Ministers were accountable not just to parliament and their constituents, but to a reading public.

Long before he became a part of Northcliffe's stable, thanks to having his newspaper sold from under him, Buckle had exemplified the power a journalist could hold in a society now increasingly reliant on newspapers as a medium of information and cockpit of discussion and debate. He was especially useful to Balfour, of whom he was a close confidant from the late 1880s onwards. Balfour had committed two political errors – one to the good of the country, the other not – that brought his party to ruin by 1905, and had greatly relied on Buckle's support to sustain him. The Education Act of 1902 had, as we have seen, alienated Non-conformists, and after their defeat in January 1906 the Unionists came to regard the Act as their undoing. The split over Imperial Preference or, specifically, over Balfour's inability to give a definitive lead on the question, was also to blame. Unlike the breed of journalists who populated the new Harmsworth papers, Buckle was a studious, scholarly and high-minded man, a product of Winchester and Oxford, with no interest in sensationalism: his one foray into it, the Pigott forgeries (discussed in Chapter 5), had cured him of that. In late 1905, with the Unionists in disarray and Balfour minded to resign, Buckle wrote telling him to stiffen his backbone. The whips had told him to stay, but Buckle saw the end was near. He felt it better for Balfour to resign than be forced into a dissolution. Buckle was also a friend of Chamberlain, and mediated between them. In a letter to Balfour of 25 November 1905, urging him to go, Buckle said Chamberlain was planning a speech to young tariff reformers at Oxford on 8 December. 'You will probably agree', he counselled his friend, 'that you should be clear of office by then?'[49]

Buckle knew Balfour's social movements, and that the prime minister and the King would be in the same party at Crichel in Dorset on 5 December, to shoot with Lord Alington. 'You can hardly blend a social visit with a political resignation. Would it not be right – if you remain in the same mind – to see the King at Sandringham before the end of this week, and so give him a few days for seeing CB [Campbell-Bannerman] before the Crichel visit?'[50] Balfour sought to reward Buckle, and on 5 December had J. S. Sandars, his private secretary, sound him out about a baronetcy. 'I was taken entirely by surprise,' Buckle replied, 'and – to be frank – the surprise was not a welcome one.'[51] While grateful for 'the kindly feeling which prompted you to make the offer', and that 'you should think that any services which, through *The Times*, I may have rendered to great causes which we both have at heart are worthy of recognition by the state', Buckle could not accept: and issued a magisterial account of why. 'The circumstances must be exceptional indeed which would justify the Editor of *The Times* in accepting any honour or title from a minister. Absolute independence of ministers and parties is one of the most cherished of our traditions in Printing House Square. Such support as *The Times* has given to your Government has been given entirely on public, and not on party grounds, and is not a suitable subject for payment with party rewards.'

That marked him out from Northcliffe, who acquired honours until his death in 1922. His later public service would justify them, but that was not the cause of his social ascent. It was also a doctrine many in Buckle's position would follow, and others ignore, in the decades ahead. Buckle's recognition, in his refusal, of the power of the press said much about a changed political climate, in which journalism was highly significant. Yet his final reason for declining was more traditional: he told Sandars that 'in any case, I had no sufficient private income to support a baronetcy.'[52] In that age, at least, journalists too knew their place.

PART IV

STRIFE

CHAPTER 14

MEN AND POWER

I

One of the towering misconceptions about the years immediately preceding the Great War is that they formed an extended Edwardian summer of calm and serenity that was shattered in August 1914. In fact, they witnessed the most socially divisive and disruptive period since the rise of Chartism in the late 1830s. Serious industrial unrest brought parts of the country to the brink of anarchy. Suffragettes turned to a militancy that verged upon terrorism in an attempt to force parliament to give them the vote. The House of Lords picked a fight with the House of Commons that brought about the worst constitutional crisis since 1688 and changed the course of British constitutional practice. Perhaps most perilous of all, agitation by Unionists over Irish Home Rule, even when the Bill granting it was about to be enacted, brought Ireland close to civil war.

The cast of men who ran Britain in the years before the Great War contains some of the most celebrated, colourful and controversial figures in the country's history. Three were of particular significance: King George V, Herbert Henry Asquith, his prime minister, and David Lloyd George, the Chancellor of the Exchequer. The contrasting strengths and weaknesses of each represented different facets of an age of rapid social, technological and political change.

II

George V's role as a constitutional monarch prevented him from espousing party politics, but in his private and public attitudes he was what later in the twentieth century would come to be known as a force of conservatism. Though he was not obdurate and would act properly on the advice of his ministers even when he violently disagreed with it, he would fight as far as he could to preserve the status quo, out of an inherent fear of radicalism that gave him more in common with his grandmother than with his father. Thus he became a stabilising figure in an age of turmoil, his public face of restraint, caution and propriety mirrored by the way he conducted his family life. No man could have been more out of tune with an age rife with hypocrisy. After the revolution in attitudes, morals and manners brought by the Great War the unchanging King would, like many of his generation, start to appear isolated and uncomprehending: hence not least the troubles he had in his relationship with his son and heir, the future King Edward VIII.

By contrast, the Liberal government that came to power in late 1905 and which King George inherited on his accession in May 1910 ruled during a period in which standards in public life declined precipitately. Private morality, too, was changing, the irregular private lives of King Edward VII and the aristocracy influencing the newly-moneyed middle classes. Despite serious infirmity brought on by cigars and gluttony, the King maintained a mistress until excess killed him: but despite the lead he set, public morals had not undergone a progressive change since the era of Dilke. Once Edward's uxorious and strait-laced son succeeded him, public tolerance of carnal improprieties went, if anything, into reverse. The new King's undiluted Victorianism meant he expected the impeccable and restrained family life he led with his beloved wife and six children to be a model for the rest of the nation. His accession, therefore, signalled a more sober age. Not only were divorced people excluded from Court; so too were separated ones. Churchill implored the King in 1911 to allow his cousin, the Duke of Marlborough, separated from the Duchess, to attend the luncheon given after the meeting of the Order of the Garter (of which the Duke was a knight) days before the Coronation: the King relented, but only after emphasising that he did not intend 'to abrogate the general rule'.

George V's interest in game shooting (at which he excelled) and philately (of which he became one of the world's foremost experts) eclipsed all else, including women. Disregarding the example of his father, his devotion to his Queen was legendary and genuine. He told Count Mensdorff, the Austrian Ambassador, with regard to the sexual mores of some of the aristocracy, 'I'm not interested in any wife except my own.'[1] His almost boring steadiness, unexcitability and predictability would, in time of severe crisis, be of great use to his country. It was a shock, therefore, when in November and December 1910, seven months after his accession, a pro-republican newspaper based in Paris called *The Liberator* three times published a story, doing the rounds since the early 1890s but with no basis in fact, claiming the King was bigamously married. It was alleged that, as a young naval officer, he had in 1890 in Malta married (Mary) Elizabeth Culme-Seymour, the daughter of an admiral in the Royal Navy, who had had children by him. The stories were written with the help of Edward Mylius, main distributor for *The Liberator* in Britain, who ensured each Member of Parliament received a copy free of charge. The paper appeared to have banked on the convention that the Royal family did not sue when libelled. The stories were not without humour. The third simply noted that 'The *Daily News* of London informs us that the King plans to visit India with his wife. Would the newspaper kindly tell us which wife?'[2]

The allegations caused outrage among those who heard them. The King asked Churchill, as Home Secretary, for advice: Churchill asked the law officers, who told him 'the paper undoubtedly contains a criminal libel on the King'.[3] Isaacs, as Attorney-General, told the Sovereign it would be unconstitutional for him to give evidence in his own court. The King decided to sue nonetheless, and this brought the allegations before a far wider audience. Had he married Miss Culme-Seymour not only would his marriage to Queen Mary have been bigamous, but his first marriage would have broken the law, being unsanctioned by the 1772 Royal Marriages Act, under which the Sovereign's permission was required before a marriage could occur involving a descendant of King George II. Also, Mylius's story suggested the Queen was not Queen and that the couple's six children were all bastards and, therefore, not in the line of succession to the Throne.

On Boxing Day 1910 Mylius was arrested and charged. The case was heard in a day, 1 February 1911, at the Old Bailey, before the Lord Chief Justice. Isaacs and Sir John Simon, the solicitor-general, prosecuted. Mylius, whom *The Times*'s correspondent described as 'a small dark man of youthful appearance', had no counsel.[4] He immediately argued with the judge, demanding the King come to court as he had a right to be faced by his accuser. The judge told him the King – who in his diary that day departed from his usual routine of discussing the weather or his game bag by describing Mylius's story as 'a damnable lie' – was not coming, and that was that.[5] Mylius justified his libels by saying they were true and that their publication 'was for the public interest'. Isaacs called the libel one of a 'gross and serious character', saying the King had not only bigamously married but had 'foully abandoned' his supposed first wife. Isaacs stressed Mylius was not being prosecuted for his republican opinions, which he was entitled to hold; but he could not call the King a bigamist without evidence.

The case was watertight. The King had not been in Malta between 1888 and some years after his marriage to the Queen. Miss Culme-Seymour had not visited the island until 1893, some months after the King and Queen had married, when her father assumed his command there. She had spoken to the King only once in her life, when she was eight years old and he was a cadet on board the *Britannia*. Maltese marriage registers showed the King had never married there; the logs of various ships proved his whereabouts during his naval career. Her father gave evidence and Mylius declined to question him; then the supposed first wife of the King, now Mrs Trevelyan Napier, said she had had never been married other than to her present husband, and had only visited Malta once the King and Queen had been married. Mylius declined to question her too, or other members of the family who swore that Elizabeth had never married anyone except Captain Napier. A representative of the Admiralty vouched for where the King had been during that part of his naval career. A Maltese functionary confirmed no such marriage had been registered on the island. Even Sir Arthur Bigge, the King's private secretary, gave evidence.

When Mylius began his defence he demanded, again, that his accuser be in court; if he would not, Mylius wanted to be tried for sedition or for defamatory, not criminal, libel. The Lord Chief Justice dismissed his claims; when he asked Mylius to continue the defendant answered: 'No, my Lord. I rest my case there, as I have been denied the Constitutional right of a fair trial.'[6] The judge made it clear in his summing-up that Mylius, having made no attempt to defend himself, deserved only one outcome. These were 'scandalous, malicious and defamatory libels . . . It is a really lamentable thing that a man should not only publish [them] but should come into Court and repeat the plea, and say it is true in the most solemn form, without having a vestige, or a scrap, or a shadow of evidence in support of the statement.' The jury did not even leave the box; in less than a minute it unanimously found the defendant guilty on all three charges. For what the judge called the 'gross and infamous libels' and 'infamous and scandalous lies' he gave Mylius a year's imprisonment, the maximum he could inflict, which he called 'wholly inadequate to the offence'. The King was relieved that 'the baseness of this cruel and abominable libel' had been proved.[7] The King's mother, Queen Alexandra, told him the whole thing had been 'too silly for words. But as the public seems to have believed it, this trial was the only way to let them hear and know the truth, and so have your good name vindicated for ever.'[8]

III

George V's virtuous example was one that Herbert Henry Asquith, whom he inherited as prime minister on his accession in May 1910, struggled to follow. A man of brilliant intellect and a lawyer by training, Asquith provided a constant challenge to the monarch, whom he could out-argue with ease but whom he treated with unfailing respect. Asquith's first wife, Helen, died of typhoid in 1891, when he was thirty-nine, leaving him to bring up five children. Helen was from the provincial middle classes, like her husband, she the daughter of a Manchester doctor and he the son of a West Riding wool merchant. In 1894 he married Margot Tennant, daughter of a Scottish baronet and landowner. Margot could not have been less like Asquith's demure, understated first wife. She was highly strung, occasionally brilliant, tiresome, interfering and ambitious for and highly protective of her husband. Her ambition for him manifested itself not least in the substitution of his second Christian name, Henry, for his first, Herbert, by which he had been known to his family for the first forty-two years of his life, but which was too plebeian for Margot.

Asquith found the enormous pressure of his work and the strict demands of marriage incompatible. He sought refuge in alcohol, an ironic departure for a leader whose party was largely rooted in Nonconformist temperance politics. But as crisis piled upon crisis, and Margot's constant micromanagement of their life became insufferable, a younger woman distracted him. Venetia Stanley, daughter of Lord Stanley of Alderley, was a close friend of Asquith's daughter Violet.

Asquith met her in 1907 when she was twenty, and for a few years she was but one of several attractive and smart young women with whom he conducted friendships – others included Viola Tree, Pamela Jekyll, Lilian Tennant and Dorothy Beresford. Asquith had long enjoyed the recreation of writing escapist and often flirtatious letters to women he met in society, and in 1910 added Venetia to his list of lucky recipients.

Nothing exceptional happened until January 1912, when suddenly the tone, and the frequency, of the letters changed. Asquith and Violet went to Sicily on holiday with Venetia and Edwin Montagu, a young Liberal MP and under-secretary of state for India, who was in the same social circle as Asquith's children and had been his private secretary. Asquith had seen off the constitutional crisis provoked by the Lords' determination to veto government policies, but was battling with Irish Home Rule, militant suffragettes and a wave of strikes. He was nearly sixty, had high blood pressure, and felt worn out. No sooner had he arrived in Sicily than his daughter saw him transformed – 'very well and bird happy'.[9]

On this holiday Asquith fell in love with Venetia. Apart from his being already married, and thirty-five years her senior, there was the difficulty that Montagu fell in love with her too. Asquith's obsession grew steadily, being at its height after the outbreak of war in 1914 when sometimes he would write to her three times a day. Venetia was polite to him, as befitted the father of a close friend, but also became fond of him. Every time she attempted to withdraw her affection – and it was never, it seems, more than that – she became so alarmed by the state into which it plunged him that she soon relented. The final break, caused by her engagement to Montagu, comes after this narrative ends, and had a devastating effect on Asquith. By contrast, his passion for her coincided with a notable improvement in his health and vigour during 1912.

He started to sign his letters to her 'Ever your loving HHA'.[10] In the spring of 1912 he took Venetia on Friday afternoons for recreational jaunts in his chauffeur-driven car; by July his letters ended 'dear love'.[11] By the following January he was even more explicit, writing of his annoyance that he had not had her to himself more during a weekend at her family's house in Cheshire. Margot, who fought to keep her jealousy in a box, was being marginalised. Many upper-middle-class marriages were in a far more irregular state than the Asquiths', but he was the King's First Minister, and must have realised that even if Venetia were to reciprocate his feelings, the only way in which they could live together was in the wake of his social and political ruin, Venetia's transformation into a scarlet woman, and substantial damage to the Liberal party.

'I purposely keep back', Asquith wrote in the same letter after the Alderley weekend, 'when we are together, so much more, I dare say, than you suspect.'[12] In the months ahead he became more open in his protestations to her. Virtually none of her letters to him survives; such as does has none of his ardour. He started to send her poetry, usually of a humorous kind, and began to make dismissive remarks about Montagu, whom he had ceased to recognise as a protégé but had started to regard as a rival, and whom he termed 'the Assyrian' – but whom he nonetheless promoted to the Treasury.

Given that he was prime minister, Asquith's conduct was outrageous. He soon began to describe the goings-on at cabinet meetings to her, and shared details of meetings with the King. The frequency of the letters stepped up to virtually daily by 1914, and in February of that year he sent her '*All* my love' – his italics.[13] Within ten days he was addressing her as 'beloved', as well as divulging the finer points of government appointments.[14] He would write to her as a distraction during cabinet meetings while his colleagues were droning on; he would write to her when he was supposed to be in cabinet meetings, keeping everyone waiting. When it appeared as though civil war might break out in Ulster in July 1914, he kept her informed of every last detail. He appeared to misread such signals as she sent him: 'I have felt ever so much happier & more hopeful since our talk yesterday,' he told her on 18 July 1914, at the height of the Ulster crisis. 'Blessed are the life-givers, of whom there is none to equal you.'[15] Had any of this become public, Asquith would have been finished; and matters became far more intense still, and wildly indiscreet, once war came. It was bad enough how much his mind was fixed on her and not on matters of state even before hostilities broke out; things would become much worse after August 1914.

IV

David Lloyd George was unquestionably the most dominant of Asquith's colleagues, and from the moment he became Chancellor on Asquith's promotion in 1908 was marked out as his obvious successor. The leader of the Liberal party's radical tradition, he spoke especially for the sizeable Non-conformist element in the party, and was also the main impetus behind the party's programme of social reform, which would lead to the creation of an embryo welfare state. However, he had also been a womaniser from adolescence, conducting a private life that, had it been exposed, would have ended his political career. He lived beyond his means, not least because of the expense of his philandering, and so constantly felt in need of money. He had been born to a Welsh family in Manchester in 1863. William George, his father, died when David was an infant. His mother went to live with her brother, Richard Lloyd, a shoemaker in Caernarvonshire, whose commitment to Liberal politics profoundly affected his nephew. Lloyd was also a Baptist minister, though his religion and its precepts would have less effect on the boy over whom he was otherwise a strong paternal influence.

There was no money for David to go to university. He was a bright, articulate and intellectually curious boy, and Lloyd encouraged his ambitions. The first was to become a solicitor, which he did after being articled to a firm in Porthmadog in the early 1880s. He set up a provincial practice, being sufficiently successful to take his brother into partnership in 1887, and to open branch offices. By this stage Lloyd George (he had, out of respect, added his uncle's name to his own) had lost his faith, though did not discuss the matter. Given his other ambition – to become a Liberal MP, also actively encouraged by his uncle – this was as well, in a part of Wales where chapel-going was central to the social fabric.

In 1888 he was adopted as Liberal candidate for Caernarvon Boroughs, and won the seat at a by-election in 1890 by nineteen votes. He had originally been a Chamberlainite radical but, now Chamberlain had left the Liberals, he joined a group of radical Welsh MPs whose main aim was to disestablish the Anglican Church in Wales. MPs were not at this date paid – a reform Lloyd George himself would introduce in 1911 – so he needed to carry on his legal work to support himself and his family. He had married Margaret Owen, a well-to-do farmer's daughter, in 1888, and they had five children. He opened a London office in 1897. However, an attempt to make some capital in the 1890s through investing in a Patagonian gold mine had ended in disaster, and his legal practice suffered because of his opposition to the Boer War. Then, though, George Cadbury's decision to pay him a 1,000-guinea commission to negotiate the purchase of the *Daily News* made up the deficit.[16]

His in-laws had opposed his marriage to Margaret. His wife was well aware of his political ambition, but preferred to live in Wales and was a reluctant visitor to London. This gave her husband plenty of opportunity to indulge his hobby. His daughter Lady Olwen Lloyd George wrote in her memoirs: 'I believe my father started having affairs with other women very soon after my parents were married.'[17] He had some close shaves. In 1897 a Montgomeryshire doctor, David Edwards, relented from naming him as co-respondent in the divorce action he was bringing against his wife, a cousin of Margaret Lloyd George, who claimed Lloyd George had fathered her child. The woman had confessed under duress but had other lovers, and Lloyd George's guilt could not be proved. A local station-master was named as co-respondent instead. No sooner was this potential disaster dealt with, however, than he became entangled with Lizzie Davies, wife of his close friend Timothy Davies, who would become a Liberal MP in 1906 with Lloyd George's help. The liaison finally, in 1899, persuaded Margaret Lloyd George to move to London.

For a time, this brought Lloyd George under control, but his womanising instinct soon prevailed. He began a liaison with Julia Henry, the American wife of another Liberal colleague, Charles Henry, who also became an MP in 1906. Henry was a big Liberal donor too, earning a baronetcy in 1911. Using her husband's money, Mrs Henry decided to build a great political salon. Lloyd George soon became a key part of it, and a regular visitor to the Henrys' houses in Oxfordshire and Shropshire. He also became keen on Mrs Henry, but there was a problem: she was interested in a long-term involvement, while he merely wanted excitement. He led her on, and took numerous favours from her husband. The relationship continued sporadically, with Lloyd George failing to recognise her increasingly proprietorial feelings towards him.

Then, shortly after he became Chancellor in 1908, there was a flurry of activity between Lloyd George and Gladys Gardner, a young woman whose family was active in Liberal politics. He engaged in a correspondence with her briefly, but then ended it after the woman suggested he might buy her a 'diamond tiara' and demanded he brief his secretaries to admit her to see him at the Treasury.[18] Miss Gardner seems to have imagined she could assume the role of political hostess in his life, something Margaret Lloyd George was unwilling to do, and expected him to agree in the interests of his social advancement. He did not, but foolishly did not reject her plans, or rather her demands, the moment she announced them. He encouraged an exchange of views over several days, which culminated in her suggesting he would prosper best by obtaining a divorce.

The anger, or loose tongue, of this scorned young woman may not have been coincidental to the appearance of an article that alluded to Lloyd George's womanising. It appeared in the *Bystander* in July 1908. When challenged, the magazine admitted there was no foundation to the story – at least, no foundation it could prove – and offered not just an unqualified apology, but paid 300 guineas' damages to charity. However, a far worse threat loomed as Lloyd George prepared his historic Budget in 1909. In January the *People* ran several articles implying that he would have been cited in another divorce had the plaintiff not been bought off with £20,000 (alleged in an article entitled 'The Price of Peace'). Lloyd George was not named, but it was obvious to whom the paper referred. To confound this career-threatening claim, he sued for libel, and wheeled out the first rank of the English Bar to represent him – Isaacs, Smith and Raymond Asquith, the prime minister's son: Sir Edward Carson, the former Unionist solicitor-general, appeared for the newspaper.

Isaacs maintained the articles 'contained the gravest possible reflections on the plaintiff's honour and moral character' and contained 'the most wicked and cruel fabrications'.[19] He said the rumours had been ventilated elsewhere and had become the talk of 'private circles'. Bringing the case had been a gamble for Lloyd George, because the allegations were put on the record in court and printed in the newspapers, including that the Chancellor had 'committed misconduct with a married lady' and would therefore face 'social and political ruin and degradation'.

Carson expressed 'profound and unqualified regret' on behalf of his clients and offered 'the frankest and fullest apology'; the £1,000 damages that accompanied this were used to build a village institute in Llanystumdwy, the village where the victim of the libel had grown up. Isaacs put Lloyd George in the witness box so that he could put on record, and on oath, his protestations of innocence: and he threatened that were such claims repeated thereafter he would pursue the matter 'to the bitter end and would accept no apology.'[20]

Thereby his reputation remained miraculously intact, although those who believed there was no smoke without fire had a field day: but it was a high-risk strategy, not least because even if innocent of these particular allegations, who could predict what else might come out? His best defence was the support of his wife; but many years later their son

Richard, whose opinion of his father was admittedly not good, said he believed his mother had been sure of Lloyd George's guilt, and that he would go to any lengths – even perjury – to salvage his political career. He wrote that 'my mother, a deeply religious woman, was in torment in giving support to the lie to be sworn on oath.'[21]

That case was settled on 12 March 1909; but on 22 March a letter was written to him by a Mrs M. Griffith, from Alexandra Park in north London, upon whom he seems to have fathered an invalid son. The letter asked for photographs Lloyd George had of the boy, and also begged for money for maintenance and treatment for him. She threatened to set a solicitor on him if money was not forthcoming. She wanted £10 to 'set us up for the year'.[22] She continued: 'You have treated me most unfairly and cruelly . . . I shall pray to God to open your heart'. She was manifestly desperate, saying, 'I appeal to you on my knees to spare me this money.' Lloyd George's biographer suggests her demands could have been actuated by the highly publicised libel action, and may have been a crude attempt at blackmail: however, it is clear she had some cause to approach him, and that he replied and, by some means, bought her silence.

Nonetheless, a second letter from Mrs Griffith accuses Lloyd George of having insulted her by his reply: the fact he was in touch with her at all strongly suggests that he had cause to be worried. 'You know in your heart', she told him, 'that to live on 30/- pay, rent, coal, food, clothes and shoes must be a fearful struggle and to add to it a little child under a specialist for years to come.' She addresses him as 'Mr George', suggesting their carnal act took place on slim acquaintance, and that she was certainly not his social equal. The story seems to be that she had met the Chancellor, asked whether he could help find her husband a job, was invited to Wandsworth, where Lloyd George then lived, to discuss this, and one thing had led to another. He may have paid her off, as there is no further evidence of contact.

He lived dangerously. It was reprehensible enough to seduce the wives of colleagues, but to seduce a casual acquaintance from the lower orders was both exploitative and utterly reckless. No wonder Sir Robert Chalmers, a senior civil servant who became Permanent Secretary to the Treasury for part of Lloyd George's Chancellorship, and who probably did not even know half of it, nicknamed him 'the Goat'.[23] Yet there were still incidents that showed Lloyd George to have been more devoted to his family than his wanton behaviour might have suggested. He was stricken by the death of his seventeen-year-old daughter Mair from appendicitis in 1907; and was what his biographer describes as 'fond' of his wife.[24] In 1911 he hired twenty-two-year-old Frances Stevenson, one of Mair's former schoolfellows, as tutor to his youngest daughter, Megan, on the advice of Mair's former headmistress from Clapham High School. At Lloyd George's suggestion Miss Stevenson learned shorthand and he found constituency work for her to do. She had realised in July 1912 that 'something serious was happening'. At the end of the year he asked her to become his private secretary and, also, his mistress.[25] Divorce was not an option, as that would end his political career. Despite having to live in the shadows, she agreed.

Whatever effect this relationship had on Margaret Lloyd George – for whom the epithet 'long-suffering' could have been coined – it was devastating to the woman who had by now become Lady Henry. She would not let go. Her main humiliation seems to have been that she could no longer show Lloyd George off at her salons: 'I can never face England again,' she told her husband, who, for his part, told Lloyd George to ignore his wife's histrionics.[26] Henry took a robustly Edwardian attitude to marital infidelity, which was just as well for Lloyd George, and it can be neither proved nor disproved that Henry's path to his baronetcy was smoothed by his tolerant approach to his wife's relationship with the Chancellor. Lady Henry continued for years to punish Lloyd George by blackguarding him to others and engineering scenes whenever they met, unconcerned about the damage this did her and, indeed, him.

On 21 January 1913, four days after his fiftieth birthday, Lloyd George and Frances Stevenson were what they would subsequently call 'married'[27]. Some have interpreted this as marking the date when they first slept together, the only evidence against that supposition being how unlike Lloyd George it would have been to have waited so long: but it is hard to see what else it could mean. Thereafter, one of the rare honourable things he did in his life was to keep his promise and marry Frances after Margaret's death in 1941, much to the outrage of his and Margaret's children. He was devoted to his mistress for the rest of his life, avoiding any further escapades. Perhaps, having passed the age of fifty, even his legendary appetite for the ladies was beginning to wane or, as his sympathetic biographer has suggested, he felt the need to devote more time to politics.[28]

He was helped to manage the affair by George Riddell, proprietor of the *News of the World*, who bought him a country house at Walton Heath in Surrey, where he could live *en famille* with Frances; Mrs Lloyd George did not have visiting rights. Riddell also gave him a car, and in return received a knighthood, a baronetcy and, in 1920, a peerage. The idea of a businessman, let alone a press baron, funding a cabinet minister in this way, not least to enable him to support a mistress, and to be honoured and ennobled for it, reflects but one of the changes in perception of the role of public figures in the last century. Since Riddell owned a newspaper, he and Lloyd George were spared the tiresome intrusion of the gutter press that might otherwise have exposed this breathtaking conduct.

V

New men needed money, and few new men needed money so much as Lloyd George, for whom the good things in life – not least his succession of mistresses – held enormous appeal. He made no money from politics until becoming a minister in 1906, and even then suffered from the salary of the President of the Board of Trade being just £2,000 a year (a huge sum nonetheless, and taxed at sixpence in the pound) rather than the £5,000 paid to other cabinet ministers. Although some colleagues were self-made and others, such as Winston Churchill, had little private money, being from cadet branches of grand families, this was still an age where politicians were expected to keep up appearances. Lloyd George's extravagant tastes would have shocked his constituents had they known of them, and extra cash was always useful. His womanising was particularly expensive. MPs needing to make money were hardly a new phenomenon, but in a House ridden by class considerations such people were often looked down upon, and were expected to behave with propriety and discretion. Although after 1908 Lloyd George was on £5,000 a year as Chancellor of the Exchequer, he still had little capital, and minded that very much. In 1909 there were rumours he had made £100,000 from share dealing in the Surrey Docks. He denied it and no documentary evidence has been found to the contrary. His next brush with financial impropriety would be less clear-cut.

In March 1910 the Marconi Company told the government that it could within three years create a wireless telegraphy network around the globe to connect up the Empire: what would be known as the Imperial

Wireless Chain. The deal would be this: it would build eighteen high-power stations, 'the licence to be for 20 years from date of completion . . . the Governments concerned to have the right to purchase the stations at the end of that time . . . The Company asked for no subsidy, and promised that telegraph rates between places in the British Dominions should be reduced so that none should exceed 1s per word.'[29]

The government rejected this progressive idea, but after the Imperial Conference of 1911 it was decided to construct the network. In March 1912 the government accepted a tender from Marconi. Each station would cost £60,000, and for twenty-eight years Marconi would take 10 per cent of the revenues. Once details of the proposed contract were given to the Commons on 19 July 1912 there were immediate concerns, since some Unionist MPs felt the terms to be far too generous to Marconi. On 1 August John Ward, the MP for Stoke-on-Trent, drew attention to the rise in price in Marconi shares since the tender's success, and another, Fred Hall, pointedly asked whether the Postmaster-General, Herbert Samuel, would lay before the House the names of the shareholders in the company. Samuel refused.

On 6 August Asquith promised a proper discussion of the contract when the House returned in the autumn. This alarmed two ministers, Samuel and Alexander Murray, the Master of Elibank (his courtesy title as heir to a Scottish peerage), the chief whip, who encouraged immediate approval on the grounds that for strategic and defence reasons the network was urgently needed, and Marconi was the only company with the expertise to do it. Asquith held the line. To general surprise, Murray chose the end of the parliamentary session to resign from the government and from the Commons. He was just forty-two, but claimed his father had made his estates over to him to manage. His friend Lord Cowdray had offered him a job, however – one that would take him all over the world, far from the estates that were now his responsibility. Murray was raised to the peerage in his own right, as Lord Murray of Elibank. It would soon become apparent, however, that he might have had other reasons for leaving Westminster.

On 8 August the *New Witness* newspaper, owned by Cecil Chesterton but featuring the journalism of his elder brother G. K. and Hilaire Belloc, accused Sir Rufus Isaacs, the Attorney-General, and Samuel of having arranged to enrich Isaacs's brother Godfrey, who happened to be managing director of Marconi. Chesterton claimed the government was paying over the odds to create a monopoly for Marconi, when other tenders would have been cheaper. And this, Chesterton said, was thanks to the 'ardent charity' of Sir Rufus Isaacs and the 'agency' of Samuel.[30] There was a strong belief in Chesterton's circle, which they wished to broadcast, that this had happened because the Isaacses and Samuel were Jewish. Cecil Chesterton was suspected of anti-Semitism, a charge that would become better founded as events played out. The 8 August article came to the thundering conclusion that 'it is the lack of even a minimum standard of honour urging even honest men to protest against such villainy that has brought us to where we are.'

Samuel wrote to Isaacs about how they should respond. The Postmaster-General was reluctant to sue, not just as the circulation of the 'contemptible rag' was so small, but because 'it would not be a good thing for the Jewish community for the first two Jews who have ever entered a British Cabinet to be enmeshed in an affair of this kind'.[31] Samuel deferred to Isaacs's legal expertise, however, and said that if Isaacs thought they should sue, he would; but Isaacs, taking the waters in Marienbad, thought it best to do nothing, a view Asquith shared. Isaacs, crucially, had confided in him about a matter that would become of central importance: he had, with Godfrey's help, invested in shares of the American Marconi company, a separate entity from the British one. Asquith saw no harm in this, but it was not made public and nor did Asquith urge it to be. Rufus Isaacs also talked Godfrey out of suing Chesterton.

Other newspapers called for an inquiry, and in the *National Review*, a magazine edited by the Unionist partisan Leo Maxse, W. R. Lawson wrote on what he called 'The Marconi Scandal'. He claimed three ministers were involved.[32] When the Commons returned on 11 October a debate was held. Sir Henry Norman, a Liberal MP and former assistant postmaster-general, called suggestions of corruption 'not only without a shadow of foundation, but . . . preposterous.'[33] He wanted the select committee being set up to investigate the matter, to haul before it those accusing 'honourable men' of corruption and having them provide evidence. Norman then attacked the government for its lack of business sense in allowing Marconi to profit so much from these stations, when they ought effectively to have been nationalised with profits going to the Treasury. 'It would be impossible,' he said, 'for this House to ratify an agreement so flagrantly opposed to the public interest.'[34] A Labour MP – George Lansbury – raised the question of 'gambling in Marconi shares . . . by people who had information in connection with this matter previous to other people'.[35] Lansbury said he hoped there would be 'no kind of shrinking' by the committee from investigating these allegations; which provoked Lloyd George, who was also featuring in rumours about the contract, to call out: 'I hope, too, there will be no shrinking on the part of those who make the allegations.'[36]

He denounced the 'sinister rumours', and demanded that Lansbury formulate his charge. Lansbury did not: but when he said no minister should make a deal on behalf of any public body with a company in which he had an interest, Samuel shot up and demanded to know whether Lansbury thought he was 'interested'.[37] Lansbury said he was suggesting nothing. It was not then forbidden for ministers of the Crown to play the Stock Exchange; but it was presumed they were sufficiently honourable only to dabble in shares whose prices the government could not influence.

Isaacs also attacked Lansbury, saying 'it would be the purest affectation for me to pretend that I am not in some way intended to be implicated by what the hon. Member said. The sole reason for the suggestion, or insinuation, that he has made, is that my brother happened to be the managing director of the Marconi Company.'[38] Even though no specific charge had been made, Isaacs denied the substance of the rumours. He said he knew nothing about the negotiations and had therefore had no part of them, until his brother had alerted him late in the proceedings; and he did not know the tender had been accepted until he read about it in a newspaper.

He then dealt with 'a worse charge': that someone with inside knowledge had bought shares that were then worth fourteen or fifteen shillings each and, once the contract was announced and they rose to £9, sold them. 'Never . . . have I had one single transaction with the shares of that company,' he intoned, referring back to the British company.[39] This disingenuous remark would lie at the heart of the ensuing scandal. He said he also spoke for Samuel and Lloyd George and denied he had used his position as Attorney-General to act in the interests of Marconi. Putting the rumours on the record, as Isaacs had done, seemed clever: Lord Robert Cecil rose to impart his own belief in Isaacs's integrity. Samuel then rose and gave his own unequivocal denial of having held shares in the company. 'It seems shameful', he said, 'that political feeling can carry men so far, that lying tongues can be found to speak and willing ears be found to listen to wicked and utterly baseless slanders such as these.'[40] Isaacs had made his gravest mistake, which was not to tell the House what he had told Asquith about the American company. This absence of candour would do him – and others – great damage.

The select committee of fifteen MPs was set up in late October 1912. Months passed without any of the ministers giving evidence. Then, however, the allegations were given a new lease of life. First, Maxse was called on 12 February 1913 and he asked why the ministers had not been heard. 'One might have conceived,' he said, 'that they would have appeared at its first sitting clamouring to state in the most categorical and emphatic manner that neither directly nor indirectly, in their own names or in other people's names, have they had any transactions whatsoever, either in London, Dublin, New York, Brussels, Amsterdam, Paris or any other financial centre, in any shares in any Marconi Company throughout the negotiations with the Government.'[41]

From the phrase 'any Marconi Company' it is clear Maxse knew more than he let on. Two days later, on 14 February, a French paper, *Le Matin*, accused Rufus and Godfrey Isaacs and Samuel of having bought shares in Marconi in an insider deal, based on a misunderstanding of what Maxse had said. Rufus Isaacs and Samuel immediately sued, and the paper rapidly withdrew its allegations. G. K. Chesterton, outraged the ministers should sue a foreign paper when they lacked the guts to sue British ones, published a poem entitled 'Song of Cosmopolitan Courage': 'I am so swift to seize affronts,/My spirit is so high,/Whoever has insulted me/Some foreigner must die.'[42]

When the libel case came to court on 19 March it appeared to be open and shut: *Le Matin* had admitted libelling the two ministers. However, Isaacs had decided to do what he should have done the previous year, and tell the whole truth. His counsel – Sir Edward Carson, who as leader of Irish Unionism was otherwise in a pitched battle with the Liberal party – made an admission on Isaacs's behalf that changed public perceptions of the controversy and the political class, and caused grave unease among many parliamentarians. He said he had bought shares in the American – not the British – company, and had sold some on to his two colleagues. This did not contradict anything Isaacs had told the Commons in October, but did prove he had not told the whole truth. Godfrey Isaacs had been responsible for placing 500,000 shares in the US company in the English market, to boost the company's capitalisation. On 9 April 1912, a month after the decision to accept the Marconi tender, he had sold 50,000 to a third Isaacs brother, Harry, a shipbroker and fruit broker in the family business, at £1 1s 3d each. Rufus Isaacs thought it improper to take the same number, which Godfrey offered him – over a lunch between the three brothers – given the government's dealings with Marconi, of which he was well aware. No public announcement had been made about the wireless network at that stage; and Rufus thought the shares overpriced.

However, on 17 April Rufus decided to buy 10,000 of Harry's shares. He felt this acceptable as they were not coming direct from Godfrey; and he also offered Harry £2 a share, a remarkable premium given he had not thought them worth a little over half that a week earlier. Rufus then offered 1,000 of his shares to Lloyd George, and 1,000 to Murray, the Master of Elibank. No money changed hands at this point, either between the Isaacs brothers or between the ministers. The next day, 18 April, the shares were issued at £3 5s; on 19 April Rufus sold 7,000 of his 8,000 remaining shares for £3 6s 6d. He later revealed there had been a pooling arrangement in his sale, in which his brother and his two colleagues were included: so what had actually happened was that he had sold 2,856 of his own shares and 357 for each of his two colleagues, the rest profiting Harry Isaacs. The three ministers still had 6,430 shares between them, Lloyd George and Murray holding 1,286 between them. The Chancellor and the chief whip sold 1,000 on 20 April for £3 3s 1d.

On 22 May, the price having dipped, Lloyd George and Murray bought 3,000 more shares between them at £2 3s 1d. During April and May Murray also bought 3,000 for the Liberal party, whose purse-strings he controlled. Much of that money had come from the sale of honours – persuading rich businessmen to part with sizeable sums as donations to the Liberal party, in return for which they would secure hereditary titles such as baronetcies and peerages – over which Murray presided, so no high estimate need be made of his moral condition. There is no documentary evidence of the original transaction, between Harry and Rufus Isaacs. It is unclear whether there were other deals, as we only have the word of those concerned, which was not always reliable. Also unclear is whether Godfrey Isaacs's offer of shares was intended simply to enrich his brother and his friends, or was meant as a bribe. There was certainly much scope for journalists to put the worst possible construction on it, not least because the massive contract for the English company enhanced the value of shares in the American one.

But then neither Isaacs nor Samuel had specified that they had not owned shares in the British company, since it would have raised the possibility they had bought shares in another. Samuel had not bought shares in the American company: but it was asserted then, and later, that he had been told his colleagues had. By the time of the libel case shares in the American company had gone down in price, and Isaacs told the court that 'I should have a loss of £1,100 or £1,200 if I sold at the present moment.'[43] He thought Lloyd George and Murray 'had lost a few hundreds each'. When the details of these transactions were made public both Isaacs and Lloyd George offered their resignations. Asquith, who had enough other problems without admitting that two senior colleagues were insider traders, refused them.

On 21 March, perhaps sensing a lucky escape at the hands of *The Times* and the *Daily Mail*, both of which had a history of attacking him, Lloyd George wrote to Northcliffe 'to thank you for the chivalrous manner in which you have treated the Attorney-General and myself over the "Marconi" case. Had we done anything of which men of honour ought to feel ashamed we could not have approached you on the subject.'[44] Northcliffe replied: 'I adopted my line about this Marconi business because five minutes' lucid explanation showed me that it was the fairest one. Moreover, I am neither a rabid party man nor an anti-semite.'[45] In keeping with his concerns about Europe, the press baron added: 'A week-end glance at the French and German newspapers convinces me that this country has before it more urgent business than personal or party issues . . . the sooner the matter is out of the way the better.' However, once Northcliffe realised there was more to the case than met the eye, he hardened his papers' line. Churchill had been buttering him up hitherto successfully, but once Northcliffe heard what came out at the committee, he told Churchill 'your Marconi friends stage-manage their affairs most damnably'.[46] However, he also told him that, for all the excitement the scandal was causing in political circles, his papers had received just three letters about it.

In a case where much would rely on circumstantial evidence, there was plenty. With Lloyd George it was his lack of money. Murray was heir to a Scottish viscountcy, but one with no great wealth attached to it, which was partly why he had left government to earn a living. Isaacs alone was well heeled, having been a highly successful barrister reputedly earning £30,000 a year, though his income had been seriously cut since he joined the government in 1910.

Andrew Bonar Law, the Leader of the Opposition, asked Asquith about the shiftiness of his ministers, as revealed by the libel action. Had he known Isaacs had told Asquith about the share purchase he might have asked whether he had ordered the cover-up in the debate of 11 October. Not only had Isaacs told him: Murray had admitted, before his resignation, buying shares in an unnamed American company, and Samuel later admitted telling Asquith in July 1912 that his colleagues had bought the shares. According to Samuels's memoirs, Asquith replied that 'our colleagues could not have done a more foolish thing'.[47] Asquith also told the King. It was announced that the ministers would give evidence to the select committee, so Law held fire. What did not come out in court was from whom Isaacs had bought the shares, or at what price, nor that Lloyd George and Murray had then dealt in shares on their own accounts.

Isaacs appeared before the committee on 25 March, with Lloyd George and Samuel watching keenly. Murray was conveniently in South America on extended business, which led to taunts of 'Bogota!' Isaacs repeated his denials of having sought to influence any colleagues over the agreement, and of having had any dealings in Marconi before 7 March, when the agreement was drawn up. He had not heard about the American company until his brother Godfrey returned from the United States on 8 April. Harry pressed the shares on him, he said, more than a week after the lunch at which he had first declined Godfrey's offer, because Harry felt he was 'unwise' not to have taken them.[48] Isaacs explained he had shared his good fortune with two colleagues 'with whom I was living on the closest terms of personal intimacy'. He also said he had volunteered to appear before the committee sooner, but had not been called until after the disclosure; which suggested the Liberal-controlled committee was trying not to expose the ministers' embarrassments.

Sir Albert Spicer, the chairman, asked Isaacs: 'When you were making your speech in the House did the thought occur to you that you could get rid of some of these rumours if you had mentioned your investment in the American Marconis? Because, being Marconis, you can easily understand that one company might be confused with another?' Isaacs replied: 'It did not occur to me, and it does not occur to me now.' Expressing, or manufacturing, outrage, he demanded to know who had written 'lies' about him. He said he had not sat in the cabinet when the deal had been discussed, and accused people of misunderstanding what the Attorney's job was if they thought he would have superintended such a thing.

Isaacs squirmed during discussion of a telegram of congratulations he had sent Marconi, as a favour to his brother, to be read out at a banquet in New York the previous March. He was asked whether it might have been unwise for a government law officer to do this, especially if he then bought Marconi shares a few weeks later. 'I must object to that,' Isaacs said. 'I was praising the enterprise of Mr Marconi, the inventor of wireless telegraphy. I do not think I referred to any company.'[49] For the Attorney-General of England to be reduced to such hair-splitting indicated the difficulties he had caused.

He was then questioned about passing on shares to Lloyd George and Murray, admitting neither of his friends had yet paid him for their shares but that 'if necessity arose' they could. He denied this was 'an unusual transaction'. Asked whether it had been 'wise' to involve his fellow ministers, he insisted there had been nothing 'wrong or improper' in doing so. It was not this purchase of shares in a company associated with one to be awarded a massive government contract that struck Isaacs as a blot on public life, but the fact that others had accused him of corruption by doing it. 'That', he protested with astonishing self-righteousness, 'was the element I never took into account. I never thought it was likely to arise in English public life.' Isaacs had, in his youth, been a stockjobber, and had been hammered on the Stock Exchange over an £8,000 debt (which he eventually repaid). His protestations of wounded virtue were preposterous.

The next day Asquith had a rough passage, when Major Martin Archer-Shee, a Unionist MP who had harried the government on the Marconi deal for months, asked him whether Lloyd George and Isaacs had informed him of their dealings before the debate the previous October; whether, had he known, he had passed the information to any of the select committee; and whether he was aware of any dealings by these or any other ministers in other wireless companies. Asquith said Murray had told him, 'at the end of July or the beginning of August' that the three ministers had bought shares in the American company.[50] With more insouciance than was perhaps advisable, he added that later in August Isaacs had repeated this 'and I believe added that they had sold some of the shares, but retained the bulk of them.'[51] He said Isaacs had told him the shares had been bought after publication of the contract –

not technically true as the contract was not published until July – and that 'the American Company had no interest direct or indirect in that contract', which was completely untrue, given the English company's huge underwriting of the American.

William Joynson-Hicks, another Unionist, put the brutally obvious question: 'May I ask the right hon. Gentleman whether he does not think it desirable that these facts should have been communicated to the House in the debate which took place at that time?' The prime minister's breathtaking response was: 'No. Sir. I confess they seemed to have no relevance whatever to the scandalous charges which were then being circulated, and I really attached no importance to them.' Given what a brilliant barrister Asquith had once been, this was a surprising response. His loyalty to his colleagues was solid throughout, but it compromised him by associating him with their lack of frankness to the Commons. In his memoirs he accused them of 'an error of judgment', but persisted in the unconvincing line that they had expected an early appearance before the select committee and intended to straighten things out then.[52]

VI

Lloyd George was the next before the committee, on 28 March. In keeping with prevailing ideas of propriety and integrity, he needed to prove he had bought the shares as an investment and not for speculation. He struggled to do this. He had urged Carson to bring out in court the exact nature of his transactions; Carson had said he would if he could (and he did), but doubted it would be within the rules of evidence. Lloyd George, as a member of the cabinet, had been well aware of the involvement of Marconi in the discussions about the Imperial Wireless Chain. He had favoured a state-owned system, but it had been Samuel's decision, he said, to accept Marconi's tender.

He then explained why Isaacs had offered him and Murray shares. Murray, he said, had lived with him in 11 Downing Street. They had been on 'the closest terms of friendship' with each other and with Isaacs.[53] All he knew about Marconi was that it was a great company exploiting a remarkable invention; it was a natural investment. Was, Lloyd George asked rhetorically, 'the fact that the British company had agreed on terms with the Government sufficient to make it improper to invest money in the company that had no contract and no negotiations for a contract with the Government?'

That he asked the question indicated the answer. He had followed precedent in the matter of ministers buying shares; and he had 'not very much to invest in spite of all the references to my prodigious fortune; it is not true; I am a comparatively poor man'. He had followed the rules in not using any confidential information obtained in his capacity as a minister; and had invested in no company whose profits or dividends relied on government contracts. He had, he said, no inside information. The cabinet knew 'absolutely nothing' about the American Marconi Company. And, as soon as he had taken the shares from Isaacs, Isaacs advised him to sell because the price was so good.

Lloyd George said he was £500 down, which as he still had not paid for the shares was a notional loss only. He pleaded poverty, rubbishing assertions that he owned 'mansions' in Wales and Surrey and a villa in the South of France. And, deploying outrage to the full, he deplored the innuendo that placed paragraphs adjacent to each other in certain publications, one asking how the Chancellor could afford such a lifestyle on £5,000 a year and another hinting he might have played the Stock Exchange with inside knowledge. 'The only house I have is a house in Wales and really, if a man fifty years of age, after working very hard, cannot have one house he can call his own it is rather hard,' he said.[54]

Spicer asked: 'Did the thought occur to you in the debate on October 11 that that was a proper place to mention your investments in the American company?' The Chancellor answered 'no, certainly not'. It would have taken up too much time, he added. When Lord Robert Cecil suggested that by the time he bought the shares he had heard Marconi executives say what a great deal they had done, he observed that 'they certainly could not go about saying they had made a very bad bargain.' Beyond that, Lloyd George affected that everything was of so little consequence that he could not always remember what had happened when, or what relations exactly were between the English and the American companies. A veil of vagueness helped keep the temperature down.

The committee adjourned over a weekend. Isaacs was unhappy with Lloyd George's performance, and coached him about his answers: 'Rufus discovered that George was still in a perfect fog as to what his transaction really had been,' Lucy Masterman, the wife of the Liberal politician

Charles Masterman, recorded.[55] 'I have never seen Rufus so nearly lose his temper, and George got extremely sulky.' Isaacs told his colleague 'to avoid technical terms and to stick as closely as possible to the plainest and most ordinary language.' When Lloyd George resumed his evidence the committee failed to unsettle him, except when pressing about why he had not yet paid for the shares. He claimed he needed to wait for Murray to return to England. He sought to turn the tables, implying the committee might have done more to discover who had spread rumours about ministers gambling in shares. He played the Liberal majority on the committee like the proverbial violin, causing Violet Asquith, the prime minister's daughter, to claim that 'he reduced his opponents to tears and himself too I believe.'[56]

It had been brave of Cecil to take on Isaacs, who had been appointed Attorney-General not least because he was a gifted lawyer. Chesterton gambled not just on the allegations having a foundation of truth – which thanks to Isaacs's disclosures during the *Le Matin* case it was now known they did – but that the politicians would be so reluctant for further dirt to be revealed that they would not sue. However, he had not counted on Godfrey Isaacs, who after an article in the *New Witness* on 9 January 1913 about his connection with no fewer than twenty bankrupt companies – and after the paper sent men bearing sandwich boards vilifying him to walk up and down outside his office and, even worse, his club – sued him not for libel, but for criminal libel. One passage may be taken as indicative of the tone: 'The files at Somerset House of the Isaacs companies cry out for vengeance on the man who created them, who manipulated them, who filled them with his own creatures, who worked them solely for his own ends, and who sought to get rid of some of them when they had served his purpose by casting the expense of burial on to the public purse.'[57]

The case began at the Old Bailey on 27 May, while the committee was considering its report, with Carson and F. E. Smith, another leading Unionist, appearing for Isaacs. Mr Justice Phillimore presided: he had been an eminent ecclesiastical lawyer, noted for his opinion on the Home Office Baby case of 1884. He had said that the Rev J. Mirehouse, Rector of Colsterworth in Lincolnshire, had committed no offence known to canon law when posting to the Home Office, for the attention of Harcourt, the Home Secretary, and in a box marked 'Perishable', the corpse of a stillborn infant, in protest at the proposed closure of a graveyard. Phillimore brought humour and almost self-parodic testiness to the proceedings, adding to the entertainment.

Chesterton's case – that the Isaacs brothers had set out to enrich each other using private knowledge based on Marconi's relationship with the government, and that Rufus had protected his brother by not having him prosecuted for various commercial outrages (notably in a motor-cab company and a mining company in Wales) – was based on circumstantial evidence. Carson claimed he had 'tried to hunt' Godfrey Isaacs.[58] Godfrey himself, in the witness box, had to admit to a string of less than successful business ventures before hitting the jackpot with Marconi's. Guglielmo Marconi gave evidence on 3 June, and testified to Isaacs's exemplary character. For those regarding the case as entertainment, however – not the least of whom was the defendant, who relished seeing Godfrey in court – the high point came on 5 June, when the duel began between Carson and Chesterton.

Part of Chesterton's defence was that the government should have considered systems other than Marconi's: but Carson made him admit he had no technical knowledge of the Marconi or any other system. Chesterton agreed he had investigated Godfrey and, because of what he had discovered about his business career, felt motivated to campaign against his company securing the contract. He felt Isaacs had elicited a favour from Samuel in having a clause in the agreement kept secret, and accused Isaacs of 'very abominable conduct between March 7 and July 19'.[59] 'Fraud?' asked Carson. 'Very near fraud,' replied Chesterton. However, when Carson pressed him to say Rufus Isaacs had influenced Samuel, he denied such an imputation.

Asked whether he accused Samuel of dishonesty or corruption, Chesterton replied that he accused him 'of having given a contract which was a byword for laxity and thereby laying himself open reasonably to the suspicion that he was conferring a favour on Mr Godfrey Isaacs because he was the Attorney-General's brother.' Pressed by Phillimore – who called him 'argumentative' and 'evasive' – Chesterton tried to avoid a question about Samuel's honesty. Eventually, asked whether he was accusing Godfrey Isaacs of corruption, Chesterton said 'no'. There was no evidence Samuel was corrupt: he had merely drawn an 'inference'. He had used 'public powers for private objects', namely 'enriching Mr Godfrey Isaacs'.

Carson then tried to have Chesterton admit he was alleging a Jewish conspiracy, reading out unpleasant references to Samuel's 'cousins in the City' that Cecil had written in an article of 23 January. Chesterton said he believed a fraud had been perpetrated with public money by giving Marconi more than was merited. 'Who were engaged in the fraud?' asked Carson. 'Mr Herbert Samuel,' Chesterton answered. He had never accused Samuel of buying shares: but had thought 'the Isaacs family was a family of a bad and corrupt type', a family 'which for two or three generations have been running different kinds of financial scandals'. This evoked the supposed Jewish conspiracy – the Samuels having a pawnbroking business in Liverpool, both families having links to moneylenders – antecedents, he implied, unsuitable for those who 'occupy places in an English executive'.

Chesterton explained that one of the most supposedly libellous references in what he had written – about someone being caught with his hand in the till – was a reference to Rufus, not Godfrey. Chesterton said he had not written the offending article on 9 January; but refused to incriminate the author – and, as editor, he was responsible for it. He admitted the article suggested Godfrey had committed a criminal offence and, pressed by the judge, said he thought he should be prosecuted. Carson asked whether Chesterton thought Godfrey should be sent to prison. 'How do I know the law?' Chesterton answered. 'Then why did you write this without knowing the law?' Carson countered. Re-examined by his own counsel, Chesterton was asked: 'What is the meaning of your reference to Jewish finance?' He replied: 'I hold very strong views about Jewish finance. I have not the slightest prejudice against the Jews as a people; but I do think Jewish finance is a dangerous thing, and should be curbed.' That may have brought matters close to the truth.

Carson insisted on putting Samuel – who had given evidence earlier – back in the box to deny having dealt in Marconi stock, or having been aware of any family member doing so: there was a specific suggestion that his first cousin, Gerald Montagu, a partner in Samuel Montagu and Co. (founded by his father), had. Montagu's bank had acted as agent in 1911 to buy some Marconi shares for a client in Amsterdam. However, there had been nothing in the register to say these shares were being held in trust, and when they were sold – at a considerable profit – the beneficiary was listed as Gerald Montagu, hence the claim. Montagu admitted this. Witnesses were called to testify to Godfrey's poor management of a Welsh mining company, and Archer-Shee reported how Samuel had pressed him the previous August to withdraw his opposition to the Marconi deal. Finally, an interesting array of character witnesses testified to Chesterton's probity: including Maurice Baring, the Reverend Conrad Noel, the radical socialist vicar of Thaxted in Essex, and Chesterton's distinguished brother, who told the court he envied Cecil 'the dignity of his present position'.[60]

The judge took three hours to sum up; the jury was out for just forty minutes. Chesterton was found guilty, a verdict with which the judge said he agreed. Phillimore felt Chesterton had been partly motivated by racial prejudice but had also been blind to the realities of business. 'Ignorance and prejudice', he intoned, 'are bad starting-points on the road to truth.'[61] Because of the damage done to Godfrey the judge had found it hard not to send Chesterton to prison. Instead he fined him £100, plus the considerable costs of the prosecution: Carson and Smith were not cheap. Some supporters paid the fine, sparing Chesterton jail.

Although the establishment had rallied round its members – even if those members, except Murray, were of relatively recent standing – the case left a smell. This was not least because, as the judge was preparing his summing-up, a new, related, fact had emerged. Murray's stockbroker, Charles Fenner, had absconded. When the public trustee looked into his business, he found that on 18 April and 14 May 1912 he had bought for his client 3,000 American Marconi shares for £9,400. It turned out that these shares had been bought not for Murray's profit, but for the Liberal party's. 'It is impossible', the paper thundered, 'to reconcile these facts, which are now fully admitted, with the attitude taken up by Ministerial spokesmen during the debate of last October.'

Once the case ended, *The Times*, speaking not with the voice of Northcliffe but of old, high-minded values, asked why the 'joint speculation' between the three ministers had not been public knowledge until the *Le Matin* trial, when it should have been clear it would be best to disclose the matter.[62] The paper concluded that what it termed the 'reticence' of the three men had not helped obtain the truth. The debate on 11 October had conveyed a false impression: there had been dealings in Marconi shares, albeit American ones. The paper was angry at how the information had been slipped out during the *Le Matin* action, as though 'trifling and irrelevant'; and was especially angry that even then it had not been made clear that Lloyd George and Murray had engaged in further speculation a few weeks later, and Asquith had been kept in the dark. 'It is impossible to reconcile these facts, which are now fully admitted, with the attitude taken up by ministerial spokesmen during the debate of last October,' the paper said. It also objected to the 'fire of recrimination, protest and objection' put up to prevent anyone getting at the facts.

The paper also attacked Murray's conspicuous absence in South America, now it was known he had bought Marconi shares for the Liberal party, and his complete failure to communicate with the committee and explain himself. It was assumed the Liberal members had failed in their inquisitorial duty by giving the ministers an easy ride. But it was precisely because Murray was 'old money', a member of the aristocracy by heredity, that his behaviour was so shocking – little better was expected of counter-jumpers such as Lloyd George and Isaacs. 'There is probably some entirely satisfactory explanation both of his absence and of his silence, but it is very desirable on public grounds that it should be put forward without delay.'

Taking their cue, the select committee asked Percy Illingworth, Murray's successor as chief whip, to explain the share purchase. Asquith was also harried about it in the Commons. He had known nothing until the previous week, when the truth had come out. Asquith was urged to order Murray to return home and appear before the committee, but said he had no power to do so. Illingworth's name had been found in Fenner's papers as co-trustee for a share purchase – though not Marconi shares. Spicer telegraphed Murray asking him to appear before it. He replied from Bogota, via his patron Lord Cowdray, that he could return in July, but had to visit Mexico and the West Indies first. Spicer said that was too late, and not to bother. Illingworth said the chief whip had sole control of party funds; and he had not been in office when the shares were bought. He described Murray as the 'most cruelly slandered man in the country'.[63]

Not all his colleagues shared that view. *The Times*'s lobby correspondent quoted other Liberal MPs' 'incredulity', and one as having said 'this is a stain upon a great party'. Another called it 'rotten'. The government's probity was called into question; but the probity of the select committee was little better, with the committee room frequently having to be cleared of strangers so that MPs from the different parties could abuse each other. It also turned out, in evidence given on 10 June, that Murray's brother Arthur, another Liberal MP, had known of the transaction – and had, indeed, been given the share certificates for safekeeping before Murray left for Bogota – but had chosen not to tell anyone in case 'political capital' were made out of the purchase.[64] Arthur Murray had not told Illingworth until the end of May; and, in keeping with the decision to play down its significance, had written to his brother telling him to conclude his 'important' business in Colombia rather than rush home. This seemed to show a studied contempt for propriety. Even the Liberal party's main organ of opinion, *The Manchester Guardian*, quoted with glee by *The Times*, said that 'the degree of unwisdom is being stretched uncomfortably far', and was appalled the three ministers had not come clean during the October debate. 'Most of the blame,' it said, 'must be put on Lord Murray'.

Chesterton and his supporters regarded the £100 fine as a moral victory. In the next issue of the *New Witness* they resumed the attack: 'Our defence is that if we had not ventured to strike in the dark, we and the people of England should be in the dark still.'[65] Despite this re-heating of the allegations no one sued, which helped make the point further. Three days after Chesterton's conviction Fenner, Murray's errant stockbroker, was declared bankrupt. His whereabouts were unknown; his brother believed he might have gone to Russia. The next day, 13 June, the select committee published its report, and divided along party lines: the eight Liberals and Irish Nationalists finding their colleagues blameless, the six Unionists reporting that the three ministers had acted 'with grave impropriety' and exposed themselves to a conflict of interest.[66]

Spicer, a Liberal, had produced a first draft in late May that had mildly criticised the ministers; but a few days later Lord Robert Cecil had produced his own draft in which the ministers were roundly castigated. The other Liberals rejected Spicer's gentle censure, and the report concluded that 'the Committee find that all the Ministers concerned have acted throughout in the sincere belief that there was nothing in their action which would in any way conflict with their duty as Ministers of the Crown.'[67] The report added that 'the Committee cannot too strongly condemn the publication . . . of unfounded charges against the honour and integrity of public men.' The press had given 'widespread currency to a slander of a particularly vile character'.

This was not, however, the unanimous view. Spicer thought Isaacs had been foolish; and all the ministers should, in his view, have come clean during the October debate. Cecil, in his draft report, went much further, damning Godfrey Isaacs's account of what happened as 'not satisfactory', implying he had lied, and regretting that a majority vote of the committee had not allowed him to be recalled to explain himself. He asserted that Rufus Isaacs had had his shares at a price far more favourable than he would have found on the open market – a highly damaging fact not known hitherto – and said that 'the statements in the Press cannot all be set down as due to mere malicious invention.' He felt the three ministers had 'failed to treat the House of Commons with the frankness or the respect to which it is entitled,' and noted that the silent and absent Murray had 'apparently intended to conceal altogether . . . that he had purchased shares on behalf of the Liberal party funds.' Cecil felt the absence of full disclosure created a feeling that, even then, the full truth was not known. He especially condemned 'the very regrettable failure of Lord Murray to present himself for examination', a failure that, whatever gloss Murray's friends offered, was an admission of guilt and an act of cowardice. Additionally, Cecil hinted at base motives on the part of Samuel in his handling of the award of the contract, and his attempt to have it approved without a proper inquiry.

The report was greeted with disdain. Newspapers published special supplements with the chairman's and Cecil's draft reports printed in full so the public could have the full background and as much of the truth as had come out. *The Times* praised Lord Robert for his 'firm and fearlessly judicial method' and said of his opponents: 'If they suppose that the public cannot see through these proceedings, or will be satisfied with the result, they are greatly mistaken.'[68] Asquith was depressed: his wife wrote to Lloyd George on 13 June to urge him and Isaacs to 'show the proper spirit' despite the 'low, vile charges made without a shadow of evidence' and apologise for what was merely a 'great indiscretion'. They had to be in earnest that 'nothing of the kind can *ever* happen again – that when you realised the folly you apologised.'[69]

On 18 June the matter was debated in the Commons, a motion of censure being moved by George Cave, a Unionist and future Home Secretary, who said he was accusing no one of personal corruption, merely of a lack of frankness about his dealings. Cave was most concerned about 'a breach of the best of our traditions' and that 'our rules have been infringed': but he was laying down a marker for the future, because he pleaded that 'they never shall with impunity be violated again.'[70] Isaacs apologised for his mistaken reticence, and said his share dealing had been a mistake too. Lloyd George – with Margot Asquith's advice ringing in his ears – concurred, though sought to argue in a way Isaacs had not, and to blame the press for his problems. 'I am conscious of having done nothing which brings a stain upon the honour of a minister of the Crown,' he protested. 'If you will, I acted thoughtlessly, I acted carelessly, I acted mistakenly, but I acted innocently, I acted openly, and I acted honestly.'[71] The House voted on party lines and a censure motion was defeated after two days of debate by 346 votes to 268, despite Cecil (whom, along with Law, Mrs Asquith accused of 'caddish behaviour') having warned the House that if they did not censure what had happened they would set a precedent for improper behaviour, with a want of frankness becoming the norm.[72] Asquith, under assault from suffragettes, Ulster Unionists and the trades unions, could do without his ministry being sunk by ministerial peculation. Backed by his Commons majority, he told the House the two ministers retained his full confidence.

Even so stern a critic as *The Times* noted Isaacs's 'obvious sincerity' but claimed that Lloyd George, more pugnacious and protesting his innocence more than was sensible, 'produced the effect of lowering the tone of the debate.'[73] The sheer impropriety of this scandal in the governing class told acute observers something disturbing about that class, and how it had changed since 1832. *The Times*, in its post-debate editorial, put it thus: 'Neither minister seems to understand how their conduct strikes the public . . . A man is not blamed for being splashed with mud. He is commiserated. But if he has stepped into a puddle which he might easily have avoided we say it is his own fault. If he protests that he did not know it was a puddle, we say that he ought to know better; but if he says that it was after all quite a clean puddle, then we judge him deficient in the sense of cleanliness. And the British people like their public men to have a very nice sense of cleanliness.'

In his *Autobiography*, published in 1936, G. K. Chesterton wrote that society should not be divided historically into pre-War and post-War, but into pre-Marconi and post-Marconi. 'It was during the agitations upon that affair that the ordinary English citizen lost his invincible ignorance; or, in ordinary language, his innocence', he wrote.[74] By then, he had seen how those with low standards could prosper, and it added venom to his pen. Lloyd George, largely because of his standing and his rhetorical power in defending what on his part had been the indefensible, survived, though he emerges well from no credible history of the scandal. The only genuine victim was Samuel, who behaved properly throughout but found himself assailed by rampant anti-Semites and tainted by association with genuine shysters.

Within four months of the committee's report Isaacs became Lord Chief Justice, a job on which the Attorney-General had traditionally had the reversion if it became available, and to which Asquith felt compelled to appoint him – to have refused would have suggested that Asquith, too, thought Isaacs a crook. The appointment outraged many, and prompted Kipling to write his poem 'Gehazi', a work of Chestertonian viciousness and anti-Semitism based on the avaricious servant of Elisha in the Book of Kings, who is punished with leprosy:

Whence comest thou, Gehazi
So reverend to behold
In scarlet and in ermine
And chain of England's gold?
From following after Naaman
To tell him all is well,
Whereby my zeal has made me
A judge in Israel.

Well done, well done, Gehazi,
Stretch forth thy ready hand,
Thou barely 'scaped from Judgment,
Take oath to judge the land.
Unswayed by gift of money
Or privy bribe more base,
Or knowledge which is profit
In any market place.

Isaacs became Lord Reading; but unusually for a Lord Chief Justice was advanced to a viscountcy in 1916 and an earldom in 1917, both thanks to Lloyd George. Nor had the patronage been exhausted then. In 1921 Lloyd George made him Viceroy of India, on his return from which he collected a marquessate, and in 1931 he was briefly Leader of the House of Lords and Foreign Secretary. He also acquired six separate knighthoods. Lloyd

George, of course, became prime minister. If mud stuck, it was hardly noticed.

Murray was a different matter. He had been popular with all factions in the Liberal party, and had been deemed a superb chief whip during the crises of 1909–11. However, his evasion of accountability had been noted, and his reputation never recovered. The hasty award of a peerage soon seemed outrageous. He died in 1920, aged just fifty, before he could inherit his father's title. The funds he had invested on his party's behalf had come from his selling of peerages and baronetcies, a practice deplored before the Great War but which would be elevated to a criminal level after it, in Lloyd George's premiership. Asquith turned a blind eye to this practice, and other ministers were well aware of it. J. B. Robinson, a South African financier and friend of King Edward VII, bought a baronetcy for £30,000, his sponsor being Churchill.

A columnist in the Liberal weekly *The Nation*, in the week of the Marconi report, observed that since so much of party funds came from peerage sales 'a taint flows from it, and it saturates the entire party system of Britain. In a purse so constituted, and a distribution of titles as lavish and undiscriminating as that which Lord Murray initiated, there lie sources of evil far beyond this incidental disclosure of recklessness.'[75] A Liberal MP, appalled not just by the conduct of ministers but by the attempt to whitewash it, told *The Times* plainly: 'Murray should be repudiated, Isaacs should resign, George should express regrets.'

Ironically, the three ended up making a loss. Isaacs was embarrassed, felt responsible, and wanted no more to do with it: but Lloyd George insisted on paying him what he owed. In December 1913 Isaacs told him he had paid £8,129 15s and had received £5,997 11s 6d, a loss of £2,132 3s 6d. Lloyd George and Murray owed a tenth of this each, £213 4s. 'Don't bother about the amount,' Isaacs wrote. 'I would not have told you but that you seemed annoyed I hadn't yet ascertained it when you last mentioned it.'[76] Asquith drew up two sets of rules – which he termed Rules of Obligation and Rules of Prudence – that began the process of preventing ministers from engaging in financial activity while in office.

In August 1911 Lloyd George had proposed payment of MPs – £400 a year – to allow those without means to stand for parliament (hitherto most Labour MPs had been funded by unions), and reduce the temptation for politicians to engage in dubious speculations. Until 1780 MPs had been given a stipend funded from local rates in their constituency; by

1911, that payment having ended, the United Kingdom had the only parliament where no contribution to the expense of doing their duties was made to its members. But the argument Lloyd George adduced was not just to allow poor men to sit in the Commons or to keep richer ones out of speculation, it was because the state had ballooned under the Asquith ministry and, as he put it, 'the work of parliament is greater, infinitely greater'.[77] The debate happened the day the Lords discussed ending their veto, and revolution was in the air. Ramsay MacDonald had made a different point: that if you didn't pay MPs, they would be more susceptible to being bribed by vested interests – what Chesterton had accused Godfrey Isaacs of having done.

The practice of augmenting Liberal party funds by selling peerages still festered. Lord Devonport, who would become an incarnation of the evils of capitalism during the period of labour troubles known as the Great Unrest and whom Ben Tillett, the veteran union leader, wanted struck dead, was a notorious example. Devonport, a plumber's son born Hudson Kearley in 1856, exemplified Victorian enterprise and social mobility. After a modest education he joined Tetley's, the tea company, aged sixteen in 1872. He founded his own tea importers in 1876 and then the International Stores. By 1890 there were 200 branches and Kearley was one of Britain's leading grocers. Two years later he became a Liberal MP, and from 1905 to 1908 served under Lloyd George at the Board of Trade as a parliamentary secretary; party patronage secured him a baronetcy in 1908, the chairmanship of the Port of London Authority in 1909 and, in 1910, a barony.

Grocers had been honoured before, and by the Unionists: though not in return for money (though they were not above rewarding brewers who helped out the party). Salisbury had had a clear sense of who was suitable to sit in the Lords. Thanks to personal services to Edward VII, the Glaswegian tea merchant Thomas Lipton acquired first a knighthood, in 1898, and then the Grand Cross of the Royal Victorian Order in 1901; Lipton was exceptionally good at entertaining the King on his yacht. In 1902 the King had asked Salisbury to agree to a peerage for Lipton, something his prime minister dismissed as 'impossible' and over which he and the monarch might, he feared, 'come to blows'.[78] A baronetcy was agreed as a compromise.

Money appeared to have changed hands for Kearley's baronetcy; but anguish was caused when, his peerage as Lord Devonport having been gazetted, he let it be known he would not pay a farthing for it. His earlier contributions had been considered a precedent for a donation to party funds. But, according to a story in *The New York Times* in July 1910, Devonport had refused to give any more because he felt his unpaid services at the Port of London, and what he had already given, were sufficient. He said he would release the correspondence demanding money to the press unless the demand were withdrawn: it was. Nonetheless Belloc wrote:

The grocer Hudson Kearley, he
When purchasing his barony
Considered first, we understand,
The title of Lord Sugarsand,
Or then again he might have been
Lord Underweight of Margarine:
But being of the nobler sort
He took the title Devonport.[79]

The controversy did Devonport no harm: he stayed at the PLA until 1925, and was advanced to a viscountcy in 1917 after serving Lloyd George as Minister of Food Control. But the reputation of the government suffered once it was known that hard cash, and not public service, was the criterion for new peerages. The puritanical wing of the Liberal party deeply deplored it. At a meeting of the Budget League – the pressure group agitating to pass the People's Budget – on 2 December 1909 a row broke out between Jack Pease, the Quaker chief whip (and Murray's predecessor), and Lloyd George over a promised £14,000 donation to the League.[80] Pease was far from satisfied that the money had not been offered in return for a peerage. On 25 August 1909 John Horsfall, a wool magnate from Keighley, had sent Churchill a cheque for £15,000 for the League: three months later he reaped a baronetcy.[81] When Murray took over the brakes came off, hence the money spent on Marconi shares. He left few traces – understandably – so the truth can only be surmised. By 1922 the traffic in honours, under Lloyd George, would create one of the great political scandals of the century. For the moment, the future prime minister was simply getting his hand in.

CHAPTER 15

DUKES AND DREADNOUGHTS

I

The end of the Boer War did not, as Unionists might have hoped, usher in a new period of political calm and accomplishment for them. Salisbury's resignation a few weeks later, around the time of Edward VII's Coronation, to make way for his nephew Balfour ushered in a new period of turbulence for the ruling party. On top of Joe Chamberlain's effective decision to split the Unionist party in 1903 between protectionists and free-traders, which ushered in two years of struggle, decline and dissension within Balfour's fading administration, there were other problems. The Russo-Japanese War of 1904–5 was of huge concern to the world's leading imperial power. The policy of importing 63,000 Chinese labourers – known as 'coolies' – to South Africa, to revive the mining industry there with cheap workers, caused a tremendous debate in Britain, not just because it was felt these people were being employed in conditions of near-slavery (which they were), but also because of a widespread prejudice against the Chinese.

The electorate's distaste for Toryism was confirmed by the landslide election defeat the party suffered in January 1906. However, the new Liberal government led by Sir Henry Campbell-Bannerman would quickly find that governing was hardly straightforward, even with their apparently commanding control of the House of Commons. A mild policy of social reform and the grant of additional rights to trades unions soon upset the Tory-dominated House of Lords. These, and the other policy challenges of early-twentieth-century Britain, brought liberalism into conflict not just with the establishment, but with conservative attitudes among many of the people, not least in the working class. With a few years the atmosphere was as far from the Edwardian myth of the perpetual tea party on the country-house lawn as it was possible to imagine.

II

Campbell-Bannerman, mortally ill after a lifelong passion for food that had caused his weight to balloon to twenty stones and triggered several heart attacks, surrendered the prime ministership of Great Britain and Ireland to his obvious successor, Herbert Henry Asquith, on 5 April 1908. He was too ill to move, so Asquith allowed him to die in Downing Street just over a fortnight later: with remarkable vision, or perhaps optimism, his last words were: 'This is not the end of me.'[1] His ministry of just over two years' duration had implemented earnest and important measures aimed at, among other things, bringing denominational schools more into the national system, changing the status of trades unions and developing the Dreadnought; it also sponsored technological progress, such as completing the electrification of London, the massive expansion of the capital's underground railways, and the spread of wireless telegraphy, but steered clear of supporting a Channel Tunnel Bill.[2] It had put a working man in the cabinet, in the shape of John Burns. He had not been sure what reception, as a former tribune of the people, he would get when meeting the Sovereign but the King oozed charm, causing Burns to tell Campbell-Bannerman that he 'was very much pleased at the way he was received by HM.'[3]

Asquith's rule would be far more vexing. The peculiarity of the handover of power was emphasised by Asquith's having to take the train to Biarritz to kiss hands with the King. He was in the resort with his mistress, Mrs Keppel, and regarded coming home to complete the constitutional proprieties as an unnecessary interruption of his carnal activities. Balfour had advised Knollys, the King's private secretary, that the opposition would accept such an unprecedented procedure.[4]

Asquith assembled the most radical cabinet in history, the tone set by the appointment of David Lloyd George as Chancellor of the Exchequer – a post Asquith had considered holding too – and Burns as head of the Local Government Board. Winston Churchill, aged just thirty-three, succeeded Lloyd George at the Board of Trade. It was said Lloyd George had, in Esher's words, 'put a pistol to Asquith's head, and asked for the Ch of the Ex with a threat of resignation.'[5] Things got off to a poor start when Asquith suspected Lloyd George of leaking details of his reshuffle to the press before they were announced, and before those affected had been consulted. The King had long seen the new Chancellor as a marked man: he had had Knollys write to Campbell-Bannerman in November 1906 complaining about 'another indecent attack on the House of Lords' after a Lloyd George speech. He had wanted the King to go to Cardiff in 1907 to open some new docks, but Knollys reported that 'the King says that nothing will induce him to visit Cardiff unless Mr Lloyd George learns how to behave with propriety as a Cabinet Minister holding an important office.'[6] The King told Asquith: 'I shall have no more to do with him than what is absolutely necessary.'[7]

The Liberals had sought to improve the conditions of the lower classes during their first two years, through the Trades Disputes Act, the Workmen's Compensation Act (both 1906), the Coal Mines Regulation Act 1908 – known as the Eight Hours Act for the time limit per day it placed on working in mines – and the Probation of Offenders Act 1907. Lloyd George and Churchill egged on Asquith to take social reform further, and there were other incentives: the Liberals lost some by-elections in 1908 and their popularity was dwindling. Part of the impetus towards reform, and behind the welfarist measures Lloyd George and Churchill would champion, was the rise of the Labour party, which was attracting support from former Liberal voters. Yet Beatrice Webb began to fear that Toryism was on the march again, and time might be running out for radical reformers. In spring 1909 she would note that 'there is coming over the country a great wave of reaction against Liberalism and Labour'.[8] The numbers working for the state, and therefore the burden on the taxpayer, also grew substantially. In 1901 there had been 130,000 civilian state employees; a decade later it was 229,900.[9]

The House of Lords, and the substantial Tory – or, as the party had now come to be known, Unionist – majority there, was used to throwing out any Liberal measure it disliked, irrespective of the government's mandate. From 1895 to 1905 the Lords posed no problem to the elected government. But when that government ceased to be Unionist, the Lords chose to ignore that fact if it suited them, and not merely revise, but veto. They were an anachronism. Their power consisted in an idea that was no longer true, that they controlled the wealth of the nation:

the Industrial Revolution had ended that. Moreover, their sway took no account of three Reform Acts and the extension of representative democracy. Worse, faced with a Liberal government of moderate (but, to the Lords, alarming) radicalism, it saw no problem in breaking two centuries of precedent, and vetoing measures earlier generations would have felt obliged to pass.

Campbell-Bannerman suggested in the summer of 1907, during cabinet discussions, that the new democratic politics dictated the Lords could not go on like this, and the elected House should be allowed to prevail in any parliament. Colleagues such as Lloyd George and Churchill were more aggressive, and wanted a showdown. Lloyd George mocked the idea that the Lords was useful. Referring to Balfour, he said the Upper House was 'the right honourable gentleman's poodle. It fetches and carries for him. It barks for him. It bites anybody that he sets it on to. And we are told that this is a great revising Chamber, the safeguard of liberty in this country. Talk about mockeries and shams.'[10] Fatally for him, Balfour ignored the dangers of the Lords' behaviour.

The Liberal government had to be mindful of the Unionist majority in the Lords. The Lords had passed what many peers considered controversial laws, such as the Eight Hours Bill – something certain Tories considered unwarranted state interference in the relationship between master and servant – but by 1908 had rejected an Education Bill and a Licensing Bill: the Unionists were the party of the brewers and distillers – 'the beerage' – whereas the Liberals were the political wing of the Temperance movement. The King had tried to persuade Lord Lansdowne, Unionist leader in the Lords, not to defeat the Licensing Bill but to amend it, not least because his own political nous and shrewdness told him that a confrontation between the two Houses might be brewing. Asquith's friend and biographer J. A. Spender said the defeat of the Licensing Bill 'added heavily to the score which the Commons were presently to settle with the Peers.'[11]

Some Tory peers were embarrassed by the party's conduct in the Upper House, and promoted schemes of reform to create a second chamber more suited to a democratic age. Campbell-Bannerman rejected an idea for joint sittings of a committee of the two Houses, favouring what John Bright had called 'the suspensory veto', which allowed for a Bill rejected by the Lords to be discussed by a 'conference' of the two Houses and, if that failed, to be introduced again. If the Lords defeated it again it became law anyway. He proposed a Bill to this effect in the 1907–8 session, but it would be another four years before such a measure, following a grave constitutional crisis, was on the statute book.

It was ironic that Asquith, when still Chancellor, had handled the ill-fated Licensing Bill; his nickname of 'Squiffy' was no mere play on words. He is thought to have been the last prime minister to sit on the front bench in the Commons while drunk, in an after-dinner sitting during the 1912–13 Home Rule crisis. There was an epidemic of drunkenness in Edwardian Britain. In the three months to 31 January 1907, 3,966 drunks were arrested in the Metropolitan Police District on Saturday nights – around 300 each week. Around 1,000 were arrested on Sundays over the thirteen-week period, but 2,000 on other nights of the week.[12] Asquith's Bill, defeated after he had become prime minister, was designed to restrict the opportunities to pursue this great national pastime by closing perhaps a third of England and Wales's 95,700 pubs.

The Lords, like Unionist MPs, objected to this assault on the brewers' business, and to the compensation they would have to be paid. Nor did they like the idea of the compensation the state would be forced to pay to those whose pubs were closed – George Younger, the Tory MP for Ayr and a brewer, said it would cause a 'financial cataclysm on the stock exchange'. They did not believe fewer pubs would mean more temperance or the lower classes spending less on alcohol, and beating their wives and children less as a result.[13] The argument was a microcosmic example of the potential effects of an interventionist state on prosperity, and the tensions between the two.

The argument of the Licensing Bill was but an aperitif to the trouble that would come with the House of Lords over the greater issue of the state providing basic welfare support for the old, sick and unemployed. Though Asquith had been a Gladstonian Chancellor in his desire to balance the books, he had realised there were the resources for an old age pension, something that had long been an aspiration of his and of many in his party. The Budget had been £5.4 million in surplus in 1906–7, and a surplus of £4 million was predicted for 1907–8. The pension would end the shame to a rich nation of its elderly poor going to the workhouse, and being stigmatised by that fate: but someone had to pay. By the 1890s only 2.6 per cent of people had Poor Law relief, and they were mainly the elderly. However, a pension would entail considerable public expenditure that, matched with the contemporaneous popular demand for a higher naval budget to allow the Royal Navy to keep pace with the expanding German fleet, required higher taxation. It was the attempt to raise this money that provoked Britain's greatest constitutional crisis of the twentieth century.

Old age pensions had been introduced in Germany in 1889; and, as with the example of the German state education system, Liberals were keen to emulate them in order to maintain Britain's reputation as an advanced and progressive nation, developing and nurturing its human capital. A Royal Commission on welfare sat from 1905 to 1909. It concluded, with a conservatism out of touch with the ruling ideology of the Liberal government, that poverty originated in moral weakness and that the Poor Law and all its harshnesses should remain, to deter those contemplating not working. The intellectual driving force of the report was Helen Bosanquet of the Charity Organisation Society, which had for decades campaigned for a distinction to be observed between the deserving and the undeserving poor, and saw no need to move with the times. She feared more state provision would reduce the charitable impulse.[14] She was the wife of the philosopher Bernard Bosanquet, a social theorist and another member of the COS. She had taken a first from Newnham in the Cambridge Moral Sciences tripos, and was one of the most formidable intellects of her generation. Her husband and she were at one on political theory, Bosanquet having argued in his *Philosophical Theory of the State* in 1899 that a state had no right to impose, in a socialist fashion, control over the lives of citizens. 'What makes and maintains States as States,' he wrote, 'is will and not force, the idea of a common good, and not greed or ambition . . . this principle cannot be overthrown by the facts of self-interest in ordinary citizens, or of selfishness in those who mould the destinies of nations.'[15]

However, Beatrice Webb published a minority report in which she took the opposite view: that paupers could not be expected to take responsibility for themselves. This at least provided the intellectual underpinning for what Asquith wished to do. Her report called for support for young people in training and education, a living wage during a person's working life, and support when sick, disabled or elderly. It was a precursor of the Beveridge Report of 1942, not least because the young William Beveridge helped Beatrice (and Sidney, who was not a member of the Royal Commission but who assisted his wife in drafting the report) research her findings, and testified in his memoirs to the influence the work had on his thinking. The Poor Law lasted until the Attlee government introduced a welfare state in the 1940s; but the split on the Royal Commission allowed the government to ignore its findings and pursue a *via media*, though one which, in establishing the principle of state intervention, steered towards the Webbs'. The government also proposed unemployment and sickness insurance, though by 1900 perhaps 4 million workers were covered for sickness by contributory schemes operated by their trades unions, friendly societies or assurance companies. The cost of even this limited welfarism would be substantial. A great economic power such as Britain should have been able to afford it, but some saw that the cost of doing so was not merely an assault on privilege, which would have to be more highly taxed, but on the incentives for wealth creation, which would undermine that economic power.

It was widely believed a state pension was affordable, because of the superfluity of young people in Britain: in the borough of West Ham in 1901 the census found that 41 per cent of people were under fifteen.[16] Asquith had intimated in the 1907 Budget that a pension was being considered; and on 7 May 1908, a month after becoming prime minister, he presented a Budget prepared before his elevation, in which he said he wished to end the 'invidious dependence' of the elderly upon Poor Law relief.[17] The Commons had discussed this for thirty years, and it was thirteen years since the Royal Commission on the Aged Poor had recommended action. Committees under the Salisbury and Balfour governments had got nowhere. The cost would be either £16 million or £27 million a year, depending whether pensionable age was sixty-five or seventy, and how many chose to claim it. It was also proposed that those with an income from other sources of ten shillings a week or more should not be eligible. There were, at the last count, 2,116,267 people over sixty-five, 1,337,984 of whom had an income of less than ten shillings a week. Those over seventy numbered 1,254,286, and 860,881 had an income of less than ten shillings. The Treasury, and not local funds, would pay the pension. This centralisation was the first sign of a welfare state.

A ten-year residence qualification would be required before the pension was paid; nor would it go to those serving prison sentences, or lunatics, or those already receiving indoor relief under the Poor Law. The scheme would be subject to revision after a year. Once paupers, criminals and all other disqualified people had been accounted for, the pension would be paid to 937,000 over sixty-five or 572,000 over seventy. If it were five shillings a week, or £13 a year, it would cost £12,180,000 if implemented at sixty-five and £7,440,000 if implemented at seventy. Administration would cost 3 per cent on top of that, with the pension being collected weekly from post offices, using a book of dated coupons. On the principle that two may live as cheaply as one, Asquith proposed a married couple's pension less than that paid to two individuals. As roughly a quarter of those of pensionable age were married, they would jointly receive 7s 6d a week, or 3s 9d each, or £9 15s a year each rather than £13. He also promised 'stringent conditions' against any attempt to obtain a pension by fraud, including forfeiture.[18]

The scheme would start on 1 January 1909. He acknowledged Tory resistance to the very idea: they thought it 'a Socialistic experiment discouraging to thrift' and a 'policy . . . of doles and largesses which was fatal to Rome.'[19] He gave that short shrift: 'If this is Socialism, it is Socialism of a kind for which both parties in this country have made themselves responsible . . . It stands, in our view, in principle on precisely the same footing as the free education of children.' If he was attempting to embarrass the Tory party into supporting the idea he would not succeed, because of the means by which he proposed to raise the money to pay for it. He told the Commons that 'I would not buy even such a boon as this for the veteran and worn-out workers of this country at the cost of free trade', in case it was imagined tariffs would pay for pensions. An increase in taxation would have to do it, and the Unionists pursued Asquith and Lloyd George – who had declared his commitment to a pension as far back as 1895 – to demand to know where the money was coming from.

With, as Austen Chamberlain pointed out on 25 May, much of the fleet in poor repair and unequal to a challenge by the German Navy, the cost of building more ships was perhaps £4 million, on top of at least £5 million for pensions in the most optimistic circumstances – that is, if many of pensionable age did not claim it. Chamberlain predicted a raid on the Sinking Fund, the repository of money set aside by successive governments to meet unexpected contingencies: to which Lloyd George countered that it would be nothing like the raid the Tory government made in 1899, of £23 million. He did not mention a war was on at the time. Chamberlain said the costs would inevitably rise: many earning over ten shillings a week would stop doing so; and to wait until seventy to pay the pension – average life expectancy was forty-seven for men and fifty for women, skewed by high infant mortality – would be deemed unfair, and the age requirement would have to be lowered. Lloyd George believed the pension should be non-contributory, in order not to deprive most women of it: and he indicated the welfare state he wanted would go much further than just a pension for the elderly – he wished to help 'a young man who is broken down and who has a wife and family to maintain . . . these problems of the sick, the infirm, of the men who cannot find means of earning a livelihood . . . are problems with which it is the business of the State to deal; they are problems which the state has neglected too long.'[20] This was a statement of radical intent.

Despite last-ditch arguments about the disincentive to thrift and the hidden costs of implementation, the Commons gave the Pensions Bill its third reading on 9 July 1908 and sent it to the Lords, with most Unionists – anxious not to appear callous or indifferent to the suffering of the elderly poor – abstaining. Asquith's original plan had been amended, with reductions in the pension once other income reached £21 a year rather than £26, a sliding scale ensuring no pension would be paid to those earning over £31 10s. Savers with friendly or provident societies would not be penalised. The age of qualification would be seventy, though many people could not prove when they were born, or simply did not know, the registration of births only having become compulsory in 1837. There would be chaotic consequences in Ireland, where registration had not begun until 1865, and where fraudulent applications for a pension became legion.

Lord St Aldwyn – as Sir Michael Hicks Beach had become – admitted that when he was Chancellor he would never have indicated his intentions so long before a Budget; but then, as he added, 'I never asked Parliament to pass a Bill that imposed burdens of this kind on future years and left them to be paid for in a way which was entirely unexplained.'[21] If Lloyd George had given a hint of his true intentions, the Lords would never have passed the Bill. But a far sterner criticism came from Rosebery. He attacked the Bill because of his profound belief that it would lead to the end of the Empire, because the creation of a welfare state would absorb money that would otherwise defend it. Although it was well known that Rosebery was still in a sulk after his political divorce from the party following his ill-fated premiership, such an objection from a former prime minister of the same party was telling.

Nonetheless, the Lords agreed to the Bill on 30 July, not least because Balfour considered it a money Bill and therefore one the Lords, by convention, should not veto. This was an interesting judgment in the light of what would happen to the following year's Budget. The Labour party felt the measure inadequate, but Asquith had reason to be satisfied.

Confirmation that a financial revolution would have to pay not just for the pension but for the expansion of the Navy came in the King's Speech on 16 February 1909. 'The expenditure of the year will be considerably in excess of that of the past twelve months,' he said. 'In these circumstances, the provision necessary for the services of the State in the ensuing year will require very serious consideration.'[22] He also announced a plan to set up labour exchanges, to get as many people into work as possible by matching vacancies with the unemployed. The Webbs and the young William Beveridge – who in 1908 joined the civil service after studying social problems at the sharp end at Toynbee Hall in the East End of London – had advised Churchill on this, and it would lead to a National Insurance principle under which the unemployed would be paid a dole and sick pay. Beveridge was a classical Liberal interventionist, admiring the Webbs' ideas on welfarism but not the socialist economics they advocated implementing to pay for them: he remained committed to the free market. T. H. Huxley, Ruskin and Rowntree were strong influences on him, as was a visit he had made to Prussia to study the kingdom's labour exchanges and social insurance system. Together with pensions, these reforms brought the end of the workhouse in sight.

III

The 1909 parliamentary session brought on the confrontation with the Lords. Asquith had told the King in late 1908 that all the main items on the Liberal party agenda that he might wish to legislate upon – Home Rule, disestablishment of the Welsh Church, land and education reform – appeared hopeless because of Unionist domination of the Upper House. There was no popular feeling against the Lords in the country, which made Asquith's task all the more difficult. There was already a problem with public spending even without the old age pension, but for the most part it was not projected social reforms that were putting pressure on the Treasury. The country wanted more Dreadnoughts to keep ahead of the Germans. In April 1908 Germany had introduced a new Navy Law, which increased their shipbuilding programme to four capital ships a year, which meant – unless Britain built more – that by about 1914 the Germans would have more such ships than the Royal Navy. The Unionists longed for naval expansion, and if that came at the cost of some of the Liberals' pet projects, so be it.

Reginald McKenna, the First Lord of the Admiralty, demanded six Dreadnoughts be built at once, on the advice of his Sea Lords. Lloyd George, whose plans might be wrecked by a huge armaments programme, thought four were enough, and the normally bellicose Churchill supported him. Lloyd George wrote to Asquith on 2 February 1909 saying the argument 'threatens to reopen all the old controversies which rent the party for years and brought us to impotence and contempt . . . I therefore earnestly pray you not to commit yourself to the very crude and ill-considered Admiralty demands'.[23] Asquith constructed a compromise to allow a programme that was 'elastic' and 'adaptable to circumstances'.[24] Four would be built at once, as planned, with the provision that four more could be built rapidly from the following April if needed. The public, whipped up by fictions about planned German invasions, were unimpressed: the cry 'We want eight, and we won't wait' passed into common usage. Not wishing for a fight on this front as well, the government agreed to build all eight: an unexpected victory for McKenna, who ended up with two more than even the Sea Lords wanted. However, Lloyd George and Churchill insisted that the extra spending must not cause a reduced welfare programme. Over the next year, as he watched how quickly Germany was developing its Navy, Churchill changed his mind about Dreadnoughts, circulating colleagues with a memorandum on 20 July 1909 advocating a full-out programme to produce twenty new ships by July 1912.[25]

Asquith told a dinner at the National Liberal Club on 11 December 1908 that 'I invite the Liberal Party tonight to treat the veto of the House of Lords as the dominating issue in politics', and added 'the Budget of next year will stand at the very centre of our work, by which we shall stand or fall, by which certainly we shall be judged in the estimation both of the present and of posterity.'[26] So concerned had Lloyd George been about the public finances when pensions were being introduced that he circulated a confidential paper to the cabinet on 19 May 1908 – ten months before the Budget – about the lengths to which the government would have to go to avoid 'the imposition of fresh taxation'.[27] His main target was defence expenditure: there had been 154,442 men in the home Army in 1893–4; now there were 185,000. The Navy had grown even more, from 76,700 in 1893–4 to 128,000. Spending had risen from £32 million to nearly £60 million in fifteen years, in a time of very low inflation. 'I need hardly remind my colleagues', he wrote, 'that we have repeatedly pledged ourselves, both before we took office and since, to a substantial reduction of the national expenditure, and particularly that which depends upon the combatant services.'

The cabinet agreed on the need for a Budget to confirm the progressive nature of modern Liberalism: but it required fourteen cabinet meetings between mid-March and the end of April to secure agreement on its contents. Defence cuts of the type Lloyd George suggested were impossible, so taxation would have to rise: but in a way that appealed to the progressive social agenda. The main opponent was Lewis 'Loulou' Harcourt, who objected to proposals to increase the rate of estate duty (invented by his father) and the super-tax that would impose a scale of heavier taxation on the rich, and become heavier the richer they were. 'I don't feel sure that the Cabinet have realised the savagery of the scale on men of *moderate means*,' he told Asquith. 'I hope we may yet be able to reconsider it.'[28] How far anyone saw at the time that it would create a trap into which the House of Lords would walk is unclear. Randolph Churchill claimed in his biography of his father that he had asked Lloyd George in the 1930s whether the land tax – a proposal to have all landholdings valued and a tax to be levied on the basis of that value – was a deliberate provocation. Lloyd George had answered that it was, and 'essential to clip the power of the Lords.'[29]

He presented that Budget on 29 April 1909. He expected a deficit, on the basis of existing taxation and estimates of spending already published, of £15,762,000.[30] Admitting this would entail a heavy increase in taxation, he said the two principal causes – the pension and the Navy – had happened 'with the unanimous assent of all political parties in this House'.[31] He alluded to the campaign to 'double and even treble' the money for Dreadnoughts, and said the government had had no moral alternative but to help the aged poor.

A pair of Dreadnoughts cost the equivalent of a penny on income tax for the two years in which they were being built. Eight would cost an increase of fourpence for each of those years. He said it would be 'lunacy' to jeopardise British naval supremacy, and had no intention of doing so. British sea power was 'so essential not only to our national existence, but, in our judgment, to the vital interests of Western Civilisation.'[32] However, to spend an extra £8 million on ships to fight 'mythical armadas' would be 'an act of criminal insanity' – 'we cannot afford to build navies against nightmares'. He intended instead to choose a 'medium path between panic and parsimony'. He would raise enough through taxation to lay down eight Dreadnoughts on 1 April 1910, and they would be ready by April 1912; but if it became clear they were not needed, the money raised would be used instead 'either in further endowment of our social programme for the benefit of the masses of the people or in giving the much-promised relief to the local ratepayer', a person much pressed by the need to improve local roads for the use of motorised vehicles, and in the provision of more schools.

His main concern was for those who, through no fault of their own, could not help themselves. The numbers who had claimed the pension – more than expected – had thrown 'a very unpleasant light' on just how many were in 'acute distress and poverty'.[33] He claimed the Unionists shared his belief that 'whichever party was in power provision would have to be made in some shape or other for those who are out of work through no fault of their own and those who are incapacitated for work owing to physical causes for which they are not responsible': the consensus had moved, and the growth in the middle and skilled working class had made the plight of those stranded at the bottom increasingly embarrassing to those at the top.[34] A symptom was the cross-party agreement that paupers over seventy, originally excluded from the pension, should from 1911 receive it as all other septuagenarians did, adding around 200,000–300,000 people to the total but with the happy effect of causing many to leave the workhouse. This additional largesse, however, only increased the problem of raising more money.

Lloyd George would not lower the pensionable age to sixty-five, which he estimated would cost another £15–20 million a year. He did wish to introduce for this age group a separate contributory social insurance scheme, as Bismarck had in Germany in the 1870s, to provide an income for those unable to work through poor health – the case of many aged between sixty-five and seventy. Some had contributed to, and were now helped by, friendly societies, but many had not, or had been unable to afford to do so. To solve this problem, he said the only sensible answer was a 'universal compulsory system'.[35] This was a momentous ideological shift, from individuals being held responsible for their welfare to the state making them contribute to a scheme, but with the state contributing too, redistributing funds from richer citizens for the benefit of poorer ones. He also wanted to provide more for the sick, invalids, widows and orphans. In the same radical vein he proposed unemployment insurance, accepting trade was often cyclical and in some trades employment was precarious. He proposed schemes of insurance by trades, on a contributory basis: an important part of the scheme being the new labour exchanges, which he and Churchill hoped would get people back into jobs quickly.

Perhaps £16.5 million might need to be raised, but creative accounting could reduce that to £13.5 million. Lloyd George promised not to raise this by any means injurious to the trade that generated Britain's wealth. As with many Chancellors, he would raise some money from motorists, with substantial taxes on big cars and threepence on each gallon of petrol. The income tax was kept at ninepence in the pound – 3.75 per cent – for those earning less than £2,000 a year. Between £2,000 and £5,000 people paid a shilling in the pound, or 5 per cent. Over £5,000, all earnings above £3,000 were taxed at an extra sixpence in the pound, a total of 7.5 per cent.

Death duties would also be increased and, most controversial of all, a land tax would be introduced, comprising a levy of 20 per cent on any increased value of land when it was sold compared with its previous price. Lloyd George also announced duties on financial transactions and, following the failure of the Licensing Bill, an increase in the cost of a licence to sell alcohol; this was accompanied by a rise in spirit duty. He also proposed a wholesale revaluation of land, the more effectively to tax it, and a rise in the tobacco tax. In a United Kingdom where only a million people out of a population (in the 1911 census) of 45 million paid income tax, he directed the burden at those who could best afford it. It was estimated that just 12,000 people would qualify for the super-tax and that 80,000 would be liable to estate duty. Unfortunately for the government, the political clout that minority had was wildly disproportionate to its numbers.

Including an adjournment, moved thoughtfully by Balfour, during which the Chancellor could rest his voice, Lloyd George spent almost five hours delivering the People's Budget. 'I am told', he said in his peroration, 'that no Chancellor of the Exchequer has ever been called on to impose such heavy taxes in a time of peace. This . . . is a War Budget. It is for raising money to wage implacable warfare against poverty and squalidness. I cannot help hoping and believing that before this generation has passed away we shall have advanced a great step towards that good time when poverty and wretchedness and human degradation which always follow in its camp will be as remote to the people of this country as the wolves which once infested its forests.'[36] On reflection after the Budget, Asquith came to feel that the land tax and the valuation system that would underpin it were 'a potential instrument for almost unlimited confiscation'.[37] He reconciled himself to the principle of the tax as it would be levied on the 'unearned increment' – the amount by which the value of land rose between valuation and sale.

It fell to Austen Chamberlain to reply for the Unionists. His father Joe, silenced by his devastating stroke in 1906, was deeply opposed to the Budget when he heard of it – not least because he saw its defeat could achieve his aim of tariff reform, the revenue from tariffs replacing those Lloyd George hoped to obtain from private property. His son, and the Unionist party, agreed. Austen said they supported adequate defence, but asked whether the proposed battleship-building was in fact adequate. They did not object in principle to some of the welfarist purposes for which money would be raised; but felt it should come from levying import duties, notably on sugar, something anathematical to free-trading Liberals. Austen concluded that Lloyd George 'is taxing again and again at different points of his Budget the same people in different ways, and those people are comparatively a very small number.'[38] It would be in the names of that very small number that the Unionists would fight the Budget. When Balfour spoke at length on it the following week he savaged it as undermining private property, not least to spread the idea that it was not only those who owned a lot of it who might have much to fear from the new ideology.

The government feared the Unionists would try to derail the measure using their Lords majority, even though such an act would be unprecedented. H. W. Wilson, the chief leader writer of the *Daily Mail*, wrote to Northcliffe, who was touring Germany, on 15 May 1909 to say that 'things here seem to be going from bad to worse. The country does not appear to realise the danger of the Budget or the position of the Navy . . . if the Budget could have been a fair and just measure, levying heavy taxes for the Navy and national defence, much could have been said for it. As it is, it is the distribution of soup-tickets provided by supertaxes to Government supporters. I fear it will profoundly damage the prosperity of the nation and thus put us more behind Germany than ever.'[39]

Wilson reflected opinion at the time – as the two general elections of 1910 would testify – that has only been made to seem reactionary in retrospect. 'The one and only hope now remaining is that the Lords will throw it out. If that brings a fight, I should say with Lincoln, "hold firm like a chain of steel; the struggle has to come now or later." Better let it come now, when there are two great issues, each making a deep appeal, the defence of the country and the issue with Socialism.' Northcliffe was pilloried for opposing the Budget through the *Mail* and *The Times*, it being suggested that his own unwillingness to pay taxes was a factor in his resistance. 'As if it mattered much to you what you paid in taxes – even in such taxes as they are now trying to impose,' commented the faithful Wilson. He was perhaps nearer the mark when he expostulated: 'As if the rich could be mercilessly taxed without the poor suffering.'

Northcliffe replied: 'I was rather sorry to hear that the powers that be in the Unionist party were against the Peers throwing out the Budget', and said that if that were so the Liberals should call an immediate general election, to gauge what people thought.[40] Wilson thought that 'if the Lords let this Budget go, there is nothing between the average man and the wild impulses of uncontrolled democracy. There will be no limit to the demands made upon us, and the uncertainty as to the future will be terrible . . . Lloyd George and Asquith use debating society arguments in the House of Commons, but deliberately refuse to face the real issues.'[41] Wilson persuaded Northcliffe that the government had no mandate for the Budget and should be 'sharply called to order,' whatever 'political battle' ensued.[42] It was not least the belligerence of the Northcliffe Press that caused the Unionists to go so far they did until August 1911.

Given the debate at home about building Dreadnoughts – and, indeed, finding the money to build them – another of Northcliffe's observations in his letter to Wilson about the visible signs of German power is pertinent. He said that he and his wife had driven 300–400 miles on their recent motor tour of Germany and 'were amazed at the vast industrial strides made in practically every town we came to. Every one of these new factory chimneys is a gun pointed at England, and in many cases a very powerful one. We have not seen one tramp on the roads or been asked for a single penny anywhere.'[43] He also noticed a vast improvement in the road and rail networks since his last visit, and how big, strong and well cared for the horses were – all liable to be requisitioned in the event of war.

Throughout the summer, while the Finance Bill spent forty-two days in committee, Liberal ministers appeared regularly on public platforms justifying it, and Unionists arranged meetings condemning it. The aristocracy, perhaps remembering how the lassitude of their class had contributed to events in France in 1789, mobilised with unusual force. The Duke of Devonshire – who had succeeded his father the previous year – became President of the Anti-Socialist Union of Great Britain, adopting a high political profile that, because of his rank, was noted by Lloyd George. Lansdowne asked Balfour to consider the possibilities of derailing at least part of the Budget: it is not clear how far either of them, at that stage, realised he might be leading his party into a trap set for it by Lloyd George. Balfour asked J. St Loe Strachey, editor of *The Spectator,* whether he could read research that Strachey had done 'in regard to the Lords' powers to reject portions of a Finance Bill.'[44] Strachey said that Gladstone's statement of 1861, defending his proposed Paper Duties, that the Lords could not amend a Finance Bill 'is based on a verbal confusion between taxes and Bills.' Amending a tax, Strachey contended, was very different from amending a tax Bill, and stemmed from the earlier practice of a separate Bill for each proposed tax. 'Your new point is extremely ingenious,' Balfour told him 'and worthy of the most careful consideration.'[45] Strachey confirmed that he had consulted several leading constitutional authorities of the day, including A. V. Dicey, Vinerian Professor of English Law at Oxford, 'and none of them seem at all inclined to challenge my argument directly'.[46]

On 16 July Lansdowne outlined his resolve to resist to the National Union of Conservative and Constitutional Associations at its annual dinner in London. 'If I cannot tell you what the House of Lords will do,' he said, 'I think I may venture to tell you what the House of Lords will not do. I do not think you will find that when the time comes the House of Lords is at all likely to proclaim that it has no responsibility for the Bill, and that because it is mixed up with the financial affairs of the nation we are obliged to swallow it whole and without hesitation. That, to my mind, would be not only a mistake, but an unconstitutional proposition.' He said he could provide proof of this from textbooks, but preferred common sense.

> It is unthinkable that either under the theory or the practice of the Constitution, in a country with two legislative chambers, it should be left to the absolute discretion of one of those chambers to impose upon the nation any burdens, however monstrous and intolerable, any taxation, however inequitable its incidence, any new financial system, however subversive of society – and I believe that to be especially true when one bears in mind, as he must, that this Government cannot claim to have received, on the occasion of the last general election, any kind or sort of mandate from the country to deal with this vast financial revolution.[47]

This was a clear declaration of intent, if not of war. Churchill, without any authority from Asquith, decided to respond to Lansdowne in kind. In an aside, Lansdowne had said the Lords were not obliged to swallow the Budget whole or without mincing. 'The House of Lords means to assert its right to mince,' Churchill jeered in a speech in Edinburgh. He said the Finance Bill could not be amended by the Lords, but would leave the Commons 'in its final form'. He amplified, to continued cheering: 'No amendments, no excision, no modifying or mutilating will be agreed to by us. We will stand no mincing, and unless Lord Lansdowne and his landlordly friends choose to eat their own mince again Parliament will be dissolved and we shall come to you in a moment of high consequence for every cause that Liberalism has ever fought.' Asquith was outraged at this pre-emption of his authority, and the presumptions it made about the exercise of the Royal prerogative as well as about party strategy. He formally rebuked Churchill at cabinet the following week: his task was difficult enough without colleagues going freelance.

However, Churchill was merely exercising his master's voice – his master being Lloyd George: and he claimed his speech was a 'mere restatement' of a speech the previous January that Asquith had approved.[48] A fortnight after Lansdowne's challenge, the Chancellor put up a defence of particular historical resonance at Limehouse in east London on a damp, cool Friday evening, 30 July, to an *ad hoc* group of Liberals calling themselves the Budget League, and in terms not far removed from Churchill's. Over 4,000 people packed into the Edinburgh Castle, the temperance hall set up by Thomas Barnardo in the 1870s to replace a public house and a music hall. Barnardo's body had lain in state there before his funeral four years earlier. A huge suffragette protest was held at bay by a small army of police, and some male supporters of female suffrage were thrown out of the hall. In every respect the occasion would become one of the great political events of the twentieth century.

The Chancellor, after what the newspapers described as an enthusiastic welcome, spoke against a backdrop of the howls of suffragettes installed not just outside the hall, but in properties surrounding it. There were Conservatives aplenty who wished for more expenditure on the Navy, he said, but who were not prepared to pay for it. But somebody had to fund the four new Dreadnoughts, and the other four that were being built. 'So we sent the hat round,' he said, provoking gales of laughter. 'We sent it round amongst the workmen, and the miners of Derbyshire and Yorkshire, the weavers of High Peak and the Scotchmen of Dumfries, who, like all their countrymen, know the value of money. They all brought in their coppers. We went round Belgravia, but there has been such a howl ever since that it has completely deafened us.'[49]

He turned on Tories who argued against pensions – none argued against Dreadnoughts – and asked why, in that case, they had promised them. And if they said they had meant contributory pensions, paid for solely by the working class who would benefit from them, why had they not said so? 'The provision for the aged and deserving poor – it was time it was done. It is rather a shame for a rich country like ours – probably the richest country in the world, if not the richest the world has ever seen – that it should allow those who have toiled all their days to end in penury and possibly starvation.' To repeated cheers, he said workmen would no longer arrive 'at the gates of the tomb, bleeding and footsore, through the brambles and thorns of poverty', but via 'a new path' widened 'so that 200,000 paupers shall be able to join in the march.' Some of the rich begrudged the poor the help they needed – not just for pensions, but for state assistance to friendly societies who wished to help widows and orphans. This was the most naked declaration of class war ever heard from a leading British statesman.

He attacked those who objected to higher land taxes, arguing that land values in areas such as east London, where he was speaking, had risen not through any effort of the landlord, but thanks to the commercial effort of the people, under free trade, who had made London so prosperous. The coming of the Underground to London suburbs – he named Golders Green – had caused property prices to rocket. The same was true in other industrial centres with better infrastructure and more businesses than previously, and where those holding land had suddenly found themselves immensely wealthy. By contrasting those who made money by effort and enterprise with those who made it by sitting back and watching their rents pile up – a tendentious comparison, but Lloyd George knew what he was doing – he was exploiting class divisions again. One passage – 'the landlord is a gentleman . . . who does not earn his wealth . . . his sole function, his chief pride, is the stately consumption of wealth produced by others' – was deemed especially inflammatory, notably by the King, who told Asquith that the Chancellor's language was 'Billingsgate'.[50]

Lloyd George mocked the rapacity of the aristocracy in its role as landowners – 'oh, these dukes! How they harass us.' He named the Duke of Northumberland, for demanding a huge sum for land where a school would stand; then the Duke of Westminster, for big increases in his ground-rents. He attacked coal-owners, deploring the dangerous conditions men worked in below ground, and accusing employers of irresponsibility in begrudging a little extra to keep the aged from the workhouse. His tone became more threatening. 'If this is an indication of the view taken by these great landlords of their responsibility to the people who at the risk of life create their wealth, then I say their day of reckoning is at hand.' He then addressed a vast overflow meeting, at which he promised that if the Lords attempted to amend the Finance Bill, the amendments would be rejected. This raised the stakes, for it seemed to invite the Lords either to accept the Budget, or reject it.

The speech's inflammatory nature hardened the view of many peers that they would have to use their veto, breaking the precedent of two centuries. The King was apoplectic, and Unionists from Balfour downwards decided the purpose of the Budget was to import socialism to the United Kingdom. In a letter to St Loe Strachey on 26 July Balfour had proclaimed that 'it seems to me quite evident that a Resolution intended to prevent a non-representative body imposing taxes cannot, by any just process of exegesis, be made to mean that the second chamber is to sit by with folded hands while the social organisation of the country is being revolutionised by financial legislation which has a political as well as a fiscal side.'[51] The new proposals divided the country, the demagoguery of Lloyd George's tone smacking of revolution. This and other such speeches helped reduce the number of Liberal MPs at the subsequent election, as many voters returned to the Tory colours.

Asquith wrote to Lloyd George on 3 August, having encountered the Sovereign at Cowes, to say he had found him 'in a state of great agitation and annoyance' and that 'I have never known him more irritated, or more difficult to appease, though I did my best.'[52] The King had found the speech 'a menace to property' and detected 'a socialistic spirit, which he thinks peculiarly inappropriate and unsettling in a holder of your office.' Asquith said the King had, thus far, taken the Budget better than expected, and it would be wise not to provoke him further and risk 'alienating his goodwill'.[53]

Asquith had also received messages of concern from committed Liberals. He told Lloyd George that what was now required was a 'reasoned appeal to moderate and reasonable men . . . my sole object is to bring our ship safely into port.' Lloyd George was unrepentant, even to the extent of writing to the King that he felt 'justified' in saying what he had at Limehouse, which he contended was not nearly so unpleasant as some of the things said by his opponents.[54] The King was no pushover, and wrote back to his Chancellor to tell him that he expressed no opinion on the Budget, but felt Lloyd George's language 'was calculated to set class against class and to inflame the passions of the working and lower orders against people who happened to be owners of property.' As for the attacks on Lloyd George, the King agreed they had been unpleasant; but holders of high office had not made them. As a holder of high office, he had to behave better than his attackers: a stricture he would make a point of ignoring.

The government took seriously the idea that the peers would veto the Budget. Asquith circulated a memorandum on 7 September to outline the effects of a rejection. Many tax increases were being levied with the authority of a simple resolution of the Commons: it was felt that the legal effect of these resolutions would end if parliament were dissolved before a Budget had confirmed them. It was also feared that 'legal proceedings would be initiated for the recovery of the amounts already paid.' Sir George Murray, the Permanent Secretary to the Treasury, said that 'I do not see what defence could be set up to any such actions.'[55] Murray predicted a deficit of £30–40 million, an awesome figure that could be covered only by borrowing, and which under the Appropriation Act would have to be repaid by 30 June 1910. This was 'practically impossible'. He argued that a provisional or incomplete Bill would have to be settled before a dissolution. Asquith agreed, and proposed a 'Taxes Continuance Bill' to ensure monies were collected.[56]

Throughout the summer and autumn of 1909 huge rallies for and against the Budget were held across the country. One speaker against it was Rosebery, who had notified Asquith in 1908 of his move to the cross-benches and who in a speech in Glasgow on 11 September attacked the taxes so uncompromisingly that Asquith felt forced to write to him about their 'parting of the political ways', announcing his resignation and that of several colleagues as vice-presidents of the Liberal League, of which Rosebery was president.[57] Rosebery replied that he had in fact resigned as president the day before the speech, and said that 'I think that you have left me rather than I have left you . . . I doubt if any of you realise the painful struggle I had to face before speaking.'

Asquith defended the Budget in terms far less inflammatory than his Chancellor's. The King was so concerned that he summoned Asquith to Balmoral in early October to ask about the constitutional propriety of his advising, and if necessary putting pressure on, Lansdowne and Balfour not to exercise the veto. Asquith assured the King this would be in order, citing the precedent of William IV pressing the Tories not to derail the Reform Bill of 1832 – 'in both cases the country was threatened with a revolution at the hands of the House of Lords'.[58] Realising the Tories would want something in return, the King suggested that after passing the Budget there would be an immediate dissolution and an election – where the country could throw the Liberals out if they disliked the Budget as fundamentally as the Unionists believed. Asquith demurred, not least because he felt peers had no right to force a dissolution; he disliked the idea of a January election, campaigning on dark days and in bad weather; and nor could he see how he would explain to his party dissolving parliament just four years into a seven-year term when they had just secured a revolutionary Budget. He also feared the outcome would be a hung parliament, with the Irish party holding the balance of power, 'a very undesirable state of things'.[59] Nothing was resolved, but the two men accepted there would have to be an immediate dissolution if the veto were used.

The King saw Lansdowne and Balfour in London on 12 October, and they led him – or, rather, misled him – to believe they had not yet decided what course the Lords would take. Others were convinced the lethal combination of tariff reformers and the landed interest would prevail, and indeed there is evidence that, whatever he told the King, Lansdowne had settled on the veto. Ten days before he saw the King, he told Lord Balfour of Burleigh – a free-trader and therefore keen to give no openings to the tariff reformers – that: 'I am in favour of rejection, upon the broad ground that the Finance Bill is a new departure of the most dangerous kind, to which the House of Lords has no right to assent until it is sure that HMG have the support of the country.'[60]

Lloyd George continued his campaign. In Newcastle-upon-Tyne the same week Asquith had been at Balmoral, he addressed two large meetings and a dinner, and ramped up his rhetoric. Asquith pleaded with him to go easy, having placated the King who, he added, objected only to the high levels of proposed death duties on moderate-sized estates. However, the Tories were holding Budget protest meetings, the theme of which was that the Budget had no mandate, and only a general election could provide one. Lloyd George felt under pressure to retaliate.

He arrived at his first meeting, in the Palace Theatre, to find the street partly barricaded, and mounted police much in evidence. This was not because of local anger at the Budget, but because of threats from suffragettes. In the event, the women held their own meeting, disrupted by what *The Times* described as 'a number of young hooligans who were cowardly as well as ruffianly'.[61] Their cause was advanced at the Chancellor's meeting by young male hecklers, who were pounced upon and thrown out, though one just in front of the stage 'fought like a maniac'. To a crowd of 4,000 Lloyd George said he had done 'five months' hard labour' on the Budget, because of the long process of amendments in the Commons, and argued that every reasonable objection had been met.

Sporadically interrupted by suffragettes, he continued by explaining how well the economy was doing, how industry had boomed and the stock market with it. He then went deep into controversy. 'Only one stock has gone down badly; there has been a great slump in dukes.' *The Times*, in its report, noted at this point 'laughter and cheers'. He continued: 'They used to stand rather high in the market, especially in the Tory market, but the Tory press has discovered that they are of no value. They have been making speeches recently. One especially expensive duke made a speech, and all the Tory press said: Well now, really, is that the sort of thing we are spending £250,000 a year upon? Because a fully-equipped duke costs as much to keep up as two Dreadnoughts; and dukes are just as great a terror and they last longer. [Laughter].'

There was more ridicule to come.

> As long as they were contented to be mere idols on their pedestals, preserving that stately silence which became their rank and their intelligence, all went well, and the average British citizen rather looked up to them and said to himself, 'well, if the worst came to the worst for this old country we have always the dukes to fall back on.' [Laughter.] But then came the Budget, they stepped off their perch, they have been scolding like omnibus drivers, purely because the Budget cart has knocked a little of the gilt off their old stage coach . . .

He delivered a gem of political philosophy.

> Most of the people who work hard for a living in the country belong to the Liberal party. I would say and think, without offence, that most of the people who never worked for a living at all belong to the Tory party. [Cheers.]

The Liberals were not an anti-property party; many had worked hard to acquire property. He branded the Unionists as 'those who are seeking to establish a complete change in the fiscal system of this country, to tax food' – raising money through tariffs, with its echoes of the Hungry Forties, before the repeal of the Corn Laws. He also renewed the attack made at Limehouse on landlords, a group he painted as indiscernible from the food-taxing Tories, and – being in Newcastle – singled out the coal-owners for special opprobrium. 'These men', he roared, 'ought to feel honoured that Providence has given them the chance to put a little into the poor box. And since they will not do it themselves, we have got to do it for them.'

He attacked the hypocrisy of the Tories in considering themselves the constitutional party; it had long been the custom under the constitution that the Commons controls supply, 'and what our fathers established through centuries of struggles and of strife, even of bloodshed, we are not going to be traitors to.' He predicted 'the Constitution is to be torn to pieces. Let them realise what they are doing. [Cheers.] They are forcing revolution.' ['Hear, hear,' and a voice, 'and they will get it.'] 'They' – the House of Lords – were merely 'five hundred men, ordinary men chosen accidentally from among the unemployed', and they were not fit to 'override the judgment – the deliberate judgment – of millions of people who are engaged in the industry which makes the wealth of the country.' This, and phrases such as 'who ordained that a few should have the land of Britain as a perquisite, who made 10,000 people owners of the soil and the rest of us trespassers in the land of our birth?' seemed pure incitement. Aware of the course the Lords could take, he told an overflow meeting of between 5,000–6,000 people that 'we may be inviting your opinion on these questions within the next few weeks – momentous weeks in the history of England.'

Lloyd George made three speeches in Newcastle, the third to a Liberal dinner that evening. *The Times*, as the voice of the status quo, analysed and savaged them all. Its leader writer felt they had been made 'in that early manner which the most hopeful observers of his career are now driven to doubt his capacity to outgrow.'[62] He had used 'the simple method of the demagogue' to 'set class against class in order to conceal his inability to do any good to either.' His 'crusade against the well to do' would, the paper argued, simply reduce employment opportunities for those lower down. 'We should like to ask the great body of honest workers to forget all about dukes for a little, and to consider what promise of betterment of any kind for themselves is contained in the Newcastle speeches.' It continued: 'The better to excite the evil passions on which the demagogue trades, Mr Lloyd George talks as if dukes were the ground landlords of the whole country. There are a round million of ground landlords in this country, and they all do just what dukes and the rest of us do – get the best price for their property in the market.'

The Budget had not been quite so well thought out as the Chancellor had maintained. While he was creating the distraction of three headline-grabbing speeches in Newcastle, the government was putting down 250 amendments to the Bill, five months into its consideration, which hardly advertised its solidity. A plan to tax unrecovered mineral deposits as part of the land tax was withdrawn after protests from Liberal MPs; many of the amendments covered the attempt to tax the brewers and distillers more highly, which would have a bad effect on the trade that exceeded the damage that might be done to these traditional Tory supporters. *The*

Times took the Tory line that it was an outrage for the Liberals 'to develop in power a policy of which they gave no hint at the election which placed them there.' It also alluded to the rumblings in the Irish party, which saw the opportunity to advance Home Rule. There was more at stake than the level at which the well-to-do would be taxed. If the Lords were neutered because of the Budget, the whole edifice of the nation could start to crack.

The clause-by-clause consideration of the Bill meant there was no autumn recess. Its third reading – when it was sent up to the Lords – was not given until 4 November, albeit by a majority of 379 to 149, after 554 divisions. Balfour called the Bill 'socialistic' and an attack on property and private enterprise.[63] Asquith and his colleagues maintained, in public, that a veto was unthinkable. The stock market was depressed. Earlier tax rises had brought no increase in revenue. There were few buyers for government stocks. Aside from the economic predicament, Lloyd George's vituperations, and attacks by his colleagues on aristocrats and plutocrats, had proved counter-productive among public opinion that disliked rabble-rousers. The prospects for an election victory were not good.

Knollys, whose mandarin reputation had not suppressed his Liberal sympathies, had by early November made the King understand the veto might be exercised. When the Lords debated the Bill on 22 November Lansdowne launched an all-out assault. The line was simple: the Lords saw no obligation to pass such a radical measure 'until it has become aware that the people of this country desire that this Bill should become law.'[64] Lansdowne cited much constitutional precedent: the Lords could not amend a money Bill, but it could throw one out. He attacked the government's fetish for free trade, urging it to raise the necessary funds from tariffs and not by taxing the wealth-creating class. The people had to be consulted; and he warned against a challenge to the fundamental rights of the Lords if it chose to veto the Bill – something, he said, successive eminent Liberal statesmen had confirmed it had a right to do.

But one prominent Liberal statesman and jurist – Lord Loreburn, the Lord Chancellor – took grave issue with Lansdowne's assertions, calling his request to reject the Finance Bill 'subversive of the traditions of parliament . . . and impossible in practice'.[65] He did not dispute that rejection would be legal: but he asserted it would not be constitutional. He pointed out that the Crown had many powers unused for centuries, which if exercised would cause constitutional upheaval. 'Custom, usage, convention . . . which by inveterate practice had so modified the hard law itself' were the key considerations, and Loreburn contended that Britain was governed 'more by custom . . . than we are even by the law'.[66] No money Bill had been rejected since 1860, when the Lords blocked Gladstone's attempt to repeal the Paper Duty; Loreburn thought no Finance Bill had been thrown out in the Lords' history, but certainly not since 1708. 'I believe,' he said, 'that the action you are asked to take is a direct invasion both of the prerogative of the Crown and of the privileges of the House of Commons.'[67] Later on a third way emerged: Rosebery said he wished he could vote against the Budget, but he would not, because the reforms that would then be inflicted on the Lords would be even worse for Britain than Lloyd George's measures.

Loreburn's predecessor as Lord Chancellor, Halsbury, countered this progressive doctrine. Halsbury was eighty-six and compiler of Halsbury's *Laws of England*. He dismissed Loreburn's citations of precedent and claimed a range of others for rejecting the Bill, saying a rejection would be entirely constitutional: otherwise there was no point having a second chamber. He urged boldness on his fellow peers, rejecting trepidation: 'I would not value a seat in a House which would yield to such paltry apprehension.'[68] These were the battle lines, and this formed the basis of an argument that would rage for two years: was it more faithful to the obligations of parliament towards the people to reject this Bill, or to pass it? And was it right the Lords should have the power to veto legislation the Commons had passed – as it had done with the Licensing Bill – or should that power be diluted or lost? For the landed interest dominating the Lords, the right to reject a money Bill was crucial, for it was through the agency of money Bills that socialism would be introduced into Britain.

On 30 November, after six nights of debate, the Lords rejected the People's Budget by 350 votes to seventy-five. Showing what they thought of Lloyd George, seventeen dukes voted against, none for it. The House passed a further resolution stating it would not be justified in approving the Bill until it had been submitted to the judgment of the country. Asquith put down a Commons motion 'that the action of the House of Lords in refusing to pass into law the financial provisions made by this House for the Service of the year is a breach of the Constitution and a usurpation of the rights of the Commons.'[69] He called what had happened 'unexampled in the history of the British Parliament.'[70] He proclaimed that 'the House of Commons would, in the judgment of His Majesty's Government, be unworthy of its past and of the traditions of which it is the custodian and the trustee if it allowed another day to pass without making it clear that it does not mean to brook the greatest indignity, and I will add the most arrogant usurpation, to which, for more than two centuries, it has been asked to submit.'[71]

There were practical problems as well as a constitutional crisis. The government would have to borrow more to meet its obligations. Asquith met the veto with threats. The unwritten constitution might not, because of the veto, last much longer: after all, the Sovereign had, but had not since Queen Anne used, the right to veto a Bill. To do so now would be unconstitutional: Asquith considered the parallel exact. 'We are living under a system of false balances and loaded dice,' he said. 'When the democracy votes Tory we are submitted to the uncontrolled domination of a single Chamber. When the democracy votes Liberal, a dormant Second Chamber wakes up from its slumbers and is able to frustrate or nullify our efforts'.[72] He would seek a dissolution: the people would show what they thought. Balfour, unblinking, responded that the Second Chamber had done simply what the Second Chamber was supposed to do. His argument was defeated by 349 to 134. Parliament was prorogued the next day. Beatrice Webb observed that 'the wisely moderate man should dread a Tory victory. The whole Liberal Party would become extremists.'[73]

IV

Knollys summoned Asquith's private secretary, Vaughan Nash, on 15 December to tell him the King's view on another stratagem: that the King might create several hundred peers to give the Liberals a majority in the Lords. This had been broached two days before the Budget's rejection, and Knollys had told Asquith that to create so many peers – the quantity imagined was 570 – was 'almost an impossibility' and 'would place the King in an awkward position'. The King would not, Nash reported, feel justified in creating hundreds of peers – the number mooted by mid-December had fallen to 300 – until after a second general election, a prospect Asquith was told not to share with his colleagues. Nash, in a memorandum to Asquith, told him that 'the King regards the policy of the Government as tantamount to the destruction of the House of Lords and he thinks that before a large creation of Peers is embarked upon or threatened the country should be acquainted with the particular project.'[74] The King really did not want a mass creation, unless they could be life peers; and he favoured shorter parliaments, reduced from seven years to five or, preferably, four, to protect against what was later termed 'elective dictatorship'. The King even sounded out Asquith on the propriety of withholding his Writ of Summons from peers who might oppose the Budget, something rejected as likely to drag the monarch into politics. Whatever Asquith might say on public platforms, this election would be about the Budget, not the veto; because the veto could only be stopped by the threat of a mass creation, and the King was not ready for that – yet.

Polling took place from 15 January to 10 February 1910. The outcome confirmed the public's distaste for Lloyd George's methods, if not for his policies. The Liberals lost 125 seats and the Unionists won 116, leaving them with 274 and 272 seats respectively. The Tories, however, had a higher proportion of the popular vote – 46.7 per cent against 43.1 per cent, a moral victory at least, and partly the result of the Tory press urging free-traders who had left the party over tariff reform to return and vote for candidates who did not share their views.[75] The Unionist victory in the popular vote, and the Liberals' reliance on seats on the Celtic fringe – away from the main engines of Britain's prosperity – would increase the idea among Unionists, and especially Unionist peers, that the government in effect had no mandate.

The election of January 1910 came at a bad time for Balfour, who was, 'by a most unhappy accident', as he told Northcliffe, in poor health.[76] He conveyed from his home in the Borders a sense that away from the conflict, hubbub and raised tempers of Westminster and society drawing rooms, nobody cared much about what was happening: 'The people I see seem cheerful.' Northcliffe sent him briefings on the Navy once the campaign was under way, but Balfour told him that 'the difficulty I feel in dealing with the Navy on platforms is that it is so hard to make the public understand the danger of the position without saying things about Germany which hardly seem discreet in the mouth of an ex-Prime Minister.'[77] This contradicted Northcliffe's belligerent anti-Germanism, which he saw as a way for the Unionists to seize the advantage over the Liberals.

The dispute that caused the election had in fact highly motivated the electorate: turnout was 86.8 per cent. While the result was ominous for the Lords – the deal the Liberals and Irish would make on Home Rule ensured that – the country was divided, socially and geographically. Beatrice Webb saw 'the South Country – the suburban, agricultural, residential England – going Tory and tariff reform, and the North Country and dense industrial populations (excluding Birmingham area) going radical socialist, a self-conscious radical socialist.'[78]

The first weeks of the parliament were fraught for the Liberals, not least because they were unsure of the Irish party. Labour had forty MPs, up from twenty-nine, but the Irish party, under John Redmond, had seventy-one and held the balance of power. Its demand for Home Rule could be met only if the Lords' veto were removed. The Irish made it known they would vote down the Budget unless a Bill ending the veto were introduced. It was a price Asquith was reluctant to pay. The battle would widen beyond the Budget: it would be about confirming the supremacy of the elected over the unelected chamber. The Liberal decision to provoke the Lords had, unhelpfully, put the toxic question of Home Rule back on the agenda.

Asquith was forced to deny that the King had promised a mass creation of peers. By late February, fearing they could not get the Budget even through the Commons, the cabinet considered resignation. The Irish party had opposed the Budget in 1909 over spirit duties, and threatened to again. Asquith told Redmond he must do as he pleased, including taking responsibility for installing a Unionist government. The Irish renewed their insistence on ending the Lords' veto. The difficulty of handling them, and predicting their moves, would make things fraught for Asquith.

The King's Speech in February promised proposals to define relations between the two Houses, settling the authority of the Commons over finance and its predominance in legislation generally. The atmosphere within the cabinet was febrile, with daily rumours of resignations. Lloyd George wanted to proceed against the veto at once; Asquith hesitated, because to abolish it required the Lords' consent. This would be forthcoming only if forced, which would cause a constitutional crisis. Asquith held off reintroducing the Budget, though said when he did it would be identical to that rejected the previous November. Whenever he was asked about the Budget he replied that 'we must wait and see', which soon became the refrain to a popular music-hall song.[79] He was not teasing the opposition, or the public: he was struggling to decide what to do, being unwilling to do anything that dragged the King into the argument. The cabinet was circulated with memoranda, about the definition of a money Bill and the wider rights of veto in the Lords, which formed the germ of a Parliament Bill. As well as preventing the veto of money Bills and of Bills the Commons had passed three times, the proposals were to limit each Parliament to five years instead of seven, and would enable 'Peers to sit as Members of the House of Commons on renouncing their right to sit in the House of Lords.'[80]

For one minister even these reforms were not enough. 'We must not deprive ourselves of the right to develop the full argument against the principle of hereditary legislators,' Churchill wrote to his colleagues on 15 February.[81] 'The time has come for the total abolition of the House of Lords.' He said there was a 'spontaneous repudiation of hereditary and aristocratic privilege' around the country and the Liberals could not 'stand outside' it. He added that 'I myself would not be frightened by having only one' chamber, but would countenance a second. The revised chamber should, he said, be a quarter of the size of the existing House; mostly it should be elected, but with some members chosen from a panel of those who had given public service or held high offices; should be elected in stages; and it should be 'subordinate . . . democratic . . . [and] fair.' The appetite for wholesale reform, when the government had no majority of its own and had battles on other fronts, was weak. On 7 March Herbert Samuel, the Chancellor of the Duchy of Lancaster, circulated extracts from the writings of great constitutional historians about what was and was not possible in regard to a mass creation of compliant peers.[82] There was much study of the crisis of 1832, when the Great Reform Bill was eventually passed.

In mid-March the government announced its plans. A two-day debate in the Commons on its relations with the Lords, which the government won comfortably, took place later that month. A committee of the House of Commons then discussed resolutions about what rights and powers the Lords should have: these resolutions would form the basis of the Parliament Bill. Of the measures proposed in cabinet in February, all were included apart from allowing peers to renounce their titles and sit in the Commons; that would have to await a later reform. This Bill, whose second reading was on 14 April, could not be passed without the

Lords' approval, and that would become the focus of the dispute. The previous day the cabinet had argued over strategy. John Morley had promised to resign if the Royal prerogative was used for a mass creation; and the question of concessions to the Irish over spirit duties was also discussed. The Unionists protested at being railroaded into change, and voted against the resolutions. When the Bill had passed its second reading, Asquith said if the Lords continued to block reform, he would request another dissolution and make the veto the issue at the ensuing election.

The Budget was reintroduced on 20 April. Asquith felt the failure of the Unionists to win the election obliged them not to reject the Budget in the Lords. Within a week it passed through all its stages – most of the Irish voting with the government – and the Lords approved it without a division on 28 April. The battle shifted to the Parliament Bill, which the King believed could not be persisted with against the Lords' wishes without consulting the country at a general election. Asquith told the King he was having a Bill drafted to provide for a referendum, but rumours of a mass creation of peers were rife.

The Unionists could not believe the prerogative would be used in this way. At Reading on 5 May 1910 Curzon, in limbo since returning from India, mocked the very thought. *The Times*'s correspondent reported that 'the idea that the House of Lords could be intimidated or coerced or cajoled by threat of the creation of 500 peers to act in a manner inconsistent with its own conviction or conscience, appeared to him a fantastic dream – nay, the idea of creating a body of peers whose first act was to be to walk into the Chamber to which they had been appointed and vote its practical extinction was a performance which was only worthy of Bedlam.'[83] Curzon's defence stimulated 'laughter and cheers', as did his sharp observation that 'heaven knows from what class they are to be drawn.' The spectacle of so many without his own inherent nobility buying robes and coronets, and voting to reduce their Chamber to a 'nullity', would be a 'pantomime' that would 'excite the inextinguishable laughter of the civilised world.' Curzon would, however, be one of the first Unionists to change his tune, once he realised Asquith was not bluffing. He was ripe for conversion, having been shocked by some of the behaviour of Unionist peers since 1906, notably obstructing the old age pension legislation and rejecting the Licensing Bill.

Curzon also attacked the government for kow-towing to the Irish –

he called Redmond 'the real prime minister', highlighting a theme that would dominate Unionist fears about where the removal of the Lords' veto would lead; and he savaged ministers for the 'indecorous' way they had dragged the King into the argument over use of the prerogative. Edward VII was an intensely political monarch; but knew the limits the constitution placed upon him, and knew too that if a second election – which was daily expected to be called – gave a mandate for a Bill to restrict the Lords' powers, he would have to use his prerogative to secure the will of the people. He would have to do this even if it meant, as he saw it, the destruction of the House of Lords (and the idea of an aristocracy) by flooding it with hundreds of counter-jumping Liberal peers. He also knew that even some of Asquith's colleagues, such as Morley, would not necessarily support this drastic solution, so anything could happen.

V

The painful duty of exercising the prerogative as it had never been exercised before would not, however, be King Edward VII's. His health wrecked by years of over-eating, over-drinking and over-smoking, he died of complications arising from bronchitis at Buckingham Palace on the evening of 6 May 1910, twenty-four hours after Curzon had defended him at Reading. His reign had been a little over nine years, but his people had come to like him, and the era to which he gave his name remains associated with what many would consider a golden age, and certainly an antidote to the sober and staid image of his mother's reign: George Dangerfield, the historian of Liberal England's 'strange death', described him, in a gem of a phrase, as 'comfortably disreputable'.[84] Asquith felt the King's death utterly transformed the political situation, not least because he felt reluctant to put pressure upon a new and inexperienced monarch to take far-reaching decisions. The new King told Asquith and Lloyd George within days of ascending the Throne that he wished to 'try his hand at conciliation'.[85] Asquith then proposed, with George V's approval, a constitutional conference between himself, Balfour and their senior colleagues, to find a way of proceeding that would enshrine the supremacy of the Commons in a way appropriate to a democratic era, without destroying the House of Lords. The idea had been floated on 8 May in a leading article in *The Observer*, written by its editor J. L. Garvin, who had then made it his business to talk senior Unionists, notably Balfour and Austen Chamberlain, into taking part.

On 1 June Asquith sent the King a note on the constitutional crisis and its causes. 'It has for a long time past,' he wrote, 'been increasingly clear to all dispassionate observers that the composition of the House of Lords, and its relations with the House of Commons, should soon call for readjustment.'[86] He gave the King a lecture on constitutional history, and on the prevailing view among constitutional experts that the Lords had no right to reject a money Bill. He told Balfour on 9 June that Edward VII's death had not affected the 'essence' of the constitutional dispute, but had 'brought about an unforeseen but undeniable change in atmosphere and perspective'.[87] Failure to reach an agreement would be 'a serious blot upon our national credit for good sense'.

Balfour agreed to meet. The conference would consider three main points: the relations of the two Houses on matters of finance; how to resolve persistent disagreements, whether by limiting the veto, holding joint sittings or referendums; and exploring the possibility of altering the composition and numbers of the Lords to make it more representative of the main parties. The conference met in Asquith's room in the Commons on 17 June. He, Lloyd George, Crewe and Augustine Birrell, the Chief Secretary for Ireland, represented the government, and Balfour, Lansdowne, Chamberlain and the Earl of Cawdor, a former First Lord of the Admiralty, attended for the Unionists. The men met a dozen times before the end of July, and the discussions were conducted in an atmosphere of mutual respect. Balfour even asked for a paper to be circulated to the cabinet in which he set out what he hoped was the common ground between the two parties; and it was.[88] After the first twelve meetings Asquith noted that the progress made was sufficient for the meetings to continue, something the participants found 'not only desirable but necessary'.[89]

However, it then proved harder to proceed than had been hoped. Lansdowne rejected the idea that, during the summer recess, the conference should meet at Crewe's country house. 'It would at once be said that the whole affair was a picnic,' he said, 'and that business of such importance ought not to be transacted in an environment of such a kind.'[90] He feared if an agreement were reached the criticism of some of their fellow Unionists would be that 'we had been "softened" by the excellence of Crewe's champagne and the other attractions of a hospitable and luxurious country house'. In the talks the sticking point was the Irish, who expected a Home Rule Bill immediately the Lords' veto was removed.

The Unionists remained deeply opposed to Home Rule – and the Liberals would rather avoid the matter. However, the alternative was a grand coalition with the Unionists, leaving the Irish stranded, which was unthinkable to Asquith. Lloyd George favoured such a coalition – provided he was a significant player in it, and not too many concessions were made to the right – and Balfour, a decidedly unpartisan party leader revolted by the extremism of some of his comrades, was briefly interested. But he told Lloyd George: 'I cannot become another Robert Peel in my party', and nothing came of it.[91] The key enthusiast on the Unionist side was F. E. Smith, who plotted with his friend Churchill, and in doing so laid the foundations of the coalition formed in 1915.

Crewe's offer to host talks having been rejected, there was a break until October. Asquith felt accord had been reached on financial questions, joint sittings and other constitutional issues. Balfour proposed that if the Lords were twice to reject a Home Rule Bill, it should be put to a referendum. Lloyd George, though admitting this was reasonable, said the government could not agree. To do so would suggest constitutional legislation differed from other legislation, which the Liberals would not concede on grounds of precedent. Asquith told the King on 14 October that the climate of the meetings had changed, and the chances of success had faded. 'I quite recognise,' the King told him, 'that the point of divergence that has now been reached is a most critical one.'[92]

Asquith showed sufficient interest in coalition – perhaps to appease the King – to charge Lloyd George with asking Crewe how far 'the settlement of the education and Welsh Church questions was a necessary preliminary to any coalition.'[93] Lloyd George did so with enthusiasm, seeking 'a wide programme of National reconstruction' through co-operation. Crewe was keen too, not least because 'we have pretty nearly got to the end of our tether as regards great reforms on party lines.'[94] The King had hoped the participants would see sense after a fortnight's adjournment; but then the other supposed points of agreement began to crumble. On 10 November 1910, after twenty-one meetings, the conference broke down. Britain was in the worst constitutional crisis in living memory. Downing Street issued a statement, and election fever broke out in the press.

The Lords wanted to debate the Parliament Bill, which had passed in the Commons. Lansdowne and his colleagues wished to advance separate proposals to prove they were happy with some reform, both of the powers of the House and of its composition. But these would be of a dilute sort unconscionable to the Liberals, and designed to engineer a symbolic government defeat. As Crewe put it: 'Our bill, we understood from the first, is to be killed. It does not matter to us whether its throat is cut or it is smothered in cotton wool.'[95] The government, unsurprisingly, wished to avoid such a debate, and on the day of the last meeting of the conference the cabinet agreed to ask the King to dissolve parliament. There was a delay while he was consulted. The impasse triggered a riot of rumour and counter-rumour – including one that a coalition would be formed without Asquith and led by Balfour and Lloyd George. Balfour, who wanted no part of any 'intrigue' by the ambitious Chancellor, scotched the idea.[96]

Asquith saw the King at Sandringham on 11 November – a journey *The Times* said proved the 'gravity' of the crisis – and told him that, as this would be the second election in a year, a final settlement had to be reached: matters could not go on like this.[97] That, he warned him, could entail the exercise of the prerogative; though the King seems not to have grasped this at first, thanks to the obliqueness of Asquith's language. Nor does Asquith seem to have impressed upon the King his duty, as a constitutional monarch, to accept his prime minister's advice; perhaps Asquith knew Knollys (whom the King had inherited from his father), and Knollys's views on the matter, so well that he felt he did not need to force the issue.

Four days later Asquith sent the King, who had been brooding, a note in the name of the cabinet advising a dissolution: but, as a concession to the Unionists, allowing a debate in the Lords on the possible reforms. The King finally grasped what might be expected of him. On 16 November, when the Lords met to demand a chance to discuss the proposed reforms, the air was already thick with rumours of dissolution. That afternoon Asquith and Crewe went to Buckingham Palace for a lengthy discussion with the King, who tried to find an alternative course to Asquith's advice to threaten use of the prerogative.

When no alternative could be found – though Asquith stressed that the threat ought to be enough, and the mass creation would not be necessary – the King asked him whether he would have given the same advice to Edward VII. Asquith replied: 'Yes, sir, and your father would have consented.'[98] Thus the King agreed, reluctantly, to accept the advice, provided the Lords could discuss the Parliament Bill before the end of the session. Asquith agreed, and promised to keep the conversation private and the King out of politics. He duly announced the dissolution two days later. The secret was well kept: Balfour did not find out that this gun was pointed at his head until the following summer. Asquith's only other option would have been to resign and have the King send for Balfour: but such an administration would never have won a vote in the Commons, so a dissolution would happen anyway. An immediate one seemed to Asquith cleaner and less likely to harm the King. Knollys knew Balfour was willing to form a government and then seek a dissolution, but, crucially, kept that to himself.

In the Lords debate about reforming the relationship between the two Houses, Lansdowne advanced his own proposals, identical to those offered during the conference. The sticking point remained the Liberals' refusal to allow different treatment for 'constitutional' Bills; but it was widely noted that the previous reluctance to contemplate reform of any sort had been tempered, and some form of compromise appeared in sight. In fact, more and more Unionists – Balfour chief among them – were realising they were in a fight they could not win, and the time for heroic obduracy was over. The Lords passed a resolution by Rosebery calling for a reformed House, partly composed of hereditary peers elected by their own number, partly of appointees, and partly some sitting by virtue of their office. A version of this plan was finally implemented in 1999.

The idea of a referendum on constitutional matters formed a key part of the Unionists' election programme. Asquith concentrated in his campaign on the importance of establishing a *modus vivendi* for the Lords that would ensure Bills such as on Home Rule and Welsh disestablishment – Bills for which the Tories argued there was no public support – could be passed. He mocked the reform plans of the Unionists as vague and the work of 'constitutional jerry-builders'.[99]

Northcliffe, his eye as usual on Berlin and the war he was certain the Germans wished against Britain, told Balfour: 'I notice, from a careful study of the German Press – of what it is printing and also what it is not printing – that our friends across the North Sea are in no wise slackening their preparations, while we are amusing ourselves with an unnecessary

General Election.'[100] The electoral weapon of the popular press was solidly against the Liberals. Balfour replied that he shared Northcliffe's concerns, and waited to see whether the government were 'more afraid of the Germans or of their own tail – an unhappy position for the rulers of a great country!'[101] Balfour had his own troubles, however, of which occasional confidants such as Northcliffe were largely unaware: the opposition to him within his own party, provoked by hard-liners who wanted to oppose the Parliament Bill to the bitter end, had been further deepened by his referendum proposal.

There was dissension in the Liberal ranks too. Violet Asquith, the prime minister's daughter, said she 'heaved over' the report of a speech by Lloyd George that she accounted 'one of his very worst', which he had made in a music hall in Mile End, a short distance from his Limehouse triumph, on 21 November, just as the Lords debated the Parliament Bill.[102] As an exercise in crude class war it could hardly be bettered. There was a reference to 'the peerages created to ennoble the indiscretions of kings', to the Lords being inferior to 'a senate of kangaroos' and, most crowd-pleasing of all, 'aristocracy is like cheese – the older it is the higher it becomes.'[103] The speech – again disrupted by suffragettes – prompted *The Times*, under Northcliffe's ownership and lacking the restraint of old, to brand Lloyd George a 'demagogue'. It argued that, like all such people, the Chancellor had tried to gain respectability by packing his platform with local worthies: and added that 'we understand that the sheer brutality and stupidity of his vituperation of aristocrats and owners of land yesterday made an impression not altogether agreeable upon those behind him.'[104]

The speech created huge strains between Lloyd George and Asquith. A week after it the Chancellor received a letter from Margot Asquith, who instructed him: 'Dont [sic] when you speak on platforms arouse what is low and sordid and violent in yr audience; it hurts those members of it that are fighting these elections with the noblest desire to see fair play . . . If yr speeches hurt and alienated lords it wd not perhaps so much matter – but they hurt and offend not only the King and men of high estate but quite poor men, Liberals of all sorts – they lose us votes.'[105] Although Mrs Asquith signed off 'Yrs in affectionate sincerity', Lloyd George was outraged. He suspected Asquith's hand in it: but the Liberal chief whip, the Master of Elibank, said the prime minister had been as surprised by the letter as anyone. It did, however, betray concerns aired between the Asquiths in private, and revealed serious tensions within the government; she had written months earlier to Churchill in similar terms.

VI

The election result was almost identical to its predecessor: the Liberals lost two seats and the Unionists one, leaving them at 272 and 271 MPs respectively. Again, the Unionists won the popular vote, a performance that caused Curzon, at a private lunch of Unionist candidates and MPs hosted by Lord Willoughby de Broke, to continue to mock the idea of the deployment of the prerogative and to advise his comrades 'to fight in the last ditch and let them make their peers if they dared': a phrase that would return to haunt him, and his party.[106] Redmond's Irishmen – seventy-four MPs – were again in the driving seat.

On 3 January 1911 Churchill wrote to Asquith to advise him 'as early as possible to make it clear that we are not a bit afraid of creating 500 peers – if necessary.'[107] Asquith had groundwork to do before he could be so belligerent. A week later Knollys, accompanied by Esher, entertained Balfour and his private secretary, J. S. Sandars, to dinner. Knollys drew Balfour out on the constitutionality of the Royal prerogative's use to create hundreds of peers – without mentioning the King's agreement to do just that if necessary – and Balfour helpfully admitted that the King could, if he wished, do so. At the end of the dinner Knollys casually remarked that it had happened with Asquith's knowledge and approval, and that what had been said at it would be reported to him.

The conversation should not have been a complete surprise to Balfour, though that 'everything I said in the freedom of friendly conversation was to be repeated to [Asquith]' was, as he noted later.[108] A fortnight earlier he had told Lansdowne he thought the pressure put on Asquith by the Irish and the Labour party would make him seek promises from the King that were against the spirit of the constitution. 'This is not,' Balfour said, 'a demand which a Constitutional Ministry should make of a Constitutional Sovereign.'[109] When Balfour realised what had happened he complained bitterly to Sir Arthur Bigge, with Knollys now joint private secretary to the King: 'Do you think it is fair that I should be asked to discuss public affairs, under circumstances which implied freedom and confidence, with an ambassador by whom I was deliberately kept in ignorance of the most essential features of the situation?'[110]

Lansdowne saw the King at Windsor on 27 January, Asquith having lifted an objection to the King talking to opposition leaders – the monarch had insisted that all he wanted was to hear their views, not seek advice. Lansdowne expressed his view, which was that it would be undesirable for the King to create 500 or so peers, but he should not assume the Lords would relieve him of this obligation: 'I gathered that Lord Knollys had told HM that he was under the impression that the Lords would in no circumstances push the King to extremities.' He was keen to disabuse the Sovereign of this, not least, one imagines, to inspire him to resist pressure from Asquith to do it.[111]

When the King opened parliament on 6 February he said that 'proposals will be submitted to you without delay for settling the relations between the two Houses of Parliament, with the object of securing the more effective working of the constitution.'[112] Asquith reintroduced the Parliament Bill on 21 February. He summarised the problem: there were around 600 peers, and when one subtracted the Bench of Bishops and some cross-benchers, around 500 of the remaining 570 were Unionists. The Lords had, he said, 'committed political suicide' on 30 November 1909, in rejecting the Budget.[113] He opposed legislating by referendum: 'we are invited to adopt . . . the principles of the Jacobins and the Napoleons, and substitute them for the well-established doctrine of the English Constitution. That is what Toryism has come to!'[114]

Balfour's view – based on what, it was unclear – was that while voters had shown in two elections that they wanted a change in the relations between the two houses, they did not wish for the one now being proposed. He called the Parliament Bill 'an instrument of revolution'; but, more contentiously, argued that change was being forced through 'not at the bidding of a real majority of this House, but at the bidding of what after all is a minority, though an important minority, coming from Ireland, and openly announcing how little they care for our institutions'.[115] Unwisely, he left little room for a later change of mind: 'We will have no part or lot with your plans, and we should think ourselves disgraced for ever if we gave our consent to it.'[116] This, though, was mild compared to what some of his followers felt: F. E. Smith, in a typically blistering performance, voiced outrage at the government's attempt to destroy the Second Chamber – the barrister's trick of putting the other side completely in the wrong was a staple of his rhetoric – and warned Asquith that 'nearly half the people of this country will support us in any resistance, however desperate, to your proposals.'[117]

By the time the second reading debate began in the Commons on 27 February the belligerence was slightly toned down, not least because the Unionists wished to appear credible when speaking of compromise. Lord Ronaldshay claimed that the 'fundamental objection' his party now had was that, if passed, the Bill 'will deprive the people of this country of an effective Second Chamber.'[118] This illustrated the continuing gulf between the parties: the Unionists' definition of 'effective' was a chamber that enabled them to defeat the elected government when its policies differed from their own.

The Bill had its second reading on 2 March by 366 votes to 243 and went into committee on 3 April. Attempts were made to amend it so it could not be used to grant Home Rule for Ireland, or Welsh disestablishment, or even the abolition of the monarchy. The pressure began to tell on the Liberal ministers. Asquith was resorting to the bottle more and more: Churchill, who could drink for England, told his wife on 22 April he had 'squirmed with embarrassment' at the state the prime minister had been in.[119] He noted that until dinner 'he is at his best – but thereafter! It is an awful pity, & only the persistent freemasonry of the House of Commons prevents a scandal.'

A more moderate section of Unionist peers, led by Curzon – whose sudden alertness to the dangers of the Lords overriding the Commons now far exceeded that of almost all his colleagues – and with the backing of the shadow cabinet, proposed plans for a reformed House. Lansdowne introduced a Bill on the subject on 8 May. It proposed a chamber of 350 men, 100 of whom would be peers elected by a panel of other peers, 120 of whom would be elected by the House of Commons, 100 of whom would be appointed by the Crown in proportion to the strength of parties in the Commons, and the rest judges and bishops. Had it been enacted, the Bill would have killed the hereditary principle. Lansdowne was heard in what his biographer, Lord Newton, called 'frigid silence'.[120] Many peers who rarely attended parliament made their objections known, and would be the main block to any resolution of the crisis. Divorced from much of public opinion – the election suggested that half of Britain, and nearly all of Ireland, were against them – and an increasing embarrassment to their leaders because of their hostility to democracy, they were branded 'backwoodsmen', 'diehards' and 'last ditchers', due to their keenness to die in that mythical place.

The Parliament Bill had its third reading on 15 May and was sent, intact, to the Lords. Morley – now Viscount Morley of Blackburn – in proposing the second reading on 23 May, illustrated the full head-in-the-sand nature of resistance to the Bill. Many Unionists, he said, did not want the measure because it would allow the Irish Home Rule, the Welsh disestablishment, the Scots to shape land law and, perhaps worst of all, the Labour interest to influence the rights of property and capital. Such 'open antagonism' of these important sectional interests would cause terrible divisions within the Kingdom and destabilise society: but that was what the diehards could not, or would not, comprehend. Peaceful completion of the long drawn-out transition from a feudal to a democratic society was at stake.[121] Without describing the means by which this would be achieved, Morley said the Lords would have to surrender their veto. A substantial hard core of Unionists decided there would now have to be a fight to the death, and they were prepared to have it.

However, Unionist peers were sufficiently nervous about the effect of defeating the Bill that on 29 May it had an unopposed second reading. This allowed the Lords to pick at it in committee and, if necessary, to defeat it on third reading. After George V's Coronation on 22 June the committee began scrutiny. It reported on 13 July, an occasion marked by an early contribution from Halsbury. He warned the government that just because the Bill had had a second reading did not mean it would get a third. It was radically amended in committee, hardly to the government's surprise but much to its annoyance. The Lords wanted a separate tribunal, not the Speaker of the Commons, to decide what was a money Bill. It proposed a new category of Bill to be settled by referendum: an example was any measure on Irish Home Rule. Asquith described the amendments as leaving the Bill 'transformed as if no General Election had been held'.[122] Those in the last ditch simply did not believe he would ask the King for a mass creation of peers, and a slowly diminishing number were prepared to call his bluff.

There were still Unionists who bitterly opposed even an amended Bill, notably Halsbury, who said that by voting against it 'I should believe that I was doing no trifling service and incurring no trifling obligation, but I should regard it as a duty, and a solemn duty, to God and to my country.'[123] The overheated rhetoric suggested the pathetic fallacy: by mid-July England was in the grip of the greatest heatwave in living memory; day after day the temperature was in the high eighties or low nineties in London, the sun shone almost continuously, and the whole pattern of life changed. Halsbury did not, however, force a vote on the third reading; the Bill was passed and sent back to the Commons.

On 14 July Asquith sent a cabinet minute to the King, branding the amendments 'destructive to the principle and purpose' of the Bill.[124] He warned the King that the Commons would reject them, creating deadlock. There having been two elections on the issue, 'a third Dissolution is wholly out of the question.' Therefore, he concluded, 'it will be the duty of Ministers to advise the Crown to exercise its Prerogative so as to get rid of the deadlock and secure the passing of the Bill.' That could mean only one thing. 'In such circumstances,' Asquith concluded, minatorily, 'Ministers cannot entertain any doubt that their sovereign would feel it to be his constitutional duty to accept their advice.' The King brooded for three days, and accepted the advice: if he wished to stay on his throne, he had no choice.

The day before that decision was relayed to Asquith, Balfour wrote to Lady Elcho – the bosom friend since the mid-1880s who may also have been his mistress – that 'I learn . . . that the govt exacted pledges about Peers from the K *before* the last election – a shocking scandal.'[125] Esher had told Balfour the truth on 6 July, and he and senior colleagues had discussed the ramifications the next day. With that intelligence, Balfour realised there was but one choice: to vote for the Bill as presented by the Commons, or reject it and risk a mass creation of peers. Balfour was not sure what the King's guarantee entailed: whether he would create 500 peers (the number bandied about in the salons of London), which would put the Lords under permanent Liberal control, or a smaller number sufficient to pass the Parliament Bill and leave the Lords subject to ebbs and flows of opinion. On 18 July, the day after the King had agreed to use his prerogative, Lloyd George told Balfour and Lansdowne the news, and Knollys confirmed it to Lansdowne the next day. Lloyd George also told him the government was reluctant to create peers, but could not see its Bill defeated.

Then, on the 20th, Asquith wrote formally to Balfour and Lansdowne to confirm that 'should the necessity arise, the Government will advise the King to exercise his prerogative to secure the passing into law of the

Bill in substantially the same form in which it left the House of Commons, and His Majesty has been pleased to signify that he will consider it his duty to accept and act on that advice.'[126] In a bellicose editorial ringing with Northcliffe's voice, *The Times* accused Asquith of being manipulated by Redmond. The paper said the prime minister 'has played a contemptible part in subservience to an avowedly disloyal faction, and his present *coup d'état* puts the seal on his dishonour.'[127] The government would announce on the 24th its plan to proceed with the Lords' amendments, but would delay the process to allow negotiations – not so much between the parties as within the Unionist camp.

The two Unionist leaders accepted the inevitable, and that it would be worse for new peers to swamp the Lords. However, the diehards dug themselves into the last ditch. They attacked Balfour, whose leadership was crumbling. Lansdowne's health was cracking under the strain. There were what Balfour termed 'violent differences' in the shadow cabinet about what the peers should do.[128] 'I personally don't much care what they do, provided they do not compel the creation of a number so great as more or less permanently to destroy such power as the House still possesses,' he told Mary Elcho on 23 July. He said he and Lansdowne, who agreed with him, were both being branded 'cowards', their internal opponents recalling the ferocity with which the leaders had earlier opposed the Bill, but recognising none of the practicalities that had caused them to temper that opposition. By this stage both men had lost control of the party they purported to lead, with the diehards – unused as most were to participating in politics – utterly unresponsive to reason. Most of Balfour's colleagues thought he was against any further opposition to the Bill. His private opinion, expressed on 21 July, was that 150 peers would be enough to make the House more responsive to the democratic climate.

Also on that date, 170 Unionist peers met in the ballroom of Lansdowne House in Berkeley Square. According to the well-briefed *Times* correspondent, the meeting was 'at times of a stormy character'.[129] Lansdowne outlined the arguments for and against voting down the Bill, coming out in favour of letting it pass. Lords Selborne, Halsbury, Salisbury, Willoughby de Broke and the Duke of Bedford all spoke forcefully against surrender. It was St Aldwyn, one of the longest-serving former ministers, who brought the meeting back down to earth by saying the Bill would eventually pass come what may, so it was best to avoid the 'deplorable consequences' of a mass creation. 'Although we might be applauded for our courage if we "died in the last ditch", the deliberate judgment of the country, when it had had time to reflect, would be against us.'[130] Lansdowne noted this 'produced a deep impression', as did a similar speech by Curzon. Lansdowne's allies felt he mishandled the meeting, by allowing the diehards to 'raise the standard of revolt', as Lord Newton put it, by encouraging them to express their opinions.[131] Curzon thought so too, and took some moderates to his house to plot how they could reduce the diehard numbers: Lansdowne seemed to have lost the energy for the fight.

Normal relations between Liberals and Tories broke down: the Tories felt there had been bad faith over the guarantees, something for which, given Knollys's role, there was some justification. Balfour refused to meet Asquith or members of his family socially, even turning down an invitation to Downing Street to meet the King and Queen, just after the Coronation, until told by Knollys it would be regarded as an unacceptable breach of protocol. Relations with some in his own party became even worse than those with the Liberals. Balfour's sense of humour had not entirely vanished: he was highly amused that Halsbury, who was eighty-seven, had told Lansdowne he would refuse to serve in another Tory ministry. On 22 July – the hottest day for thirty years, with the thermometer reaching 93 degrees in London – Asquith had a forty-minute audience of the King. He briefed him on how he would proceed when parliament met two days later, when he would outline how he would ensure the Parliament Bill was carried. Indicating the gravity of the crisis, the King contemplated cancelling his annual jaunts to Goodwood and Cowes.

On the day the Lords' amendments came before the Commons – 24 July – Curzon, now the leading moderate Unionist peer, publicly recanted his earlier pledge to die in the last ditch. In a letter to *The Times* he said it was time that Unionists, despite their detestation of the Parliament Bill, should state publicly why they did not endorse the diehards' tactics. He had succeeded the previous day in persuading Northcliffe of the sense of this position, and *The Times*'s conversion was crucial to the eventual avoidance of a *débâcle*. The diehards' plan to vote down the Bill would, he said, 'be fraught with serious injury to the interests both of our party and of the State.'[132] He said it should be the first priority of a Unionist government to remove the enacted Bill from the statute book. The Bill was certain to pass, and all that remained to be discussed was whether it did so with or without a mass creation of peers.

Curzon did not want the mass creation, for the peers could vote on much more than just the Parliament Bill – notably Home Rule and disestablishment. 'I see no surrender in refraining from pressing resistance when one knows resistance to be futile.' By voting down the Bill, he argued, 'we confer, so far as I can see, no single benefit, present or prospective, on the nation. We merely expose it to a new chapter of Constitutional outrage.' In a tone that suggested exasperation, he asked: 'It is bad enough that they [the Liberals] already have a large majority in the House of Commons. Where is either the expediency, or the common sense, or the public advantage of presenting them with a second majority in the House of Lords?'

Later that day there occurred one of the most remarkable scenes in the history of parliament: the unprecedented refusal to hear a prime minister. From the moment of Asquith's entry into the chamber his supporters cheered him and his opponents yelled at him so violently that the Speaker had to ask them to control themselves. As Asquith rose to speak some Unionist MPs, led by Lord Hugh Cecil, howled him down with cries of 'traitor'.[133] For half an hour the Speaker tried to restore calm: then members rose repeatedly to make points of order. Cecil continued to yell at Asquith: the shorthand reporters from Hansard could not catch his torrent of abuse, which included his acquitting himself of discourtesy since Asquith had 'prostituted ordinary Parliamentary usage'.[134] Then F. E. Smith, who in the Coronation honours had been made a privy counsellor on Asquith's recommendation, showed gratitude has its limits. He accused the government of having 'degraded the political life of the country'.[135] The Speaker rejected the points of order; he asked Asquith to speak, but then Sir Edward Carson, the leading Irish Unionist, tried to move the adjournment. That too was rejected, and as Asquith started again Will Crooks, a Labour MP, observed that 'many a man has been certified as insane for less than half of what the Noble Lord [Cecil] has done this afternoon'; which, from a cooper to the son of a marquess, managed in its perceived insolence to silence Cecil for a few moments.

Asquith said that but for the death of Edward VII the matter would probably have been resolved in the last session. 'Leave out the King,' shouted a Tory MP. 'Who killed him?'[136] Asquith was told that England was against him, in that he had to rely on Irish votes to pass the Bill. He ploughed on with his speech, under a constant barrage of abuse, notably cries of 'Redmond! Redmond!' He reached his main point before inviting the House to consider the Lords' amendments. 'A situation has been created from which there is only one constitutional way of escape, and that is unless the House of Lords will consent to restore this Bill, if you like with reasonable Amendments consistent with its principle and purpose, we shall be compelled to invoke and exercise the Prerogative of the Crown. I am anxious not to do so, but if we are forced – it is the determination of the Government, and, as I believe, the vast majority of the people of this country, that without further delay this Bill should take its place on the Statute Book.'[137] Asquith had his speech, largely undelivered, circulated to the newspapers, who printed it the next day, revealing the intention to use the Royal prerogative. Hansard did not record, but the newspapers did, his final remark: 'I am not going to degrade myself or my office by attempting to say more in an assembly that will not hear me.'[138]

Balfour expressed his regret at the scene, all the more sincere because his supporters had orchestrated it. The freelance behaviour of men such as Smith, Cecil and Chamberlain showed a generational revolt against Balfour and his dilute brand of Toryism; an idea of 'what we have, we hold' had taken root among these men and their friends, and made Balfour and them incompatible. He was losing control of his party, and next day would publish an open letter in which he urged support of Lansdowne's line, for the avoidance of doubt.

On 30 July he told Mary Elcho that 'fragments of the Unionist party seem to have gone temporarily crazy . . . as usual the leading lunatics are my own kith and kin' – a reference to his cousins Salisbury, Lords Hugh and Robert Cecil, and Selborne, who had signalled their willingness to fight to the death.[139] He asked for a settlement 'without a revolution, without compelling the King to destroy the whole system under which the House of Lords exists.'[140] But it was too late, and he knew it. All he could do was accuse Asquith of having 'arrogated to himself, by the advice which he has given to the Crown, powers which no Republican dictator in the world possesses . . . he has put himself above the Constitution.' Asquith retorted, fairly, that he was merely seeking powers that existed for any Tory prime minister: it was this levelling of the playing field that so many Unionists violently objected to. Once

Balfour had finished, and Grey had spoken briefly, Smith rose; but Liberals and Irish Nationalists shouted him down so volubly that the Speaker suspended the sitting because of grave disorder.

The Tory press tried to defend the scene. A *Times* correspondent wrote that 'the young Conservatives, devoted to the Crown and the Constitution, hate and detest this combination of trickery and tyranny, and they have taken the only means that lay to hand to show the Government the nature and depth of their feeling.'[141] The paper's leading article began by announcing that 'we deeply deplore the conduct of a portion of the Opposition' but added that 'the action of the Prime Minister throughout this controversy has been eminently calculated to provoke and to exasperate angry passions in the breasts of his opponents.'[142] Having kicked Asquith, the paper hoped cooler heads would prevail, taking the line that Curzon had advocated, and which was Lansdowne's and Balfour's official position. Indeed, so zealous was Curzon's conversion that he felt the party should sympathise with any Unionist who voted with the government, rather than took the official line of abstaining.

Despite the Unionist leadership's efforts, it seemed Halsbury's faction was growing: even two party whips in the Lords were said to be about to defect to it. On the evening of 25 July, the day Balfour's open letter appeared, he was undermined by a 'No Surrender' banquet in Halsbury's honour, at which (among others) Austen Chamberlain, Carson, Smith, Selborne and Halsbury spoke. All expressed their complete respect for Balfour and Lansdowne, but all expressed a determination to fight to the bitter end. Curzon tried to assess numbers, and it seemed that abstention might not be enough, given the strength of Halsbury's support: forty or fifty peers might have to vote for the government, and were lined up to do so. Balfour had talks with Lord Stamfordham – as Bigge had become in the Coronation honours – about what the King was prepared to do: he had heard from Salisbury, his cousin, that Stamfordham had expressed the opinion that '120 peers' would be sufficient to pass the Bill.[143]

Stamfordham declined to be drawn, saying it was 'not true' he had expressed a view.[144] He did say that 'the King never undertook to create an unlimited number of peers with a view to establishing a permanent Government majority in the House of Lords' – just enough to pass the Bill. This angered Balfour. 'Your reply seems quite clear,' he responded. 'It means, does it not, that whatever number of Peers were required to pass the Bill, that number would be created, even though the creation had the effect of flooding the House with 400 new members.'[145] Stamfordham denied this too, and wrote to Salisbury to tell him he had misunderstood a conversation he had had with the King on 22 July: the argument, between the leader of the opposition and the King's private secretary, showed how febrile matters had become. Knollys told Churchill – who had further complicated matters by suggesting, wrongly, that the King was party to the government's plans on Irish Home Rule – that 'the King stands in a very helpless and peculiar position, as he is unable to defend himself'.[146]

The amendments were not considered until 8 August, a day after the government survived a vote of censure over what the Unionists considered the constitutional outrage of advising the King to create hundreds of peers – Churchill, speaking in the debate, had specified perhaps 400 or 500. The debate was partly a cry of frustration, partly an opportunity for the Unionist leadership to state the reasons it objected to the government's strategy, and to accuse ministers of having put the King in an impossible position. The Commons duly overturned the amendments, apart from one preventing the Bill from applying to any attempt to extend the life of parliament beyond five years. It conceded that the Speaker could consult two senior colleagues in deciding what was a money Bill. On the boiling afternoon of 9 August the Bill was back in the Lords. It was time for the final decision: to pass it, or to veto it and await the destruction of the House of Lords. Many Unionist peers had signalled they had no wish to commit suicide. Lansdowne had pledges to abstain from 320, and Morley had 80 Liberals to vote for the Bill. It was set to be so close that it seemed impossible to predict the outcome. Curzon had been assiduous in trying to persuade peers with no party affiliation to vote for the government.

Lansdowne was determined to take defeat with dignity. 'We may be worsted in this encounter,' he said, 'but we are not going to be annihilated, and when our turn comes it will be our business to rebuild upon the ruins of the Constitution which you have wrecked a new Constitution more appropriate to the spirit of the age . . . In that great task we shall want all our resources, all our fighting strength, and above all a united Party. It is because I hope that in this great struggle your Lordships' House will play an honourable and momentous part that I do not want to see it now weakened and discredited by such a use of the Royal

Prerogative as that for which His Majesty's Government have now, in our opinion most improperly, obtained the consent of the Crown.'[147]

Halsbury felt he was being scapegoated for having been the figurehead of the resistance. He signalled his refusal to obey, comparing the government to a highwayman, and persisting in what should by then have been his unwarranted belief that the threat of a mass creation was a bluff. 'Nothing in the world,' he said, 'will induce me to vote for a Bill or to abstain from not voting against a Bill which I believe to be wrong and immoral and a scandalous example of legislation.'[148] Thus a peer of first creation, the son of a newspaper editor, was determined to die in battle while some of ancient lineage ran up the white flag. The Cecils remained steadfast, however: Salisbury said he would vote against the Bill, whatever the consequences.

Another peer of first creation, St Aldwyn, took on Halsbury, disputing his assertion that a defeat would 'kill the Bill'.[149] So did Curzon. Rosebery, an even sterner critic of the government, took the same view. This was the dead end the Unionists had reached, thanks to the King's having realised – with the help of Knollys, who in the Coronation honours had been elevated to a viscountcy – that if his prime minister asked him to create several hundred peers he had, in the circumstances of the unelected House's continued defiance of the elected one, no choice. Moreover, some peers began to feel it their patriotic duty to renounce their veto, because they believed ridicule would fall on the King if they did not. An almost tragic scene unfolded, of one Unionist peer after another expressing utter hatred of the Bill, only to end by admitting they would be voting for it.

Yet it seemed when the debate adjourned on 9 August that there were still too many who doubted the threat of a mass creation, and the government and Unionist leaders panicked. The King was asked to approve a statement, to be read out in the House by Morley, outlining the consequences of defeat in unequivocal terms. He readily agreed, and during the second day of debate – the hottest day for seventy years, with the temperature reaching 98 degrees in the shade – Morley said: 'if the Bill should be defeated tonight His Majesty would assent to a creation of Peers sufficient in number to guard against any possible combination of the different parties in opposition by which the Parliament Bill might again be exposed a second time to defeat.'[150] He stressed he said this for the avoidance of doubt, in case anyone thought the threat was 'merely made in order to inspire your Lordships with fear.' In case the message still had not sunk in – and Morley singled out Willoughby de Broke as one who still struggled to believe it – he stressed that 'every vote given tonight against my motion . . . is a vote given in favour of a large and prompt creation of Peers.'[151] Selborne, perhaps affected by the heat, could still not take it in, so Morley read it out again.

Curzon's speech, on 10 August, was addressed to the shrinking number who still followed Halsbury. It was a heartfelt plea to understand not just the inevitability of defeat, but also the extent of its consequences. He begged them to avoid 'the pollution . . . the degradation of this House' with a vote that would have 'the effect of covering it with ridicule and of destroying its power for good in the future.'[152] He continued: 'All I want is that your Lordships should clearly realise the responsibility you are assuming in this matter, because it may be that by a small majority, a majority of two or three or four of that small minority, you may impose upon the Government a course of action which may have a profound effect on the whole future of this country. I do not suppose a more momentous Division will ever have taken place in the House of Lords. It is possible that as a result of this Division 400 Peers may be created. If that is done, the Constitution is gone as we have known it. We start afresh to build up a new Constitution. God knows how we shall do it.' There was even more emotion from the diehards. Selborne asked moments before the vote: 'Shall we perish in the dark by our own hand, or in the light, killed by our enemies? For us the choice is easy.'[153]

A speech by the Archbishop of Canterbury, saying he would vote with the government because of 'the callousness – I had almost said levity – with which some noble Lords seem to contemplate the creation of some five hundred new Peers, a course of action which would make this House, and indeed our country, the laughing-stock of the British Dominions beyond the seas', brought thirteen bishops into the government's lobby. Thirty-seven Unionists followed them. The organised abstention helped the government win by 131 votes to 114. When Curzon, whose role had been crucial, went into the Carlton Club that evening he was greeted with cries of 'shame' and 'Judas!' He had abstained, feeling as a shadow cabinet member that he could not support the government: but many of his comrades identified him as the main reason for the weakening of Tory resolve, and a main agent of the defeat. He was accused of having changed his mind for reasons of snobbery, a charge for which there is no real evidence, but which shows the depth of the outrage he had provoked. His sometime friend George Wyndham, who knew a thing or two about snobbery – he once declined the offer of a Companionship of the Order of the Bath from Edward VII because he felt it was not commensurate with his idea of his social position – claimed Curzon 'could not bear to have his order contaminated with the new creations.'[154]

Balfour's mental exhaustion and disgust with politics was shown by his decision not to change his holiday plans, but to leave for the continent before the final vote. He told Mary Elcho by letter from Paris on 11 August that 'politics have been to me quite unusually odious', and that he had 'felt the situation more acutely than any in my public life – I mean from the *personal* point of view.'[155] His failure for so long to take a formal position on the question had infuriated his colleagues and turned some against him. 'Was ever a Party so badly led as ours on this occasion?' asked Chamberlain.[156] Asquith gave credit for the victory to Lloyd George, writing to him on 20 August that 'I cannot sufficiently express to you how strongly I feel the debt of obligation which I myself, and all our colleagues, owe to you for the indomitable purpose, the untiring energy, and the matchless skill with which you have brought to a settlement one of the most formidable problems we have had, as a Government, to confront.'[157] Any doubt about Asquith's natural successor appeared to be over.

Balfour's resignation as leader on 8 November had been expected, and a 'Balfour must go' campaign orchestrated by Leo Maxse, editor of the *National Review*, had not helped. Balfour showed his mettle in this personal defeat. Having announced his resignation to a meeting in his constituency, the City of London, he observed: 'I really think I must ask Leo Maxse to dinner tonight, for we are probably the two happiest men in London.'[158] Nor was it only Balfour and his party who were wounded: the King felt injured by oblique criticism of him voiced by some Unionists, though there was no lasting damage.

Earlier that year Northcliffe and Max Aitken – a Unionist MP who in January 1911 secretly invested in the *Daily Express* and would later, as Lord Beaverbrook, become its proprietor – made common cause. On 5 February Aitken wrote to Northcliffe that 'Chamberlain yesterday and Garvin today show you that our Party is in the clouds and many will be grateful if it is brought to solid earth.'[159] Aitken pushed his fellow

Canadian, Bonar Law, for the Unionist leadership when Balfour went, enlisting Northcliffe and his newspapers in support. Both men backed Imperial Preference, and among other factors saw the possibility of a Canadian prime minister of Britain as a way of binding more firmly to the mother country one of the main dominions. When Law took over in November 1911 Northcliffe told Aitken: 'I am very pleased that our prospective new leader is a Canadian . . . on the two occasions I saw Bonar Law I liked him immensely: and I do not suppose that I shall have any difficulty in giving him my full support, though I am not, as you know, a strict Party man.' Aitken arranged for Law to lunch with Northcliffe in December, and the bond was formed.

Asquith's biographer, J. A. Spender, found in his subject's papers after his death in 1928 a list of over 200 people who would have gone to the Lords had the vote gone the other way; a couple of dozen privy counsellors, a dozen and a half Liberal MPs and almost every Liberal baronet thus far unennobled; but also the Lord Mayor of London, heirs to peerages, younger sons of peers – such as Bertrand Russell and Esher's brother – soldiers, academics, retired diplomats and businessmen, such as Sir Thomas Lipton, the tea magnate, Joseph Rowntree, and Sir Abe Bailey, the diamond miner. But on the list there were also figures from more rarefied walks of life: Gilbert Murray, J. M. Barrie, Thomas Hardy and Sir Hubert Parry: and Spender. One wonders how many pangs of wistfulness there were when that list turned up.[160]

The Liberals had prevailed: but it was never glad confident morning again. The party had won its last general election. The three years until war broke out saw one desperate crisis after another. As George Dangerfield said of Asquith and his friends in his immortal account of the period: 'From that victory they never recovered.'[161]

VII

The extra revenue from taxes was duly put to work in laying the foundations of welfarism. The 1911 National Insurance Act created a contributory state insurance system to provide an income for workers when they were too sick to work, or unemployed, allowing them to escape the provisions of the Poor Law. Germany had had such a scheme since 1884, and Lloyd George had examined it when visiting in 1908; he convinced colleagues Britain should have something similar. Churchill was easily persuaded, as the Webbs had urged state insurance on him in 1908, soon after he went to the Board of Trade. He supported state intervention to alleviate poverty, with no reservations about the redistribution of wealth. He felt Liberalism helped elevate people to greater wealth while socialism depressed more people into poverty. It was a nice point.

Churchill was keen to get his plans for labour exchanges on the statute book, and keen too not to proceed with National Insurance until the Treasury had devised a means of dealing not just with unemployment, but with ill health. His son and biographer, Randolph Churchill, felt the delay 'robbed him in the public mind of a good deal of the credit for unemployment insurance', something he was, with some justification, annoyed about: not least because the credit was taken by someone he regarded as his closest friend in politics.[162] On 22 April 1911 he complained to his wife: 'Lloyd George has practically taken Unemployed Insurance to his own bosom and I am I think effectively elbowed out of this large field in which I gave so much thought and effort.' Churchill had taken a visionary view of the plan, telling Asquith it would 'justify our retention of office'.[163] He sought to persuade him that to emulate Germany would enable Asquith to 'leave a memorial which time will not deface of his administration.' Churchill also believed that an insurance scheme in tandem with labour exchanges would sort out the 'vagrant and the loafer' from the serious workman.[164]

The Act addressed a main fear of working-class, and some middle-class, people, about what happened if income was suddenly cut off. As Gissing had put it: 'To the rich, illness has none of the worst horrors only understood by the poor.'[165] Every employed person between the ages of sixteen and seventy earning under £160 a year was compelled to join. For health care, the worker contributed fourpence a week, his employer threepence and the state twopence. In return, a sick worker could receive ten shillings a week for the first thirteen weeks of an illness and five shillings a week for the next thirteen. He would also receive free medical attention and free medicine, anticipating by nearly forty years the National Health Service for the insured: Lloyd George coined the slogan 'ninepence for fourpence' to persuade workers of the benefits. Their families, unless insured as workers themselves, had to depend upon medical charities, notably local voluntary hospitals. National Insurance committees, including doctors, councillors and charity officials, administered the medical arrangements, which came into force from 15 July 1912.

Workers in seasonal or cyclical industries also paid twopence-halfpenny a week, their employers twopence and the state threepence for unemployment benefit. From 15 January 1913, after a week out of work, the worker could claim a shilling a day for up to fifteen weeks in any one year. Women workers would be eligible for maternity benefits. Unemployment benefit was payable at labour exchanges, so the claimant could, when drawing his money, learn of possible vacancies. By 1913 there were 430 labour exchanges, and 2.3 million insured. The Liberals had passed other measures to improve conditions for working people. The Workmen's Compensation Act of 1906 had provided compensation for industrial diseases or injuries. The Trade Boards Act of 1909 had established boards in certain trades, mostly in textiles and tailoring, to negotiate minimum wage rates with employers. The Shops Act of 1911 allowed a weekly half-day holiday for shop assistants, and prescribed a maximum sixty-hour week. This meant further state intervention in relations between masters and servants, which while not unprecedented – the Factories Acts had been regulating such matters since the 1830s – was beginning profoundly to alter the economic balance. A once *laissez-faire* system was taking on aspects of socialism.

The Liberals had shown their sincerity in matters of social reform not just in measures such as these, and the provision of pensions that had begun the process, but by the lengths to which they had been prepared to go to secure them. They had changed the whole constitutional history of Britain. However, they seem not to have understood the determination of the Tories to avenge their defeat, or of other groups in society that were infected with the desire to secure their rights – notably organised labour, women and the Irish. The defeat of the Lords was but the end of the beginning of their tribulations.

CHAPTER 16

THE GREAT UNREST

I

One of the great social and political changes of the nineteenth century was the rise of the trade union movement. Having begun effectively as an extension of guilds for skilled workers and craftsmen, unions developed by the 1880s into massive machines of organised labour: and what was of most concern to employers and to the ruling class was their embrace of unskilled labour, creating a mass movement that lacked only organisation and coherence before becoming a formidable political weapon. However, in the years before the Great War it achieved that status, thanks to the leadership of charismatic tribunes in the unions and in the Labour party, whose very existence became key to the workers gaining political power. The struggle that ensued between labour and capital seemed one neither side could win; but the Labour party's growing strength in the years leading up to the war was owed not least to the sense of resentment, bitterness and anger among many working-class people that grew up because they felt they could not prevail unless politically organised.

The notion that no one could win a fight between labour and capital was the basis of the plot of John Galsworthy's play *Strife*, first performed in 1909 and set in South Wales. The play might lack something in realism: Galsworthy's friend Edward Garnett noted how 'his lower-class poor people are all shown to us through the class-conscious eyes of the gentleman, who, strive as he might, could never forget the double wall of class difference, one of which was kept up . . . by the poor to keep out the rich.'[1] However, the play was a huge success, and it struck a formidable note with the liberal conscience in an era when the rich were certainly getting richer, thanks to the real growth of dividends, but the poor were falling further behind because of a failure to increase real wages.

In the play, the men of the Trenartha Tin Plate Works, which is owned and run by John Anthony, have been on strike for months, during the winter. Their women and children are starting to starve. Both sides are intransigent. One director observes that whatever hardship befalls the men and their families is hardly the management's responsibility. 'We can't go on playing ducks and drakes with the company's prosperity.'[2] Another adds that 'I'm afraid we mustn't base our policy on luxuries like sentiment' when told by Anthony's son, Edgar, that the treatment of the men is 'cruel'. A debate rages between Anthony and Harness, the representative from union headquarters, about what constitutes 'just' behaviour. The union has withheld full support from the men because even it accepts that some of their demands are exorbitant. He urges Anthony to offer concessions if the men agree to withdraw their extreme demands; Anthony's response is to say that if they don't return to work, he will recruit others to do their jobs. A director tells Harness he cannot possibly believe 'all the Socialistic claptrap' about a divergence in the interests of men and owners; Harness's view is that class differences have stopped the directors and shareholders from recognising that the workers are dignified human beings like them.[3] 'Barring the accident of money, aren't they as good men as you?' he asks.[4]

The attitudes highlight a generational problem, and echo the speed of change in Edwardian society. Anthony, who is seventy-six, recalls when hired hands did as they were told and any strike ended with their being starved back to work. The men would have no jobs at all without the employers, in his view, and therefore had to take what they were offered. His son and daughter, having grown up in an age of greater union power, and aware of the steps society has taken to empower the working class through education and a primitive welfare system, are more class-conscious, in that they see an inequality of treatment based on perceptions of social status. Anthony dismisses their views, believing they understand nothing of the realities of business; his children believe he is simply obstinate, a failing of which he accuses the men. He warns his daughter, Enid, that without the 'backbone' to stand up to the men, his children would be reduced to a state of impoverishment within a few years.[5] When Enid tells her father that 'I don't believe in barriers between classes', he listens in disbelief.

Her attempts to help the workers' starving women and children are met with naked hostility. Perceptions of class are even more entrenched among workers than owners. David Roberts, the leading militant in the workforce, tells Anthony that 'from the time that I remember anything ye have been an enemy to every man that has come into your works.'[6] His main complaint is that Anthony has 'grudged them the say of any word in their own fate'. But Roberts is callous towards wives and children, who in the depths of winter are suffering because of their breadwinners' refusal to settle as their union wishes them to. When he announces to his wife his own determination to starve rather than give in, she asks where that leaves the women. His only reply is 'this is not women's work'.[7] Mrs Roberts observes that the women's work is, in fact, to die, and indeed she does.

Both men and masters are divided. Men who would accept the union's more moderate plan are denounced as traitors; the directors who see the matter dragging on until the business implodes turn against Anthony and vote for compromise. He alienates his colleagues by his stubbornness, determined not to accept the changing dynamic of the industrial society that would culminate, forty years later, in nationalisations of businesses such as his. Just as Roberts seems to be engaged in a fight on behalf of the entire working class, Anthony is acting on behalf of his class. At the showdown with his colleagues, he says that 'we owe it to other employers to stand firm.'[8] Both men have an almost terrifying want of sentiment. When Mrs Roberts dies Anthony observes that 'war is war'.[9] Roberts's own bereavement does not divert him from his course, even though his wife had begged him to back down.

Anthony's manservant describes Roberts as 'not one of these 'ere ordinary 'armless Socialists. 'E's violent; got a fire inside 'im.'[10] In a great speech to the men before they reject his obstinacy, Roberts takes an orthodox Marxist view of the struggle. He is engaged in 'the fight o' the country's body and blood against a blood-sucker.'[11] He defines capital as 'a thing that buys the sweat o' men's brows, and the tortures o' their brains, at its own price.'[12] He claims that in return for £700 paid to him over the years for his labour, 'one hundred thousand pounds has been gained by them without the stirring of a finger'. Capital 'is a thing that will take as much and give you as little as it can.' He regards the capitalist class as obsessed with self-interest. It 'will not give one sixpence of its dividends to help you have a better time . . . for all their talk, is there one of them that will consent to another penny on the Income Tax to help the poor?' Capital is 'a white-faced, stony-hearted monster' that he rejoices in seeing hobbled; but what distresses him is his colleagues' reluctance to administer the killer blow.

What they understand better than him, however, in electing to pursue compromise, is that without capital they have no work and will starve for good; just as the directors who out-vote Anthony see that without labour, their goods stop being made and their dividends stop being paid. As Anthony fights for his place on the board and his chairmanship, he becomes ever more intransigent. 'There is only one way of treating "men" – with *the iron hand*,' he warns his directors.[13] He recognises the generational shift, and sees it as decadent. 'The half-and-half manners of this generation have brought all this upon us. Sentiment and softness, and what this young man [his son, Edgar], no doubt, would call his social policy. You can't eat cake and have it! This middle-class sentiment, or socialism, or whatever it may be, is rotten. Masters are masters, men are men! Yield one demand, and they will make it six.'

He identifies his intransigence with Roberts's. 'If I were in *their* place I should be the same. But I am not in their place.' He disclaims any self-interest. 'I am thinking of the future of this country, threatened with the black waters of confusion, threatened with mob government, threatened with what I cannot see.' It was not the Great War that began to upturn the social order; the seeds of revolt were already as well sown in Britain as anywhere else in Europe. The crowning irony of the play is that when a middle way is found, isolating only Anthony and Roberts, it is identical to a formula the union proposed at the opening of hostilities.

Galsworthy knew where the new radical politics was leading. Writing to Millicent Fawcett on 18 August 1912 he told her: 'I fancy the Labour Party can, if they so wish, paralyse and control our politics, after the next General Election, for a long time to come. It seems to me they can stand very much in the position of the Nationalists in the early eighties. I do not know if they intend to do so but I cannot see what is to prevent them if they choose to; and an alliance with the Woman's Movement would give them an additional mastery of the situation.'[14] His intuition about how Labour would advance by forming a coalition of aggrieved minorities was little short of brilliant.

II

As the Independent Labour party and the unions formed a community of interest as a movement, working-class rights became central to British political life. The ILP, led by Keir Hardie, had been born out of strife in the mills of the West Riding in the early 1890s. It had failed to win seats in the 1895 election, partly, it was felt, because of the fragmented nature of the working-class movement. Its membership fell until 1905 and many of its branches became defunct. The Trades Union Congress led the attempt to unify the movement by founding the Labour Representation Committee in 1900. It attempted to unite ILP activists, union men and members of socialist organisations such the Fabians and the Social Democratic Federation, the latter of which was dying. The union movement, by contrast, was expanding: it had around 4.1 million members by 1914.[15] Most were those to whom the rise in British prosperity had dealt a bad hand: the unskilled and women, whose sense of grievance that they were falling behind economically fed their militancy and keenness to strike.

The Labour party was formed from the LRC in 1906 thanks not least to a deal in 1903 between Ramsay MacDonald, the LRC's secretary, and Herbert Gladstone, the Liberals' chief whip. The two parties agreed to give each other a clear run in a few seats at the general election to ensure the Unionist candidate lost. Gladstone, who sent a placeman of George Cadbury, Jesse Herbert, to handle the negotiations – Cadbury was a strong believer in co-operation between the Liberals and organised labour, and also gave money to Hardie – was told the Liberals would save £15,000 in campaigning costs by standing down in these seats. The pact was secret; and secrecy could be maintained in an age when it was usual for the major parties to leave certain seats uncontested where they felt they stood no chance of winning. It served both parties well: but it served Labour better, because it helped the party win twenty-nine seats at the 1906 election, and to put it on the map. The Liberals had 400 MPs – twenty-four of whom were trade unionists, sympathetic to Labour – and the Unionists were reduced to a rump of 157, the heaviest defeat in their history. However, Labour's political muscle changed the whole climate of politics. It ushered in an era of uncertainty and strife at times reminiscent of the struggles of the 1860s, or the turbulence of the 1840s.

As far as the Labour movement was concerned, unity and cohesion were needed as never before because of increased, and successful, attempts by the forces of capital to place limits on the actions of unions and, particularly, of strikers, and to make unions responsible for any losses caused by their action. In 1901 a railway worker in South Wales, John Ewington, lobbied his employers, the Taff Vale Railway Company, for higher wages. Irritated by repeated requests, the company moved him to a different station. His union, the Amalgamated Society of Railway Servants, called a strike. The company brought in replacement workers, and in retaliation the union attacked railway property, uncoupling carriages and greasing the rails to prevent trains moving. The railway decided to sue the union for compensation; something without precedent in English law. Unions had been deemed unincorporated entities incapable of being sued. A judge found in favour of the company; the Court of Appeal overturned the verdict; but on 22 July 1901 the House of Lords restored the original judgment, led by the Lord Chancellor, Halsbury. The Lords decided that if a union could own property and take action that caused harm, it could be sued for damages to compensate. Another judge, Lord MacNaughten, observed that money was given to unions to provide benefits for the widows and orphans of its members, among other things; but if the union chose to discharge other than its benevolent role, and harm the interests of others, it had to take responsibility for that harm.

The Taff Vale judgment outraged the Labour movement. The union had to pay £23,000 plus £19,000 in costs, and it became clear that any union would be liable for commercial losses contingent upon decisions by local officials to call members out on strike. The unions realised they needed clout in parliament to meet this challenge. In the two years after the judgment, affiliation by trade unionists to the Labour Representation Committee, which existed to secure parliamentary representation for the working man, rose from 350,000 to 850,000. Balfour's administration did nothing to regularise the law by statute, happily letting the judicial decision stand while a Royal Commission deliberated. However, with the Liberals elected in 1906, the matter became live again. The radical end of the Liberal party wanted the depredations on unions to stop and the right to strike without incurring damages enshrined in statute law. Two more cases had stacked the odds against the unions since 1901. A fortnight after the Taff Vale judgment the Lords ruled, in the case of *Quinn v. Leathem*, that it was illegal to enforce a closed shop; in Ulster, a union had told a butchery business that its workers would be called out on strike if it continued to trade with a wholesaler who refused such an arrangement, but the ruling meant the union had no power to do this. Then in 1905, shortly before the Liberals' landslide victory, in the case of *The South Wales Miners' Federation v. Glamorgan Coal Company* the Lords said that it was no defence for inducing breach of contract for a union to say it sought to improve the conditions of its members and, in doing so, to have no intention of injuring the employer.

Parliament had tried and failed, in the dying years of the Unionist government, to regulate unions and the conduct of disputes. The Liberal landslide gave that government an unequivocal mandate, and at a cabinet meeting on 9 February 1906 it was agreed 'to amend the law relating to Trades Disputes.'[16] John Burns, now in the cabinet having been MP for Battersea since 1892, drove the initiative: and, fearing a loss of support for the Labour party if it did not do something for the unions, the cabinet accepted his idea. However, even before that Bill was introduced, Labour MPs including Keir Hardie and Ramsay MacDonald gave notice of their own Trade Unions and Trade Disputes Bill. In the debate on the King's Speech on 19 February Hardie stated where Labour's priorities lay. Hansard reported him saying that 'the Labour Party in the country . . . claimed absolute immunity for trade union funds from any claims for damages arising out of trade disputes . . . It was said that where the responsible officers of a trade union were responsible for an offence the funds of the union should be held liable for the loss sustained.' Their reply was, 'If an officer offends against the law, punish the officer, but do not punish the whole of the members for his indiscretion or want of judgment.' He asked 'that in particular the funds of the unions should be placed beyond the touch of employers seeking damages.'[17]

This chimed with Burns's view, but also with Campbell-Bannerman's. He and Burns had originally wanted the law to specify that unions should not be liable for damages. Campbell-Bannerman said that 'the great object is . . . to place the two rival powers of capital and labour on an equality so that the fight between them, so far as fight is necessary, should be at least a fair one.'[18] However Asquith, as a lawyer, and others with legal experience argued that this apparent introduction of the Queensberry Rules into industrial relations would tilt the balance too far in favour of the unions, and argued for a less radical option that limited the right to sue them. This formed the basis of the Bill, though angered radical MPs who introduced their own Bill advocating more widespread immunities. Ministers came into open conflict with each other, with private discussions establishing that Campbell-Bannerman wanted something far more radical, and weighted towards the unions, than many colleagues could face. In the end, he not only prevailed, but got the Bill through without the Unionists forcing a vote on either the second or third readings, and without the Lords exercising its veto.

The government's original Bill, nonetheless, had appeared generous. Introducing it, the Attorney-General, Sir John Walton, said that peaceful picketing – 'which I prefer to call the right of peaceful persuasion' – was 'an essential part of the right to strike', and he intended to enshrine that right in law.[19] Provided the picketing entailed no 'molestation or obstruction', the pickets would be immune to a charge of conspiracy. He professed that it was 'a considerable practical injustice' for employers to be able to sue a union, and to be paid damages out of its central funds, because of actions taken locally. He proposed that unless an act detrimental to an employer were undertaken by order of the governing body of the union, the union would not be liable. The unions were to be encouraged to appoint executive committees whose role would be to specify to their local agents what action may or may not be taken in a trades dispute.

Yet these concessions, which appalled some Unionists because of the impunity they extended to unions who damaged the interests of capital, were inadequate in the eyes of Labour MPs, and for some Liberals too. During the committee stage of the Bill, which because of its social and legal significance was taken on the floor of the Commons, there were constant warnings that it tipped the balance too far in favour of men and against their masters; and would imperil relations between the classes by providing a temptation to militancy. There were also concerns about what would happen to those who thought differently from their union – what a Tory MP, Sir Frederick Banbury, called the need 'to safeguard the rights of people who were to be peacefully persuaded.'[20] Banbury quoted back at Campbell-Bannerman a speech of his from 1904 defining Liberal policy as 'the policy of freedom in all things' including 'freedom from injurious privileges', saying the present Bill seemed flatly to contradict that idea in allowing coercion by unions of their members.[21]

Walton said coercion would remain an offence. However, proving that a picket's motive was to persuade peacefully rather than to coerce was another matter. To the shock of the Unionists the phrase 'peaceably and in a reasonable manner' was removed from the Bill as a description of how picketing should proceed, and effectively created over seventy years of tension as a result. F. E. Smith – a rare Tory to enter the Commons in 1906, and whose exercise of his fine legal mind, and wit, in these debates rapidly made him a legendary reputation in the House – forced Walton to concede that if a large number of pickets turned up to engage in an act of persuasion, their purpose must be intimidatory. He also argued at length that whatever the effect of the Bill on relations between employers and the employed, it threatened to put the unions beyond the reach of laws that members of the public harmed in some way by union activity might once have used.

Balfour warned that 'a great responsibility' rested on the government for having introduced the Bill, as it did on unions for how they chose to use those powers in the future.[22] The Bill included provisions that had effectively been drafted by the unions. The right to strike with apparent impunity, which would bedevil industrial relations for much of the next eighty years, thus came to be enshrined in English law; and until 1914, in utter contravention of what Balfour had hoped and Walton had promised, unions would flex their newly-acquired muscle with increasing ferocity. Spurred on by the liberties conferred by the Trades Disputes Act, they sought to confront employers and ratchet up real wages. The great beneficiary was the Labour party. Workers came to realise that the disposition of Liberal politicians to support the rights of the working class did not prevent their remaining, instinctively, on the side of the forces of capital, increasing the need for them to have their own substantial parliamentary party.

III

In the years before the Great War the growing power of the Labour movement was, after the Trades Disputes Act, characterised not by the development of political clout through institutions such as the House of Commons, but by the exercise of industrial muscle through strike action. George Dangerfield, in *The Strange Death of Liberal England*, declared that 'the date of the Unrest's beginning is, by general agreement, January 1910; and the most obvious cause of it was the continued drop in real wages.'[23] The rise in the supply of gold from South African mines had reduced the pound's purchasing power and caused a general price rise. Investment was being directed abroad, notably to the Americas. Certainly by 1911 the amount of gold coin issued by the Royal Mint had risen steadily, reaching £33 million worth in 1911 alone or, as the Mint's report noted, an amount equal to the whole issue of all the foreign coinage of the world for the same period.'[24] The Mint had issued just £14 million in gold coinage in 1909 and £24 million in 1910.[25] Inflation was the inevitable consequence of this surge in the money supply. Unemployment was less of a problem: a Board of Trade paper circulated to the cabinet in February 1910 noted a 'continuous improvement' throughout 1909.[26] Those in work, however, had grievances. The same paper showed average wages had fallen, and were back where they had been in 1900.

The sense of increasing impoverishment among the working class had created an atmosphere hostile to the forces of capital: all that was required was a trigger to unleash a wave of strike action. It duly came on 1 January 1910, when the Coal Mines Regulation Act came into force, stopping miners working more than eight hours in any twenty-four. Miners in Durham and Northumberland went on strike against the three-shift system, which played havoc with the rhythms of life the men – and their wives and mothers – were used to from the days when one of two longer shifts would be worked. Some Durham miners protested that the new system was 'detrimental to the health and welfare of the miners in the county'. Twice in 1909 a national miners' strike had been threatened, but narrowly averted. The miners were in no doubt of their economic significance, and wanted it reflected in their pay. Any other opportunity to flex their muscle would be seized upon.

Within a week 70,000 men in the two counties were idle, and there were coal shortages in the north-east. In Durham the owners tried to be conciliatory, and men returned to work after a week at around two-thirds of the county's collieries; but in Northumberland the owners' offer was deemed so derisory 'as would make the whole county rise in revolt'.[27] The men wanted a two-shift system, even if that meant pits standing idle for a third of the day. In both counties some union representatives were turned on by their men and criticised for having agreed to the three-shift system without consultation. This prompted the union to rule the strike illegal, and refuse strike pay, which in Durham helped push men back to work.

The strike caused serious collateral damage. Shipping businesses on the Tyne were badly hit because there was hardly any coal to move. There were fears the dispute might spread to South Wales, where owners were claiming compensation for loss of output. Their losses would have to be made up by miners working sixty extra hours a year, and higher prices. On 12 January twenty of the seventy pits in Northumberland, employing 12,000–13,000 men, were idle; and the call went up for Durham's miners to lay down their tools again. The owners implementing the law were nonplussed; they were suffering too, as output fell and, with it, competitiveness. In an attempt to placate the strikers, the Attorney-General, Sir William Robson, speaking in South Shields on 10 January, told the miners that the government's intention in asking parliament to pass the Act was simply 'to give more time for boys' recreation', and not to limit the output of coal, as some miners suspected.

The miners were soon without coal, in a cold winter, and on 20 January at Murton colliery near Seaham 'many hundreds' of desperate strikers tried to raid a coal-heap.[28] They overpowered the few police who tried to stop them, so sixty reinforcements were sent in. After three baton charges the riot ended, but not before the colliery office's windows, and those of the pit manager's house, had been broken. On 10 February, as the economy of the whole north-east was threatened with paralysis, the River Tyne Commissioners made a formal appeal to parliament to amend the Eight Hours Act, not least because Germany was exploiting markets starved of exports from the north-east. The Earl of Durham, one of the region's main coal owners, savaged the government for bringing forward the measure 'without for a moment considering what the consequences would be.'[29] In South Wales the situation remained tense, with 200,000 men expected to walk out, and unrest was also spreading to Warwickshire.

By late February the Miners' Federation in London took up the case. The national leadership was more moderate, which seemed to reduce the chance of a national strike; but once any action was co-ordinated centrally, the effect of a strike would be devastating. However, by mid-March tempers were cooling: in Northumberland, the owners promised to meet miners' representatives to discuss anything except the legally-binding eight hours question; and in Durham the miners voted to call not for the abolition of the three shift agreement, but for it to be amended. On 17 March, with the dispute harming the national economy, the

Board of Trade intervened, bringing on to the national stage a man whose name became synonymous with the Great Unrest: George Askwith.

Askwith, who in 1910 was in his fiftieth year, had been a successful barrister until 1907, when he joined the Board of Trade as a civil servant. He had done freelance work as an arbitrator in disputes for several years, his most notable success having been the strike in 1905 of Army bootmakers around Kettering. His great talent was settling, to the satisfaction of both sides in any dispute, the fair rate for piecework: in Kettering he had brokered a compromise about what a man should earn for making a pair of boots. At the Board of Trade he became head, or comptroller, of several departments, including its labour department, and in that capacity he was sent out to try to solve the rash of disputes that characterised the Great Unrest. In March 1910 he asked two representatives of each affected lodge – the groups of miners at each colliery – to come to London to see him. The seventeen affected lodges approved of this state intervention. Askwith soothed them by persuading them to elect a small committee to continue negotiations, and to set out their main objections to the new system.

The first was that continuous operation in the pits did not allow for the toxic fumes from explosives to clear between shifts; the second was that the danger of accidents was increased by colliers occasionally being asked to do work in which they were inexperienced – coal getters doing the work of stone cutters, for example; the third was that the new hours broke up home life, preventing evenings of education classes or recreation. Where men in the same household worked different shifts it 'would make the lives of wives and sisters a continual round of labour, equivalent almost to slavery.'[30] However, just as Askwith seemed to be making progress in the north-east through his dialogue with the strikers, South Wales called for a general strike, over the threatened termination of a wages agreement. Askwith immediately talked to the miners' representatives. He asked that a deputation come to meet the President of the Board of Trade, Sydney Buxton, who had just taken over from Churchill. On 25 March Buxton and Askwith met the deputation, and one representing the owners.

Although the Welsh miners felt underpaid, and objected to new, supposedly more efficient working practices, their liability under their supplementary agreement to the Eight Hours Act for the sixty extra hours a year remained the greatest grievance. Pushing up prices was not sustainable because of lower prices charged by other coalfields; so the owners feared lower profits, and the men lower wages, because of the new regulatory regime. After interviews at the Board of Trade both sides returned to South Wales for the matter to be put before a conciliation board in Cardiff. Nothing stirred on Tyneside: all eyes were on the Welsh dispute, awaiting its resolution; and Liberal MPs, many of whom were close to the miners, realised the Act was flawed. On 25 March the South Shields shipping magnate Sir Walter Runciman, many of whose vessels were lying empty and idle, denounced the Act as having caused 'trouble ever since it was passed into law': it operated only because masters and men had been 'bullied and cajoled into the adoption of so sinister a policy.'[31] His son, also named Walter, was President of the Board of Education, and so party to the cabinet discussions on the problem.

Around hitherto calm coalfields tempers frayed as men feared the higher costs of production would be, as one Yorkshire representative put it, 'taken out of the bone and sinew of the Welsh miners'.[32] In Staffordshire a resolution was passed calling on the Federation to call a general stoppage in support of the Welsh. The Federation used the dispute to urge more men to join its ranks, to establish solidarity against both the owners and an unsympathetic government. In 1910 818,000 men worked underground, 600,000 of whom were Federation members. The example of local agreements turning sour was an effective recruiting sergeant for a body that preferred to negotiate nationally, enhancing its clout as it did. As a Staffordshire representative was recorded saying, 'the Miners' federation had it in its power to paralyse the whole of the industries of the country.'

In Cardiff the owners, realising their livelihoods were doomed without a swift resolution, offered to scrap the supplementary agreement, and proposed other blandishments. However, at a meeting of Federation delegates from all over Britain it was initially recommended that the offer should be rejected because of insufficient extra money being offered for men working in 'abnormal places'. After some discussion, and with the Welsh miners having received almost all they had asked for, a resolution was nonetheless passed stating that 'the points of difference were not sufficient to justify either a strike in South Wales or a national struggle.'[33] The matter was put to a ballot in South Wales. Some militants wished to fight on, and 20,000 walked out before the ballot – though

180,000 were still at work. The Federation, a conservative body, made its lack of support for action quite clear.

Askwith turned back to Northumberland, where the Union had disbursed £60,000 in strike pay over the previous three months. The owners of pits that were not on strike announced an increase in wages of 1.25 per cent over the next three months. On 5 April miners' leaders saw Askwith at the Board of Trade, where he asked them why they could not accept an agreement between the Federation and the owners. The talks stalled, though some pits resumed work on an experimental four-shift system; and on 6 April further impetus was given to a settlement by a three-to-one vote in South Wales for the new arrangements. The next day all the Durham strikers returned to work; a ballot the following week ended, by a narrow margin, the dispute in Northumberland. All united in praise for the Board of Trade, in the person of Askwith.

The solution of these disputes was Askwith's greatest triumph thus far. However, perhaps because the government was so lucky to have such a gifted public servant it did not examine the underlying message of the dispute: how state intervention risked creating grievances with wide-ranging consequences, and how combustible local groups of trade unionists were, irrespective of what their national body or the TUC thought wise. Nor did the government grasp the wider point, which badly affected trades less well paid than the miners, about the continuing decline of real incomes caused by inflation. By spring 1910 only a fool could imagine the appetite among the working class for confrontation had been sated, or that it would be hard to find further causes to generate it. A dock strike in South Wales in May 1910 raised fears of rioting and caused the Army to be placed on standby, although Churchill, now Home Secretary, urged that the Metropolitan Police be deployed as a first resort.

The Miners' Federation was not the only union to dislike industrial action, and to be gainsaid by its members. In July 1910 10,000 railwaymen in the north-east, where the economy had still to recover from the coal dispute, ignored their union – the Amalgamated Society of Railway Servants – and went on strike. The cause was trivial: a shunter called Goodchild was asked to work at the east end of Park Lane sidings in Gateshead rather than at the west. He refused, for no good reason, and was sent home. The other shunters walked out, and those due to come in later refused. The general manager of the North-Eastern Railway,

Arthur Kaye-Butterworth (father of George Butterworth, the composer), warned the men they risked a suit for breach of contract, as well as losing wages. Freight traffic around Newcastle was paralysed, stopping the movement of coal to the ports and livestock to market; then drivers of passenger trains walked out too.

Even the strikers would have struggled to justify such action on the basis of a man being forced to work in a part of a goods yard different from where he had worked previously. They let it be known the *casus belli* was 'the general attitude displayed by officials towards certain men throughout the northern district.'[34] The signalmen then walked out, leaving barely enough at their posts to allow traffic from London to Edinburgh through Newcastle; there were virtually no local services. The management tried to conciliate: it promised no legal action, with nothing entered on the records of men who had walked out. Kaye-Butterworth offered to meet a deputation to hear their grievances, and to have the general superintendent meet Goodchild to discuss his. The men said they would return only if Goodchild were reinstated unconditionally, and their leader, William Allen, told the press a 'tyranny' ran the North-Eastern Railway.[35]

Even after only three days the effect on the local economy was severe. Fruit rotted in the market at Newcastle as did fish on the quayside at Hartlepool. Some pits stopped work as coal could not be moved. Even the tourist trade suffered as local excursions were cancelled, and resorts such as Filey reported a collapse in trade. The strike spread as far as Carlisle and York. But then, with a judicious intervention from the union, Kaye-Butterworth's offer was accepted. Goodchild saw the superintendent, who promised a full inquiry into his case: it upheld the original decision, there being no reason not to, and a second strike was avoided by a narrow margin. Keir Hardie, having raced to Chester-le-Street once he could find a train, crowed that 'workmen were now insisting upon having a say in the conditions of their employment . . . and they were not going to allow young whipper-snappers with a University education and a lack of acquaintance with industrial lives to order them about as if they were dogs.'[36]

If that were not a clear enough declaration of class war, Hardie added that, while he deplored stoppages, 'it was good to see the old spirit of rebellious revolt was still alive among the working classes, and that law or no law they were going to see justice done to their fellows.' As with the coal dispute the previous winter, the railwaymen had proved that organised labour could if it chose cause serious economic harm. New disputes broke out on the North British Railway and the Great Eastern, but were hastily closed down by a conciliatory management: the whipper-snappers had got the message. The ruthlessness of socialism was now infused into industrial relations, supplanting the more paternalistic role most unions had traditionally played.

IV

The rail strikes preceded an autumn of agitation in the South Wales coalfields and the cotton mills of Lancashire. In South Wales, discontent about the pay settlement the previous spring was still festering, and many miners turned on the Federation leadership for failing to secure them better terms. In some districts there were wholesale resignations from the Federation and new, more militant organisations were formed: these proved so successful that they threatened to undermine the Federation. The South Wales leaders did a U-turn, pronounced that the Federation had to be reformed – that is, made more militant – rather than abandoned, and they rejoined *en masse*. In this mood of zealotry Federation men soon refused to work alongside non-members.

However, more toxic yet was a row at the Ely Pit in Penygraig, owned by a consortium called the Cambrian Combine. A new seam was opened in 1909, but the owners soon claimed that the seventy miners employed on it were working too slowly. The miners retorted that the seam was harder to work than others at the pit; and as they were paid piece rates, there was no benefit to them in working slowly. A price for extracting coal that satisfied both sides could not be agreed. Cambrian announced on 1 September a lock-out not just of the seventy affected men, but all 950 at the mine. It imported labour, but effective picketing by the locked-out men made it hard for them to get to work. This proved incendiary. A mass meeting on 1 September at Maesteg ended in a threat to strike in sympathy with the Ely men. Two other Cambrian pits came out on 5 September. A similar issue had arisen in 1893, causing a three-month strike: neither the owners nor the Federation wished for a repeat, but matters seemed to be heading that way. On 18 September, when 8,000 men gathered at Tonypandy, they voted to strike the following morning; the total affected would be 12,000, and the strike would have the full backing of the Federation. Immediately the owners started to discuss whether to force the issue by locking out all their 200,000 men. The Federation decided to ballot its members before calling a general strike.

As the coal dispute started to overheat, so too did a hitherto localised quarrel at a Lancashire cotton mill, Fern Mill at Shaw near Oldham. The mill had been idle since 7 June. An overseer had asked George Howe, a grinder and a member of the Cardroom Amalgamation, to clean part of a machine in his charge. He refused because such work was not part of his duties, and he was sacked. His union called out the workforce, ignoring pleas by the secretary of the employers' association to visit the mill and propose a compromise. The owners were furious because there was an agreed procedure for industrial action, including a meeting of all parties concerned, but this had been ignored. The union's refusal to meet the employers remained steadfast.

One mill owner told *The Times*: 'The position is aggravated by the cardroom people setting themselves up as the sole judges as to what are and what are not new duties.'[37] The refusal to talk, or allow an investigation into the circumstances of Howe's dismissal, forced an ultimatum from the owners on 11 September: unless the operatives would agree to arbitration, the Federation of Master Cotton Spinners would lock out the whole trade. Most operatives, and indeed everyone else, thought the employers were bluffing; and the owners thought the operatives would cave in. Therefore, there was no rush to buy supplies of cotton against a future shortage. But by 25 September the operatives decided the employers might not be bluffing, and agreed to arbitration by Askwith. However, the owners refused to participate unless Fern Mill returned to work at once; otherwise, there would be a lockout at 700 mills.

Two days later the South Wales coalfield voted heavily against a general strike in support of the Cambrian miners. There was, however, a high level of abstention, which suggested the potential for trouble if matters were not resolved quickly. In Manchester the gulf between masters and men continued to widen. Not only did Fern Mill refuse to go back unless Howe were reinstated, but William Mullin, secretary of the Cardroom Workers, announced: 'We are as firmly convinced that they [the employers] are wrong as they are convinced that we are wrong. We are not going to say we are in the wrong until arbitration has proved us to be.'[38] *The Times* relayed the authentic voice of capital: 'If they overlook the disobedience of the man Howe they will be troubled with endless acts of insubordination of a similar character and they will lose control of their mills. Indeed, they say that Howe has had imitators in other mills already.'[39]

With much of Lancashire about to shut down, Askwith went to Manchester on 30 September. He put representatives of masters and men in the same room, and left them for ninety minutes: but to no avail. James Crinion, the president of the Cardroom Amalgamation, protested that 'the workers had a legitimate right to have a voice in the arrangement of the working conditions of mills, and to submit to the employers' view would reduce trade unionism to a nullity.'[40] In case that did not show sufficiently that Jack was now, in his own view, as good as his master, Crinion added: 'Workers under such conditions would become morally serfs and slaves to obey the dictates of the employers.'

The prospective cotton lock-out gripped Britain: and it distracted attention from South Wales, where by early October 20,000 men were idle because of a refusal to work with non-unionised labour. Askwith was still in Manchester, where on 2 October, hours before the lock-out was due to begin, he persuaded the operatives to offer new proposals. It was too late to avert the start of the lock-out: at noon that day 500 of the county's 700 mills closed their doors 'until further notice'.[41] Two days earlier Askwith had been asked if he had abandoned hope, and had replied: 'I never abandon hope.' His optimism was misplaced, however. The operatives asked that Howe be found a job elsewhere if he could not be reinstated at Fern Mill. The employers refused, but would urge that he be considered for the next vacancy for a grinder that arose. That was too little for the operatives. Askwith convened another conference: but by the end of the week 700 mills, and around 140,000 people, were idle.

Askwith moved into the Midland Hotel in Manchester. The union, helped with subventions from the General Federation of Trade Unions, paid strike pay to those locked out, which only hardened the strikers' resolve. The owners saw they had to take an initiative; and on 6 October Askwith had a triumph. He persuaded the Duke Mill, in Shaw, to hire Howe. The heaping of praise upon Askwith started with the Lord Mayor of Manchester lauding his 'tactful diplomacy'.[42] But Askwith could not rest: the growing rage in the South Wales coalfields would soon command his full attention.

By mid-October most men who had walked out, refusing to work with non-union labour, had returned; but Cambrian, where the issue was different, stayed out. On 26 October there was another vote, which rejected an offer from the employers; thus 12,000 men in the Rhondda would be on strike by 1 November. The men wanted 2s 6d a ton; the owners wanted to pay 1s 10½d, which the men rejected as 'starvation wages'.[43] The Federation disliked such rhetoric, and the owners felt the union had lost control of its members; suddenly, there was talk of a general strike or general lock-out to force the issue. When the Cambrian men came out on 31 October so did 8,000 men at the Powell Duffryn mine, in sympathy. Later that day 6,000 men stopped work at Maesteg, followed by several thousand at other pits. With over 30,000 out, cohorts of striking miners marched around the coalfields urging other mines to join them. This infuriated the owners, who called the police in. Then the strike spread to colliery employees who were not faceworkers, starting with the engine-men.

The Cambrian miners met in Tonypandy on 2 November, and heard their agent, David Watts Morgan, tell them that 'the fight which they had entered into must be fought with a grim determination to win.'[44] Cambrian management expected the strike to last into 1911; their men were paid a fortnight in arrears, so there was more money due, and the Federation was issuing strike pay, even though the union's official line was that the men should accept the owners' offer. Cambrian's directors, adept at public relations, gave £100 a week to the local education authority so strikers' children could be fed at school.

The strikers were marginalised not just by their employers, but by their union: and divisions over tactics worsened when, on the night of 1 November, strikers attacked a train carrying non-union miners to work in Aberdare. They broke its windows and beat up some men who fled from the train. They also smashed the windows of colliery officials' houses. The police eventually restored order, but had to guard the pit where the non-strikers were working. Within two days extra police were drafted in to the Rhondda to guard other mines. A gulf grew between the Federation's national leadership and its members in South Wales, men *The Times* described as being on 'the extreme Socialistic wing'.[45] Noting that these men held no official union position, the paper's correspondent accused them of having been 'unremitting in their crusade against the existing social order and political system and in favour of the communistic theories associated with extreme Socialism'.

Worse, 'their views have taken hold of the minds of a large number of the younger section of the workmen.'

On 4 November the owners asked Captain Lionel Lindsay, Chief Constable of Glamorgan, to do whatever was necessary to allow them to run their business; and there were suggestions that the Army might have to go in. The next day the Cambrian strikers met in Tonypandy and resolved to march, on 7 November, round other Cambrian pits to persuade men to strike. When they did, summoned by a bugle call in lashing rain and a howling gale at 4 a.m., the situation descended into disorder, with strikers attacking non-strikers. The police were sent in. The posse of strikers went from house to house, stopping men leaving for work; they chased from the pitheads men who had got in earlier, stopping only after forcing promises that they would not work until the strike was won. They also tried to close pits by sabotaging ventilation fans and pumping systems.

Now the government had to act, announcing on 7 November that the 18th Hussars would go to South Wales if necessary. Despite this threat, and the arrival of police from Swansea and Bristol, rioting broke out that afternoon. By evening it was widespread throughout the Rhondda, with hand-to-hand fighting between strikers and police, and thousands on the streets. At 10.30 p.m. men surrounded the Glamorgan Colliery at Llwynypia, outside Tonypandy, where management had manned the pumps, to storm the buildings and close the colliery down. When they smashed a wooden fence to use as weapons against the police, the police baton charged them back into Tonypandy.

The ensuing riot in the main square forced the police to implore the War Office to send in the Army. Churchill, as Home Secretary, gave the order to move troops from Salisbury Plain early on 8 November, in response to a request from Lindsay for 200 cavalry and two companies of infantry: but they were stopped at Cardiff and Swindon respectively on the understanding that disorder would end. Hoping he had made his point, and believing Lindsay had over-reacted, Churchill ordered the dispatch of seventy mounted Metropolitan policemen and 200 foot constables instead. He sent a message to Lindsay to pass on to the strikers in which he said that 'their best friends here are greatly distressed at the trouble which has broken out, and will do their best to help them get fair treatment'.[46] Although belligerence and the dramatic gesture were second nature to him, particularly at this stage in his career, he knew the dangers of sending in troops to deal with a civil disturbance, hence his assurance there would be none sent in if the rioting stopped.

His moderation backfired. *The Times* reported that, after hours of calm, there was another assault on Llwynypia. There were 'violent conflicts between the police and the strikers attempting to wreck the property of the Cambrian Coal Trust' and 'the mob got absolutely out of hand in the evening and looted the shops . . . the absence of troops which had been asked for was severely felt.' The looting, in which women and children participated, resulted in claims of £10,000 to insurance companies, including £2,000 for plate-glass windows alone. Troops had to go in, before anarchy prevailed. A squadron of cavalry arrived at Pontypridd on the evening of 8 November, and some infantry were moved to Newport. Wheeling out a yet bigger gun, Churchill asked Askwith to meet the men's representatives the following afternoon. He was vilified for decades afterwards for 'sending in the troops', something he did with the greatest reluctance and only after looting was rife; and he sent a further 200 Metropolitan Police during the night of 8/9 November to help restore peace.

All three pits in Tonypandy were idle, and almost every working man in the town was a collier. The Glamorgan Colliery was spared from flooding, and permanent damage, by management efforts to keep a steam engine running, when a battered phalanx of police stopped miners from attacking the managers who were stoking the steam engine. There was also the problem of 320 horses abandoned underground without food or proper ventilation. Flooding the mine was the objective of the rioting that broke out again late on 8 November, as the attack was launched on the power house from where the pumps were being driven. The police repelled the attackers, but that merely drove them to looting: *The Times*'s man described the events of that evening as 'an orgy of naked anarchy'.[47] It was obvious to the legion of reporters witnessing this disorder that the union leaders' pleas for calm were pointless. The evening was characterised by a series of stampedes by rioters and baton-charges by police, in some of which women and children were battered. Even though the magistrates had closed all the pubs, many rioters were drunk.

The outrages in Tonypandy caused deep disquiet around Britain. The King, who had read the account in *The Times* before a day's shooting at Sandringham, asked Churchill for an immediate report. He told the

Sovereign that 'the whole district is now in the effective control of the police', and the Army would not be needed.[48] As well as the cotton lockout and the railway disturbances, fresh in the memory, there was a long-running lockout in shipyards on Tyneside following a dispute with boilermakers. But it was the example of militant syndicalism in France, with its new fashion of *sabotage*, that caused most unease, for what was happening in Tonypandy with the attempt to disable mines seemed to follow that pattern. Everywhere militants supplanted the old union leadership; the modern syndicalist was someone with whom the forces of capital simply could not do business. The wave of disputes was, at this point, first termed 'the unrest'; it would become 'the Great Unrest': there was worse to come.[49] Over the next two years 'syndicalism' would become a notable bogey in national discourse, with fear that the trades unions were preparing to seize control of the means of production and distribution by revolutionary means, and impose a form of communism on the country.

The Rhondda quietened down with the arrival of the Army and the police reinforcements. Askwith arrived too. The strikers were not all equal. The union had endorsed the Cambrian dispute, and the men were therefore receiving strike pay. Another dispute, at the Powell Duffryn mines in nearby Aberdare, was unofficial because the union had been given the requisite notice, and the 12,000 miners were not being paid. They were thus considered more susceptible to conciliation; this proved groundless, as within days they rejected talks. Then, on 11 November, the Cambrian strikers stormed the pit where management had kept the pumps working and closed it, barricading themselves in. A magistrate was put on permanent standby to read the Riot Act. Askwith met the owners two days later, but concluded there was no scope at that point for arbitration.

It was then found that 100 pounds of saxonite – an explosive like dynamite, used for controlled explosions underground – had been stolen from Cambrian's magazine. Detonators, fuses and electric wiring were also missing. Extra soldiers were drafted in, and women and children in houses near the colliery offices were evacuated. The police removed strikers from the mine and the management restarted the pumps; Hardie, whose seat adjoined Tonypandy, visited the strike committee. In a speech he lamented that most public outrage had been directed at the plight of the horses and ponies – the King himself had telegraphed

Churchill saying 'trust that it is not true that all the horses have been lost in one of the mines' – and not at the women and children hit by truncheons.[50] However, aware of the appalling effect on the miners' reputation that the reports of looting had had, he warned them not to be 'provoked' into further violence.[51] Hardie knew – as did Churchill, who admitted as much to Lloyd George – that the problem was merely contained, not solved. The Labour leader claimed the use of troops amounted to 'Russification', evoking the hated Tsarist regime that was a universal symbol of oppression to the working-class movement

Hardie's plea was ignored. On 18 November three men tried to blow up a colliery manager's house at Gilfach Goch, just south of Tonypandy, using the stolen saxonite. Another manager had been seized that morning by strikers who tried to throw him in the river, but were thwarted when the police heard his cries. The windows of a Cambrian manager's house were broken, and other officials were assaulted in the street and on trams. Their families were also attacked. These outrages continued for several days. Hardie and others claimed reports were false or exaggerated, which according to the evidence of wrecked property and injuries they were not. Journalists noticed the police showing great restraint, and the Army was hardly visible; it was presumed, and reported, that this was on political orders from London. Whatever the miners' grievances, the intimidation, violence and destruction in which a hard core had engaged was an appalling advertisement for the Labour movement. The union leadership washed its hands of the militants, and Hardie played down events. He accused the government of siding with the owners, a useful strategy when many miners with a vote would have cast it for the Liberals: a general election was presumed to be weeks away, given the Lords' refusal to accept the Parliament Bill.

On 21 November widespread rioting broke out again in Tonypandy, and the Lancashire Fusiliers were called out; up to that point the policy of restraint had meant that not a single arrest had been made, to avoid inflaming opinion, but this now appeared unsustainable. The strikers, determined to ensure 'blackleg' labour was not imported, forced a signalman at Llwynypia Station, in the early hours, to stop all trains so pickets could search for strike-breakers. He refused, and was told that unless he relented his signal box would be wrecked and all passing trains stoned; he complied, and set the signals at 'danger' to stop the trains. During 21 November every train through Tonypandy was stopped and searched, and any suspected strike-breaker was beaten up; inevitably, most victims were not miners. The railway was outraged, and demanded the police take a firmer hand. Meanwhile, the police were stoned in the streets. That day, a conference of militants' leaders in Cardiff recommended a general strike in South Wales, to be discussed the following week.

That evening broke out what became known as 'the battle of Penygraig', the village near Tonypandy where the dispute had started. It was the worst rioting thus far, with thirty Metropolitan policemen and many local officers hurt, many with head injuries. The origins were unclear: but a riot was taking place, and police reinforcements were ordered to deal with it. They met a mob armed with sticks and stones, 'with such overwhelming numbers against them that they were in great peril.'[52] The police gave as good as they got: fifty rioters were injured in the ensuing baton charge, when strikers were driven back towards the village. A union official pleaded with the miners to stop the violence, and had to be rescued by the police. Strikers running around a warren of streets managed to attack the police from the sides and the rear, and were getting the better of them until suddenly Chief Constable Lindsay, personally leading reinforcements, arrived. He made repeated charges until the main street and the side streets were clear. Many women impeded the police, having calculated that they would act with restraint to avoid a serious incident; given what was happening to suffragette protesters in London, this was optimistic. The women threw kitchen utensils at the police, then buckets of boiling water, and, when the buckets were empty, the buckets too. Two detachments of Hussars arrived as the police had beaten off the strikers. Churchill told the King it had been 'a hard furious fight' and that, in the event of a repetition, 'the troops have full liberty to act.'[53]

Three men were charged the next day, but the press was barred from the hearing in case reports incited further unrest. The presence of soldiers was stepped up, and army officers visited pickets to warn them that any further interference with the railway, its staff, passengers or property, would not be tolerated; military pickets were posted at all stations, and anyone trying to search trains or intimidate staff would be arrested. There was further rioting in Aberdare, with youths and young men attacking the houses of mine officials. In London, Askwith talked without success to miners' representatives, and asked again to see their employers. The presence of soldiers and extra police in the Rhondda allowed enough labour to be imported to relight the furnaces at the Britannic Mine at Gilfach Goch, to restart the pumps and end its flooding. The rioting ended. A charitable appeal was started to feed the miners' children, the emergency funds for school meals having been exhausted. There was no appetite for a general strike. Miners turned on the extremists who had called them out without a ballot; not only were children hungry, but women were searching slag heaps for coal. The lower production also drove up the price of coal.

By early December most miners employed by Cambrian wanted to return to work; it was younger men, many of them radical socialists without families to support, who wanted the strike to continue. Although the rioting had stopped the collieries still had armed and police protection, an expensive situation that could not last indefinitely. Askwith went to Cardiff in mid-December to meet both sides in the Cambrian dispute, where 12,000 men had by then been striking for three months. On 19 December the 10,000 or so on strike in the Aberdare valley returned to work, but Christmas came with Cambrian's men still holding out. There was some justice in their obstinacy: as Philip Snowden, then a young Labour MP, wrote: 'In 1910 – a year of record trade – wages remained practically stationary . . . with the spread of education, with the display of wealth and luxury by the rich, it is certain that the workers will not be content. It is the duty of statesmanship to acknowledge the justice of the desire of the workers for a more human and cultured life, and to satisfy this unrest by concessions of reform.'[54]

Details of the discussions Askwith had with both sides remained, to start with, confidential; but on 2 January 1911 it was reported that the miners sought a minimum of £2 7s 7d a week, giving no undertakings about productivity in return. The management could not entertain this idea, which would mean a minimum wage two shillings a day above that demanded by the rest of the South Wales coalfield. This demand showed the gap between the Federation's view and that of the radicals who had taken over the local committee. D. A. Thomas, the head of Cambrian Coal, put it bluntly: 'In no circumstances . . . would the management concede the principle of the minimum wage.'[55] Showing a determination that should have been salutary for the government as well as the owners, the men stayed out until August, oblivious until then to entreaties from the Federation to return to work. The union was paying £3,000 a week in strike pay, but withdrew it in June. The men were, six weeks later, effectively starved back to work, for the same piece rate of 2s 3d per ton they had been offered a year earlier.

V

The emergence of aspects of syndicalism, such as sabotage, in Tonypandy came shortly before an even more politicised agitation, when on 16 December 1910 anarchists tried to hold up a jeweller's shop in the East End of London, but were surprised by the police, three of whom were shot and killed. The 'Houndsditch murders' shocked the nation. One of the gang, George Gardstein, was also killed; the others went to ground, prompting a massive manhunt. On 2 January 1911 a tip-off led the police to a house in Sidney Street, Stepney, where some of the gang were holed up. The anarchists were heavily armed and had large supplies of ammunition. Around 200 police blocked off the area, and some Scots Guards were sent from the Tower of London. There was sporadic shooting: on the morning of 3 January Churchill, who as Home Secretary had ultimate authority for the operation, decided to visit the scene, arriving just before noon.

Warming to his task, he ordered some field artillery: but as it arrived the house caught fire, and Churchill – saying 'I accept full responsibility' – refused to let the fire brigade enter until the inhabitants surrendered, and had the police poised outside with guns aimed at the door.[56] Two men burned to death inside. Churchill stayed until nearly 3 p.m. The gang leader was known as Peter the Painter, a Latvian revolutionary active in the 1905 uprising in Russia, but no trace of him was found. The two dead men were also Latvians.

Churchill's exhibitionism and interference brought him under attack. In evidence to the inquest he claimed: 'I did not in any way direct or over-ride the arrangements that the police authorities had made . . . I never directed anyone to send for a Maxim gun.'[57] On 6 February, once parliament resumed, Balfour observed:

> I understand that he did not call out the troops or assemble the police, and that he had nothing to do with the massing of artillery . . . what was the right hon. Gentleman doing? That I neither understood at the time, nor do I understand now. I must frankly say that I

should have thought that anything more embarrassing to those responsible for the operations than to have the head of the office who is over them all present with the photographer as irresponsible spectators, could not be imagined. I cannot imagine anything more embarrassing to those who had to carry out what evidently, from the result, must have been a very difficult and dangerous military operation.[58]

Such anarchy as Sidney Street derived from a syndicalism that would pile trouble on the government for much of the next three years. The strikes of 1910 had been a foretaste of what was to come, and the industrial climate was about to become far more aggressive and uncompromising. As with the disputes of 1910, those of 1911–14 were largely caused by a drop in real wages. On an index in which 1895 was 100, by 1909 it was still only at 101 and by 1911 had fallen to 96.[59] By this time Britain's reputation as the workshop of the world was being challenged by both Germany and America, and to manage the impact both those industrial powers were having on international markets, productivity had to rise to make British goods more competitive. This required more effort and output by British workers for the same pay. As a result, the number of disputes soared. In 1905 67,653 workers were involved in strikes; by 1910 it was 385,085.[60] An example of the increasingly bitter strife this caused occurred in Scotland in the spring of 1911.

One of the great technological advances of the nineteenth century had been the sewing machine; and in 1882 the Singer Company bought forty-six acres of land at Kilbowie on Clydeside, where it built the largest Singer factory in the world. From its opening in 1885 until the Great War, manufacturing levels rose steadily but supply never kept pace with demand. On 21 March 1911 the work of twelve women cabinet polishers was reorganised to include, at no extra pay, that of three sacked colleagues. Because the women were paid piece-rates it was estimated they would lose two shillings a week in earnings. They went on strike: and within two days almost all 11,000 workers had joined them. The Socialist Labour party and the Industrial Workers of Great Britain were both organising in the plant, to the annoyance of management, and were effective at mobilising the workforce.

Management's response was belligerent, saying they would close the works for good and move production to other European plants; they also issued the improbable threat that they would see to it that none of the strikers would work in Glasgow again. The threat worked: a ballot led to an overwhelming decision to return to work, which happened on 10 April. Singer then decided to settle scores: 400 workers, among them all the strike leaders and members of the IWGB, were sacked. The shockwaves resonated around the British union movement, emphasising how ruthless they would need to be in future. In Glasgow the effect was not to intimidate local labour, but to develop the ethos of 'Red Clydeside'.

Elsewhere, hitherto fragmented groups of workers coalesced to develop more industrial muscle. In November 1910 the veteran dockers' leader Ben Tillett and Tom Mann, a product of the Social Democratic Federation who had converted to communism in the 1880s, formed the National Transport Workers' Federation. This amalgamated thirty-six small unions, which included dockers and seamen, and so had the potential to paralyse the ports and the trade that kept Britain earning money. This threat first materialised on 14 June 1911 when dockers, railwaymen and sailors in Southampton declared a general transport strike, led by the National Sailors' and Firemen's Union, an affiliate of the NTWF. A measure of their militancy came when rockets were launched at several ports to signal the downing of tools, and in London a banner was unfurled saying 'War is now declared'.[61] The shipowners flatly refused an invitation to meet workers' representatives in a conciliation board.

It was aimed to make the strike not just national, but international. Strikes had started in French and Dutch ports, and lines of communication were open with New York. Seamen and firemen at Liverpool came out the same day, with Mann – who had based himself there – unfurling a banner marked 'War Declared. Strike for Liberty!' Most major British ports came out within forty-eight hours, although in some, including London, the excess of labour meant some men were happy to work for the existing rates. Even at Southampton the strike was not solid: the White Star liner *Olympic* – sister ship of the *Titanic*, then under construction – due to leave on its maiden voyage for New York, sailed only after management had surrendered to the strikers, agreeing to pay deck hands £5 5s a month and firemen £6 10s. Southampton gave much anxiety, as it was the port of departure for mail boats to America and southern Africa.

The cabinet became deeply concerned. A Board of Trade paper, which

Askwith had drafted, circulated in June 1911, considered the reasons for the latest wave of unrest: wholesale prices of staple foods were one-sixth higher than in 1896, and retail prices had risen even more. 'The advance in wages appears to have been less than the increase in the prices of food products,' the paper continued.[62] Returns on capital had increased, widening the gap between wage-earners and those living off investments: blue-chip railway shares yielded 2.75 per cent in 1897, but 3.75 per cent in 1911, and that rise was reflected elsewhere. This was because scientific and technological developments boosted profits, but left the poor behind as their wages did not increase in the way that dividends did. 'The wealthier classes', the paper suggested, 'in those types of luxurious expenditure now favoured, possibly display that luxury more than was the custom in the preceding generation.' The use of motor-cars, it said, could not fail to attract the attention of the poor; and the cheap newspapers they now read were full of stories about the rich. With working men better educated and more widely read than their fathers, and increasingly steeped in socialism, and with unions better organised, the challenges to the old order were enormous. In a conclusion written under his own name, Askwith was almost despairing, and seemed to fear revolution: 'Some effort should be made to maintain control.'

As it became increasingly desperate for freight and people to be moved, so the strikers won concessions, usually hefty bribes to get them back to work. The main public inconvenience was that the sailings of numerous steamers from south coast ports to watch the Coronation review of the Fleet at Spithead were cancelled. In most ports, including Southampton, agreements were reached by 23 June to end the strike; but in Liverpool it continued and hardened. The main cause was better wages, but there were also demands by many trades for management to recognise their union.

A strike of firemen in Hull also became problematic. The Humber was full of shipping that could not be moved without men to stoke its boilers; worse, the cargo was mainly food that was fast going off in one of the hottest summers on record. The owners were willing to fund bribes, but would not recognise Tillett's and Mann's union. So the concessions offered in Liverpool came to nothing, and food continued to rot in the mouth of the Humber. The Liverpool strike began to affect the wholesale food trade, with shortages of cheese and bacon by late June as ships from America and Canada awaited unloading. Also, Mann and his committee squashed attempts by individual firms to settle with dockers. They ordered all men to stay out until all firms had settled. By early July food was also short in the East Riding and prices were rising.

On 2 July Hardie, speaking at Wigan, demanded a national minimum wage of thirty shillings a week, but eight shillings a day for underground workers, whose work was more dangerous and arduous. He went almost as far as Mann in his rhetoric of class war. 'You working people don't realise that at the present time you are not counted as being part of the nation,' he said. 'You are "the mob". Remember all the time at election time you are "citizens", when you strike you are "the mob".'[63] Asked whether he believed in the monarchy, Hardie replied that its existence was 'proof of insanity on the part of the common people . . . the whole thing was an insult to the intelligence of the nation.'

Askwith brokered a deal in Hull, where the men went back on 4 July with a pay rise; and an initiative by shipping line owners in Liverpool got that port moving. However, the men who manned the tug boats in Liverpool then declared various grievances with their employers, and in Manchester, where dockers on the ship canal had come out the previous week, 4,000 carters went on strike for an increase in pay comparable to that sought at the coastal ports – another four shillings a week, which their employers branded 'ridiculous'.[64] There was within a couple of days a serious food shortage in the city. To get food moving non-union labour was brought in to drive lorries, under police protection, but these were immediately attacked by strikers and, in one case, pelted with raspberries. A small riot broke out, and the crowd was baton-charged.

On 7 July Askwith reached a provisional settlement between the Manchester Ship Canal Company and the dockers, in a discussion involving representatives from eighteen different unions that agreed to raise the minimum wage. It seemed the only unfinished business was a small local dispute in the Port of London, where dockers sought another penny an hour. The shipowners, roundly criticised even by the forces of capital for not having treated their men better, could easily have afforded to forestall such a damaging series of strikes, but had delayed doing so for weeks. They then published new, nationally agreed wage rates for all ports. This brought a period of calm, but Tillett said on 16 July that there would be a national strike if the demands of London's dockers who were not Port of London Authority employees, and had not therefore had the extra penny an hour, were not quickly met. A conference was convened immediately. However, seamen went on strike in Cardiff on 18 July over a refusal by their employers, the Shipping Federation, to recognise the Seamen's Union, and dock workers came out in sympathy. By 21 July *The Times*'s man in Cardiff was calling it 'a city under siege'.[65] The government sent in 600 men of the Lancashire Fusiliers. Factory hands, flour millers, brewery workers, railway packers and coal trimmers were among those who joined the strike. A lack of trucks to move coal threatened the South Wales coalfields with stoppages. By 25 July 200,000 men in the Rhondda were idle because their coal could not be moved. Rioting broke out in Penygraig, where the Cambrian miners were still on strike after ten months, when men started to throw stones at the police. Askwith, in a memorandum of 23 July, noted that society had changed – 'young men are better educated and demand a better life – labour is realising the idea of the sympathetic strike and its power'.[66]

The Cardiff strike was finally settled in the early hours of 28 July. However, no sooner was it settled than the long-running series of disputes in the Port of London reached their climax, and the NTWF called a strike there. The issue remained that Port of London Authority employees had had an increase of a penny an hour, and non-PLA workers demanded the same. On 1 August between 4,000 and 5,000 men in the Albert and Victoria Docks walked out, meaning no incoming ships were unloaded. The shipping lines said their men were already better paid than the PLA men, as their overtime rates were higher and they had a paid dinner break. The owners agreed to arbitration, but only if the men resumed work immediately. The heatwave of 1911 was at its height, with temperatures in the eighties and nineties in London most days in early August. Food rotted in the holds of unloaded ships; shortages hit London. Tillett's aim was that everyone whose work was connected with the docks should strike. He organised committees to represent each associated trade. 'This language points to an intention to call a general strike,' *The Times* observed on 3 August.[67] Hardie advised the 10,000 striking dockers to bring out every possible man they could. The watermen and lightermen, who had not yet come out, indicated they would do so in pursuit of a demand for a ten-hour day (they usually worked twelve).

The docks filled with ships. On 3 August the Surrey Docks came out as well. A process of arbitration began. Some better-paid Port of London men came out the next day, as did all railway workers connected with the docks. On 6 August the arbitrator decided in favour of the men: they should be paid eightpence an hour, and a shilling an hour overtime. The arbitrator's announcement was relayed to a Sunday afternoon rally of strikers in Trafalgar Square: 'Thereupon hats were thrown in the air, sticks and handkerchiefs were waved, and cheer after cheer was given, the audience concluding with the singing of "For he's a jolly good fellow".'[68] But the men were ordered not to return to work until their executive assured them everyone else's claims had been settled.

Until then the London docks, and everything that depended on them, would remain paralysed. Tillett magnanimously allowed ice to be moved for use in hospitals, and for rotting food to be removed before it became a health hazard; but otherwise the victory of the NTWF was complete. It showed the power organised trade unionism could exert. The Army Service Corps were brought in to unload a ship at a granary on the south bank of the river, prompting a warning from the union that there would be a 'breach of the peace' unless they desisted.[69] Askwith tried to resolve, urgently, the outstanding grievances of the coal porters, lightermen and watermen, all of which were to do with pay. The carmen also came out. The dispute was far from over.

By 9 August 100,000 men in the East End were idle, the heat was roasting – that day was the hottest ever recorded in England, with the temperature in Enfield, north-east London, reaching 98.8 degrees Fahrenheit – and tempers started to fray.[70] Pickets thronged the streets around the Tower and out towards Wapping, stopping vehicles they thought might be strike-breaking. The police frequently had to intervene. Horses were unharnessed from carts, leaving vehicles stranded and blocking the roads. Carts were overturned, blocking Tooley Street and Upper Thames Street. In the Minories, where almost every vehicle was being stopped, drivers started to attack pickets with their whips. At one point a man whose cart was being attacked fired a revolver, shooting one of his assailants in the leg.

That evening a police baton charge took place in the East India Dock. Fish, meat and fruit were becoming scarce, and very expensive: chilled and frozen meat had doubled in price, not helped by a strike of porters at Smithfield. The porters at Billingsgate decided to join them. Most alarming to the authorities, also on 9 August, was a threat by London County Council Tramway operatives to strike. That day Buxton assured a fraught House of Commons that 'the Board of Trade are using their utmost endeavours to promote a satisfactory settlement', but pleaded that 'nothing will be said or done on either side to widen the area of the dispute, or render its settlement more difficult.'[71] Churchill was outraged that some strikers claimed the Trades Disputes Act gave them the right to visit non-strikers and intimidate them into joining a dispute. One of his last acts as Home Secretary – he moved to the Admiralty on 24 October – was to send a circular to remind police to be firm on this point.[72]

'London', *The Times* editorial proclaimed on 11 August, 'is face to face with the imminent danger of actual famine'.[73] The previous day the Lords had passed the Parliament Bill; now an organised attempt by the working-class movement to starve London into submission to their will seemed to smack of revolution. Political leadership was wanting: while the Lords had been obsessed with the veto, the Commons had, the previous day, taken the momentous step of agreeing to pay a salary to MPs. Meanwhile, the public suffered. 'Thousands of tons of food are actually perishing,' the leader went on, 'but the shameful waste makes no impression upon the organisers of the strike.' It attacked the notion that until every grievance was settled no one could return to work, a principle that was holding the capital to ransom. It praised the Board of Trade's attempts to find a solution, but equated the efforts of Askwith and others with 'pouring water into a sieve'.

The paper said that 'six or seven millions of people cannot be expected to submit to starvation at the behest of a comparatively small minority who have chosen to proclaim war upon their countrymen.' It was a 'vast conspiracy to bring the life of a great capital to a standstill', an unprecedentedly co-ordinated assault by labour upon capital, and it had to stop. 'The whole thing is as insanely foolish as it is wicked', it continued, and the leaders 'hopelessly ignorant' if they imagined the poor would benefit from their destruction of wealth. The implication, though the paper did not say so, was that the Army should be sent in.

This was the moment when Dangerfield, recollecting the events a quarter-century later in *The Strange Death of Liberal England*, and referring to the union leaders, said that 'for four days Messrs Gosling, Godfrey and Tillett had the singular satisfaction of governing London.'[74] During 10 August men walked out in many railway goods yards. There were threats to blow up bridges and viaducts to stop the movement of goods.

The price of bread rose; food wholesalers spoke of impending bankruptcy; bananas were unobtainable. It was feared newspapers would cease publication because of shortages of newsprint and a strike among distributors. Private and commercial motor-vehicles were threatened by a worsening petrol shortage, and even the London Underground was in danger because of an inability to move coal to the power stations that drove it. As the violence continued, preparations were made at Aldershot to send 10,000 troops to London. Every Army Service Corps lorry was put at readiness, and each man in the Aldershot command was issued with three days' rations and ammunition.

On 11 August Askwith brought the lightermen – the one group holding up cessation of hostilities – and their employers together at the Board of Trade. At midnight the London strike was called off. In the early hours of the next morning Tillett and his committee published a statement congratulating the strikers on their 'signal victory'.[75] Askwith made an explanatory statement that suggested the union's rhetoric was not misplaced; the working day would be cut from twelve to ten hours, and the greater overtime this cut would create would be paid at ninepence an hour, or one shilling an hour between 6 p.m. and 8 p.m. Apprentices and watchmen were also to be better off. The King, who was shooting grouse, sent a telegram of congratulations to Buxton on the resolution of the strike, an indication of how far events had disturbed the ruling class. 'Trust all work will resume today,' the Royal missive concluded: it was wishful thinking.[76]

VI

Strife flared up again in Liverpool, as workers for the Lancashire and Yorkshire Railway Company went into dispute with their management over what they regarded as an inadequate pay award, and workers for six other companies whose trains served the city, but who had no grievance, came out in sympathy. Thousands of dockers working for seven steamship lines were already on strike, despite having had almost all their demands for more money met by shipowners, and in breach of agreements made earlier in the summer. On the morning of 9 August it was reported that the Joint Strike Committee in Liverpool, led by Mann, had called a general strike. Mann denied this but did issue an 'instruction' to all workers in the port 'to refuse to touch any freight or handle any merchandise for any railway wagons on the Dock Estate' to 'demonstrate our loyalty to the principles of industrial solidarity' until the railwaymen had satisfaction.[77] They had closed off the goods yards in the port, preventing cargoes from being transferred to the main line. The union movement in Liverpool had been taken over by hard-line socialists; moderate leaders were marginalised and ignored by men who saw more scope to squeeze the owners. The owners had had enough, and threatened a general lock-out from 14 August.

The government took no chances, and in response to a request from the Lord Mayor sent 400 men of the Warwickshire Regiment to the city, where they arrived just after dawn on 10 August. Police were brought in from Leeds, Birmingham and the Royal Irish Constabulary, but a further request for cavalry was not granted. However, there were mounted police, who charged a crowd on the afternoon of 10 August after wagon-loads of goods being taken to the main railway stations were attacked. The Lord Mayor pleaded for the services of Askwith, as engine-drivers and firemen of the London and North Western Railway resolved to refuse to work in conditions they deemed 'dangerous'.[78]

Mounted police quickly ended rioting on the night of 10/11 August. It was nearly as hot as in London, and it was decided to move food from one of the docks' railway stations before it rotted. A cortège of thirty-three carts, surrounded by foot and mounted police and 100 men of the Warwickshire Regiment, left the docks. A magistrate was at either end, prepared to read the Riot Act. The manoeuvre was a success, and wholesalers managed to get the food and distribute it.

Throughout the Liverpool strike there had been mass rallies on St George's Plateau, outside St George's Hall, and on Sunday 13 August a crowd estimated at 85,000 gathered there to hear an address by Mann. The police ordered a man sitting on a window ledge of the Lime Street Station Hotel to come down. When he refused, they pulled him down. Hand-to-hand fighting broke out. Street furniture was broken up and used as weapons. The police, greatly outnumbered, baton charged the crowd, and water hoses were used. The riot lasted for most of the next two days. A stipendiary magistrate, protected by soldiers, read the Riot Act; and mounted policemen were brought in, chasing the crowd into adjoining streets. The rioters set up barricades, and men on rooftops pelted the police with bricks and tiles: the officers were called 'scabs', as many were reinforcements from elsewhere. More than 350 people were injured, and ninety-six were arrested. Lime Street Station, which at one point was stormed by the mob, became a field hospital, so numerous were the injuries. Local labour leaders put the blame for the riot on the Birmingham city police, the main reinforcements.

A squadron of Scots Greys entered the city centre that evening, but by then the fighting had spread to the inner suburbs. Churchill told the King that things were worst 'in the Irish quarter' and the soldiers headed there.[79] The next day, to make matters worse, the shipowners executed their threat to lockout the cargo workers, leaving 25,000 men idle. Within hours this provoked a general strike of all transport workers in the Liverpool district, calling out another 75,000 men and paralysing the port and normal commercial life. Another major riot started late in the evening, lasting into the early hours of 15 August, with soldiers from the Yorkshire Regiment firing shots over the heads of the mob to disperse them after an outbreak of looting; they later charged with fixed bayonets, and the Riot Act was read again. The government sent in more troops from Aldershot, Dover and Salisbury, and railwaymen in Manchester announced they were coming out in support of their brothers in Liverpool.

The railway strike quickly spread to Birmingham, Bristol and Sheffield, but negotiations took place to stop it spreading to London, where the city was trying to return to normal and where the goods yards were still largely closed. It was clear by 14 August that members of the Amalgamated Society of Railway Servants were, as *The Times* put it, 'on the verge of striking in every corner of the United Kingdom' over 'low wages and excessive hours'; it was contended that many men were working for less than £1 a week.[80] The success of the dock strike encouraged the railwaymen. The initiative had passed from capital to Labour.

In Liverpool, magistrates swore in special constables, many of whom were territorial soldiers; and they issued a proclamation 'warning respectable people and sightseers against being present at scenes of actual and probable disorder.'[81] Churchill echoed that sentiment in the Commons, blaming the trouble on 'the hooligan class'.[82] They also ordered the closure of pubs in the affected areas. On 15 August, as railwaymen's leaders met in Liverpool and voted to call a general rail strike unless the employers negotiated within twenty-four hours, soldiers of the 18th Hussars fired on a crowd in Vauxhall Road, a near-slum area occupied largely by dockers, and notable as a scene of sectarian strife between Protestants and Catholics; two were killed and fifteen were injured. An angry mob had attacked a convoy of five prison vans bearing those convicted of offences during the rioting to Walton jail, and had started to stone its military escort, injuring both men and horses. The convoy reached the prison but the fighting went on for over an hour, *The Times*'s correspondent describing it as 'guerrilla warfare'.[83]

There were now 3,500 soldiers in Liverpool, and a gunboat was sent to the Mersey after the Mayors of Liverpool and Birkenhead warned Churchill that the ferry traffic could be suspended; the government prepared to send still more troops. It was then ten days since any goods traffic had gone in or out of Liverpool, and food was short. As word of events spread, railway workers across the country went on strike. With local industries closing for want of coal and supplies, the authorities in Liverpool took the course of last resort, asking the Board of Trade to send Askwith up at once.

Askwith, however, could not go. He was needed in London, for talks on 16 August, to try to prevent a national rail strike. Ramsay MacDonald was also prominently involved, trying to bring together four separate union committees of aggrieved railwaymen. The railway companies promised to run a basic service if a strike broke out, but only if the government accorded police and military protection to anyone prepared to break the strike. Cavalry units would guard all the main London railway stations. Asquith became involved, meeting employers in Downing Street with Buxton, and trying to calm down the situation.

Rioting continued in Liverpool into a third day, and by now Walton jail was so full that prisoners were shipped out to Cheshire. With liners idle in the Mersey – including the *Lusitania* – food rotting in the docks and passenger as well as goods train services packing up, Liverpool was approaching what Mann gleefully called 'a complete paralysis'.[84] The King told Churchill that 'accounts from Liverpool show that situation there more like Revolution than strike . . . strongly deprecate the half-hearted employment of troops . . . if called upon they should be given a free hand and the mob should be made to fear them.'[85] The King was not on the spot but the Lord Mayor of Liverpool, who was, told the Earl of Derby 'that it is no ordinary strike riot but . . . a revolution is in progress.'[86]

The government feared a general strike, and Buxton and Askwith convened a second day of talks, Asquith and the cabinet happy that ministers should referee the fight. The threatened rail strike portended a national emergency, if the effect of the local strikes was any guide.

Food was running out in Sheffield and Birmingham, and Bristol was not far behind. All 25,000 soldiers in the Aldershot command were stood by for work on the railways. It was reported that they would stand by the trackside with loaded rifles if necessary.

The Commons debated the unrest on 16 August, with the Unionists, led by Austen Chamberlain, accusing the government of failing to protect the rights of men who wished to work, and the property of businesses. They were also failing to ensure sufficient food was distributed to the people. Ramsay MacDonald attacked Chamberlain for not having mentioned the stagnation of wage rates after a decade in which trade had increased and the cost of living had risen. MacDonald said that 'no party . . . has been more reckless in its language of disorder' than the Unionists; and he accused the government of being heavy-handed in using police and troops against the strikers.[87] 'The persons who are mainly responsible', he concluded, 'are the employers, who used their economic power in order to crush down their workmen'.[88]

The situation worsened. On 17 August Asquith, tired and irritable after the saga with the Lords, joined discussions at the Board of Trade, after an emergency cabinet meeting, and suggested to representatives of the railwaymen that a Royal Commission be instituted to consider conciliation arrangements in their industry. The four unions' plenipotentiaries rejected the idea, since the employers had, in their view, torn up a conciliation agreement of 1907, but also because Asquith was foolish enough, in his shortness of temper, to tell them that irrespective of their decision he would do all he could to keep the trains running. The union men sent telegrams to their branches ordering a general strike from that evening: the call was widely obeyed. Asquith was as good as his word: the Army was immediately dispersed to secure rail lines, and Scotland Yard asked citizens to sign up as special constables.

To make matters even worse, in Liverpool the authorities feared a massive breakdown in public health, just as the electricity workers decided to strike. The government sent two warships, the cruisers *Antrim* and *Warrior*, to the Mersey; and magistrates, fearing an uprising, ordered the pubs to be closed. Rioting broke out, and it was indicative of the state of the people that most looting was of bakers' shops. On 18 August, 200,000 railwaymen were idle. There was a baton charge of strikers in Birmingham, and pickets occupied a signal box at York. The Army went into Leicester and Derby.

England seemed to be approaching revolution: and Wales joined in. Troops were sent to Cardiff on 18 August when railwaymen there promised to come out. On the same day in South Wales men pelted trains with bricks. The worst incident was at Llanelli, where strikers blocked a level crossing. When they heard that a train they had held up had 120 soldiers on board a disturbance broke out, eased only when the driver and other crew on the train promised to strike at once. The government panicked, sending in Lloyd George for negotiations with railwaymen and their masters. He took with him Askwith and, more pointedly, Ramsay MacDonald for a thirteen-hour session on Saturday 19 August. MacDonald persuaded the men to negotiate. Lloyd George persuaded the employers to reinstate any men sacked for striking and to start talking to union representatives. The railwaymen agreed to return to work, though the solution of their grievances was temporary. However, the return was not announced in time to stop rioting in Chesterfield on the evening of 19 August, when militants decided to wreck the Midland railway station, leaving fifty people injured and occasioning thirty arrests. There were similar scenes in Lincoln, where the Midland Railway's offices were attacked before four hours of rioting, starting at 11 p.m., in which numerous shops had their windows smashed and were looted.

Lloyd George had acted on the principle that if the Liberal party did not stand up for the railwaymen the Labour party would, with radical electoral consequences. It did not help the government that their own figures, publicised on 17 August, showed that in the six years to the end of July 1911 the wages index had risen from 97.1 to 100.3, but the price of food index for London had risen from 102.8 to 108.1. Nonetheless, the end of the strike was perceived as a considerable contribution to the nation's retreat from industrial anarchy, so much so that the King, at Bolton Abbey with the Duke of Devonshire, cancelled a plan to return to London and sent a telegram of congratulations to Buxton and to both sides in the dispute. When he learned of Lloyd George's central role in solving the dispute the King sent him a personal telegram of congratulation, which greatly repaired his standing with the monarch. 'It has caused me the greatest possible anxiety,' the King said of the strike.[89]

However, matters took an even worse turn in South Wales, where 75 per cent of drivers were striking, and in the English Midlands, where

Churchill told the King an estimated 90 per cent were out: he said a prolonged strike could cause 'the severest famine'.[90] In Llanelli, also on 19 August, a mass picket held up a train believed to be full of strike-breaking workers. The officer commanding a detachment of the Worcestershire Regiment, Major Brownlow Stuart, ordered his men to fix bayonets and disperse the strikers. The strikers immobilised the train by putting out the fire in the engine, and then turned on the soldiers in a cutting outside the station, pelting them with stones. Stuart asked the local magistrate to read the Riot Act, which he did reluctantly and inaudibly. When the stone-throwing persisted, Stuart ordered his men to fire towards the crowd. Two men were killed, one of whom had come out into his back garden to see what the commotion was about.

The effect was to bring most of Llanelli out on to the streets, and once darkness fell to launch hours of rioting in which the town centre was wrecked and shops looted. It continued until 3 a.m. on Sunday morning, and the houses of magistrates were targeted and ransacked. A train trying to pass through the station was stopped and looted. There were baton charges in the main street, but these had the effect of driving the mob back to the railway. It broke into the goods shed and looted it, doling out stocks of alcohol stored there. It then burned the shed down. At this point another striker, using dynamite to force open a freight carriage, was killed in a huge explosion. He had not realised the sealed carriage was filled with ammunition. Four other people, injured in the blast, also died. Strikers tore up parts of the main line and, later, burned a furniture warehouse, killing two horses stabled there. Only when word reached the town from London that the strike had been settled did the rioting subside, helped by a bayonet charge by the Worcestershire Regiment.

Liverpool was strewn with rubbish and wreckage, and the economic damage can be gauged by the fact that on 18 August, for the first time in its history, the city's Cotton Exchange recorded 'nil' for its daily business.[91] To help end the strike in Liverpool, the shipowners agreed to recognise their employees' union representatives, and to negotiate with them in future. However, within hours of recognition of the union the dockers voted to stay out, pending the reinstatement of every man sacked during the dispute: and until they returned, the railwaymen would stay out too. Therefore, the Lord Mayor asked Churchill to maintain the military presence in the city. He also called for special constables and volunteers to help clean it up – *The Times*'s correspondent described the streets as 'a sewage farm', posing a serious health hazard in the unusual heat. The Mayor also urged Churchill to have the law on picketing amended, as it was only the use of violence and intimidation that was, in his view, perpetuating unrest. There was by now little doubt among those in authority that the strikes were being exploited by revolutionaries. Meanwhile, on 21 August the Rhondda Valley miners formally petitioned the Miners' Federation to campaign for a minimum wage. *The Times* reported: 'it was argued that it was only by following the example of the seamen and the railwaymen that success could be achieved.'[92] The wedge was getting thicker; the next day the call was taken up by miners in Durham, and spread from there.

Churchill told the Commons on 22 August that 'all forms of intimidation and violence in furtherance of trade disputes are illegal'.[93] He and the government came under sustained attack from Labour MPs for the ready deployment of troops; Churchill did not help matters by replying that, in Britain, the authorities would send troops wherever they pleased. An unnamed MP yelled out: 'They have all gone mad.'[94] MacDonald termed what had happened 'the reckless employment of force' and said Churchill had preached a 'new doctrine' by stationing troops where civil disorder was yet to break out.[95]

As always, Churchill came out fighting. He reminded the House that the death rate in areas of Liverpool such as Toxteth had doubled during the strikes, not because of the authorities, but because of malnourished children succumbing to disease. 'The House should remember', he added, 'that the Llanelli rioters, left to themselves, with no intrusion of the police, and no assistance from the military for some hours, in a few streets of the town during the evening wrought in their drunken frenzy more havoc to life and limb, shed more blood, produced more serious injury among themselves, than all the 50,000 soldiers who have been employed on strike duty'.[96] This use of troops almost as a first resort was, indeed, a stark turn for a Liberal administration, and Labour made hay with it. Hardie, talking of the men shot dead at Llanelli, issued what sounded like a threat: 'Not only the railway men, but practically every organised trade in Great Britain will stop work until your soldiers are back into the barracks. Working men are not going to tolerate a Government using the military forces of the Crown to prevent them trying to improve their position and make their lot in life better.'[97] The seeds of Labour's post-war rise, and of Liberalism's relentless decline, had been sown: the workers now had a party that opposed capital.

It was Askwith, not the Army, who settled the Liverpool strike. On 24 August he persuaded the tramway company to reinstate some, but not all, of the men sacked for going out in sympathy with the railwaymen, which was the last sticking point. Although not a total victory, it was enough for Mann, who knew that the majority of non-militant, non-revolutionary strikers in Liverpool had had enough. He had also achieved one of his, and Labour's, main aims, of uniting disparate working-class groups. 'What we value most of all,' he said in an interview, 'is that for the first time in our history the various sections connected with the transport industry have been brought into harmonious working relations . . . solidarity has been the characteristic all through the fight and remains intact now in the hour of victory.' Mann's other achievement lay in uniting Liverpool's working-class Protestants and Catholics.

The summer's events had shaken the nation. The King wrote to Asquith on 7 September to say he was 'very much disturbed by the present unrest among the working classes' and the possibility of more strikes.[98] 'He is afraid that, if there were a renewal of the recent occurrences, the disturbances, which now appear to be inseparable from a strike, might lead to political elements being introduced into the conflict which might perhaps affect, not the existence, but the position of the Crown, independent of other evils.' He urged Asquith to use the lull in the unrest to find a way of curbing it. It was as if the very foundations of society were under threat.

VII

After some relative calm, early 1912 reawakened the prospect of a national convulsion. It was now the miners' turn to cause unrest, partly because of renewed calls for a minimum wage, and partly because the owners were feeling the pinch of the eight-hour legislation and its effects on their profitability. As before, it was owners in South Wales who wanted to abide by older agreements, and who were the obstacle to a settlement. When the Federation annual conference met at Southport on 3 October 1911 a national strike was on the agenda, but once more a conservative leadership tried to hold back militant men. Part of the conference, where the minimum wage was discussed, was held in camera, with the Northumberland miners leading the charge for a national stoppage.

Momentum built through the autumn, with one region after another expressing support for action. The Federation realised it had no choice, if unity were to be maintained, but to ballot its 700,000 members on a national strike. The ballot was set for January 1912, to allow both sides a chance to avert it. It was held after individual regions had expressed their demands: some wanted as much as eight shillings a day for underground men, down to five shillings for labourers. The Yorkshire owners' offer was typical, and showed the gap between the two sides: six shillings and sixpence for the miners, for example, when eight was sought. When polling started on 9 January, reports from the coalfields suggested the vote to strike would be carried by a large majority. This was distressing to many regional and national Federation leaders, who understood the difficulty of making a business case for a minimum wage and who feared for the security of the men's jobs. Nonetheless four out of five of those voting supported the militant line, so the Federation gave notice that the miners would walk out at the end of February.

Owners and Federation representatives met most days in the ensuing weeks. Part of the difficulty in reaching an agreement was the fragmented nature of the industry: different groups of owners and miners had different histories, relationships and economies. Parliament reassembled, and Labour demanded that the mines and the railways be nationalised because they were monopolies: an assertion (notably made by MacDonald in the Commons on 15 February 1912) that, because of the plurality of ownership in both industries, did not bear scrutiny except in the most local sense.[99] In the same debate, George Lansbury said that 'industry in this country ought to be organised not with regard to profits, but with regard to the interests of the workers.'[100] Unionists and Liberals had attacked the working-class movement for embracing syndicalism in the revolutionary continental fashion: Lansbury made no apology for this. 'Let the House remember that if it refuses to deal with the wrongs of the people; if even it is powerless to deal with them; that there is nothing else for the people to do but to attend to the matter outside this House.'[101]

On 2 February the Federation issued its demands for rates in the seventeen different regions, ranging from four shillings and elevenpence per shift in Somerset and Bristol to seven shillings and sixpence in Yorkshire, Nottinghamshire, Derbyshire and South Wales. This moderated earlier demands. There was still no agreement about what to do over work in 'abnormal places'. On 7 February representatives of owners and men met in London, but the owners insisted pay had to be related to the amount of coal produced; and therefore there could not be a minimum wage. The South Wales owners walked out. The Federation announced that 'there can be no settlement of the present dispute unless this principle is agreed to.'[102]

A national strike would have grave implications. Around 1,050,000 men and boys worked in the mines, 848,000 of them underground. It was estimated that every union member could receive modest strike pay – ten shillings a week – for four to five weeks before the money ran out.[103] Around a third of miners were not in the union and would receive no strike pay. In the new spirit of working-class solidarity, other unions might contribute to support the miners for longer; but the owners were inquiring at Lloyd's about the possibility of insuring against the effects of a strike, which suggested a painfully long haul.

The government had held off intervening; but there was scheduled for 14 February one of the thrice-yearly meetings of the Industrial Council, a thirty-strong Board of Trade committee that Askwith (who had become Sir George in the New Year's honours list) chaired. It included leading figures from both sides of industry, and expressed an overwhelming desire for the government to intervene. Buxton was in constant touch with both sides, and after being pressed by Askwith advised the government to take the initiative. On 20 February the prime minister invited representatives of both the miners and the coal owners to meet him in a conference at the Foreign Office on the 22nd. They agreed, and the meeting lasted from 10 a.m. until 7 p.m. Asquith took Sir Edward Grey, the Foreign Secretary, with him, as well as Lloyd George and Buxton. The government well understood how crucial it was to avert this strike: industry, the railways and power stations were all coal-fired, and it was the heating fuel for most houses. A national strike would be socially and economically catastrophic. Both sides outlined their positions; the Federation leaders said a national conference was happening in London the following Tuesday – 27 February – and no decisions could be reached before then.

Asquith saw the King on 23 February, after a separate and fruitless meeting with the owners. As with the other great strikes the King was agitated about the effect on the economy, but also about the stability of the social order. On the day of the national conference the government, seeking to conciliate, suggested local arrangements to ensure everyone could be decently paid, while protecting the owners from exploitation. If no agreement were possible, the government arbitrator would set a minimum wage locally. The owners in Lancashire, Yorkshire, Cumberland, North Wales and the midlands accepted these terms; Durham did too, but with deep reluctance. Northumberland rejected them, as did Scotland and South Wales, stating that they wished to stick to existing agreements. Those supporting the proposals represented 60 per cent of the nation's total output, but the failure of the large minority to agree was fatal. Without even waiting for the conference to end, miners in Derbyshire, Leicestershire and South Wales came out. The newspapers reported that in the event of a general strike there was enough coal to keep industry working for two weeks, though in some areas, such as around Coventry; supplies could last for two months. After that, the furnaces would burn out, the lights would go off and the trains would stop running.

The talks went into a third day, at the end of which all that had been achieved was that Askwith had persuaded the Northumberland owners to back the proposals. The prime minister made an impassioned speech to the miners' representatives, saying the government had become involved only as a last resort, and with great reluctance. Telling them that coal provided 'the life blood' of industry, Asquith said the determination of the two sides not to agree had left him with no choice.[104] He also said the government accepted the idea of a minimum wage; as with Lloyd George's propitiation of the railway workers, the government was taking pains not to allow Labour to have a monopoly on sympathy with the working class. Asquith told the men that they would bear 'a terrible responsibility' if the strike proceeded, because of the effect on 'the great mass of people outside whose livelihood, comfort, welfare, even existence very largely depend on you.' He spoke privately to the owners who were still refusing to accept a minimum wage.

After a morning's discussion on the fourth day the two sides were still far apart, and most British miners had walked out – an estimated 800,000 by 1 March. Railway companies reduced services, and some towns turned street lights off earlier. On 4 March Asquith made a full statement to the Commons, reporting that the owners in South Wales and Scotland stood in the way of a settlement, refusing to admit the minimum wage principle; and the men, while accepting that a minimum wage had to be set separately in each coalfield, did not accept that anyone else should set it. He also had to deny an assertion by a miner to whom he had spoken the previous week, and which had been reported in the press, that the establishment of a minimum wage for miners preceded legislation setting one for all workers: something that would have scandalised many Liberal supporters as well as the Unionists. 'I am not', Asquith said, 'in the habit of engaging in sly flirtations of this kind with Socialism and then trying to conceal from the public the manner in which I have been employing my time.'[105]

He said the owners had told him there would have to be closures of many uneconomic pits if a minimum wage were insisted upon, which would throw tens of thousands out of work. A tone of despair entered the voice of a statesman who had once been one of the leading barristers of his age. 'It has never been my good fortune to present a case which seemed to me so irresistible from the point of reason, justice, and common sense. And as I watched these men, the very flower of the mining industry of this country, while I was speaking – I was over-sanguine – I flattered myself, and I think some of my right hon. Friends shared my opinion, that I had almost persuaded them. Well, I did not.'[106] There had been no trace of bitterness in the negotiations: the situation was 'a deadlock rather than . . . a breakdown.'[107] He asked MPs with influence in the dispute – he referred, without naming them, to Labour MPs with links to the mining unions, some of whom served on the board of the Federation – to do what they could 'to minimise and shorten this terrible national calamity', or to accept 'a responsibility which history will not measure'.[108] Law, still new as leader of the opposition, endorsed Asquith's sentiments.

Railway companies trying to conserve coal to carry passengers refused to carry horses; they told their drivers to slow down; people were told to economise on electricity; the price of bread rose; shipping ground to a halt on the Tyne and elsewhere; cotton mills shut down; by mid-March 25,000 Sheffield steelworkers were idle; workers in other industries began to be laid off, or had their working hours reduced, causing immense hardship, with 250,000 idle by 6 March mainly in the north and the Black Country. The government saw that if the strike continued much longer the country would be on its knees. The Army sought to protect the minority of men who wished to continue to work, but intimidation was rife. Criminal proceedings were instituted against the editor of a leftist newspaper, the *Syndicalist*, for inciting the Army to mutiny if ordered to help break the strike.

Asquith had not wanted a Bill to introduce a minimum wage, partly because it would be precisely the sort of coercion of the employers to which he was opposed, and partly because of the precedent it would set of government intervention in the relations between masters and men, and in the labour market where liberal theory had it that wages were set according to supply and demand. But once another conference failed on 15 March, and with the country facing chaos and economic ruin – 100,000 people other than miners were, for example, now out of work in South Wales alone, and 70,000 in the Potteries – he announced he had run out of other options. At that stage neither side had signed up to the Bill, so it was a risk: but the government hoped an act of *force majeure* would bring the dispute to an end. The most the men would say was that there could be no return to work until the Bill was law – which the government deemed would be very quickly, given the agreement of the opposition – and then a return would depend on what was in the final Act.

On 19 March Asquith told the Commons he brought in the measure with 'great and unaffected reluctance'.[109] The Welsh owners had told him that if the miners' demands were to be met it would 'lead to a reduction of from 30 to 50 per cent in the output'.[110] Nonetheless, he said that passing the Bill 'within a very short period of time, is absolutely imperative in the best interests of the country', as ending the strike was 'a matter of paramount urgency'.[111] He was greeted with consensus – both Law and MacDonald signalled approval, and leave was given to introduce the Bill without a vote. While the government was taking a conciliatory line with the miners – in the national interest – it was having no truck with the revolutionary activities of syndicalists. That same day the police arrested Tom Mann in Salford for inciting soldiers to mutiny, and bail was refused, outraging Labour MPs and some Liberals. Within days minutes of a syndicalist conference in Manchester were leaked to the press, in which it was noted that Mann had said that 'the trade union movement of today is utterly incapable of effectively fighting the capitalist class and securing the economic freedom of the workers', and calling for each industry to be represented by just one union, which would join skilled and unskilled workers.[112]

The Bill's second reading opened up traditional divisions, not least because the owners were complaining that all the penalties that it allowed were to be imposed on them, not on the men. The Unionists saw the Bill as a surrender to union, and possibly syndicalist, power. Balfour, on 21 March, asked:

> We see the spectacle, the new, the strange, and the portentous spectacle of a single organisation, acting within its legal powers, practically threatening to paralyse, and in a large measure actually paralysing, the whole of the trade and manufactures of a community which lives by trade and manufactures. The power they have got, if used to the utmost, is, under our existing law, almost limitless, and there is no appearance that the leaders of the movement desire to temper the use of their legal powers with any consideration of policy or of mercy. Can anybody quote from history in respect of any of the classes on whom are visited, and often justly visited, the indignation of the historical commentator, a parallel case? Has any feudal baron ever exercised his powers in the manner in which the leaders of this great trade union are now using theirs?[113]

The second reading passed by 348 to 225, the Tories having made their point. And it was a good one: this Bill, which recognised the economy was now dependent for its success, functioning and prosperity on the co-operation of organised labour, changed the balance of society. The development of the economy and the evolution of its structure left organised labour with the whip hand, and it would become more powerful yet. Each strike concluded in favour of the unions, in recognition of the poor deal capital had given the workers for over a decade and of the strategic importance of organised labour, simply encouraged others to employ the same methods.

When the Commons scrutinised the Bill in committee there occurred perhaps the most remarkable speech of Asquith's career. Exhausted by the constitutional crisis, harried by militant suffragettes and facing insurrection in Ireland, he was at the end of his tether even before the miners threatened to close down the country. 'With the strongest sense of responsibility that any man could ever feel in the position which I hold,' he told the House on 26 March, 'I still say to both parties that if in this fifty-ninth minute of the eleventh hour they cannot come to a reasonable arrangement on a matter relatively small in its dimensions, but which is capable, if it is left unsettled, of producing infinite mischief and havoc to the community, they will have a very serious account to render to history.'[114]

He was appalled to bring in such fundamentally illiberal legislation, mocking his party's historic objection to state interference in relations between masters and men. He resented that Labour MPs felt the omission of specified rates undermined the Bill, for he knew the boards set up under the law would give the men what they sought. His voice trembled as he reached his conclusion. 'I speak under the stress of very strong feeling. I can say for myself and my colleagues we have exhausted all the powers of persuasion, argument, and negotiation at our disposal, and we press this Bill as affording the best possible solution in the great emergency with which we are confronted. With a full sense of our own shortcomings, I claim that we have done our best in the public interests with perfect fairness and impartiality.'[115] The House, and members of the press gallery, realised he was weeping. Law, who responded, proclaimed that the issue was above party politics, and affirmed his belief in Asquith's sincerity.

On 29 March the Bill had the Royal Assent. Asquith had been meeting almost daily leaders of both sides, in the hope the Bill could be abandoned and a non-statutory solution found. But the owners would not agree to a five-shilling daily minimum for men and a two-shilling one for boys, and nor would the men agree to the principle of exceptions. On 28 March, with the Bill almost enacted, the Federation agreed to ballot their men on a resumption of work: and as soon as the Bill had been enacted, even the militants in South Wales urged the men to accept the Act.

A return to work started on 1 April, though resistance in the Lancashire coalfield spread across the north of England. Their view was that the failure of the Act to specify rates was a defeat and not a victory for the miners. As it began to look as though the strike might not be over after all, food and coal prices went up. The distress among the unemployed and the striking miners was so acute that on 2 April the King sent 1,000 guineas, and the Queen and Queen Alexandra £1,000 each, to a relief fund. But by 6 April it was clear there was an overwhelming desire to resume work: the Federation ordered the men to return during the following week. For a time, Lancashire ignored the order: there were riots at Golborne, between Wigan and Manchester, where the Army was sent in after a police baton charge failed to restore order. That quelled the trouble: Lancashire, too, went back on 12 April.

The coal strike was, in terms of the economic damage it did, by far the most dangerous the country faced during the Great Unrest; but it was not the end of the sequence, as one group of workers after another followed the big battalions. In May 1912 badly paid Jewish garment workers in London's East End went on strike, encouraged by the German anarcho-syndicalist Rudolf Rocker. He brought out 13,000 sweatshop workers, demanding not just better wages but a closed shop. He had judged the mood correctly, and by 25 May the employers had conceded every point.

Two days earlier the National Transport Workers' Federation had called for a general strike of their members, with the aim of establishing closed shops throughout their industry. The dispute had begun in the London docks, where the lightermen had walked out the previous week, and union leaders in London – including Tillett – cited provocations including previous agreements, use of non-union labour and 'the general vexatious interference with the workmen of the port'.[116] The real reason was that the lightermen's employers refused to compel a worker to join the union. By now the mood of appeasement among the employers was turning, many realising that if they kept rolling over they as a class would be finished, having done the syndicalists' work for them. The general feeling, echoed in the Tory press, was that it was time to make a stand.

Tillett said the dispute would 'not be confined to the Port of London alone, but will also become national.' Any attempt to divert trade to another port would result in its closure, the Federation said. It issued two demands. One was recognition of their Federation as representing its constituent unions – an enormous and varied group covering almost every trade within the docks, canals and shipping lines – and the other uniform rates of pay, 'the best pay at present to be the standard'. Given the miners' success, there was no reason for the transport workers not to try this: and almost at once London, which a few weeks earlier had been short of coal, was now short of food. There was panic buying over the first weekend of the strike, and prices rose steeply. Troops were placed on standby; the railwaymen said they would refuse to move goods unloaded by blacklegs.

The government commissioned an independent inquiry that discovered a flagrant breach of agreements on both sides. However, the strikers made the mistake of over-reaching: there was outrage that Harry

Gosling, a dockers' leader, in decreeing that certain essential foodstuffs could be unloaded, was dictating to people what they could or could not eat; their demands expanded to reviewing all the labour practices of the Port of London; and they offered to convene a conference while dictating what representation they would countenance from the employers. It was widely felt that the unions had exceeded their normal function of bargaining on behalf of members and were instead trying to launch a syndicalist revolution.

Asquith was abroad: Lloyd George took charge. He tried to keep the militants talking, and by 4 June had apparently succeeded in having them accept a form of arbitration; but the men said that unless their terms were met immediately – prejudging the outcome of the arbitration – they would call a national strike. The East End clergy came out for the dockers, pointing out the moral failings of employers who had decided unilaterally to renege on agreements: 'Give them the certainty that this must be so in the future, and you have the remedy for that "unrest".'[117]

The government felt the clergy had a point, and asked the employers to form a federation too, so they could speak with one voice when making agreements, and keeping them. Lloyd George met Lord Devonport, the chairman of the Port of London Authority, on the evening of 6 June, and outlined proposals to avert a strike. The owners rejected them late on the evening of 10 June. The NTWF called out 300,000 workers in ports all over the Kingdom. It sent a manifesto around its members, soliciting support, which stated that, as well as ignoring agreements and spurning the government's proposals, the owners 'depend upon the use of the brutal weapons of starvation and intimidation, police and military repression, to beat us' and, more to the point, 'we have had our wages filched'.[118] There were advanced signs of hardship among the strikers' families: so much so that the Countess of Warwick, a former mistress of the late King, suggested those with large grounds set up camps for evacuated children; she set an example by establishing one for 1,000 children at her pile, Easton Park, in Essex.

By 19 June there was strike-breaking, the union was short of money, and strike pay was minimal. Some strikers sought admission to local workhouses. Throughout July men drifted back to work, despite violence and intimidation against those who did. On 12 July Asquith, Buxton and Askwith met Devonport, but the owners sensed they had won, and were in no mood to make concessions that might encourage other workers to strike. By 24 July, with defeat not just inevitable but imminent, and with many of the strikers' children being fed by charities, extensive rioting broke out in the docks, with fires started and wagons of food looted. At a meeting on Tower Hill, Tillett called for the men to pray for the death of Devonport, who he said had 'contributed to the murder by starvation of their children, their women, and their men.'[119] Asking the men to raise their hands to the skies, Tillett intoned: 'O God, strike Lord Devonport dead.' Fighting, looting and arson took place after the meeting, as between 5,000 and 6,000 men marched to the docks; there were numerous arrests after police baton charges. Tillett's and Gosling's last desperate gamble was to appeal again for a national strike. The call was rejected. On 27 July the strike committee called off the great transport strike, but their men were reluctant to agree: it took over week for a disorderly return to work. Devonport lived until 1934, dying in his seventy-ninth year, a measure of the effectiveness of trade unionism, or of the power of prayer.

The appetite for industrial action diminished after this failure. In 1912 there were 857 disputes, with 1,233,016 workers involved and 38,142,101 days lost.[120] The following year was quieter, with unions further recognised by the law in an Act that allowed them to divide their funds between political and social causes, but to enable the contracting-out of members who wished not to contribute to the political fund. A wave of caution, or conservatism, overtook the unions' leadership. When on 10 October 1913 James Larkin, an Irish union leader, in a speech in London attacked the National Union of Railwaymen for opposing sympathetic strikes, the TUC recorded their disagreement. Conditions for the very poorest also improved: by the end of 1912 163,499 fewer people qualified as paupers compared with 1910, a reduction of almost a fifth. Excluding old age pensioners, that was the lowest figure since 1873.[121] Crime also fell.

The government came under increasing criticism in 1912 for its role in the strikes, which the press and many politicians decided had only made things worse: a harsh judgment given the parlous state the country was in by the time of the Minimum Wage Act. There was a marked reluctance for ministers to intervene thereafter, though Northcliffe commissioned Wells to write a series of articles in the *Daily Mail* calling for planning to avert further unrest: Wells wrote that 'nearly all the social forces of our time seem to be in conspiracy to bring about the disappearance of a labour class as such and the rearrangement of our work and industry upon a new basis. That rearrangement demands an unprecedented national effort and the production of an adequate National Plan.'[122] The futurology was spot on, albeit fifty years too soon.

Yet by 1914 the old militancy was back. There were 937 strikes recorded from January to July, including a national agricultural labourers' strike, which started in East Anglia. The miners, railwaymen and dockers were inches from calling a general strike, with engineers and shipbuilders considering supporting them, when the Great War intervened. The working class was increasingly angry, and increasingly organised: union membership rose from just under 2.4 million in 1910 to just over 4 million in 1914. Had it not been war, it might easily have been revolution, for the government was fractious and exhausted, the prime minister was distracted and increasingly frail of judgment, the opposition opportunist, and society top-heavy with the discontented and aggrieved.

VIII

In his thoughtful book *The Social Unrest*, published when the worst of the strife was over in 1913, Ramsay MacDonald outlined his theory of why this uprising had happened in supposedly serene Edwardian Britain. He traced the class struggle in England back to the Peasants' Revolt, but argued that the greater education and political experience of contemporary workers made it more likely they would rebel. Moreover, the Industrial Revolution had created a society in which 'wealth was held without responsibility; it was in the hands of those who neither by their culture and their public services, nor their industrial merits, could command respect.'[123] Thus it became a moral question, and the moral sense of the working man – what MacDonald called his instinctive belief in equality and justice – had been deeply offended. In not fairly rewarding those whose efforts had helped to create wealth, those with it had provoked an uprising against the immoral treatment they were enduring at the hands of their masters. 'The decay of good breeding and of clean, serious living,' he observed, 'was everywhere apparent.'[124] The new rich were no longer the 'betters' of the working class: they could claim no moral superiority and had no right to command deference. And it was no wonder such self-interested people, devoid of *noblesse oblige*, refused to increase wages in line with the rise in their profits and prices in general – and had to be taught a lesson. From 1900 onwards 'the struggle to maintain the old standards of working-class life [had] been intensified', as MacDonald put it.[125] 'Could anything have happened except what actually did?'

The Great Unrest infected the conscience of the nation and intruded in its culture. We have seen Galsworthy's contribution. Forster, in *Howards End*, wrote of the working class:

> Give them a chance. Give them money. Don't dole them out poetry-books and railway-tickets like babies. Give them the wherewithal to buy these things. When your Socialism comes it may be different, and we may think in terms of commodities instead of cash. Till it comes give people cash, for it is the warp of civilization, whatever the woof may be.[126]

Later, he has this exchange between two of his upper-middle-class characters:

> 'You do admit that, if wealth was divided up equally, in a few years there would be rich and poor again just the same. The hard-working man would come to the top, the wastrel sink to the bottom.'
>
> 'Everyone admits that.'
>
> 'Your Socialists don't.'[127]

However Wells, supposedly a socialist, had a decidedly unfraternal view of the union movement because of what he saw as its opposition to progress. He saw 'the spirit of trade unionism, the conservative contagion of the old craftsmanship' as one of 'the chief obstacles in the way of the emergence . . . from the present chaos' of people who were 'equipped, organised, educated, conscious of . . . distinctive aims in the next hundred years'.[128] He conceded, however, that the ruling caste was partly to blame for the antagonism between employer and labourer, since 'in order to keep the necessary labourer submissive, it was a matter of public policy to keep him uneducated and as near the condition of a beast of burden as possible.' The labourer's response had been 'to devise elaborate rules for restricting the hours of toil, making its performance needlessly complex, and shirking with extreme ingenuity and conscientiousness.' He claimed that in older trades, notably building, where matters were made still worse by government regulations, these attitudes 'have practically arrested any advance whatever'.[129]

Wells saw a world in which technological advances would require new skills, and men would have to be trained to acquire them: but the average trade unionist viewed such a development with horror, preferring to insist 'on his position as a mere labourer' when he could have enjoyed his 'elevation . . . to the higher level of versatile educated men.'[130] He understood that if the working-class movement refused to move with the times, and with the technology, Britain's competitors would simply overtake her – as the Germans had been doing since about 1890. If manufacturers could not make new goods that would make people's lives easier, then Britain would have to import them: 'The community . . . that does least to educate its mechanics and engineers out of the base and servile tradition of the old idea of industry will in the coming years of progress simply get a disproportionate share of the rejected element, the trade will go elsewhere, and the community will be left in possession of an exceptionally large contingent for the abyss.'[131]

Wells was utilitarian in his appraisal of human resources: he attacked the education system for producing too few people of accomplishment and potential, mocking 'the shabby-genteel middle-class schoolmaster of the England of today, in – or a little way out of – orders, with his smattering of Greek, his Latin that leads nowhere, his fatuous mathematics, his gross ignorance of pedagogics, and his incomparable snobbishness', whom he considered one of the architects of the working man's unfortunate plight. He grasped a foremost concern of the Labour movement: the ability of machinery to put men out of work. He also predicted that the market for domestic service would contract as houses acquired labour-saving devices – removing another source of working-class employment. 'One always imagines a cook working with a crimsoned face and bare blackened arms,' he wrote. 'But with a neat little range, heated by electricity and provided with thermometers, with absolutely controllable temperatures and proper heat screens, cooking might very easily be made a pleasant amusement for intelligent invalid ladies.'[132]

That was all in the future. The Great Unrest had shifted the balance between masters and men. It had confirmed the superior power of organised workers in a labour-intensive economy. It had confirmed the Labour party as the natural representatives in parliament of the working-class movement, foreshadowing that party's rise at the expense of the Liberals after the Great War. The Trade Union Act of 1913 allowed unions to collect a political levy, which would greatly boost the funds of the Labour party: it reversed the House of Lords judgment of December 1909 in favour of a Liberal-supporting union member, Walter Osborne, who had objected to being forced to donate to a party he did not support. The Great Unrest forced employers to pay a fair wage: but it also showed that when unions went beyond what was fair, and tried to use their muscle for syndicalist purposes, they would lose support. The innate conservatism of the British worker, and his historically good relations with his employers, had stalled revolution. Yet it was, perhaps, as well war intervened before the next leg of the match was played.

CHAPTER 17

VOTES FOR WOMEN

I

As described in Chapter 8, women in late-Victorian Britain achieved improvements in their social and economic status: but the greatest prize of all – the right to participate in the country's governance – remained elusive. During the reign of King Edward VII, whose partiality towards the fair sex was well known, the demand for female suffrage became increasingly aggressive after years of peaceful protest. The extension of the franchise after 1832 had been limited to certain categories of males. To many men, and a considerable minority of women, it was unthinkable females should have the vote. Until shortly before the Great War, those against women's suffrage could depend on substantial public support, and had little cause to justify themselves. The arguments they adduced included the importance of domesticity, the likelihood of marital disharmony, the comparative physical weakness of women, the distraction of pregnancy and, paradoxically, the assertion that women without children were prone to neurosis.[1] Some said the English gentleman's idea of chivalry meant he could not see women as equals, with equal civil rights.[2] Such arguments indicate the Victorian cast of mind. Opposition to change was predominantly, but not exclusively, rooted in the Tory party. As with opponents to the Reform Bills of 1866 and 1867, anti-suffragists believed the beneficiaries would by education and temperament be unable to vote intelligently.

Until the Queen's death in 1901 there could be no question of any of her prime ministers – even had they believed in women's suffrage, which none did – seeking her assent to an Act that would grant it. Yet Britain's economic strength relied on an army of cheap female labour: and women knew it. So too did the comfort of the middle and upper classes, which depended on female domestic servants. In the later nineteenth century the status of women advanced. Not only did they secure property rights and local voting rights, but branched out as clerical staff, teachers, writers, administrators and in medicine and the professions allied to it.

Although women dominated teaching in the public sector – not least because elementary schools were so poorly funded that few men with the qualifications to teach wished to do the job at the salary they could command – other professions, notably the law, the Armed Forces and politics, remained closed to them. The 1911 census showed women mainly grouped in certain industries: 39 per cent in domestic service, 17.4 per cent in textiles and 15.2 per cent in clothing.[3] In textiles, they earned just over half the wage of their male colleagues.[4] But 75 per cent of the 230,000 teachers in 1901 census were women. And, naturally, as women bore more of society's burdens – something of which the Queen remained largely unaware in her detachment from her changing kingdom – so more of them sought the right to shape that society.

There was plenty of evidence that women wished to engage politically. By 1900 the Primrose League, a Unionist support group, included 500,000 women. It was obvious that women did, after all, have minds of their own; and had concluded that their lot in life would not improve without women's votes forcing governments to support wider equality. They were not alone. It was estimated that a majority in every House of Commons since 1870 had supported female suffrage, with supposedly 400 behind it in the 1910 parliament.[5]

Laws and regulations made by men tended not to consider the woman's point of view on any question – something the most formidable campaigner for women's suffrage, Emmeline Pankhurst, realised when she heard the cries of a woman giving birth in the spartan conditions of Holloway prison. Until women had the vote, the world would not be made fit for them to live in: but the political system seemed incapable of translating their economic muscle into political power. In his 1957 study *Votes for Women*, Roger Fulford described how 'rich old ladies with a train of companions, nurses and "maids", devoted daughters of professional families and stray spinsters from working-class homes looking after fading relatives were only too sadly obvious' in Edwardian Britain.[6]

As well as a fundamental desire for equality, fear that a life of domesticated unfulfilment awaited many women, and the belief that only having the vote would change this, drove on the women's movement. The way the suffrage campaign transcended class and political boundaries made change harder rather than easier to secure, because the normal forces of political action could not be mobilised in the usual way. However, as more women were educated, and worked in callings other than service and textile mills, the logic of denying them the franchise became unsustainable. The word 'feminism' is first recorded, in the political sense, in an article in the *Athenaeum* in April 1895; 'feminist', in the similar sense, came two years later.[7] The word was required, because its time had come.

II

Women's suffrage had first been discussed in the Commons in 1797, and had been regularly debated since John Stuart Mill and Jacob Bright resurrected the cause after the 1867 Reform Act.[8] Bright spoke at the first recorded campaign meeting for women's suffrage, at the Free Trade Hall in Manchester on 14 April 1868. The campaign came to London the following year, where Mill and Charles Kingsley spoke. Another speaker was twenty-two-year-old Millicent Fawcett, daughter of a Suffolk merchant and shipowner and wife of Henry Fawcett, a Liberal MP and Cambridge economist. A woman of formidable intellect, she was influenced by Frederick Denison Maurice, the Christian Socialist, and became a leader of the feminist movement. As a classical liberal she occasionally took positions that jarred with her comrades, who increasingly took their lead from the left: she felt, for example, that the oversupply of cheap labour made it dangerous for women to demand equal pay. An equal franchise was a different matter.

More meetings occurred, attracting attention because the number of women speakers increased – one of whom was Lady Amberley, daughter-in-law of Earl Russell, the former prime minister. Her parents were Lord and Lady Stanley of Alderley, the latter an outspoken campaigner for the education of women. Amberley was an atheist, when to profess such a view was to invite outrage, and both he and his wife had advanced sexual views. They practised contraception long before Marie Stopes, and advocated free love – Amberley condoned his wife's affair with the tutor of their children, one of whom was Bertrand Russell. This activism by a woman of standing horrified the leading woman in the land, the Queen. She was unique in that none of the disabilities affecting every other woman applied to her, and was unwilling to share her privileges. She wrote to Theodore Martin, her late husband's biographer, that 'the Queen is most anxious to enlist everyone who can speak or write or join in checking this mad, wicked folly of "Woman's Rights" with all its attendant horrors, on which her poor feeble sex is bent, forgetting every sense of womanly feeling and propriety. Lady Amberley ought to get a good whipping.'[9]

Sadly for the suffrage movement, many women took the Queen's view entirely, even to the extent of the proposed sanction for Lady Amberley. Once the argument started to favour the suffragists, their opponents had to organise. The most notable women's grouping was the Women's National Anti-Suffrage League, founded in July 1908, and chaired by the Countess of Jersey under the presidency of Mrs Humphry Ward, whose earnest and now largely unread novels concealed a considerable intellect. The women who opposed female suffrage were far from stupid, unlike some of their male comrades. Gertrude Bell, the writer and intrepid traveller, became the League's secretary. Another luminary was Beatrice Chamberlain, daughter of the anti-suffragist Joe and close friend of the sceptical Beatrice Webb. An ironic consequence was that by 1910 Lord Cromer, the former proconsul Evelyn Baring who put himself at the head of the male anti-suffragist movement, realised that the only women he thought fit to vote were those who led the female antis.

The League's principal argument was that women should not have the vote because 'the spheres of men and women, owing to natural causes, are essentially different, and therefore their share in the public management of the State should be different.'[10] They also argued that the things upon which the state depended for its existence – 'naval and military power, diplomacy, finance, and the great mining, constructive, shipping and transport industries' – were things in which women took no practical part; and as parliament concerned itself greatly with these issues, women should keep out of it. It was also argued that, given women's other duties, and the fact they could vote in local government, they could not possibly have the energy to participate in national matters too; that the influence they had would be diminished if they took up party politics, because they would be seen to lose their objectivity; that their increased involvement in other aspects of public life was sufficient; that political differences would intrude into family life. Giving the vote to women inexperienced in politics would be 'fraught with peril to the country'. Male opponents argued that women would vote as directed by their husbands or fathers. Where that left the substantial minority of women who had neither husbands nor extant fathers was unclear. Nor did there appear to be any evidence that women who voted in local or parochial elections did so as the proxy of an overbearing man: the Local Government Act, in force from 1 March 1894, created elected parish, rural district and urban district councils, for which women could not only vote, but stand for election. The argument contradicted that of the Women's League, which was that hearth and home would become a seat of political conflict.

The Commons – which sought to lead public opinion by even discussing this question – found it hard to agree on how female suffrage should work, rather than on its principle. Did all, or only some, women get the vote? And at what age? In 1884, as the third Reform Bill was going through, Gladstone rejected as too controversial, and too damaging to other government business, the proposal by seventy-nine of his MPs that women householders should get the vote. Henry Fawcett, who had become Postmaster-General, refused to vote against it, and Gladstone rebuked him. His sudden death shortly afterwards, aged just fifty-one, left his widow bereft, but in her grief she devoted herself to women's causes with even greater intensity, even turning down the post of Mistress of Girton in 1885.

Asquith noted in April 1892 that while 'there are some of the best women who are strongly in favour of women's suffrage', he believed 'some – I will not say a majority – of the best women . . . are strongly opposed to it.' He added that 'as to the great mass of the sex, the only thing that can be asserted with truth is that they are watching with languid and imperturbable indifference the struggle for their own emancipation.'[11] Asquith would maintain his hostility throughout his premiership, by which time some women had become violent militants.

In this speech he outlined his consistent doctrine. Anti-suffragists were asked:

> whether they will assert that a woman of genius like 'George Eliot' was unfit for the vote which was given to her butler and her

> footman. But legislation must be framed to deal not with exceptions and portents, but with average cases and normal conditions; and when this question of fitness is raised it is incumbent to realise oneself, and to remind others, that fitness is a relative term. We have not only to ask whether the average woman is fit for the franchise, but, if I may use such an expression, whether the franchise is fit for her.'[12]

He believed that women's 'natural sphere is not the turmoil and dust of politics, but the circle of social and domestic life', and asserted that 'the doctrine of democracy demands that we should equalise where inequality exists among things fundamentally alike, but not that we should identify where things are fundamentally unlike.'[13] He squared this with his liberalism thus: 'The inequalities which democracy requires that we should fight against and remove are the unearned privileges and the artificial distinction which man has made, and which man can unmake. They are not those indelible differences of faculty and function by which Nature herself has given diversity and richness to human society.'

The 1892 debate in which Asquith spoke would prove highly significant. The anti-suffragists won, but by just twenty-three votes – 175 to 152 – and the narrowness of the margin encouraged new momentum in a movement that had become moribund out of pessimism at its chances of success. A great petition was drawn up and signed by a quarter of a million people, which should have left the political class in no doubt of the popular view. In the Commons opinion shifted steadily towards extending the franchise. By 1897 a majority of seventy-one voted for change. By that point events with a strong cultural resonance in Britain had happened that helped the suffragists. On 19 September 1893 New Zealand had given women the right to vote, the first country to do so. Parts of Australia had followed the next year, and the apocalypse had not followed.

In Britain, the advances in women's education made denying them the vote seem increasingly anomalous. Ferdinand Begg, the Glasgow MP who opened the debate in February 1897, said that while it had been estimated that 73,000 illiterates had voted at the 1895 general election, approximately 500 women who had graduated from London University, 400 who had taken the tripos at Cambridge and almost 300 alumnae from Oxford, had been barred from doing so.[14] Educated women had begun to see a career as an alternative to marriage, partly to fulfil themselves intellectually, partly to avoid the restrictions conventional marriage brought upon them. A survey in 1895 showed that of the 1,486 women who up to that point had had a university education, only 208 had subsequently married.[15] Women also appeared to be more responsible citizens: the courts convicted 8,426 men in 1896, but only 1,267 women had been so degraded.

While the main force against women's suffrage came from the Unionists, Asquith's resistance to it was significant: and the Liberal leader in the Commons after Gladstone's departure, Harcourt, shared his lack of enthusiasm. There were more women than men in the United Kingdom: 106.8 women to every 100 men at the 1911 census, and in the late 1890s an estimated 1.2 million more females than males. In the 1897 debate Harcourt observed 'that it is not to be expected that all men will vote on one side and all women on the other. No man expects that, but is it not perfectly clear that where you have a majority of 1,200,000 those who possess that majority must in the long run have the determining voice?'[16] It would, he said, be 'a change upon an Amazonian basis; you are going to establish the electorate on a popular womanhood majority. In my opinion that may be a good thing or a bad thing, but it is not a thing to be disposed of on a Wednesday afternoon.'

Although the Labour movement came to be synonymous with the pursuit of equality, in the late nineteenth and early twentieth century it was nothing of the kind. The few enlightened MPs who argued for women's suffrage were outnumbered by trade unionists who saw women as a threat to their jobs and their earning power. Two well-to-do women, Esther Roper and Eva Gore-Booth (whose sister Constance, later Countess Markievicz, would be the first woman elected to the Commons), based themselves in Manchester to harness support for women's suffrage from the 96,000 women in the region who belonged to trades unions, but whose voices had thus far been silenced.

Although Misses Roper and Gore-Booth campaigned for better conditions for women in the cotton industry, theirs was not a class-based programme. They enlisted women like themselves to join in the struggle, for their own sakes as much as for that of their less privileged sisters, but their key message was that men earned far more than women for doing identical jobs because women had no votes and therefore could change nothing. They slowly persuaded local parliamentary candidates to embrace their cause; and a woman who joined their organising committee before the 1906 general election was a forty-seven-year-old Manchester woman, Emmeline Pankhurst.

Mrs Pankhurst's husband, Richard, was a radical barrister with a long history of supporting the women's movement. From a middle-class family, he had shown brilliance as a student, being awarded an LLD by London University in 1863, after which he was known as Dr Pankhurst. Twenty-two years older than his wife – he was born in either 1835 or 1836 – he was active by the 1860s in the Liberal party, the reform movement and as a sponsor of workers' educational institutes. His radicalism went beyond extending the suffrage: he was also a republican (he founded the Manchester Republican Club in 1873) and advocated disestablishment. In 1867 he was an early member of the Manchester National Society for Women's Suffrage. There he met the formidable Lydia Becker, who would assume the leadership of the movement that would, forty years later, be occupied by Pankhurst's future wife. His legal expertise was used, fruitlessly, to draft the early Women's Suffrage Bills, and to take test cases to court – such as, in 1868, demanding the vote for Manchester's female ratepayers. Just as it had with free trade thirty years earlier, the city became the crucible of another important, and ultimately successful, progressive movement. Pankhurst was also active in the parallel movement to secure women's property rights, and helped draft the Bill enacted in 1882.

In 1874 a Conservative MP, William Forsyth, had introduced a Bill that proposed to enfranchise spinsters and widows but not married women. This was acceptable to Miss Becker and her associates, but their agreement outraged Pankhurst, who resolved to have nothing more to do with them. For him, in this as in other matters, it was all or nothing. However, even if Miss Becker and her ladies presumed that married women might be told how to vote by their husbands, it was far from certain that those without husbands would be free agents. Arnold Bennett makes it clear in *Anna of the Five Towns* that the heroine remains intimidated by men and subservient to them despite her independent wealth. Her blind obedience to her husband might have been the cultural norm, but it was the natural consequence of blind obedience to her father.

Pankhurst married Emmeline Goulden, daughter of a Manchester calico printer, in 1879. Emmeline had been reading her mother's copies of the *Woman's Suffrage Journal* (edited by Miss Becker) as a precocious teenager, and hearing a rousing speech by her at a public meeting in 1872 set Emmeline on the road to militant suffragism. Shortly after her marriage, and despite the distractions of five children (one of whom died in infancy), she joined her husband on the committee of the Manchester National Society for Women's Suffrage. Dr Pankhurst fought the 1885 election for the Liberals in the London seat of Rotherhithe, which he lost partly because of the Irish vote against him, although he was a Home Ruler. However, he also lost because he had spoken in Manchester shortly before the Rotherhithe campaign about his atheism, something Mill, twenty years before, had recognised as dangerous when soliciting votes. His Tory opponents broadcast his feelings about God around the constituency. To make matters worse, Pankhurst then attempted, unsuccessfully, to sue for libel newspapers that attributed such views to him. This not only helped deplete his financial resources, but also ensured the controversy remained active.

Although angry at what she regarded as her husband's unjust defeat, Mrs Pankhurst noted both the way in which a movement – in this case for Home Rule – could cut across party lines, and how successful belligerence could be in securing political aims: the Liberals introduced their Home Rule Bill the next year. 'That was a valuable political lesson, one that years later I was destined to put into practice,' she noted in her memoirs.[17]

For seven years the Pankhursts lived in London, during which their fourth child, Frank, died of diphtheria contracted from bad drains. They stepped up their political activity. Both joined the Fabian Society. Keir Hardie became a close friend; which was followed by the Pankhursts' resignations from the Liberal party and membership of the Independent Labour party in 1893. That year the family returned to Manchester, where Mrs Pankhurst was elected to represent the ILP on the Board of Guardians of the Chorlton workhouse: female ratepayers were allowed on the electoral register for all local elections after 1869; they could also serve on school boards and boards of guardians. The conditions she observed horrified her, not least in the way they degraded young single women with children born out of wedlock. She lobbied for local improvements; but her sense of powerlessness at being unable to change the Poor Law further entrenched her determination to campaign for women's suffrage. 'These poor, unprotected mothers and their babies,' she wrote, 'I am sure were potent factors in my education as a militant.'[18]

Pankhurst's campaigning socialism in the 1890s had reduced his income as a lawyer, not merely because of the hours of paid work he lost, but because many potential clients regarded his politics as inimical to their interests. His sudden death in July 1898 left his family not just shocked but also teetering on the verge of destitution. Mrs Pankhurst did what many women in her unfortunate position had to do: she went out to work. She set up a shop – as she had unsuccessfully done earlier in her marriage – but it failed. She eventually became a registrar of births and deaths; she could not register marriages as the law stipulated that had to be done by 'a male person'.[19] Her late husband's friends set up a fund to build a memorial hall in his name in Salford, to be used as the local headquarters of the ILP. When it was opened in 1903 Mrs Pankhurst was outraged that women could not join the party there, and this prompted her to set up her own movement for women of all classes to campaign for equality in the franchise. Thus was the Women's Social and Political Union born. The first meeting was held at her house in Manchester in October 1903, and the name was chosen with various aims in mind: 'Partly to emphasise its democracy,' she recalled, 'and partly to define its object as political rather than propagandist.'[20] The founders decided not to affiliate to any party, and not to admit men as members.

The Union began by pursuing peaceful activities: marches, meetings, organising petitions and demonstrating on the fringes of the political meetings of others. To the WSPU's frustration, some MPs were prepared to give their support to the movement, but were not (with certain distinguished exceptions) prepared to upset their party whips, and their chances of advancement, by introducing a private member's Bill to obtain the vote for women. Labour sought universal suffrage – or so its leaders said – but many other MPs, even radical Liberals, felt there were still groups of unfranchised men who did not deserve the vote, let alone women. Although the WSPU started by working closely with Labour, and in Lancashire's industrial heartland, within eighteen months the limitations of Labour's support became obvious, and the urge grew to break out of the WSPU's regional base. The leadership of the movement became ever more concentrated on the Pankhursts – not just Emmeline, but her two elder daughters, Christabel and Sylvia. This would have important consequences for the governance of the WSPU, and change it within a few years from a democratic body to a form of benign and dynastic dictatorship.

III

A private member's Bill on women's suffrage was scheduled for debate on 12 May 1905, but discussion of the Bill ahead of it – the Roadway Lighting Bill, a necessity since the advent of the motor-car – was so extended by opponents of women's suffrage that there was insufficient time for a proper debate; much to the amusement of many MPs but to the disgust of the suffragists watching from the gallery. Tempers were not improved by some of the opinions expressed, such as when Henry Labouchere, seventy-four years old and from a different world, said that even John Stuart Mill would have voted against this Bill. Labouchere admitted having voted for a measure on women's suffrage Mill had proposed in 1868, but said that he had regretted it ever since, and had 'endeavoured to make up for it as a penance by opposing the Women's Franchise Bill tooth and nail ever since.'[21] Women could not, he said, be soldiers or policemen; and as civilisation had advanced, so they had stopped doing heavy manual labour. 'It was not their fault', he added, 'that they were more beautiful than muscular.'[22]

He continued: 'In domestic matters women were much more useful and understood them better than men . . . but in the consideration of the great problems which came before the Imperial Parliament they were certainly inferior intellectually to men.' And, for good measure, he noted that 'women were nervous, emotional, and had very little sense of proportion', and they were incapable of seeing when they were wrong.[23] Although the country had until recently had a Queen who had functioned tolerably well, Labouchere noted that she had always acted on the advice of her ministers, who were all men. Therefore 'it would be easier for a woman to act as Queen than to act as a simple voter.' He also feared that if women ended up in the Commons they would use feminine wiles to get their way, with 'all sorts of political flirtations going on'. Hansard recorded that when women asked to meet him Labouchere 'remembered the intelligent Ulysses closed his ears not to hear the sirens; and so he did not go to those ladies. If he had gone – man was weak – he might have been cajoled and humbugged into taking their part and voting for this measure.'[24] *The Times* report said Labouchere had spoken 'in a jocular vein'.[25]

There then followed the first of many confrontations between the suffragists and the authorities. Mrs Pankhurst went to the Central Lobby and told supporters waiting there to follow her outside, where they planned a demonstration. When the group was outside the police rushed them and moved them on. They congregated by the statue of Richard the Lionheart outside the House of Lords, but were driven away from there too. Eventually the police allowed a demonstration outside Westminster Abbey, though made a point of taking the women's names. This was the birth of suffragist militancy.

As Balfour's administration crumbled, and the prospect of a Liberal government seemed more likely, the WSPU became louder. Christabel Pankhurst and Annie Kenney, a mill worker from Oldham – the movement's first high-profile working-class recruit – disrupted a Liberal meeting at the Free Trade Hall in Manchester on 13 October 1905. Miss Kenney asked Sir Edward Grey, who would soon be Foreign Secretary: 'If the Liberal party is returned to power, will they take steps to give votes for women?'[26] The party was split on this issue, so the question was highly embarrassing. A steward covered Miss Kenney's face with his hat, after men around her had pulled her down into her seat. A commotion broke out, and when it subsided Miss Pankhurst repeated the question. Grey refused to answer. Winston Churchill, also on the platform, having just been adopted as Liberal candidate for the marginal Conservative-held seat of Manchester North-West following his desertion of the Tory party, said nothing. He had voted for women's suffrage when the matter had come before the Commons in 1904. Lady Grey was a feminist who had influenced her husband's view. It should have been easy for both men to defuse the argument. The meeting then witnessed the birth of the movement's slogan. A banner was to be unfurled asking: 'Will the Liberal Party give Votes for Women?' However, there was nowhere the large banner could be deployed, so the last three words – 'Votes for Women' – were cut out and brandished by Christabel Pankhurst as Miss Kenney spoke.

The women yelled: 'Answer the question!' The audience turned on them in rage and became, in Mrs Pankhurst's words, 'a mob'.[27] Stewards threw the two women out while Grey, Churchill and the platform party sat impassively and watched. Once the room had calmed down Grey said that he had decided not to answer 'because it is not, and I do not think it is likely to be, a party question.'[28] The women tried to address the crowd as it left the hall but were arrested for obstruction and, in Christabel's case, for assaulting the police: she threatened to spit upon them. Miss Kenney was fined five shillings or three days in jail, Miss Pankhurst ten shillings or a week inside. They refused to pay – and both refused Mrs Pankhurst's offer to pay – and were sent to prison. Churchill, who we must suppose had remained silent out of deference to a senior colleague, allowing him to take the lead, was keen for reasons of self-preservation to make amends. He went to Strangeways Prison, where the women were incarcerated, and offered to pay their fines, but the governor refused to take his money. Despite his support for them the WSPU canvassed against him in the 1906 general election, his crime having been to become a junior minister when the Liberals took power at the end of 1905. Hardie, like Churchill, realised the impact the incident would have, and sent a telegram to the women to say: 'The thing is a dastardly outrage, but do not worry it will do immense good.'[29]

This militancy caused a profound shock: Britain was not conditioned for such behaviour from women. It slowly dawned on the anti-suffrage movement that it might have underestimated the commitment of its opponents. Hitherto there had been simple, and polite, agreement to differ, as when Helen Schlegel meets the conservative Mr Wilcox in *Howards End*, and tells her sister afterwards: 'He says the most horrid things about women's suffrage so nicely, and when I said I believed in equality he just folded his arms and gave me such a setting down as I've never had.'[30] That mood was now passing. The outbreak of agitation provided a huge publicity coup for the WSPU. Suddenly the women's suffrage movement, which had almost disappeared from most of the nation, was being reported in the press and widely commented upon.

A policy not merely of questioning politicians at meetings, but heckling at them, became standard. It was at this time that the term by which the militant activists came to be known was coined; the *Oxford English Dictionary* cites the *Daily Mail* using the term 'suffragette' for the first time on 10 January 1906. When the women left prison a new, packed meeting was convened in the Free Trade Hall to welcome them back and congratulate them. This time the speaker was Hardie, who had the far from unanimous support of his party for his backing of the WSPU. Annie Kenney left her job in the mill and became a full-time campaigner, moving into the Pankhursts' house. The furore attracted recruits, and donations, to the cause.

The WSPU was not the sole suffrage movement, but it was in 1906 unique in embracing militancy. The National Union of Women's Suffrage Societies had been formed in 1897 'with a view to the more systematic and combined organisation of the work throughout the country', and its figurehead was Millicent Fawcett.[31] It was non-party political. Starting with just sixteen affiliates, 480 local societies were affiliated to it by 1914.[32] Its strategy was one of reasoned argument and rejection of extra-parliamentary agitation. It not only published leaflets and pamphlets about the cause but also offered advice to women wishing to break into predominantly masculine careers, such as medicine. It urged the admission of women to the police force (as had just happened in America) and to the law. In 1914 its information bureau listed the objections to women practising at the Bar – 'a women advocate would be irresistible with a male jury', 'the male advocate would be prejudiced in his work by a chivalrous feeling not to press the woman opponent' and 'judges would insensibly incline more favourably to the woman lawyer'.[33] It also publicised achievements by women in the arts and sciences.

The National Union had become largely invisible even before the advent of the WSPU, not through a shortage of numbers but through a failure to raise its profile. Once the campaign of militancy – and martyrdom through penal servitude – began, it started to appear increasingly redundant, having achieved precisely nothing in almost a decade of existence. In chipping away at the public consciousness the National Union steadily won converts: but it was increasingly difficult to rebut the idea that a political establishment that resolutely refused to respond to reasoned argument, and showed no sign of changing its mind, might just be persuaded by tactics akin to terrorism.

The assaults began reasonably mildly, Mrs Pankhurst leading a deputation to Campbell-Bannerman in April 1906; marching to see him, appropriately, from the statue of Boadicea on the Whitehall Embankment. She had been in regular touch with Hardie to attempt to co-ordinate the WSPU's activities with those of the ILP. The prime minister readily admitted, in response to the women's demands for an immediate Act to give them their rights, that he favoured their cause, and hoped they would continue to win converts. However, he said that much of the cabinet did not, so nothing could be done without wrecking the government: the main opponent was Asquith, then just installed as Chancellor of the Exchequer, and who would become a particular target of the suffragettes. Mrs Pankhurst threatened that she was ready to 'sacrifice life itself' to achieve her ends, a claim about which subsequent events would leave little doubt.[34] She went from the meeting to address a rally of 7,000 of her followers in Trafalgar Square.

Later in 1906 the WSPU launched a new campaign. It was computed that around 420 MPs supported women's suffrage, and the WSPU and its members saw no reason for further delay in obtaining what they wanted: though this ignored the caution of the government in supporting so radical a measure and the almost certain refusal, in those days before the 1911 Parliament Act, of the House of Lords to do so. On 23 October 200 suffragettes thronged Parliament's Central Lobby, and several tried to climb on to the plinths of statues to address the crowd. There followed what *The Times* called 'something in the nature of a tumult'.[35] The report said that 'two or three of the women stood upon one of the seats and began to harangue those present, declaring that women demanded votes and would refuse any longer to be treated as slaves.' The police intervened, impeded by women linking arms and forming a human barrier around the ringleaders. They eventually removed the protesters, though, as *The Times* continued, 'not . . . without a struggle; in fact, so violent was the resistance that in some cases it taxed the powers of a couple of constables to turn one frantic woman out of the building.' In the process, 'several of the excited women shrieked hysterically, and one or two who had to be carried out kicked with extreme vigour.' Mrs Pankhurst was knocked over.

Ten women were arrested and sent to prison for two months for refusing to find sureties of £10 each to keep the peace, imposed by the Rochester Row Police Court. This prompted a protest at the court by Sylvia Pankhurst, then aged twenty-four, who was fined twenty shillings for disorderly conduct. She refused to pay and was sent to prison too. This outraged Hardie, who twice raised the matter in parliament. He said she had been convicted 'on the uncorroborated testimony of one policeman, while three women of standing . . . contradicted that of the policeman in every essential particular'.[36] Herbert Gladstone, the Home Secretary, a supporter of women's suffrage, refused to order her release, saying she could leave prison at once if she paid her fine. Hardie then asked him to release the ten other women – their disorderly conduct, he claimed, had simply amounted to 'having asked for votes for women'. Gladstone refused to do this too.[37]

After the attempt to storm the Palace of Westminster in October 1906, Campbell-Bannerman warned the suffragettes that militancy would not change the government's view. When the women ended up in Holloway, more of their male supporters protested about their treatment. The Irish Nationalists, like most of Labour, made common cause; and one Irishman, Hugh Law, complained after the October incident that 'eleven ladies . . . have been obliged to wear prison clothes, and are otherwise being treated as ordinary criminals' – precisely the experience of Ann Veronica Stanley, heroine of Wells's 1909 novel about a young woman who flirts with suffragism.[38] Hardie complained that better treatment had been afforded to those convicted after the Jameson Raid. Even some Unionist MPs, such as Lord Robert Cecil, complained about the conditions; a Liberal MP, William Byles, was shocked that the health of two of the women had declined immediately on their entering Holloway, and complained that their treatment was too harsh 'having regard to the absence of moral delinquency in the offence for which these ladies are imprisoned'.

A class system of sorts prevailed in British jails, though not entirely based on social considerations. There was a notion of a political prisoner, and such people normally ended up in the first division, together with those whose backgrounds suggested they merited preferential treatment and who had no record of habitual offending (such as Lord Russell, convicted of bigamy in 1901 after a divorce obtained in Nevada was adjudged illegal). Such people were thereby distinguished from moderate and first offenders (second division prisoners) and common criminals (third division), did not need to wear prison clothes, associated only with their own class, and could have meals brought in. These were the privileges accorded to Dr Jameson, and which had not been given to Sylvia Pankhurst and her friends, to Hardie's outrage.

Gladstone, attacked from all sides, said that the women were not placed in the first division because the magistrate who imprisoned them had not thought to recommend it. He told the Commons he had 'brought the matter to [the magistrate's] notice; and I am glad to say he has seen his way to direct that they should be treated as first-division offenders': one can well imagine the conversation. The other consolation was that, despite not having had privileges from the start, the women 'have not associated with the ordinary criminal of the third class'.[39] Two women were released early for health reasons, and the rest would be freed halfway through their sentences. Even this would not be the end of the matter: the suffragettes soon got word out of Holloway that it was infested with rats, which ran about their cells at night while they tried to sleep.

Gladstone's refusal to bend the rules in favour of a cause he supported gave yet more impetus to militancy by creating the martyrdom of imprisonment. Even Mrs Fawcett, whose National Union repudiated violence, wrote to *The Times* to praise the way in which the WSPU had revived the debate: she condemned the tone of the press reporting, and said of one of the convicted women, Mrs Cobden-Sanderson (daughter of the Corn Laws reformer), 'I find it absolutely impossible to believe that she bit, or scratched, or screamed, or behaved otherwise than like the refined woman she is.'[40] She continued: 'Every kind of insult and abuse is hurled at the women who have adopted these methods, especially by the "reptile" Press. But I hope the more old-fashioned suffragists will stand by them; and I take this opportunity of saying that in my opinion, far from having injured the movement, they have done more during the last twelve months to bring it within the region of practical polities than we have been able to accomplish in the same number of years.' In what sounded like an incitement, she also noted: 'The real responsibility for these sensational methods lies with the politicians, misnamed statesmen, who will not attend to a demand for justice until it is accompanied by some form of violence.' When the women were free the National Union showed how close it felt to its sisters. It hosted a banquet for them at the Savoy, attended by (among others) Shaw and his wife, who dined on nut roasts.

IV

In 1907 the WSPU relocated from Manchester to London, with Mrs Pankhurst becoming a full-time paid official. It announced its arrival in the capital by organising a march from Hyde Park to the Strand on 9 February, two days before the State Opening of Parliament. Over 3,000 attended the protest, which came to be known as the Mud March because of the weather in which it occurred. Many were kept away by heavy rain, but the procession still stretched from Piccadilly Circus to Hyde Park Corner. One protester was John Maynard Keynes, aged twenty-three, who wrote to the organiser, Philippa Strachey, to say: 'I hear you may want hired roughs next Saturday', and offered his services.[41] Mrs Fawcett, using the letters columns of *The Times* to appeal for funds to continue the work, felt the meeting was a breakthrough. 'Women of all classes who had never taken part in any political demonstration before were determined, at considerable sacrifice to themselves, to show the earnestness of their demand for representation.'[42]

However, tensions were increasing between the National Union and the WSPU as the former fought to maintain its non-partisan approach while, as a confidential circular of May 1908 to its Council members pointed out, the WSPU '*invariably works* against the Government (at present Liberal) candidate'.[43] It added, in a rather wounded tone, that 'the aim of the WSPU, being not so much to educate the electors on the question of Women's Suffrage as to harass the Government into immediate action, the method of propaganda adopted by the NUWSS is far too slow in its results for this purpose.' On 13 February the WSPU again marched on parliament, this time in bright sunshine from a meeting at Caxton Hall where Mrs Pankhurst had stirred the crowd by referring to the absence of a suffrage Bill from the King's Speech. Annie Kenney moved a motion, passed with just one dissentient, to express the meeting's 'profound indignation' at the situation.[44] Apparently keen to be arrested for incitement or even sedition, Mrs Pankhurst concluded her remarks with the observation that 'if laws were broken it would not be their fault.'

The assembly then marched to Parliament Square, led by the sixty-three-year-old Mrs Charlotte Despard, sister of the Great War field marshal Sir John French. The police stopped them by St Margaret's Church, opposite parliament, and told them they could go no further. Scuffles broke out. Mrs Despard (who ended up in Holloway) and others were arrested, and Britain was shocked by reports of a pitched battle between the suffragettes and mounted police. *The Times* reported: 'The mounted [police]men . . . backed their horses on to the pavement, where the procession was, and many of the women were thrown to the ground and hurt, including Mrs Despard.' Some women had gone on ahead and were already at the entrance to Parliament. When they joined in the fight, the police threw some of them into the mud in the gutter, which prompted passers-by to yell at the police in outrage; the police manhandling apparently respectable women had not hitherto been a common sight in England. Policemen had their helmets knocked off, and some women managed to enter New Palace Yard. While being ejected, thirty-four were arrested.

They were all bailed, and that evening the WSPU assembled again at Caxton Hall. 'Mrs Despard, who was loudly cheered,' *The Times* reported, 'said she had been arrested simply and solely for endeavouring to cross the road.' Christabel Pankhurst, who took the chair, urged the meeting to march on the Commons again and demand admission. 'She advised them not to be afraid of the police, to link arms, not to break up their ranks, and if they lost sight of their leaders to become leaders themselves.' Her mother said 'it was only a question of numbers; if they were numerous enough they could settle the question in an hour.' This time the police stopped them before they could approach their objective; by 10 p.m. fifty-two women and two men had been arrested.

The defendants appeared in the Westminster police court on 14 February. There were demonstrations in the public gallery, which ended when the magistrate, Curtis Bennett, threatened to clear the court. Christabel Pankhurst, whose case came on first as she had been identified as the organiser of the march, was unrepentant. 'Yesterday was a great day in our movement,' she told the magistrate, 'and we have to take these measures to get what we want . . . if life is lost in this campaign the Liberal Government of the day is responsible.'[45] Bennett disagreed, saying the women were 'directly responsible' for 'these disgraceful scenes of disorder . . . it must be stopped.' Christabel was fined twenty shillings, or a fortnight in prison in the first division; Mrs Despard was fined forty shillings or three weeks in the first division; those convicted from the lower classes, including a factory hand from Blackburn, a servant from Leeds and a weaver from Manchester, had to be content with the second division. On her release, Mrs Despard told Mrs Fawcett: 'I do not think my health has suffered at all . . . I am thankful I have been in prison.'[46] She said that once she had won her civil rights she would campaign to reform prison, so that it stopped 'making criminals'.

Some MPs were disquieted both by the upsurge of militancy and by the authorities' response to it, and sought an immediate solution. A Liberal MP, W. H. Dickinson, introduced a private member's Bill advocating that all existing law conferring the vote on men should apply also to women, the masculine pronoun taken to include the feminine wherever necessary, and stipulating that marriage should not disqualify a woman from voting. Like so many other attempts, it got nowhere. Because of cabinet divisions the whip could not be applied, so the government could not adopt the Bill; and without that it could not become law. Its inevitable defeat inflamed the WSPU further, and increased its recruitment. On 22 March another column of suffragettes marched on parliament, causing another pitched battle; except that the government, having gauged the public's mood, kept the mounted police in their stables. An attempt, led by Christabel Pankhurst, to storm the Commons and seize the Mace – the symbol of parliamentary authority – failed.

Some women began to refuse to pay taxes unless given the vote, on the principle of no taxation without representation. One was Lady Steel, widow of Sir James Steel, the former Lord Provost of Edinburgh. Bailiffs seized her furniture and sent it to auction to recover the £18 9s she owed. A crowd of 5,000 attended the sale and the first item auctioned, a sideboard, realised almost double that amount. It was bought by a supporter and returned to the owner; the sale was stopped.

The publicity gained by such militancy brought benefits and problems. The former included the volunteering of ever more capable and better-connected women, notably the social worker and feminist activist Emmeline Pethick-Lawrence, who on becoming treasurer of the WSPU in the spring of 1906 not only used part of her husband's money to fund its activities but also enlisted some of her rich friends to do the same. It was Hardie who introduced Mrs Pethick-Lawrence to Mrs Pankhurst, a conjunction that would supercharge the activities of the WSPU. Mrs Pethick-Lawrence had been one of the eleven women sent to Holloway after the demonstration of October 1906, so established her credentials early. Her husband, to draw even more attention to her martyrdom, promised £10 to the WSPU's coffers for every day his wife was inside.

However, as the WSPU became bigger, better funded and more militant, disagreements arose about tactics and strategy. Mrs Pankhurst and Christabel (who in her mother's frequent absences in the provinces on speaking tours had taken over the organisation) were both angry at what they considered to be Labour's continuing reluctance to engage on their behalf (they had long since written off the Tories and the Liberals).

However, this split the Pankhurst family, because two other daughters, Sylvia and Adele, wished to retain links to the ILP.

In the autumn of 1907 there was an even more profound change. When the WSPU moved to London at the end of 1906 a constitution had been drawn up. It proposed quarterly meetings of an executive council. However, this council had hardly met, causing concern: not merely because of the flouting of the constitution, or the need to discuss policy, but also because of the large amounts of money now being raised – money used to pay salaries to Mrs Pankhurst and two of her daughters – for the spending of which there seemed inadequate accountability.

At the suggestion of Mrs Pethick-Lawrence and her husband Frederick, who were bankrolling the movement substantially and acting as guarantors for dozens of women on bail, Mrs Pankhurst tore up the constitution and imposed a top-down autocracy in the interests of effectiveness. There would be no annual conference after one held to establish the new regime in October 1907, but there would be a steering committee: this would, however, be comprised solely of people who agreed with Mrs Pankhurst. Most members felt that this hard-line approach would be more effective than a form of internal democracy that would simply result in endless squabbling; a few dissenters, led by Mrs Despard, left the WSPU, however, and formed what would become the Women's Freedom League, a less militant but more democratic body.

Mrs Pankhurst's success in carrying so many supporters with her in turning the WSPU into a dictatorship was down to her sincerity, her oratory, and an aura around her that allowed suspension of disbelief among many who heard her. Once the dictatorship was established, the campaign of militancy was stepped up further. The WSPU wanted to propagate the message in the provinces as well as in London, and either Mrs Pankhurst or Christabel would lead flying squads of suffragettes to harry the Liberal candidate at any by-election. Their reasoning was the old Irish Nationalist one that if the government, however full of sympathetic ministers it might be, was determined to deny time and support to a Bill, its candidates had to be defeated.

On 13 February 1908, the last day of a three-day meeting of a 'Women's Parliament' in Caxton Hall, Mrs Pankhurst was arrested for obstruction at the Commons, having led a march there to attempt to present a petition to Campbell-Bannerman. She had also allegedly smacked a constable in the face with the petition. Before leaving Caxton Hall, she had warned the government that 'she felt the time was coming when they [the WSPU] would not be able to control their forces'.[47] Numerous women begged her not to lead the deputation but, determined upon martyrdom, she ignored them. She was asked for £20 in sureties to keep the peace for year, or else sentenced to six weeks in prison. She chose the latter, serving her sentence in the second division, with criminals. Entirely unrepentant, she told the magistrate: 'I shall go to prison like the rest. But the moment I am released I shall visit you again – or, I hope, some superior court to your administration.'[48] The galleries, packed with suffragettes, erupted in applause and cheers, and the magistrate ordered the women to be thrown out. Annie Kenney, speaking in what *The Times*'s court reporter termed 'very militant tones', announced that 'I shall never give up this agitation until the women of this country get political liberty.'

Shows of support for the WSPU turned into shows of strength: on 13 June 13,000 marched from the Embankment to the Albert Hall, and on 21 June thirty special trains brought women from all over the country to join one of seven processions to Hyde Park – copying a tactic used by the Reform movement in 1866. For the first time women wore sashes in what had been deemed to be the colours of the movement – white and green, which had long been the colours of the 'constitutional' suffragettes, with the addition of purple, the colour of the militants in the WSPU and the League. *The Times* – whose editorial columns had just decreed that women were unfit for the franchise 'because they are subject to long periods of child-bearing, when they drop every other pursuit for their highest function to the state' and because 'the exercise of the franchise by women would be unfair and unequal in giving them an excessive voice in determining measures for which they would not have to bear the ultimate responsibility' – estimated the crowd at half a million, which, if true, put the meeting at seven times the size of the Reform meeting on which it was based.[49] 'All London seemed to have mustered in that stretch of green between the Serpentine and the Marble-arch,' the paper's reporter wrote. Indeed, the numbers might even, he conceded, have trebled the estimate of 250,000 set by the organisers: 'Like the distances and numbers of the stars, the facts were beyond the threshold of perception.'[50] He praised the 'remarkable' organisation and the 3,000 standard-bearers, and twenty different platforms in the park from which 100 different speakers would thrill the multitude. A bugle sounded when the speeches were to begin.

'It was a curious spectacle that now met the eye – in every direction the level flood of human faces, and above it, in every attitude of animated gesticulation, the white-robed figures of 20 lady orators.' Although no one beyond fifty yards from any speaker could hear a word that was said, *The Times* noted that 'the staple of the speeches seemed to be pungent criticism of the Government in general and of Mr Asquith in particular.' Mrs Shaw was spotted in the crowd; her husband was noted watching approvingly from the sidelines.

Just before five o'clock on a sunny summer afternoon a resolution was presented from all twenty platforms, calling upon the government to give women the vote 'without delay'. 'Immediately thousands of hands and hats were raised in enthusiastic salutation, and from thousands of voices rose a great cheer. To the eye the effect was as if the level of the great tide that flooded the Park had suddenly risen by a foot. Next, again in obedience to signal, a crescendo shout of "Votes for Women", thrice repeated, was given.' On the rally's eve, a waxwork group featuring Mrs Pankhurst, Christabel, Mrs Pethick-Lawrence and Miss Kenney was unveiled at Madame Tussaud's. The ladies depicted, conscious of the value of publicity, had granted the artist several sittings, when their attendance at Holloway permitted.

V

In Campbell-Bannerman the suffrage movement had a supporter, however timid, in 10 Downing Street. However, his resignation in April 1908 and the succession of Asquith brought a confrontation between the women and their most implacable political enemy. When one ponders upon what happened to the notion of liberalism before the Great War, this Liberal prime minister's hostility to women's suffrage is but one of the paradoxes. Hitherto the campaign had been against a whole male political class. Now it became personalised, and, as in Hyde Park, at all the great rallies of the summer of 1908, specific abuse of Asquith was notable. After another failed attempt to storm the Commons, on 30 June, two women – Marie Leigh and Edith New, both on the WSPU's payroll – threw stones at Asquith's windows, breaking some of them. At Bow

Street the next day the prosecution called for both women to be imprisoned, drawing attention to what they had allegedly said at the time of their arrests. Miss New, thirty-one, had proclaimed: 'Freedom for the women of England! We are martyrs!' while twenty-six-year-old Mrs Leigh told the police 'it would be a bomb next time'.[51] Each woman was given two months in the first division.

On 14 October Mrs Pankhurst, Christabel and Flora Drummond – a five-feet tall woman in sturdy middle age known as 'the General', who just before the Hyde Park rally had taken a motor-boat up the Thames to alongside the terrace of the Palace of Westminster, and had addressed via a megaphone those enjoying drinks on it – were charged with incitement to disorder. They had distributed leaflets at a Trafalgar Square rally the previous day, urging pro-suffragists to 'rush' the Commons. Mrs Drummond's sobriquet stemmed not just from her formidable appearance and character, but from her peerless organising skills: she had masterminded the Hyde Park rally and choreographed the processions.

A sudden but steep rise in unemployment had attracted more to the ranks of the disaffected. The authorities were anxious that the more militant end of the Labour movement might make common cause with the suffragettes, instituting anarchy. Therefore, the invitation to storm parliament was taken more seriously than previously. Some protesters did assemble in Westminster; but the closest the women got to disrupting proceedings was when Mrs Travers Symons, Keir Hardie's secretary, who was in parliament fulfilling her duties, ran into the Commons chamber while fighting continued outside and asked the Speaker to order discussion of the women's grievances. She was thrown out and banned from the precincts for two years. Hardie began to fear that the WSPU was becoming 'what the SDF had been to socialism' – an extremist group that would deter potential support.[52]

The three women spent the night before their hearing in the cells at Bow Street. Dinner was sent in from the Savoy, paid for by a sympathetic Liberal MP, Colonel James Murray, who also appeared as a friendly witness in the case. The trial was postponed for a week, in which time Herbert Gladstone and Lloyd George, who had come out and watched the demonstration (Lloyd George with his six-year-old daughter Megan) and were therefore witnesses, were made to attend under subpoena at the request of the defendants. Christabel Pankhurst, who had read law at Manchester University (she was not, of course, allowed to practise, being a woman), made a fine job of cross-examining them.

Lloyd George (who sympathised with the cause) refused to be drawn into a semantic discussion of the definition of the verb 'to rush': 'I cannot enter competition with *Chambers's Dictionary*,' he told the court.[53] Miss Pankhurst sought to persuade him to agree that 'to rush' also meant 'to be in a hurry', and said, 'There is nothing unlawful in being in a hurry.' With the Crown trying to maintain that a dangerous breach of public order had occurred, she forced Lloyd George to admit he had had no qualms about taking his daughter to witness the event. 'I trusted to the police arrangements,' he told her. Another suffragette, questioned by Christabel, said the protest had been 'like a rush at hockey'. Christabel observed, 'If you rush at hockey, it does not mean that you hit someone on the head.' Murray, giving evidence, said the crowd 'was composed of the same kind of persons who went to Church on Sunday in Scotland.'[54]

Mrs Pankhurst (who had also questioned Lloyd George – none of the women had legal representation) made a rousing two-hour speech. Having described her passionate belief in votes for women, she claimed the case against her and the others had been brought 'out of malice and for vexation'. The magistrate sentenced her to be bound over on her own recognisance for twelve months in the sum of £100, and to pay a surety of £50, or to serve three months' imprisonment. He ignored her appeal that the case be referred to a higher court or, rather, a bigger stage. There was no question of paying the sureties: the women were set on jail. The General also received three months, and Christabel ten weeks. The General warned the magistrate that 'they had left everything in working order, and while they were in prison their plan of campaign would be carried on by others exactly as they had left it.' They left the court to cheers from their supporters, who followed them to Holloway in a fleet of motor taxis.

Public opinion, and parts of the press, felt a heavy hand had been used again, not least because the women's time was to be served in the second division. The League, for its part, interrupted the Commons on 28 October, crying: 'Votes for Women!' When attendants tried to remove them, they found three suffragettes chained to the brass grille from behind which women had to watch the proceedings. The attendants had no option but to place their hands over the women's mouths, rather as a man had put his hat over Annie Kenney's face in Manchester nearly three years earlier, until someone came with a file to saw the women free. *The Times* branded the protest as 'scenes of those childish demonstrations which silly women think clever', and harrumphed at the 'downright lying and deliberate deception' the women had used to enter the gallery.[55] The same day Asquith, opening a Congregational Chapel bazaar in Highbury, was heckled relentlessly by women who had resorted to no lies or deception at all: they had entered dressed in suffragette colours and wearing 'Votes for Women' badges. 'The women of this country pay rates and taxes,' a protester yelled. 'You are their servant. What about Mrs Pankhurst in Holloway? You are responsible for that, you tyrant!'[56] She was thrown out 'amid loud hisses'. The abuse and ejections continued throughout Asquith's speech. The prime minister left to cries of: 'Traitor!'

The martyrdom of imprisonment encouraged a wider and more violent campaign, with more women being sent to prison. Muriel Matters, an Australian actress resident in London, flew over the West End in an airship and dropped pro-suffrage leaflets – an escapade parodied forty years later in the film *Kind Hearts and Coronets*. Mrs Despard was arrested again in February when trying to present a petition to Asquith in parliament. Disruptions of ministers' speeches continued throughout 1909, notably those of Asquith and Lloyd George – most famously at Limehouse in July, and the 'Dukes and Dreadnoughts' speech at Newcastle in October. A woman wielding a dog whip attacked Churchill at Temple Meads Station in Bristol.

The other side also mobilised. On 28 June a meeting of the Women's National Anti-Suffrage League took place in the WSPU's citadel of Caxton Hall. Lady Jersey presided, and many women present were the wives of peers (their husbands, therefore, not having the vote either). Some officers of the League were men. Mr Arthur Somervell, the secretary, called the League 'a body of patriotic women, who had the true welfare of their country at heart'.[57] In the eight months of the League's existence ninety-five branches had been formed, and 9,000 members recruited. Here was the proof that a substantial minority of women in Britain still knew what many men believed to be their place.

The next day Mrs Pankhurst took a deputation of eight women to the Commons. They were admitted to the precincts, but told that Asquith would not accede to their request to see him. Mrs Pankhurst's response was to smack a police inspector in the face, twice. After the women's inevitable arrest Lord Robert Cecil, a practising barrister, defended them and succeeded in getting the case sent to the High Court. It was dropped, and another attempt was made on the Commons when the news filtered through, with stones thrown at windows in Whitehall. In August, as argument raged over the People's Budget, Mrs Despard was arrested yet again for picketing in Downing Street.

In July 1909 Marion Wallace-Dunlop managed to use a printer's block to stamp a quotation from the Bill of Rights – about the right of a subject to petition the King – on a wall in the Palace of Westminster. Imprisoned in Holloway for criminal damage, she refused to eat unless transferred to the first division. Every attempt was made to get her to eat, including the authorities leaving in her cell trays of delicious food normally unknown in prison. Eventually she was released, weak from hunger, but her resolve unbroken.

She had launched the strike on her own initiative – it was a popular form of protest among political prisoners in Russia – but other women soon followed. All were released when their health became precarious. However, after two months the government changed tactics. It decided on 24 September 1909 to force-feed Mary Leigh, in Winson Green prison in Birmingham for disrupting a meeting addressed by Asquith. Force-feeding was done via a tube in the mouth or, if that proved impossible, the nostrils in order to pump liquid packed with nutrients into the body. It was not thought at the time to be dangerous, but it was deeply unpleasant, and required a doctor, nurses and several wardresses to hold the prisoner down while it was administered. It was a propaganda disaster for the government, not least because it provoked more violent disturbances in prison as the women expressed their outrage. *The Times* reported that those who were force-fed 'have become very violent, breaking the cell windows and smashing up such furniture and utensils as they are allowed. A meeting of the visiting justices has been held, and they are reported to have ordered several of them to be kept in solitary confinement and to be handcuffed to prevent further acts of violence.'[58]

Emily Wilding Davison, in jail in Manchester for disrupting a Liberal meeting, and who would become perhaps the foremost martyr of the movement, was one who refused to submit, managing to barricade herself inside her cell. The response was to turn a hose on her, at the suggestion of the prison visiting committee. Gladstone was hugely embarrassed and conceded the tactic was a mistake. Hardie was the first politician to spell out what force-feeding meant: 'Five, six or eight strong warders struggling with one helpless and weakened woman, fixing tubes in her nostrils and pumping food into her. Did not manhood revolt at such treatment?'[59]

Mrs Pankhurst led a campaign of public protest, though the outcry was, in fact, muted. She also took the message abroad, touring America and Canada in late 1909. Mrs Leigh sought to sue the government for damages, claiming force-feeding was illegal. The government argued that the procedure had been used in lunatic asylums for years, saving the lives of many patients. The jury – all male, of course – threw Mrs Leigh's case out in two minutes. Miss Davison, who sued for having the hose turned on her in Strangeways, won £2 damages. This suffering, however, hardened the hearts and the minds of the suffragettes, and increased their will to win.

Most of the public became tired of the campaign and showed increasing indifference. This emboldened the government to continue the policy of force-feeding. Some women associated with suffragism started to get cold feet, or to deplore the effect militancy was having on public perceptions of the movement. Mrs Thomas Hardy, a subscriber to the National Union, wrote to the London branch on 27 September 1909 to cancel her membership 'at least for the present' because she was 'averse to the strongly aggressive attitude of one section' which she felt wanted to 'assassinate the Prime Minister' and whose conduct was 'very *unchristian*'.[60] The National Union passed resolutions at its conference condemning violence and reassuring its members it abjured such tactics, hoping both to stop others following Mrs Hardy, and to dissociate itself from the militant minority. However, for many the greater dangers brought a sense of purpose and excitement that might hitherto have been absent from their lives. Mrs Despard proclaimed to a friend, in November 1909, that 'never was there such an era as that in which we are living now!'[61]

In the January 1910 election the WSPU implemented the lesson Mrs Pankhurst had learned from her husband's defeat in 1885, and that it had operated in by-elections: it opposed all Liberal candidates, irrespective of their views on suffrage. The party continued to govern thanks only to the Irish Nationalists, having lost seats because of general unpopularity rather than because of the activities of the WSPU. Indeed, in a Liberal seat where the campaigners made a particular effort – South Salford – the sitting MP, Hilaire Belloc, won well against the tide.

However, in the midst of the election one of the more notable suffragettes, Lady Constance Lytton, daughter of a former Viceroy of India, addressed a meeting outside Walton prison in Liverpool. Lady Constance had joined the WSPU in October 1908, when Mrs Pethick-Lawrence had welcomed her with the cry that 'the forces of destiny are behind this movement . . . you have been led to us, for the fulfilment of your own life, for the accomplishment of your destiny and for the working out of a new deliverance for humanity.'[62] She had been imprisoned twice in 1909, for a month and two days respectively, telling friends after her first sentence that her mind was 'a series of very vivid blotches' when she tried to summon up her memories of the experience.[63]

Outside Walton she was dressed as a seamstress, the disguise adopted in the interests of martyrdom – she feared special treatment if, in the event of her arrest, her finery gave her away. When arrested for leading a march on the prison she gave her name as Jane Warton. She was sentenced to a fortnight's hard labour and immediately went on hunger strike. She recalled this spell as 'intensely grim and dreadful, but now the reward seems undeservedly great'.[64] Lady Constance had been diagnosed with a weak heart. The prison doctor, however, found nothing wrong with her and ordered force-feeding. He changed his mind within a few days and recommended early release. Her other badge of suffering was a blistered heel, which laid her up, unable to walk, caused by ill-fitting prison boots.

In September 1910, aged just forty-one, she suffered a heart attack, which she survived: but was then afflicted by a series of strokes, which left her paralysed down her right side. The movement blamed her affliction on her treatment in Walton, and her suffering was yet another propaganda gift. She taught herself to write with her left hand, to compose her autobiography, in which the horrors of her experience in Walton were graphically retailed:

> He said if I resisted so much with my teeth, he would have to feed me through the nose. The pain of it was intense and at last I must have given way for he got the gag between my teeth, when he proceeded to turn it much more than necessary until my jaws were fastened wide apart, far more than they could go naturally. Then he put down my throat a tube which seemed to me much too wide and was something like four feet in length.

> The irritation of the tube was excessive. I choked the moment it touched my throat until it had got down. Then the food was poured in quickly; it made me sick a few seconds after it was down and the action of the sickness made my body and legs double up, but the wardresses instantly pressed back my head and the doctor leant on my knees.
>
> The horror of it was more than I can describe. I was sick over the doctor and wardresses, and it seemed a long time before they took the tube out. As the doctor left he gave me a slap on the cheek, not violently, but, as it were, to express his contemptuous disapproval, and he seemed to take for granted that my distress was assumed.
>
> Before long I heard the sounds of the forced feeding in the next cell to mine. It was almost more than I could bear, it was Elsie Howey, I was sure. When the ghastly process was over and all quiet, I tapped on the wall and called out at the top of my voice, which wasn't much just then, 'No surrender,' and there came the answer past any doubt in Elsie's voice, 'No surrender.'[65]

VI

The weakening of the Liberal party in the January 1910 election provided an opportunity for a new initiative. Henry Brailsford, a journalist and one of the leading voices against force-feeding, set up a Conciliation Committee for Women's Suffrage. Its president was Earl Lytton, brother of Lady Constance. Its intentions were to introduce a Bill to give the vote to women householders but not to those whose husbands could vote – a principle of one property, one vote. It had the support of fifty-four MPs from all parties, the limited nature of the proposal being designed to keep Unionists on board. This was almost exactly what had caused Richard Pankhurst to split with Miss Becker decades earlier: but the WSPU went along with it, despite Mrs Pankhurst's reservations about how few women it would enfranchise – not least that it would exclude almost all working-class women. Forster, who published *Howards End* that year, joked about this idea. After Margaret Schlegel marries she begins to understand 'why some women prefer influence to rights. Mrs Plynlimmon, condemning suffragettes, had said: "The woman who can't influence her husband to vote the way she wants ought to be ashamed of herself." '[66] Nonetheless, conceding the principle that women were not universally unsuited to exercise the franchise was a form of progress: and so on 31 January 1910 Mrs Pankhurst called a truce in the campaign of civil disobedience.

The fight over the Lords' veto meant the suffrage question receded in importance. It may also have caused Mrs Pankurst to call her truce. Yet after the Conciliation Committee's Bill's second reading on 12 July, and alarmed by the continued opposition of Asquith, Mrs Pankhurst warned that if the government obstructed it, militancy would resume. However, assaults on the Bill by Lloyd George (who claimed there were better ways to pursue women's suffrage) and Churchill – to the great surprise of the Conciliation Committee, who thought he was a supporter (he had signed a letter of support for the committee the previous April, welcoming their attempt at a cross-party solution) – suggested the government was hardening its stand against reform.

Churchill claimed: 'I do not believe that the great mass of women want a vote.'[67] He conceded there were 'numerous brilliant exceptions', but observed that 'they have made singularly little use of the immense opportunities of local and municipal government which have been thrown open to them.' Brailsford called him 'treacherous' and added: 'If you consider yourself insulted, I am at your service, and will study your convenience in making arrangements for a meeting.'[68] Churchill said he would vote for women's suffrage, but not for this Bill, and owed nothing to a movement that had disrupted almost every public meeting he had held 'for the last five years'. He had been opportunistic. Brailsford told him, 'I do not understand how a public man can say that he welcomes the formation of a Committee constituted to push a particular Bill, and then come forward as its most formidable opponent without treachery.'[69]

Asquith reiterated his hostility: 'I venture to say, and say with all sincerity and earnestness to the promoters of this movement, high-minded chivalrous men and women as I know the great bulk of them to be, that the cause which cannot win its way to public acceptance by persuasion, argument, organisation, and by the peaceful methods of agitation is a cause which has already in advance pronounced upon itself its own sentence of death.'[70] Less convinced of the terminal condition of the suffragists were Cromer and Curzon, who in the summer of 1910 started a fundraising drive for the fight against them. The women's movement was closely identified with temperance, and the two peers succeeded in raising money from the drinks industry: Lord Iveagh, the

Guinness magnate, sent £1,000 on condition the gift was anonymous.[71] A public appeal was launched, which was a gift to the suffragists, who could depict the forces against them as a conspiracy of rich aristocratic men. Within weeks, the male anti-suffrage movement and the Women's League had merged, after which the leadership became, predictably, male.

A new, trenchant and highly effective voice emerged in the debate on the Bill – that of F. E. Smith, who reminded suffragists that for all their assaults on the Liberal party, the Unionists, should they win power, might prove even more implacable. Smith mocked the Bill as anti-democratic, because it would enfranchise women of property but do nothing for the working class. He felt that neither the women of his constituency – Liverpool Walton – nor his women friends wanted the vote, and invited his fellow MPs to apply the same test before they voted. He argued that the vote was not a right; and that having to pay taxes was only one, and not the exclusive, determinant of whether someone should have the ballot. The Bill was consigned to a committee of the whole house, which killed it.

An early act of Churchill, when he succeeded Gladstone at the Home Office, was a small measure of prison reform, which ensured suffragettes received first-division treatment and were spared the harshness of a criminal jail. This was clever, because it not only made the government look more humane, but also robbed imprisoned women of automatic martyrdom. However, none of this compensated for the Bill's failure. On what became known to suffragettes as Black Friday – 18 November 1910, the day Asquith announced the year's second general election – Mrs Pankhurst led a demonstration to the Commons to protest against the government's lack of support for women's suffrage. She and Elizabeth Garrett Anderson, in her seventy-fifth year and a renowned moderate, were admitted to the precincts, where under police escort they could lobby MPs to see the Bill was put through its final stages before the dissolution. They had hoped to meet Asquith, but to the annoyance even of some of his own supporters he left the precincts without meeting them.

For six hours there were violent scenes as squads of police drove back women from the Palace of Westminster, with hand-to-hand fighting and excessive force. Women were knocked down by policemen and verbally abused; many reported being grabbed by the breasts. The change in tactics was that, in the first instance, the women were manhandled rather than simply arrested, reducing the numbers who could opt for prison.

Convicted women continued to refuse to pay fines. On 22 November Mrs Pankhurst took another demonstration to Downing Street, where fighting broke out and 156 people were arrested, including her – though no evidence was offered against her and she was discharged. However Mary Jane Clarke, her sister, who was also arrested, was badly injured and, after being force-fed in Holloway, died of heart failure on her release. Birrell, the Irish Secretary, was badly roughed up. Asquith was whisked away in a motor-car, one of whose windows was broken. Churchill, who could not resist a fight – he would soon appear in his silk hat at the siege of Sidney Street – ordered the police in his bodyguard to remove Mrs Cobden-Sanderson, who had had the temerity to walk towards him.

He was overheard by a male supporter of the suffrage movement, Hugh Franklin, who a few days later tried to attack him with a dog whip on a train from Bradford to London, calling him a 'dirty cur'.[72] Franklin had been thrown out of a meeting Churchill had addressed in Bradford for yelling: 'Votes for women!' 'Christianity survived the throwing of Christians to the lions,' Mrs Cobden-Sanderson told the press. 'Mr Churchill will not suppress the women's movement by telling his police to join up with the hooligans to make footballs of women in revolt against injustice.'[73] Mrs Despard told her friend Mrs Saul Solomon: 'I agree with you about Winston Churchill. He is our arch-foe, and he is not a straight-hitting foe. I long to have a talk with him. If only we can reduce his majority it will be something.'[74] There was also a spate of attacks on ministers' properties. Churchill told the King that 'the suffragettes have been behaving in a very naughty manner', but only those 'guilty of acts of serious violence or wanton damage' would be prosecuted, not those who were 'mere destructionists arrested for their own protection'.[75]

After the December 1910 election MPs supporting the Conciliation Committee introduced a new Bill. However, Asquith had promised there would be a suffrage Bill, on the understanding that it would be open to amendment. The new Bill would propose enfranchising women householders. However, progress was slow, as the battle over the Lords reached its climax. A new Conciliation Bill was debated in May 1911, receiving its second reading by 167 votes, but was then bogged down terminally in committee while the detail was fought over. The urgency of resolving the constitutional crisis was obvious even to the most obsessive suffragettes, and the campaign of militancy was suspended. Those not absorbed by the crisis were focusing on the Coronation: the suffragettes saw that anything they attempted to do now would at best be an irrelevance, at worst would damage them. Asquith promised Lord Lytton that a suffrage Bill would be introduced once the constitutional issue was settled.

The suffragettes were determined to remind the nation of their existence: so on the Saturday before the Coronation they massed on the Embankment between Blackfriars and Westminster and marched to Whitehall, the procession led by the General mounted on a horse. A thousand women, dressed in white, marched at the head of the procession under a banner reading 'From Prison to Citizenship' – this was the contingent who had served sentences for militant behaviour. This affability would not, however, last much longer.

In the autumn of 1911 Asquith, keeping his word to Lytton, announced that a Manhood Suffrage Bill would be included in the next King's Speech, to give the vote to all adult men, and that he would allow an amendment proposing women's suffrage. Mrs Pankhurst, on another tour of North America, sent a message of outrage to Christabel in the phrase 'protest imperative': the promise of an amendment was a joke, since it would not succeed without government support, and there would be none.[76] As the cabinet knew, there was no mandate for such a measure, and it might not be got through without a dissolution.

Mrs Pankhurst construed this as a calculated insult, and on her return to Britain in January 1912 decided to ratchet up the militancy. Christabel, who said the effect of Asquith's strategy was that 'war is declared on women', egged her on.[77] Most of the movement's Liberal supporters felt the offer quite reasonable, and that the Pankhursts and their followers risked estranging themselves from mainstream opinion if they resumed militancy. Asquith met a deputation from all the suffrage societies, and explained that although he remained personally opposed to women having the vote he would follow the judgment of the Commons, but wanted that judgment exercised as a part of overhauling the entire suffrage system. Immediately after this meeting, Lloyd George leaked through the *Daily News* his willingness to propose the amendment, something designed to impress the suffragettes: it did not.

One of the movement's more memorable tactics began: throwing rocks, stones or bricks through windows. It had started on 21 November 1911, when a group led by Mrs Pethick-Lawrence had broken windows in several government departments, the Banqueting House, the National Liberal Club and the houses of John Burns and Lord Haldane: 150 women were subsequently sent to prison. Lloyd George wrote to C. P. Scott, editor of *The Manchester Guardian*, on 30 November to describe the action of the 'Militants' as 'ruinous'.[78] He sent Scott, whom he cultivated assiduously, a copy of a letter he had written that day to Mrs Fawcett, saying that the 'indecent exhibition' the previous night of Asquith being 'howled down in a place of worship' while making a speech on behalf of a charity had, on top of everything else, created 'a grave situation'. He felt the chances of progress were only 'the slightest' unless the campaign was called off, since MPs who had supported women's suffrage were now in two minds. He knew she could not control Mrs Pankhurst: but asked her for advice.

Then, in December, Emily Wilding Davison was apprehended shortly before lighting a paraffin-soaked cloth and putting it in a letter-box in the wall of the Parliament Street post office. Mrs Pankhurst formally announced the new policy in a speech to Holloway veterans on 16 February 1912, and expected to be arrested for sedition or incitement but was not. Such wanton vandalism was anathema to many women, and further divided the movement. Mrs Pankhurst herself was taught to throw stones by Ethel Smyth, who having broken into the male preserve of composing classical music saw no reason not to have the vote too. When the vandalism started, she soon went to prison.

A few days after Mrs Pankhurst had spoken, some of her stormtroopers attended a meeting at the Albert Hall, chaired by Mrs Fawcett and addressed by Lloyd George, and disrupted it by heckling him from the moment he stood up. The catcalling became so marked that a suffragist shouted: 'Cannot you all behave like ladies for once?' which provoked 'loud cheers'.[79] No statement highlighted the class differences between the followers of Mrs Pankhurst and the followers of Mrs Fawcett quite so clearly: with the WSPU's calculated recruitment of working-class women, an appeal to behave like 'ladies' would excite only incomprehension. The WSPU militants' disruption was like an act of civil war. Other than reiterating his support for women's suffrage, Lloyd George made one significant political statement: that there was no question of a referendum. The idea had been raised not by the suffrage movement, but by the in-house journal of Asquithian Liberalism, the *Westminster Gazette*. Even the suffragists were becoming more aggressive, however. Mrs Philip Snowden, wife of a future Labour Chancellor of the Exchequer, who moved the vote of thanks to Lloyd George, said that while she would not engage in 'window-smashing and bone-breaking', she was prepared to stop paying her taxes and to go to prison. Otherwise, the National Union's view was 'our weapon is public opinion'.[80]

The same hall was packed several days later for a meeting of the anti-suffrage lobby. The meeting devoted itself to describing women's unsuitability for political life, with Violet Markham – later a distinguished public servant, social reformer and feminist – uttering the common refrain about how so few of them had participated in local government. Decades later Christabel Pankhurst, ridiculing Markham's subsequent success (she was one of the first Companions of Honour), called her 'that foul traitor – who, while suffragettes were hunger striking, appeared on the Albert Hall platform, surrounded by reactionaries like Lord Cromer and Lord Curzon, protesting against women having the vote.'[81]

Whether or not this meeting was the provocation needed to put Mrs Pankhurst's stone-throwing plan into execution is not clear. However, the next day – 1 March – random attacks took place in the West End, with women breaking shop windows in the Strand, the Haymarket, Oxford Street, Regent Street, Bond Street and Piccadilly, not with stones but with hammers secreted about their persons – 'an unprecedented campaign of wanton destruction of property', *The Times* called it.[82] The grand finale, shortly before dusk, came when Mrs Pankhurst – labelled now by *The Times* 'the notorious agitator' – and two henchwomen drove up Downing Street in a car and broke four of Asquith's windows and (a testament to their lack of cricketing skills) one in the Colonial Office opposite. They, and 121 other women, were arrested, and the West End swarmed with police guarding the remaining shop windows.

The next day she was sent to prison for two months, telling the magistrate that since the vote had not been obtained by peaceful means, the suffragists had decided to adopt methods traditionally used by men. She also launched an exercise in comparative militancy, claiming the government had settled with the miners, whereas the suffragettes' militancy was 'a mere flea-bite compared with what the miners were doing'.[83] The locking up of the movement's aristocracy alongside its foot soldiers was enormously inspirational to the rank-and-file. Myra Sadd-Brown, an Essex suffragette in Holloway for breaking windows, told her husband about having Mrs Pankhurst and Dr Smyth on the same wing as her: 'Fancy these two great women sitting sewing on garments for prisoners . . . why not put Asquith and Sir E. Grey to blacking boots?'[84] Poor Grey, a devoted suffragist, was guilty by association. The window-breaking continued for two more days, and the police raided the WSPU's offices in Clement's Inn with a warrant for the arrest of Christabel and the Pethick-Lawrences. Christabel evaded them, went into hiding and escaped to Paris, where the Princesse de Polignac gave her sanctuary. However, her mother and the Pethick-Lawrences were charged with conspiracy, and tried in May.

Mr Justice Coleridge, who presided, refused to accept the defence's point that the offences merited leniency because they were politically motivated. Mrs Pankhurst called but one witness, Ethel Smyth, who said she had broken the windows of the home of Lewis 'Loulou' Harcourt, the Colonial Secretary, not because Mrs Pankhurst had incited her, but because she had heard Harcourt make 'quite the most objectionable remark about women's suffrage that has ever been made', when he had said 'he would be very happy to give the vote to women if all women were as intelligent and well-balanced as his own wife'.[85] Dr Smyth accounted this 'the most impertinent thing I have ever heard, and also the most fatuous'.

The trial ended in the inevitable conviction of all three, and sentences of nine months in the second division, after a recommendation by the jury to leniency. Costs were awarded against them, which Pethick-Lawrence had to pay as Mrs Pankhurst had no money. He refused, and bailiffs seized the contents of his house. The convicted trio said they would go on hunger strike unless granted the status of political prisoners and allowed to serve their time in the first division. Anxious to avoid inflaming passions further, the government conceded this point.

However, the three were furious that this privilege was not conferred on their comrades already in prison, and joined a mass hunger strike that began on 19 June. The government concluded that appeasement was not an option, and began force-feeding on 22 June. When a doctor and wardresses entered Mrs Pankhurst's cell and proposed to force-feed her, she picked up a huge earthenware jug and threatened violence if they approached her. They left the cell, and two days later the government ordered her release for medical reasons. Mrs Pethick-Lawrence was force-fed once and her husband several times. They were released after five weeks. Pethick-Lawrence was ordered to pay damages won by shopkeepers for their broken windows, but elected to go bankrupt instead. Writing to a well-wisher on 1 July, after her release, Mrs Pethick-Lawrence observed that 'sorrow may endure for a night, but joy cometh in the morning!'[86]

The increasing violence not only turned some elements of public opinion, but also further emboldened anti-suffragists. On the day when another Conciliation Bill was introduced, 28 March 1912, Sir Almroth Wright, one of the country's leading immunologists and bacteriologists, wrote a long and unequivocal letter to *The Times*. Its tone was set in its opening sentences: 'Sir – For man the physiology and psychology of woman is [sic] full of difficulties. He is not a little mystified when he encounters in her periodically recurring phases of hypersensitiveness, unreasonableness, and loss of sense of proportion.'[87] Wright described the 'complete alteration of character in a woman who is child-bearing', the 'tendency of woman to morally warp when nervously ill' and the 'terrible physical havoc which the pangs of a disappointed love may work'. Then there was the 'serious and long-continued mental disorders developing in connexion with the approaching extinction of a woman's reproductive faculty'. As a doctor, he felt he understood why some women became extremists: they were not getting any sex. 'The recruiting field for the militant suffragists is the half-million of our excess female population – that half-million which had better long ago have gone out to mate with its complement of men beyond the sea.'

In case his point was insufficiently made, Wright defined these women as ones who had 'life-long been strangers to joy, women in whom instincts long suppressed have in the end broken into flame. These are the sexually embittered women in whom everything has turned into gall and bitterness of heart and hatred of men.' Having outlined the anger that women felt at their intellectual inferiority compared with men, Wright noted: 'It is not necessary in connexion with a movement which proceeds on the lines set out above any further to labour the point that there is in it an element of mental disorder. It is plain that it is there.' Not only were their arguments 'fatuous', so were their marriage prospects. And, for good measure, militant suffragism contained elements of 'dishonesty' and 'immorality'. There could be no question of women having the vote, he thought, because they were 'incompetent' to exercise it, incapable of backing up their decisions by force, and it would poison relations with men.

In most arguments adduced against the vote one usually, at least, detects chivalry towards women, however misguided and unjust the belief that they should remain unfranchised; Wright's contribution was a rare example of the naked bigotry and misogyny that the anti-suffrage movement almost always kept well hidden from public view; though it had echoes of a remark Cromer had made the previous year, implying that Western civilisation was a bar to female suffrage, since 'there is much more difference, both physically and morally, between an educated European man and woman than there is between a negro and a negress belonging to some savage Central African tribe.'[88]

Among the many who expressed their outrage at Wright's remarkable outpouring were doctors, who attacked the impropriety of a colleague discussing these matters in public. Sir Victor Horsley, an eminent physician, told Wright that 'the world is an institution in which women are human beings as much as men are, in which they have precisely the same right to work for their living and precisely the same claim to be justly paid for what they do.'[89] Lady Castlereagh mocked him, as did a lady doctor, Agnes Savill, who dismissed him as a man who 'always affords amusement to the average public'.

By far the most interesting riposte, signed with the initials 'CSC – One of the Doomed', asked Wright whether the question ought not to be 'should women have votes' but 'ought women not to be abolished altogether?' The writer continued: 'I have been so much impressed by Sir Almroth Wright's disquisition, backed as it is by so much scientific and personal experience, that I have come to the conclusion that women should be put a stop to.' The writer hoped that the world might 'look to Sir Almroth Wright to crown his many achievements by delivering mankind from the parasitic, demented, and immoral species which has infested the world for so long?' CSC was Clementine Spencer-Churchill, the twenty-six-year-old wife of the First Lord of the Admiralty.

VII

Further divisions blew up in the WSPU. The clearest evidence that the strategy of greater militancy had backfired came in parliament itself, when the Bill designed by the Conciliation Committee was defeated on its second reading. Given suffrage Bills had for years secured Commons majorities, this was a serious reverse. Nor was the movement well placed to improve matters. Christabel decided to remain in Paris indefinitely: she put Annie Kenney in charge of the WSPU. It had over £100,000 in the bank, more than enough to fund Miss Kenney's weekly trips to Paris to consult Christabel. Between them they planned a campaign of even greater militancy, with more attacks on property, including arson. However, the Pethick-Lawrences had had enough, and openly questioned this strategy – not so much because of their own unwillingness to endure any further privations, but because of the negative effect they feared the campaign would have on public opinion. They were right.

Mrs Pankhurst, by now a hardened fanatic, effectively dismissed the Pethick-Lawrences from the WSPU, announcing at a meeting in the Albert Hall in October 1912 that she and Christabel would henceforth set the movement's course. Christabel would edit a new WSPU newspaper called *The Suffragette*. All the more remarkable, in a movement dedicated to extending democracy, was how all traces of it were eliminated from the movement itself, and how compliant the rank-and-file were in this dictatorial and dynastic concentration of power. The Pethick-Lawrences went quietly. They continued to edit *Votes for Women*, established a less militant body called the Votes for Women Fellowship, and sought to bring together militants and non-militants in the common cause. Pethick-Lawrence became a Labour MP after the war, and when Attlee came to power in 1945 was made Secretary of State for India, with a peerage.

The contribution women made to the workforce and the economy was rising relentlessly, making it hard to discount or ignore. Roughly a third of women over fifteen were wage earners, including half of single women. Of women between fifteen and twenty, 66 per cent were in work, and 62 per cent of those between twenty and twenty-five. In addition, 10 per cent of married women worked, as did 30 per cent of widows; the total workforce was estimated at 4,648,241 women. Compared with 1901, there were 19 per cent more married and widowed women in work in 1911.[90] In June 1912 the Bill Asquith had promised to make the franchise more uniform was introduced. The Franchise and Registration Bill abolished plural voting and ended the property qualification. It was bitterly opposed by Conservatives, for whom the property qualification was a matter of the strictest principle – for those without a stake in the country to vote was unthinkable to the party of the landed interest. Labour was divided on whether to support the amendments giving women the vote, but at its party conference agreed to do so. However, the most vocal Labour supporter of enfranchisement, George Lansbury, who had been elected at the second 1910 election for Bow and Bromley in east London and would one day lead his party, decided against the party line to resign his seat in November 1912 and force a by-election to test support for women's suffrage. He lost.

The departure of the Pethick-Lawrences, and the damage done to public opinion by the attacks on property, hit WSPU fundraising and harmed its recruitment. Nonetheless, the Pankhursts ran a campaign that became ever more reckless, violent and militant. As well as putting hammers and bricks through windows, the women started to drop lighted objects into pillar-boxes, causing their contents to catch fire. Asquith announced early in 1913 that the Franchise Bill would be abandoned. He had responded to a question by the Speaker, who felt the amendments that would have led to women's suffrage would alter the Bill so fundamentally that under the rules of the House it would have to be withdrawn. Asquith had been badly advised by his law officers, notably Sir John Simon, the solicitor-general.

However, the suffragettes believed they had been duped and betrayed by a prime minister who had made no secret of his opposition to their aims. His claims that this had been an honest mistake, and that the government would give space immediately for a private member's Bill on women's suffrage, were treated with the deepest scepticism. The Bill was debated in May 1913, with Asquith speaking on one side and Grey on the other. It was defeated by forty-eight votes. Mrs Pankhurst considered herself and her adherents the victims of trickery, and took this as a signal to engage in the most militant campaign yet against property. In her public meetings she called for attacks to be stepped up, and said she took full responsibility for her actions: her pursuit of martyrdom was unequivocal. A series of attacks began the moment the Franchise Bill was aborted. Several Midlands golf courses had the slogan 'Votes for Women' burned into their greens with acid. The windows of the Reform Club were broken and the orchid house at Kew Gardens was trashed. A few days later, the suffragettes returned and tried to burn it down, and arson attacks were launched at two railway stations north-west of London.

Plain-clothes policemen attended Mrs Pankhurst's meetings and noted what she said. After the bombing of a house being built for Lloyd George in Surrey – the previous July militants equipped to damage Loulou Harcourt's house in Oxfordshire had been caught in the act – she accepted full responsibility for the attack. On 24 February 1913 she was arrested for incitement of others to commit offences against property, and on 2 April was sent to prison for three years. In what had become her traditional speech from the dock, she drew attention to the turpitude of the male legal profession by noting that a case had had to be retried because the judge who originally presided over it had been found dead in a brothel. The judge in her case was outraged, not least because the story was true.

Public feeling was increasingly that anyone who went on hunger strike should be allowed to starve to death. F. E. Smith's brother Harold, Unionist MP for Warrington, used the crisis to attack the weakness of Reginald McKenna, Churchill's successor as Home Secretary, saying that 'mob law' was taking hold because of releasing women whose physical weakness was self-inflicted.[91] He said that their meetings should be banned as 'a danger to the public and a great disgrace to our capital' and that the women were 'preaching war upon society'.[92] He taunted McKenna for failing to stop the outrages: but McKenna had no remedy unless he could persuade his colleagues to grant the vote to women, a policy to which Smith, like his elder brother, was vehemently opposed. He also attacked the Home Office for allowing force-feeding, 'one of the most barbaric and cruel things that could possibly be devised'.[93] His implication was that their martyrdom should be allowed to take its course without such savage interventions. The whole thing was tiresome to McKenna, who had to devote much of his time to writing letters to his smart friends whose wives were locked up in Holloway, and who were being denied the right to visit them.

That women could leave prison by imperilling their health through hunger striking mocked the law. The government therefore introduced, in April 1913, the Prisoners (Temporary Discharge) Bill, which allowed for women so released to be rearrested if they misbehaved. Lord Robert Cecil, a strong suffragist, called it 'the Cat and Mouse Bill'. It soon became the Cat and Mouse Act, and made it possible for the authorities to haul in any woman who breached conditions imposed upon her at the time of her release. Mrs Pankhurst was an early beneficiary of the Act, and in 1913 served six short spells in prison.

One of the reasons McKenna gave for not wishing to let women starve was his belief that the desire for martyrdom was so strong that for every one that died, many more would come forward to follow her example. He was right. It was during this wave of militancy that Emily Wilding Davison made the supreme sacrifice for the movement. She was highly intelligent – she had a first in English from Oxford, but had not, of course, been admitted to her degree, a right available only to men – and her record of commitment was well proven. She had been imprisoned six times since 1909, her offences including stone-throwing and setting fire to pillar-boxes (she had been an early advocate of arson), and had been force-fed. She had been locked up in Aberdeen for assaulting a Baptist minister she mistook for Lloyd George. On the night of 2 April 1911 – census day, when thousands of suffragettes stayed out all day and night to avoid having to put their names on the forms – she had locked herself in a broom cupboard in the House of Commons, so she could give it as her address on the form. Her life was the movement: she gave what money she had to the WSPU's self-denial fund, and her friends seem mainly to have been fellow suffragettes. Her death certificate records that she had 'no occupation'.[94]

In a period in Holloway, on 10 February 1912, she had written of her ideal for the future, hoping others would have the 'revelation' of 'men and women hand in hand not bound but free; both necessary, both of equal value, both the ultimate sources of life and power.'[95] She was magnificently resourceful and almost insanely courageous. Later that year she recorded that 'on Saturday June 22nd, I was fed by force about 11 a.m. I barricaded myself in my cell by force as strongly as I could but my chair had been taken from me. My barricade was however so effective that men with crowbars had to be fetched to burst in. I had a big fight at the door, pushing out the crowbars and wedges as fast as they put them in.'[96] When eventually they overcame her: 'I called out at the top of my voice, "I will not be fed by this doctor, if it must be done it must be by the senior doctor." At the same time I tried to dart out into the corridor but they seized me, and forced me into my cell, brought in the wooden armchair they use on these occasions and after a sharp and fierce struggle hauled me into it.' The wardresses having tied her into it, 'the doctor gripped my head and began to force the tube down my nostril. It hurt me very much, as though it were boring anywhere but down the right place. As it passed down behind my throat a feeling of suffocation and sickness followed . . . I commenced to cough and choke and retch . . .' When the doctor could not find 'the right passage' via one nostril, he tried the other. He ordered her to swallow, 'which of course I did not do', and she was sick all over him 'to his disgust and my satisfaction.'

Such horrific procedures quickly took a toll on her health, and even in those pre-Freudian times the doctors had rudimentary fears about her mental state, going into her cell and in the course of an 'examination and cross-examination' asking her whether she 'had any delusions, fears or fancies. I was quite calm and matter of fact, and I flatter myself stood the severe test well.'

All hunger strikers received a medal from the WSPU: in Miss Davison's papers are letters requesting her to send the medal back for a bar to be added each time she undertakes a new strike.[97] She was utterly hardened by 3 June 1913, when she laid a wreath on the statue of Joan of Arc in London. The next day, apparently without the foreknowledge of the Pankhursts, she went to Epsom and threw herself in front of Anmer, the King's horse, as it came round Tattenham Corner in the Derby. The horse was brought down, but was unhurt.

Over a century later her gesture remains the most vivid historical memory of the entire campaign. It seemed she had no intention of dying: the unused return portion of her railway ticket was found in her bag after her death. (According to the official police record, she also had about her person two suffragette flags, a memo book, a race card, some post-office counterfoils, an insurance ticket, writing paper and envelopes, eight halfpenny stamps, a handkerchief and 3s 8¾d)[98] It is also unlikely, given the speed at which the horses were moving, that she picked out the Sovereign's. She and Herbert Jones, the jockey, were both injured: neither, it seemed, fatally. Jones made a full recovery. However, Miss Davison required an operation for a head injury, which was unsuccessful. She died four days after the race, the screens around her bed draped in the suffragette colours, and the WSPU badge fixed to her headboard. 'You may take it from me', a WSPU spokeswoman told *The Daily Sketch* just after the incident, while Miss Davison clung to life, 'that if she made her mind up to do anything, the fear of death would not cause her to hesitate for a single moment.'[99] She was, the official added, 'a woman who fears nothing; permanent address Holloway Prison.' A fracture to the base of her skull was given as the cause of death, and the coroner's verdict, based not least on the unused return ticket to Victoria, was misadventure, not suicide.

Not everyone appreciated her sacrifice. The National Union refused to be officially represented at the funeral even though one of its members told Philippa Strachey that 'she suffered and died for our cause'. This was 'because she risked the lives of many innocent people and we deplore her action' and she had done 'great harm to our cause'.[100] While unconscious Miss Davison received a letter from 'An Englishman' that read: 'Miss Davison: I am glad to hear you are in hospital. I hope you suffer torture until you die. You Idiot. I consider you are a person unworthy of assistance in this world. Considering what you have done I should like the opportunity of starving and beating you to a pulp. You cat. I hope you live in torture a few years, as an example to your confederates. Why don't your people find an asylum for you?'[101] Other letters were slightly more understanding, one pointing out to her that 'two wrongs don't make a right'.[102]

The funeral was a great set-piece of the whole campaign. Thousands of women followed her coffin, which was flanked by outriders, from Victoria Station to King's Cross; the order had gone out to former hunger strikers that they would follow immediately behind the coffin, and that 'it is essential that those walking in this section are dressed in white, and that they carry a Madonna Lily.'[103] Other women dressed in the purple, green and white of the movement and carried flowers. Memorial cards given out bearing the deceased's picture stated she had 'offered up her Life for her Faith'.[104] Mrs Pankhurst was supposed to be riding in the procession, but her attendance at a suffragette function violated the terms of her release, and she was rearrested under the Cat and Mouse Act as she went to her carriage. A brief service was conducted outside St George's Church, Bloomsbury, where the congregation sang 'Nearer My God to Thee', 'Lead, Kindly Light', 'Onward Christian Soldiers' and 'Fight the Good Fight'. The cortège continued to King's Cross, and Miss Davison's mortal remains were taken by train to Northumberland for burial in the family vault at Morpeth.

VIII

The obsequies over, the campaign of arson – usually of unoccupied or vacant properties – increased. There were also attacks on commercial properties, often using crude home-made bombs packed with pieces of metal which, had anyone been in the vicinity, would have maimed or killed with ease. The suffragettes remained poor judges of public taste, perhaps because so much guidance came from Christabel, out of touch in exile in Paris. However even she should have predicted the outrage caused by the burning down of two churches, at Hatcham, near Deptford in south-east London, and Wargrave in Berkshire. These were not only sacrilegious acts but also deeply ungrateful, since many clergy had been vocal in their support of women, and had called on the government to end force-feeding. Parishes began locking churches except when needed for religious services. A bomb was placed on the Throne in Westminster Abbey, but failed to detonate. The WSPU had moved from protest to terrorism. The National Union feared this violence was wrecking its cause. At its great rally in the Albert Hall on 14 February 1914 the programme cover proclaimed that the organisation was 'non-party, non-militant'.[105] However, the National Union's telegraph address – 'Voiceless, London' – started to seem more appropriate than ever.

Part of the problem with this phase of the suffragettes' campaign was that their militancy increased the obstinacy of their opponents, which polarised the argument as between men, the exploiters, and women, the exploited. Neither side missed an opportunity to vilify the other. Christabel wrote a series of articles blaming men for an epidemic of venereal disease. The conviction of a brothel-keeper in Piccadilly in August 1913 was seized upon as propaganda, because the woman concerned (whose clients were said, without proof, to include Liberal ministers) got only three months – unlike the heavier sentences handed down to morally upright suffragettes. The edifice of male supremacy had been crumbling for decades, and another brick came out of it in June 1913, three weeks after Miss Davison jumped in front of Anmer: Miss Emily Dawson was appointed the first woman magistrate. But the vote remained the be-all and end-all: nothing could alter the suffragettes' belief that no chance of equality could exist until equality in the franchise allowed women too to shape the policies of political parties and governments. Whatever damage suffragette extremism had done to their cause, there was still a mass movement. On 26 July 50,000 women marched to Hyde Park under the aegis of the National Union. Money continued to pour in to the WSPU, funding salaries for the Pankhursts and their lieutenants. The government seems never to have considered trying to cut off the organisation's funds.

Between her conviction on 2 April 1913 and the outbreak of the Great

War, when the women's suffrage campaign was suspended, Mrs Pankhurst contrived to serve just six weeks in prison, thanks to the Cat and Mouse Act. By being almost permanently on hunger strike her health was usually sufficiently poor to merit her release. She and her daughter Sylvia, from whom she became estranged because of differences over tactics, also exploited the propaganda value of their releases, Sylvia occasionally appearing in public on a stretcher as a testament to the cruelty inflicted upon her, and Mrs Pankhurst looking gaunt and emaciated. During one release she went to America, where until President Wilson intervened she was detained as an undesirable alien. She told a New York rally that the British parliament never conceded anything without being faced with the prospect of revolution, and was re-arrested as soon as she returned home.

She was soon released, spending part of the winter of 1914 in Paris with Christabel, in whose fanatical image the suffragette movement was now cast. She went to speak in Glasgow in March and was arrested again. The next day, 10 March, her follower Mary Richardson slashed, six or seven times with a butcher's knife, the Rokeby Venus by Velázquez, in the National Gallery in London. It was not the first, but it was the most famous, work of art to be attacked. Miss Richardson, at liberty under the Cat and Mouse Act, told the crowd who watched her being led away: 'Yes, I am a suffragette. You can get another picture, but you cannot get a life, as they are killing Mrs Pankhurst.'[106] Later, she developed this into a more detailed explanation. 'I have tried to destroy the picture of the most beautiful woman in mythological history because the Government are destroying Mrs Pankhurst – the most beautiful character in modern history.'

The gallery, which had acquired the picture only in 1906 for £45,000, was closed until further notice, and other London galleries followed suit until they had reviewed their security arrangements. The attack was not unexpected: policemen, in uniform and in plain clothes, had been patrolling the gallery for the previous year, in case of such an attack. While in jail Miss Richardson was force-fed, and broadcast the details on her release in July 1914.[107] The previous month two suffragettes attacked Dr Francis Forward, the deputy governor and medical officer of Holloway, with horse whips, so the movement had some of its own back.

Over the summer the authorities hardened their campaign against the suffragettes, raiding the WSPU's premises and removing material considered likely to incite trouble. The WSPU, however, fought fire with fire. Mrs Pankhurst led some followers to Buckingham Palace on 21 May to demand to see the King and to present him with a petition. A pitched battle with the police ensued, and the newspapers the next day carried photographs of Mrs Pankhurst clasped in the embrace of a stout policeman, identified as Chief Inspector Rolfe, being carried away. 'There were some distressing scenes', reported *The Daily Mirror*, which devoted its front page to action pictures of felled suffragettes and running policemen, 'and Mrs Pankhurst, who is out on licence under the Cat and Mouse Act, was arrested almost at the gates of the Palace.'[108] Another fifty-five women were arrested with her, and when arraigned at Bow Street simply kept shouting at the bench. The General was absent in Holloway, though such was her health that she was released on the afternoon the Palace was being besieged. 'Three hours later,' *The Times* reported, laconically, 'she was arrested outside Mr McKenna's house in Smith Square, Westminster, for obstructing the police.'[109] Two days later the King, who as a constitutional monarch was bound to do what his ministers told him, was heckled at a matinee in a West End theatre by a woman who had taken the precaution of chaining herself to her seat first, and who compared His Majesty with the Autocrat of All the Russias.

IX

As can be seen from the opposition to suffrage by an impeccable Liberal such as Asquith, not all critics of women's rights were hidebound Tories: the issue proved there were conservatives in all parties, including the socialists, not all of whom believed in equality. Many did not want married women to work because they would be competing against their husbands. They wanted men to earn a living wage, to allow their wives to stay at home and bring up the children. Hardie was so exercised by Labour's attitude towards suffrage that he almost broke with it in 1906–7 when its conference decided to concentrate on universal adult suffrage – because many men still did not qualify for the vote – rather than just on votes for women. In his party, as in parliament, there was massive support for women's suffrage; but the problem was how to frame legislation that all felt able to support. The WSPU's belief that women should have the vote on the same terms as men was simply unthinkable for many of their male supporters.

H. G. Wells, despite his endorsement in 1909 of the Men's League for Women's Suffrage (he signed up on the same day as Forster and Thomas Hardy), was a socialist intellectual who took the traditional view: he deplored the idea of women in men's trades and professions, not just because they might deprive men of a living, but because it would 'prevent many women from becoming mothers of a regenerating world'.[110] Wells's unenlightened view of women was common among Edwardian men, but it took his literary gift to articulate it. 'The life of a woman is all accident,' he wrote. 'Normally she lives in relation to some specific man, and until that man is indicated her preparation for life must be of the most tentative sort. She lives, going nowhere, like a cabman on the crawl, and at any time she may find it open to her to assist some pleasure-loving millionaire to spend his millions . . . with the continued growth of the shareholding class, the brighter looking matrimonial chances, not to speak of the glittering opportunities that are not matrimonial, will increase.'[111] He feared literacy was encouraging women to imagine 'wide possibilities of luxury and freedom'. 'The whole mass of modern fiction written by women for women, indeed, down to the cheapest novelettes, is saturated with the romance of *mésalliance*.' How difficult it would be for young women whose minds had been thus turned to reconcile themselves to child-rearing and ordering the domestic arrangements of an engineer, or some other significant male.

He expanded on these thoughts in *Ann Veronica*, which cynics can and do read as an exposition of the Wellsian ideal of females: that women, especially pretty and intelligent ones, lived to give pleasure to men rather like Wells. Ann Veronica is spirited, beautiful, and has men prostrating themselves before her. She is also intelligent, but not sufficiently so to realise what men want from her, and such cynicism as she has is suspended when she meets Capes, a biology teacher of strong passions who bears a remarkable resemblance to Wells, a biology teacher of strong passions. The story of *Ann Veronica* is about a young woman who seeks to assert her independence and to 'live'. Her father, who confines her to their house rather than let her attend a party – even though she is of age – is the first man she seeks to defy. She does this by leaving home and setting herself up in a bedsit. However, her dreams of finding work in London prove ill founded: her lack of qualifications and experience leave her desperate for money. Wells shows Ann Veronica can survive only with the help of a man: something her brother tells her.

'You got to take the world as it is, and the only possible trade for a girl that isn't sweated is to get hold of a man and make him do it for her.'[112] He adds that 'Providence . . . has arranged it so that men will keep you.'[113]

To pay her rent and fees at her college, where she hopes to obtain a biology degree to qualify her for a career, she takes a loan from Ramage, a neighbour of her father who has taken a shine to her and sees her as a leisure pursuit (he has an invalid wife). When she rejects Ramage's advances she agrees to marry a simpering romantic, who has the means to keep her in the style to which she is accustomed. Then, however, she realises she doesn't love her fiancé but loves Capes, and runs off with him. They mostly live happily ever after, though only once Ann Veronica's dependence on men has been confirmed.

Ann Veronica's intelligence had been spotted at school, and 'she made a valiant fight for Somerville or Newnham, but her father had met and argued with a Somerville girl at a friend's dinner-table, and he thought that sort of thing unsexed a woman.'[114] That is what she is up against. Her father later says to Ramage that 'I'm not sure whether we don't rather overdo all this higher education'.[115] Ann Veronica and her friends, inevitably, take a violently opposing point of view. One says: ' . . . we're not toys, toys isn't the word; we're litter. We're handfuls. We're regarded as inflammable litter that mustn't be left about. We are the species and maternity is our game.'[116] Ann Veronica cries out, at the height of her frustration, 'I'm a human being – not a timid female.'[117] Only the vote can solve this, and she eventually becomes militant in her pursuit of it, martyring herself by going to prison after storming the Commons. *The Spectator*, in a review written by its editor, St Loe Strachey, called *Ann Veronica* 'a poisonous book' that was 'based on the negation of women's purity and of man's good faith in the relations of sex . . . the muddy world of Mr Wells's imagination . . . is a community of scuffling stoats and ferrets.'[118] He thought it sought something far worse than female suffrage: the destruction of family life. 'Unless the institution of the family is firmly founded and assured, the State will not continue.'

Wells's own private life may have been known to Strachey when he wrote his review, giving him detailed knowledge of where much of the source material for *Ann Veronica* had come from. The well-to-do progressives in London's literary world had radical views on sexuality and sexual behaviour, but these were not universally shared. The nascent Bloomsbury set, with its open regard for free love and homosexuality, was at one extreme, and Wells emulated them: the Webbs, with their austere and correct lives, at the other. It was therefore ironic that it was one of the Webbs' friends, by 1910 one of the most-widely read writers and thinkers in Britain, who threatened the most serious scandal, routinely behaving at odds with the puritanical nature of the working-class movement he claimed to support.

Wells's futurism did not anticipate feminism or women's liberation; he seems to have believed the purpose of women was principally to make men happy, and to make Wells happy above all. He inherited his priapic approach to women from his father, whose career as a cricket coach was ended when he fell off a ladder and broke his leg while helping a lady friend escape unseen from his house. A reading of *Ann Veronica* gives an accurate picture: the heroine's militant suffragism is not a success, her life serene only once she is properly married – and subjugated – to a man.

Wells married his cousin Isabel, 'very soberly', aged twenty-five, in 1891, the relationship having started when he lodged with his aunt.[119] He claimed to have been 'prey to a secret but uncontrollable urge towards early marriage.'[120] However, they separated within three years because of his affair with Amy Robbins, a pupil in his science class at a tutorial college in Holborn. Writing in his late sixties, Wells (who did not usually respect taboos, especially concerning sex) attributed the break-up of his first marriage solely to intellectual forces: 'She became the gently firm champion of all that I felt suppressing me,' he said. He did, however, admit that, as a result, he 'began to find an increasing interest in the suggestions of personality in the girls and women who flitted across the background of my restless, toilsome little world.'[121]

He found Amy – or Jane, as he nicknamed her, and as she soon became known to their friends – intellectually exciting, at least. 'She was breaking away from the tepid, shallow, sentimental Church of England Christianity in which she had been brought up,' he wrote.[122] Such free-thinking excited him: 'It came to me quite suddenly one night that I wanted the sort of life Amy Catherine Robbins symbolised for me and that my present life was unendurable.' He added: 'And the sexual element in this shift of desire was very small.'

Isabel divorced him and he married Jane, with whom he had two children; and Jane tolerated his affairs. In his novel *In the Days of the Comet* he set out a utopian vision of free love, which Mrs Wells, it seems, was left to take at face value. He claimed to have developed a 'compromise' with her about his philandering after 1900.[123] He attributed his loucheness to the growth of 'individuality' inevitable in an 'advancing' world, rather than to his moral weakness. He also seems to have regarded it as an inevitable by-product of the 'socialist world state' he desired.[124] He excused himself by belittling his affairs. 'The French', he wrote, 'with their absurd logicality distinguish between the *passade*, a stroke of mutual attraction that may happen to any couple, and a real love affair. In theory, I was now to have *passades*.' Before the Great War Wells made himself the talk of literary London by pursuing two other novelists, Dorothy Miller Richardson – 'she and I took a special grave interest in each other' – and Elizabeth von Arnim, who would marry Bertrand Russell's elder brother Earl Russell.[125] Wells impregnated Dorothy, to whom he had also acted as a literary mentor, but she miscarried and had a serious breakdown in 1907.

Another affair was more serious. It was with Amber Reeves, whose parents – William and Maud Pember Reeves – were friends of Wells through the Fabian Society, having been introduced to each other by the Webbs. William Pember Reeves had been Agent-General for New Zealand, but by 1908 was director of the London School of Economics. Wells's son Anthony West, in his life of his father, described the Reeveses as having 'advanced views' – they would need them – and their daughter as being 'the embodiment of my father's ideal of what a liberated woman should be.'[126] Reeves offered Amber the choice between being presented at Court or going to Cambridge. She chose the latter, becoming an ardent socialist while at Newnham, and was co-founder and treasurer of the Cambridge University Fabian Society. As a family friend, Wells was invited to address the society, and from then on Amber conceived a passion for him.

With his rampant egotism, Wells described Amber as 'my adherent and a great propagandist of Wellsism at Newnham College.'[127] He recalled her as 'a girl of brilliant and precocious promise. She had a sharp, bright, Levantine face under a shock of very fine abundant black hair, a slender nimble body very much alive, and a quick greedy mind.' He believed his mentoring helped her to a double first, and noted that 'she conceived the pretty fancy of calling me by the flattering name of "Master"'.[128] Amber, the inspiration for Ann Veronica, was nineteen when Wells, then forty-one, met her in 1907. He claimed Mrs Reeves 'encouraged' their 'very intimate' friendship.[129] Amber threw herself at him and Wells obliged. The liaison was consummated in Soho. Shortly before her finals, Amber had 'some days of insatiable mutual appreciation' with Wells in that haven of romance, Southend-on-Sea: 'And I remember also that, after our luggage had gone down to the waiting cab, we hesitated on the landing, lifted our eyebrows, and went back gleefully for a last cheerful encounter in the room we were leaving.'[130]

During the early phase of the relationship Wells wrote a work of philosophy – largely ignored on its publication in the autumn of 1908 – called *First and Last Things*. In the chapter entitled 'Sex', he reflects that 'for most of us half the friendships and intimacies from which we derive the daily interest and sustaining force in our lives, draw mysterious elements from sexual attraction, and depend and hesitate upon our conception of the liberties and limits we must give to that force.'[131] For Wells, it was more liberties than limits. In a chapter on 'The Institution of Marriage' he advocated easier divorce, suggesting monogamy was the result of there being almost as many females as males in the population: and 'marriage . . . does not necessarily mean cohabitation.'[132]

After Newnham, Amber returned to her parents in Kensington, and visited Wells regularly at his flat near Victoria Station. He called what ensued 'one great storm of intensely physical sexual passion and desire'.[133] As with all his affairs he wanted it kept secret, but made a poor job of doing so: he took Amber to a Fabian dinner party and those present put two and two together. Also, she was keen to broadcast her conquest – to her friends, her dons and her mother, who did her best to take an enlightened view. Wells would discover there were after all limits to the Fabian spirit of tolerance, which thus far had coped with him divorcing, remarrying and philandering *seriatim*. Amber 'was neither frightened nor upset', Anthony West recorded, 'when it became apparent to her, after they had been lovers for some time, that she was going to have a baby.'[134]

Amber's father, predictably and for all his 'advanced' views, was scandalised, and 'became all that an eighteenth-century father should be', even to the extent of threatening to shoot Wells.[135] So was Beatrice Webb, who raged over the scandal. This was not just because of the association of the Reeveses and Wells with the Fabians, but out of guilt at having – she believed – introduced the Reeveses to Amber's seducer, as well as because of her prudishness. (Wells claimed he had met Reeves not through the Webbs, but at a Royal Society dinner.)[136]

West, whose account is mostly factually reliable even if his commentary shows a bias towards Wells and a credulity towards his mother's version of events, says that the Reeveses 'had never meant their daughter to confuse principles with practice.'[137] It would not be the last time in the progressive movement that hypocrisy was the inevitable response to the application of doctrine: women asserting themselves and practising free love was, the Reeveses seem to have decided, something to advocate for others but not for a daughter who might have been presented at Court. Impregnation by a libidinous middle-aged novelist was definitely not what they had expected for Amber.

They felt Wells had ruthlessly exploited her idealism and naïvete, and were outraged by his conduct. Wells retaliated by accusing Reeves of having 'a badly adjusted nervous system' and 'a good, but unoriginal, mind'.[138] Her parents and another suitor, Rivers Blanco White, a lawyer, did all they could to persuade Amber to end the affair long before they received the news of her pregnancy. She was teaching at Morley College – at around the same time as, among others, Gustav von Holst – but as soon as her parents realised what was happening Wells took her away to Le Touquet, blithely unconcerned by what even his progressive circle regarded as a massive scandal.

Life at Le Touquet was a shock for Amber. No sooner had she arrived than she learned the real nature of Wells's commitment to radical feminism. In their *ménage*, he expected her to act as housekeeper and to attend to his every need: she had no intention of doing so. Wells returned temporarily to Kent, to the handsome house Voysey had built him and where Jane and his legitimate children were installed. While he was away, according to West, Amber fell down the stairs and lay there for a night until the cleaning woman found her; miraculously the baby was unharmed. On Wells's return there was a volcanic row, culminating in his telling her to marry Blanco White, since the young man seemed keen on that outcome. This outraged Amber still further – to her, the suggestion that to avoid a social embarrassment she should marry a man for whom she felt little was not far off suggesting a life of prostitution. Wells's response was to accuse her of being 'childish' and 'unrealistic' and of being 'a damned fool'.[139]

He then, effectively, deserted her. She took the ferry to Newhaven by herself and asked Blanco White (who had no idea she was pregnant) to meet her there. West writes (and his source may be Wells's own account, which if not fabricated might well have been embroidered) that Amber's behaviour on the crossing was so agitated that a steward locked her in an empty cabin, fearing she would jump overboard. Blanco White brushed aside the difficulty; he married her within weeks and the last half of her pregnancy was passed as a married woman. She (and, more to the point, Wells) avoided public scandal, though in Fabian circles his name was blackened. It appeared that, for once, Wells had gone too far. Some of his friends dropped him, and he felt obliged to resign from his club, the Savile, for which Reeves had proposed him. Amber gave birth to a daughter, Anna-Jane, on the last day of 1909, and Blanco White brought up the child as his own. Not until she was eighteen would she know who her father was.

That, though, was not the end of the saga. The Blanco Whites were still living in the cottage in Surrey where Wells had installed Amber, and he remained a regular visitor. Her parents were shocked to hear this, as they had assumed their daughter's marriage to mean the end of her unwholesome involvement with him. Reeves felt personally betrayed by Wells, whose side he had taken in the earlier row over the direction of the Fabian Society. He broadcast his sense of betrayal to anyone who would listen, and among his willing audience was Beatrice Webb, who took it upon herself to propagate the news further. West attributes her behaviour to her repressed lust for Wells, but that is a matter of conjecture; Beatrice, in her early fifties by then, remained a handsome woman, but was thirty years too old for Wells's tastes.

Whatever the tensions, Beatrice felt it her duty after learning of this 'sordid intrigue' to write to friends and fellow Fabians with teenage daughters, warning them to keep the girls away from Wells.[140] It was a vicious ploy, but Wells could hardly sue for libel. She started with Sydney Olivier, who had four nubile daughters, and who (to Beatrice's bemusement) told Wells about the warning; Wells had already told Olivier about Amber and said, when it came to unmarried motherhood, 'we were much too timid about these things.' He wrote in rage to Beatrice: thereafter, for safety's sake, the attack on his morals was delivered by word of mouth instead. Beatrice stood by Amber, and dropped Wells, who 'will doubtless drift into other circles – probably the only person of his own *ménage* who will suffer is his patient and all-enduring little wife, who, having entered into that position illicitly herself at the cost of another woman, cannot complain.'[141]

Beatrice was alert to the contradictions – as Wells seems not to have been – between the progressive attitude to free love and the rights of women, and its effects in practice. To her, Amber's case was 'a striking example of the tangle into which we have got on the sex question.' Their society had accepted the divorced Wells out of tolerance, and, seeing he and his new wife were happy, 'ordinary enlightened principles' dictated acceptance of the new arrangement. 'And Mrs Reeves,' Beatrice wrote, 'claiming to be "advanced" in her opinions . . . [was] very intimate with him and allowed him to become Amber's guide, philosopher and friend. Amber being a little heathen, and HG being a sensualist, they both let themselves go'. She felt Amber had, out of 'panic', married the first man to come along, leaving 'the Reeves parents looking on in tragic sorrow, and Reeves calling HG a "vile impudent blackguard".'

Beatrice was unquestionably right when she wrote: 'All this arises because we none of us know what exactly is the sexual code we believe in, approving of many things on paper which we violently object to when they are practised by those we care about.' What further revolted her was that the 'deceit and secrecy' she felt were 'the inevitable condition today of any "sexual experiments"' made 'any divergence from the conventional morality so sordid and lowering.' She felt men who wished to experiment should do so in the 'accustomed way', with prostitutes, not on a 'young girl, fresh from college' upon whom one then imposes 'a polygamous relationship': 'That is not playing the game of sexual irregularity even according to the rules of a game full of hazards, at any rate, for the woman.'[142]

Amber stayed friends with the Webbs, even though Beatrice regarded her as 'a little liar, she is superlatively vain, and has little or no pity in her nature.' Beatrice believed their support might stop the 'rot' in Amber's character going further. As for Wells, Beatrice pronounced him 'distinctly on the down-grade, and unless he can pull himself up he will soon be little more than a ruined reputation.'[143] She felt partly responsible for Wells's degeneracy, by introducing him to her smart friends, which had 'whetted his social ambition and upset his growing bourgeois morality.' Then, in September 1909, Beatrice was further outraged, as she learned from the Reeveses more details of the affair. 'The blackguardism of Wells is every day more apparent. He seduced Amber within the very walls of Newnham, having been permitted, as an old friend, to go to her room. He continued the relationship during her visits at his own house, apparently with the connivance of his wife, whilst he was on the most intimate terms of friendship with her parents. He taught her to lie . . .'[144] Reeves also told Beatrice that Wells had written him an 'impudent' letter suggesting that Mrs Reeves, because of her admiration of his novel *In the Days of the Comet*, must have condoned his affair with Amber. News that Reeves was contributing £300 a year to keep Amber in the Surrey cottage, because Wells was not paying enough, magnified Beatrice's outrage. She advised both Reeves and Blanco White to put a solicitor on to Wells, to ensure he was punished both socially and financially.

Beatrice saw herself as an agent of that punishment, and continued to blacken Wells's name. Shaw refereed the fight, by trying to explain to Beatrice that Amber had not been a naïve victim, and shocking her by saying that the only remarkable feature of the episode was that Wells had resisted so long as he had. He advised Beatrice to shut up, or face Wells and his friends exposing the carnal irregularities of other Fabians, and making the society a laughing stock. Shaw also told Reeves and Blanco White 'to condone everything and accept the situation in order to avoid a public smash'.[145] Wells's revenge on the Webbs would be to mock them brutally in *The New Machiavelli*.

However, despite growing competition, Wells was his own worst enemy. In the summer of 1909 he started to show his friends the manuscript of *Ann Veronica*, and they recognised the barely-veiled portrait of Amber in its eponymous heroine. Some implored him not to publish it. Anthony West later recognised that there was a danger of the book being seen as 'a self-serving justification of [Wells's] own scandalous behaviour.'[146] St Loe Strachey's excoriating review in *The Spectator* – in his spare time he ran the National Social Purity Crusade – did Wells huge damage in literary circles but, worse, deeply upset Amber and, more to the point, her husband.

Blanco White, as a lawyer, saw that this picture of Amber was defamatory, given it was then a grave libel to imply a woman had had sex before marriage. He was in any case livid with Wells because Amber was becoming close to him again, while keeping her husband at arm's length. He would not sue Wells because of the effect of the adverse publicity on Amber; but, urged on by the Webbs and his father-in-law, he found enough people willing to swear on oath that they had identified Amber with Ann Veronica to force Wells to sign a solemn and binding undertaking, in default of libel proceedings, not to have any further contact with her. Wells did this days before his daughter was born, and used it to repudiate financial responsibility.

'HGW has been frightened off,' Beatrice Webb noted in her diary on 20 March 1910.[147] 'It is one of those rare cases where the punishment will fall far more heavily on the man than on the woman. Amber, if she behaves well, will be taken back by her friends. HG and his wife will be permanently dropped by most of his old acquaintances. He is too old to live it down. The scandals have revealed the moral rottenness of his life. I am sorry for Jane Wells, but she pandered to him and deceived friends like the Reeveses, I wish we had never known them.'

Amber's subsequent detachment from Wells created a vacancy. A *passade* with Elizabeth von Arnim ended in 1913, but another opportunity arose. Cicely Fairfield had grown up in an intellectual household that was short of funds. The family moved to Edinburgh, where Cicely attended George Watson's Ladies' College, but the family money ran out when she was sixteen. She came to London, trained as an actress, and chose Rebecca West – the name of a grim character from a grim Ibsen play – as her *nom de guerre*. Together with her sister Letitia she became a suffragette. She began to write regularly for the *Freewoman*, a feminist weekly, and in September 1912 nineteen-year-old Rebecca wrote a disobliging review of Wells's novel *Marriage*. He and his wife saw the review and invited her for a weekend at Easton Glebe, their tasteful old rectory in north Essex. By late 1913, despite Wells noting 'a curious mixture of maturity and infantilism' in her, she was his mistress, their affair lasting until 1922.[148] Once more Wells left his mark, with their son, Anthony West, who would also become a novelist, being born just as war broke out in 1914.

West – who had better relations with his father than with his mother – described in his biography of Wells how he thought his mother had pursued the man of letters. 'It is evident that my mother took the initiative,' he wrote.[149] 'She was determined to be involved, and monumentally so, with my father. She was urging a *grand amour* upon him, the sort of thing from which the substance of romantic biographies of great and famous persons are made.' Wells said she 'flamed up into open and declared passion'.[150] She got what she wished for: but also became an unmarried mother, in a society that deplored such conduct and inflicted social ruination on women who indulged in it. The ethos of Wellsian free love would eventually prevail, but not in his lifetime.

West found the correspondence between his parents from 1913, which begins by showing Wells trying not to become involved. However, once this attractive young woman said that she wouldn't take no for an answer, he decided, as usual, to oblige. He did, though, hedge his acceptance of her favours by specifying limits to their engagement. He also made it clear that if he became bored, he would be off. He then, according to West, found her 'affected, silly and pretentious', and told her, by letter, to go away.[151] West excuses his father by arguing that he was still in love with Amber Reeves – 'he had loved Amber . . . as fully as he was capable of loving anyone' – and therefore incapable of imagining a new commitment. It was ironic, then, that it should have been Rebecca's second review of a Wells novel – *The Passionate Friends*, written by him to try and get over Amber – that should have brought her and Wells together finally.

He tried, and failed, to persuade Rebecca to have an abortion when he discovered that she was pregnant. As history repeated itself Wells, who claimed to have impregnated her on their second private encounter, determined nothing should change after the birth of the child: if he hoped for another Blanco White to turn up in shining armour, he would be disappointed. Given the catastrophes resulting from Amber's broadcasting the details of her pregnancy, Wells decided that this time there would have to be deep secrecy, with only a select few aware of the facts. Jane Wells knew of the affair from the start, as part of the new contract she had had her husband make with her: he could sleep with whomever he wished provided she was kept informed, and provided she liked the woman concerned. In return, she would confine herself to pitying the women Wells seduced.

He determined to find somewhere obscure where Rebecca could give birth and, having rejected Llandudno, settled on the tiny resort of Hunstanton in north-west Norfolk, as there it would be almost impossible to encounter anyone he or Rebecca knew. She was installed in what their son calls 'the rawly ugly and somewhat poky late-Victorian villa called Brig-y-Don' before the end of February, having to endure five months of isolation and house arrest to prevent word reaching literary society of her condition and the man responsible.[152] Wells visited her sporadically and briefly, but wrote copious letters telling her all would be well, hinting that she would in time become Mrs Wells.

He had no intention of doing that, and of all the monstrous aspects of his behaviour, that was perhaps the worst. He had, indeed, made no plan for what would happen to Rebecca after the child was born. She ended up in a grim estate cottage in a Hertfordshire hamlet twenty miles from Wells's old rectory, before fleeing to the smart west London home of Violet Hunt, the novelist and literary hostess, herself a former *inamorata* of Wells, who was by then embroiled in an affair with Ford Madox Hueffer. It was a suitably circular conclusion to an episode that proved how for all Edwardian society's power to exercise shame, there would always be some utterly immune to it. Wells was unrepentant. Writing of the time before Amber and Rebecca when the 'compromise' had been made with his wife, he said her 'humour and charity, and the fundamental human love between us, were to be tried out very severely in the years that lay ahead. Suffice it here to say that they stood the test.'[153] That essential subservience that Wells expected, indeed demanded, of his women, was entirely at odds with the world the suffragists and suffragettes were making for themselves, in which they would stand on equal terms with men in everything, not just in the matter of the vote.

X

On 4 June 1914 – the anniversary of Miss Davison's sacrifice – Mary Blomfield, daughter of the late Sir Arthur, one of the most distinguished church architects of the late-Victorian era, was being presented at Court. She asked the King, while curtseying to him, to stop force-feeding, and threw herself on her knees before him. *The Times* reported that she 'fell on both knees while passing the Royal presence and cried in a loud shrill voice, which could be heard throughout the Throne room, "Your Majesty, won't you stop torturing the women?"'[154] The good news was that 'eye-witnesses describe the bearing of their Majesties, and the continuance of the ceremony, as a masterpiece of dignity and composure' in the face of this 'deplorable act of discourtesy'.

Such was the sensation that the story flashed around the world: *The New York Times* carrying a story headlined 'QUEEN UNRUFFLED BY SUFFRAGE PLEA – Would Forgive Invasion of Royal Court – Miss Bloomfield's [sic] Mother Apologizes'.[155] Lady Blomfield had suspected that her daughters, who were both to be presented, would attempt an act of militancy if presented at Court, so decided not to accompany them. She was presenting another young woman, however, and was in another room at the Palace when word reached her of the incident. She fainted. Revived, she issued a statement to the press, disowning her flesh and blood: 'Lady Blomfield desires to state that her daughters did not accompany her to court on June 4, but arrived later, without her knowledge. The appeal was entirely Miss Blomfield's own idea. Lady Blomfield saw nothing of the incident, which she and her whole family deeply deplore. Lady Blomfield wishes further to state that she is in no way connected with the militant suffragists.'[156] Another member of her family, unnamed, put it even more strongly: 'I should like it as widely known as possible that we dissociate ourselves entirely from this girl's misguided act. We are sick and disgusted to a degree.'

The Palace tightened up its scrutiny of debutantes. 'All the officials in the Palace yesterday morning were in consultation, and the list of guests for last night's court was being vigorously examined. As a result invitations extended to three women were withdrawn by special messenger.' Queen Mary, according to the paper, observed that 'if this had been the worst thing the women had done, they might perhaps be forgiven.' In his diary the King noted, with his customary analytical force, 'I don't know what we are coming to'.[157] *The New York Times* told its readers that in this climate of militancy there would be no Royal garden party that summer, in case 'wild women' sought to attack the Sovereign.[158]

The incident forced the government to examine what could be done to hamstring the militants. Although not so grave as arson and vandalism, the high profile the incident commanded was a propaganda coup that could not go unpunished – although the press reported its negative effect on public opinion. At last, WSPU funding came under scrutiny. *The Times* reported that 'the Law Officers of the Crown . . . are of the opinion that the subscribers to the funds of militant organizations come within the reach of the law and that their property may be attached in respect of damage done.'[159] This would end the careers of 'paid agitators': though how the government would trace those throwing half-crowns or sovereigns into collecting buckets at suffragette rallies was not discussed.

When war was declared on 4 August the suffrage battle was at its height, with little sign that reform would come. Sylvia Pankhurst had opened up a new front in the East End of London, living there and recruiting not just women but as much of the working-class movement as she could. She preached revolution, having learned from methods the Bolsheviks were using in Russia to overthrow an authority that ignored them. Asquith thought it prudent to meet her and a deputation of women from Bromley-by-Bow, days before Franz Ferdinand was shot in Sarajevo, and to make it clear that his views on the question were susceptible to change. The war accelerated the reform, but it would have been inevitable even before it, because of progress in other institutions and in social attitudes.

As it turned out, it was not revolution, but the war to end all wars that finally secured the women of Britain the vote. The campaign ended two days after war was declared. Women worked as nurses, in munitions factories and in numerous other callings. Their patriotism was beyond question. As mothers, wives, sisters and daughters, they were bereaved in their hundreds of thousands, and on many fell the responsibility of raising families. Many men – including Asquith – expressed surprise, when the war was under way, at what an enormous contribution women made by taking over jobs in hitherto male preserves so that men could go to the front. When the proposal to enfranchise women was debated at the end of the war this was duly recognised, but there were also signs that the campaign of militancy had had its effect: some surmised, probably rightly, that a refusal to grant the franchise to women after the part they had played in the war would have caused a massive outbreak of civil disobedience, and perhaps on a worse scale than before 1914. Nonetheless, women had proved their point. The vote was given to all of them over thirty in 1918; and on an equal basis with men in 1928. In November 1918 a separate Act allowed women to stand for parliament. When Mrs Pankhurst finally had the right to cast her ballot, she cast it for the Conservative party.

CHAPTER 18

REBELLION

I

The price of keeping the Unionists out of office at the 1910 elections was paid to the Irish party, and the currency was Home Rule. Therefore, as well as militant suffragettes, militant trade unionists and militant peers, Asquith also had to handle divisions created by his Irish policy. The result was that he succeeded not merely in provoking militancy among Unionists, but in bringing elements of the British establishment closer to rebellion than at any time since the Glorious Revolution.

This problem dominated the three years before the Great War, beginning the moment the Lords lost their veto, with leading Unionists such as Andrew Bonar Law, F. E. Smith and Sir Edward Carson inciting Ulster to oppose a Home Rule Bill that, thanks to the combination of the Liberals' need for Irish support to get their whole programme through, and the 1911 Parliament Act neutering the Unionist majority in the Lords, would inevitably become law. Because of this inevitability, the agitation came from those whose definition of loyalty to the Crown was to support the maintenance of the Union with Ireland. Then, as the enactment of the Bill approached – after its third passage in three successive sessions of parliament, the Lords' veto ended – the Army was plunged into near mutiny, when British soldiers stationed in Ireland refused to move against Ulster Loyalists. This provocation triggered Nationalist opposition to partition, in an Ireland gaining self-confidence from a flowering of its culture and a growing, and increasingly sophisticated, sense of national identity. It left Asquith with his greatest crisis of all, until war came.

II

John Redmond entered parliament in 1881, aged twenty-five, and led the Irish National party from 1900. He was from a Wexford Catholic gentry family, educated at Clongowes College, which in the generation after him produced two of Ireland's finest writers, James Joyce and Oliver St John Gogarty. Redmond read law at Trinity College Dublin, leaving without a degree. Several kinsmen, notably his father, were or had been MPs; his mother had converted to Catholicism on her marriage but rejected her son's Nationalist politics. Redmond worked for his father at Westminster and, shortly after his father's death, secured through a connection with Parnell the Irish party nomination for a seat at a by-election. He was called to the Irish bar in 1887 and to the English one the following year.

After visiting Australia in 1883 Redmond had acquired both a wife – who died six years later, having borne him three children – and a commitment to the British Empire. This would set him apart from more ardent Nationalists and, later on, from Sinn Féin. He saw the Empire as something in which the Irish had had a serious hand, and wished to retain the Irish voice in its development. Therefore, though advocating Home Rule, he wanted to retain Irish MPs at Westminster, with Ireland a self-governing part of the United Kingdom. Unionist resistance to this, in retrospect, remarkably moderate ideal would provoke something far more radical and divisive.

After Parnell's death in 1891 Redmond led the small group of Parnellites, most of the party following John Dillon, the much-imprisoned former land reform agitator who had disapproved of Parnell because of his relative political moderation and his scandalous private life. After the failure of the second Home Rule Bill, and during the first period of Unionist rule after 1895, Redmond worked with the government to secure such innovations as an agricultural department for Ireland. When Nationalism's factions reunited in 1900, Redmond became leader as a compromise candidate because of a split among the anti-Parnellites. Serving until 1918, he never enjoyed complete authority because he never commanded the anti-Parnellites' respect. He had a tense relationship with Dillon, his effective and more radical deputy.

At the 1900 election Redmond's party won seventy-seven of the eighty-three seats it fought; in 1906 eighty-two of eighty-four, but just seventy-one and seventy-four at the two 1910 elections – although these were ample to call the tune with Asquith. Redmond grew in stature, not least because of his moderation and willingness to work with ministers to secure advantages for Ireland. However, the ideological division in his movement between the minority of which he was a member, who wanted to stay within the imperial family, and those who did not, formed the basis of a tension unresolved until independence.

One of Redmond's main achievements was his part in the Irish Land Act of 1903. It was mainly the work of the Nationalist MP and agrarian agitator William O'Brien, and was brought to the statute book by George Wyndham, the Unionist Chief Secretary. In talks from December 1902 O'Brien represented Ireland's tenants, and Redmond was one of three other negotiators. O'Brien had wanted a scheme of compulsory purchase, but it was agreed sales would be made attractive by the government paying the difference between the price landlords wanted and what tenants could afford. This caused substantial acreages to be put on the market and created a new class of proprietors. It also diminished the Anglo-Irish Ascendancy. George Dangerfield, an earlier historian of the period and no admirer of the Unionist government, called the Act 'the most constructive piece of legislation in the history of England's relations with Ireland'.[1]

Redmond was delighted. Dillon, however, opposed the Act because it entailed co-operation with landlords. The veteran agitator Michael Davitt went further, repudiating it because it did not, as he had wanted, nationalise land. The Irish Parliamentary party embraced all economic doctrines between liberal capitalism and back-to-the-land Marxism. But Redmond and O'Brien were right: by 1914 9 million acres had been transferred to ownership by former tenants, and landlordism was effectively over. As a next step in improving Irish living standards the Liberal government passed an Act in 1906 that led to the building of 40,000 cottages for labourers in the Irish countryside, upgrading the housing of around a quarter of a million who had lived in buildings little better than those used by livestock.

Nationalism faced an organised challenge from the Republicans. Arthur Griffith, editor of the *United Irishman*, called in March 1900 for unity among opponents of British rule in an organisation he called *Cumman na nGaedheal*, or the Society of Gaels. By 1902, under its auspices, Griffith demanded a boycott by Irish MPs of the parliament at Westminster. The next year Edward VII visited Ireland; Griffith was part of another organisation, the National Council, that successfully lobbied Dublin Corporation not to present a loyal address to him. Griffith stepped up his campaign to disengage Ireland from Britain, citing as his example the passive resistance in Hungary in the 1860s that had led to the establishment of a dual monarchy with Austria instead of Austrian control.

The phrase *Sinn Féin* – we ourselves – had served as a separatist slogan since the 1880s. Now Griffith, on the suggestion of his friend Mary Ellen Butler, adopted it to describe his 'Hungarian' policy. At the National Council's first annual convention on 28 November 1905 he called it his 'Sinn Féin policy': the party's foundation is regarded as having happened on that date, when the National Council also – against Griffith's wishes – announced it was founding a network of branches to organise throughout Ireland. By 1907 the Society of Gaels, the National Council and an Ulster-based movement, the Dungannon Clubs, had merged as Sinn Féin.

The new party was potentially a threat to Redmond. C. J. Dolan, one of his MPs, announced late in 1907 his decision to resign his Leitrim seat and fight it for Sinn Féin. He lost, but with 27 per cent of the vote. This would be the party's high water mark in the pre-war period. Thanks to land reform and better housing, its membership tailed off and funds declined. It secured the election of some councillors in 1911, but by 1915 could not pay the rent on its offices in Dublin. It would not be until after the 1916 Easter Rising (in which it played no part), when taken over by Éamon de Valera and his associates, that it would become significant, superseding the Nationalists at the 1918 general election.

III

On the last day of the first 1910 general election, 10 February, Redmond said in Dublin that the Liberal party had 'come back to the standard of Gladstone and Home Rule.'[2] This was a surprise – and not an entirely pleasant one – to most Liberal MPs. Of the 272 elected, 188 had ignored Home Rule in their election addresses. This absence of a popular mandate would underpin Unionist objections to the third Home Rule Bill. We have seen how the Liberals' need to placate the Irish drove Lords reform, as Nationalists understood how removal of the Lords' veto could deliver a Home Rule Bill. Later in 1910 Redmond tightened the screw by stating that 'we stand in this question precisely where Parnell stood.'[3] This dismayed Asquith, though he knew it was the inevitable consequence of keeping his party in power. He had in 1901 stated that the Liberals should reject office if the only means to it were the support of the Irish party, and in 1906 had discouraged Campbell-Bannerman from committing the Liberals to Home Rule.

In this he had been at one with the King. Knollys wrote to Campbell-Bannerman on 1 November 1906 to say that 'the King has been hearing in private Society and reading in the press about a measure of what is called 'devolution' for Ireland being under consideration by the Cabinet – as however you have not mentioned the matter in your Cabinet letters to him he presumes there is no truth in the statement.'[4] For the moment there was not, but Redmond had seen his opportunity. Lloyd George and he talked in February 1910 to see what common ground there might be. The Liberals were, for the moment, intransigent. After a final meeting on 17 February Redmond wrote to Lloyd George to say: 'I take it for granted you have no further suggestions to make in the direction of easing the situation and therefore we stand, I am sorry to say, where we did at the commencement of our interchanges of opinions some days ago.'[5]

The Unionists had hoped that the land reforms, particularly those championed by Wyndham during the Balfour government, would be sufficient to convince the Irish that they were better off inside the Union. When that proved not to be so, and robbed of the Lords' veto on which they had hitherto relied, they cynically joined with the Orangemen of Ulster to whip up popular feeling in trying to stop Home Rule. The threat of civil war was their instrument of blackmail, and would become tantamount to treason, forcing the Liberals to treat with Redmond. Once it was clear in 1910 that Asquith needed Redmond, and that the Liberals were unconcerned about the aspirations of Ulster, Ulster Protestants clove to the Unionist party. They revived near-moribund Orange lodges and formed an Ulster Unionist Council, led by Carson. In England there was deep sympathy among Tories for Ireland's Protestants, and resistance to Home Rule not least because of the vulnerability of those outside Ulster who would be left behind as a minority in the Home Rule state, and for whom the possibility of geographical exclusion was not an option.

Carson was now fifty-five and MP for Dublin University, and although from the predominantly Catholic south of Ireland was a devout Unionist. From 1900 to 1905 he had been in the Unionist government as solicitor-general; and in 1911 assisted Halsbury in managing resistance to the Parliament Bill. Once that battle was lost Carson, in the autumn of 1911, turned to the defence of Ulster. For him as for many other middle- and upper-middle-class Unionists, the motivation was not purely religious. Belfast and its environs had been the only part of Ireland affected by the Industrial Revolution, and its inhabitants accounted for much of Ireland's wealth. Businessmen and industrialists in Ulster feared Home Rule would undermine their prosperity, and they would be required to support the rest of the nation – a nation, more to the point, largely out of sympathy with them culturally. For the lower classes, however, the main problem was religious, and deep bigotries were nursed against each other.

Pope Pius X had issued the decree *Ne Temere* in 1908, which declared that marriages between Roman Catholics and Protestants that had not been solemnised by the Catholic church would be considered void. It also stipulated that the children of marriages thus solemnised should be brought up as Roman Catholics. Together with frequent pronouncements by Catholic divines that Ireland was and would continue to be a Catholic country, Protestants feared the laws of an Ireland under Home Rule being shaped to provide what some called 'Rome rule'. Augustine Birrell, the Chief Secretary for Ireland, tried to persuade Nationalist politicians to defend pluralism against Catholic hegemony, but little notice was taken. Birrell was a type now largely unknown to politics; a lawyer, essayist and professor, he was the longest-serving Chief Secretary, in office from January 1907 until resigning in despair after the Easter Rising in 1916. After 1911 he lost his grip on Irish policy because of the illness of his wife, a granddaughter of Tennyson, who went insane as a consequence of an inoperable brain tumour. He became an administrator rather than a policy-maker, and in complex discussions during 1913–14 was marginalised completely, Lloyd George having supplanted him as Asquith's confidant. His attempts to moderate the influence of Catholicism were then set back by a Papal decree *(motu proprio)*, late in 1911, which stated that no layman could bring a Catholic cleric before a civil court.

On 23 September 1911 between 50,000 and 100,000 people attended a meeting at Craigavon, the house of Captain James Craig, MP, that

Belfast Unionists had organised ostensibly to *fête* Carson but in effect to show the government in London, and the Nationalists, that Ulster would mobilise against Home Rule and, as Lord Randolph Churchill had put it twenty-five years earlier, fight. Craig gave a private luncheon party for the leadership, the menu cards for which featured crossed rifles and the motto 'The Arming of Ulster'.[6] The procession that marched the four miles from Belfast City Hall was so vast that the last marchers did not leave until two hours after the head of the column. The platform was packed with Unionist MPs and peers, with the Duke of Abercorn sending regrets because of a family bereavement, and the Marquess of Londonderry sending a lavish tribute to Carson of 'my admiration for you as leader of the Irish Unionist Party in the House of Commons.'[7] Before Carson spoke a resolution was passed, thanking him for his services and inviting English MPs present (Smith had been expected, but was absent) to carry back to London a plea for aid in resisting Home Rule. The seconder of the resolution warned the British government that if it were to 'lay a finger on any man for asserting the principles of freedom in civil and religious matters . . . they would light a fire in Protestant Ulster that would never be put out.' That set the tone.

Carson did not disappoint. He spoke of the 'grave responsibility' his fellow Unionists had thrown upon him, and entered into a 'solemn compact' with them to discharge it in the 'great struggle' ahead. They shared a 'grim determination to fight this question to the finish.' His argument could not be construed as based on bigotry: he said Ireland's economic progress was greater than ever, and this was an absurd time for the government to choose to cause 'disastrous strife, dissension and turmoil'. But civil and religious liberties would be at stake too, he said, under Home Rule: for it would constitute 'a tyranny to which they never could and never would submit.' Unionists should go to such lengths – which were not specified – as to make any Home Rule Bill ineffective against Ulster, and Ulster would govern itself if necessary.

After this meeting five senior Orangemen – Captain Craig, MP, Colonel Sharman Crawford, MP, Thomas Sinclair, Colonel R. H. Wallace and Edward Sclater – were entrusted with drawing up a constitution for the provisional government of Ulster. Carson found the Orange Order distasteful, but was ready to harness it for Protestant Ulster. Groups of Orangemen started drilling, and bands of Ulster Volunteers were formed early in 1912. The Coercion Act, which had banned the import of arms, was no longer in force, so Volunteers could be armed: and with money from sympathisers in Britain, they soon were. Meanwhile the government spent much of the winter of 1911–12 trying to frame a Bill to keep Nationalists happy while offering safeguards to the Unionists. Redmond undertook a speaking tour of Britain to seek to win support, his strategy being mainly to accuse Carson and his friends of bigotry and scaremongering.

The Bill was almost identical to Gladstone's 1893 measure, dividing responsibilities between the Irish and imperial parliaments, and allowing Dublin limited tax-raising powers. However, there was much cabinet discussion over whether to allow Ulster counties with majority Protestant populations to opt out, or whether such an offer should be retained as a bargaining chip for later in a process that, with the Lords allowed to reject the Bill twice, could last over two years. Lloyd George and Churchill alone, sensing trouble ahead, argued for the exclusion. On 6 February the cabinet told the King that while the Bill would apply to all of Ireland, Redmond would be warned that 'the Government held themselves free to make changes, if it became clear that special treatment must be provided for the Ulster Counties'.[8]

British Unionists took up the cause, not least because it might destabilise, and possibly remove, the Liberal government. On 26 January 1912 Law, the son of an Ulster-born clergyman, addressed a Unionist meeting in a packed Albert Hall in London. He was about to start his first parliamentary session as Unionist leader, and the meeting was partly to acclaim him. He showed how different he was from Balfour, and how different the Unionists would be without a brake on their militancy. He said the promise of a Home Rule Bill was 'the most glaring example of political trickery', because he professed – unconvincingly, one suspects, even to those present – that no one had expected the Parliament Act to lead to this.[9] (The fear it would lead precisely to this had driven the fight to retain the veto.) He denounced Churchill, about to speak in Belfast, for having planned to speak in the Ulster Hall, the temple of Unionism where Lord Randolph had announced in 1886 that 'Ulster will fight, and Ulster will be right.' Law, taking his line from Lord Londonderry, who had called for Ulster Unionists to prevent the meeting, saw this as a deliberate provocation, threatening a breach of the peace; there were plenty of other places where Churchill could speak, if he wished. So angry was public opinion that, after a barely civil correspondence between Churchill and Londonderry and a rebuke from Birrell about 'how lightly and how inconsiderately the whole matter has been treated', his hosts moved the venue.[10]

Dangerfield claims of the Unionists that:

> everything they did in the next two years was aimed, not against Home Rule, but against the very existence of Parliament. Because Liberalism was already almost moribund, in spite of its appearance of health, their conscious aim was to destroy Liberalism: because the whole mood of that pre-war England was sullen, sombre, and violent, their unconscious desire was to ruin an institution which they were pledged to protect. An utterly constitutional party, they set out to wreck the Constitution; and they very nearly succeeded.[11]

Certainly, the cabinet had not reckoned upon the Unionists' militant encouragement of Ulster Protestants to rebel.

On 8 February Churchill reached Belfast. The Unionists, though despising what he said, were determined to show that, apart from in the Ulster Hall, there was freedom of speech. The authorities were prepared for trouble: 'The police report that great quantities of bolts and rivets have been abstracted from the yards, and many revolvers have been taken out of pawn,' the Master of Elibank told him. He was not expecting a 'serious riot' but 'isolated disturbance'.[12]

The First Lord of the Admiralty addressed an audience of around 5,000 in a chilly marquee on a football ground, sharing the platform with Redmond, who had hauled himself from the bed where he had spent a month recuperating from an unfortunate modern phenomenon, the car crash. From the moment Churchill landed at Larne he encountered what one report called 'profound hostility', which, as soon as he passed into the Catholic part of Belfast, changed to 'vociferous demonstrations in the opposite sense'.[13] He and his wife – whom he had been implored not to bring – left their boat in a port festooned with Union flags, the walls covered with anti-Home Rule slogans. The Churchills were booed, after which the crowd sang 'Rule, Britannia' and 'God Save the King'. They travelled to Belfast by train, and anti-Home Rule placards were posted all along the line, as were many members of the Royal Irish Constabulary. Extensive preparations to maintain order around Churchill's visit prevented mass disturbances, as did the vile weather and the fact that Churchill, having spoken, was spirited away through the back streets to a special train that took him quickly to Larne, and thence England.

Before speaking, he spent the morning at the Grand Central Hotel. By the time he left for his meeting 10,000 people, apparently all Unionists, had lined the street outside. The crowd almost overturned his car, but the police intervened. Churchill, typically, did not blink at a predicament far more dangerous than he might have expected to encounter. The mood changed once he reached the Falls Road, where effigies of Carson and Londonderry hung from lampposts. Once he reached the marquee Churchill found a crowd mainly, but not exclusively, composed of Home Rulers: some Unionists had paid between a shilling and half-a-crown to hear him. They were well-behaved: the only disturbances were from supporters of women's suffrage.

In a seventy-five-minute speech, Churchill discussed self-rule in Canada and South Africa, and asked why it should not be possible in Ireland. He called the Ulster Protestants' fears 'groundless'. He confirmed a policy leaked a week earlier, that one of the great social changes since the last attempt to legislate in 1893 – the old age pension – would be funded by the Exchequer in London. That this would give Ireland the status of a dependent relative seemed not to trouble the Nationalists. More troubling to Unionists were things that neither Churchill, nor anyone else in the cabinet, was saying: such as about the composition and constitution of the two chambers of the Irish legislature; what would happen to Irish peers; what limits would be imposed on Irish MPs at Westminster; how Home Rule would affect Customs and Excise, and the Royal Irish Constabulary.

Churchill did say that the legislative assemblies would represent Protestants and Catholics 'fully and fairly' and ensure the rights of minorities, notably religious freedoms.[14] He promised the Privy Council would declare void any Bill passed by the Irish legislature that exceeded its competence, but said that the legislature would have 'real responsibility in Irish finance.' The Crown would retain the ultimate power over Ireland. 'Would not', he asked, 'the arrival of an Irish parliament upon the brilliantly lighted stage of the modern world be an enrichment and an added glory to the treasures of the British Empire? . . . The Separation of Ireland from Great Britain is absolutely impossible. The interests and affairs of the two islands are eternally interwoven.' Churchill attempted to prove continuity with his father's stance while believing the complete opposite. He ended by saying Ulster would fight 'for the reconciliation of races and the forgiveness of ancient wrongs'. Redmond stated that he accepted every word of Churchill's speech.

Nationalists held a huge rally in O'Connell Street in Dublin on 31 March to demonstrate Ireland's support for the Bill. The crowd had been brought in from all over the country in sixty-four special trains. Four different platforms were put up in the street, and leading Nationalists addressed the crowd. 'It is no exaggeration to say that this meeting is Ireland,' Redmond proclaimed.[15] He called for unity: 'We have not one word of reproach or one word of bitter feeling . . . one feeling only – an earnest longing for the arrival of the day of reconciliation.' Nothing was further from Ulster's thoughts. Eight days later Law and seventy Unionist MPs arrived at Larne for what *The Times* termed a 'triumphal progress'.[16] It was, indeed, believed the ecstatic scenes exceeded anything seen when visiting Unionists came in 1886 and 1893, as well they might: for in those two earlier years the Unionists had known that the Lords' veto would save them. Law was, as the son of an Ulsterman, coming home, which added fervour to the occasion: though he had never lived in Ireland, his father's home and resting place.

The Times's correspondent made several observations that need to be viewed with caution since they were written for a Northcliffe paper, pursuing Northcliffe's ideal of Unionism. The reporter said he believed feelings were running higher than ever, a fair judgment. Other claims he made may or may not have been true, but they would certainly have played to Northcliffe's prejudices. 'There are all the indications of a community which is preparing for a great crisis in its history,' he wrote. Perhaps more worryingly for the government, he observed that 'organisation has been carried to a high pitch of perfection' and that 'the effects of drill and discipline are now beginning to be seen in the demeanour and appearance of the crowd.' What was being created was a paramilitary state. Men 'of stalwart presence and resolute faces' provided Law's guard of honour, and large crowds cheered him from Larne to Belfast. Before he left Larne he promised that 'this great injustice shall not be inflicted on the people of the north of Ireland'; his train stopped at stations along the way to Belfast for him to receive addresses from Unionists.

After a night with Lord Londonderry at Mount Stewart, Law attended a rally at Balmoral outside Belfast. 'It was more than a political meeting,' *The Times* reported, 'more even than a demonstration on an unprecedented scale; it was the assemblage of a nation to defend its existence, to plead against an attempt to suppress its identity, to plead and also to warn.'[17] The paper quoted one of the seventy or eighty Unionist MPs present: 'If one-tenth of the electors of Great Britain could only see this, it would be an end of Home Rule.' Law stood on a saluting platform and between 80,000 and 100,000 men 'in military order and showing in their carriage the effects of drill and discipline' marched past. Most were Ulstermen, but all four provinces were represented. Another 100,000 or so were in the agricultural show ground where the rally was held, and tens of thousands more had lined the route from central Belfast.

Carson introduced Law after having the whole meeting repeat the mantra that 'we will never, in any circumstances, submit to Home Rule.' The Unionist leader delivered a dense, dour speech rubbishing Nationalist aspirations and criticising their obstruction of land purchase under the 1903 Act. He also argued that it would be an economic catastrophe for Ireland to separate from Britain, and that the 'Redmondite' policy was one of 'poverty'. He echoed Chamberlain's famous remarks of 1886: 'Ireland is not, and never has been, a nation. There are two peoples in Ireland, separated from each other by a gulf of religion, of race, and, above all, of prejudice, far deeper than that which separates Ireland as a whole from the rest of the United Kingdom.'[18] He enunciated the fears of his audience precisely: 'You believe not only that your industrial prosperity would be ruined, but, what is far more serious, that under such a government neither your civil nor your religious liberty would be safe.'

The Protestants were perhaps a quarter of Ireland's population; but he asserted that two-thirds of Ireland's customs dues were collected in Belfast, and that the minority paid half the taxes and did half the trade of Ireland. He felt it 'impossible' for any government to overcome the opposition of the Protestant minority in defence of its birthright. He acknowledged that the loss of the Lords' veto meant that what he considered the will of the majority of the British people to resist Home Rule would be disregarded; instead, the Liberals had 'sold the Constitution' to the Nationalists to retain power. He urged resistance: but paid no heed to the fact that he was a constitutional politician, the leader of His Majesty's Loyal Opposition, and that the means of resistance was the illegal army of paramilitaries whose salute he had taken earlier.

Two days later Asquith introduced the third Home Rule Bill, delayed by his preoccupation with the coal strike. He placed it in the context of a similar devolutionary process for other parts of the Kingdom. He said the term 'Ulster' was misleading: the province returned thirty-three MPs, of whom seventeen were Unionists and sixteen Home Rulers. He also sought to reassure Unionists that what was proposed was but a small step. He quoted the first clause of the Bill: 'Notwithstanding the establishment of the Irish Parliament or anything contained in this Act, the supreme power and authority of Parliament in the United Kingdom shall remain unaffected and undiminished over all persons, matters and things within His Majesty's Dominions.'[19] Home Rule would give the Irish control of matters local to Ireland, as the 1893 Bill had proposed, while United Kingdom matters such as defence and foreign affairs would remain at Westminster. Asquith also promised religious equality, and stressed that the Lord Lieutenant would be able to veto any Bill violating the principles of legislation passed at Westminster.

He outlined a bicameral system for Ireland – a House of Commons and a Senate. The Senate would be nominated, not least to ensure the representation of minorities. The Commons would have 164 members, fifty-nine of them from Ulster. The 103 MPs currently at Westminster would be cut to forty-two. He detailed how Ireland would raise taxes for matters such as defence that would be provided by Britain, with the Treasury in London sending part of what was raised to Ireland to discharge obligations imposed upon it by Westminster. Ireland would be allowed to raise taxes for things Ireland had to do for itself; to spend more, it would have to raise more. Carson said that 'more ridiculous or fantastic proposals than those . . . have never been put before this or any other parliament.'[20] He called the safeguards Asquith had offered 'simply delusions'. Redmond and his followers were happy with the Bill, seeing it as a great act of reconciliation. Redmond said Asquith had 'again extended the hand of friendship to Ireland.'[21]

The Bill had its second reading on 9 May 1912 by 372 votes to 271, after seven days of discussion. With debates almost daily on the industrial anarchy, and about the consequences for public safety at sea of the sinking of the *Titanic* in April and its enormous loss of life, it was 11 June before scrutiny of the Bill in committee started. Thomas Agar-Robartes, Liberal

MP for St Austell, raised an amendment 'as an honest attempt to solve one of the most complex questions in connection with the government of Ireland': namely, to exclude the four Ulster counties of Antrim, Armagh, Down and Londonderry, all of which had Protestant majorities, from Home Rule.[22] Law and Balfour supported this; but in doing so they seemed to accept Home Rule for the rest of Ireland, and to be casting adrift Unionists in the other twenty-eight counties. Birrell rejected the amendment, and Asquith pointed out the trap into which the Unionists would walk if it were accepted: 'You will take out from Ireland just that body of the Protestant minority which is best able to protect itself, and you will leave without any kind of redress or protection not only the scattered Protestant minority in the south and west, but the Protestants in the remaining parts of the province of Ulster. Was there ever such a self-stultifying amendment?'[23] Maybe not: but more would be heard of this idea.

Each point was argued over for weeks, to no avail: the government and the Nationalists would thwart attempts to wreck the legislation; and with the Lords no longer able to veto the Bill, only extra-parliamentary action could stop it. The focus moved, therefore, away from Westminster. The anniversary of the Battle of the Boyne, 12 July, a sacred day for Orangemen, saw another great manifestation of Unionist resistance to Home Rule. Despite 'penetrating rain that defeated all artificial protection less defensive than an oilskin', scores of thousands of men, watched by scores of thousands of women and children, marched from all over Ulster to a field three miles outside Belfast.[24] It took four hours from the marchers setting off until the last man arrived in the field. Once a message of support had been read out from 40,000 Scottish Orangemen – a worrying sign for the government – the star turn rose to speak: F. E. Smith. *The Times*'s correspondent felt that at first his speech 'seemed to be a little above the heads of the people he was addressing'; but once they had detected what Smith's theme was, they quickly warmed to it.

With justification, he accused Asquith of supporting Home Rule only from necessity: there had been no mention of it until the Liberals lost their majority. But Smith knew accusations of hypocrisy could get him only so far. So, alluding to the supremacy of the threat of violence over the exercise of democracy, he spoke of 'a Bill which you know and I know, and Mr Asquith knows, will never become operative in Ulster.'[25] He referred to the futility of the Westminster debate, such as three days spent discussing the possibility of exclusion for Ulster; something Smith said the Redmondites would never accept because it would leave them with 'no-one to tax and no-one to persecute.'

It was not his last colourful turn of phrase, as he showed in attacking Joseph Devlin, rabble-rousing Nationalist MP for Belfast West, who in some respects was a mirror-image of Smith. 'If I were an Ulster Protestant I would rather be ruled from Constantinople, by the Sultan of Turkey, than by a politician like Mr Devlin who, if he were as effective as he is defamatory, or as resourceful as he is malignant, would be a considerable demagogue.' In parliament for just six years, Smith – not least because of how he had been talked up by his close friend Churchill, but also because of his superb rhetorical skills – had become a leading Unionist. In the harsher, more ruthless party that had developed since Balfour, he would make his political fortune easily, and exploiting Home Rule was a highly effective way in which to do so.

Asquith too could play public relations, and on 19 July went to Dublin to speak about his policy, the first serving United Kingdom prime minister to visit Ireland. Sharing a platform with Birrell, Redmond, Devlin and others, he told an enthusiastic crowd of 3,000 that whatever the Lords might do that year, or the next, the Bill would reach the statute book. Brushing aside interruptions by suffragettes, he said Home Rule would be 'the first step in the new constitutional development for the Empire', starting a process of decluttering the Imperial Parliament of matters that could be discussed elsewhere, and leaving it to debate only the most far-reaching questions.[26] He affirmed that Ireland was one, not two, nations, and its destiny would be fulfilled as such. He called those who argued that the four counties of Ulster with Protestant majorities would suffer under an Irish parliament 'contemptible', deriding the notion that it would ever 'do wrong and injustice and be guilty of religious, civil and political oppression.'

He expressed his exasperation that the Belfast Chamber of Commerce had just told him that whatever he did to the Bill, they could not support it, despite his assurances of safeguards. And 'not one word of suggestion was made by any member of the deputation,' he added. It was a perfect illustration of what he was up against. 'I am not, however, in the least embarrassed when asked, as I constantly am, what are you going to do in the event of civil war? [Laughter]. I tell you quite frankly I do not believe in the prospect of civil war.' Such complacency was ill-judged.

The Unionists strove to mobilise British public opinion behind them as well as managing regular shows of force in Ulster. When Ireland was eventually partitioned in 1922 it was beyond doubt the threat of bloody civil war waged determinedly by aggrieved Protestants that brought it about: so much was clear even by 1914. However, it helped the Unionists to be able to argue that majority opinion elsewhere in the Kingdom was against Ulster being ruled from Dublin. Law, Smith and Carson addressed 3,000 delegates from Unionist associations at Blenheim, the estate of the fiercely Unionist Duke of Marlborough, on 27 July 1912, who had been brought in by fleets of special trains from all over Britain. Once the delegates had been given luncheon and a guided tour, around 10,000 others from the neighbouring district were let in and filled the courtyard, where speeches were made.

Law's argument was that the Parliament Act, itself passed using the votes of those who wished to break up the Kingdom, had conferred 'despotic power' on the government.[27] He came closer than ever to advocating unconstitutional action. 'We do not acknowledge their right to carry such a revolution by such means. We do not recognise that any such action is the constitutional government of a free people.' As if that were not clear enough, he added: '[W]e shall use any means [loud cheers], whatever means seem to us likely to be most effective . . . we shall use any means to deprive them of the power which they have usurped and to compel them to face the people they have deceived. Even if the Home Rule Bill passes through the House of Commons, what then? . . . there are things stronger than Parliamentary majorities.'

This was a dangerous doctrine. The government had never concealed what it would do to keep the support of the Nationalists, and Nationalist votes in the Commons were as valid as any others. The Parliament Act had been passed legitimately. That it was needed was the fault of the Unionists, for voting down the People's Budget. For Law, as leader of the opposition, to announce that, if it chose, his party would disregard the decision of the Commons and take some as yet undefined action to resist Home Rule, was unheard of. He tried to justify it by saying that Asquith's contention that there were not two nations in Ireland was wrong, and that the Commons had the eternal duty to act as 'arbiter' between those two nations.[28] But his was a naked call for rebellion nonetheless.

He raised the stakes in a way that would have serious consequences and expose the weakness of the government. 'Does anyone imagine that British troops will be used to shoot down men who demand no privilege which is not enjoyed by you and me and no privilege which any one of us would ever surrender?' This would resonate with the Army. 'No nation will ever take up arms to compel loyal subjects to leave the community,' he said. If one tried, it 'would succeed only in lighting fires of civil war which would shatter the Empire to its foundations.' He added: 'I can imagine no length of resistance to which Ulster will go in which I shall not be ready to support them and in which they will not be supported by the overwhelming majority of the British people.' The audience, *The Times* reported, 'rose from their seats and cheered this declaration for some minutes.' For once Law, not rated for his charisma or force, outplayed Smith and Carson. But he had also stimulated those in Ireland who went beyond Redmond's moderate point of view to see that moderation might not, in the long run, work. His biographer, Lord Blake, observed that 'such a tone had not been heard in England since the debates of the Long Parliament', and it came oddly from the leader of the party that stood for law and order.[29] Churchill told J. L. Garvin of *The Observer*: 'I am shocked at these threats of Ulster violence which are made by Conservative leaders. Do they think they will never come back to power? Have they no policy for Ireland except to make it ungovernable?'[30]

IV

Ambitious ministers saw Ireland as a means to make or advance reputations; and Asquith's collegiate style of leadership encouraged them to weigh in. To Churchill, who had a long history of looking for trouble, it was irresistible. On 12 September 1912, during what was, in a different age, described as his 'annual visit to his constituents in Dundee', and stressing that he spoke personally and not for the government, he tried to resolve the Ulster problem. In a speech interrupted by suffragettes, he advanced an idea he had first put to Asquith eighteen months earlier. Brushing aside a cry of 'How dare you show your face here while women are being murdered?' he said a federal system could make Irish Home Rule easier to swallow.[31]

Developing a point Asquith had made in April, he claimed Home Rule was intended 'to be a forerunner and a preliminary to a genuine system of self-government in all the four countries', united under the imperial parliament. He saw no difficulty for Scotland and Wales, but because of the size of England it would need regional assemblies – for 'an

English Parliament, whatever its functions or limitations might be, could not fail in the nature of things to be almost as powerful as the Imperial Parliament' and 'the quarrel between these two tremendously powerful bodies might tear the State in half': a quarrel that survived the intervening century. He advocated separate legislatures in densely populated areas such as Greater London, Lancashire, Yorkshire and the midlands; perhaps ten or twelve in England, answering to Westminster, creating a federal system such as in Australia, Canada and South Africa, and a Scottish parliament. He was vague about Ulster, but saw his proposals as a means of convincing the Protestant minority that they, too, could rule themselves according to their own traditions.

Unionists rubbished his ideas. *The Times*, under Northcliffe the official organ of Unionism, said passing the Bill would not be, as Churchill had said, the preliminary to a federal system, but 'the greatest conceivable obstacle' to it; it was 'utterly uncalled for by public opinion'.[32] It was also – correctly, as it turned out – interpreted as a sign that the government knew it could not win the battle to have Ulster ruled from Dublin. *The Times* accused Churchill of admitting as much: 'He has totally knocked the bottom out of every argument for placing Protestant Ulster under the same local Parliament as the Roman Catholic South of Ireland.' Nationalists, some of whom questioned Churchill's support on the grounds of heredity, detected a split in the government. Churchill was signalling, in the view of the *Cork Free Press*, that he would not support coercing Ulster.[33] He had, indeed, written to Lloyd George on 21 August to say 'we ought to give any Irish county the option of remaining at Westminster for a period of five to ten years, or some variant of this', and urged this to be put to the Irish before parliament reassembled.[34]

Churchill had been attempting to talk Redmond round on Ulster since the end of August. He had written to him on 31 August that 'the opposition of three or four counties is the only obstacle which now stands in the way of Home Rule. You and your friends ought to be thinking of some way round this.'[35] He asserted that the Unionists were not otherwise opposed to Home Rule, but saw the Ulster issue as a way to weaken a government they opposed. 'Something should be done to afford the characteristically Protestant and Orange counties the option of a moratorium of several years before acceding to an Irish Parliament. I think the time approaches when such an offer should be made – and it would come much better from the Irish leaders than from the

Government.' Redmond, however, would not split his party by suggesting this.

Also in September 1912 the King invited Law to Balmoral, and Law prepared a memorandum reiterating his view that when Royal Assent was required for the Bill, the position would be 'very serious' and 'almost an impossible one for the Crown'.[36] No longer urging the Royal veto, Law instead said the King should insist on Home Rule being confirmed at a general election. The alternative was for half his people to attack him, and the institution of the Crown, if he gave assent, and for the other half to attack him if he didn't. Only an election could resolve the issue, providing new ministers to advise the King, if that was the electorate's wish. Law had consulted A. V. Dicey, the constitutional historian, and had his support. However, to insist on a dissolution might mean the King exercising his right, also rendered obsolete by disuse, to dismiss Asquith. The most he could do, while retaining legitimacy, was to persuade him to take a certain course.

The next step in Loyalist resistance was Ulster's Solemn League and Covenant. This oath of determination to resist Home Rule was Craig's idea, based on the Scottish Covenant of 1638, with Carson as front man. The threat of Home Rule had intensified interest in Ulster's Scottish connections, so the allusion in the covenant was appropriate. A huge demonstration thronged Enniskillen on 18 September, where the official party arrived with a mounted paramilitary escort. Lord Hugh Cecil made an impassioned speech supporting Ulster's right to resist the parliament in which he sat. Carson had approved the text in mid-August, and on 19 September read it out on the steps of Craigavon, Craig's country house, to invited journalists, who noted he was bare-headed and smoking a cigarette. The Ulster Unionist Council approved the wording four days later, and people were urged to sign up on what had been designated 'Ulster Day', 28 September. Until then, Carson and Craig whipped up support by undertaking a tour of the Province, recruiting signatories. At Coleraine on 21 September Carson, sensitive to accusations by such as Churchill that the Ulstermen were advocating treason, called the Parliament Act 'the greatest act of treason that had ever been recorded in history'.[37]

Smith accompanied him on the tour, loving every moment. His role drew mockery. The Liberal MP Frederick Kellaway noted that in February 1911, on the second reading of the Parliament Bill, Smith had said that 'nearly half the people of this country will support us in any resistance, however desperate, to your proposals'.[38] He was using similar language about the Home Rule Bill. Kellaway further noted that 'the most bloodthirsty expedient adopted by Mr Smith and the other terrible fellows who fought with him was the Die-Hard dinner at the Hotel Cecil.' In the days before the signing of the covenant Smith was always at Carson's side, earning the derisive nickname 'Galloper Smith' as he was like Carson's aide-de-camp: there are pictures of him walking behind the cemetery-faced Carson as they inspect the upright ranks of Ulstermen, armed and ready.

Carson was the first to sign the covenant, on 'Ulster Day' in Belfast City Hall, on a round table spread with a Union flag. People converged on the hall from a hundred different religious services around Belfast at which specially written prayers were said. Lord Londonderry signed second; Smith was also present. Carson had marched at the head of a procession from a religious service in the Ulster Hall to City Hall behind a yellow silk banner said to have been carried at the Battle of the Boyne. Others were then admitted in groups of 500 to sign, on desks set up along a third of a mile of corridors, the doors left open until nearly midnight. People signed at around 500 other places in the Province. A total of 237,268 men signed the covenant, which pledged them to defend their place in the Kingdom and to use 'all means which may be found necessary to defeat the present conspiracy to set up a Home Rule Parliament in Ireland', and to 'refuse to recognise its authority'.[39] As well as this, 234,046 women signed a declaration, associating themselves with the menfolk and 'praying that from this calamity God will save Ireland'. That day Ulstermen in London, Glasgow, Liverpool, Manchester and other British cities signed too, bringing the total signatories for the covenant and the declaration to over half a million. In 1914 another 2 million in Britain signed a corresponding covenant, among them Elgar and Kipling; Kipling wrote a poem, 'Ulster 1912', in which he romanticised the solidarity of the anti-Home Rulers.

That evening the Lord Mayor of Belfast hosted a public dinner for Carson. Two toasts were proposed: 'The King' and 'The Fighting Democracy of Ulster'.[40] With the SS *Patriotic* getting up steam at Donegal Quay in Belfast, waiting to take Carson, Smith and others to Liverpool, there was no time for speeches but the Lord Mayor and his guests did have time to proclaim 'No surrender!' and 'A fight to a finish'. Between

70,000 and 100,000 people lined the short route to the quay, and the paramilitary guard that escorted the Unionist party on board fired a salute of revolver shots. When the boat docked at Liverpool before dawn the next morning thousands, many in Orange regalia, lined the quayside in welcome, and both Carson and Smith made impromptu speeches before a spontaneous rendition of 'O God, Our Help in Ages Past'.

An estimated 150,000 filled the streets of Liverpool, through which the men proceeded before a celebratory breakfast. Although the whole procedure, from the meeting at Enniskillen to the arrival at Liverpool, verged on the ridiculous in its elaborate theatre, there could be no doubt that as an exercise in intimidation it worked superbly. Asquith came under increasing pressure to use the criminal law against those who led, encouraged or engaged in paramilitary displays in Ulster, using effectively a private army to resist the will of parliament. He wrote in his memoirs over a decade later that 'no Irish jury would convict' – he meant an Ulster jury – and the rule of law would be undermined.[41] He also wished for 'the birth of the new State' to be 'under the star of Peace', something that would not be achieved by the coercion of anyone involved.

In October the Home Rule Bill was back in the Commons, and proceeded with bad-tempered inevitability until, just after four o'clock on the afternoon of 11 November, the government lost by 227 votes to 206 on an amendment to a financial resolution complementary to the Bill. The amendment embodied an important principle: that, in the words of the Unionist MP who moved it, Sir Frederick Banbury, it should 'prevent the taxpayers of England being called upon by the Government to provide money for a country in whose Government they shall have no share.'[42] The lump sum the government proposed to give Ireland was reduced from £6 million to £2.5 million. Given its majority, the government should not have lost: it was a simple failure by the whips to ensure enough MPs turned up.

The Commons was adjourned; the cabinet decided not to resign. The government announced that evening that as the defeat followed a 'snap division' – the motion had not been on the Order Paper, and it overturned the substance of a resolution passed the previous week by 121 votes – it would press on. Twelve Nationalist MPs had not voted. The next afternoon Asquith made a statement that the House would have an opportunity the next day to rescind the resolution. When it did, the mood was tense and angry, the Unionists claiming it broke the rules for the government to try to reverse its defeat. There was protracted procedural argument, but the Speaker, James Lowther, backed the government, inviting the House to tell him otherwise. The debate started, and continued for three hours, during which a Unionist, Sir William Bull, was ordered out for repeatedly shouting 'Traitor!' at Asquith. Then when Isaacs, the Attorney-General, rose to speak Unionists shouted him down. The Speaker adjourned the House for an hour to allow tempers to cool. However, they did not, and pronouncing it 'useless to continue' he said that 'a state of grave disorder has arisen', and adjourned the House for the day.[43]

Churchill left the chamber to cries of 'Rats!', which prompted him to take out his handkerchief and wave it at the opposition. At this Ronald McNeill, the Unionist MP for St Augustine's, picked up a copy of Standing Orders from by the Speaker's chair and threw it at Churchill, 'hitting him on the cheek and bruising him'.[44] It seemed as though Churchill would confront McNeill until two Liberal MPs rushed him out. Order papers were also thrown across the floor, and a riot appeared imminent until Will Crooks, the Labour MP, shouted out 'Should auld acquaintance be forgot', provoking laughter. In 1925, McNeill – who the next day apologised in the Commons unreservedly to his victim – would serve under Churchill at the Treasury, as Financial Secretary.

The following day, 14 November, Speaker Lowther took the unusual step of suggesting the question be delayed for further reflection. He did this, he said, not merely to avoid more ugly scenes, but to protect the rights of minorities in the House. Lowther wanted the government to find another way around its difficulties. Asquith and Law, who pointedly refused to condemn his MPs' behaviour, agreed to an adjournment until 18 November. When the House met that day Asquith asked for a rescission of the resolution on condition that the government offered a new one that would meet some of Banbury's concerns about excessive funding by the English taxpayer. The House agreed to act as though the vote of 11 November had never happened: thus the resignation of the government and the collapse of the legislation were avoided.

The Bill spent fifty-two days on the floor of the Commons in all its stages, with no more alarms for the government after the money resolution was rescinded. Carson's hope rested in an amendment he moved on New Year's Day 1913, to the first clause of the Bill that talked of establishing a parliament 'in Ireland'. He wished to add 'except in the Province of Ulster' immediately afterwards.[45] He spoke for almost an hour, and was answered in respectful detail by Asquith – who accused him of trying to veto Home Rule simply because a minority in Ulster did not want it – and then by Redmond, who said Ulster was as much a part of Ireland as any other, and could not be sundered from it. He noted that in five of Ulster's nine counties Roman Catholics formed a majority; and he wished to avoid 'a sharp and eternal and dividing line between Irish Catholics and Irish Protestants'.[46] He turned the question of coercion round: for it would hardly be easier to let Ulster have its way and to coerce the rest of the nation, determined as it was to have Home Rule. The amendment was lost by 294 votes to 197.

On 15 January 1913 Northcliffe wrote to Aitken – intending his feelings to be passed on to Law – that 'the objections to the present Home Rule Bill are not understood by the people at large, except perhaps in Lancashire, and that they are in consequence extremely apathetic'.[47] The Bill had its third reading that day, and the one following, with Unionists – notably Smith, in a powerful speech – demanding to know in what circumstances the government would consider the exclusion of Ulster: but it was too late for that, or so it seemed. McNeill, who had thrown the book at Churchill, said that the result of the Bill would be 'the effusion of blood', blood that would be on the government's hands.[48] But Birrell told the Unionists that 'the right you demand is an arrogant right. It is the right to defeat this great national solution of the problem . . . the coercion of Ulster is terrible; so is the coercion of the rest of Ireland.'[49] He recognised the agony would continue. The third reading was given by 367 votes to 257. On 30 January, after three days' debate, the Lords threw the Bill out by 326 votes to sixty-nine. Halsbury, in the last ditch eighteen months earlier over the Parliament Act, summed up the futility now the veto had gone: 'We are merely called upon for a barren expression of opinion which can have no operation whatever.'[50]

Carson took no part in the parliamentary proceedings after his attempt to have Ulster excluded failed, not purely because he lacked constitutional means to achieve his aims but because his wife was mortally ill: she would die in April. Meanwhile, on 13 January, the Ulster Unionist Council formally announced the creation of the Ulster Volunteer Force. A militia had existed since before the covenant: the UVF would be composed initially of the men who had signed that document. Carson announced that the establishment would be limited initially to 100,000 men aged between seventeen and sixty-five. Lieutenant-General Sir George Richardson, a veteran of the Boxer Rising and a retired Indian Army officer, was placed in command. The Ulster Volunteers were, at this stage, unarmed, and their activities limited to physical training and drilling. In that respect they were little different from boy scouts; but this was a substantial private army raised in the most febrile part of the United Kingdom. It was a pledge for the future: it was a demonstration that Ulster had the numbers to resist rule from Dublin, and so any threat to do so was not idle. Asquith and his colleagues, who remained determined not to use the criminal law against Carson and his followers, had no excuse not to know that if they chose to put Home Rule on the statute book and impose it on Ulster, Ulster would resist to the point of rebellion and civil war. More to the point, in doing so they would have the unqualified support of His Majesty's Loyal Opposition.

In May 1912 Law had suggested to the King that the removal of the 'buffer' of the Lords' veto meant he could now constitutionally refuse Royal Assent to the Bill.[51] Rosebery denounced this in anticipation as being like 'a *coup d'état*'.[52] That Law could suggest it shows how detached from reality, and how recklessly irresponsible, some Unionists had become. On 2 February 1913 Hensley Henson, just appointed Dean of Durham (of which he would be Bishop from 1920 to 1939), was invited to preach before the Royal family at St George's Chapel, Windsor. He recorded in his journal that at dinner that evening the King 'expressed himself with astonishing freedom.'[53] Henson continued: 'He is evidently very bitter about the humiliation which the Government inflicted on him by exacting "pledges": and talks darkly about "something he has up his sleeve", which, at the eleventh hour, shall prevent the Home Rule Bill from becoming law.'

Stamfordham had a similar conversation with Henson, a strong Unionist, and Henson then proceeded to egg the King on into this highly unconstitutional position. Displaying 'distress of mind' the King told Henson that 'I was basely treated in that matter of guarantees. They knew I was in a difficult position, and forced my hand.'[54] He described Asquith as 'weak' and Grey as 'a sentimental radical'. Henson found his Sovereign 'a well-intentioned but weak man, who was conscious of an obligation to take some decisive action, but unable to determine what precise action that should be.'[55] He told the King that the veto no longer exercised by the Lords 'must now be claimed and used by the Crown: that if he used it in the case of the Home Rule Bill, he would be supported by the country'. Whether or not the monarchy would have survived such a reversion to a practice abandoned under Queen Anne did not seem to trouble Henson.

The Government of Ireland Bill began its second passage on 9 June 1913 in a mood as far from compromise as imaginable. The Nationalists wanted the whole Bill; the Unionists wanted no Bill at all. No constitutional measure since the Great Reform Bill had absorbed so much Commons time. Thanks to Labour MPs augmenting the Liberals, there was a 'very substantial British majority' for the Bill, which only the Lords were holding up.[56] Asquith admitted a problem with four counties in Ulster; but invited suggestions of what to do with the other five counties, and three provinces. 'The exclusion of Ulster', he proclaimed, referring to the great argument that had come to the fore in the preceding eighteen months, 'affords no solution of any sort or kind whatever.'[57] He rounded on the covenant. 'It is a claim to interpose an absolute veto. I say to the House of Commons there is no legislative assembly that would tolerate such a claim.'[58]

Carson challenged him by alleging people were being driven out of the polity against their will; Asquith countered by reciting the safeguards to religious and civil liberties. Coercion was no longer possible. Carson accused him again of betrayal, and promised militancy would continue. 'Our duty upon this question is not here. Our duty is to help our own people to organise, and also to ask those people of Great Britain who would never be a party to your wretched, miserable and scandalous betrayal, to organise for our assistance.'[59] He would take responsibility for any resistance Ulster made; he rubbished the idea that the government would dare put down a rebellion by force; he was, in effect, daring it to start a civil war, or to allow Ulster to exercise the very veto Asquith had denied it possessed.

The Bill passed its second reading by 370 votes to 268, and on 7 July its third reading by a similar margin. On 15 July the Lords threw it out by 302 votes to sixty-four, knowing if they did the same in 1914 it would be enacted anyway. In private, the Unionists began to talk about the King possibly forcing a dissolution, which some – notably Lansdowne – argued would be acceptable given the Lords' emasculation. This was wishful thinking, and a misunderstanding of the Parliament Act, which confirmed the supremacy of the Commons and had not installed the King as an arbiter. Despite what he had said to Henson, the King was now sensibly reluctant to be dragged into this consequent horror.

V

For the next six months the focus moved from parliament to extensive private discussions between ministers and Unionists, the details of which were kept so secret that the press and the public had no clue about them; and to action by the people of Ireland. Here, too, the focus moved from Ulster, where the drilling and training of the UVF continued, to Dublin, where unrest broke out with a massive industrial dispute.

For all its Georgian grandeur, and place as the seat of government, Dublin had since the Industrial Revolution been the poor relation, economically, to Belfast. Unionists feared Home Rule would compromise their prosperity. Most of the working class lived in grim, vast slums. Nearly a quarter of families in the city lived in one-room households, tuberculosis was rife and infant mortality high. In 1905 – a good year – general mortality in Dublin was 22.3 per 1,000, compared with 15.6 in London.[60] There was high unemployment, and trades union organisation lagged far behind Britain's. Insofar as there was a Marxist strain to resurgent Irish republicanism after 1916, its seeds lay in the 1913 Dublin lock-out, which began with a dispute among workers at the United Tramways Company. The owner, William Martin Murphy, also owned Independent Newspapers, a big Dublin department store, a shipping line, and numerous other businesses; he was a substantial slum landlord besides. He was not known for benign treatment of his staff: in some of his companies workers had little time off and were expected to work far beyond the statutory hours. United Tramways was vulnerable to the union movement because its operatives' pay was far below that in comparable cities, notably Belfast. Murphy would dock his staff's wages for the slightest transgression, which managers discovered through a network of informers.

Like many Irish capitalists, Murphy was alarmed by the growth of trade unionism, and his main target was the Irish Transport and General Workers' Union, founded in 1909 by James Larkin. Murphy took on the TGWU in July 1913, calling a meeting of over 300 employers who resolved to ask their workers to agree not to join a union, and to sack dissidents. This was what Larkin, a seasoned and feared agitator who regarded the union movement as the means towards a socialist revolution, wanted: Dangerfield called him 'preposterous and powerful, half genius and half lunatic'.[61] It was a tactic no English employer would have contemplated, partly because – Tonypandy aside – the Liberal state would be unlikely to support it, but also because the superior muscle of English unions and the Trades Disputes Act might defeat the employers. The TGWU's response to the employers' initiative was, first, to recruit members at United Tramways. For good measure, it advocated a boycott of Murphy's newspapers, with newsboys in Dublin and, soon, other Irish towns refusing to sell them.

Larkin's ambition was for a wider, paralysing strike to bring the forces of capitalism to their knees. Murphy played into his hands when, on 15 August, he sacked forty tramways workers he believed to be union men. The TGWU members wished to strike at once, but Larkin stopped them: he was still trying to recruit operatives at Dublin's main Ringsend power station, so as to be able to close down all the businesses reliant on electricity. The following week Murphy sacked another 300 workers, including men and boys in his newspaper's dispatch department, which forced Larkin's hand. On 24 August he made a speech in which he reserved the strike weapon, but denounced Murphy for saying he 'would spend £100,000' to defeat Larkin.[62] He asked: 'If Mr Murphy was going to starve men, by what authority had the government promised to support him?' Murphy and his friends crowed that Larkin had failed to bring out the tram workers, but soon ate their words. The following evening Larkin called a meeting of his members at United Tramways – just as the Ascendancy and the Quality were packing the city for the Dublin Horse Show – and called them out on strike from the next morning. At 10 a.m. on 26 August around 150 drivers stopped their trams where they were – often in the middle of busy streets – and walked away from them. A skeleton service ran during the afternoon, manned by inspectors and management, but the threat of rioting caused even that to be suspended. Matters swiftly became inflamed, with 200 extra officers drafted in from the RIC to support the Dublin Metropolitan Police. The strike spread: within two days around 20,000 people working for 300 or so employers were out.

Larkin had, the previous year, formed the Irish Labour party with Jim

Connolly, a Marxist who in 1896 had founded the Irish Socialist Republican party, and who would be executed after the Easter Rising. As the name Irish Labour party suggests, the organisation had two prongs, which made it easy for Larkin and Connolly to make common cause. After destroying the power of capitalism, Connolly wanted an Irish Republic ruled by workers. The movement had, however, a formidable opponent not so much in Murphy as in the Roman Catholic Church, which regarded its leaders as revolutionaries; the dispute divided Irish society. The British union movement offered full assistance, with the TUC sending £150,000 to help feed strikers' families, and offering to board the families of its members' children who were, effectively, evacuated from Dublin: but the church denounced the idea, fearing children would be corrupted by anti-Catholic, or even anti-Christian, influences once over the water. Capitalism was also divided: the Guinness brewery, Dublin's major employer, refused to lock out its workers.

As picketing became more aggressive, so too did policing. A few trams were still operating on Saturday 30 August and some suffered violent attacks. That evening a riot in central Dublin left thirty police and 200 civilians injured, and led to eighty arrests. Larkin turned up – in a false beard and a frock coat – to address a rally in Sackville Street the next afternoon. The chief divisional magistrate had banned it. Larkin burned a copy of the proclamation and said he would be there 'alive or dead'.[63] He was arrested as he arrived on the balcony of the Imperial Hotel. This provoked a riot and police baton charges that left two dead and 400 injured, and resulted in 210 arrests. The police were showered with stones and broken bottles, and the Army was called in. Later that evening another riot broke out in Inchicore, a suburb of Dublin, when three tramcars were attacked and vandalised; a police escort saw the trams safely back to their depot, but was assailed by the mob. Again, the Army was summoned.

These were events that, not for the last time in Irish history, earned the label 'Bloody Sunday'. Two others – a woman shot by a strike breaker and a union official beaten up in a police station – died in the unrest. The rioting resumed on 1 September, though not on the scale of the previous day. The employers, refusing to be cowed, started to sack workers supporting Larkin. MPs accused the police of having used 'unnecessary brutality'. One, Handel Booth, the Liberal MP for Pontefract, who had witnessed the scenes, said he could not understand 'why people were kicked when lying prostrate on the ground'.[64] Count Markievicz, whose wife would in 1918 become a Sinn Féin MP and the first woman elected to the Commons, compared what he had seen with 'Red Sunday' in St Petersburg: *The Times*, where this was reported, hinted that its readers should not take this too seriously, on account of the Countess's being renowned for her 'extreme Nationalist tendencies'.

Larkin and Connolly formed the Irish Citizen Army to protect strikers. It was under the command of a former army officer, Jack White, son of a field marshal from County Antrim, who had conceived a loathing of the British ruling class while serving heroically in the Boer War, and become an Irish republican. However, Irish society remained divided. One Nationalist, at a meeting of the Dublin Corporation, said that 'when the lowest dregs of Dublin were incited to riot the authorities were justified in taking action.'[65] Although there was an anti-British element to what happened, with the syndicalist movement under Larkin using the dispute to organise republicans too, the lockout also pitted middle-class Nationalists against working-class ones.

Once Larkin was arrested and the riots were over the situation returned to normal, the tramways mostly running with the help of labour from Britain and elsewhere in Ireland. Sackings continued at factories where TGWU members supported Larkin; shortly after the riots Jacob's, the biscuit factory, locked out its union members. Tedcastle, a coal merchant, paid off 100 men; and then paid off 100 carters who went out in sympathy. Other Dublin coal merchants followed their example. Larkin appeared in court on 1 September, in his frock coat and silk hat, charged with inciting others to commit assault and murder, and with uttering seditious words and libels.

Nationalist MPs, distracted by a bigger issue, were reluctant to support Larkin, whom they regarded as an extremist. A parliamentarian with no such reservations was Keir Hardie, who arrived in Dublin on 2 September to visit him in jail. By 5 September shipping companies had locked out TGWU members, leaving 6,000 men on strike across the city. Exporting people and goods from Ireland became problematic, with a rapid effect on agriculture. Then, a week after the riots, the building trade locked out union members. A meeting of employers, 'while asserting its friendly feelings towards trade unionism', declared that 'the position created by the Irish Transport and General Workers' Union (which is a union in name only) is a menace to all trade organisations and has become intolerable.'[66] As the lockout spread a delegation of English trades unionists visited Dublin to try to mediate: they failed, as attitudes hardened on both sides. The price of coal rose because little was being shipped, and the price of meat too. By the end of the month food was scarce, for those who still had the means to pay for it. Employers using British labour became indifferent to whether their workers returned or not.

The lockout would last until spring 1914, when the strikers were starved back to work, and into agreements not to join a union. Many in the middle-class intelligentsia who supported the TGWU would lead the Republican movement after the Easter Rising, which (together with the establishment of organised labour in Ireland) gave the lockout a historical resonance. But it also confirmed to London how volatile Irish society was, and supplied a further reason not to aggravate the problem by delaying Home Rule. On 1 November 1913 the argument crossed the Irish Sea, with a huge meeting being held in the Albert Hall in support of Larkin, who was in jail for sedition. He was released on 13 November.

VI

In September another suggestion was made for dealing with Ulster, and one to which Asquith gave serious thought. Lord Loreburn, who had retired in 1912 as Lord Chancellor after nearly seven years on the Woolsack, wrote a lengthy letter to *The Times* advocating a conference of all the parties. His premise was that once the Bill was enacted in 1914 it would be followed by 'serious rioting' in Ulster, a conflict he said would be further inflamed 'if the Conservative party in England is prepared to condone if not to approve of it', which it was widely believed it would.[67] The refusal of juries to convict after such disturbances, and the creation of an idea of 'impunity', would be further encouragement, together with the idea that the government would not use force against rioters. He felt a conference would serve Redmond's interests as the man most likely to be leading an independent Ireland, as it would help succour the hostile minority he would have to govern, and perhaps end misunderstandings. There could be no reason for refusing to meet and see 'if . . . Irish self-government can be amicably adjusted.'[68] Politicians were excited by Loreburn's proposals: with the exception, however, of Asquith, who having thought about it had reached the conclusion that neither

Redmond nor Carson would find such a conference satisfactory, and nor would they command the confidence of their supporters in agreeing to one. Nationalist opinion felt Carson could only act as he did because of the weakness of the government, and the suggestion was made that he, and possibly other Unionists, should be removed from the Privy Council.[69]

On 23 September a 500-strong meeting of the Ulster Unionist Council discussed arrangements for a provisional government if Home Rule were implemented. Carson would lead it, daring London to stop it: the Unionists were convinced no force would be used. This was done with the full knowledge of Law, who admitted to Crewe – whom he met while staying with the King at Balmoral – that it would be terrible for the country. He was happy to agree to a conference if that would ease matters. Crucially, and to avoid a catastrophe, he hinted that Ulster's exclusion might placate his party, allowing them to accept Home Rule for the rest of Ireland. Law had also to manage tensions, with Lansdowne outraged at Smith's behaviour in making claims that seemed to incite anarchy, in the name of the Unionist party. 'Are you not a little horrified,' Lansdowne asked Law on 23 September, 'at the manner in which F. E. Smith is pledging not only himself but the whole Unionist party to violent action in Ulster?'[70]

Churchill was also at Balmoral, and Law tried to convince him the position was 'desperate' for both parties, but worse for the Liberals, who might have to deal with a provisional government in Ulster under Carson and sustained by an armed militia.[71] He warned that the Army might not obey orders to coerce Ulster, and threatened that Unionists might disrupt the Commons. Churchill reported this to Asquith, who admitted: 'I always thought (and said) that, in the end, we should probably have to make some sort of bargain about Ulster as the price of Home Rule.'[72] The threats of disruption he saw as 'puerile in their crudity'. Law told Carson exclusion had to be an option, and its acceptability would hinge on whether it betrayed Unionists in the rest of Ireland. Lansdowne thought it would, but Carson said that southern Unionists – and he spoke as one – would not agitate against Home Rule: not just because they realised the game was up, but because their financial interests could be compromised.

Asquith went to Balmoral and with the King's approval – and to his relief – wrote to Law to suggest they meet. He also admitted to the King that the Bill was unlikely to be enacted in its original form, and that there might be a delay in implementing it. On 14 October he met Law at the Surrey home of the leader of the opposition's friend, fellow Unionist MP and co-conspirator, Sir Max Aitken, the first of three meetings. It was agreed the choice of coercing either Ulster or the rest of Ireland would present huge problems for whoever was in power, and that coercing neither would be preferable. But while the two men agreed, they doubted how far they could convince their parties. Law, who wanted at least four and possibly six Ulster counties excluded, on the understanding they could opt in later, was unsure he could persuade Lansdowne – who as a big Irish landowner fretted about the plight of Unionists in the south – of this. Asquith and Law agreed that he would swallow some form of exclusion provided his senior colleagues agreed, and there was no outcry from Unionists in Ireland outside Ulster.

A form was sent round Ulster's men to ask them to volunteer for duties in a militia, if needed: by 23 September 60,000 had signed, and within weeks 100,000. The government was vexed by the notion of Ireland's capital being paralysed by a general strike, and its second city controlled by an illegal militia. Askwith was sent to Dublin to see whether he could help. But as the employers saw it, the workers had no bargaining power. They could work or starve: and in the end starvation would send them back to work – which it did.

Redmond came under increasing criticism from his own side for a lack of imagination in dealing with Home Rule and the unrest in Dublin – they felt he was rather inert when it came to dealing with the Unionist threat to derail proceedings, and that his failure to engage with a crippling general strike did not bode well for a Nationalist government in Ireland after Home Rule. The political realities were too much for Lloyd George, who once more, on 12 November, raised at cabinet the question of excluding Ulster. The exact area to be excluded was yet to be settled, but a time limit of five or six years should be set, allowing at least one or possibly two general elections. Asquith and his colleagues, faced with the far worse option of a potential civil war, agreed to the proposal. Thus partition became inevitable, and Lloyd George took charge of it. He set up two meetings with Dillon, identified as the most obstinate part of the Nationalist leadership, and Asquith tried to bring round Redmond.

On 15 November Churchill said at Alexandra Palace in north London that: 'Nationalist Ireland should receive her freedom and her own self-government, with the means and the money to make that self-government a success.'[73] But he added, in the first public hint of compromise, 'Protestant Ulster should, somehow or other, be satisfied and comforted.' This reversed the Liberal dogma that Ireland was not, as the Unionists maintained, two nations. Two days later *The Times* published, without attribution, the exclusion proposals: Lloyd George had briefed it. He hinted that the British taxpayer would compensate the Irish government with revenues to make up for those lost from Ulster.

However, Nationalists remained fervently opposed to Ulster's exclusion. Redmond, speaking at Northampton, announced that 'we would welcome with open arms a settlement of this question by consent; but we are not going to sacrifice in the moment of victory the fruits of our long battle.'[74] He was equally opposed to talks, complaining that he was being asked to 'go into a conference where the whole question of the principle of Home Rule would be put back once again into the melting pot. This we cannot and will not do.'[75] Carson said he would wait until the proposals were official, and then gauge the opinion of his clientele. A short exclusion would, it was felt, make little or no difference to Ulster's sentiments: a permanent exclusion was now the desired end. The government used its proposals, which resembled Churchill's federation idea, as a basis for further private discussions with the Unionists. They, meanwhile, used every opportunity to call for an early general election: such as in a speech Lansdowne made in Brighton on 18 November, in which he also said exclusion would not stop the injustice of Home Rule for Unionists outside Ulster, nor prevent a Nationalist government being 'a source of weakness and danger to the United Kingdom.'[76] He suggested federation might be the only solution; but there was still no appetite for that, for it would mean completely redesigning the Home Rule Bill.

The Nationalists, seeing how Ulster had assembled a potential militia, decided they needed one too. In late 1913 several Nationalist or republican groups – Sinn Féin, the Ancient Order of Hibernians and the Gaelic League notably, but also, undeclared, the secret Irish Republican Brotherhood – coalesced to recruit this militia. The initiative came from the IRB. Determined to show a moderate face, the Volunteers persuaded Eoin MacNeill, Professor of Early and Medieval History at University College Dublin to be its figurehead. The IRB, however, saw an opportunity to create the force that would gain Irish independence, founded under the guise of a response to the UVF. After several meetings the Volunteers were launched on 25 November, with a recruitment rally in Dublin, organised by the IRB. The same day Lloyd George told Redmond that the authorities would seize 95,000 rounds of ammunition from the UVF in Belfast.

The IRB's hidden agenda for the Volunteers, which for its first few months recruited thousands of members every week, was handicapped by the strong involvement of Redmond's moderate followers, who did not share the IRB ideology of republicanism inherited from the Fenians. MacNeill also outlined moderate aims for the movement, wishing the force to be mobilised only in response to any British attempt to repress the Irish people. This moderation and commitment to a partnership with Britain would be proved within a year, when an estimated 90 per cent of the Volunteers joined the British Army on the outbreak of the Great War.

The UVF and, now, the Volunteers were not acting illegally; the Arms Act, which had banned the importation into and carrying of arms within Ireland, had been repealed years earlier. The UVF had licences for their weapons: that was all the law asked. They had drilled regularly under the eyes of the police. This could not go on, and shortly after the formation of the Volunteers a proclamation was issued banning the importing of arms to Ireland. However, the UVF was already heavily armed, and was believed to have 10,000 rifles; the Volunteers were not. Also, the creation of this militia focused attention in London on the reliability of the Army. On 16 December, as fears rose about its enforcing the government's will in Ulster, Jack Seely, the Secretary of State for War, summoned the six generals in charge of the Home commands to discuss what to do if officers tried to resign their commissions rather than obey lawful orders. Sir John French, the Chief of the Imperial General Staff, and Sir Spencer Ewart, the Adjutant-General, were also present. Seely, a colonel on the Reserve, said officers could not 'pick and choose' which orders to obey; but he promised there would be no order for 'outrageous action, for instance, to massacre a demonstration of Orangemen.'[77]

On 25 November the cabinet agreed to hold the idea of exclusion in reserve. The King became more optimistic, believing (on Asquith's advice) that the six-year exclusion would be offered when parliament met in February, and that 'Mr Redmond will probably be induced to accept the proposal.'[78] Asquith met Carson in December and tried to persuade him that a mechanism could be devised whereby the imperial parliament alone would be able to override the wishes of a majority of Ulster representatives. Carson did not budge, and Asquith told the cabinet on 22 January 1914 that he was 'flatly refusing anything short of the exclusion of Ulster.'[79] A paper was circulated to the cabinet describing how a separate Ulster might be governed.[80] But at least now exclusion appeared a possibility, and the prospect would underpin policy from then on. Asquith was further jolted in this direction by what he told Venetia Stanley was 'a letter (of rather a neurotic kind) from the highest quarters': the King told him that 'Ulster will never agree to send representatives to an Irish parliament in Dublin.'[81]

But the King also urged Law to keep talking to Asquith. Stamfordham, his private secretary, told Law on 20 January that 'His Majesty still clings to the belief in British common sense and trusts that by "give and take" by all parties an amicable solution may yet be found.'[82] Asquith frequently, in private asides to his wife, commented on how decent the King was, but how much better it would be had he been properly educated. Law was even more direct. Though his own stance had become more conciliatory, Asquith was still resisting Ulster's counties voting to exclude themselves, so he told Stamfordham: 'There are now only two courses open to the Government: they must either submit their Bill to the judgment of the people, or prepare to face the consequences of civil war.'[83]

Asquith told Redmond on 2 February of the obstinate position of the Unionists, and warned him that if taken to its logical conclusion it would force a general election. Even if the Liberals won, the end of the 1910 parliament would also end the process under the Parliament Act by which the Home Rule Bill would become law: the process would have to start all over again. The only way to avert this was by the Nationalists agreeing to concessions; they would have to offer the exclusion of Ulster, which would rob the Unionists of the moral high ground if they rejected such an offer. Redmond replied on 4 February that his colleagues felt the effect of any hint of concessions would be 'grave'.[84] Ulster's belief that it could bully Britain into submission 'would make the Bill not the end but the reopening of the whole Irish problem.' It would seem as though the government had admitted it faced a civil war – a threat Redmond believed 'exaggerated' – and that would lead to 'some serious explosion of violence' in Ulster. He also felt that it would be disastrous for his party, which would be accused of 'betrayal' of the Nationalists of Ulster; and he believed it would weaken the government. He pleaded with Asquith not to commit himself in the debate on the address when parliament reassembled, and promised his wholehearted support if he did not.

VII

The King's Speech, on 10 February 1914, promised the Government of Ireland Bill would be submitted again. Asquith bowed to Redmond, deciding the time was still not right to mention the possible exclusion of Ulster. His Majesty expressed regret that the question had not been settled; and warned that this was a matter 'which, unless handled now with foresight, judgment, and in the spirit of mutual concession, threatens grave future difficulties.'[85] His speech also promised proposals for reforming the Lords, indicating where the government felt the blame lay for such a meal having been made of the Irish question.

Unionists sought ways to derail the Bill. Having dropped the idea of the King withholding consent or forcing Asquith to accept a dissolution, they thought of having the Lords defeat the annual Army Bill, which would stop the government deploying troops in Ireland. It would, however, also stop them being deployed everywhere else, which would have been catastrophic. Nonetheless, this plan was given serious consideration. In the debate on the King's Speech Walter Long, Chief Secretary for Ireland under Balfour and, next to Carson, possibly the most militant anti-Home Ruler, proposed an amendment calling for an immediate general election – he had attempted something similar in 1913. Reflecting his party's desperation at the imminence of the legislation – this was its third and final passage – he said 'there is predominating and overwhelming all classes the knowledge that for the first time for centuries in the history in this country we are threatened with the worst form of internal disturbance, civil war within the United Kingdom.'[86]

He added: 'In Ulster every man knows today that there is a force training, arming, equipping and preparing itself for action, numbering something like one hundred thousand men, and they are determined if necessary at the cost of their lives to resist this Bill.'[87] Calling this 'the first fruits of your Parliament Act, which was to do so much for the privileges and liberties of the people', he warned the government that if it were to proceed, it would have 'to meet force with force'. That meant 'you are going to have to carry your first great measure in Ireland by using British bayonets and British bullets.'

Long mocked the idea of federalism, and that the UVF was bluffing. He dismissed the safeguards, saying the Westminster parliament would never overturn any decision made by Dublin. He made a dark threat: 'Are you quite sure that this trouble will be confined to Ireland itself? Are you quite sure it will not extend to the United Kingdom, and even beyond the confines of the United Kingdom to distant parts of the Empire – are you quite sure of this?'[88] The implication that unrest would extend to Glasgow, Liverpool, Birmingham, possibly London, anywhere with a big Irish population, was chilling.

He believed the government would not meet force with force, because the Army and the Royal Irish Constabulary simply would not act against the resistance: 'Many a soldier would send in his commission rather than fight against the people of Ulster.' He quoted a letter sent to the Duke of Cambridge, as commander-in-chief, at the time of the 1893 Bill, in which a senior officer had warned him: 'If ever our troops are brought into a collision with the loyalists of Ulster and blood is shed it will shake the whole foundations upon which our Army rests to such an extent that I fear our Army will never be the same again.'[89] Long redefined the argument: 'It will be a crime of the first magnitude to use the forces of the Crown to shoot down the people of Ulster, who will be fighting in defence of the same flag and of their own religion.'

Asquith asked: 'Is there any evidence in what has since taken place, particularly in what has taken place since the House rose last August, to show that the country has really changed its mind?'[90] This was dangerous ground, for since the House had risen there had been seven by-elections, and the Liberals had lost two seats. Casuistically, Asquith said both defeats were three-cornered fights in which the anti-Home Rule parties – his own and Labour – had more votes than the Unionist who had been elected. The Unionists would give no guarantee that if the Liberals won a general election they would let the Bill pass: the whole Parliament Act process would have to start again. They did concede that they would, if they lost an election, withdraw their support for the Ulster Unionists, but that was a separate matter. Asquith also regarded an election as irrelevant because a Liberal victory would not change the outlook of the Ulstermen. There was a fundamental refusal to accept the democratic will unless it coincided with the principles of the Unionist party; it was not a satisfactory basis on which to proceed.

Pressed on his refusal to exclude Ulster, Asquith referred to a letter in that morning's *Times* from Sir Horace Plunkett, a highly respected former Unionist MP and prominent Irish agricultural reformer, who had converted to Home Rule. Plunkett was busy behind the scenes trying, and failing, to reconcile his Unionist friends to the Bill, and his letter was a public expression of the doubts about exclusion he was expressing in private. He suggested including Ulster now, but allowing it the option to seek exclusion if its worst fears were fulfilled. Asquith announced he was happy with such a solution, confident his safeguards would work and that there would be no demand for exclusion. He urged that the Plunkett plan be, at least, 'respectfully entertained'.[91]

Asquith thus admitted things had changed; he said so, explicitly, moments later. What he did not say explicitly was that what had also changed was the arrival of a committed paramilitary force that would resist Home Rule to the death, and which Asquith had no certain force at his disposal to counteract. A note almost of desperation entered into his language. 'Every one of us must desire to avoid civil war and bloodshed, and there is nothing we will not do, consistently with the maintenance of our fundamental principles in regard to the solution of this question, to avoid that terrible calamity,' he said.[92] The lawyerly parenthesis in that sentence was, however, a further indication of how limited Asquith's course of action would be. Craig called out to him to make suggestions; Asquith had nothing to say other than that he would bring the measure forward again without delay. This went down badly: Arthur Salter, the Unionist MP who spoke next, accused him of 'appalling levity' and of deploying a strategy in which he 'drifts on and presses for time.'[93]

The next day the Unionists, after a powerful speech by Carson in which he accused the Nationalists of never having tried to win over Ulster, but having merely wanted it for its tax revenues, forced a division on whether the Bill should be delayed until after an election. Lloyd George promised proposals aimed at allaying Unionist fears; Law pressed the government to reveal whether it would commit troops to coerce Ulster, but received no answer. The attempt to force an election failed by 333 votes to 255. The one hope Asquith took from the proceedings was that Carson seemed to accept the exclusion of Ulster, and to regard it as a possible alternative to the wholesale obstruction of Home Rule. A fortnight later a vote, which also failed, was held to ask the government to bring forward its new proposals for the Government of Ireland Bill: Asquith said it would happen before the Easter recess.

The government was still struggling to persuade its erstwhile supporters in the Irish Parliamentary party to accept exclusion. Lloyd George and Birrell worked on Redmond and Dillon, and on 4 March told their cabinet colleagues that the Irish had been 'reluctantly persuaded as the price of a peaceful settlement' to give Ulster – or a part of it, to be determined – the right to exclude itself, after a referendum, for six years.[94] Redmond saw that this put the burden on the Unionists to accept or reject the offer. This plan leaked immediately, the *Daily News* publishing it on 5 March: Lloyd George suspected Churchill to be the culprit. On 9 March Asquith announced it formally in the Commons, hoping it would be seen as progress. But Law asked what would happen if, after six years, Ulster still wanted no part of an Ireland under Home Rule; the Unionists decided the idea was unworkable.

In early March, as civil war was openly discussed, intelligence reports suggested that the UVF were about to storm Carrickfergus Castle, take the ammunition stored there, and march on Dublin. A paper circulated by Birrell to the cabinet reported that 81,410 men in the nine counties of Ulster were signed up to the UVF: and that there were 467,500 rounds of ammunition in the Province outside Belfast, which had 403,400 rounds. There were an estimated 9,500 rifles, and over 3,600 swords. Birrell added that the UVF were on manoeuvres and organising 'surprise mobilisations'.[95] It was widely believed that the moment a Home Rule Bill became law, the UVF would seize police barracks and take control of the infrastructure.

Seely, on Asquith's instructions, therefore on 15 March ordered General Sir Arthur Paget, the commander-in-chief, Ireland, to move troops not just to Carrickfergus but to Armagh, Omagh and Enniskillen – all with concentrations of military stores and notably of ammunition – to protect them, as he later put it, 'from the possibility of attack by evilly-disposed persons'.[96] Paget was grandson of the Marquess of Anglesey, had married an American heiress, owned a string of steeplechasers but was not heavy with brains, evoking the officer corps before the Cardwell reforms in which he had begun his service, in the days when the aristocracy and the well-to-do could buy commissions in the Army rather than need to rely on advancement by merit. Unfortunately, Seely was rather dim: the meeting of two such minds made misunderstanding inevitable. After discussions with Seely, Paget ordered troops to remove the stores, rather than staying put and reinforcing the depots. Worse, the orders given to Paget were couched to suggest the cabinet wanted such measures applied to the whole of Ireland, not just Ulster. He passed them on to officers at the main depot in the south, at the Curragh in County Kildare, a mistake that would have huge consequences.

Paget also undertook a survey of the growing Nationalist volunteer strength. In a document marked 'Secret' he reported to the War Office that in Clare 'conviction [of militant nationalists] almost impossible owing to corruption of Magistrates and intimidation of juries'.[97] In Limerick the Volunteers were 'generally of better class and stamp than usual' with 'many rifles'. 'Religious intolerance' was 'very great', with the locals ready to start attacking Protestants if Ulster rebelled. Cork and Kerry were relatively quiet, but there was a 'raw mob' in Wexford that raised fears of a 'general massacre of Protestants' if there was a rising in Ulster. Paget felt 'the greatest danger to the peace of the country is the demoralisation and discontent of the police', many of whom were preparing to resign rather than confront armed bands from either side.

Meanwhile Churchill decided, without notifying Asquith, to deploy the Navy to the Ulster coast. The First Lord thought the 3rd Battle Squadron, which was due for some practice, could have it off Lamlash on the Isle of Arran, about three hours' sail from Larne, in case it was needed to ship in reinforcements. A cruiser was going to Carrickfergus and two destroyers would steam up the Irish Sea; and the admiral in command of those waters was reinforcing coastguard stations. The cabinet endorsed this, and agreed to centralise the command structure of the police in Ulster. Later, Churchill's readiness to deploy the Navy was seen as proving he wished to provoke a Unionist uprising, to force the issue. The naval dispositions and Paget's clumsy handling of troop movements seemed to Ulstermen proof that they would be coerced.

Churchill seemed to be spoiling for a fight; but he had mishandled the naval estimates, leading to a projected £5 million budget deficit, a row with his friend Lloyd George and the prospect of Churchill's having to resign. His stock was low in the party. Championing Home Rule helped rebuild his political credit. At Bradford on 14 March, angered by the Unionists' rejection of a compromise, he told an audience of 3,000 that the government had conceded as much as it could. In a speech peppered with interruptions from suffragists, he hardened the tone and seemed to issue a threat. He told Ulster to obey the law; and that if they didn't like the law, they could campaign for a party pledged to repeal it at the next election. An offer had been made, he said, 'in all friendship and goodwill, an offer going beyond anything which, on a strict interpretation of our rights, was required of us . . . as an earnest effort to procure agreement and lasting peace.'[98]

He mocked the response the offer – the six-year exclusion to allow for two general elections to be held – had had. 'Unless they had exclusion or a General Election, they said, there would be civil war. They have got both, and they still say there is going to be civil war.' He said rebellion was justifiable only where there was real oppression, and where no remedy other than resort to arms was possible: but this was not the case with Ulster. He accused Carson of 'bitterness' and described the Ulster Convention as a 'treasonable conspiracy'. He accused Law of using Ulster to force an early election. Most provocatively, he seemed to dare Ulster to rise up. 'There are things worse than bloodshed, even on an extensive scale. The collapse of the Central Government of the British Empire would be worse . . . the trampling down of that law and order which under the conditions of a civilised state assure to millions life, liberty and the pursuit of happiness – all this would be worse than bloodshed.' (A few months earlier he had insisted to cabinet colleagues that he would never agree to 'the shooting down of Orangemen'.[99]) If, he concluded, events in Ulster were down to a 'sinister and revolutionary purpose', then 'let us go forward together and put these grave matters to the proof.' The speech incensed Unionists, but secured Churchill's rehabilitation: Asquith noted that at cabinet three days later 'Winston preened himself and was stroked by the others'.[100]

On 18 March Paget went to the War Office to warn Seely that many officers in Ireland would refuse to take up arms against the Ulster Volunteers, if that was the government's order. The next day French and Ewart agreed, with Seely's approval, that officers domiciled in Ulster could 'disappear' for the duration of such operations. The rest would have to do their duty or resign. At another meeting that day Seely told Paget the government had no intention of allowing a civil war, which further reinforced Paget's view that the Army – which in Ireland was easily outnumbered by the UVF – would have to secure Ulster. Seely told him that all troop movements had to be finished by 31 March, extending them to Dundalk and an empty barracks in Newry. These were both in Nationalist areas, but strategically too important to be allowed to fall into the hands of the UVF. That day the King told Asquith of his concerns about the capabilities of the UVF, which Asquith dismissed to Venetia Stanley as 'exaggerated'.[101]

The next day the Unionists tabled a vote of censure against the government, which Law warned risked destroying the Army. Carson walked out of the chamber, provoking lengthy Unionist cheers; not just to make a dramatic exit, but to get back to Ulster in case rumours that Asquith had had enough, and was about to issue a warrant for his arrest, were true. It was certainly the case that many Liberals feared Carson would proclaim a provisional government – unlikely given the Home Rule Bill was not yet law. Then on 20 March Paget, who had returned to Ireland overnight, ordered senior officers under his command to his headquarters in Dublin. In a long memorandum he sent to the King the following week, Paget said he thought this meeting necessary 'since I was not certain all my Brigadiers were of my own opinion that duty came before any other consideration.'[102] He added: 'I knew that all troops were loyal to their Sovereign, but I had doubts as to their loyalty to his advisers.'

Paget managed to misrepresent – or perhaps deliberately exceed – his orders from London, causing the officers to believe that, as Seely later told the Commons, 'there was a plan to treat Ulster as an enemy's country, and to overwhelm her with a surprise attack.'[103] Paget informed the King he had told his officers that any troop movements would be 'only in support of law and order', but might cause 'great excitement'; and that 'a situation might then rapidly evolve which might set Ireland ablaze by Saturday, and would lead to something more serious than quelling of local disturbances'.[104] He outlined the options open to officers from Ulster: those from elsewhere who were reluctant to fight were told, Paget added, that they 'will at once be dismissed from the Service'.[105] He seemed to be offering his officers an ultimatum, and many responded accordingly.

Rumours abounded in Ulster, and the atmosphere was febrile. It was said that the 200 most prominent men in the anti-Home Rule movement were about to be arrested, and warrants had been drawn up; then that a secret movement would move in and disarm the UVF. One who thought he would be asked to suppress Ulster was Brigadier-General Hubert

Gough, who had commanded the 3rd Cavalry Brigade at the Curragh since 1911, and who recorded Paget's address in his memoirs. Gough did not live in Ulster but had family there. He decided to resign, not least because he felt Paget had threatened him. He maintained he had obeyed orders: he had been ordered to make a choice, and had done so. He returned to the Curragh to speak to a regiment under his command, the 5th Lancers. As a result, he missed a second meeting in Dublin that afternoon when Paget clarified his earlier statement, in which he claimed the plan was to intimidate Ulster rather than to fight.

Paget telegraphed the War Office later that day saying that large numbers of officers were resigning, and that 'Brigadier and fifty-seven officers Third Cavalry Brigade prefer to accept dismissal if ordered north.'[106] When Seely addressed the Commons he said he had been told that all officers except two – and one was doubtful – from the 5th Lancers were resigning, and the 16th Lancers were in a similar position. Paget had also told Seely: 'Fear men will refuse to move.'[107] Seely ordered him to relieve senior officers of their command and send them to London; others would replace them. Asquith, whose game of bridge at Lord Sheffield's on the evening of 20 March was interrupted by the news, realised any prospect of the Army quelling Ulster was impossible. He made the mistake of not telling the King, who learned of the incident from his newspaper the next morning and sent Stamfordham to issue a rebuke in person. Asquith went to the King, and the editor of *The Times*, the next day, to try to calm these two key constitutional figures.

However, calm was not universal: Churchill, his bellicosity barely restrained, told French on the evening of Lord Sheffield's bridge party that whatever the Army might do, if Belfast rose up 'his fleet would have the town in ruins in 24 hours'.[108] Paget, apparently nearing hysteria, went to the Curragh on 21 March to berate Gough and his brother officers, spraying out threats that included 'no resignations would be accepted' and 'senior officers would be tried by court martial'.[109] According to some present, Paget said the possibility of moving on Ulster was 'the direct order of the Sovereign', which it was not (and Paget later denied saying it, and was supported by others present in doing so): the King was only just learning of the crisis from *The Times*. Paget supposedly claimed that the King's was the order he was obeying, and not that of 'those swine of politicians'. He later told the King he had offered 'concessions' to the officers 'to save the reputation of these three Regiments and the credit of the Forces in Ireland.'[110] He admitted he should not have made the 'concessions' – he told the King verbally what they were, but did not put them in his memo, though they appear to have been about the promise of 'disappearing' followed by reinstatement. He admitted, too, to the King that he had not expected Gough and his brother officers to decline the offer, and complained that, if they had not, the whole crisis could have been averted.

On 22 March Gough arrived in London with two of his colonels. It was now that the Curragh incident – not quite a mutiny, since no serving officer had refused to obey orders – threatened to spiral out of control, and undermine the whole Army. If the intention was to make an example of Gough, it failed. French, hearing Gough had been suspended, threatened to resign unless he was reinstated. Gough also saw Major-General Henry Wilson, Director of Military Operations at the War Office. Wilson was a fanatical anti-Home Ruler – the IRA assassinated him on the doorstep of his London house in 1922 – and one who used his position to feed information to Law and other senior Unionists, to further the cause, as well as secretly advising the UVF. Between 21 and 31 March Wilson met Law ten times, either in his or Law's house, telling him government secrets. Wilson persuaded Gough to demand from French a written guarantee that the Army would not be used against Ulster; Wilson had already made such a suggestion to Seely, who rejected it. Gough also saw Seely who, when he failed to persuade Gough to change his view and perhaps realising he was out of his depth, acted on French's idea that the Army Council should publish a document saying the Curragh incident had been a misunderstanding – which it had not – and that it was 'the duty of all soldiers to obey lawful commands'.

The next day the cabinet, fearing French's resignation and that of many other officers who sympathised with Gough, approved the wording of this document, absurdly in Seely's absence: he had delivered it to the meeting and then had had to go to an audience of the King, to explain why the War Office had not kept the enraged Sovereign better informed. In his attempt to bring Gough to heel Seely had, however, given him an undertaking that the government's right to use the forces of the Crown in Ireland and elsewhere did not include the intention 'to crush political opposition to the policy or principles of the Home Rule Bill' – something that would have outraged Nationalists had they known of it.[111] However Gough insisted, on Wilson's advice, on this being added to the document, with the clarification that the Army would not be used to impose Home Rule *on Ulster.* French endorsed this, not least because he had learned that all officers of the Aldershot command would resign if Gough were not reinstated.

Seely, without consulting the cabinet but with the help of Morley, the Lord President of the Council, the only colleague he could find, acquiesced in putting his verbal assurance in writing. Morley felt nothing had happened at the cabinet meeting to prevent this. However Asquith, vexed by what he called 'Paget's tactless blundering, and Seely's clumsy phrases', was outraged to discover this change had been made; while realising the Army could not coerce Ulster, he was alarmed that Seely, backed by French, had signed away the government's right to have it do so, and had thereby risked losing Nationalist support.[112] Asquith sent for Seely and questioned him. Seely may have been dim but he was honourable and, in the Great War, won a reputation for astonishing bravery. He explained he had given his word to Gough and had felt obliged to add the guarantee to the document. Asquith demanded Gough should return it, and publicly repudiated what Balfour called 'the peccant paragraphs'.

Gough had already left for Ireland, however. Worse, Asquith had Grey telling him that before the Home Rule Bill was implemented, he should call an election to test the mood of the country. French and Seely insisted upon resigning. Gough went on to become a leading commander in the Great War, though was made a scapegoat for Passchendaele and sacked. French returned within months to command the British Expeditionary Force. Seely went to the front in 1914 and finished the war as a General, commanding the Canadian Cavalry Brigade. In the short term, Gough's reinstatement meant that he, and the officers under him, could not be used against Ulster, so the government could not enforce Home Rule.

In the Commons on 25 March Churchill admitted moving ships to the coast of Ireland 'in case of serious disorders occurring'.[113] He referred to the 'precautionary' movements of troops that had been 'effected without opposition from the army of 100,000 which has been raised to resist the authority of the Crown and Parliament', a remark that caused uproar. Later that day Seely had to explain himself, and the government, to parliament. He admitted that while, until the Curragh incident, no officer had tried to resign, fourteen on the retired list had written to the

War Office qualifying their promise to serve if mobilised: the government should have seen what was coming.

Seely admitted that as all communication was by telegram, and events were moving so quickly, there was room for misunderstanding.[114] He said Paget had told him reports of his remarks on the morning of 20 March were not accurate, and that Gough had said that had he known he and his men would be ordered to Ulster to support the civil authority there, rather than fight, he would have obeyed without question. The statements appeared contradictory. If what Paget claimed he said were true Gough would have known the score, and Paget would not have had to call his clarificatory second meeting on 20 March. Seely also described his meeting with Gough, in which Gough had told him he thought he was being told to coerce Ulster, which he did not feel would have been lawful; though on what grounds it is hard to tell. But Seely also said he told Gough that in asking the Army merely to support the civil authority, the government 'would not take advantage of the right to protect the civil power . . . in order to crush political opposition.'[115] It was then that Gough, conscious of earlier 'misunderstandings', asked for this to be put in writing.

Agreeing, Seely asked Ewart, who as the man in charge of Army discipline had also been present, to draw up a draft. It was this document Ewart had delivered to the cabinet in Seely's absence at Buckingham Palace. When Seely saw it he realised it did not reflect the promise he had made Gough. He exonerated French and Ewart from any responsibility for the 'peccant paragraphs'. 'Blame does rest,' he said, 'and it rests upon me, and I will tell the House for what. I added to a document, which the Cabinet had considered, my version of what I thought should be said . . . I did not apprehend that the Cabinet had seriously considered this document, and regarded a document of this kind as a matter of vital concern.'[116] Seely was either indulging in rare disingenuousness, or was exceptionally stupid: the document was crucial, given that it threatened to remove the power to coerce Ulster and enforce a Home Rule Act.

It had been an idiotic time for the King to demand to see Seely, and the private secretaries who arranged the meeting were gravely at fault in thus exposing him. The pressure on him had been enormous. Yet Seely said nothing altered the fact that: 'I am to blame, and gravely to blame in my judgment, and for that reason, while I ask the House to believe that throughout this difficult business I have acted with the sincere desire to be loyal to my colleagues, and to see fair play to the Army, I have felt it my duty to ask the Prime Minister to accept my resignation of my office.'[117] This stratagem was agreed between him and Asquith, who promised to refuse the resignation. Mrs Asquith was less charitable: she regarded Seely as a 'jackass' and feared that 'between him Paget and Winston I can see Henry will be smashed up and all the Gov so also.'[118]

However once French and Ewart insisted on going, Seely felt he had no choice but to insist too. Morley did not resign, and justified not doing so by saying he felt what Seely was adding was consistent with the document. Asquith took over the War Office, conscious the government he led had been exposed as being unable to control the Army. Rumours circulated that the troop movements Paget had been told to make, and the deployment of the battle squadron, had been part of a conspiracy by Seely and Churchill to goad the UVF into action, creating the *casus belli* to allow the rebellion to be crushed. Balfour, responding to Seely, mentioned this in the Commons.[119] Seely repudiated the claim, for which there is no evidence, as did the prime minister.

Asquith exonerated Paget, who remained in charge in Ireland until the outbreak of war. Churchill had told Asquith that Paget 'resolved to observe every conceivable precaution which courage and humanity could suggest, to avoid a collision and to prevent bloodshed'.[120] Controversy continued, however, about whether he had taken the King's name in vain when putting pressure on his senior officers. One, Angus Mackintosh, wrote to Asquith to confirm Paget did not 'at any time refer to the King in any personal sense.'[121] Another, O. C. Woolley-Dod, agreed he was 'quite sure' Paget had said nothing about the King. However Stamfordham was convinced Paget had exceeded his remit: 'I cannot disguise . . . ,' he wrote on 20 June 1914, 'the fact that from numerous communications which have reached me there was an unmistakable impression among the troops at the Curragh that the instructions given to them had been approved of by the King.'[122] One of the messages Stamfordham had seen was from Lieutenant-Colonel C. Brett, commanding the 2nd Suffolk Regiment, saying his officers had agreed to do their duty because Major-General Sir Charles Fergusson told them on the morning of 21 March that Paget assured them: 'the action of the Ministry in ordering the Army to take part in operations against Ulster has the full approval of His Majesty the King. The King has given the order, and we, one and all, obey him.'[123]

Fergusson had exceeded his remit: he took responsibility and offered his resignation, which Paget refused. He felt the responsibility was his, and told Stamfordham on 1 July: 'I, therefore, feel it incumbent on me to tender my own resignation on the same grounds.'[124] The matter was becoming absurd: Stamfordham replied that the King did not feel it was 'possible for him to express an opinion on your contemplated action.'[125] The question, within days, became subsumed into the abyss of war. What was clear, however, was that the Army had, for the moment, prevailed, and defeated Asquith and the government. Ramsay MacDonald suggested, with enough truth to make the assertion painful, that the Unionist party had replaced the Lords' veto with that of the officer corps of the Army; though many whom MacDonald would have considered his natural supporters were just as partisan towards Ulster as their officers.

VIII

Asquith, distressed and exhausted by relentless adversity from the Irish, the Army, the Unionists, the peers, the suffragettes and the trades unions, was far from having the clarity of mind and energy needed to deal with the burdens of the War Office as well as those of the premiership. Not all his colleagues approved of his intentions to act in this capacity. When he announced it to the cabinet: 'Winston's eyes blazed, and his polysyllables rolled, and his gestures were those of a man possessed.'[126] The prime minister seems to have felt that only by superintending the Army could he keep them under control, and avoid them engaging in any further, unhelpful, policy-making. He told the Commons on 30 March, after confirming Seely's departure, that he acted 'only in deference to what I believe to be a great public emergency'.[127]

The Unionists were livid, because the law required an MP who accepted a new cabinet post to seek his constituents' approval by offering himself as a candidate at a by-election, which would put Asquith out of the Commons during the third passage of the Government of Ireland Bill. Some Unionists disputed that Asquith, as he already held a cabinet office, had to do this – Gladstone had not done so in 1873 when assuming the office of Chancellor – but Sir John Simon, the Attorney-General, told him he had to go. However, when this row was at its height, the prime minister was not in the Commons to be pressed about it.

Unionists saw, or thought they saw, evil tidings in the dispatch of

General Nevil Macready to Belfast as the officer commanding that district, and as a putative military governor if civil war broke out. Leo Amery asked on 6 April – the aftermath of the Curragh incident was lengthy – whether Macready 'was intended to act as military governor of Belfast in case of the proclamation of martial law'.[128] McKenna, who answered, said the orders given to Macready were confidential, but there was 'no question' of martial law being proclaimed. Much was read into Paget's order to remove arms and ammunition from the depots he had reinforced; and there was a widespread belief among Unionists that warrants were being prepared for the arrest of Ulster covenanters – something McKenna also denied. On 6 April the Government of Ireland Bill was given its second reading by 356 votes to 272.

In the debate, Carson recorded why Unionists had rejected the offer of six years' exclusion: 'I refused to take a ticket of leave for six years, and I will tell you why. I would far prefer to advise the people of Ulster to go in and be included in the Dublin Parliament and let you commence your coercion to-morrow. I believe it would be shorter in the long run, but I am perfectly certain . . . that to adopt this six years' limit in relation to the exclusion of Ulster would be to make a hell of Ulster for six years.'[129] The King wrote Asquith what the latter called 'rather a hysterical letter' asking for the six-year limit to be removed. Asquith replied that he did not think he would get such a measure through the Commons; he knew he would never get it past Redmond.

On the night of 24–25 April between 25,000 and 35,000 German rifles and 3 million rounds of ammunition were landed at Larne for the UVF, to whom they were quickly distributed. There was nothing amateur about the exercise. Telegraph and telephone wires were cut to prevent anyone raising the alarm. Armed Ulster Volunteers – 12,000 were involved in the operation – surrounded the harbour to ensure the landing was not interfered with. Asquith called what happened a 'grave and unprecedented outrage'.[130] Yet on 11 May, pressed by MPs about what steps the government would take against the gun-runners, he rejected criminal proceedings: 'Other steps are being taken that I do not think it desirable for the present to make public.'[131] He, and the cabinet, knew no jury would convict anyone of this flagrant breach of the law – Carson knew of the operation, but deliberately did not inform Law. A week earlier, in a secret meeting in the house of Asquith's junior colleague and former private secretary, Edwin Montagu, the prime minister had talked to Carson and Law, who warned him the compulsory incorporation of Ulster into a Home Rule state after six years would be 'impossible'. They sought an amendment to the Bill making incorporation optional.[132] Asquith reluctantly agreed to this as a last resort, with the full details of Ulster's exclusion to be thrashed out later. The alternative was Ulster erupting once the Bill was enacted, which Asquith could not contemplate.

Accordingly, on 12 May he announced an Amending Bill to the Home Rule Bill; it would allow for the temporary exclusion of Ulster, with the exact area to be excluded – four, six or all nine counties – to be discussed once the Bill and the Amending Bill were passed. The cabinet had considered a paper suggesting excluding six counties.[133] This put Redmond, who felt cornered, in an invidious position. After his meeting with Carson and Law, Asquith had informed Redmond that there would be an Amending Bill, but had gone into no detail. By this point there were 100,000 Nationalist Volunteers, a third of them in Ulster, the most effective recruiting sergeants being men such as Carson proclaiming that Home Rule would not be allowed to happen. Redmond's determination to have all Ireland included, even if parts of Ulster joined later, would be supported by the Volunteers; he faced having to stick to his principles, and possibly risk armed confrontation that could lead to civil war, or abandon his leadership. Also, the sheer numbers of Nationalist Volunteers started to make the Unionists realise they could not hope to continue to rule most of Ireland. It simply seems not to have occurred to most of them that the Nationalists would, like those opposed to Home Rule, raise their own militia in defence against a Unionist one, and to see that the constitutional promise of Home Rule was carried through.

By the time the Bill had its third reading on 21 May there were still no exact details of what the Amending Bill would do. Therefore the Unionists sought to have the debate adjourned. When that failed the uproar was such that the Speaker had to suspend the sitting. The Commons passed the Home Rule Bill on 25 May; squabbling immediately started about which Ulster counties might be excluded. During June the numbers of National Volunteers increased by 15,000 a week, pitching Ireland towards the civil war the Liberals had striven to avoid. This so alarmed Redmond that he demanded the Volunteers be answerable to him, to which their leaders reluctantly acceded. Meanwhile, although some Unionists were retreating, others, notably Lansdowne, wanted no

Home Rule at all, and Carson was putting no pressure on his adherents in Ulster to moderate their line.

The Amending Bill was introduced on 23 June, allowing any county in Ulster that wished to exclude itself from Home Rule for six years to do so. The Lords contemplated wrecking it, so the Government of Ireland Bill could not be amended before Royal Assent and, therefore, that Assent would not be sought; and the qualifying period within the Parliament Act would run out, forcing the process to start all over again. Despite protracted negotiations designed to resolve the issue – which in the end came down to the eligibility of Fermanagh and Tyrone to be included, because of their large Catholic populations – the Lords amended the Amending Bill to exclude Ulster, making a nonsense of it.

It was Redmond, and not the Unionists, who was now the obstacle. Edwin Montagu suggested Asquith make common cause with Law to press Redmond. Asquith refused, noting on 6 July: 'I felt that we might both have been tempted to say things which we should afterwards wish unsaid. But I may very likely have a secret talk with Carson.'[134] That happened the next day; Carson was keen to settle, but pleaded intransigence on the part of his supporters. Asquith noted that Carson now favoured six and not all nine Ulster counties being excluded, in case the large numbers of Catholics Ulster would contain pushed it easily towards the Home Rule state.

All were at the end of their tethers. 'We had a long and dreary Cabinet this morning,' Asquith wrote on 8 July, 'trying to solve the old problem of how to get a quart into a pint pot.' The Tory press was disparaging the government's efforts, which Asquith started to see as an outright incitement to civil war. On 13 July he saw Northcliffe 'and tried to impress on him the importance of making *The Times* a responsible newspaper.'[135] The previous day Carson had presented colours to three UVF battalions, telling them: 'if they could not have peace with honour it must be war with honour.'[136]

Asquith tried to make Law see that if an election were called – the aim of many Unionists, and not entirely because of Ireland – there would be 'a very difficult situation' for the winner. He said it would be 'a crime' if a civil war broke out because of a failure to agree about the division of Tyrone.[137] The cabinet, having exhausted all other options, and with the Amending Bill compromised, considered the Loreburn strategy, and decided to convene a conference of the interested parties. To help ensure its success, they resolved to ask the King, who had long pressed Asquith to have such a meeting, to host it at Buckingham Palace. The King readily agreed, and suggested the Speaker of the Commons, Lowther, should chair it. News leaked out in the Northcliffe press before the King was ready: 'There is absolutely no doubt', Lloyd George told his ally Robert Donald, editor of the *Daily Chronicle*, 'that the other side gave it away'; his evidence for that was that the story made no mention of the Speaker's chairmanship, the one detail to which the Unionists were not then privy.[138]

The constitutional conference was held from 21 to 24 July; the Amending Bill's progress was delayed until after it. 'My intervention at this moment may be regarded as a new departure,' the King told the participants. 'But the exceptional circumstances under which you are brought together justify my action.'[139] There were eight attendees besides Lowther: Asquith, Lloyd George, Law, Lansdowne, Redmond, Dillon, Carson and Craig. Carson, capriciously, now wanted all nine counties of Ulster. Redmond told him that would alienate Nationalists throughout Ireland. After four meetings on successive days at which, as Asquith told the Commons, 'the possibility of defining an area for exclusion from the operations of the Government of Ireland Bill was considered', no agreement was reached 'either in principle or detail' so 'it brought its meetings to a conclusion.'[140] Asquith noted in his memoirs that it was the 'geographical demarcation' – Tyrone, which both Carson and Redmond demanded for themselves – that was the problem.[141]

'I have rarely felt more hopeless in any practical affair,' Asquith told Venetia Stanley: 'An impasse, with unspeakable consequences, upon a matter which to English eyes seems inconceivably small, & to Irish eyes immeasurably big. Isn't it a real tragedy?'[142] It was agreed to proceed with the Amending Bill, and Redmond and Dillon reluctantly backed Asquith's suggestion that the six-year time limit should be removed – agreeing, effectively, to permanent partition, though with individual counties giving their view through plebiscites. Some legal opinion claimed the Amending Bill would change the Government of Ireland Bill so much that it would no longer qualify under the Parliament Act, which required the same Bill to be passed three times. The King knew this; Asquith feared he might insist on an election before Home Rule could be imposed. Discussion of the Amending Bill, and its implications, was scheduled for the following week. Events, however, intervened.

When the conference broke up on 24 July Asquith returned to Downing Street to chair a cabinet meeting, to report the lack of progress. He noted in his journal: 'There was a lot of talk about Ulster, but the real interest was Grey's statement of the European situation, which is about as bad as it can possibly be.'[143] Ireland had until then – eleven days before Britain's declaration of war on Germany and almost four weeks after the assassination of Archduke Franz Ferdinand in Sarajevo, on 28 June – distracted Asquith's attention from Europe, so much so that Grey's report of the 'bullying' ultimatum Austria had sent to Serbia, the country deemed responsible for the murder of the heir to the Austro-Hungarian thrones, and its likely consequences (what Asquith called, with obvious awe, 'real Armageddon'), seems just to have come to him in a *moment révélateur.* One can only speculate on how British policy and diplomacy might have evolved during July 1914 had Ireland not been an issue, and had Asquith been better placed to monitor Grey's command of the situation.

Nor was the distraction at an end. On Sunday 26 July, at about 1 p.m., more than 1,000 National Volunteers met a yacht at Howth that was packed with arms, sent from Germany by Erskine Childers, author of *The Riddle of the Sands* and an active Home Ruler, who within weeks would be commissioned into the Royal Navy: and, having unloaded them, the men marched to Dublin through Clontarf. The coastguards alerted the police, and as the Volunteers marched a number of officers of the Dublin Metropolitan Police met them, as did 160 men of the King's Own Scottish Borderers. A struggle occurred when the police tried to disarm the Volunteers. The soldiers did not fire, but two were shot and wounded in the legs; three Volunteers were injured too. Word reached Dublin Castle and, fearing an incident, the duty under-secretary sent a message to the assistant commissioner of police that the 'forcible disarmament of the men now marching into Dublin with these arms should not in all the circumstances be attempted, but the names of the men carrying arms should, as far as possible, be taken and watch should be kept to ascertain the destination of the arms illegally imported. His Excellency cannot authorise any further steps in this matter at present.'[144]

The practicalities of the order were absurd, but it was acted upon. The soldiers returned to their barracks, but were attacked in Bachelor's Walk by what Birrell, reporting to the Commons the next day, called 'an angry crowd'.[145] An officer, a Major Haig, tried to order the crowd back; but 'several soldiers in the rear of the column, becoming exasperated, fired without orders'. Thirty-one rounds were let off before the men were ordered to stop. Birrell said that 'a considerable number of soldiers had by this time received severe injuries', but three Volunteers had been killed and thirty-two others injured. He promised an immediate inquiry into the soldiers' conduct.

Harrel, the assistant commissioner, had demanded the rifles as well as the names of the men. He had been told he could have the names, but not the rifles, so ordered a bayonet charge; this provoked some Volunteers to fire on the soldiers; the police refused to obey Harrel's order to disarm the Volunteers. Harrel then talked to the leaders, who said they were doing only what men in Belfast had been doing for months. Harrel realised he was beaten and arranged for the men to slip away into Dublin, which they did; only a few rifles were taken from the men nearest him and his forces.

The Nationalists were outraged, not merely by the loss of life, but because on the preceding day 5,000 members of the UVF had marched unimpeded through Belfast, openly displaying five machine guns. Neither the Army nor the RIC tried to stop the men or confiscate their weapons, nor indeed to note their names. Nor had action been taken against those who arranged the importation of arms into Larne earlier in the year. The Proclamation against arms imports had been entirely disregarded in Ulster, whereas in the south and west of Ireland it was being rigidly enforced, to prevent arms falling into the hands of the Catholic majority. As the Nationalists sought to arm themselves and the police strove to stop them, the dangers of a full-scale confrontation were apparent. Asquith, in the middle of yet another game of bridge when the news was brought to him on the Sunday evening, cursed 'the malignity of fortune', and said the engagement of soldiers in the action and their decision to open fire 'passes my comprehension'.[146]

Redmond demanded to know 'who is responsible for this monstrous attempt to discriminate in the administration of the law between various classes of His Majesty's subjects in Ireland?'[147] The answer was the police, notably Harrel and his superior, Sir John Ross, whom Redmond branded 'a well-known political partisan', 'a thoroughly incompetent officer', and whose removal he demanded. The truth of the two nations in Ireland seemed to be laid bare by these incidents: that those who wished to be British could do as they pleased; those who wished to be Irish could not. Redmond was unequivocal:

> I ask that the law shall be administered impartially, and that what is regarded as lawful in Ulster shall not be regarded as a crime in Munster, Leinster or Connaught. I ask that so long as the Ulster Volunteers are allowed to arm and drill and march with fixed bayonets and machine guns, Nationalist Volunteers must be given the same freedom, and I conclude by saying, let the House clearly understand that four-fifths of the Irish people will not submit any longer to be bullied, or punished, or penalised, or shot, for conduct which is permitted to go scot-free in the open light of day in every county in Ulster by other sections of their fellow countrymen.[148]

Law suggested that the old Irish hatred of the Army had come out into the open, and was being exploited; and that 'the Government have abrogated authority in Ireland and have ceased to govern.'[149]

For the moment, the issue would not be forced. Before the Amending Bill could continue, war broke out between Austria and Serbia. One by one the great powers were sucked into it, with alarming speed. Law and Carson agreed to call off their dogs, to present a face of national unity in a time of severe crisis. Instead of the Amending Bill there was a Suspensory Bill, which delayed Home Rule indefinitely, pending the end of the war. Redmond also played the unity card, pledging Protestant and Nationalist volunteers would fight together to defend Ireland against a foreign invader, but wrote to Lloyd George the day war was declared begging for the Bill to be enacted at once: 'If the Home Rule Bill is postponed my people will say they are sold. I will be unable to hold them and deplorable things will be said and done in Ireland and the Irish cause may be lost for our time . . . Don't fail us now.'[150] Redmond was more accurate than perhaps even he realised.

By 1914, even before the horrific expenditure of blood and treasure in the war to end all wars, British power was in decline. A ruling class whose decadence had provoked the often successful challenges of the Labour movement, and which had struggled to contain a private army of militant women, displayed the symptoms of weakness: but nothing was so emblematic of its decline as Britain's inability to control what was happening in Ireland. The integrity of the United Kingdom was compromised, not by the overwhelming desire in Ireland for Home Rule, but by Asquith's capitulation to Ulster, a surrender that was inevitable if he wished to cling on to power. He was diminished; the government he led was diminished; Britain was diminished, because his, the administration's and the state's authority were diminished. A nation so recently not just great, but the greatest power the world had ever known, sustained in its greatness by a rule of law and parliamentary democracy, had begun its decay.

ENVOI:

ONE AFTERNOON OF HEAT

On 24 June 1914, four days before Gavrilo Princip shot Archduke Franz Ferdinand of Austria-Hungary and his morganatic wife in Sarajevo, beginning the crisis that caused the Great War, Edward Thomas and his family took the train from London to Worcester. At 12.45 p.m., according to his notes, it made an unscheduled stop at a station just before Moreton-in-Marsh. From his seat Thomas noted the name of the halt. That evening he dined with, among others, Rupert Brooke.

Seven months later, laid up with a sprained ankle just before he volunteered for the Army, he recalled the event in a poem that continues the theme of Edwardian nostalgia, deepening it to represent a pastoral England holding out not just against change, but against an assault on civilisation. The dominance of nature in the poem suggests a world whose innocence was already out of reach when Thomas wrote it in January 1915, and obliterated when peace returned in November 1918. Thomas was killed at the battle of Arras on 9 April 1917, by a direct hit in the chest from a 77mm shell.

Yes, I remember Adlestrop –
The name, because one afternoon
Of heat the express-train drew up there
Unwontedly. It was late June.

The steam hissed. Someone cleared his throat.
No one left and no one came
On the bare platform. What I saw
Was Adlestrop – only the name

And willows, willow-herb, and grass,
And meadowsweet, and haycocks dry,
No whit less still and lonely fair
Than the high cloudlets in the sky.

And for that minute a blackbird sang
Close by, and round him, mistier,
Farther and farther, all the birds
Of Oxfordshire and Gloucestershire.

BIBLIOGRAPHY

Primary Sources

H. H. Asquith: Bodleian; Parliamentary Archive (PA).
A. J. Balfour: British Library (BL).
Hilaire Belloc: British Library.
Arnold Bennett: British Library.
G. E. Buckle: British Library.
Cabinet Papers: National Archives (NA).
Sir Henry Campbell-Bannerman: British Library.
Joseph Chamberlain: British Library; Hatfield House; Bodleian; Cambridge University Library (CUL).
G. K. Chesterton: British Library.
Lord Randolph Churchill: Cambridge University Library (Add. MS 9248).
Director of Public Prosecution's Papers: National Archives.
2nd Viscount Esher: Churchill College, Cambridge (ESHR).
Millicent Fawcett: LSE; British Library; Churchill College, Cambridge.
Roger Fry: British Library.
W. E. Gladstone: British Library.
Sir William Harcourt: Bodleian; British Library; Churchill College, Cambridge.
Hensley Henson: Durham Cathedral Archives.
Gustav Holst: British Library.
David Lloyd George: Parliamentary Archive; British Library.
Lord Chamberlain's Papers: British Library.
1st Earl of Midleton (St John Brodrick): British Library.
William Morris: British Library.
1st Viscount Northcliffe: British Library.
Sir Arthur Paget: British Library; Bodleian.
Emmeline Pankhurst: LSE.
Sir C. H. H. Parry: Shulbrede; Royal College of Music.

Lt-Col Charles à Court Repington: British Library.
3rd Marquess of Salisbury: Hatfield House; British Library.
5th Earl Spencer: British Library.
George Bernard Shaw: British Library; LSE.
Ralph Vaughan Williams: British Library; Cambridge University Library.
H. G. Wells: British Library; LSE.
H. W. Wilson: British Library.

Secondary Sources

A&E: *The Growth of Public Employment in Great Britain*, edited by Moses Abramovitz and Vera F. Eliasberg (Princeton University Press, 1957).

ACE: *Arts and Crafts Essays*, by Members of the Arts and Crafts Society (Rivington, Percival, 1893).

Adams, *Balfour*: *Balfour: The Last Grandee*, by R. J. Q. Adams (John Murray, 2007).

Adams, *Law*: *Bonar Law*, by R. J. Q. Adams (John Murray, 1999).

Allfrey: *Edward VII and His Jewish Court*, by Anthony Allfrey (Weidenfeld & Nicolson, 1991).

Aronson: *Prince Eddy and the Homosexual Underworld*, by Theo Aronson (John Murray, 1994).

Askwith: *Industrial Problems and Disputes*, by Lord Askwith (John Murray, 1920).

Asquith, *FY*: *Fifty Years of Parliament*, by the Earl of Oxford and Asquith KG (Cassell, 2 Vols, 1926).

Asquith, *MR*: *Memories and Reflections 1852–1927*, by the Earl of Oxford and Asquith KG (Cassell, 2 Vols, 1928).

Asquith, *VS*: *H. H. Asquith: Letters to Venetia Stanley*, selected and edited by Michael and Eleanor Brock (OUP, 1982).

B-P: *Scouting for Boys: A Handbook for Instruction in Good Citizenship*, by Robert Baden-Powell, edited by Elleke Boehmer (OUP, 2004).

B-P *Guides*: *The Handbook for Girl Guides: How Girls Can Help to Build Up the Empire*, by Miss Baden-Powell and Sir R. Baden-Powell (Thomas Nelson, 1912).

Baker: *The History of the Marconi Company 1874–1965*, by W. J. Baker (Routledge, 1998).

Balfour, *Decadence*: *Decadence: The Henry Sidgwick Memorial Lecture*, by the Rt Hon. Arthur James Balfour, MP (CUP, 1908).

Balfour, *Letters*: *The Letters of Arthur Balfour and Lady Elcho, 1885–1917*, edited by Jane Ridley and Clayre Percy (Hamish Hamilton, 1992).

Barker: *Plays by Harley Granville Barker*, edited by Dennis Kennedy (Cambridge University Press, 1987).

Belloc: *The Old Road*, by Hilaire Belloc (Constable, 1904).

Belloc, *Verse*: *Complete Verse*, by Hilaire Belloc (Random House, 2011).

Bennett, *Anna*: *Anna of the Five Towns*, by Arnold Bennett (Methuen, Cheap Edition, 1929).

Bennett, *Card*: *The Card*, by Arnold Bennett (Methuen, Cheap Edition, 1932).

Bennett, *Clayhanger*: *The Clayhanger Family*, by Arnold Bennett (Methuen, 1925).

Bennett, *Letters* II: *Letters of Arnold Bennett*, Volume II, edited by James Hepburn (OUP, 1968).

Bennett, *WGHJ*: *Whom God Hath Joined*, by Arnold Bennett (Methuen, Fountain Library Edition, 1935).

Bew: *Enigma: A New Life of Charles Stewart Parnell*, by Paul Bew (Gill and Macmillan, 2011).

Blake: *The Unknown Prime Minister: The Life and Times of Andrew Bonar Law 1858–1923*, by Robert Blake (Eyre & Spottiswoode, 1955).

Bolsterli: *The Early Community at Bedford Park: The Pursuit of "Corporate Happiness" in the First Garden Suburb*, by Margaret Jones Bolsterli (Routledge & Kegan Paul, 1977).

Bonner: *Charles Bradlaugh: A Record of His Life and Work*, by Hypatia Bradlaugh Bonner (T. Fisher Unwin, 7th Edition, 2 Vols, 1908).

Bosanquet: *The Philosophical Theory of the State*, by Bernard Bosanquet (Batoche Books, 2nd Edition, 2001).

Bostridge: *The Fateful Year: England 1914*, by Mark Bostridge (Penguin Viking, 2014).

Broadhurst: *Henry Broadhurst, MP: The Story of His Life from a Stonemason's Bench to the Treasury Bench*, by Henry Broadhurst (Hutchinson, 1901).

Brooke, *Letters*: *The Letters of Rupert Brooke*, edited by Sir Geoffrey Keynes (Faber, 1968).

Brooke, *Poems*: *The Poetical Works of Rupert Brooke*, edited by Geoffrey Keynes (Faber, 1946).

C&G: *Winston S. Churchill*, by Randolph Churchill and Martin Gilbert (Heinemann, 8 Vols, 1966–88).

Carlebach: *Caring for Children in Trouble*, by Julius Carlebach (Routledge & Kegan Paul, 1970).

Campbell: *F. E. Smith, First Earl of Birkenhead*, by John Campbell (Jonathan Cape, 1983).

Cannadine, *D&F*: *The Decline and Fall of the British Aristocracy*, by David Cannadine (Yale, 1990).

Carey: *The Intellectuals and the Masses: Pride and Prejudice Among the Literary Intelligentsia, 1880–1939*, by John Carey (Faber, 1992).

Carey Evans: *Lloyd George Was My Father*, by Lady Olwen Carey Evans (Gomer Press, 1985).

Carlebach: *Caring for Children in Trouble*, by Julius Carlebach (Routledge, 1970).

Chesterton: *Autobiography*, by G. K. Chesterton (Hutchinson, 1936).

Chitty: *Playing the Game: A Biography of Sir Henry Newbolt*, by Susan Chitty (Quartet, 1997).

Chothia: *English Drama of the Early Modern Period, 1890–1940*, by Jean Chothia (Longmans, 1996).

Churchill, *Companion*: *Winston S. Churchill*, by Randolph S. Churchill: Volume II: *Companion* (Heinemann, 3 Parts, 1969).

Cohen: *Lady Rothschild and Her Daughters*, by Lucy Cohen (John Murray, 1935).

Cox: *Take a Cold Tub, Sir! The Story of the Boy's Own Paper*, by Jack Cox (Lutterworth Press, 1982).

Crosland: *The Suburbans*, by T. W. H. Crosland (John Long, 1905).

Crossick: *The Lower Middle Class in Britain 1870–1914*, edited by Geoffrey Crossick (Croom Helm, 1977).

Cust: *King Edward VII and His Court: Some Reminiscences*, by Sir Lionel Cust KCVO (John Murray, 1930).

Dangerfield: *The Strange Death of Liberal England*, by George Dangerfield (Constable, 1936).

Davey: *Arts and Crafts Architecture: The Search for Earthly Paradise*, by Peter Davey (The Architectural Press, 1980).

Dibble: *C. Hubert H. Parry: His Life and Music*, by Jeremy Dibble (Oxford University Press, 1992).

Dugdale: *Arthur James Balfour*, by Blanche E. C. Dugdale (Hutchinson, 2 Vols, 1939).

Ellmann: *Oscar Wilde*, by Richard Ellmann (Hamish Hamilton, 1987).

Esher: *The Journals and Letters of Reginald, 2nd Viscount Esher*, edited by Maurice V. Brett (Ivor Nicholson & Watson, 4 Vols, 1934–8).

Fanning: *Fatal Path: British Government and Irish Revolution 1910–1922*, by Ronan Fanning (Faber, 2013).

Ferris: *The House of Northcliffe: The Harmsworths of Fleet Street*, by Paul Ferris (Weidenfeld & Nicolson, 1971).

Foot: *The History of Mr Wells*, by Michael Foot (Doubleday, 1995).

Forster, *HE*: *Howards End*, by E. M. Forster (Edward Arnold, Pocket Edition, 1947).

Foster: *Vivid Faces: The Revolutionary Generation in Ireland, 1890–1923*, by R. F. Foster (Allen Lane, 2014).

Fry: *Life Worth Living: Some Phases of an Englishman*, by C. B. Fry (Eyre & Spottiswoode, 1939).

Fulford: *Votes for Women: The Story of a Straggle*, by Roger Fulford (Faber, 1957).

G&A: *The Life of Joseph Chamberlain*, by J. L. Garvin and Julian Amery (Macmillan, 6 Vols, 1933–69).

Galsworthy, *Letters*: *Letters from John Galsworthy 1900–1932*, edited by Edward Garnett (Jonathan Cape, 1934).

Galsworthy, *Strife*: *Strife*, in *Ten Famous Plays*, by John Galsworthy (Duckworth, 1941).

Galsworthy, *TCH*: *The Country House*, by John Galsworthy (Heinemann, The Grove Edition, 1927).

Galton, *Inquiries*: *Inquiries into Human Faculty*, by Francis Galton (1883).

Gardiner: *The Life of Sir William Harcourt*, by A. G. Gardiner (Constable, 2 Vols, 1923).

Garnett: *A Censured Play: The Breaking Point*, by Edward Garnett (Duckworth, 1907).

Gilmour: *Curzon*, by David Gilmour (John Murray, 1994).

Girouard: *Victorian Pubs*, by Mark Girouard (Yale University Press, 1984).

Gissing: *New Grub Street*, by George Gissing (Oxford World's Classics, 1958).

Gladstone, *Diaries*: *The Gladstone Diaries*, edited by M. R. D. Foot and H. C. G. Matthew (OUP, 14 Vols, 1968–1994).

Gray: *Edwardian Architecture: A Biographical Dictionary*, by A. Stuart Gray (Duckworth, 1985).

Grigg, *Champion*: *Lloyd George: The People's Champion 1902–1911*, by John Grigg (Eyre Methuen, 1978).

Grigg, *PW*: *Lloyd George: From Peace to War 1912–1916*, by John Grigg (Methuen, 1985).

Grigg, *YLG*: *The Young Lloyd George*, by John Grigg (Eyre Methuen, 1973).

Hague: *The Pain and the Privilege: The Women in Lloyd George's Life*, by Ffion Hague (Harper Press, 2008).

Hamilton: *The Diary of Sir Edward Walter Hamilton 1880–1885*, edited by D. W. Bahlman (OUP, 2 Vols, 1972).

Hardy, *TL*: *Time's Laughingstocks, and Other Verses*, by Thomas Hardy (Macmillan, 1909).

Harris: *Private Lives, Public Spirit: A Social History of Britain, 1870–1914*, by José Harris (OUP, 1993).

Harrison: *Separate Spheres: The Opposition to Women's Suffrage in Britain*, by Brian Harrison (Croom Helm, 1978).

Harrison M: *Bournville: Model Village to Garden Suburb*, by Michael Harrison (Phillimore, 1999).

Hassall: *Rupert Brooke: A Biography*, by Christopher Hassall (Faber, 1964).

Healy: *Letters and Leaders of My Day*, by T. M. Healy, KC (Thornton Butterworth, 2 Vols, 1928).

Heffer, *HM*: *High Minds: The Victorians and the Birth of Modern Britain,* by Simon Heffer (Random House, 2013).

Heffer, *PP*: *Power and Place: The Political Consequences of King Edward VII*, by Simon Heffer (Weidenfeld & Nicolson, 1998).

Henley: *Poems*, by William Ernest Henley (David Nutt, 5th Edition, 1901).

Henty: *St George for England: A Tale of Cressy and Poitiers*, by G. A. Henty (Dean's Classics No. 75, undated).

Holmes, *EM*: *Eleanor Marx: A Life*, by Rachel Holmes (Bloomsbury, 2014).

Holmes, *LFM*: *The Little Field Marshal: A Life of Sir John French*, by Richard Holmes (Weidenfeld & Nicolson, 2004).

Holroyd, *Shaw*: *Bernard Shaw*, by Michael Holroyd (Chatto & Windus, 3 Vols, 1988–91).

Holroyd, *Strachey*: *Lytton Strachey: A Critical Biography*, by Michael Holroyd (Heinemann, 2 Vols, 1967–8).

Holt: *Sport and the British*, by Richard Holt (OUP, 1989).

Housman: *A Shropshire Lad*, by A. E. Housman (The Richards Press, 1896).

Howard 1898: *Tomorrow: A Peaceful Path to Real Reform*, by Ebenezer Howard (Swan Sonnenschein, 1898).

Howard 1902: *Garden Cities of Tomorrow*, by Ebenezer Howard (Swan Sonnenschein, 1902).

Hyde: *The Cleveland Street Scandal*, by H. Montgomery Hyde (W. H. Allen, 1976).

Hynes: *The Edwardian Turn of Mind*, by Samuel Hynes (Princeton University Press, 1968).

ICPD: *Report of the Inter-Departmental Committee on Physical Deterioration* (HMSO, 3 Vols, 1904).

Jackson: *Victorian Theatre: The Theatre in Its Time*, by Russell Jackson (New Amsterdam, 1989).

James: *The Middle Class: A History*, by Lawrence James (Little, Brown, 2006).

James, *Portrait*: *The Portrait of a Lady*, by Henry James (Oxford World's Classics, 1947).

Jenkins: *Sir Charles Dilke: A Victorian Tragedy*, by Roy Jenkins (Collins, 1958).

Jones: *The Last Great Quest: Captain Scott's Antarctic Sacrifice*, by Max Jones (OUP, 2003).

Jones J: *Fifty Years in the Fiction Factory: The Working Life of Herbert Allingham*, by Julia Jones (Golden Duck, 2012).

JSC: *Report from the Joint Select Committee of the House of Lords and the House of Commons on the Stage Plays (Censorship)* (HMSO, 1909).

Judd: *Lord Reading: Rufus Isaacs, First Marquess of Reading, Lord Chief Justice and Viceroy of India, 1860–1935*, by Denis Judd (Weidenfeld & Nicolson, 1982).

Kapila: *An Intellectual History for India*, edited by Shruti Kapila (CUP, 2010).

Kennedy, *E*: *Portrait of Elgar*, by Michael Kennedy (3rd Edition, OUP, 1987).

Kennedy, *VW*: *The Works of Ralph Vaughan Williams*, by Michael Kennedy (OUP, 2nd Edition, 1980).

Kipling: *Something of Myself*, by Rudyard Kipling (Macmillan, 1937).

Kipling, *Verse*: *Rudyard Kipling's Verse: Inclusive Edition, 1885–1932* (Hodder & Stoughton (4th Edition, 1933).

L&A: *The Men Behind Boys' Fiction*, by W. O. Lofts and D. J. Adley (Howard Baker, 1970).

Lees-Milne: *The Enigmatic Edwardian: The Life of Reginald, 2nd Viscount Esher*, by James Lees-Milne (Sidgwick & Jackson, 1986).

Le Queux: *The Invasion of 1910: With a Full Account of the Siege of London*, by William Le Queux (Eveleigh Nash, 1906).

Lewis: *Women in England 1870–1950: Sexual Divisions and Social Change*, by Jane Lewis (Wheatsheaf Books, 1984).

Lloyd George: *Lloyd George*, by Richard Lloyd George (Frederick Muller, 1960).

Long: *The Edwardian House: The Middle-Class Home in Britain 1880–1914*, by Helen C. Long (Manchester University Press, 1993).

Longford: *Victoria R.I.*, by Elizabeth Longford (Weidenfeld & Nicolson, 1964).

Lucas: *Arnold Bennett: A Study of His Fiction*, by John Lucas (Methuen, 1974).

Lyons, *Dillon*: *John Dillon*, by F. S. L. Lyons (Chicago University Press, 1968).

Lyons, *Parnell*: *Charles Stewart Parnell*, by F. S. L. Lyons (Gill & Macmillan, 1973).

Lytton: *Prisons and Prisoners: Some Personal Experiences*, by Constance Lytton and Jane Warton, Spinster (William Heinemann, 1914).

MacDonald: *The Social Unrest: Its Cause and Solution*, by J. Ramsay MacDonald (T. N. Foulis, 1913).

MacCarthy: *William Morris*, by Fiona MacCarthy (Faber, 1994).

McKinstry: *Rosebery: Statesman in Turmoil*, by Leo McKinstry (John Murray, 2005).

Magnus: *King Edward VII*, by Philip Magnus (John Murray, 1964).

Marrot: *The Life and Letters of John Galsworthy*, by H. V. Marrot (Heinemann, 1935).

Martin: *TUC: The Growth of a Pressure Group, 1868–1976*, by Ross M. Martin (Clarendon Press, 1980).

Meleady: *John Redmond: The National Leader*, by Dermot Meleady (Merrion, 2014).

Miller: *Letchworth: The First Garden City*, by Mervyn Miller (Phillimore, 1989).

Morgan: *Keir Hardie: Radical and Socialist*, by Kenneth O. Morgan (Weidenfeld & Nicolson, 1975).

Morley: *The Life of W. E. Gladstone*, by John Morley (Macmillan, 2 Vols., 1905).

Morris: *The Collected Letters of William Morris*, edited by Norman Kelvin (Princeton University Press, 4 vols, 1984–96).

Nankivell: *Stamp Collecting as a Pastime*, by Edward J. Nankivell (Stanley Gibbons, 1902).

Nesbit: *The Railway Children*, by E. Nesbit (Wells Gardner, 1906).

Newbolt: *Collected Poems 1897–1907*, by Henry Newbolt (Thomas Nelson, undated).

Newsinger: *Rebel City: Larkin, Connolly and the Dublin Labour Movement*, by John Newsinger (Merlin Press, 2004).

Newton: *Lord Lansdowne, A Biography*, by Lord Newton (Macmillan, 1929).

Nicolson: *King George the Fifth: His Life and Reign*, by Harold Nicolson (Constable, 1952).

Nowell-Smith: *Edwardian England 1901–1914*, edited by Simon Nowell-Smith (OUP, 1964).

O'Brien: *Milner*, by Terence H. O'Brien (Constable, 1979).

O'Day: *Irish Home Rule, 1867–1921*, by Alan O'Day (Manchester University Press, 1998).

OHBE: *The Oxford History of the British Empire* (General Editor: William Roger Louis) (OUP, 5 Vols, 1998–9).

P&H: *Northcliffe*, by Reginald Pound and Geoffrey Harmsworth (Cassell, 1959).

Pakenham: *The Scramble for Africa 1876–1912*, by Thomas Pakenham (Weidenfeld & Nicolson, 1991).

Pankhurst: *My Own Story*, by Emmeline Pankhurst (Eveleigh Nash, 1914).

Pevsner, *Lancashire LSW*: *The Buildings of England: Lancashire: Liverpool and the South-West*, by Richard Pollard and Nikolaus Pevsner (Yale University Press, 2006).

Pevsner, *London C*: *The Buildings of England: London 1: The City of London*, by Simon Bradley and Nikolaus Pevsner (Yale University Press, 2002).

Pevsner, *London N*: *The Buildings of England: London 4: North*, by Bridget Cherry and Nikolaus Pevsner (Penguin, 1998).

Pevsner, *London W*: *The Buildings of England: London 6: Westminster*, by Simon Bradley and Nikolaus Pevsner (Yale University Press, 2003).

Phelps: *Selected Articles on Woman Suffrage*, by Edith M. Phelps (Forgotten Books, 2013).

Pinero, *SMT*: *The Second Mrs Tanqueray*, by Arthur Wing Pinero (Heinemann, 1895).

Pinero, *TCM*: *The Cabinet Minister*, by Arthur Wing Pinero (Heinemann, 1892).

Pollock: *Gordon: The Man Behind the Legend*, by John Pollock (Constable, 1993).

Ponsonby: *Recollections of Three Reigns*, by Sir Frederick Ponsonby (Eyre & Spottiswoode, 1951).

Pope: *Queen of the Music Halls: Being the Dramatized Story of Marie Lloyd*, by W. Macqueen-Pope (Oldbourne, undated).

QV2: *The Letters of Queen Victoria: Second Series: A Selection from Her Majesty's Correspondence and Journal Between the Years 1862 and 1885*, edited by George Earle Buckle (John Murray, 3 Vols, 1926–8).

QV3: *The Letters of Queen Victoria: Third Series: A Selection from Her Majesty's Correspondence and Journal Between the Years 1886 and 1901*, edited by George Earle Buckle (John Murray, 3 Vols, 1930–32).

Ranelagh: *A Short History of Ireland*, by John Ranelagh (CUP, 2012).

RCHM: *Royal Commission on Historical Monuments (England): An Inventory of the Historical Monuments in Essex*, Vol. I (HMSO, 1916).

Reid: *Life of the Right Honourable William Edward Forster*, by T. Wemyss Reid (Chapman & Hall, 2 Vols, 1888).

Rhodes: *The Last Will and Testament of Cecil John Rhodes, with Elucidatory Notes*, edited by W. T. Stead (Review of Reviews, 1902).

Rhodes James: *Lord Randolph Churchill*, by Robert Rhodes James (Weidenfeld & Nicolson, 1959).

Ridley: *Bertie: A Life of Edward VII*, by Jane Ridley (Chatto & Windus, 2012).

Roberts: *Salisbury: Victorian Titan*, by Andrew Roberts (Weidenfeld & Nicolson, 1999).

Ronaldshay: *The Life of Lord Curzon*, by the Earl of Ronaldshay (Ernest Benn, 3 Vols, 1928).

Rose, *GV*: *King George V*, by Kenneth Rose (Weidenfeld & Nicolson, 1983).

Rose, *LC*: *The Later Cecils*, by Kenneth Rose (Weidenfeld & Nicolson, 1975).

Rose J: *The Intellectual Life of the British Working Classes*, by Jonathan Rose (Yale University Press, 2001).

Rosebery: *Lord Randolph Churchill*, by Lord Rosebery (Arthur C. Humphreys, 1906).

Rowntree: *Poverty: A Study of Town Life*, by B. Seebohm Rowntree (Macmillan, 4th Edition, 1902).

S&A: *Life of Herbert Henry Asquith, Lord Oxford and Asquith*, by J. A. Spender and Cyril Asquith (Hutchinson, 2 Vols, 1932).

St Aubyn: *Edward VII: Prince and King*, by Giles St Aubyn (Collins, 1979).

Saki: *The Novels and Plays of Saki* (H. H. Munro) (Bodley Head, 1933).

Samuel: *Memoirs*, by Viscount Samuel (Crescent Press, 1945).

Scott: *Journals: Scott's Last Expedition*, by Robert Falcon Scott (Oxford University Press, 2005).

Searle: *A New England: Peace and War 1886–1918 (The New Oxford History of England)*, by G. R. Searle (Clarendon Press, 2004).

Seeley: *The Expansion of England*, by J. R. Seeley (Macmillan, 1883).

Service: *Edwardian Architecture: A Handbook to Building Design in Britain 1890–1914*, by Alastair Service (OUP, 1977).

Sharpe: *A Fiery & Furious People: A History of Violence in England*, by James Sharpe (Random House, 2016).

Shaw, *Plays*: *The Complete Plays of Bernard Shaw*, by George Bernard Shaw (Odhams, 1934).

Shaw, *Prefaces*: *Prefaces*, by Bernard Shaw (Constable, 1934).

SL: *Survey of London: Vol. I: Bromley-by-Bow* (HMSO, 1900).

Spencer: *The Red Earl: The Papers of the Fifth Earl Spencer*, edited by Peter Gordon (Northamptonshire Record Society, 2 Vols, 1981–6).

Spinner: *George Joachim Goschen: The Transformation of a Victorian Liberal*, by Thomas J. Spinner Jr (CUP, 1973).

Springhall: *Coming of Age: Adolescence in Britain*, 1860–1960, by John Springhall (Gill & Macmillan, 1986).

Stevenson: *Lloyd George: A Diary*, by Frances Stevenson, edited by A. J. P. Taylor (Hutchinson, 1971).

Thomas: *The Heart of England*, by Edward Thomas (OUP, 1982).

Thompson: *The Poems of Francis Thompson*, edited by Wilfred Meynell (OUP, 1937).

Thomson: *Cricketers of My Times*, by A. A. Thomson (Stanley Paul, 1967).

UVW: *A Biography of Ralph Vaughan Williams*, by Ursula Vaughan Williams (OUP, 1964).

Vamplew: *Pay Up and Play the Game: Professional Sport in Britain 1875–1914*, by Wray Vamplew (CUP, 1988).

VBC: *Lantern Slides: The Diaries and Letters of Violet Bonham Carter, 1904–1914*, edited by Mark Bonham Carter and Mark Pottle (Weidenfeld & Nicolson, 1996).

Vicinus: *Suffer and Be Still: Women in the Victorian Age*, edited by Martha Vicinus (Methuen, 1980).

VW: *National Music, and Other Essays*, by Ralph Vaughan Williams (OUP, 2nd Edition, 1987).

Ward: *Gilbert Keith Chesterton*, by Maisie Ward (Sheed & Ward, 1944).

Webb, *Diaries*: *The Diaries of Beatrice Webb*, edited by Norman and Jeanne MacKenzie (Virago, 4 Vols, 1982).

Weeks: *Sex, Politics and Society: The Regulation of Sexuality Since 1800*, by Jeffrey Weeks (Pearson, 1981).

Wells, *Anticipations*: *Anticipations*, by H. G. Wells (Chapman & Hall, 1902).

Wells, *AV*: *Ann Veronica*, by H. G. Wells (Dent, 1943).

Wells, *EA*: *Experiments in Autobiography*, by H. G. Wells (Faber & Faber, 2 Vols, 1984).

Wells, *FLT*: *First and Last Things*, by H. G. Wells (Constable, 1908).

Wells, *NM*: *The New Machiavelli*, by H. G. Wells (Odhams, undated).

Wells, *PEA*: *H. G. Wells in Love: Postscript to an Experiment in Autobiography*, edited by G. P. Wells (Faber & Faber, 1984).

Wells, *TB*: *Tono-Bungay*, by H. G. Wells (Odhams, undated).

Wells, *Utopia*: *A Modern Utopia*, by H. G. Wells (Odhams, undated).

West: *H. G. Wells: Aspects of a Life*, by Anthony West (Hutchinson, 1984).

Wilde, *DP*: *De Profundis*, by Oscar Wilde, edited by Vyvyan Holland (Methuen, 1949).

Wilde, *Letters*: *The Complete Letters of Oscar Wilde*, edited by Merlin Holland and Rupert Hart-Davis (Fourth Estate, 2000).

Williams: *Made in Germany*, by E. E. Williams (Heinemann, 1896).

Wilson: *CB: A Life of Sir Henry Campbell-Bannerman*, by John Wilson (Purnell, 1973).

Winstanley: *Ireland and the Land Question, 1800–1922*, by Michael Winstanley (Lancaster Pamphlets, 2007).

Woolf, *B&B*: *Mr Bennett and Mrs Brown*, by Virginia Woolf (Hogarth Press, 1924).

Young: *Arthur James Balfour*, by Kenneth Young (G. Bell & Sons, 1963).

Periodicals

The Agricultural History Review

The Boy's Own Paper

British Tax Review

The Daily Mirror

The Daily Sketch

The Daily Telegraph

The Girl's Own Paper

Journal of the Royal Society of Medicine

The Link

The Magnet

The Manchester Guardian

The New York Times
The Nineteenth Century
The Pall Mall Gazette
The Spectator
The Times
Victorian Studies

Reference Works

The Dictionary of National Biography
Dod's Parliamentary Companion
Hansard 1880 to 1914: Series 3 ends with Vol. 356, 5 August 1891; Series 4 begins with Vol. 1, 9 February 1892 and ends with Vol. 198 on 21 December 1908; Series 5 begins on 16 February 1909.
Journals of the House of Commons
The Oxford English Dictionary
Wisden's Cricketers' Almanack

NOTES

Abbreviations may be found in the Bibliography on page 827.

Prologue: Swagger

1. BL Add. MS 49684 f. 143.
2. BL Add. MS 49684 f. 144.
3. BL Add. MS 49684 f. 158.
4. ESHR:12/6, ff. 4, 8, 24, 26.
5. *The Times*, 9 June 1897, p. 6.
6. *Ibid.* 17 June 1897, p. 8.
7. *Ibid.*
8. QV3, III, p. 172.
9. *Ibid.* p. 174.
10. *The Times*, 23 June 1897, p. 9.
11. QV3, III, p. 175.
12. *Ibid.*
13. *The Times*, 23 June 1897, p. 11.
14. *Ibid.* p. 10.
15. QV3, III, p. 181.
16. *Ibid.* p. 176.
17. Cohen, p. 270.
18. *The Times*, 4 February 1901, p. 5.
19. *Ibid.* 4 February 1901, p. 8.
20. *Ibid.*
21. Cust, p. 135.
22. *Ibid.* p. 139.
23. *The Times*, 27 May 1887, p. 10.
24. Heffer, *HM*, p. 357ff.
25. *The Times*, 25 July 1887, p. 3.
26. Hansard, Vol. 90 cols 1031–2.
27. *Ibid.* col. 829.
28. *The Times*, 28 February 1901, p. 7.
29. *Ibid.* 7 March 1901, p. 8.
30. Hansard, Vol. 90 col. 1343.
31. *The Times*, 15 January 1902, p. 7.
32. Service, p. 142.
33. For details of the reluctance with which Scott built the Foreign Office in the classical style he despised see Heffer, *HM*, p. 735ff.
34. Pevsner, *London W*, p. 645.
35. Heffer, *HM*, p. 372.
36. Pevsner, *London W*, p. 211.
37. Pevsner, *London C*, p. 121.
38. Pevsner, *London W*, p. 559.
39. *Ibid.* p. 460.
40. St Aubyn, p. 146.
41. Ridley, p. 91.
42. Magnus, p. 365.
43. St Aubyn, p. 147.
44. *Ibid.* p.146.
45. Magnus, p. 364.
46. Ellman, p. 4.
47. *Ibid.* p. 196.
48. *Ibid.* p. 276.
49. Wilde, *Letters*, p. 465.
50. Rosebery, pp. 31–2.
51. Rhodes James, p. 53.
52. Rose, *LC*, pp. 46–7.
53. Rose, *GV*, p. 80.
54. *Ibid.* p. 102.
55. Kennedy, *E*, p. 168.
56. *Ibid.* p. 169.
57. *Ibid.* p. 225.
58. Forster, *HE*, pp. 37–8.
59. Kennedy, *E*, p. 236.
60. *Ibid.* p. 238.
61. James, *Portrait*, p. 1.
62. Bennett, *WGHJ*, p. 13.

63. Wells, *TB*, p. 69.
64. Searle, p. 89.
65. Harris, pp. 11–12.
66. Retrieved from http://www.britishtelephones.com/histuk.htm
67. Searle, p. 85.
68. *Ibid.*
69. *The Times*, 9 February 1912, p. 6.

Part I: The World of the Late Victorians

Chapter 1: The Decline of the Pallisers

1. Harris, p. 99.
2. Ridley, p. 233.
3. Gladstone, *Diaries*, IX, p. 508.
4. QV2, III, p. 165.
5. G&A, I, p. 386.
6. BL Add. MS 44225, f. 158.
7. BL, Chamberlain MSS 5/34/1.
8. QV2, III, p. 88.
9. *Ibid.* p. 87; BL Add. MS 44258 f. 163.
10. Gladstone, *Diaries*, IX, p. 526.
11. Gladstone, *Diaries*, IX, p. 564.
12. QV2, III, p. 181.
13. Jackson, p. 332.
14. G&A, I, p. 386.
15. QV2, III, p. 298.
16. *The Times*, 31 March 1883, p. 10.
17. *Ibid.* 4 April 1883, p. 11.
18. *Ibid.* 16 April 1883, p. 8.
19. *Ibid.* 14 June 1883, p. 6.
20. BL Add. MS 44546 f. 128.
21. Gladstone, *Diaries*, XI, p. 1.
22. *Ibid.* p. 2.
23. QV2, III, p. 431.
24. BL Add. MS 44546 f. 166.
25. BL Add. MS 44546 f. 173.
26. BL Add. MS 44546 f. 179.
27. Gladstone, *Diaries*, XI, p. 59.
28. Hamilton, II, p. 514.
29. Gladstone, *Diaries*, XI, p. 70.
30. BL Add. MS 44146 f. 239.
31. Gladstone, *Diaries*, XI, p. 80.
32. BL Add. MS 44547 f. 24.
33. Hansard, Vol. 285 col. 108.
34. *Ibid.* col. 129.
35. *Ibid.* col. 133.
36. *Ibid.* col. 113.
37. Gladstone, *Diaries*, XI, p. 119.
38. Hansard, Vol. 285 col. 150.
39. *Ibid.* col. 431.
40. *Ibid.* col. 625.
41. *Ibid.* Vol. 287 col. 769.
42. *Ibid.* col. 773.
43. *Ibid.* col. 1437.
44. *Ibid.* col. 1438.
45. BL Add. MS 44109 f. 97.
46. BL Add. MS 44547 f. 78.
47. BL Add. MS 44487 f. 42.
48. BL Add. MS 44547 f. 81.
49. *Ibid.*
50. Hansard, Vol. 290 col. 112.
51. *Ibid.* col. 143.
52. *Ibid.* col. 395.
53. *Ibid.* col. 407.
54. *Ibid.* col. 408.
55. *Ibid.* col. 414.
56. *Ibid.* col. 416.
57. *Ibid.* col. 468.
58. Gladstone, *Diaries*, XI, p. 171.
59. Roberts, p. 297.
60. Hansard, Vol. 290 col. 692.
61. *Ibid.* col. 798.
62. Jenkins, p. 187.
63. Hansard, Vol. 290 col. 1342.
64. *Ibid.* col. 1343.
65. *Ibid.* cols 690–91
66. Broadhurst, p. 126.
67. G&A, I, p. 465.
68. QV2, III, p. 523, Letters, Vol. 2, p. 253.
69. BL Add. MS 44547 f. 90.
70. G&A, I, p. 467.
71. *Ibid.* p. 470.
72. Gladstone, *Diaries*, XI, p. 191.
73. *Ibid.* p. 192.
74. *Ibid.* p. 193.
75. *Ibid.* p. 201.
76. Morley, II, p. 370.
77. BL Add. MS 44547 f. 116.
78. BL Add. MS 43875 f. 177.
79. Gladstone, *Diaries*, XI, p. 216.
80. *National Review*, October 1884, Vol. IV, p. 157.

81. BL Add. MS 44147 f. 149.
82. Gladstone, *Diaries*, XI, p. 217.
83. *The Times*, 4 October 1884, p. 7.
84. *Ibid.* p. 9.
85. Rosebery, pp. 87–8.
86. *The Times*, 4 October 1884, p. 10.
87. Gladstone, *Diaries*, XI, p. 220.
88. *Ibid.* p. 221.
89. *The Times*, 8 October 1884, p. 6.
90. G&A, I p. 472.
91. QV2, *Letters*, Vol. III, p. 548.
92. *The Times*, 14 October 1884, p. 6.
93. *Ibid.* 15 October 1884, p. 6.
94. *Ibid.* 20 October 1884, p. 10.
95. QV2, *Letters*, Vol. III, p. 554.
96. *Ibid.* p. 555.
97. G&A, I p. 474.
98. QV2, *Letters*, Vol. III, p. 557.
99. G&A, I p. 474.
100. QV2, Letters, Vol. III, p. 558.
101. BL Add. MS 44547 f. 124.
102. Gladstone, *Diaries*, XI, p. 225.
103. BL Add. MS 44487 f. 290.
104. Hansard, Vol. 293 col. 544.
105. Morley, II, p. 375.
106. BL Add. MS 43875 f. 192.
107. BL Add. MS 44645 f. 203.
108. BL Add. MS 50014 f. 274.
109. Morley, II, p. 379.
110. Jenkins, p. 192.
111. McKinstry, p. 273.
112. BL Add. MS 76936, Harcourt-Spencer, 26.ii.1894.
113. Gardiner, II, p. 285. Rosebery's own family seat at Mentmore, which came with his marriage into the Rothschild family, itself had to be sold with some of its contents to pay death duties in 1976.
114. McKinstry, p. 312.
115. *Ibid.* p. 313.
116. Harris, pp. 101–3.
117. Hansard, Vol. 24 col. 511.
118. *Ibid.* col. 1186.
119. *Ibid.* col. 1274.
120. *Ibid.* col. 1524.
121. *Ibid.* col. 513.
122. *Ibid.* col. 524.
123. *Ibid.* col. 634.
124. *Ibid.* col. 635.
125. *Ibid.* Vol. 25 col. 816.
126. *Ibid.* cols 817–18.
127. *The Times*, 9 June 1894, p. 8.
128. Hansard, Vol. 25 col. 831.
129. *Ibid.* col. 851.
130. *The Times*, 9 June 1894, p. 8.
131. Hansard, Vol. 27 col. 959.
132. *Ibid.* col. 954.
133. *Ibid.* col. 957.
134. *Ibid.* col. 958.
135. *Ibid.* col. 960.
136. See Giles Worsley, 'Country houses: the lost legacy' (*The Daily Telegraph*, 15 June 2002), at http://www.telegraph.co.uk/culture/art/3578853/Country-houses-the-lost-legacy.html
137. Searle, p. 83.
138. Galsworthy, *TCH*, p. 133.
139. *Ibid.* p. 177.
140. *Ibid.* p. 241.
141. *Ibid.* p. 277.
142. Galsworthy, *Letters*, p. 5.
143. Marrot, p. 185.
144. BL Add. MS 45291 f. 158.
145. Galsworthy, *Letters*, p. 6.
146. *Ibid.* p. 75.
147. Pinero, *TCM*, p. 56.
148. *Ibid.* p. 17.
149. *Ibid.* p. 24.
150. *Ibid.* p. 54.
151. Rose, *GV*, p. 87.
152. *The Times*, 19 February 1870, p. 13.
153. Ridley, p. 130.
154. Galsworthy, *TCH*, p. 136.
155. *The Times*, 27 October 1879, p. 4.
156. Salisbury Papers: Hatfield House, 3M: Series E, Beresford correspondence 12 July 1891.
157. *Ibid.* 3 August 1891.
158. *Ibid.* 30 November 1891.
159. *Ibid.* 17 December 1891.
160. *Ibid.* 18 December 1891.
161. *Ibid.* 19 December 1891.
162. *Ibid.* 21 December 1891.
163. *The Times*, 2 June 1891, p. 11.
164. *Ibid.* 10 June 1891, p. 9.

165. Ridley, p. 285.
166. *The Times*, 10 June 1891, p. 9.
167. Longford, p. 512.
168. Allfrey, p. 23.
169. BL Add. MS 52513 f. 98.
170. BL Add. MS 52513 f. 102.
171. Jenkins, p. 220.
172. Healy, I, p. 215.
173. McKinstry, p. 151.
174. *The Times*, 13 February 1886, p. 12.
175. *Ibid.* 4 May 1886, p. 8.
176. BL Add. MS 43874 f. 73.
177. *The Times*, 27 November 1889, p. 7.
178. NA: DPP 1/95/3.
179. See Aronson, p. 27.
180. Hyde, p. 30.
181. NA: DPP 1/95/1.
182. NA: DPP 1/95/1.
183. ESHR: 12/3/1.
184. NA: DPP 1/95/1.
185. ESHR: 12/3/4.
186. ESHR: 12/3/7.
187. ESHR: 12/3/18.
188. NA: DPP 1/95/1.
189. NA: DPP1/95/1.
190. Hyde, pp. 59–60.
191. Lees-Milne, p. 80.
192. NA: DPP 1/95/3.
193. *The Times*, 7 January 1890, p. 13.
194. Hyde, p. 53.
195. Salisbury Papers: Hatfield House, 3M: Series E, Webster correspondence, 18 September 1889.
196. ESHR: 12/3/31.
197. ESHR: 12/3/166.
198. NA: DPP 1/95/3.
199. NA: DPP 1/95/1.
200. Lees-Milne, p. 79.
201. NA: DPP 1/95/1.
202. ESHR: 12/3/48.
203. ESHR: 12/3/49.
204. ESHR:12/3/57.
205. ESHR: 12/3/55.
206. NA: DPP 1/95/1.
207. NA: DPP 1/95/1.
208. Salisbury Papers: Hatfield House 3M: Series F, Probyn correspondence, 19 October 1889.
209. Hyde, p. 96.
210. ESHR: 12/3/59.
211. ESHR: 12/3/58.
212. NA: DPP 1/95/3.
213. *The Times*, 16 January 1890, p. 6.
214. ESHR: 2/8, journal entry for 5 November 1890.
215. *The Times*, 24 December 1889, p. 10.
216. *New York Herald*, 22 December 1889, p. 8.
217. *The Times*, 16 January 1890, p. 6.
218. *Ibid.* 17 January 1890, p. 7.
219. Hansard, Vol. 341 col. 1534.
220. Salisbury Papers: Hatfield House, 3M: Series F, Knollys Correspondence, 2 March 1890.
221. ESHR: 12/3/141.
222. Hansard, Vol. 341 col. 1535.
223. *Ibid.* col. 1536.
224. *Ibid.* col. 1537.
225. NA: DPP 1/95/1.
226. Hansard, Vol. 341 col. 1538.
227. *Ibid.* col. 1539.
228. *Ibid.* col. 1543.
229. *Ibid.* col. 1544.
230. *Ibid.* col. 1546.
231. *Ibid.* col. 1548.
232. See Chapter 5.
233. Hansard, Vol. 341 col. 1619.
234. Roberts, pp. 545–6.
235. Ridley, p. 275.
236. ESHR: 12/3/99.

Chapter 2: The Rise of the Pooters

1. Crossick, p. 19.
2. Lewis, p. 75.
3. Harris, p. 9.
4. Bennett, *Anna*, p. 25.
5. Bennett, *Clayhanger*, p. 417.
6. Bennett, *Card*, p. 18.
7. Bennett, *WGHJ*, p. 126.
8. Crossick, p. 107.
9. Wells, *EA*, I, p. 285.
10. Nowell-Smith, p. 148.
11. Nesbit, p. 10.
12. Michael Heller, 'Work, income and stability: the Victorian and Edwardian male clerk revisited', *Business History*, Vol. 50, No. 3, p. 256.

13. *Ibid.* pp. 44–5.
14. *Ibid.* p. 44; p. 40.
15. Bennett, *Card*, p. 256.
16. See Heffer, *HM*, pp. 445–62.
17. Rose J, p. 61.
18. Jones J, p. 105.
19. Cox, p. 24.
20. Gissing, p. 400.
21. Jones J, p. 73.
22. *The Girl's Own Paper*, 30 October 1886, p. 79.
23. Jones J, pp. 79–80.
24. *The Boy's Own Paper*, 22 November 1890, p. 128.
25. L&A, p. 170.
26. *The Magnet*, Vol. 2, No. 46, p. 3.
27. *Ibid.* p. 6.
28. *Ibid.* p. 10.
29. *Ibid.* p. 14.
30. *Ibid.* pp. 4–5.
31. Retrieved from http://www.orwell.ru/library/essays/boys/english/e_boys
32. Retrieved from http://www.friardale.co.uk/Ephemera/Newspapers/George%20Orwell_Horizon_Reply.pdf
33. Henty, p. 119.
34. *Ibid.* p. 58.
35. *Ibid.* pp. 152–3.
36. *Ibid.* p. 162.
37. Chothia, p. 23.
38. BL Add. MS 45291 ff. 142–3.
39. Holroyd, *Shaw*, II, p. 93.
40. BL Add. MS 45290 f. 39.
41. Retrieved from http://www.nationaltheatre.org.uk/discover-more/welcome-to-the-national-theatre/the-history-of-the-national-theatre/stage-by-stage/the
42. *Ibid.*
43. See Heffer, *HM*, pp. 285–339.
44. BL Add. MS 43874 f. 22.
45. Parry papers, Shulbrede: Grove to Parry, 30 December 1882.
46. Parry papers, Shulbrede: Grove to Parry, 18 March 1886.
47. Kennedy, *VW*, p. 15.
48. Dibble, p. 258.
49. Fry, p. 44.
50. Holt, p. 76.
51. Vamplew, p. 60.
52. Fry, p. 216.
53. *Wisden*, 1896, p. 367.
54. *Ibid.* p. 376.
55. I am grateful to Mr David Frith for this information.
56. *Wisden*, 1896, p. liii.
57. Fry, p. 107.
58. Thomson, p. 167.
59. *Ibid.* p. 159.
60. *Wisden*, 1903, p. 283.
61. Fry, p. 235.
62. Thomson, p. 159
63. Newbolt, p. 131.
64. Vamplew, p. 55.
65. Long, p. 5.
66. Nankivell, p. 3.
67. *Ibid.* p. 21.
68. *Ibid.* p. 10.
69. Nicolson, p. 61.
70. Ponsonby, p. 281.
71. Crosland, p. 80.
72. *Ibid.* p. 9.
73. Shaw, *Prefaces*, p. 193.
74. Shaw, *Plays*, p. 729.
75. Shaw, *Prefaces*, p. 118.
76. *Ibid.* p. 119.
77. Wells, *EA*, I, p. 247.
78. Webb, *Diaries*, I, p. 111.
79. *Ibid.* p. 115.
80. *Ibid.* p. 118.
81. *Ibid.* p. 211.
82. Webb, *Diaries*, II, p. 190.
83. Lewis, p. 96.
84. Webb, *Diaries*, I, p. 322.
85. Holroyd, *Shaw*, I, p. 172.
86. *Ibid.* p. 125.
87. *Ibid.* p. 127.
88. Webb, *Diaries*, I, p. 329.
89. *Ibid.* pp. 329–30.
90. *Ibid.* p. 354.
91. *Ibid.* pp. 355–6.
92. Wells, *NM*, p. 131.
93. *Ibid.* p. 135.
94. *Ibid.* p. 198.

95. Wells, *AV*, p. 110.
96. Roberts, p. 501.
97. Holroyd, *Shaw*, I, p. 410.
98. Webb, *Diaries*, II, p. 16.
99. *Ibid.*

Chapter 3: The Workers' Struggle

1. For an analysis of the true unemployment situation in Britain during the period leading up to the Great War, see George R. Boyer and Timothy J. Hatton, 'New estimates of British unemployment 1870–1913', *The Journal of Economic History*, Vol. 62, No. 3, p. 643ff.
2. Rowntree, p. viii.
3. *Ibid.* p. 11.
4. *Ibid.* p. 25.
5. *Ibid.* p. 31.
6. *Ibid.* p. 33.
7. *Ibid.* p. 39.
8. *Ibid.* p. 36.
9. *Ibid.* p. 77.
10. *Ibid.* p. 78.
11. *Ibid.* p. 135.
12. Girouard, p. 2.
13. Girouard, p. 5.
14. Retrieved from http://www.nationalarchives.gov.uk/pathways/census/living/food/beer.htm
15. Figures retrieved from http://www.historyandpolicy.org/opinion-articles/articles/the-highs-and-lows-of-drinking-in-britain
16. Pope, p. 9.
17. *Ibid.* p. 140.
18. *Ibid.* p. 141.
19. *Ibid.* p. 38.
20. *Ibid.* p. 148.
21. Bennett, *Anna*, pp. 18–19.
22. Holt, p. 170.
23. *Ibid.* p. 135.
24. Bennett, *Clayhanger*, p. 155.
25. *The Link*, No. 21, 23 June 1888, p. 1.
26. *Ibid.* No. 22, 30 June 1888, p. 2.
27. Holmes, *EM*, p. 322.
28. *The Times*, 24 September 1889, p. 10.
29. See http://www.tuc.org.uk/about-tuc/union-history/section-why-not-have-congress-our-own
30. Martin, p. 31.
31. Broadhurst, p. 79.
32. *Ibid.* p. 186.
33. *Ibid.* p. 111.
34. *Ibid.* p. 153.
35. *Ibid.* p. 206.
36. Holmes, *EM*, p. 233.
37. BL Add. MS 45341 f. 57.
38. Broadhurst, p. 82.
39. MacCarthy, pp. 422–3.
40. Morris, *IIA*, p. 356, p. 590.
41. BL Add. MS 45341 f. 45.
42. BL Add. MS 45341 f. 48.
43. BL Add. MS 45341 f. 87.
44. *The Times*, 9 February 1886, p. 6.
45. *Ibid.*
46. *Ibid.* p. 9.
47. *Ibid.* 13 February 1886, p. 7.
48. *Ibid.*
49. *Ibid.* 18 February 1886, p. 7.
50. Holroyd, *Shaw*, I, p. 183.
51. *The Times*, 22 February 1886, p. 7.
52. *Ibid.* 25 February 1886, p. 12.
53. *Ibid.* 10 April 1886, p. 5.
54. *Ibid.* 12 April 1886, p. 7.
55. Holroyd, *Shaw*, I, p. 186.
56. Morgan, p. 18.
57. *Ibid.* p. 33.
58. *Ibid.* p. 54.
59. *The Times*, 13 April 1891, p. 10.
60. *Ibid.* 14 April 1891, p. 10.
61. *Ibid.* 14 January 1893, p. 7.
62. Hansard, Vol. 19 col. 1180.
63. Wells, *NM*, p. 94.
64. *Ibid.* p. 96.
65. *Ibid.* p. 204.
66. *Ibid.* p. 206.

Part II: Coming Storms

Chapter 4: Imperial Tensions

1. OHBE, III, p. 349.
2. Seeley, p. 1.
3. *Ibid.* p. 2.

4. *Ibid.* p. 10.
5. *Ibid.* p. 12.
6. *Ibid.* p. 13.
7. *Ibid.* p. 14.
8. *Ibid.* p. 16.
9. *Ibid.* p. 37.
10. *Ibid.* p. 59.
11. *Ibid.* p. 65.
12. *Ibid.* p. 66.
13. *Ibid.* pp. 45–6.
14. *Ibid.* p. 55.
15. *Ibid.* p. 166.
16. *Ibid.* p. 234.
17. Gladstone, *Diaries*, IX, p. 522.
18. BL Add. MS 44644 f. 124.
19. BL Add. MS 44644 f. 126.
20. BL Add. MS 44645 f. 8.
21. Lees-Milne, p. 56.
22. Pollock, p. 202.
23. *Ibid.* p. 264.
24. *Ibid.* p. 265.
25. *Ibid.* p. 264.
26. *Ibid.* p. 266.
27. *The Pall Mall Gazette*, Vol. 39, No. 5879, p. 11.
28. *Ibid.* p. 1.
29. QV2, III, p. 477.
30. Gladstone, *Diaries*, XI, p. 111 (n).
31. Hansard, Vol. 284 col. 696.
32. *Ibid.* cols 697–8.
33. BL Add. MS 44645 f. 46.
34. Hamilton, II, p. 584.
35. Hansard, Vol. 286 col. 1528.
36. Pollock, p. 297.
37. Hamilton, II, p. 602.
38. Gladstone, *Diaries*, XI, p. 145.
39. Hansard, Vol. 288 col. 35.
40. *Ibid.* col. 52.
41. BL Add. MS 44645 f. 138.
42. BL Add. MS 44645 f. 150.
43. Gladstone, *Diaries*, XI, p. 181.
44. *Ibid.* p. 190.
45. Pollock, p. 300.
46. *Ibid.* p. 306.
47. Hamilton, I, p. 686.
48. Pakenham, p. 223.
49. Hansard, Vol. 294 col. 438.
50. Pollock, p. 311.
51. Pakenham, p. 234.
52. BL Add. MS 44147 f. 218.
53. Recorded in Pollock, p. 317.
54. *The Times*, 6 February 1885, p. 5.
55. Gladstone, *Diaries*, XI, p. 291 (n).
56. *Ibid.* p. 289.
57. Hamilton, II, p. 789.
58. QV2, III, p. 597.
59. Pollock, pp. 303–4.
60. QV2, III, p. 598.
61. *Ibid.* p. 603.
62. *The Times*, 6 February 1885, p. 5.
63. *Ibid.* p. 9.
64. Pakenham, p. 264.
65. Gladstone, *Diaries*, XI, p. 295.
66. QV2, III, p. 608.
67. Hamilton, II, p. 798.
68. BL Add. MS 44547 f. 181.
69. Hansard, Vol. 294 col. 1080.
70. *Ibid.* col. 1100.
71. *Ibid.* col. 1114.
72. *Ibid.* col. 1628.
73. Morley, II, p. 416.
74. *The Times*, 28 February 1885, p. 13.
75. Morley, II, p. 417.
76. Seeley, p. 10.
77. Wells, *NM*, p. 223.
78. Webb, *Diaries*, II, p. 31.
79. G&A, III, p. 5.
80. *The Times*, 25 May 1912, p. 9.
81. *Ibid.* p. 5.
82. BL Add. MS 49683 ff. 56–57.
83. BL Add. MS 49683 f. 61.
84. *The Times*, 12 November 1895, p. 6.
85. G&A, III, p. 11.
86. A&E, p. 34.
87. Hansard, Vol. 72 col. 172.
88. Kipling, *Verse*, p. 320.
89. Hansard, Vol. 258 col. 1954.
90. G&A, III, p. 44.
91. *The Times*, 12 November 1895, p. 6.
92. G&A, III, p. 55.
93. Kipling, p. 191.
94. G&A, III, p. 73.
95. Salisbury Papers: Hatfield House, 3M, Series A, Chamberlain correspondence, 26 December 1895.

96. Salisbury Papers: Hatfield House, 3M: Series A, Jameson Raid Telegrams, 30 December 1895.
97. *Ibid.* 29 December 1895.
98. Salisbury Papers: Hatfield House, 3M: Series A, Jameson Raid Telegrams, 29 December 1895.
99. Salisbury Papers: Hatfield House, 3M: Series A, Chamberlain Correspondence, 31 December 1895.
100. Salisbury Papers: Hatfield House, 3M: Series A, Jameson Raid Telegrams, 30 December 1895.
101. G&A, III, p. 89.
102. Salisbury Papers: Hatfield House, 3M: Series A, Jameson Raid Telegrams, 31 December 1895.
103. *Ibid.*
104. Pakenham, p. 503.
105. Hansard, Vol. 37 col. 90.
106. Bennett, *Clayhanger*, p. 371.
107. Hansard, Vol. 72 col. 598.
108. *The Times*, 10 October 1899, p. 3.
109. Webb, *Diaries*, II, p. 164.
110. *The Times*, 11 October 1899, p. 7.
111. Pakenham, p. 571.
112. Spencer, II, p. 279.
113. Cost estimated by National Archives at http://www.nationalarchives.gov.uk/pathways/census/events/britain7.htm
114. Hansard, Vol. 89 col. 397.
115. *Ibid.* col. 401.
116. *Ibid.* col. 404.
117. *Ibid.* col. 405.
118. *Ibid.* col. 1180.
119. *Ibid.* col. 1240.
120. *Ibid.* col. 1247.
121. *The Times*, 15 June 1901, p. 12.
122. *Ibid.* p. 11.
123. Hansard, Vol. 95 col. 574.
124. *Ibid.* col. 583.
125. *The Times*, 19 June 1901, p. 10.
126. See Heffer, *PP*, p. 120ff.
127. *The Times*, 4 January 1902, p. 9.
128. Wells, *NM*, p. 211.
129. Grigg, *YLG*, p. 293.
130. Rhodes, p. 51.
131. *Ibid.* p. 58.

Chapter 5: Ireland

1. This and other statistics in this section are to be found at http://www.historyhome.co.uk/c-eight/ireland/ire-land.htm, quoted in Winstanley, *op cit.*
2. Searle, p. 8.
3. Morley, I, p. 886.
4. BL Add. MS 44544 f. 5.
5. Bew, p. 115.
6. Ranelagh, p. 153.
7. *The Spectator*, 14 August 1880, p. 2.
8. *The Times*, 2 October 1880, p. 11.
9. BL Add. MS 44544 f. 71.
10. *The Times*, 18 October 1880, p. 6.
11. QV2, III, p. 149.
12. *The Times*, 18 October 1880, p. 9.
13. *Ibid.* 1 November 1880, p. 6.
14. BL Add. MS 44157 f. 186.
15. *The Times*, 4 November 1880, p. 6.
16. *Ibid.* 5 November 1880, p. 4.
17. *Ibid.* 8 November 1880, p. 6.
18. *Ibid.* 9 November 1880, p. 6.
19. *Ibid.* 10 November 1880, p 10.
20. QV2, III, p. 168.
21. Gladstone, *Diaries*, IX, p. 616.
22. BL Add. MS 44625 f. 19.
23. Gladstone, *Diaries*, IX, p. 647 (n).
24. QV2, III, p. 165.
25. *Ibid.* p. 166.
26. Gladstone, *Diaries*, IX, p. 655.
27. *The Times*, 29 December 1880, p. 8.
28. *Ibid.* 30 December 1880, p. 10.
29. *Ibid.* 31 December 1880, p. 8.
30. *Ibid.* 26 January 1881, p. 10.
31. *Ibid.* 25 January 1881, p. 7.
32. *Journals of the House of Commons*, Vol. 136, p. 50.
33. Hamilton, I, p. 104.
34. *The Times*, 4 February 1881, p. 10.
35. Gladstone, *Diaries*, X, p. 17.
36. Hansard, Vol. 258 col. 68.
37. *Ibid.* Vol. 259 col. 829.
38. BL Add. MS 44544 f. 148.

39. Hansard, Vol. 260 col. 890.
40. Lyons, p. 49.
41. Hansard, Vol. 260 col. 909.
42. *Ibid.* col. 923.
43. *Ibid.* col. 1104.
44. *Ibid.* cols 1322–3.
45. *Ibid.* col. 1612.
46. *Ibid.* Vol. 261 col. 95.
47. *Ibid.* col. 661.
48. BL Add. MS 44545 f. 11.
49. CUL: Churchill papers, Add. MS 9248/618
50. Bew, p. 81.
51. *The Times*, 27 September 1881, p. 5.
52. BL Add. MS 44159 f. 27.
53. Bew, p. 82.
54. BL Add. MS 43385 f. 298.
55. Reid, II, p. 341.
56. *The Times*, 8 October 1881, p. 7.
57. *Ibid.* 14 October 1881, p. 5.
58. QV2, III, p. 244.
59. BL Add. MS 44545 f. 35.
60. Reid, II, p. 362.
61. *Ibid.* p. 368.
62. Salisbury Papers: Hatfield House, 3M: Series D, Waterford Correspondence, 9 November 1881.
63. BL Add. MS 62114 f. 4.
64. Bew, p. 93.
65. Reid, II, p. 428.
66. BL Add. MS 62114 f. 5.
67. BL Add. MS 62114 f. 6.
68. BL Add. MS 44160 f. 160.
69. Gladstone, *Diaries*, X, p. 247.
70. Reid, II, p. 441.
71. *Ibid.* pp. 442–3.
72. Gladstone, *Diaries*, X, p. 247.
73. Hamilton, I, p. 263.
74. QV2, III, p. 278.
75. *Ibid.* p. 281.
76. *The Times*, 5 May 1882, p. 9.
77. Spencer, I, p. 184.
78. Gladstone, *Diaries*, X, p 253.
79. Hamilton, I, p. 265.
80. QV2, III, p. 283.
81. Spencer, I, p. 189.
82. Gladstone, *Diaries*, X, p. 255.
83. BL Add. MS 44545 f. 132.
84. BL Add. MS 44545 f. 132.
85. Hansard, Vol. 269 col. 323.
86. *The Times*, 8 May 1882, p. 7.
87. Gladstone, *Diaries*, X, p. 257.
88. BL Add. MS 43874 ff. 42–43.
89. Hamilton, I, p. 267.
90. Gladstone, *Diaries*, X, p. 256.
91. *The Times*, 8 May 1882, p. 11.
92. QV2, III, pp. 298–9.
93. *The Times*, 13 May 1882, p. 7.
94. *Ibid.* 22 January 1885, p. 10.
95. Morley, II, p. 434.
96. Gladstone, *Diaries*, IX, p. 337.
97. Hansard, Vol. 299 col. 1098.
98. *Ibid.* col. 1119.
99. Gladstone, *Diaries*, XI, p. 372.
100. Roberts, p. 348.
101. BL Add. MS 44769 f. 217.
102. G&A, II, p. 5.
103. *Ibid.* p. 11.
104. BL Add. MS 44316 f. 27.
105. Gladstone, *Diaries*, XI, p. 389.
106. BL Add. MS 44148 f. 132.
107. Gladstone, *Diaries*, XI, p. 394.
108. *Ibid.* p. 395.
109. *Ibid.* p. 403.
110. BL Add. MS 44269 ff. 234–6.
111. *The Times*, 10 November 1885, p. 6.
112. Gladstone, *Diaries*, XI, p. 448.
113. Morley, II, p. 501.
114. BL Add. MS 56445 f. 144.
115. Gladstone, *Diaries*, XI, p. 451.
116. Spencer, II, p. 94.
117. G&A, II, p. 145.
118. Spencer, II, p. 96.
119. CUL: Churchill papers, Add. MS 9248/1210.
120. Gladstone, *Diaries*, XI, p. 481.
121. G&A, II, p. 166.
122. Morley, II, pp. 527–8.
123. QV3, I, p. 26.
124. *Ibid.* p. 32.
125. Gladstone, *Diaries*, XI, p. 487.
126. Bennett, *Clayhanger*, p. 366.
127. BL Add. MS 44255 f. 54.
128. QV3, I, pp. 35–6.

129. *The Times*, 23 February 1886, p. 10.
130. G&A, II, p. 185.
131. QV3, I, p. 84.
132. BL Add. MS 44647 f. 41.
133. Gladstone, *Diaries*, XI, p. 519.
134. Hansard, Vol. 304 col. 1038.
135. *Ibid*. col. 1054.
136. *Ibid*. col. 1057.
137. *Ibid*. col. 1085.
138. *Ibid*. col. 1086.
139. *Ibid*. col. 1089.
140. *Ibid*. col. 1104.
141. *Ibid*. col. 1200.
142. *Ibid*. col. 1201.
143. Webb, *Diaries*, I, p. 162.
144. Hansard, Vol. 304 col. 1244.
145. QV3, I, p. 102.
146. Hansard, Vol. 304 col. 1344.
147. Gladstone, *Diaries*, XI, p. 549.
148. Hansard, Vol. 305 col. 602.
149. *Ibid*. col. 666.
150. ESHR 2/8: Journal entry for 20 May 1886.
151. Hansard, Vol. 306 col. 1239.
152. Gladstone, *Diaries*, XI, p. 566.
153. Wilde, *Letters*, p. 369.
154. CUL: Churchill papers, Add. MS 9248/502.
155. CUL: Churchill papers, Add. MS 9248/1261a.
156. Spinner, p. 127.
157. QV3, I, p. 162.
158. ESHR: 2/8, journal entry for 25 December 1886.
159. Rosebery, p. 181.
160. *Ibid*. p. 72.
161. Adams, *Balfour*, p. 80.
162. Hansard, Vol. 321 col. 231.
163. Dugdale, I, p. 108.
164. *Ibid*. p. 109.
165. Hansard, Vol. 321 col. 239.
166. *Ibid*. col. 289.
167. *Ibid*. col. 290.
168. *Ibid*. col. 305.
169. *Ibid*. col. 310.
170. *Ibid*. col. 356.
171. *The Times*, 15 November 1887, p. 8.
172. Balfour, *Letters*, p. 46.
173. Adams, *Balfour*, p. 95.
174. *The Times*, 18 April 1887, p. 8.
175. Bew, p. 157.
176. S&A, I, p. 59.
177. Adams, *Balfour*, p. 93.
178. BL Add. MS 62114 f. 9.
179. BL Add. MS 44773 f. 48ff.
180. Gladstone, *Diaries*, XII, p. 254.
181. BL Add. MS 44773 f. 170.
182. Gladstone, *Diaries*, XII, p. 271.
183. BL Add. MS 564448 f. 45.
184. Gardiner, II, p. 83.
185. ESHR: 2/8, journal entry for 2 December 1890.
186. Gladstone, *Diaries*, XIII, p. 59.
187. QV3, II, p. 132.
188. BL Add. MS 44774 f. 41.
189. Gladstone, *Diaries*, XIII, p. 126.
190. Asquith, *MR*, I, p. 133.
191. BL Add. MS 44648 f. 28.
192. *The Nineteenth Century*, No. CLXXXVIII, p. 509.
193. *Ibid*. p. 510.
194. *Ibid*. p. 522.
195. BL Add. MS 44549 f. 44.
196. Hansard (Fourth Series) Vol. 8 col. 1243.
197. *Ibid*. col. 1275.
198. *Ibid*. col. 1298.
199. *Ibid*. col. 1299.
200. *Ibid*. col. 1411.
201. *Ibid*. col. 1734.
202. *Ibid*. cols 1743–4.
203. BL Add. MS 44648 f. 92.
204. Gladstone, *Diaries*, XIII, p. 235.
205. Hansard, Vol. 15 col. 727.
206. Gardiner, II, p. 224.
207. QV3, II, p. 290.
208. Hansard, Vol. 16 col. 1838.
209. Spencer, II, p. 221.
210. Hansard, Vol. 17 col. 48.
211. *Ibid*. col. 640.
212. BL Add. MS 44258 f. 328.
213. BL Add. MS 44137 f. 486.
214. BL Add. MS 44776 f. 57.
215. Gladstone, *Diaries*, XIII, p. 439.

216. *Ibid*. p. 440.
217. BL Add. MS 44776 f. 64.
218. Rose, *GV*, p. 240.

Chapter 6: The Death of God

1. Hansard, Vol. 252 col. 20ff.
2. Bonner, II, 211.
3. QV2, III, p. 100.
4. *The Times*, 21 May 1880, p. 4.
5. Hansard, Vol. 252 cols 188–9.
6. *Ibid*. col. 191.
7. Gladstone, *Diaries*, IX, p. 529.
8. Hansard, Vol. 252 cols 200–201.
9. *Ibid*. col. 215.
10. *Ibid*. col. 315.
11. Bonner, II, p. 227.
12. *Ibid*. pp. 229–30.
13. QV2, III, p. 103.
14. Gladstone, *Diaries*, IX, p. 533.
15. BL Add. MS 441944 f. 202.
16. Bennett, *Clayhanger*, p. 702.
17. *Ibid*. p. 155.
18. *Ibid*. pp. 201–2.
19. *The Times*, 17 June 1880, p. 10.
20. Bonner, II, p. 231.
21. *The Times*, 22 June 1880, p. 9.
22. Gladstone, *Diaries*, IX, p. 543.
23. Hansard, Vol. 253 col. 462.
24. *Ibid*. col. 506.
25. *Ibid*. col. 564.
26. *Ibid*. col. 571.
27. *Ibid*. col. 572.
28. *Ibid*. col. 573.
29. Ibid col. 631.
30. *Ibid*. col. 634.
31. *Ibid*. col. 637.
32. *Ibid*. col. 638.
33. *Ibid*. col. 647.
34. *Ibid*. col. 648.
35. *Ibid*. col. 649.
36. Bonner, II, p. 244.
37. Hansard, Vol. 253 col. 651.
38. *Ibid*. col. 658.
39. *The Times*, 24 June 1880, p. 10.
40. Bonner, II, p. 245 (n).
41. Hansard, Vol. 253 col. 835.
42. Hamilton, I, p. 21.
43. Gladstone, *Diaries*, X, p. 45.
44. Hansard, Vol. 260 col. 1187.
45. *Ibid*. col. 1194.
46. *Ibid*. col. 1199.
47. *Ibid*. col. 1204.
48. *Ibid*. col. 1208.
49. *Ibid*. col. 1209.
50. *Ibid*. col. 1211.
51. *Ibid*. col. 1212.
52. *Ibid*. col. 1216.
53. Gladstone, *Diaries*, X, p. 58.
54. Hamilton, I, p. 134.
55. Hansard, Vol. 260 col. 1244.
56. *The Times*, 27 April 1881, p. 11.
57. Bonner, II, p. 250.
58. Gladstone, *Diaries*, X, p. 65.
59. Hansard, Vol. 260 col. 1559.
60. Gladstone, *Diaries*, X, p. 80.
61. *Ibid*. p. 91.
62. Hansard, Vol. 266 col. 74.
63. *The Times*, 22 February 1882, p. 9.
64. BL Add. MS 44545 f. 113.
65. Bonner, II, p. 310.
66. BL Add. MS 44546 f. 100.
67. Hansard, Vol. 278 col. 956.
68. *Ibid*. col. 965.
69. *Ibid*. col. 967.
70. *Ibid*. col. 973.
71. *Ibid*. col. 1196.
72. *Ibid*. col. 1603.
73. CUL: Churchill papers, Add. MS 2948/1279–1281.
74. Hansard, Vol. 302 col. 23.
75. Bennett, *Clayhanger*, p. 156.
76. See https://faithsurvey.co.uk/download/csintro.pdf
77. BL Add. MS 45291 f. 157.
78. Heffer, *PP*, p. 108.
79. *The Times*, 24 November 1880, p. 10.
80. *Ibid*. 14 January 1881, p. 8.
81. Gladstone, *Diaries*, X, p. 121.
82. BL Add. MS 44196 f. 216.
83. Gladstone, *Diaries*, X, p. 125.
84. *The Times*, 13 February 1889, p. 4.
85. *Ibid*. 5 February 1890, pp. 3–5.
86. *Ibid*. 22 November 1890, p. 4.
87. *Ibid*. p. 6.

Chapter 7: The Civilising Mission

1. QV2, III, p. 118.
2. BL Add. MS 44544 f. 59.
3. QV2, III, p. 108.
4. *Ibid.* p. 130.
5. *Ibid.* p. 131.
6. See Heffer, *HM*, pp. 663–7.
7. Harrison M, p. 26.
8. *Ibid.* p. 31.
9. *Ibid.* p. 11.
10. LG/C/11/1/39.
11. *The Times*, 27 October 1883, p. 9.
12. Hamilton, II, p. 499.
13. See Heffer, *HM*, p. 675ff.
14. Heffer, *PP*, p. 60.
15. *Ibid.*
16. Hansard, Vol. 284 col. 1686.
17. *Ibid.* cols 1688–9.
18. *Ibid.* col. 1694.
19. *Ibid.* col. 1698.
20. *Ibid.* Vol. 299 col. 889.
21. *Ibid.* col. 890.
22. *Ibid.* col. 891.
23. Gray, p. 22.
24. See Heffer, *HM*, p. 800–802.
25. Hansard, Vol. 299 col. 892.
26. *Ibid.* col. 893.
27. *Ibid.* col. 1170.
28. *Ibid.* col. 1171.
29. *Ibid.* col. 1177.
30. *Ibid.* col. 1771.
31. *Ibid.* Vol. 300 col. 1596.
32. *Ibid.* (Fourth Series) Vol. 3 col. 739.
33. Gray, p. 23.
34. Hansard, Vol. 4 col. 675.
35. ESHR: 2/8, journal entry for 26 January 1889.
36. CUL: Churchill papers, Add. MS 9248/1422.
37. Rose J, p. 149.
38. See for example Rose J, p. 169.
39. Hansard, Vol. 183 col. 1540.
40. *Ibid.* Vol. 185 col. 343.
41. Hansard, Vol. 335 col. 194.
42. *Ibid.* col. 197.
43. *Ibid.* col. 201.
44. *Ibid.* col. 1442.
45. *Ibid.* col. 1443.
46. *Ibid.* Vol. 338 col. 950.
47. *Ibid.* Vol. 339 col. 301.
48. Hansard (Lords), Vol. 25 col. 1609.
49. Hansard, Vol. 183 col. 1434.
50. *Ibid.* col. 1436.
51. *Ibid.* Vol. 141, col. 776.
52. *Ibid.* Vol. 184 col. 30.
53. Carlebach, p. 83.
54. NA: HO 45/9396/50134.
55. Hansard, Vol. 21 col. 2163.
56. *Ibid.* Vol. 21 col. 2165.
57. *Ibid.* Vol. 21 col. 2172.
58. *Ibid.* Vol. 21 col. 2176.
59. *Ibid.* Vol. 21 col. 2177.
60. *Ibid.* Vol. 22 col. 1152.
61. *Ibid.* Vol. 22 col. 2003.
62. Churchill, *Companion*, II, II, p. 1199.

Chapter 8: Protecting Women

1. Lewis, p. 5.
2. Geoffrey Chamberlain, 'British maternal mortality in the nineteenth and early twentieth centuries', *Journal of the Royal Society of Medicine*, November 2006, pp. 559–63.
3. Retrieved from http://visual.ons.gov.uk/how-has-life-expectancy-changed-over-time
4. Hansard, Vol. 107 col. 408.
5. Lewis, p. 5.
6. Sharpe, p. 457.
7. *Ibid.* p. 218.
8. *The Times*, 4 May 1896, p. 9.
9. *Ibid.* 23 May 1896, p. 15.
10. Lewis, p. 17.
11. Retrieved from http://www.portcities.org.uk/london/server/show/ConNarrative.111/chapterId/2347/Prostitution-in-maritime-London.html
12. Hansard, Vol. 266 col. 1827.
13. *The Pall Mall Gazette*, 4 July 1885: reproduced at http://www.attackingthedevil.co.uk/pmg/tribute/notice.php

14. Reproduced at http://www.attackingthedevil.co.uk/pmg/tribute/mt1.php
15. Hansard, Vol. 298 col. 1827.
16. *Ibid*. Vol. 299 col. 199.
17. *Ibid*. col. 281.
18. *Ibid*. col. 910.
19. *Ibid*. Vol. 300 col. 579.
20. *Ibid*. col. 580.
21. *Ibid*. col. 582.
22. *Ibid*. col. 587.
23. *Ibid*. col. 1397.
24. *The Times*, 24 October 1885, p. 4.
25. *Ibid*. 4 November 1885, p. 3.
26. *Ibid*. 5 November 1885, p. 4.
27. *Ibid*. 9 November 1885, p. 3.
28. See Heffer, *HM*, pp. 534–5.
29. Vicinus, p. 77.
30. Hansard, Vol. 279 col. 65.
31. *Ibid*. Vol. 303 col. 981.
32. *Ibid*. col. 983.
33. *Ibid*. col. 1912.
34. *Ibid*. col. 1914.
35. *Ibid*. Vol. 43 col. 1949.
36. *The Times*, 20 May 1912, p. 6.
37. *Ibid*. 22 May 1912, p. 13.
38. *Ibid*. 11 July 1912, p. 4.
39. *Ibid*. 17 July 1912, p. 10.
40. *Ibid*. 24 July 1912, p. 4.
41. Hansard, Vol. 43 col. 1857.
42. *The Times*, 25 October 1912, p. 3.
43. *Ibid*. 13 November 1912, p. 16.
44. Hansard, Vol. 43 col. 1901.
45. *Ibid*. col. 1927.
46. *The Times*, 25 November 1912, p. 6.
47. Hansard, Vol. 43 col. 1928.
48. *The Times*, 14 December 1912, p. 6.
49. *Ibid*. 20 January 1913, p. 3.
50. *Ibid*. 27 November 1912, p. 6.
51. See Heffer, *HM*, p. 544ff.
52. Hansard, Vol. 273 col. 1604.
53. Gissing, p. 374.
54. Searle, p. 47.
55. *Ibid*. p. 73.
56. Weeks, Ch. 3.
57. Wells, *Anticipations*, p. 126.

Part III: Public Debates, Public Doubts

Chapter 9: The Future

1. BL Add. MS 76936, Harcourt-Spencer 6.viii.1895.
2. Holroyd, *Shaw*, II, p. 131.
3. Wells, *Anticipations*, p. 14.
4. *Ibid*. p. 15.
5. *Ibid*. p. 57.
6. *Ibid*. pp. 128–9.
7. *Ibid*. p. 135.
8. *Ibid*. p. 147.
9. *Ibid*. p. 171.
10. *Ibid*. p. 32(n).
11. *Ibid*. p. 191.
12. *Ibid*. p. 195.
13. Wells, *Utopia*, p. 400.
14. Churchill, *Companion*, I, p. 98.
15. Galton, *Inquiries*, pp. 24–5.
16. Hynes, p. 32.
17. *The Times*, 5 June 1873, p. 8.
18. Quoted in Victoria Brignell, 'The eugenics movement Britain wants to forget', *New Statesman*, 9 December 2010.
19. See article by Sir Martin Gilbert at http://www.winstonchurchill.org/publications/finest-hour/finest-hour-152/leading-churchill-myths-churchills-campaign-against-the-feeble-minded-was-deliberately-omitted-by-his-biographers
20. For a detailed discussion of Keane's ideas see *Victorian Studies*, Vol. 31, p. 426 ff.
21. ICPD, p. 3.
22. *Ibid*. p. 13.
23. *Ibid*. p. 17.
24. *Ibid*.
25. *Ibid*. p. 22.
26. *Ibid*. p. 26.
27. Shaw, *Prefaces*, p. 170.
28. *Ibid*. p. 296.
29. *Ibid*. p 299.
30. Wells, *Anticipations*, pp. 252–3.
31. *Ibid*. p. 254.

32. *Ibid.* pp. 254–5.
33. *Ibid.* p. 256.
34. See Heffer, *PP*, p. 155ff.
35. Wells, *Anticipations*, p. 279.
36. *Ibid.* p. 311.
37. Williams, p. 1.
38. *Ibid.* pp. 10–11.
39. Balfour, *Decadence*, pp. 6–7.
40. *Ibid.* p. 59.
41. Hansard, Vol. 160 col. 656.
42. *Ibid.* col. 662.
43. *Ibid.* col.658.
44. Bostridge, p. 120.
45. Le Queux, pp. 85–6.
46. Churchill, *Companion*, II, II, p. 1127.
47. *Ibid.* p. 1108.
48. Le Queux, p. 542.
49. Saki, p. 169.
50. *Ibid.* pp. 170–71.
51. *Ibid.* p. 172.
52. *Ibid.* p. 158.
53. *Ibid.* p. 175.
54. *Ibid.* p. 229.
55. *Ibid.* p. 203.
56. *Ibid.* p. 259.

Chapter 10: Nostalgia

1. Bennett, *Clayhanger*, p. 658.
2. *Ibid.* p. 663.
3. Pevsner, *London N*, p. 547.
4. Wells, *NM*, p. 33.
5. *Ibid.* p. 35.
6. *Ibid.* p. 36.
7. *Ibid.* p. 37.
8. *Ibid.* p. 38.
9. Forster, *HE*, p. 15.
10. *Ibid.* p. 23.
11. *Ibid.* pp. 113–14.
12. Hansard (Lords), Vol. 272 col. 833.
13. *Ibid.* (Commons), Vol. 273 col. 1599.
14. RCHM, p xi.
15. SL, p. 3.
16. London County Council (General Powers) Act, 1898, Section 60.
17. SL, p. 5.
18. See Heffer, *HM*, p. 675ff.
19. *The Times*, 4 May 1882, p. 10.
20. Retrieved from https://en.wikisource.org/wiki/The_Preservation_of_Places_of_Interest_or_Beauty
21. Pevsner, *Lancashire LSW*, p. 344.
22. Davey, p. 24.
23. *Ibid.* p. 84.
24. Wells, *EA*, II, p. 638.
25. ACE, p. 88.
26. Bolsterli, p. 8.
27. ACE, p. 12.
28. *Ibid.* pp. 13–14.
29. *Ibid.* p. 18.
30. Howard 1898, p. 9.
31. *Ibid.* p. 10.
32. Howard 1902, p. 167.
33. Miller, p. 5.
34. *Ibid.* p. 61.
35. Davey, p. 171.
36. Davey, p. 175.
37. Belloc, p. 3.
38. *Ibid.* p. 9.
39. *Ibid.* p. 21.
40. Thomas, p. 33.
41. Hardy, *TL*, p. 128.
42. *Ibid.* p. 27.
43. *Ibid.* p. 99.
44. *Ibid.* p. 168.
45. Housman, p. 57.
46. *Ibid.* p. 30.
47. *Ibid.* p. 83.
48. Henley, p. 166.
49. Brooke, *Poems*, p. 67.
50. *Ibid.* p. 68.
51. *Ibid.* p. 70.
52. *Ibid.* p. 71.
53. *Ibid.* p. 67.
54. *Ibid.* pp. 71–2.
55. Thompson, p. 138.
56. UVW, p. 66.
57. *Ibid.* p. 69.
58. *Ibid.* p. 70.

Chapter 11: Imperial Consequences

1. Wells, *NM*, p. 211.
2. Churchill, *Companion*, II, I, p. 195.
3. *Ibid.* p. 219.

4. *Ibid*. p. 223.
5. *Ibid*. p. 237.
6. Webb, *Diaries*, I, p. 266.
7. Nowell-Smith, p. 61.
8. OHBE, III, p. 429.
9. *Ibid*. p. 432.
10. *Ibid*. pp. 434–5.
11. Gilmour, p. 30.
12. BL Add. MS 50074.
13. BL Add. MS 49683 f. 164.
14. BL Add. MS 49685 f. 13.
15. BL Add. MS 49685 f. 26.
16. BL Add. MS 49685 ff. 33–4.
17. BL Add. MS 49685 f. 42.
18. BL Add. MS 49685 f. 43
19. BL Add. MS 49685 f. 44.
20. BL Add. MS 49685 ff. 50–51.
21. BL Add. MS 49685 ff. 98–9.
22. In his Rectorial Address at Glasgow University, 7 November 1923.
23. Hansard (Lords), Vol. 154 col. 1443.
24. B-P, p. 15.
25. *Ibid*. p. 9.
26. *Ibid*. p. 19.
27. *Ibid*. p. 22.
28. *Ibid*. p. 25.
29. *Ibid*. pp. 25–6.
30. *Ibid*. p. 28.
31. *Ibid*. p. 45.
32. *Ibid*. p. 149.
33. See Heffer, *HM*, pp. 205–10.
34. B-P, p. 295.
35. *Ibid*. p. 273.
36. Hynes, p. 29.
37. B-P *Guides*, p. 340.
38. Wells, NM, p. 211.
39. Wells, *NM*, p. 87.
40. *Ibid*. p. 88.
41. Newbolt, pp. 131–3.
42. OHBE, IV, p. 47.
43. *Ibid*. pp. 543–4.
44. Scott, p. 592.
45. *Ibid*. p. 595.
46. Hansard, Vol. 48 cols 717–18.
47. *Ibid*. (Lords), Vol. 13 cols 1013–14.
48. Jones, p. 204.
49. Scott, p. 422.

Chapter 12: Art and Life

1. Wilde, *Letters*, p. 632.
2. Ellmann, p. 414.
3. Hyde, p. 240.
4. Wilde, *Letters*, pp. 559–60.
5. *Ibid*. p. 594.
6. *Ibid*. p. 646.
7. *The Times*, 27 May 1895, p. 4.
8. Wilde, *DP*, pp. 117–18.
9. *Ibid*. p. 87.
10. *Ibid*. p. 90.
11. Hansard, Vol. 325 col. 1708.
12. *Ibid*. col. 1709.
13. *Ibid*. col. 1710.
14. *Ibid*. col. 1719.
15. Hynes, p. 307.
16. BL Add. MS 49685 f. 2.
17. BL Add. MS 49685 f. 3.
18. BL Add. MS 73198 f. 9.
19. BL Add. MS 45291 f 146.
20. BL Add. MS 45291 f. 147.
21. BL Add. MS 45291 f. 150.
22. Galsworthy, *Letters*, p. 145.
23. BL Add. MS 45291 f. 153.
24. *The Times*, 29 October 1907, p. 15.
25. Garnett, p. ix.
26. *Ibid*. p. x.
27. *Ibid*. p. xiv.
28. Barker, p. 17.
29. Barker, p. 229.
30. Holroyd, *Shaw*, II, p. 226.
31. Garnett, p. xv.
32. *Ibid*. p. xxi.
33. *Ibid*. p. xxvii.
34. *The Times*, 27 November 1907, p. 8.
35. JSC, p. 198.
36. *The Times*, 29 June 1909, p. 12.
37. *Ibid*. 30 June 1909, p. 10.
38. JSC, p ix.
39. *Ibid*. p. 15.
40. *Ibid*. p. 16.
41. *Ibid*. p. 17.
42. *Ibid*. p. 19.
43. *Ibid*. p. 24.
44. *Ibid*. p. 26.
45. *Ibid*. p. 28.
46. *Ibid*. p. 35.

47. *Ibid.* p. 38.
48. *Ibid.* p. 39.
49. *Ibid.* p. 47.
50. *Ibid.* p. 48.
51. *Ibid.* p. 49.
52. *Ibid.* p. 50.
53. *Ibid.* p. 71.
54. *Ibid.* p. 72.
55. *Ibid.* p. 73.
56. *Ibid.* p. 75.
57. *Ibid.* p. 77.
58. *Ibid.* p. 93.
59. *Ibid.* p. 101.
60. *Ibid.* p. 102.
61. *Ibid.* p. 127.
62. *Ibid.* p. 128.
63. *Ibid.* p. 129.
64. *Ibid.* p. 151.
65. *Ibid.* p. 153.
66. *Ibid.* p viii.
67. *Ibid.* pp. viii–ix.
68. *Ibid.* p. x.
69. *Ibid.* p. xiii.
70. *The Times*, 16 February 1912, p. 8.
71. Shaw, *Plays*, p. 729.
72. *Ibid.* p. 736.
73. *The Times*, 21 March 1913, p. 2.
74. Woolf, *B&B*, p. 4.
75. *Ibid.* p. 5.
76. *Ibid.* p. 12.
77. See http://www.papalencyclicals.net/Pius10/p. 10moath.htm
78. Quoted in Holroyd, *Strachey*, I, p. 395.
79. BL Add. MS 50534 f. 86.
80. BL Add. MS 50534 f. 88.
81. BL Add. MS 50534 f. 89.
82. BL Add. MS 50534 ff. 91–3.
83. BL Add. MS 50534 f. 94.
84. BL Add. MS 50534 f. 95.
85. BL Add. MS 50534 f. 96.

Chapter 13: The Uses of Literacy

1. Bennett, *Letters* II, p. 90.
2. *Ibid.* p. 115.
3. *Ibid.* p. 318.
4. Holroyd, *Shaw*, I, p. 205.
5. James, p. 281.
6. Carey, p. 5.
7. Wells, *EA*, I, p. 323.
8. *Ibid.* p. 328.
9. P&H, p. 79.
10. Ferris, p. 36.
11. P&H, p. 115.
12. *Ibid.* p. 122.
13. Gissing, p. 485.
14. *Ibid.* p. 505.
15. Ferris, p. 72.
16. P&H, p. 200.
17. BL Add. MS 62384, entries for 3 and 4 May 1896.
18. Ferris, p. 83.
19. Roberts, p. 311; BL Add. MS 62292A ff. 14–15.
20. BL Add. MS 62292A ff. 4–5.
21. Roberts, p. 668.
22. BL Add. MS 62153 ff. 1–2.
23. BL Add. MS 62292A f. 13.
24. BL Add. MS 62153 ff. 3–4.
25. Bennett, *Letters* II, p. 73.
26. BL Add. MS 62153 ff. 9.
27. BL Add. MS 62391 entry for 1 November 1903.
28. BL Add. MS 62153 f. 18.
29. BL Add. MS 62153 f. 20.
30. BL Add. MS 62201 ff. 20–21.
31. BL Add. MS 62201 f. 1.
32. BL Add. MS 62391, entry for 4 November 1903.
33. BL Add. MS 62201 f. 88.
34. BL Add. MS 62201 f. 24.
35. BL Add. MS 62243 ff. 2–3.
36. P&H, p. 309.
37. BL Add. MS 62243 f. 11.
38. BL Add. MS 49797 f. 49.
39. BL Add. MS 62243 f. 156.
40. BL Add. MS 62243 f. 168.
41. BL Add. MS 62253 f. 10.
42. BL Add. MS 62243 f. 222.
43. BL Add. MS 62253 f. 12.
44. BL Add. MS 62253 f. 14.
45. BL Add. MS 62157 ff. 1–2.
46. BL Add. MS 62157 ff. 7.
47. Ferris, p. 142.
48. *Ibid.* p. 143.
49. BL Add. MS 49797 f. 39.
50. BL Add. MS 49797 f. 40.

51. BL Add. MS 49797 f. 42.
52. BL Add. MS 49797 f. 43.

Part IV: Strife

Chapter 14: Men and Power

1. Rose, *GV*, p. 96.
2. *The Times*, 2 February 1911, p. 6.
3. Churchill, *Companion*, II, II, p. 1217.
4. *The Times*, 2 February 1911, p. 6.
5. Nicolson, p. 143.
6. *The Times*, 2 February 1911, p. 7.
7. Churchill, *Companion*, II, II, p. 1237.
8. Nicolson, p. 144.
9. VBC, p. 296.
10. Asquith, *VS*, p. 19.
11. *Ibid.* p. 21.
12. *Ibid.* p. 24.
13. *Ibid.* p. 45.
14. *Ibid.* p. 49.
15. *Ibid.* p. 107.
16. See Grigg, *PW*, pp. 44–5.
17. Carey Evans, pp. 63–4.
18. Grigg, *Champion*, p. 185.
19. *The Times*, 13 March 1909, p. 3.
20. *Ibid.* p. 4.
21. Lloyd George, p. 112.
22. Grigg, *Champion*, p. 187.
23. *Ibid.* p. 146.
24. Grigg, *PW*, p. 73.
25. Stevenson, p. 217.
26. Hague, p. 231.
27. Grigg, *PW*, p. 73.
28. *Ibid.* p. 80.
29. NA: CAB 37/107/63.
30. Ward, p. 288.
31. Judd, p. 96.
32. *The Times*, 1 October 1912, p. 4.
33. Hansard, Vol. 42 col. 667.
34. *Ibid.* col. 672.
35. *Ibid.* col. 712.
36. *Ibid.* col. 713.
37. *Ibid.* col. 715.
38. *Ibid.* col. 716.
39. *Ibid.* col. 718.
40. *Ibid.* col. 726.
41. Ward, p. 292.
42. *Ibid.* p. 293.
43. *The Times*, 20 March 1913, p. 8.
44. BL Add. MS 62157 ff. 22–3.
45. BL Add. MS 62157 f. 24.
46. Judd, p. 102.
47. Samuel, p. 75.
48. *The Times*, 26 March 1913, p. 3.
49. *Ibid.* p. 4.
50. Hansard, Vol. 50 col. 1629.
51. *Ibid.* col. 1630.
52. Asquith, *MR*, I, p. 210.
53. *The Times*, 29 March 1913, p. 3.
54. *Ibid.* p. 4.
55. Ward, p. 296.
56. VBC, p. 382
57. *The Times*, 6 June 1913, p. 4.
58. *Ibid.* 28 May 1913, p. 4.
59. *Ibid.* 6 June 1913, p. 4.
60. *Ibid.* 7 June 1913, p. 5.
61. *Ibid.* 9 June 1913, p. 4.
62. *Ibid.* p. 9.
63. *Ibid.* 10 June 1913, p. 8.
64. *Ibid.* 11 June 1913, p. 8.
65. Ward, p. 302
66. Baker, p. 146.
67. *The Times*, 14 June 1913, p. 8.
68. *Ibid.* 14 June 1913, p. 9.
69. PA: LG/C/6/12/2.
70. Hansard, Vol. 54 col. 405.
71. *Ibid.* cols 448–9.
72. PA: LG/C/6/12/2.
73. *The Times*, 19 June 1913, p. 9.
74. Chesterton, p. 205.
75. *The Times*, 14 June 1913, p. 8.
76. PA: LG/C/7/2/7.
77. Hansard, Vol. 29 col. 1368.
78. Heffer, *PP*, p. 125.
79. Belloc, *Verse*, p. 232.
80. Grigg, *Champion*, p. 250.
81. Churchill, *Companion*, II, II, p. 905.

Chapter 15: Dukes and Dreadnoughts

1. Retrieved from http://www.quarterly-review.org/famous-last-words/
2. BL Add. MS 52512 f. 110.
3. BL Add. MS 52513 f. 60.

4. BL Add. MS 49685 f. 112.
5. Esher, II, p. 303.
6. BL Add. MS 52513 ff. 67–8.
7. Nowell-Smith, p. 27.
8. Webb, *Diaries*, III, p. 110.
9. A&E, p. 34.
10. Hansard, Vol. 176 col. 1429.
11. S&A, I, p. 232.
12. Hansard, Vol. 184 col. 1748.
13. Hansard, Vol. 185 col. 175.
14. For a detailed discussion of the COS, see Heffer, pp. 668–75.
15. Bosanquet, p. 184.
16. Springhall, p 48.
17. Hansard, Vol. 188 col. 463.
18. *Ibid.* col. 472.
19. *Ibid.* col. 475.
20. *Ibid.* Vol. 190, cols 564–86.
21. *Ibid.* Vol. 192 col. 1377.
22. *Ibid.* (Fourth Series), Vol. 1 col.13.
23. PA: LG/C/6/11/6.
24. PA: LG/C/6/11/4.
25. NA: CAB 37/100/99.
26. S&A, I, p. 241.
27. PA: LG/C/14/1/2.
28. Grigg, *Champion*, p. 177.
29. C&G, II, p. 323.
30. Hansard, Vol. 4 col. 473.
31. *Ibid.* col. 475.
32. *Ibid.* col. 480.
33. *Ibid.* col. 481.
34. *Ibid.* col. 482.
35. *Ibid.* col. 486.
36. *Ibid.* col. 548.
37. S&A, I, p. 255.
38. Hansard, Vol. 4 col. 560.
39. BL Add. MS 62201 ff. 35–6.
40. BL Add. MS 62201 f. 36.
41. BL Add. MS 62201 f. 40.
42. BL Add. MS 62201 f. 41.
43. BL Add. MS 62201 ff. 36–7.
44. BL Add. MS 49797 f. 188.
45. BL Add. MS 49797 f. 190.
46. BL Add. MS 49797 f. 192.
47. *The Times*, 17 July 1909, p. 6.
48. Churchill, *Companion*, II, II, p. 900.
49. *The Times*, 31 July 1909, p. 9.
50. S&A, I, p. 256.
51. BL Add. MS 49797 f. 196.
52. Grigg, *Champion*, p. 208.
53. *Ibid.* p. 209.
54. *Ibid.* p. 210.
55. NA: CAB 37/100/121.
56. NA: CAB 37/100/123.
57. S&A, I, pp. 263–4.
58. *Ibid.* p. 257.
59. *Ibid.* p. 258.
60. Newton, p. 378.
61. *The Times*, 11 October 1909, p. 6.
62. *Ibid.* p. 9.
63. Hansard, Vol. 12 col. 2115.
64. Hansard, (Lords) Vol. 4 col. 731.
65. *Ibid.* col. 750.
66. *Ibid.* col. 751.
67. *Ibid.* col. 754.
68. *Ibid.* col. 767.
69. Hansard, Vol. 13 col. 501.
70. *Ibid.* col. 546.
71. *Ibid.* col. 547.
72. *Ibid.* col. 558.
73. Webb, *Diaries*, III, pp. 131–2.
74. S&A, I, p. 261.
75. See, for example, a letter from J. St Loe Strachey to A. J. Balfour, BL Add. MS 49797 f. 201, in which he urges this reconciliation in the wider interest of defeating the government.
76. BL Add. MS 62153 f. 36.
77. BL Add. MS 62153 ff. 39–40.
78. Webb, *Diaries*, III, p. 134.
79. Hansard, Vol. 16 col. 25, for example.
80. NA: CAB 37/102/1.
81. NA: CAB 37/102/3.
82. NA: CAB 37/102/7.
83. *The Times*, 6 May 1910, p. 10.
84. Dangerfield, p. 31.
85. Grigg, *Champion*, p. 259.
86. NA: CAB 37/102/20.
87. BL Add. MS 49692 f. 101.
88. NA: CAB 37/102/23.
89. S&A, Vol. I, p. 286.
90. Newton, p. 401.
91. Adams, *Balfour*, p. 245.

92. BL Add. MS 49692 f. 102.
93. PA: LG/C/4/1/1.
94. PA: LG/C/4/1/2.
95. Hansard (Lords) Vol. 6 col. 850.
96. S&A, I, p. 287.
97. *The Times*, 12 November 1910, p. 11.
98. Dangerfield, p. 39.
99. *The Times*, 26 November 1910, p. 10.
100. BL Add. MS 62153 f. 41.
101. BL Add. MS 62153 ff. 42–3.
102. VBC, p. 228.
103. *The Times*, 22 November 1910, p. 8.
104. *Ibid.* p. 11.
105. Grigg, *Champion*, p. 283.
106. Ronaldshay, III, p. 56.
107. Churchill, *Companion*, II, II, p. 1031.
108. BL Add. MS 49686 f. 67.
109. Newton, p. 408.
110. BL Add. MS 49686 f. 68.
111. Newton, p. 411.
112. Hansard (Lords), Vol. 7 col. 4.
113. Hansard, Vol. 21 col. 1746.
114. *Ibid.* col. 1748.
115. *Ibid.* col. 1764.
116. *Ibid.* col. 1765.
117. *Ibid.* col. 1934.
118. *Ibid.* Vol. 22 col. 110.
119. C&G, II, p. 344.
120. Newton, p. 415.
121. Hansard (Lords), Vol. 8 cols 703–4.
122. S&A, I, p. 309.
123. Hansard (Lords), Vol. 9 col. 596.
124. S&A, I, p. 310.
125. Balfour, *Letters*, p. 266.
126. *The Times*, 22 July 1911, p. 8.
127. *Ibid.* p. 9.
128. Balfour, *Letters*, p. 267.
129. *The Times*, 22 July 1911, p. 8.
130. Newton, p. 422.
131. *Ibid.* p. 423.
132. *The Times*, 24 July 1911, p. 8.
133. Hansard, Vol. 28 col. 1467.
134. *Ibid.* col. 1468.
135. *Ibid.* col. 1469.
136. *Ibid.* col. 1470
137. *Ibid.* col. 1473.
138. *The Times*, 25 July 1911, p. 8.
139. Balfour, *Letters*, p. 268.
140. Hansard, Vol. 28 cols 1478–9.
141. *The Times*, 25 July 1911, p. 8.
142. *Ibid.* p. 9.
143. BL Add. MS 49686 f. 40.
144. BL Add. MS 49686 f. 42.
145. BL Add. MS 49686 f. 44.
146. Churchill, *Companion*, II, II, p. 1111.
147. Hansard (Lords), Vol. 9 col. 896.
148. *Ibid.* col. 900.
149. *Ibid.* col. 920.
150. *Ibid.* col. 999.
151. *Ibid.* col. 1000.
152. *Ibid.* col. 1069.
153. *Ibid.* col. 1073.
154. Gilmour, p. 394.
155. Balfour, *Letters*, pp. 269–70.
156. Adams, *Balfour*, p. 255.
157. PA: LG/C/6/11/9.
158. Grigg, *Champion*, p. 289.
159. BL Add. MS 62161 f. 4.
160. The list is an appendix in S&A, I, pp. 329–31.
161. Dangerfield, p. 6.
162. C&G, II, pp. 305–6.
163. *Ibid.* p. 307.
164. *Ibid.* pp. 309–10.
165. Gissing, p. 471.

Chapter 16: The Great Unrest

1. Garnett, p. 7.
2. Galsworthy, *Strife*, p. 9.
3. *Ibid.* p. 13.
4. *Ibid.* p. 14.
5. *Ibid.* p. 22.
6. *Ibid.* p. 20.
7. *Ibid.* p. 36.
8. *Ibid.* p. 62.
9. *Ibid.* p. 63.
10. *Ibid.* p. 58.
11. *Ibid.* p. 48.
12. *Ibid.* p. 49.
13. *Ibid.* p. 67.
14. LSE, Fawcett letters, 9/01.
15. James, p. 285.
16. BL Add. MS 52512 f. 13.
17. Hansard, Vol. 152 col. 196.

18. Wilson, p. 505.
19. Hansard, Vol. 154 cols 1301–2.
20. Hansard, Vol. 163 col. 1460.
21. *Ibid.* col. 1461.
22. *Ibid.* Vol. 164 col. 911.
23. Dangerfield, p. 209.
24. Hansard, Vol. 43 col. 1790.
25. *Ibid.* col. 1725.
26. NA: CAB 37/102/4.
27. *The Times*, 11 January 1910, p. 10.
28. *Ibid.* 21 January 1910, p. 12.
29. *Ibid.* 14 February 1910, p. 12.
30. *Ibid.* 23 March 1910, p. 10.
31. *Ibid.* 25 March 1910, p. 6.
32. *Ibid.* 26 March 1910, p. 10.
33. *Ibid.* 31 March 1910, p. 10.
34. *Ibid.* 20 July 1910, p. 8.
35. *Ibid.* 21 July 1910, p. 9.
36. *Ibid.* 25 July 1910, p. 8.
37. *Ibid.* 12 September 1910, p. 8.
38. *Ibid.* 28 September 1910, p. 8.
39. *Ibid.* 29 September 1910, p. 10.
40. *Ibid.* 1 October 1910, p. 12.
41. *Ibid.* 3 October 1910, p. 10.
42. *Ibid.* 7 October 1910, p. 8.
43. *Ibid.* 27 October 1910, p. 10.
44. *Ibid.* 3 November 1910, p. 7.
45. *Ibid.* 4 November 1910, p. 9.
46. *Ibid.* 9 November 1910, p. 10.
47. *Ibid.*
48. Churchill, *Companion*, II, II, p. 1207.
49. *The Times*, 10 November 1910, p. 10.
50. Churchill, *Companion*, II, II, p. 1207.
51. *The Times*, 14 November 1910, p. 6.
52. *Ibid.* 23 November 1910, p. 12.
53. Churchill, *Companion*, II, II, p. 1213.
54. Askwith, p. 146.
55. *The Times*, 2 January 1911, p. 6.
56. Churchill, *Companion*, II, II, p. 1243.
57. *Ibid.* pp. 1243–4.
58. Hansard, Vol. 21 col. 56.
59. Retrieved from http://www.lse.ac.uk/assets/richmedia/channels/publicLecturesAndEvents/slides/20120228_1830_comparingRealWagesTheMcWageIndex_sl.pdf
60. Grigg, *Champion*, p. 291.
61. *The Times*, 15 June 1911, p. 9.
62. NA: CAB 37/102/70.
63. *Ibid.* 3 July 1911, p. 10.
64. *Ibid.* 5 July 1911, p. 9.
65. *Ibid.* 22 July 1911, p. 10.
66. Churchill, *Companion*, II, II, p. 1265.
67. *The Times*, 3 August 1911, p. 6.
68. *Ibid.* 7 August 1911, p. 6.
69. *Ibid.* 8 August 1911, p. 9.
70. *Ibid.* 10 August 1911, p. 6.
71. Hansard, Vol. 29 col. 1150.
72. NA: CAB 37/107/97.
73. *The Times*, 11 August 1911, p. 7.
74. Dangerfield, p. 251.
75. *The Times*, 12 August 1911, p. 7.
76. *Ibid.* 14 August 1911, p. 6.
77. *The Manchester Guardian*, 10 August 1911, p. 9.
78. *The Times*, 11 August 1911, p. 8.
79. Churchill, *Companion*, II, II, p. 1268.
80. *The Times*, 14 August 1911, p. 6.
81. *Ibid.* 15 August 1911, p. 6.
82. Hansard, Vol. 29 col. 1547.
83. *The Times*, 16 August 1911, p. 6.
84. Hansard, 17 August 1911, p. 6.
85. Churchill, *Companion*, II, II, p. 1274.
86. *Ibid.*
87. Hansard, Vol. 29 col. 1950.
88. *Ibid.* col. 1959.
89. *Ibid.* 22 August 1911, p. 4.
90. Churchill, *Companion*, II, II, p. 1287.
91. *The Times*, 21 August 1911, p. 5.
92. *Ibid.* 22 August 1911, p. 6.
93. Hansard, Vol. 29 col. 2283.
94. *Ibid.* col. 2286.
95. *Ibid.* col. 2296.
96. *Ibid.* col. 2332.
97. *Ibid.* col. 2340.
98. NA: CAB 37/107/107.
99. Hansard, Vol. 34 col. 52.
100. *Ibid.* col. 86.
101. *Ibid.* col. 88.
102. *The Times*, 8 February 1912, p. 7.
103. *Ibid.* 9 February 1912, p. 8.

104. *Ibid.* 1 March 1912, p. 10.
105. Hansard, Vol. 35 col. 42.
106. *Ibid.* col. 46.
107. *Ibid.* col. 47.
108. *Ibid.* col. 48.
109. *Ibid.* col. 1723.
110. *The Times*, 18 March 1912, p. 9.
111. Hansard, Vol. 35 col. 1723.
112. *The Times*, 26 March 1912, p. 8.
113. Hansard, Vol. 35 col. 2078.
114. *Ibid.* Vol. 36 col. 233.
115. *Ibid.* Vol. 36 col. 234.
116. *The Times*, 24 May 1912, p. 57.
117. *The Times*, 7 June 1912, p. 8.
118. *Ibid.* 11 June 1912, p. 9.
119. *Ibid.* 25 July 1912, p. 6.
120. Dangerfield, p. 296.
121. *The Times*, 22 February 1913, p. 10.
122. Wells, *EA*, II, p. 665.
123. MacDonald, p. 35.
124. *Ibid.* p. 36.
125. *Ibid.* p. 57.
126. Forster, *HE*, p. 134.
127. *Ibid.* pp. 164–5.
128. Wells, *Anticipations*, p. 88.
129. *Ibid.* p. 89.
130. *Ibid.* p. 90.
131. *Ibid.* p. 92.
132. *Ibid.* p. 109.

Chapter 17: Votes for Women

1. Harrison, p. 63.
2. *Ibid.* p. 71.
3. Searle, p. 56 (n).
4. *Ibid.* p. 57.
5. Churchill, *Companion*, II, III, p. 1431.
6. Fulford, p. 14.
7. Citations in the *Oxford English Dictionary*.
8. See Heffer, *HM*, p. 526ff.
9. Fulford, p. 75.
10. Phelps, p. 257.
11. Hansard, Vol. 3 col. 1510.
12. *Ibid.* col. 1512
13. *Ibid.* col. 1513.
14. Hansard, Vol. 45 col. 1175.
15. Searle, p. 69.
16. Hansard, Vol. 45 cols 1227–8.
17. Pankhurst, p. 18.
18. *Ibid.* p. 28.
19. *Ibid.* p. 31.
20. *Ibid.* p. 38.
21. Hansard, Vol. 146 col. 226.
22. *Ibid.* col. 227.
23. *Ibid.* col. 228.
24. *Ibid.* col. 230.
25. *The Times*, 13 May 1905, p. 11.
26. Pankhurst, p. 46.
27. *Ibid.* p. 48.
28. Fulford, p. 128.
29. *Ibid.*
30. Forster, *HE*, p. 5.
31. LSE 2/NWS/C1.
32. LSE 2/NWS/C4/2/25.
33. LSE 2/NWS/C4/2/30.
34. Fulford, p. 140.
35. *The Times*, 24 October 1906, p. 11.
36. Hansard, Vol. 163 col. 518.
37. *Ibid.* col. 519.
38. *Ibid.* cols 1108–9.
39. *Ibid.* col. 1110.
40. *The Times*, 27 October 1906, p. 8.
41. LSE 9/27/F/025.
42. *The Times*, 13 February 1907, p. 4.
43. LSE 2/NWS/D1/5.
44. *The Times*, 14 February 1907, p. 10.
45. *Ibid.* 15 February 1907, p. 4.
46. LSE 9/20.
47. *The Times*, 14 February 1908, p. 11.
48. *Ibid.* 15 February 1908, p. 4.
49. *Ibid.* 15 June 1908, p. 11.
50. *Ibid.* 22 June 1908, p. 9.
51. *Ibid.* 2 July 1908, p. 4.
52. Morgan, p. 221.
53. *The Times*, 22 October 1908, p. 2.
54. *Ibid.* 26 October 1908, p. 3.
55. *Ibid.* 29 October 1908, p. 9.
56. *Ibid.* p. 10.
57. *Ibid.* 29 June 1909, p. 9.
58. *Ibid.* 25 September 1909, p. 8.
59. *Ibid.* 27 September 1909, p. 7.
60. LSE 9/01.
61. LSE 9/20.
62. LSE 9/20

63. LSE 9/20.
64. LSE 9/20.
65. Lytton, p. 264.
66. Forster, *HE*, p. 243.
67. Hansard, Vol. 19, col. 221.
68. Churchill, *Companion*, II, III, pp. 1436–7.
69. *Ibid.* p. 1439.
70. Hansard, Vol. 19, col. 254.
71. Harrison, p. 127.
72. Churchill, *Companion*, II, III, p. 1458.
73. *The Times*, 24 November 1910.
74. LSE 9/20.
75. Churchill, *Companion*, II, II, p. 1214.
76. Dangerfield, p. 158.
77. Fulford, p. 243.
78. PA: LG/C/8/1/1.
79. *The Times*, 24 February 1912, p. 8.
80. LSE 2/NWS/D1/3.
81. Harrison, p. 13.
82. *The Times*, 2 March 1912, p. 8.
83. *Ibid.* 4 March 1912, p. 4.
84. LSE 9/20.
85. Fulford, p. 252.
86. LSE 9/20.
87. *The Times*, 28 March 1912, pp. 7–8.
88. Harrison, p. 60.
89. *The Times*, 1 April 1912, p. 9.
90. LSE 2/NWS/C4/2.
91. Hansard, Vol. 50 col. 873.
92. *Ibid.* col. 877.
93. *Ibid.* col. 879.
94. LSE 7/EWD/A7/3.
95. LSE 7/EWD/A4/3.
96. LSE 7/EWD/A4/4/2.
97. See, for example, LSE 7/EWD/A6/2.
98. LSE 7/EWD/A7/2.
99. *The Daily Sketch*, 5 June 1913, p. 1.
100. LSE 9/20.
101. LSE 7/EWD/A7/5.
102. LSE 7/EWD/A7/7.
103. LSE 7/EWD/A8/1.
104. LSE 7/EWD/A8/3/1.
105. LSE 2/NWS/D3/2.
106. *The Times*, 11 March 1914, p. 9.
107. Bostridge, p. 58.
108. *The Daily Mirror*, 22 May 1914, p. 1.
109. *The Times*, 22 May 1914, p. 8.
110. Wells, *Anticipations*, p. 118.
111. *Ibid.* p. 119.
112. Wells, *AV*, p. 100.
113. *Ibid.* p. 101.
114. *Ibid.* p. 5.
115. *Ibid.* p. 18.
116. *Ibid.* p. 32.
117. *Ibid.* p. 129.
118. *The Spectator*, 20 November 1909, pp. 846–7.
119. Wells, *EA*, I, p. 337.
120. *Ibid.* p. 345.
121. *Ibid.* p. 361.
122. *Ibid.* p. 363.
123. *Ibid.* II, p. 465.
124. Wells, *PEA*, p. 55.
125. *Ibid.* p. 61.
126. West, p. 7.
127. Wells, *PEA*, p. 73.
128. *Ibid.* p. 74.
129. *Ibid.*
130. *Ibid.* p. 75.
131. Wells, *FLT*, p. 209.
132. *Ibid.* p. 217.
133. Wells, *PEA*, p. 61.
134. West, p. 7.
135. Wells, *PEA*, p. 79.
136. *Ibid.* p. 71.
137. West, p. 7.
138. Wells, PEA, p. 73 and p. 69.
139. West, p. 7.
140. Webb, *Diaries*, III, p. 120.
141. *Ibid.* p. 121.
142. *Ibid.* p. 122.
143. *Ibid.* pp. 122–3.
144. *Ibid.* p. 125.
145. *Ibid.* p. 128.
146. West, p. 15.
147. Webb, *Diaries*, III, p. 138.
148. Wells, *PEA*, p. 94.
149. West, p. 5.
150. Wells, *PEA*, p. 95.
151. West, p. 6.
152. *Ibid.* p. 20.
153. Wells, *EA*, II, p. 466.

154. *Ibid.* 5 June 1914, p. 8.
155. *The New York Times*, 6 June 1914, p. 1.
156. *Ibid.*
157. Fulford, p. 297.
158. *The New York Times*, 6 June 1914.
159. *The Times*, 5 June 1914, p. 8.

Chapter 18: Rebellion

1. Dangerfield, p. 71.
2. S&A, I, p. 271.
3. Meleady, p. 184.
4. BL Add. MS 52513 f. 67.
5. PA: LG/C/7/3/2.
6. Fanning, p. 51.
7. *The Times*, 25 September 1911, p. 5.
8. S&A, II, p. 15.
9. *The Times*, 27 January 1912, p. 9.
10. Churchill, *Companion*, II, III, p. 1388.
11. Dangerfield, p. 91.
12. Churchill, *Companion*, II, III, p. 1390.
13. *The Times*, 9 February 1912, p. 9.
14. *Ibid.* p. 10.
15. Meleady, p. 211.
16. *The Times*, 7 April 1912, p. 7.
17. *Ibid.* 10 April 1912, p. 7.
18. *Ibid.* p. 8.
19. Hansard, Vol. 36 cols 1407–8.
20. *Ibid.* col. 1427.
21. *Ibid.* col. 1452.
22. *Ibid.* Vol. 39 col. 771.
23. *Ibid.* col. 786.
24. *The Times*, 13 July 1912, p. 9.
25. *Ibid.* p. 10.
26. *Ibid.* 20 July 1912, p. 10.
27. *Ibid.* 29 July 1912, p. 7.
28. *Ibid.* p. 8.
29. Blake, pp. 130–1.
30. Churchill, *Companion*, II, III, p. 1393.
31. *The Times*, 13 September 1912, p. 4.
32. *Ibid.* 16 September 1912, p. 5.
33. *Ibid.* 19 September 1912, p. 7.
34. Churchill, *Companion*, II, III, p. 1396.
35. C&G, II, p. 470.
36. Blake, p. 151.
37. *The Times*, 23 September 1912, p. 5.
38. *Ibid.* 25 September 1912, p. 4.
39. *Ibid.* 20 September 1912, p. 5.
40. *Ibid.* 30 September 1912, p. 10.
41. *Asquith*, *FY*, II, pp. 141–2.
42. Hansard, Vol. 43 col. 1766.
43. *Ibid.* col. 2054.
44. *The Times*, 14 November 1912, p. 6.
45. Hansard Vol. 46 col. 377.
46. *Ibid.* col. 406.
47. BL Add. MS 62161 f. 18.
48. Hansard Vol. 46 col. 2381.
49. *Ibid.* col. 2410.
50. Hansard (Lords) Vol. 13 col. 769.
51. Blake, p. 133.
52. S&A, II, p. 26.
53. Henson Journal, Vol. 18, p. 273.
54. *Ibid.* p. 274.
55. *Ibid.* p. 275.
56. Hansard, Vol. 53 col. 1284.
57. *Ibid.* col. 1292.
58. *Ibid.* col. 1293.
59. *Ibid.* col. 1467.
60. Newsinger, p. 5.
61. Dangerfield, p. 304.
62. *The Times*, 25 August 1913, p. 8.
63. *Ibid.* 1 September 1913, p. 6.
64. *Ibid.* 2 September 1913, p. 6.
65. *Ibid.*
66. *Ibid.* 6 September 1913, p. 6.
67. *Ibid.* 11 September 1913, p. 7.
68. *Ibid.* p. 8.
69. PA: LG/C/4/8/9.
70. Blake, p. 157.
71. *Ibid.* pp. 155–6.
72. Churchill, *Companion*, II, III, pp. 1400–1401.
73. *The Times*, 17 November 1913, p. 9.
74. *Ibid.* 18 November 1913, p. 8.
75. Meleady, p. 247.
76. *The Times*, 19 November 1913, p. 8.
77. Holmes, *LFM*, p. 170.
78. Fanning, p. 94.
79. S&A, II, p. 37.
80. NA: CAB 37/119/20.
81. Asquith, *VS*, pp. 42–3.
82. Blake, p. 168.
83. *Ibid.* p. 169.
84. NA: CAB 37/119/22.
85. Hansard, Vol. 58 col. 52.

86. *Ibid.* col. 60.
87. *Ibid.* col. 62.
88. *Ibid.* col. 68.
89. *Ibid.* col. 70.
90. *Ibid.* col. 75.
91. *Ibid.* col. 81.
92. *Ibid.* col. 82.
93. *Ibid.* col. 84.
94. S&A, II, p. 37.
95. NA: CAB 37/119/36.
96. Hansard, Vol. 60 col. 393.
97. BL Add. MS 51250 f. 88.
98. *The Times*, 16 March 1914, p. 13.
99. Meleady, p. 248.
100. Asquith, *VS*, p. 55.
101. *Ibid.* p. 56.
102. BL Add. MS 51250 f. 94.
103. Hansard, Vol. 60 col. 396.
104. BL Add. MS 51250 f. 95.
105. BL Add. MS 51250 f. 96.
106. Dangerfield, p. 331.
107. Hansard, Vol. 60 col. 395.
108. Blake, p. 189.
109. *Ibid.* p. 193.
110. BL Add. MS 51250 f. 97.
111. Blake, p. 198.
112. Asquith, *VS*, p. 60.
113. Hansard, Vol. 60 col. 378.
114. *Ibid.* col. 396.
115. *Ibid.* col. 399.
116. *Ibid.* col. 401.
117. *Ibid.* col. 403.
118. PA: LG/C/6/12/8.
119. Hansard, Vol. 60 col. 406.
120. Churchill, *Companion*, II, III, p. 1413.
121. BL Add. MS 51250 f. 112.
122. BL Add. MS 51250 f. 120.
123. BL Add. MS 51250 f. 122.
124. BL Add. MS 51250 f. 125.
125. BL Add. MS 51250 f. 131.
126. Asquith, *VS*, p. 62.
127. Hansard, Vol. 60 col. 843.
128. *Ibid.* col. 1622.
129. *Ibid.* col. 1668.
130. *Ibid.* Vol. 61 col. 1348.
131. *Ibid.* Vol. 62 col. 711.
132. S&A, II, 50.
133. NA: CAB 37/119/53.
134. Asquith, *MR*, II, p. 3.
135. *Ibid.* p. 4.
136. Meleady, p. 278.
137. Asquith, *VS*, p. 83.
138. PA: LG/C/4/8/6.
139. S&A, II, 53.
140. Hansard, Vol. 65 col. 897.
141. Asquith, *FY*, II, p. 156.
142. Asquith, *VS*, p. 109.
143. Asquith, *MR*, II, p. 5.
144. Hansard, Vol. 65 col. 934.
145. *Ibid.* col. 935.
146. Asquith, *VS*, p. 127.
147. Hansard, Vol. 65 col. 1026.
148. *Ibid.* col. 1030.
149. *Ibid.* col. 1040.
150. PA: LG/C/7/3/11.

INDEX

PICTURE ACKNOWLEDGEMENTS

Images are reproduced by kind permission of: Alamy: Cecil Sharp with singer (Heritage Image Partnership Ltd), Empire Day poster (Chronicle), family at the seaside (Amoret Tanner), Labour Exchange (Chronicle), Lord Curzon (Archive Pics), Selfridge's (Chronicle). Bridgeman Images: H. G. Wells (© Granger), house by C. F. A. Voysey (Private Collection / The Stapleton Collection), Marie Lloyd poster (Private Collection / © Look and Learn / Peter Jackson Collection), riots during dock strike (© SZ Photo / Scherl), Robert Baden Powell (National Portrait Gallery, London, UK / Photo © Stefano Baldini). Getty Images: Charles Boycott (Sean Sexton), Charles Gordon (Time Life Pictures), Daimler advertisement (Heritage Images), Emmeline Pankhurst arrested (Jimmy Sime / Stringer), eviction in Ireland (Sean Sexton), Flora Drummond arrested (Universal History Archive), Hornsey suburb (Hulton Archive / Stringer), man collecting pension (Hulton Archive / Stringer), Northampton school (Popperfoto), Rowntree's factory (Heritage Images), 'The Dawn of Hope' poster (Hulton Archive), Tranby Croft (Hulton Archive / Stringer). © National Portrait Gallery, London: Charles Parnell in prison, David Lloyd George, Lord Northcliffe. Wikimedia Commons: A. E. Housman, Arthur Balfour, Baron Ribblesdale, George V, H. H. Asquith, John Burns, Lady Colin Campbell, Lord Salisbury. All other images author's own or from publisher's collection.